THE OXFORD HANDBOOK OF

ISLAM AND WOMEN

THE OXFORD HANDBOOK OF

ISLAM AND WOMEN

Edited by

ASMA AFSARUDDIN

OXFORD
UNIVERSITY PRESS

OXFORD
UNIVERSITY PRESS

Oxford University Press is a department of the University of Oxford. It furthers the University's objective of excellence in research, scholarship, and education by publishing worldwide. Oxford is a registered trade mark of Oxford University Press in the UK and certain other countries.

Published in the United States of America by Oxford University Press
198 Madison Avenue, New York, NY 10016, United States of America.

Library of Congress Cataloging-in-Publication Data
Names: Afsaruddin, Asma, 1958– editor.
Title: The Oxford handbook of Islam and women / Asma Afsaruddin.
Description: 1. | New York : Oxford University Press, 2023. |
Includes bibliographical references and index.
Identifiers: LCCN 2023017630 (print) | LCCN 2023017631 (ebook) |
ISBN 9780190638771 (hardback) | ISBN 9780190638795 (epub) |
ISBN 9780190638801
Subjects: LCSH: Women in Islam. | Muslim women.
Classification: LCC BP173.4.O945 2023 (print) | LCC BP173.4 (ebook) |
DDC 297.082—dc23/eng/20230508
LC record available at https://lccn.loc.gov/2023017630
LC ebook record available at https://lccn.loc.gov/2023017631

DOI: 10.1093/oxfordhb/9780190638771.001.0001

Printed by Sheridan Books, Inc., United States of America

Contents

Acknowledgments ix
List of Contributors xi

A. DECIPHERING MUSLIM WOMEN'S LIVES: RELIGION, AGENCY, AND DIVERSITY
ASMA AFSARUDDIN

B. FOUNDATIONAL TEXTS AND THEIR INTERPRETATIONS

1. The Qur'ān and Woman 21
HIBBA ABUGIDEIRI

2. Classical Exegeses on Key Qur'ānic Verses Concerning Women 39
HADIA MUBARAK

3. Women in the *Ḥadīth* Literature 61
FERYAL SALEM

4. Modern Rereadings of the Qur'ān through a Gendered Lens 80
ASMA AFSARUDDIN

5. Modern Rereadings of the *Ḥadīth* through a Gendered Lens 119
KHALED ABOU EL FADL

C. WOMEN AND ISLAMIC LAW

6. Marriage, Divorce, and Inheritance in Classical Islamic Law and Premodern Practice 155
MARIAM SHEIBANI

7. Status of Muslim Women in Modern Family and Personal Law 181
SOHAIRA SIDDIQUI

8. Women's Rights and Duties in Classical Legal Texts: Modern Rereadings 200
Natana J. DeLong-Bas

D. DECIPHERING WOMEN'S LIVES: WOMEN IN HISTORY AND TEXTS

9. Early Muslim Women as Moral Paragons in Classical Islamic Literature: *al-Mubashsharāt bi-l-janna* 223
Yasmin Amin

10. Women as Moral Exemplars in Twelver Shīʿism 245
Maria Dakake

11. Women as Transmitters of Knowledge 259
Asma Sayeed

12. Muslim Women and Devotional Life 275
Zahra Ayubi and Iman Abdoulkarim

13. Women as Littérateurs in the Premodern Period 289
Samer M. Ali

14. Women as Economic Actors in the Premodern Islamic World 304
Amira Sonbol

E. WOMEN'S LIVED REALITIES AND THEIR RELIGIOUS AND SOCIAL ACTIVISM IN THE MODERN PERIOD

15. Women in the Mosque: Contesting Public Space and Religious Authority 323
Marion Katz

16. Negotiating Motherhood, Religion, and Modern Lived Realities 338
Margaret Aziza Pappano

17. Women as Modern Heads of State 354
Tamara Sonn

18. Women's Religious and Social Activism in Palestine, Lebanon, and Syria 367
Elizabeth Brownson

19. Women's Religious and Social Activism in Egypt and North Africa 380
Nermin Allam

20. Women's Religious and Social Activism in Iran 397
Seema Golestaneh

21. Women's Religious and Social Activism in Turkey 415
Chiara Maritato

22. Women's Religious and Social Activism in South Asia 428
Elora Shehabuddin

23. Women's Religious and Social Activism in Southeast Asia 444
Nelly van Doorn-Harder

24. Muslim Women's Religious and Social Activism in China 462
Maria Jaschok and Man Ke

25. Muslim Women's Religious and Social Activism in South Africa 478
Nina Hoel

26. Muslim Women's Religious and Social Activism in the United States 489
Juliane Hammer

27. Muslim Women's Religious and Social Activism in Western Europe 503
Jeanette S. Jouili

28. Women's Religious and Social Activism in Saudi Arabia and the Gulf Countries 519
Alainna Liloia

F. MODERN NARRATIVES OF THE GENDERED SELF: WOMEN WRITING ABOUT WOMEN

29. Modern Representations of the Wives of the Prophet Muḥammad 537
Ruqayya Y. Khan

30. Modern and Contemporary Muslim Feminist Literature: An Overview 549
Miriam Cooke

G. ISLAM, WOMEN, AND THE GLOBAL PUBLIC ARENA

31. Women's Sartorial Agency: The History and Politics of Veiling 571
ANNA PIELA

32. Muslim Women as a Cultural Trope: Global Discourses and the Politics of Victimhood 590
KATHERINE BULLOCK

Index 609

Acknowledgments

THIS work owes its existence to Theodore Calderara, Editor-in-Chief of History and Religion, who approached me several years ago with the suggestion of editing a volume on the topic of "Islam and Women" for Oxford University Press's renowned Handbook series. Although I could not assume the task right away, the suggestion planted in my mind shortly blossomed into a conviction that this was a project that I would dearly like to take on. My profound thanks, therefore, to Theodore for getting the ball rolling on editing this volume and for his patient and skillful shepherding of this project from start to finish.

I also recognize Paloma Escoveda, project editor at OUP, who efficiently took care of the logistical details related to the final production of the volume.

Thanks are also due to the College Arts and Humanities Institute (CAHI) at Indiana University which provided me with a grant to defray the expenses of index preparation.

And last but absolutely not least, I acknowledge my fellow collaborators on the Handbook and their learned contributions, without which it simply would not exist. The years between March 2020 and summer 2022 were particularly challenging as a global pandemic shut down universities and colleges, along with other institutions, altering the course of our lives in completely unexpected ways. Many of the contributors were delayed in submitting their final chapters because their institution's libraries had closed down and essential services, like interlibrary loan, were not available. Some of them struggled to find childcare while business was supposed to go on as usual; some had to look after sick loved ones, and a few among them fell prey to COVID themselves. Many of us scrambled to revise syllabi on the fly and master the art of holding online classes and worse, hybrid classes, where we had to lecture in class and allow students to Zoom in as well! For those of us who were a bit technologically challenged at the beginning (as I certainly was), it was quite a learning curve.

But all rose superbly to the occasion and made the herculean effort to get us collectively to the finish line. After unavoidable delays, here we are. So a very robust shout-out to the contributors to this volume, who persevered through a very challenging period indeed with exemplary collegiality and patience.

Asma Afsaruddin
Bloomington, Indiana

Contributors

Iman AbdoulKarim is a PhD candidate in the Departments of Religious Studies and African American Studies at Yale University.

Khaled Abou El Fadl is Distinguished Professor of Law and Omar and Azmeralda Alfi Chair in Islamic Law at the UCLA School of Law.

Hibba Abugideiri is Associate Professor of History in the Department of History at Villanova University.

Asma Afsaruddin is Class of 1950 Herman B Wells Endowed Professor and Professor of Middle Eastern Languages and Cultures at Indiana University, Bloomington.

Samer M. Ali is Associate Professor of Arabic Language and Literature in the Departments of Middle East Studies and Comparative Literature at the University of Michigan.

Nermin Allam is Associate Professor of Politics at Rutgers University, Newark.

Yasmin Amin is the Representative of the Orient-Institut Beirut (Max-Weber-Stiftung) in Cairo, Egypt.

Zahra Ayubi is Associate Professor of Islamic Studies in the Department of Religion at Dartmouth College.

Elizabeth Brownson is Associate Professor of History at the University of Wisconsin-Parkside, Kenosha.

Katherine Bullock teaches Islamic Politics in the Department of Political Science at the University of Toronto, Mississauga.

miriam cooke is Braxton Craven Distinguished Professor Emerita of Arab Cultures in the Department of Asian and Middle Eastern Studies at Duke University.

Maria Dakake is Associate Professor of Religion at George Mason University.

Natana J. DeLong-Bas is Professor of the Practice in the Theology Department and Islamic Civilization and Societies Program at Boston College.

Seema Golestaneh is Assistant Professor in the Department of Near Eastern Studies at Cornell University.

Juliane Hammer is Professor of Religious Studies at the University of North Carolina, Chapel Hill.

Nina Hoel is Associate Professor in Religion & Society in the Faculty of Theology, University of Oslo, Norway and Visiting Researcher at the Centre for Contemporary Islam, Department for the Study of Religions, University of Cape Town, South Africa.

Maria Jaschok is a Senior Research Associate of the Contemporary China Studies Program in the Oxford School of Global & Area Studies and a Life Fellow of The Global China Academy, London.

Jeanette S. Jouili is Associate Professor in the Department of Religion at Syracuse University, Syracuse, New York.

Marion Katz is Professor of Middle Eastern and Islamic Studies at New York University.

Man Ke is Professor of Anthropology and Ethnology in the School of Ethnology and Sociology at Northwest Minzu University, Lanzhou, China.

Ruqayya Y. Khan is Malas Professor of Islamic Studies in the Department of Religion, School of Arts and Humanities, at Claremont Graduate University in Claremont, California.

Alainna Liloia completed her PhD in Middle Eastern & North African Studies at the University of Arizona in 2022, focusing on the role of Qatari women in nation-building and branding through the lens of transnational feminist theory.

Chiara Maritato is Post-Doctoral Research Fellow in the Department of Cultures, Politics and Society at the University of Turin, Italy.

Hadia Mubarak is Assistant Professor of Religion at Queens University of Charlotte.

Margaret Aziza Pappano is Associate Professor in the Department of English Language and Literature at Queen's University, Canada.

Anna Piela is Visiting Scholar in the Department of Religious Studies at Northwestern University.

Feryal Salem is Associate Professor of Arabic and Islamic Studies at American Islamic College in Chicago.

Asma Sayeed is Associate Professor of Islamic Studies in the Department of Near Eastern Languages and Cultures at the University of California, Los Angeles.

Elora Shehabuddin is Professor of Gender & Women's Studies and Global Studies at the University of California, Berkeley.

Mariam Sheibani is Assistant Professor of Islamic Studies in the Department of Near Eastern and Judaic Studies at Brandeis University.

Sohaira Siddiqui is Associate Professor of Theology at Georgetown University, Qatar.

Amira Sonbol is Professor of History at Georgetown University, Qatar and in the College of Arts and Sciences at Georgetown University, Washington, D.C.

Tamara Sonn is Hamad bin Khalifa al-Thani Professor Emerita in the History of Islam in the School of Foreign Service, Georgetown University.

Nelly van Doorn-Harder is Professor of Religious Studies at Wake Forest University, North Carolina.

A

DECIPHERING MUSLIM WOMEN'S LIVES

Religion, Agency, and Diversity

ASMA AFSARUDDIN

"ISLAM and Women" is a very broad topic and as complex as the lives of women that it encompasses in a broad swath of the world. It is a topic that is of great interest to variegated audiences—to scholars of Islam and of Muslim societies, to academics and intellectuals concerned with the premodern and modern Middle East in general from different disciplinary backgrounds, legal specialists with a focus on human rights, and also to a large "lay" audience of public intellectuals, policymakers, "talking heads," social justice and feminist activists, and opinion-makers of all sorts.

In recent times, the topic of Islam and women has become highly "ideologized" in many spheres, acquiring a certain political valency that inevitably casts a shadow as we approach this complex topic in the contemporary period. To engage and countervail this contemporary "ideologization" which sometimes threatens to derail level-headed conversations on the topic, it is important to adopt a historical, longue-durée approach that provides appropriate contextualization for a number of these contemporary debates. This is among the primary purposes of this *Handbook*.

In its wide-ranging coverage of issues subsumed under the umbrella topic of Islam and women, this volume is purposefully multidisciplinary. Its various chapters are authoritative contributions from well-known scholars from the humanities and the social sciences, and who are at the cutting-edge of scholarship on, inter alia, the topics of Qur'ānic hermeneutics; *ḥadīth* analysis; Islamic law, especially as it pertains to women's legal and social rights; the scholarly and literary activities of Muslim women in the premodern Islamic world, and their activism and lived realities in contemporary Muslim-majority societies. These chapters delineate a broad spectrum of views on these key issues and the contestations of some of these views that are prevalent inside and outside of academia. They provide sophisticated and often innovative analysis of textual sources and of broad sociological and political trends within Muslim-majority societies. Many of these chapters emphasize above all the diversity present in Muslim women's lives, both in the premodern and modern periods, and pay close attention to the historical and political contexts that shaped their lives and framed the thinking and actions of key figures throughout Islamic history. Such an approach results in fine-grained macro- and microstudies of Muslim women's lives that problematize reified assumptions of gender and agency in the context of Muslim-majority societies, as is all too common.

Following this Introduction, the *Handbook* is divided into six sections: B. Foundational Texts and Their Interpretations; C. Women and Islamic Law; D. Deciphering Women's Lives: Women in History and Texts; E. Women's Lived Realities and Their Religious and Social Activism in the Modern Period; F. Modern Narratives of the Gendered Self: Women Writing about Women; and G. Islam, Women, and the Global Public Arena. Under each of these rubrics experts weigh in on diverse topics related to that particular theme, creating wide-ranging narratives that attempt to do justice to complex, sometimes interrelated, issues.

In the first section, the lead chapter is written by Hibba Abugideiri, who foregrounds "the question of woman" in the Qur'ān by focusing on three prominent female figures within it: Mary, the mother of Jesus; Bilqīs, the queen of Sheba (who is otherwise not named in the Qur'ān); and Zulaykha, the wife of 'Azīz, the Egyptian pharaoh's viceroy. In her study of these women, Abugideiri adopts the "*tawḥīdic* approach," which allows her "to interpret the Qur'ān as Divine Discourse that must, by its own logic, reflect God's Self Disclosure, starting with *tawḥīd* (unicity)." This is an approach previously made famous by two distinguished gender scholars, amina wadud and Asma Barlas, who are regarded as pioneers in the field of modern Qur'ānic hermeneutics through a woman-centered, gender-egalitarian lens. Abugideiri puts this approach to great use in her chapter. Through this lens, she proceeds to offer us a penetrating analysis of the portrayals of these women that allows her to arrive at highly significant and original conclusions regarding the relation between the masculine and the feminine in the Qur'ān. Rather than being characterized by *duality*, which implies exclusion and separation, she finds that women and men in the Qur'ānic text are characterized by *polarity*, which implies interconnectedness, reciprocity, and complementarity.

The *tawḥīdic* approach, furthermore, allows Abugideiri to stress not just God's transcendence but also his immanence so that one may thereby "authenticate female and male subjectivities through God's intimacy with humanity, women and men." Applying this *tawḥīdic* paradigm allows her to discern that in the Qur'ānic text woman and man are ontological equals who synergistically point to the unicity of God and his larger purpose for humankind. The moral lessons we derive from the lives of Mary, Bilqīs, and Zulaykha parallel the lessons we extrapolate from the lives of Jesus, Solomon, and Joseph, the male figures to whom their lives are linked respectively, so much so that "their narratives can be deemed 'un-gendered' examples of undifferentiated spirituality." The emphasis on polarity rather than duality ultimately helps us view woman and man in the Qur'ānic text as coeval agents in the staging of the human struggle on earth in all its various aspects, concludes Abugideiri.

Hadia Mubarak contributes the second chapter in this section, which focuses on influential commentaries written by some of the most prominent premodern male exegetes on key verses in the Qur'ān that are frequently cited in the context of women's and gender issues. These verses are Qur'ān 4:1; 2:228; 4:34; and 4:128. Mubarak's rigorous and nuanced analysis of a wide range of exegetical works allows her to exhume far from monolithic views recorded in these sources in the premodern period. Her survey of these influential commentaries leads her to conclude that works of *tafsīr* (exegesis) are characterized far more by polysemy and diverse approaches than is usually conceded in modern studies of this important genre. She remarks significantly, "this [hermeneutical] tradition is not a hermetically sealed box nor are its contents fixed," and therefore it remains "amenable to a multiplicity of readings." Her careful, in-depth analysis leads her to conclude that it is not always productive to read exegetical works along a sharp patriarchal-egalitarian divide; one is often able to discern on the part of the premodern male exegete a deep concern for the well-being of women, a notion that was inflected by the exigencies of their particular historical circumstances. It is, therefore, important to keep in mind, Mubarak reminds, that the sociocultural and intellectual milieu in which exegetes lived considerably impacted their hermeneutical maneuvers and interpretive proclivities, allowing us to question the normativity of their exegetical discourses and opening up space in the modern world today for alternative, "revisionist" interpretations that similarly foreground the welfare of women, especially from egalitarian and gender-just perspectives.

After the Qur'ān, the *ḥadīth*—statements attributed to the Prophet Muḥammad—is the most important source for recreating the lives and roles of the first generation of Muslim women, the celebrated *Ṣaḥabiyyāt* or women Companions of the Prophet. In chapter 3, Feryal Salem insightfully discusses a number of significant *ḥadīth* that have been and continue to be frequently cited to establish mimetic precedents for subsequent generations of Muslim women. A number of these *ḥadīth* also serve as "causes/occasions of revelation" for key Qur'ānic verses and therefore provide important contextualization for understanding their larger moral and normative implications. Salem makes the significant observation that when women scholars engage these prophetic reports they often extrapolate levels of meanings that were occluded from their male counterparts. Life experiences, especially as shaped by gender, and the sociopolitical milieux of those who explicated *ḥadīth* in the premodern period heavily influenced their perspectives—pointing to how our own radically altered circumstances in the twenty-first century can shape our readings of the *ḥadīth* corpus and allow us to variously endorse or question the lessons that our male predecessors derived from it. Furthermore, she points out, a holistic engagement with the *ḥadīth* corpus, along with the Qurʾān, allows Muslims to critically engage a number of reports with misogynistic content and assess their reliability as well as their credibility.

It is to modern readings of sacred, foundational texts that we turn next. In my own chapter that focuses on woman-centered and feminist exegeses of the Qurʾān in the contemporary period, these divergences in reading strategies that ultimately lead to dramatically different interpretations of key verses become clearly apparent. The chapter outlines the pioneering efforts of early Muslim women exegetes of the twentieth century to read the Qurʾānic text on its own terms rather than engage it through the prism of the rich commentarial tradition generated by learned male scholars through the generations. The results in some cases have been downright revolutionary. These gender scholars—some of whom self-consciously identify as "feminist" while others do not—have very cogently questioned some of the interpretive strategies of premodern Qurʾān commentators and the highly gendered, hierarchical understandings to which they often led. Through their own careful, cross-referential reading of the Qurʾānic text and exploration of the semantic layers of key terms, such as *qānitāt*/*qānitūn*, *nushūz*, *daraja*, and *faḍTl*, modern women exegetes are able to mount a trenchant critique of androcentric construals of the Qurʾān that continue to impact the lives of Muslim women to this day. In the chapter, I also discuss some recent critiques of their position by a small coterie of gender scholars and assess their validity.

In chapter 5, Khaled Abou El Fadl focuses on modern rereadings of the *ḥadīth* literature and the *sunna* of the Prophet, which refer to his sayings and practices respectively, as recorded by his closest Companions and transmitted by succeeding generations of Muslims. As the author points out, the *ḥadīth* corpus documents certain events in the earliest history of Islam that have been interpreted as empowering and liberating for Muslim women. At the same time, he notes, a number of the reports recorded in this corpus can also be understood to advocate patriarchal values and structures that sanction male dominance over women. The chapter begins by exploring what Abou El Fadl terms "tension reports" "that are alleged historical memories of the exercise of women's agency in a fashion that challenged or defied the institutions of patriarchy at the time of the Prophet or his companions." The tension arises when these reports are contraposed to what Abou El Fadl describes as "misogynistic reports" that uphold patriarchal institutions and mores. Their content has been critically analyzed and challenged by several Muslim women scholars in the modern period.

The bulk of the chapter is then taken up by a rich and thoughtful account of the three main interpretive or thematic stratagems that have been employed by Muslim women scholars, who write in English, in their engagement with the *ḥadīth* literature and the interpretation of various reports in the modern world. Abou El Fadl concludes that although patriarchy is a trial (*ibtilāʾ*) and the content of certain reports remain problematic to this day, one cannot advocate the wholesale jettisoning of the *ḥadīth* corpus, as some have proposed. Rather, he says, a more circumspect and credible approach is to continue to regard the *ḥadīth* and *sunna* as "critical components of the Islamic tradition," and to recognize that "this tradition must continue to serve as the source for dynamic and inventive solutions, even to deeply entrenched challenges such as patriarchy."

In the next section, "Women and Islamic Law," Mariam Sheibani provides a broad overview of how classical jurists (from the second/eighth to twelfth/eighteenth century) conceived of the rights and duties of Muslim women, particularly in regard to marriage, divorce, and inheritance rights, and especially within the four Sunnī *madhāhib*, with occasional comparisons with Shi'i legal positions, particularly within the Imāmī or Ja'farī school. The chapter also explores the reasoning behind these legal pronouncements, the sources that the jurists drew from, and the assumptions they made about women's agency and sexuality that informed such legal positions. The strength of the chapter lies in its skillful highlighting, wherever relevant, of the diversity of views among the classical jurists themselves on these key issues of marriage, divorce, and inheritance. Sheibani stresses that there was always a complex and contested relationship between the formal articulation of rights and obligations in legal manuals and moral and religious duties that were not enforceable by the courts. In reality, therefore, legal rulings pertaining to women's rights and obligations were always subjected to accommodation of realities on the ground and the negotiation of diverse local customs and social practices which allowed for various inflections of legal norms to emerge in specific settings. Specific case studies provided in this chapter helpfully illustrate this highly significant point which allow us to question monochromatic representations of Islamic law and its application throughout history.

In her meticulously researched chapter, Sohaira Siddiqui points out how Islamic family law (IFL; *al-aḥwāl al-shakhṢiyya*) in the modern period is often used as a litmus test for both modernization and Islamization. Starting in the period of European colonial occupation, a general awareness that IFL was in need of reform took shape, especially as women's status and roles began to be reconceptualized in Organization of Islamic Conference (OIC) countries. The ideological tug-of-war that ensued created a series of dichotomies—traditional versus modern, religious versus secular, state versus civil society, and tradition versus reform—that continue to "frame legal and policy debates on Islamic family law." Siddiqui provides a rich historical backdrop to the phases of codification of IFL that took place in a number of Muslim-majority countries, starting in 1917, when the Ottoman Law of Family Rights was passed. The variable factors that determined the process of legislative reform were constituted by "the colonial legacy, state politics, the relationship between the state and religion, and the dominant political actors on the scene." Siddiqui provides a sweeping overview of these historical developments and assesses the efficacy of the historical-legal, anthropological, sociological, and political approaches adopted by scholars to study IFL. Some of the challenges inherent in effecting legislative reforms, especially in regard to the promotion of gender equality, are brought into sharp relief in Siddiqui's discussion of Malaysia and Morocco as case studies.

In chapter 8, Natana J. Delong-Bas traces the history and content of modern scholars' engagement with classical Islamic law, adroitly guiding us through debates about its origins and development through time in order to trace "how normative roles of women and their accompanying rights and duties came about." In her valuable review of relevant literature, she contextualizes a number of these debates and critically interrogates the terms "women," "rights and duties," and "classical legal literature," pointing to the imprecise nature of such terminologies and the plural ways they can be understood. Issues of methodology also are paramount and leads her to ask, "To what degree do the theoretical descriptions match actual legal practice and how best to understand differences between the two?" Delong-Bas advocates that both qualitative and quantitative approaches to the classical legal literature be adopted. This would lead to a more holistic approach to the study of classical Islamic law and "help to reassert the mutuality that is supposed to be at the heart of the husband–wife relationship, rather than the unidirectionality implied in a hierarchical relationship of obedience." At the same time, she warns, reformers should not downplay the real problems inherent in highly patriarchal formulations of classical legal precepts concerning women and the family that have led to pronounced gender inequalities in Muslim-majority societies.

The next section is titled "Deciphering Women's Lives: Women in History and Texts." In this section, Yasmin Amin in chapter 9 focuses on biographical and prosopographical literature that records entries on the ten women Companions promised paradise by Muḥammad on account of their moral excellences and exceptional accomplishments, on a par with the ten male Companions who were similarly assured of paradise. Over time, it is the names of these male Companions that have been given prominence and that have predominated in the literature written about the first generation of Muslims, so much so that most Muslims would be hard put to name these illustrious female Companions. Through her foray into this rich literary genre, Amin retrieves the names of these women and dwells on their individual accomplishments that brought them this kind of prophetic recognition during their own lifetimes. At the same time, she ponders what social-political-historical factors contributed to the eclipse of their names and of the memory of their distinguished status when the opposite trend is clearly discernible in regard to their male counterparts. Modern, especially women, scholars, are beginning to reverse this trend by exhuming the details of the lives of these prominent women Companions and assessing the different ways in which the significance of such details has been interpreted and reinterpreted by male biographers. After her careful, diachronic examination of these various sources, Amin concludes that "such reinterpretations and re-assessments have been used to justify a great variety of cultural attitudes toward women and gendered norms of behavior," a process that, in fact, continues to our very day.

Maria Dakake's chapter nicely complements that of Amin by focusing more narrowly on two prominent women from the first century of Islam. They are Fāṭima, Muḥammad's daughter, one of the women promised Paradise and greatly revered by both the Sunnīs and Shī'a; and Zaynab, the female protagonist of the battle of Karbalā' fought in 61/680 between an Umayyad army and al-Ḥusayn, the beloved grandson of the Prophet.

Both Fāṭima's and Zaynab's lives are assessed through pro-ʿAlid and pro-Shīʿī eyes, allowing for the tragic suffering and heroic forbearance of these two iconic women to be foregrounded above all other attributes. Dakake's thoughtful reading of their lives as depicted in Shīʿī sources brings into sharp relief the different yet complementary ways in which these women are valorized: Fāṭima, the long-suffering daughter of Muḥammad and mother of his famous grandsons, al-Ḥasan and al-Ḥusayn, often regarded as passive; and Zaynab, the stalwart and activist heroine who goads the menfolk into battle, single-handedly saves the life of the future Shīʿī Imām, and fearlessly speaks truth to corrupt power as represented by the Umayyad caliph Yazīd ibn Muʿāwiya (d. 64/683). Yet, as Dakake, points out, they share a number of similar attributes. Through a judicious sifting of the relevant sources, Fāṭima is clearly revealed to also be a fearless critic of injustice and unflinching in her championship of the rights of the *ahl al-bayt*, the family of the Prophet. Ultimately, Dakake observes, "as models of devotion, obedience, courage, and conviction, they serve as virtuous examples, not only for Shīʿī women, but for all Shīʿīs, regardless of gender."

In chapter 11, Asma Sayeed focuses on the roles played by Muslim women in the transmission of knowledge, particularly of *ḥadīth*, since the first century of Islam. She traces the ebb and flow in women's participation in *ḥadīth* transmission, linking them to specific historical factors that impacted such trends and provides a useful review of the scholarly literature on the topic to date. Modern scholarly interest in this topic has only grown in recent times, since, as Sayeed reminds us, "women's religious learning is indelibly bound up with questions of their agency, authority, and empowerment." Although the focus has typically been on Sunnī women scholars, the terrain has recently begun to change with more studies now emerging that discuss the contributions of learned Shīʿī women from the Imāmī branch; however, similar studies of female education within the Zaydī and Ismāʿīlī traditions are currently lacking. Sayeed concludes her chapter by reflecting on the future of scholarship focused on women's transmission of learning and the directions it might assume. She suggests that "stronger interdisciplinary, transregional, and historical connections" be forged among scholars to do full justice to this promising field of inquiry and that there be a conscious attempt to connect modern Muslim women's scholarship to that of the past.

In chapter 12, which discusses how Muslim women's devotional lives tend to be portrayed in scholarly studies, Zahra Ayubi and Iman Abdoulkarim observe that two principal paradigms tend to be invoked: one posits women's practices as alternatives to those of men while the other focuses on the historical and contemporary recovery of women's religious learning and authority. Ayubi and Abdoulkarim proceed to interrogate both these paradigms and uncover the assumptions and tensions inherent in each of them. A perennial tension apparent in both paradigms is between hierarchical and egalitarian conceptions of gendered relations and norms in Muslim-majority societies that continue to spark debate into the contemporary period. This tension becomes evident in certain types of literature that focus on issues of women's empowerment, especially through the pursuit of devotional activities and the acquisition of religious knowledge, that are sometimes subversive of men's traditional authority and sometimes not.

In his highly illuminating and provocative chapter, Samer Ali resurrects the contributions of Arab and Muslim women to Islamic literary production in the premodern period, generously documented in collections of poetry (*dīwān*); verse segments (*qiṭʿas*), orations (*khuṭabs*), and stories (*akhbār*) that he analyzes. The seminal contributions of these gifted women are, however, hardly known in the West and have been obscured by Orientalist authors who approached the Islamic East through the prism of European imperialism. Such an "approach sidelined evidence of phenomena that defied preconceived categories and constrained a rigorous understanding of women's roles as littérateurs and agents in society," says Ali. Using the broad category of "speech" and the umbrella category of "women's rhetoric," Ali is able to cogently establish centuries of women's literary imprint on genres, such as poetry, verse fragments, oration, and stories. Women's prominence in literature should not be considered surprising, he says; women were valorized in pre-Islamic poetry, for example, as the beloved subject of the male poet and women played robust, public roles during the early, formative period of Islam, both during and after the time of the Prophet. Subsequent generations of women, he says, "implicitly benefited from the legacy of autochthonous feminist counter-culture, and the record of these women's deeds in sources attests to the interests, even admiration, of later generations, including men." Through cultural and literary productions of various kinds and their mastery of rhetoric, women from different levels of society established their agency that contributed to their sense of dignity, Ali notes, and even allowed them to assume positions of cultural leadership, sometimes through the medium of the literary salon.

In chapter 14, Amira Sonbol focuses on the topic of Muslim women's participation in the economies of their communities in the premodern period and unearths a wealth, so to speak, of information regarding their contributions from primary sources. The sources that she relied on for this research are multiple and varied: records of financial transactions concerning trade, mortgage, and litigation of various kinds; documents of financial settlements during marriage and divorce; inheritance records; and records of charitable endowments and trusts (*awqāf*) established by women. Sonbol's survey of these documents reveals that some women were economically very engaged and made critical contributions to their local economies that were recognized as important and essential in their own time. Their economic productivity enjoyed legitimacy because women along with men are given the right to own property under Islamic law and "neither was forbidden from being financially active, investing, holding or spending wealth inherited or earned." In the life of the community, Sonbol describes the socioeconomic relationship between male and female as "rhizomatic," that is to say, "interconnected" horizontally characterized by communality and mutual dependence. By citing real cases drawn from these myriad documents, she brings to life the impressive range of economic activities Muslim women engaged in, continuing a tradition that extends back to the early formative period of Islam and to the pre-Islamic period. Based on her valuable study, Sonbol observes that the "diversity of financial transactions that women were involved in, as registered in premodern courts, shows how integral women were to the economies of their communities and families," and notes that such economic participation was even considered normative.

The following section is titled "Women's Lived Realities and Their Religious and Social Activism in the Modern Period," In chapter 15, Marion Katz provides a notable intervention in academic debates about how to assess the significance of women's increased mosque participation in the modern period in terms of agency and access to "public" space. Saba Mahmood's highly influential work *Politics of Piety: The Islamic Revival and the Feminist Subject*, published in 2005, in many ways set the terms for these academic conversations. To a large extent, these conversations have been shaped by Mahmood's analysis of women's mosque movements as largely counterhegemonic, especially in their efforts to expand women's religious authority, despite the conservative gender ideology to which many of these women subscribe. This leads Katz to fruitfully interrogate the "public–private dichotomy" and the traditional framing of the mosque as "public space." Her research leads her to conclude that "women's use of mosque space has not historically conformed to the model of "public" religious activity" and "that women's religious activities inside and outside of the mosque do not fit a simple public/private dichotomy." This observation leads to further reflection on how the mosque in the contemporary period is increasingly becoming a site for debates about citizenship and reconceptualized as an arm of the state, all of which affect women's access to the mosque in different sociopolitical contexts.

Chapter 16 focuses on motherhood and mothering in modern Muslim-majority societies. As the author Margaret Aziza Pappano observes, these terms refer to a constellation of "multiple meanings, social formations, and diversity of practices" that has global and transhistorical resonance. While motherhood is ostensibly revered in practically every society, its importance is more often than not obscured within patriarchal institutions and cultural mores, she says. Pappano notes that although the Qur'ān and the *ḥadīth* exalt the status of mothers above that of fathers without implying that childbearing was the primary function of women, Islamic patriarchal societies, as they evolved since the seventh century of the common era, came to depict motherhood as essential to a woman's identity and position in society. This tendency appears to have intensified in the modern period. Pappano surveys certain modern Muslim-majority countries and notes that women in such societies are often marginalized and stigmatized if they do not bear children. A complicating factor that arose in the modern period was that motherhood and "motherwork" became implicated in issues of nationalism and mobilized as a tactic of resistance to European colonialism in the nineteenth and twentieth centuries. In the more recent period, the role of Muslim mothers has become the object of sharp scrutiny in the context of the rise of religiopolitical radicalism in many Muslim-majority societies and in the so-called War on Terror launched by Western governments.

In her highly informative study of Muslim women heads-of-state in chapter 17, Tamara Sonn identifies several such rulers, who, varyingly, cite their religious background and/or commitments as a source of political empowerment. They include Qudsia or Gohar Begum, Sikander, Shah Jahan, Sultan Jahan Begum, all of Bhopal, India; Benazir Bhutto of Pakistan; Khaleda Zia and Sheikh Hasina of Bangladesh, Megawati Sukarnoputri of

Indonesia; Tansu Çiller of Turkey; and Sibel Siber of the Republic of Northern Cyprus. Sonn discusses how these influential women leaders, when acceding to power, made concerted efforts in their different milieux to improve the situation of women in general. With the exception of Çiller, they referred to Islam as empowering them to work for social and political justice, and especially in the postcolonial period, to work to establish democracy in their respective societies. Bhutto is notable in having left behind publications in which she strongly asserts the congruence between foundational Islamic principles and the establishment of democratic, civil societies that guarantee the rights of women and of all citizens equally. Sonn concludes by observing that the women heads-of-state she focused on, in general, did not regard their positions as anomalous; rather they considered themselves as continuing the legacy of exercising multiple roles of leadership as evident in the lives of the first generation of prominent Muslim women.

In the next chapter, Elizabeth Brownson provides a masterly survey of how women in Palestine, Lebanon, and Syria derive empowerment and agency from their religious and social activism in these specific milieux. She reminds us that social, economic, historical, and political factors specific to a particular context must always be taken into consideration when conducting a survey of this sort. This allows her to reveal the complexities inherent in the lives of the women she studied in these three different locales and the ways in which they do not map neatly onto preconceived notions of empowerment and agency. For example, the Hamas women leaders Brownson studied in Palestine proved to be quite effective in parlaying their political appointments into opportunities for seeking better access to education and employment for all women, often using religious arguments to make their case. Their situation, Brownson argues, challenges the assumptions of some enthocentric Western observers that women who wear the hijab and practice gender segregation are automatically to be regarded as disenfranchised. Careful attention to facts on the ground and nuances in details also allows Brownson to revisit an assumed ready tension between Islamist and secular women activists. Her research brings to light instead some common ground between these two groups on key issues like work, education, and political participation, although different conceptualizations of human rights continue to be a source of disagreement.

In chapter 19, Nermin Allam provides an account of women's religious and social activism in Egypt and, more broadly, North Africa, and makes the critical point that the range of women's activism in this region challenges an assumed bifurcation between the secular and religious realms, on the one hand, and between the social and political, on the other. This is to be expected, she affirms, since these women are from different socioeconomic backgrounds and have differential access to key resources and positions of power. Moreover, whether such activism is fueled by Islamic volunteerism or not, women's public engagement challenges preconceived notions of agency and self-empowerment current in the West. Despite such complexities inherent in their lived realities, Allam is nevertheless able to identify some common themes and patterns that marked women's social and religious activism, including the rise of a Qur'ān-based Islamic feminism, and shaped its trajectory specifically in Egypt, reflecting broader trends in North Africa. These themes include the framing of women's social and religious activities, particularly in the early period; the frequent overlap in the intellectual roots of secular and Islamic discourses; and a tendency toward what Islah Jad has termed "NGO-ization:" that is to say, the tendency to form nongovernmental organizations, whose track record over the years has at best been mixed.

Seema Golestaneh's chapter on women's activism in Iran since the nineteenth century provides a vivid and detailed description of the different trajectories these modes of activism have assumed over the years in changing sociopolitical circumstances. She surveys the intellectual histories and ethnographies of Iranian women's religious and political engagements and rehearses some of the key debates in the field regarding the origins and nature of such engagements. In the course of her extensive literature review, she delves into writings generated by women activists themselves, retrieved from influential periodicals, such as *Zanān* and others, and surveys as well the secondary literature that studies such activism. The policing of women's apparel, as apparent in the various unveiling/veiling measures adopted under different governments, is explored to reveal how women learn to navigate these sartorial restrictions. Golestan further questions the efficacy of "unfortunate binaries, pitting 'feminist' against 'Islamic fundamentalism' or 'Islamists' against 'secularists,'" noting that the scholarly trend now is "to document the ways in which women, of varying personal pieties, have used religious discourses in order to influence legislation and issues they view as favorable to women." As a result, religious and secular feminists have formed alliances to promote cooperation on shared concerns and more effectively campaign for legislative reform, leading to what some have called "the secularization of Islam."

In chapter 21, Chiara Maritato explores the changes that have occurred in the last three decades in women's movements in Turkey, a key site for women's activism in the MENA region. Her study is based on ethnographic research that she conducted there between 2013 and 2019, which focused on the Islamist women who were employed as religious officers by the Presidency of Religious Affairs (Diyanet) after the repeal of the headscarf ban by the AKP government. Maritato adopts a perspective "that considers women's religious activism beyond the feminism–antifeminism dichotomy," making it possible to shed light on different forms of women's agency. She discovered that while most of the women employed by the Diyanet had been politically and religiously active against previous governments, their activism became attenuated after attaining their Diyanet positions, and they largely became transformed into compliant bureaucrats under the AKP. More critical voices emanating from Muslim and secular feminists have become marginalized since 2010 and has contributed to a more "religious-conservative gender climate," in which the historic cooperation between these two groups has become diluted.

Elora Shehabuddin's chapter highlights the religious activism of women in Pakistan and Bangladesh, two populous Muslim-majority countries in South Asia. Shehabuddin focuses on their membership in two important Islamic pietist organizations—the Tabligh-i Jamaat (TJ) and the Jamaat-i Islami (JI), which established a women's wing known as the Halq-e Khawateen. Interestingly, as she notes, the TJ has eroded certain markers of gendered behavioral differences between women and men by emphasizing moral virtues, such as humility and modesty, equally for women and men. Both are equally called to engage in proselytizing activity and both are expected to contribute to domestic chores, like cooking, etc., raising alarm among some that young men are being feminized. Like the TJ women, the JI women also participate in proselytization; however, at the same time, they are guided by the vision of Abu al-Ala Mawdudi, the founder of the JI, that a woman's primary realm of activity was her home. Nevertheless, with rising rates of literacy and, especially for the JI, increased focus on gaining political leverage, these religious women have also mobilized themselves on college and university campuses and often run for political office and parliamentary seats. Despite these tangible gains and the acquisition of skills in social activism and political organization, Shehabuddin notes that these women have not inaugurated movements that can be considered progressive and ultimately, they have "supported policies and laws that discriminate against [other] women" who do not dress or observe the same practices as they do.

In chapter 23, dealing with Muslim women's activism in Southeast Asia, Nelly van Doorn-Harder focuses on Indonesia and Malaysia, two of the largest Muslim-majority countries today, which are the sites of robust women's engagement with the key social and political concerns of the day. Many of these women activists are avid participants in religious discourses that contest classical interpretations of key Qurʾānic verses and of relevant *ḥadīth* concerning women and the family that have been deployed to restrict women's rights. They frequently join NGO's, like the women's wings of the influential Muhammadiyah and Nahdlatul Ulama groups in Indonesia. There are also women-led NGOs, like Sisters in Islam, and its successor organization Musawah in Malaysia, that have gained national and international recognition for their concerted efforts to challenge discriminatory laws against women through scriptural hermeneutics. In a Muslim-minority context in the Philippines, Muslim women activists are similarly campaigning for social and legal change, employing many of the same hermeneutical tools and reformist rhetoric as their counterparts in Indonesia and Malaysia, and establishing NGOs like the Philippine Center for Islam and Democracy. In each of these contexts, as Van Doorn-Harder points out, "vibrant groups advocating for the rights of Muslim women are creating new models and repertoires of Muslim feminism."

It has long been known that there has been a proud tradition of female imams and female-led mosques in China for almost 300 years. Maria Jaschok's and Man Ke's well-researched and timely chapter reminds the reader of this proud tradition of Muslim women's contributions to Islam in China, especially among the Hui people. But they rightly caution us that in order to retrieve instances of women's empowerment, we should focus on not only organized campaigns and movements geared toward this end but also women's quotidian activities that create new social opportunities and forms of social interaction that "expand their presence in the public space." Living as a religious minority in an often hostile sociopolitical milieu (the current dire predicament of the Uighur Chinese readily come to mind), Chinese Muslim women's access to the public sphere and their potential activism are, as the authors remind us, "inscribed by gender, culture, time, and place." They express concern that in our desire to find overt manifestations of religious and social activism in a perilous environment, we may overlook activities that are more pragmatically geared toward existential well-being and communal solidarity. Such activities illustrate the importance of the concept of *bande* among Muslim women, "which means taking responsibility for socializing, constructing and maintaining interpersonal relationships," that allow for "the first building-blocks of civil society" to be introduced into their world and thereby "foster local and translocal social/religious networks." Ultimately, Jaschok and Ke remind us that change does not always come through organized radical movements, but often through individual and group activities that more modestly and incrementally create greater access to public and social goods, especially in less than congenial, if not downright dangerous, circumstances that have to be carefully navigated.

In chapter 25, Nina Hoel describes Muslim women's activism in South Africa as constituting a "rich and composite terrain." In covering this terrain, Hoel presents three case studies that illustrate the nexus of "theoretical issues and strategies prevalent in the South African context."' They are: women in the mosque; the struggle to establish a Muslim personal law; and the negotiation of queerness in the Muslim context, presenting examples from the activism of the organization The Inner Circle. Experience, intersectionality, and the *tafsīr* of praxis, a phrase introduced by the South African scholar Sa'diyya Shaikh, are three theoretical concepts that render Muslim women's activism in the South African context distinctive, observes Hoel. A careful analysis of the South African landscape through these lens allows the author to reveal the complex ways in which religion, law, the state, individuals, and organizational actors interact with one another and contribute to the distinctiveness of South African Muslim women's activism.

In the next chapter, Juliane Hammer outlines four theoretical considerations that undergird her survey of Muslim women's activism in the United States: the relationship between Islam and feminism; the effect of anti-Muslim hostility on activism and the scholarly literature on it; the relationship between practice and discourse; and the extension of the purview of women's activism well beyond that of "women's issues." She applies these considerations to her study of various movements, organizations, and individuals that are prominent in the American Muslim community in order to allow for their particularities embedded in their sociohistorical context to emerge and to reveal the diversity of their approaches to a wide gamut of issues, such as grassroots community-building, women's education, sexual violence, mosque participation, and racial and religious discrimination. At the same time, Hammer is able to identify broader patterns of responses to the challenges Muslims face in the larger American society and the networks of cooperation and solidarity that have developed among a number of these organizations and individuals, both in national and international contexts.

In chapter 27, Jeannette Jouili discusses how Muslim women's activism has evolved in Europe since the second half of the twentieth century and examines four principal kinds of such activism: (1) activism that focuses on empowering women within Muslim communities and within the broader societies, (2) religious activism within Islamic communities and institutions, (3) activism centered on religious minority rights and gaining public recognition, and (4) activism on larger social and political issues. In the course of pursuing such activisms, Muslim women face considerable challenges both from within their own communities and from the larger, frequently hostile, non-Muslim society they inhabit. Given the variegated sociopolitical and economic contexts in which they operate, their agendas and methods of negotiating specific challenges vary quite a bit, especially in "response to the political discourses constructed about them in their respective societies." One activity common to these women is their constant battle against the cultural and religious stereotypes of Muslims, and of Muslim women in particular, that are endemic in the larger society, reinforced by the "hegemonic structure of the 'liberal grammar' within debates on European Islam"—all of which prevent them from enjoying the full benefits of citizenship.

Alainna Liloia is among a handful of specialists today who study women's religious and social activism in Saudi Arabia and the Gulf region. In her chapter, she reveals how standard stereotypes concerning the relationship between religion, secularism, and women's feminist consciousness are challenged by research like hers that probe the complex relationship between these variables, as evident in the lives of Saudi and Gulf women. Liloia particularly draws attention to the "intersection of political agendas, religious expectations, and social pressures [that] have impacted women in the Gulf and shaped their subjectivities and identities in different ways." As a consequence, women express their agency in different ways through their level of engagement with the various educational, political, religious, and social institutions that impact their lives. Specific state initiatives and agendas directly affect their attempts to achieve social and political equality with men. Through her insightful analysis, Liloia reminds that women's activism can be gauged not only through their participation in public organized campaigns that focus, for example, on the right to drive in Saudi Arabia, but also in the myriad ways they negotiate, challenge, and resist mundane social and political norms that impact their daily lives.

Chapter 29 is the first of two chapters in the fifth section, titled "Modern Narratives of the Gendered Self: Women Writing about Women." In this chapter, Ruqayya Y. Khan examines modern portrayals of the Wives of Muḥammad, particularly by women authors, against the backdrop of Muslim reverence for "the Mothers of the Believers" on the one hand, and Western polemics against Islam and its prophet, on the other. As Khan explains, much of early Islamic history cannot be fully understood unless we study the lives of the Prophet's wives (Wives) as well, who, by virtue of who they were, were witnesses to all the major events in Muḥammad's life and became key transmitters of his sayings (*ḥadīth*) that assumed normative status for subsequent generations of Muslims. Studying the lives of the Wives as Wives (rather than as "Mothers of the Believers") also humanizes Muḥammad and allows for a more honest and critical appraisal of his legacy to emerge, she says. Khan stresses the need to go beyond the traditional focus on Khadīja and 'Ā'isha, who are the best-known among the Prophet's wives, and pleads for "a freshness in approaches and methods to the study and examination of the Wives," in order to dismantle "the tried and typical approaches." She provides a helpful review of primary sources and secondary scholarship on the topic and suggests that new studies employing innovative approaches to the sources be undertaken "that can highlight the egalitarian undertones in the history and the biographical corpus of these prominent Muslim female figures."

In her chapter, miriam cooke surveys various forms of literature—specifically novels, short stories, memoirs, and poems—produced by Arab, Iranian, and American Muslim women authors in which they highlight the gendered inequalities that they are subjected to in their respective societies. She traces the rise of this genre of feminist writing to the early twentieth century, when the Arabic word *nisā'iyya* began to circulate to refer to this woman-centered consciousness. The term "feminism" itself, however, had the stigma of being attached to the kind of colonial feminism being promoted by European imperialists, cooke notes; in this shadow, Muslim reformers, men at first starting in the nineteenth century and joined by women in the next century, struggled to mount a campaign to root out discriminatory practices against women. In her survey of Muslim women's feminist writings, she focuses on five themes that recur in such literature and that evidences resistance to the following: (1) a *ḥadīth* that claims that women are lacking in reason (*'aql*); (2) another *ḥadīth* that claims that women's voice is pudendal (*'awra*) and should not be heard in public; (3) imposition of the veil (without maligning women who adopt the practice); (4) the creation of patriarchal societies; and (5) the exclusion of women from ritual spaces. Cooke documents the way these women writers have proceeded to engage with these themes, providing evocative examples from their work to illustrate the eloquence and poignancy of their protest against patriarchy and against the suppression of their rights in the name of religion.

The sixth and final section of the *Handbook* is titled "Islam, Women, and the Global Public Arena." There is no doubt that if there is one single issue connected with Muslim women that frequently exercises the collective Western imaginary in the modern period and leaves its imprint on the global public sphere, it is the *ḥijāb* or headscarf. Muslim women's sartorial choices and their intense politicization in the contemporary period is therefore, appropriately, the focus of the penultimate chapter (chapter 31) by Anna Piela. To do justice to this broad topic, Piela focuses on four distinctive historical periods when this process of politicization starts to become apparent: the early twentieth century; the last two decades of the twentieth century; the decade immediately following the September 11 attacks; and the decade following the 2010 Belgian burqa ban. Through her investigation of these four critical periods, Piela allows us to see how women's sartorial choices became considered an essential "signifier of modern nation-making" after a specific "discourse of the veil" emerged by the late nineteenth century during the period of European colonial occupation of a broad swath of the Muslim-majority world. This obsession with the veil provided "the lens through which developments in global politics could be interpreted and understood," as she remarks. The headscarf—"ostensibly a piece of cloth"—became anything but; indeed, it has become *the* lightning rod in heated global debates about Muslim women's agency, national identity, and broader issues of cultural/civilizational compatibility. These debates took a more sinister and grave turn during the launching of the "War on Terror" under the George W. Bush presidency, when Muslim women's bodies became commandeered by Western cultural warriors in order to reshape the Middle East and "reform" Islam, as they imagined it. In this scenario, these culture warriors pitted a reified West against a reified Islamic world that are deemed to be utterly incompatible in terms of their religious values, cultural norms, and, above all, treatment of women. It is a discourse that has been launched to justify military intervention in the Muslim-majority world and to cast a moral veneer on otherwise morally indefensible actions. Piela provides a compelling account of how Muslim women's bodies are appropriated to stage these global culture wars and to justify the use of lethal force against the societies they inhabit.

The final chapter, by Katherine Bullock, provides a fitting continuation of and closure to some of the themes foregrounded by Piela. Like Piela, Bullock provides an eloquent and jarringly blunt portrayal of how Muslim women and their lives have been weaponized on the global stage as part of what many continue to consider to be a "clash of civilizations." The veiled Muslim female becomes the convenient straw-woman for these ideologues in their construction of destructive binaries that are meant to dehumanize Muslims *qua* Muslims and to question the very legitimacy of their presence in the West. This fear and hatred of Muslims—Islamophobia—gains oxygen by specifically targeting Muslim women and playing up their assumed "victimhood" in order to create a contrast to "liberated" non-Muslim Western women as a mark of the "civilized" West. Particularly in the United States and western Europe, the post–September 11 period has seen the emergence of a specific kind of "culture talk" that uses Muslim women, especially those who wear headscarves, as a trope to highlight a fundamental cultural divide. Much of this mentality and usage of this trope can be traced back to the entrenchment of Orientalism during the European colonial period. Bullock adroitly traces this genealogy to reveal how deeply ensconced this kind of "culture talk" has become in many parts of the North Atlantic region and how it colors the depictions of Muslim women as monolithic figures who are to be constantly pitied. The chapter dissects these multiple discourses in order to understand how they are deployed for specific political and military projects in the contemporary world, often with the active connivance of Western feminists.

* * *

These chapters in the aggregate, therefore, provide much material for deep reflection when contemplating the broad topic of "Islam and Women." Neither "Islam" nor "women" proves to be a predictable and monothetic category. The chapters make clear that each has to be parsed with careful attention to the various contexts in which these terms are used at a given time and locale. The various analytic lens adopted to study this topic generates different ways of engaging it. No single volume can do justice when attempting to capture these polysemies. But the chapters together tell us much about the impact of Islam in all its facets—as a mode of worship; as a constellation of beliefs about the human relationship to God; as a set of distinctive practices that creates a confessional community; and above all, as a discursive tradition that grows, changes, and adapts to changing human conditions—on the lives of Muslim women who inhabit practically every corner of the globe. What I hope the reader will ultimately take away from these chapters is the conviction that Muslim women have been involved in the shaping of the Islamic tradition from its very inception in the seventh century of the common era until today. Only by reinstating their experiences, contributions, and perspectives as an integral part of this tradition can we begin to claim to fully understand it.

B

FOUNDATIONAL TEXTS AND THEIR INTERPRETATIONS

THE first part of this section focuses on foundational religious texts within Islam and the portrayal of women and their roles in them. These foundational texts are the Qurʾān, believed by Muslims to be an exact transcript of the divine revelations received by the Prophet Muḥammad in the first/seventh century in the Arabian peninsula, and the *ḥadīth* literature, which records the sayings of the Prophet as attributed to him by his close associates, known collectively as the Companions (the *Ṣaḥāba* in Arabic). The *ḥadīth* is part of the *sunna* or the overall practices and customs of Muḥammad for which he expressed either explicit or tacit approval. As the very word of God, the Qurʾān takes precedence over the *ḥadīth* in matters of faith and worship and in the derivation of law and ethics, while the latter is considered to be necessary for explaining the meaning and intent of the former. The *ḥadīth* is also essential for legislation and the ordering of the daily lives of Muslims.

The second part of this section deals with the interpretations of these foundational texts that have seminally shaped women's lives, even as women have been historically excluded from formally engaging in such hermeneutic activity, especially in the classical and postclassical periods of Islam (from the third/ninth century onward). The discussion of the variegated historical contexts that shaped the interpretations of the Qurʾān by male exegetes is a key component of this section. No text, after all, is interpreted in a historical vacuum. The vast commentary literature on the Qurʾān (*tafsīr*) is a highly valuable source for reconstructing the shifting interpretive landscape as it pertains to women from the first century of Islam (seventh century of the common era) until the modern period.

The same is true for the voluminous *ḥadīth* corpus containing prophetic reports that deal with women's religious, social, and legal issues. These reports are of varying degrees of reliability, according to the standards developed by the premodern *ḥadīth* scholars;

those reports deemed to be "sound" (*Ṣaḥīḥ*) are regarded as normative and held to be second in status only to the Qurʾān for the purposes of deriving moral and ethical precepts and for drawing up legal regulations.

The modern phenomenon of women playing a key role in the interpretation of these foundational texts and their revisitation of traditional male exegeses and scholarship in general are highlighted in this chapter. Such women exegetes are extrapolating a much more egalitarian and women-friendly message from the Qurʾān in particular that mounts a clear challenge to the hierarchical and androcentric perspectives that inform the commentaries of the premodern male exegetes. Such hermeneutic activities have launched what has become known as "Islamic feminism" in Western academic circles. Many of these Muslim feminists and gender scholars are also rereading the *ḥadīth* literature through a sharp critical lens. They home in on specific reports that convey misogynistic perceptions and mandate discriminatory practices toward women and are subjecting the reliability of such reports to critical reappraisals. The potentially revolutionary consequences of such feminist/womanist perspectives and analyses and what they may portend for the future are indicated in this section.

CHAPTER 1

THE QUR'ĀN AND WOMAN

HIBBA ABUGIDEIRI*

THE gender contestations revolving around the Qur'ān would not weigh so heavily if not for the Muslim belief in the Qur'ān's divine provenance. The Qur'ān, God's Word revealed to Muḥammad, teaches the believers the doctrine of its own nature.[1] This includes the belief in the Qur'ān as God's literal Word as revealed verbatim and seriatim to Muḥammad, the Seal of the Prophets, and that the Qur'ān is God's final message to the world, and thus a guidance for humankind.[2] As the embodiment of Divine Discourse, the Qur'ān is "inimitable, inviolate, inerrant, and incontrovertible."[3] Yet its divine nature is at the heart of the problem. The apparent disparities in how the Qur'ān scripturally treats woman in contrast to man not only loom large but also raise fundamental questions, if not serious doubt, about the Qur'ān's transcendental claims of divine justice. Similar to the other Abrahamic scriptures of the Old and New Testament, no issue has plagued the Qur'ān's scriptural standing with such persistence and intensity more than the question of woman.

As an exercise in self-reflexive criticality and in the spirit of scholarly debate pursuant of Islamic social justice and specifically gender justice, this chapter explores the Qur'ān's textual references to certain women figures who populate the many stories of the Qur'ān, including Eve, Mary, Bilqīs, Zulaykha, the wife of ʿAzīz (who is identified with the biblical Potiphar, the Pharaoh's viceroy), and the women surrounding the lives of Abraham, Moses, Noah, Lot, and Muḥammad. This reading, however, focuses solely on Mary, Bilqīs, and Zulaykha, arguably three of the most powerful female figures in the Qur'ān. The first two have proven elusive and difficult for premodern exegetes to "paradigmatize," while Zulaykha has been made the Qur'ān's archetypal "femme fatale." Their signification is also underdeveloped and undertheorized within modernist and particularly feminist exegeses.

This commentary (*tafsīr*) situates its interpretation of verses regarding these three women within a broader God–human relationship and therefore adopts a *tawḥīdic* paradigmatic approach. The "*tawḥīdic* paradigm" is the interpretive approach of choice for feminist exegetes as a basis for desacralizing male supremacy. Based on this approach made famous by amina wadud[4] and Asma Barlas,[5] this *tafsīr* proceeds to interpret the

Qur'ān as Divine Discourse that must, by its own logic, reflect God's Self Disclosure, starting with *tawḥīd* (unicity).

> *Tawhid* relates to the transcendent and yet eminent divinity or ultimate reality, the "unicity" of Allah. Allah is not only one and unique, Allah is uniform, and unites existing multiplicities or seeming dualities in both the corporeal and the metaphysical realm. . . . Because of *tawhid*, Islam exists along the lines of the irrefutable and unconditional notion of Allah's oneness. . . . That which emanates from Allah participates in this unity.[6]

Reading through the prism of *tawḥīd* demonstrates an undifferentiated spirituality within the Qur'ānic text that endows women with the same moral capacity as men. *Tawḥīd* signifies a "multiplicity in unity, meaning that all principles (masculine or feminine) are interconnected in the totality of God's Being."[7] This understanding of *tawḥīd* enables a contingency between woman and man as ontologically relational and inextricably equal, characterized not by duality, which implies exclusion, separateness, and closedness, but rather by polarity, characterized by interconnectedness, interdependence, openness, mutuality, indeterminateness, complementarity, correlativity, coexistensiveness—"a world in which continuous foci are intrinsically related to each other."[8] Woman and man, then, do not embody mutually exclusive or opposite attributes; rather, they incorporate both masculine and feminine attributes; "each manifests the whole."[9]

Also critical to this *tawḥīdic* approach is a broadening of the limited imaginary of a transcendent God, which abounds in *tafsīr*, to also emphasize God's immanence. As rightly argued by Sa'diyya Shaikh, patriarchal notions of a transcendent God sustained through the "discriminatory structures and values embedded within texts emerging from an exclusively male experiential reality," can be destabilized by resuscitating images of God's immanence. We thereby restore balance and inclusivity to the divine symbolic economy and authenticate female and male subjectivities through God's intimacy with humanity, women and men.[10] This view of *tawḥīd* guides how the God–human relationship is applied to this reading of Mary, Bilqīs, and Zulaykha, and allows us to see how woman in her ontological contingency with man operates at different levels of the text.

Woman in and through the Qur'ān

The stories of the Qur'ān's female figures offer lessons of women's undifferentiated spirituality to highlight the precept the Qur'ān is teaching its reader (or listener); "they are non-gender specific examples . . . of the individual responsibility towards belief."[11] Stopping there, however, limits woman's signification to Qur'ānic moral instruction and overlooks its engagement of woman and the feminine at other levels of the text.[12] In addition to being "ungendered," these women's signification is also *gendered* in the sense that they illuminate the necessity of woman and the feminine in the Qur'ān, meaning at the scriptural level, and through the Qur'ān, meaning at the metaphysical level of meaning, and therefore and ultimately to the Qur'ān. Put differently, we see woman *in* the Qur'ān, but we can also see her *through* the Qur'ān, but always in a contingent relationality with man as ontologically equal parts (4:1; 2:187; 30:21; 3:195; 4:124; 9:71; 33:35; etc.). Let us start, not with the allegorical figure of Eve, but with Mary.

Mary (Maryam) and Abraham (Ibrāhīm)

Mary, the only female identified by name in the Qur'ān and to have an entire chapter named after her, is the celebrated mother of Jesus who is mentioned more frequently in the Qur'ān than in the entire New Testament.[13] Collectively all of the revelations about Mary, according to the *tafsīr* literature, serve as both divine clarification of the true nature of Jesus and Mary and another sign of God's Oneness and Omnipotence. Interestingly, Mary's problematic "Islamic paradigmatization" for premodern exegetes rests in deciding which facets of her model status are suited for emulation by Muslim women.[14]

Reduced to a female archetype for only Muslim women, Mary's Qur'ānic signification is wholly missed. Yet the story of Mary is best compared—not to Eve, the Pharoah's (unnamed) wife, Khadīja and ʿĀʾisha (wives of Muḥammad), or Faṭima (daughter of Muḥammad) as found in the *ḥadīth* literature, or Zacharia, Mary's guardian and whose Qur'ānic story is intertwined with hers, as found in Qur'ānic *tafsīr*[15]—but rather to Abraham. In fact, their stories bear such resemblance by the most critical scriptural markers as to render Mary a prophet.

First, both Mary and Abraham, each after whom a chapter is named, are the only two figures to whom the adjective *qānitīn* (complete obedience to God) is ascribed by name, rather than as a quality of the faithful more broadly. The second half of Qur'ān 66:12 reads: "And [Mary] put faith in the words of her Lord and His scriptures, and was of the obedient" (*qānitīn*, in the masculine plural form).[16] Rightly pointed out by wadud, "there is no reason not to use the feminine plural form—except to emphasize that the significance of Mary's example is for all who believe."[17] But it also suggests that Mary stands in mixed company in the text. "Verily, Abraham was a man who combined within himself all virtues, devoutly obeying God's will, turning away from all that is false and not being of those who ascribe divinity to aught beside God" (16:120). The Arabic root, *qanata*, means full and complete obedience to God alone. Mary and Abraham are bestowed this exclusive distinction in parallel stories that ultimately stress *tawḥīd* and their absolute devotion and obedience to God, arguably the most central dimension of the God-human relationship.

Second, both go into seclusion. Mary "withdrew from her family to an eastern place and kept herself in seclusion from them" (19:16–17), whereas Abraham, after confronting his father and people about their polytheistic beliefs to no avail, leaves his homeland: "And [Abraham] said: 'Verily, I shall (leave this land and) go wherever my Sustainer will guide me!'" (37:99). Third, following their respective seclusion, both are visited by, not one angel which typifies prophethood, but multiple angels. For Mary, not all of these visits were an annunciation. For example, Mary is visited by a group of angels arguably to announce her prophetic appointment: "And lo! The angels said: 'O Mary! Behold, God has elected thee (*iṣṭafāki*) and made thee pure (*ṭahharaki*), and raised thee (*waṣṭafāki*) above all women in all of creation'" (3:42).[18] Interestingly, prophets are divinely chosen (*iṣṭafā*)—"God chooses (*yaṣṭafī*) message-bearers from among the angels as well as from among people" (*min al-nās*, not "from men" as this is typically translated, 22:75). The translation "chosen" and "to choose" here are inadequate; *iṣṭafā* denotes being chosen and given a special rank or status due to one's devotion and exemplary behavior. This meaning better reflects the honorific nature of this distinction in light of being completely devoted (*qānitīn*) to God.

The remaining visits relate to the annunciation, in Qur'ān 19:17 by a single angel and a group of angels in Qur'ān 3:45: "Lo! The angels said: 'O Mary! Behold, God sends thee the glad tiding, through a word from Him, [of a son] who shall become known as the Christ Jesus.'" Abraham too received angelic guests: "There came unto Abraham Our [heavenly] messengers, bearing a glad tiding. They bade him peace; [and] he answered, '[And upon you be] peace!'" (11:69). Zacharia (19:7) and Lot (11:81; 15:61) were also visited by multiple angels. To put this distinction into perspective, the Qur'ān mentions the honor of receiving visits from multiple angels at once as a reward for the faithful in the Hereafter: "And the angels will come unto them from every gate [and will say]: 'Peace be upon you, because you have persevered!'" (13:23–24). Only prophets receive angels on earth.

There are two noteworthy points before proceeding. Mary is chosen not once, but twice in Qur'ān 3:42: the first time confirms her rank among other chosen prophets and the second grants her an absolute rank above "all women in all of creation." This distinction works in concert with three others: Mary's consecration, her purification, and the Divine spirit (*rūḥ*) breathed into her. First, Mary was born to Ḥanna, "a woman of 'Imrān,"[19] thus a prestigious priestly family who, due to her own devout piety, dedicated her unborn child—thought to be male and described as *muḥarrar*, or "freed from all world affairs"—to God's service (3:35). When the child was born female, to Ḥanna's surprise, God, knowing the child was female ("God had been fully aware of what she would give birth to."), honored Ḥanna's prayer and "accepted the girl-child with goodly acceptance, and caused her to grow up in goodly growth" (3:36–37). This is in contrast to the Jewish tradition that maintains that only dedicated sons could be consecrated to the service of the sanctuary.[20] Furthermore, despite the fact that the status of *muḥarrar* was reserved for boys alone, God chose a girl and granted her a highly coveted religious distinction typically accorded to only the select males of the time.[21] It could also be read as a foreshadowing of and preparation for Mary's appointment to another exclusively male distinction: prophethood.

Second, the Arabic root, *ṭahara*, to purify, is only used in the Qur'ān to describe Mary and Jesus by name.[22] To understand this status, we find clues in its usage elsewhere in the text: it is the state of people in heaven (2:25), it is a state loved by God (2:222), and it is an aspirational state by "men desirous of growing in purity" who stand forth in prayer in the mosque (9:108). Jesus but more notably Mary had *already* reached this state, as indicated by the use of the past tense of *ṭahara*. Therefore, and uncoincidentally, Mary and Jesus are the only two people to be "a Sign for all of creation" (*āya lil ʿālamīn*, 21:91). Yet her distinction rests in being the only person purified while living; Jesus is to be purified in the future (3:55). This purification occurs in preparation for the divine *rūḥ* or "spirit" (21:91; 66:12): "Mary, the daughter of ʿImrān, who guarded her chastity, whereupon We breathed of Our spirit into that [which was in her womb]" (*farjiha*, 66:12). What could be more majestic and immanent than the moment when God blows His Spirit into Mary's most intimate part (*farjiha*, literally crack or split, which carries a more consistent meaning when applied to its references to the sky in Qur'ān 50:6 and 77:9). The Qur'ān recognizes this miraculous moment in only one other instance, namely with Adam: "Then He forms [Adam] in accordance with what he is meant to be, and breathes into him of His spirit" (32:9)—a verse that when read, requires prostration (*sajda*), similar to the angels' prostration to Adam by divine decree after Adam was created (Qur'ān 15:29; 38:72). The gender symmetry here is stunning: God breathes His Spirit into Mary and Adam at different moments that similarly invoke His Majesty and Mercy as a way of deepening the connection between God and humanity, female and male. Thus, Mary's distinctions parallel those of other prophets, here Jesus and Adam.

Fifth, and more notably, is the miraculous birth preceded by "glad tidings." Striking is how the miracle surrounding the conception of Jesus and Jacob, respectively, shares a similar narrative structure. Mary and Abraham's wife are each visited by an angel that gives "glad tidings" of a son; each questions the possibility of a birth given their different states: Mary defends her chastity as "no man has ever touched [her]" while Abraham's wife claims their old age; and finally, both are told that their conception is a matter of divine decree (Qur'ān 19:19–21 and Qur'ān 11:71–73, respectively).

Sixth, Mary and Abraham are each "gifted" (*wahaba*) a son who would become a prophet, but not without undergoing great trials to complete their divine mission. We see their humanity in full display in two stunningly emotional scenes, narrated at length to draw in and deepen the reader's connection to God:

> So she conceived [Jesus] and she retired with him to a remote place. And the pains of childbirth drove her to the trunk of a palm tree. She cried (in her anguish): "Ah! Would that I had died before this! Would that I had been a thing forgotten and out of sight!" But (a voice) cried to her from beneath (the palm tree): "Grieve not! For your Lord has provided a rivulet beneath you. And shake towards yourself the trunk of the palm tree. It will let fresh ripe dates fall upon you. So eat and drink and cool your eye." (19:22–26)

Mary, the chosen and most purified from "all women in all of creation," was left to suffer childbirth on her own, in isolation, with no human help. "She is like every other woman who bears a child," says wadud.[23] She also faced what must have been an insurmountable challenge of facing her people with a newborn, risking the disgrace of her priestly lineage to "the house of Aaron" (19:28). Yet, in both instances, God intervened and "consoled" her miraculously with food, water, and His Nearness ("Grieve not!"), as well as vindicated her through Jesus's miraculous speech from the cradle (19:30–33). Most notably, she received "the gift of a holy son" (19:19).

Similarly, in the same chapter as Mary's narrative (*Sūrat Maryam*), Abraham, in an exceptionally moving plea, beseeches his father to accept the one true God:

> "Oh my father! Why worship that which hears not nor sees, nor can it avail you anything? Oh my father! Do not serve the devil. The devil is a rebel to the Beneficent. Oh my father! I fear that a punishment from the Beneficent may overtake you so that you become a comrade of the devil." [His father] said: "Do you reject my gods, O Abraham! If you do not cease, I shall surely stone you. Depart from me a long while!" [Abraham] said: "Peace be to you! I shall ask forgiveness of my Lord for you. He was ever gracious to me. I shall withdraw from you and that to which you pray beside God, and I shall pray to my Lord. It may be that, in prayer to my Lord, I shall not be unblest." So, when he had withdrawn from them and what they were worshipping beside God, We gifted him Isaac and Jacob. Each of them We made a prophet. (19:42–49)

Interestingly, this story is narrated elsewhere in the Qur'ān (21:51–75) but does not evoke the same emotion since, as is typical of Qur'ānic narration, the same stories can operate differently in other parts of the text. Abraham, the only person that the Qur'ān refers to as *ḥanīf* (one who never deviates from the Truth, thus from monotheism, 3:67) and holds the distinction of being the "Father of the line of Semitic prophecy,"[24] is tried with the test of familial dissociation, only to be "gifted" (*wahaba*) a son and grandson: "We gave him (*wa wahabnā lahu*) Isaac and Jacob. . . . Thus do We reward those who do good" (6:84). Mary and Abraham are not the only two; other prophets too were "gifted" loved ones: Zacharia is given a son, John (21:90), and Moses his brother, Aaron (19:53). But it is Mary and Abraham, the only two identified by name as *qānitīn* in the Qur'ān, who are tested with the most intimate bond of parent and child and consequently "rewarded" with "the gift" of a prophetic son.

Importantly Mary and Abraham stand among other prophets who suffered—proof of their humanity—and then were consoled by God. This only strengthens the case for Mary's prophetic appointment. The Qur'ān captures their hardships as intimate moments made real and accessible to the reader by their rawness and humanness—a confirmation of God's immanence and nearness to His chosen servants, and, therefore, to the reader. In the chapter "The Prophets" (*Sūrat al-Anbiyā'*), using the same grammatical construction, the Qur'ān mentions "remembering" a prophet who "cried out to Us"—Noah (21:76), Job (21:83), Dhū al-Nūn, who "cried through the depths of darkness" (21:87), and Zacharia (21:89). In each instance God "helped him" (21:77), "listened to him" and "removed the distress" (21:84), "listened to him and delivered him from distress" (21:88), and "listened to him and We granted him (*wahabnā*) John (Yaḥyā)" (21:90). This list of prophets ends strikingly with Mary (21:91).

Directly after, God confirms their prophethood, which collectively brought a single message to form a single community—that must therefore include women and men—to worship a single God (*tawḥīd*): "Verily, this community of yours is one single community (*inna hādhihi ummatukum umma wāḥida*), since I am the Sustainer of you all, worship, then, Me [alone]!" (21:92). Also, throughout Sūrat Maryam, we see God's self-referential *al-Raḥmān* ("the Merciful One") used in verses to highlight His connection to His devoted servants, starting with Mary (19:18), Abraham (19:44–45), Moses (19:51), and culminating in the verse: "These were some of the prophets upon whom God bestowed His blessings. . . . Whenever the messages of the Most Gracious (*āyāt al-Raḥmān*) were conveyed unto them, they would fall down [before Him], prostrating themselves weeping" (19:58).

Based on the above Qur'ānic evidence, Mary is undeniably a prophet. Such a claim is not new, though it is radical. Classical Muslim theologians debated the issue, especially after it was championed by the Ẓāhirī school,[25] represented by Ibn Ḥazm of Cordoba (d. 456/1064), who argued in favor of Mary's prophethood, a doctrine that was ultimately rejected by consensus-based Sunnī theology and even labeled "heretical innovation."[26] However, the well-known medieval Shāfi'ī scholar Ibn Ḥajar (d. 852/1449) mentions in his *tafsīr* other Sunnī scholars who at different points argued for Mary's prophethood, including Abū Mūsa al-Ash'arī (d. ca. 42/662 or 52/672) and the Mālikī jurist al-Qurṭubī (d. 671/1273).[27] Ultimately, a consensus emerged that there were no women prophets.[28]

Yet, when using the Qur'ān and specifically its own criteria for prophethood to interpret Mary's signification, it is difficult to refute such a claim. She cannot simply be relegated to a female archetype (even then, this is problematic). Her many honorific distinctions make this implausible, and in fact place her at the highest levels of prophethood, "the elect, the truly good" (*al-muṣṭafayn al-akhyār*, 38:47), including Abraham—higher than those prophets at the level of "the truly good" (*al-akhyār*, 38:48). As such, God's confirmation of all the prophets, cited above, applies equally to Mary, in which case Muslims could make no distinction among God's chosen ones: "To those who believe in God and His Messengers and make no distinction between any of the messengers, We shall soon give their (due) reward; for God is Oft-Forgiving, Most Merciful" (4:152). Mary's prophethood, then, would not only make spiritual belief in God (*īmān*) contingent on her acceptance, it would reconfigure how we understand belief itself.

Bilqīs and Solomon (Sulaymān)

If Mary's signification offers us an ultimate spiritual model, Bilqīs, another powerful Qur'ānic figure, offers us an ultimate political model. Like Mary, Bilqīs's strong presence in the Qur'ān resists paradigmatization, but here because exegetes found her story to be obscure, since the notion of female political sovereignty lay outside of the accepted paradigm of women's societal status. She ably governed as a woman, according to the Qur'ānic account, and yet she was pagan. For this reason, of the Qur'ān's women figures, Bilqīs has remained the most elusive and enigmatic for Muslim exegetes to grasp. They were content with providing legendary materials for their interpretations without searching for the story's "applicability" or sociomoral lesson for Islamic society. Consequently, the Qur'ānic image of the queen of Sheba has on the whole been more productive in fanciful storytelling than scholarly *tafsīr*.[29]

Much is lost in her problematic paradigmatization. Bilqīs, the queen of a pagan sun-worshipping nation, offers a powerful lesson in ideal political leadership—a claim made ironic by exegetical interpretations of female political incompetence tied to a weak but popular *ḥadīth* ("a people who entrust their command to a woman will not thrive") attributed to Muḥammad "when Bilqīs was mentioned in his presence."[30] Unlike Mary, Bilqīs is never named in the Qur'ān; like other unnamed female figures in the Qur'ān, they are named in *tafsīr*. Unlike Mary's, Bilqīs's story is narrated in a series of verses, not across the Qur'ān, but in a single chapter (27:23–44). However, like Mary's, its meaning is grasped more fully when juxtaposed to a prophet, namely Solomon. His prophetic career "unfolded mainly in the arena of public life, where he became renowned for his wise and skillful administration of justice and also his God-given knowledge and powers."[31] The Qur'ān presents him as one who commanded the gift of diplomacy and great leadership: he was endowed by God with knowledge of the speech of animals (27:16, 19), the ability to rule the wind(s) and subdue "the evil ones" (*shayāṭīn*, 21:81–82; 38:36–37), and the power to employ jinn (34:12–13).[32] When Bilqīs's story is narrated, however, Solomon's powers form the backdrop against which we read her many gifts, which take center stage.

Though it is Solomon who has divinely inspired esoteric knowledge, the Qur'ān, through its narrative structure, builds up the character of Bilqīs, gradually unfolding her unrivaled powers of understanding as a political leader. There are four noteworthy moments in her story, each building on the previous one. First, after receiving Solomon's letter of invitation to Islam, Bilqīs is quoted as noticing the invocation, "In the name of God, Most Gracious, Most Merciful" (27:30), hinting at a level of awareness and perception that sets the scene. Wadud sees some indication of her perspective in her characterization of Solomon's letter as *karīm* (noble).[33]

Second, Bilqīs consults with her advisors, an act that confirms, not female weakness, but the political acumen and necessity of power-sharing for the successful directing of especially stately affairs—a point amplified by the shortsighted position of her ministers. They advocate for either the excessive use of military power because "[they] are endued with strength and given to vehement war" or blindly follow her command (27:33). Their position however falls flat, as seen in her pointed critique of them and their position: "She said: 'Verily, whenever kings enter a country they corrupt it, and turn the noblest of its people into the most abject'" (27:34). The Qur'ānic juxtaposition here of Bilqīs's approach compared to her ministers' and her use of power as queen in contrast to that of kings is rich; in both is a critique of power and its misuse, which explains her deliberative and cautionary style of governance. Here we come to a stunning moment in the story's narration: God's confirmation of Bilqīs's stance on the destructive abuse of power found at the end of Qur'ān 27:34: "And this is the way they (always) behave" (*wa kadhālika yaf'alūn*). Put differently, God confirms that Truth inheres in her position—an interpretive view found widely in the *tafsīr* literature.

Third, Bilqīs opts for prudence, an extolled political virtue, by testing Solomon with gifts "and await[ing] whatever [answer] the envoys bring back" (27:35), that is, to better understand his motivations. While the test insults Solomon, we gain through this tense moment a clearer sense of her discernment and approach to diplomacy in the face of the unknown. Finally, after Solomon has Bilqīs's throne miraculously brought to him and disguised to test her openness to guidance, she is asked if it is hers. She offers not merely a diplomatic response (she neither affirms nor denies), but arguably one that outsmarts Solomon's question: "It is as though it were the same!" (*ka'annahu huwa*, 27:42). Ultimately, the miracles of her transported throne and the slabs of glass made to appear as water in the palace, performed through Solomon, allow Bilqīs to see the Truth: "O my Sustainer! I have been sinning against myself: but (now) I have surrendered myself, with Solomon, unto the Sustainer of all the worlds!" (27:44). Here, she shows an independent ability to govern wisely, but also *be* governed wisely in spiritual matters.[34] This verse brings Bilqīs (and the reader) full circle back to the verse on *tawḥīd* that directly precedes her story: "God, there is no god but He!—Lord of the Throne, Supreme!" (27:26). The reference to God and "His Supreme Throne," again a verse that frames Bilqīs's story, invokes God's transcendence as the ultimate judge and arbiter of humanity. It also reminds the reader of the prominent "throne verse" (*āyat al-kursī*, 2:255), said to capture the virtues of the Qur'ān, that references both God's "chair" (*kursī*), associated with Solomon (38:34), and His "throne" (*'arsh*) associated here with Bilqīs. Thus, a symbolic connection between these two figures is expressed through the text, with God's seat "over" His creation always reigning supreme.

Sight—physical and symbolic—is central to discerning the story of Bilqīs, and uncoincidentally constitutes a key metaphor of Sufism as a mode of discerning the Truth. Seeing, not seeing, being tested to determine how you see, and ultimately seeing the Unseen (with the heart) are central aspects of the Qur'ān's storytelling about the queen of Sheba. We are to presume from its unfolding that her conversion would not have been possible if not for her political virtues that the Qur'ān clearly extolls. While most of the medieval exegetes acknowledge Bilqīs's wisdom before her conversion, there still remains a great deal of ambivalence, even misogyny, surrounding her rulership. Al-Qurṭubī, for instance, commends Bilqīs for her use of consultation (*shūra*), and her ability to discern Solomon's letter as "noble" (27:29) and test Solomon's motives (27:35), yet calls her "an ignorant woman" who "worships the sun."[35] Ibn Kathīr, by contrast, sees Bilqīs's test of Solomon as evidence of her "conciliation, reconciliation, deceit, and craftiness."[36]

Strikingly, while there is a general consensus among exegetes that God, rather than Bilqīs, made the critical statement, "And this is the way they (always) behave," in Qur'ān 27:34 above, the question was nevertheless debated. While some like Ibn 'Abbās (d. 67/687), Muqātil ibn Sulaymān (d. 150/767), al-Ṭabarī (d. 311/923), and Ibn Kathīr favored God as the speaker without engaging the debate, others, like al-Qurṭubī and al-Rāzī (d. 606/1210), presented both positions before offering their own. While al-Qurṭubī favored God, al-Rāzī claimed it was Bilqīs who confirmed her own critique about power, implying that her paganness was grounds for her incompetent, if not illegitimate, rule.[37]

Bilqīs's political leadership as a woman also proved problematic for some exegetes, as the renowned Medinan exegete al-Ḥasan al-Baṣrī (d. 110/728) makes clear. He is said to have critiqued Bilqīs's ministers for "delegating the decision to a crude infidel (*'ālja*) whose breasts shake."[38] Notable here is the application of the term *'ālja* (feminine form)—an insult reserved for "infidels" who were typically men and understood to be crude, primitive, and certainly inferior to the Muslims they fought— and its juxtaposition to Bilqīs's "shaking breasts." In this quote, al-Baṣrī leaves little doubt that Bilqīs's incompetence as a sovereign is inseparable from, if not attributable to, her sex—an interpretation that illustrates how exegetes, despite their acknowledgments, continued to struggle with Bilqīs's Islamic paradigmatization.

Yet Bilqīs is the only figure in a state of disbelief (*kufr*, 27:43) whose *qualities* are nevertheless praised by the Qur'ān. Her foil here is Pharaoh, a male pagan sovereign. Despite Moses's miracles inviting Pharaoh and his people to the Truth, Pharaoh refuses and even threatens those who convert with extreme punishment (7:103–127). In contrast to Pharaoh, whose oppressive abuse of power places him among the "rebellious" (*fāsiqīn*, 7:102; *ṭāghūt*, 89:11), "those who make mischief" (*al-mufsidīn*, 7:103), and "multiply iniquity [in the land]" (*fa aktharu fīhā al-fasād*, with "*fīhā*" referring to the land, 89:12), Bilqīs's defining character(istics), which revolve around the ethical use of power, which God confirms, make her obstinate against politically oppressing others. Indeed, "the blame is only against those who oppress people" (42:42). Through her negotiations with Solomon, we watch her come to the realization of her own spiritual self-oppression, one she cannot accept. It is her intelligence and leadership qualities that enable her to come to this spiritual awakening and ultimately confirm the Truth. Read as such, we not only get a great political leader in the figure of Bilqīs—one worthy of emulation, we also simultaneously restore an exemplary leader, an exemplary *woman* leader, back to the Qur'ānic text.

Zulaykha and Joseph (Yūsuf)

If Mary and Bilqīs can be regarded as exemplary (female) models for all Muslims, what do we do with Zulaykha—another powerful female figure but whose story is associated in the *tafsīr* literature with female seductiveness and cunning? In fact, she appears in the *ḥadīth* literature as a symbol of the concept of *fitna* (social anarchy and temptation), which indicates that to be female is to be sexually aggressive and hence dangerous to social stability.[39] In contrast to Joseph's holy, purified, and prophetic self, exegetes emphasize Zulaykha as "the cunning woman" and thus her nature as symbolic of the sexually aggressive, destabilizing, and dangerous nature of women as a whole; as a Qur'ānic figure, therefore, she has lost much of her human fullness.[40] At the heart of such misreadings is a failure to contextualize Zulaykha within the chapter's broader story of

Joseph or its reccurring themes. To do so would produce a very different meaning of her signification.

Unnamed, Zulaykha is called "the 'Azīz's wife" in the Qur'ān, referring to the title of the supervisor of Egypt's treasury at the court of the Egyptian king al-Rayyān ibn al-Walīd of the Amalekites.[41] Broadly speaking, the story of Joseph, and the many cast members who populate it, invoke themes of heedlessness, love, jealousy, deception, evil, and forgiveness, all of which revolve around the *nafs* ("the genderless self") and its enticement. Zulaykha's story is traditionally said to begin with verse 22, when the Azīz purchases Joseph as a slave and brings him home, after which she attempts to seduce him. Actually, Zulaykha's signification begins much earlier in the chapter, specifically with Joseph's brothers, who plot against him (12:5) because they are jealous of their father's (Jacob's) love for him (12:8). At the end of verse 5, Jacob reminds Joseph, in light of his brother's concocted plan, that "Satan is to humanity an avowed enemy" (*inna al-shayṭān lil nās 'adū mubīn*). Thus, a connection between "plotting" and Satan is established early on, which is crystallized first through the actions of the brothers and later Zulaykha. We watch as the brothers contrive a plan against Joseph, lie to and deceive Jacob, and delude themselves into thinking that after they get rid of Joseph, they will regain Jacob's favor and "be righteous after that" (12:9–14). Once they return, having abandoned Joseph in a well, they feign grief and lie to and deceive Jacob again, claiming a wolf had devoured him and produce "his shirt with false blood" as evidence (12:15–18). From the outset, then, the story involving Joseph's brothers establishes themes of delusional love, jealousy, lies, and deception, all of which make Jacob suspicious and cause him to remark to his sons, "Nay, indeed! Your selves have enticed you into an affair" (*bal sawwalat lakum anfusukum amr*) (12:18; 12:83). It is within this context that Zulaykha enters the scene.

It is verse 28 that has produced the most troubling *tafsīr* of Zulaykha: the 'Azīz, after realizing her guilt, remarks: "Indeed, it is of your [sc. the women's] plot. Indeed your plot is great" (*innahu min kaydikunna inna kaydakunna 'aẓīm*). The feminine second-person plural is used here, despite speaking only to Zulaykha, and thus becomes the basis on the part of medieval Qur'ān commentators for generalizing Zulaykha's "cunning" to her nature and thus to that of all women. The classical Muslim exegete al-Rāzī (d. 606/1210), for instance, interprets Qur'ān 12:28 as: "The plotting of women compared to men's is great (*'aẓīm*) . . . for women possess in this respect wiliness and craftiness that men do not possess, and because their plotting brings a level of shame that men's plotting does not."[42] The verb *kāyada*, however, denotes plotting, not cunning, as is often used in translations. We see the same form of the word used in the fifth verse to describe Joseph's brothers. In fact, the word in its derivative forms is used a total of nine times in this chapter and not all refer to Zulaykha. Its usage elsewhere in the Qur'ān often invokes a struggle between disbelievers who plot against believers: the Quraysh against the Muslims before the Battles of Uḥud and Badr (3:120), Satan against "those who believe" (4:76), the polytheists against Muḥammad (7:195), and Pharaoh against Moses (20:60). Therefore, it is not used exclusively for woman to characterize her "cunning" nature.

The Azīz, a notable, is now put in a dishonorable position where he has to ask his wrongly accused slave to "turn away," that is, forget the matter, and tell his wife to ask for forgiveness for "[her] sin (*lidhanbiki*, literally "your intentionally committed sin"), "for truly you are among the wrongdoers" (*innaki kunti min al-khāṭi'īn*, 12:29). But this does not end the saga of Joseph's seduction. Zulaykha gathers the city's women who thought lowly of her for "seducing her slave boy against his will" (*turāwidu fatāha 'an nafsihi*) in order to vindicate herself and her high standing. When they see Joseph, they understand her attraction (12:31). Joseph is "seduced" again, this time by the group of women (12:51); he understands that he will be among the *jāhilīn* (ignorant, misled, foolish, 12:33) unless God helps him, and He does so again by averting their plot against him (*faṣarafa 'anhu kaydahunna*, 12:34). Thus, based on Qur'ānic terminology, Zulaykha and the city women are equally guilty as the brothers for their "plotting." However, there is no judgment of woman's nature because of their scheming, just as there is no judgment of the brothers' nature due to theirs. It is the nature of their plotting that render them both "betrayers" (*kayd al-khā'inīn*, 12:52). This may relate to their respective positions of power over, or responsibility for, Joseph and thus its possible abuse. This is subtly suggested when the older group of brothers pressure their elderly father to let Joseph come with them "to play" (12:11, 14) and then betray the trust of their father and especially their younger brother (12:11–14). It is also suggested in the reference to Zulaykha when she attempts to seduce Joseph: "And she, in whose house [Joseph] was" (*allatī huwa fī baytihā*, 12:23). She treats him, not "honorably" as instructed and done by the Azīz himself (12:21), but rather as one "who oppresses" (*al-ẓālimūn*, 12:23), and thus betrays her husband and especially her slave. Lies and betrayal by those with power foreground both narratives.

Yet the nature of their "wrongdoing" differs in ways that explains Zulaykha's greater culpability. The brothers eventually recognize their wayward ways and declare to Joseph: "By God! Most certainly has God raised you high above us, and we were indeed but sinners!" (*wa in kunnā la khāṭi'īn*, 12:91). They admit to this same wrongdoing to Jacob, using the same expression, *innā kunnā khāṭi'īn* (12:97). This phrasing, to recall, is also used for Zulaykha's wrongdoing cited in 12:29 above. But she also commits a *dhanb*, which means a sin committed intentionally, in contrast to *khāṭi'īn*, which denotes a sin committed either intentionally or unintentionally. Because Zulaykha's seduction was directed and intentional throughout the story, but more notably because her plotting against Joseph enticed his *nafs*, her culpability is weightier than that of the brothers whose plot against Joseph was based on their own "enticed" *nafs*.

The brothers seek forgiveness from both Joseph and Jacob (12:92, 98).[43] The chapter is unclear about Zulaykha's forgiveness (but she also does not ask for it in the story). What is certain is her recognition of her sin (*dhanb*): "Now has the truth come to light! It was I who sought to make him yield himself unto me—whereas he, behold, was indeed speaking the truth!" (12:51). Ultimately it is Joseph who puts Zulaykha's story into perspective when he accepts partial blame: "I am not trying to absolve myself" (12:53). He takes responsibility for whatever desire he initially felt, despite not acting on it—a point that reveals his weakness but also his humanness in the face of his trials as a prophet. Both stories are brought together at the end of verse 53: "The human *nafs* is certainly prone to evil, unless my Lord do bestow His Mercy" (12:53). Despite Joseph's *nafs* being plotted against by both his brothers and Zulaykha, it is ultimately protected thanks to prayers to his "Merciful" Lord. More than this, both narratives unfold around the central theme of how the *nafs* can be corrupted by delusional love, deception, and lies through plotting—one plot of a near-murder and the other a seduction, one by men and the other by women.

The chapter comes full circle, however, when the narration returns to Muḥammad, with whom it began (12:3), and highlights the transcendental lesson:

> This account of something that was beyond the reach of your perception We now reveal unto you [O Prophet]. For you were not with Joseph's brothers when they resolved upon what they were going to do and wove their schemes [against him]. . . . And how many Signs are there in the heavens and on earth which they pass by [unthinkingly] and on which they turn their backs! (12:102, 105)

Joseph's complex story is fundamentally about the undifferentiated *nafs* and its corruptibility unless one remains steadfast and perseveres against "heedlessness" (*ghafl*, 12:3) and ignorance (*jahl*, 12:33), with the guidance of the "Oft-Forgiving and Merciful."

Conclusion

This chapter has made a number of interrelated arguments about how we can read woman, here as Qur'ānic female figures, in and through the text to derive her signification within the Qur'ān. Thanks to a *tawḥīdic* approach, we can better discern a contingent female–male polarity expressed in and through the text. The stories of Mary, Bilqīs, and Zulaykha offer us powerful lessons in moral instruction that are worthy of emulation by all Muslims. In the case of Mary, this would in fact be a requirement by virtue of her prophethood—a claim with major implications and transformative potential for established Islam. The stories of Mary, Bilqis, and Zulaykha offer, each in different ways, exemplary lessons that are fundamentally about, not themselves, but God. Indeed, the overarching precept that takes precedence in all three stories is *tawḥīd*, and the role each woman plays in the story, like the men they are narratively connected to, are instructional in order to lift up and highlight God's Unity and, therefore, God Himself. Through their stories, we are offered lessons for deepening the God–human relationship. It is in this sense that their narratives can be deemed "ungendered" examples of undifferentiated spirituality.

However, to "ungender" or decouple the didactic function of a Qur'ānic story from the embodied identity of its female figures overlooks another signification of woman to the Qur'ān, namely a necessary female–male polarity that expresses itself in and through the text. The interpretation of each woman's story becomes scripturally generative when related to those of men: Mary's signification is illuminated by her juxtaposition to that of Abraham (and Adam), Bilqīs's to Solomon's (and Pharaoh's), and Zulaykha's to Joseph's brothers. I am not arguing that woman's value can only be determined when compared to man's; such an argument imposes an essentialist hierarchy that presupposes male supremacy. I am also not suggesting that woman and man as ontological categories have essentially distinct natures; both are created from a single *nafs*, as mentioned in Qur'ān 4:1. Rather, I am suggesting that, methodologically speaking, their signification in Qur'ānic revelation is unveiled when juxtaposed to the signification of man. After all, woman and man, feminine and masculine, as ontological equals, are expressed in and through the Qur'ān in a multiplicity of ways but always based on polarity. Their multiplicity is unified by *tawḥīd* since polarity defines not only God's Reality but also human reality.[44] Such a view opens up new possibilities for different or more expansive understandings of woman and man and their relationality in the Qur'ān.[45]

The lesson of *tawḥīd* could have been narrated through stories populated only by men as main characters, prophet or otherwise. But they are not. Mary's story did not have to include divinely appointed distinctions unrelated to the miraculous birth of Jesus (read: her maternity or her body). But it does. Bilqīs's leadership qualities as a queen did not have to be extolled in light of her pagan status. But they are. Zulaykha's nature could have been indicted for her womanly guile. But it is not. Mary, Bilqīs, and Zulaykha matter as women in and to these Qur'ānic narratives for good reason. To restrict their importance to supporting cast members whose performance only matters to an all-female audience, because of their bodies, defies the Qur'ān, if one uses the Qur'ān to understand itself. But disembodying these women in order to stress lessons of spiritual undifferentiation, thus equality, also ignores the ways in which woman matters to the text's contents, to its very narration, by virtue of being in the text, but only to the extent that man matters textually. This is not an argument for perfect symmetry in women and men's representation as Qur'ānic figures in the text; that would impose a certain gender regime on the Qur'ān. Rather, it is an argument that when woman is chosen to "appear" in the text—including the many unnamed female figures, like Eve or Hagar, with less prominent roles in a story—their presence and actions leave powerful imprints that are better illuminated when read in correlativity with those of men. This reading proposes, then, a hermeneutic dialectic of seeing and unseeing gender that necessarily appears and must also necessarily disappear to remain faithful to the text.[46] When read as such, we are able to break the women of the Qur'ān out of their symbolic confines that perpetually hover them *over* the text as archetypes and restore them back *into* the text where their humanness and moral capacity for both virtue and sin can be reinterpreted anew.

The correlative nature of their stories—Mary/Abraham, Bilqīs/Solomon, Zulaykha/Joseph's brothers—also reveals the criticality of woman and man as ontologically contingent and equal parts to the meaning of the text, as reflective of God's Truth. Their relationality is a necessary reflection of the female-male contingency designed by the Creator. "And all things We have created by pairs, that perhaps you may reflect" (51:49). Even the Qur'ān's chapters occur in pairs.[47] As Divine Speech, the Qur'ān expresses these metaphysical dimensions through its text, and not only through stories. This same female-male polarity, for instance, is also expressed through Qur'ānic language itself. As Michael Sells describes it:

> Within the nuances of Qur'anic language one encounters a balanced and powerful gender dynamic. Arabic, like French, is based on grammatical gender; even inanimate objects are masculine and feminine. The Qur'an uses this grammatical gender in a way that allows the masculine and feminine to move beyond the grammatical gender and form a kind of subtle gender interplay. Using condensed masculine and feminine grammatical constructions, fitting them into key places of rhyme and rhythm, and aligning them with certain implicit metaphors (the earth—grammatically feminine—giving birth to her final secret), the Qur'an generates a sense of gender interplay that always hovers at the edge of personification.[48]

This necessary male–female relational contingency, which works at different levels of the text, serve both to reveal and reflect God's immanence. By drawing out images of divine immanence from especially Mary's and Zulaykha's story, we restore balance to the divine symbolic field. By doing so, we are able to authenticate female and male human subjectivities through God's intimacy with humanity, both women and men.[49] It is at the nexus of God, the God-creation/human relationship, and a male–female polarity, unified through the principle of *tawḥīd*, that we find more egalitarian modes of relationality between woman and man expressed in and through the Qur'ān.

NOTES

* I am indebted to Murtada Elkhalifa whose mastery of Qur'anic Arabic was critical in shaping this essay.
For *tafsīr* works cited in the notes, I consulted the online source: https://altafsir.com.

1. Barbara Freyer Stowasser, *Women in the Qur'an, Traditions, and Interpretation* (New York: Oxford University Press, 1994), 13.
2. Ibid.
3. Asma Barlas, *"Believing Women" in Islam: Unreading Patriarchal Interpretations of the Qur'an* (Austin: University of Texas Press, 2002), 32–33.
4. Amina wadud, *Qur'ān and Woman: Rereading the Sacred Text from a Woman's Perspective* (New York: Oxford University Press, 1999), 34.
5. Barlas, *Believing Women*.
6. Amina wadud, *Inside the Gender Jihad: Women's Reform in Islam* (Oxford: Oneworld Publications, 2006), 28–29.
7. Barlas, *Believing Women*, 102.
8. Sachiko Murata, *The Tao of Islam: A Sourcebook on Gender Relationships in Islamic Thought* (Albany: State University of New York Press, 1992), 10; quoted in Barlas, *Believing Women*, 102.
9. Murata, *The Tao of Islam*, 43; quoted in Barlas, *Believing Women*, 103.
10. I am deriving these hermeneutical principles regarding God's immanence from Sa'diyya Shaikh's work on Ibn 'Arabi; see Sa'diyya Shaikh, *Sufi Narratives of Intimacy: Ibn 'Arabi, Gender, and Sexuality* (Chapel Hill: University of North Carolina Press, 2014), 26–27.
11. Wadud, *Qur'ān and Woman*, 34.

12. I am not suggesting that woman as an ontological category is synonymous with femininity if by the latter we are referring to culturally derived gender constructions. I am attempting to identify and link how the Qur'ān itself presents polarity, here meaning a certain relationality between woman and man on an ontological level and masculine and feminine at the linguistic and symbolic level that work together to reveal a deeper metaphysical understanding and contingency of these relational modes in the Qur'ān.
13. Stowasser, *Women in the Qur'an*, 67. Mary is mentioned thirty-four times in thirty-three total verses.
14. Ibid., 72–73.
15. Ibid., 67, 73.
16. I am relying largely on the following translations: Muḥammad Asad's *The Message of the Qur'ān* (London: The Book Foundation, 2005); Jane McAuliffe, *The Qur'ān* (New York: W. W. Norton & Co., 2017), 'Abdullah Yusuf 'Ali, *The Meaning of the Holy Qur'an* (Beltsville, MD: Amana Publications, 2001), and Arthur Jefferey, *The Koran: Selected Suras* (Mineola, NY: Dover Publications, 1958), depending on which translation offered the most clarity and best flow.
17. Wadud, *Qur'an and Woman*, 40.
18. Asad translates the last part of the verse as "above all the women of the world," but a closer translation of the Arabic, *'ālamīn*, is "above all the women of all creation," which would then allow for the inclusion of *jinn*, which further emphasizes her distinction.
19. Her biblical name is Hanna, and in the *tafsīr* literature Ḥanna bint Qa'ūd ibn Qabīl; see the *tafsīr* for Qur'ān 3:35 by both al-Ṭabarī and al-Qurṭubī in www.altafsir.com.
20. The first-century Jewish historian Flavius Josephus mentions this in his *Antiquities of the Jews*, trans. William Whiston, Project Gutenberg, 2009, Book XV, chapter 11, section 5. This point is further emphasized by Asma Lamrabet, *Women in the Qur'an: An Emancipatory Reading* (Leicestershire, UK: Square View, 2016), 72.
21. Lamrabet, *Women in the Qur'an*, 74. Lamrabet interprets Mary, then, as a "remedy" to the gender discrimination of that era.
22. Importantly, others are characterized as such, like Muḥammad's family, but they remain unnamed in the Qur'ān.
23. Wadud, *Qur'an and Woman*, 39.
24. 'Ali, *Meaning of the Holy Qur'an*, 546.
25. The Zāhirī school (Arabic: *al-Zāhirīyya*), named after its founder Dāwūd al-Zāhirī (third/ninth century), is often characterized as Islam's fifth legal school of thought that especially flourished in Cordoba, the capital of Islamic Spain, under the leadership of the famous Muslim scholar Ibn Ḥazm, but declined by the tenth/fourth century due to its rejection of analogical reasoning as part of the standard methodology of Islamic jurisprudence.
26. Stowasser, *Women in the Qur'an*, 69.
27. He notes these views in the discussion of *ḥadīth* no. 3411; see Ibn Ḥajar al-'Asqalāni, *Fatḥ al-bārī bi sharḥ ṣaḥīḥ al-Bukhārī* (Cairo: al-Maktaba al-Salafiyya, n.d.), 6: 447–448.
28. Ibn Ḥajar, *Fatḥ al-bārī*, 473.
29. Stowasser, *Women in the Qur'an*, 65.
30. Ibid., 65.
31. Ibid., 63.
32. Jinn, rendered in English as "genie," are described in the Qur'ān (15:25; 38:76; 55:15) as a species of sentient and rational beings, like humans. They are semispirit beings that the

Qur'ān affirms as a fundamental aspect of the created world and like humans, can embrace or refuse Islam; see Michael Sells, *Approaching the Qur'an: The Early Revelations* (Ashland, OR: White Cloud Press, 1999), 37–38.

33. Wadud, *Qur'an and Woman*, 41.
34. Ibid., 41 (emphasis mine).
35. Al-Qurṭubī connects 27:32 with two verses on *shūra*—3:159, which commands Muḥammad to "consult with the believers," and 42:38, which describes the conduct of the believers "and whose affairs are settled with mutual consultation." Al-Qurṭubī considers 27:32 as upholding the "validity" of *shūra* based on 3:159 and 42:38. https://altafsir.com/Tafasir.asp?tMadhNo=1&tTafsirNo=5&tSoraNo=27&tAyahNo=32&tDisplay=yes&Page=1&Size=1&LanguageId=1.
36. https://altafsir.com/Tafasir.asp?tMadhNo=1&tTafsirNo=7&tSoraNo=27&tAyahNo=35&tDisplay=yes&UserProfile=0&LanguageId=1.
37. On Ibn 'Abbās and Muqātil, see https://altafsir.com/Tafasir.asp?tMadhNo=1&tTafsirNo=7&tSoraNo=27&tAyahNo=34&tDisplay=yes&UserProfile=0&LanguageId=1; on al-Ṭabarī, see https://altafsir.com/Tafasir.asp?tMadhNo=1&tTafsirNo=1&tSoraNo=27&tAyahNo=34&tDisplay=yes&UserProfile=0&LanguageId=1; on Ibn Kathīr, see https://altafsir.com/Tafasir.asp?tMadhNo=1&tTafsirNo=7&tSoraNo=27&tAyahNo=34&tDisplay=yes&UserProfile=0&LanguageId=1; on al-Qurṭubī, see https://altafsir.com/Tafasir.asp?tMadhNo=1&tTafsirNo=5&tSoraNo=27&tAyahNo=34&tDisplay=yes&Page=2&Size=1&LanguageId=1; on al-Rāzī, see https://altafsir.com/Tafasir.asp?tMadhNo=1&tTafsirNo=4&tSoraNo=27&tAyahNo=34&tDisplay=yes&UserProfile=0&LanguageId=1.
38. Cited in the *tafsīr* of Ibn Kathīr on Qur'ān 27:32. https://altafsir.com/Tafasir.asp?tMadhNo=1&tTafsirNo=7&tSoraNo=27&tAyahNo=32&tDisplay=yes&UserProfile=0&LanguageId=1.
39. Stowasser, *Women in the Qur'an*, 50. To see how notions of *fitna*, as associated with female cunning in the *ḥadīth* literature, is applied to other female figures in the Qur'ān, see Hibba Abugideiri, "Allegorical Gender: The Figure of Eve Revisited," *American Journal of Islamic Social Sciences* 13, no. 4 (Winter 1996): 518–535.
40. Stowasser, *Women in the Qur'an*, 50, 54–55.
41. Ibid., 52.
42. https://altafsir.com/Tafasir.asp?tMadhNo=1&tTafsirNo=4&tSoraNo=12&tAyahNo=28&tDisplay=yes&Page=3&Size=1&LanguageId=1.
43. From Joseph: "May God forgive you your sins: for He is the most Merciful of the Merciful!" (12:92); from Jacob: "O our father! Ask God to forgive us our sins, for, verily we were sinners." [Jacob] said: "I shall ask my Sustainer to forgive you: He alone is truly forgiving, a true dispenser of grace!" (12:98).
44. Barlas, *Believing Women*, 103.
45. I recognize that this approach must be tested and applied to those scriptural references to woman that relate to rights and roles, especially pertaining to marriage, divorce, inheritance, and testimony. Due to space constraints and the topic assigned for this chapter, I was unable to undertake such a reading here, which leaves this chapter open to the critique of the limitations of my interpretive approach.
46. I am currently working on an article that elucidates this hermeneutic approach more fully.
47. Raymond Farrin, *Structure and Qur'anic Interpretation: A Study of Symmetry and Coherence in Islam's Holy Text* (Ashland, OR: White Cloud Press, 2014), xv.

48. Sells, *Approaching the Qur'an*, 19–20.
49. Shaikh, *Sufi Narratives of Intimacy*, 26.

Bibliography

Abugideiri, Hibba. "Allegorical Gender: The Figure of Eve Revisited." *American Journal of Islamic Social Sciences* 13, no. 4 (Winter 1996): 518–535.

'Ali, Abdullah Yusuf. *The Meaning of the Holy Qur'ān*. Beltsville, MD: Amana Publications, 2001.

Asad, Muḥammad. *The Message of the Qur'ān*. Bristol, UK: The Book Foundation, 2005.

Barlas, Asma. *"Believing Women" in Islam: Unreading Patriarchal Interpretations of the Qur'an*. Austin: University of Texas Press, 2002.

Farrin, Raymond. *Structure and Qur'anic Interpretation: A Study of Symmetry and Coherence in Islam's Holy Text*. Ashland, OR: White Cloud Press, 2014.

Ibn Ḥajar al-'Asqalāni. *Fatḥ al-Bārī bi Sharḥ Saḥiḥ al-Bukhārī*. Cairo: al-Maktaba al-Salafiyya, n.d.

Jefferey, Arthur. *The Koran: Selected Suras*. Mineola, NY: Dover Publications, 1958.

Lamrabet, Asma. *Women in the Qur'an: An Emancipatory Reading*. Leicestershire, UK: Square View, 2016.

McAuliffe, Jane. *The Qur'ān*. New York: W. W. Norton, 2017.

Murata, Sachiko. *The Tao of Islam: A Sourcebook on Gender Relationships in Islamic Thought*. Albany: State University of New York Press, 1992.

Sells, Michael. *Approaching the Qur'ān: The Early Revelations*. Ashland, OR: White Cloud Press, 1999.

Shaikh, Sa'diyya. *Sufi Narratives of Intimacy: Ibn 'Arabi, Gender, and Sexuality*. Chapel Hill: University of North Carolina Press, 2014.

Stowasser, Barbara Freyer. *Women in the Qur'an, Traditions, and Interpretations*. New York: Oxford University Press, 1994.

Wadud, amina. *Inside the Gender Jihad: Women's Reform in Islam*. Oxford: Oneworld Publications, 2006.

Wadud, amina. *Qur'ān and Woman: Rereading the Sacred Text from a Woman's Perspective*. New York: Oxford University Press, 1999.

CHAPTER 2

CLASSICAL EXEGESES ON KEY QUR'ĀNIC VERSES CONCERNING WOMEN

HADIA MUBARAK

One should bear in mind three significant and interrelated points regarding the nature of the genre of *tafsīr* (exegesis) when analyzing classical exegeses of key Qurʾānic verses concerning women. First, the divine origins of the Qurʾān—as Muslims believe—in contrast to the potential fallibility of human interpretation, has long instilled an open-endedness to the scholarly production of Qurʾānic exegesis. Unlike law, the genre of *tafsīr* created a broader spectrum of interpretation, in which the realm of possible meanings was more expansive than it could be for a discipline like law, which by its nature, needed to be exact and precise. No exegete could claim that he or she had conclusively exhausted the Qurʾān's meanings nor could an exegete curtail the "open market" of *tafsīr*. Classical exegetes wrestled with the hermeneutical tensions that exist between recognizing that the Qurʾān has an inherent meaning, on one hand, and the multiplicity of interpretations that exegesis offered on the Qurʾān's meaning, on the other. As the sixth/twelfth-century theologian and exegete Abū Ḥāmid al-Ghazālī (d. 505/1111) argued, "One of the impediments to understanding [the Qurʾān] is to read a particular interpretation and then assume that no further meaning could be added to the Qurʾān... this is among the greatest veils [to understanding the Qurʾān]."[1] An exegete's decision to embark on writing a *tafsīr* was, therefore, embedded in the recognition that the scholarly tradition of *tafsīr* has not fully exhausted the Qurʾān's intended meanings or the significance of those meanings to human societies.

Second, a corollary to the first point is that the exegetical tradition, far from being monolithic, has been marked by a diversity in both methodology and interpretation. The Islamic exegetical tradition underscored textual polysemy as an inherent feature of the Qurʾān, rendering it amenable to a multiplicity of readings.[2] This pluralism was a byproduct of the very function of *tafsīr*, which was to establish a discursive space through which to elucidate the Qurʾān's meaning. While the exegetical tradition has been the bearer of interpretive authority over the Qurʾān's meaning, this tradition is not a hermetically sealed box, nor are its contents fixed.

Third, two sets of influences play a direct role in exegetes' interpretive differences. The first one, and perhaps the most obvious, are the hermeneutics that exegetes applied, which bore a direct relationship to the meanings they derived and the issues that most preoccupied their attention. The second significant influence, and the most relevant to the subject at hand, is the intellectual, cultural, and social milieu in which an exegete was trained and socialized. There is no question that an exegete's predominant sociocultural reality bore a direct influence on his/her interpretation of the text, especially as it pertained to women's issues, as will become evident in our ensuing discussion.

In this chapter, I examine classical exegeses of specific "gender verses" that have had significant consequences for conceptualizations of gendered identities and roles in Muslim-majority societies: Qurʾān 4:1, 2:228, 4:34, and 4:128. Qurʾān 4:1 is central to the Qurʾān's portrayal of the ontology of both sexes and the presumed chronology of the first primal parents, Eve and Adam. Qurʾān 2:228 is central to the debate on gender hierarchy in the Qurʾān, as the latter part of the verse establishes that although men and women have reciprocal rights, men have a "degree" of sorts over women. Qurʾān 4:34, the subject of even greater controversy, grants husbands the function of *qiwāma* over women due to "what God has preferred some over others" and men's financial maintenance of women. Among other themes, it also prescribes three measures for dealing with a wife who is guilty of *nushūz*, often interpreted as disobedience. Whereas Qurʾān 4:34 has been the subject of countless articles and books, another verse in the same chapter, Qurʾān 4:128, which describes the process of resolution when the husband is guilty of *nushūz*, has been almost entirely overlooked.[3] In contrast to Qurʾān 4:34, which identifies wives as the source of marital turbulence, Qurʾān 4:128 identifies husbands as the source of marital conflict. By exploring interpretations of men and women's *nushūz* in tandem (Qurʾān 4:34 and Qurʾān 4:128), I illustrate the discrepancies that arise in premodern exegetes' gendered definitions of *nushūz*, a term that has been subjected to much contestation in the modern period.

Qurʾān 4:1: Qurʾānic Narrative on Human Creation

The Qurʾānic narrative on human creation is one of the best illustrations of the Qurʾān's capacity to be read in drastically different ways by its readers, even when they share the same faith, tradition, and history. One of the key verses that deals with the issue of human creation is Qurʾān 4:1 which declares, "People, be mindful of your Lord, who created you from a single soul, and from it created its mate, and from the pair of them spread countless men and women far and wide; be mindful of God, in whose name you make requests of one another. Beware of severing the ties of kinship: God is always watching over you."[4]

In clear contrast to many contemporary scholars who read the Qurʾān's description that all human beings are created from a single *nafs* (Qurʾān 4:1) as a declaration of ontological sexual equality,[5] most medieval exegetes understood the same verse to indicate that all human beings derive from Adam, the first human creation. The main point of contention among classical exegetes on this verse—from a gendered perspective—revolves around the origin of Eve's creation. It should be pointed out that the Qurʾān does not mention Eve by name nor does it provide details on how she was created. It simply tells us, in 4:1, 7:189, and 39:6, that God created the human from a single *nafs* (soul/spirit) and created the mate "from it."[6] This invites the question: does the pronoun "it" here signify Adam or does it signify the same substance from which Adam was created?

According to the fourth/tenth-century exegete, Muḥammad ibn Jarīr al-Ṭabarī (d. 310/923), Eve was created from Adam's rib; he cites six different reports to support this interpretation.[7] These reports, as scholars have pointed out, provide a level of detail that the Qurʾān itself omits. Further, the exegetical narratives are a near replication of biblical ones. For example, one report indicates that Eve was created from his lowermost rib;[8] others specify that God creates Eve from Adam's left rib while he was asleep, and then awakens to find Eve next to him, at which point he exclaims, "my flesh, my blood, my wife."[9] The resemblance of these reports to Genesis 2:21–23 is unmistakable. In fact, al-Ṭabarī explicitly states that his last report—that Eve was created from Adam's rib while he was asleep—comes from Ibn Isḥāq,[10] who attributes it to "the People of the Torah."[11] The verse stands primarily as evidence for al-Ṭabarī of humanity's collective responsibility to one another, as siblings who originate from a single set of parents.[12]

The theme of Eve's creation from Adam's rib persists throughout medieval Sunnī and Shīʿī exegesis.[13] Many significant Sunnī commentators cite this interpretation, ranging from ʿAbdallāh ibn ʿUmar al-Bayḍāwī (d. 685/1286 or 710/1310)[14] and Maḥmūd ibn ʿUmar al-Zamakhsharī (d. 538/1144) to Ismāʿīl Ibn Kathīr (d. 773/1371), Jalāl al-Dīn al-Maḥallī (d. 864/1460) and Jalāl al-Dīn al-Suyūṭī (d. 911/1505).[15] Both Abū al-Ḥasan al-Māwardī (d. 450/1058) and Abū ʿAbd Allāh al-Qurṭubī (d. 671/1273) cite this opinion and attribute it to early exegetical authorities, yet it is unclear whether or not they agree with this opinion.[16] The polyvalent nature of Qurʾānic exegesis meant that exegetes often cited opinions to establish the spectrum of interpretations without necessarily endorsing those opinions. Incidentally, early Sufi commentators, such as al-Sulamī (d. 412/1021), al-Qushayrī (d. 465/1072), al-Baqlī (d. 606/1209), and al-Jaylānī (d. 713/1166) are strikingly silent on the origin of Eve's creation, as the narrative of her creation from Adam's rib is entirely dropped.[17] However, this interpretation makes a comeback in the Sufi commentaries of the Ottoman scholar, Ismāʿīl Ḥaqqī al-Burūsawī (d. 1127/1725) and Ibn ʿAjība (d. 1224/1809).[18] Al-Burūsawī narrates a similar interpretation to al-Ṭabarī, indicating that God created Eve from Adam's lowermost rib while Adam was in a midstate between sleep and wakefulness. When he discovers Eve by his side, he feels an inclination toward her and finds her familiar to him, since she is created from him.[19]

Despite this dominant interpretation regarding the source of Eve's creation, we find a few outliers throughout the centuries. The first comes from Muḥammad al-Bāqir (d. 117/733), also known as Abū Jaʿfar, who is identified by the Twelver Shīʿa as the fifth imam and as a scholar by Sunnīs. According to a narration cited in the exegesis of Abū al-Naṣr al-ʿAyyāshī (d. 320/932), a man identified as the father of ʿAmr b. Miqdām asks Abū Jaʿfar, "From what thing did God create Eve?" to which the latter responds, "What does this creation say?"[20] The man responds, "They say, God created her from one of Adam's ribs." Abū Jaʿfar retorts, "They have lied (*kadhabū*). Was He incapable of creating her from anything other than a rib?"[21] At this point, he clarifies that Eve was in fact created from leftover earth, not Adam.[22] Later Shīʿī scholars, such as Abū Jaʿfar Muḥammad Ibn Ḥasan al-Ṭūsī (d. 406/1068) and Faḍl ibn Ḥasan al-Ṭabarsī (d. 548/1153)[23] pick up al-Bāqir's argument and cite it side-by-side with the prophetic report, "Women were created from a rib. . . ."[24]

A meticulous consideration of theology produces a similar reinterpretation of the verse by the Ashʿarī theologian, Fakhr al-Dīn al-Rāzī (d. 606/1210). Like al-Bāqir, he contests the notion that Eve was created from Adam's rib. Yet for al-Rāzī, the gender implications of this interpretation are irrelevant. Known for his logical dialecticism, al-Rāzī is most concerned with the theological implications of interpreting Eve as created from Adam's rib. More specifically, al-Rāzī is keen on refuting the arguments of a theological faction, the naturalists (*al-Ṭabāʾiʿiyyīn*), who believed that all created things were created from preexisting matter, not from "total nonexistence."[25] Al-Rāzī argues that a created being cannot derive from another created being, yet fundamentally differ in its composition. It becomes evident that al-Rāzī's interpretation is informed by his adherence to Ashʿarī doctrine, according to which, all creation is created from total nonexistence because there can be no other preexisting matter (*qadīm*) in the universe other than God, the origin of all creation.[26] Citing the Muʿtazilī exegete Abū Muslim al-Iṣfahānī (d. 322/934), al-Rāzī notes that *min* in the verse denotes the point of origin or initiation, not a literal extraction of one substance from the other.[27] Accordingly, al-Rāzī argues, "If it is proven that God is capable of creating Adam from clay, then He is also capable of creating Eve from clay, and if this is the case, then what benefit is there in her being created from one of Adam's ribs?"[28] Although al-Iṣfahānī is regarded as the source of the argument that *min* in Qurʾān 4:1 is not literal, this interpretation takes on a new theological dimension in al-Rāzī's exegesis.

Despite these outliers, the dominant strand of interpretation in Qurʾānic exegesis is that Eve was created from Adam's rib. Based on this creation narrative, Ibn Kathīr derives a justification for restricting women's public movements. Citing a report attributed to Ibn ʿAbbās (d. 687/1288), he writes, "Woman was created from man so her desire is in men, whereas man was created from earth, so his desire is in the earth, so confine your women."[29] As Ibn Kathīr acknowledges, he does not rely on the canonical *ḥadīth* collections for this report, but on the fourth/tenth-century commentary of a fellow Shafiʿī, Ibn Abī Ḥātim al-Rāzī (d. 327/938). Ibn Kathīr's decision to incorporate this *ḥadīth* is likely a reflection of the cultural sensibilities of his eighth/

fourteenth-century Mamluk milieu, which appear to have promoted the cloistering of women in their homes, according to some scholars.[30]

Qur'ān 2:228: Men and Women's Reciprocal, Yet Unequal, Rights

One of the most critical verses for scholars engaging the Qurʾān through a gendered lens is Qurʾān 2:228. This verse states:

> And divorced women shall wait concerning themselves for three cycles. It is not lawful for them to conceal what God has created in their wombs, if they believe in God and the Day of Judgment. And their husbands have a greater right to take them back if they [men] desire reconciliation, and they [women] have rights like the rights upon them, according to honorable norms [*bi'l-maʿrūf*] and men have a degree [*daraja*] over them, and God is powerful and wise.[31]

Qurʾān 2:228 is one of 350–500 legal verses of the scripture's approximate 6,236 verses.[32] It establishes the legal process following a man's unilateral pronouncement of divorce. A husband's ability to revoke or retract his pronouncement of divorce stood as the primary marker of distinction between two broad categories of divorce in Islam: revocable divorce (*talāq rajʿī*) and nonrevocable divorce (*talāq bāʾin*). Qurʾān 2:228 established the husband's right to revoke his pronouncement of divorce during the wife's waiting period (*ʿidda*), as long as he had initiated the divorce, rather than the wife, and as long as this was his first or second pronouncement of divorce. The husband forfeited the right to revoke a divorce after a third pronouncement of divorce or in the case of a female-initiated divorce (*khulʿ*) or judicial annulment (*faskh*) of marriage.

More specifically, Qurʾān 2:228 makes three distinct legal prescriptions: First, it establishes a three-cycle[33] waiting period for a wife whose husband has pronounced a single, unilateral divorce. Second, it allows the husband to take back his wife (i.e., retract his divorce) during this waiting period. Third, it obliges the wife to disclose her pregnancy or menstrual cycle during this period. These prescriptions have a number of significant legal implications: First, the termination of a woman's three-cycle waiting period signals her eligibility to marry another man. Until then, her husband's right to take her back precedes the right of any other man's wish to marry her. Second, a woman's discovery that she is pregnant changes the timing of her waiting period from three menstrual cycles to the full duration of her pregnancy, during which her husband must maintain her.[34] Third, the conditional phrase "*in arādū iṣlāḥ*[an]," specifies that a man's right to take back his wife after pronouncing divorce is premised on the intention for *iṣlāḥ*, which has been frequently translated as "reconciliation."[35] The legal nature of this verse led exegetes to primarily delve into issues of law.

The legal aspects of this verse have received much less attention from gender scholars than the last part of the verse, which declares that "women have rights like the rights unto them, according to honorable norms, and men have a degree over them." Yet premodern exegetes' interpretation of men and women's mutual rights were largely informed by law. They oscillated between viewing men's and women's rights as equal or as reciprocal, but different. For the most part, premodern exegetes interpreted this Qur'ānic phrase in a way that suggests that although men and women may have reciprocal rights, these rights are not the same. Some, however, suggest that men and women's reciprocal rights share the same objective; yet the concrete manifestations of these rights diverge. For example, in one of the earliest published Qur'ānic exegeses, al-Ṭabarī notes the meaning of "women have rights like the rights upon them" as follows: Men should not take back their wives (during the waiting period) unless they intend reconciliation and do not wish to harm them, while women should not conceal their pregnancies with the intention of harming their husbands if their husbands decide to take them back (during the waiting period).[36] For al-Ṭabarī, the reciprocal right that women and men enjoy is the right not to be harmed by one's spouse during the process of divorce. Both spouses have an *equal* right to be safe from the other spouse.

Yet the ways in which each spouse could inflict harm on the other differs based on the explicit wording of this verse. Since men exclusively hold the prerogative to take back their wives during their three-cycle waiting periods, then the way men harm their wives is by taking them back without an intent to reconcile, but simply to exact revenge or afflict harm. Women, who uniquely possess the capacity for reproduction, inflict harm on their husbands by concealing their pregnancy or menstruation in order to forfeit their husbands' right to take them back or to extend the waiting period unnecessarily, during which husbands are obliged to financially support their wives.[37] Al-Ṭabarī's interpretation clearly links men and women's mutual rights to the particular legal context of divorce.

Like al-Ṭabarī, the fifth/eleventh-century Andalusian scholar Abū Bakr ibn al-ʿArabī (d. 543/1148) also believed that men and women's reciprocal rights referenced in the verse were particular to the legal context of divorce. He argues, "Since men's right over women is to revoke the divorce, women's right over men is kind companionship."[38] Similarly, the seventh/thirteenth-century theologian and exegete al-Rāzī interprets this Qur'ānic statement within the legal context of the waiting period. Applying an intertextual hermeneutic, he connects the first and second parts of the verse. He writes, "Realize that when God clarified that the aim of taking back one's wife is to improve her affairs, not to harm her, He established that each spouse has a right upon the other. And realize that the very purpose of marriage cannot be fulfilled except when each spouse considers the right of the other."[39] According to al-Rāzī, spouses have the mutual responsibility to refrain from harming the other; men therefore should not take back their wives unless they intend reconciliation and women should not conceal their pregnancies during their waiting period.[40]

Exegetes entertained the possibility that a man could take back his wife simply to harm her. Recognizing the legal limitations of discerning human intent, al-Ṭabarī argues that if a man takes back his wife simply to harm her, he is sinful before God. Yet the courts cannot ascertain the intent of his action, so it is legally valid for him to retract his divorce within the three-cycle period, until his third pronouncement of divorce.[41] Al-Rāzī follows in suit: "One's intent is a hidden condition that we cannot know, so legislation (*al-shar*ʿ) does not prevent the validity of retraction based on it [intent]; yet its validity between him and God is based upon this intent, such that if he takes her back with the intent to harm her, then he deserves to be punished."[42] Both exegetes' interpretations reflect the legal principle that the law can only prosecute actions, not intentions.

Two premodern Mālikī exegetes, Ibn al-ʿArabī and al-Qurṭubī, both concede that men's real intentions cannot always be known. However, they add, if a judge discovers that a man retracted his divorce in order to harm his wife, then the judge will divorce him from his wife.[43] This interpretation reflects the particularities of their legal school, since the Mālikī school identified the affliction of spousal harm as a legitimate cause for judicial annulment.[44] Exegetes' emphasis on the ethical considerations involved in taking back one's wife and protecting women from potential harm reflects a general concern with women's well-being, which defies common depictions of the genre as monolithically patriarchal.

Exegetes also underscored a woman's agency in disclosing whether she was menstruating or pregnant during this waiting period. As in the case of a husband whose innermost intentions cannot be legally determined, divorced women were not subject to a bodily check if they claimed they had menstruated three times or not. Legal definitions on the minimum and maximum lengths of purity and menstruation, however, could regulate such claims. Al-Rāzī affirms that the law takes the woman's statement at face-value if she claims that her waiting period has ended, so long as it meets the legal limits of possibility.[45] According to the Shafiʿī legal school, he notes this would be a minimum of thirty-two days and one hour. "Whenever she claims this minimum or more than this, her statement is accepted," he writes. "Similarly, if she was pregnant and claims she miscarried, then her statement is accepted, since the default is her trustworthiness (*ʿalā aṣl amānatihā*)."[46] In a similar vein, al-Qurṭubī writes that only women are able to ascertain whether they are pregnant or menstruating. Since she has been "entrusted" with disclosing this, "her statement is made the default one if she claims her waiting period is finished or not."[47] He cites the Successor[48] Sulaymān ibn Yasār (d. 107/725) to argue that men are not responsible for ascertaining whether or not their divorcées are menstruating (while awaiting the termination of a waiting period), "but that has been delegated to them (women)."[49] Al-Ṭabarī cites an early exegetical authority, al-Ḍaḥḥāk ibn Muzāḥim (d. 102 /720), who states, "women have been entrusted with (disclosing) menstruation and the child (i.e. pregnancy)."[50] They recognized the possibility that a woman could conceal her pregnancy and then attribute it to a second man she marries after her waiting period.[51] Despite these significant ramifications, women's claims about their own biological cycles were not to be second guessed.

The concept of mutual, but different rights permeates the exegetical interpretation of the Qurʾānic phrase, "*and women shall have rights similar to the rights against them, according to honorable terms.*" This is most evident in the exegesis of al-Zamakhsharī and al-Bayḍāwī, whose exegeses are separated by over a century. Al-Zamakhsharī notes that the reciprocity of men and women's rights is a reciprocity of equal obligation to fulfill them, not the type of rights (*lā fī jins al-fiʿl*). "If she washes his clothes or bakes bread for him, this does not mean he is obliged to do the same," al-Zamakhsharī writes.[52] The objective of reciprocity (*mumāthala*) in this verse is that each spouse should reciprocate good deeds to the other, because fulfilling a right is a good deed (*ḥasana*), he states.[53]

Al-Baydāwī is also explicit in his belief that men and women's rights are not the same. He writes, "Women have rights like men's rights in terms of the necessity [for men] to fulfill them and women's right to demand them [their rights], *but not in the type* [of rights] (*lā fī 'l jins*)."[54] In his interpretation of "*men have a degree over them*," he elaborates what he means by the "different type of rights" that each gender possesses. Informed by his Shafiʿī legal persuasion, he explains that husbands' rights are to women's bodies [*fī anfusihinna*], meaning the right to demand sexual intercourse and control their mobility. Al-Baydāwī elaborates that women's rights are that their husbands pay them a marital dowry, financially support them, abstain from harming them, and other similar rights.[55] His interpretation implies that women, unlike men, do not have a sexual claim over their husbands' bodies.

The notion that women cannot "legally" demand sex from their husbands also emerges in al-Rāzī's interpretation of Qurʾān 4:128, a verse discussed below. Exegetes' interpretations of the Qurʾān are often mediated by their legal school's doctrine.[56] Al-Rāzī, a Shafiʿī exegete like al-Bayḍāwī, writes that a wife's right over her husband is her marital dower, financial maintenance and *qism* (a fair allotment of nights). "These three are the rights a woman is able to demand from her husband, whether he wishes or refuses; as for sex, this is not the case, because the husband cannot be compelled to have sex."[57] The views of both al-Bayḍāwī and al-Rāzī reflect a legal definition of rights, rather than what is morally required. It is worth pointing out that Prophet Muḥammad encouraged men not to rush women during the act of sexual intercourse and to help women attain sexual satisfaction.[58]

We find a significant departure from this view in the exegesis of the seventh/thirteenth-century Mālikī exegete, al-Qurṭubī. Three of the four mutual rights he identifies equally apply to both spouses.[59] His interpretation comes closest to rendering these rights as equal rather than merely reciprocal. Al-Qurṭubī's exegesis is also unique in acknowledging men's sexual responsibilities toward their wives. For example, one reciprocal right, according to al-Qurṭubī, is that both spouses should attempt to look pleasing to the other. He later elaborates extensively on the ways in which men can adorn themselves, concluding that "if a man finds himself unable to fulfill his wife's sexual rights, then he should take medicine to increase his [sexual] capability and strengthen his desire in order to protect her [from fulfilling her sexual needs elsewhere]."[60]

Qurʾān 2:228: The "Degree" of Men

How do classical exegetes reconcile the notion of men and women's reciprocal but different rights with the verse's description that men have a degree over women? The most distinct premodern interpretation of men's degree comes from al-Ṭabarī. While mentioning five possible meanings for men's degree over women, based on the opinions of four Successors and one Companion, al-Ṭabarī explicitly champions the most egalitarian interpretation of the five possible meanings. He argues that men's degree over women is the responsibility to pardon women if they fail to fulfill their responsibilities while still fulfilling the rights of their wives. For evidence, he cites a tradition from Ibn ʿAbbās, a foremost authority on Qurʾānic interpretation and the cousin of the Prophet, to legitimate this meaning. Ibn ʿAbbās states, "I do not wish to exhaust all of my rights from my wife because God said, 'and men have a degree over them.' "[61]

Maintaining the textual polysemy that is characteristic of al-Ṭabarī's work, the fifth/eleventh-century Shīʿī scholar and exegete Shaykh al-Ṭāʾifa Muḥammad ibn al-Ḥasan al-Ṭūsī (d. 460/1067) presents three possible meanings for men's degree. He notes that men's degree has been interpreted as men's greater merit by obliging their wives' obedience, or second, as men's greater merit by forgoing some of their rights over their wives, or finally, men's greater share of inheritance and the obligation to perform *jihād*.[62] Unlike al-Ṭabarī, he does not champion a specific meaning as being the correct one. He cites a modified version of Ibn ʿAbbās's statement that is found in al-Ṭabarī: "I do not like to exhaust all of my rights from my wife, so that I have merit with her."[63] Over a century later, Faḍl ibn Ḥasan al-Ṭabarsī (548/1153) cites an interpretation nearly identical to that of al-Ṭūsī. Yet he adds to this interpretation a report attributed to Prophet Muḥammad, cited by the fifth Shīʿī imam Muḥammad al-Bāqir (d. 114/732), that reinforces a patriarchal understanding of this verse by listing the ways in which women must obey their husbands, including never leaving their homes without the husband's permission or else they will be cursed by the angels of the heavens and earth and the angels of wrath and mercy.[64]

Known for his dialectical mode of argumentation, al-Rāzī cites two possible meanings for men's degree, each reflecting the opposite outcome. The first appears to resemble the interpretation championed by al-Ṭabarī. After identifying eight reasons[65]—based on his own reasoning—for men's merit or virtue (*faḍīla*)[66] over women, he writes:

> If all these male prerogatives are proven, this would make women like feeble hostages in the hands of men. For this reason, the Prophet peace be upon him said, "take care of women for they are in your care (*ʿawān*)." . . . And the meaning of the verse is that due to the degree that God gave men over women in capability, they are entrusted with fulfilling more of women's rights. Therefore, the mention of this [degree] is to warn men against encroaching upon women to harm or hurt them.[67]

On the other hand, it is possible that men might be on the losing end of this equation, notes al-Rāzī. One could also argue that women possess the greater fortune of rights, al-Rāzī points out, because God has assigned men the duty of paying women their marital dower (*mahr*), financially supporting them, defending them, looking out for their interests, and preventing them from places of harm.[68] If this is the case, "then a woman's duty to serve her husband is a confirmed obligation, in consideration of the greater rights" she enjoys, he writes.[69] As further evidence of women's need to obey their husbands, he cites Qur'ān 4:34 and a *ḥadīth*, "if I were to order anyone to prostrate to one other than God, I would have ordered the woman to prostrate to her husband."[70]

Reflecting textual polyvalence, the seventh/thirteenth-century Andalusian Mālikī exegete al-Qurṭubī draws on several sources for the meaning of "men's degree." A careful analysis of the diverse interpretations he cites reflects a logic to their order; it appears as if he lists the opinions in order of strength, with the first being the weakest and the last being the strongest. Therefore, he first cites the opinion of Ḥumayd[71] (d. 244/858) that men's degree is their beard, although al-Qurṭubī is quick to dismiss this as unsuitable to the context of the verse.[72] Despite its weakness, several exegetes go out of their way to cite Ḥumayd's opinion, such as al-Ṭabarī, Ibn al-ʿArabī, al-Māwardī, and Abū Muḥammad ibn ʿAṭiyya (d. 541/1147), only to reject it.[73]

Displaying an interpretive pluralism, al-Qurṭubī also cites a statement by Ibn ʿAbbās to the effect that men should be kind to women and magnanimous to them with their money and character.[74] Yet unlike al-Ṭabarī, it does not appear as though al-Qurṭubī interprets men's degree as a greater responsibility to be magnanimous to women. Rather, he writes that "a woman should feel that her husband's right upon her is more deserving of being fulfilled than her right upon him."[75] Al-Qurṭubī cites the opinion of the Shafiʿī legal judge, al-Māwardī, who interprets men's degree as follows: "he can divorce her at will [i.e., without her consent or the need to go to a court]; and she is obliged to respond to his sexual requests, but he is not obliged to respond to hers."[76] This interpretation parallels al-Bayḍāwī's position that men have claims over their wives' bodies, which is *not* a mutual right.

The eighth/fourteenth-century exegete Ibn Kathīr intensifies the concept of male superiority to women, as he introduces an ontological component to men's advantage over women. In his view, men's "degree" over women in this verse is "in their merit (*faḍīla*), physical constitution (*khalq*), character (*khuluq*), status (*manzila*), the right to be obeyed (*ṭāʿat al-amr*), the responsibility of financial maintenance, overseeing women's interests, and their preference in this world and the next (*al-faḍl fīl-dunya wal-ākhira*).[77] In other words, men's degree over women is their superiority in all these matters. Whereas earlier exegetes like al-Ṭabarī, al-Rāzī, and al-Qurṭubī confined the discussion of *daraja* to the fulfillment of rights by one party or the other, later exegetes like Ibn Kathīr take the discussion outside of the context of legal rights and responsibilities. Further, he turns women's rights, such as the right of financial maintenance and fulfilling women's interests, as an affirmation of men's advantage over women. He cites Qur'ān 4:34, as a basis for the interpretation he provides. This limited intratextual reading, however, imparts on both verses a similar hierarchal interpretation to the advantage of men. This survey of selected exegeses of Qur'ān 2:228 invites us to ponder the following questions: What considerations guide Qur'ānic exegetes as they determine which sources to bring into the fold of their interpretive ventures? Why do some exegetes, like al-Ṭabarī, find Ibn ʿAbbās's statement to be central to a correct understanding of men's degree, while other exegetes, like al-Rāzī and al-Qurṭubī, find a prophetic tradition about wives prostrating to husbands a more relevant source for their interpretation of men's "degree"? It becomes clear that a scholar's reliance on a particular source to interpret the Qurʾan may be mediated by preconceived notions or beliefs regarding the suitability of that source to the verse in question.

Gendered Definitions of *Nushūz*: Qurʾān 4:34 and Qurʾān 4:128

No other verse in the Qurʾān has garnered as much controversy in modern scholarship on gender in the Qurʾān as Qurʾān 4:34. Whereas Qurʾān 4:34 has been the subject of countless articles and books, another verse in the same chapter, Qurʾān 4:128, which describes the process of resolution when the husband is guilty of *nushūz*, has been almost entirely overlooked. The lack of scholarly attention to a Qurʾānic verse that speaks of men's *nushūz* is a perfect illustration of the disproportionate emphasis given to verses that have been understood to refer to male privilege or female passivity as opposed to verses that focus on the duties that men owe to women. To arrive at a more holistic understanding of exegetes' approaches to the foundational text of the Qurʾān, we should consider exegetical discussions on both genders in tandem, as I proceed to do.

Premodern exegetes in general acknowledged that the term *nushūz* in Qurʾān 4:34 and Qurʾān 4:128 derives from one semantic wellspring. For example, the fourth/tenth-century exegete al-Ṭabarī uses the terms "elevation" (*istiʿlāʾ*) and "rising" (*irtifāʿ*) to interpret *nushūz* in both verses. In the context of marital discord, this *nushūz* is a type of haughtiness or arrogance that one spouse displays toward the other. Yet for al-Ṭabarī, the way that men and women display haughtiness is clearly gendered. A woman's *nushūz*, according to al-Ṭabarī, is her refusal to have sex with her husband, due to "her disobedience," and her defiance in other matters in which she should obey him, either out of hatred or disregard for the husband.[78] A husband's *nushūz* is his disregard for his wife and his preference for another woman either due to his hatred or dislike of one of her characteristics.[79]

The gendered ways in which al-Ṭabarī describes the sexual disinterest of both spouses is grounded in Islamic legal conceptions of marriage as an exchange of rights. In both cases, the *nushūz* that he describes constitutes a spouse reneging on one of the rights he/she owes the other. Al-Ṭabarī uses the term disobedience "*ʿiṣyanan minhunna*" to characterize the wife's abandonment of her husband's bed due to legal conceptions of sex as a right that a wife owes to her husband. On the other hand, al-Ṭabarī uses the phrase "giving preference to another" (*atharatan ʿalayhā*) to characterize the husband's sexual abandonment of his wife. The equal treatment of co-wives was regarded as a legitimate right that a woman could demand from her husband.[80] A man's sexual neglect of his wife, therefore, was not regarded as "disobedience," but as a violation of a wife's right to be treated on par with other wives, based on Qurʾan 4:3 "and if you fear that you will not be just, then marry only one (woman) or your female slaves." Therefore, al-Ṭabarī's understanding of *nushūz* is grounded in his legal conception of marriage as an exchange of rights.

This gendered definition of *nushūz*, informed by the different legal rights that each spouse owes the other, continues with exegetes from subsequent centuries. The sixth/twelfth-century exegete al-Zamakhsharī interprets a woman's *nushūz* as her disobedience and truculence toward her husband.[81] On the other hand, he interprets a man's *nushūz* as being harsh toward his wife "by depriving her of sexual intercourse, finances, love, and mercy, which should be between a man and woman" and verbal or physical abuse.[82]

In the seventh/thirteenth century, al-Rāzī acknowledges that the term *nushūz* shares one linguistic origin in both verses. He writes, "*nushūz* could stem from either of the spouses and it is the hatred of one for the other."[83] Despite this initial concession, al-Rāzī proceeds to define the markers of *nushūz* for men and women in distinct ways. For al-Rāzī, a woman's *nushūz* is grounded in her disobedience toward her husband.[84] The husband's *nushūz*, on the other hand, is marked by his disinterest in his wife or ill-treatment of her. Al-Rāzī writes, "A man's *nushūz* against his wife's right is that he neglects her, frowns in her face, ceases to have sex with her, and treats her badly (*yusīʾ ʿushratahā*)."[85] In both cases, the spouse evinces disinterest in the other. Yet in the case of women, al-Rāzī characterizes this as disobedience; in the case of men, he characterizes it as bad companionship.

Qurʾān 4:34: Consequences of Women's *Nushūz*

The Qurʾānic text prescribes two different scenarios for resolving cases of *nushūz*, depending on whether the wife or husband is the source of turbulence. To remedy a wife's *nushūz*, Qurʾān 4:34 establishes a three-step process. According to a face-value interpretation, husbands are first advised to counsel their wives, then to abandon them sexually, and third, to "hit them."

As early as al-Ṭabarī, premodern exegetes reflected a general discomfort with the idea that a man could hit his wife without any restriction or qualification. Most premodern exegetes attempted to qualify the verse's third injunction "to hit" women who were in a state of *nushūz*. The most common qualifier of "hitting" for premodern exegetes was that it cannot be injurious or leave marks. Al-Ṭabarī, for example, cites eighteen different reports that place conditions on wife-beating so that it is not harmful or does not leave marks. The most frequent opinion of those eighteen citations is that hitting must be noninjurious (*ghayr mubarriḥ*). Two other terms used to describe this noninjurious type of hitting was *ghayr shāʾin*, "nondisfiguring," and *ghayr muʾaththir*, "not leaving marks or traces."[86] In three of the eighteen reports, ʿAṭāʾ ibn Abī Rabāḥ (d. 115/733) seeks more information on the meaning of *ghayr mubarriḥ* from Ibn ʿAbbās, who clarifies that it means to hit with a *siwāk*[87] or a similar object.[88] Al-Ṭabarī's insertion of these citations seeks to restrict or diminish the effect of the hitting, although not eliminate it.[89]

While none of the classical exegetes argued that it was impermissible for a husband to discipline his wife, a few of them argued that it was preferable that a husband *not* hit his wife. The Mālikī exegete Abū Bakr ibn al-ʿArabī adopted this position, based on the legal opinion of the Meccan mufti, ʿAṭāʾ ibn Abī Rabāḥ. ʿAṭāʾ said, "The husband does not hit his wife even if he commands and forbids her and she refuses [to obey]; rather, he gets angry with her."[90] Ibn al-ʿArabī praises ʿAṭāʾ's legal rigor: "This (interpretation) is due to ʿAṭāʾ's insight and (correct) understanding of *sharīʿa*."[91] ʿAṭāʾ determines that hitting one's wife takes the ruling of *karāhiyya* (reprehensibility) rather than *ibāḥa* (permissibility), based on the following *ḥadīth*, "I verily hate that a man would hit his female slave when angry [with her] and then attempt to sleep with her in the day."[92] By making this argument, Ibn al-ʿArabī attempts, like ʿAṭāʾ before him, to argue that the legal norm is to avoid hitting.

A century later, al-Rāzī emerges as another proponent for the legal position that a husband should refrain from physically chastising a wife who is guilty of *nushūz*. He relies on al-Shāfiʿī's legal opinion that although a symbolic hitting is permitted as a third measure, it is legally preferable not to hit ("*wa tarkuhu afḍal*").[93] He bases this opinion on an authentic *ḥadīth* which states, "Certainly those [who beat] are not the best among you."[94] In his *tafsīr*, al-Rāzī cites the entire report and al-Shāfiʿī's commentary on it.[95] The effect of both Ibn al-ʿArabī's and al-Rāzī's commentary is to turn the function of the imperative "hit them" into a disliked action.

Qurʾan 4:128: Consequences of Men's *Nushūz*

> If a woman fears *nushūz* or neglect from her husband, there is no blame upon them if they settle and settlement (*al-ṣulḥ*) is good (*khayr*); and selfishness is ever-present in human souls. But if you do good and are conscious of Him, God is indeed aware of all that you do. (Qurʾān 4:128)

The corollary to men's *nushūz*, based on a literal reading of the verse, is for both spouses to reach a compromise. The verse uses the dual form of the Arabic verb "to settle"—*yuṣliḥā*—which denotes a level of mutuality. Despite the explicit wording of the Qurʾānic text, premodern exegetes disproportionately lay the onus to settle on the wife. For the most part, they recommended she relinquish some of her financial rights or nights allotted to her in order to salvage her marriage. Considering the fact that women who were guilty of *nushūz* bore the consequences of their "deviation" or recalcitrance in premodern interpretations of Qurʾān 4:34, it is not unusual to find premodern exegetes disproportionately lay the consequences of men's *nushūz* on women as well.

The explicit wording of the clause "there is no blame upon them if they settle" led most of the premodern exegetes to read this as permission for a compromise that entails the relinquishment of one or a few of the legal rights that spouses owed each other, based on Islamic legal norms. They based this interpretation on reports from early authorities, including the Prophet's wife, ʿĀʾisha, regarding the occasion of this verse's revelation. With some variation in the main characters, the primary narrative of these reports remained the same: a wife fears that her husband may divorce her, an outcome she wants to preempt, so she relinquishes her right to a fair allotment of nights to remain married. For example, al-Ṭabarī cites twenty-two reports in which the wife compromises her rights to reach a settlement with her spouse. The nature of this compromise, according to seventeen of these reports, is to relinquish either some or all of her *qisma*, a specific allotment of nights.[96] By interpreting "settlement" in terms of a wife fully or partially relinquishing her right to have her husband spend the night with her (*ḥaqq al-mabīt*), which implies sexual intimacy, these reports underscored that the husband's *nushūz* stems from his loss of sexual interest in his wife. However, al-Ṭabarī cites four reports that place the responsibility to compromise on the husband. In contrast to twenty-two reports, these four reports use the Arabic term *yuṣāliḥuhā*—"he makes amends with her." Three of these reports describe the husband as making amends by giving her a predictable allotment of nights; two of them also mention monetary compensation.[97]

The later exegetes al-Zamakhsharī and al-Rāzī make no mention of the opinion that the husband should compromise anything. Rather, in both cases, the onus to compromise is on the wife, if she desires to remain married. For al-Zamakhsharī, the woman's compromise consists of renouncing her right to *qisma*—the allotment of specific nights a man should spend with his wife. Similarly, al-Rāzī writes, "this settlement is like a wife giving back all or some of her marital dower (*mahr*) to the husband, dropping the right to financial provision or dropping the right to *qism*, an allotment of nights" out of a desire to remain married.[98] This interpretation is nearly identical in the exegesis of a later commentator, al-Bayḍāwī. Although the Qurʾān uses the dual form "they (dual) settle," he proceeds to interpret this in terms of the singular feminine: "She drops some of her marital dower or allotment of nights for him, or she gifts him something to win his affection."[99]

The notion that husbands should be the ones to compromise for their *nushūz* makes a comeback in the seventh/thirteenth-century exegesis of al-Qurṭubī. Whereas al-Rāzī and al-Zamakhsharī interpret the meaning of settlement only in terms of a wife's relinquishment of rights, al-Qurṭubī concludes there could be four distinct outcomes of the "settlement" described in this verse: first, the husband compensates the wife in exchange for her patience; second, she compensates him and he does not give preference to another over her; third, she compensates him in exchange for him to hold on to the marriage (i.e., does not divorce her) and prefer another wife over her; and fourth, they mutually agree to settle on the following terms: the wife will be patient; the husband will prefer another over her, without compensation from either side.[100]

One must question, however, why would classical exegetes suggest that a wife give up some of her rights in order to remain married to a man who no longer desires her? The answer to this question is embedded in the way exegetes interpreted the phrase *wa'l-ṣulḥ khayr*, "and reconciliation is better." The comparative form, "better," indicated that reconciliation was a superior alternative to something else. Thus, exegetes presumed that it was "better" for an aged woman to remain within a marriage in which her husband financially provided for her—even if she had to forgo sexual rights—than to be divorced.

Conclusion

This chapter finds that premodern exegetes' interpretations on women were influenced by two distinct set of factors: their hermeneutics and their intellectual, cultural, and social milieu. Their views on women were often embedded in their historical, sociocultural realities, which—at times—informed their understanding of certain Qur'ānic phrases on women. The hermeneutics that exegetes applied—including an application of disciplines or subfields such as philology, law, theology, and *ḥadīth*—also determined the range of possible meanings a verse could hold. An exegete's selection of evidence to support a specific meaning was not inconsequential to his interpretation. For example, whereas al-Ṭabarī cites a report by Ibn ʿAbbās to argue that "men's degree" meant a responsibility to be magnanimous to women, Ibn Kathīr instead points to gender differences in Islamic legal rulings to argue that "men's degree" means they are preferred over women in this world and the next. The significant variation one finds among medieval exegetes illustrates the ways in which they conferred egalitarian or patriarchal dimensions on certain verses, depending on the extra-Qur'ānic material they employed to interpret it.

Second, a closer engagement with *tafsīr* reveals a more complex image of classical and modern exegetes' attitude toward women, a byproduct of the genre's interpretive pluralism. Although medieval male exegetes do not appear to place a premium on notions of gender justice, as we may understand these concepts in our contemporary context, this does not mean that medieval exegetes and jurists were not attuned to other notions of significance to those invested in gender justice.[101] For example, one finds that the themes of justice, rights, and men's responsibility to provide good companionship to their wives (*ḥusn al-muʿāshara*) were also central to their understanding of marriage and divorce in the Qur'ān. The medieval exegetical tradition, despite its patriarchal bent, simultaneously reflects a consistent concern for women's welfare and well-being. This is not an attempt to absolve the exegetical tradition of the patriarchy it has imposed on Qur'ānic scripture at different junctures. Rather, it is an argument for understanding the historical and intellectual processes that govern the *tafsīr* tradition. The textual polysemy of this tradition suggests that a binary approach to the exegetical tradition as either "patriarchal" or "egalitarian" is neither useful nor accurate. As Shuruq Naguib suggests, scholarship on gender in the Qur'ān should begin to consider more creative ways of thinking about and engaging the *tafsīr* tradition.[102]

Third, the project of determining the Qur'ān's meaning, known as Qur'ānic exegesis, has been far from monolithic, static, or conclusive. Despite the divergent methods and orientations of classical exegetes, they found a level of acceptance in Muslim scholarship by anchoring their interpretations within established methodological norms, not by reaching the same conclusions as previous exegetes, as some scholars have suggested.[103] Among its many functions, the genre of *tafsīr* created an interpretive space for understanding the Qur'ānic text, which exegetes viewed as polysemic and capable of accommodating multiple meanings.[104] The capacity to bring new meanings and reflections to bear on the Qur'ān is, therefore, inherent to the Qur'ānic exegetical tradition.

Notes

1. Muḥammad al-Ṭāhir Ibn ʿĀshūr, *al-Taḥrīr wa'l-tanwīr* (Tunis: al-Dār al-Tūnisiyya li-l-Nashr, 1984), 1:29.
2. Norman Calder, "*Tafsīr* from Tabarī to Ibn Kathīr: Problems in the Description of a Genre, Illustrated with Reference to the Story of Abraham," in *Approaches to the Qur'ān*, ed. G. R. Hawting and Abdul-Kader A. Shareef (London: Routledge, 1993), 103.
3. Ayesha Chaudhry's *Domestic Violence and the Islamic Tradition* (Oxford: Oxford University Press, 2014), 62–67, is one of the few works that give some attention to the way premodern exegetes interpreted men's *nushūz* in comparison to women's *nushūz*.
4. Muhammad Abdel-Haleem, *The Qur'ān: A New Translation*, Oxford World Classics (New York: Oxford University Press, 2004), 50.
5. Modern interpretations of these "gender verses" will be discussed in the next chapter.
6. For a detailed assessment of the significance of these terms, see amina wadud, *Qur'ān and Woman* (New York: Oxford University Press, 1999), 15–23.
7. Abū Jaʿfar Muḥammad ibn Jarīr al-Ṭabarī, *Jāmiʿ al-bayān ʿan taʾwīl al-Qur'ān* (Beirut: Dār al-Kutub al-ʿilmiyya, 2014), 3:566.
8. Attributed to the Successor, Mujāhid ibn Jabr (d. 102/720), al-Ṭabarī, *Jāmiʿ al-bayān* (2014), 3:566.
9. Al-Ṭabarī, *Jāmiʿ al-bayān* (2014), 3:566.
10. This is most likely the historian Abū Bakr Muḥammad ibn Isḥāq ibn Yasār (d. 151/768).
11. Al-Ṭabarī, *Jāmiʿ al-bayān* (2014), 3:566.
12. Ibid., 3:565.
13. For a comparative study of Shīʿī, Sunnī, and Ismāʿīlī exegesis on Qur'ān 4:1, see Karen Bauer, *Gender Hierarchy in the Qur'ān: Medieval Interpretations, Modern Responses* (New York: Cambridge University Press, 2015).
14. Al-Bayḍāwī's date of death is disputed in modern scholarship. For a detailed summary of this, see Farid Suleiman, "A Note on al-Bayḍāwī's Years of Birth and Death," *Journal of Qur'ānic Studies* 22, no. 2 (2020): 105–115.
15. ʿAbdallāh ibn ʿUmar al-Bayḍāwī, *Anwār al-tanzīl wa asrār al-taʾwīl*, ed. Muḥammad Khallāq and Mahmūd Aḥmad al-Aṭrash (Damascus: Dār al-Rashīd, 2000) 1:329; Ismāʿīl ibn ʿUmar Ibn Kathīr, *Tafsīr al-Qur'ān al-ʿaẓīm* (Riyadh: Dār al-Salām, 1999), 1:558–559; Maḥmūd ibn ʿUmar al-Zamakhsharī, *al-Kashshāf ʿan ḥaqāʾiq al-tanzīl wa ʿuyūn al-aqāwīl fī wujūh al-taʾwīl*, ed. Al-Shuraybīnī Sharīda (Cairo: Dār al-Ḥadīth, 2012), 1:429; Jalāl al-Dīn al-Maḥallī and Jalāl al-Dīn al-Suyūṭī, *Tafsīr al-Jalālayn* (Damascus: Dār Ibn Kathīr, 2011), 77.

16. Abū ʿAbdullāh Muḥammad ibn Aḥmad al-Anṣārī al-Qurṭubī, *al-Jāmiʿ li-aḥkām al-Qurʾān*, ed. ʿAbdullāh ibn ʿAbd al-Ḥasan al-Turkī (Beirut: Muʾassasat al-Risāla, 2006), 6:6; Abū al-Ḥasan ʿAlī ibn Muḥammad ibn Ḥabīb al-Māwardī, *al-Nukat wa-l-ʿuyūn* (Beirut: Dār al-Kutub al-ʿIlmiyya, n.d.) 1:446.
17. Abū ʿAbd al-Raḥmān al-Azadī al-Sulamī, *Ḥaqāʾiq al-Tafsīr*, ed. Sayyid ʿImrān (Beirut: Dār al-Kutub al-ʿIlmiyya, 2001), 1:139–140;ʿAbd al-Karīm ibn Huwāzin Abū al-Qāsim al-Qushayrī, *Laṭāʾif al-Ishārāt*, 3rd ed. (Cairo: al-Hayʾa al-Miṣriyya al-ʿĀmma li-l-Kitāb, 2000), 1:312; Ṣadr al-Dīn al-Baqlī, *ʿArāʾis al-Bayān fī Ḥaqāʾiq al-Qurʾān*, 1st ed., ed. Aḥmad Farīd al-Mazīdī (Beirut: Dār al-Kutub al-ʿIlmiyya, 2008), 1:229–230; ʿAbd al-Qādir al-Jaylānī, *Tafsīr al-Jaylānī*, rev. ed., ed. Aḥmad Farīd al-Mazīdī (Quetta, Pakistan: al-Makataba al-Maʿrūfiyya, 2010), 1:339.
18. Aḥmad Ibn Muḥammad Ibn ʿAjība, *al-Baḥr al-Madīd fī Tafsīr al-Qurʾān al-Majīd*, ed. Aḥmad ʿAbdullāh al-Qurashī Raslān (Cairo: n. publ, 1999), 1:459; Ismāʿīl Ḥaqqī al-Burūsawī, *Rūḥ al-Bayān fī Tafsīr al-Qurʾān* (Istanbul: al-Maṭbaʿa al-ʿUthmāniyya, 1911), 2:159. Since al-Burūsawī hailed from Bursa, Turkey, there are many distinct transliterations of his name, including al-Bursevî, al-Bursawī, and Burūsawī. I have adopted the transliteration used by the editors of *The Study Quran* (New York: HarperOne, 2015).
19. Al-Burūsawī, *Rūḥ al-Bayān*, 2:159.
20. Abū al-Naṣr Muḥammad ibn Masʿūd al-ʿAyyāshī, *al-Tafsīr* (Qum: Muʾassasat al-Biʿtha, 2000), 1:363.
21. Ibid. I use Bauer's translation of this sentence; see Bauer, *Gender Hierarchy*, 124.
22. Al-ʿAyyāshī, *al-Tafsīr*, 1:363.
23. Muḥammad Abū Jaʿfar ibn al-Ḥasan al-Ṭūsī, *al-Tibyān fī Tafsīr al-Qurʾān* (Beirut, Lebanon: Dār Iḥyāʾ al-Turāth al-ʿArabī, 1985) 3:100–101; Faḍl ibn Ḥasan al-Ṭabarsī, *Majmaʿ al-Bayān fī -Tafsīr al-Quʾrān* (Beirut: Dār al-Murtaḍā, 2006), 3:7.
24. The narration of this *ḥadīth* differs from one exegete to the other. In al-Bukhārī's compilation of *ḥadīth*, it appears accordingly: "The Prophet said, 'Whoever believes in Allah and the Last Day should not hurt (trouble) his neighbor. And I advise you to take care of the women, for they are created from a rib and the most crooked portion of the rib is its upper part; if you try to straighten it, it will break, and if you leave it, it will remain crooked, so I urge you to take care of the women' " ("Book of Marriage, Chapter 80: The exhortation of taking care of the women," *ḥadīth* no. 5185, *Ṣaḥīḥ al-Bukhārī*, Sunnah.com, accessed October 10, 2020, https://sunnah.com/bukhari/67/120).
25. Al-Rāzī, *Mafātīḥ al-Ghayb*, 4th ed., ed. Ibrāhīm Shams al-Dīn and Aḥmad Shams al-Dīn (Beirut: Dār al-Kutub al-ʿIlmiyya, 2013), 9:131–132.
26. Ibid., 9:132. I thank Abdullah Heyari for his critical insight in understanding al-Rāzī's complicated theological dialectic on this issue.
27. Ibid.
28. Ibid., 9:131.
29. Ibn Kathīr, *Tafsīr al-Qurʾān al-ʿAẓīm*, 1:557–558.
30. Asma Afsaruddin, "Early Women Exemplars and the Construction of Gendered Space: (Re-)Defining Feminine Moral Excellence," in *Harem Histories: Envisioning Places and Living Spaces*, ed. Marilyn Booth (Durham, NC: Duke University Press, 2010), 42–43. As she notes, two chapter headings in the work of ʿAbd al-Raḥmān Ibn al-Jawzī (d. 597/1201) best illustrate this point: "Cautioning women from going outside the Home" and "Mention of the Merit of (Staying) Home for Women." Karen Bauer finds that patriarchal

interpretations of the Qurʾān became more entrenched in the genre of *tafsīr* by the sixth/twelfth century; see Bauer, *Gender Hierarchy*, 272.

31. Qurʾān, 2:228. This is a slight modification of Yusuf Ali's translation.
32. This numbering of verses is based on the Kufi count, which is one of the seven canonical Qurʾānic recitations. Schools of Islamic law differ on the exact number of verses in the Qurʾān due to a number of factors, including whether or not one includes the *basmala* (referring to the statement *Bismillāh al-Raḥmān al-Raḥīm*)—and disjointed letters at the beginning of twenty-nine chapters.
33. There is a difference of opinion among the legal schools regarding whether three *qurūʾ* means three cycles of purity or menstruation. The Mālikī and Shāfiʿī position is that *qurʾ* (sing.) is a cycle of purity, whereas the Ḥanbalīs and Ḥanafīs argued that *qurʾ* is a menstrual cycle.
34. Jurists based this on Qurʾānic verse 65:4, which partially reads, "for those who carry (life within their wombs), their period is until they deliver their burdens."
35. Mustafa Khattab, Talal Itani, Muhammad Asad, Yusuf Ali, M. H. Shakir, and Marmaduke Pickthal all translate *islāḥ* as "reconciliation" in this verse.
36. Al-Ṭabarī, *Jāmiʿ al-Bayān* (2014), 2:467.
37. Ibid., 2:462–465.
38. Abū Bakr ibn al-ʿArabī, *Aḥkām al-Qurʾān* (Beirut: Dār al-Kutub al-ʿIlmiyya, 2012), 1:256.
39. Al-Rāzī, *Mafātīḥ al-Ghayb*, 6:81.
40. Ibid.
41. Al-Ṭabarī, *Jāmiʿ al-Bayān* (2014), 2:465–466.
42. Al-Rāzī, *Mafātīḥ al-Ghayb*, 6:81.
43. Ibn al-ʿArabī, *Aḥkam al-Qurʾān*, 1:256; al-Qurṭubī, *al-Jāmiʿ li-aḥkām al-Qurʾān*, 4:51.
44. According to Mālik ibn Anas, the founder of the Mālikī school, if a woman ransoms herself from her marriage (i.e., *iftidāʾ*) due to her husband harming or constraining her, the divorce is in effect and her money is returned to her; see *Sharḥ al-Zurqānī ʿalā Muwaṭṭaʾ al-Imām Mālik*, 4th ed. (Lebanon: Dar al-Kutub al-ʿIlmiyya, 2011), 3:240. See also the earlier Mālikī text, Khalīl ibn Isḥāq, *al-Tawḍīḥ: Sharḥ Mukhtaṣar ibn al-Ḥājib fī Fiqh al-Imām Mālik* (Lebanon: Dār al-Kutub al-ʿIlmiyya, 2011), 4:14.
45. Al-Rāzī, *Mafātīḥ al-Ghayb*, 6:79.
46. Ibid.
47. Al-Qurṭubī, *al-Jāmiʿ li-aḥkām al-Qurʾān*, 4:44.
48. A contemporary of the Prophet's companions; that is, from the second generation of Muslims.
49. Al-Qurṭubī, *al-Jāmiʿ li-aḥkām al-Qurʾān*, 4:44.
50. Al-Ṭabarī, *Jāmiʿ al-Bayān* (2014), 2:461.
51. Ibid., 2:462; al-Rāzī, *Mafātīḥ al-Ghayb*, 6:80; al-Qurṭubī, *al-Jāmiʿ li-aḥkām al-Qurʾān*, 4:45.
52. Al-Zamakhsharī, *al-Kashshāf*, 1:255.
53. Ibid.
54. Al-Bayḍāwī, *Anwār al-Tanzīl*, 1:196. My emphasis.
55. Ibid.
56. Bauer, *Gender Hierarchy*, 120, 163.
57. Al-Rāzī, *Mafātīḥ al-Ghayb*, 11:53.
58. According to a report in the early *ḥadīth* collection known as the *Muṣannaf* of ʿAbd al-Razzāq al-Ṣanʿānī (d. 211/827), the Prophet stated, "When one of you has intercourse with his wife, let him not rush away from her (*falyaṣduqhā*), after having attained his own

climax, until she is satisfied" ('Abd al-Razzāq al-Ṣan'ānī, *al-Muṣannaf* [Beirut: al-Maktāb al-Islāmī, 1983], 6:194, ḥadīth no. 10,466). A similar *ḥadīth*, although designated as *munkar* ("defective") due to its chain of transmission, is the following: "It is not appropriate that you fall upon your wives like a beast but you must send a message of love beforehand." It was narrated by al-Daylamī in his collection, *Musnad al-Firdaws*, and cited in Abū Ḥāmid al-Ghazālī, *Iḥyā' 'Ulūm al-Dīn* (Beirut: Dār al-Ma'rifa, 1982), 2:50.

59. The first reciprocal right, according to al-Qurṭubī, is that both spouses should attempt to look pleasing to the other. The second reciprocal right diverges from an understanding of equal rights for spouses, as he mentions that men should provide benevolent friendship and companionship to their wives, while women should obey their husbands in those matters that God has ordained for women to obey them. Like al-Ṭabarī, al-Qurṭubī constricts wifely obedience to the realm of legal responsibilities, rather than leaving it open-ended. The third and fourth reciprocal right of both spouses is not to harm the other and to be mindful of God in their treatment of each other (*al-Jāmi' li-Aḥkām al-Qur'ān*, 4:52).
60. Al-Qurṭubī, *al-Jāmi' li-aḥkām al-Qur'ān*, 4:52-53. He writes, "*wa 'in ra'ā al-rajul min nafsihi 'ajzan 'an iqāmati ḥaqqihā fī maḍji'ihā akhadha min al-adwiya allatī tazīd fī bāhihi wa tuqawwī shahwatahu ḥattā ya'ifuhā.*"
61. Al-Ṭabarī, *Jāmi' al-Bayān* (2014), 2:468.
62. Al-Ṭūsī, *al-Tibyān fī Tafsīr al-Qur'ān*, 2:241.
63. Ibid.
64. Al-Ṭabarsī, *Majma' al-Bayān*, 2:83-84.
65. Al-Rāzī cites the following eight reasons that give men an advantage over women (*azyad fī al-faḍīla*): (1) his mind; (2) the blood money to be paid to his family for his murder [which is supposedly less for a woman]; (3) his share of inheritance; (4) his suitability to serve as an imam [leader of prayers], a judge, and a witness; (5) he can marry another woman, have sexual relations with a concubine, while she cannot do so; (6) as a spouse, he will inherit more from her when she dies than she will inherit from him when he dies; (7) he has the right to divorce her and then retract the divorce [during the waiting period], whether or not she wants to return, whereas she does not share this right; and (8) his share of war spoils is greater (al-Rāzī, *Mafātīḥ al-Ghayb*, 6:82).
66. Al-Rāzī's statement that men are *azyad fī al- faḍīla* is a paraphrase of al-Zamakhsharī's interpretation that men have a *ziyāda fī al-ḥaqq wa faḍīla*; see al-Zamakhsharī, *al-Kashshāf*, 1:255.
67. Al-Rāzī, *Mafātīḥ al-Ghayb*, 6:82.
68. Ibid.
69. Ibid.
70. Ibid., 6:82. Different narrations of this *ḥadīth* exist in various collections, but this exact narration is found in *Sunan al-Tirmidhī*, no. 1159, and is narrated by Abū Hurayra.
71. Although none of the exegetes fully identify Ḥumayd, he is most likely Ḥumayd ibn Mas'ada al-Bāhilī al-Baṣrī from the third/ninth century, one of the narrators of *Ṣaḥiḥ al-Bukhārī*. I thank Hatim Yousef for his assistance in identifying this narrator.
72. Al-Qurṭubī, *al-Jāmi' li-aḥkām al-Qur'ān*, 4:53.
73. Al-Ṭabarī, *Jāmi' al-Bayān* (2014), 2:468; al-Māwardī, *al-Nukat wa-l-'uyūn*, 1:293; Abū Muḥammad 'Abd al-Ḥaqq ibn Ghālib Ibn 'Aṭiyya, *al-Muḥarrar al-Wajīz fī Tafsīr al-Kitāb al-'Azīz* (Beirut: Dār al-Kutub al-'Ilmiyya, 2001), 1:306; Abū Bakr ibn al-'Arabī, *Aḥkām al-Qur'ān*, 1:256; al-Qurṭubī, *Al-Jāmi' li-aḥkām al-Qur'ān*, 4:53.
74. Al-Qurṭubī, *Al-Jāmi' li-aḥkām al-Qur'ān*, 4:53.

75. Ibid., 4:54.
76. Ibid., 4:54.
77. Ibn Kathīr, *Tafsīr al-Qurʾān al-ʿAẓīm*, 1:271.
78. Al-Ṭabarī, *Jāmiʿ al-Bayān* (2014), 4:64.
79. Ibid., 4:304.
80. Women's legal right to equal treatment with co-wives is discussed in all four legal schools based on Qurʾānic verse 4:3 and the Prophetic tradition: "If a person has two wives and he is inclined towards one of them, he will appear on the Day of Judgement with one of his sides paralyzed" (*Sunan Abī Dawūd*, "Book of Marriage" [Kitāb al-Nikāḥ], *ḥadīth* no. 88); I use Imran Nyazee's translation of this *ḥadīth*, as cited in Burhān al-Dīn al-Marghīnānī, *al-Hidāyah*, trans. Imran Khan Nyazee (Bristol, England: Amal Press, 2006), 1:545.
81. Al-Zamakhsharī, *al-Kashshāf*, 1:473.
82. Ibid., 1:532.
83. Al-Rāzī, *Mafātīḥ al-Ghayb*, 11:52.
84. Ibid., 10:73.
85. Ibid., 11:52.
86. Al-Ṭabarī, *Jāmiʿ al-Bayān ʿan Taʾwīl al-Qurʾān*, 2nd ed., ed. Maḥmūd Shākir and Aḥmad Shākir (Cairo: Dār al-Maʿārif, 1961), 8:314–315. See reports #9385 and #9389. Other editions of al Ṭabarī's work omitted the terms *ghayr shāʾin* and *ghayr muʾaththir*.
87. A small twig of the *arak* tree, traditionally used as a toothbrush and recommended for hygienic use by the Prophet. It is also referred to as *miswāk*.
88. Al-Ṭabarī, *Jāmiʿ al-Bayān* (1961 ed.), 8:314–315. See reports #9368, #9387, and #9388. In the last one, ʿAṭāʾ does not identify Ibn ʿAbbās as the source of this information.
89. Ayesha Chaudhry lists twenty-eight other exegetes who qualify that any hitting must be *ghayr mubarriḥ*; see *Domestic Violence*, appendix 24, 232.
90. Ibn al-ʿArabī, *Aḥkām al-Qurān*, 1:536.
91. Ibid.
92. Ibid. See also al-Bukhārī, *Ṣaḥiḥ al-Bukhārī*, Chapter on Marriage, #94.
93. Al-Rāzī, *Mafātīḥ al-Ghayb*, 10:73.
94. Classified as *ṣaḥīḥ* and narrated by Aḥmad ibn Ḥanbal, Abū Dawūd, al-Nasāʾī, Ibn Ḥibbān, and al-Ḥākim; see *Mawsūʿat al-Sunna*, "Abū Dawūd," 8, no. 2146 (Tunis: Dār al-Saḥnūn and Dār al-Daʿwa, 1992), 608.
95. The tradition narrated by al-Rāzī is: "It has been related that ʿUmar b. al-Khaṭṭāb said: 'We, the people of Quraysh, our men used to dominate our women, but when we came to Medina, we found that their women dominated their men. Then our women mingled [with their women] and they began to snub (*dhaʾirna*) their husbands, meaning they committed *nushūz* and became audacious. So, I went to the Prophet and said: the women have snubbed (or turned away from) their husbands, so permit us to strike them. Thereafter, a gathering of women surrounded the apartments of the wives of the Prophet, all of them complaining about their husbands. So [the Prophet] said: "The family of Muhammad was surrounded tonight by seventy women, all of them complaining about their husbands. You will not find those [who hit their women] the best among you," (al-Rāzī, *Mafātīḥ al-Ghayb*, 10:73). Most legal manuals and *ḥadīth* collections cite a slightly different narration by ʿUmar. See *ḥadīth* no. 14775, *Sunan al-Bayhaqī al-Kubrā*, 3rd ed. (Beirut: Dār al-Kutub al-ʿIlmiyya, 2003), 7:496 and al-Shāfiʿī, *al-Umm*, 6:423–424.
96. Al-Ṭabarī, *Jāmiʿ al-Bayān* (2014 ed.), 4:305–308.
97. Ibid.

98. Al-Rāzī, *Mafātīḥ al-Ghayb*, 11:53.
99. Al-Bayḍāwī, *Anwār al-Tanzīl*, 1:397.
100. Al-Qurṭubī, *al-Jāmiʿ li-Aḥkām al-Qurʾān*, 7:164.
101. Bauer, *Gender Hierarchy*, 119, 166; Shuruq Naguib, "Horizons and Limitations of Muslim Feminist Hermeneutics: Reflections on the Menstruation Verse," *New Topics in Feminist Philosophy of Religion*, ed. Pamela Anderson (Netherlands: Springer, 2010), 38–43.
102. Shuruq Naguib, "Horizons and Limitations," 47.
103. Aysha Hidayatullah, *Feminist Edges of the Qurʾān* (New York: Oxford University Press, 2014), 179–180; Ayesha Chaudhry, "The Ethics of Marital Discipline in Pre-Modern Qurʾānic Exegesis," *Journal of the Society of Christian Ethics* 30, no. 2 (Fall/Winter 2010), 128.
104. Calder, "*Tafsīr* from Ṭabarī to Ibn Kathīr," 103.

Bibliography

Afsaruddin, Asma. "Early Women Exemplars and the Construction of Gendered Space: (Re)Defining Feminine Moral Excellence." In *Harem Histories: Envisioning Places and Living Spaces*, edited by Marilyn Booth, 42–43. Durham, NC: Duke University Press, 2010.

ʿAyyāshī, Abū al-Naṣr Muḥammad ibn Masʿūd al-. *Al-Tafsīr*. Edited by Qism al-Dirāsāt al-Islāmiyya. Qom: Muʾassasat al-Biʿtha, 2000.

Baqlī, Ṣadr al-Dīn al-. *ʿArāʾis al-Bayān fī Ḥaqāʾiq al-Qurʾān*. 1st ed. Edited by Aḥmad Farīd al-Mazīdī. Beirut: Dār al-Kutub al-ʿIlmiyya, 2008.

Bauer, Karen. *Gender Hierarchy in the Qurʾān: Medieval Interpretations, Modern Responses*. New York: Cambridge University Press, 2015.

Bayḍāwī, ʿAbdallāh ibn ʿUmar al-. *Anwār al-Tanzīl wa Asrār al-Taʾwīl*. Edited by Muḥammad Khallāq and Mahmūd Aḥmad al-Aṭrash. Damascus: Dār al-Rashīd, 2000.

Burūsawī, Ismāʿīl Ḥaqqī al-. *Rūḥ al-Bayān fī Tafsīr al-Qurʾān*. Istanbul: al-Maṭbaʿa al-ʿUthmāniyya, 1911.

Calder, Norman. "Tafsir from Tabarī to Ibn Kathīr: Problems in the Description of a Genre, Illustrated with Reference to the Story of Abraham." In *Approaches to the Quran*, edited by G. R. Hawting and Abdul-Kader A. Shareef, 101–140. London: Routledge, 1993.

Chaudhry, Ayesha S. *Domestic Violence and the Islamic Tradition*. Oxford: Oxford University Press, 2014.

Chaudhry, Ayesha S. "The Ethics of Marital Discipline in Premodern Qurʾānic Exegesis." *Journal of the Society of Christian Ethics* 30, no. 2 (Fall/Winter 2010): 123–130.

Hidayatullah, Aysha. *Feminist Edges of the Qurʾān*. New York: Oxford University Press, 2014.

Ibn ʿAjība, Aḥmad Ibn Muḥammad. *Al-Baḥr al-Madīd fī Tafsīr al-Qurʾān al-Majīd*. Edited by Aḥmad ʿAbdullāh al-Qurashī Raslān. Cairo: No publisher, 1999.

Ibn al-ʿArabī, Abū Bakr. *Aḥkām al-Qurʾān*. 5th ed. Edited by Muḥammad ʿAbd al-Qādir ʿAṭā. Beirut: Dār al-Kutub al-ʿIlmiyya, 1971.

Ibn al-Jawzī, Jamāl al-Dīn al-Qurashī al-Baghdādī. *Tafsīr Zād al-Masīr fī ʿIlm al-Tafsīr*. Beirut: Dār ibn Ḥazm, 2002.

Ibn ʿĀshūr, Muḥammad al-Ṭāhir. *Al-Taḥrīr wa-l-tanwīr*. Tunis: al-Dār al-Tūnisiyya li-l-Nashr, 1984.

Ibn ʿAṭiyya, Abū Muḥammad ʿAbd al-Ḥaqq ibn Ghālib. *Al-Muḥarrar al-Wajīz fī Tafsīr al-Kitāb al-ʿAzīz*. Beirut: Dār al-Kutub al-ʿIlmiyya, 2001.
Ibn Isḥāq, Khalīl. *Al-Tawḍīḥ: Sharḥ Mukhtaṣar ibn al-Ḥājib fī Fiqh al-Imām Mālik*. Lebanon: Dār al-Kutub al-ʿIlmiyya, 2011.
Ibn Kathīr, Ismāʿīl ibn ʿUmar. *Tafsīr al-Qurʾān al-ʿAẓīm*. Riyadh: Dār al-Salām li-l-Nashr wa-l-Tawzīʿ, 1999.
Jaylānī, ʿAbd al-Qādir al-. *Tafsīr al-Jaylānī*. Rev. ed. Edited by Aḥmad Farīd al-Mazīdī. Quetta, Pakistan: al-Makataba al-Maʿrūfiyya, 2010.
Maḥallī, Jalāl al-Dīn al-, and Jalāl al-Dīn al-Suyūṭī. *Tafsīr al-Jalālayn*. Damascus: Dār Ibn Kathīr, 2011.
Marghīnānī, Burhān al-Dīn al-. *Al-Hidāyah*. Translated by Imran Nyazee. Bristol, England: Amal Press, 2006.
Māwardī, Abū al-Ḥasan ʿAlī ibn Muḥammad ibn Ḥabīb al-. *Al-Nukat wa-l-ʿuyūn*. Beirut: Dār al-Kutub al-ʿIlmiyya, 1992.
Naguib, Shuruq. "Horizons and Limitations of Feminist Hermeneutics." In *New Topics in Feminist Philosophy of* Religion, edited by Pamela Anderson, 33–49. Netherlands: Springer, 2010.
Qurṭubī, Abū ʿAbdullāh Muḥammad ibn Aḥmad al-Anṣārī al-. *Al-Jāmiʿ li-Aḥkām al-Qurʾān*. Edited by ʿAbdullāh ibn ʿAbd al-Ḥasan al-Turkī. Beirut: Muʾassasat al-Risāla, 2006.
Qushayrī, ʿAbd al-Karīm ibn Huwāzin Abū al-Qāsim al-. *Laṭāʾif al-Ishārāt*. 3rd ed. Cairo: al-Hayʾa al-Maṣriyya al-ʿĀmma li-l-Kitāb, 2000.
Rāzī, Fakhr al-Dīn al-. *Al-Tafsīr al-Kabīr (Mafātīḥ al-Ghayb)*. 4th ed. Edited by Ibrāhīm Shams al-Dīn and Aḥmad Shams al-Dīn. Beirut: Dār al-Kutub al-ʿIlmiyya, 2013.
Saleh, Walid. *The Formation of the Classical Tafsīr Tradition*. Leiden: Brill, 2004.
Ṣanʿānī, ʿAbd al-Razzāq al-. *Al-Muṣannaf*. Beirut: al-Maktab al-Islāmī, 1983.
Sulamī, Abū ʿAbd al-Raḥmān al-Azadī al-. *Ḥaqāʾiq al-Tafsīr*, edited by Sayyid ʿImrān. Beirut: Dār al-Kutub al-ʿIlmiyya, 2001.
Ṭabarī, Abū Jaʿfar Muḥammad ibn Jarīr al-. *Jāmiʿ al-Bayān ʿan Taʾwīl al-Qurʾān*. 6th ed. Beirut: Dār al-Kutub al-ʿIlmiyya, 2014.
Ṭabarī, Abū Jaʿfar Muḥammad ibn Jarīr al-. *Jāmiʿ al-Bayān ʿan Taʾwīl al-Qurʾān*. 2nd ed. Edited by Maḥmūd Shākir and Aḥmad Shākir. Cairo: Dār a-Maʿārif, 1961.
Ṭabarsī, Faḍl ibn Ḥasan al-. *Majmaʿ al-Bayān fī Tafsīr al-Quʾrān*. 1st ed. Beirut: Dār al-Murtaḍā, 2006.
Ṭūsī, Muḥammad Abū Jaʿfar Ibn al-Ḥasan al-. *al-Tibyān fī Tafsīr al-Qurʾān*. Edited by Aḥmad Ḥabīb al-Quṣayr al-ʿĀmilī. Beirut, Lebanon: Dār Iḥyāʾ al-Turāth al-ʿArabī, 1985.
Wadud, amina. *Qurʾān and Woman*. New York: Oxford University Press, 1999.
Zamakhsharī, Maḥmūd ibn ʿUmar al-. *al-Kashshāf ʿan Ḥaqāʾiq al-Tanzīl Wa ʿUyūn al-Aqāwīl fī Wujūh al-Taʾwīl*. Edited by al-Shuraybīnī Sharīda. Cairo: Dār al-Ḥadīth, 2012.
Zurqānī, Muḥammad ibn ʿAbd al-Bāqī al-. *Sharḥ al-Zurqānī ʿalā Muwaṭṭaʾ Imām Mālik*. 4th ed. Lebanon: Dār al-Kutub al-ʿIlmiyya, 2011.

CHAPTER 3

WOMEN IN THE *ḤADĪTH* LITERATURE

FERYAL SALEM

Ḥadīth literature is rich with its references to women from the ancient past as well as those from the Prophet Muḥammad's contemporary period. A study of the way in which women are portrayed and referenced in *ḥadīth* texts provides a unique glimpse into the roles women played for the narrators of these prophetic traditions. Women in the *ḥadīth* literature can be divided into four primary categories: (1) women whose stories are told from the past; (2) stories, narratives, and references to the wives of the Prophet whose rank as "Mothers of the Believers (*ummahāt al-muʾminīn*)," earned them a distinctive role as instructional models; (3) women who were considered Companions of the Prophet or *saḥābiyyāt*; and finally (4) statements and references to women as a general category without specific references to any particular individual.

While not an exhaustive study, bringing together all of these types of occurrences of women in *ḥadīth* texts helps us have a more accurate understanding of women's roles and contributions to early Islam through examining the *ḥadīth* corpus holistically. This is especially so since selective readings of *ḥadīths* can convey the biases of the reader, transmitter, or the memory of the individual narrator. A broad study of the different ways in which women are portrayed in early *ḥadīth* reports creates a significantly more nuanced perspective that acknowledges complexity and the human element in the transmission process.

The *Ḥadīth* of Umm Zarʿ

Among the most well-known *ḥadīths* in which women feature prominently is what is famously known as the "*Ḥadīth* Umm Zarʿ." This *ḥadīth* has received so much attention by Muslim scholars that numerous commentaries and studies of this one prophetic tradition can be found in Islamic sources.[1] What is noteworthy however, is that despite the focus of this *ḥadīth* on women and its narration by a woman, this woman-centric perspective present in the narration is commonly overlooked by male scholars. This perspective tends to be restored when women are present in scholarly circles of interpretation, which leads to a more sustained reflection on the spiritual significance of this *ḥadīth*.

The *ḥadīth* of Umm Zarʿ begins with the Prophet's wife ʿĀʾisha telling the story of eleven women from the pre-Islamic period, gathering to speak about their husbands and promising each other that they would be completely honest. The first woman begins by characterizing her husband as a piece of emaciated flesh on a camel that is neither easy to climb on nor flexible enough to move on its own. The second woman said that she would not start talking about her husband's flaws because if she started, she feared she would not be able to stop.[2] The third woman said her husband was rough and if she dared speak, he would either divorce her or keep her in limbo.[3] The fourth woman compared her husband to the "night of Tihāma," which was neither too hot nor too cold. He was neither menacing nor demanding. The fifth woman praised her husband saying that he was like a lynx in the house and a lion when he was in public. He also does not hold his family to account for gifts and provisions he has generously given them. The sixth woman said that when her husband eats, he feasts and when he drinks, he empties the jug. When he lies down, he curls up to himself without extending a hand of comfort to his wife. The seventh woman said her husband was a buffoon who had every illness. He will either hurt you or wound you or both. The eighth woman said her husband had the gentle touch of a rabbit and a fragrant smell. The ninth woman described her husband as being refined and of tall stature. His home is near the center of congregation. The tenth woman talked about her husband's extensive wealth beyond the average imagination.

These ten women precede the eleventh woman, who is known as Umm Zarʿ. Although this lengthy and much-cited prophetic tradition is better known by its second segment, which focuses on the story of Umm Zarʿ, the inclusion of all of the detailed descriptions of the various types of husbands above is significant. In recalling this incident while with the Prophet, ʿĀʾisha could have omitted the first ten women's stories, considering them superfluous. But the narrative indicates that she explicitly chose not to do so. This general structure of ten women's descriptions preceding the story of Umm Zarʿ has also been preserved in a number of chains of transmission in different *ḥadīth* texts with little variation. While some commentators on the *ḥadīth* have highlighted the peculiar Arabic vocabulary in this narrative and others have commented on the Prophet's patience with his family in his willingness to listen to what may be deemed as an old wives tale, what is often missing in examinations of this *ḥadīth* is its instructional relevance for men seeking to understand prophetic ideals of male companionship through analyzing the allusions and connotations of each of the ten women's depictions of what constitutes a good husband and a bad one as portrayed by ʿĀʾisha to the Prophet Muḥammad.

Each of these ten women's husbands personify both vices and virtues that women look for and desire in marriage companions. The first two women describe bad husbands who are either so difficult to live with that they are like "insurmountable pieces of flesh on a camel," or they are full of so many flaws that if their wives began to speak about them in public, they "fear they would not stop." It would appear that through using metaphor and indirect critique of specific models of male companionship which do injustice to their female counterparts, ʿĀʾisha is using this *ḥadīth* as a medium of instruction to men who will later hear this *ḥadīth*. Furthermore, if ʿĀʾisha is perceived as the scholar and teacher to the early Muslim community that she was commonly believed to be, it would seem reasonable to assume that every part of the *ḥadīth*, including that of the first ten women, is deliberately included for instructional purposes, with particular attention to male listeners.

ʿĀʾisha's role as a leader and teacher to men is reminiscent of another *ḥadīth* in which she instructs men in a far more personal matter to follow the Prophet's example by telling them, "If someone relates to you that the Messenger of Allah urinated while standing, do not believe him."[4] The other *ḥadīths* on this specific issue are considered weak by *ḥadīth* transmitters. The exception is in ʿĀʾisha's narration of the *ḥadīth* whose transmission has been relied on to derive preferred practices from a legal perspective (*fiqhī*) that ensure male modesty in these circumstances. Although there are numerous other examples of ʿĀʾisha's religious authority, her ability to instruct men in such intimate matters reflects her strength of leadership in addressing an even more urgent matter for the cohesiveness of family structures in the early Muslim community by teaching men about good male companionship and what may be termed in contemporary contexts as "positive masculinity" through her story telling in the *Ḥadīth* of Umm Zarʿ.

The third and seventh women similarly describe men who are abusive toward their wives, either emotionally or physically. The placement of these qualities and vices is also tactfully instructive. When the tale of the eleventh woman begins, the listener may assume by the third woman that all of the men are villains in this narrative. However, this pattern is abruptly broken by the fourth woman, who in describing her husband as a lynx at home and a lion in public is alluding to his flexible and mild nature among his family members and his firmness among those who are unrelated to him. This gentleness among kin and firmness among strangers is reminiscent of the Qur'ānic verse in which believers are described as "firm towards the disbelievers and merciful among themselves" (Qur'ān, 48:29). The fifth woman's husband follows in stark contrast by being a slothful and lazy husband at home who eats and drinks too much. She also describes her husband as curling up when he sleeps and not extending a hand to "uncover any sorrow." Lest the implications of the absence of his intimate companionship be lost on the listener, the eighth husband is admired for his smooth touch and good smell.

The inclusion of these references to women's appreciation or lack thereof of the intimate companionship of their husbands is significant in that they affirm women's sexuality. This is explicitly mentioned in the *ḥadīth* of Umm Zarʿ, in addition to other positive qualities of the husband, such as his ability to support his wife emotionally, and thereby affirming her humanity as another integral element of a marital partnership. The ninth and tenth women expand further on the qualities that women seek in husbands through highlighting the generosity and material support that each of these men provided their wives.

The eleventh woman shifts the focus of this story to another chapter when she begins by saying that her husband was Abū Zarʿ. She is the first woman to actually name her husband. She then proceeds to ask the question, "And who was this Abū Zarʿ?"—after which she begins a lengthy description of her marriage that is notably longer than that of all of the ten women who came before. Abū Zarʿ gave his wife much jewelry and her earrings swung back and forth on her ears. Her arms became fleshy and Abū Zarʿ praised his wife until she began to praise herself. He married his wife from a modest family and brought her into luxury and comfort, indicating that he did not marry her for her family connections. The eleventh woman, whom we will learn is named Umm Zarʿ, says that when she spoke her husband listened and did not turn her away. She slept until the morning and drank her fill.

The story describes in equal detail all of the comforts and luxuries that each of their children and members of their household enjoyed. But the story takes a turn in that one day, Abū Zarʿ went out and met a woman with two boys. Abū Zarʿ divorced Umm Zarʿ and married this other woman. Umm Zarʿ says that after Abū Zarʿ, she too remarried and that her new husband was a noble and generous man who told her to eat and drink to her fill. He gave her various pairs of cattle and showered her with all the gifts she might desire. He also gave her everything she needed to support her family. After emphasizing the generosity of her new husband, Umm Zarʿ says that "If I combined everything he gave me, it would not have equaled the smallest vessel from Abū Zarʿ." Upon finishing the story, ʿĀʾisha relates that the Prophet Muḥammad said to his wife, "I am to you what Abū Zarʿ was to Umm Zarʿ, except that he divorced her and I will never divorce you."[5]

While many commentators have studied this *ḥadīth* for its rhetoric, Arabic folklore, and legal implications, such as the permissibility of relating stories about others when the identities of the participants are unnamed, there is a dearth of studies that examine the implications this report has for women's roles and representation in the early Islamic tradition. Considering that the silence of the Prophet toward words and actions done in his presence is considered by *ḥadīth* scholars as an act of approval and hence a part of the prophetic Sunna from which Muslims can draw ethical guidelines, the lack of correction or condemnation of the Prophet as he listened to his wife tell this tale is more than simply instructive of what constitutes backbiting (*ghība*) and whether the anonymity of characters in a story makes exposing their negative actions permissible, as has commonly been discussed in legal (*fiqh*) commentaries on the *ḥadīth*.

It goes further to indicate what kinds of behaviors and companionship models in husbands are regarded as encompassing prophetic ideals. This is even more pressing when one juxtaposes this *ḥadīth* to another in which the Prophet states, "the best among you are those who are best to their wives, and I am the best among you to my wife."[6] Furthermore, we see in this *ḥadīth* that the Prophet is not only silent as ʿĀʾisha relays the story to him, he himself becomes an active participant in the narrative by comparing himself to Abū Zarʿ in his relationship to ʿĀʾisha with the important exception that he will never leave her. Thus, the absence of a rigorous discussion of the significance of this *ḥadīth* to understanding gender dynamics by both past and present scholars is a conspicuous shortcoming in the study of this *ḥadīth* in particular, as well as the depiction of women in *ḥadīth* literature in general.

As mentioned, it would appear that in relaying this story ʿĀʾisha is seeking to convey an instructive message to the men of the early Muslim community about what women seek in their male companions. The prophetic approval and participation in this narrative, and its later reporting in the canonical *ḥadīth* books of al-Bukhārī, Muslim, and Tirmidhī, make this a tradition that cannot be ignored and forgotten.[7] Umm Zarʿ's depiction of Abū Zarʿ "praising her until she started praising herself," signifies the importance of men showing respect and value to their wives as a way to help them feel comfortable about their own self-worth. Abū Zarʿ also listened to his wife when she spoke and "did not turn her away." This is another Islamic ideal of male interaction with the women in their lives that is personified in the actions of Abū Zarʿ. He let her "sleep until the morning" and gave her everything she needed, indicating that an ideal husband takes responsibility for taking care of the needs of his wife and makes her comfort a priority. Abū Zarʿ married a woman who came from a materially less privileged background and elevated her in rank through her shared life with him. This too is an indication that a husband who is following the model set out by the Prophet in this *ḥadīth* does not belittle his wife in their marriage and ensures that their marital bond is one of a mutual relationship that encompasses a shared identity rather than a woman being regarded as still affiliated with her parental family unit while the children and husband are affiliated with the man, as happens in some traditional cultures.

All of this behavior is then explicitly endorsed by the Prophet when he tells ʿĀʾisha that he is Abū Zarʿ to her with the one major exception which is that he will never divorce her. It appears that even in this interaction is an instructive lesson to Muslim men who seek to emulate prophetic models of masculinity. The Prophet in this *ḥadīth* did not leave his wife "hanging" or cultivate in her a sense of insecurity as a form of domination. The Prophet is endorsing Abū Zarʿ's benevolence to his wife and then surpassing it through giving his wife ʿĀʾisha a sense of permanence in her irreplaceable position in the Prophet Muḥammad's life. In doing so, the Prophet appears to be exemplifying another *ḥadīth* in which he states that women are the other halves of men (*al-nisāʾ shaqāʾiq al-rijāl*)[8] and teaching men through his example how to make the women in their lives feel valued, loved, respected, and secure in their status. This challenges conceptions of masculinity that are sometimes framed as Islamic, but commonly transcend religious affiliation in which the expression of deep commitment to one woman, interacting with her on the basis of love, respect, and devotion are deemed as either weaknesses or imports from romanticized relationship models that are alien to Islamic norms.

Furthermore, the framing of Umm Zarʿ's description of the events leading to their breakup is also significant. When Abū Zarʿ went out and fell in love with another woman, he did not simply marry her as another wife in a polygamous relationship. Abū Zarʿ divorced Umm Zarʿ and married this other woman. The theme of monogamous relationships in this narrative is noteworthy in that it challenges assumptions that the idea of a man and a woman having a monogamous loving relationship is alien to the early Islamic community.

Once again, the Prophet did not interrupt to ask why Abū Zarʿ needed to divorce Umm Zarʿ to marry the other woman, as some contemporary Muslim men may ask. Instead, the prophetic correction to this story is that unlike Abū Zarʿ, the Prophet would never divorce ʿĀʾisha. This also challenges modern male conceptions of masculinity in which polygamy in some modern Muslim movements has taken on an ideological form and even considered by some as a religiously mandated manifestation of masculinity. For Muslims who rely on the *ḥadīth* tradition to derive the Sunna or prophetic precedent, the Prophet Muḥammad's conspicuous silence on the option of polygamy is instructive. His corrective role in this story can also be instructive for Muslims. The Prophet makes no mention of polygamy as a corrective to Abū Zarʿ's behavior but rather mentions a superior form of loyalty to his wife as the corrective. It is, after all, noteworthy that the Prophet Muḥammad emphasizes that, unlike Abū Zarʿ, he would never abandon his wife ʿĀʾisha to whom he expressed his love.

Other significant elements of the *ḥadīth* from the perspective of gender is that the woman whom Abū Zarʿ leaves Umm Zarʿ for is not a younger woman who had never been married. Instead, she is either a divorced or widowed woman with two male children at her feet when he sees her and falls in love with her. The lack of stigma for a woman in this stage in her life and her ability to tempt Abū Zarʿ away from his wife is in sharp contrast to later cultural norms that developed in many parts of the Muslim world in which a previously married woman with children, let alone male children, would be regarded as undesirable for marriage. In addition, Umm Zarʿ also remarries. The *ḥadīth* describes both characters, "he married her and I also remarried," without alluding to any stigma associated with a woman remarrying after divorcing a husband. This too is in sharp contrast to the cultural norms that developed in Muslim lands that make it challenging for women to remarry after divorce.

The Four Women of Paradise

Another well-known *ḥadīth* that refers to women of the past while maintaining an element of relevance to the period contemporary to the Prophet Muḥammad is, "The best of women among the people of Paradise are Khadīja bint Khuwaylid, Fatima bint Muḥammad, Maryam bint ʿImrān, and Āsiya bint Muzāḥim, the wife of Pharaoh."[9] The role of Khadīja in both the *ḥadīth* literature and historical reports is significant. One such tradition narrates that she had once gathered with her friends near the Kaʿba when she was a young woman when a wandering old man came to them prophesizing, "O women of Tayma, a prophet named Ahmad will be sent from your city with a divine message. Whoever has the ability to be his wife, should not hesitate."[10]

This report in Ibn Saʿd's *Ṭabaqāt* continues by stating that all of the women laughed at this man and turned him away with the exception of Khadīja, who pondered these words and considered that they may possibly be true. The portrayal of Khadīja as anticipating Muḥammad's prophecy when she married him based on this report is a valuable glimpse into her character, yet it is commonly overlooked by contemporary scholars who often depict the significance of the historical accounts of her life as relevant to the extent that they reveal elements of the prophetic biography (*sīra*). Comparing this report to the numerous other *ḥadīths* that describe Khadīja as having been exceptionally calm and supportive of the Prophet when he came to her for comfort during the time he is said to have first received Qur'ānic revelation, supports this portrayal of her expectations from her future husband.[11]

Various other *ḥadīths* portray Khadīja as the bedrock of support for the Prophet in the earliest phases of Islamic history. She was a twice-widowed older woman with two children from a previous marriage before marrying the Prophet. She had the financial means to build a new family with Muḥammad, with whom she had six children. When Muḥammad used to retreat to the outskirts of Mecca, the *ḥadīth* literature presents Khadīja as supportive of her husband's contemplative practices through regularly sending food to make his lengthy seclusion possible. *Ḥadīths* also assert that when the Prophet was first approached by the angel Gabriel, he was afraid and that it was in the bosom of Khadīja that he found reassurance and support.[12]

According to the *ḥadīth* literature, Khadīja has the distinction of being the first convert to Islam and having the rank of the first Companion (*ṣaḥābiyya*), which is regarded as a distinctive religious status with implications for *ḥadīth* transmission and religious leadership. Khadīja is also depicted in the *ḥadīth* literature as being the only person who received greetings of peace from God transmitted through the angel Gabriel to her husband. It is reported that:

> One day Gabriel delivered a salutation to Muḥammad, peace be upon him, saying: "Present Khadīja with *salām* [i.e., greetings of peace] from her Lord." The Prophet, peace be upon him, declared: "O Khadīja, that was Gabriel. He has delivered a salutation from your Lord!" Khadīja replied: "God is peace and from Him comes peace and upon Gabriel I wish peace."[13]

Based on this narration, Khadīja's response in the *ḥadīth* above has become a commonly recited supplication to this day after the completion of the five daily Muslim ritual prayers. The year that Khadīja died is memorialized by Muslims as "The Year of Sadness (*ʿām al-ḥuzn*)." The *ḥadīth* literature depicts the Prophet as continuing to send gifts to Khadīja's family and maintaining connections with them until he died. When this became a point of contention at one point with his wife ʿĀʾisha, he replied in a well-known *ḥadīth*, "She believed in me when nobody believed in me. She believed the truth when people thought I was a liar. She supported me with her wealth when nobody gave me. And God granted me children from nobody else."[14]

For Muslims who regard the Prophet as an ethical model, this is another source for defining positive masculinity. While many men might deem such an eternal loyalty to one woman as compromising their manliness or while some may find pleasing a newer and younger wife more expedient, the character of the Prophet in his interactions with Khadīja's relatives, even after her death, challenge such notions of masculinity. Loyalty and love to a woman based on her inward qualities rather than her outward beauty is demonstrated throughout *ḥadīth* literature as a model of virtue for men who look to the Prophet Muḥammad for defining ideals that establish masculine norms for interacting with female partners.

Faṭima, who is the second figure mentioned in the "four women of Paradise *ḥadīth*," was the daughter of the Prophet Muḥammad. She is known in *ḥadīth* literature to have received the nickname the "mother of her father,"[15] due to the extent of the attentiveness she gave to her father after her mother's death. She is known to have emigrated to Abyssinia and then emigrated again to Medina. Several accounts of her marriage to ʿAlī and her children are also extant in *ḥadīth* literature. The Prophet is reported to have had a special place in his heart for Faṭima. *Ḥadīths* mention that whenever she would come into a room, the Prophet would stand to greet her, then kiss her and hold her hand, and then seat her in his place. It is said that when the Prophet would enter a room, Faṭima would reciprocate by doing the same.[16] Faṭima is said to have been the last person to whom the Prophet would bid farewell before leaving for a trip and the first person that he would visit upon his return.[17] The detailed descriptions of the extent of the reverence and affection that the Prophet showed his daughter provides further insight into gender relations based on the Muḥammadan model, according to which female family members were treated with the highest levels of respect and devotion.

While the *ḥadīth* literature is scarce in its portrayals of the other two women, Maryam and Āsiya, in the "four women of Paradise *ḥadīth*," most of what can be gleaned about their significance to Muslims can be found in Qur'ānic narratives. The verses from the Qur'ān of special relevance are:

> And God sets forth as an example for those who believe the wife of Pharaoh when she said, "My Lord, build for me a house near unto Thee in the Garden, deliver me from Pharaoh and his deeds, and deliver me from the wrongdoing people." And Mary, the daughter of ʿImrān, who preserved her chastity. Then We breathed therein of Our Spirit, and she confirmed the Words of her Lord and His Books; and she was among the devoutly obedient. (Qur'ān 66:1–12).[18]

The *ḥadīth* that cites the two women mentioned in this verse as among "the four women of Paradise" is making an implied statement about the extent of their virtue. The verse from the Qur'ān above clarifies an essential question regarding the gender specific nature of the four women of Paradise *ḥadīth*. Namely one may ask, is the capacity for virtue by these women limited by their gender? Do Muslim sources conceive that women can also exceed men in their virtue and piety?

It is worthy of note that the Qur'ān refers to Āsiya and Maryam as models of virtue for all of humanity, rather than as models exclusively for women. Thus, the final verses of the Qur'ānic chapter *al-Taḥrīm* explicitly indicate a Qur'ānic vision of vice and virtue that is not gendered. In other words, both men and women are depicted as being able to attain equal ranks of vice or virtue, regardless of their gender. Based on this context of Qur'ānic references to the same women in the "four women of Paradise *ḥadīth*," it can be argued that the femaleness of the four characters is not intended to delimit the extent of their piety as distinctively inferior to that of male counterparts, but rather to highlight the extent to which women can attain piety that can exceed that of men while also being independent of them. This latter point will be further elucidated below.

Another significant feature of women as they appear both in this *ḥadīth* and the corresponding Qur'ānic references is that Āsiya is considered to have a holy status in Islam that is emblematic of universal virtue, not because of her adherence to her husband's beliefs but because of her pious and principled defiance of him. Her husband was the Pharaoh of Egypt who ignored the warnings of Moses. She believed in Moses despite the tyranny of her powerful husband and her precarious position as his wife in the cultural context of this ancient time period.

The second woman perceived to be emblematic of virtue in the "four women *ḥadīth*" is Maryam, who is deemed as saintly by Muslims without having any husband at all. In the Islamic narrative, there is no report of her ever marrying and there is no mention anywhere of Joseph, as there is in Christian narratives. This does not deny the possibility that she did later marry; but the lack of explicit reference to her marital status indicates the irrelevance of such a status for the story of Mary and Jesus within the Islamic tradition. According to the Qur'ānic narrative, Maryam is a single mother who faces the hardships and taunts from her community single-handedly without a male counterpart to save her. Her perseverance and sincere devotion to God then earns her a rank among those closest to God—hence, in the Qur'ān, Maryam represents a model of piety and goodness for all of humanity to follow. Furthermore, her son, Jesus or ʿĪsā, is honored in the Qur'ān by being known through his affiliation to her as "ʿIsā ibn Maryam" or "Jesus, the Son of Mary." Furthermore, God in the Qur'ān corrects Maryam's mother's assumption that "a male is not like a female" (Qur'ān, 3: 36) in terms of spiritual capacity and status in this Qur'ānic narrative in which this girl, that was mistakenly believed to not be as good as a male child, supersedes all the boys and men of her time in virtue and becomes a model of piety for both men and women—not only women—as indicated the verses from *al-Taḥrīm* mentioned above.

The two women mentioned in the verses before those referencing Maryam and Āsiya in the Qur'ān are the wives of Lot and Noah.[19] The Qur'ān juxtaposes them against the virtuous models of Āsiya and Maryam as models of vice of whom humanity is exhorted to be wary. These women were also married to men who were considered among the most pious individuals in Islam through their ranks as Prophets. Yet despite the righteousness of their husbands, they are presented as being their opposite in moral standing by virtue of their individual actions.

Thus, one of the lessons of these Qur'ānic narratives is that they indicate women's free agency in becoming either agents of vice or virtue without connection to their husbands or lack thereof (as in the case of Maryam). Since many elements of *ḥadīth* literature are fundamentally linked to Qur'ānic narratives that further explicate their significance within *ḥadīths*, it is essential to examine related Qur'ānic verses to have a better understanding of the scriptural contexts in which these women in *ḥadīths* are referenced.

Ḥadīths about Women Whose Queries Are Answered by the Qur'ān

Among examples of *ḥadīth* reports linked to Qur'ānic references related to women are the *ḥadīths* that depict the context for the verse in *Sūrat al-Aḥzāb* that explicate the principle of spiritual equality of men and women. Among the various reports on this, it said that ʿUmāra al-Anṣāriyya came to the Prophet and said, "I do not see but that everything is about men, and I do not find the women mentioned with regard to anything."[20] Another account relates that Umm Salama came to the Prophet and asked, "Why is it that we are not mentioned in the Qur'ān as are the men?"[21] After this query, the *ḥadīth* literature indicates that the following verse was revealed to the Prophet:

> For submitting men and submitting women, believing men and believing women, devout men and devout women, truthful men and truthful women, patient men and patient women, humble men and humble women, charitable men and charitable women, men who fast and women who fast, men who guard their private parts and women who guard [their private parts], men who remember God often and women who remember [God often], God has prepared forgiveness and great reward. (Qur'ān, 33:35)[22]

Similarly, we find the contextual information within the *ḥadīth* literature for a Qura'nic chapter named after a woman who complained to the Prophet (*Sūrat al-Mujādila*). Khawla bint Thaʿlaba is reported to have come to the Prophet after her husband initiated a pre-Islamic practice known as *ẓihār*. This practice entailed a man telling his wife that she is the equivalent of "his mother's back." This meant that he would neither approach her in marital relations nor divorce her. The woman was said to be "suspended" between these two states.

When Khawla bint Thaʿlaba's husband declared that she was now the "equivalent of his mother's back," it is reported in the *ḥadīth* literature that she went to the Prophet saying: "He has worn out my youth and I let him enjoy me. But when I grew older and could no longer bear children, he put me away saying that I am as his mother's back. O God, I complain to Thee!"[23] One version of the story relates that she did not move until the angel Gabriel came down with the verses from the Qur'ān:

> God has indeed heard the words of she who disputes with thee concerning her husband and complains to God. And God hears your conversation. Truly God is Hearing, Seeing. Those among you who commit *ẓihār* against their wives, those are

> not their mothers. None are their mothers save those who gave birth to them. Truly they speak indecent words and calumny. And truly God is Pardoning, Forgiving. (Qur'ān, 58:1–2).

Another version of the *ḥadīth* relates that the Prophet sought to resolve the conflict by pronouncing the *ẓihār* as an equivalent of a divorce. This was not satisfactory to Khawla, who argued that her husband did not actually declare a divorce and that a *ẓihār* was not the equivalent of a divorce. They argued about this matter back and forth, until it is reported that this portion of the Qur'ān was later revealed. The rest of the *ḥadīths* on this matter relate to the penalty that her elderly husband had to pay in order to restore the marriage.[24]

Both of these narratives in the *ḥadīth* literature portray an active presence of women around the Prophet in establishing the early Muslim community and participating in the revelatory process. Women's voices were heard and acknowledged as such in reports on sections of the Qur'ān that become known as providing the "cause of revelation" or *sabab al-nuzūl* for specific verses. In the cases above, we find that these specific causes that instigated the revelation of certain verses (*asbāb al-nuzūl*) referred to women who sought equality with men or were wronged by their husbands and sought justice. Just like Āsiya, who is honored for the defiance of her husband, Khawla bint Tha'laba becomes immortalized in Islamic narratives as having been a woman who not only challenged her husband but argued with the Prophet who was overruled by God in her favor.

We find the strong voices of women consistently in numerous other depictions of figures close to the Prophet within *ḥadīth* literature. Asmā' bint Yazīd was a woman from the Anṣār of Medina who participated in the oath of allegiance that the nascent Muslim community of Medina gave the Prophet. She had been known for excelling in learning and understanding of the Prophet's mission. She was also commended for her sense of modesty not preventing her in asking about intimately personal matters related to religious practice, such as menstruation and ritual cleansing. Asmā' was so esteemed among her female peers for her forthrightness and knowledge that they appointed her as their spokeswoman in asking the Prophet about matters related to the equality of men and women in religious status. It is reported in a well-known *ḥadīth* that Asmā' bint Yazīd approached the Prophet when he was seated among a group of his male Companions one day saying:

> You are my mother and father O Messenger of God! I am a representative sent on behalf of the women to you. There is not a woman east or west who heard of my coming to you except that she holds the same opinion as me. God sent you to the entirety of men and women. Hence, we believed in you and in God. But we—the body of women—are deprived (*maqṣūrāt*) and limited (*maḥṣūrāt*) [while] sitting in your homes, fulfilling your needs, raising your children. While you—O men—have been favored with [greater access] to gatherings and meetings, visiting the sick, witnessing funerals, and pilgrimage (Ḥajj) after pilgrimage. Even better than that is fighting in the path of God. When a man from among you set out for greater or lesser pilgrimage

> or martial engagement, we protect your property, mend your clothes, and raise your children. Do we not share in divine reward with you O Messenger of God?[25]

The Prophet Muḥammad is reported to have turned to the men in his presence upon hearing Asmāʾ's question saying to them, "Have you ever heard a woman's speech better than this one asking about her faith?" The men responded saying, "No, O Messenger of God. We did not think women could lead in this way." The Prophet then turned to Asmāʾ and said, "Return O Asmāʾ, and inform the women behind you that the good companionship of one of you to her spouse and seeking his contentment and her following that which he concurs with, equals all of that [you have listed from the actions of men]."[26] The report finishes by saying that the woman left exultant (*tahallal*), jubilant, and ready to report back the good news to the women she represented. Different versions of this narrative have slight variations in their wording. However, the general framework of the *ḥadīth* remains the same.

Considering that this incident is reported to have taken place in the first/seventh century, a woman coming to the "populace" of men from the "populace" of women sounds much like a grassroots protest. The word used in the *ḥadīth* is *maʿshar*, which has the connotation of a large community of people. Here we have a *ḥadīth* in which the entire female community has expressed concern to the Prophet regarding their access to equal opportunities for spiritual advancement in their faith. It is worthy of note that the women were not rebelling against their roles in running the household and raising a family, but rather they were concerned that these extra responsibilities were obstacles to their striving to have equal spiritual ranks before God through extra worship. This is indicated in the inclusion of the state of being *maqṣūr* or "falling short" in their opportunities for the same types of worshipful acts that men had, as presented in their list of concerns.

The women also complained about their being "limited" or "excluded" (*maḥṣūrāt*) from participation in the many public rituals that men were involved in by virtue of their household responsibilities. Such a case being brought to the Prophet and representing the unified voice of women in the first century of Islam and its subsequent preservation in *ḥadīth* literature is quite extraordinary in revealing the extent of women's courage to speak with strength, not only privately to the Prophet, but to also do so in front of all of the male Companions who were gathered around the Prophet.

The Prophet's response, as transmitted in the *ḥadīth*, is also informative. He did not find this kind of challenge from the women in his community as threatening. He did not ridicule Asmāʾ nor did he attempt to "put her back in her place." Instead, he elevated her and used this woman's strength as a teaching moment for the males of his community to acknowledge her and commend her for her words. Before addressing Asmāʾ, the *ḥadīth* indicates that the Prophet turned to the men around him first and asked them a rhetorical question, "Have you ever heard a woman deliver a speech inquiring about her faith better than this?" The *ḥadīth* seems to indicate that the Prophet is highlighting both the eloquence of her words as well as the extent of her sense of urgency in practicing her faith.

The response of the Companions to the Prophet supports this interpretation. They respond saying they did not know that women could lead in this way. This ignorance was remedied with the Prophet's affirmation of this woman and the women's concerns she brought to him. In telling women that in performing different responsibilities, that are of course determined by societal limitations and norms of the seventh century, they receive the same reward as all the things that men do, he is setting a prophetic precedent (*sunna*).

The tone of the Prophet Muḥammad's words is positive and uplifting. When a woman came to him on behalf of the entire community of women with concerns regarding equity, his response was to assure her that men had no preference over women in matters of faith. The detail at the end of the report in which she left the gathering with her head held high and with good news for the women, is consistent with the portrayal of the response of the Prophet Muḥammad in the rest of this tradition. He does not let her down or belittle her in front of his male Companions, in fact the Prophet does the opposite by elevating this female Companion in front of the male Companions.

In the details of this story, we see parallel patterns of behavior with the narrative of Umm Zarʿ in terms of the Prophet's response to his wife ʿĀʾisha in which he uplifts her and responds with affirmation. These details in *ḥadīth* literature have contemporary relevance for Muslims who look to prophetic precedents (*sunna*) for guidance regarding ideals of male interactions with women based on the Muḥammadan model.

Furthermore, Asmāʾ bint Yazīd is given the title of "orator" or *khaṭība* for her eloquence. This is significant in that it demonstrates that women were praised for public speaking and that there is a precedent for women speaking in front of a group of men during the lifetime of the Prophet. As Muslim practices began to limit women's public appearance including her public speech in later centuries, these types of reports of women in *ḥadīth* literature highlight the subjectivity of the reliance on *ʿurf* or customary practice to inform Islamic law based on changing gender norms that may contradict Muḥammadan principles depicted in hadith literature about the early Muslim community.[27]

Contemporary analysis of these types of reports leaves room for revision of gender related practices that are commonly assumed to be based on prophetic precedent, but closer analysis reveals that they are legal positions that were informed by the cultural context of later times. This does not discredit the ruling per se, as consideration of context is a hallmark of the genius of a skilled *fiqh* specialist. Rather, it simply highlights the need to revisit ossified *fiqh* rulings related to daily life (*muʿāmalāt*)—including matters related to marriage and gender relations—as contexts change.

Like Asmāʾ bint Yazīd, Nusayba bint Kaʿb was another woman of the Anṣār who exemplifies in her life women's desires to participate in public ritual and observances. Her most well-known role in *ḥadīth* literature is her active participation in battle. It is known in Islamic practice that women are not required to take arms when men are called to do so. Thus, it can be said that Nusayba was a woman in the seventh century who joined Muslims in battle out of her own choice. This is not only an indicator of her own initiative but also an indicator of an early Muslim community that was open to and allowed for women to make choices about their public roles.

Nusayba bint Kaʿb's leadership started in her representation of women through her participation in the oath of ʿAqaba (622 CE) in which the new Muslim converts of Medina promised allegiance to and protection of the Meccan Muslim community. After her conversion to Islam, Nusayba bint Kaʿb is known to have played an active role in every major battle that the Muslims were involved in. She was known to have been a veteran of the battles of Uḥud, Ḥunayn, Khaybar, and Yamāma. Even more worthy of note is the report in which it is said that when Muslims were surrounded during the battle of Uḥud and a large number of Muslims dispersed or fled, Nusayba was among a group who surrounded the Prophet and fought with him. Such courage on the battlefield attributed to Muslim women and preserved in *ḥadīth* literature is significant. Later, ʿUmar was reported to have testified to her courage during his rule through favoring her with gifts and saying that he heard the Prophet say of the Battle of Uḥud, "I never turned right or left without seeing her fighting to defend me."[28]

Furthermore, Nusayba bint Kaʿb is among the Companions of the Prophet who witnessed the two most consequential events of this historic period, namely that of the Treaty of Ḥudaybiyya and the Conquest of Mecca. Among the events that led to the Treaty of Ḥudaybiyya in which the early Muslim community was first recognized by the Meccans through a truce, was the disappearance of ʿUthmān ibn ʿAffān after he had been sent to the Meccans to negotiate. At this point, the Muslims believed that he had been killed and as a result upheld the unity of their community through renewing their allegiance of loyalty to the Prophet. This is said to be the context in which a verse from the Qur'ān was revealed saying, "Truly those who pledge allegiance unto thee pledge allegiance only unto God. The Hand of God is over their hands." (Qur'ān, 48: 10). Nusayba bint Kaʿb, through her participation in this oath, was therefore included among those who pledged her allegiance and whose hands are said to have had the "hand of God" over them. A common interpretation for this expression of God's "hand being over theirs" is that God's protection and empowerment was granted to the likes of Nusayba when she pledged allegiance to God's messenger, Muḥammad.

Ḥadīths Composed of Short Statements

Perhaps, better known than the many detailed *ḥadīth* reports depicting women's lived experiences of Islamic practice and their interactions with the Prophet Muḥammad mentioned above, are numerous short statement *ḥadīths* that make references to women in ways that can be perceived as either positive or negative.

Examples of *ḥadīths* that may be regarded as positive are the following. "Whoever has three girls and is patient with them, feeds them, gives them drink, and clothes them to the best of his ability, he will be veiled from hellfire on the Day of Judgment, even if it were one [daughter]."[29] There are a number of different variations of this well-known *ḥadīth*. One states that one who raises two daughters and treats them well will accompany the Prophet Muḥammad in Heaven like two fingers stuck to one another. Another version of this tradition explicitly states that if a parent does not favor his sons above his daughters and treats them with tenderness, they will be granted Heaven as their final abode.[30]

In another *ḥadīth*, a man approached the Prophet and asked him who is most worthy of his good companionship. The Prophet responded saying, "Your mother." He asked, and then whom? The Prophet responded, "Your mother." He asked again, and then whom? The Prophet said, "Your mother." The man asked the Prophet one final time, "And then whom?" The Prophet responded, "Your father."[31] This *ḥadīth* is viewed as highlighting the greater importance of showing love, kindness, and loyalty to a mother over a father by threefold.

Another (previously mentioned) *ḥadīth* reports that the "Best of you is he who is best to his wife. And I am the best to my wife." The term *ahl* used here is interpreted to mean wife in the context of the Prophet's time. Another exhortation to men to treat women well is contained in the famous final sermon of the Prophet Muḥammad in which he is reported to have said:

> Fear God in your [relations] with women and deal with them in goodness. For they are under your custody and they possess nothing of their own. When you took them, you did so as a trust from God. Intimacy with them became permissible through the word of God. So, ponder my words, O people![32]

It is worthy of note that the Prophet dedicated a significant portion of his last testament before his imminent death to emphasize the importance of men treating women with kindness and respect. While the outward form of this type of behavior is inevitably portrayed through what is considered good treatment within the norms of the seventh century, the broader message of a man's responsibility to show respect and compassion toward women is highlighted by the choice of the inclusion of this injunction in what is memorialized as the Prophet's Farewell Sermon (*khuṭbat al-wadāʿ*).

There are other *ḥadīths* that are similarly short statements that have been deemed controversial in modern times and that appear to challenge the content of women-friendly reports discussed above when singled out and read selectively. Among those that are viewed by some as "problematic" *ḥadīths* is one in which the Companions of the Prophet are said to have observed Christians in Syria prostrating to their bishops. When asked whether they should prostrate similarly to the Prophet, he told them that a Muslim should not prostrate to anyone but God. Upon informing his Companions it is impermissible for a Muslim to prostrate to anyone except God, it is reported he said, "If I were to order anyone to prostrate to anyone else, I would order a woman to prostrate to her husband."[33]

Another *ḥadīth* along these lines states that women make up the majority of the inhabitants of Hell due to their ungratefulness to their husbands. It also states that women are deficient in intellect and religion.[34] In a separate *ḥadīth* in which the Prophet was told that the Persian King Khosrow was succeeded by his daughter after his death, the Prophet is said to have stated that "No people will ever prosper who entrust their leadership to a woman."[35]

These single short-statement *ḥadīths* can be subjected to methods of scrutiny so that apparent meanings that appear unfair to women can be measured in light of the larger *ḥadīth* and Qur'ānic corpus to determine the validity of such possible interpretations. For instance the *ḥadīth* apparently claiming to discourage women's leadership abilities is challenged by portrayals of the Queen of Sheba in the Qur'ān[36] or the Prophet himself having sought advice from his wife Umm Salama during the signing of the Treaty of al-Ḥudaybiyya (630 CE), which was a milestone event in early Islamic history. The meanings of the *ḥadīth* claiming that the majority of the dwellers in hell is composed of women can be challenged along similar lines.[37] While a comprehensive overview of each *ḥadīth* is beyond the scope of this particular study, the method by which misogynistic meanings derived from some interpretations of *ḥadīths* can be challenged by holistic readings of the larger corpus of Islamic scriptures is worthy of further study.[38]

Conclusion

Ḥadīth literature is a valuable source for analyzing the roles Muslim women played in the early history of Islam. *Ḥadīths* often portray women as leaders, teachers, and models of virtue; they further depict them as having challenged assumptions of inequality during their time in ways that are believed to have been later affirmed by Qur'ānic revelation. The various interactions of the Prophet Muḥammad with women recorded in a substantial number of *ḥadīths* also indicate a pattern of respect for women and concern on his part for their well-being.

Ḥadīths made up of solitary statements constitute a category of reports that can be perceived as including both favorable and unfavorable depictions of women. It can be argued that the latter have received disproportionate attention in the modern period due to atomistic readings of the *ḥadīth* corpus, a tendency that has arisen in recent times with the loss of traditional institutions of learning that required a contextualization of *ḥadīths* with lived practice and the consistency of interpretations with the larger corpus of Islamic scripture. While the invention of the printing press and the loss of access to educational models that ensured contextual readings of scriptures had the benefits of making knowledge more readily accessible, the social harms associated with the misuse of the large *ḥadīth* corpus through selective readings defined by contemporary political and social movements also became more likely.

A significant aspect of this shift has been a result of the historical context of European colonialism in Muslim lands in which family law became perceived as the last bastion of Islamic practice which elicited a reactionary response from various modern Muslim movements that made women's rights an ideological issue. This was exacerbated by

European colonizers and Christian missionaries who often presented themselves as saviors of Muslim women who needed to be rescued from the control of Muslim male dominance and backward religious practices. With the disintegration of the classical educational systems, many self-made Muslim religious leaders who lacked the sophistication of thought engendered through classical training in the Islamic intellectual tradition rooted in pragmatism and rationalism, clung to elements of what may be perceived as outdated patriarchal cultural norms practiced by some Muslims as "social hooks." This led them to regard such norms as essential (*dhātī*) to Muslim practice rather than incidental (*ʿaraḍī*), in an attempt to preserve a misconceived presumption of Islamic orthodoxy.

Notes

1. See, for example, Ibn Ḥajar al-ʿAsqalānī, *Fatḥ al-Bārī sharḥ Ṣaḥīḥ al-Bukhārī*, ed. ʿAbd al-ʿAzīẓ ibn Bāz and Ayman Fuʾād ʿAbd al-Bāqī (Beirut: Dār al-Kutub al-ʿIlmiyya, 1997), *Kitāb al-nikāḥ: bāb ḥusn al-muʿāshara maʿa al-ahl*, 9:163 (al-Bukhārī *ḥadīth* no. 5189); and Muḥyī al-Dīn al-Nawawī, *al-Minhāj fī sharḥ Ṣaḥīḥ Muslim ibn al-Ḥajjāj* (Damascus: Dār al-Khayr, 1999), *Kitāb faḍāʾil al-ṣaḥāba: bāb faḍl ʿĀʾisha*, 15:579 (Muslim *ḥadīth* no. 2448).
2. Another interpretation of this section of the *ḥadīth* states that she feared getting divorced. However, the above interpretation appears to fit the context of the rest of the sentence in the original *ḥadīth* better, see Ibn Ḥajar al-ʿAsqalānī, *Fatḥ al-Bārī*, 9:169.
3. Commentators say this may mean an incomplete divorce, which would mean she was neither married nor free to remarry; see Ibn Ḥajar al-ʿAsqalānī, *Fatḥ al-Bārī*, 9:170.
4. Al-Nasāʾī, *Sunan al-Nasāʾī, Kitāb al-Ṭahāra*, *ḥadīth* no. 29; and al-Tirmidhī, *Jāmiʿ al-Tirmidhī, Kitāb al-Ṭahāra*, *ḥadīth* no. 12.
5. This is one of the variations in wording in which this *ḥadīth* has been transmitted. Most chains of narration report the Prophet as having said, "I am to you like Abū Zarʿ." For the wording mentioned above, see: Sulaymān ibn Aḥmad al-Ṭabarānī, *al-Muʿjam al-kabīr*, ed. Ḥamdī ʿAbd al-Majīd al-Salafī (Cairo: Maktabat Ibn Taymiyya, n.d.), 23:173 (*ḥadīth* number 270).
6. The term used in the *ḥadīth* is *ahl*. This has been explained to mean "wives" by commentators on the *ḥadīth*.
7. *Ṣaḥīḥ al-Bukhārī, Kitāb al-nikāḥ: bāb ḥusn al-muʿāshara maʿa al-ahl, ḥadīth* no. 123; *Ṣaḥīḥ Muslim, Kitāb faḍāʾil al-ṣaḥāba, ḥadīth* no. 5998; *Jāmiʿ al-Tirmidhī, Kitāb manāqib ʿan rasūl Allāh, ḥadīth* no. 4156.
8. See *Sunan Abī Dāwūd, Kitāb al-Ṭahāra, ḥadīth* no. 236.
9. Al-Ḥākim al-Naysābūrī, *al-Mustadrak ʿalā al-Ṣaḥīhayn* (Cairo: Dār al-Taʾṣīl, 2018), 5:473 (*ḥadīth* no. 3882).
10. Muḥammad ibn Saʿd, *Ṭabaqāt al-kubrā*, ed. ʿAlī Muḥammad ʿUmar (Cairo: Maktabat al-Khānjī, 2001), 10:16.
11. See *Ṣaḥīḥ al-Bukhārī, Bāb kayfa kāna badaʾa al-waḥy*.
12. ʿAbd al-Malik ibn Hishām, *Sīrat al-nabī* (Cairo: Maktabat Muḥammad ʿAlī Ṣabīḥ, 1963), 1:259.
13. Al-Ḥākim, *al-Mustadrak*, 3:186.

14. *Ṣaḥīḥ al-Bukhārī, Kitāb manāqib al-Anṣār: Bāb tazwīj al-nabī ṣalla Allāhu ʿalayhi wa sallam Khadīja wa faḍlihā raḍiya Allāhu ʿanhā, ḥadīth* no. 3607.
15. Ibn al-Athīr, *Usd al-ghāba fī maʿrifat al-ṣaḥāba* (Cairo: Dār al-Shaʿb, 1970–1973), 5:520.
16. Al-Ḥākim, *al-Mustadrak*, 3:160.
17. Abū Dāwūd al-Sijistānī, *al-Sunan*, ed. Shuʿayb al-Arnaʾūṭ (Damascus: Dār al-Risāla al-ʿĀlamiyya, 2009), 4:87.
18. Seyyed Hossein Nasr et al., *Study Quran* (New York: Harper Collins Publishers, 2015), 1392.
19. Qur'an, 66:10.
20. See commentary in Nasr, *Study Quran*, 1029–1030.
21. Both versions of the narrative are found in the commentary of Nasr, *Study Qur'an*, 1029–1030.
22. Nasr, *Study Qur'an*, 1029–1030.
23. al-Ḥākim, *al-Mustadrak*, 5:447 (*ḥadīth* no. 3837).
24. See discussion in Nasr, *Study Quran*, 1341–1343.
25. Ibn al-Athīr, *Usd al-ghāba*, 7:19.
26. Ibid.
27. For research on how Hanafi *fiqh* shifts on the issue of women leading women in prayer, see: Behnam Sadeghi, *The Logic of Lawmaking in Islam* (Cambridge: Cambridge Studies in Islamic Civilization, 2015).
28. Ibn Saʿd, *Ṭabaqāt al-Kubrā*, 10:386.
29. *Sunan Ibn Mājah, ḥadīth* no. 3669; *Musnad Aḥmad, ḥadīth* no. 17439.
30. *Ḥadīth* s related to the virtues of raising daughters can be found in the following sources: *Jāmiʿ al-Tirmidhī, Kitāb al-birr wa ṣila ʿan rasūl Allāh, ḥadīth* no. 22 (or *Jāmiʿ al-Tirmidhī, ḥadīth* no. 1916); *Sunan Abī Dāwūd, Kitāb al-adab, ḥadīth* no. 374 (*Sunan Abī Dāwūd, ḥadīth* no. 5146); *Musnad Ibn Ḥanbal, ḥadīth* no. 11706.
31. *Ṣaḥīḥ al-Bukhārī, Kitāb al-adab: bāb man aḥaqq al-nās bi ḥusn al-ṣuḥba, ḥadīth* no. 5626.
32. Ibn Hishām, *Sīrat al-nabī*, 4:277.
33. *Sunan Abī Dāwūd, Kitāb al-nikāḥ: Bāb fi ḥaqq al-zawj ʿalā al-marʾa*, no. 95 (*Sunan Abī Dāwūd, ḥadīth* no. 2140).
34. *Ṣaḥīḥ Al-Bukhārī, Kitāb al-ḥayḍ: Bāb tark al-ḥāʾiḍ al-ṣawm, ḥadīth* no. 9 (al-Bukhārī, *ḥadīth* no. 304).
35. See Ulrike Mitter, "The Majority of Dwellers in Hell-Fire Are Women: A Short Analysis of A Much Discussed *Ḥadīth*," in *The Transmission and Dynamics of Textual Sources in Islam*, ed. Nicolet Boekhoff-van der Voort, Kees Versteegh, and Joas Wagemakers (Leiden: Brill, 2011), 443–473.
36. See for example, Qur'ān, 27:22–44.
37. Mitter, "Majority of Dwellers."
38. Modern rereadings and critiques of a number of these *ḥadīths* are discussed in chapter 5, by Khaled Abou El Fadl.

Bibliography

Abū Dāwūd, Sulaymān ibn Ashʿath al-Sijistānī. *Al-Sunan*. Edited by Shuʿayb al-Arnaʾūṭ. 6 vols. Damascus: Dār al-Risāla al-ʿĀlamiyya, 2009.

Bukhārī, Muḥammad ibn Ismāʿīl al-. *Al-Jāmiʿ al-ṣaḥīḥ*. Edited by Muḥibb al-Dīn al-Khaṭīb and Muḥammad Fuʾād ʿAbd al-Bāqī. 4 vols. Cairo: al-Maṭbaʿa al-Salafiyya, 1980.

Ḥākim al-Naysābūrī, Muḥammad ibn ʿAbdallāh al-. *Al-Mustadrak ʿalā al-Ṣaḥīḥayn*. 9 vols. Cairo: Dār al-Taʾṣīl, 2018.
Ibn al-Athīr, ʿIzz al-Dīn. *Usd al-ghāba fī maʿrifat al-ṣaḥāba*. 7 vols. Cairo: Dār al-Shaʿb, 1970–1973.
Ibn Ḥajar al-ʿAsqalānī, Shihāb al-Dīn. *Fatḥ al-Bārī sharḥ Ṣaḥīḥ al-Bukhārī*. Edited by ʿAbd al-ʿAzīẓ ibn Bāz and Ayman Fuʾād ʿAbd al-Bāqī. Beirut: Dār al-Kutub al-ʿIlmiyya, 1997.
Ibn Ḥanbal, Aḥmad. *Al-Musnad*. Edited by Shuʿayb al-Arnaʾūṭ. 50 vols. Beirut: Muʾassasat al-Risāla, 1993–2001.
Ibn Hishām, ʿAbd al-Malik. *Sīrat al-nabī*. Cairo: Maktabat Muḥammad ʿAlī Ṣabīḥ, 1963.
Ibn Saʿd, Muḥammad. *Ṭabaqāt al-kubrā*. Edited by ʿAlī Muḥammad ʿUmar. 11 vols. Cairo: Dār al-Khānjī, 2001.
Mitter, Ulrike. "The Majority of Dwellers in Hell-Fire Are Women: A Short Analysis of a Much Discussed *Ḥadīth*." In *The Transmission and Dynamics of Textual Sources in Islam*, edited by Nicolet Boekhoff-van der Voort, Kees Versteegh, and Joas Wagemakers, 443–473. Leiden: Brill, 2011.
Muslim ibn al-Ḥajjāj al-Nīshapūrī. *Al-Jāmiʿ al-ṣaḥīḥ*. Edited by Muḥammad Fuʾād ʿAbd al-Bāqī. 5 vols. Cairo: ʿĪsā al-Bābī al-Ḥalabī wa-Shurakāʾuh, 1955–1956.
Nasāʾī, Aḥmad ibn Shuʿayb al-. *Kitāb al-sunan al-kubrā*. Edited by Ḥasan ʿAbd al-Munʿim Shalabī. 12 vols. Beirut: Muʾassasat al-Risālah, 2001.
Nasr, Seyyed Hossein et al. *Study Quran*. New York: Harper Collins Publishers, 2015.
Nawawī, Muḥyī al-Dīn al-. *al-Minhāj fī sharḥ ṣaḥīḥ Muslim ibn al-Ḥajjāj*. Damascus: Dār al-Khayr, 1999.
Sadeghi, Behnam. *The Logic of Lawmaking in Islam*. Cambridge: Cambridge Studies in Islamic Civilization, 2015.
Ṭabarānī, Abū al-Qāsim Sulaymān ibn Aḥmad al-. *al-Muʿjam al-kabīr*. Edited by Ḥamdī ʿAbd al-Majīd al-Salafī. 25 vols. Cairo: Maktabat Ibn Taymiyya, n.d..
Tirmidhī, Abū ʿĪsā al-. *al-Jāmiʿ al-kabīr*. Edited by Bashshār ʿAwwād Maʿrūf. 6 vols. Beirut: Dār al-Gharb al-Islāmī, 1996.

CHAPTER 4

MODERN REREADINGS OF THE QUR'ĀN THROUGH A GENDERED LENS

ASMA AFSARUDDIN

CAN the Qur'ān only be read in a patriarchal way? Does the fact that the Qur'ān has been read primarily through a patriarchal lens by premodern male exegetes prevent nonpatriarchal readings of it in the modern period? Are such nonpatriarchal readings non"authentic," simply because they depart from classical ones and because such readings have been generated by mainly modern Muslim women scholars?

These questions form the backdrop to this chapter, which explores the writings of modern women exegetes, who self-identify as Muslim, on the issue of women and gender in the Qur'ān. Many of these exegetes read the Qur'ān through a lens of self-empowerment in order to challenge what they consider to be patriarchal readings of the Qur'ānic text by male exegetes that have been deployed to undermine women's social and legal rights through the centuries. They are motivated by the desire to generate in their stead interpretations that affirm women's ontological, social, and legal equality to men, their intrinsic dignity as humans, and their right to live flourishing lives in accordance with the moral and just injunctions they retrieve from the Qur'ān. A presentation and analysis of the arguments and methodologies offered by a number of these scholars will be provided in this chapter, along with certain critiques that have been launched against their positions. In the final section of the chapter, I offer my assessment of these perspectives and present the conclusions I arrive at regarding the question that continues to be asked: Does the Qur'ān promote patriarchy or undermine it?

Even though some of the scholars I discuss may consciously reject the label "feminist," and do not necessarily describe their hermeneutic projects as falling under the rubric of "Islamic feminism,"[1] and even robustly reject this term,[2] I frequently and interchangeably refer to them as "feminist" or "women exegetes," and also more broadly as "gender scholars." When I refer to "feminist exegetes," I intend to highlight their conscious centering of women's experiences and sensibilities in the reading of the Qur'ān, particularly in order to retrieve gender egalitarianism from its text. Invoked in this way, "feminist" does not imply ipso facto a secular orientation, as might be assumed in a Western academic context, or complicity with Western orientalizing and paternalistic, sometimes violent, projects of colonial feminism.[3] Rather, in this chapter, the default assumption is that gynocentric readings of the Qur'ān that are the focus of my discussion are generated by women exegetes who explicitly acknowledge their Muslim religious identity and adopt the lens of self-empowerment in their personal and scholarly engagement primarily with the Qur'ān.[4]

Pioneers of Nonpatriarchal Exegesis of the Qur'ān

In 1992, a slim volume published by an American Muslim scholar, amina wadud, by a little-known Malaysian publisher under the title of *Qur'ān and Woman* quickly gained the recognition it deserved. Written from the perspective of a female scholar of Islam, it was the first monograph-length treatment of specifically "the woman question" in Islam's holiest text (later reissued by Oxford University Press in 1999).[5] Wadud's work proved to be groundbreaking, not only because it was produced by a female scholar but also because it insisted on going back to the actual wording of the original Qur'ānic verses, bypassing, as it were, the learned but highly masculinist exegeses of the classical male commentators, in order to retrieve a gender-egalitarian perspective.

Wadud's hermeneutical approach to the Qur'ān appealed to established Islamic hermeneutical principles but was also revolutionary in challenging conventional interpretive methodologies and reading strategies. She suggested adopting what she called a "hermeneutics of *tawhid*," referring to a holistic method of reading the Qur'ān that affirms the singularity and uniqueness of the Divine Being and challenges the gendered hierarchy blatantly evident in most of the premodern classical exegetical literature. Wadud specifically challenged the line-by-line atomistic method of interpretation that was popular among many classical exegetes. If the Qur'ānic claim of establishing a "universal basis for moral guidance" is to be taken seriously, asserted wadud, then Muslim exegetes must develop a hermeneutical framework that leads to "a systematic rationale for making correlations [among Qur'ānic verses] and [that] sufficiently exemplifies the full impact of Qur'ānic coherence."[6] Universals and particulars must be distinguished from one another; time- and place-bound interpretations must be recognized as such and their limited applicability recognized. Wadud's interpretive venture was fundamentally concerned with retrieving an unending "trajectory of social, political, and moral possibilities" that remain consistent with the overall "Qur'ānic ethos of equity, justice, and human dignity" in changing historical and sociopolitical circumstances.[7]

Another prominent gender scholar, Asma Barlas, who was influenced by wadud's interpretive approaches, similarly emphasized the development of a new

Qur'ānic hermeneutics that would effectively challenge and undermine traditional understandings of key Qur'ānic verses related to gender and women's roles in society. In her influential book *"Believing Women" in Islam: Unreading Patriarchal Interpretations of the Qur'ān*, first published in 2004, Barlas says,

> Even though a Qur'ānic hermeneutics cannot by itself put an end to patriarchal, authoritarian, and undemocratic regimes and practices, it nonetheless remains crucial for various reasons. First, hermeneutic and existential questions are ineluctably *connected* [emphasis in text]. As the concept of sexual/textual oppression suggests, there is a relationship between what we read texts to be saying and how we think about and treat real women. This insight, though associated with feminists because of their work on reading and representation, is at the core of revelation albeit in the form of the reverse premise: that there is a relationship between reading (sacred texts) and liberation. . . . Accordingly, if we wish to ensure Muslim women their rights, we not only need to contest readings of the Qur'ān that justify the abuse and degradation of women, we also need to establish the legitimacy of liberatory readings. Even if such readings do not succeed in effecting a radical change in Muslim societies. It is safe to say that no meaningful change can occur in these societies that does not derive its legitimacy from the Qur'ān's teachings, a lesson secular Muslims everywhere are having to learn to their own detriment.[8]

This rereading of the Qur'ānic text has allowed Muslim women exegetes to recuperate what they understand to be a gender-egalitarian Qur'ānic worldview, eclipsed by centuries of culturally-inflected androcentric and hierarchical interpretations of the Qur'ān. Nowhere is this more evident than in the sharply divergent readings of a critical verse— Qur'ān 4:34—that continues to pit feminist exegetes against conservative/traditionalist ones. As Hadia Mubarak comments in chapter 2, "No other verse has garnered as much controversy in modern scholarship on gender in the Qur'ān as Qur'ān 4:34."[9] It has, therefore, almost become de rigueur to start with a discussion of this controversial verse when engaging with the topic of the Qur'ān's perspectives on women. I too bow to tradition and proceed next to a discussion of this verse.[10]

Qur'ān 4:34—Creating a Fault Line between Feminist and Traditionalist Exegeses

Qur'ān 4:34 states,

> Men are *qawwāmūn* over women because God has preferred some of them over others and because of what they spend of their wealth. Virtuous women are *qānitāt*, guarding the unseen with what God has guarded. As for those whose *nushūz* may be

feared, reprimand them, banish them to their beds, and lightly tap them. And if they obey you, then do not seek a way against them; indeed God is majestic and great.[11]

The two Arabic words in italics above are deliberately left untranslated since their meanings are highly contested and open to interpretation. As for the locution *waḍribuhunna*, whose meaning is similarly contested, I have chosen to translate/interpret it as "lightly tap them," for reasons that will become evident below.

A quick, diachronic survey of the views of some of the most prominent male exegetes from the second/eighth century to the modern period yields the following results. The early exegetes, Muqātil ibn Sulaymān (d. 150/767) and al-Ṭabarī (d. 310/923), understand Qur'ān 4:34 to be applicable exclusively in the domestic context, so that the husband enjoys his "preferential" status by virtue of his role as economic provider. *Qānitāt* is understood by both of them to refer to women who are obedient to God *and* their husbands while *nushūz* is interpreted as a general wifely disobedience to the husband by Muqātil[12] and the expression of a haughty repugnance by the wife toward her husband by al-Ṭabarī.[13] By the time we get to al-Wāḥidī (d. 468/1076) in the fifth/eleventh century, it is evident, however, that male exegetes had made up their minds that a generic male superiority over women is also to be assumed on the basis of this verse, rather than a more limited, functional one restricted to the domestic sphere. To this end, al-Wāḥidī compiles a lengthy list of the superior essential attributes that men enjoy *qua* men and the weighty sociopolitical roles they consequently play that are denied to women. Significantly, al-Wāḥidī glosses *qānitāt* only as women who are obedient to their husbands.[14] Fakhr al-Dīn al-Rāzī (d. 606/1210) in the late sixth/twelfth century adds even more laudable traits to the list produced by al-Wāḥidī to underscore the male's intrinsic superiority over the female.[15]

There is one outlier in my survey: 'Abd Allāh ibn 'Umar al-Bayḍāwī (d. ca. 685/1286), who, in the seventh/thirteenth century, notably glosses *qānitāt* as a reference to virtuous women who, while mindful of their obligations to their husbands, owe their obedience only to God (*muṭī'āt li-llāh*).[16] His seems to be a minority, dissenting voice in the late medieval period when an overwhelming majority of male exegetes had convinced themselves that the Arabic root *qnt* in relation to women referred either to obedience on their part to both God and their husbands or exclusively to their husbands, while the same root in relation to men referred to their obedience to God alone.

In the early twentieth century, Rashīd Riḍā (d. 1935) emphasizes not so much a hierarchical relationship between husbands and wives as complementarity in their roles vis-à-vis one another in his reading of Qur'ān 4:34. The functional superiority of the husband within the family resides in his greater physical ability to defend and protect those in his care and to financially provide for his family, he says. The "degree" of superiority that is accorded to men as a consequence of their familial responsibilities is, however, *not* interpreted by Riḍā to indicate a general superiority of men over women.[17]

A generation later, the Egyptian Islamist ideologue Sayyid Quṭb (d. 1966), similarly emphasizes in his *tafsīr* work the complementarity of the roles of men and women within marriage that reflect their different physical and biological endowments. Outside of the domestic domain, he says, women and men are the exact spiritual equals of one another, since the Qur'ān promises equal recompense to the faithful for their good deeds regardless of gender. Surprisingly, it is Quṭb with his reputation for radical Islamist views who stresses that *qānitāt* refers to believing women who place their faith exclusively in God and that the word contains no suggestion of obedience to human beings. He comments—perceptively—that if obedience was owed to humans, then the corresponding adjective applied to women would have been *muṭīʿāt*.[18]

While the overwhelming majority of the classical male exegetes understood *nushūz* in Qur'ān 4:34 to be an exclusive reference to a woman's arrogant demeanor and behavior toward her husband, there is one exception in this survey. This is indicated by al-Ṭabarī, who takes note of the more egalitarian understanding of a very early authority—the pious abstemious scholar from the late first/seventh–early second/eighth century ʿAṭā' ibn Abī Rabāḥ (d. 115/733)—who notes that *nushūz* applies equally to the husband and wife and was a basic reference to the desire of either party to separate from the other.[19]

ʿAṭā' may have been among our very early "feminist" readers of the Qur'ān who preferred to read the text cross-referentially because the Qur'ān does in fact refer to *nushūz* on the part of both men and women. The corresponding verse in regard to men is Qur'ān 4:128, which states, "If a woman fears *nushūz* or rejection (*iʿrāḍ*) from her husband, there is no blame on them if they reach a settlement, and settlement is better, even though people's souls lack magnanimity." In his exegesis of this verse, al-Ṭabarī understands *nushūz* on the part of the husband to be similar to *nushūz* on the part of the wife—that it is an attitude of haughtiness and pride toward one's spouse. The *nāshiz* is also one who expresses distaste toward his wife, whether it is on account of her lack of comeliness, advancing years, or other reasons. *Iʿrāḍ* consists of turning away from her with his face or withholding certain benefits that she is accustomed to receiving from him. In such cases, the couple is exhorted to seek arbitration and reconciliation which, al-Ṭabarī comments, is better than separation and/or divorce.[20]

It is noteworthy that even though the same term is used in both verses and may be understood to imply the same basic meaning in relation to the husband and wife, other than al-Ṭabarī, none of the male exegetes mentioned above referred to Qur'ān 4:128 in connection with Qur'ān 4:34. Instead, they showed a clear preference for explaining the term *nushūz* solely as it occurs in the latter verse to sharply demarcate gendered differences, with the earliest commentators in our survey—Muqātil and al-Ṭabarī—delineating these differences within the domestic sphere, progressing to al-Wāḥidī and his successors who extrapolated broad ontological differences between the male and the female. The result was the construction of a highly patriarchal family in the later period with *nushūz* implying primarily the wife's disobedience to her husband, who wielded considerable authority over her physical and emotional well-being. In contrast, reading the two verses that contain the term *nushūz* together allows one to derive a more reciprocal concept of marital rights and duties.

The imperative *waḍribuhunna* in Qur'ān 4:34 continues to provoke considerable anxiety among modern gender scholars, as Ayesha Chaudhry has noted in her extensive study of the verse.[21] The command elicited similar concern on the part of the classical male jurists and they took great care to explain the imperative *waḍribuhunna* as referring at most to a light tapping that causes no physical injury.[22] This was the maximum discipline that was considered permissible by them as a last resort. The practice of this husbandly "duty" did not then amount to wife battery, as the concept is understood today in reference to physical injury inflicted on the wife by an abusive husband. Such battery was overwhelmingly regarded by male scholars as a reprehensible activity for which the husband would be held criminally liable and required to pay a compensation to his wife.[23]

The term *ḍaraba* in the sense of beating continues to remain problematic for feminist exegetes today. Many of them, therefore, tend to seek a solution in the rich polysemy of the Arabic root *ḍrb*: besides to beat, the root in its various derivative forms can also mean to avoid or shun someone; to have sexual relations with a person; and to set an example, among others. Two alternate meanings that have been favored in feminist exegeses for *waḍribuhunna* are as follows (indicated in bold): (a) as for those women whose *nushūz* may be feared, reprimand them, banish them to their beds and **have sex with them**; and (b) as for those women whose *nushūz* may be feared, reprimand them, banish them to their beds and **depart from them/leave them alone**.[24] The second meaning is generated by understanding the imperative as being derived from the fourth verbal form *'aḍraba* rather than from the first verbal form *ḍaraba*; a slight change in orthography (with the addition of the *hamza* to the initial *alif*) credibly leads to the meaning of "leave them alone."[25]

This last reinterpretation is quite popular among many feminist exegetes, women and men, because it further satisfactorily accords with what is known of Muḥammad's own conduct toward his wives, whom he is not known to have ever struck or addressed harshly. The Prophet after all was the living sunna,[26] and his behavior is understood to exemplify the essence of the Qur'ānic message (cf. Qur'ān 33:21). Hadia Mubarak has noted that the Andalusian Mālikī exegete Abū Bakr Ibn al-ʿArabī (d. 543/1148), argued that "the legal norm is to avoid hitting [the wife]," basing his opinion on the views of the early second/eighth-century scholar 'Aṭā' ibn Abī Rabāḥ, who maintained that wives should never be beaten even when they disobeyed their husbands; at most the latter should only express anger.[27] Jonathan Brown has further documented that the prominent scholar 'Abd Allāh al-Dārimī (d. 255/869) was adamant that striking women was completely forbidden and *ḥadīth*s that permitted it were to be regarded as fabrications.[28]

Feminist Exegetical Challenges to Classical Androcentric Interpretations

Typically, feminist exegetes have been highly critical of the traditional interpretive methodologies of classical male exegetes, which, for the most part, consisted of line-by-line analysis of Qur'ānic verses. These feminist exegetes insist that the Qur'ān must instead be read holistically—that is to say, as an integrated text in which the various verses are read cross-referentially on a given theme and/or when similar vocabulary or concepts are employed. This emphasis on a holistic reading of the Qur'ānic text is a hallmark of modernist and feminist exegeses in general, which stresses that single verses, especially those that appear to be promoting gender inequality, should be read in conjunction with other verses that are thematically and semantically related, allowing for the emergence of other interpretive possibilities, an approach that was at best inconsistently followed by premodern exegetes.[29]

Because of their primarily atomistic approach to the Qur'ānic text, classical exegetes have been further criticized by modern scholars for their inability to distinguish between the general or universal commandments of the Qur'ān and the particular, contextualized applications of them. In the discipline of *tafsīr* (exegesis), this division is well-recognized in regard to the meaning of verses—*'āmm* (general) vs. *khāṣṣ* (particular)—but not necessarily applied in a consistent manner. This has led to what a number of gender scholars today consider to be misreadings of the Qur'ān, especially when it concerns women.[30] This is particularly evident in discussions of Qur'ān 4:34 which prima facie refers to the differentiated roles of men and women within the specific context of the family. However, as my brief diachronic survey revealed above, most premodern exegetes after the third/ninth century derived a theory of the general superior status of the male versus the female from this verse and interpreted what was a functional and contingent description of the male's status within the family as an ontological and universal one, applicable to all time and place.

As a number of gender scholars argue, a holistic reading of the Qur'ān would allow for a fuller sense of the equal, complementary roles that men and women are expected to assume within an Islamic marriage to emerge when other Qur'ānic verses that are relevant to this discussion are brought in. Prominent among such relevant verses is Qur'ān 2:187, which states, "wives] are your garments and you [husbands] are their garments." According to al-Ṭabarī, early prominent exegetes from the second generation of Muslims (known as "Successors"), like Mujāhid, Qatāda, al-Suddī, and 'Amr ibn Dinār, as well as the Companion Ibn 'Abbās, understood "garments" to be a metaphor for the comfort and tranquility (*sakn/sukūn*) that wives and husbands seek and find in one another.[31] Another relevant verse is Qur'ān 30:21, which states, "And among His signs is this, that He has created for you mates from among yourselves, that you may dwell in tranquility with them; and He has put love and mercy between you." Such loving, reciprocal marital relationships between partners who are equally a source of comfort to the other challenge a patriarchal familial paradigm which conceives of the husband as his wife's overlord, who unilaterally sets the terms for their relationship.

Other Qur'ānic concepts and terms which have been interpreted to convey gender inequality by classical male jurists are similarly being revisited by feminist exegetes. Among these concepts is the term *ḥarth*, which in its basic signification refers to a tilth or land suitable for cultivation. The relevant verse (Qur'ān 2:223) containing this term in relation to women states: "Your women are a *ḥarth* for you, so approach your *ḥarth* as you will and send [good deeds] in advance for your souls; and fear God and know that you will meet [Him]." An example of classical exegesis of this verse can be found in al-Ṭabarī's commentary. He explains this verse as, "Your women are the 'tilling ground' of your children (*nisā'ukum muzdara' awlādikum*), so approach your tilling ground however you wish and wherever you wish." This notion of women as the "tilling-ground" of men—generally understood to point to their biological and reproductive functions—is the pervasive one in al-Ṭabarī's exegesis. He refers to several early authorities like Ibn 'Abbās (d. ca. 68/687) and al-Suddī (d. 128/745) who corroborate this understanding. According to al- Ṭabarī, the sexual union between husband and wife which is expected to result in children is to be considered among the good deeds carried out by humans; the continuation of the same verse—"send [good deeds] in advance for your souls"—confirms this understanding. Thus, as al-Ṭabarī documents, Ibn 'Abbās counseled people to utter the *basmala* ("In the name of God, the Merciful, the Compassionate") before commencing sexual relations, as one would with any positive and licit act.[32] On the whole, al-Ṭabarī's exegesis of this verse conveys a positive valuation of the sexual and procreative functions of marriage that are regarded as good deeds for which the spouses will earn heavenly rewards in the hereafter.

As Barlas points out, this verse has, however, been typically construed by male jurists to imply that women are the sexual property of men and that men have the right to sexual relations with their wives whenever and however they want. Read atomistically through a masculinist lens, the term *ḥarth* in this verse can then be understood to imply sexual possession of women by men, highlighting as it does the sexual and reproductive roles of women. Barlas seeks to circumvent this reading by going on to invoke another verse (Qur'ān 42:20), which uses the term *ḥarth* but not in relation to women. The verse states: "To any that desires the [*ḥarth*] of the Hereafter, We give increase in his [*ḥarth*]; and to any that desires the [*ḥarth*] of this world, We grant somewhat thereof, but he has no share or lot in the hereafter." In this verse, *ḥarth* is clearly what humans reap according to their intention and deeds in this world. If humans perform good deeds with a view to pleasing God, then their *ḥarth*—equaling "recompense" or "harvest," if one wishes to maintain the agricultural metaphor—is paradise. If one carries out certain deeds with the simple objective of profiting in this world, then the recompense will be in accordance with one's intentions. The larger point that Barlas makes in comparing these two verses is that the term *ḥarth* does not ipso facto imply any kind of property that can be owned.[33]

Read in conjunction with Qur'ān 2:187 and Qur'ān 30:21, both of which emphasize a mutually loving and nurturing marital relationship as the ideal, Qur'ān 2:223 then is more properly interpreted not as mandating an unequal relationship between husbands and wives, says Barlas, but pointing to two of the fundamental purposes of the marital union within Islam—the enjoyment of licit sexual pleasure and production of offspring. Here women's distinctive biological functions are emphasized because only they are capable of conceiving and giving birth to children, just as men's distinctive biological functions are also highlighted in this verse because only they are capable of impregnating women—both participate in the process of procreation. There is nothing in the specific language of the verse to indicate that biological differences in themselves amount to an unequal relationship between the husband and wife. As Barlas says memorably, "the Qur'ān does not use sex to construct ontological or sociological hierarchies that discriminate against women;" and that "the Qur'ān recognizes sexual specificity but does not assign it gender symbolism."[34] In other words, one would have to deliberately impose a gendered, hierarchical understanding on the verse by specifically subscribing to the view that the act of male impregnation is somehow morally and biologically superior to the female act of giving birth. The entire thrust of the Islamic tradition—which has glorified the status of the mother considerably over that of the father—would militate against this particular interpretation.[35]

Ḥadīths Used as Exegetical Reports on Specific Qur'ānic Verses

In addition to Qur'ānic exegeses, gender scholars have also critically scrutinized certain *ḥadīths*, sayings attributed to the Prophet, that have been deployed by male exegetes to restrict, transform, and, in many cases, undermine the prima facie meanings of specific Qur'ānic verses so as to conform to certain gendered perspectives that lead to gender inequality and discrimination. Modernist scholars in general, and feminist scholars in particular, are concerned with maintaining the primacy of the Qur'ān over the *ḥadīth* literature, especially when certain tendentious *ḥadīths* directly contradict either the specific wording of Qur'ānic verses or the overall ethos of the Qur'ān.

A case in point is the importation of the biblical rib story into the exegetical literature to impute secondary status to the female in relation to the male, in direct contravention of the Qur'ānic accounts of the creation of Adam and his wife which make no such reference and do not specifically grant the male primacy in creation. Thus if we look at the verses in the Qur'ān that refer to the creation of Adam and his wife before their earthly existence, we are struck by how the Qur'ān either (a) blames Adam exclusively for the Fall or (b) blames Adam and his wife equally for giving in to the blandishments of Satan. Readers from a Judeo-Christian background will be struck by the fact that Adam's wife (named Ḥawwā' [Eve] in the exegetical literature) is not singled out for exclusive blame in the Qur'ān, in contrast to the principal biblical creation account contained in the Book of Genesis (2:21–3:21) which makes Eve, created from Adam's rib, the sole culprit in the events that lead up to the banishment of the couple from Paradise. On balance, Adam in the Qur'ān is the one who is morally culpable for failing to heed God's injunctions and succumbing to wrongdoing. He is, however, forgiven by God, and he and his wife are given the opportunity to start over with a clean slate on earth. In its creation accounts (Qur'ān 2:30–39; 7:11–27; 15:26–43; 20: 115–124; and 38:71–85), the Qur'ān does not, therefore, assign any kind of ontological moral failing to the woman companion of Adam and thus by extension to womankind in general.[36]

This point has been underscored by Muslim feminists[37] in particular as they argue from within the Islamic tradition for gender egalitarianism. Recuperation of the meanings of the original Qur'ānic verses concerning Adam and Eve is highly important in feminist discourses as a corrective to a very different story that emerges from the prolific exegetical literature on this topic. Qur'ān commentaries from after the third/ninth century reveal that the Qur'ānic assignment of blame to either Adam alone or to Adam and his wife together proved unpalatable to a number of later Muslim male exegetes and they deliberately imported the biblical creation story into their interpretations to reassign the blame exclusively to Ḥawwā'/Eve. Earlier commentators, including al-Ṭabarī, stayed closer to the Qur'ānic text and noted that Adam in the Qur'ān bore the brunt of the blame for having caused the "Fall." However, later exegetes—roughly after the fifth/tenth century—began to show a marked preference for the biblical version, which mandates the wife's subjugation to her husband as a result of her sin, an interpretation that was more in line with the growing patriarchal nature of society. Not surprisingly, in the late sixth/twelfth century, Fakhr al-Dīn al-Rāzī (d. 606/1210) embellishes his narrative with the story of woman's creation from the rib of Adam to drive home the point that the female is secondary to the male as a human being, a biblical literary motif that by his time had taken deep root in Muslim exegeses.[38]

Such construals are markedly in contrast to what the Qur'ān actually states concerning the creation of humankind. One such relevant verse is:

> O humankind! Be careful of your duty to your Lord Who created you from a single soul (*nafs wāḥida*) and from it created its mate (*zawj*) and from them the two has spread abroad a multitude of men and women. (Qur'ān 4:1)

Simultaneous creation from the *nafs wāḥida* negates the possibility of the male being granted an ontologically superior status by virtue of having been created first, from whose body is then derived the female's. Here the Qur'ān clearly undermines the notion of a hierarchical relationship between male and female. In spite of this fundamental Qur'ānic worldview or perhaps because of it, the rib story entered the *ḥadīth* literature and became a favorite of most of the later male exegetes as a way of justifying the woman's assumed inferior social and legal status compared to that of the man. Their interpretations provide a valuable window into the gradual "patriarchalization" of Muslim society and the elaborate arguments constructed to support this project—all couched in a legitimizing religious idiom.

Recent Critiques of Antipatriarchal Readings of the Qur'ān

Wadud's and Barlas's interpretations have become quite well-known and influential among gender scholars, particularly within the Western academy, and they are considered to be the best-known representatives of the nonpatriarchal, egalitarian approach to the Qur'ān. In recent times, their positions have attracted a measure of criticism from a few Muslim feminist scholars who have taken issue with what they consider to be wadud's and Barlas's overly optimistic characterization of the Qur'ān as a fundamentally woman-friendly egalitarian text that undermines patriarchy. Two of these scholars are Kecia Ali and Aysha Hidayatullah, whose counterarguments are summarized below.

Ali's main argument is that in making their case for a nonpatriarchal reading of the Qur'ān, wadud and Barlas overlook or downplay certain verses that she claims are inconvenient for maintaining their position. The Qur'ān, Ali says, has verses that are alternately egalitarian and hierarchical, so that one cannot describe the text as being exclusively one or the other. Verses that, according to her, confirm patriarchy include Qur'ān 4:34 and 2:187, which address men and in which "women are spoken of but men are spoken to."[39] For Ali, "the very mode of address presumes a privileged position for men as the audience for divine guidance."[40] In Qur'ān 2:228 (often referred to as the *daraja* verse, discussed below), both women and men are spoken of but treated as unequals, she says. She recognizes the validity of wadud's and Barlas's arguments that the Qur'ān exclusively addresses men in these verses because it was responding in the context of the sociohistorical circumstances of seventh-century Arabia, during which patriarchal families prevailed and men exercised complete authority over women's lives. But she finds problematic the assumption, as she sees it, in Qur'ān 2:187 and Qur'ān 2:222–223, that only men initiate sexual intimacy so that women are depicted as the passive recipients of their sexual overtures. She regards Qur'ān 2:223 as "objectifying women" when it refers to wives as *ḥarth*.[41] Interestingly—and inconsistently—she does not, however, similarly regard Qur'ān 2:187 as objectifying both men and women as each other's "garments." Ali appears to reduce the Qur'ān's deployment of metaphors and similitudes as part of its rich, evocative language to mere "objectification" in regard to women but not in regard to men or men and women together.[42]

In her thoughtful discussion of Qur'ān 4:34, Ali dwells on what she sees as some conundrums emerging from the text for a feminist reader like herself. She correctly recognizes that the *qānitāt* must be understood as a reference to pious women who are obedient to God alone on par with the *qānitūn*, pious men who owe their obedience to God, despite the general medieval exegetical understanding of *qānitāt* as referring to women who are obedient to both God and husbands. With regard to *nushūz*, however, Ali finds it problematic that the consequences for female *nushūz* are markedly different in Qur'ān 4:34 in comparison with the consequences for male *nushūz* in Qur'ān 4:128.[43] She also accuses Asghar Engineer and John Esposito of conveniently sidestepping a discussion of the *daraja* verse (Qur'ān 2:228) because, she surmises, that would undermine their position that the Qur'ān fundamentally upholds gender egalitarianism and undermines the patriarchal family.[44]

Ali concludes that the Qur'ān is a "thoroughly androcentric" but not a misogynist text, because, in her understanding, it privileges male sexual agency while promoting at the same time mutual affection between husbands and wives. In her view, scholars like wadud and Barlas have not made an irrefutable case for gender egalitarianism in the

Qur'ān, and she fears that they may be reading such egalitarianism into the text which ultimately cannot support such an interpretation.[45]

Hidayatullah's arguments against wadud and Barlas closely echo those deployed by Ali, whom she often references in her book. Like Ali, she is not convinced that the Qur'ān is resolutely antipatriarchal and fears that Muslim women exegetes are misguided in their efforts to extrapolate gender egalitarianism from specific Qur'ānic verses. She recognizes that the Qur'ān advocates kind and loving relations between husbands and wives in specific verses, but that in others, she says, men are granted financial, social, and sexual control over women. In her opinion, the content of such verses cannot be reconciled, and she fears that, ultimately, the Qur'ān cannot be called on to support the kind of gender equality "as we define it today." Furthermore, she says, "no amount of interpretation can make the text definitively cohere with our contemporary sense of justice."[46] Hidayatullah does not offer a definition of gender equality "as we define it today"; the concept is rather asserted as a nebulous assumption regarding which a (universal?) consensus is presumed to exist. Nor does she explicitly mention which audience or readership is intended in her appeal to "our" sense of justice. If she has in mind a contemporary Western, particularly American, secular audience—the obvious one to infer for a book published in English by a Western academic press—then this raises highly complex questions regarding what constitutes justice at the intersection of race, gender, religion and socioeconomic status in the contemporary West, where these identity markers have led to gross social and political inequities and a spectacular rise in racial and religious animosities in recent times. Political commitments and ideological affiliation heavily color notions of "justice" in the North Atlantic region today, especially as applied to non-European peoples in general, attitudes which also influence foreign policy measures adopted by certain Western countries.[47] In her 2018 book *Sex and Secularism*, Joan Scott mounts a compelling critique of Western secular feminist arguments that have been deployed to legitimize various Western imperial projects in the name of "justice" and "liberation" that have brought untold misery to women, including Muslim women, in the Global South.[48] Some of these projects have been launched with the grandiose objective of "saving" Muslim women," as tellingly criticized by Lila Abu-Lughod;[49] a point also cogently underscored by Joseph Massad and others.[50]

Not surprisingly, Hidayatullah spends some time discussing Qur'ān 4:34, since, as must be evident by now, this verse has become the lightning rod within virtually all Muslim feminist discussions. She challenges wadud's and Barlas's interpretations of this verse by maintaining that contrary to their assertions, the verse does mandate specific gendered roles, going so far as to suggest that the assignment of such gendered roles has implications even for the ontological equality of men and women. She says, "Thus, when function is related to being, functional inequality will be necessarily rooted in ontological inequality.[51]

Hidayatullah levels charges of anachronism and the willful manipulation of texts at those gender scholars she disagrees with.[52] She questions wadud's and Barlas's understanding of mutuality and hierarchy as contradictory notions and asserts that she holds "patriarchal characteristics to be central to many of the Qur'ān's hierarchy verses."[53] Proceeding from this vantage point, her interpretation of *qānitāt* in Qur'ān 4:34 is that it is a reference to "those who are deferential (*qānitātun*) to something/ someone unspecified" and that "the verse commands that if the women defer to their husbands (*fa-in aṭa'nakum*), then the men should not engage in unspecified action against them."[54] Hidayatullah understands this verse to mandate the obedience of *all* wives to *all* husbands in conformity with her preference for a patriarchal reading.[55]

Assessing the Antipatriarchal Position and Its Critiques

The debate about whether the Qur'ān upholds patriarchy or undermines it has not abated since wadud first published *Qur'ān and Woman* in 1992. More broadly, the question continues to be asked as to whether the Qur'ānic text can be understood to support an ethics of egalitarianism, in which gender is not a marker of moral, social, and legal difference. Here I weigh in based on my own reading of the Qur'ān and the exegetical literature around it.

On the general topic of equality and egalitarianism, it cannot be said that the Qur'ān is not concerned with it, as some have maintained. On the contrary, the Qur'ān evidences a strong concern for setting up certain criteria for gauging equality versus inequality—gender, however, is not one of them, neither is race, ethnicity, color of one's skin, or socioeconomic background, criteria that we usually invoke in the modern period, especially in the West, to discuss issues of inequality. Rather, the possession or nonpossession of specific moral attributes and the commission of certain pious acts establish the essential and *only* criteria for comparing and describing people who are unequal to one another. In other words, the issue of the equality of human beings in the Qur'ān has nothing to do with ontological, physical attributes like race, gender, and skin color. Humans, by virtue of being human, are fundamentally equal—this is an incontestable part of the Qur'ānic ethos by default.

There is in fact a specific vocabulary employed by the Qur'ān to discuss equality and inequality among human beings; verbal and adjectival derivatives from the Arabic root *swy* are used to launch these comparisons. Two such significant verses ask, "Are the blind and the seeing person or darkness and light to be deemed equal (*tastawī*)?" Qur'ān 13:16 (see also 6:50; 35:19; 40:58; 59:20); asks, "Are those who know and those who do not know equal?" Other verses posit inequality between (a) good and evil (41:34; 5:100); (b) the believers who do good deeds and the unrighteous who do not (32:18; 9:19); (c) those who are able to give away their wealth in charity and those not (16:75); (d) believers who actively strive to do good and those believers who do not, despite having the capacity to do so (4:95); (e) those who command justice and those who do not (16:76); (f) those who spent in charity and fought before the fall of Mecca (8/630) and those who did not (57:10); (g) those who will be heaven-dwellers versus hell-dwellers (59:20); and (h) those among the People of the Book who are upright and are prayerful and those among them who are not (3:113–114).[56]

This survey makes clear that in the Qur'ān, it is the cultivation of personal virtues, such as righteousness, adherence to justice, and devoutness, as well as sedulousness in practicing charity and other good deeds, that are the ultimate criteria for determining a person's moral worth and standing. The one attribute that is most prominently invoked as demarcating difference in status among humans is possession of knowledge in the broadest sense; knowledge confers "sight" and "insight" so that the difference between those who know and those who do not know is like the difference between the seeing person and the one who is blind. None of these attributes is gendered (or racialized, ethnicized, tribalized)—each and every human being is capable of acquiring knowledge and carrying out acts of piety to the best of their ability (for example, Qur'ān 2:286). For those who need to be assured of the nongendered nature of the Qur'ānic discourse on the equality of human beings based on their personal righteousness (*taqwā*) and the commission of good deeds, their attention can be drawn particularly to Qur'ān 33:35, which asserts that women and men earn the same heavenly rewards for the same acts of faith and piety.[57] In relation to the manifestation of piety in social and political settings, Qur'ān 9:71 declares men and women to be partners or allies of one another in "commanding good and forbidding wrong"—the fundamental moral imperative that undergirds Islamic morality and ethics. (I will be returning to a discussion of these last two verses toward the end of this chapter.)

So where would patriarchy which flagrantly posits the unequal status of women vis-à-vis men fit into the Qur'ānic ethos? We can all agree that "patriarchy," in the words of the Canadian sociologist Dorothy E. Smith, refers to "men's political and personal domination over women."[58] It would be very difficult, if not impossible, to aver that the Qur'ān endorses such a patriarchal regime predicated on *all* women's acquiescence to *all* men's control over their lives. There is, after all, not a single Qur'ānic verse that commands the unquestioning obedience of women *qua* women to men *qua* men, or of wives *qua* wives to husbands *qua* husbands.[59] Although it may come as a surprise to many, Qur'ān 4:34 is actually the best evidence for arriving at this conclusion, as I explain below.

Along with Qur'ān 4:34, I discuss below another verse—Qur'ān 2:228—that is frequently cited to make the case for patriarchy and to point to a lack of gender egalitarianism within the Qur'ān.

Qur'ān 4:34

In her 2006 book, *Inside the Gender Jihad*, amina wadud bluntly counsels that we should say no to the command *waḍribūhunna* in Qur'ān 4:34.[60] Khaled Abou El Fadl similarly expresses his discomfort with the specific wording of Qur'ān 4:34 and says it should give us "a conscientious pause."[61] This is, however, not just a modern reaction. Classical male exegetes themselves appeared to be taken aback when encountering the verb *ḍaraba* so that they went to great lengths to explain that the verb referred to a light, symbolic tapping at best that in no way should cause the errant wife any physical harm. The term *ḍaraba* in the sense of "physical beating," after all, is highly discordant with the rest of the Qur'ānic text, which shows considerable solicitousness toward women and other groups of people prone to being victimized by those who are stronger and more powerful in society—traditionally these have been adult males. This apparent dissonance continues to haunt us into the modern day.

The verse further provokes feminist anxiety that it may be interpreted as mandating the submission of *all* women to *all* men and of *all* wives to *all* husbands. This anxiety can be allayed by taking seriously the profound semantic difference between the description of women as *qānitāt* in the earlier part of the verse and the verb *aṭaʿna* (meaning "they [feminine] obey") in the latter part of the verse. The conflation of the two lexemes allows for the interpretation that first, women should be obedient to men in general and second, that wives should be obedient to their husbands in general. But this conflation elides the fact that the verse specifically uses the verb *aṭaʿna only* in connection with the *nāshizāt* who are clearly guilty of a flagrant violation of their marital obligations,[62] and not with women or wives in general. If marriage is a partnership, as is certainly indicated in Qur'ān 2:187, that is infused with love, mercy, and tranquility (Qur'ān 30:21), and men and women in general are partners and allies in promoting what is good and preventing what is wrong (Qur'ān 9:71), then a wife's failure to uphold her end of marital responsibilities must invite censure, as it would for the husband. In other words, the wife's "obedience" to her husband in this specific instance is not contingent on her gender but is a consequence of her grievous misconduct that threatens to undermine their marriage for which she is morally accountable. Her husband is not her overlord who commands her unquestioning obedience but her partner to whom specific obligations are due (Qur'ān 2:228). This kind of cross-referential reading of relevant verses allows the nongendered nature of a human being's moral accountability and agency to emerge from within the Qur'ān and allows us to avoid the trap of superimposing culturally mediated notions of gendered hierarchical roles on the language of the Qur'ān.[63]

The verse furthermore indicates that the Qur'ān prefers that such instances of marital discord be first resolved by the couple themselves. The protocol that is outlined for the husband to correct the erring wife's behavior in such cases is geared toward this end. When the three steps fail to convince the wife to amend her errant ways, the next verse 4:35 counsels the couple to seek arbitration. Within this ethos of seeking to set things right between the estranged couple, we must be willing to consider the potential multiple meanings of the verb *ḍaraba*, which would accord better with the overall tenor of the Qur'ān; the very polyvalence of the lexeme's root invites us to do so. The Qur'ān is, after all, very protective of a woman's rights within a marriage as well as in larger social contexts and anxious to protect her from harassment and harm. One may be reminded here of certain verses, such as Qur'ān 2:231, which warns husbands against mistreating their wives during divorce proceedings; Qur'ān 24:23, which protects women from slander against them; Qur'ān 24:4, which mandates punishment against those who resort to such slander; and Qur'ān 81:8, which condemns the practice of female infanticide in the pre-Islamic period when daughters were valued less than sons, and severely chides fathers who resorted to this reprehensible practice (Qur'ān 16:58–59). Those feminist exegetes who question the understanding of *ḍaraba* in Qur'ān 4:34 as "to beat/

strike" are in fact responsibly exercising their moral imagination and responding to the invitation extended by Qur'ān 39:18 to the reader to find the "best meaning" from its text[64] that is in accordance with its overall ethos.

Canvassing a broader range of sources that use the lexeme *ḍaraba* in variegated contexts is helpful in illustrating the more capacious semantic landscape around this word. Such an exhaustive survey is not possible in this chapter, but let us consider a well-known *ḥadīth* from which a specific meaning of *ḍaraba* can be extrapolated. In this report, Muḥammad is described as getting ready to dispatch Mu'ādh ibn Jabal to Yemen as its governor and asks the latter how he will govern. When Mu'adh's reply pleased him, the Prophet is said to have "struck him on the breast" (*fa-ḍaraba ṣadrahu*). Clearly, here the "striking" is out of joy and connotes no intent of causing physical harm, and best rendered as "patting."[65] The overwhelming majority of premodern exegetes who emphasized the symbolic nature of *ḍaraba* in Qur'ān 4:34 and modernist exegetes today who push back against the understanding of this verse as commanding injurious "wife-beating" are actually on very firm semantic ground based on a good grasp of this lexeme's polyvalence and its deployment in multiple contexts. My preference for the translation/interpretation of *waḍribuhunna* as "and lightly tap them" is based on these considerations.

It is highly significant that similar to the directive contained in Qur'ān 4:35, husbands described as guilty of *nushūz* in Qur'ān 4:128 are also instructed to seek arbitration. It may be argued that wives are not told to directly censure such behavioral infractions on the part of their errant husbands because of their obvious vulnerability in such situations, especially if these husbands are already physically abusive toward them. Here it is appropriate to interject into our discussion the need to balance the demand for strict equality with the demand for justice.[66] A strict, literal understanding of equality would have us looking for a similar directive in Qur'ān 4:128 allowing the aggrieved wife to discipline her husband in some manner. This allows us to ask if it would be just to impose this duty of disciplining the erring spouse on the victim of abuse (here the wife), which could have life-threatening consequences for her. The moral and just answer has to be no. Society must step in to protect victims of injustice and oppression; the appeal to arbitration in Qur'ān 4:128 is just such a measure to be undertaken by the collectivity in order to protect those who are vulnerable to abuse by those who are more powerful.[67]

Considerations of justice and equity may be similarly invoked when discussing the topics of inheritance and polygamy in the Qur'ān.[68] With regard to inheritance, if we were to adopt a purely bean-counting approach, then the division of inheritance shares as described in Qur'ān 4:11–12 would strike us as unfair, since the male is generally given two shares compared to the female, except in the case of parents who receive equal shares. This last exception—often given scant attention in discussions of inheritance—compels us to think of the rationale behind the apportionment of shares, ostensibly on the basis of gender. The Qur'ān in its own milieu underscores the responsibility of men as the sole breadwinners to support their families; in other words, their economic dependents—traditionally wives and children—have a claim on whatever wealth they inherit. Women have no such economic obligations mandated for them;

as is well known, married Muslim women hold on to their property in their own names and are not required to spend any part of it to support their families.[69] The extra share apportioned for men can then be understood to take into consideration their additional economic responsibilities toward their families. This *ratio legis* (legal rationale) for the disparity in inheritance shares would not apply to parents who need to be equally supported, especially in their old age.[70] Similar considerations of justice arise in regard to polygyny, where men, once again, as the principal breadwinner in the premodern period, had the economic responsibility to look after especially widows and their orphaned children, as the larger context of Qur'ān 4:3 indicates.[71]

Hidayatullah's reading of Qur'ān 4:34, particularly centered on the meanings of *qānitāt*, is highly problematic. She understands *qānitāt* to be a reference to those who are deferential to "something/someone unspecified," thereby ignoring well-established meanings for this word readily retrievable from classical dictionaries, as well as from internal evidence derived from the Qur'ān itself. Lexemes derived from the root *qnt* are not used in the Qur'ān to describe in general women's obedience to men or of humans to other humans; the one exception is Qur'ān 33:31, where obedience to Muḥammad is included along with obedience to God. In reference to Qur'ān 30:26 (also Qur'ān 2:116), which states, "To God belongs the earth and the heavens and all are *qānitūn* to him," *Lane's Lexicon*, which draws from classical Arabic dictionaries, explicates the nature of obedience implied in *qānitūn*, as occurs in this verse, as "obedience to the will [of God]," and that the *qānit* is "the performer of the commands of God."[72] The well-known seventh/thirteenth-century dictionary *Lisān al-ʿArab* describes the *qānit* as one who mentions God [constantly] (*al-dhākir li-llāh taʿālā*) and equates the *qānitūn* with "devout worshippers" (*al-ʿābidūn*).[73] Even the Hans Wehr dictionary that a college undergraduate typically uses in first-year Arabic classes in the United States documents that *qunūt* (the verbal noun from the root *qnt*) means "obedience to God" and "humility before God."[74] To ascribe semantic ambiguity to this important word despite the wealth of lexical material available for it is disingenuous to say the least.

Here we may seize the opportunity to reflect on our own sociocultural biases and preconceptions about normative gendered roles that allow many of us to automatically read not just wives' but women's general obedience to men into this verse (as did a majority of the premodern male exegetes)—when such obedience in a general sense is not only *not* explicitly stated in this verse but is clearly undermined by the usage of a word—*qānitāt*—that in the Qur'ānic milieu signals all women's direct obedience to God on an equal footing with that of all men.[75] When Qur'ān 4:34 in its latter part switches to the verb *aṭaʿna*, only the *nāshizāt*, that is to say, only specific erring wives are indicated, *not women or wives in general.*

Beside the Prophet, the only human beings to whom believing men and women owe their obedience are, in the Qur'ān, the *ulū 'l-amr* (Qur'ān 4:59);[76] obedience in such instances is indicated by the use of verbal derivatives specifically from the root *ṭwʿ*. Since we are not told otherwise, and since Qur'ān 9:71 describes men and women as being endowed with equal moral agency, the *ulū 'l-amr* would include both men and women who have the requisite qualifications for holding positions of authority—namely knowledge and piety. In the Qur'ān, these attributes are held to be attainable equally by women and men and confer on both groups moral and religious authority.[77] The late first/seventh-century exegete Mujāhid ibn Jabr (d. 104/722) understands *ulū 'l-amr* to be a reference to all the Companions of the Prophet, which would, naturally, include both women and men.[78] From this cross-referential reading of relevant verses, it becomes clear that obedience in the Qur'ān is not due to humans based on their social status and gender but rather contingent on the proper and righteous behavior of the people involved and their attendant moral authority grounded in knowledge and understanding, as applicable to specific situations.

To make the case for a Qur'ān-based patriarchy, we would also have to ignore the example set by the pious wife of the Pharaoh of Egypt (called Āsiya in the exegetical literature), who famously defied her tyrannical husband, as mentioned in Qur'ān 66:11; this act of defiance is glorified in the Qur'ān as an act of righteous resistance to evil and injustice.[79] Āsiya is furthermore held up as an exemplar of righteousness for all those who believe (*lilladhīna āmanū*), not only for women, as emphasized by Feryal Salem in Chapter 3 of this *Handbook*. This is precisely because she upheld the Qur'ānic ideals of piety and God-consciousness (*taqwā*) and heroically carried out the moral imperative of enjoining what is right and just against what is wrong and unjust, an imperative binding on both women and men (Qur'ān 9:71). Praise for such wifely disobedience would be unthinkable within a patriarchy that is predicated on the unqualified domination of men over women—that is to say, regardless of the former's personal attributes or adherence to norms of justice. Whether such moral activism is pleasing to a woman's husband or not is utterly irrelevant; the Qur'ān recognizes the woman believer's primary fealty to God as it does for a male believer.[80] It should be noted that jurists in the later period sometimes recognized and upheld this foundational principle; for example, Ibn al-Ḥajj al-'Abdarī (d. 737/1336) in his legal work *Madkhal al-Shar' al-Sharīf* expressed the opinion that if a husband were to forbid his wife from acquiring a religious education, as she is entitled to, she had the right to seek legal redress against him in order to carry out this essential duty.[81]

And let us not forget to note that Sūrat al-Mujādila (chapter 58 of the Qur'ān) takes a woman's complaint against her husband's conduct seriously and takes steps to ameliorate the situation of wives by forbidding specific divorce pronouncements by husbands.[82] There is no reprimand directed at the aggrieved wife for protesting the husband's treatment of her; instead, the chapter launches into a critique of husbands who resort to unfair divorce practices carried over from the pre-Islamic period. Sūrat al-Mujādila can therefore be read as a clear and explicit endorsement of a wife's right to lodge a complaint against her husband for unjust behavior on his part and to expect that her grievance will receive a fair hearing.

And, finally, it is highly significant that in the cluster of verses in Qur'an 24:6–10 (sometimes referred to as the *li'ān* verses or verses of "mutual imprecation"), when a husband resorts to accusing his wife of adultery and he has no witnesses, the wife's assertion of her innocence based on her own testimony is understood to override the husband's accusation. In other words, she has the last word and no further action can be taken against her (although the marriage is assumed to have irretrievably broken down). In a patriarchy, where the wife's obedience to her husband and women's general subjugation to men is a sine qua non, the Qur'an's affirmation of the independent moral and legal agency of women in general that can be exercised against an unjust husband, ruler, or any other male authoritative figure in this and other verses, should be read as striking a mortal blow against patriarchal regimes.

Faḍḍala and *Daraja* as an Indication of Divine Preference for Men over Women?

To push back against egalitarianism, one may conceivably remonstrate (as many have and continue to do) that the verb *faḍḍala* as used in the first part of Qur'ān 4:34 and the noun *daraja* in Qur'ān 2:228 may be interpreted to mean that men *as a whole* have been given preference over women *as a whole*. My examination below of the first part of Qur'ān 4:34 is followed by a discussion of Qur'ān 2:228 in order to assess the credibility of this remonstrance.

Faḍḍala in Qur'ān 4:34

To refresh our memory, the first part of this verse states: "Men are the economic providers[83] for women because God has preferred (*faḍḍala*) some of them over others and because of what they spend of their wealth."

Men's general preferential status over women has been traditionally extrapolated by the classical male exegetes from the verb *faḍḍala*. One can see how this meaning might be extracted in a decontextualized manner: the verb *faḍḍala* is derived from the Arabic root *fḍl*, which implies an excess of something and can connote preference. The noun *faḍl* derived from the same root used in relation to God refers to his bounty and grace. In relation to humans, *faḍl* can refer to their specific attributes or endowments as conferred by God.

The Qur'ān uses *faḍḍala* with different conjugations in seventeen verses without any gendered connotations and without implying any ontologically superior status for those who are the recipients of divine *faḍl* or bounty. The conferral of God's bounty always occurs selectively—some humans are the recipients of specific forms of divine bounty while others are not. Nowhere do we sense the implication that as a result these groups of people are always superior to other groups of people or that men as a whole are superior to women (or the reverse). For example, if we look at Qur'ān 4:32—two verses before the much-discussed 4:34—we note that the verse refers to some men and women who have been given more by God than others; both women and men in this case earn the same reward for the meritorious actions they carry out as a result of this *faḍl*.[84] The larger, obvious implication of this verse is that those women who have been so favored enjoy a preferential status over *other men and women* who are not the recipients of such bounties—gender is not a determinant of such a favored status at all.

Furthermore, two significant verses referring to the same group of people taken together disabuse us of the notion that certain kinds of divine *faḍl* conferred on some implies an inferior *ontological* status for those who are not recipients of the same. For example, in reference to prophets as a collectivity, Qur'ān 17:55 states, "We have preferred some of the prophets over others." In another longer verse, Qur'ān 2:253 says, "As for those Messengers, we preferred some to others; to some of them God spoke (directly); others He raised to degrees (*darajāt*); and to 'Īsā (Jesus), the son of Maryam (Mary), we gave clear proofs and strengthened him with the holy spirit."

Compare these verses to Qur'ān 2:285:

> The Messenger believes in what has been sent down to him from his Lord, as do the believers. Each one believes in God, His Angels, His Books, and His Messengers. They say, "*We make no distinction between any of His Messengers*" [emphasis mine]—and they say, "We hear and we obey; [we seek] your forgiveness, our Lord, and to you is the return."[85]

Reading these verses together allows us to arrive at the conclusion that although different prophets were endowed with different qualities and aptitudes and thereby attained varying degrees of distinction (*darajāt*), Muslims are not supposed to make any distinction between them because they were equally faithful and devout.[86] In other words, having access to God's specific bounties and consequently raised to earthly stations of honor on their basis do not make particular individuals intrinsically superior to others—that is to say, the ontological and religious/moral equality of human beings is not compromised in any way on account of the different endowments that humans possess. Needless to say, all humans are differently endowed. With regard to natural attributes, some are more intelligent/more analytical/more courageous than others. With regard to physical attributes, some are more attractive/stronger/more graceful than others. God's *faḍl* is bestowed in different ways on human beings which may bring them varying degrees of earthly honor and enable some to carry out distinctive functions—none of which, however, affects their fundamental, ontological equality as humans.

The classical male exegetes understood and accepted this implication of *faḍl* when discussing Qur'ān 2:253, but many fell back on atavistic cultural assumptions when discussing the connotations of *faḍl* in Qur'ān 4:34. We see this clearly when we compare the commentary of the eighth/fourteenth-century exegete Ibn Kathīr (d. 774/1373) on the meanings and implication of *faḍḍala* in Qur'ān 2:253 with his commentary on Qur'ān 4:34. In his exegesis of Qur'ān 2:253, Ibn Kathīr refers to a *ḥadīth* narrated by Abū Hurayra, according to which a Muslim and a Jewish man wrangled over the status of Muḥammad vis-à-vis Moses. When the Jewish man asserted that God had preferred Moses over all creation, the Muslim was outraged and struck him in the face. The Jewish man went to the Prophet and complained about the Muslim's conduct, upon which

Muḥammad instructed, "Do not give preference to me over [other] prophets." In a variant report, he is quoted as saying, "Do not make distinctions among the prophets"[87] (this would be in accordance with Qur'ān 2:285, referenced above). Among the inferences one can derive from this prophetic counsel, says Ibn Kathīr, is that one should not base one's preferences merely on opinion and partisan sentiment and that the calculation of any implied superiority based on such preferences is best left to the judgment of God.[88]

Ibn Kathīr, however, fails to heed this counsel himself when he proceeds to comment on Qur'ān 4:34. Instead he has made up his mind that *faḍḍala* in this verse, in contrast to its meaning in Qur'ān 2:253, must mean that the group described as having a specific *faḍl* (men) has an undisputed and inherently superior status vis-à-vis the group which lacks this specific *faḍl* (women). Ibn Kathīr arrogates to himself the right to make such a judgment, despite his warning that only God can pronounce on such assumed superiority. Thus, he goes on to declare that the man—in general—must be regarded as the woman's "head" (*ra'īsuhā*), her "elder" (*kabīruhā*), her "ruler/judge" (*al-ḥākim 'alayhā*), and her "discipliner (*mu'addibuhā*) if she should stray." On the basis of this understanding, Ibn Kathīr proceeds to baldly assert that "the male is superior to the female by virtue of being male" (*fa-'l-rajul afḍal min al-mar'a fī nafsihi*).[89] This assumed ontological superiority of the male over the female is connected with his understanding of *qānitāt* in Qur'ān 4:34 as a reference to wives' unconditional obedience *only* to their husbands; like al-Wāḥidī before him, he removes God altogether as the object of women's devotion here. Lest the reader miss the significance of this point, he deploys the *ḥadīth* in which Muḥammad is said to have declared, "If I were to command anyone to prostrate himself before another [person], it would be the wife before her husband on account of the rights he enjoys in relation to her."[90] Ibn Kathīr's inclusion of this report here proves to us that male authoritarian attitudes toward women in the later period were frequently projected back to the time of the Prophet in the form of *ḥadīth*s, creating a powerful legitimizing source for such changed sensibilities.[91]

Ibn Kathīr's differential understanding of the verb *faḍḍala* in the two verses referenced above illustrates for us how strongly cultural notions of gendered identities had come to prevail in Muslim-majority realms by the eighth/fourteenth century when he lived, allowing for an ontologically superior status for the male over the female to be read back into Qur'ān 4:34 in the later period, in contrast to the earlier period (roughly before the fourth/tenth century). Such an exegetical process all but completely occluded the gender-egalitarian ethos of the Qur'ān and the imprint it had left on early Islamic societies.

Before we leave this section, it is worth pointing out that those prophets to whom God spoke to directly are not considered to be superior to those who were denied such a privilege, according to Qur'ān 2:253. This is a relevant observation in view of the fact that a few feminist scholars are of the opinion that because God addresses men more than women in the Qur'ān and/or directly addresses men only (although Mary would be the exception), then women's status should be considered diminished in comparison with that of men. Clearly, this conclusion cannot be supported on the basis of the internal evidence provided by the Qur'ān itself, derived from a cross-referential reading of relevant verses.

Daraja

Besides Qur'ān 2:253, the word *daraja* famously occurs in Qur'ān 2:228, which states:

> Divorced women remain in waiting for three periods, and it is not lawful for them to conceal what God has created in their wombs if they believe in God and the Last Day. And their husbands have the right to take them back in this [period] if they want reconciliation. And the rights due to the women are similar to the rights upon them (or the responsibilities they owe) with regard to what is good and equitable (*ma'rūf*), and the men have a "degree" (*daraja*) over them. And God is Exalted in Might and Wise.

This is another verse popular with those who want to retrieve a gendered hierarchy from within the Qur'ān. *Daraja* occurring in this verse has been traditionally understood by premodern exegetes to refer to a man's "degree" over a woman, implying, according to them, a fundamental superiority of the former over the latter. One may again resort to a cross-referential reading of the Qur'ānic text in order to determine whether this understanding can be supported on the basis of other verses in the Qur'ān that use the term *daraja*.

There are eighteen verses that contain either the singular *daraja* or its plural *darajāt*; two of them are Qur'ān 2:253 and 2:228, as referenced above; I now mention a few additional ones. Qur'ān 46:19 says, "Everyone has a rank/degree" (*li-kullin daraja*); and Qur'ān 9:20 states, "The ones who believed, emigrated and strove in the cause of God with their wealth and their lives are greater in rank (*a'ẓam daraja*) in the sight of God. And it is they who attain [success]." Another verse, Qur'ān 6:165, states, "For He it is who has appointed you vicegerent over the earth, and has elevated some of you over others in degrees (*darajāt*) that He may try you in what He has bestowed upon you. Indeed your Lord is swift in retribution, and He is certainly all-forgiving, all-compassionate." A fourth verse (Qur'ān 43:32) says:, "Is it they who apportion the mercy of your Lord? It is We who have apportioned their livelihood among them in the life of this world, and have raised some above others in rank (*daraja*) so that some of them may harness others to their service. Your Lord's mercy is better than all the treasures that they hoard."

The first verse refers to the simple fact that everyone (regardless of gender) has a rank or degree in respect to others on the basis of the characteristics they possess and the merit of their actions. The second verse underscores the greater merit that accrues to those who embraced Islam in the early period and rendered great service to the Muslim community—the assignment of such a merit-based rank (*sābiqa*) is not gendered since both the male and the female Companions who emigrated to Medina are the clear referent in this verse.[92] The third verse refers to *darajāt* as a trial from God, since humans who attain to certain ranks on earth also acquire certain responsibilities along with them that they are expected to discharge. The fourth verse refers to those who have greater financial resources and therefore have an "edge" or "advantage" over others who are not similarly monetarily privileged. These verses also do not link *daraja* to gender.

This broader perspective is helpful for better appreciating the contextualized meaning of *daraja* in Qur'ān 2:228. The relevant part of the verse asserts that wives (since the context is clearly domestic) have rights and duties vis-à-vis their husbands that are the equal of the rights and duties of husbands toward their wives. Husbands, however, have an edge or advantage over their wives. Given my earlier discussion of *daraja* as it occurs in several verses, I am interpreting this "edge," as indicated in Qur'ān 2:228, as a reference to men's greater ability to earn money and provide financial maintenance for their families.[93] This "edge" is therefore, purely functional and monetary in nature, and gendered only to the extent that in the premodern world, men were the principal breadwinners.[94] There is not a whiff of ontological superiority attached to this functional and historically contingent edge that men typically have enjoyed over women in the domestic sphere. More broadly, no Qur'ānic verse that deploys the term *daraja/darajāt* makes any ontological claims about those who possess such ranks/degrees.[95] Based on the Qur'ān, Hidayatullah's remonstrance that functional difference can imply an ontological one has to be categorically rejected.

The reciprocity of rights and duties that wives and husbands enjoy should also be understood to include access to sex. Both Ali and Hidayatullah lament that while husbands are depicted as initiating sex in the Qur'ān, wives are not so described. This leads them to conclude that the Qur'ān deprives women of sexual agency. But one may more cogently argue that once the Qur'ān states that married couples have equal rights vis-à-vis one another, then this general proclamation should be understood to subsume specifics, such as sexual agency for both parties; there would be no need to belabor the obvious. No verse, after all, prohibits wives from making sexual overtures to their husbands. The verses in which men are taught the ethics of sexually approaching their wives may be read as correcting the former's behavior that may have smacked of sexual predatoriness in the prerevelation period. This is indicated in a *ḥadīth* in which Muḥammad counsels his followers regarding the proper way to make sexual overtures:

> "Do not fall on your women like animals. Send a 'messenger' first." When the Companions wished to know what he meant by "a messenger," the Prophet replied, "Kisses and words of endearment."[96]

Regardless of whether this *ḥadīth* is reliable or not, it appears to encode a general awareness that Muslim sexual ethics requires that marital intimacy be based on gentle and affectionate behavior toward one's spouse.[97]

Women Outside of the Domestic Sphere: Qur'ān 33:35 and 9:71

We may well ask: why, out of the over 6,000 verses in the Qur'ān, has one part of a single verse (Qur'ān 4:34), which deals with an anomalous minority of wives[98] who do not honor their marriage commitments in some egregious way, been generalized to *all* women and *all* wives over time? We can perhaps full well understand why a majority of the premodern male exegetes did so—this segment of a Qur'ānic pericope confirmed their patriarchal worldview that had become predominant by the third/ninth century in Islamic realms. One can almost imagine their *aha!* moment when they encountered this verse. But it should make us wonder why a handful of gender scholars in the contemporary period have also embraced this interpretation as reflecting an assumed overall patriarchal thrust to the Qur'ānic text. Their proclivity should invite us to take stock of the kind of social and political precommitments that predispose at least a handful of Muslim gender scholars to expect and then read back into this verse women's general obedience to men (in tandem with a majority of the premodern male exegetes). This unusual congruence in medieval and modern feminist exegetical views, at least as held by a few, is rather ironical to say the very least.

Focusing primarily on Qur'ān 4:34 and Qur'ān 2:228 when talking about women in the Islamic milieu fosters the notion, perhaps inadvertently, that women are only sexual and domestic beings. Yet, women in the Qur'ān are also cerebral, moral, ethical, and productive human beings who take part and are expected to take part in the grand human drama of human agency, fulfillment, and salvation unfolding throughout history. They are necessary actors in this drama without whose participation Islamic history—as part of this universal human story—is inconceivable. This is not just an ideological assertion. The Qur'ān addresses them along with men in its frequent vocatives—"O those who believe" (*ya ayyuhā alladhīna āmanū*) and "O humankind" (*ya ayyuhā al-nās*)—as it instructs how humans should worship their Creator and serve as stewards (*khalīfa*/*khulafā'*) of the earth.

Two verses that celebrate women as actors in multiple spheres of life now need to be foregrounded as a corrective to an excessive emphasis on their familial and reproductive roles. First, Qur'ān 33:35 remains the verse par excellence that establishes the equality of women and men in the sight of God on the basis of their moral excellences and deeds. It states:

> Those who have surrendered to God among males and females; those who believe among males and females; those who are devout among males and females; those who are truthful among males and females; those who are patient among males and females; those who fear God among males and females; those who give in charity among males and females; those who fast among males and females; those who remember God often among males and females—God has prepared for them forgiveness and great reward.

This verse has been embraced particularly by many modern Muslim women exegetes who draw self-empowerment and self-validation from within the Qur'ān itself. The verse, after all, asserts the complete spiritual and moral equality of men and women, based on their faith, practice of specific virtues, and observance of their religious duties. Most exegetes record the following cause of revelation: In roughly the third or fourth year of the Islamic era (corresponding to 625–626 CE), the Medinan woman Companion Umm 'Umāra remarked to Muḥammad in connection with the Qur'ānic revelations he had received up to that point, "I see that everything pertains to men; I do not see the mention of women."[99] Umm 'Umara was commenting on the fact that Qur'ānic verses that had come down so far primarily referred to men and their good deeds and the rewards that they were consequently promised in the hereafter. Were women believers not to be recognized as equal participants in the grand human and cosmic drama unfolding before them? The subsequent revelation of this verse proceeded to settle the question once and for all: women and men have equal moral agency in their quest for the good and righteous life in this world for which they reap identical rewards in the afterlife. Gender had no role to play in the salvific efficacy offered by the Qur'ān through its prescription for the well-ordered moral and spiritual existence on earth. It is worth noting that this message of complete parity in the moral worth of actions, regardless of gender, is also repeated in a briefer form in Qur'ān 3:195 in which God speaks, "I will not let the work of any of you, whether male or female, to be lost; each of you is from the other."

The second verse is Qur'ān 9:71, which, like Qur'ān 33:35, may be understood to have a broad, general applicability (*'amm*) and to cover the whole gamut of activities that women are able to take part in as part of their God-given mandate to command what is right and good and prevent what is wrong and evil. Pre-modern exegetes did not pay much attention to it; it has been "rediscovered," so to speak, by Muslim women exegetes who discern its empowering message that is particularly resonant in the modern period.

The verse states:

> (Male) believers (*al-mu'minūn*) and (female) believers (*al-mu'mināt*) are the partners/allies (*awliyā'*) of one another; they command the good and forbid wrong and they perform prayer, give the obligatory alms, and obey God and His messenger. They are those upon whom God has mercy; indeed God is Almighty, Wise.

The obvious intent of the verse, based on its plain sense, is to establish parity between men and women as partners in the common venture to promote the good, righteous society on earth and to fulfill their individual and communal obligations toward God.[100] But a majority of male interpreters from the premodern and modern periods understood this verse in ways that were consonant with their own particularist views of women's roles in the social and political contexts of their day. A sampling of the perspectives of a number of influential exegetes is now provided below to offer a glimpse into the conceptualization of such gendered identities in variegated historical circumstances.[101]

Premodern Exegeses of Qur'ān 9:71

In the first half of the second/eighth century during the late Umayyad and early 'Abbasid periods, the exegete Muqātil ibn Sulaymān (d. 150/767) asserts the full and equal partnership of female and male believers in matters of religion (*fī al-dīn*) and highlights their mutually reinforcing obedience to God in Qur'ān 9:71.[102] Al-Ṭabarī from the 'Abbasid period in the early fourth/tenth century similarly emphasizes that righteous men and women "who believe in God, His messenger and the verses of His book" are each other's helpers (*anṣār*) and supporters (*a'wān*). Their fundamental duty to promote what is right and prevent what is wrong consists in inviting people to believe in one God and abandon the worship of idols, and to carry out their fundamental religious obligations, such as offering prayers and paying alms.[103]

The fifth/eleventh-century exegete al-Wāḥidī similarly underscores the complementarity of men and women's religious and familial roles to be indicated in this verse. He quotes from the famous Companion Ibn 'Abbās, who stated that believing women and men were allies of one another "in regard to mercy and affection" (*fī al-raḥma wa al-maḥabba*). Al-Wāḥidī understands this statement to mean that they were like "one hand in supporting [one another]" and, like al-Ṭabarī, stresses that they were particularly called to invite people to worship the one God and to themselves observe the fundamental tenets of Islam.[104] Very similar views are expressed by the well-known Andalusian exegete Muḥammad b. Aḥmad al-Qurṭubī (d. 671/1273), who, on the basis of this verse, characterizes the relationship between men and women as one of "hearts united in mutual affection, love, and empathy."[105]

The eighth/fourteenth-century exegete Ibn Kathīr, whom we met earlier, also comments on this special bond existing among believers in his exegesis of Qur'ān 9:71 and invokes the *ḥadīth* in which the Prophet describes the faithful as constituting "a [single] edifice in which each strengthens the other" in this context.[106] Worthy of note is that Ibn Kathīr uses however only the masculine noun for believers (*al-mu'minīn*) in his commentary; this is in stark contrast to our earlier commentators who repeated in their exegeses the masculine and the feminine plural nouns occurring in Qur'ān 9:71 that refer explicitly to male and female believers.

In the twentieth century, Rashīd Riḍā provides a more detailed explanation of the nature of *wilāya*[107] (partnership) indicated in the verse and how that applies to men and women, both equally and differentially. As far as their fundamental relationship is concerned, Riḍā states, the *wilāya* that exists between believing women and men, according to this verse, has to do "in general with mutual support, solidarity and affection" (*ta'umm wilāyat al-nuṣra wa-wilāyat al-ikhwa wa al-mawadda*). He also invokes *ḥadīth*s as proof-texts, one in which Muḥammad describes the community of Muslims as "one body" (*al-jasad al-wāḥid*) and another (previously quoted by Ibn Kathīr) in which the *umma* constitutes a "single edifice in which each strengthens the other." The alliance of support (*wilāyat al-nuṣra*) is specifically constituted so that all may collaborate in defending truth, justice, the religious community, and the nation.[108]

Where gender does make a difference is in the realm of military defense of the polity, says Riḍā; in this realm, women offer their help in everything short of actual combat. He points to the example of the women Companions during the lifetime of the Prophet who provided water for thirsty combatants, prepared food, and tended to the wounded on the battlefield.[109] Aside from this difference, Riḍā appears to consider men and women to be equally engaged in their efforts to promote what is right and prevent what is wrong in different spheres of life.

The fairly brief comments on the whole recorded by premodern male exegetes on what otherwise strikes many Muslim feminists today as a radically egalitarian verse with potentially revolutionary sociopolitical implications are perhaps telling. They underscore for us that the medieval male imaginary was not capable of extrapolating from this verse a larger scriptural mandate for women and men to work together companionably and on an equal footing in all spheres of life. They restrict the *wilāya* indicated in Qur'ān 9:71 to essentially the religious sphere and do not (and perhaps could not) derive a broader empowerment of women and men equally in the larger society around them. Riḍā in the twentieth century has a more capacious understanding of *wilāya* in connection with both men and women. He, however, places one restriction on the purview of the *wilāya* of women—that it does not extend to fighting on the battlefield, which remains a male preserve. By default, all other activities that constitute the promotion of truth, justice, and righteousness are available equally to women and men by virtue of the Qur'ānic mandate to serve as "allies of one another."

In the twenty-first century, we are able to question the need to place a cap on what activities women may engage in, since many of the previous sociocultural constraints that influenced the interpretations of this verse have begun to (mostly) recede; additionally, economic necessity in particular requires women to join the labor force in modern societies. Qur'ān 9:71 remains the verse par excellence that in our contemporary world may be understood to provide an explicit mandate for the equal partnership of women and men and to endow them with equal agency in all spheres of life—there are, after all, no qualifiers indicated in the verse. It should be noted that despite Riḍā's reservations about women taking part in active combat, some of the women Companions did fight on the battlefield during the lifetime of Muḥammad and in the early period after his death, for which activity they earned effusive praise from the Prophet himself and won considerable renown in their own lifetimes.[110] Their participation in the early battles, whether as combatants or as providers of humanitarian assistance, entitled them to shares of the war-spoils equal to those of men, an egalitarian practice that, not surprisingly, would become vigorously contested in the later period.[111]

This mutual alliance (*wilāya*) for the common good—however that common good may be interpreted in various times and places—may be seen as more than subversive of patriarchy; it may, in fact, be understood to completely dismantle it. Not surprisingly, this notion of *wilāya* is robustly invoked by many Muslim gender scholars and feminist practitioners today to underscore what they understand to be the Qur'ān's prescient gender egalitarianism that is particularly resonant today. As Asma Lamrabet, a prominent Moroccan reformer and advocate of women's rights remarks, "In today's social context, it is time to reclaim the Qur'ānic concept of *wilāyah* as a principle that dictates responsible and constructive membership and participation of women and men in society."[112]

Qur'ān 2:282—One Last Attempt to Restrict Women

Those who are determined to find evidence in the Qur'ān of a woman's ontologically inferior status vis-à-vis that of a man have another favorite verse to point to: Qur'ān

2:282. This verse states, "Set up two witnesses from your own men, and if there are not two men, then choose a man and two women as witnesses, so that if one makes a mistake, then the other can remind her." Despite the fact that the context in which this verse is embedded refers to a very specific kind of financial enterprise—a loan transaction (*dayn*)—the verse has been invoked by some as a proof-text to establish that a woman's legal testimony in general is worth half that of a man. This disparity is assumed to stem from her tendency to be forgetful and to be not as mentally competent as a man. Interestingly, al-Ṭabarī in the early fourth/tenth century does not indulge in this kind of gendered generalization in his comments on this verse but rather focuses on a linguistic and semantic analysis of the key terms involved in legal testimony. But two centuries later, al-Rāzī (d. 606/1210) discerns in this verse a reference to the woman being more prone to forgetfulness (*al-nisyān*) "because of the predominance of cold and moisture in her basic temperament." And, not surprisingly, Ibn Kathīr in the eighth/fourteenth century goes even further and says that two women take the place of one man in legal testimony because of the "deficient intelligence of the woman" (*li-nuqṣān ʿaql al-marʾa*).[113]

Although this view appears to have been taken hold among many premodern male exegetes after the fourth/tenth century, it cannot be attributed uniformly to the medieval *fuqahaʾ* (jurists), as Mohammad Fadel has shown. Instead, he documents that a number of premodern jurists had much more complex and sophisticated views on the validity of women's testimony; in fact, two of the most prominent premodern Ḥanbalī jurists, Ibn Taymiyya (d. 728/1328) and his student Ibn Qayyim al-Jawziyya (d. 751/1350) (both of whom incidentally are highly regarded in conservative circles today), came very close to articulating the equal valid testimony of women compared to men. These two jurists clearly understood that the general cannot be derived from the particular.[114]

Many gender scholars emphasize this distinction between the general and the particular. In this vein, they typically argue that the specific context of Qur'ān 2:282 highly circumscribes its applicability, especially in the modern world. The assumption of a woman's incompetence in financial transactions in the premodern world, where such competence would have been rare, had no bearing in other matters where she may have competency equal or superior to a man's—in *ḥadīth* transmission and childbearing matters, for example. In fact, in the field of *ḥadīth* transmission with its rigorous standards of moral probity and accurate oral transmission, the individual testimony of women narrators about the reliability of *ḥadīth*s they related from the Prophet was frequently and freely accepted when they met this high bar, especially in the early period.[115]

It should also be noted that according to Qur'an 24:6–9, should a wife be accused of adultery by her husband and there are no witnesses, the wife's sole testimony on behalf of her innocence prevails over the husband's accusation. Returning to Qur'ān 2:282, both the Qur'ānic context and the historical practices or the living *sunna* of the early community provide irrefutable proof that this verse was not meant to constitute a generalizable rule about the value of a woman's legal testimony. Here the maintenance of a distinction between the general (*ʿamm*) and particular (*khāṣṣ*) becomes particularly acute, as does recourse to cross-referential reading of Qur'ānic verses. Thus we see that when Qur'ān 2:282 is read along with Qur'ān 33:35 and 9:71, it allows us to make the case that the general proclamation of women's equality to men in faith and deed and affirmation of their independent moral agency in the latter two verses trump the particularist understanding of feminine limitations, as indicated in the first, that are attributable to mere historical contingency.

Conclusion

At the beginning of this chapter I posed certain questions that are often asked by gender scholars about the Qur'ānic worldview concerning women. The prime concern is whether the Qur'ān may be understood to be a gender-egalitarian text or one that ultimately condones patriarchy and upholds a form of gendered hierarchy in which men are deemed to be ontologically and morally superior to women. My analysis of relevant texts and arguments emanating from both proegalitarian and prohierarchical stances leads me to the conclusion that the proegalitarian position is the more credible and cogent one. I find no incontrovertible proof or persuasive argument that makes the case for a patriarchal and hierarchical ethos within the Qur'ān. To support such an ethos, the Qur'ān would have to posit the ontological inferiority of women to men; stipulate that all women/wives obey all men/husbands—a sine qua non of patriarchy; value male worship and deeds higher than women's; and restrict the acquisition of knowledge and access to moral and social goods only to men. In my exploration of this issue, I find that the Qur'ān affirms the exact opposite of these positions.

Through a cross-referential reading of related verses, I furthermore arrive at the conclusion that the construction of a divinely mandated gender hierarchy based on specific locutions occurring in the Qur'ānic text—*faḍḍala 'alā* and *daraja*—cannot withstand careful scrutiny. Ibn Kathīr's specious reasoning to extrapolate such a hierarchy from Qur'ān 4:34 in contrast to Qur'ān 2:253, where he discounts the possibility of such a hierarchy existing among humans—despite the occurrence of the same relevant vocabulary in both—is revealing of the lengths to which certain male exegetes were prepared to go in the late premodern period to preserve masculine privilege.

I perceive three main problems in prohierarchy discourses, as follows: (1) the functional, circumscribed "superiority" of the male, especially within the domestic sphere, that is contingent on his status as the sole financial provider in the premodern period, has been mistaken for a general and ontological superiority; (2) the subversive function of *qunūt* in establishing women's direct access to God without the mediation of men established throughout the Qur'ān and as powerfully evident, for example, in the case of Āsiya, the pious *disobedient* wife of the Pharaoh, receives scant attention; and (3) the revolutionary potential of Qur'ān 9:71 as the gender-egalitarian verse par excellence that has broad, sweeping applicability, particularly in the modern period, has not been fully appreciated. Instead, the fixation with Qur'ān 4:34 and what I understand to be its misreadings continue to dominate and derail conversations on the topic of "Islam and Women."

There is no doubt that believing Muslim women who are seeking empowerment and self-actualization from within their own faith tradition will continue to engage primarily with the Qur'ān, because they understand that only God's words can transcend the banality of gendered inequality constructed by humans and thereby ensure their rights. Already in the first century of Islam, we see a clear articulation of this conviction when a Qurayshī woman—who is unnamed in the sources I have looked at—stood up to challenge the second caliph 'Umar ibn al-Khaṭṭāb (d. 24/644) in the Prophet's mosque at Medina when he wished to restrict the amount of *mahr* (marital dower or gift) for women. She protested that he was overstepping his bounds and cited Qur'ān 4:20,[116] which warns against placing a cap on the *mahr*, thereby clearly implying that no man could take away from women what God had already given them.[117] Her words are poignantly resonant in our own time as learned Muslim women, based on their own readings of the Qur'ān, mount challenges to entrenched patriarchies and critique the unequal relationships that they foster between women and men.

The story has a happy epilogue: the woman's remonstrance had the intended effect—it gave 'Umar pause and caused him to rethink and declare publicly from the pulpit that he had reversed his earlier pronouncement. More importantly perhaps, he was forced to concede that a woman's exegesis was better than his. That can only be considered a positive augury.

Notes

1. For a detailed overview of the rise of what is termed "Islamic feminism" in Western academic scholarship since the nineteenth century, see Margot Badran, *Feminism in Islam: Secular and Religious Convergences* (Oxford: Oneworld Publication 2009). However, this term in English is not coined out of whole cloth; the Arabic term *nisāwiyya* or *nisā'iyya* was in circulation already in the late nineteenth century in Muslim women's writings, and can be understood as referring to a "womanist" or "feminist" consciousness, particularly when approaching and reevaluating religious and legal issues pertaining to women; see further Margot Badran and miriam cooke, *Opening the Gates: An Anthology of Arab Feminist Writing*, 2nd ed. (Bloomington: Indiana University Press, 2004). Ziba Mir-Hosseini has observed that although there is no exact term connoting feminism in Persian, "as a consciousness it has always existed"; see her chapter, "Women and Politics in Post-Khomeini Iran: Divorce, Veiling, and Emerging Feminist Voices," in *Women and Politics in the Third World*, ed. Haleh Afshar (London and New York: Routledge, 1996), 144–173.
2. See, notably, Asma Barlas, "Engaging Islamic Feminism: Provincialising Feminism as a Master Narrative," in *Islamic Feminism: Current Perspectives*, ed. Anitta Kynsilehto (Tampere, Finland: Tampere Peace Research Institute, 2008), 15–24. This resistance can also be retrieved from Omaima Abou-Bakr, ed., *Feminist and Islamic Perspectives: New Horizons of Knowledge and Reform*, trans. Y. Motawy (Cairo: The Women and Memory Forum, 2013), 4–8, where the editor questions the need for an "Islamic feminism."
3. Thus Barlas remonstrates, "To the extent that feminism in any form is complicit with this violence—which I believe it is when it reads oppression into Islam and reads liberation out of the West's imperialist depredations—I feel the need to resist it in all its forms;" Barlas,

"Engaging Islamic Feminism," 20. Leila Ahmed defines "colonial feminism" as a Western project of political and cultural domination which is predicated on "the notion that an intrinsic connection existed between the issue of culture and the status of women, and . . . that progress for women could be achieved only through abandoning the native culture"; see her well-known study *Women in Islam: Historical Roots of a Modern Debate* (New Haven: Yale University Press, 1992), 244.

4. This chapter draws to a certain extent from my previously published chapters as follows: Asma Afsaruddin, *Contemporary Issues in Islam* (Edinburgh: Edinburgh University Press, 2015), chapter 4, 86–114; and "Reading the Qur'an through a Gendered, Egalitarian Lens: Revisiting the Concept of *Wilāya* in Q. 9:71," in *Islamic Interpretive Tradition and Gender Justice*, ed. Nevin Reda and Yasmin Amin (Montreal: McGill-Queens University Press, 2020), 100–124.
5. Amina wadud, *Qur'ān and Woman: Rereading the Sacred Text from a Woman's Perspective* (New York: Oxford University Press, 1999).
6. Ibid., xii.
7. Ibid., xii–xiii.
8. Asma Barlas, *"Believing Women" in Islam: Unreading Patriarchal Interpretations of the Qur'ān* (Austin: University of Texas Press, 2004), 3. When I reference Barlas's views, I am referring to the 2004 edition of her book, unless stated differently.
9. See chapter 2 by Hadia Mubarak in this *Handbook*.
10. See further Mubarak's extensive discussion of classical exegeses of this verse in chapter 2, which provides more details. My discussion is meant to supplement the analysis she provides there of key points that emerge from her survey of select, well-known premodern commentaries.
11. Unless stated otherwise, translations of the Qur'ān are mine, although I have freely consulted a number of published English translations.
12. Muqātil ibn Sulaymān, *Tafsīr Muqātil ibn Sulaymān* (Cairo: Mu'assasat al-ḥalabī washurakā'uh, 1969), 1:370–371.
13. Al-Ṭabarī, *Tafsīr* (Beirut: Dār al-kutub al-'ilmiyya, 1997), 4:64.
14. Al-Wāḥidī, *al-Wāsiṭ fī tafsīr al-Qur'ān*, ed. 'Ādil Aḥmad 'Abd al-Mawjūd (Beirut: Dār al-kutub al-'ilmiyya, 1994), 2:45–47.
15. Al-Rāzī, *al-Tafsīr al-kabīr* (Beirut: Dār iḥyā' al-turāth al-'arabī, 1999), 4:70
16. Al-Bayḍāwī, *Tafsīr al-Bayḍāwī* (Beirut: Dār al-kutub al-'ilmiyya, 1988), 1:213.
17. Rashīd Riḍā, *Tafsīr al-Manār* (Beirut: Dār al-kutub al-'ilmiyya, 1999), 5:55–57. For more modern readings of this verse, see now Hadia Mubarak's comprehensive new study *Rebellious Wives, Neglectful Husbands: Controversies in Modern Qur'anic Commentaries* (Oxford: Oxford University Press, 2022), chapter 5, 126–161.
18. Sayyid Quṭb, *Fī ẓilal al-Qur'ān* (Cairo: Dār al-Shurūq, 2001), 2:652–653.
19. Al-Ṭabarī, *Tafsīr*, 4:64.
20. Al-Ṭabarī, *Tafsīr*, 4:304 ff. For a discussion of how jurists understood *nushūz* in relation to both husbands and wives, see Mariam Sheibani's discussion of this topic in chapter 6 of this *Handbook*.
21. See this discussion in Ayesha S. Chaudhry, *Domestic Violence and the Islamic Tradition* (Oxford: Oxford University Press, 2014), 1–22.
22. See this discussion by Hadia Mubarak in chapter 2 of this *Handbook*.
23. See, for example, al-Ṭabarī, *Tafsīr*, 4:70.
24. See this discussion in Chaudhry, *Domestic Violence*, 182–183.

25. This interpretation however does not address the grammatical problem generated by not having the expected Arabic pronoun *'an* before the pronominal suffix *hunna* in *waḍribuhunna* to convey the meaning of "depart **from** them" (*aḍribū 'an hunna*).
26. For example, Fazlur Rahman, *Islamic Methodology in History* (Islamabad: Central Institute of Islamic Research, 1984).
27. Mubarak, chapter 2 of this *Handbook*. See also Manuela Marin, "Disciplining Wives: A Historical Reading of Qur'ān 4:34," *Studia Islamica* 97 (2003): 5–40.
28. Jonathan Brown, *Misquoting Muhammad: The Challenges and Choices of Interpreting the Prophet's Legacy* (London: Oneworld Publications, 2014), 275–276. For a useful overview and assessment of *ḥadīths* that have been used as exegetical material for 4:34, see John Andrew Morrow, *The Most Controversial Qur'anic Verse: Why 4:34 Does Not Promote Violence against Women* (Lanham, MD: Rowman and Littlefield, 2020), chapter 5, 105–156.
29. On this topic, see Nevin Reda, "Holistic Approaches to the Qur'an: A Historical Background," *Religion Compass* 4, no. 8 (2010): 495–506; and Mustansir Mir, "The Surah as a Unity: A 20th Century Development in Qur'anic Exegesis," in *Approaches to the Qur'an*, ed. G. Hawting and A. A. Shareef (London: Routledge, 1993), 211–224.
30. An insightful discussion of the interpretive importance and cogency of the principle of *takhṣīṣ al-'amm*, especially in connection with the *ḥadīth* that has the Prophet declare that a community ruled by a woman would never prosper, is offered by Mohammad Fadel in his article, "Is Historicism a Viable Strategy for Islamic Law Reform? The Case of 'Never Shall a Folk Prosper Who Have Appointed a Woman to Rule Them,'" *Islamic Law and Society* 18 (2011): 131–176.
31. Al-Ṭabarī, *Tafsīr*, 2:169.
32. Ibid., 2:404–411.
33. Barlas, *Believing Women*, 163–165.
34. Ibid., 165.
35. One is reminded here of the well-known *ḥadīth* in which the Prophet counsels one of his Companions, "Stay with her [your mother] because paradise lies beneath her feet," recorded by Aḥmad b. Ḥanbal and al-Nasā'ī in their *ḥadīth* collections; see A. J. Wensinck, *Concordance et Indices de la Tradition Musulmane* (Leiden: E.J. Brill, 1967), 6:113. Further, the nineteenth chapter of the Qur'ān on Mary (Maryam) describes her act of giving birth to Jesus with great compassion and reverence, detailing tenderly her birth pangs and investing the whole event with great cosmic and moral significance.
36. Barbara Stowasser, "The Chapter of Eve," in *Women in the Qur'ān, Traditions, and Interpretation* (Oxford: Oxford University Press, 1994), 25–38. See further Hadia Mubarak's discussion in chapter 2 of this *Handbook*.
37. I reserve the term "Muslim" when referring to people, and "Islamic" when describing non-human referents. Therefore my usage of the phrase "Muslim feminists" overlaps with other scholars' usage of the phrase "Islamic feminists"; I make no distinction between the two.
38. Rifaat Hassan, "'Made from Adam's Rib': The Woman's Creation Question," *al-Mushir* (1985): 124–155; Stowasser, *Women in the Qur'ān*, 28--37.
39. Kecia Ali, *Sexual Ethics and Islam: Feminist Reflections on Qur'ān, Ḥadīth, and Jurisprudence* (Oxford: Oneworld Publications, 2016), 160.
40. Ibid.,161.
41. Ibid., 162–164.
42. In Qur'ān 24:35, God is described as "the light of the heavens and the earth," and charitable humans are likened to ears of grain that yield a bountiful harvest (Qur'ān 2:261). The

Qur'ān proclaims that it consciously employs such metaphorical expressions and similes for humans (24:35) so that they may reflect on the larger meaning of these locutions (59:21) and be mindful of the truth (39:27). To reduce such figures of speech to mere "objectification" and unnecessarily gendering them clearly misses the point and trivializes the aesthetic and didactic dimensions of the Qur'ānic discourse.

43. Ali, *Sexual Ethics*, 152–157.
44. Ibid., 158.
45. Ibid., 166–167.
46. Aysha A. Hidayatullah, *Feminist Edges of the Qur'an* (Oxford: Oxford University Press, 2014), 153.
47. With the recent resurgence of blatant nativism and virulent racial and religious bigotry in broad swaths of the Global North—one is especially reminded in this context of the Black Lives Matter movement that gained special momentum in 2020 revealing deep fissures in the US along racial and socio-economic lines -- , an appeal to a generalized contemporary American and/or European sense of social justice and equality smacks of a certain naiveté— surely we can do much better!
48. Joan Wallach Scott, *Sex and Secularism* (Princeton: Princeton University Press, 2018).
49. See now the classic work by Lila Abu-Lughod, *Do Muslim Women Need Saving?* (Cambridge, MA: Harvard University Press, 2015).
50. Joseph Massad, *Islam in Liberalism* (Chicago: University of Chicago Press, 2015), 110–212; see also Katherine Bullock's chapter in this *Handbook*.
51. Hidayatullah, *Feminist Edges*, 171.
52. Ibid., 153–154.
53. Ibid., 165.
54. Ibid., 162.
55. For Barlas's response to Ali's and Hidayatullah's critiques, see her article, "Secular and Feminist Critiques of the Qur'ān: Anti-Hermeneutics as Liberation?," *Journal of Feminist Studies in Religion* 32, no. 2 (2016): 121–126; and, more recently, in the new edition of *Believing Women in Islam: Unreading Patriarchal Interpretations of the Qur'ān*, rev. ed. (Austin: University of Texas Press, 2019), 237–264.
56. See further my chapter "Egalitarianism in the Qur'an," in *The Cambridge History of Socialism*, ed. Marcel van Linden (Cambridge: Cambridge University Press, 2023), 56–78.
57. For the importance of *taqwā* in dissolving assumed gendered differences, see wadud, *Qur'an and Woman*, 63–64; Barlas, *Believing Women* (2004 ed.), 142–146.
58. Dorothy E. Smith, "Women, Class and Family," *Socialist Register* 20 (1983): 1–44, at 36.
59. Also emphasized by wadud, *Qur'an and Woman*, 77; and Barlas, *Believing Women*, 184–189.
60. Amina wadud, *Inside the Gender Jihad: Women's Reform in Islam* (Oxford: OneWorld Publications, 2006), 203.
61. Khaled Abou El Fadl, *Speaking in God's Name: Islamic Law, Authority and Women* (Oxford: Oneworld Publications, 2001), 94.
62. For jurists' views on the nature of such violations, see the chapter by Mariam Sheibani in this *Handbook*.
63. This point has been similarly emphasized by wadud, *Qur'an and Woman*, 36–37; and Barlas, *Believing Women* (2004 ed.), 140. More recently, Celene Ibrahim came to a similar conclusion after studying the way key female figures are portrayed in the Qur'ān, leading her to state, "If there is one common element to these disparate figures, it is that the Qur'an depicts them with the agency and responsibility to shape their destinies, for better or

worse"; see her *Women and Gender in the Qur'an* (Oxford: Oxford University Press, 2020), 146. These perspectives are reflected in the conclusions that Hibba Abugideiri arrives at in chapter 1 of this *Handbook*, where she notes, after her careful study of three principal female figures in the Qur'ān, that woman and man in the Qur'ānic text are coeval agents in fulfilling the mission they are called to carry out on earth in positive synergy with one another.

64. Barlas, *Believing Women* (2004 ed.), 16.
65. Abū Dāwud, *Sunan*, trans. Ahmad Hasan (Lahore: Muhammad Ashraf, 1984), 3:1019, #3585, where the translator correctly renders *ḍaraba* as "patting."
66. As Abou El Fadl points out perceptively in chapter 5 of this *Handbook*, "Equality is a theoretically elusive concept, and the relationship of equality to justice is ever more complex."
67. See Sheibani's chapter in this *Handbook*, where she documents how jurists, especially from the Mālikī school of law, invoked the concept of *ḍarar* (harm) "that can be broadly interpreted to include cruelty and physical harm to a wife" in order to effect a judicial divorce between the wife and her abusive husband.
68. Wadud, *Qur'an and Woman*, 80–85.
69. See further Mariam Sheibani, chapter 6, in this *Handbook*.
70. Sheibani points out (ibid.) that if one anticipates unjust treatment of female relatives in the apportioning of inheritance shares, a number of legal stratagems—gifts and the establishment of charitable endowments, for example—could be employed to protect their rights. As she notes, legal obligations were frequently counterbalanced by moral and religious obligations that could be invoked for the benefit of women.
71. The verse states: "If you fear that you will not be able to deal justly with the orphans, marry women of your choice, two, three, or four. But if you fear that you will not be able to deal justly, then only one or those that your right hand possesses; that is more proper so that you do not incline to injustice."
72. E. W. Lane, *Arabic-English Lexicon* (Cambridge: Islamic Texts Society, 1984), 2:2566.
73. May be retrieved from: http://ejtaal.net/aa/#hw4=14,ll=38,ls=1,la=1,sg=20,ha=21,br=26,pr=9,aan=24,mgf=33,vi=51,kz=10,mr=25,mn=1,uqw=106,umr=26,ums=14,umj=34,ulq=247,uqa=17,uqq=2,bdw=h19,amr=h7,asb=h17,auh=h37,dhq=h2,mht=h6,msb=h8,tla=h8,amj=h22,ens=h1,mis=h1.
74. Hans Wehr, *A Dictionary of Modern Written Arabic* (*Arabic-English*), ed. J. M. Cowan (Urbana, IL: Spoken Language Services, Inc., 1979), 926.
75. In chapter 1 of this *Handbook*, Hibba Abugideiri rightly emphasizes this understanding of *qunūt* as referring to exclusive and sincere devotion to God, praised in the Qur'ān as an attribute of the truly righteous, regardless of gender.
76. See my detailed discussion of the term *ulū 'l-amr* and its various interpretations in Asma Afsaruddin, "Obedience to Political Authority: An Evolutionary Concept," in *Islamic Democratic Discourse: Theory, Debates, and Directions*, ed. Muqtedar Khan (Lanham, MD: Lexington Books, 2006), 37–60. In the early period, *ulū 'l-amr* referred in general to "people of knowledge and discernment" (*ahl al-'ilm wa al-fiqh*) as well as to "military commanders." This would explain why so many men were willing to follow 'Ā'isha, the Prophet's widow, into the battlefield and obey her commands; gender, clearly, had very little to do with her status as one of the *ulū 'l-amr*.
77. See Asma Afsaruddin, "Authority, Religious," *Encyclopaedia of Islam*, 3rd ed. (Leiden: E.J. Brill, 2010–2011), 57–62.
78. See al-Ṭabarī, *Tafsīr*, 4:152.

79. This exaltation of Āsiya's pious act of defiance toward her husband carries over into the *ḥadīth* literature, as discussed by Feryal Salem in chapter 3 of this *Handbook*.
80. Ibrahim makes a similar observation in her *Women and Gender in the Qur'an*, 109, where she states that Qur'ān 66:11 "links the ill treatment of one woman to the corruption of society more generally and is yet another occasion in which a woman experiencing a trial cries out to God for solace."
81. Mentioned in Asma Sayeed, "Women and Ḥadīth Transmission: Two Case Studies from Mamluk Damascus," *Studia Islamica* 95 (2002): 71–94; at 91.
82. See further chapter 5 by Khaled Abou El Fadl in this *Handbook*.
83. Here I have come to the conclusion that "economic providers" is the appropriate translation of *qawwāmūn* in the specific context of this verse.
84. Qur'ān 4:32 states, "Do not hanker after the bounties that God grants some of you over others; for men there is a portion from what they earn and for women there is a portion from what they earn; ask God for His bounties; indeed God is aware of all matters."
85. See also Qur'ān 3:84, which states, "Say, "We believe in God and in what is revealed to us and what was revealed to Abraham, Ishmael, Isaac, Jacob, and the tribes, and in what was given to Moses and Jesus and to the prophets from their Lord. *We make no distinction between any of them* (emphasis mine), and we submit to Him;" similarly in Qur'ān 2:136.
86. This is also briefly noted by wadud, *Qur'an and Woman*, 69.
87. Ibn Kathīr, *Tafsīr al-Qur'ān al-'aẓīm* (Beirut: Dār al-jīl, 1990), 1:287.
88. Ibid., 1:287–288.
89. Ibid., 1:465.
90. Ibid., 1:466. For a trenchant critique of the reliability of this *ḥadīth*, see Khaled M. Abou El Fadl, *And God Knows the Soldiers: The Authoritative and Authoritarian in Islamic Discourses* (Lanham, MD: University Press of America, 2001), 62–82.
91. See Afsaruddin, *Contemporary Issues in Islam*, 92–101.
92. The concept of *sābiqa* (precedence in faith and good deeds) was a highly important factor in establishing the moral excellence of both the female and male Companions; see my study "Early Women Exemplars and the Construction of Gendered Space: (Re-)Defining Feminine Moral Excellence," in *Harem Histories: Envisioning Places and Living Spaces*, ed. Marilyn Booth (Durham, NC: Duke University Press, 2010), 23–48; and chapter 9 by Yasmin Amin in this *Handbook*. For a general study of *sābiqa*, see my earlier monograph *Excellence and Precedence: Medieval Islamic Discourse on Legitimate Leadership* (Leiden: E.J. Brill, 2002).
93. Others have interpreted this "edge" to consist of men's ability to divorce with greater ease, since the verse deals with divorce; see wadud, *Qur'an and Woman*, 68.
94. See further Azizah al-Hibri, "A Study of Islamic Herstory?," in "Women and Islam," special issue, *Women's Studies International Forum* 5 (1982): 207–19.
95. Fazlur Rahman, *Major Themes of the Qur'ān* (Minneapolis: Bibliotheca Islamica, 1980), 49.
96. Cited in Abū Hāmid al-Ghazālī, *Iḥyā' 'ulūm al-dīn* (Beirut: Dār al-Ma'rifa, 1982), 2:50; see also Hadia Mubarak's reference to this *ḥadīth* and its status in chapter 2 of this *Handbook*, note 57.
97. The Umm Zar' *ḥadīth* discussed by Feryal Salem in chapter 3 describes the qualities of the ideal husband, which include generosity and emotional tenderness toward his wife.
98. As must be assumed—otherwise, the default assumption is that all or most wives are ipso facto incapable of honoring their marriage commitments and living congenially with

their husbands, which is certainly not the common sense meaning of the verse nor can it be considered an accurate reflection of reality.

99. Ibn Ḥajar, *al-Iṣāba fī tamyīz al-ṣaḥāba* (Beirut: Dār a-jīl, n.d.), 8:262. A variant report credits this statement to Umm Salama; see Ibn Saʿd, *al-Ṭabaqāt al-kubrā*, ed. Muḥammad ʿAbd al-Qādir ʿAṭā' (Beirut: Dār Ṣādir, 1997), 8:161.
100. Al-Hibri, "A Study of Islamic Herstory," 207–219.
101. Azadeh Aghighi recently completed a PhD dissertation in Islamic Studies at Indiana University, Bloomington, in which she undertakes a detailed study of the exegeses of Qur'ān 9:71 by both Sunnī and Shīʿī commentators in premodern and modern Arabic and Persian sources; see her "The Hermeneutics of Egalitarianism: A Comparative Study of Traditionalist Male Exegeses and Modernist Muslim Feminists' Interpretations of Qur'ān 9:71" (PhD diss.: Indiana University, 2023). My brief survey below is restricted to Sunnī Arabic sources.
102. Muqātil, *Tafsīr*, 2:181.
103. Al-Ṭabarī, *Tafsīr*, 6:415.
104. Al-Wāḥidī, *WāsiṬ*, 2:509.
105. Al-Qurṭubī, *al-Jāmiʿ li-aḥkām al-Qur'ān*, ed. ʿAbd al-Razzāq al-Mahdī (Beirut: Dār al-kitāb al-ʿarabī, 2001), 8:186.
106. Ibn Kathīr, *Tafsīr*, 2:353.
107. *Wilāya* is the verbal noun related to *awliyā'* ("partners/allies") derived from a common verbal root.
108. Riḍā, *Tafsīr*, 10:471.
109. Ibid.
110. See Yasmin Amin's chapter in this *Handbook*.
111. Asma Afsaruddin, "Jihād, Gender, and Religious Minorities in the *Siyar* Literature: The Diachronic View," *Studia Islamica* 114 (2019): 1–26.
112. Asma Lamrabet, "An Egalitarian Reading of the Concepts of *Khilafah*, *Wilayah* and *Qiwama*," in *Men in Charge? Rethinking Authority in Muslim Legal Tradition*, ed. Ziba Mir-Hosseini, Mulki al-Sharmani, and Jana Rumminger (Oxford: Oneworld Publications, 2015), 86. Other chapters in this edited volume also deserve attention for challenging androcentric interpretations of *wilāya* and *qiwāma* through time.
113. Ibn Kathīr, *Tafsīr*, 1:317.
114. Mohammad Fadel, "Two Women, One Man: Knowledge, Power and Gender in Medieval Sunni Legal Thought," *International Journal of Middle East Studies* 29 (1997): 185–204; see also Abdulaziz Sachedina, "Woman Half-the Man? Crisis of Male Epistemology in Islamic Jurisprudence," in *Intellectual Traditions in Islam*, ed. Farhad Daftary (New York: I.B. Tauris, 2000), 160–178.
115. See Asma Sayeed, "Gender and Legal Authority: An Examination of Early Juristic Opposition to Women's Ḥadīth Transmission," *Islamic Law and Society* 16 (2009): 115–150, in which she shows that a number of medieval jurists, like Abū Ḥanīfa (d. 150/767) and his student al-Shaybānī (d. 189/804), were opposed to *ḥadīth* transmission by women scholars, which may be correlated to the decline in the number of women engaging in this activity in the third/ninth century, compared to the first two centuries of Islam, when women transmitters were more plentiful.
116. The verse states, "But if you want to replace one wife with another and you have given one of them an exorbitant amount (*qinṭār*) [as dower], do not take back from it anything.

Would you take from it when that would constitute an act of disgrace and flagrant wrong-doing?"

117. Al-Shawkānī, *Fatḥ al-qadīr: al-jāmiʿ bayn fannay al-riwāya wa-l-dirāya min ʿilm al-tafsīr* (Cairo: Sharikat maktaba wa maktabat muṣṭafā al-bābī al-ḥalabī wa awlāduh, 1963), 1:443. This account is attributed to Jalāl al-Dīn al-Suyūṭī (d. 911/1505), and its *isnād* is deemed "good" (*jayyid*); other variants exist.

Bibliography

Abou-Bakr, Omaima, ed. *Feminist and Islamic Perspectives: New Horizons of Knowledge and Reform*. Translated by Yasmin Motawy. Cairo: The Women and Memory Forum, 2013.

Abou El Fadl, Khaled. *Speaking in God's Name: Islamic Law, Authority and Women*. Oxford: Oneworld Publications, 2001.

Abou El Fadl, Khaled M. *And God Knows the Soldiers: The Authoritative and Authoritarian in Islamic Discourses*. Lanham, MD: University Press of America, 2001.

Abū Dāwūd. *Sunan*. Translated by Ahmad Hasan. Lahore: Muhammad Ashraf, 1984.

Abu-Lughod, Lila. *Do Muslim Women Need Saving?* Cambridge, MA: Harvard University Press, 2015.

Afsaruddin, Asma. "Authority, Religious." In *Encyclopaedia of Islam*, 3rd ed., edited by Gudrun Krämer et al., 57–62. Leiden: E.J. Brill, 2010–2011.

Afsaruddin, Asma. "Early Women Exemplars and the Construction of Gendered Space: (Re-) Defining Feminine Moral Excellence." In *Harem Histories: Envisioning Places and Living Spaces*, edited by Marilyn Booth, 23–48. Durham, NC: Duke University Press, 2010.

Afsaruddin, Asma. "Egalitarianism in the Qur'an." In *The Cambridge History of Socialism*, edited by Marcel van Linden, 56–78. Cambridge, UK: Cambridge University Press, 2022.

Afsaruddin, Asma. *Excellence and Precedence: Medieval Islamic Discourse on Legitimate Leadership*. Leiden: E.J. Brill, 2002.

Afsaruddin, Asma. "Jihād, Gender, and Religious Minorities in the *Siyar* Literature: The Diachronic View." *Studia Islamica* 114 (2019): 1–26.

Afsaruddin, Asma. "Obedience to Political Authority: An Evolutionary Concept." In *Islamic Democratic Discourse: Theory, Debates, and Directions*, edited by Muqtedar Khan, 37–60. Lanham, MD: Lexington Books, 2006.

Afsaruddin, Asma. "Reading the Qur'an through a Gendered, Egalitarian Lens: Revisiting the Concept of *Wilāya* in Q. 9:71." In *Islamic Interpretive Tradition and Gender Justice*, edited by Nevin Reda and Yasmin Amin, 100–124. Montreal: McGill-Queens University Press, 2020.

Afsaruddin, Asma. *Contemporary Issues in Islam*. Edinburgh: Edinburgh University Press, 2015.

Ali, Kecia. *Sexual Ethics and Islam: Feminist Reflections on Qur'ān, Ḥadīth, and Jurisprudence*. Oxford: Oneworld Publications, 2016.

Badran, Margot. *Feminism in Islam: Secular and Religious Convergences*. Oxford: Oneworld Publications, 2009.

Badran, Margot, and miriam cooke. *Opening the Gates: An Anthology of Arab Feminist Writing*. 2nd ed. Bloomington: Indiana University Press, 2004.

Barlas, Asma. *"Believing Women" in Islam: Unreading Patriarchal Interpretations of the* Qur'ān. Austin, TX: University of Texas Press, 2004.

Barlas, Asma. *Believing Women in Islam: Unreading Patriarchal Interpretations of the Qur'ān*. Rev. ed. Austin: University of Texas Press, 2019.
Barlas, Asma. "Engaging Islamic Feminism: Provincialising Feminism as a Master Narrative." In *Islamic Feminism: Current Perspectives*. Edited by Anitta Kynsilehto, 15–24. Tampere, Finland: Tampere Peace Research Institute, 2008.
Barlas, Asma. "Secular and Feminist Critiques of the Qur'ān: Anti-Hermeneutics as Liberation?" *Journal of Feminist Studies in Religion* 32, no. 2 (2016): 121–126.
Bayḍāwī, 'Abd Allāh ibn 'Umar al-. *Tafsīr al-Bayḍāwī*. Beirut: Dār al-kutub al-'ilmiyya, 1988.
Brown, Jonathan. *Misquoting Muhammad: The Challenges and Choices of Interpreting the Prophet's Legacy*. London: Oneworld Publications, 2014.
Chaudhry, Ayesha S. *Domestic Violence and the Islamic Tradition*. Oxford: Oxford University Press, 2014.
Fadel, Mohammad. "Is Historicism a Viable Strategy for Islamic Law Reform? The Case of 'Never Shall a Folk Prosper Who Have Appointed a Woman to Rule Them.'" *Islamic Law and Society* 18 (2011): 131–176.
Fadel, Mohammad. "Two Women, One Man: Knowledge, Power and Gender in Medieval Sunni Legal Thought." *International Journal of Middle East Studies* 29 (1997): 185–204.
Ghazālī, Abū Hāmid al-. *Iḥyā' 'ulūm al-dīn*. Beirut: Dār al-Ma'rifa, 1982.
Hassan, Rifaat. "'Made from Adam's Rib': The Woman's Creation Question." *Al-Mushir* 27 (1985): 124–155.
Hibri, Azizah al-. "A Study of Islamic Herstory?" In "Women and Islam," special issue, *Women's Studies International Forum* 5, no. 2 (1982): 207–219.
Hidayatullah, Aysha A. *Feminist Edges of the Qur'an*. Oxford: Oxford University Press, 2014.
Ibn Ḥajar al-'Asqalānī. *Al-Iṣāba fī tamyīz al-ṣaḥāba*. Beirut: Dār a-jīl, n.d.
Ibn Kathīr, Ismā'īl ibn 'Umar. *Tafsīr al-Qur'ān al-'aẓīm*. Beirut: Dār al-jīl, 1990.
Ibn Sa'd, Muḥammad. *Al-Ṭabaqāt al-kubrā*. Edited by Muḥammad 'Abd al-Qādir 'Aṭā'. Beirut: Dār ṣādir, 1997.
Ibrahim, Celene. *Women and Gender in the Qur'an*. Oxford: Oxford University Press, 2020.
Lamrabet, Asma. "An Egalitarian Reading of the Concepts of *Khilafah*, *Wilayah* and *Qiwama*." In *Men in Charge? Rethinking Authority in Muslim Legal Tradition*, edited by Ziba Mir-Hosseini, Mulki al-Sharmani, and Jana Rumminger, 65–87. Oxford: Oneworld Publications, 2015.
Lane, E. W. *Arabic-English Lexicon*. Cambridge: Islamic Texts Society, 1984.
Marin, Manuela. "Disciplining Wives: A Historical Reading of Qur'ān 4:34." *Studia Islamica* 97 (2003): 5–40.
Massad, Joseph. *Islam in Liberalism*. Chicago: University of Chicago Press, 2015.
Mir, Mustansir. "The Surah as a Unity: A 20th Century Development in Qur'anic Exegesis." In *Approaches to the Qur'an*, edited by G. Hawting and A. A. Shareef, 211–224. London: Routledge, 1993.
Mir-Hosseini, Ziba. "Women and Politics in Post-Khomeini Iran: Divorce, Veiling, and Emerging Feminist Voices." In *Women and Politics in the Third World*, edited by Haleh Afshar, 144–173. London and New York: Routledge, 1996.
Morrow, John Andrew. *The Most Controversial Qur'anic Verse: Why 4:34 Does Not Promote Violence against Women*. Lanham, MD: Rowman and Littlefield, 2020.
Mubarak, Hadia. *Rebellious Wives, Neglectful Husbands: Controversies in Modern Qur'anic Commentaries*. Oxford: Oxford University Press, 2022.

Muqātil ibn Sulaymān. *Tafsīr Muqātil ibn Sulaymān*. Cairo: Mu'assasat al-Ḥalabī wa-Shurakā'uh, 1969.
Qurṭubī, Muḥammad al-. *Al-Jāmiʿ li-aḥkām al-Qur'ān*. Edited by ʿAbd al-Razzāq al-Mahdī. Beirut: Dār al-kitāb al-ʿarabī, 2001.
Quṭb, Sayyid. *Fī ẓilal al-Qur'ān*. Cairo: Dār al-Shurūq, 2001.
Rahman, Fazlur. *Islamic Methodology in History*. Islamabad: Central Institute of Islamic Research, 1984.
Rahman, Fazlur. *Major Themes of the Qur'ān*. Minneapolis: Bibliotheca Islamica, 1980.
Rāzī, Fakhr al-Dīn al-. *Al-Tafsīr al-kabīr*. Beirut: Dār iḥyā' al-turāth al-ʿarabī, 1999.
Reda, Nevin. "Holistic Approaches to the Qur'an: A Historical Background." *Religion Compass* 4, no. 8 (2010): 495–506.
Riḍā, Rashīd. *Tafsīr al-Manār*. Beirut: Dār al-kutub al-ʿilmiyya, 1999.
Sachedina, Abdulaziz. "Woman Half-the Man? Crisis of Male Epistemology in Islamic Jurisprudence." In *Intellectual Traditions in Islam*, edited by Farhad Daftary, 160–178. New York: I.B. Tauris, 2000.
Stowasser, Barbara. *Women in the Qur'ān, Traditions, and Interpretation*. Oxford: Oxford University Press, 1994.
Sayeed, Asma. "Gender and Legal Authority: An Examination of Early Juristic Opposition to Women's Ḥadīth Transmission." *Islamic Law and Society* 16 (2009): 115–150.
Sayeed, Asma. "Women and Ḥadīth Transmission Two Case Studies from Mamluk Damascus." *Studia Islamica* 95 (2002): 71–94.
Scott, Joan Wallach. *Sex and Secularism*. Princeton: Princeton University Press, 2018.
Shawkānī, Muḥammad al-. *Fatḥ al-qadīr: al-jāmiʿ bayn fannay al-riwāya wa-l-dirāya min ʿilm al-tafsīr*. Cairo: Sharikat maktaba wa maktabat muṣṭafā al-bābī al-ḥalabī wa awlāduh, 1963.
Smith, Dorothy E. "Women, Class and Family." *The Socialist Register* 20 (1983): 1–44.
Ṭabarī, Muḥammad ibn Jarir al-. *Tafsīr*. Beirut: Dār al-kutub al-ʿilmiyya, 1997.
Wadud, amina. *Inside the Gender Jihad: Women's Reform in Islam*. Oxford: OneWorld Publications, 2006.
Wadud, amina. *Qur'ān and Woman: Rereading the Sacred Text from a Woman's Perspective* New York: Oxford University Press, 1999.
Wāḥidī, ʿAlī ibn Aḥmad al-. *al-Wāsiṭ fī tafsīr al-Qur'ān*. Edited by ʿĀdil Aḥmad ʿAbd al-Mawjūd. Beirut: Dār al-kutub al-ʿilmiyya, 1994.
Wehr, Hans. *A Dictionary of Modern Written Arabic (Arabic-English)*. Translated and edited by J. M. Cowan. Urbana, IL: Spoken Language Services, 1979.
Wensinck, A. J. *Concordance et indices de la tradition Musulmane*. Leiden: E.J. Brill, 1967.

CHAPTER 5

MODERN REREADINGS OF THE *ḤADĪTH* THROUGH A GENDERED LENS

KHALED ABOU EL FADL*

THIS chapter focuses on modern rereadings of the *ḥadīth* literature. The *ḥadīth* tradition and the *sunna* of the Prophet have played an inestimable role in shaping the theology and law of Islam. However, the *ḥadīth* and *sunna* are the repository of conflicting momentums that could be read to support or undermine patriarchy. While the *ḥadīth* and *sunna* preserved the collective memory of liberating moments for Muslim women, much of this tradition also upholds and perpetuates the institutions of patriarchy and male dominance. This chapter starts out by exploring what I describe as "tension reports" in the Islamic narrative tradition. Tension reports are alleged historical memories of the exercise of women's agency in a fashion that challenged or defied the institutions of patriarchy at the time of the Prophet or his Companions. As explained below, tension reports are parts of the tradition that offer potentially liberating moments from the institutions of patriarchy. Next, I briefly discuss what I describe as the misogynistic traditions in the *ḥadīth* literature and the three main interpretive or thematic stratagems employed by Muslim women scholars in wrestling with the Prophetic tradition and its meaning in the modern world. To limit the scope of this article, I focused mostly on the scholarship of Muslim women writing in the English language. The last section of this article offers concluding remarks on the main interpretive or thematic stratagems discussed below. While some scholars have called for the wholesale rejection of the *ḥadīth* and *sunna* as hopelessly patriarchal and misogynistic, I argue for a far more circumspect approach. In my view, the *ḥadīth* and *sunna* are critical components of the Islamic tradition, and this tradition must continue to serve as the source for dynamic and inventive solutions, even to deeply entrenched challenges such as patriarchy. As argued below, the tradition must continue to be the basis for revelation-based interpretive solutions even to the most intractable temporal problems.

Tension Reports and Moments of Possible Liberation

The earliest traditions of Islam provide many examples of socially active and inspiring women.[1] Among them is the iconic figure of Sukayna bint al-Ḥusayn b. ʿAlī (d. 117/735) the great-granddaughter of the Prophet Muḥammad and the granddaughter of the Prophet's daughter Fāṭima and the Prophet's cousin ʿAlī. In Islamic historical sources, Sukayna was celebrated for her purported beauty, wit, and intelligence, and for her patronage of poets. Sukayna's exact date of birth is not known, but she must have been very young when she witnessed the massacre of her family in Karbala, an event that marked her for life. Sukayna was very proud of her lineage and was persistently indignant toward the ruling Umayyad dynasty that was responsible for killing her father and other members of her family. But what makes Sukayna particularly noteworthy was her social visibility and mobility, and also the jealousy with which she guarded her autonomy. As a young woman in the Hijaz, Sukayna was a fashion-setter who became famous for an attractive hairdo, labeled *al-ṭurra al-sukayniyya*. The historical sources do not agree on how many times Sukayna married, but reportedly it was anywhere from two to six times. Sukayna rejected many marriage proposals from men she considered inferior, and even in her marriages, she is consistently portrayed as anything but subservient or timidly obedient to her husbands.[2]

After her first husband died, Sukayna refused to marry for a long time. Sukayna's servant urged her to consider the proposal of ʿAbd Allāh (the grandson of ʿUthmān), and so Sukayna finally instructed her servant to go to ʿAbd Allāh and inform him that she was interested in his proposal. Abū Zahra, the clan of ʿAbd Allāh, was excited about the possible union with the tribe of Banū Hāshim (Sukayna's tribe) and so they went to make the formal proposal. But as the report goes, Sukayna kept making demands of Abū Zahra until, at some point, ʿAbd Allāh and his clan realized that Sukayna was not serious and that she had no intention of marrying ʿAbd Allāh. As the narrative goes, this eventually led to a fight and violence between the clans of Abū Zahra and Banū Hāshim. After the fight broke out, Sukayna announced that she was no longer interested in marrying ʿAbd Allāh. Other than a desire to show off her desirability and social influence, it is suspected that Sukayna intended to insult the clan of Abū Zahra. In about a year, Zayd ibn ʿUmar ibn ʿUthmān is said to have proposed marriage to Sukayna; the latter agreed to marry him as long as he would agree to three conditions: (1) he would not touch any other woman; (2) he would not prevent her from spending any of his money; (3) he would not restrict her movement by prohibiting her from going wherever she pleased. If he violated any of these conditions, the marriage would be automatically dissolved. Commentators on this narrative typically note that these stipulations were unusual because breaching them would have rendered the marriage null and void. The more common practice was to make the marriage voidable—in other words, the violation of the conditions would create an option that the wife could exercise if she chose to do so. Commentators note that Sukayna's innovation was the fact that if Zayd violated the conditions, then there would be no options and no choice, the marriage would be dissolved. According to all versions of this event, Zayd accepted Sukayna's conditions and married her. On one occasion, Zayd announced that his family was going for Hajj and he asked Sukayna for permission to leave for Mecca so as to meet with his family. She responded that she would not agree to his departure unless Ashar, a male servant, went along with him. Ostensibly, Ashar was supposed to act as Sukayna's spy, but on the trip to Mecca, Zayd had sexual intercourse with a slave girl and bribed Ashar not to inform his wife. Upon their return, Sukayna intensely interrogated both Ashar and Zayd. Finally, Zayd gave in and confessed to his affair with a slave girl and promptly begged for her forgiveness. To prove his goodwill, he offered to free all of his slave girls. Sukayna refused her husband's apology and offer, and proclaimed the dissolution of her marriage. The dispute continued until 'Umar ibn ʿAbd al-'Azīz (the Umayyad caliph) came to power, and Zayd went to court to attempt to force a settlement. Reluctantly, Sukayna appeared in court but she informed the judge that she would not accept his jurisdiction because this matter had been resolved and the marriage had already been dissolved. The judge responded, "God likes moderation in everything." Sukayna responded, "What wrong have I done? Your problem is like seeing a splinter in someone's eye, my problem is that I see a whole log in someone's eye," meaning that the judge thinks that the moral failure of her husband can be negotiated because it is like a splinter, but she sees it as a devastating log in his eye, i.e., a resounding failure. The judge and Sukayna argued back and forth, and Sukayna continued to refuse Zayd's plea for forgiveness. Ultimately, Sukayna stormed out of the courtroom and although the judge issued an order attempting to compel her cooperation, she refused the judge's order and insisted that this matter had been settled.[3]

For many Muslim women, figures like Sukayna provide the possibility of, as Fatima Mernissi described it, "liberating memories."[4] Sukayna could be part of the time-mirror wherein Muslim women can foresee themselves crafting a different future. Sukayna's historical image, as contested as many of the details about her life may be, is not that of a docile, subservient, or submissive woman. She, like the figures of the more famous ʿĀʾisha or Umm Salama, is a woman with an undeniable degree of moral agency and autonomy.[5] This does not mean that early Muslim women liberated themselves from the burdens of patriarchy or that the historical moment in which these women lived was less androcentric than any other moment in the past. I believe that patriarchy, androcentricity, and male dominance, simply put, was a fact in the past and remains a fact in the present. Gender egalitarianism, as an ideology and as an epistemological consciousness, is a byproduct of social and economic forces born in modernity. However, one cannot deny that throughout history, Muslim women negotiated their moral agency in complex and creative ways that often challenged or at least restrained the institutions of patriarchy.

Consider the historical precedent of another prominent Muslim woman from the late first/seventh century, 'Ā'isha bint Ṭalḥa (d.101/719), who was a contemporary of Sukayna, and granddaughter of Abū Bakr (the first caliph) and daughter of the famous

Companions Umm Kulthūm bint Abī Bakr and Ṭalḥa ibn ʿUbayd Allāh (d. 36/656).[6] ʿĀʾisha bint Ṭalḥa's aunt was no other than the illustrious ʿĀʾisha, the wife of the Prophet (d. 58/678).[7] ʿĀʾisha bint Ṭalḥa was reportedly known for her piety and for teaching the *ḥadīth* of the Prophet. But she was also famous for being a notoriously defiant and argumentative wife. ʿĀʾisha bint Ṭalḥa married three times, and her disputes, especially with her first and second husbands, became the stuff of legends. After a fight with her first husband, ʿAbd Allāh bin ʿAbd al-Rahmān, her maternal cousin and the grandchild of Abū Bakr, she left her home and resided with her aunt ʿĀʾisha and refused to speak to or reconcile with her husband until he passed away.

ʿĀʾisha bint Ṭalḥa was very proud of her beauty. When her second husband Muṣʿab asked her to cover her face in public, she refused, stating:

> God the Almighty has gifted me with the highly praised attribute of beauty, and I want people to see my beauty, so that people will know that by making me beautiful and allowing me to be seen that God has done them a favor. Therefore, I am not going to cover. By God, there is no moral defect in this.

She vowed never to wear the ḥijāb—a vow she apparently kept.[8] What emerges from ʿĀʾisha bint Ṭalḥa's legacy is the image of a woman who was not traditionally obedient and subservient toward men. Like her famous aunt, ʿĀʾisha bint Ṭalḥa exercised her moral agency in ways that often clashed and negotiated with the institutions of societal patriarchy. To pretend that ʿĀʾisha bint Ṭalḥa was a paragon of women's liberation is anachronistic, but to ignore the nuanced complexity of her historical legacy would be no less a distortion of historical memory. Women such as Sukayna and the two ʿĀʾishas were not outliers. Their historical legacies point to the fact that the social realities of Muslim women were far more complex and nuanced than the prescriptive books of *ḥadīth* and law would indicate.[9]

I think it is undeniable that the Prophet's legacy, especially in Medina, empowered and animated the women of his time, and that this legacy or historical memory resounded with a continuing momentum throughout Islamic history.[10] As Fatima Mernissi and others have shown, the energetic social involvement of Muslim women at the time of the Prophet led to considerable tension with the embedded institutions of patriarchy in Medina.[11] This tension was memorialized in ʿUmar ibn al-Khaṭṭāb's famous declaration: "We men of Quraysh used to dominate our women. When we arrived in Medina, we saw that the Anṣār let themselves be dominated by theirs, but then our women began to copy their habits."[12] Reportedly, ʿUmar's complaint came after his wife was defiant and argued with him. When ʿUmar attempted to discipline his wife, she protested that the Prophet's own wives defy and argue with him and the Prophet did not object. In fact, one of the Prophet's wives, Hafṣa, was ʿUmar's own daughter. When ʿUmar attempted to reproach his daughter Hafṣa and the Prophet's other wives for arguing with the Prophet, he was rebuked by the strong-willed Umm Salama. Moreover, when the Prophet had a disagreement with Hafṣa, they asked her father to arbitrate between them. In ʿUmar's presence, the Prophet invited Hafṣa to make her case. Hafṣa declined to be the first to speak commenting: "No Prophet, you speak first but only speak the truth!" 'Umar was shocked by what he saw as his daughter's insolence, for how could she imply that the Prophet would say anything but the truth? Enraged, 'Umar raised his hand to discipline his daughter, but the Prophet intervened to stop him.[13]

Tension Reports in the *Ḥadīth* Literature

Although this is not the place to fully explore the issue, it is important to note that the Islamic tradition is replete with what I described as "tension reports." These are reports that evidence an exercise of moral agency and activism by women that most likely resulted in tension or that challenged the institutions of patriarchy at some level.[14] For example, it is reported that women complained to the Prophet that men tended to monopolize his time, and thus, requested that the Prophet set out specific days and times exclusively for them.[15] Although the historical record does not show any evidence that men objected to the setting aside of a time exclusively for women, the very articulation of the request and the Prophet's accommodation of it is evidence of the exercise of moral agency. Whether they intended to do so or not, and whether consciously or subconsciously, by exercising their moral agency, women challenged and negotiated the settled institutions of societal patriarchy. Even fairly innocuous events would have the same effect and play the same function. Take, for example, the reports that assert that women would walk up to the Prophet, take him by the hand, and escort him to settle disputes with their spouses or to resolve one problem or another.[16] The historical record does not mention that this conduct resulted in overt social tensions in Medina. However, it is reasonable to imagine that every time a woman took the initiative to solicit the Prophet's intervention in a marital dispute, such initiatives would establish a precedent in the collective social imagination. Every exercise of free moral agency threatens the institutions of power and creates the potential for change. Whether that potential eventually results in change or is ultimately aborted is altogether a different matter.

Perhaps the most famous of the tension reports have to do with ḥadīth or narrations that assert that God directly responded to the concerns or complaints of women at the time of the Prophet. Among the most influential and impactful were the various narrations explaining the circumstances that led to the revelation of Qur'ān 33:35.[17] Reportedly, Umm Salama complained to the Prophet, "Why is it that the Qur'ān only mentions men and not women?" God responded to Umm Salama's concerns by revealing the above verse. Other *ḥadīth* narrations report that this same verse was revealed because Asmā' bint 'Umays (who was married to Ja'far ibn Abī Ṭālib) told the Prophet, "O Messenger of God, women are disappointed and despondent!" The Prophet inquired why this was the case, and Asmā' replied, "Women are not mentioned in the Qur'ān in goodness as are the men." In response, Qur'ān 33:35 was revealed. Yet other narrations report that Qur'ān 33:35 was revealed because Umm 'Umara al-Ansariyya came to the Prophet and proclaimed, "I see that everything [in the Qur'ān] is about men, and I do not find women mentioned with regard to anything!"[18] Importantly, this verse is not the only part of the Qur'ān that explicitly addresses women's piety, but it is certainly the most famous.[19] As discussed below, many modern interpreters believe that Qur'ān 33:35 was a direct response to Umm Salama's strong personality and her outspoken exercise of moral and social agency. However, considering the many divergent narrations about the circumstances surrounding the revelation of this verse, it is likely that a number of women sought assurances from the Prophet that God was cognizant of their contributions and wanted the divine text to explicitly acknowledge their moral worth and the value of their piety.

Another set of tension reports that have become no less important among modern interpreters revolve around the circumstances that led to the revelation of the chapter titled *al-Mujādila* ("the arguing or disputing woman").[20] Qur'ān 58:1–2 states:

> God indeed has heard the words of the woman who argued with you about her husband, and who complained to God, for God hears your conversations, and truly, God is All-Hearing and All-Seeing. Those among you who commit *ẓihār* against their wives, those are not their mothers for none are their mothers save those who gave birth to them. Verily, what they say is indecent and calumny, and God is pardoning and most forgiving.

Ẓihār was a pre-Islamic practice according to which a man would swear at his wife, "you are to me as my mother's back," a pronouncement that would count as an irrevocable divorce. There are divergent reports as to the name of the disputant woman, but most sources state that it was Khawla bint Tha'laba. Reportedly, Khawla complained to the Prophet that her husband swore *ẓihār* at her, and the Prophet responded, "You are now forbidden to him," which means that they are irrevocably divorced. Khawla continued to argue with the Prophet that her husband's *ẓihār* was not intended as a divorce, and that her marriage should not be dissolved. At some point, in desperation, Khawla redirected her appeals from the Prophet to God, saying, "O God, I complain to You!" Other reports assert that having despaired of getting a different answer from the Prophet, Khawla stood in the direction of Ka'ba, and uttered a long prayer appealing to God for a solution. Ultimately, the Qur'ānic revelation supported Khawla's position and proclaimed that *ẓihār* is not a divorce. The Qur'ān stated that *ẓihār* is a serious sin and demanded expatiation. Those who commit *ẓihār* must free a slave or fast two months or feed sixty poor people. Khawla, however, complained that her husband did not own slaves, was too old and frail to fast two months, and was too poor to feed sixty poor people. At this point, the Prophet raised the donations necessary for expatiation and gave it to Khawla to feed the poor on her husband's behalf.[21]

One could reasonably suspect that Qur'ānic interventions on behalf of women, such as Khawla, must have created tensions with the traditional institutions of patriarchy in early Islam. In fact, Khawla herself was sufficiently empowered by the Qur'ānic intervention on her behalf to the point that she continued to play an active social and political role in the life of the nascent Muslim community. Reportedly, later on in her life, after the Prophet died, Khawla accosted the caliph ʿUmar Ibn al- al-Khaṭāb when he passed by her while riding his donkey and firmly lectured him on his duties as the people's leader. When some of ʿUmar's companions inquired why he stood by as this old woman sternly lectured him, ʿUmar retorted that he would humbly listen to this woman for as long as she desired because she is no other than Khawla, the woman who was the subject of Qur'ānic revelation.[22] Perhaps the strongest statement of the role of Qur'ānic interventions in empowering women and in becoming the locus for tension reports is that which has been narrated by ʿUmar's son, ʿAbdullah Ibn Umar (d. 73/692). He reportedly said, "When the Prophet was alive, we were cautious when speaking and dealing with our women in fear that a revelation would come [from God] concerning our behavior. But when the Prophet died, we were able to speak and deal with them [more freely]."[23]

I will give one more example of the tension reports found in the tradition before moving on. In the incident known as *ḥadīth al-ʿifk*, ʿĀ'isha was slandered and falsely accused of inappropriate conduct with a man named Ṣafwān. The Prophet did not believe the accusations against ʿĀ'isha, but she was hurt by what she perceived to be a lack of full support by the Prophet. The Qur'ān eventually vindicated ʿĀ'isha against her accusers, and those who slandered her were punished. After the Qur'ānic revelation defended ʿĀ'isha and proclaimed her innocence, ʿĀ'isha's parents, her father Abū Bakr and mother Umm Rumān, exhorted her to thank the Prophet. However, ʿĀ'isha insisted that gratitude was owed to God alone because only God (and not the Prophet) had properly vindicated her.[24] Throughout Islamic history, the *ḥadīth al-ʿifk* incident and ʿĀ'isha's responses to the Prophet have been the subject of numerous interpretations. Regardless of the interpretation one accepts, it is indisputable that in insisting that it is God, and God alone, who has vindicated her, and that gratitude is owed only to God, ʿĀ'isha was exercising her moral agency and setting a powerful precedent that resonated throughout Islamic history. Her exercise of moral agency negotiated the institutionalized patriarchy in her society in ways that were not intended or even foreseeable by ʿĀ'isha or by those who witnessed and first narrated these events. Most significantly, as discussed below, these tension reports were co-opted and adapted by contemporary Muslims in developing gendered reinterpretations of the tradition designed to empower women against the entrenched institutions of patriarchy and male dominance.

The Misogynistic Traditions

In proportion to, and to the extent that the Islamic tradition generated "liberating memories" and tension reports that had the potential of challenging patriarchy, the same tradition also generated deeply chauvinistic reports. Considering that institutions of patriarchy are deeply embedded in all of human history, the existence of misogynistic reports or narrations attributed to the Prophet or his companions is hardly surprising. But as I have argued elsewhere,[25] and as Mernissi has shown,[26] some of the most misogynistic reports were born in direct response to early social debates about the role and place of women, either at the time of the Prophet or shortly after his death. Examples of such reports include traditions that claim that women are not fit for positions of leadership and reports that attempt to seclude women from involvement in public life.[27] But before delving into what I am describing as misogynistic traditions, it is important to make three prefatory points: the first has to do with the definition of misogynistic reports; the second with the sources of such reports; and the third with the historical context of such reports.

What I mean by misogynistic reports are traditions attributed to the Prophet or the Companions that demean women by describing them as inherently defective, flawed, or inferior to men. Most often, these reports offer a dogmatic view of women that is bigoted, indiscriminate, unreflective, and uncritical. In these traditions, women, as a gender, are often described as defective or flawed, and should, therefore, be subservient to men. Having said this, it is important to note that historical context matters—and it matters a great deal. Thus, reports that strike the modern reader as demeaning toward women might not have always been considered as such. Moreover, it is not always possible to ascertain the intention behind many of the narrated reports found in the tradition. Take, for instance, traditions that portray women as a constant source of *fitna* (sexual seduction and enticement) to men—would such reports have been considered demeaning or degrading for women of the first/seventh or second/eighth centuries? Similarly, there are reports that do not allow women to lead congregational prayers—at the time in which these narratives emerged, were these narratives intended to be degrading or demeaning to women? Yet from the time of the Prophet to this very day, women in congregational prayers stand behind men. Is this a misogynistic practice? These questions raise complex historical and methodological issues that are beyond the scope of this article.[28] To the extent possible, I have avoided discussing reports that on their face do not appear to be degrading or demeaning to women.

There is often a thin line separating reports that discriminate against women and reports that can be described as misogynistic. The purported intentionality behind a particular report or the historical context that might have produced the report cannot be considered dispositive as to whether a particular narration or another is misogynistic. Again, whether the practice of having women stand behind men in congregational prayers could be considered misogynistic depends on numerous contextual factors, including whether women who follow this practice feel demeaned or degraded by it. The same can be said about the practice of hijab or wearing a veil covering a woman's hair or face. So as not to succumb to the temptations of orientalism, we can ask the same questions regarding the Christian and Jewish traditions. In the Roman Catholic and Anglican orders, nuns often wear a habit and veil, and in Jewish law, the veiling of women's hair is part of *tzniuth*, or the law of modesty. According to some schools of thought, a woman's hair and other parts of a woman's body are considered *ervah* ("erotic enticement") and must therefore be covered. Moreover, according to some interpretations of Jewish law, a married woman may not appear in public with her hair uncovered, and a virgin bride is required to veil her face.[29] Are these veiling practices misogynistic? It seems to me that whether the veiling of women may be considered misogynistic depends on numerous cultural and epistemological factors or contingencies. Addressing these traditions that apply exclusively to women and that single out women with special burdens or accommodations require a more systematic and comprehensive approach that is beyond the scope of this chapter.

The final prefatory remark, a point I will return to later, has to do with the textual sources in which misogynistic reports are found. It is important to note that the same sources that contain the misogynistic reports also contain the tension-reports or the reports embodying liberating memories. The historical memory of the Prophet and the early Muslim generations are contained in the texts of the Qur'ān, *sunna*, *ḥadīth*, and *sīra*, and these texts contain narratives that can potentially both oppress and liberate Muslims.[30] The very same texts that preserved memories that strike modern readers as oppressive and unjust also preserved historical memories that are surprisingly egalitarian, equitable, or liberating. As we will discuss later, some scholars have attempted to deal with the problems of patriarchy and misogyny in the tradition by arguing that Muslims should rely solely on the Qur'ān and dismiss all other texts as unreliable or as hopelessly prejudiced against women. What may be called "Qur'ān-only" approaches (those who adopt such approaches are known in Arabic as *al-qur'āniyyūn*) raise serious methodological problems that I will address later.

The Misogynistic *Ḥadīth* Reports

The Turkish female theologian Hidayet Tuksal divided misogynistic *ḥadīth* into five main categories. The first three categories are as follows: (1) *ḥadīth* that state that women were created from Adam's rib; (2) *ḥadīth* that claim that the majority of the inhabitants of hell will be women; (3) *ḥadīth* that assert that women are deficient or lacking in religion and intellect, and that they lead men astray. According to Tuksal, *fitan* (sing. *fitna*) reports, such as "I have not left to you any *fitna* ("trial") greater than women," are included in this third category. The fourth category includes: (4) *ḥadīth* that claim that women are a bad omen or inauspicious; and the final fifth category includes: (5) *ḥadīth* that claim that if dogs, donkeys, or women pass in front of a man performing ritual prayer, they will invalidate this prayer.[31] I agree with Tuksal's categorizations, although these five are not exhaustive. I will briefly comment on each of the five categories before discussing some of the traditions Tuksal might have missed.[32]

Women Created from a Rib

The *ḥadīth* states: "Be kind to women for they are created from a rib, and the most curved portion of the rib is its upper portion. If you should try to straighten it, it will break, but if you leave it as it is, it will remain bent. So be kind to women."[33] Some medieval scholars have taken this *ḥadīth* to affirm the biblical perspective that Eve was created from Adam's rib.[34]

Although the *ḥadīth*, in its many versions, counsels the kind treatment of women, modern scholars who considered it misogynistic have done so on account of it describing women as having a crooked nature.[35] Contemporary Muslims who have defended this report have argued that crooked does not mean flawed but simply different, and therefore, the *ḥadīth* was intended to espouse deference to women's distinct and unique nature. I think it is very difficult to ascertain the actual authorial intent behind this report. However, as far as I am aware, all ribs by definition are crooked because there are no straight ribs. The reasonable import of the words is that women have been created from something derivative, and that women require special treatment because, to put it simply, something is wrong with their very nature. It is as if women are fragile and flawed, or like children, i.e., women need especially benevolent treatment so as not to offend their delicate nature. It should be recalled that in Islamic theology, straightness, such as in the expression "the straight path" (*al-ṣirāṭ al-mustaqīm*), is equated with goodness and justness. At the same time, crookedness holds the exact opposite connotation, meaning "deviance" or "corruption." Hence, one can easily understand why many modern interpreters of *ḥadīth* considered the crooked rib traditions misogynistic. Moreover, the crooked rib traditions have been exploited in contemporary abusive practices against women.[36]

The Majority of the Inhabitants of Hellfire and Deficiency in Religion and Intellect

The same *ḥadīth* that claim that women are the majority of the inhabitants of hellfire also claim that women are deficient in religion and intellect. In other words, they are not two separate categories of *ḥadīth* but rather belong to the same strand of *ḥadīth*. This same basic report is related in a number of different versions,[37] too many to adequately discuss here. In essence, the *ḥadīth* claims that the Prophet advised women to be generous in giving alms and to be fervent in asking God for forgiveness because women will be the majority of the inhabitants of hell. Reportedly, when women asked the Prophet why this is so, he explained that this is because women tend to be ungrateful, especially to their husbands, and because women curse too often. The Prophet then purportedly adds that although women infatuate men, often leading men astray, women are deficient in religion and intellect. Women then inquire in what way are they deficient in religion and intellect, and the Prophet reportedly replies that women lack religion because they do not pray or fast while menstruating, and that they lack intellect because in certain situations, the testimony of a woman equals only half that of a man's.[38] The authenticity and meaning of this *ḥadīth*, in its many different versions, has been widely debated throughout Islamic history. The *ḥadīth* has been repeatedly cited in the context of many of the most misogynistic discourses in Islamic theology and jurisprudence. Some such discourses went so far as recommending that men should always consult with women only to do the exact opposite of their advice.[39] Meanwhile, other sources attempted to marginalize and limit the impact of this *ḥadīth* by insisting that the Prophet was only joking and that the entire report was intended as a pun.[40]

Bad Omens, Donkeys, Dogs, and Women

There are a number of competing versions of the *ḥadīth* attributed to the Prophet stating that if bad omens existed then they are to be found in houses, horses, and women.[41] Most medieval scholars raised questions about the authenticity of this particular strand of *ḥadīth* while others argued that the *ḥadīth* was intended to describe beliefs and practices of the pre-Islamic period (*jāhilīyya*).[42] These scholars often cite a version of the *ḥadīth* that claims that the Prophet said, "Bad omens do not exist, but if good omens existed in anything then it would be in women, homes, and horses."[43] 'Ā'isha strongly opposed the bad omen traditions. When two men informed 'Ā'isha that Abū Hurayra had claimed that the Prophet said that women and mounts could be bad omens, 'Ā'isha was outraged. She responded: "By God Who revealed the Qur'ān to Abū al-Qāsim (that is, Muḥammad to whom this teknonym was applied), whoever attributes this to the Prophet, they have lied!"[44]

Very similar dynamics surround the *ḥadīth* that claims that if a donkey, black dog, or woman passes in front of a person performing ritual prayer, then the prayer is voided.[45] The *ḥadīth* exists in many divergent versions, but most medieval scholars raised serious questions about the authenticity of this *ḥadīth*.[46] This *ḥadīth*, with its different versions, became the subject of very contentious debates because it was opposed by the Prophet's wives Umm Salama and 'Ā'isha, who insisted that the Prophet never said such a thing.[47] 'Ā'isha is reported to have been outraged when she heard this *ḥadīth* and exclaimed, "God confound you! You have made women the same as dogs and donkeys! By God, I used to lie down in front of the Prophet while on my menstrual cycle, as he continued to pray."[48]

Other Misogynistic *Ḥadīth*: The Obedience and Subservience Reports

Other misogynistic reports make the autonomy or moral agency of women wholly subservient to that of men. One can label this cluster of *ḥadīth* the "obedience and subservience" reports.[49] For example, some of these reports state that a woman will not enter Heaven unless she pleases her husband, and in one such *ḥadīth*, the Prophet is reported to have said, "A woman's prayers or good deeds will not be accepted [by God] as long as her husband is upset with her."[50] Other *ḥadīth* attributed to the Prophet claim that God will not gaze upon a woman who is not grateful to her husband, and yet other *ḥadīth* assert that the angels will curse a woman who rejects her husband's sexual advances until she accedes to his demands.[51] However, perhaps the most misogynistic narrations of this kind are what I have called the "prostration *ḥadīth*." This genre has been narrated in many variants, however one example will convey the basic idea. It is reported that the Prophet said, "No human may prostrate before another, but if it were permissible for a human to do so, I would have ordered a wife to prostrate before her husband because of the enormity of his rights over her. By God, if there were an ulcer excreting pus from his feet to the top of his head, and she licked it (for him) she would not fulfill his rights."[52] Other versions of this *ḥadīth* do not include the reference to ulcers but instead state that if a husband demands sexual gratification from his wife, even while on the back of a camel, she must oblige him.[53] One hardly needs to comment on the misogyny that is characteristic of the "obedience and subservience" cluster of *ḥadīth*. These *ḥadīth* are often cited by contemporary scholars to underscore that women owe their husbands gratitude, obedience, and servitude, especially of the sexual kind.[54]

A sizable number of Muslim women scholars have endeavored to challenge patriarchal and misogynistic interpretations of the Islamic tradition. However, among those writing in the English language, not as many have focused specifically on the Prophetic traditions in Islam. Many works by Muslim women scholars writing on gender equality deal with the *ḥadīth* traditions indirectly or incidentally, but only a few have *ḥadīth* as their primary or main interest. It is fair to say that most Muslim women scholars writing on gender equality are explicitly or implicitly skeptical of the historical authenticity of misogynistic traditions attributed to the Prophet. Most of these scholars agree that gender equality cannot be achieved unless the religious texts that preserved and sanctified the misogynistic reports are read critically and with a great deal of historical skepticism. And again, most of these scholars either explicitly reject or simply ignore the classical method of authenticating *ḥadīth* known as *isnād* analysis. In the classical tradition, *ḥadīth* scholars would painstakingly document biographical information about the narrators who reported and transmitted *ḥadīth* attributed to the Prophet. The chains of transmission of each *ḥadīth* would be evaluated, and the *ḥadīth* scholar would then adjudge a *ḥadīth* as sound or unsound, or some degree in between. For the most part, contemporary scholars interested in gender egalitarianism in Islam do not feel bound by the determinations of classical *ḥadīth* scholars as to the soundness of a report. Therefore, although a *ḥadīth* may have been declared "sound" (*ṣaḥīḥ*) in classical *ḥadīth* collections, the scholars discussed in this chapter do not treat such determinations as binding or dispositive.[55]

Main Stratagems for Rereading the *Ḥadīth* and Sunna

In response to patriarchal and misogynistic *ḥadīth* traditions, we can identify three main thematic stratagems adopted by Muslim women scholars. In this context, what I have called thematic stratagems are pedagogical or hermeneutic approaches designed to interrogate and challenge the authority of *ḥadīth* traditions that appear to promote gender inequity in Islam. The reason I have chosen to call these approaches thematic stratagems, instead of interpretive methods, is that approaches of the scholars discussed below are not necessarily designed to reconstruct the meaning of the *ḥadīth*. As noted above, very few scholars have adopted a gendered approach to *ḥadīth* exclusively from a hermeneutical perspective. The issue that challenges gendered approaches is not so much the meaning of *ḥadīth* but the role or authority of *ḥadīth* in the first place. To one extent or another, all gendered approaches to the *ḥadīth* literature deconstruct or impeach the credibility or authenticity of narratives attributed to the Prophet that are seen as chauvinistic or misogynistic. The thematic stratagems discussed below outline different reasons or methodologies for critically evaluating the weight and authority that ought to be given to problematic *ḥadīth*. Alternatively, the stratagems employed in gendered approaches to *ḥadīth* seek to explain the role and function of patriarchal institutions in the production of Islamic knowledge. The net effect of these approaches is to raise serious doubts as to whether reports attributed to the Prophet can in fact be reliability believed to have come from him.

These three thematic stratagems to gendered approaches to *ḥadīth* tend to focus on (1) the limited role that women played in the production of Islamic knowledge; (2) the historicism of Islamic religious text; and (3) the supremacy of the Qur'ānic message as well as the centrality of universal ethical values to any historical or hermeneutical analytical project. As discussed below, these thematic stratagems are not mutually exclusive, and various scholars adopt one or more of them to one extent or another. Of those discussed below, no scholar has relied exclusively on one stratagem, but it is also clear that scholars tend to underscore particular stratagems, and not others, as partially responsible for gender inequality or as the best way to achieve gender egalitarianism. Below, I will discuss each of the stratagems employed by Muslim women scholars, and in the final part of this chapter, I will outline my own approach to problematic traditions.

The Limited Role of Women in the Production of Knowledge

As noted earlier, Muslim scholars have emphasized that women played a prominent role in the preservation and promotion of Islamic knowledge. Women, such as the Prophet's wives 'Ā'isha and Umm Salama, were among the earliest narrators of *ḥadīth*. As Leila Ahmed has shown, at the time of the Prophet, women openly exercised their agency by playing an active role in political and religious life.[56] In his very detailed study, Mohammad Nadwi has shown that the extent to which women were involved in the preservation and production of Islamic knowledge varied greatly from one region and period to another.[57] At least one-third of the corpus of religious knowledge known as the *ḥadīth* and *sunna* was transmitted by women during the formative first century of Islam. The traditional position is that the gender of the narrator did not affect the ultimate judgment as to the soundness or authenticity of a report. Put differently, until recently it was believed that it did not matter whether a man or woman narrated a *ḥadīth* because both men and women were treated equally for the purposes of evaluating the authenticity and authority of a *ḥadīth*.[58]

In this context, the relatively recent contributions of Asma Sayeed and Nimat Barazangi are most significant. Sayeed argues that while women participated in the process of transmission of knowledge and *ḥadīth* in the first Islamic century, the role of women sharply decreased with the professionalization of the field of *ḥadīth* transmission in the early second/eighth century. Sayeed demonstrates that, contrary to the inherited traditional position, gender was indeed a factor in evaluating the credibility and legal impact of the first *ḥadīth* narrations. In other words, the gender of the *ḥadīth* narrator could affect whether a particular report was deemed sound, and could also diminish the weight and value given to particular traditions in legal determinations.[59] Building on Sayeed's scholarship, Barazangi argues that despite the fact that many reports were narrated on the authority of women, women were excluded from participating in the formation and development of the *ḥadīth* sciences. According to Barazangi, women *ḥadīth* narrators were consistently marginalized by male-dominated institutions and were excluded from developing what Barazangi calls "the theology of the Sunna." Barazangi contends that since the *ḥadīth* literature was mostly developed, read, and interpreted by men, this entire corpus of inherited traditions clearly bear the imprint of male perspectives and biases.[60]

Both Sayeed and Barazangi do not dismiss the entire corpus of *ḥadīth* and *sunna* as a mere invention or fabrication of a male patriarchy. However, their scholarship does desacralize the *ḥadīth* and *sunna* by underscoring the role of human interpretive agency in the preservation and reproduction of this corpus of religious knowledge. As Barazangi puts it rather bluntly,

> I am neither discrediting the reported Hadith, nor refuting its central value and importance for Muslim thought and life. Rather, I want to demystify the divine halo that has been cast over Hadith literature and that has caused injustices, especially to the Muslim woman by misusing and abusing the theology of sunnah.[61]

Of course, the main challenge to this argument is that the institutions that preserved all sacred texts, and indeed all of history, has been largely shaped by men. The dominance of patriarchy and the prevalence of the male voice in the institutions that preserved the human past is a universal and cross-cultural reality. One would be hard-pressed to find an inherited tradition that did not privilege the male perspective and a gendered male voice. In fact, as Leila Ahmed has pointed out, Islam is the only major religion to include the participatory voices of women in its foundational religious texts.[62] Gender bias was not the only form of prejudice at play in the formative moments of history—all formative moments are plagued by the prejudices of power and privilege, whatever they may be. In my view, to the extent that Sayeed and Barazangi's arguments entail a healthy dose of skepticism and critical insight when analyzing institutions that perpetuated prejudice and privilege, I think these arguments are reasonable. However, employing critical historical insights to deconstruct and dismiss tradition creates rather intractable theological and jurisprudential problems. I will return to this point later.

Arguments from Historical Contexts

Historical contextualization is a common interpretive stratagem that is widely employed by Muslim women scholars in dealing with the *ḥadīth* tradition. Perhaps the most famous and influential of these efforts is that of Fatima Mernissi in *The Veil and the Male Elite*. Mernissi analyzes the dynamics of power in relation to the formation of the *ḥadīth*, and what she describes as the use of sacred text as a political weapon.[63] Mernissi undertakes a close analysis of a number of what she describes as misogynistic reports in order to demonstrate that these *ḥadīth* came into being as part and parcel of the schismatic political conflicts shortly after the death of the Prophet. The misogynistic *ḥadīth* Mernissi analyzes were invented as a direct response to ʿĀʾisha's political activism and her rebellion against the fourth caliph, ʿAlī.[64] As significantly, Mernissi contends that the Prophet embraced an egalitarian project in which he tried to accommodate and support women's self-empowerment and self-assertion. However, the male elite of the nascent Prophetic state resisted his egalitarian project as they found their patriarchal privileges increasingly threatened. Ultimately, the Prophet's egalitarian project failed when the law of the *Ḥijāb* (seclusion) was decreed, giving the upper hand to ʿUmar's patriarchal faction. Nevertheless, after the Prophet's death, women such as ʿĀʾisha continued to resist the *Ḥijāb* and resist other patriarchal efforts to exclude women from public life.[65]

Other historical arguments focused on exploring the influx of cultural influences on Muslims after the early Islamic conquests. Ahmed and others argued that following the Islamic conquests, local Byzantium and Sassanid cultures were assimilated and integrated into Islamic practices. These cultures constructed the image of women as religiously and intellectually defective, and this image was readily integrated into Islamic theology and law, especially through the medium of the *ḥadīth* literature.[66] As Barbara Stowasser states, "Bible-related traditions, including their symbolic images of the female's defective nature, were seamlessly integrated into an Islamic framework."[67] Through Qur'ānic exegesis and the canonization of *ḥadīth*, the image of women as at once defective and flawed, and alluring and dangerous became woven into the fabric of Islamic orthodoxy.[68]

In this context, we must take note of the work of the scholarship of amina wadud and Asma Barlas, who argue that all religious texts, including the Qur'ān and *sunna*, must be read within the historical contexts in which they came into being. This means that one must distinguish between text that was intended to apply universally and in perpetuity (*al-ʿāmm*), and text that was bound to a specific time and a particular set of circumstances (*al-khāṣṣ*).[69] Using this method of historical contextualization, scholars such as wadud, Barlas, and Kecia Ali argue for a thorough and critical rereading of the Islamic traditions dealing with, among other topics, polygamy, veiling and seclusion, and laws of marriage and divorce.[70] For Muslim women scholars, the rereading of history to understand the ways in which the Prophet and early generations negotiated gender relations act as a source of hermeneutic inspiration. It is not an exaggeration to say that these scholars resist the oppressive momentum of history by insisting on their right to take ownership of the past. For instance, Barlas finds considerable inspiration in the character of the Prophet's wife Umm Salama, and this inspiration drives her entire hermeneutical project. As mentioned above, Umm Salama complained to the Prophet that the Qur'ān spoke to men and did not address women directly. In response, the revelation responded to Umm Salama's concerns by directly addressing women. With impressive transparency, Barlas comments on this incident: "As a believer, I interpret this incident to mean not that a woman corrected God, but rather that, by God's Grace, Umm Salama's critique became the way for God to correct an entire community."[71]

I do not believe that a believer living in the modern world can avoid the weight and trajectory of history in any way. Trying to avoid understanding the historical context that shaped and molded so many of the Prophetic traditions invariably amounts to putting one's proverbial head in the ground and trying to pretend that history does not exist. Nevertheless, it is important to deal briefly with the often-heard challenges to the historical approach. Among the common challenges raised in response to the historically contextualized approach is that it superimposes the value system of the interpreting historian on the body of sacred religious dogma. Without clear moral foundations, or a precise theological frame of reference, the historically contextual approach risks becoming a thinly veiled secular reconstruction of the Divine law. Historically contextualized approaches could systematically deconstruct the idea of Divine intent, but it does not necessarily replace it with a coherent religious outlook. For example, Mernissi argues that the *ḥijāb* was imposed largely in response to repressive patriarchal demands by the male elite at the time of the Prophet. However, this begs the question: Why did God accommodate the repressive demands of the male elite? What are the implications of the Divine accommodating the demands of patriarchy at the expense of women? While Mernissi offers a critical method that appeals to secular outlooks, her approach could be far less appealing to those who consider the Qur'ān and *sunna* to be the repository of the Divine Will. If by imposing the *ḥijāb*, God ultimately accommodated the demands of the male elite, as Mernissi argues, what are the theological implications of such a move? Does this mean that at the time of the Prophet, God sided with the male elite against the demands of socially active women? As a theological and moral imperative, does this mean that the male scholarly elite was espousing the Islamically correct position? Mernissi's historical analysis does not provide convincing responses to these intractable theological questions.

Historically informed approaches often challenge the normative assumptions of theology and law with uncomfortable and disquieting questions. Understandably, this raises considerable anxiety among believers, who are forced to confront disconcerting questions about the implications of historical memory for theology and law. The *ḥadīth* and *sunna* cover a broad array of topics, including prayer, fasting, the giving of alms, pilgrimage to Mecca, prohibition against usury, etc. The most common anxiety voiced by believers is that if critical analytical methods are applied to deconstruct the substantive tradition attributed to the Prophet on the grounds of inequity between genders, what does this imply for other issues, such as class, race, sexual liberties, and so on? At what point does one succumb to self-idolatry as opposed to submitting to the will of God?

Objections to historically contextualized interpretations often boil down to an argument not only about the relevance of the Divine Will but also about how the Divine Will is discoverable. Did God intend to assign roles to men and women, and were these roles intended to be different and distinct? Did God intend to privilege males? And how do we know what God wills? I will return to these questions later, but for now, there is a more concrete objection to historically contextualized approaches to the *ḥadīth* and *sunna*. Such approaches are often accused of being both selective and dismissive toward the *ḥadīth* and *sunna*. For example, Shadaab Rahemtulla in his *Qur'an of the Oppressed* claims that Barlas is largely dismissive of the *ḥadīth* literature precisely because of its questionable reliability, and that she is equally dismissive of the Sharīʿa because of its sexism.[72] The charge of dismissiveness is an often-heard challenge made in response to all reform-oriented scholars who attempt to historicize the huge corpus of *ḥadīth* reports and *sunna*. Historical approaches to the *ḥadīth* and *sunna* often imply that this religious corpus is the byproduct of material conditions that shaped and crafted this body of literature. As such, the *ḥadīth* and *sunna* become the repository of the subjective and negotiated human agency, and not the Divine Will.

In his review of the scholarship of Barlas, Rahemtulla also echoes the often-repeated charge of selectivity.[73] Of course, this charge is made not just against Barlas but also against all Muslim women reformers—if not against all reformers. In reviewing the scholarship of those she calls "exegetes," Aysha Hidayatullah writes:

> In some cases, the exegetes are inclined to cite certain Hadith reports positively without scrutinizing their historical authenticity when they support the just treatment of women, and they use them to buttress their interpretations of the Qur'an. In other cases, they argue for the inauthenticity of Hadith reports that demean women, rejecting those reports, and maintaining that the Qur'an must be prioritized over them.[74]

Hidayatullah's criticism is basically sound, but the reality is that selectivity is essential to any reform project. Any pretense to objectively interpret history is just that: a pretense. As discussed below, moral and ethical commitments are important in any interpretive project, but what matters is that one be transparent and honest about one's normative commitments. Especially when one claims to engage the Divine Will, one must offer an understanding of that Will and lay bare one's own teleological commitments. This sets an engagement with the reader that is honest and transparent. Often, this does mean that the reformer must sift through the often chaotically inconsistent *ḥadīth* reports in the tradition arguing for the credibility of some reports while rejecting the credibility of others.

The Qur'ānic Guidance Arguments

Most women scholars who critically engage the *ḥadīth* and *sunna* anchor their approach on the hermeneutics of the Qur'ān. Scholars such as wadud, Barlas, Barazangi, and Riffat Hassan argue for a thematic and holistic reading of the Qur'ān in order to systematically understand its moral and ethical universe.[75] The Qur'ān is interpreted to support the autonomy, dignity, and equality of women, and then *ḥadīths* are substantively analyzed to assess whether the reports in question are consistent with these values. Part of this methodological stratagem is not to read the Qur'ān in a piecemeal fashion or as a code of law, but to emerge with a coherent Qur'ānic outlook on gender equality. Perhaps the most prominent of these approaches is wadud's "Tawhidic Paradigm." *Tawḥīd* is the belief in God's unity, indivisibility, singularity, and immutability. For wadud, God alone is sovereign, and all human beings are equal moral agents before God. God alone is supreme, and this means that all human beings, regardless of gender, race, or class, are equal before God. Therefore, according to wadud's approach, the entire Islamic tradition ought to be scrutinized and interpreted in order to achieve this egalitarian moral vision.[76] Importantly, scholars such as wadud and Barlas do not argue that their reading of the Qur'ān is the only possible hermeneutical engagement or interpretation of the text. Rather, their reading represents an affirmative moral commitment toward human autonomy, dignity, and gender egalitarianism. While readily conceding that the Qur'ān can be read in patriarchal ways that further male dominance and the oppression of women, these interpreters appeal to their readers to share an understanding of the Divine Will that is committed to the principles of justice and equality, especially between genders.

Kecia Ali charges that Qur'ānically based approaches by some of the scholars mentioned above suffer from both dogmatism and lack of transparency. After conceding the strength of some scriptural interpretations positing a privileged role for males in society and family, Ali goes on to write:

> One must debunk and counter aggressively patriarchal and indeed misogynist interpretations, but also justify the project of egalitarian interpretation. In the process, one must acknowledge that esteeming equality as the most important interpersonal value is a peculiarity of some modern Muslims and not something inherent in the text of the Qur'ān. Feminist exegetes must take care not to be as blinded by the commitment to equality, and the presumption that equality is necessary for justice, as classical exegetes were by their assumptions about the naturalness of male superiority and dominance in family and society.[77]

Although I am not sure Ali's own commitment to justice and sexual freedom is better justified than the approaches to equality she criticizes, she does raise an important objection that is often made in response to Qur'ānically committed approaches. Equality is a theoretically elusive concept, and the relationship of equality to justice is ever more complex.[78] What is the proper balance between respecting the integrity and authority of the text, with all its historical peculiarities, and the subjectivities and idiosyncrasies of the interpreter of the text? If one accepts the *ḥadīth* and *sunna* only when they affirm one's interpretation of the Qur'ānic text, does not this mean that one is cherrypicking the tradition for whatever the reader finds agreeable, while disregarding whatever is disagreeable? Is not this, as some have charged, inconsistently selective?[79] Many Muslim women scholars argue that *ḥadīth* should be accepted only to the extent that the specific Prophetic narrations are corroborated by the Qur'ān. *Ḥadīth* and *sunna* that are inconsistent with the purported Qur'ānic *tawḥidic* principles or the Qur'ānic principles of self-determination, liberation, autonomy, or self-identity should be rejected as inauthentic or unreliable.[80] What unites these approaches is that they derive from the Qur'ān's foundational moral principles that support gender egalitarianism, and then *Ḥadīth* and *sunna* are scrutinized and either accepted or rejected in light of these principles. However, these approaches are open to the same criticism of subjectivity and selectivity, and of cherrypicking through the tradition.

I must admit that I do not find the charge of selectivity particularly compelling or persuasive. In fact, selectivity in approaching an inherited tradition is necessary because embracing a tradition in its entirety as if its epistemological universe applies in perpetuity is nothing short of unfettered irrationalism. The real issue is transparency and honesty in selectivity. Before dealing with this argument, however, I need to deal with some of the basic foundational issues that arise in this context.

Reasonability in Approaching the *Ḥadīth* and *Sunna*

As noted earlier, in response to the patriarchy and misogyny found in some of the *ḥadīth* and *sunna* traditions, some scholars have either altogether rejected the authority of the Sharīʿa or tried to dilute its authority by arguing that the Sharīʿa is a morally guided path and not law.[81] I think the unspoken assumption is that a morally guided path is less constraining and more flexible and negotiable than law or a legal system. While it is true that Sharīʿa is a morally guided path, this does not mean that this moral guidance does not necessitate or even mandate firm, binding obligations (*taklīf*). The entire edifice of *fiqh* (Islamic jurisprudence) is based on the foundational premise that the moral path of Sharīʿa cannot be fulfilled unless the follower of the path (*al-mukallaf*) pursues the exploration of the *adilla* (evidence or indicators of the Divine Will) in order to comprehend and apply the obligations (*taklīf*) that follow from that path. While we can define Sharīʿa as the normative commitments commanded by God, the Sovereign, *fiqh* is the human effort at comprehending and giving effect to Sharīʿa. Although the abstract and practical boundaries between Sharīʿa and *fiqh* are often blurry and unclear, the expressions "Islamic law" or "Sharīʿa law" usually refer to both the Sharīʿa and *fiqh*. This is not the place to discuss whether Islamic law, as many Muslim reformers have claimed, is not real law, but it is sufficient to note that this necessarily depends on how we define the concept of law.

I have argued elsewhere that what constitutes law is a deliberative and cumulative interpretive practice that forms a narrative community that shares a common linguistic practice, interpretive and expository methodologies, and instrumentalities of authoritativeness.[82] Islamic law is not law in the positivistic sense and not even in the "natural law" meaning of law, but it is law in the sense of structures and processes of generating authority, obligation, and the need for deference. The idea that what constitutes law is the command of the sovereign backed up by the threat of the use of force is deeply flawed. In essence, law is premised on the idea of the creation of obligations that earn deference and obedience whether force is used or not. In a nonpositivistic sense of law, the very basic dynamic at play in the construction of obligation is founded on authority and deference. The person claiming authority and the person deferring to this authority share an epistemological presupposition based on a common framework of meaning, reference, and a shared heritage or tradition.[83] In the Islamic context, the epistemological presupposition for the construction of what is authoritative is the Divine Will—what God arguably demands from a believing and committed Muslim. Whether acknowledged or not, and whether the interpreter admits as much or not, all arguments about Islamic reform and Islamically driven reconstruction of gender roles are indeed arguments about the Divine Will and what the purported reformer imagines God expects from Muslims.

Now, the epistemological presuppositions of Sharīʿa law as currently constructed include the Qur'ān and *ḥadīth* and *sunna*, as well as the cumulative interpretive communities that reasoned through the fields of *uṣūl al-fiqh* ("sources of jurisprudence"), *al-qawāʿid al-fiqhiyya* ("legal maxims"), and *fiqh* (as came to be recorded in books of positive legal opinions). As currently constituted, when we negotiate the Divine Will, we rely on concepts such as *ijtihād*, *qiyās* (reasoning through similarities or analogy), consensus (*ijmāʿ*), *maṣlaḥa* (public interest or welfare), and *ḍarūra* (necessity)—all of which come from the universe of cumulative interpretive communities of the past. Hence, whether consciously or not, reformers negotiate the Divine Will through a shared epistemic universe with their readers—this universe is derived directly from the inherited cumulative interpretive communities of the past who worked through and constructed such foundational concepts such as *ikhtilāf* (diversity of opinions), *tarjīḥ* (preponderance of evidence or opinion), and *shubūhat* (doubt or lack of certitude or lack of evidence), among many other concepts.[84]

My point is that there is an epistemic universe in which those who belong to the Islamic tradition dwell, and this epistemic universe generates meaning, authoritativeness, and persuasiveness. The question that interests me here is whether it makes sense to expunge, delete, or remove the *ḥadīth* or *sunna* from this epistemic universe. In order to institute a proper Islamic reform, should we rely on the Qur'ān only and abrogate or ignore the traditions attributed to the Prophet? In my view, this would be a serious error, because if we abrogate the past (the traditions attributed to the Prophet are part of the past), we deconstruct the tapestry of authority that binds and maintains the Islamic tradition. The serious risk in subverting and unraveling the Islamic tradition is that the very venues for communication and deference among Muslims will entirely disintegrate. The *ḥadīth* and *sunna* are at the very heart of the epistemic communities of Islam—if they are abolished, the entire edifice of Islamic meanings and communication is torn down as well. Not even the Qur'ān will have meaning without the traditions of the past that give the semantics of the Qur'ān a range of meanings and that give a historical context to so much of the revelation. Without reliance on the communities of interpretation that accumulated around the Divine text and that created what might be called a tradition, all that remains is a purely phenomenological approach that most likely will be too subjective and even idiosyncratic to be persuasive or authoritative.

To recapitulate, my argument thus far is that the core issue in any reform project is the question of Divine Will, as in what obligations are owed to God. We explore the question of *taklīf* (obligation) within a world of epistemic presuppositions that define the authoritative within the Islamic tradition. The authoritative is whatever earns the deference of the agent who is searching for the Divine Will. If we abolish or dismiss the *ḥadīth* and *sunna*, the epistemic presuppositions or the world of meaning in which Muslims dwell will cease to have meaning. There is no meaningful way where we can talk about what the Qur'an means when it uses words such as *ṣalāh*, *ṣawm*, *zakat*, or *ḥajj*, let alone words such as *maʿrūf*, *qisṭ*, *ʿadl*, or *iḥsān*, unless we anchor our discourse in the epistemic world of the Islamic tradition. Worlds of meaning are always anchored in interpretive traditions, and without its interpretive tradition, not only Sharīʿa but Islam itself will not have an authoritative frame of reference.

Much of the *ḥadīth* and *sunna*, however, is not only sexist, and at times misogynistic, but also contradictory and inconsistent. This is precisely why it is important to be both principled and selective when negotiating this tradition. Approaching this tradition with a selective and principled methodology mandates the adoption of the interpretive values of honesty, self-restraint, diligence, comprehensiveness, and reasonableness. I will have more to say about these values below, but for now I want to elaborate on the issue of moral agency in dealing with the Islamic tradition and reconstituting gender roles.

Conclusion

As discussed earlier, on a number of occasions, the Qur'ān and its accompanying interpretive tradition document occasions in which God hears and responds to complaints made to the Prophet. For instance, in one such occasion the Qur'ān states, '*wa yastaftūnaka fī al-nisā*' (and they ask you about issues that involve women),[85] and as discussed above, on another occasion, the Qur'ān states that God heard the woman who argued with the Prophet about her husband and appealed to God.[86] On these occasions, among others, God responds to inquiries by women or about women—the Divine responds to contexts initiated by human activity. The human agent initiated the query eliciting a Divine response—to use the Qur'ānic expression, the human agent did an *istiftā'* (asked for a fatwa), and the Divine responded. But this raises the question: What if these human agents had not acted so that the cycle of revelation could be completed? I think, however, this is the wrong question. The dynamic here is illustrative of the fact that the Divine Will is discoverable through, to use the phrase from the tradition, *'ilāqat al-'aql bi-l-ma'qūl*—an active dynamic between the rationalizing agent and the subject of that agency.

The negotiation between the rational and the comprehended (*'aql* and *ma'qūl* respectively), or the epistemology that is the product of the negotiation and renegotiation between the active agent and subject of the agency, must be able to mine the tradition for inspiration for solutions, and not just for formulas. Revelation has come to an end, but there has to be an alternative process by which to undertake the *'istiftā'*, a process by which the rational agent can pose questions to the tradition and derive divinely inspired responses to these questions. Consider the following illustrative example. Aḥmad Ibn Ḥanbal (d. 241/855) narrated a *ḥadīth* in which the Prophet is reported to have said, "Whoever has a daughter and does not bury her alive (*ya'iduhā*), does not insult her, nor favor his son over her, God will reward him with Paradise."[87] In this tradition, parents should not give preference to boys over girls, and should not bury their daughters.[88] However, if this *ḥadīth* is read in conjunction with the Qur'ānic condemnation of *istikrāh* (coercion and compulsion) and *istiḍ'āf* (oppression), the expression *ya'iduhā* could be read to mean to suffocate or oppress her in addition to bury her alive.[89] In earlier generations Muslim women would go to the Prophet with problems, and the Prophet responded with open revelation.

This revelation is a text that is historically contingent and circumstantial, and it is a text that is responding to the specific moral demands made by active agents. But at the same time, this text is open-ended in the sense that, from a religious perspective, it is intended to have perpetual relevance. The text does not just memorialize specific determinations but also, as significantly, serves important anecdotal purposes. The text contains anecdotes of empowerment. If this is the case, it seems to me that the *taklīf* is not simply one of obedience. Rather, the *taklīf* is to pose questions, make moral demands from this tradition, and generate a methodology for constructing meaning that is responsive to the rationalizing agent and the subject of this agency. Hence, burying girls (*wa'd al-banāt*) could be reconstructed and renegotiated to mean the oppressing and suffocating of girls so that their souls and intellects, and not just their physical bodies, are murdered. If women are rendered powerless and systematically oppressed so that they cannot exercise their moral agency, it seems to be the essence of burying human beings alive. *Wa'd al-banāt* was a pre-Islamic practice in which families killed their daughters by burying them alive. The above-quoted *ḥadīth*, however, goes beyond the prohibition of murder to calling for the kind treatment of daughters and for not favoring boys over girls. Considering the modern moral challenges and epistemological demands, the concept of *wa'd al-banāt* should be reconceptualized and reinterpreted to mean soul-murder and all that leads to suffocating the souls of young girls.

Returning to the issue of Sharīʿa and Islamic law, to the extent that the *ḥadīth* above supports a *taklīf* (obligation) on the agent who chooses to defer to the evidence of this obligation, this *ḥadīth* is part of Sharīʿa. At the same time, this *ḥadīth* and the cumulative interpretative efforts that engaged it are part of Islamic law. But it is a part of the Islamic law only as long as this interpretive effort is focused on the ultimate question of *taklīf*, and as long as it engages the linguistic practice and deliberative mechanics of Islamic jurisprudence. If, for one reason or another, the interpretive effort is not interested in the question of Divine Will and *taklīf*, and if it does not employ the mechanics and linguistic practice of jurisprudence then, by definition, it is not a part of Islamic law or the Islamic legal tradition. However, just because determinations are part of Islamic law or the Islamic legal tradition does not mean it is moral or ethical. To assume that Islamic legal determinations are moral or ethical is to lapse the Divine truth with subjective efforts struggling to reach this truth. Everything in the created world must be rationalized by a rationalizing agent, and the two are engaged in a dynamic in which they mold and shape each other. This is especially the case when it comes to law; the law is a concerted effort at fulfilling the Divine Will, but it is not the Divine Will. The most that legal determinations can hope to be are authoritative without abusing or usurping the Divine Will. Importantly, no tradition speaks in a single moral voice—all interpretive efforts that are embedded in any tradition whatsoever are necessarily selective and discriminate. However, in order to discharge one's duty to be as authoritative as possible without abusing or usurping this interpretive authority the interpreting agent should make best efforts to uphold the values of honesty, self-restraint, diligence, comprehensiveness, and reasonableness.[90] The role of ethics is to interrogate, scrutinize, and at times, shame the law so that the law will not be allowed to slip into the comfortable assumption that justice, fairness, and equity have indeed been achieved. Ethical critiques of the law, and also critiques of the representatives of a legal system, should force the agents functioning on behalf of this legal system to reconsider and re-evaluate their interpretive efforts and determinations.

I must close this chapter with a comment about the fact that I am a male interpreter writing about women interpreters of the religious tradition. As a male interpreter, I am necessarily constrained and limited by the subjectivities and selectivities of my own gender. No matter how much I try to elevate myself beyond these constraints and read the tradition with a principled commitment to egalitarianism between genders, I am limited by the subjectivities of my male perspective. I am committed to the Islamic tradition, including the *ḥadīth* and *sunna*, because I believe that this tradition, with all its inconsistencies, contradictions, and paradoxes, is the repository of Islamic meaning and authoritativeness. However, as a male interpretive agent, I am fully cognizant of the fact that patriarchy is, as Asma Barlas warned, an ingrained cultural habit; it is a bad habit at that, and bad habits veil the truth.[91] No one is better positioned to break the habits of patriarchy and of male dominance in the Islamic tradition than Muslim women acting as interpretive agents. With feet firmly planted in this tradition, these interpretive agents can then act to authoritatively represent, but at the same time, reconstruct and reinvent it. Like the women who made demands of the Prophet and sought Divine intervention, Muslim women must make demands on this tradition. Yet because revelation has come to an end, it is Muslim women scholars who must intervene on their own behalf and renegotiate and reinterpret the tradition to generate persuasive responses. The challenge is always relevance and authoritativeness—in order for determinations to be persuasive and earn the deference of believing Muslims, these determinations must authoritatively negotiate the Divine Will. To authoritatively work through the demands of the Divine Will, in my view, necessarily means wrestling with the interpretive traditions of Islam even if these interpretive traditions were formed and shaped by men.

From a theological perspective and from a tradition-based point of view, I would argue that patriarchy is not just a bad habit, but it is an *ibtilāʾ* (trial, plight, or challenge). Like all trials given to us by God, it is there to test our ability as Muslims to persevere and overcome by achieving justice and equity (*al-ʿadl wa-l-iḥsān*). Patriarchy, like other endemic forms of *ibtilāʾ*, like racism, ethnocentrism, nationalism, and classicism, is a malady of the human condition that is, like so many human follies, both natural and wrong. One of the firmly anchored principles in Islamic jurisprudence, and possibly Islamic ethics, is that suffering, and harm (*ḍarar*) must be removed or brought to an end.[92] To the extent that any *ḥadīth* or *sunna* results in suffering and harm, there is a proportional duty (*taklīf*) to rethink the normative application of this tradition to end the suffering. Patriarchy is a plight or *ibtilāʾ* in every age; however, the harm and suffering that results from this challenge differs a great deal from one age and place to another. But here is where the imperative of Muslim women's agency becomes particularly compelling. It is Muslim women who must testify to their own suffering, and it is the women scholars of Sharīʿa who must become the medium through which revelation speaks to the demands of each place and age.

Notes

* I am very grateful to Zezen Zaenal Mutazin, Robert O'Brien, and my wife, Grace Song, for their invaluable feedback and assistance.

1. Jennifer Heath, *The Scimitar and the Veil: Extraordinary Women of Islam* (Mahwah, NJ: Hidden Spring, 2004); Aisha Abdurrahman Bewley, *Muslim Women: A Biographical Dictionary* (London: Ta-Ha Publishers, 2004); ʿUmar Riḍā Kaḥḥāla, *Aʿlām al-Nisāʾ fī ʿĀlamī al-ʿArabī wa al-Islām* (Beirut: Muʾassasat al-Risāla, 1959).
2. ʿĀʾisha ʿAbd al-Rahmān Bint al-Shāṭiʾ, *Tarājim Sayyidāt Bayt Al-Nubuwwa* (Cairo: Dār al-Rayyān li Turāth, 1987), 936–939.
3. Bint al-Shāṭiʾ, *Tarājim*, 936–939; Heath, *Scimitar*, 245–247; Bewley, *Muslim Women*, 151–152.
4. Fatima Mernissi, *The Veil and The Male Elite: A Feminist Interpretation of Women's Rights in Islam*, trans. Mary Jo Lakeland (New York: Basic Books, 1991), 195.
5. Denise A. Spellberg, *Politics, Gender, and the Islamic Past: The Legacy of ʿAʾisha Bint Abi Bakr* (New York: Columbia University Press, 1994); Ruth Roded, "Umm Salama Hind," in *The Encyclopaedia of Islam*, ed. P. J Bearman et al. (Leiden: E.J. Brill, 2000), 10:856; Asma Afsaruddin, "ʿĀʾisha Bint Abī Bakr," in *The Encyclopaedia of Islam*, ed. Kate Fleet et al.,

3rd ed. (Leiden: E.J. Brill, 2010-11), available at https://referenceworks-brillonline-com.proxyiub.uits.iu.edu/entries/encyclopaedia-of-islam-3/aisha-bt-abi-bakr-COM_23459?s.num=6&s.f.s2_parent=s.f.book.encyclopaedia-of-islam-3&s.q=afsaruddin 'Ā'isha bint Abī Bakr was a prominent wife of Muḥammad and the daughter of Abū Bakr (d. 13/634), a Companion and political Successor of the Prophet. She is remembered as a favored wife of the Prophet, the most prolific female transmitter of *ḥadīth* (*muḥadditha*), and a jurist in her own right (*faqīha*). Umm Salama (also known by her birth name Hind bint Abī Umayya) is credited with being the second-most prolific female in *ḥadīth* transmissions after 'Ā'isha. She married the Prophet Muḥammad after the death of her first husband at the Battle of Uḥud (3/625), and was a leading figure among the Prophet's co-wives.

6. Reportedly, ʿĀʾisha bint Ṭalḥa and Sukayna were both married (at different times) to Mus'ab bin al-Zubayr, the governor of Basra. Mus'ab was ʿĀʾisha's second husband. See Bewley, *Muslim Women*, 9–10.
7. Resit Haylamaz, *Aisha: The Wife, The Companion, The Scholar* (Clifton, NJ: Tughra Books, 2014).
8. Bint al-Shāṭiʾ, *Tarājim*, 904; Heath, *Scimitar*, 240–244; Abū al-Faraj al-Iṣfahānī, *Kitāb Al-Aghānī*, ed. Iḥsān ʿAbbās, Ibrāhīm al-Sa'āfīn, and Bakr ʿAbbās (Beirut: Dār Sādir, 2008), 11:122.
9. Asma Afsaruddin, "Early Women Exemplars and the Construction of Gendered Space: (Re-) Defining Feminine Moral Excellence," in *Harem Histories: Envisioning Places and Living Space*, ed. Marilyn Booth (Durham, NC: Duke University Press, 2010): 23–48; Benedikt Koehler, "Female Entrepreneurship in Early Islam." *Economic Affairs* 31, no. 2 (2011): 93–95; Pernilla Myrn, *Female Sexuality in the Early Medieval Islamic World: Gender and Sex in Arabic Literature* (New York: Bloomsbury Publishing, 2019).
10. Barbara Freyer Stowasser, "The Status of Women in Early Islam," in *Muslim Women*, ed. Freda Hussain (London: Routledge, 2016), 11–43; Mernissi, *The Veil and The Male Elite*, 115–140; Leila Ahmed, *Women and Gender in Islam: Historical Roots of a Modern Debate* (New Haven, CT: Yale University Press, 1992), 72; Asma Sayeed, *Women and the Transmission of Religious Knowledge in Islam* (Cambridge: Cambridge University Press, 2013). A good comprehensive source is ʿAbd al-Ḥalīm Abū Shuqqa, *Taḥrīr al-Marʾa fī ʿAṣi al-Risāla*, 2 vols. (Cairo: Dār al-Qalam, 1999), vols. 1 and 2.
11. Mernissi, *Veil and The Male Elite*, 115-140; Ednan Aslan, "Early Community Politics and the Marginalization of Women in Islamic Intellectual History," in *Muslima Theology: The Voices of Muslim Women Theologians*, ed. Ednan Aslan and Marcia K. Hermansen (Frankfurt am Main: Peter Lang, 2013), 35–43; Asma Lamrabet, *Women in the Qur'an: An Emancipatory Reading* (Leister,UK: Porter Square Books, 2016), 91–159.
12. Khaled Abou El Fadl, *Speaking in God's Name: Islamic Law, Authority and Women* (Oxford: Oneworld, 2010), 232; Mernissi, *Veil and The Male Elite*, 142–143.
13. Abou El Fadl, *Speaking in God's Name*, 232; Mernissi, *Veil and The Male Elite*, 143–144; Abī ʿAbd al-Raḥmān Aḥmad b. Shuʿayb al-Nasāʾī, *Kitāb 'Ishrat al-nisā'* (Cairo: Maktabat al-Sunna, 1998), 159–160.
14. Abou El Fadl, *Speaking in God's Name*, 223.
15. Abū Shuqqa, *Taḥrīr al-Marʾa*, 2:42. See also chapter 3 in this *Handbook* by Feryal Salem.
16. Abū Shuqqa, *Taḥrīr al-Marʾa*, 2:45.
17. Qur'ān 33:35: "Indeed, the Muslim men and Muslim women, the believing men and believing women, the obedient men and obedient women, the truthful men and truthful women, the patient men and patient women, the humble men and humble women, the

charitable men and charitable women, the fasting men and fasting women, the men who guard their private parts and the women who do so, and the men who remember Allah often and the women who do so— for them Allah has prepared forgiveness and a great reward."

18. Muḥammad b. Jarīr al-Ṭabarī, *Tafsīr al-Ṭabarī Jāmiʿ al-Bayān ʿan Taʾwīl Ayy al-Qurʾān*, ed. ʿAbd Allāh ʿAbd al-Muḥsīn al-Turkī (Cairo: Dār Hijr, 2001) 19:111; Abū ʿAbd Allāh Muḥammad al-Qurṭubī, *al-Jāmiʿ li-Aḥkām al-Qurʾān*, ed. ʿAbd Allāh ʿAbd al-Muḥsīn al-Turkī (Beirut: Mu'assasat al-Risāla, 2006) 17:149; Abū al-Ḥasan al-Māwardī, *al-Nukat wa al-ʿUyūn Tafsīr al-Māwardī* (Beirut: Dār al-Kutub al-ʿIlmiyya, n.d), 4:402.
19. See also 4:32 and 3:195, where the Qur'ān affirms that women bear equal moral responsibility to that of men.
20. This title is often misread as *al-mujādala* ("the disputation") instead of *al-Mujādila* ("the woman who disputes").
21. Al-Ṭabarī, *Tafsīr*, 21:446–456; al-Māwardī, *Nukat*, 5:487–488; al-Qurṭubī, *Jāmiʿ*, 20:280–282; Fakhr al-Dīn al-Rāzī, *Tafsīr al-Fakhr al-Rāzī* (Beirut: Dār al-Fikr, 1981) 29:250–253.
22. Al-Qurṭubī, *Jāmiʿ*, 20:280; Muḥammad Ibrāhim Salīm, *Nisāʾ Ḥawl al-Rasūl* (Cairo: Maktabat Ibn Sinā, 1990) 49–51; Abū ʿAbd Allāh Muḥammad Ibn Saʿd, *Kitāb al-Ṭabaqāt al-Kabīr*, ed. ʿAlī Muḥammad ʿAmr (Cairo: Maktaba al-Khānjī, 2001), 10:353–355; Ibn Ḥajar al-ʿAsqalānī, *Fatḥ al-Bārī Sharḥ Ṣaḥīḥ al-Bukhārī* (Cairo: al-Maktaba al-Salafiyya, n.d.) 9:433; Badr al-Dīn al-ʿAynī, *ʿUmda al-Qārī Sharḥ Ṣaḥīḥ al-Bukhārī* (Beirut: Dār al-Fikr, n.d) 20:280; Aḥmad Ibn Ḥanbal, *Musnad al-Imām Aḥmad Ibn Ḥanbal*, ed. Shuʿayb al-Arnāʾūṭī (Beirut: Mu'assasat al-Risāla, 1996), 45:280.
23. Abou El Fadl, *Speaking in God's Name*, 223; Ibn Ḥajar al-ʿAsqalānī, *Fatḥ al-Bārī*, 9:253–254.
24. Abou El Fadl, *Speaking in God's Name*, 230; Mernissi, *Veil and The Male Elite*, 180–188.
25. See Abou El Fadl, *Speaking in God's Name*.
26. Mernissi, *Veil and The Male Elite*, 85–189, esp. 102–115.
27. Abou El Fadl, *Speaking in God's Name*, 111–115, 228–231. See also, Mohammad Fadel, "Is Historicism a Viable Strategy for Islamic Law Reform? The Case of 'Never Shall a Folk Prosper Who Have Appointed a Woman to Rule Them,'" *Islamic Law and Society* 18, no. 2 (2011): 131–176.
28. For a discussion of the *fitna* traditions, see Abou El Fadl, *Speaking in God's Name*, 232–247. On women leading prayer, see amina wadud, *Inside the Gender Jihad: Women's Reform in Islam* (New York: Simon and Schuster, 2013), 177–186.
29. Barbara Goldman Carrel, "Shattered Vessels That Contain Divine Sparks: Unveiling Hasidic Women's Dress Code," in *The Veil: Women Writers on Its History, Lore and Politics*, ed. Jennifer Heath (Berkeley: University of California Press, 2008), 44–59; Michael J. Broyde, "Hair Covering and Jewish Law: Biblical and Objective (Dat Moshe) or Rabbinic and Subjective (Dat Yehudit)?," *Tradition: A Journal of Orthodox Jewish Thought* 42, no. 3 (2009): 97–179; Joshua Schwartz, "Hair's the Thing: Women's Hairstyle and Care in Ancient Jewish Society," in *Strength to Strength: Essays in Honor of Shaye J. D.*, ed. Michael L. Satlow (Atlanta: Society of Biblical Literature, 2018), 341–358; Susan Weiss, "Under Cover: Demystification of Women's Head Covering in Jewish Law," *Nashim: A Journal of Jewish Women's Studies & Gender Issues* 17 (2009): 89–115.
30. On *sunna* and *ḥadīth*, see Abou El Fadl, *Speaking in God's Name*, 98–132.
31. Hideyat Sefkatli Tuksal, "Misogynistic Reports in the Ḥadīth Literature," in *Muslima Theology*, 133–154.

32. Asma Barlas writes, "it is ironic that even though there are only about six misogynistic AḤadīth accepted as Sahih (reliable) out of a collection of 70,000, it is these six that men trot out when they want to argue against sexual equality"; see Asma Barlas, *Believing Women in Islam: Unreading Patriarchal Interpretations of the Qur'ān* (Austin: University of Texas Press, 2002), 46.
33. Abī ʿAbd Allāh Muḥammad al-Bukhārī, *Ṣaḥīḥ al-Bukhārī* (Beirut: Dār Ibn Kathīr, 2002), 819; Muslim ibn al-Ḥajjāj, *Ṣaḥīḥ Muslim* (Riyaḍ: Dār Ṭayba, 2006), 683; Abū ʿAbd Allāh Muḥammad b. Yazīd Ibn Māja, *Sunan Ibn Māja*, ed. Rāʾid b. Ṣabr Abī ʿAlafa (Riyaḍ: Dār al-Ḥaḍāra, 2015), 279; Abī ʿAbd al-Raḥmān Aḥmad b. Shuʿayb al-Nasāʾī, *Kitāb al-Sunan al-Kubrā* (Beirut: Mu'assasat al-Risāla, 2001), 8:251.
34. Tuksal, "Misogynistic Reports," 137.
35. Ibid. On the bent rib *ḥadīth*, its patriarchal interpretations, and what the author calls "deficiency *Ḥadīth*," see Karen Bauer, *Gender Hierarchy in the Qur'ān: Medieval Interpretations, Modern Responses* (Cambridge: Cambridge University Press, 2015), 36–49, 123–134.
36. "From a Crooked Rib," became the title of Nuruddin Farah's strongly critical novel of gender roles in Somalia. Originally published in 1970, the novel continues to attract scholarly attention from the Islamic gender studies community, particularly from those writing from the geographic perspective of Africa; see Nuruddin Farah, *From a Crooked Rib* (London: Heinemann Educational, 1970). See also Ifeoma Einne Odinye, "Violence against Girls: A Feminist Perspective on Nuruddin Farah's From a Crooked Rib," *Journal of Linguistics, Language and Culture* 6, no. 1 (Spring 2019): 113–139; Mohd Anuar bin Ramli et al., "Muslim Exegeses Perspective on Creation of the First Woman: A Brief Discussion," *Middle-East Journal of Scientific Research* 13, no. 1 (Spring 2013): 41–44; Riffat Hassan, "Feminist Theology: The Challenges for Muslim Women," *Critique: Journal for Critical Studies in the Middle East* 5, no. 9 (1996): 53–65.
37. Abou El Fadl, *Speaking in God's Name*, 225.
38. Al-Bukhārī, *Ṣaḥīḥ*, 84, 356; Muslim ibn al-Ḥajjāj, *Ṣaḥīḥ Muslim*, 51; Ibn Ḥanbal, *Musnad*, 9:245–246; Abū Dāwud al-Sijistānī, *Sunan Abī Dāwud*, ed. Shu'ayb al-Arnā'ūṯī (Damascus: Dār al-Risāla al-'Ālamiyya, 2009), 7:68.
39. Abou El Fadl, *Speaking in God's Name*, 222–229; Tuksal, "Misogynistic Reports," 140–148.
40. Abou El Fadl, *Speaking in God's Name*, 229.
41. Muslim ibn al-Ḥajjāj, *Ṣaḥīḥ Muslim*, 1059–1060; Ibn Ḥanbal, *Musnad*, 10:262; al-Bukhārī, *Ṣaḥīḥ*, 1299, 1456; Abī Dāwūd, *Sunan Abī Dāwūd*, ed. Shu'ayb Al- Arnā'ūṯī (Damascus: Dār al-Risāla al-'Ālamiyya, 2009), 6:63–64; al-Nasāʾī, *Kitāb al-Sunan*, 4:315–316.
42. See discussion in Tuksal, "Misogynistic Reports," 148–149.
43. Ibn Qayyim al-Jawziyya, *ʿAwn al-Ma ʿbūd Sharḥ Sunan Abī Dāwud*, ed. ʿAbd al-Raḥmān Muḥammad ʿUthmān (Medina: Muḥammad ʿAbd al-Muḥsin, n.d.), 10:419–420.
44. ʿAbd al-Raḥmān ʿAbd Allāh al-Zarʿī, *Abū Hurayra wa Aqlām Al-Ḥāqidīn* (Kuwait: Dār al-Arqam, 1984), 65–66; Ibn Ḥajar al-ʿAsqalānī, *Fatḥ al-Bārī*, 6:61–62.
45. Muslim ibn al-Ḥajjāj, *Ṣaḥīḥ Muslim*, 510–11; Ibn Ḥanbal, *Musnad*, 35:272; al-Sijistānī, *Sunan Abī Dāwud*, 2009, 6:32. See further discussion in Tuksal, "Misogynistic Reports," 150–152.
46. See discussion in Abou El Fadl, *Speaking in God's Name*, 226–227.
47. Abou El Fadl, *Speaking in God's Name*, 226–227.
48. Muslim ibn al-Ḥajjāj, *Ṣaḥīḥ Muslim*, 232–233; Ibn Ḥanbal, *Musnad*, 41:423; al-Bukhārī, *Ṣaḥīḥ*, 134, 1566–1567.

49. Most of these reports can be found in Muḥammad Ṣadīq Khān al-Qanūjī, *Ḥusn Al-Uswa bi-mā Thabata min Allāh wa Rasūlihi fī al-Niswa* (Beirut: Mu'assasat al-Risāla, 1981), 553–562.
50. Abou El Fadl, *Speaking in God's Name*, 219–220.
51. Abou El Fadl, *Speaking in God's Name*, 220.
52. Ibn al-Jawzī, *Kitāb Aḥkām al-Nisā'*, ed. 'Umar 'Abd al-Mun'im Salīm (Cairo: Maktabat Ibn Taymiyya, 1997), 208–214; 'Alī al-Muttaqī al-Hindī, *Kanz al-'Ummāl fī Sunan al-Āqwāl wa al-Af'āl* (Beirut: Mu'assasat al-Risāla, 1985), 16:337–338; al-Nasā'ī, *Sunan*, 8:253; Ibn Qayyim al-Jawziyya, *'Awn al-Ma'būd*, 6:178.
53. On the prostration *ḥadīth* and its variants, see Abou El Fadl, *Speaking in God's Name*, 210–218.
54. Khaled Abou El Fadl, *And God Knows The Soldiers: The Authoritative and Authoritarian in Islamic Discourses* (Lanham, MD: University Press of America, 2001), 62–66.
55. In the Sunnī tradition, the main *ḥadīth* collections are by al-Bukhārī, Muslim, al-Nasā'i, Abū Dāwūd, al-Tirmidhī, and Ibn Māja.
56. Ahmed, *Women and Gender*, 72.
57. Muhammad Akram Nadwi, *Al-Muḥaddithāt: The Women Scholars in Islam* (London: Interface Publications, 2007), 245–272. Also see, Asma Sayeed, "Shifting Fortunes: Women and *Ḥadīth* Transmission in Islamic history (First to Eighth Centuries)" (PhD diss., Princeton University, 2005).
58. Nadwi, *al-Muḥaddithāt*, 18–22.
59. Sayeed, *Women and the Transmission of Religious Knowledge*, 188. Also see, Asma Sayeed, "Gender and Legal Authority: An Examination of Early Juristic Opposition to Women's Hadīth Transmission," *Islamic Law and Society* 16, no. 2 (2009): 115–150.
60. Nimat Hafez Barazangi, *Woman's Identity and Rethinking the Ḥadīth* (Burlington: Routledge, 2016), 19–27, 160–161.
61. Barazangi, *Woman's Identity*, 7–8.
62. Ahmed, *Women and Gender*, 73.
63. Mernissi, *Veil and The Male Elite*, 25–48.
64. Mernissi, *Veil and The Male Elite*, 49–81.
65. Mernissi, *Veil and The Male Elite*, 85–188.
66. Ahmed, *Women and Gender*, 11–36.
67. Barbara Freyer Stowasser, *Women in the Qur'ān, Traditions, and Interpretation* (New York: Oxford University Press, 1994), 23.
68. Barlas, *Believing Women*, 45; Ahmed, *Women and Gender*, 65–68.
69. Wadud, *Inside the Gender Jihad*, 196–197.
70. Aysha Hidayatullah, "Muslim Feminist Theology in the United States," in *Muslima Theology*, 86–90; Barlas, *Believing Women*, 129, 167; amina wadud, *Qur'ān and Women: Rereading the Sacred Text from a Woman's Perspective* (New York: Oxford University Press, 1999), 62; Kecia Ali, *Sexual Ethics and Islam: Feminist Reflections on Qur'ān, Ḥadīth, and Jurisprudence* (Oxford: Oneworld, 2006). For a detailed study of the thought of amina wadud and Asma Barlas, see Shadaab Rahemtulla, *Qur'an of the Oppressed: Liberation Theology and Gender Justice in Islam* (New York: Oxford University Press, 2017), 96–225.
71. Barlas, *Believing Women*, 20.
72. Rahemtulla, *Qur'an of the Oppressed*, 167–169.
73. Ibid., 190–191.

74. Aysha A. Hidayatullah, *Feminist Edges of the Qur'ān* (Oxford: Oxford University Press, 2014), 81.
75. Barazangi, *Woman's Identity Ḥadīth*, 33–57; Riffat Hassan, "Muslim Women and Post-Patriarchal Islam," in *After Patriarchy: Feminist Transformations of the World Religions*, ed. Paula M. Cooey, William R. Eakin, and Jay Byrd McDaniel (Maryknoll, NY: Orbis Books, 1991), 47; Riffat Hassan, "An Islamic Perspective," in *Women, Religion, and Sexuality: Studies on the Impact of Religious Teachings on Women*, ed. Jeanne Becher (Philadelphia: Trinity Press International, 1991); wadud, *Qur'ān and Women*, x, 1–2; Barlas, *Believing Women*, 9.
76. Wadud, *Inside the Gender Jihad*, 32–48; Hidayatullah, "Muslim Feminist Theology," 94–97.
77. Ali, *Sexual Ethics*, 133.
78. On the complex and many possible meanings of equality, see Douglas W. Rae and Douglas Yates, *Equalities* (Cambridge, MA: Harvard University Press, 1981).
79. For Kecia Ali's criticism of Asma Barlas, see Ali, *Sexual Ethics and Islam*, 116. Also see Rahemtulla, *Qur'an of the Oppressed*, 204–207.
80. Barazangi, *Woman's Identity*, 77–87; Maysam J. al-Faruqi, "Women's Self-Identity in the Qur'ān and Islamic Law," in *Windows of Faith: Muslim Women Scholar-Activists in North America*, ed. Gisela Webb (Syracuse: Syracuse University Press, 2000), 72–101; Aminah Beverly McCloud, "The Scholar and the Fatwa: Legal Issues Facing African-American and Immigrant Muslim Communities in the United States," in *Windows of Faith*, 136–144; Riffat Hassan, "Muslim Feminist Hermeneutics," in *In Our Own Voices: Four Centuries of American Women's Religious Writing*, ed. Rosemary Skinner Keller and Rosemary Radford Ruether (Louisville, KY: Westminster John Knox Press, 2000), 455–459.
81. See for example, Barazangi, *Woman's Identity*, 7.
82. Khaled Abou El Fadl, "What Type of Law Is Islamic Law?," in *Routledge Handbook of Islamic Law*, ed. Khaled Abou El Fadl, Ahmad Atif Ahmad, and Said Fares Hassan (New York: Routledge, 2019), 32.
83. For detailed argument, see Abou El Fadl, *Speaking in God's Name*, 18–69.
84. For this, see, for example, Intisar A. Rabb, *Doubt in Islamic Law: A History of Legal Maxims, Interpretation, and Islamic Criminal Law*, Cambridge Studies in Islamic Civilization (New York: Cambridge University Press, 2015).
85. Qur'ān 4:127.
86. Qur'ān 58:1. For the occasion of the revelation of this verse, see, for example, Seyyed Hossein Nasr et al., *The Study Quran: A New Translation and Commentary* (New York: Harper Collins, 2015), 1342.
87. Ibn Ḥanbal, *Musnad*, 3:426, no 1957.
88. Also see Qur'ān 59:58.
89. On coercion, see Qur'ān 10:99; and for the theology of coercion and oppression in the Qur'ān, see Abou El Fadl, *Reasoning with God*, 382–389.
90. Reasonableness is the effort and ability to negotiate determinations within the framework of accepted cultural norms and socially recognized conceptions of justice. Unreasonable determinations are issued without regard either to their profound and turbulent social and cultural impact or to the internal cohesiveness and systematic application of a system of law. I argue that the necessary values of reasonableness are three: (1) proportionality (*tanāsub*) between means and ends, (2) balance (*tawāzun*) between all valid interests and roles, and (3) measuredness (*talāzum*) in which the processes of law are systematized and rendered both accessible and accountable. See Abou El Fadl, *Reasoning with God*, 52–54.

91. Barlas, *Believing Women*, 210.
92. Khaleel Mohammed, "The Islamic Legal Maxims," *Islamic Studies* 44, no. 2 (Summer 2005), 191–207; Mohammad Hashim Kamali, "Legal Maxims and Other Genres of Literature in Islamic Jurisprudence," *Arab Law Quarterly* 20, no. 1 (Spring 2006): 77–101; Sobhi Mahmassani, *Falsafat al-Tashri' fī al-Islām* (Leiden: E.J. Brill, 1961).

Bibliography

Abou El Fadl, Khaled. *And God Knows The Soldiers: The Authoritative and Authoritarian in Islamic Discourses*. Lanham, MD: University Press of America, 2001.

Abou El Fadl, Khaled. *Reasoning with God: Reclaiming Shari'ah in the Modern Age*. Lanham, MD: Rowman & Littlefield, 2014.

Abou El Fadl, Khaled. *Speaking in God's Name: Islamic Law, Authority and Women*. Oxford: Oneworld, 2010.

Abū Shuqqa, ʿAbd al-Ḥalīm. *Taḥrīr al-Marʾa fī ʿAṣr al-Risāla*. Cairo: Dār al-Qalam, 1999.

Afsaruddin, Asma. "Early Women Exemplars and the Construction of Gendered Space: (Re-) Defining Feminine Moral Excellence." In *Harem Histories: Envisioning Places and Living Space*, edited by Marilyn Booth, 23–48. Durham, NC: Duke University Press, 2010.

Afsaruddin, Asma. "ʿĀʾisha Bint Abī Bakr." In *The Encyclopaedia of Islam*, edited by Kate Fleet et al., 3rd ed., 22–27. Leiden: E.J. Brill, 2010–2011. https://referenceworks-brillonline-com.proxyiub.uits.iu.edu/entries/encyclopaedia-of-islam-3/aisha-bt-abi-bakr-COM_23459?s.num=6&s.f.s2_parent=s.f.book.encyclopaedia-of-islam-3&s.q=afsaruddin.

Ahmed, Leila. *Women and Gender in Islam: Historical Roots of a Modern Debate*. New Haven, CT: Yale University Press, 1992.

Ali, Kecia. *Sexual Ethics and Islam: Feminist Reflections on Qur'an, Hadith, and Jurisprudence*. Oxford: Oneworld, 2006.

Aslan, Ednan. "Early Community Politics and the Marginalization of Women in Islamic Intellectual History." In *Muslima Theology: The Voices of Muslim Women Theologians*, edited by Ednan Aslan and Marcia K. Hermansen, 35–43. Frankfurt am Main: Peter Lang, 2013.

Aslan, Ednan, and Marcia K. Hermansen, eds. *Muslima Theology: The Voices of Muslim Women Theologians*. Frankfurt am Main: Peter Lang, 2013.

ʿAsqalānī, Aḥmad b. al-. *ʿAlī b. Ḥajar, Fatḥ al-Bārī Sharḥ Ṣaḥīḥ al-Bukhārī*. 13 vols. Cairo: al-Maktaba al-Salafiyya, n.d.

ʿAynī, Badr al-Dīn al-. *ʿUmda al-Qārī Sharḥ Ṣaḥīḥ al-Bukhārī*. 25 vols. Beirut: Dār al-Fikr, n.d.

Barazangi, Nimat Hafez. *Woman's Identity and Rethinking the Hadith*. New York: Routledge, 2016.

Barlas, Asma. *Believing Women in Islam: Unreading Patriarchal Interpretations of the Qur'an*. Austin: University of Texas Press, 2002.

Bauer, Karen. *Gender Hierarchy in the Qur'ān: Medieval Interpretations, Modern Responses*. Cambridge: Cambridge University Press, 2015.

Becher, Jeanne. *Women, Religion, and Sexuality: Studies on the Impact of Religious Teachings on Women*. Valley Forge, PA: Trinity Press International, 1991.

Benda-Beckmann, Franz von. *Property in Social Continuity: Continuity and Change in the Maintenance of Property*. N.p.: Springer, 2013.

Bewley, Aisha Abdurrahman. *Muslim Women: A Biographical Dictionary*. London: Ta-Ha, 2004.

Bint al-Shāṭi', 'Ā'isha 'Abd al-Rahmān. *Tarājim Sayyidāt Bayt al-Nubuwwah*. Cairo: Dār al-Rayyān li-Turāth, 1987.

Bourchier, David. *Illiberal Democracy in Indonesia: The Ideology of the Family State*. London and New York: Routledge, 2016.

Bowen, John R. *Islam, Law, and Equality in Indonesia: An Anthropology of Public Reasoning*. Cambridge: Cambridge University Press, 2006.

Brenner, Suzanne April. *The Domestication of Desire Women, Wealth, and Modernity in Java*. Princeton: Princeton University Press, 2012.

Broyde, Michael J. "Hair Covering and Jewish Law: Biblical and Objective (Dat Moshe) or Rabbinic and Subjective (Dat Yehudit)?" *Tradition: A Journal of Orthodox Jewish Thought* 42, no. 3 (2009): 97–179.

Bukhārī, Abī 'Abd Allāh Muḥammad al-. *Ṣaḥīḥ al-Bukhārī*. Beirut: Dār Ibn Kathīr, 2002.

Carrel, Barbara Goldman. "Shattered Vessels That Contain Divine Sparks: Unveiling Hasidic Women's Dress Code." In *The Veil: Women Writers on Its History, Lore and Politics*, edited by Jennifer Heath, 44–59. Berkeley: University of California Press, 2008.

Cooey, Paula M., William R. Eakin, and Jay Byrd McDaniel, eds. *After Patriarchy: Feminist Transformations of the World Religions*. Maryknoll, NY: Orbis Books, 1991.

Fadel, Mohammad. "Is Historicism a Viable Strategy for Islamic Law Reform? The Case of 'Never Shall a Folk Prosper Who Have Appointed a Woman to Rule Them.'" *Islamic Law and Society* 18, no. 2 (January 1, 2011): 131–176.

Farah, Nuruddin. *From a Crooked Rib*. London: Heinemann Educational, 1970.

Faruki, Maysam J. al-. "Women's Self-Identity in the Qur'an and Islamic Law." In *Windows of Faith: Muslim Women Scholar-Activists in North America*, edited by Gisela Webb, 72–101. Syracuse: Syracuse University Press, 2000.

Halevi, Leor. "Wailing for the Dead: The Role of Women in Early Islamic Funerals." *Past and Present*, no. 183 (May 2004): 3–39.

Ḥanbal, Aḥmad b. *Musnad Imām Aḥmad Bin Ḥanbal*. Edited by Muḥammad Ẓafar Iqbāl. Al-Ghāt: Maktaba Raḥmānīya, n.d.

Hassan, Riffat. "An Islamic Perspective." In *Women, Religion, and Sexuality: Studies on the Impact of Religious Teachings on Women*, edited by Jeanne Becher, 93–128. Philadelphia: Trinity Press International, 1991.

Hassan, Riffat. "Feminist Theology: The Challenges for Muslim Women." *Critique: Journal for Critical Studies in the Middle East* 5, no. 9 (1996): 53–63.

Hassan, Riffat. "Muslim Feminist Hermeneutics." In *In Our Own Voices: Four Centuries of American Women's Religious Writing*, edited by Rosemary Skinner Keller and Rosemary Radford Ruether, 455–459. Louisville, KY: Westminster John Knox Press, 2000.

Hassan, Riffat. "Muslim Women and Post-Patriarchal Islam." In *After Patriarchy: Feminist Transformations of the World Religions*, edited by Paula M. Cooey, William R. Eakin, and Jay Byrd McDaniel, 39–64. Maryknoll, NY: Orbis Books, 1991.

Haylamaz, Resit. *Aisha: The Wife, The Companion, The Scholar*. Clifton, NJ: Tughra Books, 2014.

Heath, Jennifer. *The Scimitar and the Veil: Extraordinary Women of Islam*. Mahwah, NJ: Hidden Spring, 2004.

Hidayatullah, Aysha. "Muslim Feminist Theology in the United States." In *Muslima Theology: The Voices of Muslim Women Theologians*, edited by Ednan Aslan and Marcia K. Hermansen, 81–100. Frankfurt am Main: Peter Lang, 2013.

Hidayatullah, Aysha A. *Feminist Edges of the Qur'an*. Oxford: Oxford University Press, 2014.

Hindī, ʿAlaʾ al-Dīn ʿAlī al-Muttaqī al-. *Kanz al-ʿUmmāl fi Sunan al-Aqwāl wa al-Afʿāl*. Vol. 16. Beirut: Mu'assasat al-Risāla, 1985.

Hussain, Freda. *Muslim Women*. London and New York: Routledge, 2016.

Ibn al-Jawzī. *Kitāb Aḥkām Al-Nisāʾ*. Edited by ʿUmar ʿAbd al-Munʿim Salīm. Cairo: Maktabat Ibn Taymiyya, 1997.

Ibn Ḥajar al-ʿAsqalānī. *Fatḥ al-Bārī Sharḥ Ṣaḥīḥ al-Bukhārī*. Cairo: al-Maktaba al-Salafiyya, n.d.

Ibn Ḥanbal, Aḥmad. *Musnad al-Imām Aḥmad Ibn Ḥanbal*. Edited by Shu'ayb al- Arnā'ūṭī. Beirut: Mu'assasat al-Risāla, 1996.

Ibn Māja, Abū ʿAbd Allāh Muḥammad b. Yazīd. *Sunan Ibn Māja*. Edited by Rāʾid b. Ṣabr Abī ʿAlafa. Riyaḍ: Dār al-Ḥaḍāra, 2015.

Ibn Sa'd, Abū ʿAbd Allāh Muḥammad. *Kitāb al-Ṭabaqāt al-Kabīr*, edited by ʿAlī Muḥammad ʿAmr. 11 vols. Cairo: Maktabat al-Khānjī, 2001.

Iṣfahānī, Abū al-Faraj al-. *Kitāb al-Aghānī*. 24 vols. Edited by Iḥsān ʿAbbās, Ibrāhīm al-Sa'āfīn, and Bakr ʿAbbās. Beirut: Dār Sādir, 2008.

Jawziyya, Ibn Qayyim al-. *ʿAwn al-Ma'būd Sharḥ Sunan Abī Dāwud*. Edited by ʿAbd al-Raḥmān Muḥammad ʿUthmān. Medina: Muḥammad ʿAbd al-Muḥsin, n.d.

Kaḥḥāla, ʿUmar Riḍā. *A'lām Al-Nisāʾ fī ʿĀlamī al-ʿArabi wa al-Islām*. 5 vols. Beirut: Mu'assasat al-Risāla, 1959.

Kamali, Mohammad Hashim. "Legal Maxims and Other Genres of Literatures in Islamic Jurisprudence." *Arab Law Quarterly* 20, no. 1 (Spring 2006): 77–101.

Koehler, Benedikt. "Female Entrepreneurship in Early Islam." *Economic Affairs* 31, no. 2 (June 2011): 93–95.

Lamrabet, Asma. *Women in the Qur'an: An Emancipatory Reading*. Cambridge, MA.: Porter Square Books, 2016.

Mahmassani, Sobhi. *The Philosophy of Jurisprudence in Islam*. Leiden: E.J. Brill, 1961.

Māwardī, Abū al-Ḥasan al-. *Al-Nukat wa al-ʿUyūn: Tafsīr al-Māwardī*. 6 vols. Beirut: Dār al-Kutub al-ʿIlmiyya, n.d.

McCloud, Aminah Beverly. "The Scholar and the Fatwa: Legal Issues Facing African-American and Immigrant Muslim Communities in the United States." In *Windows of Faith: Muslim Women Scholar-Activists in North America*, edited by Gisela Webb, 136–144. Syracuse: Syracuse University Press, 2000.

Mernissi, Fatima. *The Veil and The Male Elite: A Feminist Interpretation of Women's Rights in Islam*. Translated by Mary Jo Lakeland. New York: Basic Books, 1991.

Mohammed, Khaleel. "The Islamic Legal Maxims." *Islamic Studies* 44, no. 2 (Summer 2005): 191–207.

Muslim ibn al-Ḥajjāj al-Naysābūrī. *Ṣaḥīḥ Muslim*. Riyaḍ: Dār Ṭayba, 2006.

Myrne, Pernilla. *Female Sexuality in the Early Medieval Islamic World: Gender and Sex in Arabic Literature*. New York: Bloomsbury Publishing, 2019.

Nadwi, Muhammad Akram. *Al-Muḥaddithāt: The Women Scholars in Islam*. London: Interface Publications, 2007.

Nasāʾī, Abī ʿAbd al-Raḥmān Aḥmad b. Shuʿayb al-. *Kitāb al-Sunan al-Kubrā*. Beirut: Mu'assasat al-Risāla, 2001.

Nasāʾī, Abī ʿAbd al-Raḥmān Aḥmad b. Shuʿayb al-. *Kitāb 'Ishrat al-Nisāʾ*. Cairo: Maktabat al-Sunna, 1998.

Odinye, Ifeoma Einne. "Violence against Girls: A Feminist Perspective on Nuruddin Farah's From a Crooked Rib." *Journal of Linguistics, Language and Culture* 6, no. 1 (Spring 2019): 113–139.
Qanūjī, Muḥammad Ṣadīq Khān al-. *Ḥusn al-Uswa bi-mā Thabata min Allāh wa Rasūlihi fī al-Niswa*. Beirut: Mu'assasat al-Risāla, 1981.
Qurṭubī, Abū ʿAbd Allāh Muḥammad al-. *Al-Jāmiʿ al-Aḥkām al-Qurʾān*. 24 vols. Edited by ʿAbd Allāh ʿAbd al-Muḥsīn al-Turkī. Beirut: Mu'assasat al-Risāla, 2006.
Rae, Douglas W., and Douglas Yates. *Equalities*. Cambridge, MA: Harvard University Press, 1981.
Rahemtulla, Shadaab. *Qur'an of the Oppressed: Liberation Theology and Gender Justice in Islam*. New York: Oxford University Press, 2017.
Ramli, Mohd Anuar, Shahidra Abdul Khalil, Mohammad Aizat Jamaludin, Saadan Man, Ahmad Badri Abdullah, and Mohd Roslan Mohd Nor. "Muslim Exegeses (sic) Perspective on Creation of the First Woman: A Brief Discussion." *Middle-East Journal of Scientific Research* 13, no. 1 (Spring 2013): 41–44.
Rāzī, Fakhr al-Dīn al-, *Tafsīr al-Fakhr al-Rāzī*. 31 vols. Beirut: Dār al-Fikr, 1981.
Roded, Ruth. "Umm Salama Hind." In *The Encyclopaedia of Islam*, edited by P. J Bearman, Th. Bianquis, C. E. Bosworth, E. van Donzel, and W. P. Heinrichs, 10:856. Leiden: E.J. Brill, 2000.
Safi, Omid. *Progressive Muslims: On Justice, Gender and Pluralism*. Oxford: Oneworld, 2006.
Salim, Muḥammad Ibrāhim. *Nisāʾ Ḥawl al-Rasūl*. Cairo: Maktaba ibn Sinā, 1990.
Sayeed, Asma. "Gender and Legal Authority: An Examination of Early Juristic Opposition to Women's Hadīth Transmission." *Islamic Law and Society* 16, no. 2 (2009): 115–150.
Sayeed, Asma. "Shifting Fortunate: Women and Hadith Transmission in Islamic History (First to Eighth Centuries)." PhD diss., Princeton University, 2005.
Sayeed, Asma. *Women and the Transmission of Religious Knowledge in Islam*. Cambridge University Press, 2013.
Schwartz, Joshua. "Hair's the Thing: Women's Hairstyle and Care in Ancient Jewish Society." In *Strength to Strength: Essays in Honor of Shaye J. D. Cohen*, edited by Michael L. Satlow, 341–358. Atlanta: Society of Biblical Literature, 2018.
Shīrāzī, Ṣadr al-Dīn Muḥammad. *Ittiḥād al-ʿĀqil wa al-Maʿqūl*. Baghdad: Dār al-Mada, 2004.
Sijistānī, Abī Dāwud al-. *Sunan Abī Dāwud*. Edited by Shu'ayb al-Arnuʿūṭ. Damascus: Dār al-Risāla al-ʿĀlamiyya, 2009.
Spellberg, Denise A. *Politics, Gender, and the Islamic Past: The Legacy of ʿAʾisha Bint Abi Bakr*. New York: Columbia University Press, 1994.
Stowasser, Barbara Freyer. "The Status of Women in Early Islam." In *Muslim Women*, edited by Freda Hussain, 11–43. London and New York: Routledge, 2016.
Stowasser, Barbara Freyer. *Women in the Qur'an, Traditions, and Interpretation*. New York: Oxford University Press, 1994.
Ṭabarī, Muḥammad b. Jarīr al-. *Tafsīr al-Ṭabarī Jāmiʿ al-Bayān ʿan Taʾwīl Ayy al-Qurʾān*. 25 vols. Vol. 19. Edited by ʿAbd Allāh ʿAbd al-Muḥsīn al-Turkī. Cairo: Dār Hijr, 2001.
Tuksal, Hideyat Sefkatli. "Misogynistic Reports in the Hadith Literature." In *Muslima Theology: The Voices of Muslim Women Theologians*, edited by Ednan Aslan and Marcia K. Hermansen, 133–154. Frankfurt am Main: Peter Lang, 2013.
Wadud, amina. *Inside the Gender Jihad: Women's Reform in Islam*. Simon and Schuster, 2013.

Wadud, amina. *Qur'an and Women: Rereading the Sacred Text from a Woman's Perspective*. New York: Oxford University Press, 1999.

Watt, W. Montgomery. "ʿĀʾisha Bint Abī Bakr." In *The Encyclopaedia of Islam*, edited by H. A. R Gibb, E. Levi-Provencal, and Joseph Schacht, 1:307–308. Leiden: E.J. Brill, 2000.

Webb, Gisela, ed. *Windows of Faith: Muslim Women Scholar-Activists in North America*. Syracuse: Syracuse University Press, 2000.

Weiss, Susan. "Under Cover: Demystification of Women's Head Covering in Jewish Law." *Nashim: A Journal of Jewish Women's Studies and Gender Issues*, no. 17 (2009): 89–115.

Zarʿī, ʿAbd al-Raḥmān ʿAbd Allāh al-. *Abū Hurayra Wa Aqlām Al-Ḥāqidīn*. Kuwait: Dār al-Arqam, 1984.

C

WOMEN AND ISLAMIC LAW

The Qur'ān and the *sunna*, the two most important sources of Islamic legislation, were interpreted in particular ways in specific sociohistorical circumstances by male legal scholars. Such scholars also resorted to analogical reasoning (*qiyās*), which became an important source of legislation, in addition to *ijmā'* or juridical consensus on key legal issues. Jurists further took into consideration local custom and practices (*'āda/'urf*) and, increasingly, notions of *maṣlaḥa*, or "public benefit/common good." Legal rulings (*aḥkām*) were always articulated through a constant process of negotiation between scriptural prescriptions and their variegated interpretations, on the one hand, and the specific sociopolitical contexts as well as notions of the common good, on the other, that allowed for a healthy measure of pragmatism in the implementation of such rulings. This juridical propensity allowed for what may be termed "legal pluralism" to flourish, certainly in the formative period, that mitigated doctrinal dogmatism and allowed for multiple and what were deemed to be equally valid legal perspectives to emerge on a number of critical issues. This becomes strongly evident when we look particularly at legal responsa (*fatāwā*; sing. *fatwā*) and court records from the classical period that document considerable legal flexibility in the application of specific legal rulings.

The flurry of juridical activity, starting already in the second/eighth century, resulted in an influential juridical corpus that increasingly dealt in a detailed manner with women's legal status, which began to crystallize by the fourth/tenth century when formal schools of law began to take shape. Many of these classical views formulated in distinctive sociohistorical circumstances in the premodern period have remained influential until today, and such legal texts continue to hold sway in Muslim-majority societies, understood to contain authoritative prescriptions for the ordering of proper gender relations and roles in society. In the realm of personal and family law, these prescriptions with some modifications have become codified as part of modern constitutional law in contemporary Muslim nation-states.

This section discusses women's rights and obligations in classical legal literature, especially as they pertain to marriage, divorce, and inheritance issues, in the four principal

Sunnī *madhāhib* (legal schools): Ḥanafī, Mālikī, Shāfiʿī, and Ḥanbalī, as well as in the Twelver Shīʿī (Imāmī/Jaʿfarī) legal school. These legal articulations continue to influence modern conceptualizations of women's rights and duties in contemporary Muslim-majority societies, as codified in modern legal texts under the rubric of Islamic Family Law. An account of modern Muslim women scholars rereading and engaging classical legal texts, often in a highly critical vein, is also included in this section. While such rereadings have begun to spur animated debates and instigate legal reform in a modest number of Muslim-majority countries included within the Organization of Islamic Cooperation (OIC), in others they provoke considerable anxiety in the challenges they pose to the legal status quo, and thereby invite considerable pushback and outright resistance.

CHAPTER 6

MARRIAGE, DIVORCE, AND INHERITANCE IN CLASSICAL ISLAMIC LAW AND PREMODERN PRACTICE

MARIAM SHEIBANI

THIS chapter provides a broad overview of premodern juridical perspectives (from the second/eighth to twelfth/eighteenth century) on women's rights and obligations as they pertain to marriage, divorce, and inheritance. Legal doctrines on these topics are deeply gendered and provide differing obligations and entitlements for men and women. This chapter discusses some of the rationales for these differentiated rules by exploring their scriptural foundations, underlying assumptions, and animating legal logic. The chapter equally endeavors to draw out the differences of opinion about these rules as they exist among the four Sunnī schools of law (Ḥanafī, Mālikī, Shāfiʿī, and Ḥanbalī) and the Twelver Shīʿī (Imāmī; also known as Jaʿfarī) legal tradition.[1] While this study centers on substantive legal doctrines (*furūʿ al-fiqh*), it is important to bear in mind two points about what such a study reveals and what it conceals about women's quotidian lives in premodern societies and their encounters with the law as social and institutional practice.

First, the formal rules encountered in legal manuals are generally prescriptive rather than descriptive accounts of women's lives in premodern Muslim societies. These doctrinal rules are elaborated in specialized handbooks and commentaries intended for the training and consultation of legal professionals who were educated in a particular way of asking questions and interpreting answers, not unlike lawyers, judges, and law professors today. In contrast, legal practice in premodern Islam negotiated the law's formal rules with varied sociocultural customs. Drawing on court records, legal responsa (*fatāwā*; sing. *fatwā*), notarial manuals, and other historical sources, historians of diverse Muslim societies have shown how legal procedures and social strategies around marriage, divorce, and inheritance accommodated, circumvented, and interfered with the application of formal legal rules. To provide a more historically accurate picture, this chapter will examine doctrinal rules alongside legal practice as a window onto how Muslims have interpreted and at times reshaped Islamic legal norms in response to changing sociohistorical conditions.

Second, while Islamic law is a normative discourse that is central to Muslim practice, it is not univocal in its prescriptions, nor is it the only normative discourse governing Muslim life. As this chapter demonstrates, there are often a variety of views among, and even within, the legal schools concerning marriage, divorce, and inheritance. Furthermore, while Islamic law makes a moral claim as a representation of the Divine Will, Islamic law is not the only normative discourse governing behavior and thus women's experience in family life. Jurists themselves acknowledged that legal obligations did not necessarily represent religious ideals or the virtuous behavior of spouses within a functioning marriage; they recognized that other moral obligations existed beyond those enforceable in court that were in keeping with the exemplary model (*Sunna*) of the Prophet Muḥammad, and thus were in the domain of religion and morality rather than law, as will be discussed below. This meant that legal obligations could sit alongside, or even contradict, a religious duty or moral imperative. In premodern Muslim discourse, Islamic law operated alongside other ethicoreligious discourses that articulated alternative ideals and values for human conduct, such as Sufism, philosophical ethics (*akhlāq*), *zuhd* literature, and commentaries on the Prophet Muḥammad's exemplary conduct (*sunna*) and characteristics (*shamāʾil*).

With these two considerations in mind—the ongoing negotiation between formal rules and legal practice, on the one hand, and between law and morality, on the other—this chapter will examine how Islamic law's marital claims, divorce procedures, and rules for the transmission of property sat at the intersection of a complex web of social customs, judicially enforceable legal norms debated among the legal schools, and nonlitigable moral and religious duties.

Marriage

The Marital Contract: The Bride's Guardian and Her Consent

Many of the rights and obligations impacting women's lives are triggered by entering into a contract of marriage.[2] Jurists differed on the precise conditions for the validity of the marriage contract, though elements considered essential or strongly recommended by all jurists include the consent of both parties, a marriage guardian (*walī*) for the bride, the spoken contract, a dower gifted by the husband to the wife, two witnesses attesting to the union, and public proclamation of the marriage.[3]

Of these conditions, worthy of note here is the bride's consent to her marriage and the role of her guardian (*walī*) in compelling her marriage. According to all legal schools, fathers can marry off their minor children, girls and boys, without requiring their consent.[4] According to Shāfiʿīs, Mālikīs, and some Ḥanbalīs, this prerogative persists for virgin girls who reach majority. Jurists from these three schools consider the guardian's involvement necessary for a previously unmarried woman's marriage, on the basis of such statements of the Prophet Muḥammad as "There is no marriage without a guardian" and "The marriage of any woman who marries without a guardian is void." However, they consider the guardian's consultation with the bride and her approval a moral imperative that is highly recommended (*mandūb*), albeit not necessary for the contract's legal validity. In contrast, the non-virgin female who reaches majority has to articulate her spoken consent to a marriage. This distinction between the virgin and non-virgin is based on the report in which the Prophet Muḥammad instructed, "The non-virgin is not married until her permission is sought, and the virgin until she is consulted." Someone objected: "The virgin is shy." He replied: "Her permission is her silence."[5]

Jurists nonetheless stipulate safeguards to ensure that a marriage chosen or compelled by the guardian is in the bride's best interest. For the minor child, the Mālikīs and Ḥanbalīs allow only the father to contract his or her marriage, to which the Shāfiʿīs add the paternal grandfather, thereby excluding any other male member of the child's agnatic kin to whom guardianship would devolve from marrying off the minor child. The rationale they offer is that only the fullness of a father's loving care (*shafaqa*) can be counted on to tend to the child's best interest.[6] Jurists further stipulate that the guardian marry his ward to a suitable mate (*kuf*) and that there be no enmity between the bride and the guardian.[7] A woman whose guardian refuses to marry her to a suitable groom of her choice can seek to have a more distant guardian marry her according to the Ḥanbalīs, or have a judge intervene on her behalf, with the judge potentially serving as marriage guardian himself according to all three schools.[8] Court records show that women sometimes registered their opposition to a marriage contracted for them by their fathers without their consent in the court's communal record, or sought a dissolution of a marriage arranged for them on the basis of it not being suitable or desirable to them.[9]

In opposition to this majority juristic view, the dominant opinion in the Ḥanafī and Imāmī Twelver Shīʿī schools is that a female who has attained majority can marry independently without the permission of a guardian, regardless of whether she was previously married, and she may contract her own marriage just as she freely concludes financial contracts. Nonetheless, they deem it recommended that she ask her father's permission and appoint him, or another close male relative if he is deceased, as her agent for the contract.[10] Ḥanafī jurists further place limitations on a woman's autonomy by allowing her guardian to dissolve her marriage through judicial intervention if she marries an unsuitable groom inferior to her in lineage or socioeconomic status (*kafāʾa*).[11] Ḥanafī practice could be even more restrictive: A tenth/sixteenth-century Ottoman sultanic order put in force a minority view within the Ḥanafī school that prohibited women from concluding a marriage without a guardian's consent, apparently aimed at imposing greater familial control over women and buttressing existing mufti practice.[12]

Legal Consequences: Marital Rights and Obligations

In Islamic law, marriage is treated as a contract of exchange that entails a number of legal consequences. Jurists generally framed the exchange effectuated by the marriage contract as lawful sexual access to the wife for the husband's dower, and her continued sexual availability for his material support.[13] The contract further entails benefits shared by both spouses: it makes sex licit, establishes the husband's paternity of any children his wife bears, introduces mutual rights of inheritance, and obligates each spouse to treat the other well. In addition to these shared duties and benefits, marriage gives rise to a range of gender-differentiated but interconnected claims (*ḥuqūq*, sing. *ḥaqq*) in which the obligations of the husband are the rights of his wife, and vice versa.

The wife's rights, which correspond to the husband's duties, are first and foremost material support in the form of the dower and maintenance. The dower (*mahr* or *ṣadāq*) is a marriage gift pledged by the groom at the time of the marriage contract and gifted to the bride rather than her family.[14] Maintenance (*nafaqa*) is the husband's primary duty during marriage, which consists of providing his wife with food, clothing, and lodging. The legal schools differ concerning the details of what is included in maintenance, when it begins, conditions for its suspension and cessation (e.g., what happens if the wife leaves the marital bed or home), the consequences if the husband neglects to provide maintenance, and how her entitlement varies based on her status and/or his means.[15] Jurists equally debate the wife's entitlement to receive domestic help. Sunni and Shīʿī jurists obligate the husband to provide a wife who is accustomed to being served with domestic help or to serve her himself.[16] Marital support is owed to the wife regardless of her need or her husband's ability to pay, unlike other dependents, like children, parents, and distant relatives, for whom financial support was contingent on their need.[17]

Social historians have shown the diverse ways that Muslims at times incorporated local traditions into legal practices, some of which enabled women to leverage their financial entitlements to gain economic independence and power in their marriages. One area of negotiation from early Islamic times was the dower. While Islamic law only requires that the husband give his bride a dower, Muslims in early Islamic Egypt absorbed the local Near Eastern practice of dividing the dower into immediate and deferred portions, which was incorporated into Islamic legal discourse, despite early objections by some jurists.[18] In second/eighth-century Egypt, it was customary practice for the advanced portion of the dower to be paid when the marriage contract was concluded, while payment of the deferred portion, usually equal to or greater than the advanced portion, was paid on a fixed date or upon divorce or death of the husband.[19] These practices persisted in the Mamluk period, when the deferred portion was commonly divided into yearly installments, to which was added a portion of the dower designated as due debt (*ḥāll*), or payable upon demand, which allowed the wife to request payment at any time during the marriage, and if the husband refused to pay, the judge would send him to jail.[20]

As Yossef Rapoport shows, the obligation of maintenance also underwent significant change during the Mamluk period. Up to the end of the seventh/thirteenth century, husbands supported their wives by buying food in the market—quite literally by putting food on the table. During the eighth/fourteenth century, this norm gradually gave way to marital support being paid as a variety of cash payments: a daily cash allowance to their wives for sustenance and annual payments for clothing. The routinization of cash payments and allowances made it such that

> a fifteenth-century husband would have usually owed his wife the deferred part of the marriage gift, an annual payment for her clothing, a daily allowance, and perhaps the rent for living in her house. In addition, she may have been entitled to demand a due portion of the marriage gift at any point during the marriage.[21]

The cumulative effect of these formalized social customs, which Rapoport aptly describes as "the monetization of marriage," was to empower the wife in the relationship and to make it difficult for men to initiate a unilateral divorce (*ṭalāq*) because they would be required to immediately repay all of their debts to their wives. The prominent medieval jurist Ibn al-Qayyim (d. 751/1350) bemoans the resultant inversion of power in marital relationships in the following way:

> Only God knows how much evil and corruption have spread since women were given the power to demand the deferred portions of their marriage gift, and to cause the imprisonment of their husbands. If a husband scolds his wife for her housekeeping, or prevents her from stepping out or leaving his house, or does not let her go wherever she wishes, the wife then demands her marriage gift. The husband is sent to prison, while she goes wherever she wants. The husband is writhing and wriggling in jail, while she spends the night wherever she pleases.[22]

In addition to her right to financial maintenance, the wife also has sexual rights, which translate into a corresponding duty on her husband to keep her sexually satisfied. This religious duty finds its basis in *ḥadīth*, such as the report in which the Prophet Muḥammad exhorts a Companion, "Your wife has a right over you," and another in which he counsels husbands "not to fall upon their wives like beasts," but rather to send "an emissary" prior to the sexual act. When questioned, Muḥammad clarified that this "messenger" was foreplay, or "kissing and conversation."[23] The implications of these exhortations were elaborated in religious and literary sources that stress men's responsibility for making their wives' sexual experiences pleasurable, emphasizing foreplay to ensure readiness for penetration and prolonged stimulation to ensure that she attains climax.[24]

Scholarly consensus upholds the husband's moral duty to provide his wife with ongoing sexual enjoyment, and some jurists recommend that men have intercourse with their wives once every four nights and mandate that they do so at least once every four or six months.[25] However, enforcement mechanisms for these directives are scarce, and jurists generally did not entitle a wife to dissolve her marriage on grounds of sexual dissatisfaction if the husband had consummated the marriage.[26] In other words, as a legal right, juristic analysis of women's sexual rights was limited to court-enforceable claims that entitle her to have her marriage annulled through judicial intervention. For instance, if the husband is impotent or fails to consummate the marriage, jurists concur that a wife can have her marriage dissolved.[27] However, in practice, a wife whose husband left her sexually unfulfilled either because of a long absence or some physical impediment could appeal to the courts to have her marriage annulled, to which judges would typically oblige because mutual sexual enjoyment was understood to be a primary purpose of marriage.[28] Related to the wife's right to sexual enjoyment is her right to progeny. Most jurists held that a wife must consent to the use of coitus interruptus as a method of birth control as it can interfere with both her pleasure and her right to offspring.[29]

Unrelated to and separate from the wife's right to sexual satisfaction and progeny is a claim the wife has on her husband for companionship. As a legal entitlement, this right is primarily discussed in relation to the division of time between co-wives (*qasam*). Most jurists apportion each wife an equal share of the husband's time, regardless of whether that time entails sexual contact or not,[30] while Twelver Shīʿī jurists allow the husband a certain amount of discretion once each wife receives a minimum of one in four nights.[31] Finally, a wife has a right to good treatment (*maʿrūf*) beyond the basic fulfillment of her material needs, which entails amicable and honorable dealings and not being subject to injury or oppression.[32]

In exchange for financial maintenance, the husband's primary legal claim in marriage is to derive sexual enjoyment from his wife. The husband's right to sexual intimacy is considered unrestricted, meaning that he can demand sex whenever he wants, so long as he does not harm his wife or prevent her from her religious duties, and that he avoid penetration during menstruation. This far-reaching husbandly claim finds its basis in Prophetic reports that tie a wife's fulfillment of sexual duties toward her husband to divine approval, such as the Prophet's statement, "By Him in Whose Hand is my soul, when a man calls his wife to his bed, and she does not respond, the One Who is in the heaven is displeased with her until he (her husband) is pleased with her."[33] Admonitions like these toward the wife found their counterpart in the Prophet's exhortations directed at the husband to ensure that he make sexual intimacy enjoyable to the wife (e.g., "send forth an emissary," as referred to in text above) and that he treat her well: "The best of you is he who is best to his family."[34]

The husband's right to sexual enjoyment translates into a duty on the wife to make herself sexually available to her husband. It is also linked to her claim for maintenance, which some jurists consider compensation for the opportunity cost of her constant availability, analogizing it to the wages paid to the tax collector or the judge for the time they spend in public service that prevents them from earning an independent income.[35] Refusing her husband sexual intimacy is, according to most jurists, grounds for suspension of marital support, though the Ḥanafīs maintain that so long as the wife remains in the marital home, her husband is obliged to support her even if she refuses him sex.[36] The husband's right to sexual enjoyment of his wife frames many of his secondary prerogatives, such as taking her with him when he travels and the stipulation that she seek his permission to leave the marital home or to fast a supererogatory fast.[37] These prerogatives are further reinforced by the wife's general duty of obedience to her husband in all matters that do not harm her and do not conflict with her religious and broader familial duties.[38] To mitigate these husbandly privileges, in many Muslim societies women customarily included conditions in their marital contracts to ensure that they maintained certain freedoms of mobility and association, such as the allowance to visit their family and neighbors and entertain their visits, and a guarantee that they would not be compelled to move from the city in which they resided when they married.

Jurists debate whether the wife is obligated to perform domestic service or nurse her offspring, with the majority holding that she did not have a legal obligation to undertake these duties—even if some affirm them as a moral, religious, or social obligation.[39] In terms of legal obligation, Shāfiʿī, Ḥanbalī, and some Mālikī jurists consider it nonobligatory for wives to undertake household chores or to nurse her offspring. Some jurists even affirm that a wife can validly contract to receive wages from her husband for her domestic labor or to nurse their children.[40] The role of social class and custom are most evident in the dominant Mālikī view, which obligates the wife to undertake domestic service only if her husband is poor or if she belongs to a nonelite class for whom domestic labor is customary.[41] While contesting domestic labor as a universal legal obligation on women, early Mālikīs are nonetheless committed to it as a moral or a social obligation for nonelite women, albeit one that is not enforceable in court.[42] Similarly, although Ḥanafī jurists do not consider the wife's domestic labor to be a legal obligation, they consider it a non-compulsory or unenforceable religious obligation.[43] Thus, while jurists routinely distinguish between the legal parameters of the marriage contract (which did not require wives to do housework) and the religious ideals or social customs of wifely conduct (which did), the latter are more fully treated in other discourses, such as *zuhd*, Sufism, and philosophical ethics, even if they are at times mentioned in legal writings.[44]

Jurists deliberate nonfulfillment of marital rights through the lens of the Qur'ānic doctrine of ill-conduct (*nushūz*), discussed as it pertains to the wife in Qur'ān 4:34 and to the husband in Qur'ān 4:128. Ill-conduct amounts to behavior on the part of either spouse that violates or fails to fulfill the rights of the other. Ill-conduct arising from the wife consists of refusing her husband sexual intercourse, leaving the marital home, or some other gross disobedience or rebelliousness. Such ill-conduct on the part of the wife gives rise to a husband's right to discipline his wife according to an ascending scale set out in Qur'ān 4:34, first by admonishing her, then suspending conjugal relations, and finally applying mild physical punishment.[45] As noted above, jurists also debate whether her ill-conduct entails a suspension of financial maintenance, particularly if the wife left the marital home. The *nushūz* of the husband towards his wife comprises behavior that violates her rights, such as harming her, treating her badly, physically abusing her, or failing to fulfill any of her rights such as financial maintenance or sexual intercourse.

However, as the subordinate party in the relationship, the wife's recourse is by appeal to a judge to admonish her husband and to compel him to fulfill her rights or to cease harming her. The judge is empowered to punish him physically as a discretionary punishment (*taʿzīr*), separate between them, or oblige the husband to relocate next to a court-appointed agent who can supervise him and prevent him from harming his wife.[46] It is in the context of ill-conduct on the part of the husband toward the wife that the Qur'ān discusses a wife seeking separation from her husband (Qur'ān 4:128), the topic to which we now turn.

Divorce

The Sunnī and Twelver Shīʿī schools of law recognize three types of divorce: (1) Unilateral repudiation by the husband (*ṭalāq*), (2) Consensual separation (*khulʿ*), and (3) judicial divorce for cause (referred to variously as *faskh*, *firāq*, and *taṭlīq*). This section first analyzes the legal doctrine and practice of *ṭalāq* as the exclusive prerogative of the husband, then turns to three procedures that the wife can pursue to end her marriage: delegated *ṭalāq* from the husband or through stipulation in her marriage contract, consensual separation, and judicial divorce. The overview of substantive doctrines will be supplemented by a discussion of divorce procedures in practice in such diverse societies as eighth/fourteenth century Egypt and North Africa, ninth/fifteenth century Spain, tenth/sixteenth century Palestine and Syria, and twelfth/eighteenth century Ottoman Istanbul and the Balkans.

Regardless of how a divorce is initiated, a number of consequences ensue upon the dissolution of the marital bond. The wife is entitled to maintenance during the waiting period (*nafaqat al-ʿidda*) lasting three menstrual cycles if she remains in her marital home (Qur'ān 65:1) unless she waives this maintenance as part of her *khulʿ* compensation.[47] Property in the marital home is considered separate; each spouse retains ownership of the property he or she acquired before or during the marriage. As for child custody, the wife obtains custody of children (*ḥaḍāna*), or their nurture, while the father retains guardianship (*wilāya*), or care for their education, discipline, and general acculturation.[48] The mother's legal custody ends when children reach a particular age, at which point they live with their father. The legal schools differ concerning the age at which the mother's custody ends: for Ḥanafīs, at age seven for boys and puberty for girls; for Mālikīs, at puberty for boys and upon marrying for girls; for Ḥanbalīs and Shāfiʿīs, children remain in the mother's custody until they reach the age of discernment (*rushd*) when they choose the parent with whom they wish to reside; and for Imāmī Shīʿīs, custody ends at two years for boys and seven years for girls.[49] However, if a mother remarries before her children reach these ages, custody rights are typically transferred to her mother or another female relative, such as the father's mother. As we will see, maintenance during the waiting period and child custody were among the issues informally negotiated in the most common type of divorce in medieval Islam: consensual separation.

Ṭalāq-Divorce

According to Islamic law, unilateral repudiation (*ṭalāq*, literally "releasing") was a discretionary right granted to the husband alone to unilaterally end his marriage, requiring neither cause nor the consent of the wife or a judge. In Sunnī law, the husband pronounces a declaration of divorce three times, such as "I divorce you," or a similar pronouncement of one of several divorce formulae accepted by jurists, typically done out of court.[50] Shīʿī law, in contrast, requires the presence of witnesses and that the formula take a specific and fairly unambiguous form.[51]

Ṭalāq-divorce was sanctioned in the Qur'ān in verses that both set out its legal procedures, coupled with strong moral admonition to men undertaking divorce to fear God and be mindful of their duty before Him by treating their wives honorably throughout the process of divorce (e.g., Qur'ān 65). The Qur'ān introduced a number of procedures meant to protect a woman from abandonment and to establish the paternity of any unborn children should she be pregnant. Foremost of these is the waiting period (*ʿidda*), an interval that begins as soon as the husband pronounces the divorce and during which he must continue to provide for her. The waiting period also presents an opportunity for the couple to be reconciled; the husband can revoke the *ṭalāq* during the waiting period if he has regrets (Qur'ān 2:228; 2:234; 33:49; 65:4).[52] However, he can only do this twice: "Divorce must be pronounced twice and then (a woman) must be retained in honor or released in kindness" (Qur'ān 2:229). After the third repudiation, a bar to remarriage arises between the spouses until the ex-wife marries another man, consummates that marriage, and then that marriage ends in either divorce or the husband's death, a process known as *taḥlīl* (Qur'ān 2:230).[53] By limiting the number of repudiations that a man can pronounce against his wife to three (Qur'ān 2:230), the Qur'ān put an end to the pre-Islamic practice in which men kept their wives in an indeterminate limbo by continuously repudiating them and taking them back at will.

While the basis for *ṭalāq*-repudiation was Qur'ānic, the husband's prerogative to end the marriage was rationalized by jurists on the basis that Islamic law imposes financial obligations only on the husband—including in the event of divorce—and therefore were the wife able to divorce him at will, that would place unwarranted financial burdens on him. In keeping with their cultural milieu, some medieval jurists also justified the disparity between the spouses to end their marriage on the basis of the female nature being wanting in rationality and self-control.[54] On the social plane, the husband's unilateral prerogative to pronounce *ṭalāq* was seen as a symbol of his patriarchal authority, on par with other male privileges like polygamy, concubinage, and the right to discipline his wife for her ill-conduct.[55]

Despite its ease and simplicity, repudiation was not as common in medieval Muslim societies as one would expect. As Rapoport has shown in his study of Mamluk society, men were deterred by the financial cost of *ṭalāq*, which entails paying all remaining financial obligations—the deferred and due portions of their dower, any arrears in payments of maintenance, and other debts they may have incurred during the marriage—in addition to maintenance during the waiting period and a supplementary compensation gift to their divorcées (*mutʿa*).[56] Moreover, for a husband to divorce his wife without a good reason was socially stigmatized as an impropriety, as it deprived his wife of financial support and protection and could prevent her from remarriage if she had children whose custody she wanted to retain.[57]

Historians have argued that rather than being a major mechanism of actual divorce in premodern Muslim societies, *ṭalāq* was used to control women's behaviors and as a threat against an insubordinate wife. Sunnī law recognizes divorce oaths that allow a husband to attach conditions (*taʿlīq*) to a repudiation, such that when the specified condition occurs, *ṭalāq* automatically ensues.[58] For example, many a *fatwā* and court case involve a husband who threatened to divorce his wife if she left his house without his permission or if she divulged a family secret. Strained relations with the mother-in-law were also a common reason for pronouncing oaths of repudiation.[59] While *ṭalāq* was the most informal type of divorce that did not require court intervention, divorced women appealed to the court to certify a *ṭalāq*, to sue for payment of their financial entitlements,[60] or inversely, to try to render a *ṭalāq* invalid by claiming that the husband had shown signs of "diminished rationality" owing to a mental illness at the time he had pronounced the divorce.[61]

Contract Stipulations and Delegated Conditional Divorce

Unlike the husband who has the ability to divorce his wife with ease, a wife who wants to end her marriage has more limited and less immediate options: she can stipulate conditions in her marital contract or negotiate a conditional or delegated divorce; pursue a consensual divorce; or seek the intervention of the court for a judicial divorce.

Stipulations in the marriage contract have been employed by Muslim women throughout history to preemptively protect their rights and to facilitate divorce.[62] Typically, this involves the wife setting down stipulations that would allow her to choose a divorce in the event that her husband took another wife or a concubine, beat her, or failed to sustain her (the prevalence of clauses in historical contracts are as ordered here).[63] There is considerable disagreement among the schools concerning which stipulations are enforceable, which are void, and which conditions void a contract altogether. Stipulations that void a marriage contract to which they are attached are those that contravene a basic purpose of marriage, such as stipulating that the groom will divorce the bride after "making her lawful" for a previous husband who had repudiated her triply (*taḥlīl*) or specifying an explicit end date to the union that undermines lasting intimacy as a fundamental purpose of marriage, though an expiration date was valid in a temporary marriage (*mutʿa*) under Twelver Shīʿī law.[64] Short of such conditions undermining the purpose of marriage, jurists disagree concerning which stipulations are enforceable and which are void. There is general agreement that accepted stipulations include which family members will live with the couple, the amount of maintenance the wife will receive, and the financial maintenance of a wife's children from another marriage.[65] The Ḥanbalīs, who espouse the most flexible approach to contract law in general, allow the broadest scope for enforceable stipulations, including those against polygyny or relocation of the wife, that if breached, allows the wife to opt for divorce.[66]

Extant marriage contracts from Egypt and Greater Syria from as early as the third/ninth century up to the Ottoman period show that it was customary for contracts to contain stipulations and that they were considered legally binding.[67] Standard clauses sought to mitigate the most potentially damaging male privileges—most to protect against polygamy and abuse—and granted the wife automatic divorce, or the option of divorce, should the husband violate any of the stipulated conditions.[68] Some contracts even delegated to the wife the power to cause the divorce of any other woman whom her husband marries or to sell any concubine he owns.[69] Contracts from seventh/thirteenth- to tenth/sixteenth-century Muslim Spain customarily stipulate five acts that the husband pledged not to do: marry a second wife or take a concubine without the permission and consent of his first wife, absent himself for more than six consecutive months, mistreat his wife physically or financially, force her to relocate, or forbid her from visiting her relatives and receiving their visits.[70] Formulary works consistently enumerate these five conditions as standard clauses, preceded by an acknowledgment that the husband promises to uphold the stipulations "in order to seek her friendship and trying to keep her happiness," and empowering the wife to free herself from the marriage if he breaches any of these clauses.[71] Sometimes the conditions were unique, such as a woman detailing the furnishings expected in her marital home or specifying where they would live (e.g., not with his family or near hers).[72] By stipulating conditions in her contract, a wife secured the ability to easily get a divorce in circumstances that would otherwise not be recognized grounds for her to seek a judicial divorce.

A similar outcome can be achieved through the negotiation of contingent repudiations, which could take one of two forms: the husband attaching conditions to a repudiation (*taʿlīq*, discussed above) or a contingent delegated *ṭalāq*, in which the husband empowers his wife to divorce herself if a specified event occurs. In the former, the husband voluntarily pronounces a divorce-oath constraining his behavior, such as "If I ever hit you, if I am absent for more than 6 months, if I take a co-wife, or if I drink wine again, you are divorced." If the contingent event or behavior occurs, his wife is automatically divorced. In a contingent delegated *ṭalāq*, in contrast, the divorce does not automatically take place upon the occurrence of the event specified in the oath, rather it grants the wife the option to divorce herself.[73] For example, if he hits her or is absent for more than six months, she has the choice to release herself from the marriage. The Ḥanafī school allows for a broader option in which the husband grants his wife an option to divorce herself whenever she likes.[74] Both the contingent and the delegated divorce were used by couples to restrict the husband's behavior in ways similar to stipulations, and among Mālikīs, they were the typical method used to restrict the husband from polygyny or relocation.[75]

Contingent delegated *ṭalāq* was institutionalized as social practice in medieval Islam. Before traveling or embarking on a military campaign, it was customary for husbands in Mamluk and Ottoman lands and in the medieval Islamic West to deposit or register a conditional bill of divorce empowering their wives to seek a divorce. In this bill, the husband states that if he fails to return in a specified period of time—in cases from the ninth/fifteenth century after a very short absence of two months or even ten days—his wife has the right to confirm the divorce in court.[76]

Consensual Separation (*Khulʿ*, *ibrāʾ*, or *hul*)

Consensual divorce (*khulʿ*, literally "ransom"), historically the most common method of divorce, is initiated by the wife and negotiated with the husband, who must consent to the separation, according to most jurists. Consensual divorce is a procedure that predates Islam and is affirmed by the Qurʾān, which instructs that if the spouses fear breaking the limits set by God, the husband should release his wife in exchange for compensation (Qurʾān 2:229). This verse is often explained by reference to a *ḥadīth* in which the wife of Thābit b. Qays came to the Prophet complaining of her dissatisfaction with Thābit and her unhappiness in the marriage. The Prophet ordered her to return to Thābit the garden he had given her as a dower and ordered Thābit to separate from her.[77] *Khulʿ* typically involves the wife exchanging a countervalue or financial compensation for her release from the marriage—just as the Prophet instructed Thābit's wife to return the garden in exchange for separation. This compensation may consist of repayment of the dower or it can entail an amount that is more or less than it.[78] It usually also includes waiving outstanding financial claims against her husband, such as the unpaid portion of the dower or maintenance during the waiting period (*nafaqat al-ʿidda*).

In Sunnī law, the *khulʿ* agreement is negotiated between the wife and her family and the husband outside of court, after which they appear together in front of the judge to register (rather than litigate) the divorce in court to ensure that its occurrence is documented and its terms are enforceable.[79] Shīʿī jurists require the presence of witnesses for the *khulʿ*, as they do for a husband's *ṭalāq* pronouncement.[80] Consensual separation is a definite and irrevocable divorce (*bāʾin*), meaning that the husband cannot take back his wife during her waiting period (*ʿidda*) and once the waiting period expires, a new marriage contract is necessary if the former couple wishes to resume conjugal life.[81]

Historians have shown that *khulʿ* was the legal form of the majority of actual divorces under the Mamluks, a trend that historians believe continued during Ottoman times, at least among divorces that appear in court records.[82] Women whose husbands were reluctant to give their assent to a consensual divorce employed various strategies that made marital life difficult in order to induce their husbands to agree to divorce, such as forfeiting marital duties, like housekeeping or sexual relations, or claiming the remaining part of dower from a husband unable to pay, who would then agree to divorce to avoid prison for violation of the contract.[83] On the other hand, husbands frequently exacted favorable divorce settlements by demanding that wives waive all their financial rights, including the balance of their dowries, any due debts, maintenance during the waiting period, the return of the initial dowry, and some demanded an additional sum of money even though this was considered reprehensible (*makrūh*).[84]

By the Ottoman period, "generous compensation for *khulʿ* was the norm in both theory and practice."[85] Many women also gave up additional rights in order to acquire custody of their children; *khulʿ* settlements commonly saw women agreeing to finance the upkeep of children, which was the father's responsibility, in exchange for maintaining custody even if they remarried.[86]

Due to the very high cost of *khulʿ* divorce for women, Ottoman muftis in eleventh/seventeenth- and twelfth/eighteenth-century Palestine and Syria would ensure that women did not unjustifiably compensate the husband: "if the wife contracted the *khulʿ*, the mufti would call witnesses to establish if the divorce had not actually been a *ṭalāq*, in the sense that the husband had proposed to divorce his wife if she compensated him. In such cases muftis would tell the woman that she was not obliged to pay anything and could even claim her deferred dower."[87] Could a woman obtain a *khulʿ* without the husband's acceptance? While the vast majority of court proceedings documenting *khulʿ* settlements note the agreement of the husband, two historians of Ottoman Cairo have identified a handful of cases in which the judge granted a *khulʿ* divorce over the husband's refusal, though this does not seem to have been standard practice.[88]

Judicial Divorce (*ṭatlīq*, *tafrīq*, or *faskh*)

In medieval Muslim societies, divorcing couples typically appeared before judges or notaries in the court to register their divorce, which was necessary to confirm their financial settlements and to register future marriages.[89] But to what extent could and did judges intervene to authorize a divorce when one party did not agree to a divorce or when the initiating party claimed grounds for annulling the marriage? The grounds for judicial divorce (*ṭatlīq*, *tafrīq*, *faskh*) differed from one legal school to another, as did judges' activism in applying them from society to society.

In terms of the legitimate grounds for judicial divorce, the discovery of a significant defect in either spouse after the marriage contract was agreed on as constituting grounds for its annulment. Most jurists limit these defects to four: insanity, leprosy, *baraṣ* (a skin disease similar to leprosy), and any condition of the sexual organ that prevents intercourse.[90] Beyond these rare defects that constitute absolute impediments to lawful sex as a primary purpose of marriage, the legal schools vary significantly in determining the scope of valid grounds allowing women to initiate divorce for cause. In the Ḥanafī school, the grounds for judicial divorce are circumscribed to such extreme circumstances as long-term abandonment, meaning until her husband could be presumed dead, defined variously as 99, 120 years, or until all members of his peer group had died—none of which was likely to be of use to an abandoned wife. The Shāfiʿī and Ḥanbalī schools fall in the middle of the spectrum: they consider the husband's failure to pay maintenance as acceptable grounds for divorce, and the Ḥanbalīs allow a wife whose husband is absent for more than six months to obtain a divorce.[91] The Mālikī school recognizes the most expansive grounds for judicial divorce, which encompasses circumstances of desertion or failure to provide, in addition to a unique doctrine of "harm" (*ḍarar*) that can be broadly interpreted to include cruelty and physical harm to a wife, offering significant discretion to the judge, who determines what acts and behaviors qualify as harmful.[92]

Judicial divorce was accepted and widely practiced in premodern Muslim societies, albeit employed somewhat unevenly depending on the society in question. In medieval Spain and North Africa, where Mālikī law was implemented, we find numerous cases of women appearing in court to seek redress against abuse from their husbands.[93] Rapoport finds that judicial divorce was comparatively rare in Mamluk Egypt and Greater Syria, and that it was generally reserved for abandoned wives who appealed to Ḥanbalī or Mālikī judges to testify that their husbands had been absent for at least six months and had left them without support.[94]

In the Ottoman empire, where Ḥanafī law was applied, judges sidestepped restrictive Ḥanafī doctrine by relying on the doctrines of other schools to annul marriages in cases of abandonment and harm. Ottoman judges referred cases of husband desertion to deputy Shāfiʿī and Ḥanbalī judges, opening the door to a widespread practice of women going to court to obtain annulments when their husbands abandoned them or failed to provide for them financially.[95] Similarly, Ottoman judges in Egypt seemed to rely on Mālikī law to annul marriages in which a wife had suffered harm, which typically entailed beating, fear of abuse, mistreatment of a wife's family members, lack of financial support, a husband's constant absence from the marital home, or sexual dissatisfaction.[96] If a wife could show lack of piety or the nonperformance of Islamic duties, this lent proof to her case against her husband.[97] Women who could prove that their husbands had blasphemed could gain annulment on that basis alone because it established the husband's apostasy, which was an act that automatically dissolved his marriage.[98] By privileging the less restrictive annulment doctrines of other legal schools, Ottoman Ḥanafī jurists institutionalized a pragmatic concession to social needs, enabling a woman in a difficult marriage to obtain a divorce without her husband's consent and without relinquishing her rights to dower and maintenance.

"The Science of the Shares": Islamic Law of Inheritance

The Islamic law of inheritance (*mīrāth*) is founded in Qur'ānic injunctions detailing extensive rules for how the estate of the deceased should be distributed across a range of immediate, near, and distant relatives.[99] Qur'ān 4:11–12 and 4:176 award compulsory fractional shares of the deceased's estate (*farāʾiḍ*) to specified heirs: children, parents, siblings, husbands, and wives. Qur'ān 4:8 establishes an entitlement for both men and women to inherit: "Men have a share in what parents and relatives leave behind at death and women have a share in what parents and relatives leave behind. Be it large or small, a legal share is fixed." This Qur'ānic mandate replaced the tribal customary law of pre-Islamic West Arabia in which women did not inherit but were themselves inherited by their husband's male relatives (Qur'an 4:19), while the rest of his property devolved to the male members of the *ʿaṣaba* (relatives more than one degree removed from the deceased who are connected to the deceased through male ties). The Qur'an allowed women to inherit for the first time as widows, daughters, sisters, mothers, or grandmothers, although in most instances, their shares amount to half of those of a male inheriting in the same capacity.[100] The Qur'ānic framework is complemented and clarified by Prophetic guidance indicating that inheritance does not cross confessional boundaries; a murderer does not inherit from his victim; an enslaved person does not inherit from his/her master; an illegitimate child has no claim on the estate of his/her father; and clientage creates mutual rights of inheritance between patron and client.[101]

The Qur'ān also instructs a person contemplating death to leave a testamentary bequest (*waṣiyya*) for parents and close relatives (Qur'ān 2:180–82, 240; 5:106–108). The Prophet Muḥammad clarified the relationship between the inheritance share and the bequest through two stipulations: bequests are limited to one-third of the net assets of the estate and there is "no bequest to an heir," meaning that a person entitled to a fractional share cannot receive a bequest (unless the other heirs consent). Bequests were typically reserved as charitable gifts, though they played a role in providing for orphaned grandchildren who did not receive a fractional share of their grandparent's estate.[102]

These provisions from the Qur'ān and Sunna formed the textual foundation of the "science of the shares" (*ʿilm al-farāʾiḍ*), a set of legal rules of great precision and mathematical complexity regulating the devolution of property formulated by Muslim jurists during the first/seventh century. In the Sunnī inheritance system, following the repayment of debts, funeral expenses, and bequests (not exceeding one-third), the remaining property of the deceased is divided among two categories of heirs: qualifying sharers (*dhawū al-farāʾiḍ*) and agnates (*ʿaṣaba*).[103] Sharers are heirs designated by the Qur'ān as recipients of a fractional share of the estate: son(s), daughter(s), parent(s), a spouse, and in the absence of children, sibling(s).[104] Agnates, who are persons related to the deceased exclusively through male ties, are ordered in a series of hierarchical classes and degrees of relationship to the deceased, with the person nearest in degree excluding all others, such as the son excluding the grandson.[105]

The division of the estate begins by distributing to sharers their Qur'ānic entitlements, after which the closest surviving agnate inherits whatever remains. For example, ʿAlī dies leaving a wife, daughter, son, and two brothers and his estate comprises a house, a plot of land, and a mill. According to the science of the shares, ʿAlī's wife will inherit 1/8 of the house, plot of land, and mill; his daughter 7/24; and his son 7/12. As for ʿAlī's brothers, they are excluded from inheriting by ʿAlī's children, who are the closest surviving agnates. While the same shares are applied in all cases, the divisions differ in each case according to the unique constellation of heirs surviving the deceased. This general framework is applied by all the Sunnī schools, who differ only concerning minor points and scenarios not explicitly covered by Qur'ānic and Sunnaic injunctions.

For example, Ibn Ḥanbal alone was of the view that the paternal grandmother is not excluded from inheritance by her son, who is the father, but inherits a share of one sixth, either alone or shared evenly with the mother.[106]

In contrast, the law of inheritance among the Twelver Shīʿīs displays some marked divergences from the Sunnī framework. Most consequential was Shīʿī rejection of a special status for the agnatic relationship and their conferral of equal status to the maternal and paternal relatives, which placed females in a more favorable position than the Sunnī inheritance system.[107] For example, if Aḥmad is survived by his wife, his daughter's son, and a distant agnatic cousin, Sunnī law would allot the wife one-fourth of the inheritance and exclude the grandson, and the cousin would inherit the remaining three-fourths of the estate. Although Shīʿī law would similarly apportion a quarter of the estate to the wife, the remaining three-fourths would go to the daughter's son, or her daughter, while the agnatic cousin would be excluded from inheriting.

Inheritance in Practice: The Islamic Inheritance System

Since inheritance rules are rooted in the Qur'ān, Muslims consider them a universal and timeless expression of the Divine Will. Nevertheless, Islamic inheritance laws could undermine the social consolidation of property and its economic utility through both the progressive fragmentation of property as fractional shares become smaller and smaller over time and the alienation of property by females marrying outside the family. For these reasons, throughout Islamic history, inheritance law remained in tension with local customs, especially in regions in which property was controlled by the male patriline.

Some Muslim societies responded to these challenges by ignoring inheritance shares and distributing property according to local norms and customs. This commonly involved the disinheritance of women, especially from real property, while allowing them to inherit gold, silver, and movable property.[108] In many societies, sociocultural pressures and familial demands induced women not to claim a property share, to relinquish their inheritance shares in land in return for monetary compensation, or to cede their inheritance rights to male relatives, most often brothers, in return for nonmonetary compensation, like protection in the event of divorce or the death of a husband.[109] Anthropological studies have shown that some of these customs have persisted into the twentieth century.[110]

Rather than jettisoning inheritance shares altogether, more typical across Muslim societies from al-Andalus to Indonesia was the development of social and legal strategies that made it possible to circumvent the letter of the law without violating its spirit, typified by three strategies: the family endowment/trust (*waqf ahlī* or *dhurrī*), gifts, and nominal sales. These strategies effectively negotiated between Islamic inheritance law, local customs, and economic needs and had the potential to both benefit or disadvantage women vis-à-vis Islamic inheritance rules, depending on how they were employed.

A popular method to side-step limited inheritance shares was the family endowment, by which the owner (*wāqif/wāqifa*) ties the income of her endowment established for a specified purpose to herself, then her descendants in perpetuity. Only when her descendants become extinct does the endowment devolve to charitable purposes. Historically, family endowments were used successfully to shelter property from the effects of Islamic inheritance law, thereby protecting it from fragmentation upon the owner's death. While some family endowments could be used to deprive women of their inheritance rights as initial beneficiaries or award them half shares vis-à-vis male counterparts, studies of family endowment deeds from eighth/fourteenth-century Morocco and ninth/fifteenth-century Damascus show that female beneficiaries were often deliberately given portions at rates explicitly higher than their Qur'ānic shares or awarded entitlements equal to their male counterparts.[111] In his comparative study of family endowments in two nineteenth-century Ottoman provincial towns in Greater Syria, Tripoli (Lebanon) and Nablus (Palestine), Beshara Doumani shows how family endowments could be established to accommodate disparate social ends. Doumani documents that while endowments in Tripoli overwhelmingly included female children and their progeny (98.3%) and hardly ever excluded them (1.2%), in Nablus female children were rarely included (12.1%) and were customarily excluded (87.2%).[112] Thus while family endowments could be used to reinforce and supplement women's rights to inherit property or to intentionally circumvent Islamic inheritance laws to improve the fortunes of daughters and granddaughters, the opposite could also be true.

Another way in which an individual could determine how to transmit his property was by gifting it, in whole or in part, to children or other relatives of his choosing. So long as this was not done during an illness that caused the fear of death (*maraḍ al-mawt*), a simple gift (*hiba*), a charitable gift (*ṣadaqa*) given to the orphans, the poor, or female relatives, or a lifetime gift (*'umra*) conferring usufructuary rights on the recipient could be made even to someone who would be among the Qur'ānic heirs upon the donor's death. While gifting property allows a proprietor to arrange the devolution of his property in light of long-term goals while he is still alive, it also entails the obvious drawback of having to immediately relinquish control of property, which would normally pose a disadvantage to the owner's short-term interests. To mitigate this difficulty, the owner could retain use of his property which is the subject of the gift (according to Mālikī jurists) or stipulate that the recipient must maintain the donor during his or her lifetime (according to the Ḥanafī school).[113] Another compromise involves the owner limiting the gift to a fractional portion of a property, as in the case of a sixth/twelfth-century Cordoban who retained 10 percent of the revenues of a property he had gifted to his daughters as a charitable gift.[114]

The custom of gifting property has the potential to benefit women or to partially or wholly disinherit them. In rural and agricultural contexts, lifetime gifts were often used to concentrate land within the hands of the most active son(s). Studies of Ottoman urban societies have shown that men routinely gave houses to their sons to evade the splitting of property among numerous heirs and to preempt conflict among male siblings over the division of inherited homes. This meant that women infrequently inherited shares of houses.[115] In contrast, social customs in other societies institutionalized gifts to daughters that amounted to sums equal to or more than their brothers as a form of "pre-mortem inheritance." Elites in Mamluk society institutionalized a gender-specific premortem inheritance model for transmitting property: sons inherited their father's office with land grants (*iqṭāʿ*) while daughters inherited a share in their parents' wealth in the form of a trousseau of personal items and heirlooms, which functioned as a form of premortem inheritance reserved exclusively for daughters.[116] Similarly, in Indonesia to the present day, women and girls customarily receive gifts as compensation for the perceived disadvantages of their lesser inheritance shares.[117]

A final method of circumventing the effects of the law of inheritance is the fictitious or nominal sale. This strategy is best illustrated by the following case: A grandmother sold one-fourth of her estate for an unspecified but artificially low price to her granddaughter's fiancée, on condition that he immediately transfer the property to his fiancée as her dower. At the same time, the grandmother gifted her granddaughter one-fourth of her estate. These two separate but simultaneous transactions enabled the grandmother to transfer half of her estate to her granddaughter, effectively disinheriting her own son (the bride's father) and her daughter in the process. When the grandmother died one year later, after her granddaughter's marriage had been arranged but before it was consummated, all of the interested parties became involved in litigation, leaving us with a fortuitous paper trail.[118]

These various mechanisms together form the backbone of what David Powers has dubbed the "Islamic inheritance system," a combination of various modes of transmitting property that include inheritance law, bequests, family endowments, gifts, donations, customary exchanges, land tenure rights, and settlement restrictions that have regulated the division of land and property throughout the Muslim world, from al-Andalus to Indonesia, for a millennium (from the third/ninth century to the middle of the thirteenth/nineteenth-century). David Powers summarizes these customary processes in the following way:

> typically, several years before he died, the head of a family will transfer title to a house or apartment to his wife or daughters in the form of a gift; designate certain fields, orchards, gardens and other revenue-producing properties as an endowment for a lineal descent group; and make other alienations of property so that little or none of the immovable property that he has accumulated over the course of a lifetime will be subject to the effects of the law of inheritance when he dies. Such decisions presumably are based upon many considerations, including individual need, personal sympathy, and regard for social and business relationships.[119]

Within this inheritance system, mandatory inheritance shares play a subordinate role to other categories of law and social processes, and their application is often the last and least important stage in property transmission from generation to generation.[120]

CONCLUSION

This chapter reviewed women's rights and duties in classical marriage, divorce, and inheritance law. It highlighted salient differences of opinion between Sunnī and Twelver Shīʿī jurists and discussed some of the textual and rational proofs underpinning contested legal rules. The analysis presented distinguished between legal obligations as court-enforceable rights, on the one hand, and moral, religious, and social duties, on the other. The chapter sought to historicize the application of legal rules by exploring how customary practices in diverse Muslim societies accommodated, negotiated, and circumvented legal rules, in ways both beneficial and detrimental to women. In sum, the chapter emphasized the complex and shifting relationships between formal rights and obligations developed by jurists and enshrined in legal manuals, sociolegal practices institutionalized in diverse Muslim societies, and moral or religious duties beyond the scope of court-enforceable legal claims.

NOTES

1. Ḥanafī legal doctrines are drawn from Abū al-Ḥasan ʿAlī al-Marghīnānī, *al-Hidāya sharḥ Bidāyat al-mubtadī*, ed. Naʿīm Ashraf Nūr Aḥmad, 8 vols. (Karachi: Idārat al-Qur'ān Wa-l-ʿUlūm al-Islāmiyya, 1417/1996 or 1997) and Abū Bakr al-Kāsānī, *Badāʾiʿ al-ṣanāʾiʿ fī tartīb al-sharāʾiʿ*, ed. ʿAlī Muḥammad Muʿawwaḍ and ʿĀdil Aḥmad ʿAbd al-Mawjūd, 10 vols. (Beirut: Dār al-Kutub al-ʿIlmiyya, 2003). Mālikī law is drawn from Ibn Rushd, *Bidāyat al-mujtahid wa-nihāyat al-muqtaṣid*, ed. Muḥammad Ṣubḥī Ḥallāq, 4 vols. (Cairo: Maktabat Ibn Taymiyya, 1415/1994 or 1995). I draw on two Shāfiʿī commentaries on al-Nawawī's *Minhāj al-Ṭalibīn*: Jalāl al-Dīn al-Maḥallī, *Kanz al-rāghibīn sharḥ Minhāj al-ṭalibīn*, ed. Maḥmūd Ṣāliḥ al-Ḥadīdī, 2 vols. (Jeddah: Dār al-Minhāj, 2013) and Muḥammad al-Shirbīnī, *Mughnī al-muḥtāj ilā maʿrifat maʿānī alfāẓ al-Minhāj*, ed. Muḥammad Khalīl ʿAytānī, 4 vols. (Beirut: Dār al-Maʿrifa, 1997). For Ḥanbalī law, I use Muwaffaq al-Dīn Ibn Qudāma, *al-Mughnī*, ed. ʿAbd Allāh al-Turkī and ʿAbd al-Fattāḥ al-Ḥulw, 3rd ed., 15 vols. (Riyadh: Dār ʿĀlam al-Kutub, 1997). Finally, Twelver Shīʿī law draws on al-Muḥaqqaq al-Ḥillī, *Sharāʾiʿ al-Islām fī masāʾil al-ḥalāl wa-l-ḥarām*, ed. Ṣādiq al-Ḥussainī al-Shīrāzī, 2 vols. (Beirut: Dār al-Qāriʾ, 2004).
2. For a detailed overview of rules of the marriage contract, see Kecia Ali, "Marriage in Classical Islamic Jurisprudence: A Survey of Doctrines," in *The Islamic Marriage Contract: Case Studies in Islamic Family Law*, ed. Asifa Quraishi and Frank E. Vogel (Cambridge, MA: Islamic Legal Studies Program at Harvard Law School and Harvard University Press, 2008), 13–21.
3. Al-Ḥillī, *Sharāʾiʿ al-Islām*, 1:511–515; al-Kāsānī, *Badāʾiʿ al-ṣanāʾiʿ*, 3:317f; Ibn Qudāma, *al-Mughnī*, 9:344–10:220; Ibn Rushd, *Bidāyat al-mujtahid*, 3:12–31; al-Maḥallī, *Kanz al-rāghibīn*, 2:210.
4. Al-Ḥillī, *Sharāʾiʿ al-Islām*, 1:519; Ibn Qudāma, *al-Mughnī*, 9:398, 402–404, 415; al-Maḥallī, *Kanz al-rāghibīn*, 2:215; al-Marghīnānī, *al-Hidāya*, 3:39–46. On minor marriage in Islamic law, see Carolyn Baugh, *Minor Marriage in Early Islamic Law* (Leiden: Brill, 2017).

5. Ibn Qudāma, *al-Mughnī*, 9:344–347, 398–413; Ibn Rushd, *Bidāyat al-mujtahid*, 3:12–13, 15–18; al-Maḥallī, *Kanz al-rāghibīn*, 2:214.
6. Ibn Qudāma, *al-Mughnī*, 9:402–405, 415–416; Ibn Rushd, *Bidāyat al-mujtahid*, 3:17–19.
7. Al-Shirbīnī, *Mughnī al-muḥtāj*, 3:200–201.
8. Ibn Qudāma, *al-Mughnī*, 9:387–390; Ibn Rushd, *Bidāyat al-mujtahid*, 3:31–34; al-Shirbīnī, *Mughnī al-muḥtāj*, 3:206–207.
9. See, for example, Leslie P. Peirce, *Morality Tales: Law and Gender in the Ottoman Court of Aintab* (Berkeley: University of California Press, 2003), 88.
10. Al-Ḥillī, *Sharāʾiʿ al-Islām*, 1:513, 517; al-Kāsānī, *Badāʾiʿ al-ṣanāʾiʿ*, 3:348, 369–376; al-Marghīnānī, *al-Hidāya*, 3:31–36.
11. Al-Kāsānī, *Badāʾiʿ al-ṣanāʾiʿ*, 3:573–585; al-Marghīnānī, *al-Hidāya*, 3:32–33. On the notion of *kafāʾa* generally, see, for example, al-Marghīnānī, *al-Hidāya*, 3:50–56.
12. Rudolph Peters, *Shariʿa, Justice and Legal Order, Egyptian and Islamic Law: Selected Essays* (Leiden: Brill, 2020), 590–592.
13. For a book-length study examining this reciprocal exchange, see Kecia Ali, *Marriage and Slavery in Early Islam* (Cambridge, MA: Harvard University Press, 2010).
14. On the dower, see, for example, al-Marghīnānī, *al-Hidāya*, 3:63–105; al-Shirbīnī, *Mughnī al-muḥtāj*, 3:291–330.
15. On maintenance, see, for example, al-Ḥillī, *Sharāʾiʿ al-Islām*, 1:585–590; Ibn Qudāma, *al-Mughnī*, 11:347–382; Ibn Rushd, *Bidāyat al-mujtahid*, 3:103; al-Marghīnānī, *al-Hidāya*, 3:374–392; al-Shirbīnī, *Mughnī al-muḥtāj*, 3:558–570.
16. Al-Ḥillī, *Sharāʾiʿ al-Islām*, 1:587; Ibn Rushd, *Bidāyat al-mujtahid*, 3:104–108; Ibn Qudāma, *al-Mughnī*, 11:355–357; al-Marghīnānī, *al-Hidāya*, 3:381–382.
17. Al-Marghīnānī, *al-Hidāya*, 3:395–399.
18. Yossef Rapoport, "Matrimonial Gifts in Early Islamic Egypt," *Islamic Law and Society* 4, no. 1 (2000), 1–36.
19. Rapoport, "Matrimonial Gifts," 6–16.
20. Yossef Rapoport, *Marriage, Money and Divorce in Medieval Islamic Society* (Cambridge: Cambridge University Press, 2005), 16–17.
21. Yossef Rapoport, "Women and Gender in Mamluk Society: An Overview," *Mamluk Studies Review* 11, no. 2 (2007): 28.
22. Rapoport, *Marriage, Money and Divorce*, 57.
23. Ibn Qudāma, *al-Mughnī*, 10:232–233.
24. Ibid., for example.
25. Al-Ḥillī, *Sharāʾiʿ al-Islām*, 1:510, 573; Ibn Qudāma, *al-Mughnī*, 10:240–241; al-Shirbīnī, *Mughnī al-muḥtāj*, 3:332.
26. Ibn Qudāma, *al-Mughnī*, 10:55–57, 88–90.
27. Ibid., 10:55–57, 88–90, 237.
28. Ibid., 10:240–242; Amira Sonbol, "A History of Marriage Contracts in Egypt," in Quraishi and Vogel, *The Islamic Marriage Contract*, 97, 105.
29. Al-Ḥillī, *Sharāʾiʿ al-Islām*, 1:509–510; Ibn Qudāma, *al-Mughnī*, 10:228–230.
30. Al-Ḥillī, *Sharāʾiʿ al-Islām*, 1:573; Ibn Qudāma, *al-Mughnī*, 10:245–246; al-Shirbīnī, *Mughnī al-muḥtāj*, 3:331–341.
31. Al-Ḥillī, *Sharāʾiʿ al-Islām*, 1:574.
32. Al-Shirbīnī, *Mughnī al-muḥtāj*, 3:334.
33. This *ḥadīth* can be found in Muḥammad b. Ismaʿīl al-Bukhārī, *Ṣaḥīḥ al-Bukhārī: kitāb badʾ al-khalq, bāb idhā qāl aḥadukum āmīn wa-l-malāʾika fī al-samāʾ āmīn fa-wāfaqat*

iḥdāhumā al-ukhrā ghufira lahu mā taqaddama min dhanbih (#3237) and Muslim b. al-Hajjāj, *Ṣāḥīḥ Muslim: Kitāb al-nikāḥ, bāb taḥrīm imtināʿihā min firāsh zawjihā* (#1436).

34. This *ḥadīth* can be found in Muḥammad b. ʿĪsā al-Tirmidhī, *al-Jāmiʿ: bāb faḍl azwāj al-nabī* (#3895).
35. Marion Katz, *Wives and Work: Islamic Law and Ethics Before Modernity* (New York: Columbia University Press, 2022), chap. 3.
36. Al-Ḥillī, *Sharāʾiʿ al-Islām*, 1:585–586; Ibn Qudāma, *al-Mughnī*, 10:259–260; al-Marghīnānī, *al-Hidāya*, 3:378; al-Shirbīnī, *Mughnī al-muḥtāj*, 3:572.
37. Ibn Qudāma, *al-Mughnī*, 10:224–226; Ibn Rushd, *Bidāyat al-mujtahid*, 3:104–107.
38. Ibn Qudāma, *al-Mughnī*, 10:259–260; al-Shirbīnī, *Mughnī al-muḥtāj*, 3:572.
39. See, for example, Ibn Qudāma, *al-Mughnī*, 10:226, who frames the wife's domestic labor as a moral obligation and social custom rather than a legal obligation.
40. Al-Ḥillī, *Sharāʾiʿ al-Islām*, 1:583; Marion Katz, *Wives and Work*, chap. 4: "The Ḥanbalīs: Reframing Marriage Law in Damascus, 14th century C.E."
41. Ibn Rushd, *Bidāyat al-mujtahid*, 3: 104–105.
42. Katz, *Wives and Work*, chap. 1.
43. Katz, *Wives and Work*, chap. 3.
44. For a book-length study exploring legal and religious discourses on wives' domestic service, see Marion Katz, *Wives and Work*. Katz identifies key tensions between legal rights that could be upheld in court and religious or moral obligations that were at times also discussed in juristic literature, and were explored more extensively in other religious discourses like *zuhd*, Sufism, and philosophical ethics.
45. Ibn Qudāma, *al-Mughnī*, 10:259–261; al-Shirbīnī, *Mughnī al-muḥtāj*, 3:342–346, 572–575.
46. Al-Ḥillī, *Sharāʾiʿ al-Islām*, 1:577; al-Shirbīnī, *Mughnī al-muḥtāj*, 3:344, 571.
47. Ibn Rushd, *Bidāyat al-mujtahid*, 3:170–182; al-Marghīnānī, *al-Hidāya*, 3:330–344.
48. On this distinction, and on child custody more broadly, see Ahmed Fekry Ibrahim, *Child Custody in Islamic Law: Theory and Practice in Egypt since the Sixteenth Century* (Cambridge: Cambridge University Press, 2018).
49. Al-Ḥillī, *Sharāʾiʿ al-Islām*, 1:584; Ibn Qudāma, *al-Mughnī*, 11:412–422; Ibn Rushd, *Bidāyat al-mujtahid*, 3:107–108; al-Marghīnānī, *al-Hidāya*, 3:366–372; al-Shirbīnī, *Mughnī al-muḥtāj*, 3:592–601.
50. Ibn Qudāma, *al-Mughnī*, 10:355–363; Ibn Rushd, *Bidāyat al-mujtahid*, 3:143–150; al-Marghīnānī, *al-Hidāya*, 3:165–176; al-Shirbīnī, *Mughnī al-muḥtāj*, 3:370–376.
51. Al-Ḥillī, *Sharāʾiʿ al-Islām*, 2:9–11, 13–14.
52. Ibn Qudāma, *al-Mughnī*, 10:537–577; Ibn Rushd, *Bidāyat al-mujtahid*, 3:163–168.
53. Ibn Qudāma, *al-Mughnī*, 10:334; al-Ḥillī, *Sharāʾiʿ al-Islām*, 2:19–21.
54. See, for example, Ibn Qayyim al-Jawziyya, *Iʿlām al-muwaqqiʿīn ʿan rabb al-ʿālamīn*, ed. Abū ʿUbayda b. al-Ḥasan Āl Salmān, 7 vols. (Jeddah: Dār Ibn al-Jawzī, 2002), 5:218.
55. Rapoport, *Marriage, Money and Divorce*, 69.
56. Ibn Rushd, *Bidāyat al-mujtahid*, 3:183–184; Rapoport, *Marriage, Money and Divorce*, 70–71; Abdal-Rehim Abdal-Rahman Abdal-Rehim, "The Family and Gender Laws in Egypt during the Ottoman Period," in *Women, the Family, and Divorce Laws in Islamic History*, ed. Amira el-Azhar Sonbol (Syracuse, NY: Syracuse University Press, 1996), 104.
57. Rapoport, *Marriage, Money and Divorce*, 69.
58. Ibn Qudāma, *al-Mughnī*, 10:452–486; Ibn Rushd, *Bidāyat al-mujtahid*, 3:159–162; al-Shirbīnī, *Mughnī al-muḥtāj*, 3:411–438.
59. Rapoport, "Women and Gender in Mamluk Society," 32–33.

60. Abdal-Rehim, "The Family and Gender Laws," 104; Madeline C. Zilfi, "'We Don't Get Along': Women and *Hul* Divorce in the Eighteenth Century," in *Women in the Ottoman Empire: Middle Eastern Women in the Early Modern Era*, ed. Madeline C. Zilfi (Leiden: Brill, 1997), 270.
61. Judith E. Tucker, *In the House of the Law: Gender and Islamic Law in Ottoman Syria and Palestine* (Berkeley: University of California Press, 1998), 88–90.
62. While the husband could also add conditions to the contract, this was less prevalent since he could easily end his marriage through *ṭalāq*. Court records include instances of husbands stipulating in their marriage contract an allowance to live in a wife's house without compensating her (see, e.g., Sonbol, "A History of Marriage Contracts in Egypt," 96, 102; Abdal-Rehim, "The Family and Gender Laws," 100).
63. Sonbol, "A History of Marriage Contracts in Egypt," 101.
64. Ibn Qudāma, *al-Mughnī*, 9:488. On temporary marriage in Twelver Shīʿī law, see al-Ḥillī, *Sharāʾiʿ al-Islām*, 1:532–537, and Shahla Haeri, *Law of Desire: Temporary Marriage in Shiʾi Iran* (Syracuse: Syracuse University Press, 2014).
65. Sonbol, "A History of Marriage Contracts in Egypt," 87.
66. Ibn Qudāma, *al-Mughnī*, 9:483–487. Twelver Shīʿī law did not permit conditions prohibiting polygyny or concubinage; see al-Ḥillī, *Sharāʾiʿ al-Islām*, 1:567–568.
67. Abdal-Rehim, "The Family and Gender Laws," 101. About Ottoman Egypt, Abdal-Rehim states, "the general rule was the inclusion of preconditions."
68. See, e.g., Sonbol, "A History of Marriage Contracts in Egypt," 87–122; Amalia Zomeño, "The Islamic Marriage Contract in al-Andalus," in Quraishi and Vogel, *The Islamic Marriage Contract*, 136–155; Mohammad Fadel, "Reinterpreting the Guardian's Role in the Islamic Contract of Marriage: The Case of the Mālikī School," *Journal of Islamic Law* 4, no. 1 (1998), 1–26.
69. Sonbol, "A History of Marriage Contracts in Egypt," 95.
70. Zomeño, "The Islamic Marriage Contract in al-Andalus," 144.
71. Ibid., 144–145.
72. Sonbol, "A History of Marriage Contracts in Egypt," 99.
73. Ibn Qudāma, *al-Mughnī*, 10:381–384; Ibn Rushd, *Bidāyat al-mujtahid*, 3:139–142; al-Shirbīnī, *Mughnī al-muḥtāj*, 3:377–378.
74. Al-Marghīnānī, *al-Hidāya*, 3:206–227.
75. For further details on contingent and delegated divorces, see Ali, "Marriage in Classical Islamic Jurisprudence," 24–27.
76. See, for example, Rapoport, "Women and Gender in Mamluk Society," 34, n. 167; Tucker, *Women, Family, and Gender in Islamic Law*, 106; Svetlana Ivanova, "The Divorce between Zubaida Hatun and Esseid Osman Ağa: Women in the Eighteenth-Century Sharia Court of Rumelia," in Sonbol, *Women, the Family, and Divorce Laws in Islamic History*, 120; Abdal-Rehim, "The Family and Gender Laws," 102; David Powers, "Women and Divorce in the Islamic West: Three Cases," *Hawwa* 1, no. 1 (2003): 39–42; Sonbol, "A History of Marriage Contracts in Egypt," 105; Peirce, *Morality Tales*, 81.
77. Ibn Qudāma, *al-Mughnī*, 10:267–268; Ibn Rushd, *Bidāyat al-mujtahid*, 3:130–131. Thābit's wife is identified variously as Ḥabība bint Sahl and Jamīla bint ʿAbd Allāh. For discussion of these reports, see Susan A. Spectorsky, *Women in Classical Islamic Law: A Survey of the Sources* (Leiden: Brill, 2010), 125–126, 171–172.
78. Al-Ḥillī, *Sharāʾiʿ al-Islām*, 2:43–47; Ibn Rushd, *Bidāyat al-mujtahid*, 3:132.
79. Ibn Qudāma, *al-Mughnī*, 10:268–269; Abdal-Rehim, "The Family and Gender Laws," 106.

80. Al-Ḥillī, *Sharāʾiʿ al-Islām*, 2:48.
81. Ibn Qudāma, *al-Mughnī*, 10:274–275; al-Marghīnānī, *al-Hidāya*, 3:280–283; al-Ḥillī, *Sharāʾiʿ al-Islām*, 2:49.
82. Rapoport, *Marriage, Money and Divorce*, 69; Ivanova, "Divorce," 118; Zilfi, "'We Don't Get Along,'" 272, 275; Tucker, *In the House*, 97–100; Peirce, *Morality Tales*, 231. It is difficult to precisely determine incidences of *khulʿ* relative to *ṭalāq*, because the former was routinely registered in court while the latter could be effectuated without recourse to the courts.
83. Rapoport, *Marriage, Money and Divorce*, 72–73.
84. Ibn Qudāma, *al-Mughnī*, 10:269–270, 281–282; Tucker, *Women, Family, and Gender in Islamic Law*, 110.
85. Abdal-Rehim, "The Family and Gender Laws," 105; Tucker, *Women, Family, and Gender in Islamic Law*, 110.
86. Rapoport, "Women and Gender in Mamluk Society," 34; Peirce, *Morality Tales*, 231–232; Zilfi, "'We Don't Get Along,'" 285–291.
87. Tucker, *In the House of the Law*, 96–97.
88. Abdal-Rehim, "The Family and Gender Laws," 106; Sonbol,"A History of Marriage Contracts in Egypt," 107.
89. Rapoport, *Marriage, Money and Divorce*, 78.
90. Al-Ḥillī, *Sharāʾiʿ al-Islām*, 1:555–561; Ibn Qudāma, *al-Mughnī*, 10:57–58; al-Marghīnānī, *al-Hidāya*, 3:325–330.
91. Ibn Qudāma, *al-Mughnī*, 10:240–242.
92. Ibn Rushd, *Bidāyat al-mujtahid*, 3:185–186.
93. See, for example, Powers, "Women and Divorce in the Islamic West."
94. Rapoport, *Marriage, Money and Divorce*, 76
95. Tucker, *Women, Family, and Gender in Islamic Law*, 107–109.
96. Sonbol, "A History of Marriage Contracts in Egypt," 97, 105.
97. Abdal-Rehim, "The Family and Gender Laws," 105.
98. Tucker, *Women, Family, and Gender in Islamic Law*, 107–108.
99. Al-Shirbīnī, *Mughnī al-muḥtāj*, 3:5–7.
100. Ibn Qudāma, *al-Mughnī*, 9:6.
101. Al-Ḥillī, *Sharāʾiʿ al-Islām*, 2:261–264; Ibn Qudāma, *al-Mughnī*, 9:6–36; Ibn Rushd, *Bidāyat al-mujtahid*, 4:185–187; al-Shirbīnī, *Mughnī al-muḥtāj*, 3:10–14.
102. On the rules governing bequests, see, for example, Ibn Qudāma, *al-Mughnī*, 8:389–579; al-Shirbīnī, *Mughnī al-muḥtāj*, 3:52–62.
103. Al-Shirbīnī, *Mughnī al-muḥtāj*, 3:7–8.
104. Ibn Rushd, *Bidāyat al-mujtahid*, 4:185–228.
105. Ibid.
106. Ibn Qudāma, *al-Mughnī*, 9:60–61; Ibn Rushd, *Bidāyat al-mujtahid*, 4:203–205.
107. Al-Ḥillī, *Sharāʾiʿ al-Islām*, 2:261–314.
108. David Powers, "Law and Custom in the Maghrib, 1475–1500: On the Disinheritance of Women," in *Law, Custom, and Statute in the Muslim World: Studies in Honor of Aharon Layish*, ed. Ron Shaham (Leiden: Brill, 2006), 17–40.
109. Ibid., 34; Peirce, *Morality Tales*, 227–231.
110. See, for example, Annelies Moors, "Women, Gender and Inheritance: Arab States," in *Encyclopedia of Women in Islamic Countries* (Leiden: Brill, 2004), 2:299–302.

111. David Powers, "The Mālikī Family Endowment: Legal Norms and Social Practices," *International Journal of Middle Eastern Studies* 25, no. 3 (1993): 379–406; Michael Winter, "Mamluks and Their Households in Late Mamluk Damascus: A *waqf* Study," in *The Mamluks in Egyptian and Syrian Politics and History*, eds. Amalia Levanoni and Michael Winter (Leiden: Brill, 2004), 297–316.
112. Beshara Doumani, "Endowing Family: Waqf, Property Devolution, and Gender in Greater Syria, 1800 to 1860," *Comparative Studies in Society and History* 40, no. 1 (1998): 3–41.
113. Ibn Rushd, *Bidāyat al-mujtahid*, 4:165–167; al-Marghīnānī, *al-Hidāya*, 3:39–46.
114. David Powers, "The Islamic Inheritance System: A Socio-Historical Approach," in *Islamic Family Law and the State*, ed. Chibli Mallat and Jane Conners (London: Trotman, 1990), 25.
115. Peirce, *Morality Tales*, 226–227.
116. Rapoport, "Women and Gender in Mamluk Society," 18.
117. John R. Bowen, *Islam, Law and Equality in Indonesia: An Anthropology of Public Reasoning* (Cambridge: Cambridge University Press, 2003).
118. Powers, "The Islamic Inheritance system," 26.
119. Ibid., 23.
120. Ibid., 29.

Bibliography

Abdal-Rehim, Abdal-Rehim Abdal-Rahman. "The Family and Gender Laws in Egypt during the Ottoman Period." In *Women, the Family, and Divorce Laws in Islamic History*, edited by Amira El Azhary Sonbol, 96–111. Syracuse, NY: Syracuse University Press, 1996.

Ali, Kecia. *Marriage and Slavery in Early Islam*. Cambridge, MA: Harvard University Press, 2010.

Ali, Kecia. "Marriage in Classical Islamic Jurisprudence: A Survey of Doctrines." In *The Islamic Marriage Contract: Case Studies in Islamic Family Law*, edited by Asifa Quraishi and Frank E. Vogel, 11–45. Cambridge, MA: Islamic Legal Studies Program at Harvard Law School and Harvard University Press, 2008.

Baugh, Carolyn. *Minor Marriage in Early Islamic Law*. Leiden: Brill, 2017.

Bukhārī, Muḥammad b. Isma'īl al-. *Ṣaḥīḥ al-Bukhārī*. Cited by chapter, subchapter system.

Bowen, John R. *Islam, Law and Equality in Indonesia: An Anthropology of Public Reasoning*. Cambridge: Cambridge University Press, 2003.

Doumani, Beshara. "Endowing Family: Waqf, Property Devolution, and Gender in Greater Syria, 1800 to 1860." *Comparative Studies in Society and History* 40, no. 1 (1998): 3–41.

Fadel, Mohammad. "Reinterpreting the Guardian's Role in the Islamic Contract of Marriage: The Case of the Mālikī School." *Journal of Islamic Law* 4, no. 1 (1998): 1–26.

Haeri, Shahla. *Law of Desire: Temporary Marriage in Shi'i Iran*. Syracuse, NY: Syracuse University Press, 2014.

Ḥillī, al-Muḥaqqaq al-. *Sharā'i' al-Islām fī masā'il al-ḥalāl wa-l-ḥarām*. Edited by Ṣādiq al-Ḥussainī al-Shīrāzī. 2 vols. Beirut: Dār al-Qāri', 2004.

Ibn al-Hajjāj, Muslim. *Ṣāḥīḥ Muslim*. Cited by chapter, subchapter system.

Ibn Qayyim, al-Jawziyya. *I'lām al-muwaqqi'īn 'an rabb al-'ālamīn*. Edited by Abū 'Ubayda b. al-Ḥasan Āl Salmān. 7 vols. Jeddah: Dār Ibn al-Jawzī, 2002.

Ibn Qudāma, Muwaffaq al-Dīn. *al-Mughnī*. 3rd ed. Edited by ʿAbd Allāh b. ʿAbd al-Muḥsin al-Turkī and ʿAbd al-Fattāḥ Muḥammad al-Ḥulw. 15 vols. Riyadh: Dār ʿĀlam al-Kutub, 1997.

Ibn Rushd al-Ḥafīd, Muḥammad b. Aḥmad. *Bidāyat al-mujtahid wa-nihāyat al-muqtaṣid*. Edited by Muḥammad Ṣubḥī Ḥallāq. 4 vols. Cairo: Maktabat Ibn Taymiyya, 1415/1994 or 1995.

Ivanova, Svetlana. "The Divorce between Zubaida Hatun and Esseid Osman Ağa: Women in the Eighteenth-Century Sharia Court of Rumelia." In *Women, the Family, and Divorce Laws in Islamic History*, edited by Amira El Azhary Sonbol, 112–125. Syracuse, NY: Syracuse University Press, 1996.

Kāsānī, Abū Bakr al-. *Badāʾiʿ al-ṣanāʾiʿ fī tartīb al-sharāiʿ*. Edited by ʿAlī Muḥammad Muʿawwaḍ and ʿĀdil Aḥmad ʿAbd al-Mawjūd. 10 vols. Beirut: Dār al-Kutub al-ʿIlmiyya, 2003.

Katz, Marion. *Wives and Work: Islamic Law and Ethics Before Modernity*. New York: Columbia University Press, 2022.

Maḥallī, Jalāl al-Dīn al-. *Kanz al-rāghibīn sharḥ Minhāj al-Ṭalibīn*. Edited by Maḥmūd Ṣāliḥ al-Ḥadīdī. 2 vols. Jeddah: Dār al-Minhāj, 2013.

Marghīnānī, Abū al-Ḥasan ʿAlī al-. *Al-Hidāya sharḥ Bidāyat al-Mubtadī*. Edited by Naʿīm Ashraf Nūr Aḥmad. 8 vols. Karachi: Idārat al-Qurʾān Wa-l-ʿUlūm al-Islāmiyya, 1417/1996 or 1997.

Moors, Annelies. "Women, Gender and Inheritance: Arab States." In *Encyclopedia of Women in Islamic Countries*, 2:299–302. Leiden: Brill, 2004.

Peirce, Leslie P. *Morality Tales: Law and Gender in the Ottoman Court of Aintab*. Berkeley: University of California Press, 2003.

Peters, Rudolph. *Sharīʿa, Justice and Legal Order, Egyptian and Islamic Law: Selected Essays*. Leiden: Brill, 2020.

Powers, David. "Law and Custom in the Maghrib, 1475–1500: On the Disinheritance of Women." In *Law, Custom, and Statute in the Muslim World: Studies in Honor of Aharon Layish*, edited by Ron Shaham, 17–40. Leiden: Brill, 2006.

Powers, David. "The Mālikī Family Endowment: Legal Norms and Social Practices." *International Journal of Middle Eastern Studies* 25, no. 3 (1993): 379–406.

Powers, David. "The Islamic Inheritance System: A Socio-Historical Approach." In *Islamic Family Law and the State*, edited by Chibli Mallat and Jane Conners, 11–29. London: Trotman, 1990.

Powers, David. "Women and Divorce in the Islamic West: Three Cases." *Hawwa* 1, no. 1 (2003): 29–45.

Rapoport, Yossef. *Marriage, Money and Divorce in Medieval Islamic Society*. Cambridge: Cambridge University Press, 2005.

Rapoport, Yossef. "Women and Gender in Mamluk Society: An Overview." *Mamluk Studies Review* 11, no. 2 (2007): 1–47.

Rapoport, Yossef. "Matrimonial Gifts in Early Islamic Egypt." *Islamic Law and Society* 4, no. 1 (2000): 1–36.

Shirbīnī, Muḥammad al-. *Mughnī al-muḥtāj ilā maʿrifat maʿānī alfāẓ al-Minhāj*. Edited by Muḥammad Khalīl ʿAytānī. 4 vols. Beirut: Dār al-Maʿrifa, 1997.

Sonbol, Amira. "A History of Marriage Contracts in Egypt." In *The Islamic Marriage Contract: Case Studies in Islamic Family Law*, edited by Asifa Quraishi and Frank E. Vogel, 87–122. Cambridge, MA: Islamic Legal Studies Program at Harvard Law School and Harvard University Press, 2008.

Spectorsky, Susan A. *Women in Classical Islamic Law: A Survey of the Sources.* Leiden: Brill, 2010.
Tirmidhī, Muḥammad b. al-.ʿĪsā. *Al-Jāmiʿ*. Cited by chapter, subchapter system.
Tucker, Judith E. *In the House of the Law: Gender and Islamic Law in Ottoman Syria and Palestine.* Berkeley: University of California Press, 1998.
Tucker, Judith E. *Women, Family, and Gender in Islamic Law.* Cambridge: Cambridge University Press, 2008.
Zilfi, Madeline C. "'We Don't Get Along': Women and *Hul* Divorce in the Eighteenth Century." In *Women in the Ottoman Empire: Middle Eastern Women in the Early Modern Era*, edited by Madeline C. Zilfi, 264–296. Leiden: Brill, 1997.
Zomeño, Amalia. "The Islamic Marriage Contract in al-Andalus." In *The Islamic Marriage Contract: Case Studies in Islamic Family Law*, edited by Asifa Quraishi and Frank E. Vogel, 136–155. Cambridge, MA: Islamic Legal Studies Program at Harvard Law School and Harvard University Press, 2008.
Winter, Michael. "Mamluks and Th eir Households in Late Mamluk Damascus: A *Waqf* Study." In *The Mamluks in Egyptian and Syrian Politics and History*, edited by Amalia Levanoni and Michael Winter, 297–316. Leiden: Brill, 2004.

CHAPTER 7

STATUS OF MUSLIM WOMEN IN MODERN FAMILY AND PERSONAL LAW

SOHAIRA SIDDIQUI

ISLAMIC family law (*al-aḥwāl al-shakhṣiyya*; henceforth, IFL) is often used as both the litmus test for modernization and Islamization.[1] Advocates for the modernization of Muslim societies conflate modernization with secularization, resulting in an opposition to the presence of IFL. They support replacement with secular laws in accordance with international law and the United Nation's Declaration of Human Rights on the basis that IFL distinguishes between men and women, almost exclusively to the disadvantage of the latter. Regardless of incremental reforms in the Muslim world, women continue to receive unequal rights under regimes that enforce IFL. In opposition, advocates of Islamization argue that the sine qua non of Muslim societies is IFL: It accords with the religious and social customs of the governed populace, and reflects the values of states that enshrine Islamic law in the constitution itself. Nevertheless, proponents of IFL recognize that it is in need of reform as the place of women in Muslim societies has changed significantly over the last century.

Islamic family law forms part of the laws of all OIC member countries,[2] and each country has amended these laws to varying degrees. Incidentally, non-OIC countries such as India and Israel have partially adopted IFL, precluding definitive generalizations about these laws across countries.[3] This chapter provides some general insights and illuminating examples that will enable the reader to navigate the terrain of modern IFL. The first part of the chapter will provide a brief history of IFL, focusing on its genesis and early implementation. The second part will transition to surveying the various approaches to the study of IFL by scholars, researchers, and activists. What will become apparent is that there are various ways to approach IFL. The third part will shift to modern IFL surveying reform proposals within IFL, highlighting mechanisms and strategies employed by key stakeholders, such as politicians, women's groups, and activists. The fourth part will provide an in-depth comparative analysis of IFL and the reform of IFL in Morocco and Malaysia. These two countries are chosen to demonstrate how advocates of reform face drastically different challenges based on their socio-political circumstances. The fifth and final part of this article will look at the future of IFL and the challenges that arise from the reality that legislative changes and social changes often do not move at parallel speeds.

A Brief History of Islamic Family Law

The history of IFL is one of the most fascinating cases of colonial endurance and legal development in the world. When the colonial powers began indirect rule, most emblematically in the case of the British in both India and Egypt, instead of completely removing Islamic law, Islamic law was retained in certain spheres—namely criminal law and family law, or personal status law. Eventually, criminal law was brought under the remit of English law, leaving Islamic family law as the only element of Islamic law to exist alongside colonial legal systems. This formed a pluralistic legal model which gave colonial powers a greater degree of legitimacy. But when states acquired independence, legal unification was desired as both legal monism and the state's monopoly over the law was considered central to the project of nationhood.

The development of IFL as a codified law within the legislative structure developed over three phases, according to Lynn Welchman.[4] Welchman traces the first phase of IFL and codification to the Ottoman Law of Family Rights (OLFR) passed in 1917. While the OLFR predominately relied on legal opinions from the Ḥanafī school, legal opinions from other schools were incorporated on certain matters. The aim was to standardize IFL, but the OLFR was abandoned after the abolishment of the Ottoman Empire in 1922 and the newly formed Turkish Republic adopted family laws on the basis of the 1926 Swiss Civil Code.[5] Though this milestone is often read as part of Kemal Ataturk's singular pursuit of a secular, modern Turkey, the incorporation of Western laws, such as the Swiss Code, actually began much earlier, in 1839, with the Ottomans. Starting with their adoption of criminal, commercial, and procedural laws from various European countries, the Ottoman incorporation of these codes already signaled a thrust toward circumscribing the role of the Sharīʿa in lawmaking. After 1926, the OLFR no longer held any legislative weight in Turkey, although Welchman notes that the OLFR continued to apply in some Ottoman successor states. In Israel, a version of the code continues to apply to its Muslim citizens.[6]

The second phase of IFL began in the 1950s, when legal codification gathered momentum in Jordan, Syria, Tunisia, Morocco, Pakistan, Mali, and Iraq.[7] The mode and time taken to codify and implement IFL in these various states depended on the colonial legacy, state politics, the relationship between the state and religion, and the dominant political actors on the scene. In Yuksel Sezgin's assessment, there were three ways the state managed the process of codification: (1) some states "aimed to redefine the provisions of membership in the political community,"[8] (2) some states "aimed to redefine the role of religious norms and institutions in public life, "[9] and (3) some states "were initiated with purely mechanical or non-ideological considerations such as systemization of law and justice administration, or reclamation of full sovereignty by terminating non-state jurisdictions on the national territory."[10] Sezgin highlights that although *all* states intervened in the matter of IFL, the *mechanisms* and *modes* of intervention depended on the exact nature of the state project, the sociopolitical environment, and the realities of both political and public life. Based on the scope of interventions undertaken by the state, Sezgin classifies state intervention as three: normative intervention, institutional intervention, and substantive intervention,[11] with the first being the most exhaustive with an eye toward unification, and the final being focused on the actual material laws with less concern for unification.

Sezgin notes that these three modes of state intervention resulted in three distinct models of IFL: fragmented confessional, unified confessional, and unified semiconfessional. In fragmented confessional systems, states recognize different religious and ethnic groups and also allow them a network of courts backed by the power of the state to apply the approved state laws. States adopting the fragmented confessional model desire to accommodate religious and ethnic groups, but maintain a segmented and stratified community. The two countries that adopt this model are Israel and India. In both countries, IFL is applied to the minority Muslim population through a state-controlled judiciary and legislative process. In unified confessional systems, the state formally incorporates IFL, but the application of it is through secular state courts run by state-appointed civil judges. The main distinction between fragmented confessional and unified confessional systems is the judicial network. In fragmented confessional systems, a network of state-sanctioned courts implement IFL, whereas in unified confessional systems, secular civil courts replace previously existing religious courts.[12] The most prominent example of a unified confessional system is Egypt, where IFL is implemented through secular courts as Sharīʿa courts were abolished in the 1950s. The final system, a unified semiconfessional system, has a unified judiciary and a single code, with exceptions being granted to certain segments of the population to be governed by their own religious laws. Though no exact model of a unified semiconfessional system in IFL exists, as will be seen, Malaysia's federalist system comes close. By emphasizing the different modes of intervention and the different systems that result, Sezgin demonstrates that in the process of nation-building and legal unification, postcolonial nations did not adopt a singular approach to codifying and implementing IFL. Their approaches were varied, and were not driven primarily by religious motivations but by the political actors involved in the debate and the degree of unification desired.

Aside from the distinct institutional models adopted by states in phase two of the codification of IFL, there were important political and social shifts that resulted in challenges to these early codes and attempts to reform them. One of the first shifts that had to be attended to by various states was the decrease of secular nationalism and the rise of Islamist movements starting in the 1970s. Sezgin convincingly argues that the incorporation and codification of IFL was not necessarily a religious project, but often a political and secular one. Thus, Islamist groups questioned the scope of state control and interference, even while not wanting to remove IFL.[13] From the 1980s, Annelies Moors notes that the participation of women, secular reformers, and NGOs greatly increased. This shifted the discourse away from a discussion on codification and implementation toward a focus on reform.[14] Importantly for Moors, not all three groups—women, secular reformers, and NGOs—aligned in their visions. For example, she notes that while some women wanted to remove IFL and adopt secular codes which they believed would achieve gender equality, other women aligned themselves with Islamist platforms, paradoxically advocating for certain rights for women, while continuing to "embrace the positions propagated by the male leadership."[15]

Given the sheer number of states that adopted IFL, phase two of Welchman's periodization is undoubtedly one of the most important periods in the history of IFL. It is also the period in which conversations regarding reform of marriage, divorce, guardianship, and polygamy most vociferously took place. This phase extends until the 2000s, when the third phase of codification began with the creation of codes in countries that previously were without them: The United Arab Emirates (2005), Qatar (2006), and Bahrain (2009). Welchman's periodization model is indeed a useful one for analyzing both codification and legislative reform, and aids scholars in understanding the manner in which legislative discourse around IFL evolved. Even so, as Sezgin, Moors, and others have demonstrated, there are many ways to approach the study of IFL, from the historical, to the sociopolitical, to the judicial and anthropological. In the next section we will survey some of these approaches to better understand how they illuminate the functioning of IFL on the ground.

Approaches to the Study of Islamic Family Law

As noted previously, the study of IFL has been approached from a multitude of perspectives. For the purposes of this chapter, I will categorize four scholarly approaches and present some of the most salient methods and conclusions within each approach. The first method, a historical-legal one, analyzes the legal developments of IFL from state legislative and constitutional perspectives after the fall of the Ottoman Empire until today. The second method, an anthropological one, focuses on the actual implementation of IFL in courtrooms and competing understandings of IFL by lawmakers, judges, and citizens alike. The third method, a sociological one, shifts the focus from courtrooms to society and accentuates the various stakeholders and their discourses regarding IFL. The fourth approach, a political science one, focuses on the political factors impacting IFL and the measurable outcomes with regard to the rights of women. Each of these approaches highlights a specific element of IFL, and together they provide a more robust account of how IFL developed, functions, and continues to remain a contested terrain.

Starting with the historical-legal approach, scholars focus on how IFL is incorporated into the state constitution, the specifics of substantive laws, the introduction of new laws, and methods of legal reform. Scholars adopting this approach identify trends and note comparative similarities and differences. An example is Welchman's periodization of IFL, which analyzes the historical development of IFL and state law. Welchman notes some of the shortcomings of the "state-law-focused analysis" in her preface, stating, "It is abundantly clear that statutory law tells either only part of the story of 'the law,' or only one story among many. That (part of the) story is still worth telling."[16] Responding to those who have critiqued a positivist or state-centric approach to the study of IFL, Welchman opines this approach is still valuable as it remains one of the primary modes of studying the *actual* laws. By exploring IFL diachronically, historical-legal scholars are able to provide key insights into how various laws developed and how they changed as well as new trends in IFL.[17] Welchman further argues that while each country has a unique set of factors to negotiate with regards to IFL, countries often look to one another, and therefore it is imperative for scholars to understand broad historical trends and developments. For example, John Eposito's work *Women in Muslim Family Law* compares substantive legal developments across countries in the Middle East, North Africa, and South/Southeast Asia to argue that while each country is negotiating a unique set of circumstances, there are trends, especially regarding reform, that can be mapped onto one another.[18] Beyond historical developments and legislative changes, the historical-legal approach unravels judicial organization and implementation, and strategies for legal reform, although, given that both implementation and reform necessarily involve institutions and individuals beyond the confines of the state, other methodological perspectives are often employed.

The anthropological approach investigates the judicial implementation of IFL through a focus on the courtroom, the various actors within it, such as judges and litigants, judicial education, the functioning of the Sharīʿa courts, and the various modes of legal reasoning employed by judges. The inception of this approach was in some ways a response to characterizations of Islamic law, and *fatwas*, as being rigid and solely to the disadvantage of women. One of the first scholars to study *fatwas* in family law was Amira Sonbol, who focuses on the marriage and divorce of minors in Ottoman Egypt. She argues that the Ottoman recognition of various legal schools (*madhhabs*) ushered in a greater deal of legal flexibility and also allowed litigants greater choice in adjudication.[19] Judith Tucker, who focuses on the judicial decisions in Syria and Palestine during the seventeenth and eighteenth century, reaches similar conclusions: Islamic law, as opposed to being rigid, was in fact very flexible and fluid, and the agency of women was apparent in court documents which showcase women as advocates of their legal rights. Tucker notes that the codification of Islamic law actually stripped Islamic law of this flexibility because "codified law cannot, by definition, be flexible and fluid law."[20] Codification, coupled with a rigid interpretive framework, reduced the room for judges to be attentive to customs and norms. Lawrence Rosen disagrees with Sonbol and Tucker. He argues that judicial reasoning is shaped by cultural assumptions, so even with the codification of IFL, the manner in which it is interpreted will differ based on context. Furthermore, concepts such as "equity" and "justice" are so open-ended that they naturally allow for an element of judicial discretion that cannot be tightly controlled by any codified law.[21] Rosen articulates five elements that influence the application of IFL in Morocco: (1) the political environment, (2) the cultural context, (3) the judges' subjectivity, (4) the education of the judges, and (5) the legal principles employed by judges.[22] Thus, while codified IFL indeed ushers in a degree of rigidity due to the presence of a textually bound law, codification cannot stymie plurality when it comes to practice, or flexibility when it comes to judicial interpretation. Nahda Shehada reinforces Rosen's arguments through extensive fieldwork focusing on Sharīʿa courts. Based on the Sharīʿa courts in Palestine, Shehada argues that "contextual elements such as the sociopolitical milieu, litigants' power, and judges' discretion are decisive"[23] and play a crucial role within the courtroom. She finds that irrespective of a codified IFL, social practice has changed despite the law remaining unmodified. The judiciary, even outside of Palestine, adopts a flexible interpretive framework despite the rigidity of the codified law.[24] Overall, scholars note that understanding the substantive changes in the law only gives scholars insight into legal change in *theory*, whereas practice may in fact be different. Moreover, and perhaps most importantly, the anthropological approach demonstrates the ways in which both judges and individuals challenge the actual codified laws and find ways to adapt laws to social change when legislative change is not enacted in a timely manner.

The sociological approach shifts from focusing on the substantive letter of the law and the enactment of the law, to analyzing the various stakeholders in the debates surrounding IFL. Codification of IFL is a project of the state, but it is influenced by NGOs, both local and international, civil society groups, religious groups, and women's groups. Thus, scholars adopting a sociological lens attempt to understand how these groups interact with one another in order to uncover the sociological factors that influence IFL. Those adopting this approach often focus on two time periods. The first period is the early nineteenth century during the initial formulation of a codified IFL. Differing trajectories in countries are traced to specific colonial histories, the varying importance given to Islam when crafting national identities, the strength of tribal groups, and the desire for secular nationalism.[25] The second period is after the 1990s, when calls to reform IFL were widespread, spearheaded by NGOs and women's groups. Although one may be tempted to view these various groups as being unified, scholars emphasize that within each interest group, a great deal of variance exists, precluding simple characterization. For example, Mervat Hatem analyzes the rise of women's groups in Egypt and notes how the Egyptian state introduced "economic, social and ideological divisions among Egyptian women that make it increasingly difficult to develop a single organization and/or program for action that can represent their conflicting needs and aspirations."[26] Hatem argues that the government promoted "state feminism" which sought to replace female dependency on male members of the family with female dependency on the state. In this way, women became productive members of the state's work force, to the advantage of the state, but left public and private patriarchy unchallenged.[27] Lower-middle class women did not benefit from the state's new economic policies toward women, leaving them increasingly disenfranchised. This alienation of lower-middle class women was capitalized on by "Islamic ideologues" who emphasized a return to traditional models of public versus private life as a way to address the social and economic challenges faced by families. In the picture painted by Hatem, state policies interacted with women's groups and interests, and these interests became increasingly diverse and often challenged one another.

Turning to Morocco, Leon Buskens analyzes the debates surrounding the reform of the *Mudawwana*, an IFL code adopted in 1958. In tracing the codification of the *Mudawwana* and the reforms that took place in the 1990s, Buskens discusses how the rise in democratization processes, challenges to the monarchy, and the rise of opposition parties all contributed to the discourse surrounding reform. He argues that IFL should be analyzed as a "political phenomenon" because "family law and gender serve as powerful political symbols in the modern Muslim world."[28] Looking at the first instance of reform of the *Mudawwana* in 1993, Buskens wonders whether the substance of the actual reforms was rather limited as it was subsumed under King Hassan II's larger agenda for political reform and democratization.[29] Juxtaposing this to the reform discussions that started in 1998, the presence of Islamists, women's groups, and opposing political parties, all resulted in reforms that were not simply meant to accord with a broader political goal, but were indeed substantive in nature and engaged with the various civil society actors that advocated for legal change. What Hatem, Buskens, and other scholars demonstrate by adopting a sociological approach is that debates surrounding IFL are not merely debates regarding Islamic law in which the only interested actors are Islamists and reformers, but are larger political debates that force one to contend with interest groups, individuals, and even international bodies that all have a stake in the discussion on IFL.[30] While both Buskens and Hatem are interested in the historical development of IFL, and the substantive legal changes brought about through reform, they remain primarily interested in the sociopolitical and religious mechanisms that inform changes and development in IFL.

The final method, the political science approach, is concerned with measurable outcomes resulting from the implementation of IFL. Though this approach is probably the least common, it is perhaps the most useful in tracing the impact of IFL on society. It is also particularly useful in noting the efficacy of certain reforms, and providing worldwide comparative analysis. In a recent study, Mala Htun and Lauren Weldon gathered data on family law in seventy-one countries in 1975, 1985, 1995, and 2005. Thirteen different metrics were analyzed: (1) minimum marriage age, (2) consent, (3) marriage ban, (4) spousal rights and duties, (5) guardianship, (6) name change, (7) marital property, (8) right to work, (9) divorce, (10) custody after divorce, (11) property after divorce, (12) adultery, and (13) inheritance.[31] Each country was assigned a score in each metric. Countries with higher scores were considered less discriminatory. The goal of the study was to rank countries in order of those that eliminated inequalities in family law. The study concludes that the majority of countries with high scores, and thus the absence of gender discrimination, were in Latin American and European countries. The scholars concluded this is likely due to a confluence of factors including the feminist movement, political liberalization, and change in public attitudes regarding gender roles.[32] The eight countries with the lowest scores are countries that all implement IFL.[33] Many of these countries, such as Jordan, Malaysia, Pakistan, and Egypt, all underwent reform of IFL in the 1990s, but are likely to retain their low scores because the laws on guardianship, inheritance, divorce, and custody, to name but a few, continue to distinguish on the basis of gender. However, this does not mean that reform in IFL is not registered by these types of studies. In fact, the scholars also rank those countries that underwent the greatest legal changes from 1975 until 2005. At the forefront were Morocco and Turkey, both countries that have codified IFL.

One shortcoming of the political science approach is that the decision on whether a specific law is discriminatory or not is solely based on the letter of the law itself, whereas the anthropological approach reveals that while the substantive laws may continue to be discriminatory, judges and litigants often find ways to circumvent these discriminatory laws. Notwithstanding this deficiency, it is useful in highlighting the elements of IFL that reformists should focus on. Moreover, given that Morocco and Turkey, both countries with IFL, were the ones that enacted the greatest change, civil society actors advocating for the change of IFL can look at these two countries as potential models for change. At the same time, the sociological approach to IFL has demonstrated that the terrain of IFL in each country varies, and thus programs for reform must take into consideration local circumstances.

This brief overview of approaches to IFL is by no means exhaustive—rather, it is meant to highlight the varying ways in which scholars have approached, and continue to approach, IFL. While the historical-legal approach is undoubtedly the starting point for understanding the substantive elements of IFL, how IFL is implemented, how it changes and develops, and how it impacts individuals within society, these are all facets of IFL that are explored through other approaches. Thus, to have a comprehensive understanding and presentation of IFL, scholars need to engage with all of these approaches. A final note—despite these approaches being distinct—these various approaches tend to focus on a specific country, or a specific set of countries, as opposed to drawing sweeping conclusions about IFL. This does not mean that comparative works do not exist, but they either focus on a few select countries, or they focus on select metrics, as with the political science approach. While the limited comparative lens signals the sheer amount of diversity present within IFL, one element that connects experience in different countries is the actual mechanisms and strategies used to advocate for reform, which is what we turn to next.

Mechanisms and Strategies for Reforming Codified Islamic Family Law

Although the reform of IFL in various Muslim majority countries has not been uniform, it is possible to identify central issues and modes of argument that connect otherwise differing landscapes. Before delving into these specifics, it should be noted that advocates of reform are divided between proponents of equity and proponents of equality. Proponents of equity seek to change certain elements of IFL but remain committed to religious interpretations that acknowledge gender distinctions on the basis of biology. Reform by proponents of equity usually emphasize the educational, economic, and political rights of women, but do not seek to change substantive laws regarding inheritance, marriage, and other gender-based laws. As a result, they address specific laws within IFL deemed problematic, but are open to accepting others. On the other hand, proponents of equality advocate for complete equality between the sexes and do not acknowledge gender distinctions on the basis of biology and/or religious interpretations. Proponents of equality often adopt a piecemeal approach to the reform of IFL because they view it as the most effective way of reforming IFL. On a legislative and judicial level, the desire for equality dominates. According to Chibli Mallat in his study on Middle Eastern legal systems, "legislators and judges in the twentieth century operate with an expressed or muted awareness of the legal equality between two individuals across the gender divide of the nuclear family."[34] In the classical Islamic legal world, the concept of equality between the genders did not exist, and this understanding was canonized in IFL through the process of codification. Thus, "when an egalitarian prism is used for the assessment of gender-based rights, it stands in sharp contrast to an overall framework of classical law which is indifferent to gender equality."[35] Crucially for Mallat, contemporary judges and legislators operating within the twentieth-century prism of legal equality have been instrumental in reforming IFL.

Chibli Mallat traces these judicial and legislative reformers to the early twentieth century when codification after colonization in countries such as Syria, Iraq, Tunisia, and Morocco was taking place. The primary legal method adopted by these early legal reformers was what he refers to as eclecticism (*takhayyur*). Instead of drafters adopting legal opinions from only one of the four major schools (Hanafī, Shafīʿī, Mālikī, or Hanbalī), in creating these family law codes they mined opinions from various schools to determine which ruling was most appropriate.[36] Some have negatively dubbed this contemporary phenomenon as "legal forum shopping." However, Ahmed Fekry has recently demonstrated legal eclecticism was not an entirely modern phenomenon. He notes that in the classical period, in addition to choosing opinions from varying schools, scholars also combined two opinions within the same school, and often gave dispensations to individuals to follow a less stringent opinion in certain circumstances. All of these methods fall under the banner of what he labels as "pragmatic eclecticism."[37] He does note, however, that "legal forum shopping" became more dominant in the modern period. In explaining this shift, "with the dominance of the codification episteme, which emphasized stability and determinancy of rules over flexibility, and centralization over local contingencies, there was an institutional need for more flexibility to accommodate the evolving needs of society and empire."[38] According to Fekry, because codification limited flexibility within the law, both legislators at the time of drafting, and judges during adjudication, increasingly turned to pragmatic eclecticism as a way of issuing laws that were conducive to the social milieu that litigants inhabit. Moreover, as the law is still derived from within the parameters of Islamic law, it is more likely that proponents of equity, who continue to champion religious interpretations, would readily assent to it. In this way, pragmatic eclecticism represents one of the most efficacious ways to enact lasting legal change and balance between competing voices of equality and equity.

The landmark example of eclecticism, according to Mallat, was the 1986 Arab Family Law Project, which sought to create a unified family law code for all Arab countries. Drafting of the code began in the 1970s and continued all the way until 1986. In deriving laws, the drafters would return to classical Islamic legal texts in order to find precedents that would support improving the legal status of women. Some of the main reforms suggested in the project included increasing the minimum age of marriage, restricting polygamy, introducing spousal support, restricting the right of divorce for men, and increasing the custody rights of women.[39] Although the resulting Unified Arab Code of Personal Status was never formally adopted, it provided a roadmap for legal reform for IFL.

Stepping outside legislative reforms and into the world of civil society modes of advocating reform, the picture is complicated due to the number of actors present. Aside from the division between proponents of equity and proponents of equality indicated above, specific arguments for the reform of IFL differ. Some groups voice their desire for legal and social reform through the paradigm of the Universal Declaration of Human Rights in 1948. This is most pursued by proponents of equality and international NGOs present in various Muslim majority countries.[40] Other groups focus on the economic contributions of women to both society and their families, as well as their social and political contributions.[41] The economic agency of women has led to arguments regarding the equalization of inheritance, the right of maintenance after divorce, and restriction on polygamy. To embed these changes legislatively, legal eclecticism remains the dominant mode. In some cases, judges also invoke arguments based on public interest (*maṣlaḥa*) in order to effect changes in the economic and social status of women, but these arguments are still couched within a religious vernacular. Thus, while awareness of the need to reform IFL can be credited to grassroots civil society groups, resultant changes emerged legislatively.[42]

Since the reform of IFL differs from country to country, the next section will provide a comparative example of reform between Morocco and Malaysia. Morocco has adopted a comprehensive approach to reforming IFL, with much of it being facilitated by politics and governmental structures that are conducive to reform. On the other hand, realizing reform in Malaysia has been much more difficult. These examples will aptly demonstrate the diversity of reform projects related to IFL, and the complex social, political, and religious variables at play.

Comparative Reform in Morocco and Malaysia

Htun and Weldon observe that in the thirty-year period between 1975 and 2005, Morocco made the most substantive legal changes addressing gender inequalities.

According to the same study, in 2005 Malaysia remained one of the countries with the most discriminatory laws toward women. What allowed for such sweeping reforms in Morocco and not in Malaysia? And what do these differences reveal about prospects and challenges of reforming IFL moving forward? These are some of the questions explored in this section.

Morocco, a constitutional monarchy, underwent the first set of reforms to its personal status code, the *Mudawwana*, in the early 1990s under the leadership of King Hassan II, although calls for reform began in the 1970s. In 1991, a million signatures were gathered by L'Union de l'Action Feminine (UAF), a women's group, demanding reform. Responding, the king assembled a committee consisting of twenty men, a woman, and one member of the royal court to discuss reforms. The committee suggested a number of changes focusing on consent, male guardianship, and polygamy that were enacted in 1993 by decree of the king.[43] The changes made, however, were considered unsatisfactory by most, so when his son, King Muhammad VI, ascended to the throne in 1999, the debate regarding reforms resumed. After his ascension to the throne, a series of rallies demanding changes to the *Mudawwana* culminated in Muhammad VI announcing the creation of a commission in 2001 to reform the law. This commission was more expansive than the one assembled by his father—consisting of members of the judiciary, religious scholars, politicians, and most crucially, women from a variety of different women's groups. After two years the king announced sweeping changes that would address almost every element of the *Mudawwana* that was seen as promoting injustice and inequality. Unlike the reforms of his father, which were enacted by royal decree when Parliament was dissolved, the reforms suggested by Muhammad VI were deliberated in Parliament and the reforms were not finalized until January 2004. The reforms were praised internationally for affirming equality between the genders and for providing a legislative roadmap for other countries seeking to reform IFL.[44]

The sweeping reforms of 2004 revealed a political determination hitherto unseen. According to some scholars, increasing political opposition against Muhammad VI after his ascendency to the throne impelled the king to use the reform of the *Mudawwana* as a way of placating various ruling elites in order to maintain power. Catalano goes as far as arguing that the power of the king, and his title of "Commander of the Faithful" played an important role.[45] This has led other scholars to note that civil society activism, while essential, is not necessarily the main determinant of reform. Indeed, some scholars contend that the eventual push to reform was primarily driven by the king's desire to remain in power. Thus, counterintuitively, Cavatorta has argued that civil society activism can result in the entrenching of authoritarianism when the reforms are facilitated by a constitutional monarch.[46]

The other challenges to achieving reform are implementation and enforcement. While legal reform has taken place, long-term efficacy depends on the judiciary's commitment to consistent implementation. Dorthe Engelcke analyzes the implementation of the 2004 reforms, concluding that cultural resistance to the reforms and bureaucratic inertia prevents the creation of a single "normative legal order" that mirrors the reforms set forth in the *Mudawwana*.[47] These various scholars all highlight that the further entrenchment of monarchical power, the absence of uniform mechanisms of implementation, and cultural and civil society resistance all circumscribed the efficacy of these reforms. These obstacles also reveal the shortcoming in concentrating on legal change without considering the praxis outcomes of those legal changes.

Shifting now to Malaysia, the lack of reforming IFL is surprising since Malaysia is often heralded as one of the more progressive Muslim countries. Malaysia is considered a federalist constitutional republic composed of thirteen federal states. Although Islam is ordained in the constitution by virtue of Article 3, the extent to which Islamic law governs the lives of individuals is a *state* question, not a federal one. There have been various attempts at unification, but each state continues to exercise its own administration of IFL. Civil and Sharīʿa courts are separated, and are overseen by two high courts that have jurisdiction over all courts. Any attempts at reforming Islamic law depends on convergence of state and state custom.[48] There was one semisuccessful attempt in 1984 to unify IFL though the Islamic Family Law (Federal Territory Act). This act was seen to reform many of the central issues of concern for women; however, given that states continued to have legislative and judicial power, the enforcement of the Act was patchy. To complicate matters further, in 1988, the Sharīʿa courts received even more independence when Article 121 was introduced, which eliminated the power of the civil courts to hear appeals from the Sharīʿa courts. The lack of appeals to the civil courts meant that state Sharīʿa courts could increasingly function within a vacuum.[49]

Nevertheless, civil society groups persisted in advocating for the rights of women. The most famous to date is Sisters in Islam (SIS).[50] Created in 1988, the group was founded by seven women advocating for reform and also providing alternative religious explanations for certain gender-biased religious interpretations of the Quran. SIS a held a variety of seminars and eventually presented a memorandum to the federal government in 1997 that requested comprehensive reforms to the 1984 Act and provided proposals for substantive legal reforms.[51] In 1997 the Department of Islamic Development in Malaysia was created in order to standardize IFL laws, and the following year the Department of Syariah Judiciary Malaysia was created to ensure that citizens were given equal legal rights.[52] Though these were not legal reforms, they were considered victories by the SIS, who noted that equal access to legal rights was a problem across the states.

SIS also champions for adequate judicial training in the Sharīʿa, the appointment of female judges, and equity in the application of laws. It furthermore focuses on procedural reform relating to implementation and raising awareness of the various ways in which women are disadvantaged in the Sharīʿa courts. While there have been some reforms relating to consent, divorce, and polygamy, many issues remain relating to domestic violence, inheritance, the bias of male judges, and the accessibility of rights that SIS and other women's groups continue to champion.[53] Given that the implementation and adjudication of IFL continues to be a state issue, the advocacy of SIS must to some extent also be state-specific.

When comparing the experiences of Morocco and Malaysia, it is clear that the ability to reform IFL is directly connected to the arrangement of political power within nation-states. Morocco is a constitutional monarchy, so legislative decrees from the king are absolute, even if the Parliament resists. On the other hand, even if federal laws are passed in

Malaysia, states can find ways to circumnavigate these laws, decreasing their authority. Second, political actors are reactive to social pressures, so despite civil society actors not having direct legislative power, they are able to affect change through campaigns for awareness, protests, and petitions. Crucially, however, it is important that these civil society groups remain cognizant of the political terrain in which they advocate reforms.

Conclusion

This brief overview of IFL scrapes the surface of a very large and complicated topic that continues to unfold in varying ways in the countries that implement it. While some reform attempts have been successful, many issues continue to challenge advocates of both equality and equity. In the reforms that have taken place in various countries, the focus has been on questions of polygamy, divorce, consent and coercion, and the right of women to work. Contemporary reform debates seek to tackle a new set of issues—equal inheritance, custody of children after remarriage, and domestic violence. In addition to focusing on substantive reforms, there is increasing awareness that substantive reforms do not always translate into *actual* reforms, thus attention must be given to mechanisms of ensuring enforcement, equal access to the law, and widespread civil society support for any legal changes enacted.

Notes

1. By "Islamization" I am referring to the formal legislation of Islamic law in Muslim-majority countries, regardless of whether Islam is the official religion of the state or not.
2. OIC stands for the Organization of Islamic Cooperation, which was founded in 1969 to provide a unified global voice for the concern of Muslims. In 2023, the Cooperation had fifty-seven members, and forty-seven of these members are Muslim-majority countries. For more on the OIC, see Turan Kayaoglu, *The Organization of Islamic Cooperation: Politics, Problems and Potential* (New York: Routledge, 2015).
3. For a comparative study of IFL, see Abdullahi An-Na'im, *Islamic Family Law in a Changing World: A Global Resource Book* (New York: Zed Books, 2002).
4. For her exhaustive study on the development of IFL, see Lynn Welchman, *Women and Muslim Family Law in Arab States* (Amsterdam: Amsterdam University Press, 2007).
5. Ibid., 12. Muhammad Rashid Feroze, "Family Laws of the Turkish Republish," *Islamic Studies* 1, no. 2 (1962): 131.
6. Welchmann, *Women and Muslim Family Law*, 13.
7. Ibid.
8. Yuksel Sezgin, *Human Rights under State-Enforced Religious Family Laws in Israel, Egypt and India* (Cambridge: Cambridge University Press, 2015), 27
9. Ibid., 27.
10. Ibid., 27.
11. Ibid., 33–34.

12. Ibid., 39.
13. Annelies Moors, "Public Debates on Family Law Reform: Participants, Positions and Styles of Argument in the 1990s," *Islamic Law and Society* 10, no. 1 (2003): 4.
14. Ibid., 4, 7.
15. Ibid., 8.
16. Welchman, *Women and Muslim Family Laws*, 9.
17. Other notable works within this approach include: Jamal Nasir, *The Islamic Law of Personal Status* (Leiden: Brill, 2009) and Nasir, *The Status of Women under Islamic Law* (Leiden: Brill, 2009); Fawzi Najjar, "Egypt's Laws of Personal Status," *Arab Studies Quarterly* 10 (1988): 319–344; Ebrahim Moosa, "The Poetics and Politics of Law after Empire: Reading Women's Rights in the Contestation of Law," *UCLA Journal of Near Eastern Law* 1 (2001–2): 1–46; Ruth Mitchell, "Family Law in Algeria before and after the 1984 Family Code," in *Islamic Law, Theory and Practice*, ed. Robert Gleave (London: I.B. Tauris, 1997), 194–204; Chibli Mallat, "Shi'ism and Sunnism in Iraq: Revisiting the Codes," in *Islamic Family Law*, eds. Chibli Mallat and Jane Connors (London: Springer, 1991), 71–91; Tahir Mahmood, *Statutes of Personal Law in Islamic Countries: History, Texts and Analysis* (New Delhi: Institute of Objective Studies, 1995); Naila Hamadeh, "Islamic Family Legislation. The Authoritarian Discourse of Silence," in *Feminism and Islam*, ed. Mai Yamani (Ithaca: Ithaca University Press, 1996), 331–349.
18. John L. Esposito and Natana J. DeLong-Bas, *Women in Muslim Family Law* (Syracuse: Syracuse University Press, 2001).
19. Amira Sonbol, "Adults and Minors in Ottoman Sharīʿa Courts," in *Women, The Family and Divorce Laws in Islamic History*, ed. Amira Sonbol (Syracuse: Syracuse University Press, 1996), 236–258. Also see Sonbol, "Women in Sharīʿa courts: A Historical and Methodological Discussion," *Fordham International Law Journal* 27 (2003): 225–253.
20. Judith Tucker, *In the House of the Law: Gender and Islamic Law in Ottoman Syria and Palestine* (Berkeley and Los Angeles: University of California Press, 1998).
21. Lawrence Rosen, "Equity and Discretion in a Modern Legal System," *Law and Society Review* 15, no. 2 (1980): 217–246. Also see Rob Shaham, "An Egyptian Judge in a Period of Change: Qadi Ahmad Muhammad Shakir 1892–1958," *Journal of the American Oriental Society* 119, no. 3 (1999): 440–456.
22. Lawrence Rosen, *The Anthropology of Justice: Law as Culture in Islamic Society* (Cambridge: Cambridge University Press, 2008).
23. Nahda Shehada, "House of Obedience: Social Norms, Individual Agency and Historical Contingency," *Journal of Middle East Women's Studies* 5, no. 1 (2009): 24. Also see Shehada, "Flexibility versus Rigidity in the Practice of Islamic Family Law" in *Political and Legal Anthropology Review* 32, no. 1 (2009): 28–46.
24. For other notable studies, see Ziba Mir-Hosseini, *Marriage on Trial: A Study of Islamic Family Law* (London: I. B. Tauris, 2000); Susan Hirsch, *Pronouncing and Preserving: Gender and the Discourses of Disputing in an African Islamic Court* (Chicago: Chicago University Press, 1998); Barbara Stowasser and Zeineb Abdul-Magd, "*Tahlil* Marriage in *Shariʿa:* Legal Codes and the Contemporary Fatawa Literature," in *Islamic Law and the Challenges of Modernity*, ed. Yvonne Haddad and Barbara Stowasser (Walnut Creek: AltaMira Press, 2004), 161–181; Ron Shaham, *Family and the Courts in Modern Egypt: A Study Based on Decisions by the Shariʿa Courts* (Leiden: Brill, 1997); Anna Wurth, "A Sana'a Court: The Family and the Ability to Negotiate," *Islamic Law and Society* 2, no. 3 (1995): 320–340.

25. Annelies Moors, "Public Debates," 4.
26. Mervat F. Hatem, "Economic and Political Liberation in Egypt and the Demise of State Feminism," *International Journal of Middle East Studies* 24 (1992): 231.
27. Ibid., 233, 239.
28. Leon Buskens, "Recent Debates on Family Law Reform in Morocco: Islamic Law as Politics in an Emerging Public Sphere," *Islamic Law and Society* 10, no. 1 (2003): 71.
29. Ibid., 79–80.
30. The sociological approach builds on studies of the Muslim world that focus on the emergence of a public sphere. For this, see Dale Eickelman and Jon Anderson, *New Media in the Muslim World: The Emerging Public Sphere* (Bloomington and Indianapolis: Indiana University Press, 1999). For further sociological approaches, see Mounira Charrad, *States and Women's Rights: The Making of Postcolonial Tunisia, Algeria and Morocco* (Berkeley: University of California Press, 2001); Laurie Brand, *Women, The State and Political Liberalization: Middle Eastern and North African Experiences* (New York: Columbia University Press, 1998); Karima Bennoune, "Between Betrayal and Betrayal: Fundamentalism, Family Law and Feminist Struggle in Algeria," *Arab Studies Quarterly* 17 (1995): 51–76; Margot Badran, *Feminists, Islam and Nation: Gender and the Making of Modern Egypt* (Princeton: Princeton University Press, 1996).
31. Mala Htun and S. Laurel Weldon, "State Power, Religion and Women's Rights: A Comparative Analysis of Family Law," *Indiana Journal of Global Legal Studies* 18, no. 1 (2011): 151–153.
32. Ibid., 155.
33. Ibid., 158.
34. Chibli Mallat, *Introduction to Middle East Law* (Oxford: Oxford University Press, 2009), 355.
35. Ibid., 356.
36. Ibid., 367–368. John L. Esposito also notes the early use of *takhayyur* during the Ottoman period. See Esposito, *Women in Muslim Family Law*, 53–54.
37. Ahmed Fekry, *Pragmatism in Islamic Law: A Social and Intellectual History* (Syracuse: Syracuse University Press, 2015), 1–31, 167–201.
38. Ibid., 15.
39. Mallat, *Introduction*, 368 ff.
40. See, for example, Human Rights Watch, *Divorced from Justice: Women's Unequal Access to Divorce in Egypt, Human Rights Watch Reports* 1, no. 8 (2004); Ann Elizabeth Mayer, "Islamic Reservations to the Human Rights Convention," *Recht van de Islam* 15 (1998): 25–45 and Mayer, "Internationalizing the Conversation on Arab Women's Rights: Arab Countries Face the CEDAW Committee," in *Islamic Law and the Challenges of Modernity* (Walnut Creek: AltaMira Press, 2004), 133–160.
41. See, for example, Bruce Maddy-Weitzman, "Women, Islam and the Moroccan State: The Struggle over the Personal Status Law," *Middle East Journal* 59, no. 3 (2005): 393–410; Tahir Mahmood, *Family Law Reform in the Muslim World* (Bombay: N.M. Tripathi, 1972); Valentine Moghadam, ed., *Gender and National Identity: Women and Politics in Muslim Societies* (New York: Zed Books, 1994).
42. For an important overview of reform in different countries, see Nadjma Yassari, *Changing God's Law: The Dynamics of Middle Eastern Family Law* (London: Routledge, 2018); Fazlur Rahman, "A Survey of the Modernization of Muslim Family Law," *International Journal of Middle East Studies* 11 (1980): 451–465; and Lynn Welchmann, ed., *Women's Rights and*

Islamic Family Law: Perspectives on Reform (New York: Zed Books, 2004). For the use of Islamic law in reform, see Ziba Mir-Hosseini, "The Construction of Gender in Islamic Legal Thought and Strategies for Reform," *Hawwa: Journal of Women of the Middle East and the Islamic World* 1, no. 1 (2003): 1–28; and John Hursh, "Advancing Women's Rights through Islamic Law: The Example of Morocco," *Berkeley Journal of Gender, Law and Justice* 22, no. 2 (2012): 252–305.

43. For an overview of the development of IFL in Morocco, see Leon Buskens, "Sharīʿa and National Law in Morocco," in *Sharīʿa Incorporated*, ed. Jan Otto (Chicago: Chicago University Press), 89–138; and Buskens, "Recent Debates on Family Law Reform," 70–131. For the involvement of women's groups in this process, see Amy Evrad, *The Moroccan Women's Rights Movement* (Syracuse, NY: Syracuse University Press, 2014), 176–226.
44. See Buskens, "Recent Debates on Family Law Reform"; and Katie Zoglin, "Morocco's Family Code: Improving Equality for Women," *Human Rights Quarterly*, 31 (2009): 964–984.
45. Serida Catalano, "Islamists and the Regime: Applying a New Framework for Analysis to the Case of Family Code Reforms in Morocco," *Party Politics*, 19, no. 3 (2001): 408–431.
46. Francesco Cavatorta, "Liberal Outcomes through Undemocratic Means: The Reform of the Code de statut personnel in Morocco," *Journal of Modern African Studies* 47, no. 4 (2009): 487–506.
47. Dorthe Engelcke, "Interpreting the 2004 Moroccan Family Law: Street-Level Bureaucrats, Women's Groups and the Preservation of Multiple Normativities," *Law and Social Inquiry* (2017): 1–28. Also see Ann Eisenberg, "Law on the Books vs. Law in Action: Under-Enforcement of Morocco's Reformed 2004 Family Law," *Cornell International Law Journal*, 44 (2011): 694–728.
48. Andrew Harding, "Islamic Law in Malaysia," *Yearbook of Islamic and Middle Eastern Law Online* (1995): 61–72; Harding, "Sharia and National Law in Malaysia," in *Sharīʿa Incorporated*, 491–528.
49. Farid Shuaib, "The Islamic Legal System in Malaysia," *Pacific Rim Law and Policy Journal* 21, no. 1 (2012): 85–113.
50. They continue to have an active online presence and have a rich archive of their activism. See http://www.sistersinislam.org.my/.
51. Rebecca Foley, "Muslim Women's Challenges to Islamic Law: The Case of Malaysia," *International Feminist Journal of Politics* 6, no. 1 (2004): 53–84, 67.
52. Shuaib, "The Islamic Legal System," 93.
53. Foley, "Muslim Women's Challenges," 69–72.

Bibliography

An-Na'im, Abdullah. *Islamic Family Law in a Changing World: A Global Resource Book*. New York: Zed Books, 2002.

Badran, Margot. *Feminists, Islam and Nation: Gender and the Making of Modern Egypt*. Princeton: Princeton University Press, 1996.

Bennoune, Karima. "Between Betrayal and Betrayal: Fundamentalism, Family Law and Feminist Struggle in Algeria." *Arab Studies Quarterly* 17 (1995): 51–76.

Brand, Laurie. *Women, The State and Political Liberalization: Middle Eastern and North African Experiences*. New York: Columbia University Press, 1998.

Buskens, Leon. "Recent Debates on Family Law Reform in Morocco: Islamic Law as Politics in an Emerging Public Sphere." *Islamic Law and Society* 10, no. 1 (2003): 70–131.
Buskens, Leon. "Sharīʿa and National Law in Morocco." In *Sharīʿa Incorporated*, edited by Jan Otto, 89–138. Chicago: Chicago University Press, 2010.
Catalano, Serida. "Islamists and the Regime: Applying a New Framework for Analysis to the Case of Family Code Reforms in Morocco." *Party Politics* 19, no. 3 (2001): 408–431.
Cavatorta, Francesco. "Liberal Outcomes through Undemocratic Means: The Reform of the Code de statut personnel in Morocco." *Journal of Modern African Studies* 47, no. 4 (2009): 487–506.
Charrad, Mounira. *States and Women's Rights: The Making of Postcolonial Tunisia, Algeria and Morocco.* Berkeley: University of California Press, 2001.
DeLong-Bas, Natana J., and John L. Esposito. *Women in Muslim Family Law.* Syracuse: Syracuse University Press, 2001.
Eickelman, Dale, and Jon Anderson. *New Media in the Muslim World: The Emerging Public Sphere.* Bloomington and Indianapolis: Indiana University Press, 1999.
Eisenberg, Ann. "Law on the Books vs. Law in Action: Under-Enforcement of Morocco's Reformed 2004 Family Law." *Cornell International Law Journal* 44 (2011): 694–728.
Engelcke, Dorthe. "Interpreting the 2004 Moroccan Family Law: Street-Level Bureaucrats, Women's Groups and the Preservation of Multiple Normativities." *Law and Social Inquiry* (2017): 1–28.
Evrad, Amy. *The Moroccan Women's Rights Movement.* Syracuse, NY: Syracuse University Press, 2014.
Fekry, Ahmed. *Pragmatism in Islamic Law: A Social and Intellectual History.* Syracuse, NY: Syracuse University Press, 2015.
Feroze, Muhammad Rashid. "Family Laws of the Turkish Republish." *Islamic Studies* 1, no. 2 (1962): 131–147.
Foley, Rebecca. "Muslim Women's Challenges to Islamic Law: The Case of Malaysia." *International Feminist Journal of Politics* 6, no. 1 (2004): 53–84.
Hamadeh, Naila. "Islamic Family Legislation. The Authoritarian Discourse of Silence." In *Feminism and Islam*, edited by Mai Yamani, 331–349. Ithaca, NY: Ithaca University Press, 1996.
Harding, Andrew. "Islamic Law in Malaysia." Yearbook of Islamic and Middle Eastern Law Online 2, no. 1 (1995): 61–72.
Harding, Andrew. "Sharia and National Law in Malaysia." In *Sharīʿa Incorporated*, edited by Jan Otto, 491–528. Chicago: Chicago University Press, 2010.
Hatem, Mervat F. "Economic and Political Liberation in Egypt and the Demise of State Feminism." *International Journal of Middle East Studies* 24 (1992): 231–251.
Hirsch, Susan. *Pronouncing and Preserving: Gender and the Discourses of Disputing in an African Islamic Court.* Chicago: Chicago University Press, 1998.
Htun, Mala, and S. Laurel Weldon. "State Power, Religion and Women's Rights: A Comparative Analysis of Family Law." *Indiana Journal of Global Legal Studies* 18, no. 1 (2011): 151–153.
Hursh, John. "Advancing Women's Rights through Islamic Law: The Example of Morocco." *Berkeley Journal of Gender, Law and Justice* 22, no. 2 (2012): 252–305.
Maddy-Weitzman, Bruce. "Women, Islam and the Moroccan State: The Struggle over the Personal Status Law." *Middle East Journal* 59, no. 3 (2005): 393–410.
Mahmood, Tahir. *Statutes of Personal Law in Islamic Countries: History, Texts and Analysis.* New Delhi: Institute of Objective Studies, 1995.

Mahmood, Tahir. *Family Law Reform in the Muslim World*. Bombay: N.M. Tripathi, 1972.
Mallat, Chibli. *Introduction to Middle East* Law. Oxford: Oxford University Press, 2009.
Mallat, Chibli. "Shi'ism and Sunnism in Iraq: Revisiting the Codes." In *Islamic Family Law*, edited by Chibli Mallat and Jane Connor, 71–91. London: Springer, 1991.
Mayer, Ann Elizabeth. "Internationalizing the Conversation on Arab Women's Rights: Arab Countries Face the CEDAW Committee." In *Islamic Law and the Challenges of Modernity*, edited by Yvonne Haddad and Barbara Stowasser, 133–160. Walnut Creek: AltaMira Press, 2004.
Mayer, Ann Elizabeth. "Islamic Reservations to the Human Rights Convention." *Recht van de Islam* 15 (1998): 25–45.
Mitchell, Ruth. "Family Law in Algeria before and after the 1984 Family Code." In *Islamic Law, Theory and Practice*, edited by Robert Gleave, 194–204. London: I.B. Tauris, 1997.
Mir-Hosseini, Ziba. "The Construction of Gender in Islamic Legal Thought and Strategies for Reform." *Hawwa: Journal of Women of the Middle East and the Islamic World* 1, no. 1 (2003): 1–28.
Mir-Hosseini, Ziba. *Marriage on Trial: A Study of Islamic Family Law*. London: I. B. Tauris, 2000.
Moghadam, Valentine, ed. *Gender and National Identity: Women and Politics in Muslim Societies*. New York: Zed Books, 1994.
Moors, Annelies. "Public Debates on Family Law Reform: Participants, Positions and Styles of Argument in the 1990s." *Islamic Law and Society* 10, no. 1 (2003): 1–11.
Moosa, Ebrahim. "The Poetics and Politics of Law after Empire: Reading Women's Rights in the Contestation of Law." *UCLA Journal of Near Eastern Law* 1 (2001–2): 1–46.
Najjar, Fawzi. "Egypt's Laws of Personal Status." *Arab Studies Quarterly* 10 (1988): 319–344.
Nasir, Jamal. *The Islamic Law of Personal Status*. Leiden: Brill, 2009.
Nasir, Jamal. *The Status of Women under Islamic Law*. Leiden: Brill, 2009.
Rahman, Fazlur. "A Survey of the Modernization of Muslim Family Law." *International Journal of Middle East Studies* 11 (1980): 451–465.
Rosen, Lawrence. *The Anthropology of Justice: Law as Culture in Islamic Society*. Cambridge: Cambridge University Press, 2008.
Rosen, Lawrence. "Equity and Discretion in a Modern Legal System." *Law and Society Review* 15, no. 2 (1980): 217–246.
Sezgin, Sezgin. *Human Rights under State-Enforced Religious Family Laws in Israel, Egypt and India*. Cambridge: Cambridge University Press, 2015.
Shaham, Ron. "An Egyptian Judge in a Period of Change: Qadi Ahmad Muhammad Shakir 1892–1958." *Journal of the American Oriental Society* 119, no. 3 (1999): 440–456.
Shaham, Ron. *Family and the Courts in Modern Egypt: A Study Based on Decisions by the Shariʿa Courts*. Leiden: Brill, 1997.
Shehada, Nahda, "Flexibility versus Rigidity in the Practice of Islamic Family Law" in *Political and Legal Anthropology Review* 32, no. 1 (2009): 28–46.
Shehada, Nahda. "House of Obedience: Social Norms, Individual Agency and Historical Contingency." *Journal of Middle East Women's Studies* 5, no. 1 (2009): 24–49.
Shuaib, Farid. "The Islamic Legal System in Malaysia." *Pacific Rim Law and Policy Journal* 21, no. 1 (2012): 85–113.
Sonbol, Amira. "Adults and Minors in Ottoman Sharīʿa Courts." In *Women, The Family and Divorce Laws in Islamic History*, edited by Amira Sonbol, 236–258. Syracuse, NY: Syracuse University Press, 1996.

Sonbol, Amira. "Women in Sharīʿa Courts: A Historical and Methodological Discussion." *Fordham International Law Journal* 27 (2003): 225–253.
Stowasser, Barbara, and Zeineb Abdul-Magd. "*Tahlil* marriage in *Shariʿa:* Legal Codes and the Contemporary Fatawa Literature." In *Islamic Law and the Challenges of Modernity*, edited by Yvonne Haddad and Barbara Stowasser, 161–181. Walnut Creek: AltaMira Press, 2004.
Tucker Judith. *In the House of the Law: Gender and Islamic Law in Ottoman Syria and Palestine.* Berkeley and Los Angeles: University of California Press, 1998.
Welchman, Lynn. *Women and Muslim Family Law in Arab States*. Amsterdam: Amsterdam University Press, 2007.
Welchman, Lynn. *Women's Rights and Islamic Family Law: Perspectives on Reform*. New York: Zed Books, 2004.
Wurth, Anna. "A Sana'a Court: The Family and the Ability to Negotiate." *Islamic Law and Society* 2, no. 3 (1995): 320–340.
Yassari, Nadjma. *Changing God's Law: The Dynamics of Middle Eastern Family Law*. London: Routledge, 2018.
Zoglin, Katie. "Morocco's Family Code: Improving Equality for Women." *Human Rights Quarterly* 31 (2009): 964–984.

CHAPTER 8

WOMEN'S RIGHTS AND DUTIES IN CLASSICAL LEGAL TEXTS

Modern Rereadings

NATANA J. DELONG-BAS

Introduction

The broad outlining and quantification of what is often formulated as "women's rights and duties in classical legal literature" has long been a preoccupation of scholars seeking to define and portray an ideal Islamic society in which "women" are a legal category and in which gender roles carry social and political implications. Classical legal scholars operated within patriarchal family and social structures and political hierarchies in which people were presumed to have specified gender roles and assigned status in society. While theory described "ideal" societies and conditions, practice varied according to location, placement in socioeconomic and political hierarchies, free or slave status, ethnic background (particularly Arab vs. non-Arab), and religious affiliation. These categories serve as guideposts for contemporary scholars, although with caution not to use them in a reductionist, unidimensional way that assumes that all "women," "female slaves," or "mothers," for example, are inherently the same. Contemporary scholars are further challenged to engage the classical literature based on the context in which it was written, but also with an eye toward methodologies designed to unveil the underlying purposes and objectives of the legal literature. This is particularly true where positive views of a diversity of opinions and conceptions of justice and the common good (*maslaha*) are concerned,[1] which require that they be placed within the broader sphere of complex and changing political, legal, social, and cultural contexts, looking for continuity and change over time and space, and comparing and contrasting them with other surrounding societies and structures.

Constructing the Field of Islamic Law

While a comprehensive review of the construction and development of the field of Islamic law is not possible here, some understanding of the history and context in which Western scholarship has engaged the topic is critical as a lens for understanding how and why the field developed as it did. Islamic law became a topic of serious scholarly Western interest during the era of Orientalist scholarship (late nineteenth through mid-twentieth century). Such interest was largely driven by concerns previously raised in the field of biblical studies, namely origins of religious belief and practice; tracing what were described as borrowings or even thefts across religious traditions; the discovery of the historicity of foundational figures outside of religious texts; the development of scripture as a crafted and redacted human product; and dismissal of oral tradition as inherently unreliable.[2] While these lines of inquiry opened new, non-faith-based methodologies and approaches to the study of Islam and Islamic law, they also tended to carry heavy Western, Christian and colonial biases that presumed falsity and shortcomings in the topics under study, as well as the inferiority of Muḥammad as spiritual and political/military leader and polygynous husband, in contrast to the purely spiritual Jesus. These early works on Islamic law must be read and analyzed with that context in mind.

During the era of Orientalist scholarship, women's rights and duties were not a separate topic of study, but were subsumed into larger questions about when and in what form Islamic law first emerged. Scholars such as Joseph Schacht[3] and Ignaz Goldziher[4] argued that Islamic law as we know it, along with the *ḥadīth* literature recording Muḥammad's statements and example, existed neither during Muḥammad's lifetime nor for the greater part of the first Islamic century, but instead were established later and then projected backward to Muḥammad and the Companions. Such assertions served to desacralize, at least for Western scholars, both Islamic law and the sources on which it was based, rendering both deliberately constructed sources with purely human origins. The resulting controversy over the nature and origins of Islamic law and its sources sparked intense scholarly debate in both Western and Muslim scholarship that continues until today.[5]

Early studies of Islamic law are characterized by their focus on mechanics—what it said, how it operated, what rules and regulations it established, and what rights and duties were assigned to different groups of people. This constituted a first stage in the Western study of Islamic law, establishing a database of theoretical knowledge at the same time that it enshrined a methodology of critique that presumed Western superiority in the provision of justice and highlighted perceived failures of the Islamic system, such as the capacity of individuals to bribe and otherwise circumvent the system. While neither Schacht nor Goldziher gave specific attention to women and gender issues as such, their methodology of classifying groups of individuals according to rights and duties, particularly within family law, established the framework for how the field was approached for decades, whether in support or opposition, and focused attention on documenting and authenticating the earliest versions of various writings and sources. At the same time, particular topics, such as family law, were deemed worthy of study, while others, such as worship and ritual, were not, despite being quantitatively more important.

A second stage in the modern study of Islamic law sought to analyze it through the broader underlying values of the system, the construction of gender roles, and variances between theory and practice. Wael Hallaq[6] connected Islamic law to the community it practiced and served, rendering it a matter of social morality embedded in the social order, not just a judicial system connected to power structures.[7] Because the law is not intended to stand alone, Hallaq argues that it should not be reduced to the simple study of texts, but must necessarily include attention to the surrounding social realities. He accuses the colonial era of reducing *Sharīʿa* to family law with a patriarchal flavor—a reduction from which Islamic law as it is implemented and practiced today has never recovered. Although he does not engage women and gender as a field of study, Hallaq nevertheless finds an abundance of material that highlights the presence and active voices of women as community members and court litigants, ranging from women defending their reputation, honor, status, and material interests to managing financial affairs and property and serving as guardians of minors, all of which belies theoretical legal literature reducing women to victims or objects of contract. Instead, Hallaq argues that women wielded considerable financial power and capably used the courts to bolster their own positions. These kinds of transactions in commercial law and court records are clearly in need of more comprehensive research, particularly in comparison and contrast to jurisprudential writings from the same time and place.[8]

Added to these two stages of study in Islamic law have been case studies enhancing the database of knowledge, particularly through comparative analyses of different locations, times and cultures, especially different parts of the Ottoman Empire and comparisons and contrasts between Europe and the Middle East. There remains ample room for expansion of such comparative scholarship focused on the classical period, examining developments in different locations during the same time, tracing the spread and cross-pollination of ideas and their retranslation into different contexts, particularly urban-rural dynamics and varying relationships to power in the center versus the periphery,[9] and reading legal literature against other literature from the same time and place to uncover a fuller picture of women's lives.[10]

Although debates about the origins and dating of foundational texts can be tedious, they have shaped the field of study of Islamic law from its inception and are particularly important in raising questions about how normative roles of women and their accompanying rights and duties came about.[11] Do they date to Muḥammad's lifetime, which would indicate his approval or at least acceptance, or are they developments from later points in time that were projected backwards in the quest for legitimacy? As Muslim women today seek to recover, reclaim, and even rediscover their rights and duties, these questions have ongoing significance, particularly because only serious, rigorous, scholarly analysis and questioning of those foundations can lead to substantive change.

Rediscovering the Foundational Texts

The call for rediscovery of the foundational texts of Islam with respect to "women's rights and duties in classical legal literature" began with two pivotal articles by Azizah al-Hibri[12] that established the questions, methodologies, and objectives for the field as it has developed. Al-Hibri posed the challenge of trying to separate culture from religious interpretation, arguing that patriarchy and authoritarianism came from the surrounding culture, rather than being inherent to the religion, but have become so embedded in religious interpretation over time that they have come to be considered authentic, despite their detrimental impact on women, a conclusion also reached by Leila Ahmed.[13] Ahmed's work strove to restore women to the historical record, arguing that Islamic civilization and culture as they developed owed much to adoption of surrounding Persianate culture, ultimately to the detriment of women as they were gradually erased from public life, a sharp contrast to the foundational Islamic era when women and men were equally present and participated in community life and decision-making. Making this distinction between the Islam of the Qur'ān and "institutional" Islam as it developed, particularly in the classical era, is intended to enable the removal of these cultural accretions, a daunting task that has shaped the fields of women and gender studies and Islamic legal studies ever since, in large part by encouraging women scholars, in particular, to engage in deeper studies of the Qur'ān, *ḥadīth* sciences, and the principles of jurisprudence (*uṣūl al-fiqh*).

Riffat Hassan[14] was one of the first to respond to this challenge, seeking to establish a hierarchy within the "Islamic sources," beginning with the assertion of the Qur'ān, rather than the *ḥadīth* or tradition, as the absolute authority in Islam and calling for rejection of any *ḥadīth* inconsistent with the Qur'ān's teachings, particularly when it has a detrimental impact on women. David Powers[15] engaged in a study of Islamic legal principles related to female inheritance as outlined in three sets of Qur'ān verses and then compared them against actual practice in medieval Spain, finding that many legal loopholes had been developed to circumvent clear Qur'ānic statements to the detriment of women. Ultimately, he argued that, although the origins of Islamic law are clearly found within the Qur'ān, Islamic law as it developed did not adhere to those teachings, particularly as the Islamic Empire expanded and large portions of wealth and property were at stake. Amina wadud[16] also explored disconnects between what the Qur'ān says and how certain matters have been treated in Islamic law with the goal of reconceptualizing gender roles to include lived experience, not just theorizing.

Feminist legal scholars have insisted on the centrality of the Qur'ān as a source of Islamic law[17] at the same time that they have called for use of the lens of gender in interrogating it, including detailed examination of gendered grammar, attention to the patriarchal context in which the Qur'ān was revealed and to the contexts of its interpretation over time, distinction between universal and particular statements about women and gender, and prioritizing passages discussing women's relationships to God over those assigning social or family roles.[18] The ultimate purpose is a restoration of women's humanity and dignity rooted in a values-based approach to social and legal matters that gives attention to outcomes, not just mechanics. From this perspective, any reading of the Qur'ān that justifies the degradation and abuse of women or supports sexual inequality or misogyny is rejected as inconsistent with the Qur'ānic intent toward justice and egalitarianism.[19]

Hassan insisted on the growth of scholarship among women, particularly in theology, as the main field in which to engage change in the status of women. She particularly denounced the tendency of Muslim men to arrogate to themselves the right to define the ontological, theological, eschatological, and sociological status of women, confining women physically, mentally, and emotionally, and depriving them of their right to realize their own full human potential, analyze their own life experiences, and fully participate in their religion as a liberatory, rather than oppressive, instrument,[20] themes most recently picked up by Asma Lamrabet.[21]

Ḥadīth as a source of legal material has also undergone scholarly reanalysis and repurposing. Fatima Mernissi's[22] pioneering work in examining *ḥadīth* selected to support state and religious policies with respect to women compared against the entire corpus of *ḥadīth* raised important methodological questions that remain relevant today. On the one hand, despite the questions raised about why certain *ḥadīth* are privileged over others, weaknesses of the content, chains of transmission and initial transmitters, as well as the likelihood that some transmitters would be more credible than others on certain topics, the reality remains that scholarly challenges and analyses have not necessarily led to concrete changes in the law or even a revisiting of certain legal parameters where the status of women is concerned. The bridge between scholarship and policy remains largely uncrossed, despite evidence from the foundational sources for issues ranging from female autonomy in religious affiliation, assured protection from sexual harassment and violence, and claimed membership and participation in public affairs during Muḥammad's lifetime. Rather than finding religion and particularly the foundational sources of Islam to blame for women's status, Mernissi found that women's rights, duties, and status had come to be defined by the interests of male elites in preserving and expanding their own power.

Methodological Issues

From a methodological perspective, any analysis of "women's rights and duties in classical legal literature" requires definition of what is meant by "women," "rights and duties," and "classical legal literature." All of these categories have come to be problematized by academics, given that assumptions of singular, definitive categories tend to mask variations in experiences, rather than foregrounding them.

Deconstructing "Women"

Building on the three waves of feminism frequently cited in academic literature,[23] scholars of women and gender in Islam are problematizing the study of "women" as a category, questioning what the defining characteristics of "women" are, whether all women share these characteristics, and to what degree differences such as socioeconomic status, race, sexual orientation, political views, educational levels, age, and marital status, among others, must be taken into account when defining or discussing "women."[24] Primary questions about "women" in Islamic law include: whether "women" are autonomous, moral agents with goals, aspirations, and achievements that stand independently,[25] or if "women" are only acted up on—and potentially victimized—whether by men, the family, or the state;[26] whether "women" can only be approached through their relationships with others, such as wife or mother, or are considered separate, complete beings in their own right;[27] whether being a "woman" is defined by biology and the ability to reproduce, by status within a group, or by being able to hear and respond individually to God;[28] whether "women" are to be studied only as people who make mistakes and cause social disorder,[29] or if they can be considered contributors to broader society;[30] and whether categorization as a "woman" inherently implies ability or disability.[31]

Al-Hibri[32] argues that, structurally, all of these issues are rooted in questions of autonomy and authority, namely who has it and who does not, all of which connect back to the central concern of patriarchy and male control over the female body. They also reflect attention to assignment of gendered roles as a matter of social order, lumping "women" back into a broad and largely undifferentiated category, other than their status as virgin or deflowered. Al-Hibri notes the tendency to assume that at least some females, namely minors and those who had not been married before, were understood to be in need of protection from unscrupulous and predatory men and from their own emotional, impulsive, and dependent natures. She also observes the overtones of classism often used to justify the need for male control over female marriage contracts, as socioeconomic incompatibility constituted grounds for nullification of a marriage not approved by the male guardian. She then challenges the relevance of those assumptions for contemporary circumstances, as many women today have independent social standing, experience, and education—to the extent that she argues that laws must be changed to reflect these new realities.

Among the most central concerns in such debates is the prioritization of presumed roles for "women." If "women" are supposed to be defined by their ideal roles as wives and mothers, then questions that must be asked in this context include: which role takes priority, why, what happens in the event that a woman is unable to fulfill one or both roles, and what do the answers to these questions tell us about underlying assumptions about power and agency? Ahmed[33] has argued that family law is based on male sexual desire as the controlling feature of marriage, rendering the dower and the marriage contract a contract of sale and control, rather than a relationship of mutuality. Kecia Ali's[34] investigation of classical legal literature similarly finds that the spousal relationship is prioritized over the parental one because the legal regulations overseeing marriage and divorce are rooted in male control and dominion over women, not in women's obligations toward their children.[35] Although legal literature justifies this as a matter of "protection" and "welfare" for both women and society,[36] Ali sees it as a reflection of the power dynamics of the patriarchal context in which it was written, raising questions about the prescriptive versus descriptive nature of the material and who determines what an "ideal" society and gender roles look like. These power dynamics become even more pronounced when adding in the realities of slavery and concubinage that, although objectionable by contemporary standards due to the lack of agency and bodily and sexual autonomy, were nevertheless part of the sociosexual patterns of life in the classical Mediterranean region.[37] Basim Musallam has found mention of slaves throughout juridical literature and court records, including in bringing property claims to court, and as benefactors of charitable endowments (*waqf*).[38]

Ali[39] further engages the complexity of multiple categories of belonging and the challenges that rigid categories can create. On the one hand, she argues that femaleness and enslavement both qualified as legal disabilities in classical legal literature. Yet, on the other hand, she found that Islamic conceptions of slavery differed from those of other surrounding cultures, particularly where privileges and restrictions related to sexual access, sexual codes of conduct, and property ownership, were concerned. In some cases, the same standards were applicable to both slaves and free persons, blurring the boundaries of autonomy, while, in others, there were variations among slaves and/or free persons based on gender, relationships, and status. Ali's work demonstrates the importance of an intersectional and variegated approach to "women." Similarly, Judith Tucker[40] has noted that legal literature on family law generally considers women to be less fully subjects than men, rendering femaleness a legal disability, at the same time that women are considered equal to men and capable of expressing their agency in matters related to property rights and commerce, particularly as plaintiffs in court. She further found that, inasmuch as judges were likely to uphold limitations on women's personal autonomy and agency within marriage and the family, they nevertheless were also likely to defend women's property rights. Tucker therefore argues that the degree to which femaleness is associated with disability depends on the issue under consideration—family status versus property, rather than "women" constituting a broad legal category of inherently and permanently disabled persons.[41] Works such as Ali and Tucker make clear the need to continue to problematize the category of "women" and to read court records and juridical literature in light of each other toward the goal of establishing a more expansive composite image of "women."

Deconstructing "Rights and Duties"

"Rights and duties" as a category in classical Islamic legal literature tends to reduce women to a single identity before the law with respect to the family—"wife," "mother," "sister," "daughter," "widow," etc. All of these roles are relational—i.e., defining a woman through her relationship to a specific person, typically a man, and hierarchical with respect to both male and female family members. These roles further carry the expectation that there is an "ideal" family role that every woman within that category is expected to fulfill, regardless of her personal story or circumstances—and regardless of how "ideal" the husband is or is not in reality.[42] It also suggests that the only "rights and duties" women have are those outlined in the legal literature, regardless of whether these produce justice and fairness as outcomes. Locating women's "rights and duties" within their relationships to men establishes power, rather than mutuality or the fulfillment of needs, as the basis of the relationship, solidifying and sacralizing patriarchy without questioning whether patriarchy is intended as a divine imperative. It also serves to focus on women's "rights and duties" as separate entities from men's "obligations" by focusing exclusively on one gender.[43] Claims such as the need to treat women with tenderness, affection, kindness, and honor do not respond to this underlying power structure, as they ultimately leave fulfillment to individual conscience and even risk reducing rights and duties to purely mechanical parameters, such as paying maintenance, without acknowledging the emotional dimension of relationships.

Feminist scholars beginning with al-Hibri[44] have proposed as a solution reclaiming the original egalitarian message of the Qur'ān while also giving attention to the reality that the Qur'ān was revealed to a society rooted in patriarchy and hierarchies—to the point that even Muḥammad had to compromise. Thus, even the foundational era may not represent the original revelation in its fullness. By positing the argument in this way, al-Hibri effectively pushes back against tradition, even that of the foundational period, in favor of a direct return to the foundational sources in order to reclaim the original message. Any attempt to discuss "women's rights and duties in classical legal literature" must, in her opinion, necessarily include interrogation and rediscovery of the Qur'ān and *ḥadīth* as a priority, rather than relying on *fiqh*, which is human interpretation of the divine message.[45]

The greatest difficulty with "rights and duties" as a category is that it implies a "one size fits all" approach to any family matter, as well as projecting only one single acceptable model for women—being raised within one family with the expectation of marrying into another and producing children. Because all classifications of women's rights and duties revolve around her place within a given family, the category of "rights and duties of women in classical legal literature" is designed to locate women exclusively within the family from the outset, essentially removing them from the public sphere. Scholars such as Asma Barlas have expressed concern that the "rights and duties" approach tends to conflate the roles of wives and mothers, a conflation that does not appear in the Qur'ān.[46]

Such an approach is clearly overly narrow, as it does not account for the fullness of women's experiences within the family or even for a variety of family models beyond the traditional, such as the reality of women serving as de facto heads of household, or their participation as active members of society, particularly where commerce and property ownership are concerned, even though court records of actual practice make it clear that women have bought, sold, and owned property, businesses, and wealth; sought justice; and founded charitable institutions (*waqf*) throughout Islamic history.[47]

Furthermore, the conflation of "women's rights and duties" with reproductive and sexual obligations has complicated contemporary work toward greater gender equality in many Islamic contexts, as documented by Jocelyne Cesari and Jose Casanova,[48] although scholars such as Musallam[49] and Sa'diyya Shaikh[50] have argued for strong historical and legal precedents for female bodily autonomy with respect to contraception, including the right of both the man and the woman to use it, particularly when already nursing an infant or due to concern about a child being born into enslavement, and the necessity of the free woman's consent to its use based on her inherent right to sexual fulfillment and children.[51] An alternative approach to issues of rights and duties rooted in common humanity, rather than gender roles in marriage and the family, is used by Abdulaziz Sachedina[52] in identifying ethical approaches to Sharīʿa principles related to life, death and the responsibility to care for the human body—both one's own and those of others—as a matter of respecting human dignity and the human body as God's creation.

For all of the clarity that the legal literature is intended to project in defining each person's gender-designated role within the family and society, there are nevertheless numerous instances that appear increasingly murky today. Sometimes rights and duties clash, such as child custody following divorce. On the one hand, women are raised with the expectation that they will become wives and mothers and that motherhood is a respected and even venerated role in Islamic societies. Yet, in the event of divorce, according to classical Islamic law, fathers automatically receive custody of children over a certain age (seven for boys, nine for girls), based on legal argumentation highlighting the father's role as guardian, responsible for the child's education, property, and marriage. Not only does such a blanket ruling assume certain conduct on the part of the father, it also does not take into consideration the conduct or quality of parenting provided by the mother. The rights and duties of women are simply subordinated to the rights and duties of men as a matter of process. Nor does the legal literature address the now confused status of the mother, who remains mother in name and relationship but is unable to fulfill her responsibilities for nurturing and care unless the former husband allows it. It seems that the relationship with and control by the husband/ex-husband takes priority over the relationship to the child where the mother is concerned, even though the relationship to the child cannot be broken, while the relationship with the spouse can. While this is in keeping with prioritizing the relationship with the spouse over the relationship with the child discussed above, it does not necessarily reflect the best interests of the child—or the parents. It also may not reflect the historical reality, at least in some places, of custom (*ʿurf*) placing the welfare of the child at the center of child custody matters. Ahmad Fekry Ibrahim[53] provides a case study for Egypt in this regard. Topics highlighting such disconnects with "rights and duties" are in need of additional research.

Deconstructing "Classical Legal Literature"

Major questions facing scholars about how effectively to approach the classical legal literature concern both content and methodology. Questions about content include the following: Does "classical legal literature" include the foundational sources of the Qur'ān and *ḥadīth*, neither of which are *fiqh*, but both of which are omnipresent in *fiqh* and central to determination of doctrine and practice, particularly given that feminist scholars and women's rights activists insist on the centrality of the Qur'ān and *ḥadīth* to their reform programs?[54] Is classical legal literature designed to be prescriptive of an "ideal" society that believers should strive to implement, or is it better understood as a description of what society was like at the time when it was written?[55] To what degree is knowledge of the author, the surrounding context—social, political, economic, religious, and cultural—and the author's relationship to surrounding power structures necessary or important for analyzing the author's output?[56] Should this literature be read exclusively for its legal content or should it be read to discover the underlying assumptions and values it was intended to uphold?[57] To what degree is it important to compare and contrast this literature with what came before and after it or to other jurists within the same law school (*madhhab*)?[58]

Susan Spectorsky[59] wrote one of the first comparative analyses, examining three third/ninth-century Ḥanbalī texts on marriage and divorce, arguing for dynamic and flexible legal reasoning even within the context of their mechanics. Although her approach followed the "rights and duties" model, her analysis showed that Ibn Ḥanbal tended to prefer doctrines that protected women from exploitation based on the guiding principle of words and actions having consequences as a matter of justice. This stands in marked contrast to other law schools that allowed for the "doubt canon" to serve as a mechanism for avoiding consequences,[60] often at the expense of women. At the same time, while Spectorsky's work added to the knowledge base, it did so largely through reportage on the content of what is and is not lawful and who legally owns and is entitled to what, rather than addressing broader issues of worldviews or contextualization. A later work by Spectorsky[61] engaged a deeper level of analysis, examining the development of juridical questions between the first/seventh through the sixth/twelfth centuries for Sunnī jurists and how Qur'ān verses and *ḥadīth* were used for different legal purposes. A parallel work for early Mālikī law was engaged by Jonathan Brockopp,[62] albeit with the purpose of tracing the compilation and canonization of sources in parallel to other legal codes in the same area of study.

Other questions concern methodology: To what degree do the theoretical descriptions match actual legal practice and how best to understand differences between the two?[63] Can legal literature be read as "stand alone" material or must it be read in conjunction with theological literature of the same time, given the religious nature of both?[64] How best to interpret gender roles as described within this literature—as reflections of society, reflections of the jurist's personal views and experiences, as a guideline for individuals, or a guideline for society? How important is it that the authors of classical *fiqh* were all male, and how should that influence our understanding of the material? How might we best understand periodic references to women in evidentiary support for legal doctrines and how might those insights be used to interrogate the sources in new ways? To what degree should the literature be read against the values, objectives, and principles it is intended to uphold and what insights might this provide about changing understandings of those values, objectives, and principles?[65] How much impact can the literature be presumed to have had? How might the researcher best contextualize her/himself with respect to this literature? Are there inherent risks in approaching classical literature with contemporary questions and concerns, such as the potential for reading something into the text that is not there?[66] How to assure that analysis of the literature accurately reflects the intent of the jurist, rather than the researcher? Given that legal literature is not written in a vacuum, it should not be read or analyzed in one, either.

A concrete example of many of these potential pitfalls is the strong presence of material dealing with hermaphrodites in classical legal literature. While one might be tempted to assume that the level of attention assigned to the topic is indicative of its social importance or even a reflection of realities of the time, such a reading would be mistaken. The issue at stake was one of social structure. If rights and duties are based on assigned gender roles, then identification of gender as something assigned externally, rather than determined by the individual, is considered central to the functioning of the broader society. Hermaphrodites represented a social conundrum because the typical physical markers of sex were unclear, adding a potential third gender into a legal system constructed on the basis of gendered binaries. Rather than seeking to add a third gender, legal literature was concerned with mechanisms for determining which of the two legally recognized genders was to be assigned to the hermaphrodite in question. Legal literature thus must be read according to its purpose—the encounter of legal questions or concerns for which either definitive solutions or mechanisms for determining the most likely solution were to be found or outlined. Legal literature is concerned with order, matters of right and wrong, and the dispensation of justice—whether in the form of compensation or punishment—that serves the community, not individual or personal interests.

At the same time, quantitative approaches to the classical legal literature could be instructive. For example, the overwhelming majority of content in Islamic legal literature addresses worship matters (*ʿibādāt*), sending a clear message of the primacy of human responsibilities toward God over responsibilities toward human beings (*muʿāmalāt*), yet there is very little scholarly analysis of this literature being undertaken today.[67] Most studies of worship material tend to be written in a laundry list format of do's and don'ts, rather than more analytically with respect to how gender is or is not addressed within those requirements. Holistic studies that engage the full literature, rather than simply family law, could provide an avenue for reordering the standard approach of focusing on women's rights and duties with respect to men by reasserting the primacy of women's rights and duties with respect to God, thereby redesigning power structures so as to place God at the top and men and women on a level below God but equal to each other, in keeping with the Qur'ān's teaching that male and female were created from a single soul and are therefore of the same nature.[68] Such reassertion of the relationship with God as primary for both women and men would render analyses of the classical literature more in keeping with the priorities the classical jurists themselves assigned to these relationships and pushing back against claims that men are in charge of women to the point of claiming responsibility for their relationship to God.[69] It could also help to reassert the mutuality that is supposed to be at the heart of the husband–wife relationship, rather than the unidirectionality implied in a hierarchical relationship of obedience.[70] At the same time, such an approach should not be misused to ignore or downplay the very real problems represented by issues such as polygamy, presumed supremacy of men over women, bearing witness, inheritance, and personal status codes that deny women the right to contract their own marriages, initiate divorce, and require her to obey her husband.[71]

Looking Ahead—Future Trajectories of Research

Future directions for research and analysis should continue to expand the knowledge base through case studies and comparative analyses at the same time that intertextual readings of legal literature, court records and other sources should be encouraged, particularly where there are disconnects between what the legal literature describes and the realities reflected in court records. For example, Yosef Rapoport's[72] comparative study of marriage and divorce in late medieval Cairo, Damascus, and Jerusalem finds that women successfully initiated divorce as often as men did and that women had access to waged labor, owned property, and successfully claimed their dowers so that assumptions of women's legal inferiority to and economic dependence on men portrayed in the literature simply does not match lived reality. Like Beshara Doumani,[73] he further documents a variety of family models that included working women, single women, and women as heads of households and even *ribats*, demonstrating the need for a more in-depth and deliberate interrogation of the historical record with respect to women and gender. Reinstatement of *ikhtilaf* as a normal, expected, and healthy part of legal debate could create space for inclusion of a wider diversity of voices, including those of women. Expanding appointment of female judges in Shariah courts could also help with that pursuit.[74]

New fields of study might include attention to interconnection of different categories of law, as initially engaged by Ali and Tucker, in comparing and contrasting court attitudes toward women in family matters versus property cases. Intersection of family and criminal law might prove to be particularly informative, examining whether certain behaviors exhibited by a woman in one situation might be considered laudatory and consequently carry over to other areas. For example, an expanded understanding of women as property owners and proprietors combined with Qur'ānic assurances of their right to be such could provide more solid ground for contemporary women to maintain control over their assets and inheritances and push back against family pressure to defer in favor of a male relative.[75] Greater attention to sexual violence in criminal law historically could prove useful in holding perpetrators, rather than victims, accountable, particularly if more attention was focused on intent and violence, rather than male ownership and control of the female body.[76]

Challenging past precedent simply as past precedent by seeking the original purpose, meaning, or values serves as an important means of keeping Islamic law alive and relevant to contemporary Muslim communities at the same time that it seeks to reinsert justice, rather than power, into the equation. It could also serve to reinstate the law as an open, rather than closed, system as greater attention could be given to a variety of interpretations and contexts, rather than asserting a presumed comprehensive, self-contained, and immutable normative system.

Notes

1. Azizah al-Hibri, "Islam, Law and Custom: Redefining Muslim Women's Rights," *American University International Law Review* 12, no. 1 (1997): 1–44, first identified the centrality of these issues with respect to family law. Scholars working to distinguish between *Sharīʿa* and *fiqh* (jurisprudence) also point to the importance of looking at intent versus outcomes in engaging reform; see Wael B. Hallaq, *A History of Islamic Legal Theories: An Introduction to Sunnī uṣūl al-fiqh* (New York: Cambridge University Press, 1997); Felicitas Opwis, *Maṣlaḥa and the Purpose of the Law: Islamic Discourse on Legal Change from the 4th/10th to 8th/14th Century* (Leiden: Brill, 2010); John L. Esposito and Natana J. DeLong-Bas, *Shariah: What Everyone Needs to Know* (New York: Oxford University Press, 2018); and Idris Nassery, Rumee Ahmed, and Muna Tatari, eds., *The Objectives of Islamic Law: The Promises and Challenges of the Maqāṣid al- Sharīʿa* (Landham, MD: Lexington Books, 2018).
2. See, for example, W. Montgomery Watt, *Muhammad: Prophet and Statesman* (New York: Oxford University Press, 1974).
3. Joseph Schacht, *The Origins of Muhammadan Jurisprudence* (Oxford: Clarendon Press, 1950); and Joseph Schacht, *An Introduction to Islamic Law* (New York: Oxford University Press, 1964).
4. Ignaz Goldziher, *Introduction to Islamic Theology and Law*, trans. Andras and Ruth Hamori (Princeton: Princeton University Press, 1981).
5. For challenges to Schacht's timeline and rejection of a direct connection between Islamic law and Muḥammad's practices, see G. H. A. Juynboll, *Muslim Tradition: Studies in Chronology, Provenance, and Authorship of Early Hadith* (New York: Cambridge University

Press, 1983); Nabia Abbott, *Studies in Early Arabic Literary Papyri*, vol. 2 (University of Chicago Press, 1964); Fuat Sezgin, *Geschichte des arabishcen Schrifttums* (Leiden: Brill, 1996); M. M. Azami, *Studies in Early Hadith Literature* (Oak Brook, IL: American Trust Publications, 1978), and others. Ultimately, there remains no broad scholarly consensus on questions of origins. Instead of addressing the complete body of literature, current studies, such as Asma Afsaruddin, *Striving in the Path of God: Jihad and Martyrdom in Islamic Thought* (New York: Oxford University Press, 2013), choose to focus on challenging the origins of specific *ḥadīth* related to a given theme or which enjoy great popularity today, such as apocalyptic events, martyrdom for death in battle, and purported citations of naval warfare, rather than the entire body of literature, acknowledging that certain *ḥadīth* seem very convenient to particular political agendas in a given time and place.

6. Wael B. Hallaq, *An Introduction to Islamic Law* (New York: Cambridge University Press, 2009).
7. Some scholars have critiqued Hallaq's work as painting an overly rosy picture of the pre-colonial functioning of Islamic law. See, for example, Mohammed Fadel, "A Tragedy of Politics or an Apolitical Tragedy? Review," *Journal of the American Oriental Society* 131, no. 1 (January–March 2011): 109–127.
8. See further Amira Sonbol's chapter in this *Handbook*.
9. Some studies of this kind exist, such as Rudolph Peters, *Crime and Punishment in Islamic Law: Theory and Practice from the Sixteenth to the Twenty-First Century* (New York: Cambridge University Press, 2005), which highlights some differences in practice between local and central courts, albeit rooted in jurisdiction, and more specific attention to the shaping of gender roles in different parts of the Ottoman Empire in Judith Tucker, *In the House of Law: Gender and Islamic Law in Ottoman Syria and Palestine* (Berkeley: University of California Press, 2000). However, these studies concern later time periods. More attention to the classical era is needed.
10. Manuela Marin and Randi Deguilhem, eds., *Writing the Feminine: Women in Arab Sources* (London and New York: I. B. Tauris, 2002).
11. Asma Afsaruddin, *The First Muslims: History and Memory* (Oxford: OneWorld Publications, 2007), engages one of the most comprehensive approaches to study of the early Muslim community, sorting out history from memory.
12. Azizah al-Hibri, "A Study of Islamic Herstory: Or, How Did We Ever Get into This Mess?" in "Women and Islam," special issue, *Women's Studies International Forum*, 5, no. 2 (1982): 207–219, and al-Hibri, "Islam, Law and Custom," 1–44.
13. Leila Ahmed, *Women and Gender in Islam* (New Haven, CT: Yale University Press, 1992).
14. Riffat Hassan, "An Islamic Perspective," in *Women, Religion and Sexuality: Studies on the Impact of Religious Teachings on Women*, ed. Jeanne Becher (Geneva: World Council of Churches Publications, Geneva, 1990), 96. Although this came across as a daring methodology at the time, it was really just a reassertion of the methodology that was popular in eighteenth-century Islamic revival and reform movements. See Natana J. DeLong-Bas, *Wahhabi Islam: From Revival and Reform to Global Jihad*, rev. ed. (New York: Oxford University Press, 2008), 45–54, for details on *ḥadīth* methodology.
15. David S. Powers, *Studies in Qur'an and Hadith: The Formation of the Islamic Law of Inheritance* (Berkeley: University of California Press, 1986).
16. Amina wadud, *Qur'an and Woman: Rereading the Sacred Text from a Woman's Perspective* (New York: Oxford University Press, 1999).
17. This stands in contrast to Schacht, who spent only 4 pages out of 312 discussing the Qur'ān.

18. Pioneers in this field include al-Hibri, Hassan, wadud, and Asma Barlas, *"Believing Women" in Islam: Unreading Patriarchal Interpretations of the Qur'an* (Austin: University of Texas Press, 2002).
19. This argument is made by wadud, Barlas, Ahmed, and Barbara Stowasser, *Women in the Qur'an, Traditions, and Interpretation* (New York: Oxford University Press, 1994). Blame for inequality is assigned to the *tafsīr* (exegetical) literature and *ḥadīth*, rather than the Qur'ān.
20. Hassan, "An Islamic Perspective."
21. Asma Lamrabet, *Women in the Qur'an: An Emancipatory Reading*, trans. Myriam Francois-Cerrah (Leicestershire, UK: Square View, 2016).
22. Fatima Mernissi, *The Veil and the Male Elite: A Feminist Interpretation of Women's Rights in Islam*, trans. Mary Jo Lakeland (Reading, MA: Addison-Wesley Publishing, 1991).
23. For a brief history, see Margaret Walters, *Feminism: A Very Short Introduction* (New York: Oxford University Press, 2006).
24. For a broad overview of varying roles for women, including both obstacles and opportunities, in legal discussions and throughout Islamic history, see Irene Schneider, *Women in the Islamic World: From Earliest Times to the Arab Spring*, trans. Steven Rendall (Princeton: Markus Wiener, 2012).
25. See, for example, wadud, *Qur'an and Woman* and Barlas, *"Believing Women" in Islam.*
26. See Hassan, "An Islamic Perspective," and Madawi Al-Rasheed, *A Most Masculine State: Gender, Politics and Religion in Saudi Arabia* (New York: Cambridge University Press, 2013).
27. Hassan, "An Islamic Perspective," poignantly raises this question. See also Nimat Hafez Barazangi, *Woman's Identity and Rethinking the Hadith* (New York: Routledge, 2015), particularly the discussions of women's autonomous authority. At the same time, wadud, *Qur'an and Woman*, calls for respect and valorization of the nurturing and protective roles played by mothers as a matter of human dignity.
28. See Kathryn M. Kueny, *Conceiving Identities: Maternity in Medieval Muslim Discourse and Practice* (Albany: State University of New York Press, 2013). Basim F. Musallam, *Sex and Society in Islam* (New York: Cambridge University Press, 1983), details juridical discussions of sexual intercourse rooted in questions of right to sexual satisfaction and children, consent and contraception, violations of which could result in monetary compensation to the aggrieved party.
29. See Stowasser, *Women in the Qur'an.*
30. See Asma Sayeed, *Women and the Transmission of Religious Knowledge in Islam* (New York: Cambridge University Press, 2015).
31. See Kecia Ali, *Marriage and Slavery in Early Islam* (Cambridge, MA: Harvard University Press, 2010) and Judith Tucker, *Women, Family, and Gender in Islamic Law* (New York: Cambridge University Press, 2008). David Solomon Jalajel, *Women and Leadership in Islamic Law: A Critical Analysis of Classical Legal Texts (Culture and Civilization in the Middle East* (Abingdon and New York: Routledge, 2016), also discusses classical assumptions about women's deficient natures and their impact on gender hierarchies. Hassan, "An Islamic Perspective," 123, cites consideration of women as "disadvantaged persons," in the legal literature, despite the egalitarian ethic of the Qur'ān.
32. Al-Hibri, *Islam, Law and Custom.*
33. Ahmed, *Women and Gender in Islam.*
34. Ali, *Marriage and Slavery in Early Islam.*

35. Ali, *Marriage and Slavery in Early Islam*, focuses on the mechanics of marriage and slavery as matters of property rights. For an alternative view of sexual intercourse as a matter of eroticism and pleasure, see Habeeb Akanda, *A Taste of Honey: Sexuality and Erotology in Islam* (London: Rabaah Publishers, 2015).
36. Hassan, "An Islamic Perspective," 115. Even some feminist commentators make this argument. For example, Hassan argues that men must care for women because only women are capable of bearing children and that women with dependent children who are not cared for by men are subject to economic, social, psychological, and other ills. At the same time, she insists that this should not be misinterpreted to place the husband in a position of superiority over his wife.
37. For details on slave and master rights, particularly with respect to sexual access, and childbearing, see Basim F. Musallam, *Sex and Society in Islam*. Careful attention to context is needed as the lived realities of slaves varied considerably by location and cannot necessarily be read through the lens of the African American experience, as demonstrated by Jonathan A. C. Brown, *Slavery in Islam* (Oxford: OneWorld Publications, 2019).
38. See Musallam, *Sex and Society in Islam*, for details.
39. Ali, *Marriage and Slavery in Early Islam*.
40. Tucker, *Women, Family, and Gender in Islamic Law*.
41. Although Ali, *Marriage and Slavery in Early Islam*, agrees with Tucker, *Women, Family, and Gender in Islamic Law*, that women often appeared in court to claim their property rights, Ali concludes that this is because women's property rights were those that were most frequently flouted. Had they been respected, there would not have been a need to go to court.
42. Outlines of these rights and duties based on categories in classical Islamic law and contemporary challenges to them based upon lived realities can be found in John L. Esposito with Natana J. DeLong-Bas, *Women in Muslim Family Law*, 2nd ed. (Syracuse: Syracuse University Press, 2001).
43. See Barlas, *"Believing Women" in Islam*.
44. al-Hibri, "A Study of Islamic Herstory."
45. Ibid.
46. Barlas, *"Believing Women" in Islam*, cites the example of Muḥammad's wife, 'Ā'isha, who did not bear any children, observing that this did not invalidate or even have any negative impact on her position as wife, scholar, or pillar of the community.
47. See, for example, the case studies in Amira El Azhary Sonbol, ed., *Women, the Family, and Divorce Laws in Islamic History* (Syracuse, NY: Syracuse University Press, 1996); and Amira El Azhary Sonbol, ed., *Beyond the Exotic: Women's Histories in Islamic Societies* (Syracuse, NY: Syracuse University Press, 2005). The most recent and innovative study of this kind, albeit for a later time period, is Beshara Doumani, *Family Life in the Ottoman Mediterranean: A Social History* (New York: Cambridge University Press, 2017), which provides detailed and nuanced pictures of different family models and uses women's management of *waqf* to challenge assumptions about concepts of the family, application of *Sharīʿa*, and legal discrimination.
48. Jocelyne Cesari and Jose Casanova, eds., *Islam, Gender, and Democracy in Comparative Perspective* (New York: Oxford University Press, 2017).
49. Musallam, *Sex and Society in Islam*.
50. Saʿdiyya Shaikh, "Family Planning, Contraception, and Abortion in Islam: Undertaking Khalifah," in Daniel C. Maguire, ed. *Sacred Rights: The Case for Contraception and Abortion*

in World Religions (New York: Oxford University Press, 2003), 105–128. Shaikh has noted that eight out of the nine classical legal schools permitted contraception and that there were a variety of opinions about abortion, guided by the Qur'ān and teachings of the different law schools, based on the gestation period.

51. Because any child produced in a union between a slave woman and her master would be the master's legal heir, the master retained control over use of contraception. Slave women were not considered to have an inherent right to children in classical Islamic law; see Musallam, *Sex and Society in Islam*, for details.
52. Abdulaziz Sachedina, *Islamic Biomedical Ethics: Principles and Application* (New York: Oxford University Press, 2009).
53. Ahmed Fekry Ibrahim, *Child Custody in Islamic Law: Theory and Practice in Egypt since the Sixteenth Century* (New York: Cambridge University Press, 2018).
54. For many feminist scholars of Islam and Islamic law, including those already cited, the Qur'ān and *ḥadīth* are the ultimate battlegrounds in the quest for meaning and redirection of the tradition. See also Fatima Mernissi, *Beyond the Veil: Male-Female Dynamics in a Modern Muslim Society* (Hoboken, NJ: John Wiley & Sons, 1975).
55. Ahmed, *Women and Gender in Islam*, engages both sides of the question, demonstrating how the "ideals" of classical Islamic law were elaborated in conjunction with patriarchal understandings of what an "ideal" society should look like and came to be implemented gradually with the expansion of Islamic civilization and culture, at the same time that she highlights borrowing from surrounding cultures and legal structures.
56. For an example of such contextualization with respect to both scholarly circles and political power structures, see DeLong-Bas, *Wahhabi Islam*.
57. Ali, *Marriage and Slavery in Early Islam*, is a good example of this type.
58. Although there are a few examples of this kind of comparative work, they remain few and far-between. Examples include Susan A. Spectorsky, *Chapters on Marriage and Divorce: Responses of Ibn Hanbal and Ibn Rahwayh* (Austin: University of Texas Press, 1993); Jonathan Brockopp, *Early Mālik ī Law: Ibn 'Abd al-Hakam and His Major Compendium of Jurisprudence* (Leiden: Brill, 2000); Susan Spectorsky, *Women in Classical Islamic Law: A Survey of the Sources* (Leiden: Brill, 2010); and Jalajel, *Women and Leadership in Islamic Law*. Examples of tracing a single issue across multiple authors and time periods include Asifa Quraishi and Frank E. Vogel, eds., *The Islamic Marriage Contract: Case Studies in Islamic Family Law* (Cambridge, MA: Harvard University Press, 2008), and Ayesha S. Chaudhry, *Domestic Violence and the Islamic Tradition* (New York: Oxford University Press, 2013).
59. Spectorsky, *Chapters on Marriage and Divorce*.
60. For use of the "doubt canon" in the Ottoman Empire, see Peters, *Crime and Punishment in Islamic Law*. For a comprehensive study of the "doubt canon" in both Sunnī and Shī'ī law schools, see Intisar A. Rabb, *Doubt in Islamic Law: A History of Legal Maxims, Interpretation, and Islamic Criminal Law* (New York: Cambridge University Press, 2015). Briefly, the "doubt canon" permitted a judge to avoid punishment in cases where doubt remained, such as with respect to factual discrepancies, legal ambiguities, or moral concerns.
61. Spectorsky, *Women in Classical Islamic Law*.
62. Brockopp, *Early Mālik ī Law*.
63. Sonbol in her *Women, the Family, and Divorce Laws* and *Beyond the Exotic*, repeatedly raises this question, noting the disconnect that often exists between theory and practice.

She argues that legal literature must be read in conjunction with court records and archival materials to gain an understanding of social reality.

64. Again, this is an important issue for feminist scholars today who are rooting their arguments in reinterpretation of the Qur'ān, in particular.
65. Many legal scholars note this distinction between *Sharīʿa* as values, objectives, and principles versus *fiqh* as human elaboration of the same. While *Sharīʿa* is unchanging, *fiqh* is expected to change as human needs, contexts, and understandings change; see Esposito and DeLong-Bas, *Shariah*.
66. For example, this question has been raised with respect to contemporary questions about human sexuality and their projection into classical sources. See Scott Siraj al-Haqq Kugle, *Homosexuality in Islam: Critical Reflection on Gay, Lesbian, and Transgender Muslims* (Oxford: Oneworld Publications, 2010).
67. Relatively rare examples include Behnam Sadeghi, *The Logic of Law Making in Islam: Women and Prayer in the Legal Tradition* (New York: Cambridge University Press, 2015), and Jalajel, *Women and Leadership in Islamic Law*.
68. Al-Hibri, "Islam, Law and Custom," and wadud, *Qur'an and Woman*.
69. Al-Hibri, "Islam, Law and Custom" first pointed to this concern, noting that insistence on a wife's obedience to her husband to the detriment of her obedience to God inappropriately places the husband in the position of God. On this question of authority over women, see Ziba Mir-Hosseini, Mulki al-Sharmani, and Jana Rumminger, eds., *Men in Charge? Rethinking Authority in Muslim Legal Tradition* (Oxford: OneWorld Publications, 2015).
70. Al-Hibri, "A Study of Islamic Herstory"; al-Hibri, "Islam, Law and Custom"; wadud, *Qur'an and Woman*; and Barlas, *"Believing Women" in Islam*. Hassan, "An Islamic Perspective," refers to it as "interdependence."
71. These issues were identified as the most important with respect to working for reforms in al-Hibri, "A Study of Islamic Herstory," and al-Hibri, "Islam, Law and Custom."
72. Yossef Rapoport, *Marriage, Money, and Divorce in Medieval Islamic Society* (Cambridge: Cambridge University Press, 2005).
73. Doumani, *Family Life in the Ottoman Mediterranean*.
74. See Nadia Sonneveld and Monika Lindbekk, eds., *Women Judges in the Muslim World: A Comparative Study of Discourse and Practice*. (Leiden: Brill, 2017).
75. For excellent work already being undertaken in this regard, see chapter 14 in this *Handbook* by Amira Sonbol.
76. See Hina Azam, *Sexual Violation in Islamic Law: Substance, Evidence, and Procedure* (New York: Cambridge University Press, 2015); and Asifa Quraishi, "Her Honor: An Islamic Critique of the Rape Laws of Pakistan from a Woman-Sensitive Perspective," in *Windows of Faith: Muslim Women Scholar-Activists in North America*, ed. Gisela Webb (Syracuse, NY: Syracuse University Press, 2000), 102–135, for useful models.

Bibliography

Abbott, Nabia. *Studies in Early Arabic Literary Papyri*. Vol. 2. Chicago: University of Chicago Press, 1964.

Afsaruddin, Asma. *The First Muslims: History and Memory*. Oxford: OneWorld Publications, 2007.

Afsaruddin, Asma. *Striving in the Path of God: Jihad and Martyrdom in Islamic Thought*. New York: Oxford University Press, 2013.

Ahmed, Leila. *Women and Gender in Islam*. New Haven, CT: Yale University Press, 1992.

Akanda, Habeeb. *A Taste of Honey: Sexuality and Erotology in Islam*. London: Rabaah Publishers, 2015.

Ali, Kecia. *Marriage and Slavery in Early Islam*. Cambridge, MA: Harvard University Press, 2010.

Azam, Hina. *Sexual Violation in Islamic Law: Substance, Evidence, and Procedure*. New York: Cambridge University Press, 2015.

Azami, M. M. *Studies in Early Hadith Literature*. Oak Brook, IL: American Trust Publications, 1978.

Barazangi, Nimat Hafez. *Woman's Identity and Rethinking the Hadith*. New York: Routledge, 2015.

Barlas, Asma. *"Believing Women" in Islam: Unreading Patriarchal Interpretations of the Qur'an*. Austin: University of Texas Press, 2002.

Brockopp, Jonathan. *Early Mālik ī Law: Ibn 'Abd al-Hakam and His Major Compendium of Jurisprudence*. Leiden: Brill, 2000.

Brown, Jonathan A. C. *Slavery in Islam*. Oxford: OneWorld Publications, 2019.

Cesari, Jocelyne, and Jose Casanova, eds. *Islam, Gender, and Democracy in Comparative Perspective*. New York: Oxford University Press, 2017.

Chaudhry, Ayesha S. *Domestic Violence and the Islamic Tradition*. New York: Oxford University Press, 2013.

DeLong-Bas, Natana J. *Wahhabi Islam: From Revival and Reform to Global Jihad*. Rev. ed. New York: Oxford University Press, 2008.

Doumani, Beshara. *Family Life in the Ottoman Mediterranean: A Social History*. New York: Cambridge University Press, 2017.

Esposito, John L., and Natana J. DeLong-Bas. *Shariah: What Everyone Needs to Know*. New York: Oxford University Press, 2018.

Esposito, John L., with Natana J. DeLong-Bas. *Women in Muslim Family Law*. 2nd ed. Syracuse: Syracuse University Press, 2001.

Fadel, Mohammed. "A Tragedy of Politics or an Apolitical Tragedy? Review." *Journal of the American Oriental Society* 131, no. 1 (January–March 2011): 109–127.

Goldziher, Ignaz. *Introduction to Islamic Theology and Law*. Translated by Andras Hamori and Ruth Hamori. Princeton: Princeton University Press, 1981.

Hallaq, Wael B. *A History of Islamic Legal Theories: An Introduction to Sunnī uṣūl al-fiqh*. New York: Cambridge University Press, 1997.

Hallaq, Wael B. *An Introduction to Islamic Law*. New York: Cambridge University Press, 2009.

Hassan, Riffat. "An Islamic Perspective." In *Women, Religion and Sexuality: Studies on the Impact of Religious Teachings on Women*, edited by Jeanne Becher, 93–128. Geneva: World Council of Churches Publications, 1990.

Hibri, Azizah al-. "A Study of Islamic Herstory: Or, How Did We Ever Get into This Mess?" *Women's Studies International Forum, Special Issue: Women and Islam* 5, no. 2 (1982): 207–219.

Hibri, Azizah al-. "Islam, Law and Custom: Redefining Muslim Women's Rights." *American University International Law Review* 12, no. 1 (1997): 1–44.

Ibrahim, Ahmed Fekry. *Child Custody in Islamic Law: Theory and Practice in Egypt Since the Sixteenth Century*. New York: Cambridge University Press, 2018.

Jalajel, David Solomon. *Women and Leadership in Islamic Law: A Critical Analysis of Classical Legal Texts (Culture and Civilization in the Middle East)*. Abingdon and New York: Routledge, 2016.
Juynboll, G. H. A. *Muslim Tradition: Studies in Chronology, Provenance, and Authorship of Early Hadith*. New York: Cambridge University Press, 1983.
Kueny, Kathryn M. *Conceiving Identities: Maternity in Medieval Muslim Discourse and Practice*. Albany: State University of New York Press, 2013.
Kugle, Scott Siraj al-Haqq. *Homosexuality in Islam: Critical Reflection on Gay, Lesbian, and Transgender Muslims*. Oxford: OneWorld Publications, 2010.
Lamrabet, Asma. *Women in the Qur'an: An Emancipatory Reading*. Translated by Myriam Francois-Cerrah. Leicestershire, UK: Square View, 2016.
Marin, Manuela, and Randi Deguilhem, eds. *Writing the Feminine: Women in Arab Sources*. London and New York: I. B. Tauris, 2002.
Mernissi, Fatima. *Beyond the Veil: Male-Female Dynamics in a Modern Muslim Society*. Hoboken, NJ: John Wiley & Sons, 1975.
Mernissi, Fatima. *The Veil and the Male Elite: A Feminist Interpretation of Women's Rights in Islam*. Translated by Mary Jo Lakeland. Reading, MA: Addison-Wesley Publishing, 1991.
Mir-Hosseini, Ziba, Mulki al-Sharmani, and Jana Rumminger, eds. *Men in Charge? Rethinking Authority in Muslim Legal Tradition*. Oxford: OneWorld Publications, 2015.
Musallam, Basim F. *Sex and Society in Islam*. New York: Cambridge University Press, 1983.
Nassery, Idris, Rumee Ahmed, and Muna Tatari, eds. *The Objectives of Islamic Law: The Promises and Challenges of the Maqāṣid al- Sharīʿa*. Landham, MD: Lexington Books, 2018.
Opwis, Felicitas. *Maṣlaḥa and the Purpose of the Law: Islamic Discourse on Legal Change from the 4th/10th to 8th/14th Century*. Leiden: Brill, 2010.
Peters, Rudolph. *Crime and Punishment in Islamic Law: Theory and Practice from the Sixteenth to the Twenty-First Century*. New York: Cambridge University Press, 2005.
Powers, David S. *Studies in Qur'an and Hadith: The Formation of the Islamic Law of Inheritance*. Berkeley: University of California Press, 1986.
Quraishi, Asifa. "Her Honor: An Islamic Critique of the Rape Laws of Pakistan from a Woman-Sensitive Perspective." In *Windows of Faith: Muslim Women Scholar-Activists in North America*, edited by Gisela Webb, 102–135. Syracuse, NY: Syracuse University Press, 2000.
Quraishi, Asifa, and Frank E. Vogel, eds. *The Islamic Marriage Contract: Case Studies in Islamic Family Law*. Cambridge, MA: Harvard University Press, 2008.
Rabb, Intisar A. *Doubt in Islamic Law: A History of Legal Maxims, Interpretation, and Islamic Criminal Law*. New York: Cambridge University Press, 2015.
Rapoport, Yossef. *Marriage, Money, and Divorce in Medieval Islamic Society*. Cambridge: Cambridge University Press, 2005.
Rasheed, Madawi al-. *A Most Masculine State: Gender, Politics and Religion in Saudi Arabia*. New York: Cambridge University Press, 2013.
Sachedina, Abdulaziz. *Islamic Biomedical Ethics: Principles and Application*. New York: Oxford University Press, 2009.
Sadeghi, Behnam. *The Logic of Law Making in Islam: Women and Prayer in the Legal Tradition*. New York: Cambridge University Press, 2015.
Sayeed, Asma. *Women and the Transmission of Religious Knowledge in Islam*. New York: Cambridge University Press, 2015.
Schacht, Joseph. *An Introduction to Islamic Law*. New York: Oxford University Press, 1964.
Schacht, Joseph. *The Origins of Muhammadan Jurisprudence*. Oxford: Clarendon Press, 1950.

Schneider, Irene. *Women in the Islamic World: From Earliest Times to the Arab Spring.* Translated by Steven Rendall. Princeton: Markus Wiener Publishers, 2012.

Sezgin, Fuat. *Geschichte des arabishcen Schrifttums.* Leiden: Brill, 1996.

Shaikh, Sa'diyya. "Family Planning, Contraception, and Abortion in Islam: Undertaking Khalifah." In *Sacred Rights: The Case for Contraception and Abortion in World Religions*, edited by Daniel C. Maguire, 105–128. New York: Oxford University Press, 2003.

Sonbol, Amira El Azhary, ed. *Beyond the Exotic: Women's Histories in Islamic Societies.* Syracuse, NY: Syracuse University Press, 2005.

Sonbol, Amira El Azhary, ed. *Women, the Family, and Divorce Laws in Islamic History.* Syracuse, NY: Syracuse University Press, 1996.

Sonneveld, Nadia, and Monika Lindbekk, eds. *Women Judges in the Muslim World: A Comparative Study of Discourse and Practice.* Leiden: Brill, 2017.

Spectorsky, Susan A. *Chapters on Marriage and Divorce: Responses of Ibn Hanbal and Ibn Rahwayh.* Austin: University of Texas Press, 1993.

Spectorsky, Susan. *Women in Classical Islamic Law: A Survey of the Sources.* Leiden: Brill, 2010.

Stowasser, Barbara. *Women in the Qur'an, Traditions, and Interpretation.* New York: Oxford University Press, 1994.

Tucker, Judith. *In the House of Law: Gender and Islamic Law in Ottoman Syria and Palestine.* Berkeley: University of California Press, 2000.

Tucker, Judith. *Women, Family, and Gender in Islamic Law.* New York: Cambridge University Press, 2008.

Wadud, amina. *Qur'an and Woman: Rereading the Sacred Text from a Woman's Perspective.* New York: Oxford University Press, 1999.

Walters, Margaret. *Feminism: A Very Short Introduction.* New York: Oxford University Press, 2006.

Watt, W. Montgomery. *Muhammad: Prophet and Statesman.* New York: Oxford University Press, 1974.

D

DECIPHERING WOMEN'S LIVES

Women in History and Texts

UPON reading official chronicles in general, one would be tempted to conclude that the occlusion of women from these narratives reflect the overall marginalization of women in society, starting during the Abbasid period (750–1258). Fortunately for us, however, we also have at our disposal a rich biographical literature from the premodern period that occasionally included sections on the lives of prominent women. Typically, these prominent women belonged to the first generation of Muslims, collectively called the *Saḥabiyyāt* or the women Companions of the Prophet. Less frequently, biographical dictionaries and prosopographical works from the postclassical period contain entries on the most notable women of the period who were religious scholars, littérateurs, and philanthropists. Foraging through these works allows us to retrieve the lives of these all-but-forgotten women and to reinsert them into the master narrative about the Islamic intellectual tradition and sociocultural history.

In this section, the discussion focuses on how the most prominent women of early Islam have been portrayed in biographical and prosopographical sources, as well as in devotional writings and literary works. In both Sunnī and Shīʿī sources, certain members of the *Ṣaḥabiyyāt* are held up as exceptional paragons of virtue who serve as role models for women as well as men. One chapter discusses how the treatment of the lives of these prominent women, who were assured of Paradise in tandem with certain male Companions, tends to change over time: from an acknowledgment of their full moral and societal agency to a slow attrition in such acknowledgment, as becomes evident in some Sunnī biographical works composed in the later period.

Another chapter traces the contributions of women scholars in the transmission of *ḥadīth* and related areas of scholarship, a fact widely recognized but not studied as much. Women have also been recognized for their devotional activities; their effort to gain access to public spaces of worship, however, have frequently been a site of contestation, a phenomenon that continues to characterize the lives of modern Muslim women, as we learn in one chapter.

In the premodern period, educated, literary-minded women often composed poetry and women singers and musicians entertained at caliphal courts, making major contributions to the cultural production of their time. Their participation in the stunning efflorescence of literature, music, and the arts during the "golden age" of Islamic civilization is vividly captured in one chapter and brings to life a nearly eclipsed facet of women's critical shaping of the cultural and intellectual life of the premodern Muslim world.

The section ends with an account of women's economic activities in the premodern field, another relatively understudied phenomenon. Careful scholarly research into primary sources unearths a wealth of evidence for women's roles, sometimes quite robust, as economic actors. Their participation was made possible through intricate networks of familial and communal relationships, which these women entrepreneurs were quite willing and able to take advantage of not only for their own economic benefit but also for the benefit of their larger communities.

CHAPTER 9

EARLY MUSLIM WOMEN AS MORAL PARAGONS IN CLASSICAL ISLAMIC LITERATURE

al-Mubashsharāt bi-l-janna

YASMIN AMIN

MUCH has been written about the early Muslim community and its women, who serve as exemplary figures and role models for later Muslim generations. Biographical dictionaries, as well as *sīra* works, provide numerous accounts of the lives of the *Ṣaḥābiyyāt* (female companions) and the Prophet's female family members, so that they may serve as moral exemplars for the community to emulate. Yet, while specific collections devoted countless pages to the ten male Companions to whom the Prophet is said to have promised paradise (*al-mubashsharūn al-ʿashara*)—namely the four "Rightly Guided" caliphs: Abū Bakr, ʿUmar ibn al-Khaṭṭāb, ʿUthmān ibn ʿAffān, and ʿAlī ibn Abī Ṭālib; in addition to Ṭalḥa ibn ʿUbayd Allāh, al-Zubayr ibn al-ʿAwwām, ʿAbd al-Raḥmān ibn ʿAwf, Saʿd ibn Mālik, Saʿīd ibn Zayd, and Abū ʿUbayda ibn al-Jarrāḥ—there exists no such list for the *Ṣaḥābiyyāt*, even though the Prophet gave glad tidings of Paradise to more than ten women.

This chapter will focus on *al-Mubashsharat bi-l-janna* ("women who were promised paradise") as moral paragons for all Muslim women. They are Khadīja, the first wife of Muḥammad, and her daughter Fāṭima, as well as twelve female companions, namely Umm Rumān, Asmāʾ bint Abī Bakr, Umm Sulaym, Umm Ḥarām, Umm Zafar or Umm Zakhar, Umm ʿUmāra, Umm Ayman, al-Rabīʿ bint Maʿūdh, Sumayya bint Khayyāṭ, Umm Waraqa, Umm Saʿd/Kabsha bint Rāfiʿ, and Umm Kulthūm bint ʿUqba. They were among those regarded as *sābiqāt* (women who preceded others in embracing Islam) who are praised as a collectivity in Qurʾān 56:10–14, which consequently elevated their status in the Muslim community. Many of them migrated, thereby combining both migration and precedence in Islam (*sābiqa*), and are applauded in Qur'ān 9:100. Most endured hardship or injustice, for which they are also commended in Qur'ān 16:41, 110; and most pledged their allegiance (*bay'a*) to the Prophet in the very early days.

The following section delves into greater details about the lives of these remarkable women and focuses on the qualities that earned them the coveted title of *al-Mubashsharāt bi-l-janna*, as they are described in some of the most prominent biographical works of the premodern period, as well as *ḥadīth* compendia and *sīra* works. These works include: *al-Ṭabaqāt al-kubrā*, *al-Istīʿāb fī maʿrifat al-aṣḥāb*, *Usd al-ghāba fī maʿrifat al-sahaba*, and *al-Iṣāba fī tamyyīz al-saḥāba* as well as *al-Ṣaḥīḥayn*, the two *ḥadīth* collections of al-Bukhārī and Muslim regarded as the most reliable by the majority of Muslims, among other classical works.

WOMEN OF PARADISE

Khadīja bint Khuwaylid

Her name was Khadīja bint Khuwaylid ibn Asad ibn ʿAbd al-ʿUzza ibn Qussay ibn Kilāb. Her great-grandfather ʿAbd al-ʿUzza was the brother of Prophet Muḥammad's great-grandfather ʿAbd Manāf ibn Qusayy. Her father was Khuwaylid, a successful merchant, and her mother was Fāṭima bint Zāʾida ibn al-Aṣamm ibn Harim ibn Ruwāḥa ibn Luʾay.[1]

In her youth, Khadīja was promised to her cousin Waraqa ibn Nawfal, but the marriage did not take place. Instead she married Hind ibn al-Nabash ibn Zarāra ibn Waqdān ibn Tamīm, with whom she had two sons, Hāla and Hind. After the marriage ended, she married ʿĀtiq ibn ʿĀbid ibn ʿAbd Allah ibn ʿUmar ibn Makhzūm, with whom she had a daughter also named Hind.[2] The information about both marriages is contradictory in the sources. While some sources say that she was widowed twice, others claim she was widowed once and divorced once.

Khadīja was a successful merchant, and her caravans are said to have equaled all Meccan caravans put together. As she did not travel herself, she employed traders, among whom was the young Muḥammad before his call to prophethood.[3] She is said to have been impressed by his honesty and proposed marriage to him through her trusted friend Nafīsa. Though Muḥammad hesitated at first because he could not afford the wedding expenses, he consulted his uncles, who encouraged this union.[4] The sources do not agree whether they had eight, seven, or six children together, though they agree that four of them—Zaynab, Ruqayya, Umm Kulthūm, and Fāṭima—were female and that none of their sons survived past infancy. She is said to have married Muḥammad at the age of forty, when she was fifteen years his senior.

Khadīja received her glad tidings directly from angel Jibrīl (Gabriel), who is reported to have told the Prophet: "Give Khadīja, the Mother of the Believers, peace from her Almighty Lord and from me, and give her glad tidings of a house in Paradise, without clamor or exertion."[5] These happy tidings are linked to the days when Muḥammad would meditate in the cave of Hirāʾ before his call to prophethood and Khadīja would bring him *ḥays*[6] as sustenance. Jibrīl alerted him to her coming and said, "God orders you to give her His greetings." Khadīja replied, "God is peace, from God comes peace and peace be upon Jibrīl."[7] The promised dwelling in Paradise is described as being without clamor and hardship, because when the Prophet called to Islam, it involved hardship and exertion and Khadīja helped him voluntarily with all her might, effort, and wealth; comforted him; alleviated his exhaustion and fatigue; and supported him beyond the call of duty; therefore, the house promised to her reflects the extent of her contributions and sacrifices.[8]

Another *ḥadīth* reports that Muḥammad drew four lines on the ground and explained that these lines referred to the most excellent women of Paradise: Khadīja bint Khuwaylid, Fāṭima bint Muḥammad, Maryam bint ʿImrān, and Āsiya bint Muzāḥim, wife of the Egyptian pharaoh.[9] What Āsiya, Maryam, and Khadīja had in common was their belief in a prophet, support for him, and promotion of his message: Āsiya supported Mūsā (Moses), Maryam (Mary) raised ʿĪsā (Jesus), and Khadīja sought out Muḥammad to marry him, putting all her wealth at his disposal.[10] It is not surprising that Khadīja, the first Muslim to believe in the Prophet and his message, would receive this news. The story of how she comforted him after the first revelation and how she provided confirmation that it was indeed a revelation from God through her cousin Waraqa ibn Nawfal is well known in Islamic history and tradition.[11]

Fāṭima bint Muḥammad

As for Fāṭima, her fame rests mainly on her famous lineage: she was the Prophet's daughter by Khadīja, the wife of ʿAlī ibn Abī Ṭālib, and the mother of al-Ḥasan and al-Ḥusayn. Her preeminence in early Islamic history is, therefore, primarily due to the historical importance of her father, husband, and sons. The Sunnī biographical dictionaries do not ascribe any outstanding deeds to her personally, other than her attentiveness toward her father, yet there are many discussions concerning the glad tidings she received. The discussion centers on her date of birth due to the unusual report transmitted by the Syrian scholar al-Ṭabarānī, (d. 360/971), in which ʿĀʾisha bint Abī Bakr relates that the Prophet said, "When I was taken to heaven I walked around and saw a tree unlike any I had ever seen, with fruits unlike any I had ever seen. I ate one of the fruits which became a sperm in my loin. When I descended back to earth I had intercourse with Khadīja and she became pregnant with Fāṭima."[12] This report alleges that the *Isrāʾ* (the Prophet's ascension to Jerusalem) and the *Miʿrāj* (his night journey to the heavens) were before Fāṭima was born, though she is said to have been born before the *baʿth* ("call to Prophethood").[13] Al-Ṭabarānī himself reports that Fāṭima was born seven years before the call to Prophethood, whereas *al-Isrāʾ wa-al-Miʿrāj* took place in the first year after the call, but he does not attempt to reconcile the conflicting information.[14] Al-Ṭabarānī adds that she was called *Umm Abīha* ("her father's mother") for her attentive care of her father, tending to his wounds and consoling him when he was insulted and harmed by the Meccans.[15]

In the *Ṣaḥīḥayn* there is an addendum explaining that each one (Maryam bint ʿImrān and Khadīja) was the best woman of her time. Moreover, Khadīja's house in heaven is described as being carved out of hollowed pearls.[16] Al-Ḥaḍramī (d. 489/1095) reports a qualification that Fāṭima is the mistress of women in paradise after Maryam. He then engages with the question of who is preferred: ʿĀʾisha, Khadīja, or Fāṭima, concluding that Fāṭima came from the Prophet's loins, therefore, nobody is preferred over her, then Khadīja followed by ʿĀʾisha.[17] Yet no entry anywhere explicitly mentions that ʿĀʾisha, who is said to have been the Prophet's most beloved wife, was among the *Mubashsharāt bi-l-janna*.

Umm Rumān

In contrast to ʿĀʾisha, Umm Rumān, the wife of Abū Bakr (the first Rightly Guided caliph) and ʿĀʾisha's mother, is mentioned in the sources as having received the glad tidings of Paradise.

Umm Rumān (which was her *kunya* or paedonymic)[18] was named Zaynab bint ʿĀmir ʿUmayr ibn Dahmān. Before marrying Abū Bakr she was married to ʿAbd Allah ibn al-Ḥārith, who fathered one son, al-Ṭufayl, with her. She had two children with Abū Bakr: ʿĀʾisha and ʿAbd al-Raḥmān. She is described as a good and very charitable woman.[19] She accepted Islam among the first Muslims, immediately after her husband Abū Bakr, and pledged her allegiance to the Prophet.[20] Ibn Saʿd, the famous early biographer (d. 230/845), reports that the Prophet gave Umm Rumān glad tidings saying, "Whoever wants to see the *ḥūr* (a reference to the dark-eyed female inhabitants) of Paradise, should look at Umm Rumān."[21]

She died six years after the *hijra*, during the Prophet's lifetime, and he personally carried her to her grave and laid her to rest, asking forgiveness for her, and saying: "Oh merciful God, you know what she endured for You and Your Prophet."[22] Muḥammad ibn Yūsuf al-Ṣāliḥī, the tenth/sixteenth-century Syrian scholar (d. 942/1536) commends her support for ʿĀʾisha during the event known as *ḥadīth al-ifk*[23] ("the episode of the slander").[24]

Asmāʾ bint Abī Bakr

As for ʿĀʾisha's half-sister, Asmāʾ, her mother was Qutayla bint ʿAbd al-ʿUzza, Abū Bakr's first wife. She bore him Asmāʾ and ʿAbd Allah, after which he divorced her. Asmāʾ is famous in the history of early Islam for having carried food and water concealed in her belt, that she had cut into two, to the Prophet and Abū Bakr, when they were hiding in the Cave of Thawr on their way to Medina during the *hijra* (an event alluded to in Qurʾān 9:40). On account of that, the Prophet named her *dhāt al-niṭāqayn* ("she of the two belts") and gave her glad tidings of Paradise and told her that God will grant her two belts there.[25]

Ibn Saʿd reports that every time she fell ill, Asmāʾ would manumit all her slaves and that she encouraged her children to spend in charity without expecting anything in return.[26] The famous Damascene scholar al-Ṣafadī (d. 764/1363) lists another sobriquet for her: namely *ʿajūz al-janna* ("the elderly lady of Paradise"), as she was the last of the immigrants to die. He states that she died after her son, ʿAbd Allah, was killed, when she was a hundred years old in 73/692. However, he adds that she had neither lost a single tooth nor her sharp wit.[27] The Egyptian scholar al-Qasṭallānī (d. 923/1517) reports that she was the fourth woman to accept Islam after Khadīja, Sumayya, and Umm al-Faḍl, making her among the first twenty people who accepted Islam.[28]

Umm Sulaym

Her name is al-Rumaysāʾ bint Milḥān, and she was one of the earliest women to accept Islam in Medina. She is said to have acquired the name al-Rumayṣāʾ or al-ʿUmayṣāʾ, because of a discharge from her eyes. She is described as a slender pretty woman who was from the al-Khazraj tribe and was first married to Mālik ibn al-Naḍr, with whom she had a son, Anas, who served the Prophet. Mālik left her because she became a Muslim. After he left, she vowed not to remarry until Anas became a man. The Prophet would ask God to bless her for such a superb upbringing and guardianship (*wilāya*) of her son.[29]

Abū Ṭalḥa al-Anṣārī, one of the Prophet's companions, was impressed with her steadfastness and told her: "Now Anas is grown up and is speaking at gatherings (*majālis*), it is time for you to remarry." She replied saying that he is worshipping what can neither benefit nor harm him and that he should follow the man she believes in, the Messenger of God.[30] She asks him if he was not ashamed to prostrate to a useless piece of wood. The conversation is reproduced in detail in the sources and ends with her convincing him to accept Islam.[31] When Abū Ṭalḥa went to the Prophet to announce his acceptance of Islam, the Prophet saw him coming and said: "There comes Abū Ṭalḥa with Islam in his eyes." When he heard about Umm Sulaym's condition he remarked that this was the greatest dowry ever paid, because she had asked for Islam as dowry.[32]

Umm Sulaym participated in the *bayʿa* (the giving of allegiance to the Prophet) and in the Battle of Uḥud, where she nursed the wounded and distributed water.[33] She also went to the Battle of Ḥunayn with her husband Abū Ṭalḥa while she was pregnant with her son ʿAbd Allah ibn Abī Ṭalḥa.[34] She carried a dagger, and when she was asked what she intended to do with it, she replied, "I will disembowel any polytheist who comes close." When the Prophet heard that he laughed. Her moral excellence is indicated by a report in *Ṣaḥīḥ al-Bukhārī* in which the Prophet states that he went to heaven and heard a scuffing sound, whose source turned out to be Umm Sulaym.[35] The Prophet remarked that God was pleased with her and she had preceded all women and men to Paradise.[36]

Umm Ḥarām

The sources do not mention a variant name for Umm Ḥarām, though they mention that she was Umm Sulaym's sister. She was from the Anṣārī elite, and like her sister accepted Islam early and was therefore one of the *sābiqāt*. The Prophet used to visit her and her sister before the *ḥijāb* became mandatory and he used to sleep with his head in her lap.[37] On those visits, she fed and deloused him.[38] The Prophet used to pray with her and her sister, sometimes adding extra or supererogatory prayers.[39]

Umm Ḥarām was married to ʿUbāda ibn al-Ṣāmit, who was one of the first Anṣārī men to take part in the Pledge of al-ʿAqaba. They had two sons, Qays and ʿAbd Allah.[40] The Prophet said that the first army of his *umma* to conquer the seas will all go to Paradise as martyrs. Umm Ḥarām asked if she would be among them and the Prophet affirmed that she would.[41] This came to pass when her husband ʿUbāda ibn al-Ṣāmit took her with him on a naval expedition to Cyprus and she died after breaking her neck while trying to get on her mount upon disembarking from the ship.[42]

She is described as one of the wise, reasonable voices of her time and a trustworthy *ḥadīth* narrator who narrated a number of reports from the Prophet.[43] Her narrations are included in all collections except *Jāmiʿ Abī ʿĪsā*.[44] Many people narrated the Prophet's sayings from her, among them two of the Mothers of the Believers, ʿĀʾisha and Umm Salama.[45]

Umm Zafar or Umm Zakhar

Umm Zafar or Umm Zakhar remains mostly unnamed in the sources, though al-Bukhārī (d. 256/810) offers two names for her, either Suʿayra or Shuqayra al-Asadiyya.[46] Al-Bukhārī refers to Umm Zafar as a believing black woman whose given name cannot be known with certainty. She is said to have suffered from epilepsy, on account of which she asked the Prophet to make supplications for her. Prophet Muḥammad gave her the choice between suffering from epilepsy now or being rewarded with Paradise for her *ṣabr* (patience) later. She chose Paradise, but asked him to pray that she not be exposed during one of her fits; her prayer was granted and she was never exposed during any seizure.[47] In his *Ṣaḥīḥ*, al-Bukhārī further mentions that she was often found clinging to the Kaʿba coverings.[48]

Muslim ibn Ḥajjāj (d. 261/875) adds that Umm Zafar was Khadīja's *māshiṭa* (*coiffeuse*), who used to frequently visit the Prophet after Khadīja's death.[49] Ibn Bashkawāl, the Andalusian historian (d. 578/1183), adds that she was from Abyssinia.[50] Ibn al-Athīr, the famous historian (d. 630/1233), reports that she was believed to have been possessed by Jinn and was slightly insane. When her brothers brought her to the Prophet to be cured, he tapped her chest so as to induce the Jinn to leave her body, but apparently, he failed to cure her. Ibn al-Athīr describes her as a tall, big, *samrāʾ* (dark) woman, who used to frequently sit on the stairs of the Kaʿba. The choice between earthly suffering and the heavenly reward of Paradise and bypassing judgment, according to Ibn al-Athīr, was given not to her, but to her brothers; however, she is said to have interrupted them and chosen the latter option for herself.[51]

Ibn Ḥajar, the Egyptian polymath (d. 852/1449) quotes the Prophet as saying that her earthly ʿ*ayb* (defect) had ensured her entrance into Paradise. He also mentions that it was her brothers who gave her the choice between earthly suffering and entrance into Paradise after consulting the Prophet.[52]

It is noteworthy how this account evolved over time—the earliest version given by al-Bukhārī describes Umm Zafar as directly responding to the Prophet when he offered her the choice between enduring her epilepsy and ready admission into Paradise as compensation for her suffering. In Ibn al-Athir's version, the Prophet addresses her brothers instead of Umm Zafar; when the latter inserts herself into the process and prevents her brothers from speaking on her behalf, we are led to believe that her action was somewhat presumptuous, since the Prophet had not spoken to her directly. By the time of Ibn Ḥajar's account in the ninth/fifteenth century, Umm Zafar has been robbed of all agency and her brothers preempt the role of Muḥammad in offering her the choice between earthly suffering and Paradise. Comparison of these three accounts is highly revealing of diachronic changes regarding conceptualizations of women's agency and gendered roles by the Mamluk period and of the perceived need to retroject these changes back to the time of the female Companions so as to grant them at least a veneer of legitimacy.

Umm ʿUmāra

Umm ʿUmāra's name was Nusayba bint Kaʿb. She was from the tribe of Banū Māzin b. al-Najjār and was married to Zayd ibn ʿĀṣim ibn Kaʿb, with whom she had two sons, Ḥabīb and ʿAbd Allah.[53] Ibn Saʿd claims that she married three times and gave each husband a son.[54] She was one of two women offering her *bayʿa* at al-ʿAqaba,[55] from among sixty-two Anṣār. The second woman was her sister, though there is a claim that the second woman was Asmāʾ bint ʿAmr ibn ʿAdiy, known as Umm Manīʿ.[56]

Umm ʿUmāra's heroic feats on the battlefield during the Battle of Uḥud (fought in 3/625), during which she protected Muḥammad with sword, bow, and arrow, are legendary.[57] She is said to have initially only tended to the wounded, and distributed water, but she began to fight when she saw the Prophet besieged by his enemies. She is quoted as saying that she had to save him, because without him they would all be doomed.[58] She herself suffered a dozen penetrating injuries and deep wounds that left a deep gash beside her shoulder and caused her to bleed profusely and which took a whole year to heal.[59] The Prophet is said to have tended to her wounds at Uḥud and bandaged them.[60]

The Prophet is quoted as saying that wherever he turned on the battlefield, there she was, fighting left and right, protecting him. Muḥammad praised her courage and valor, beyond that of some men who are only named as *fulān* and *fulān* (so-and-so).[61] He is said to have smiled at her during the battle, saying that nobody endured what she had endured. She received her glad tidings during the Battle of Uḥud, when she asked to be one of the Prophet's companions in Paradise because she did not care about this world. After a prophetic supplication to make her one of his companions in Paradise, the Prophet told her that her wish had been granted.[62] Her courage at the Battle of Yamāma, where she lost her hand and received eleven wounds, has also been praised.[63]

Umm Ayman

Umm Ayman's name is given as Baraka bint Tha'laba ibn ʿAmr ibn al-Nuʿmān, and she is also known by another *kunya*, Umm al-Ẓibāʾ. She was the Prophet's dry-nurse in his childhood, establishing such a close bond with Muḥammad that he came to regard her as his second mother. She is said to have been an enslaved person and was manumitted by Muḥammad when he married Khadīja. He wed Umm Ayman to ʿUbayd ibn Zayd, who fathered her son Ayman after the call to Prophethood. The Prophet used to count her, like Nusayba, from among his *ahl al-bayt* (family).[64]

It is reported that she had a lisp, which used to make the Prophet smile, when she failed to utter the greeting '*salām*' correctly. Muḥammad used to tell her lovingly to keep quiet, because of her lisp. When the Prophet died, she cried piteously, saying she was crying over the revelation coming to an end.

Sources report that she immigrated twice, first to Abyssinya and then to Medina, and that she was black. She lost her son, Ayman, at the Battle of Uḥud. Her designation as one of the *mubashsharāt bi-l-janna* occurred when the Prophet remarked, "Whoever wants to marry a woman of Paradise, should marry Umm Ayman." Thereafter, Zayd ibn Ḥāritha (d. 8/629), Muḥammad's adopted son, married her and she bore him a son, Usāma. She is described as walking on foot during her immigration to Medina while fasting and suffering tremendously from thirst, since she was without any sustenance. She almost died, but when the sun set, she heard a noise, raised her head and found a bucket dangling from heaven.[65] She drank from it and is said to have never felt thirsty again in her life.[66] She died in the early days of ʿUthmān's reign.[67] The Syrian historian and *ḥadīth* scholar al-Dhahabī (d. 748/1348), adds that she narrated *aḥādīth* from the Prophet which are found in the standard collections.[68]

Al-Rabīʿ bint Maʿūdh al-Anṣāriyya

Al-Rabīʿ bint Maʿūdh al-Anṣāriyya was one of the two women who pledged allegiance to the Prophet at al-Riḍwān. Ibn Ḥanbal, the eponymous founder of the Ḥanbalī school of jurisprudence (d. 241/855), quotes the Prophet as asserting that all those who had pledged allegiance "under the tree"[69] would escape hellfire and go to Paradise.[70] Ibn Abī Khaythama (d. 279/892) attests to her being among those who pledged allegience under the tree.[71]

Al-Rabīʿ is reported to have narrated many *aḥādīth* from the Prophet, found in most of the standard collections, one in particular describing the perfect ablution.[72] She accompanied the Prophet on battles, where she tended to the wounded and helped to transport them back to Medina.[73] In addition to both daughters of Milḥān (Umm Sulaym and Umm Ḥarām, mentioned above) she was also one of the women the Prophet used to visit alone.[74] She died during the reign of the Umayyad ruler ʿAbd al-Malik (r. 66/685–86/705).[75]

Sumayya bint Khayyāṭ

Sumayya bint Khayyāṭ was the first martyr in Islam. It is worthy of note in this context that the first believer and the first martyr in Islam were both women, a fact that does not receive sufficient emphasis in the sources. Sumayya was an enslaved woman belonging to Abū Ḥudhayfa ibn al-Mughīra of the Banū Makhzūm, who gave her in marriage to Yāsir ibn ʿĀmir ibn Mālik al-ʿAnsīy, an early Companion of the Prophet.[76] Ibn Hishām (d. 218/833), most famous for his biography of the Prophet, reports that Sumayya and her son ʿAmmār were tortured brutally by the Meccan polytheists in order to make them renounce Islam. When ʿAmmār recanted publicly, the polytheists ceased tormenting him. This caused the revelation of Qurʾān 16:106, which promises forgiveness to those who apostasize outwardly under duress but remain firm in their faith inwardly.[77] Sumayya, however, remained steadfast and continued to be tortured inhumanely[78] until Abū Jahl finally stabbed her in the heart.[79] Other biographers detail the torture Sumayya was subjected to in her old age and also describe her strength and endurance in refusing to renounce Islam. The famous jurist and traditionist al-Bayhaqī (d. 458/1066), adds that she was one of the first seven to accept Islam and the second woman to do so after Khadīja, which made her one of the earliest and most famous *Ṣaḥābiyyāt*.[80] Some report that Abū Jahl did not stab her in the heart, but inserted a lance into her private parts tearing her apart, making her the first martyr.[81] When the Prophet saw the entire family being tortured, he prayed to God to have mercy on them. He then gave them glad tidings of Paradise saying: "Be patient Āl (family of) Yāsir, for you have a date with Paradise."[82]

Umm Waraqa

Umm Waraqa bint ʿAbd Allah ibn al-Ḥārith al-Anṣārī, one of the Medinan Muslims, was known for her knowledge of the Qurʾān, which she had memorized in its entirety. When the Prophet was leaving to fight at Badr, she asked to join him to tend to the wounded, hoping to be martyred. The Prophet refused, citing her age. However, he told her that God would grant her martyrdom and gave her glad tidings of Paradise, calling her *al-shahīda* (the martyr) thereafter. He ordered her to lead the prayers of her household (*dār*) and appointed a muezzin for her.[83] Two of her slaves subsequently murdered her, suffocating her with a velvet cloth, and then escaped.[84] They were later caught and crucified, being the first to be subjected to such a punishment in Medina. She was one of the renowned Companions and was killed during ʿUmar's reign.[85]

Umm Waraqa's fame does not derive from her martyrdom but rather from having been asked by the Prophet to lead the prayers in her mixed-gender household, because of her knowledge and for having memorized the entire Qur'an. Early sources attest to this fact; however, later sources starting in the later third/ninth century begin to minimize or elide these references to her superior knowledge of the Qur'an and her role as a prayer leader. Thus we find that in the first half of the third/ninth century, Aḥmad ibn Ḥanbal (d. 241/855) cites a prophetic tradition stating that she had memorized the entire Qur'an, on account of which the Prophet ordered her to lead the prayers in her household and assigned her a muezzin.[86] Abū Dāwūd (d. 275/889) cites the same tradition verbatim,[87] and lists another one where he adds that the muezzin was an elderly man (*shaykh*).[88] In the late third/ninth century, however, al-Marwazī (d. 294/909) glosses over her knowledge of the Qur'an and only mentions that she used to lead the prayers in her household and had a muezzin. He neither mentions that the Prophet asked her to do so, nor that he assigned her a muezzin, though he lists other instances of women leading prayer, like the Prophet's wives, ʿĀʾisha and Umm Salama, and emphasizes that women can only lead women and not a mixed-gender congregation. He writes extensively about the prohibition of women leading men in prayer and goes as far as prohibiting pregnant women from leading prayers or participating in a prayer led by a woman, in case the fetus is male.[89]

In the following century, al-Ṭabarānī (d. 360/971) mentions in a summary that she had memorized the entire Qur'an, that the Prophet had assigned her a muezzin, and that she led prayers. His main focus, however, is on her request to join the Battle of Badr that was denied, the Prophet giving her glad tidings of martyrdom, and on her subsequent murder.[90] Al-Dāraquṭnī, the famous *ḥadīth* scholar (d. 385/995), reports that the Prophet gave her glad tidings of martyrdom and refers to her subsequent murder. He further mentions that she led the prayers in her household, and was allowed to hire a muezzin, omitting the detail that the Prophet had asked her to do so and had appointed the muezzin for her.[91] Ibn al-Jawzī (d. 597/1201) returns to the original narrative, stating that she had memorized the entire Qur'an and that the Prophet ordered her to lead the prayers for her entire household. He, however, does not mention the appointment of the muezzin but narrates the other details regarding her wish to take part in battle and that she was called a martyr by the Prophet, without referencing her subsequent murder.[92] Ibn Ḥajar (d. 852/1449) mentions Umm Waraqa twice: the first time he mentions that she had "read" the Qur'an, not memorized it, and that the Prophet allowed her to lead prayers in her household. He omits any reference to the muezzin and classifies the report as weak.[93] In the second account, which is much longer, he starts with the story of her asking to join battle and her being named al-*shahīda* and her murder, focusing on how the culprits were crucified, being the first to face this punishment. He does not, however, mention her knowledge of the Qur'an nor her leading prayers.[94] Clearly, Ibn

Ḥajar manipulated the details of Umm Waraqa's life to reflect the juristic developments and preferences concerning gendered roles during his time.

Umm Saʿd

Umm Saʿd's name is Kabsha bint Rāfiʿ. She was from the al-Ḥārith clan of the al-Khazraj tribe and among the first to convert to Islam. She was married to Muʿādh ibn al-Nuʿmān, of the al-Aws tribe, with whom she had five sons and one daughter. Kabsha was among the first women of Medina to give the oath of allegiance to the Prophet after his arrival in Medina with Umm ʿĀmir bint Yazīd, her sister Ḥawwāʾ, Layla bint ʿAwf, and Mariam bint Abī Sufyān and her sister Tamīma.[95] Kabsha's entire family committed themselves with great dedication to the defense of Islam and the Prophet.[96]

Kabsha lost eleven of her sons, brothers, and relatives in one battle. When she was told about that, she remained composed and went to see the Prophet. When she found him safe, she said this alleviated her loss. The Prophet gave her glad tidings then, saying that they will all be together, including her, in heaven.[97] The Prophet left a share of the booty to the women who attended the battle, fighting and tending the wounded: Ṣafiyya bint ʿAbū Ṭālib, Umm ʿUmāra, Umm Salīṭ, al-Sumayrāʾ bint Qays, and Kabsha, Umm Saʿd ibn Muʿādh.[98] When her son Saʿd ibn Muʿādh was martyred Kabsha is said to have wept heartbreakingly. People advised her not to, because lamentations were a *Jāhilī* habit that Islam had rejected. The Prophet told her to rejoice, for God will greet Saʿd ibn Muʿādh laughing, because He was pleased with him.[99] When she lamented her son, the Prophet is said to have remarked, "every weeper, mourner and lamenter lies, except the one lamenting Saʿd ibn Muʿādh, meaning her [sc. Kabsha]."[100]

Umm Kulthūm

Umm Kulthūm bint ʿUqba is renowned in early Islamic history as the woman who migrated despite the objections of her family and regarding whom Qur'ān 60:10 was revealed.[101] She had pledged her allegiance to Muḥammad at al-Riḍwān, because she was one of the women who accepted Islam very early on.[102] She was the half-sister of ʿUthmān ibn 'Affān (d. 36/656), the third Rightly Guided caliph (r. 23/644–36/656).[103]

Umm Kulthūm was married to al-Zubayr ibn al-ʿAwwām (d. 36/656), a cousin and Companion of the Prophet, one of the first converts to Islam and one of his main military leaders, who was known to be very harsh and violent. She asked him to divorce her several times, which he did not. She was pregnant and about to deliver, which he did not know. When she kept insisting that he divorce her, al-Zubayr finally acceded to her wish while he was performing his ablutions. Thereafter, she left him and gave birth to their daughter Zaynab. Someone gave him the news that she had just given birth and he went to the Prophet to complain furiously that she had tricked him. The Prophet replied,

"God's holy book mentions her, make up with her," but he swore never to take her back. She later married ʿAbd al-Raḥmān ibn ʿAwf and bore him two sons.[104]

Not only was Umm Kulthūm one of the renowned companions, but also she narrated many reports from the Prophet. When she defied her family and migrated to Medina on her own, she was met halfway by a Muslim from the tribe of Khuzāʿa who traveled with her for protection. The Prophet trusted her for her wisdom and the strength of her faith and took her on battles to tend the wounded. She is described as one of the few women of her time who could read and write and who taught other Muslims.[105]

Summary of the Exemplary Traits of the *Mubashsharāt*

All the *Ṣaḥābiyyāt* mentioned above suffered and endured grief, torture, and tragedy because of their early acceptance of Islam. This precedence in embracing the new faith made them part of a distinguished religious and spiritual elite, signified by the term *sābiqāt*, applied to all of them. Some bore witness to something beyond tragedy, yet sowed the seeds of hope and consolation in God's eternal justice, showing that goodness and truth cannot be erased, and redemption may be found through the sting of suffering. They all displayed courage, power and grace through the feminine; though gender did not define them exclusively and, therefore, they became role models for all Muslims to emulate. Some of the medieval biographers ascribed miracles to a number of them, like Umm Sulaym and Umm Ayman, to highlight their status and privileged position. Many of them showed exceptional abilities in memorizing the Prophet's words and transmitting them to the community, so they were regarded as trustworthy *ḥadīth* transmitters; they included Umm Ayman, Umm Ḥarām, al-Rabīʿ bint Maʿūdh, and Umm Kulthūm. Others, most notably Umm Waraqa, memorized the Qur'ān in its entirety or a great portion of it and led prayers at the Prophet's request. On account of their personal qualities and accomplishments, they are to be regarded as being among the foremost Companions of the Prophet, as the early sources, in particular from before the fourth/tenth century, often attest.

Modern Scholarship on the Lives of the Female Companions

Even though neither traditional nor modern scholars have compiled a list of the *Mubashsharāt*, much has been written about the *Ṣaḥābiyyāt* in general. Modern scholars, especially feminists, have been and still are keen on studying the lives of these exemplary women as a way of understanding the roles of women in early Muslim society and what lessons could be derived from their lives for modern times. The "Mothers of the Believers"—an honorific reserved for the wives of the Prophet—received ample attention in particular, due to their rank and the special status awarded to them in the Qur'ān, for example in Qur'ān 33:32. Each period had its own interpretations about the significance of the lives of the Mothers of the Believers; such interpretations were further affected by popular, cultural, and moral values of the time. The emphasis on the status and roles of the Prophet's wives originated not only from their historical personalities but also from the continuous modifications and revisions in the interpretations of the details of their lives and assessment of their significance.[106] As the survey above indicates, such reinterpretations and reassessments have been used to justify a great variety of cultural attitudes toward women and gendered norms of behavior.[107]

As for the *Ṣaḥābiyyāt*, modern scholarship has engaged with a select few, not in the context of being *Mubashsharāt*, but in other contexts as warriors, teachers, and role-models. Asma Afsaruddin mentions three of the women given glad tidings in a chapter discussing the normative behavioral precedents set by the *Ṣaḥābiyyat*, studying their conduct and actions as recorded in official biographies as morally exemplary and prescriptive for later generations of Muslim women.[108] She mentions the moral excellence, precedence, and service to Islam of Kulthūm bint ʿUqba, Nusayba bint Kaʾb and Umm Waraqa, among others.[109] She also notes the well-known report promising paradise to ten prominent male Companions, and that entries on individual *Ṣaḥābiyyāt* also promise them Paradise for their exceptional standing within Islam, clearly singling out pious women as destined for heavenly reward on par with the distinguished male Companions. Afsaruddin further notes that their names are not grouped together as a list, which this chapter attempted to provide.[110]

Umm Waraqa has also received much attention, mainly in the context of prayer leadership. Nevin Reda published an extensive article in 2004 detailing the historical and textual evidence supporting the permissibility of woman-led prayers, using Umm Waraqa's example.[111] Hina Azam criticized Reda's article and explained that though she herself supported women leading prayers in principle, she found Reda's argument and methodology flawed, concluding that there was no traditional legal support for her position.[112] More refutations and counter-refutations were written in response.[113] Aisha Geissinger notes that several Muslim feminists in the late twentieth century highlighted the precedent created by Umm Waraqa of a woman leading a mixed-gender prayer in early Islamic history.[114] Simonetta Calderini devoted an entire book to women leading prayers, in which Umm Waraqa features prominently.[115]

Marilyn Booth argues that there was a flood of biographical compendia on women of early Islamic history available in bookstores across the Middle East in the 1990s, echoing and shaping rival agendas on women's roles "crucial to alternative models of national(ist) state-building."[116] Geissinger discusses several early Muslim women, and examines the roles that they "have been made to play" in some Muslim feminist discourses.[117] She studies a wide range of classical Arabic texts, such as *sīra* works, *ḥadīth* compilations, biographical dictionaries, Qurʾān commentaries, historical works, and legal compendia showing that Muslim discourses since the nineteenth century looked to the past to legitimate actions in the present, particularly regarding controversial issues, and to provide cultural and/or religious legitimation for their respective "stances in contemporary debates about gender roles, family, and sexuality."[118] Afsaruddin also notes how the images of the *Ṣaḥābiyyāt* were amended or reworked over time and discussed what insights can be gained about changing conceptions of women's roles in Muslim societies.[119]

Ruth Roded examined women in Islamic literature over the centuries through the eyes of Muslim authors.[120] She shows that until the tenth/sixteenth century, compilers of biographical dictionaries usually included a separate section at the end of their works on women or interspersed a number of women's biographies among those of men.[121]

Though Fāṭima, the Prophet's daughter, is the object of great veneration by all Muslims, there are only a few modern studies dealing with her life that are not from a Shīʿī perspective.[122]

This chapter aimed at filling the existing gap about *al-Mubashsharāt bi-l-janna*, the early Muslim female companions of the Prophet, who serve as moral paragons in classical and modern literature. The highest reward to be aspired to by all believers, male and female, is a place in Paradise. The sacrifice, steadfastness, courage, and unshakable faith of these exceptional women earned them this distinction in the classical sources, and made them into role models to be emulated by modern Muslims.

Notes

1. Muḥammad Ibn Saʿd, *al-Ṭabaqāt al-kubrā*, ed. Muḥammad ʿAbd al-Qādir (Beirut: Dār al-Kutub al-ʿIlmiyya, 1990), 1:16.
2. Ibid., 8:11.
3. Ibid., 1:105.
4. Ibid., 8:11.
5. This is found in various *ḥadīth* compendia, for example in Muḥammad ibn Ismāʿīl al-Bukhārī, *al-Jāmiʿ al-musnad al-ṣaḥīḥ (Ṣaḥīḥ al-Bukhārī)* (Beirut: Dār Ṭawq al-Najāh, 2001), 3:6, #1792.
6. Name for a stew made out of dates, buttermilk, and ghee.
7. Abū al-Walīd Muḥammad ibn ʿAbd Allah ibn Aḥmad al-Azraqī, *Akhbār Makka wa mā jāʾa fīha min al-āthār* (Beirut: Dār al-Andalus, 1983), 2:204.
8. Mūsa ibn Rāshid al-ʿĀzimī, *al-Luʾluʾ al-maknūn fī sīrat al-nabī al-maʾmūn*, ed. Muḥammad Rawās Qalʿajī (Kuwait: al-Maktaba al-ʿamiriyya li-l-iʿlān wa-l-nashr wa-l-tawzīʿ, 2011), 1:418.
9. Aḥmad Ibn Ḥanbal, *Faḍāʾil al-ṣaḥāba* (Beirut: Muʾasassat al-Risāla, 1983), 2:760, #1339.
10. Ismāʿīl ibn ʿUmar Ibn Kathīr, *al-Bidāya wa-l-nihāya* (Beirut: Dār Iḥyāʾ al-Turāth al-ʿArabī, 1988), 3:141.
11. For details, see Muḥammad Ibn Isḥāq, *Sīrat Ibn Isḥāq (Kitāb al-siyar wa-l-maghāzī)* (Beirut: Dār al-Fikr, 1978), 128–133.
12. Abū al-Qāsim Sulaymān ibn Aḥmad al-Ṭabarānī, *al-Muʿjam al-kabīr* (Cairo: Maktabat Ibn Taymiya, 1983), 22:401.
13. For more on the Isrāʾ and Miʿrāj, see Muḥammad Ibn Isāq, *al-Sīra al-nabawiyya li Ibn Isḥāq* (Beirut: Dār al-Kutub al-ʿIlmiyya, n.d.), 309–310.

14. al-Ṭabarānī, *al-Mu'jam*, 22:399.
15. Ibid., 22:397.
16. See al-Bukhārī, *al-Jāmi'*, 4:158, #3411; 4:164, #3433; 5:29, #3769; and Ibn al-Ḥajjāj al-Naysābūrī Muslim, *Ṣaḥīḥ Muslim* (Beirut: Dār Iḥyā' al-Turāth al-'Arabī, 1991), 4:1886. #2431.
17. Abū Bakr 'Abd Allah ibn Sa'īd al-Ḥaḍramī, *Muntahā al-su'āl 'alā wasā'il al-wuṣūl ilā shamā'il al-rasūl* (Jeddah: Dār al-Minhāj, 2005), 2:155–156.
18. *Kunya* or paedonymic refers to a parent's name based on their firstborn (usually male) child's name. Thus, Umm Rumān means "Mother of Rumān," though she had no son named Rumān.
19. Yūsuf ibn Qizughlī Sibṭ Ibn al-Jawzī, *Mir'āt al-zamān fī tārīkh al-a'yān* (Damascus: Dār al-Risāla al-'Ilmiyya, 2013), 3:409.
20. Ḥusayn ibn Rahaway Muḥāmad Diyār Bakrī, *Tārīkh al-khamīs fī aḥwāl anfas nafīs* (Beirut: Dār Ṣādir 1973), 2:26.
21. Ibn Sa'd, *al-Ṭabaqāt*, 8:216.
22. Taqī al-Dīn al-Maqrīzī, *Imtā' al-asmā' bimā li-l-nabī min al-aḥwāl wa-l-amwāl wa-l-ḥafada wa-l-mitā'* (Beirut: Dār al-Kutub al-'Ilmiyya, 1999), 6:181–182.
23. In the fifth year after the migration, the Prophet was returning from the Battle of Banū al-Muṣtaliq, when the caravan departed without 'Ā'isha, who had gone off to relieve herself and, having lost her necklace, began searching for it and was delayed. She was accidentally left behind, as they thought she was in her *hawdaj* (palanquin) and moved on without her. Ṣafwān ibn al-Mu'aṭṭal al-Sulamī, a Companion, found her, and escorted her back to Medina, where scandalous rumors had spread accusing her of infidelity. Qur'ānic verses 24:11–26 were said to have been revealed to exonerate her. Al-Bukhārī reports a long *ḥadīth* on 'Ā'isha's authority (5:62, #3910) about this episode and again (5:116, #4141) about the exegesis of Qur'ān 24:11–26. The episode is described in detail in 'Abd al-Malak Ibn Hishām, *al-Sīra al-nabawiyya* (Beirut: Dār al-Jīl, 1990), 2:302.
24. Muḥammad ibn Yūsuf al-Ṣāliḥī, *Subul al-hudā wa-l-rashād fī sirat khayr al-'ibād* (Beirut: Dār al-Kutub al-'ilmiyya, 1993), 11:164.
25. 'Alī ibn Ibrāhīm al-Ḥalabī, *Insān al-'uyūn fī sīrat al-amīn al-ma'mūn (al-Sīra al-Ḥalabiyya)* (Beirut: Dār al-Kutub al-'Ilmiyya, 2006), 2:44–45.
26. Ibn Sa'd, *al-Ṭabaqāt*, 8:198.
27. Ṣalāḥ al-Dīn Khalīl al-Ṣafadī, *al-Wāfī bi-l-Wafayāt* (Beirut: Dār Iḥyā' al-Turāth, 2000), 9:36.
28. Aḥmad ibn Muḥammad al-Qasṭallānī, *al-Mawāhib al-laduniyya bi-al-minaḥ al-Muḥammadiyya* (Cairo: al-Maktaba al-Tawfīqiyya, 1907), 1:134.
29. Abū Dāwūd ibn al-Jārūd al-Ṭayālisī, *Musnad Abī Dāwūd al-Ṭayālisī* (Cairo: Dār Hājar, 1999), 3:534, #2168.
30. Ibn Sa'd, *al-Ṭabaqāt*, 8:313.
31. Ibid., 8:314.
32. Al-Ṭayālisī, *Musnad*, 3:534, #2168.
33. Ibn Sa'd, *al-Ṭabaqāt*, 8:424.
34. Ibid.
35. al-Bukhārī, *al-Jāmi'*, 4:180, #3509.
36. Majd al-Dīn ibn Muḥammad Ibn al-Athīr, *Jāmi' al-uṣūl fī aḥādīth al-rasūl* (Damascus: Maktabat al-Ḥalawānī, 1969–1972), 8:575.

37. Ibid., #2788.
38. Aḥmad ibn Muḥammad al-ʿAsqalānī Ibn Ḥajar, *al-Iṣāba fī tamyīz al-Ṣaḥāba* (Beirut: Dār al-Kutub al-ʿIlmiyya, 1994), 8:375, #11971.
39. Shams al-Dīn Muḥammad ibn ʿUthmān al-Dhahabī, *Siyar aʿlām al-nubalāʾ* (Beirut: Muʾasassat al-Risāla, 1985), 3:537.
40. Ibn Saʿd, *al-Ṭabaqāt*, 8:434.
41. Mālik ibn Anas, *al-Muwaṭṭaʾ* (Abu Dhabi: Muʾasasat Zāyid ibn Sulṭān Āl-Nahyān li-l-aʿmāl al-khayriyya, 2004), 3:661.
42. Yūsuf ibn ʿAbd Allah Ibn ʿAbd al-Barr, *al-Istiʿāb fī maʿrifat al-aṣḥāb* (Beirut: Dār al-Jīl, 1992), 4:1931, #4137.
43. Ibid., 4:1940, #4163.
44. al-Dhahabī, *Siyar Aʿlām*, 3:537.
45. ʿIzz al-Dīn Ibn al-Athīr, *Usd al-ghāba fī maʿrifat al-ṣaḥaba* (Beirut: Dār al-Kutub al-ʿIlmiyya, 1994), 7:120, #6939.
46. al-Bukhārī, *al-Jāmiʿ*, 7:116, #5652.
47. Muḥammad ibn Ismāʿīl al-Bukhārī, *al-Adab al-Mufrad* (Beirut: Dār al-Bashāʾir al-Islāmiyya, 1989), 1:178.
48. al-Bukhārī, *al-Jāmiʿ*, 7:116, #5652.
49. Muslim, *Ṣaḥīḥ Muslim*, 4:1994, #2576.
50. Khalaf ibn ʿAbd al-Malak ibn Masʿūd Ibn Bashkawāl, *Ghawāmiḍ al-Asmāʾ al-mubhama al-Wāqiʿa fī mutūn al-aḥādith al-musnada* (Beirut: ʿĀlam al-Kutub, 1986), 2:801.
51. Ibn al-Athīr, *Usd al-Ghāba*, 7:322.
52. Ibn Ḥajar, *al-Iṣāba*, 8:395.
53. Abī Ja'far Muḥammad ibn Jarīr al-Ṭabarī, *Tārīkh al-Ṭabarī: tārīkh al-rusul wa-al-mulūk li-Abī Ja'far Muḥammad ibn Jarīr al-Ṭabarī* (Beirut: Dār ādir, 2008), 2:362
54. Ibn Saʿd, *al-Ṭabaqāt*, 8:303–305.
55. The second pledge at al-ʿAqaba, in the month of Dhū l-Ḥijja of the year prior to the Hijra in 622 CE, when seventy-two men and two women pledged to defend the Prophet, recognizing him as their leader.
56. Ibn al-Athīr, *Usd al-ghāba*, 6:280, #7311.
57. al-Maqrīzī, *Imtāʿ al-asmāʿ*, 1:163.
58. Ibn Saʿd, *al-Ṭabaqāt*, 8:303–305.
59. Ibid.
60. al-Dhahabī, *Siyar*, 3:515–517.
61. al-Maqrīzī, *Imtāʿ al-asmāʿ*, 1:163.
62. Ibid.
63. Ibn Saʿd, *al-Ṭabaqāt*, 8:303–305.
64. al-Maqrīzī, *Imtāʿ al-asmāʿ*, 9:167.
65. Sibṭ Ibn al-Jawzī, *Mir'āt al-zamān*, 5:428–430.
66. Ibn Saʿd, *al-Ṭabaqāt*, 8:179.
67. Ibid.
68. al-Dhahabī, *Siyar*, 3:480–481.
69. *Bay'at al-shajarah* (Pledge of the Tree), also known as *Bay'at al-riḍwān* (Pledge of Satisfaction) took place in 6/628, in which the Companions swore their allegiance to the Prophet under a tree. See Ibn Isāq, *al-Sīra al-Nabawiyya*, 460–461.
70. Aḥmad Ibn Ḥanbal, *Musnad al-Imām Aḥmad ibn Ḥanbal* (Cairo: Dār al-Ḥadīth, 1995), 23:93, #14778.

71. Abū Bakr Ibn Abī Khaythama, *al-Tārīkh al-Kabīr* (Cairo: al-Fārūq al-Ḥadītha li-l-Ṭibā'a wa-l-Nashr, 2006), 2:801, #3468.
72. Isḥāq ibn Ibrāhīm Ibn Rahawayh, *Musnad Isḥāq ibn Rahawayh* (Medina: Maktabat al-Imān, 1991), 5:141, #2264.
73. Abū-l-Faraj 'Abd al-Raḥmān Ibn al-Jawzī, *al-Muntaẓam fī tārīkh al-umam wa-l-mulūk* (Beirut: Dār al-Kutub al-'Ilmiyya, 1992), 5:137.
74. al-Ḥalabī, *Insān al-'uyūn*, 2:179.
75. al-Dhahabī, *Siyar*, 4:300.
76. Ibn Sa'd, *al-Ṭabaqāt*, 3:101
77. [16:106] "he who is compelled while his heart is at rest on account of faith . . . ."
78. Ibn Hishām, *al-Sīra al-nabawiyya*, 1:261.
79. Ibn al-Jawzī, *al-Muntaẓam*, 2:384.
80. Abū Bakr al-Bayhaqī, *Dalā'il al-nubuwwa wa ma'rifat aḥwāl ṣāḥib al-sharī'a* (Beirut: Dār al-Kutub al-'Ilmiyya Beirut, 1984), 2:170.
81. Abū 'Umar Muḥammad ibn Ḥammād al-Ṣawānī, *al-Sīra al-nabawiyya kama jā'at fī al-aḥādīth al-ṣaḥīḥa* (Jeddah: Maktabat al-'Ubaykān, 2004), 1:96.
82. Ibn Sa'd, *al-Ṭabaqāt*, 4:101–102.
83. Ibn Rahawayh, *Musnad Isḥāq ibn Rahawayh*, 5:234, #2381.
84. Ibn Ḥajar, *al-Iṣāba*, 8:489, #12298.
85. Ibn al-Jawzī, *al-Muntaẓam*, 4:305–306.
86. Ibn Ḥanbal, *Musnad*, #27283.
87. Abū Dāwūd Sulaymān ibn al-Ash'ath al-Sijistānī, *Sunan Abī Dāwūd* (Beirut: al-Maktaba al-'Aṣriyya, 2007), 1:161 #591.
88. Ibid., #592.
89. Abū 'Abd Allah Muḥammad ibn Naṣr al-Marwazī, *Mukhtaṣar qiyām al-layl wa qiyām Ramaḍān wa kutub al-witr* (Faisalabad: Ḥadīth Akadimī, 1988), 1:227.
90. al-Ṭabarānī, *al-Mu'jam al-kabīr*, #326.
91. 'Alī Ibn 'Umar al-Dāraquṭnī, *Sunan al-Dāraquṭnī* (Beirut: Mu'assassat al- Risāla, 2004), 2:21, #1084.
92. Ibn al-Jawzī, *al-Muntaẓam*, 4:305 #226.
93. Ibn Ḥajar, *al-Iṣāba*, 2:287.
94. Ibid., 8:489.
95. Ibn Sa'd, *al-Ṭabaqāt*, 8:9.
96. Diyār Bakrī, *Tārīkh al-Khamīs*, 1:500.
97. al-Maqrīzī, *Imtā' al-asmā'*,1:175.
98. Ibid., 1:253.
99. 'Abd al-Qādir ibn Muḥammad al-Shanqīṭī, *Nuzhat al-afkār fī sharḥ qurrat al-abṣār* (Buraydah: Markaz al-Nukhab al-'Ilmiyya. n.d.), 1:274.
100. Ibn Kathīr, *al-Bidāya wa-l-nihāya*, ed. 'Alī Shīrī, 15 vols. (Beirut: Dār Iḥyā' al-Turāth al-'Arabī, 1988), 4:148.
101. [60.10] O you who believe! when believing women come to you fleeing, then examine them; God knows best their faith; then if you find them to be believing women, do not send them back to the unbelievers, neither are these (women) lawful for them, nor are those (men) lawful for them, and give them what they have spent; and no blame attaches to you in marrying them when you give them their dowries; and hold not to the ties of marriage of unbelieving women, and ask for what you have spent, and let them ask

for what they have spent. That is God's judgment; He judges between you, and God is Knowing, Wise.

102. Ibn al-Jawzī, *al-Muntaẓam*, 19:424.
103. Ibn Kathīr, *al-Bidāya*, 9:160.
104. Shams al-Dīn Muḥammad ibn ʿUthmān al-Dhahabī, *Tārīkh al-Islām wa wafayyāt al-mashāhīr wa-l-aʿlām* (Tunis: Dār al-Gharb al-Islāmī, 2003), 2:279.
105. Sibṭ Ibn al-Jawzī, *Mirʾāt al-zamān*, 4:53.
106. Yasmin Amin, "The Prophet's Wives," in *The Oxford Encyclopedia of Islam and Women*, ed. Natana J. DeLong-Bas (Oxford: Oxford University Press, 2013), 429.
107. Ascha Ghassan, "The Mothers of the Believers': Stereotypes of the Prophet Muhammad's Wives," in *Female Stereotypes in Religious Traditions*, ed. Ria Hanegraaf Kloppenborg and Wouter J. Hanegraaf Kloppenborg (Leiden: E. J. Brill, 1995), 107.
108. Asma Afsaruddin, "Early Muslim Women Exemplars and the Construction of Gendered Space," in *Harem Histories—Envisioning Places and Living Spaces*, ed. Marilyn Booth (Durham, NC: Duke University Press, 2010), 23–24.
109. Ibid., 29.
110. Ibid., 44.
111. Juliane Hammer, *American Muslim Women, Religious Authority, and Activism: More Than a Prayer* (Austin: University of Texas Press, 2012), 42.
112. Ibid., 46.
113. See, for example, A. Elewa and L. Silvers, "'I Am One of the People': A Survey and Analysis of Legal Arguments on Woman-Led Prayer in Islam," *Journal of Law and Religion* 26 (2010–2011): 141–171.
114. Aisha Geissinger, "Feminist Muslim (Re)interpretations of Early Islam," in *Routledge Handbook on Early Islam*, ed. Herbert Berg (Abingdon, Oxon: Routledge, 2017), 303.
115. Simonetta Calderini, *Women as Imams: Classical Islamic Sources and Modern Debates on Leading Prayer* (London: I. B. Tauris, 2021), 99–116.
116. Marilyn Booth, "Women's Biographies and Political Agendas: Who's Who in Islamic History," *Gender and History* 8 (1996): 133–137.
117. Geissinger, "Feminist Muslim (re)interpretations," 297.
118. Ibid., 296.
119. Asma Afsaruddin, "Reconstituting Women's Lives: Gender and the Poetics of Narrative in Medieval Biographical Collections," *Muslim World* 92, nos. 3–4 (2002): 461.
120. Ruth M. Roded, *Women in Islamic Biographical Collections: from Ibn Saʿd to Who's Who* (Boulder, CO: Lynne Rienner, 1994).
121. Ibid., viii.
122. See, for example, Bärbel Beinhauer-Köhler, *Fāṭima bint Muḥammad: Metamorphosen einer frühislamischen Frauengestalt* (Wiesbaden: Harrassowitz, 2002); and Christopher Paul Clohessy, *Fatima, Daughter of Muhammad* (Piscataway, NJ: Gorgias Press, 2018).

Bibliography

Primary Sources

Abū Dāwūd, Sulaymān ibn al-Ashʿath al-Sijistānī. *Sunan Abī Dāwūd*. Beirut: al-Maktaba al-ʿAṣriyya, 2007.

ʿĀzimī, Mūsa ibn Rāshid al-. *Al-Luʾluʾ al-maknūn fī sīrat al-nabī al-maʾmūn*. Edited by Muḥammad Rawās Qalʿajī. 4 vols. Kuwait: al-Maktaba al-ʿamiriyya li-l-iʿlan wa-l-nashr wa-l-tawzīʿ, 2011.

Azraqī, Abū-l-Walīd Muḥammad ibn ʿAbd Allāh ibn Aḥmad al-. *Akhbār Makka wa mā jāʾa fīha min al-athār*. Edited by Rushdī al-Ṣāliḥ Milḥis. 2 vols. Beirut: Dār al-Andalus, 1983.

Bayhaqī, Abū Bakr al-. *Dalāʾil al-nubuwwa wa maʿrifat aḥwāl ṣāḥib al-sharīʿa*. 7 vols. Beirut: Dār al-Kutub al-ʿIlmiyya Beirut, 1984.

Bukhārī, Muḥammad ibn Ismāʿīl al-. *al-Adab al-Mufrad*. Edited by Muḥammad Fuʾād ʿAbd al-Bāqī. Beirut: Dār al-Bashāʾir al-Islāmiyya, 1989.

Bukhārī, Muḥammad ibn Ismāʿīl al-. *al-Jāmiʿ al-musnad al-ṣaḥīḥ (Ṣaḥīḥ al-Bukhārī)*. 9 vols. Beirut: Dār Ṭawq al-Najāh, 2001.

Dāraquṭnī, ʿAlī Ibn ʿUmar al-. *Sunan al-Dāraquṭnī*. Beirut: Muʾassassat al- Risāla, 2004.

Dhahabī, Shams al-Dīn Muḥammad ibn ʿUthmān al-. *Siyar Aʿlām al-Nubalāʾ*. Edited by Shuʿayb al-Arnaʾūṭ. 25 vols. Beirut: Muʾasassat al-Risāla, 1985.

Dhahabī, Shams al-Dīn Muḥammad ibn ʿUthmān al-. *Tārīkh al-Islām wa wafayyāt al-mashāhīr wa-l-aʿlām*. Edited by Bashār ʿAwaḍ Maʿrūf. 15 vols. Tunis: Dār al-Gharb al-Islāmī, 2003.

Diyār Bakrī, Ḥusayn ibn Muḥāmad. *Tārīkh al-Khamīs fī Aḥwāl Anfas Nafīs*. 2 vols. Beirut: Dār Ṣādir, 1973.

Ḥaḍramī, Abū Bakr ʿAbd Allah ibn Saʿīd al-. *Muntahā al-suʾāl ʿalā wasāʾil al-wuṣūl ilā shamāʾil al-rasūl*. 4 vols. Jeddah: Dār al-Minhāj, 2005.

Ḥaḍramī, Muḥammad ibn ʿAmr ibn Mubārak al-Ḥimyarī al-. *Hadāʾiq al-anwār wa maṭāliʿ al-asrār fī sirat al-nabī al-mukhtār*. Jeddah: Dār al-Minhāj, 1998.

Ḥalabī, ʿAlī ibn Ibrāhīm al-. *Insān al-ʿUyūn fī sirat al-amīn al-maʾmūn (al-Sīra al-Ḥalabiyya)*. 3 vols. Beirut: Dār al-Kutub al-ʿIlmiyya, 2006.

Ibn ʿAbd al-Barr, Yūsuf ibn ʿAbd Allah. *al-Istiʿāb fī maʿrifat al-Aṣḥāibn*. Edited by ʿAlī Muḥammad al-Bajāwī. 4 vols. Beirut: Dār al-Jīl, 1992.

Ibn Abī ʿĀṣim, Abū Bakr. *al-Āḥād wa-l-Mathānā*. Edited by Bāsim Fayṣal Aḥmad al-Jawābira. 6 vols. Riyadh: Dār al-Rāya, 1991.

Ibn Abī Khaythama, Abū Bakr. *al-Tārīkh al-Kabīr*. Edited by Ṣalāḥ ibn Fatḥī Hilāl. 2 vols. Cairo: al-Fārūq al-Ḥadītha li-l-Ṭibāʿa wa-l-Nashr, 2006.

Ibn Anas, Mālik. *Al-Muwaṭṭaʾ*. Edited by Muḥammad Musṭafa al-Aʿzamī. 8 vols. Abu Dhabi: Muʾassasat Zāyid ibn Sulṭān Āl-Nahyān li-l-Aʿmāl al-Khayriyya, 2004.

Ibn al-Athīr, Ezz al-Dīn. *Usd al-Ghāba fī Maʿrifat al-Ṣaḥaba*. Edited by ʿAlī Muḥammad Muʿawwaḍ. 8 vols. Beirut: Dār al-Kutub al-ʿIlmiyya, 1994.

Ibn al-Athīr, ʻIzz al-Dīn. *Usd al-Ghāba*. 8 vols. Beirut: Dār al-Fikr, 1989.

Ibn al-Athīr, Majd al-Dīn ibn Muḥammad. *Jāmiʿ al-uṣūl fī aḥādīth al-rasūl*. Edited by ʿAbd al-Qādir al-Arnaʾūṭ. 12 vols. Damascus: Maktabat al-Ḥalawānī, 1969–1972.

Ibn Bashkawāl, Khalaf ibn ʿAbd al-Malak ibn Masʿūd. *Ghawāmiḍ al-Asmāʾ al-mubhama al-Wāqiʿa fī mutūn al-aḥādith al-musnada*. Edited by ʿIzz al-Dīn ʿAlī al-Sayyid. 2 vols. Beirut: Beirut, 1986.

Ibn Ḥajar, Aḥmad ibn Muḥammad al-ʿAsqalānī. *al-Iṣāba fī tamyīz al-ṣaḥāba*. 8 vols. Beirut: Dār al-Kutub al-ʿIlmiyya, 1994.

Ibn Ḥanbal, Aḥmad. *Faḍāʾil al-Ṣaḥāba*. 2 vols. Beirut: Muʾasassat al-Risāla, 1983.

Ibn Ḥanbal, Aḥmad. *Musnad Aḥmad ibn Ḥanbal*. Beirut: Muʾassassat al-Risāla, 2001.

Ibn Ḥanbal, Aḥmad. *Musnad al-Imām Aḥmad ibn Ḥanbal*. Edited by Aḥmad Muḥammad Shākir. 8 vols. Cairo: Dār al-Ḥadīth, 1995.

Ibn Hishām, ʿAbd al-Malak. *al-Sīra al-nabawiyya*. Edited by Ṭaha ʿAbd al-Raʾūf Saʿd. 2 vols. Beirut: Dār al-Jīl, 1990.

Ibn Isāq, Muḥammad. *al-Sīra al-nabawiyya li Ibn Isḥāq*. Beirut: Dār al-Kutub al-ʿIlmiyya, n.d.

Ibn Isḥāq, Muḥammad. *Sīrat Ibn Isḥāq (Kitāb al-iyar wa-l-maghāzī)*. Beirut: Dār al-Fikr, 1978.

Ibn al-Jawzī, Abū-l-Faraj ʿAbd al-Raḥmān. *al-Muntazim fī tārīkh al-umam wa-l-mulūk*. 19 vols. Beirut: Dār al-Kutub al-ʿIlmiyya, 1992.

Ibn al-Jawzī, Abū-l-Faraj ʿAbd al-Raḥmān. *Talqīḥ fuhūm ahl al-athar fī ʿuyūn al-tārīkh wa-l-siyar*. Beirut: Dār al-Arqam, 1997.

Ibn Kathīr, Ismāʿīl ibn ʿUmar. *al-Bidāya wa-l-nihāya*. Edited by ʿAlī Shīrī. 15 vols. Beirut: Dār Iḥḥyāʾ al-Turāth al-ʿArabī, 1988.

Ibn Rahawayh, Isḥāq ibn Ibrāhīm. *Musnad Isḥāq ibn Rahawayh*. Edited by ʿAbd al-Ghafūr al-Balūshī. 5 vols. Medina: Maktabat al-Imān, 1991.

Ibn Saʿd, Muḥammad. *al-Ṭabaqāt al-kubrā*. Edited by Muḥammad ʿAbd al-Qādir ʿAṭā. 8 vols. Beirut: Dār al-Kutub al-ʿIlmiyya, 1990.

Iṣbahānī, Abū Nuʿaym al-. *Maʿrifat al-Ṣaḥāba*. Edited by ʿĀdil ibn Yūsuf al-ʿAzzāzī. 7 vols. Riyadh: Dār al-Waṭan li-l-Nashr, 1998.

Maqrīzī, Taqiyy al-Dīn al-. *Imtāʿ al-asmāʿ bimā li-l-nabiy min al-aḥwāl wa-l-amwāl wa-l-ḥafada wa-l-mitāʿ*. Edited by Muḥammad ʿAbd al-Ḥamīd al-Namīsī. 15 vols. Beirut: Dār al-Kutub al-ʿIlmiyya, 1999.

Marwazī, Abū ʿAbd Allah Muḥammad ibn Naṣr al-. *Mukhtaṣar qiyām al-layl wa qiyām Ramaḍān wa kutub al-witr*. Faisalabad: Ḥadīth Akadimī, 1988.

Muslim, Ibn al-Ḥajjāj al-Naysābūrī. *Ṣaḥīḥ Muslim*. Edited by Muḥammad Fuʾād ʿAbd al-Bāqī. 5 vols. Beirut: Dār Iḥyāʾ al-Turāth al-ʿArabī, 1991.

Nasāʾī, Aḥmad ibn Shuʿayb ibn ʿAlī al-. *Al-Sunnan al-Kubra*. Edited by Ḥasan Muḥamad ʿAbd al-Munʿim Shalabī. 12 vols. Beirut: Muʾasassat al-Risāla, 2001.

Nawawī, Muḥiyy al-Dīn al-. *Tahdhīb al-Asmāʾ wa-l-lughāt*. Beirut: Dār al-Fikr, 1996.

Qasṭallānī, Aḥmad ibn Muḥammad al-. *al-Mawāhib al-laduniyya bi-al-minaḥ al-Muḥammadiyya*. Cairo: al-Maktaba al-Tawfīqiyya, 1907.

Ṣafadī, Ṣalāḥ al-Dīn Khalīl al-. *al-Wāfī bi-l-Wafiyyāt*. Edited by Aḥmad Arnaʾūṭ. 29 vols. Beirut: Dār Iḥyāʾ al-Turāth, 2000.

Ṣāliḥī, Muḥammad ibn Yūsuf al-. *Subul al-hudā wa-l-rashād fī sīrat khayr al-ʿibād*. 12 vols. Beirut: Dār al-Kutub al-ʿilmiyya, 1993.

Ṣawānī, Abū ʿUmar Muḥammad ibn Ḥammād al-. *al-Sīra al-Nabawiyya kama jāʾat fī al-aḥādīth al-ṣaḥīḥa*. 4 vols. Jeddah: Maktabat al-ʿUbaykān, 2004.

Shanqīṭī, ʿAbd al-Qādir ibn Muḥammad al-. *Nuzhat al-afkār fī sharḥ qurrat al-abṣār*. Edited by al-Sharīf Aʿzīzī ibn al-Māmī al-Sibāʿī. 2 vols. Burayda: Markaz al-Nukhab al-ʿIlmiyya, n.d.

Sibṭ Ibn al-Jawzī, Yūsuf ibn Qizughlī. *Mirʾāt al-zamān fī tārīkh al-aʿyān*. 23 vols. Damascus: Dār al-Risāla al-ʿIlmiyya, 2013.

Ṭabarānī, Abū-l-Qāsim Sulaymān ibn Aḥmad al-. *al-Muʿjam al-Kabīr*. Edited by Ḥamdī ʿAbd al-Majīd al-Salafī. 23 vols. Cairo: Maktabat Ibn Taymiyya, 1983.

Ṭabarī, Abī Jaʿfar Muḥammad ibn Jarīr al-. *Tārīkh al-Ṭabarī: tārīkh al-rusul wa-al-mulūk li-Abī Jaʿfar Muḥammad ibn Jarīr al-Ṭabarī*. Beirut: Dār ādir, 2008.

Ṭayālsī, Abū Dāwūd ibn al-Jārūd al-. *Musnad Abī Dāwūd al-Ṭayālsī*. Edited by Muḥammad ibn ʿAbd al-Muḥsin al-Turkī. 4 vols. Cairo: Dār Hājar, 1999.

Yaḥṣabī, al-Qādī ʿAyāḍ ibn Mūsā al-. *Muzīl al-khafāʾ ʿan alfāẓ al-shifāʾ*. Beirut: Dār al-Kutub al-ʿIlmiyya, 2009.

Secondary Sources

Abbott, Nabia. *Aishah: The Beloved of Mohammed*. Chicago: University of Chicago Press, 1944.

Afsaruddin, Asma. "Early Muslim Women Exemplars and the Construction of Gendered Space." In *Harem Histories—Envisioning Places and Living Spaces*, edited by Marilyn Booth, 23–48. Durham, NC: Duke University Press, 2010.

Afsaruddin, Asma. "Reconstituting Women's Lives: Gender and the Poetics of Narrative in Medieval Biographical Collections." *Muslim World* 92, no. 3–4 (2002): 461–480.

Ahad, Abdul. *The Honourable Wives of the Prophet*. Riyadh and New York: Darussalam Publications, 2004.

Amin, Yasmin. "The Prophet's Wives." In *The Oxford Encyclopedia of Islam and Women*, edited by Natana J. DeLong-Bas, 426–429. Oxford: Oxford University Press, 2013.

Amin, Yasmin. "Umm Salama's Contributions: Qur'an, Hadith, and Early Muslim History as Sources for Gender Justice." In *Muslim Women and Gender Justice: Concepts, Sources, and Histories*, edited by Dina el Omari, Juliane Hammer, and Mouhanad Khorchide, 185–203. London: Routledge, 2019.

Ascha, Ghassan. "'The Mothers of the Believers': Stereotypes of the Prophet Muḥammad's Wives." In *Female Stereotypes in Religious Traditions*, edited by Ria Hanegraaf Kloppenborg, and Wouter J. Hanegraaf Kloppenborg, 89–107. Leiden: E. J. Brill, 1995.

Beinhauer-Köhler, Bärbel. *Fāṭima bint Muḥammad: Metamorphosen einer frühislamischen Frauengestalt*. Wiesbaden: Harrassowitz, 2002.

Bint al-Shāṭiʾ, ʿĀʾisha ʿAbd al-Raḥmān. *Al-Sayyida Zaynab, baṭalat karbalāʾ*. Cairo: Dār al-Hilāl, 1972.

Bint al-Shāṭiʾ, ʿĀʾisha ʿAbd al-Raḥmān. *Nisāʾ al-nabī ʿalayhi al-ṣalāt wa-alāāalt wa—salm*. Cairo: Dār al-Maʿārif, 2009.

Bint al-Shāṭiʾ, ʿĀʾisha ʿAbd al-Raḥmān. *Tarājim sayyidāt bayt al-nubuwwa*. Beirut: Dār al-Kitāb al-ʿArābī, 1988.

Bint al-Shāṭi', 'Ā'isha 'Abd al-Raḥmān. *The Wives of the Prophet*. Translated by Matti Moosa. Piscataway, NJ: Gorgias Press, 2006.

Booth, Marilyn. "Women's Biographies and Political Agendas: Who's Who in Islamic History." *Gender and History* 8, no. 1 (1996): 133–137.

Calderini, Simonetta. *Women as Imams: Classical Islamic Sources and Modern Debates on Leading Prayer*. London: I. B. Tauris, 2021.

Clohessy, Christopher Paul. *Fatima, Daughter of Muḥammad*. Piscataway, NJ: Gorgias Press, 2018.

Debas, Faridah Mas'ood. *The Wives of Prophet Muḥammad*. Translated by Sameh Strauch. Riyadh: International Islamic Publishing House, 2009.

Decker, Doris. *Frauen als Trägerinnen religiösen Wissens: Konzeptionen von Frauenbildern in frühislamischen Überlieferungen bis zum 9. Jahrhundert*. Stuttgart: Verlag W. Kohlhammer, 2013.

Decker, Doris. "Weibliche Politik im Frühislam am Beispiel von Muḥammads Frau Umm Salama." *Marburg Journal of Religion* 19, no. 1 (2017): 1–22.

Dukhayyil, ʿAlī Muḥammad ʿAlī. *Umm Salama*. Tehran: Amīr Kabīr, 1982.

Elewa, A., and L. Silvers. "'I Am One of the People': A Survey and Analysis of Legal Arguments on Woman-Led Prayer in Islam." *Journal of Law and Religion* 26, no. 1 (2010–2011): 141–171.

Geissinger, Aisha. "Feminist Muslim (re)interpretations of Early Islam." In *Routledge Handbook on Early Islam*, edited by Herbert Berg, 296–308. Abingdon, Oxon: Routledge, 2017.

Hammer, Juliane. *American Muslim Women, Religious Authority, and Activism—More Than a Prayer*. Austin: University of Texas Press, 2012.
Ḥasanī, Amīna Amzīyān al-. *Umm Salama: Umm al-mū'minīn*. 2 vols. Al-Muḥammadīya, al-Mamlaka al-Maġribīya: Wizārat al-Awqāf wa-l-Shu'ūn al-Islāmiyya, 1998.
Imā'illāh, Amtunnūr Tayyab, et al. *Ḥazrat Umm-i Salmā*. London: Islam International Publications, 2008.
Qureshi, Zafar Ali. *The Mothers of the Believers*. Islamabad: National Hijra Council, 1986.
Rhouni, Raja. *Secular and Islamic Feminist Critiques in the Work of Fatima Mernissi*. Leiden: Brill, 2009.
Roded, Ruth M. *Women in Islamic Biographical Collections: From Ibn Sa'd to Who's Who*. Boulder, CO: Lynne Rienner, 1994.
Spellberg, Denise A. "Political Action and Public Example: 'A'isha and the Battle of the Camel." In *Women in Middle Eastern History: Shifting Boudaires in Sex and Gender*, edited by Beth Baron and Nikki R. Keddie, 45–57. New Haven, CT: Yale University Press, 1991.
Spellberg, Denise A. *Politics, Gender and the Islamic Past the Legacy of 'A'isha bint Abi Bakr*. New York: Columbia University Press, 1994.
Sunbul, Nizār Muḥammad Shawqī al-. *Wārithat Khadīja: Umm Salama umm al-mū'minīn; (ḥayātuhā, mawāqifuhā, aādīthuhā)*. Beirut: Dār al-Muṣṭafā li-Iḥyā' al-Turāth, 2002.
Thomson, Ahmad. *The Wives of the Prophet Muḥammad*. London: Ta-Ha Publishers, 2012.
Zayd, Ḥuṣṣa bint 'Abd al-Karīm al-. *Sīrat umm al-mū'minīn Umm Salama wa-juhūdihā al-da'wīyya*. Riyadh: Maktabat al-'Ubaykān, 2001.
Zirkilī, Khayr al-Dīn al-. *al-A'lām*. 10 vols. Beirut: Dār al-'Ilm li-l-Malāyīn, 2002.

CHAPTER 10

WOMEN AS MORAL EXEMPLARS IN TWELVER SHĪʿĪSM

MARIA DAKAKE

In the history of the Twelver Shīʿī tradition, there are relatively few well-known female participants in, or significant contributors to, its religiopolitical formation or its religious scholarship. There is no Shīʿī female figure who plays a role quite comparable, in these particular dimensions, to that of the Prophet's wife ʿĀʾisha bint Abī Bakr in the Sunnī tradition. ʿĀʾisha's closeness to the Prophet Muḥammad, her status as daughter of the first caliph, Abū Bakr, and her strong personality and wit made her an influential participant in the history of the early Islamic caliphate and a major contributor to Islam's body of religious literature, and the *sunna* in particular. However, two figures in the Shīʿī tradition who are clearly comparable to ʿĀʾisha in terms of closeness to the Prophet Muḥammad and subsequent political outspokenness, respectively, are the Prophet's daughter, Fāṭima, and his granddaughter, Zaynab bint ʿAlī. In this chapter, I will look closely at the figures of Fāṭima and Zaynab as they are remembered in the Twelver Shīʿī tradition, the relationship between the particular qualities that are celebrated in these women and particular Shīʿī readings of both religion and history, and the ways in which they serve not only as moral exemplars for other Shīʿī women but also as models of devotion and commitment for all Shīʿīs, regardless of gender.

At first glance, Fāṭima and Zaynab seem to represent different and complementary aspects of Shīʿī constructions of moral excellence—passive and active embodiments of the Shīʿī moral ideal, respectively. Fāṭima's excellence is traditionally understood to reflect primarily the "passive" aspect of this ideal, the confident, but generally quiet, endurance of injustice and suffering, which, when borne with dignity, testifies to the purity and nobility of the victim and the wrongs of the oppressor. It is martyrdom in its most fundamental meaning as "witness."[1] Zaynab, by contrast, is usually considered to embody the more active pole of the Shīʿī ideal: steadfast and selfless defense of the innocent and powerless, the public condemnation and thus historical memorialization of injustice, and the courage and eloquence to speak truth to oppressive power in a way that demolishes the latter's claim to any real moral authority, even when public rebuke fails to dislodge its worldly power. As we shall see, this distinction is not absolute—Fāṭima openly protests her and her husband's treatment, and Zaynab, too, is a passive victim of the brutalities of Karbala. This serves to underscore how interrelated and inseparable these two aspects of the Shīʿī moral ideal are in Shīʿī history and hagiography, leading to an intellectual and political dynamic marked by both quietism and activism, each propelling the other throughout Shīʿī history.

Fāṭima: Daughter of the Prophet, Wife and Mother of the Imams

A widely cited *ḥadīth* of the Prophet Muḥammad identifies by name the "four greatest women of the world."[2] These women are, as is well known, Mary the mother of Jesus; Āsiya the wife of Pharaoh; the Prophet's first wife, Khadīja; and his youngest daughter, Fāṭima. Even among the perfect, however, some have suggested a hierarchy. Of these four women, only one has her story told and her superior status explicitly mentioned in the Qur'ān—Mary, the mother of Jesus, whom the Qur'ān describes as "chosen . . . above all the women of the worlds."[3] The Qur'ān's unique endorsement of Mary's position would seem to make her, indeed, the greatest woman in an absolute sense. For Shīʿīs, however, Mary's superior position is limited to her own time, and was matched and ultimately surpassed by that of Fāṭima after the coming of Islam.[4] Indeed, Fāṭima's title as *sayyida* ("noble mistress" or "queen") of the Muslim community, of the worlds, or of the people of paradise is invoked widely in both Sunnī and Shīʿī sources.

Fāṭima as an Exemplar of Filial Piety and Devotion

While Fāṭima's inimitable purity and sacred lineage cannot be matched or imitated by other pious women, she also displays characteristics that make her a model for emulation by other Shīʿī women, as well as by all Shīʿīs. The extraordinary devotion displayed by Fāṭima toward her father, the Prophet, and her sons, al-Ḥasan and al-Ḥusayn makes Fāṭima, as a woman, a model for women of filial and maternal piety. On the basis of her support for her husband, ʿAlī's, claims to leadership after the Prophet's death, and her devotion toward her own special family, the *ahl al-bayt* (family of the Prophet), she serves as a model of Shīʿī religious devotion for all Shīʿīs, regardless of gender, as Matthew Pierce insightfully explains in his study on Shīʿī hagiography.[5]

It is Fāṭima's devotional attention to her father and sons that receives the greatest attention in Shīʿī hagiographical sources, but almost always in a tragic register. Fāṭima's presence during the more triumphal moments of the Prophet's life is rarely mentioned;

rather, the tradition focuses on her care for her father during some of his most difficult moments. When Muḥammad's enemies among the Quraysh threw camel entrails on him while he was praying, it was the young Fāṭima who was there to witness it, to sadly but lovingly remove the filth from her father, and to curse those who had humiliated him.[6] She suffered along with the rest of the Hashimite clan during their temporary banishment by the Quraysh. Accounts of her tears at the death of her mother, Khadīja, whose final illness is usually attributed to the hunger and exposure she endured during this time, adds pathos to accounts of the Prophet's loss.[7] Both Fāṭima and ʿAlī were said to be present to nurse the Prophet when he was injured during the Battle of Uḥud,[8] and of course, Fāṭima is an important presence during the Prophet's final illness and death. At one point, Fāṭima drew near to her dying father and he whispered to her a private communication, unheard by the other Companions gathered around him. During this intimate conversation, the Prophet is said to have confided to Fāṭima that she would be the first of his community to join him in the hereafter, which prompted some joy in his daughter, otherwise deeply distraught over his imminent death.[9] The episode indicates that any sadness she might have felt about the prospect of dying and leaving her husband and young children was easily displaced by the thought of reuniting with her father.

Fāṭima is also portrayed and imagined as a deeply sympathetic mother to her young children, particularly the future Imams, al-Ḥasan and al-Ḥusayn, even if stories of her maternal care of her children are rivaled or surpassed by accounts of her love for her father. This may well be because she had only a few years to mother her own children before her early death, when her children were still under the age of ten. Importantly, though, Shīʿī accounts indicate that she was made aware through her own spiritual premonition, or through a foretelling by the Prophet, of the violent death that awaited her younger son, al-Ḥusayn,[10] and so endured the terrible pain that any mother would feel at the suffering of her child.[11] In this way, Fāṭima serves as an image and model of the suffering mother, forced to contemplate her son murdered unjustly and dying in the cause of righteousness, even if she herself had passed away long before the event of Karbala. In fact, in the Shīʿī *taʿziya*, or passion play reenacting the Battle of Karbala, Fāṭima herself is present at the scene to mourn and comfort her martyred son and her other descendants. It is this role of Fāṭima as both chief mourner and comforter that is often invoked in modern Shīʿī devotion, and a number of cemeteries in Iran that house the modern "martyrs" of recent military conflicts, such as the Iran-Iraq War are named after her—for example, the large *Behesht-i Zahrā*'[12] in Tehran.

Fāṭima's marriage to her husband, ʿAlī, is portrayed in Shīʿī literature as providential,[13] and Shīʿī tradition often indicates that ʿAlī was the only possible spiritual match for Fāṭima,[14] although Fāṭima is sometimes said to have refused the proposal until she was told it was divinely arranged, which serves to further burnish her image as devoutly obedient to God above all else.[15] Even as their marriage is celebrated by Shīʿīs as spiritually foreordained, it is also presented as a natural, almost familial arrangement,[16] grounded in their shared love of the Prophet: both ʿAlī and Fāṭima are raised (almost like siblings) in the house of the Prophet, and when Fāṭima references ʿAlī in her public discourse, she refers to him as her "cousin" rather than her spouse.[17] In Sunnī sources, there are hints that the relationship was not without its difficulties. The widely acknowledged poverty and material deprivation that they endured as a married couple is extolled in Shīʿī sources as a moral example of asceticism and patience in adversity,[18] but various reports in Sunnī sources suggest that Fāṭima was not always content with this situation. Some indicate that she complained to her father about their poverty and (unsuccessfully) sought assistance from him.[19] Other reports suggest occasional marital disagreements between the couple,[20] or indicate that ʿAlī once considered marrying another woman while Fāṭima was alive, but that the Prophet forbade this.[21] Shīʿīs strongly dispute accounts of difficulty or discontent in the marriage,[22] but also rarely discuss their relationship in terms of personal closeness or love between the two. Rather, ʿAlī and Fāṭima, who both had independent claims of closeness to Muḥammad, seem to be united most clearly in their common love of the Prophet, and their relationship is celebrated in Shīʿī sources primarily as the collective wellspring of the Prophet's genealogical legacy and of the *ahl al-bayt* in its most specific sense. Matthew Pierce has observed in his research on Shīʿī hagiographies of the Imams that women in these accounts play important roles primarily as dutiful daughters or mothers of the Imams, rather than as wives. Indeed, the respect accorded to the wives of the Prophet in Sunnism is more ambiguous in the case of Shīʿism, and even the wives of the Imams themselves are not typically the subject of hagiographical narratives *as wives*.[23] The focus on Fāṭima as the daughter of the Prophet and the mother of the second and third Imams, al-Ḥasan and al-Ḥusayn, thus seems to be in keeping with the greater Shīʿī concern with issues of lineage and propagation in the agnatic line of the *ahl al-bayt*, than with the marital lives of the Prophet or the Imams.

Fāṭima as Both Exceptional and Exemplary

More than merely daughter to the Prophet and wife and mother to the Imams, Fāṭima is herself included along with Muḥammad and the twelve Imams as one of the "Fourteen Infallible/Protected (*maʿṣūm*) Ones," and she is considered to possess many of the extraordinary spiritual qualities of the Imams themselves. In addition to representing a physical link between the Prophet, ʿAlī, and the rest of the Imams, Fāṭima is also said to be the bearer of the Prophet's *waṣiyya* (final will and testament). Some accounts indicate that the Prophet received knowledge of his successors, the future Imams, from the Angel Gabriel, and that he told this to Fāṭima during his lifetime. She later dictated it to ʿAlī to put into writing.[24] Other accounts assert that Fāṭima personally received this as a revelation from the angel shortly after the death of her father. This "revelation" was recorded in what is known as the *muṣḥaf* or *lawḥ* (codex or tablet) of Fāṭima, which is often described in glorious terms in Shīʿī *ḥadīth* as an emerald book whose pages radiated light like the sun.[25] Even leaving aside the more fantastical aspects of this tradition, the account establishes Fāṭima as the bearer of the Prophet's *waṣiyya*, as well as the recipient of a divinely granted knowledge of the future, something otherwise limited to the Prophet and the Imams in Shīʿī tradition.

Although a woman, and not an Imam herself, Fāṭima shares a number of other important characteristics with the Imams. Like them she suffers oppression and injustice at the hands of those who took political control of the community after the Prophet's death; and like many of them, she is said to have died a martyr. She is said to have suffered, according to a common but polemical Shīʿī account, an ultimately fatal injury and miscarriage when members of the tribe of Quraysh, including ʿUmar, forced their way through the door of her house to compel ʿAlī's *bayʿa* ("allegiance") to Abū Bakr after the Prophet's death.[26] Suffering oppression, injustice, and martyrdom, however, are a legacy not only of Fāṭima and the Imams, but also of many of their devoted followers, who took the heroic suffering and martyrdom of members of the *ahl al-bayt* as an example of activism and self-sacrifice to be emulated. In this way as in others, Fāṭima, like the Imams, is not only exceptional but also exemplary. Aspects of her life that are capable and worthy of imitation include her selfless devotion to the Prophet and her family, the *ahl al-bayt*. In this case, she is both a model of filial, wifely, and maternal devotion for all women, and an exemplar of spiritual devotion to the *ahl al-bayt* for all Shīʿīs. There are also the numerous Shīʿī anecdotes about her steadfast endurance of hardship and poverty, as well as reports of her charity toward others despite the severe limits of her own means, serving as admirable examples of patience, humility, and generosity. Her example of bearing injustice and mistreatment with patience provides an important moral lesson for a minority community that would suffer in various ways throughout its history.

Despite the image of Fāṭima as quiet and obedient, her response to persecution and injustice was not always silence and stoic patience. In particular, the Shīʿī tradition is clear that Fāṭima was in no way inclined to hide her displeasure regarding the events that followed the death of her father, the Prophet Muhammad, or to accept them quietly. According to at least one Shīʿī report, ʿAlī was dragged out of his house after the Prophet's death in an attempt to force his *bayʿa* to Abū Bakr, Fāṭima followed behind him, and delivered a powerful protest near the grave of her father. She demanded that ʿAlī be released and threatened to tear her shirt in anger, warning them that she and her children were dearer to God than the she-camel of the Prophet Ṣāliḥ (whose slaughter brought divine destruction upon Ṣāliḥ's recalcitrant people).[27] Her words are said to have nearly shaken the walls of the Medinan mosque from their foundations, until Salmān al-Fārsī—a Persian companion of the Prophet strongly sympathetic to ʿAlī's claims—gently persuaded her to abandon her threats.[28] More well-known is Fāṭima's response to Abū Bakr's denial of her inheritance from the Prophet, which was reportedly an eloquent speech, calling on Abū Bakr to acknowledge her right on the basis of Qur'ānic evidence, as well as her standing as the Prophet's only surviving daughter. Abū Bakr had reportedly denied Fāṭima her inheritance because of a statement he claimed the Prophet once made, indicating that prophets have no heirs; but Fāṭima challenged this report with a commonsense argument that also carried emotional impact so soon after her father's death: Why should everyone else be allowed to inherit from their fathers, except for her?[29] Fāṭima also cited the Qur'ān itself to demonstrate that prophets do indeed have heirs, including verses about Solomon inheriting from his father, David; the line of inheritance from Abraham to his sons and grandsons; and the prophet Zakariya praying for a son in his old age who would be his heir (*walī*)—a request that God grants.[30]

Fāṭima is said to have made this speech herself not only in front of Abū Bakr but also before a large group of companions who were with him at the time. This would seem to set the example that speaking truth to power takes precedence over any existing concerns or social conventions regarding female modesty. However, in this case, as well as in the case of Zaynab bt. ʿAlī discussed below, what might seem to the contemporary reader to be historical demonstrations of female agency, voice, and self-possession, may have been understood by the original Shīʿī narrators of these accounts as further examples of the wrongs suffered by the family of the Prophet. Instead of being able to carry on more dignified private lives, the closest female relatives of the Prophet were forced into unusually public roles by the need to react to the outrageous injustices against themselves and their family members. Yet accounts of Fāṭima and Zaynab's outspokenness and strength are there for contemporary Shīʿī women to reclaim. Even if some of the arguments articulated in Fāṭima's speech may represent later developments in Shīʿī polemical thought retroactively attributed to her, the fact that she issued a public protest against the denial of her rights can hardly be doubted.

Zaynab bint ʿAlī

The second-most-celebrated woman in Shiʿi history is undoubtedly Fāṭima and ʿAlī's daughter, Zaynab, granddaughter to the Prophet and sister to al-Ḥasan and al-Ḥusayn. Zaynab is a far more "human" and heroic figure than Fāṭima. Her story does not contain the mythological and hagiographical elements found in traditions about her mother, but Zaynab is an extraordinary figure in her own right. Her exemplary qualities include her devoted love for her family, the *ahl al-bayt*; her unwavering loyalty to her brother, al-Ḥusayn, and her extended family, even at great personal sacrifice; her dignity and strength in the face of suffering; her ability to assume leadership in moments of great crisis; her courage and eloquence in speaking truth to power; and the role that all of these virtues played in preserving the lineage, honor, and tragic history of the *ahl al-bayt*.

Devotion to the Family

As with Fāṭima, Zaynab's role as devoted daughter, sister, and aunt to the Imams is emphasized over her role as wife to her husband, ʿAbdullāh ibn Jaʿfar ibn Abī Ṭālib (also her first cousin, d. ca. 80/699), or even mother to her own children. Her life is guided by devotion to her father, ʿAlī; her brother, al-Ḥusayn; and her extended ʿAlid family.

She and her husband abandoned their life in Medina to follow her father, ʿAlī, when he moved the caliphate to Kufa to confront the rebellion that had emerged against him in 35/656. She and her family returned to Medina after the First Civil War ended in 40/661. Many years later, she would leave her husband behind in Medina to join her brother and their extended family on the fateful journey to Karbalaʾ, bringing along two of her sons, ʿAwn and Muḥammad, both of whom were killed along with the other adult males in the tragic event. Yet, in her moving speeches after the massacre of her family, it is not her own sons who are the focus of her anguished mourning, but her brother, al-Ḥusayn—to whose surviving children she becomes an honorary "mother."[31] Zaynab's devotion to family is directed primarily toward her agnatic family, and especially the Imams among her kin, rather than to her marital family. Like Fāṭima, Zaynab's familial devotion is a model on two levels. For women, she exemplifies devotion to, and at times fierce defense of her family; but more generally, her devotion to *her particular family*, makes her more than just a model sister, daughter, and aunt. She is also a model devotee of the Imams and the *ahl al-bayt*.

Zaynab is best known for her fearless actions at the Battle of Karbala and its aftermath. She was determined to follow her brother (and the third Shīʿī Imam), al-Ḥusayn, as he embarked on his dangerous and ultimately fatal challenge to the second Umayyad caliph Yazīd ibn Muʿāwiya (d. 64/683). She did so without her husband (although reportedly with his permission). She knew that she was putting her own life at risk, as well as the lives of her own two sons, who accompanied her. Her complete lack of regard for her own personal safety is clear, for example, in the account that at one point she ran onto the battlefield in her zeal to fight to defend her kinsmen. Her unusual courage was no match for her perfect deference to her brother, al-Ḥusayn, however. When he told her to return to her tent, she obeyed,[32] indicating that her courage was both passionately driven and restrained by her loyalty to the Imam. Throughout the battle, her nephew and future Imam, ʿAlī ibn al-Ḥusayn Zayn al-ʿĀbidīn (d. 95/713), had been too ill to participate, and remained in her tent. Later, when the battle had concluded with all of al-Ḥusayn's men slaughtered, the besieging army raided the camp and found the ailing ʿAlī among the women in Zaynab's tent. Zaynab protected him, however, and the soldiers decided to spare him, and bring him with the remaining female members of al-Ḥusayn's camp to face first the Iraqi governor, Ibn Ziyād (d. 67/686), and later the caliph, Yazīd. Unable to defend one Imam, her brother al-Ḥusayn, Zaynab's brave actions nonetheless preserved the life of his successor, ensuring that the line of Imams would continue.

One of the striking qualities attributed to Zaynab in the accounts of Karbala is her ability, even in the face of her own suffering and loss, and despite the historical limitations and vulnerabilities of women in this historical context, to assume the position of leader of her family at a tremendously dangerous and uncertain time. When Zaynab was brought to the court of the Iraqi governor, Ibn Ziyād in Kufa, he displayed no sympathy for her or her family, and attempted cruelly to rub salt in her emotional wounds by exclaiming, "Praise be to God who has shamed you and fought you and shown your words to be lies!"[33] She responded by directly inverting and challenging the assertions of the governor, who quite literally held her life in his hands, saying, "Praise be to God who has ennobled us through Muḥammad and purified us completely. It is not as you say. For it is only the iniquitous who are brought to shame and only the corrupt who are shown to be liars!"[34] Her words impressed Ibn Ziyād, who remarked that she was courageous like her father, but she dismissed the comparison, saying, "What do women have to do with courage?"[35] Yet only shortly after this exchange, Zaynab offered further evidence of her extraordinary courage, when Ibn Ziyād, upon realizing that the only male survivor, ʿAlī ibn Al-Ḥusayn, had reached maturity, ordered him to be killed. Zaynab immediately embraced her nephew and told Ibn Ziyād that he would have to kill her along with him, if he was intent on doing so. Ibn Ziyād relented, and Zaynab had saved the life of her nephew, and future Imam, for the second time.[36]

After the encounter with the Iraqi governor, the captives were taken to the court of the caliph, Yazīd, whose desire to procure an oath of allegiance from al-Ḥusayn had initially prompted the events of Karbala. When one of Yazīd's men insultingly indicated his desire to take al-Ḥusayn's captive young daughter, Umm Kulthum, for himself, and Yazīd directed one of his men to bring her to him, Zaynab objected that he was unworthy of someone who possessed her niece's noble lineage.[37] She rebuked Yazīd for his hubris, challenging his own self-regard, and his apparent belief that his defeat of al-Ḥusayn had constituted a sign that God and right were on his side. She asked him rhetorically, "Do you think that because we are dragged along like prisoners that we have become weak and you have become noble in God's eyes? Or that this gives you such importance that you can look condescendingly upon us, taking joy in seeing everything now ordered according to your liking . . . even though you have merely been granted a temporary respite from God?" She warned him against seeing this respite as a sign of divine favor, quoting Qur'ān 3:178: "And let not those who disbelieve suppose that the respite We grant them is good for them. We only grant them respite that they may increase in sin, and theirs shall be a humiliating punishment."[38]

Zaynab's speech was not only courageous and persuasive—the members of Yazīd's court, including Yazīd's own family members are said to have been brought to tears—but also effectively changes the narrative and perception of the situation, offering an interpretation of Karbala and its aftermath that would ultimately become the judgment of Muslim history itself: God's favor was not on the side of the victor, but the victim; defeat cannot stain the honor of the family of the Prophet, but rather, the shedding of their blood would remain a permanent stain on Yazīd and his caliphate. The chains of Zaynab's captivity could not hold back her tongue; rather, her words captivated all who heard them, and shamed Yazīd into freeing Zaynab and the rest of the Karbala survivors. The nobility and freedom of the *ahl al-bayt* were reestablished through her words, even as they stood in chains before Yazīd, while all of the pomp of his court could not conceal, even from his own family, his baseness and the monstrous nature of what he had wrought upon the family of Muḥammad.

Commemoration of Zaynab in Shīʿī Devotion

Despite the memory of Zaynab's courageous actions and words in a number of relatively early accounts of Karbala, the interpretation of her actions has not always been constant. While some accounts emphasize her strength in a desperate moment, others suggest a certain lack of self-control on her part in the face of overwhelming grief. For example, in the very early Shīʿī historical work of Yaʿqūbī, Zaynab's defiant speeches in the courts of Ibn Ziyād and Yazīd are not reported. Rather, there is an account of Zaynab at Karbala, when al-Ḥusayn gives her the news that death and defeat seem inevitable for him, where she seems beside herself with grief and almost self-pity, lamenting that she has already lost her mother, her father, and her older brother al-Ḥasan, and now seems poised to lose al-Ḥusayn as well.[39] It would be easy to surmise that the traditional portrayal of Zaynab as both victim and victor, both vulnerable and strong is similar to other paradoxical and inconsistent hagiographical representations of spiritual women, whether it be Joan of Arc or Rābiʿa al- ʿAdawiyya, which can seem to vacillate between portraying them as women whose weak constitutions make them unusually sensitive to spiritual matters, and that of women whose inner strength and public fearlessness make them truly exceptional among the people of their time. But it is at least as likely that this representation reflects a central theme of the Shīʿī perspective: suffering is not weakness and defeat in this world may be nothing short of spiritual victory. With lives marked simultaneously by tragedy and heroism, Zaynab and other members of the *ahl al-bayt* inspire among Shīʿīs both bitter and mournful commemoration, as well as confident and determined emulation. Several field studies of contemporary women's Shīʿī devotional rituals related to Zaynab have demonstrated that embracing Zaynab as an example of courageous activism, rather than as a pitiable victim, is a conscious choice that many female Shīʿī devotees seem aware of and are eager to articulate.[40]

Conclusion

Given the dominance of men as protagonists of Shīʿī history, and as its main chroniclers and commentators, one might assume that the role of early Shīʿī heroines and important female figures serve primarily as examples of filial piety, purity, and selfless devotion for other Shīʿī women in particular. Given that celebrated Shīʿī female figures, such as Fāṭima and Zaynab, were themselves members of the *ahl al-bayt*, one might also expect that they function more naturally as objects of veneration than as models of emulation for real or contemporary Shīʿī women. To some extent, both assumptions are true, but not entirely, and these assumptions can obscure the extent to which these women model personal qualities that can be emulated by all Shīʿīs, not just women.

The selfless devotion, sacrifice, and responsible care for family celebrated in the lives and actions of Fāṭima and Zaynab may seem largely maternal in nature. Such qualities, however, are not always associated with *biological* motherhood; symbolic, surrogate, or spiritual motherhood is of at least equal importance. Fāṭima is an important maternal figure for her own children, but she is also extolled as "the mother of her father," because her loving attention to the Prophet approached the selfless devotion of a mother toward her children. Zaynab is a mother to her own children, but weeps more profusely for the death of her brother, al-Ḥusayn (to whom she is said to have acted like a mother after their own mother's death) than for her own two sons, also slain on the field of Karbala. Moreover, it is her fierce motherly protection of her nieces that prevents their violation by Yazīd and his men, rather than any intervention by their own mothers (at least one of whom was said to be present on the occasion). She is also credited with raising these children after the death of her brother, al-Ḥusayn.

When comparing Fāṭima and Zaynab we noted that Fāṭima is often considered to embody an example of obedience and patient suffering, borne with dignity and resignation. Her resistance to injustice is sometimes portrayed as primarily existential or symbolic in nature. Simply the sight of Fāṭima shortly after the death of her father is enough to bring his companions, assembled around the new caliph, Abū Bakr, to tears, even before her speech begins. Zaynab, on the other hand, seems to embody a more active and outspoken ideal of resistance to the oppressors and opponents of her family that requires her to assume a role not typical for the women of her time. However, this reflects a difference of emphasis, rather than a stark opposition. A more nuanced assessment would recognize that both Fāṭima and Zaynab manifest a traditional demeanor of respectful obedience to the men in their family—that is, to those who hold legitimate spiritual authority in the Shīʿī view—and defiance and resistance to those whom they regard as illegitimate or spiritually corrupt (Abū Bakr, Ibn Ziyād, Yazīd)—a dynamic clearly identified by Kamran Scott Aghaie in a recent study of contemporary Shīʿī devotion.[41] Their stories can and have been invoked differentially as manifesting a traditional ideal of feminine submissiveness or as an inspiring model of female activism and outspokenness. In both cases, however, we see that these women display unfailing and selfless devotion to the rightful authority of their family members, who are also the Shīʿī Imams, and fearless criticism and resistance to the illegitimate authority of those who persecute or dispossess them. In this way, they are models for all Shīʿīs of unquestioning loyalty and obedience to the Imams and implacable resistance to their enemies.

Finally, many of the female protagonists of Shīʿī tradition enact the role of preserver of the line and lineage of the *ahl al-bayt* and the Imams in particular. Zaynab, for example, twice saves her nephew and the fourth Imam, ʿAlī Zayn al-ʿĀbidīn, from execution, thus preserving the lineage of Imams for the future as well. These women also serve as the repositories and transmitters of the *waṣāya* of the Prophet (Fāṭima) and of the Imams (Zaynab).[42] Zaynab, in particular, is largely responsible for preserving the memory of the tragedy of Karbala, both through her powerful rebukes to Ibn Ziyād and Yazīd, and through her commitment to relating and publicizing these events when she returned home to Medina, helping to ensure that these events were never forgotten within the Muslim community. This instinct for the preservation of the *ahl al-bayt*, their lineage, their honor, and their tragic history is, again, hardly a model for women alone, even if women, for various practical reasons, sometimes played this role. Rather it is an example to the whole of the Shīʿī community, men as well as women, about the importance of remembering the suffering and victimhood of the *ahl al-bayt*, while celebrating—and when necessary, emulating—their heroism and spiritual conviction.

Notes

1. Of course, the Greek origin of the word "martyr" has "witness" as one of its root meanings, analogous to the term's Arabic counterpart, *shahīd*, which can mean both martyr and witness. For a discussion of the variant understanding of this term as martyr and witness in its Qur'ānic usage, see Asma Afsaruddin, *Striving in the Path of God: Jihad and Martyrdom in Islamic Thought* (Oxford: Oxford University Press, 2013), 95–96.
2. Muḥammad ibn ʿIsā al-Tirmidhī, *Sunan al-Tirmidhī* (Liechtenstein: Thesaurus Islamicus Foundation, 2000) 2:980, no. 4252.
3. Qur'ān 3:42.
4. Abū Jaʿfar Muḥammad ibn Abi'l-Qāsim al-Ṭabarī, *Bishārat al-muṣṭafā li-shīʿat al-murtaḍā*, ed. J. al-Qayyūmī al-Isfahānī (Qum: Mu'assasa al-Nashr al-Islāmī, 2004), 274. See also Ibid., 307, where the Qur'ānic statement that Mary was chosen above all the women of the world is also said to pertain to Fāṭima.
5. Pierce discusses this extensively, examining its gendered symbolism, and asserting that Fāṭima and other Shīʿī women offered a model of "feminized devotion" that served as an example for both Shīʿī and men and women in their mode of approaching the Imams; see Matthew Pierce, *Twelve Infallible Men: The Imams and the Making of Shiʿism* (Cambridge, MA: Harvard University Press, 2016), esp. 121–123.
6. Muḥammad ibn Ismāʿīl al-Bukhārī, *Ṣaḥīḥ al-Bukhārī* (Liechtenstein: Thesaurus Islamicus, 2000) 2:568, no. 2971.
7. In one Shīʿī account, the young Fāṭima, clinging to the Prophet and crying for her deceased mother, is comforted by a revelation brought by the Angel Gabriel to Muḥammad, assuring Fāṭima that Khadīja is in paradise; see Aḥmad ibn Abī Yaʿqūb al-Yaʿqūbī, *Tarīkh al-Yaʿqūbī*, ed. ʿAbd al-Amīr al-Muhannā (Beirut: Muʿassasat al-Aʿlamī, 1993) 1:354.
8. Al-Bukhārī, *Ṣaḥīḥ*, 3:1185, no. 5781.
9. Muslim Ibn Hajjāj, *Ṣaḥīḥ Muslim*, (Liechtenstein: Thesaurus Islamicus, 2000) 2:1047, no. 6466.
10. Abū Jaʿfar Muḥammad ibn Yaʿqūb al-Kulaynī, *al-Kāfī*, ed. Muḥammad Jaʿfar Shams al-Dīn (Beirut: Dār al-Taʿāruf li-l-Maṭbūʿāt, 1990) 1:530, 536–537.
11. Foreknowledge of al-Ḥusayn's terrible future demise made Fāṭima's bearing and delivery of the infant al-Ḥusayn particularly painful and difficult (al-Kulaynī, *al-Kāfī*, 1:536); another tradition claims that she did not even nurse him, but rather he was fed by the Prophet himself in infancy (Ibid., 1:537), although this may be in keeping with a common Shīʿī hagiographical trope in which the Imams are "nursed" by their fathers or the preceding Imam (see Pierce, *Twelve Infallible Men*, 139). See also Mary Thurkill, *Chosen among Women: Mary and Fatima in Medieval Christianity and Shiʿite Islam* (Notre Dame, IN: University of Notre Dame Press, 2008) 77, 123–124; and for a modern devotional account of Fāṭima weeping for al-Ḥusayn, even before his death, see Negar Mottahedeh, "Taʿziyeh: A Twist of History in Everyday Life," in *Women of Karbala: Ritual Performance and Symbolic*

Discourses in Modern Shiʿi Islam, ed. Kamran Scott Aghaie (Austin: University of Texas Press, 2009), 34–35.

12. Zahrā'—meaning "the radiant" in Arabic—is perhaps the most common honorific name for Fāṭima.
13. al-Kulaynī, *al-Kāfī*, 1:533; see also Abū Manṣūr Aḥmad ibn ʿAlī al-Ṭabarsī, *al-Iḥtijāj*, ed. I. Bahādurī and M. Hādī (Qum: Intashārāt Uswa, 2004), 1:309.
14. al-Kulaynī, *al-Kāfī*, 1:33.
15. See Thurkill, *Chosen among Women*, 76.
16. For a dramatic elaboration of this idea, seeʿAli Shariati, *Fatima Is Fatima*, trans. Laleh Bakhtiar, accessed March 14, 2021 (https://www.al-islam.org/fatima-fatima-ali-shariati#comment-0), 85, where ʿAli is described as having been "nourished in the lap of Khadīja."
17. See, for example, al-Ṭabarsī, *al-Iḥtijāj*, 1:223.
18. This is sometimes seen in Shīʿī piety as an implied critique of the ostentatious wealth of her female Qurayshī contemporaries, see Kamran Scott Aghaie, "The Gender Dynamics of Moharram Symbols and Rituals in the Latter Years of Qajar Rule," in *Women of Karbala*, 49–50.
19. See, e.g., al-Bukhārī, *Ṣaḥīḥ*, 3:1123, no. 5415; Muslim, *Ṣaḥīḥ*, 2:1149, no. 7094.
20. See al-Bukhārī, *Ṣaḥīḥ*, 2:732–733, no. 3750, and 3:1262–1263, no. 6275.
21. The report that ʿAlī had considered taking another wife is found in Sunnī sources (see, e.g., al-Bukhārī, *Ṣaḥīḥ*, 3:1095, no. 5275; and Muslim, *Ṣaḥīḥ*, 2:1047, no. 6466), although the idea that the Prophet would have prohibited such a thing is mentioned in some Shīʿī works as well; see Abū Jaʿfar Muḥammad ibn Abī'l-Qāsim al-Ṭabarī, *Bishārat al-muṣṭafā*, ed. Jawād al-Qayyūmī (Qum: Muʾassasat al-Nashr al-Islāmī, 2003), 381.
22. Thurkill, *Chosen among Women*, 94.
23. Pierce, *Twelve Infallible Men*, 82–83, 114–116, 134–135.
24. Al-Ṣaffār al-Qummī, *Baṣāʾir al-darajāt fī faḍāʾil Āl Muḥammad* (Dār Jawād al-A'imma, 2007), 1:319, 325.
25. See al-Kulaynī, *al-Kāfī*, 1:605–606, 611; al-Ṣaffār al-Qummī, *Baṣā'ir al-darajāt*, 1:306–310; al-Ṭabarsī, *al-Iḥtijāj*, 1:162–166; al-Ṭabarī, *Bishārat al-muṣṭafā*, 283–284.
26. Al-Yaʿqūbī, *Tārīkh* 2:11; and al-Ṭabarsī, *al-Iḥtijāj*, 1:210–212, where Fāṭima is explicitly said to have died as a *shahīda* (female martyr); see also al-Kulaynī, *al-Kāfī*, 1:530. Other ʿAlid women, such as Khadīja, Zaynab, and al-Ḥusayn's daughter, Ruqayya, are sometimes said to have been martyrs, often dying of "grief" (see Aghaie, "Gender Dynamics," 52). Edith Szanto has mentioned regular Shīʿī gatherings in Syria to commemorate the death/martyrdom of Fāṭima; see her unpublished dissertation,"Szanto, "Following Sayyida Zaynab: Twelver Shiʿism in Contemporary Syria" (PhD diss., University of Toronto, 2012), 111–113.
27. Al-Ṭabarsī, *al-Iḥtijāj*, 1:222–223; for the Qur'ānic account of the prophet Ṣāliḥ, which she invokes, see Qur'ān 7:73–78.
28. Al-Ṭabarsī, *al-Iḥtijāj*, 1:222–223.
29. Al-Yaʿqūbī, *Tārīkh*, 2:12.
30. Al-Ṭabarsī, *al-Iḥtijāj*, 1:253–274; a shorter version can be found in Ibn Abī Ṭāhir Ṭayfūr, *Balāghāt al-nisā'* (Beirut: Dār al-Ḥadātha, 1987), 26–28.
31. In Shīʿī piety, Zaynab is often seen as a second mother to her brother al-Ḥusayn after their mother, Fāṭima's, death, and a foster mother to ʿAlī Zayn al-ʿĀbidīn, even prior to Karbala; see Syed Akbar Hyder, *Reliving Karbala: Martyrdom in South Asian Memory* (Oxford:

Oxford University Press, 2006) 164. See also Faegheh Shirazi, "Daughters of Karbala: Images of Women in Popular Shiʿi Culture in Iran," in *Women of Karbala*, 110.

32. Aghaie, "Gender Dynamics," in *Women of Karbala*, 50–51.
33. Here clearly referring to the ʿAlīd legitimist cause in general, which lay behind al-Ḥusayn's revolt.
34. Ibn al-Athīr, *al-Kāmil fī-l-tārīkh* (Beirut: Dār Ṣādir, 1965), 4:82.
35. Ibid., 4:82.
36. Ibid., 4:82.
37. Ibid., 4:86.
38. Ibid., 4:86–87.
39. al-Yaʿqūbī, *Tārīkh*, 2:157.
40. See Lara Deeb, "From Mourning to Activism: Sayyedeh Zaynab, Lebanese Shiʿi Women, and the Transformation of Ashura," in *The Women of Karbala* 255–257; and Szanto, "Following Sayyida Zaynab," 36–37.
41. Aghaie, "Gender Dynamics," 48.
42. Umm Salama, and some of the other women of the Imams' households, are also said to have borne witness to the birth of some of the Imams. Even some otherwise relatively unknown or unremarkable women were sometimes said in Shīʿī accounts to have transmitted information about the Imams' successors or the *waṣāya* from one Imam to another; see Maria Massi Dakake, *The Charismatic Community: Shiʿite Identity in Early Islam* (Albany: State University of New York Press, 2007), 220–222.

Bibliography

Afsaruddin, Asma. *Striving in the Path of God: Jihad and Martyrdom in Islamic Thought*. Oxford: Oxford University Press, 2013.

Aghaie, Kamran Scot, ed. *The Women of Karbala: Ritual Performance and Symbolic Discourses in Modern Shiʿi Islam*. Austin: University of Texas Press, 2009.

Aghaie, Kamran Scot. "The Gender Dynamics of Moharram Symbols and Rituals in the Latter Years of Qajar Rule." In *The Women of Karbala: Ritual Performance and Symbolic Discourses in Modern Shiʿi Islam*, edited by Kamran Scot Aghaie, 45–64. Austin: University of Texas Press, 2009.

Bukhārī, Muḥammad ibn Ismāʿīl al-. *Ṣaḥīḥ al-Bukhārī*. Liechtenstein: Thesaurus Islamicus, 2000.

Dakake, Maria Massi. *The Charistmatic Community: Shiʿite Identity in Early Islam*. Albany: State University of New York Press, 2007.

Deeb, Lara. "From Mourning to Activism: Sayyedeh Zaynab, Lebanese Shiʿi Women, and the Transformation of Ashura." In *The Women of Karbala: Ritual Performance and Symbolic Discourses in Modern Shiʿi Islam*, edited by Kamran Scot Aghaie, 241–266. Austin: University of Texas Press, 2009.

Hyder, Syed Akbar. *Reliving Karbala: Martyrdom in South Asian Memory*. Oxford: Oxford University Press, 2006.

Ibn al-Athīr, ʿIzz al-Dīn. *Al-Kāmil fī-l-tārīkh*. Beirut: Dār Ṣādir, 1965.

Ibn Hajjāj, Muslim. *Ṣaḥīḥ Muslim*. Liechtenstein: Thesaurus Islamicus, 2000.

Kulaynī, Abū Jaʿfar Muḥammad ibn Yaʿqūb al-. *al-Kāfī*. Edited by Muḥammad Jaʿfar Shams al-Dīn. Beirut: Dār al-Taʿāruf li-l-Maṭbūʿāt, 1990.

Mottahedeh, Negar. "Ta'ziyeh: A Twist of History in Everyday Life." In *The Women of Karbala: Ritual Performance and Symbolic Discourses in Modern Shi'i Islam*, edited by Kamran Scot Aghaie, 25–44. Austin: University of Texas Press, 2009.

Pierce, Matthew. *Twelve Infallible Men: The Imams and the Making of Shi'ism*. Cambridge, MA: Harvard University Press, 2016.

Ṣaffār al-Qummī, Abū Ja'far Muḥammad ibn al-Ḥasan al-. *Baṣā'ir al-darajāt fī faḍā'il Āl Muḥammad*. Beirut: Dār Jawād al-A'imma, 2007.

Shariati, 'Ali. *Fatima Is Fatima*. Translated by Laleh Bakhtiar. Accessed March 14, 2021. https://www.al-islam.org/fatima-fatima-ali-shariati#comment-0.

Shirazi, Faegheh. "Daughters of Karbala: Images of Women in Popular Shi'i Culture in Iran." In *The Women of Karbala: Ritual Performance and Symbolic Discourses in Modern Shi'i Islam*, edited by Kamran Scot Aghaie, 93–118. Austin: University of Texas Press, 2009.

Szanto, Edith. "Following Sayyida Zaynab: Twelver Shi'ism in Contemporary Syria." PhD diss., University of Toronto, 2012.

Ṭabarī, Abū Ja'far Muḥammad ibn Abī'l-Qāsim al-. *Bishārat al-muṣṭafā li-shī'at al-murtaḍā*. Edited by J. al-Qayyūmī al-Isfahānī. Qum: Mu'assasa al-Nashr al-Islāmī, 2004.

Ṭabarsī, Abū Manṣūr Aḥmad ibn 'Alī al-. *al-Iḥtijāj*. Edited by I. Bahādurī and M. Hādī. Qum: Intashārāt Uswa, 2004.

Ṭayfūr, Ibn Abī Ṭāhir. *Balāghāt al-nisā'*. Beirut: Dār al-Ḥadātha, 1987.

Thurkill, Mary. *Chosen among Women: Mary and Fatima in Medieval Christianity and Shi'ite Islam*. Notre Dame, IN: University of Notre Dame Press, 2008.

Tirmidhī, Muḥammad ibn 'Isā al-. *Sunan al-Tirmidhī*. Liechtenstein: Thesaurus Islamicus, 2000.

Ya'qūbī, Aḥmad ibn Abī Ya'qūb al-. *Tarīkh al-Ya'qūbī*. Edited by 'Abd al-Amīr al-Muhannā. Beirut: Mu'assasat al-A'lamī, 1993.

CHAPTER 11

WOMEN AS TRANSMITTERS OF KNOWLEDGE

ASMA SAYEED

Literature Review and Navigating the State of Field

SINCE the late twentieth century, the number of studies relating to Muslim women's religious knowledge has increased exponentially. A simple search for "Muslim women's religious knowledge," in library catalogs of major research universities yields approximately 4,800 publications that mention these terms.[1] The vast majority of these have been published within the past three decades. Notwithstanding the fact that such a broad search yields numerous publications that are only tangentially related to the topic, it is telling that there has been a substantial increase in publications which include some reference to this topic in recent decades. News coverage of sanctions against women's education by the Taliban in Afghanistan and Boko Haram in Nigeria has fueled some of this interest. More broadly, and perhaps unsurprisingly, women's religious learning is indelibly bound up with questions of their agency, authority, and empowerment. As such, questions of how women acquire religious learning and whether they are able to authoritatively transmit that knowledge intersect with contemporary debates on the status of Muslim women, a proxy battleground for assorted ideological contestations between Muslims and non-Muslims as well as among Muslims themselves. The issue of women's religious knowledge also intersects with seemingly tangential concerns, such as how Muslim communities assimilate knowledge about sundry matters from mammograms to reproductive health to terrorism. The overview below focuses on English-language academic publications[2] that deal substantively with the transmission of religious knowledge by Muslim women and serves as an entry point and an aid to navigating this burgeoning subfield.

A number of salient characteristics are immediately apparent in a survey of academic publications. First, the chronological coverage of women and the transmission of religious knowledge is uneven. The bulk of analyses focus on the modern period (ca. nineteenth century) onwards and comparatively few studies cover the earliest eras of Islamic history (ca. first/seventh to seventh/thirteenth). The Ottoman, Safavid, and Mughal periods have received minimal attention. Historical studies on the earliest eras are primarily documentary and have relied on published sources, especially biographical dictionaries and chronicles. By contrast, for modern women's studies, the source base has expanded to include periodicals, poetry and other literary productions, folklore, autobiography, art, and film. Scholars working on the modern era have employed a range of disciplinary methods including ethnographic research, literary analysis, sociological surveys, and historical and historiographical methodologies. As inquiries into contemporary women's religious learning have multiplied in recent years, it is crucial that researchers be mindful of conceptual, disciplinary, and methodological divergences between the study of premodern Muslim women and contemporary ones, especially insofar as the discontinuities are bound up with complex, intertwined histories of Islamic education, colonialism, nationalist and Islamic reformist movements, and evolutions in Islamic studies itself as an increasingly global, interdisciplinary field.

Regional and sectarian coverage also shows distinct patterns. For premodern Muslim societies, studies cluster around the central Islamic areas including Egypt, Syria, Iraq, and Iran, with only a few that have forayed into North and West Africa, al-Andalus, or east to South Asia and East Asia. For the modern period, the geographic range has expanded to include West Africa, Sub-Saharan Africa, South Asia, and East Asia as well as communities in Europe and North America.[3] Finally, a vast majority of the studies focus on Sunnī women's engagement, though there are now a handful that also examine Shīʿī women's learning and religious authority. Devin Stewart's article and my own have analyzed the representation of Imāmī Shīʿī women up to the Safavid era in selected biographical compendia.[4] For the modern period, there are several studies on the rise of women's religious learning in the decades after the Iranian revolution. Among these are studies of Nusrat Amin (1886–1983), a leading female jurist (*mujtahida*) and research on women in the *hawza* system, which has facilitated the spread of Shīʿī doctrines across global Muslim communities.[5] Unfortunately, similar studies on Ismāʿīlī or Zaydī female education have not yet been published.

In keeping with the chronological organization of this *Handbook*, the remainder of this chapter focuses on early and classical history. An analysis of primary themes is followed by an overview of historical patterns within one of those domains, namely, *ḥadīth* transmission. Historical studies typically evince two major concerns: historicity and representation across time. The former concern relates to the challenge of accurately reconstructing the activities of historical figures such as ʿĀʾisha bint Abī Bakr (d. ca. 58/678) or Umm Salama (d. ca. 59/679), both wives of the Prophet, who played significant roles in the transmission of religious knowledge. The latter relates to analyzing how Muslims across time have represented early or classical Muslim women in different genres of literary production. In this vein, the biographical writings of Zaynab Fawwāz (1860–1914) and ʿĀʾisha bint ʿAbd al-Raḥmān (1913–1998), have been analyzed for how their histories of early Muslim female exemplars impact contemporary feminist and political discourses.[6] Alternatively, Hanan el-Sayyid examines Assia Djebar's modern literary portrayal of women in early Muslim historiography, and concludes that her representation reflects Western/French perceptions and expectations of Muslim women rather than the earliest sources themselves.[7] While these scholarly concerns of historicity and representation are not mutually exclusive, the methodology and analytical goals of each are distinct, and few studies are able to balance and integrate both impulses effectively in a single study.

History and Historicity

In excavating and reconstructing the history of early Muslim women's religious learning, several studies focus on women's *ḥadīth* transmission and Sufism. Women's engagement with theology, law, philosophy, history, and scriptural exegesis has left fewer traces in the published primary sources at our disposal, and this lacunae is, in turn, reflected in current scholarship. Among Western academics, Ignaz Goldziher (d. 1921) was among the first to draw attention to the regular mention of female scholars of *ḥadīth* in his famed *Muslim Studies*.[8] His brief anecdotal survey leaves the task of a fuller study to future scholars. Similarly, M. Z. Siddiqi devotes a chapter to the topic in his *Hadith Literature*, a monograph intended as a primer for Western audiences on the sciences of *ḥadīth* from a Muslim critical perspective.[9]

Subsequent decades witnessed the publication of a handful of articles and book chapters which explored the phenomenon more closely. Yet, it was not until the early twenty-first century that two English monographs were devoted to the topic, namely M. Akram Nadwi's *Muḥaddithāt* and my own *Women and the Transmission of Religious Knowledge in Islam*.[10] Each of these works takes a divergent approach to the phenomenon of female *ḥadīth* scholars. Nadwi's work is written as the introduction to his as yet unpublished but extensive Arabic compilation of biographies devoted to female scholars across Islamic history. Nadwi offers chapters on legal conditions for narrating *ḥadīth*, scholarly networks (teachers and students), travel, and educational venues, but his aim is not to present a historical synthesis or narrative.[11] *Women and the Transmission of Religious Knowledge*, on the other hand, synthesizes the history of female participation in this domain across ten centuries and contextualizes the evidence in terms of Muslim social and intellectual history. Generally, the historical method of these studies is to mine biographical dictionaries, chronicles, and *ḥadīth* compilations, such as the leading Sunnī collections for information about women and their achievements.[12] Piecemeal and formulaic evidence in such sources necessitates not only advanced language competency (generally in Arabic) but also an understanding of the diverse genres of historical literature to avoid misinterpretation of evidence. Further, inquiries into the first century and a half of Islamic history must also engage with the thorny, at times polemical, debates about the authenticity of early Muslim sources.

A few studies have drawn our attention to women in the arenas of Sufism, law, and Qurʾān. With respect to Sufism, Rkia Cornell's translation of al-Sulamī's (d. 412/1021) *Dhikr al-Niswa al-mutaʿabbidāt as-Ṣūfiyyāt* and her introduction to this volume and Homerin's annotated translation of ʿĀʾisha al-Bāʿūnīya's (d. 1516) *Principles of Sufism* are particularly significant contributions which allow us to hear women's voices through primary sources.[13] With respect to women's engagement with *sharīʿa* and the Qurʾān, published historical sources offer less evidence. Even in the case of a woman as celebrated as ʿĀʾisha bint Abī Bakr, it is more difficult to piece together her contributions to scriptural and legal exegesis. Her niece, ʿAmra bint ʿAbd al-Raḥmān (d. 98/716), though less well known, and a few other female Companions and Successors were also known for their exegetical and legal authority. In this regard, Aisha Geissinger's analyses of women's exegetical reports are exemplary in their careful readings and renditions of available source material.[14] The issue of how or whether Ḥafṣa bint ʿUmar (d. 45/665), a wife of Prophet Muḥammad, preserved the Qurʾān has recently sparked interesting methodological debates that highlight the diversity of academic approaches and the challenges of early source material. Prompted by Ruqayya Khan's assertion that Ḥafṣa did indeed play a significant role in "editing" the Qurʾān, a few other scholars have questioned the role of contemporary feminist discourses in shaping our understanding of the participation of early Muslim women as well as what may be credibly read into the sources.[15] Overall, historical studies have made significant progress in answering questions such as these: What is the history of women's transmission of religious knowledge; what does women's scholarly participation tell us about gender norms in early and classical Islam; and more broadly what can women's participation show us about the history of Islamic education itself?

A final point is that studies on women's rhetorical, literary, and poetic accomplishments in the early and classical eras have not considered the intersections between religious knowledge and literary production, a distinction which is not necessarily mirrored in the primary sources themselves. Such divisions, unfortunately, have impeded full understanding of the contributions of women such as ʿĀʾisha bint Ṭalḥa (d. 100/719) and Sukayna bint al-Ḥusayn (d. 117/736), both known for their literary and poetic skills and in a more limited capacity for narrating reports.[16] For the modern period, this divide has been more successfully bridged in the studies of Bint al-Shāṭī, ʿĀʾisha al-Bāʿūnīyya, Zaynab Fawwāz, and Nana Asmāʾu, whose literary production has been examined in conjunction with their accomplishments as religious scholars.

Memory and Representation

In contrast to studies that attempt to write the biographies of learned women or about the historical phenomenon of Muslim women's religious learning, some analyses are more concerned with how the female figures are represented by later authors or by contemporary Muslims themselves. Such scholarship asks questions related to *reception history* and how the memory and reimagination of pious female exemplars intersects with the broader project of the social constructions of gender across Muslim communities. The example of ʿĀʾisha bint Abī Bakr is instructive here as well. Spellberg's study of ʿĀʾisha's role in the early Muslim community considers the ways in which Muslims of later centuries remembered ʿĀʾisha as an exemplar in terms of her religious knowledge and discernment but were conflicted about her political legacy.[17] Similarly, Marilyn Booth and Ruth Roded have examined the writings of Zaynab Fawwāz and Bint al-Shāṭī, modern female scholars, who wrote about early Muslim women not just in the interests of historical writing but to uphold them as models for contemporary Muslim women.[18] In a study which combines exciting transregional, historical, and interdisciplinary research, Beverly Mack's analysis considers how American Muslims, especially women, recreate the legacy of Nana Asma'u (1793–1864), a legendary female Qādiriyya scholar and daughter of Uthman dan Fodio (d. 1817), the reformist shaykh and founder of the West African Sokoto caliphate.[19]

Women's *Ḥadīth* Transmission: Overview and Historical Analysis

The increasingly expansive scope of research on Muslim women's religious learning as well as the title of this chapter, namely "Women as Transmitters of Knowledge," can conjure a broad set of associations with respect to women and knowledge. Yet, this chapter limits itself to *religious knowledge*. Furthermore, the sections below focus on women's engagement *within a specific arena* of religious learning. These authorial decisions are related to historical patterns and understandings within Arabo-Muslim communities. Thus, it is important first to clarify the connotations of "knowledge" and "transmission," in the early and classical Muslim tradition. Indeed, these meanings continue to exercise an influence today in the understandings of women and religious learning across the Muslim world. The Arabic term *ʿilm* is often used to signify religious knowledge. While there is no single agreed upon definition of the fields that constitute the arena of "religious knowledge," there is broad historical consensus that they minimally include the following: the Qurʾān and its interpretation; sayings attributed to Prophet Muḥammad (*ḥadīth*); Arabic grammar and philology; Islamic law; and theology. Fields such as astronomy, physics, medicine, history, philosophy, and math were sometimes included in the premodern curricula of religious scholars. In the modern era, however, it is more common to see a division between "religious knowledge" and "secular knowledge." Social sciences and humanistic disciplines, including history, philosophy, anthropology, art, and literature are often classified as secular fields and do not come within the purview of religious learning. By extension, an *ʿālim* (masc.) or *ʿālima* (fem.) designates one who has acquired religious knowledge either through institutional training or informal networks. Throughout Islamic history and into the modern period, the process of both becoming and being publically recognized as an *ʿālim* or *ʿālima* has not been a standardized, linear one. A combination of factors, therefore, helps to ascertain those who merit the appellation of *ʿālim*/*ʿālima*. These include a basic training in the aforementioned requisite religious sciences and the acquisition of expertise in one or more of them, as well as public recognition that one is capable of preserving and authoritatively transmitting that knowledge.

In premodern Islamic history, "transmission" is a term most often associated with the field of *ḥadīth* studies, an arena governed by specific guidelines for authoritative, reliable transmission of the reports attributed to Muḥammad and the early generations of Muslims. Arabic terms associated with this arena of learning include "*taḥammul al-ʿilm*" (the conveying/reproduction of religious knowledge), *riwāya* (the memorization and narration of reports attributed to the Prophet and early Muslims), and *ʿulūm al-ḥadīth* (the sciences of *ḥadīth* transmission). When historical sources record female participation in the transmission of religious knowledge, the field of religious learning being referenced is usually *ḥadīth* and **not** Islamic substantive jurisprudence and its methodology (*fiqh* and *uṣūl*), Qurʾānic commentary (*tafsīr*), or theology (*kalām*). This is notwithstanding the fact that female scholars may well have been proficient in fields other than *ḥadīth*. Such terminological distinctions of premodern contexts are critically important because each subfield is associated with distinct methods and its own culture and vocabulary of knowledge transmission. Furthermore, contemporary feminist discourse has probed the distinct significance and valence of women's *reproduction* of religious knowledge (most often associated with *ḥadīth* transmission) as opposed to their acts of *creation* or *authorship* and *interpretation* (associated with law, *tafsīr*, and theology).

Women's participation from the rise of Islam to the modern period fluctuated considerably and shows disparate patterns in sectarian milieus. The overview offered here draws on Sunnī and Imāmī Shīʿī sources to reconstruct this chronology. Among Sunnī circles of learning, women's prominence as *ḥadīth* scholars rises or falls in correlation with the professionalization of the field of *ḥadīth* transmission, the formation of the *ʿulamāʾ* (scholars, broadly designated) as a social class, and the entrenchment of Sunnī traditionalism across the classical Muslim world.[20] Among the first generation of Muslims (i.e., Companions), women regularly participated in transmitting information about Prophet Muḥammad. The major Sunnī *ḥadīth* collections contain reports attributed to approximately 112 female Companions. The proportion of female Companions in these compilations is significant and varies from approximately 12 to 20 percent depending on the compilation. There are no scriptural or legal proscriptions against women's religious learning, and since there were leading female Companions who transmitted numerous reports, we may expect that women's *ḥadīth* transmission would persist across the centuries. Yet, the sources at our disposal paint a different picture. The second/eighth century witnessed a sharp decline, followed by the near disappearance of women from the chains of transmission of major Sunnī collections in the third/ninth century.[21]

This demise, however, was temporary. Beginning in the fourth/tenth century, women re-engaged as students and teachers of *ḥadīth* across urban centers such as Marv, Nishapur, and Isfahan. Over the next few centuries, their numbers steadily increased. Al-Sakhāwī's (d. 902/1497) tenth/fifteenth-century Egyptian biographical dictionary titled *al-Ḍawʾ al-Lāmiʿ li-Ahl al-Qarn al-Tāsiʿ* [*A Lustrous Light upon the Notables of the Ninth-Century [AH]*] contains an entire volume of over a thousand entries devoted to women who were known for their piety and/or religious learning.[22] Damascus, Aleppo, and Baghdad experienced similar activity on the part of women from the ninth to the fifteen centuries. Women are regularly mentioned as teachers and students of *ḥadīth* not just in published biographical compendia and local histories but also in certificates of transmission (*ijāzāt* and *samāʿāt*), many of which remain in manuscript form.

This revival of female *ḥadīth* participation was diffuse and spanned nearly four centuries. The late fifteenth and early sixteenth centuries, however, witnessed another contraction. This turn, however, did not mark a broader marginalization of women from religious learning in the Ottoman era. Rather, women appear to have increasingly availed opportunities for participation in Sufi institutions and informal organizations, and some also earned fame for their legal learning. Although women's participation in *ḥadīth* learning after the Mamluk era (648/1250–922/1517) is recorded at lower levels, it persists to this day as an arena for women's engagement.

Explanations for the aforementioned patterns of women's *ḥadīth* learning are best found in the domains of social and intellectual Islamic history. It is worth noting here that feminism and feminist consciousness cannot be projected back to the premodern eras to explain the rise or decline of female *ḥadīth* learning. This point is critical to contextualizing the impetuses for women's successes. Further, the contents of the texts that women learned and taught for most of Islamic history bear little relation to feminist discourses about the place of *ḥadīth* in determining women's status.

In the earliest decades of Islamic history, female Companions shared in building the first Muslim community. They not only witnessed Prophet's actions and decision-making, but were direct participants in shaping discussions and events. After Muḥammad's death, these Companions became sought-after sources of knowledge about him. Men and women both contributed to an informal, unregulated exchange of information about him. This environment supported regular participation on the part of several women such as ʿĀʾisha bint Abī Bakr (d. 58/678), a beloved wife of Muḥammad. She was one of the most prolific Companion transmitters and also displayed legal discernment in her understanding of Muhammad's precedents. The historical records also attest to the contributions of lesser-known women, such as Salāma bint al-Ḥurr, who is known for a single report. The variation in the levels of women's participation and the spectrum of topics they cover, from ritual actions to eschatology, is likely a result of the informal, ad hoc nature of *ḥadīth* learning in these early decades and also attests to the absence of restrictions on female Companions' participation.

In the second/eighth and third/ninth centuries, the steep decline and near disappearance of women from this domain maps onto a number of developments in social and intellectual history as the fledgling *umma* expanded exhibiting markers of socioeconomic and intellectual differentiation. Among these was the professionalization of different spheres of learning, a development that generated new challenges for female transmitters. The best scholars demonstrated specialized legal knowledge in transmitting texts, could boast of direct oral transmission from their teachers, and were able to undertake rigorous, often solitary, journeys to learn *ḥadīth* from scholars across the Muslim world. Women were at a disadvantage in this evolving environment. Although legal prescriptions do not prohibit or even discourage women from acquiring and disseminating knowledge, they do paradoxically curtail male–female interactions among those not related by blood or marriage. Negotiating the normative terrain was likely especially challenging in the context of early *ḥadīth* transmission due to the heightened emphasis on face-to-face oral transmission of reports as opposed to learning texts on one's own or by written correspondence. Domestic obligations and the hazards of travel further dampened women's prospects for succeeding as *ḥadīth* transmitters. It is not surprising that the precedent established by female Companions was interrupted given that the Companions' activity was localized and less regulated and their participation owed more to happenstance than systematic training.

The fourth/tenth-century reemergence of women can be similarly contextualized with respect to developments in the field of *ḥadīth* transmission, including the canonization of *ḥadīth* collections, and the growing acceptance of written transmission accompanied by a decreased reliance on oral transmission. From the sixth/twelfth to the ninth/fifteenth centuries, the spread of Sunnī traditionalism from North Africa to Transoxania generated a demand for the reproduction of *ḥadīth*-based compilations. Works transmitted through short *isnād*s (*isnād ʿālī*) were especially valuable. Long-lived women (and men) who embodied the virtues of religious learning, piety, and a scholarly lineage and who had procured certificates of transmission were in high demand. Not surprisingly, therefore, the rise in women's participation as *ḥadīth* transmitters coincides with a rising demand for short *isnād*s.

In addition to these factors, women's religious learning benefited from new sociocultural factors related to the growth and development of Muslim scholarly classes, the detailed history of which remains to be written. Nevertheless, local histories and specific case studies attest that around the fifth/eleventh century, the *ʿulamāʾ* increasingly relied on kinship networks to perpetuate their status and traditions of learning. The education of daughters in the religious sciences, and especially in *ḥadīth* transmission, which could be more easily balanced with the demands of marriage and childrearing, became an established means of confirming such status. The combination of these factors created a hospitable environment over a period of four centuries for women's *ḥadīth* participation and left measurable traces in the historical sources. The marked increase and flourishing in the numbers of women who attained enviable reputations in this arena is therefore among the outcomes of this broader social evolution.

The contraction in the late ninth/fifteenth and early tenth/sixteenth centuries is also correlated with variables in the history of religious education as well as evolutions in the forms of social organization. Thus, a deemphasis on *ḥadīth* and a growing legal orientation in religious learning coincides with the declining numbers of female *ḥadīth* transmitters in this period. Women appear to be increasingly involved with organized Sufism as adepts or teachers within Sufi brotherhoods (*ṭarīqa*s).

Female engagement with *ḥadīth* continues in the modern period. Yet, its forms and purposes vary. *Ḥadīth* learning, in some cases, upholds individual women's pietistic practices and provides a compelling avenue for connecting with pious early exemplars. Such learning also serves to preserve the tradition of the short *isnād*, through which seekers can affirm their place in a broader network of knowledge-seekers with connectedness to pious, learned forbears. By contrast, some contemporary institutions which are either devoted to *ḥadīth* study or incorporate it into their curricula, seem only superficially connected to early and classical Islamic precedents. The Madrasa al-Ḥadīth al-Nūriya, adjacent to the Damascene Umayyad mosque, for example, was established in 2001. Expressly for women's religious education, the compound houses classrooms, a library, a computer center, and a cafeteria much like contemporary schools. The curriculum centers on *ḥadīth* sciences and the study and memorization of Qurʾānic readings. In addition to memorization of canonical texts such as the *Ṣaḥīḥ* of al-Bukhārī, students listen to exegetical lectures on these compilations which provide practical lessons in the interpretation and application of traditional texts in contemporary circumstances. A final difference relates to the minimum age requirement at this institute, where students are permitted to enroll only after the age of sixteen and the acquisition of elementary education. By contrast, the more classically oriented model promoted the certification of female *ḥadīth* transmitters from childhood, and formal institutions had far less impact on the educational trajectory of these students. Ultimately, the Madrasa *al-Ḥadīth* al-Nūriya conforms to a particularly modern purpose, namely the accommodation of conservative piety within a secure institutional harbor. Such institutions permit expressions of piety and fulfill a desire for women's religious learning even as the state maintains vigilance and institutional oversight.

The survey above offered a portrait of the transmission of religious knowledge in premodern Sunnī communities. It would be a mistake, however, to assume similarities in Shīʿī women's participation. Imāmī sources, for example, reveal their own patterns shaped by sectarian considerations as well as legal debates within Shīʿism itself.[23] The overall rates of Imāmī Shīʿī female *ḥadīth* participation are significantly lower, and the fluctuations themselves also vary. To contextualize the patterns that emerge from Shīʿī sources, we must first start with a chronological framework that is more relevant to this sectarian context as follows: (1) the pre-Occultation period (that is, during the lifetime of the twelve Imams [10/632–260/872]); (2) the beginning of Occultation to the Safavid period (260/874–907/1501); and (3) the Safavid era itself (907/1501–1135/1722). Within these three broadly demarcated periods, it is possible to discern evolving positions concerning the epistemology of religious knowledge that in turn are likely to have impacted women's participation. For example, during the first period (10/632–260/874), when the

Imāms provided religious guidance themselves, women did not function prominently as authoritative transmitters.[24] Rather, the male disciples of the Imāms appear more often in the Shīʿī chains of transmission of their reports. In the second phase (after the Occultation and up to the Safavid period), which overlaps to a degree with the revival of women in Sunnī communities, there are still only a few women who are commended for religious learning in Shīʿī sources. It is not until the Safavid era that we see more engagement with *ḥadīth* learning among women. Intriguingly, the few female religious scholars who are mentioned in the biographical sources are described as being interpreters and commentators and not as transmitters of religious texts.

An explanation for discrepancies between Sunnī and Imāmī Shīʿī portraits turns our attention to the many variables that have shaped women's intellectual and spiritual endeavors across Islamic history. The overall lower numbers of Imāmī women is due undoubtedly in part to the minority status of Shīʿīs. Given the persecution of Shīʿīs in the early centuries, it is not likely that many women would have been tasked with the public dissemination of religious knowledge. This is especially pertinent before the rise of the Safavids, who were themselves a Shīʿī dynasty committed to the patronage of Shīʿī *ʿulamāʾ*.[25] Yet, the significantly lower incidence of female participation in *ḥadīth* learning has other causes as well. As mentioned earlier, Shīʿī biographical dictionaries evince greater concern with women who were recognized for their expertise in law and *tafsīr*. This may be attributed to the differing place of *ḥadīth* transmission itself in Sunnī and Imāmī Shīʿī cultures. In the former, as explained above, the culture of traditionalism, in which *ḥadīth* transmission evolved as a public activity, as well as the evolution of the *ʿulamāʾ* as a social class drew in scores of female scholars from the fourth/tenth century onward.

In Imāmī Shīʿism, on the other hand, scholarly contestations concerning the evaluation of transmitted religious knowledge followed their own course. Here, the struggles concerned inclinations which have come to be known as "traditionism" and "rationalism." The latter as a legal and theological inclination places greater emphasis on the primacy of reason in ascertaining the validity and application of reports attributed to the Prophet and the Imāms. Traditionism, on the other hand, advocates a reliance on the apparent meaning of reports tending to minimize the use of human agency (e.g., faculties of reason and interpretation) in determining their significance. Rationalism necessitated a higher level of interpretive engagement with texts, whereas traditionism promoted the faithful transmission of them. In contrast to Sunnī intellectual history, rationalist (*uṣūlī*) scholars exercised a pervasive influence across premodern Imāmī communities. Their ascendancy, in turn, is likely to have had a broader impact on the value associated with different spheres of religious learning. In this vein, it appears that religious education consistent with a rationalist view, that is, a focus on legal and interpretive engagement with texts was promoted and extolled. While the transmission of reports attributed to the Prophet and Imāms is valuable among Uṣūlīs, it was not an end in and of itself.

Our historical sources do not discuss how the broader intellectual milieu may have shaped the educational preferences and value assigned to different fields of learning.

Nevertheless, recent theoretical and historical studies on the development and entrenchment of orthodox views across Muslim history have highlighted the broad social processes of asserting dominance in doctrinal debates which extend well beyond the intellectual and ruling elite. With respect to the history of women's transmission of religious knowledge, the impact of contestations between Imāmī rationalists and traditionists seems to have left its traces in biographical literature. When Imāmī Shīʿī communities did experience a rise in the influence of a more traditionist-oriented body of scholars, there are increased numbers of female scholars who are known for their learning in this arena. The most significant period of traditionist-influence, from the eleventh/seventeenth century to the latter half of the twelfth/eighteenth century, was known as the Akhbārī revival. During this era, Imāmī scholars such as Muḥammad b. ʿAlī al-Ardabīlī (d. 1001/1593), compiler of *Jāmiʿ al-Ruwāt* and Mīrzā ʿAbd Allāh al-Iṣfahānī (d. 1130/1718), author of *Riyāḍ al-ʿulamāʾ wa-ḥiyāḍ al-fuḍalāʾ*, were concerned with thoroughly documenting male and female narrators of reports, and their works contain more complete lists of female narrators than the compilations of their predecessors. Yet, even in these works, the tenor of the descriptions of female transmitters of reports is entirely different from that in classical Sunnī biographical works that extoll the contributions and piety of *muḥaddithas*. Imāmī biographical literature, by contrast, dwells more on women's oratorical defenses of the family of the Prophet (such as that of Zaynab bint ʿAlī [d. 62/682]), and also with legal/hermeneutical engagement with texts (such as that of Āmina Khātūn [fl. eleventh/seventeenth century]), the daughter of Muḥammad Taqī al-Majlisī.[26] This overview of Imāmī biographical literature on women highlights some of the ways in which sectarian considerations shaped women's intellectual endeavors and underscores the importance of not universalizing premodern Muslim women's experiences on the basis of Sunnī sources and discourses alone.

Directions for Future Research

The unabated interest in Muslim women and their religious authority heralds a trajectory of growth and disciplinary and regional diversification in the decades ahead. Given the divergent interests in this area and the requisite expertise to conduct studies, there is significant risk that researchers will remain confined to their geographic, linguistic, or temporal silos. Future research ideally should aim to benefit from previous scholarship and to forge stronger interdisciplinary, transregional, and historical connections. Among the desiderata are studies on Andalusia, Northwest Africa, West Africa, Sub-Saharan Africa, and South Asia. While published primary sources, especially biographical dictionaries and chronicles have been used in prior studies, their utility is far from exhausted. Digital humanities has made it possible for us to search textual corpora and not rely solely on indices compiled by authors or editors. Mining historical sources in their entirety for references to women's religious learning is likely to yield a complete picture of their activities and intellectual networks. Similarly, sustained manuscript research would allow us to build and expand on the existing framework and open new methodological and analytical frontiers. Examining marginal notes, certificates of transmission and hearing, and even evidence of women's calligraphy can also add to our substantive knowledge of how women participated as teachers and students of different Islamic sciences.

Finally, the proliferation of studies on modern female piety movements and activism raises the question of what the connections are between premodern movements and contemporary ones. For example, although *ḥadīth* transmission persists as a field of religious learning, there are no academic studies of women's contemporary engagement with it. Rather, studies display greater concern with women's exegetical endeavors and authority in the areas of Qurʾān and Islamic law. Contemporary Sufism has also received attention. Another intriguing avenue of inquiry has been female religious authority in popular or folk contexts. Longue durée analyses, which can both meaningfully engage with the well-established practices and habitus of female religious scholars historically and also inform us about how contemporary Muslim women conceive of their own history and lineage, would be welcome additions to the field.

Notes

1. This figure is based on a search conducted in July 2019 on Melvyl, the University of California search engine, which searches major research libraries worldwide.
2. The vast majority of publications on this topic are in English. Far few studies have been published in French, Spanish, German, and other European languages.
3. Some of these studies are listed as suggested sources in the bibliography.
4. Devin Stewart, "Women's Biographies in Islamic Societies: Mīrzā ʿAbd Allāh al-Iṣfahānī's *Riyāḍ al-ʿUlamāʾ*," in *Rhetoric of Biography: Narrating Lives in Persianate Societies*, ed. Louise Marlow (Boston: Ilex Foundation, 2011), 106–139; and Asma Sayeed, "Women in Imāmī Biographical Collections," in *Law and Tradition in Classical Islamic Thought: Studies in Honor of Professor Hossein Modarressi*, ed. Michael Cook et al. (New York: Palgrave Macmillan, 2013), 81–97.
5. See, for example, Bahar Davary, "In Search of Female Authority in Islam: A Contemporary Shiʿa Mojtahede," *Pakistan Journal of Women's Studies: Alam-e-Niswan* 20, no. 1 (2013): 19–33; Mirjam Künkler and Roja Fazaeli, "The Life of Two Mujtahidahs: Female Religious in Twentieth Century Iran," in *Women, Leadership, and Mosques: Changes in Contemporary Islamic Authority*, ed. Masooda Bano and Hilary Kalmbach (Boston: Brill, 2012), 127–160; Maryam Rutner, "Religious Authority, Gendered Recognition, and Instrumentalization of Nusrat Amin in Life and after Death," *Journal of Middle East Women's Studies* 11, no. 1 (2015): 24–41; Mirjam Künkler and Devin Stewart, *Female Religious Authority in Shiʿi Islam: Past and Present* (Edinburgh: Edinburgh University Press, 2021).
6. Marilyn Booth has written extensively on Zaynab Fawwāz; see, for example, *May Her Likes Be Multiplied* (Los Angeles: University of California Press, 2001); and *Classes of Ladies of Cloistered Spaces* (Edinburgh: Edinburgh University Press, 2015). See also, Hoda Elsadda, "Discourses on Women's Biographies and Cultural Identity: Twentieth Century Representations of the Life of ʿĀʾisha bint Abi Bakr," *Feminist Studies* 27, no. 1 (2001):

37–64; and Ruth Roded, "Bint al-Shati's 'Wives of the Prophet': Feminist or Feminine?" *British Journal of Middle Eastern Studies* 33, no. 1 (2006): 51–66.

7. Hanan Elsayed, "'Silence' and Historical Tradition in Assia Djebar's Loin de Médine," *Research in African Literatures* 44, no. 1 (2013): 91–105.
8. Ignaz Goldziher, *Muslim Studies*, ed.S. M. Stern, tr. C. R. Barber and S. M. Stern (London: Aldine Publishing Co., 1966), 2:366–368
9. Muhammad Z. Siddiqi, *Ḥadīth Literature: Its Origin, Development, and Special Features*, ed. A. H. Murad (Cambridge: Islamic Texts Society, 1993), 117–123.
10. Mohammad Akram Nadwi, *al-Muhaddithat: The Women Scholars in Islam* (London: Interface, 2007); and Asma Sayeed, *Women and the Transmission of Religious Knowledge in Islam* (New York: Cambridge University Press, 2013).
11. Nadwi himself characterizes his work as more of: "[A] *listing*; it is . . . much nearer to 'words' than 'sentences', and far from 'paragraphs' linked into an 'essay'." *al-Muhaddithat*, xi.
12. These include compilations such as the *Ṣaḥīḥ* collections of al-Bukhārī (d. 256/870) and Muslim (d. 261/875) and the *Sunan*s of Ibn Māja (d. 273/887), Abū Dāwūd (d. 275/889), al-Tirmidhī (d. 279/892) and al-Nasā'ī (d. 303/915), as well as the *Musnad* of Ibn Ḥanbal (d. 241/855).
13. Rkia E. Cornell, ed. and trans., *Early Sufi Women: Dhikr an-Niswa al-Muta'abbidāt aṣ-Ṣūfiyyāt* (Louisville: Fons Vitae, 1999); and Th. Emil Homerin, ed. and trans., *Principles of Sufism* (New York: New York University Press, 2014). See also, Arezou Azad, "Female Mystics in Medieval Islam: The Quiet Legacy," *Journal of Economic and Social History of the Orient* 56, no. 1 (2013): 53–88.
14. Aisha Geissinger, *Gender and Muslim Constructions of Exegetical Authority: A Rereading of the Classical Genre of Qur'ān Commentary*. For an overview on 'Ā'isha, see Geissinger, "'Aisha bint Abi Bakr and her Contributions to the Formation of the Islamic Tradition," *Religion Compass* 5, no. 1 (2011):37–49; and Geissinger, "Portrayal of the Ḥajj as a Context for Women's Exegesis: Textual Evidence in al-Bukhārī's (d. 870) *al-Ṣaḥīḥ*," in *Ideas, Images, and Methods of Portrayal*, ed. Sebastian Guenther (Leiden: Brill, 2005), 153–179. For an insightful examination of 'Amra bint 'Abd al-Raḥmān, see the article by Mona Hassan, "Relations, Narrations, and Judgements: The Scholarly Networks and Contributions of an Early Female Muslim Jurist," *Islamic Law and Society* 22 (2015): 323–351.
15. Ruqayya Khan, "Did a Woman Edit the Qur'ān: Hafṣa and Her Famed Codex," *Journal of the American Academy of Religion* 82, no. 1 (2014): 174–216. The responses are as follows: Sean Anthony and Catherine Bronson, "Did Ḥafṣah Edit the Qur'ān? A Response with Notes on the Codices of the Prophet's Wives," *Journal of the International Qur'ānic Studies Association* 1 (2016): 93–125; and Aisha Geissinger, "No a Woman Did Not 'Edit the Quran,' Towards a Methodologically Coherent Approach Portraying a Woman and Written Qur'ānic Materials," *Journal of the American Academy of Religion* 85, no. 2 (2017): 416-445.
16. See Sayeed, *Women and Transmission*, 68–69, 86–87, for further information and references about 'Ā'isha and Sukayna respectively.
17. Denise Spellberg, *Politics, Gender, and the Islamic Past: The Legacy of 'A'isha bint Abi Bakr* (New York: Columbia University Press, 1994). See also, Asma Afsaruddin, "Literature, Scholarship and Piety: Negotiating Gender and Authority in the Medieval Muslim World," *Religion and Literature* 42, no. 1/2 (2010): 111–131.
18. See note 6 above.
19. Beverly Mack, "Nana Asma'u's Instruction and Poetry for Present-Day American Muslimahs," *History in Africa* 38 (2011): 153–168; Mack, "Fodiology: African American

Heritage Connections to West African Islam," *Journal of West African History* 4 (2): 103–130; and Jean Boyd and Beverly B. Mack, eds., *Collected Works of Nana Asma'u, Daughter of Usman dan Fodiyo (1793–1864)* (East Lansing: Michigan State University Press, 1997).

20. See Sayeed, *Women and the Transmission*, for a more complete historical analysis of female *ḥadīth* participation and for an explanation of the methodology used to derive this chronological overview.
21. Sayeed, *Women and Transmission*, chap. 2.
22. For a recent study of these female scholars in al-Sakhāwī's biographical work, see Asma Afsaruddin, "Knowledge, Piety, and Religious Leadership in the Late Middle Ages: Reinstating Women in the Master Narrative," in *Knowledge and Education in Classical Islam*, ed. Sebastian Guenther (Leiden: E. J. Brill, 2020), 941–959.
23. This summary draws on my chapter, "Women in Imāmī Biographical Collections." Further research on Zaydī and Ismāʿīlī sources is necessary to understand women's religious education within these Shīʿī subsects.
24. These observations are based on an examination of the three earliest extant Imāmī works devoted to transmitters of reports (i.e., *rijāl* works) which contain some reference to women. These are al-Ṭūsī's (d. 460/1067), *Ikhtiyār Maʿrifat al-Rijāl*; al-Najāshī's (d. 450/1058–9) *Rijāl*; and al-Ṭūsī's *Rijāl*. There are approximately seventy women who have brief, anecdotal entries in the selected Imāmī sources; see Sayeed, "Women in Imāmī Biographical Collections," 82–84, for a more detailed overview of the listing of female authorities in these works.
25. The impact of the Fāṭimids, as an Ismāʿīlī Shīʿī dynasty, on female *ḥadīth* transmission has yet to be examined.
26. For an evocative biography of Zaynab, see, Muḥsin al-Amīn al-ʿĀmilī, *Aʿyān al-Shīʿa* (Beirut: Dār al-Taʿāruf, 1986) 7:137–142; and for Āmina Khātūn's biography, see Mīrzā al-Iṣfahānī, *Riyāḍ al-ʿulamāʾ wa-ḥiyāḍ al-fuḍalāʾ* (Qum: Maktabat Āyat Allāh al-Marʿashī al-ʿĀmma, 1980–81), 5:407.

Bibliography

Afsaruddin, Asma. "Knowledge, Piety, and Religious Leadership in the Late Middle Ages: Reinstating Women in the Master Narrative." In *Knowledge and Education in Classical Islam*, edited by Sebastian Guenther, 941–959. Leiden: E. J. Brill, 2020.

Afsaruddin, Asma. "Literature, Scholarship, and Piety: Negotiating Gender and Authority in the Medieval Muslim World." *Religion and Literature* 42, no. 1/2 (2010): 111–131.

Alwani, Zainab. "Muslim Women as Religious Scholars: A Historical Survey." In *Muslima Theology, The Voices of Muslim Women Theologians*, edited by Ednan Aslan, Marcia Hermansen, and Elif Medeni, 45–58. Frankfurt am Main: Peter Lang, 2013.

Anthony, Sean W., and Catherine L. Bronson. "Did Ḥafṣah Edit the Qurʾān? A Response with Notes on the Codices of the Prophet's Wives." *Journal of the International Qur'anic Studies Association* 1 (2016): 93–125.

Asma'u, Nana. *Collected Works of Nana Asma'u, Daughter of Usman Dan Fodiyo, (1793–1864)*. African Historical Sources, No. 9. East Lansing: Michigan State University Press, 1997.

Azad, Arezou. "Female Mystics in Mediaeval Islam: The Quiet Legacy." *Journal of the Economic and Social History of the Orient* 56, no. 1 (2013): 53–88.

Bāʿūnīyah, ʿĀʾishah bint Yūsuf. *The Principles of Sufism*. Translated by Th. Emil Homerin. Library of Arabic Literature. New York: New York University Press, 2014.

Bano, Masooda. *Female Islamic Education Movements: The Re-Democratisation of Islamic Knowledge*. Cambridge: Cambridge University Press, 2017.

Booth, Marilyn. *Classes of Ladies of Cloistered Spaces: Writing Feminist History through Biography in Fin de Siècle Egypt*. Edinburgh: Edinburgh University Press, 2015.

Booth, Marilyn. "Exemplary Lives, Feminist Aspirations: Zaynab Fawwāz and the Arabic Biographical Tradition." *Journal of Arabic Literature* 26, no. 1/2 (1995): 120–146.

Booth, Marilyn. *May Her Likes Be Multiplied: Biography and Gender Politics in Egypt*. Berkeley: University of California Press, 2001.

Boyd, Jean. *Educating Muslim Women: The West African Legacy of Nana Asma'u 1793-1864*. Leicestershire: Kube Publishing, 2013.

Cornell, Rkia. *Rabi'a from Narrative to Myth: The Many Faces of Islam's Most Famous Woman Saint, Rabi'a al-'Adawiyya*. London: OneWorld Academic, 2019.

Davary, Bahar. "In Search of Female Authority in Islam: A Contemporary Shiʿa Mojtahede." *Pakistan Journal of Women's Studies Alam-e-Niswan; Karachi* 20, no. 1 (2013): 19–33.

Elsadda, Hoda. "Discourses on Women's Biographies and Cultural Identity: Twentieth-Century Representations of the Life of ʿAʾisha Bint Abi Bakr." *Feminist Studies* 27, no. 1 (2001): 37–64.

Elsayed, Hanan. "'Silence' and Historical Tradition in Assia Djebar's Loin de Médine." *Research in African Literatures* 44, no. 1 (2013): 91–105.

Geissinger, Aisha. " 'A'isha Bint Abi Bakr and Her Contributions to the Formation of the Islamic Tradition." *Religion Compass* 5, no. 1 (2011): 37–49.

Geissinger, Aisha. *Gender and Muslim Constructions of Exegetical Authority: A Rereading of the Classical Genre of Qurʾān Commentary*. Leiden: Brill, 2015.

Geissinger, Aisha. "No, a Woman Did Not 'Edit the Qurʾān': Towards a Methodologically Coherent Approach to a Tradition Portraying a Woman and Written Quranic Materials." *Journal of the American Academy of Religion* 85, no. 2 (January 4, 2017): 416–445.

Geissinger, Aisha. "Portrayal of the Ḥajj as a Context for Women's Exegesis: Textual Evidence in al-Bukhārī's (d. 870) *al-Ṣaḥīḥ*." In *Ideas, Images, and Methods of Portrayal: Insights into Classical Arabic Literature and Islam*, edited by Sebastian Guenther, 153–179. Vol. 58, *Islamic History and Civilization*. Boston and Leiden: Brill, 2005.

Goldziher, Ignaz. *Muslim Studies*, edited by S. M. Stern and translated by C. R. Barber and S. M. Stern. London: Aldine Publishing Co., 1966.

Hassan, Mona F. "Relations, Narrations, and Judgments: The Scholarly Networks and Contributions of an Early Female Muslim Jurist." *Islamic Law and Society* 22 (2015): 323–351.

Kaḥḥāla, ʿUmar Riḍā. *Aʿlām Al-Nisāʾ fī ʿālamay al-ʿArab wa-al-Islām*. Beirut: Muʾassasat al-Risālah, 1977.

Kalmbach, Hilary. "Social and Religious Change in Damascus: One Case of Female Islamic Religious Authority." *British Journal of Middle Eastern Studies* 35, no. 1 (2008): 37–57.

Khan, Ruqayya. "Did a Woman Edit the Qur'an? Hafsa and Her Famed 'Codex.'" *Journal of the American Academy of Religion* 82 (March 1, 2014): 174–216.

Künkler, Mirjam, and Roja Fazaeli. "Life of Two Mujtahidahs: Female Religious Authority in Twentieth Century Iran." In *Women, Leadership and Mosques: Changes in Contemporary Islamic Authority*, edited by Masooda Bano and Hilary Kalmbach. Women and Gender, 11. Boston: Brill, 2012.

Künkler, Mirjam, and Devin Stewart, eds. *Female Religious Authority in Shi'i Islam: Past and Present*. Edinburgh: Edinburgh University Press, 2021.

Mack, Beverly. "Fodiology: African American Heritage Connections to West African Islam." *Journal of West African History* 4, no. 2 (2018): 103–130.

Mack, Beverly. "Nana Asma'u's Instruction and Poetry for Present-Day American Muslimahs." *History in Africa* 38 (2011): 153–168.

Nadwi, Muhammad Akram. *Muḥaddithāt: The Women Scholars in Islam*. Oxford: Interface Publications, 2007.

Ragab, Ahmed. "Epistemic Authority of Women in the Medieval Middle East." *Hawwa* 8, no. 2 (2010): 181–216.

Renne, Elisha P. "Educating Muslim Women and the Izala Movement in Zaria City, Nigeria." *Islamic Africa* 3, no. 1 (2012): 55–86.

Roded, Ruth. "Bint Al-Shati's 'Wives of the Prophet': Feminist or Feminine?" *British Journal of Middle Eastern Studies* 33, no. 1 (2006): 51–66.

Rutner, Maryam. "Religious Authority, Gendered Recognition, and Instrumentalization of Nusrat Amin in Life and after Death." *Journal of Middle East Women's Studies* 11, no. 1 (March 1, 2015): 24–41.

Sayeed, Asma. "Gender and Legal Authority: An Examination of Early Juristic Opposition to Women's Hadith Transmission." *Islamic Law and Society* 16 (2009): 115–150.

Sayeed, Asma. "Women and Ḥadīth Transmission Two Case Studies from Mamluk Damascus." *Studia Islamica*, no. 95 (2002): 71–94.

Sayeed, Asma. *Women and the Transmission of Religious Knowledge in Islam*. New York: Cambridge University Press, 2013.

Sayeed, Asma. "Women in Imāmī Biographical Collections." In *Law and Tradition in Classical Islamic Thought: Studies in Honor of Professor Hossein Modarressi*, edited by Michael Cook et al., 81–97. New York: Palgrave Macmillan, 2013.

Siddiqi, Muhammad Zubair, and Abdal Hakim Murad. *Ḥadīth Literature: Its Origin, Development and Special Features*. Rev. ed. Cambridge: Islamic Texts Society, 1993.

Spellberg, Denise A. *Politics, Gender, and the Islamic Past: The Legacy of 'A'isha Bint Abi Bakr*. New York: Columbia University Press, 1994.

Stewart, Devin. "Women's Biographies in Islamic Societies: Mīrzā ʿAbd Allāh al-Iṣfahānī's Riyāḍ al-ʿUlamāʾ." In *Rhetoric of Biography: Narrating Lives in Persianate Societies*, edited by Louise Marlow, 106–139. Boston: Ilex Foundation, 2011.

Sulamī, Muḥammad ibn al-Ḥusayn. *Early Sufi Women: Dhikr an-Niswa al-Mutaʿabbidāt aṣ-Ṣūfiyyāt*. Translated by Rkia Cornell. Louisville, KY: Fons Vitae, 1999.

CHAPTER 12

MUSLIM WOMEN AND DEVOTIONAL LIFE

ZAHRA AYUBI AND IMAN ABDOULKARIM

MUSLIM women's devotional lives have been subject to broad political, historical, personal, societal, and familial gender dynamics. Historians of Muslim ritual and devotional practices have described women's devotions using at least two dominant paradigms. The first is what we call the "women's alternative practices" paradigm that was most prominently theorized in Leila Ahmed's landmark thesis that following the Prophet Muḥammad's death, there was a systematic marginalization of women from public ritual and religious authority that resulted in separate gendered experiences of Islam. Namely, men live the law and public ritual, while women live ethics and private devotion.[1] Several scholars extend this idea in their description of Muslim women's public rituals (whether based on historical records or ethnographic observation) as a form of resistance that seeks alternatives to normative men's rituals, i.e., congregational daily prayers, Friday, Eid, or funerary prayers from which they might be barred. Examples of women's alternative public or private rituals might be women's visits to Sufi shrines, women's-only Shīʿī gatherings (*majālis*), devotional chanting of Sufi *dhikr/zikr* or singing of devotional poetry, such as the Burda (celebrating the Prophet Muḥammad's birth), and poetry in praise of God, the Prophet, or Islamic beliefs (variously known as *ḥamd*, *naʿat* or *nashīd*).

The second paradigm with which scholars have described Muslim women's devotional lives attempts to recover their religious learning and scholarly authority. Specifically, this scholarship demonstrates that women have long had an independent devotional life as accomplished Sufis, *shaykhas* or religious leaders, and scholars. Scholars often use the phrase "in their own right" to describe women's independent devotional lives as a means to address a historical wrong that assumes religious/devotional women rode the coattails of pious/learned men. Some of these forms of authority fit into the "women's alternative practices" paradigm, while others seek to recover women's authority in normative male traditions of learning.

At the heart of these paradigms of describing women's devotional life are two deeply underlying ontological issues. The first issue concerns beliefs about the Divine intention for women's roles in this life, i.e., whether or not they ought to appear in public, how their sexuality and appearance factor into their participation in the mosque and other ritual/devotional spaces, and what alternatives normative discourses have planned for them. Research on these questions inevitably encounters the issue of how women's sexuality and appearance affect their participation in public rituals. While this may not appear to be an ontological issue, it speaks to many Muslims' deeply held beliefs about the relationship between women's bodies and women's status as decreed by the Creator.

The second ontological issue deals with Muslim beliefs about the nature of women's own relationship with the Divine, i.e., how have women determined this in their expressions of devotion? Is it dependent on men's normative plans for them based on their subordinate status? Or perhaps the question should be whether there is such a thing as women's own relationship with the Divine that is not in some way controlled either by men, overtly or indirectly through gender norms that prohibit women from fully realizing their relationship to the Divine while they still maintain beliefs and practices with varying intensity and ability.

Common in these historiographical accounts of women's devotions is the normative gendered expectation that women are pious when they stay home, observe silently, and devote themselves to God by devoting themselves to their husbands and children, an expectation that appears to have gained ground after the second/eighth century. There is a tension between socially upheld gender norms, such as the patriarchal expectations of wife/motherhood, and the cultivation of the personal devotional life that runs up against the legal literature that attempts to curb women's public religious life. As we discuss below, this tension is apparent in the social history of mosque participation and the division of male and female domains/forms of devotional life. Finally, that tension has come to a head with new Muslim women's-only mosque movements that emerge out of women's historical frustration with their marginalization in public devotional life. More importantly, its language of empowerment additionally serves the dual purpose of asserting religious authority and speaking against patriarchy on a broader scheme, i.e., using devotional life as a medium to address larger ontological questions of women's existence as divine subjects (alongside men), who have rights to spirituality as well as responsibilities to fulfill them. Taking on the obligation to attend prayer is to claim an equal ontological standing with men and proposing that women have the ability to lead prayer is to reimagine markers of Islamic religious authority traditionally unavailable to women.

The rest of this chapter examines the ontological questions and challenges featured in scholarship on Muslim women's otherworldly relationship to the Divine as influenced by the worldly issues of gender norms, authority, and access by: first, accounting for dominant discourses on women's participation in normative practices; next, introducing "women's alternative practices" paradigm used by scholars to examine traditionally unexamined practices and spaces that define women's religious agency; and then examining how parallel movements to recover women's religious learning and religious authority grapple with questions of normativity, agency, and women's engagement with Islamic religious knowledge in complementary and, at times, divergent ways.

Women in Normative Devotional Practices and Spaces

Before we discuss the two paradigms of women's alternative practices and the recovery of their religious learning and authority, it is important to account for discourses on women's participation in normative ritual practices, such as required prayers, attending the mosque, and performing religious pilgrimages. Shampa and Sanjoy Mazumdar have argued that sacred structures communicate what is important in a religion; namely, mandatory Friday congregational prayer (*jumuʿa*) for Muslim men reaffirms their commitment to Islam and religious communities, and male–female sections in mosque communicate the importance of gender segregation for maintaining ritual purity.[2] Prayers in mosques—the five daily prayers and *jumuʿa* prayers—are a focal point for examinations of Muslims' public devotional life. By and large, legal/jurisprudential (*fiqh*) discourses on women's participation and presence in ritual life are preoccupied with the issue of how to manage women's sexual appeal and the maintenance of male integrity in religious spaces. As such they discuss proper age, dress, behavior, and location of women, among other related issues, to maintain acceptable gender segregation. Furthermore, there is a preoccupation with the possible pollution caused to religious or sacred spaces by women's bodies, such as if they are menstruating or taking up space that could be allocated to men. The historical roots of legal and religious pronouncements on women's limited access to the mosque can be traced back to classical *ḥadīth* literature on the topic. Nevin Reda identifies three trends in *ḥadīth* literature following the Prophet's death in 11/632, one of which attempted to keep women from mosques based on a "better than" formula rather than any normative principle. This formula was derived from *ḥadīths* in which the Prophet is reported to have stated that women praying in their homes is better than praying in a mosque. Such *ḥadīths* would ultimately "provide a basis for scholars to prevent women's access to any mosque."[3] The far-reaching extent to which such discourses inform contemporary religious thought and Muslim women's present-day experiences is evidenced in ethnographic research, such as Pia Karlsson Minganti's survey of Muslim women's activism in mosques in Sweden. Activists challenged the equation of women in mosques with *fitna* by emphasizing women's role as "bearers of Islam," reframing *fitna* as passive temptation rather than an active temptress, and attributing *fitna* to both men and women.[4] These strategies aimed to dissolve the link between "woman" and *fitna* and recognize women as "religious subjects, with the right—or rather duty—to attend mosques."[5]

Contemporary discourses that inhibit women's participation in public devotional practices rely on (re)imaginings of women's roles in Islamic history. Understanding

Muslim women's participation, or lack thereof, requires contextualizing their devotion in social and political climates, colonial history, sectarian differences, and more. Consequently, normative Muslim practices become inherently male practices if women are viewed as absent from their inception. For example, Marion Katz has proposed that, during early Islamic history, Muslim women's participation in mosques and public ritual life were not defined by legal jurisprudence, but the inverse. Her survey of the major Sunni schools of jurisprudence demonstrated that jurists often ruled against women's presence in mosques in response to their vigorous participation in real life, as demonstrated by their elaboration on the finer points of women's sexuality and their ability to cause *fitna*, or social upheaval, at various ages.[6]

Depictions of prominent women figures in Islamic history within the domestic roles of wife and mother are essential to locating women's devotional lives within the private sphere. In particular, the wives of Prophet Muḥammad serve as archetypes of women's devotion, but not without rhetorical maneuvering to fit them into such archetypes. For example, Kecia Ali's survey of how the Prophet's narrative has been told over the past two centuries, noted that modern authors build on "ancient descriptions of Khadīja as comforter to depict the act of comforting as a wifely duty."[7] Frequently cited depictions of Khadīja as an "angel" assign religious overtones to marital intimacy, imagery that "links the spiritual and the domestic."[8] However, as Ali has noted, "These ways of speaking about Khadīja draw on early texts that celebrate her pivotal role, yet they are decisively modern in their view of marriage as the center of one's emotional life, and the couple and nuclear household as the proper pattern for family living."[9] In her examination of the legacy of ʿĀʾisha bint Abī Bakr in political and gendered discussions in the medieval period, Denise Spellberg examined how constructions of ʿĀʾisha's direct involvement in the politics of succession and the first Muslim civil war became increasingly crucial during the fourth/tenth century and after, as her role in Islamic history was cited to define conceptions of legitimate leadership among Sunnī and Shīʿī Muslims. However, Spellberg noted that "although Sunni and Shīʿī Muslims disagreed about ʿĀʾisha's responsibility and culpability in the first civil war, they agreed fundamentally about her potential as a negative example for all women."[10] Thus, while ʿĀʾisha is extolled as the Prophet's favorite wife, her political legacy was used by medieval scholars to justify women's exclusion from politics based on their ability to create chaos in the public sphere.

Noting these historical imaginings of women's roles in Islamic history is not to suggest that gender relations in early Islamic history reflect contemporary notions of equality. On the contrary, as Leila Ahmed noted, rulings on hierarchical marriage structures during the time of the Prophet exemplified the tension between the pragmatism that marked rulings during early Islamic history and the "stubborn egalitarianism" that defines the ethical vision of Islam.[11] The lives of women in early Islamic history are sites where this tension plays out, bringing into relief women's contributions to Islam as active agents in the formation of Islamic political and intellectual history on the one hand, and, on the other, women's erasure from current public ritual life on the assumption that women were similarly marginalized in early Islamic history. For example, Kamran Aghaie has attributed the exclusion of women from Shīʿī Muharram rituals, like *ta'zīya* (theatrical performances depicting the Battle of Karbala), as not only the result of expressed governmental contempt for televising women actresses or male actors dressing up as women, but historical accounts that center male martyrs at the expense of pivotal female characters in the narrative.[12] Research on Muharram rituals has often focused entirely on male self-flagellation during the central procession, resulting in the erasure of women from both historical depictions of Muharram and contemporary rituals in its honor.[13] Asma Afsaruddin has studied early biographical accounts of the first Muslims, such as those by Ibn Sa'd (d. 230/845) and retrieved examples of women Companions as active members in public, political, and devotional life—like Umm Waraqa, who led both men and women in prayer. When these accounts are compared with those of later biographers, she discovered that the latter often "had to 'doctor' to a certain extent the early accounts of the lives of the women Companions since, unedited, they conveyed an image somewhat seditiously different from the desired one" and presented women as "anything but cloistered beings residing in grand seclusion in their homes."[14] Thus, modern constructions of the roles of prominent women in Islamic history are useful for illustrating the tension between contemporary restrictive legal/jurisprudential discourses concerning women's participation in public rituals and the ethical vision of Islam.

However, women's limited roles in public rituals, as Mazumdar and Mazumdar have noted, does not equate to a lack of participation in ritual practices or an inability to create meaningful religious lives for themselves, their families, and other women.[15] Expressions of women's religious agency outside of congregational prayer include the reclamation of public ritual spaces for alternative events, development of expertise in Islamic scholarship, occupying roles as preservers of their faith within their homes and among their children, and active engagement in religious holidays.[16] These alternative expressions of religious agency illustrate that an impact of women's limited roles in the public sphere is the formation of devotional practices influenced by women's domestic roles. For example, Mohammad Maaruf examined the gendered aspects of Berber women's participation in public rituals in Morocco and concluded that it is women's influence in the domestic sphere and importance in the household that "is ritually accentuated in socially accepted avenues such as marriage ceremonies, carnivals of *ashura*, carnivals of the Great feast/Bilmawn, jinn evictions and other ritual practices."[17] Although Maaruf's examination highlighted women's participation in public ritual practices, the symbolism and significance of such rituals reiterate normative discourses that synonymize women's devotional status with their roles in the domestic sphere. However, and more importantly, devotional practices informed by women's domestic roles are assigned equal religious significance and meaning as normative public rituals and enhance women's relationship with the Creator.

Gender norms are not the only identity-based discourses that have informed the relationship between women's devotional practices and the private sphere. Sylvia Chan-Malik's notion of "insurgent domesticity" has accounted for how race-based discourses complicate depictions of Muslim women in the domestic sphere. Popular images of US Muslim women as wives and mothers in discourses on the Nation of Islam (NOI) during the Cold War era depicted an "insurgent domesticity" that "performed a specific type of ideological work that rendered the domestic lives of Muslim women as sites of political struggle."[18] In constructing marriage and motherhood as Islamic rituals and essential to *being* Muslim amid the "crisis of masculinity" for white American men during the Cold War era, US Muslim women were "engaged historical actors who rendered acts of gendered 'submission' into forms of religious ritual, political protest, and national threat."[19] Depictions of women's devotional lives as intimately connected to fulfilling their domestic roles countered negative depictions of broken black families and feminized black men and, as Su'ad Abdul Khabeer noted, challenged constructions of blackness as "surplus, excess, and lack" while simultaneously illustrating the influence of gendered and sexualized class tensions within NOI politics.[20] The domestic insurgency that underscored US women's devotional lives in the Cold War era demonstrates the need to consider how gender, race, and women's other intersectional identities challenge logics surrounding their participation in normative Muslim practices.

Women's Alternative Religious Practices

Despite Muslim women's overall historical marginalization or absence from congregational prayer, they have been active participants in mosques across time periods and locations. Drawing on nineteenth-century accounts of travel to Ottoman Istanbul that describe women's frequent visits to mosques in between prayers and increased presence during the month of Ramadan, Marion Katz has concluded that "the relative absence of women appears to have applied more to the specific ritual activity of congregational prayers than to mosque space per se."[21] Thus, it was not the gendering of space that necessarily defined Muslim women's relationship to the mosque, but the gendering of activities.[22] The argument that gendered activities have historically played a significant role in determining women's access to devotional spaces and rituals has led scholars to examine women's religious agency through examples of alternative devotional practices that cultivate their relationship to the Creator in spite of restrictive gender norms.

Much of Muslim women's alternative religious practices fall under the rubric of mystical or Sufi devotions. Although it is debatable whether Sufi practices are an alternative or mainstream aspect of Muslim devotional life, they constitute a major part of women's devotional lives historically and now. Examples of alternative practices include the recitation of devotional songs and poems, visits to Sufi shrines, and membership in historically male and more recently women-led Sufi orders or *ṭarīqas*. The aim of these alternative practices is progression along the spiritual path with the goal of achieving a direct relationship with the Creator and knowledge of the world's essential truths. However, scholars have questioned whether Sufi devotional practices offer women unmediated knowledge of the Divine or if Sufi spiritual paths are inherently gendered.

While Margaret Smith has argued that mystical devotion is the only Islamic discourse in which women have the potential to become equals because of the influential legacy of women mystics, Annemarie Schimmel, and more recently, Scott Kugle and Rkia Cornell have shown there is great complexity in the way women have figured in Sufi discourses.[23] Attitudes toward women's mystical activities have ranged from tolerance of women who are related to male saints to championing women who are teachers and *shaykhas* (spiritual leaders) themselves. Amila Butorovic has noted that women mystics have "left a powerful legacy that adds to the Sufi path a new metaphoric depth and a great symbolic diversity."[24] However, she has concluded that such a legacy "does not affect in any transformative way Muslim women's social status" because Sufism is not a social reform movement.[25] Unlike male mystics, women maintain their social, familial, and household responsibilities while being on a devotional path in creative ways that show their agency but do not revise the totality of gender roles within the Sufi realm.

Sectarian *ziyārāt*, or pilgrimages, to sites of local religious importance have typically served as alternative devotional practices in which gender and the free-mixing of bodies have played a crucial role in their formation.[26] For example, Anne Betteridge's ethnographic work has noted that women in Shiraz, Iran, are more likely to make pilgrimages to local Shīʿī shrines than their male peers. Reasons for women's increased involvement are twofold: first, men are more likely to make pilgrimages to larger shrines considered more legitimate by religious authorities, second, the informal nature of local pilgrimages has served as an alternative to more formalized religious practices often denied to women due to concerns of their sexual appeal in religious spaces.[27] Pilgrimage to local shrines has created a religious space for events such as Qur'an classes, prayer sessions, funerals, and other religious events in which women are likely to be more involved.[28] Similarly, Nancy Tapper in her ethnographic examination of *ziyārāt*, in Eğirdir, Turkey, notes women's comparatively active participation in local pilgrimages to religiously significant shrines compared to that of men's, who often regard the practice as "verging on heresy."[29] However, women's visits to shrines provide an opportunity to exercise significant autonomy in their ability "to choose their company, to manage the outing, and to construct a personal relationship with God via the saint."[30]

While the women's alternative practices paradigm has recovered women's religious agency by examining the unique ways they cultivate a relationship with the Creator despite their restricted access to public religious spaces and practices, this paradigm is complicated when considering whether different, gender-based devotional practices equate to different, gender-based statuses as devotional beings. Scholar-activist amina wadud, author of the first women-inclusive reading of the Quran, put forward the *tawhidic* (unity of God) paradigm to argue that gender restrictions on women's devotional practices and roles have undermined the unity or oneness of God as the sole Creator. In other words, it is the equivalent of idolatry to say that men are the mediators between women and God or have an ontological superiority over women—as suggested by men's increased responsibility to perform normative devotional acts—because it would suggest that men have a God-like status. Thus, "if human beings really are horizontally equal, independent, and mutually codependent, each has the same potential for performing any social, religious, political, or economic task."[31] It is the tension between women's ontological equality as devotional beings and restrictions placed upon them as developers, practitioners, and leaders of Islamic devotional life that has catalyzed women-led hermeneutical and jurisprudential inquiries into the justification for women's marginalization within the public religious sphere. Such inquiries, most notably by those like wadud, have challenged suggestions that women are not able to cultivate a relationship to the Divine, fulfill the same devotional obligations, and know Islam in the same way as men. This suggests a different and equally important question at the center of inquiries into women's devotional lives, one that examines not only how women engage with alternative practices to exercise religious agency but also why such alternative practices are needed in the first place. Varying engagements and answers to these questions have been offered by women's revivalist movements in particular and are explored in the following section.

Recovery of Women's Religious Learning and Authority: Academics, Reformists, and Revivalists

A second paradigm used to understand Muslim women's devotional lives centers on the recovery of their access to religious knowledge and ability to exercise equal religious authority as men. This recovery is being carried out by three distinct but sometimes overlapping groups of women: academics, reformists, and revivalists. Contemporary Muslim women's feminist movements as well as religious revivalist movements (which are interestingly at odds) aim to enhance women's religious education and highlight the impact of gender norms on women's devotional life. Conversations surrounding contemporary women's movements are contextualized by discourses on early Islamic history that assess women's access to religious education, their contributions to Islamic religious knowledge, and their long-held roles as religious educators within their communities and families. Muslim academic scholars, often in a devotional, faithful move, ask gender-critical questions of Muslim history in order to either recover or assert women's access to the Islamic intellectual tradition.

Scholars like Leila Ahmed, and more recently Asma Sayeed, have offered accounts of the learning of early Muslim women that seek to recover their religious authority. Sayeed's work supports Leila Ahmed's assertion that early Muslim women "were important contributors to the verbal texts of Islam, the texts that, transcribed eventually into written form by men, became part of the official history of Islam and of the literature that established the normative practices of Islamic society."[32] Sayeed analyzed women's status as *ḥadīth* transmitters in the first ten centuries of Islamic history. Her findings note that women's participation in *ḥadīth* transmission in the first century and a half after the death of the Prophet was curtailed by the professionalization of *ḥadīth* transmission during the second and third century. However, women's roles as extolled *ḥadīth* transmitters reemerged during the fourth century of Islamic history (tenth century of the common era) due to the rise of Sunni Islam, and then witnessed a sharp reduction during the early Ottoman period.[33] The ebbs and flows of women's access to religious knowledge as *ḥadīth* transmitters is contextualized by the shifting sociopolitical and cultural shifts that marked the first ten centuries of Islamic history. Sayeed argued that her chronology challenges two dominant discourses, one that views Muslim women's religious education in Islamic history as always marked by oppression, and the other that "promotes an unfailingly positive account of educational access and opportunities for Muslim women throughout history" by referencing the achievements of well-known early figures, such as ʿĀʾisha bint Abī Bakr.[34]

Contemporary approaches toward women-led Islamic reform movements draw on women's long-held status as contributors to Islamic religious knowledge, which has led to a resurgence of women's formalized religious education and a growing number of prominent *shaykhas* or women religious scholars with transnational platforms. It is important to note that these movements are not unified, nor do they share the same ideas about gender roles in Islam. Many women's groups are trying to address the issue of women in Islam, often in response to Western critiques that Muslim women are oppressed. Their approaches vary widely from assertions of women's religious authority in order to support or defend what they view as Islamic, complementary gender roles to absolute, unequivocal gender equality. The question of women's religious authority has been approached in at least two ways: revivalist and reformist. Revivalist movements have focused on increasing women's access to religious knowledge as supported by Islamic texts and early Islamic history, while reformist approaches have aimed to reimagine women's status in Islam and offer, at times, historically unprecedented approaches toward Islamic religious knowledge and visions for women's status as religious leaders.

Among these three groups, the revivalist movements are arguably the most prominent and have exerted the most influence at the grassroots level in a number of Muslim-majority societies. The following section briefly examines how some of these contemporary revivalist movements advocate for women's increased access to religious learning, but offer distinct constructions and approaches toward women's religious authority.

Popular Women's Revivalist Movements

An example of a revivalist movement that aims to increase women's access to religious education is Farhat Hashmi's Pakistan-based, international conservative Islamic revivalist movement. Her organization, Al-Huda ("the Guidance"), is a transnational network of female students and preachers who have created formal spaces for women's religious learning in twenty-eight cities in Pakistan as well as in Canada, and informally through the use of Al-Huda publications in London, Damascus, and the

United States.[35] Similarly, the Qubaysī movement, originally based in Syria, has established itself as one of the largest women's piety movements in the world. Before the war in Syria, Qubaysī managed over half of the female madrasas, or religious schools, in Damascus with over 75,000 students, and their publications have spread internationally.[36] As with all expressions of Islam, women's piety movements and organizations are highly contextualized by the sociopolitical climates in which they function. While scholars may look down at these women and their movements, the result of generations of Muslim women with direct access to religious thought, coupled with their own life experiences, will inevitably threaten, deviate from, or otherwise compete with the male monopoly over interpretations of Islamic scriptural sources and their applications.

Though women's revivalist movements advance women's access to religious education, the aim of such efforts is not necessarily the disruption of the status quo but the enhancement of women's piety. Scholars have noted that the absence of an explicitly resistant stance toward the social norms or systems of power that curtail women's religious education complicate constructions of revivalist movements as social reform initiatives. Saba Mahmood famously articulated the questions at the heart of this assessment in her ethnography of the Women's Mosque Movement in Egypt:

> How do we conceive of individual freedom in a context where the distinction between the subject's own desires and socially prescribed performance cannot be easily presumed, and where submission to certain forms of (external) authority is a constitution for achieving the subject's potentiality? In other words, how does one make the question of politics integral to the analysis of the architecture of the self?[37]

For the women in Mahmood's ethnography, and likely for women in other female-led Islamic revivalist movements, the primary objective is not challenging established social structures but leading a life of devotion and piety. This forces one to question the importance of social structures and politics when the goal of revivalist movements is to promote women's full self-actualization as devotional beings. Sayeed echoes Mahmood's skepticism toward contemporary frameworks of subordination versus resistance to account for women's piety. Although communal norms informed women's actions and access to education during the classical era, which was marked by the revival of women *ḥadīth* transmitters, "it is through embracing and upholding those norms, not subverting them, that they acquired stature and, in all likelihood, personal fulfillment."[38]

Critiques of contemporary revivalist movements highlight a similar relationship between women's religious learning and gendered social norms. Based on her ethnographic research at Al-Huda headquarters, Khanum Shaikh has critiqued the organization and Hashmi's scholarship for placing women's religious obligations within the domestic sphere and that of men within the public arena. She notes that Hashmi and teachers at Al-Huda respond to such critiques by justifying their teachings as the word of the Qur'an. However, Shaikh has argued that such a defense is a "problematic assertion of a direct, unmediated relationship to the Divine text, and a subsequent denial that for centuries there has been a diversity of approaches to reading and interpreting the Qur'an and Hadith."[39] Shaikh's criticism of Al-Huda has identified a contradiction in the organization's lack of critical engagement with social norms when notions of women's piety, women's status as devotional beings, and the organization's interpretations of Islamic texts is informed by them.

Sayeed's historiography, Mahmood's theoretical critique of binary understandings of subordination versus resistance, and Shaikh's assessment of Al-Huda have exposed complicated ontological questions at the heart of revivalist movements. Revivalist movements do not challenge hierarchical constructions of women as subordinate devotional beings by emphasizing their right to religious knowledge; but, such initiatives place Muslim women's full self-actualization as pious, devotional subjects as their interest, even though it risks perpetuating their status as subordinate subjects within their respective sociopolitical contexts or communities. Thus, revivalist movements normalize women's possession of religious authority.

Conclusion

There are two main paradigms scholars have used to understand Muslim women's devotional lives. First, the "women's alternative practices" paradigm accounts for the alternative practices and spaces women use to cultivate a relationship to the Divine and exercise their religious agency, despite their marginalization within public ritual practices and spaces. Many of these alternative practices and spaces fall under the mystical or Sufi realm of practice, which raises the question of whether they are truly "alternative" to normative Muslim devotion, since mysticism is so widespread in Muslim history and geography. The second paradigm accounts for efforts at recovery of women's access to religious learning and authority, which adopt divergent approaches for grappling with the relationship between women's devotional lives and the gender norms and systems of power that inform their lived realities and the Islamic religious tradition. Some Islamic revivalist women's movements are focused on responding to "Western" influence that has dismantled traditional gender roles and simultaneously reclaiming women's religious authority to do so. In outlining these paradigms, it becomes clear that the category of gender blurs the line drawn between the physical, embodied world and the Divine, making women's devotional lives critical sites for examining the interdependent relationship between the characteristics that define this world and the qualities of the next. This creates opportunities to take a philosophical approach to studying what devotion to the Divine tells us about ontological understandings of gender.

Notes

1. Leila Ahmed, *Women and Gender in Islam* (New Haven, CT: Yale University Press, 1992), 66; Leila Ahmed, *A Border Passage: From Cairo to America—A Woman's Journey* (New York: Farrar, Straus and Giroux, 1999), 123–124.
2. Shampa Mazumdar and Sanjoy Mazumdar, "Religion and Place Attachment: A Study of Sacred Places," *Journal of Environmental Psychology* 24, no. 3 (2004): 390.
3. Nevin Reda, "Women in the Mosque: Historical Perspectives on Segregation," *American Journal of Islamic Social Sciences* 21, no. 2 (2004): 94.
4. Pia Karlsson Minganti," Challenging from Within: Youth Associations and Female Leadership in Swedish Mosques," in *Women, Leadership, and Mosques*, ed. Masooda Bano and Hilary E. Kalmbach (Leiden: Brill, 2012), 377.
5. Ibid.
6. Marion Holmes Katz, *Women in the Mosque: A History of Legal Thought and Social Practice* (New York: Columbia University Press, 2014).
7. Kecia Ali, *The Lives of Muhammad* (Cambridge, MA: Harvard University Press, 2014), 121.
8. Ibid., 122.
9. Ibid., 122–123.
10. Denise A. Spellberg, *Politics, Gender, and the Islamic Past: The Legacy of Aisha Bint Abi Bakr* (New York: Columbia University Press, 2012), 149.
11. Leila Ahmed, *Women and Gender in Islam*. (New Haven, CT: Yale University Press, 1992), 63.
12. Kamran Scot Aghaie, *The Women of Karbala: Ritual Performance and Symbolic Discourses in Modern Shi'i Islam* (Austin: University of Texas Press, 2005), 14.
13. Ibid.
14. Asma Afsaruddin, *The First Muslims: History and Memory* (Oxford: Oneworld Publications, 2008), 190; see also her article "Early Women Exemplars and the Construction of Gendered Space: (Re-)Defining Feminine Moral Excellence," in *Harem Histories: Envisioning Places and Living Spaces*, ed. Marilyn Booth (Durham, NC: Duke University Press, 2010), 23–48.
15. Shampa Mazumdar and Sanjoy Mazumdar, "Ritual Lives of Muslim Women: Agency in Everyday Life," *Journal of Ritual Studies* (1999): 58–70.
16. Ibid.
17. Mohammed Maarouf, "'Āšūrā' as a Female Ritual Challenge to Masculinity," *Arabica* 56, no. 4 (2009): 443.
18. Sylvia Chan-Malik, *Being Muslim: A Cultural History of Women of Color in American Islam* (New York: New York University Press, 2018), 77.
19. Ibid., 98.
20. Su'ad Abdul Khabeer, *Muslim Cool: Race, Religion, and Hip Hop in America* (New York University Press, 2016), 224.
21. Katz, *A History of Women's Mosque Access*, 192.
22. Ibid., 194.
23. Margaret Smith, *Rábi'a: The Life and Work of Rábi'a and Other Women Mystics in Islam* (Oxford: Oneworld, 1994); Annemarie Schimmel, *My Soul Is a Woman: The Feminine in Islam* (New York: Continuum, 1997); Scott Kugle, *Sufis and Saints' Bodies: Mysticism, Corporeality, and Sacred Power in Islam* (Chapel Hill: University of North Carolina Press,

2007); Rkia Cornell, *Rabi`a from Narrative to Myth: The Many Faces of Islam's Most Famous Woman Saint, Rabi`a al-`Adawiyya* (Oxford: Oneworld, 2019).

24. Amila Butorovic, "Between the Tariqa and the Shari'a: The Making of the Female Self," in *Feminist Poetics of the Sacred: Creative Suspicion*, ed. Frances Devlin-Glass and Lyn McCredden (Oxford: Oxford University Press, 2001), 135.
25. Ibid.
26. Sophia Rose Arjana, *Pilgrimage in Islam: Traditional and Modern Practices* (London: Oneworld, 2017).
27. Anne H. Betteridge, "Muslim Women and Shrines in Shiraz," in *Everyday Life in the Muslim Middle East*, ed. Donna L. Bowen and Evelyn A. Early (Bloomington: Indiana University Press, 2014), 277.
28. Ibid., 280–283.
29. Nancy Tapper, "Ziyaret: Gender, Movement, and Exchange in a Turkish Community," in *Muslim Travellers: Pilgrimage, Migration and the Religious Imagination*, ed. Dale F. Eickelman and James Piscatori (London: Routledge, 1990), 247.
30. Ibid., 248.
31. Amina wadud, *Inside the Gender Jihad: Women's Reform in Islam* (Oxford: Oneworld, 2008), 168–169.
32. Ahmed, *Women and Gender in Islam*, 43.
33. Asma Sayeed, *Women and the Transmission of Religious Knowledge in Islam* (New York: Cambridge University Press, 2013).
34. Ibid., 2.
35. Khanum Shaikh, "New Expressions of Religiosity: Al-Huda International and the Expansion of Islamic Education for Pakistani Muslim Women," in *Women and Islam*, ed. Zayn R. Kassam (Santa Barbara, CA: Praeger, 2010), 166.
36. Katherine Zoepf, "Islamic Revival in Syria Is Led by Women," *New York Times*, August 29, 2006, accessed December 3, 2018, https://archive.nytimes.com/www.nytimes.com/ref/world/middleeast/29syria.html.
37. Saba Mahmood, *Politics of Piety: The Islamic Revival and the Feminist Subject* (Princeton, NJ: Princeton University Press, 2012), 31.
38. Sayeed, *Women and the Transmission of Religious Knowledge in Islam*,18.
39. Shaikh, "New Expressions of Religiosity," 180.

Bibliography

Abdul Khabeer, Su'ad. *Muslim Cool: Race, Religion, and Hip Hop in America.* New York: New York University Press, 2016.

Afsaruddin, Asma. *The First Muslims: History and Memory.* Oxford: Oneworld Publications, 2008.

Afsaruddin, Asma. "Early Women Exemplars and the Construction of Gendered Space: (Re-)Defining Feminine Moral Excellence." In *Harem Histories: Envisioning Places and Living Spaces*, edited by Marilyn Booth, 23–48. Durham, NC: Duke University Press, 2010.

Aghaie, Kamran Scot, ed. *The Women of Karbala: Ritual Performance and Symbolic Discourses in Modern Shi'i Islam.* Austin: University of Texas Press, 2005.

Ahmed, Leila. *A Border Passage: From Cairo to America—A Woman's Journey.* New York: Penguin Books, 2012.

Ahmed, Leila. *Women and Gender in Islam: Historical Roots of a Modern Debate*. Philadelphia: University of Pennsylvania Press, 2011.

Ali, Kecia. *The Lives of Muhammad*. Cambridge, MA: Harvard University Press, 2014.

Arjana, Sophia Rose. *Pilgrimage in Islam: Traditional and Modern Practices*. London: Oneworld Publications, 2017.

Betteridge, Anne H. "Muslim Women and Shrines in Shiraz." In *Everyday Life in the Muslim Middle East*, edited by Donna L. Bowen and Evelyn A. Early, 276–289. Bloomington: Indiana University Press, 2014.

Butorovic, Amila. "Between the Tariqa and the Shari'a: The Making of the Female Self." In *Feminist Poetics of the Sacred: Creative Suspicions*, edited by Frances Devlin-Glass and Lyn McCredden, 135–150. Oxford: Oxford University Press, 2001.

Chan-Malik, Sylvia. *Being Muslim: A Cultural History of Women of Color in American Islam*. New York: New York University Press, 2018.

Cornell, Rkia. *Rabi`a From Narrative to Myth: The Many Faces of Islam's Most Famous Woman Saint, Rabi`a al-`Adawiyya*. Oxford: Oneworld, 2019.

Katz, Marion Holmes. *Women in the Mosque: A History of Legal Thought and Social Practice*. New York: Columbia University Press, 2014.

Kugle, Scott. *Sufis and Saints' Bodies: Mysticism, Corporeality, and Sacred Power in Islam*. Chapel Hill: University of North Carolina Press, 2007.

Maarouf, Mohammed. "Āšūrā'as a Female Ritual Challenge to Masculinity." *Arabica* 54, no. 4 (2009): 400–439.

Mahmood, Saba. *Politics of Piety: The Islamic Revival and the Feminist Subject*. Princeton, NJ: Princeton University Press, 2012.

Mazumdar, Shampa, and Sanjoy Mazumdar. "Religion and Place Attachment: A Study of Sacred Places." *Journal of Environmental Psychology* 24, no. 3 (2004): 385–397.

Mazumdar, Shampa, and Sanjoy Mazumdar. "Ritual Lives of Muslim Women: Agency in Everyday Life." *Journal of Ritual Studies* 13, no. 2 (1999): 58–70.

Minganti, Pia Karlsson. "Challenging from Within: Youth Associations and Female Leadership in Swedish Mosques." In *Women, Leadership, and Mosques*, edited by Masooda Bano and Hilary E. Kalmbach, 371–391. Leiden: Brill, 2012.

Reda, Nevin. "Women in the Mosque: Historical Perspectives on Segregation." *American Journal of Islamic Social Sciences* 21, no. 2 (2004): 77–97.

Sayeed, Asma. *Women and the Transmission of Religious Knowledge in Islam*. New York: Cambridge University Press, 2013.

Schimmel, Annemarie. *My Soul Is a Woman: The Feminine in Islam*. New York: Continuum, 1997.

Shaikh, Khanum. "New Expressions of Religiosity: Al-Huda International and the Expansion of Islamic Education for Pakistani Muslim Women." In *Women and Islam*, edited by Zayn R. Kassam, 163–184. Santa Barbara, CA: Praeger, 2010.

Smith, Margaret. *Rábi'a: The Life and Work of Rábi'a and Other Women Mystics in Islam*. Oxford: Oneworld, 1994.

Spellberg, Denise A. *Politics, Gender, and the Islamic Past: The Legacy of Aisha Bint Abi Bakr*. New York: Columbia University Press, 2012.

Tapper, Nancy. "Ziyaret: Gender, Movement, and Exchange in a Turkish Community." In *Muslim Travellers: Pilgrimage, Migration and the Religious Imagination*, edited by Dale F. Eickelman and James Piscatori, 236–255. London: Routledge, 1990.

Wadud, amina. *Inside the Gender Jihad: Women's Reform in Islam*. Oxford: Oneworld, 2008.

Zoepf, Katherine. "Islamic Revival in Syria Is Led by Women." *New York Times*. August 29, 2006. Accessed December 3, 2018. https://archive.nytimes.com/www.nytimes.com/ref/world/middleeast/29syria.html.

CHAPTER 13

WOMEN AS LITTÉRATEURS IN THE PREMODERN PERIOD

SAMER M. ALI

Challenges in Writing about Women Littérateurs in the Premodern Period

WOMEN produced and consumed literature in premodern Arabo-Islamic cultures in ways that have scarcely been explored, much less understood, in the contemporary West.

Centuries of condescending attitudes in the West, called "Orientalism," have explicitly or implicitly served the interests of imperialism in Africa and Asia, thus inquiry into Arabo-Islamic cultures began with preconceptions about the abject otherness of the amorphous "Orient," incapable of self-representation.[1] This approach sidelined evidence of phenomena that defied preconceived categories and constrained a rigorous understanding of women's roles as littérateurs and agents in society. Europe's biases stemmed from displacements and projections of anxieties about sex, gender, and miscegenation of races; thus when the West saw itself as chaste and restrained, the "Orient" was otherized as the opposite: a canvas of barbarous hypersexuality and bawdiness, depicted by scores of orientalist writers and painters dreaming of harems; bathhouses; nude men, women, and children; and belly-dancers, as in the writings of T. E. Lawrence, Gertrude Bell, and Edward Lane and the paintings of Ingres, Delacroix, Gérôme, Matisse, and Chassériau.[2] In the mid-twentieth century, when European sexual mores relaxed with the liberation movements of the 1960s, orientalists reotherized the Orient largely as an abject place of sexless, repressed, and frustrated men and women. In assessing the impact of preconceptions on our subject, their injustice lies in their casual power to simplify and immobilize the complexity of human phenomena, rather than engage in open-ended discovery leading to deeper levels of understandings.

Sources for Writing about Women Littérateurs in the Premodern Period

Given the history of the field, it is no wonder that many people assume that women contributed little to Islamic literary production, or that little remains of such production. However, based on current assessments, medieval authors have transmitted and recorded the speech of some 400 women, mostly poets. We use the broad category of speech, since women's works include many overlapping types of speech, such as poetry (*shiʿr*), verse fragment (*qiṭʿa*), stories (*akhbār*), and orations (*khuṭab*) among others, and medieval and modern scholars often use the umbrella category of "women's rhetoric" (*balāghāt al-nisāʾ*; literally, "women's persuasive speech") to indicate performative efficacy in situ. The extent and quality of rhetoric might be deemed surprising when compared to the corpora of other medieval world cultures, and more discoveries are possible. The primary sources of evidence for women's rhetoric are three types: (1) collections of poetry (sg. *dīwān*) that gather and transmit verse ascribed to individually named women poets, such as the collection of al-Khansāʾ, ʿUlayya bint al-Mahdī, Wallāda bint al-Mustakfī, and Mashhadānī's curation of Ḥujayja's works; or (2) mixed-gender anthologies of poetry that feature the literature of women, named and unnamed, presented side by side with that of men, such as the *Book of Songs* (*Kitāb al-Aghānī*) by al-Iṣfahānī; or (3) literary compendia particularly dedicated to rhetoric by women, such as those curated by Ibn Abī Ṭāhir Ṭayfūr, al-Marzubānī, al-Suyūṭī, Yamūt, or Muhannā. The latter category suggests that, from the pre-Islamic to the modern period, the concept of women's rhetoric (*balāghāt al-nisāʾ*) fascinated literary experts and amateurs alike, as thought, discourse, and social practice, evidenced in Arabic sources.

One might note two particular reasons for this robust legacy: (1) since the earliest pagan poetry, women were depicted as the limerent poet's love interest in romantic poetry (*ghazal*), tragic-lyrical poetry (*ʿudhrī*), as well as the lyrical opening (*nasīb*) of the classical ode (*qaṣīda*); and (2) the leitmotif of the Arabic literary tradition was the power of rhetoric (*balāgha, bayān, khiṭāb*) to alter social circumstances, particularly hierarchical relations. Thus, women littérateurs were one of many test cases, along with other marginalized groups, that demonstrated the power of rhetoric to challenge the biases, misogyny, and abuses of patriarchy. A third reason is the fact that the Prophet's household comprised primarily womenfolk, and he had no sons who survived childhood, which ipso facto expressed the will of God and surely troubled male triumphalism. Despite opposition in some quarters, his wives and daughters did in fact rise to prominence as key eyewitnesses to the Prophet's conduct in his private life. Their prominence indicates early Muslim recognition of their access and authority to speak and to report *ḥadīth* from an unparalleled perspective of privilege. A fourth reason is that despite obvious gender-specific threats, like maternal mortality, women who survived those perils could lay claim to the power of fertility and longevity: In youth, women had a distinctive bodily connection with conception and life, and in seniority enjoyed longer life spans on average, thus outliving men and being in a better position to contend for credibility in speech in a cultural system that favored age and precedence.

Beyond these practical realities, it is important to note common beliefs that favored women: (a) longevity was traditionally associated with insight, wisdom, and prophecy in Semitic cultures; despite stories of aged male prophets, to the contrary, more women than men lived into their seventies and beyond; (b) the sacrality of women ancestors and deities in Near Eastern cultures, no doubt, augmented the stature of women's speech; and (c) robust roles for women, either as heroines, protagonists, or in supporting roles, were particularly featured in Arabic folk epics, such as al-Amīra Dhāt al-Himma, ʿAbla in the Epic of ʿAntara, and ʿAntara's daughter who succeeds him as heir, and Shahrazad in the *1001 Nights*, all of which suggest that folk/vernacular Islam established inspiring role models for girls and women as a countercurrent to male dominance in culture. These women in literature held and expended various forms of power (*yad* or *sulṭa*) and legitimacy (*sharʿiyya* or *masdaqiyya*), which conferred on them "power to do things" (*malaka* or capacity), and granted them "power over" (*mulk* or dominance) and "power with" (*tamāsuk* or solidarity) others. Most importantly, these literary depictions suggest a theory in narrative form positing the ways that social and rhetorical power mutually constitute one another, which offered new possibilities of exercising agency and pride in the everyday lives of women. A final reason is that beyond that, the Qur'anic text and its legacy planted in popular imagination the legitimacy of women as prophets (Mary) and queens (Bilqīs of Sheba), while affirming the equality and dignity of women before God and his law, at least in principle. Powerful women in history, such as the ruler of Egypt Shajarat al-Durr (d. 655/1257) and the women poets discussed below, implicitly benefited from the legacy of autochthonous feminist counterculture. The record of these women's deeds in sources attests to the interests, even admiration, of later generations, including that of men.

Reorientations

Many scholars have found it helpful to use "emic" critical terms for analysis rather than "etic" ones. Drawn from anthropology, emic terms are the ones used in the local culture to reflect lived experience, as opposed to etic ones imported from a modern Western context. As such, the French term "belle-lettres" poses problems by connoting and denoting high-class, formal (not functional) literature, which aligns with the Romantic notion of art for art's sake, while the premodern Arabic term *adab* included a wider range of artistic and literary productions. *Adab* might correspond functionally to our educational term "humanities," since it encompasses a broad array of artistic pursuits, blending genres, registers, and aims. *Adab* in reality was more complex than simple terms like "belle-lettres," "literature," or "writings." Typically, premodern littérateurs from the pagan to the late Ottoman periods made sport out of blending categories, by interlacing form and function, and braiding class, Bedouin, and urban registers of language, as well as integrating brainy-bawdy sensibilities (ascetic wisdom *and* bacchic wine-poetry, for example) and oral-written modes of composition and transmission. No doubt, *adab* texts were taken as prestige models for education and self-cultivation, but the breadth of those models contained an eclectic diversity that reflected a surprisingly wide spectrum of voices drawing on class, gender, homo- and heteroerotic, and other social differences.

Most importantly, medieval Arabic sources articulate a theory of literature that posits *adab* humanities as sculpting human excellence and leadership. Al-Thaʿālibī (d. 429/1038) notes, for example, "He who does not study *adab* in youth leads no one in adulthood."[3] The poet Abū Tammām (d. ca. 232/846) likewise observed the vital role of poetry in defining the catalog of virtues that inspire leadership: "Were it not for a *sunna*-precedent set by poetry, those seeking greatness would know not how to attain excellence"; here, his use of *sunna* hints at the semiprophetic status of poets.[4] Far beyond European Romantic notions of art for art's sake, *adab* in Arabic was seen as formative of character (personally), polis (socially), and leadership (politically). Thus, women's acculturation in *adab* knowledge—as audiences, amateurs, or professionals—was fundamentally political, and potentially threatening to patriarchy. *Adab* education in this context sowed the seeds of women's excellence and leadership.

Survey of the Literature

The earliest extant Arabic poetry comes from the pre-Islamic pagan era (approximately the sixth century). Though most Arabs at the time must have lived in the verdant highlands of Yemen or oasis towns, like Mecca and Medina (formerly Yathrib), where many earned a livelihood from farming or trade, a small but key percentage lived a rustic life as tribal nomads of the desert, called Bedouins, widely lyricized in poetry, legend, and lore. The desert environment was intense, and left no room for a central government, thus, disputes needed to be resolved locally with recourse to enduring codes of honor. Violations of codes would need to be enforced by respected tribes or federations that would initiate either statecraft or warfare. Elite women, who were veiled and sheltered from the public eye, had a vested interest in influencing the proceedings of war and peace, since violent attack would often mean not only swift death for men but also the unthinkable risks of rape, concubinage, or slavery for women and girls. In effect, elite women had a gender-based obligation to voice their interests as a constituency, using ritual genres such as inciting (*taḥrīd*) men to go fight, when necessary, sometimes by calling out cowards and questioning their sense of honor, or offering encouragement (*tashjīʿ*), if men happened to be on the right course, and hold out the promise of elegy (*marthiyya*) for brave men killed in the line of duty, as the ultimate act of fealty in memoriam. Beyond the aims of the moment, in the long term, these lamentations revitalized a code of honor that served as the regulatory framework for the Bedouin system of self-governance. Women's poetry was therefore crucial to maintaining checks and balances on inter- and intratribal governance and to preventing timidity or incompetence from prevailing, when common defense was needed. Due to vested interests, women did much of the memorial work to pass on values to the next generation. Their poetry was marked by the use of memorable sobriquets, indicated here with title caps, such as those in the outraged elegy of al-Khirniq bint Badr: "Let my kinsmen never perish! Men who are the Enemy's Poison, The Slaughter Camels' Bane [i.e., mark of generosity], The Leaders in Every Battle . . . The Sword Strikers in the Thick of Battle, The Lance Thrusters."[5]

Poetic practices over time established gender norms and rituals, much like gender-specific clothing. However, certain poetic figures, men and women alike, made it a point to transgress those norms, and their work thus displayed a type of poetic cross-dressing, which served poetic and political aims. One example was the male poet, Muhalhil ibn Abī Rabīʿa, whom lore depicted as not conforming to masculine gender expectations and thus unable or unwilling to take up the mantle of his fallen brother, Kulayb Wāʾil, who was a fearsome figure in pre-Islamic lore and one of the most storied victims of the War of Basūs, one of the tribal wars of the pre-Islamic period mentioned in the *Ayyām al-ʿArab*.[6] Muhalhil's example illustrates better than most how poetry, like clothing, became associated with gender expectations, but could be borrowed for the sake of poetic cross-dressing. Evoking an oedipal struggle, Kulayb had taunted Muhalhil for his dalliances and gender ambiguity, and upon the death of Kulayb, the latter could not bring himself to avenge his brother's blood. Muhalhil's poetry placed Kulayb in limbo, ebbing and flowing on a continuum of gender. According to tradition, his poetry employed motifs such as tears and cries of "Let him not perish," evoking those of women's lamentations and at times committing himself to blood vengeance and impetuous grandeur befitting putatively masculine heroism. But, these fluctuations were cyclical not linear, giving an impression of upward (or downward) spiral, hesitation, and doubt. After a few cycles, his poetry eventually depicted a disproportionate show of force in vengeance for Kulayb and wild heroism in the past tense, as he alludes to his brother's former taunts, which gives the impression of overcompensation for something still gnawing within.

Another example of poetic crossdressing comes in the persona of Ḥujayja. In Arabia, these self-organizing Bedouin tribes often engaged in relations of conflict or cooperation with the more settled Arab Kingdoms of the Lakhmids (in Mesopotamia) or Ghassanids (in Syria), as is the case with the Bedouin tribe of the Banū Shaybān, and their heroine Ḥujayja. Through her poetry, we obtain one of several versions of events that led up to the epic Battle of Dhū Qār between her tribe and the Sasanians of Iran, in an existential drama that prefigured the rise of the Arabs over the Persians, and to some, the ascendance of a kind of Arabo-Islamic feminism in Muḥammad's new world order. In this version of events, al-Ḥurqa, the daughter of the Lakhmid king Mundhir, flees after the Sasanian king Anushirwan murders her father for refusing to allow the forced marriage of his daughter to the Persian king. Al-Ḥurqa as the refugee-bride-to-be flees to the protection of Ḥujayja and recites a lament (*marthīya*), beseeching her to intervene on behalf of her just cause. Ḥujayja is moved by her words. She, in turn, calls on the tribal code of hospitality-protection (*ijāra*) to compel her tribesmen to take an ethical and courageous stand against a tyrant, despite the apparent odds, in a David–Goliath match-up. In due time, Ḥujayja of the Banū Shaybān built a military confederation of tribes to defend their collective interests and dignity against the villainy of the Sasanian emperor in the Battle of Dhū Qār, a monumental battle in early Islamic memory that dispelled the Sasanian's aura of invincibility.[7] This Arabo-Islamic feminist ethos echoes the early sensibilities of Muḥammad reflected in the Qur'an's limits on patriarchy and polygyny, as well as the historical role of women in the *ḥadīth* literature, in the epics mentioned above, and later in the *Arabian Nights* folk cycles, where matrons and dowagers deployed stories of heroines to embolden and prepare their daughters for a misogynistic world. Again, it's important to note the role of these cultural productions in the formation and acculturation of women, supporting their everyday dignity, and in many cases leadership.[8]

Moreover, women were not only agents of their own poetry but also subjects of men's poetry that opened up a discourse on existential issues of life, love, and belonging, early in the pre-Islamic era. In praise poetry, the feminine beloved was often an avatar for the masculine patron, such as a king or other father figure, through whom the poet might protest his treatment at the hands of a cold beloved as a coded critique of political authority.[9] In tragic love poetry, a series of couples emerged, such as Dhul-Rumma-Mayya and Majnūn-Laylā, where the poet projects the beloved as indifferent and toying with his vulnerabilities, dramatizing a range of maddening discontents. This tragic love poetry was particularly meaningful in the Umayyad era, which saw a dizzying military expansion from Andalusia to the Indus Valley, but also gross mismanagement of civil strife, and unprecedented trauma that scarred a putatively sacred *umma* (the Muslim community). Dhul-Rumma (d. ca. 117/735) embodies the ambivalence of empire that many felt when he says of Mayya, "She is the cure, she is the disease," evoking the continuum (not binary) of attraction and repulsion in matters of love and war.[10] Conversely, in triumphant-romantic love poetry (*ghazal*), the figure of the beloved was often deployed to connote hopeful attainment of an object desired.

In the Umayyad era, Laylā al-Akhyaliyya (d. ca. 85/704) emerged as a rebel in the face of establishment rivals, whether professional or political.[11] She was famous for using her poetic skill to shame the Umayyad court into making costly concessions, to lampoon a rival poet, al-Nābigha al-Jaʿdī (d. 64/684), and to immortalize her deceased lover, Tawba.[12] Lore about Laylā trumpets her capacity to overwhelm with her sharp wit any man naïve enough to cross her: When the Umayyad ʿAbd al-Malik (d. 86/705)—a caliph, no less, and the grand builder of the Dome of the Rock—asked her publicly, "What did Tawba see in you that made him love you?" She parried, "What did people see in you that they made *you* caliph?"[13]

During the early Abbasid era, a new type of poetess emerged in the person of Rābiʿa al-ʿAdawiyya (d. 185/801), who gives herself in complete fidelity to her one true love, God, enabling her to gain the status of a saint and master teacher in the Sufi tradition.[14] Though no vows of celibacy are stated explicitly, an exclusive devotion to the divine is implied by Ibn Khallikān (d. 681/1282) in his biography of her:

> When the dark of night would fall, she would climb to the rooftop and cry out, "My Deity, the hustle is now ceased and the bustle hushed, and each lover seeks intimacy with his beloved. And I seek intimacy with you, O Beloved. May you render my intimacy with you tonight a redemption from Inferno."[15]

Betrothal to God is further implied, as she rejects multiple marriage proposals from leading men, preserving her independence. When an admirer of great means sent a letter of proposal to her, she replied,

> No doubt, asceticism in this world is relief from want for both body and soul, and desire for it [things] bequeaths worry and sorrow. When my letter arrives, prepare yourself for your fate, and be your own advisor and give not advice to others, fast for your fate and let death be your first bread. God has given me multiples [in wealth] of what he gave you, keeping me occupied.[16]

Her response in many ways places the expectations of a patriarchal society [i.e., marriage and children] in tension with ascetic monotheism, and uses the latter to reject the former. In another example of her ethics, Ibn Khallikān notes her spirit of forgiveness, when he quotes her prayer: "O God, I give unto you [i.e., absolve] those who have wronged me. Give unto me those I have wronged."[17] It is interesting to observe that, whereas using the command form with an earthly king would constitute a perilous violation of court protocol, here it suggests a deep level of intimacy with the divine king.

Rābiʿa's senior years overlapped with the youth of a poetess who pioneered a contrasting poetic persona. Far from asceticism, ʿUlayya (d. ca. 210/825) made a name for herself navigating the challenges and opportunities of the imperial court. Born into great privilege as the daughter of the Abbasid caliph al-Mahdī (d. 169/785) and sister of the famous caliph Hārūn al-Rashīd (d. 193/809), she carefully developed her persona as a princess but her poetry toyed with propriety and taboos. According to *Kitāb al-Aghānī* (*The Book of Songs*), we are reminded of her position as a leading woman and a creative inspiration to others, when the author notes that ʿUlayya had a blemish on her forehead and thus took to wearing jeweled headbands, setting trends in Abbasid high society. She embraced a gender-specific embodied style of poetry: She was said to transgress into singing poetry and drinking wine for nonpraying times of the month (i.e., during her menses), but would return to prayer, Qur'an, and books, thereafter. Thus, her poetic behavior correlated with ritual bodily states in outward deference to religion and patriarchy. Moreover, we are told that she never needed to repent for violations of taboos depicted in her poetry, since such verses were only said in jest (*ʿabathan*). These stylized caveats provided plausible deniability, while nearly all of her poetry in effect parries patriarchal and caliphal prerogatives, as she often locked horns with her brothers, the prince Ibrāhīm and the caliph Hārūn al-Rashīd.[18] Indeed, the efficacy of her poetry was often measured by her capacity to walk into and out of trouble almost at will, while exposing the breach between monotheism and patriarchy with wit and serenity.

In one instance, she was caught by her brother al-Rashīd reciting love poetry for a servant of the caliph, Ṭall (meaning "gentle rain" or "drizzle"), whom she engaged in several exchanges of poetry. However when the romance came to light, the caliph forced her to promise never to mention his name again. Later in the story, we find her innocently reciting the second chapter of the Qur'ān, Sūrat al-Baqara, where inevitably the word Ṭall appears in verse 265. In deference to her brother, she distorts the word of God and says, "and the one whose [name] the Commander of the Faithful forbids," putting the caliph's will in tension with God's. The caliph overheard this workaround, entered the room, kissed her forehead apologetically, and said, "I shall not deny thereafter anything you want."[19] Unlike Ḥujayja, who used alliances and warfare to corner and defeat her enemies, or Rābiʿa who rejected the trappings of the world altogether, ʿUlayya modeled an engaged style of resistance appropriate to civilian life in the new imperial capital, while laying bare the inherent tensions between Islam's emerging version of monotheism and monarchy.

Much of her poetry also played with breaches in language usage, with metapoetic twists. In one example, ʿUlayya knew to code the name of a different beloved, Rashaʾ, a man, as a woman named Zaynab, which was then discovered, so she changed it to *Rayb* meaning "doubt." And she said, playing with language and theology, "The heart craves Doubt; O Lord, is that a sin? It has held my heart captive; I can do nothing but weep, O Knower of All Secrets. I hid the name of my lover in my verse, like a pip in my purse."[20] We are told, furthermore, that she sung these infectious verses while wandering the palace, thus making her petition to God noticeable to others, and implying a critique of caliphal and familial restrictions, while teasing apart the tensions between apparent and substantive meanings of language.

In retrospect, scholars today can discern four overlapping types of persona for poetesses in premodern culture: the grieving mother/sister/daughter (al-Khansāʾ, al-Khirniq bint Badr and al-Fāriʿa bint Shaddād), the warrior-diplomat (al-Ḥujayja), the princess (al-Ḥurqa, ʿUlayya bint al-Mahdī and Wallāda bint al-Mustakfī), and the courtesan-ascetic (ʿArīb, Shāriya, and Rābiʿa al-ʿAdawiyya). We can imagine the impact of these types and models when we recognize the perennial human pattern that young boys and girls learn modes of being and living by observing the adults around them, whether actual or depicted. It would strain credulity to think that captivating literary figures would go unnoticed as boys and girls gained cultural literacy and became men and women. From the early Abbasid period onward, this poetry increasingly reached a broader public that was ethnically more diverse and included socially mobile men and women who rose to noble status, as well as an emerging subnobility, sometimes referred to as "those of merit" (*ḥasab*) or "of new money" (*ṭarīf*), who were "neither royalty nor rabble," according to Ibn Qutayba (d. 276/889).[21] This subnobility included chancery workers, judges, and a burgeoning class of merchants, who earned their wealth from retail shops and/or long-distance trade routes. By the fourth/tenth century, it became obvious that court poetry was no longer primarily the preserve of the court. However, rather than aping courtly culture, the subnobility adapted and largely democratized the aesthetics and interests reflected in the literature. For example, salons spread rhizomatically in the ninth and tenth centuries among the subnobility in major cities, like Cordoba, Qayrawān, Cairo, Aleppo, and Baghdad; they were less hierarchical than those at royal courts and more egalitarian; there was greater emphasis on turn-taking, tolerance of foibles, and a warm sociability leavened by wine, flowers, fruits, and the occasional sprig of basil to awaken the senses. The *Romance of Bayāḍ and Riyāḍ* illustrates how, in Andalusia, women too hosted single-sex and mixed salons, where men and women could declaim court poetry or sing it to the plucking of lute strings. Evidence from late medieval bourgeois homes in Cairo and Aleppo also suggests that the private section (*ḥarāmlak*) of the home, used primarily by women, featured large, as well as more cozy, salon spaces.[22]

These salon spaces gave ordinary women access to educational opportunity, where they could witness poetry and narrative come to life in performance, and earn or seize the chance to perfect their skills. The famous ʿAbbasid littérateur al-Tanūkhī (d. 384/994), for example, tells a salon-type story about an Egyptian woman who uses her skills to check the abuses of caliphal power (manifested as monarchy, patriarchy, and misogyny) embodied in the misconduct of the seventh ʿAbbasid caliph al-Maʾmūn (d. 218/833). Implicitly, such narratives inscribe great rhetoric as a necessary counterbalance to state power. It was said that al-Maʾmūn was passing by an Egyptian village estate, when the owner of that estate, named Maria the Copt, invited him to sojourn for the night and thus honor the estate with his presence. Barely containing his arrogance, he obliged while still dismissing her capacity to host generously and properly. That evening, Maria offered grand shows of country hospitality for the whole retinue, but at daybreak, the caliph and his entourage hurried to depart without a proper farewell to the host, depriving her of the honor of displaying further hospitality in the morning. The woman, tamping down her frustration, intercepted him with a train of her own servants, but the caliph condescendingly whispered to his entourage, "Here comes the Coptic lady, bringing you gifts of the countryside: vinegar-sauce, salt fish, and bitter aloes." To the contrary, the gifts turned out to be nuggets of pure gold—a universal not local good—befitting prophets and kings. In one fell swoop, Maria the Copt was able to force God's deputy on earth to acknowledge the gift's value and eat his words. Shocked, he asked her to take them back; suddenly, he was bereft of speech. With some righteous indignation, Maria replied, "No!" she said, "I swear to God, I won't!" In this courtly chess game, it was apparent to all that he had underestimated his opponent's skills. In contrast to the caliph's unforced error, Maria initiated her closing maneuver entailing a mix of charm (*luṭf*) and reproach (*ʿitāb*): she knelt and grabbed a handful of soil, then cried out that this black dirt turns to gold, day after day of farming, and it compels her to display her munificence as any man would. Admonishing the caliph, she said, "O Commander of the Faithful, do not break our hearts, or deride us." Finally chastened, the caliph became "amazed at the magnitude of her 'manliness' [*murūʾa*, intended as a pun on her Christian name], and the extent of her wealth."[23] Stories such as these illustrate the capacity of women to gain rhetorical skills (and wealth) and use them in high-stakes encounters; they also demonstrate the interest men and women littérateurs of subsequent generations showed in narrating these tales.

The most renowned poetess of Andalusia was no doubt Wallāda bint al-Mustakfī, (d. 484/1091) the daughter of the caliph of Cordoba, who was famous for attending and hosting mixed-gender literary salons and developing a corpus of poetry of love (*ghazal*) and lampoon (*hijāʾ*), though only a fraction of it survives. In these salons, she was wooed by many men, especially two high profile viziers, Ibn ʿAbdūs (d. 472/1080) and Ibn Zaydūn (d. 463/1070; also a poet). From her poetry we learn that she initially rejected the former and chose the latter, thus publicly signaling her status. Only about ten poems or fragments of hers have come down to us, and most of them involve Ibn Zaydūn. Their poetic interactions, writ flamboyantly in history, span a spectrum of emotions from love to a war of words, and stand as daring reflections on passion and pain. Her early poetry composed for Ibn Zaydūn offers examples of unguarded love. In one instance, she almost whispers: "Wait, when night falls, for my visit. For I find night best keeps secrets. My thing for you, if the sun had it, it would not shine, nor moon glow, nor stars rise."[24] Her confessions, putatively secret, but consciously made public through the medium of catchy verse seems all the more risky because Ibn Zaydūn's loyalty to her royal family—the Umayyads—was suspect. In a sense, positioned as star-crossed lovers with diverging politics, the seeds of their theatrical breakup were planted from the beginning. At mid-saga, her poetry begins to show strain, when she alludes to both sexual and political disappointments, but not without some humor: "Ibn Zaydūn, despite his virtues, distrusts me unfairly, and he looks at me askance when I come to him, as if I come to castrate him."[25] The final episode of their breakup, involved "another woman." It is not clear whether this was a reference to a physical person or a figurative device standing in for an ineffable reason. "If in love you were just, you would not fall for my girlfriend, and choose her. You would not abandon a lush branch in all its beauty and fall for a twig, now dry."[26] Interestingly, tradition has it that Ibn Zaydūn apologetically offered his famous Nūn-Ode to Wallāda but she refused his gestures, in a dramatic display of her autonomy. Though she never married, she lived the rest of her life with Ibn ʿAbdūs.

As noted earlier, salons in Andalusia were often of mixed gender and the *Romance of Bayāḍ and Riyāḍ* illustrates how women might have managed the responsibility of hosting. In the *Romance*, the male protagonist, Bayāḍ, is invited to recite poetry at a garden salon to win the heart of Riyāḍ. In the beginning, Bayāḍ realizes that the matron and host of the salon is the all-important facilitator, called "al-Sayyida" meaning the dame or matron, an early rather courtly version of the Celistina figure of Iberian literature. He thus seeks to earn the favor and affection of the kindly matron and host to facilitate his courtship of Riyāḍ. The matron advises him to focus on his performance: "My son, I don't need this [deference] from you, rather prepare your mind, consider your speech, and sequence your utterances for your introduction to a proper Matron's palace." His response conveys performance anxiety (in love and art): "If all of this, all of what you say, is as you describe, then I can't enter her palace ever."[27]

In due course, Bayāḍ recovers and impresses his audience, and the matron of the house lauds him with the label "a poet genius and winning littérateur" ("*shāʿir mufliq wa adīb arīb*") and explains the basis for her admiration, rooted in performance style:

"[W]e recite what we have related, memorized, and overheard from others, but you recite what you improvise from within yourself."[28] She does not rest, however, without raising the stakes for Bayāḍ when she says, "We all humbly ask and suggest, show us the breadth of your soul, the freshness of your mind and your perceptiveness of poetry. We would like you to describe the garden that we are in. It will not be difficult for you."[29] To which, Bayāḍ responds with a tilt of his head, an impromptu composition of poetry and melody, eliciting rousing compliments and more requests.

As we have seen, the core element of Arabic poetry and other literature is nothing less than existence itself: love, belonging, friendship, and the traumas of life. These emotional issues are not only present in the content of poetry, but in the culture of salons as well, where aficionados performed texts that came to life before friends. As we talk about practical functions, it deserves to be mentioned that salons fulfilled a deeply emotional purpose for both men and women. They helped explore perennial human fears about loss in life, and the risks of oblivion after death. In short, salons enabled people to voluntarily form "communities of love" that sustain social bonds by asserting life against the vagaries of time. The ʿAbbasid poet al-Buḥturī (d. 284/897) composed an elegy on a friend's death and said,

> May showers bless our salons that you made intimate,
> Alas to our salon that you left bereft.
> You made our salon by your legacy lively;
> You now attend hereafter another [salon] forever.
> Your legacy is a friend among us present,
> Only your body you yield to others.[30]

In a similarly lyrical vein, emphasizing love despite mortality, the physician Ibn Buṭlān (d. 458/1066)—having neither wife nor child—put his hopes in his salon community: "If I die, no one will weep over my death except for my salon of medicine and books; they will weep."[31] While we do not have such direct sentiments about women's experiences, we have evidence that mixed- and single-gender salons existed, and the *Romance of Bayāḍ and Riyāḍ* suggests that we have no reason to assume a lower horizon of possibility for the experiences of women in literary salons.

It should be noted that in the modern era, salons continue to serve as key social institutions for creatively responding to the challenges of modernity, colonialism, and European supremacy. Most visibly, the Cairo-based salon of Mayy Ziyāda (d. 1941) flourished and gathered the luminaries of the Arabic Nahda (Renaissance), and introduced Egypt to the work of New York–based Arab émigré author, Kahlil Gibran. These days, the entertainment and educational functions of the salons are fulfilled by modern broadcast media and formal education, but the need to socialize and politick still continues to propel salons under the name *umsiyya* in Egypt and *dīwān* or *dīwāniyya* in Kuwait and other Gulf States. In Kuwait's 2009 parliamentary elections, sixteen women candidates ran as MPs representing various districts. Four women were elected that year—Aseel Alawadhi, Rola Dashti, Massouma al-Mubarak, and Salwa al-Jassar—largely by visiting and hosting salons and delivering stirring speeches to single-gender and mixed audiences.

Conclusion

Our starting point was Orientalism of the nineteenth and twentieth centuries. Orientalist preconceptions and prejudices limited the kinds of questions Western scholars asked and not surprisingly sidelined evidence of women's *adab*. *Adab* was a heterogeneous corpus of cultural knowledge that constituted a well-rounded education in the humanities designed to promote eloquence in high-stakes social settings. It included poetry, prose, and samples of persuasive speech. What is noteworthy, in light of stereotypical assumptions, is that the Arabic literary tradition curated, preserved, and transmitted the work of women, despite the predominance of men. For more than a millennium, each instance of collection and preservation de facto implied that the verbal achievements of women were worth recording for posterity. Many works that recorded those moments survived to this day, and their inclusion as part of the *adab*-humanities curriculum further implied that women's eloquence circulated in informal salons and became a part of the lived culture of youths as they themselves came of age and filled roles in society as competent adults. For youth, the examples of lived culture drawn from past generations was not of one size to fit all. As we observed, at least four archetypes of woman poet existed, providing for girls and women options for role models: the grieving poetess like al-Khansāʾ, the warrior-diplomat like al-Ḥujayja, the princess like ʿUlayya, and the courtesan-ascetic like Rābiʿa. Based on *adab* principles, each became a model that inspired generations to cultivate a personal, social, and political voice, and not seldom to engage in social issues of their time. Inevitably, such engagement caused controversy, but each type spawned a socioconceptual category that made women of that archetype at least familiar and recognizable to broader society, if no less edgy. Without that legibility, Muslim women would certainly have had fewer opportunities to project their dignity and sovereignty as social beings in public spaces.

Given the challenges of our dysfunctional politics today, basic human compassion and coexistence have risen to the fore as minimum prerequisites for intercultural cooperation and problem-solving. Far from a luxury, knowledge of our human past and cultural heritage plays a crucial role in not only cultivating a respect for cultural differences but enriching our lives, society, and political systems with fresh ideas. Perhaps one of the most exciting insights from the history of Arab women littérateurs is the connections between eloquence and personal sovereignty. Stories of verbal prowess in Islamicate sources demonstrate a conception of sovereignty that is rooted not in land, wealth, or peoplehood, but in language and being able to use it for a personal or collective good. Every example of women's rhetorical skill illustrates a gendered sovereignty that inspires others.

Notes

1. Edward W. Said, *Orientalism* (New York: Vintage Books, 1978), 123, 283.
2. Ibid.; Lynne Thornton, *Women as Portrayed in Orientalist Painting* (Paris: ACR Edition, 1994); Edward William Lane, *An Account of the Manners and Customs of the Modern Egyptians Written in Egypt during the Years 1833–34, and –35* (London: Charles Knight, 1836), 1:221–241, 388, 397.
3. ʿAbd al-Malik Al-Thaʿālabī, *Al-Tamthīl Wal-Muḥaḍara Fī ʿIlm al-Ḥikam Wal-Munāẓara*, ed. Muḥammad Ḥulw ʿAbd al-Fattāḥ (Tunis: al-Dār al-ʿArabiyya lil-Kitāb, 1983), 163. For more on al-Thaʿālibi, see Bilal Orfali, *The Anthologist's Art: Abū Manṣūr al-Thaʿālibī and His Yatīmat al-Dahr* (Leiden: Brill, 2016).
4. All translations are the author's unless indicated. For the Arabic original, see: Ḥabīb b. Aws Abū Tammām, *Dīwān Abī Tammām: bi-Sharḥ al-Khaṭīb al-Tibrīzī [Poetry Collection of Abū Tammām with the Commentary of al-Tabrīzī]*, ed. Muḥammad ʿAbduh ʿAzzām (Cairo: Dār al-Maʿārif, 1982), 3:183. For more on the poet, see Margaret Larkin, "Abu Tammam (circa 805–845)," in *Arabic Literary Culture, 500–25*, ed. Michael Cooperson and Shawkat M. Toorawa (Detroit, MI: Gale, 2005), 33–52, http://link.gale.com/apps/doc/UNTBGS540615893/DLBC?u=umuser&sid=zotero&xid=92b30da0.
5. Suzanne Pinckney Stetkevych, *The Mute Immortals Speak: Pre-Islamic Poetry and the Poetics of Ritual* (Ithaca, NY: Cornell University Press, 1993), 168. For a biography of al-Khirniq, see Khayr al-Dīn al-Ziriklī, *Al-Aʿlām: Qāmūs Tarājim Li-Ashhar al-Rijal Wa-al-Nisa Min al-ʿArab Wa-al-Mustaʿribīn Wa-al-Mustashriqīn*, 15th ed., 13 vols. (Beirut: Dār al-ʿIlm lil-Malāyīn, 2002), 2:303.
6. Usually translated as "The Battle-Days of the Arabs," which documents these intertribal violent encounters among the pagan Arabs.
7. Muḥammad J. H. Mashhadānī, *Ḥarb Banī Shaybān Maʿa Kisrā Ānūshirwān,narrated by Bishr ibn Marwān al-Asadī.* (Baghdad: n. publ., 1988).
8. Samer M. Ali, *Arabic Literary Salons in the Islamic Middle Ages: Poetry, Public Performance, and the Presentation of the Past* (Notre Dame, IN: University of Notre Dame Press, 2010), 30–31; Samer Ali, "Literary Salons," in *The Oxford Encyclopedia of Islam and Women*, ed. Natana J. DeLong Bas (Oxford: Oxford University Press, 2013), http://www.oxfordreference.com/view/10.1093/acref:oiso/9780199764464.001.0001/acref-9780199764464-e-0153.
9. For examples, see Julie Scott Meisami, *Medieval Persian Court Poetry* (Princeton, NJ: Princeton University Press, 1987), 8–9, 22–23, 24–25, chap. 2; Ali, *Arabic Literary Salons*, 94–98.
10. Michael A. Sells, *Desert Tracings: Six Classic Arabian Odes by ʿAlqama, Shánfara, Labíd, ʿAntara, Al-Aʿsha, and Dhu Al-Rúmma* (Middletown, CT: Wesleyan University Press, 1989), 72; Geert Jan van Gelder, "Dhu Al-Rummah (circa 696–circa 735)," in *Arabic Literary Culture, 500–925*, ed. Michael Cooperson and Shawkat M. Toorawa (Detroit, MI: Gale, 2005), http://link.gale.com/apps/doc/UNXGBM896673329/DLBC?u=umuser&sid=zotero&xid=d1390af1.
11. F. Gabrieli, "Laylā Al-Akhyaliyya," in *Encyclopaedia of Islam*, 2nd ed. (Leiden: E. J. Brill, April 24, 2012), http://referenceworks.brillonline.com/entries/encyclopaedia-of-islam-2/layla-al-akhyaliyya-SIM_4652?s.num=0&s.f.s2_parent=s.f.cluster.Encyclopaedia+of+Islam&s.q=akhyaliyya.
12. A. Arazi, "Al-Nābigha al-Djaʿdī," in *Encyclopaedia of Islam*, 2nd ed. (Brill, April 24, 2012), http://referenceworks.brillonline.com/entries/encyclopaedia-of-islam-2/al-nabigha-al-djadi-SIM_5704?s.num=2&s.f.s2_parent=s.f.cluster.Encyclopaedia+of+Islam&s.q=nabigah.

13. Arabic text from Abū al-Faraj al-Isbahānī, *Kitāb al-Aghānī*, ed. Ibrāhīm Ibyārī, 31 vols. (Cairo: Dār al-Sha'b, 1969), 11:4026; and 'Abd al-Amīr 'Alī Muhannā, *Mu'jam Al-Nisā' al-Shā'irāt Fī al-Jāhiliyya Wa-al-Islām* (Beirut: Dār al-Kutub al-'Ilmiyya, 1990), 220; for analysis, see Dana Al-Sajdi, "Trespassing the Male Domain: The Qasīdah of Laylā Al-Akhyaliyyah," *Journal of Arabic Literature* 31, no. 2 (2000): 121–146.
14. Rkia Elaroui Cornell, "Rabi'ah al-'Adawiyyah (circa 720–801)," in *Arabic Literary Culture*, 500–925, http://link.gale.com/apps/doc/UOHUGX779579911/DLBC?u=umuser&sid=zotero&xid=3140a9f6.
15. Abū al-'Abbās Shams al-Dīn Ibn Khallikān, *Wafayāt al-A'yān wa Anbā Abnā' al-Zamān*, ed. Iḥsān 'Abbās (Beirut: Dār al-Thaqāfa, 1968), 2:285–286.
16. Ibid., 2:286.
17. Ibid.
18. 'Ulayya Bint al-Mahdī, *Dīwān 'Ulayya Bint Al-Mahdī, Ukht Hārūn al-Rashīd* (Beirut: Dār Ṣādir, 1997), 84–108.
19. Ibid., 86.
20. Ibid., 88–89.
21. Samer Mahdy Ali, "The Rise of the Abbasid Public Sphere: The Case of al-Mutanabbī and Three Middle Ranking Patrons," *Al-Qanṭara* 29, no. 2 (December 30, 2008): 467–494.
22. Ali, *Arabic Literary Salons*, 30.
23. Ibid., 30–31.
24. Wallāda Bint al-Mustakfī, "Taraqqab Idhā Janna al-Ẓalāmu Ziyāratī," accessed May 27, 2020, http://www.adab.com/modules.php?name=Sh3er&doWhat=shqas&qid=73319&r=&rc=.
25. Wallāda Bint al-Mustakfī, "Inna Ibn Zaydūn 'Alā Faḍlihi," accessed May 27, 2020, http://www.adab.com/modules.php?name=Sh3er&doWhat=shqas&qid=73326&r=&rc=.
26. Wallāda Bint al-Mustakfī, "Law Kunta Tanṣifu Fil-Hawā," accessed May 27, 2020, http://www.adab.com/modules.php?name=Sh3er&doWhat=shqas&qid=73318&r=&rc=.
27. Ali, *Arabic Literary Salons*, 29. Based on the original Arabic in Alois Richard Nykl, ed., *Historia de Los Amores de Bayad y Riyad / Qissat Bayāḍ Wa Riyāḍ* (New York: Trustees of the Hispanic Society of America, 1941).
28. Ali, *Arabic Literary Salons*, 30.
29. Ibid., 30.
30. Ibid., 47.
31. Ibid., 46.

Bibliography

Primary Sources

Bū Falāqa, Sa'd, and Wallāda bint al-Mustakfī. *Wallāda Bint al-Mustakfī: al-amīra al-shā'ira*. Cairo: al-Maktab al-'Arabī lil-Ma'ārif, 2016.

Ibn Abī āhir Ṭayfūr, Aḥmad. *Balāghāt al-nisā': wa-ṭarā'if kalāmihinna wa-milḥ nawādirihinna wa-akhbār dhawāt al-rā'yi minhunna wa-ash'ārihinna fī al-Jāhiliyya wa-al-Islām*. Sidon: al-Maktaba 'Aṣriyya, 2000.

Iṣfahānī, Abū al-Faraj al-. *al-Imā' al-shawā'ir*. Beirut: 'ālam al-Kutub, 1984.

Iṣfahānī, Abū al-Faraj al-. *Kitāb al-Aghānī*. Edited by al-Najdī Nāṣif and Muḥammad Abū al-Faḍl Ibrāhīm. 24 vols. Cairo: al-Hay'a al-Maṣriyya al-'Āmma lil-Kitāb, 1992–1993.
Khansā' al-. *Dīwān* [poetry collection]. 'Ammān: Dār 'Ammār, 1988.
Mahdī, 'Ulayya bint al-. *Dīwān*. Beirut: 'ālam al-Kutub, 1997.
Ma'mūniyya, 'Arīb al-. *'Arīb al-Ma'mūniyya: akhbāruhā wa-ash'āruhā*. Irbid: Dār al-Mutanabbī, 2009.
Marzubānī, Muḥammad ibn 'Imrān. *Ash'ār al-nisā'*. Beirut: 'ālam al-Kutub, 1995.
Marzubānī, Muḥammad ibn 'Imrān al-. *Shā'irāt al-qabā'il al-'Arabiyya*. Beirut: al-Dār al-'Arabiyya lil-Mawsū'āt, 2007.
Mashhadānī, Muḥammad J. H., ed. *Ḥarb Banī Shaybān Ma'a Kisraā Ānūshirwān*. Narrated by Bishr Ibn Marwān al-Asadī. Baghdad: n. publ., 1988.
Muhannā, 'Abd al-Amīr 'Alī. *Mu'jam al-nisā' al-shā'irāt fī al-Jāhiliyya wa-al-Islām*. Beirut: Dār al-Kutub al-'Ilmiyya, 1990.
Nykl, Alois Richard, ed. *Historia de Los Amores de Bayad y Riyad / Qissat Bayāḍ Wa Riyāḍ*. New York: Trustees of the Hispanic Society of America, 1941.
Sells, Michael A. *Desert Tracings: Six Classic Arabian Odes by 'Alqama, Shánfara, Labíd, 'Antara, Al-A'sha, and Dhu Al-Rúmma*. Middletown, CT: Wesleyan University Press, 1989.
Suyūṭī, Jalāl al-Dīn al-. *Nuzhat al-julasā' fī ash'ār al-nisā'*. Beirut: Dār al-Makshūf, 1958.
Yamūt, Bashīr. *Shā'irāt al-'Arab fī al-Jāhiliyya wa-al-Islām*. Beirut: Maktaba al-Ahliyya, 1934.

Secondary Sources

Ali, Samer M. *Arabic Literary Salons in the Islamic Middle Ages: Poetry, Public Performance, and the Presentation of the Past*. ND Poetics of Orality and Literacy. Notre Dame, IN: University of Notre Dame Press, 2010.
Ali, Samer M. "The Rise of the Abbasid Public Sphere: The Case of al-Mutanabbi and Three Middle Ranking Patrons." *Al-Qantara: Revista de Estudios Árabes: Special Issue on Patronage in Islamic History* 29, no. 2 (2008): 467–494.
Cooperson, Michael, and Shawkat M. Toorawa. *Arabic Literary Culture, 500–925*. Detroit, MI: Gale, 2005.
DeLong-Bas, Natana J., ed. *The Oxford Encyclopedia of Islam and Women*. Oxford: Oxford University Press, 2013.
Hammond, Marlé. *Beyond Elegy: Classical Arabic Women's Poetry in Context*. Oxford: Oxford University Press, 2010.
Mernissi, Fatima. *The Forgotten Queens of Islam*. Translated by Mary Jo Lakeland. Minneapolis: University of Minnesota Press, 1993.
Said, Edward W. *Orientalism*. New York: Vintage Books, 1978.
Steinberg, Amanda Hannoosh. "Wives, Witches, and Warriors: Women in Arabic Popular Epic." PhD diss., University of Pennsylvania, 2018.
Stetkevych, Jaroslav. *The Zephyrs of Najd: The Poetics of Nostalgia in the Classical Arabic Nasīb*. Chicago: University of Chicago Press, 1993.
Stetkevych, Suzanne Pinckney. *The Mute Immortals Speak: Pre-Islamic Poetry and the Poetics of Ritual*. Ithaca, NY: Cornell University Press, 1993.
Stetkevych, Suzanne Pinckney. *The Poetics of Islamic Legitimacy: Myth, Gender, and Ceremony in the Classical Arabic Ode*. Bloomington: Indiana University Press, 2002.

CHAPTER 14

WOMEN AS ECONOMIC ACTORS IN THE PREMODERN ISLAMIC WORLD

AMIRA SONBOL

This chapter explores the topic of Muslim women's participation in their communities' economy during the premodern period. Sources containing records of financial transactions involving women were relied on for this research. These include financial settlements related to marriage, such as dowries and various types of divorce settlements and support; inheritance records detailing what women inherited or left to their heirs in their estates, records of *awqāf* set up by women or to which women were assigned as overseers or beneficiaries, and multiple types of transactions, such as buying, selling, mortgaging, and various disputes over trade or earnings that involved women as defendants or accusers. A general conclusion of the chapter is that women's participation in the economic life of their communities was normative and their contributions were essential to the continuity and vitality of their communities and families. Depending on class, place, and environment, women invested in agricultural land, or urban businesses, such as retail shops or coffee-houses. Others united together to invest in buying real estate and rentals or production and sale of goods like butter or olive oil. Still others worked as vendors and peddlers, often taking on goods on commission and peddling them for a profit. Hard labor was also usual for women who worked as domestics in agriculture, stone quarries, or factories. Islam guaranteed the right to own property for both men and women, and neither was forbidden from being financially active, investing, holding, or spending wealth inherited or earned. Therefore, as this chapter shows, the social system was actually rhizomatic, relations were interconnected, and business and financial undertakings were shared and depended on the community as a whole.

Introduction

Acclaimed as a house that "made history," the home of Zaynab Khātūn (d. 1836) stands today as a memorial to a woman of influence who lived through turbulent times and was witness to momentous events with far-reaching impact. The building actually dates back to before 1486 and was renovated in 1713, as the sign standing at its gate informs visitors.[1] A large medieval building with multiple floors and courtyards, it provides testimony to the wealth and power of its owners. Its original builder was another woman, Shaqrā', granddaughter of the Mamluk sultan Ḥasan ibn Qalawūn (d. 762/1361) who himself was a powerful benefactor renowned as the builder of the Qalawūn hospital that was still serving Cairo's population when the French occupation army arrived in 1212/1798. Shaqrā' may have been a princess with access to wealth, but Zaynab started her career as an enslaved person who was manumitted and married a *mamlūk* who purchased Shaqrā's house for her. Zaynab was famous for her influence and for the wealth she had accumulated. When the French invaded Egypt, their soldiers looted her house in search of treasure and in pursuit of Egyptian fighters resisting French occupation whom she protected in the basement. The house therefore memorializes important events in Egypt's history and symbolizes the centrality of women in their communities.

Not far from the Khātūn house is located the mausoleum of Shajar al-Durr (d. 654/1257) built in commemoration of the first sulṭān (ruler) and founder of the Mamluk dynasty. This was the dynasty that held political leadership in Egypt from the end of the Ayyubid period in 649/1249 until the arrival in 1798 of Napoleon's French army, which invaded Egypt and defeated the Mamluks. Shajar and Zaynab share a history: one began the age of the Mamluks and the other witnessed its end. They both started their lives as enslaved women and ended up as powerful women in command of significant power and wealth. Cairo, the city where they both lived, celebrates its other female citizens as well, including naming three districts after 'Aisha bint Ja'far al-Ṣādiq (d. 145/924), Zaynab bint 'Alī ibn Abī Ṭālib (d. 62/682), and Nafīsa bint al-Ḥassān ibn Zayd (d. 208/830), all direct descendants of 'Ali ibn Abī Ṭālib (d. 40/661), the fourth caliph of Islam, and who are said to have taken refuge in Egypt after the martyrdom of `Ali's son al-Ḥusayn (d. 61/680), grandson of the Prophet Muḥammad.

That women commanded respect and exercised influence in their premodern communities was a common phenomenon in cities and towns from one province of the Islamic world to another. Islamic historical works that chronicle the achievements and legacy of Islamic civilization (*turāth*) are replete with information about women. Unfortunately, however, much of what we learn about them in these sources is narrated in reference to where they stood in relationship to a male relative. This is particularly the case when it concerns an important Islamic figure like the Prophet, his early Companions, or political leaders. When the woman is mentioned in her own right, it is usually not as informative as when a man's biography is being narrated. We are therefore dependent on literary material, court records, *awqāf*, and other sources to give us information about the lived realities of women, and we have to reach conclusions regarding their economic agency and the wealth they possessed based on these sources. As this chapter shows, much can be learned about women's economic activities by widening research to include various types of transactions and relationships. We may not often see women titled as Shāhbandār ("grand merchant"), although the rare mention does exist, nor do we see *wikālas* (trade depots/caravansarais) named after women when tens of *wikālas* existed throughout the Islamic world often named after male founders—e.g., Wikālat al-Ghūrī in Cairo.[2] But records of courts of law yield information regarding women: for example, wage labor and inheritance records record the wealth women held and passed on to their families at various levels within the social classes to which they belonged. Marriage and divorce records give an idea of the dowries expected by women when marriage was transacted and the actual settlements they received as divorce settlements. Furthermore, legal records, particularly those related to litigation, show the extent and diversity of resources that women held, properties they invested in, and work they undertook, as will become evident below.

How involved were women in wage labor? Did wage labor provide the main source of income for women or were they largely dependent on inheritance or money received as dowry? If one depended solely on *fiqh* sources that focus on issues such as women leaving the home with or without a spouse's permission, or highlighted specific duties for which women were compensated, like breast-feeding, then information about wage labor and economic investments undertaken by women become very limited and even questionable. Instead, women's dependence on inheritance and dowries as their only real source of income is given credibility. At first glance, court records do lend support to this last hypothesis, since much of what we see in these records involves suing for denied inheritance or delayed dowries or marriage contracts. It must be pointed out that details regarding inheritance, dowries, and living support that women received in the form of room and board, plus amounts paid as divorce settlements, actually constitute important resources for women that they often used wisely for investing and acquiring property. The importance of these resources cannot be underestimated, given the negotiations and legal cases brought to court by women, personally or through their agents, to ensure that they received what belonged to them. Moreover, the dimensions of the estates left by deceased women and the *waqf*s they set up that are recorded in courts, show that women often managed to accumulate substantial wealth during their lifetime that could not have been solely received through inheritance and marriage settlements. Some of these issues are discussed in greater detail below.

Inheritance and Guardianship

Inheritance constituted a major source of wealth for both men and women, as did control of family property, which was a significant reason for litigation before the courts in the premodern period. Acting as guardians (*walī* or *waṣī*) to orphans was also an important source and both men and women acted as guardians. The various types of records left to us provide good examples of the actual dynamics of family finances and the role of different players in them. A seventeenth-century *sijill* (court register) from Jerusalem helps illustrate the frequency and diversity of family financial disputes brought forward for litigation.[3] The *sijill* consists of 221 pages containing altogether 1,859 entries concerning litigation about various issues ranging from manumission to marriage and divorce, sales and business disputes, registration of property, and disputes over unpaid debts or financial rights. A survey of the first one hundred pages of the *sijill* shows that 241 cases out of a total of 714 (over one-third) involved females, including a number of cases concerning orphans whose gender is not indicated. A good percentage of the cases deal with inheritance, child custody and guardianship, and marriage and divorce, while another significant number represents disputes over property and cases involving other forms of financial rights.

While this *sijill* may not be an exact representation of similar courts during the premodern Islamic world, it presents an image of lived realities that illustrate a life where gender plays little role. Instead of being a hierarchical system in which a patriarch seems to reign and financial power and business are the domain of men, the system was actually quite rhizomatic: that is to say, it was very interconnected in regard to the people involved, the relations between them, the shared and exchanged properties, and the various details involved in holding on to and accumulating and investing wealth. Some examples, as follows, may be illustrative.

> Maryam bint Ḥasan al-Turkumānī, assigned as *waṣī* for ʿAbd Allāh and ʿAbd al-Qādir, the orphans of ʿAlī al-Turkumānī, claimed that Luṭfī bint Muṣṭafā received on behalf of her husband's deceased daughter, Fāṭima bint Bākīr, whose inheritance was bequeathed to the mentioned underage boys. . . .[4]
>
> The woman Khadīja bint al-ʿAttār . . . received in her hands the amount of fifty and half piasters . . . from Muḥammad al-Ḥājj ʿAlī . . . ten piasters of which being the price of *gūkh* (felt/type of fabric) that she sold and gave to him . . . the remainder was to [remain as debt] for a full year . . . and he mortgaged the house located . . . under her hands . . . including the rights of usage.[5]
>
> Shaʿbān ibn Muḥammad al-Hibl and Khalaf ibn al-Ḥājj Ibrāhīm al-Hibl rented from al-Ḥājj ʿAwwād ibn al- Ḥājj Shāhīn al-Muqartam, proxy on behalf of his sister-in-law ʿAdīla bint Muṣal al-Nābulsī, wife of Mūsā bin ʿĀbid, and Fakhr al-Dīn al-Murastaq, representing himself, and Ḥassan ibn Ghānim, and Maḥmūd ibn Ṣāliḥ al-Fuqāʿī, proxy for bint ʿĀbid, who rented to them sixteen and one fifth *qirāṭ*, the rest of the seven and nineteenth *qirāṭ* being sold to partners whose names are known to them. [Rent] for a full year for the amount of seven piasters to be paid at the end of the period as accepted rent.[6]

In the first case above, a wife is made *waṣī* (guardian) of the two sons of her deceased husband's deceased daughter. She is suing for the two boy's inheritance from their mother. Such arrangements were not unusual as a similar case from Egypt shows.

> Fāṭima al-Shāmiyya, the named defendant has seized the named building without any legal rights. I ask that she take her hand off my share of the building and the share of Mu'mina, the minor who is under my *wiṣāya* (guardianship) and to deliver the share of Mu'mina to me since I am her legal guardian, as established by the legal document in my hand.[7]

In this case from Egypt the wife was made the *waṣī* over the young second wife of her deceased husband and was suing for her rights on her behalf. This was the nature of these families: the most capable, male or female, took the lead and became the overseer of the family rights. In the second case, referred to above, from the Jerusalem *sijill*, a woman is involved in litigation concerning sale of goods and property and the last case shows women engaged in real estate investments involving a group of investors, mostly men not directly related to them. The three cases are illustrative of the roles women played, their activities and investments and connections with others from whom they bought, sold, or entered into financial partnerships usual for Jerusalem during the Ottoman period.

Women's financial investments and labor will be discussed in the second section of this chapter. Here the focus is on family property, inheritance, guardianship, and family investments. In regard to guardianship, it should be pointed out that control of family inheritance was and continues to be a very important matter, as court records demonstrate. Women's control over their children's inheritance extended their authority over the larger family. We see this practice in many places in the Islamic world, in both urban and rural areas. James Reilly discusses this financial power of women and their activities in preserving the property of their children and investing it to increase their value. One example he gives is from 1848 Damascus, where

> two women, two widows of one man, appeared personally in court to sell their late husband's one-quarter share of the *gedik* (breach, crevice) of a water mill. The widows not only had inherited shares of the mill themselves, but one of them was also the guardian of her two minor children from her husband. Therefore, she had the right to sell the minors' shares of the mill as well, subject to court certification that the sale was in the best interests of the minors. Women also used legal guardianship to invest minors' money in commercial properties.[8]

There also seems to have been differences in regard to women's abilities to control family finances depending on the class to which they belonged: "evidence from the *sharīʿa* law court registers of Damascus indicate that women of the middle and upper classes dealt in residential, commercial and agricultural properties."[9]

While being a *waṣī* involved orphans of various classes, frequently *wiṣāya* involved control over substantial wealth as in the case of children who were sons or daughters of wealthy merchants. Here too mothers were often chosen as *waṣī*s who came to court to sue for what belonged to their underaged charges. A good example is that of a woman in sixteenth-century Nablus who sued her deceased husband's business partner for a share of the trade that should have gone to her children who were under her guardianship.[10] Sometimes the guardianship of a mother was placed under the supervision of a male relative, but at other times the opposite situation took place. In the following two cases we see how this worked, the first involves the *wiṣāya* of a woman under the *wilāya* of the grandfather, while in the second the grandfather is the *waṣī* with the mother as *walī*[11] (both terms refer to guardianship: the *walī* is a general guardian, usually a blood relative, who is given the guardianship of orphans and their property, while the *waṣī* is a specific legal executor assigned to manage the affairs of minors.)

> The Qassām (the judicial authority who decides inheritance shares) . . . assigned the woman . . . as guardian and spokesperson for her two sons. . . . She is to watch over them, make decisions on their behalf regarding buying and selling . . . handling all legal matters expected of a legal guardian . . . until they are old enough to handle their religious duties and their money . . . [witnessed by] the paternal grandfather . . . the *khawāja* [big merchant] . . . the honorable . . . the Qassām appointed the grandfather . . . as *nāẓir* [supervisor/warden] . . . on behalf of the boys over the guardian [who] cannot undertake transactions without his prior knowledge. . . .[12]
>
> Sheikh Ahmad . . . the legal *waṣī* over the named orphans . . . and the *nāẓir* over them . . . is to take no general or specific action regarding their property without the knowledge of the *nāẓira* [female supervisor/warden].[13]

The *sijills* from Jerusalem and from Egypt show that inheritance in the form of money or property could have been small or quite substantial depending on the class to which the woman belonged. Sometimes inheritance situations involving rich estates were a matter of generational disputes with increasingly branching out sections of wealthy families that clashed over inherited property that had not been equitably divided. Beshara Doumani's study of family life in Nablus of the seventeenth and eighteenth centuries makes extensive use of court records to recreate the life of one such family, its properties, and the disputes related to them. As he recounts, in 1117/1706, two brothers sued their uncles in court demanding property and *waqf* income that constituted their true inheritance from their mother who died almost two decades earlier. In the detailed list of the properties mentioned in the court case were included shops in which the mother held from 2 to 25 percent ownership, residential houses of which she owned various percentages, and agricultural land again in certain percentages. From the percentages and the previous ownership of the property, it appears that in most cases the mother inherited the property; however, in several cases where no inheritance was mentioned, she could have been one of the purchasers of the property.[14]

From the extensive records involving inheritance disputes in premodern courts it is clear that inheritance constituted a major source of wealth for both men and women, as did control of family property. At the same time, given the frequency of cases brought to court by women in pursuit of inheritance, it must be assumed that fair and lawful division of inherited property due to each member of the family from the estate of a deceased family member was not always guaranteed. The same can be said for the rights of minors and even adult younger brothers, perhaps because it was usually the eldest male who controlled the estate and it was through him that the division took place. A great diversity of situations is represented in inheritance disputes, many of which are cases involving women who came to court to complain of being denied their inherited property, or to dispute amounts actually received, usually in the presence of the male relative or the one responsible for the estate. Women also came to court to document that they paid shares belonging to other family members who inherited when they were the ones holding the property, or to document that they had received all the money due to them as heirs. A typical example of the last is that of Barka bint ʿĀbid al-Nābulsī, who declared and documented in court that she had received ten piasters from her brother Ḥassān as the price of her share amounting to one and one-fifth *qirāṭ* (twenty-four *qirāṭ*s are equal to one acre of land) for the house that she inherited from her father.[15]

The amounts inherited by women recorded in court records vary between the very modest to the very generous, depending on the socioeconomic class to which the women belonged. The same can be said about the marriage settlements women received in the form of dowry (*mahr*, total amount gifted to the bride), delayed dowry (*mahr muʾakhkhar*, previously agreed on part of the dowry to be paid at the time of divorce or husband's death), *nafaqa* (alimony/support), *ʿidda* (waiting period of three months following divorce during which a divorced wife cannot remarry and all her housing and living expenses are paid by the husband; the word also refers to the financial settlement received by the divorcée to cover expenses during the three months), or *mutʿa* (compensation to a divorced wife for a no-fault divorce), the latter four being various types of payments that can fall under alimony following divorce.

At the modest end is a mid-sixteenth-century marriage contract from Alexandria, Egypt, detailing a debt due to the wife from her husband that remained from her dowry: "fifty and a half *niṣf* and clothes allowance for three years, and a silver bracelet12 to 20 percent and a gold dinar."[16] At a more lucrative level from the same Alexandria *sijill* is a complicated settlement involving cash dowry and delayed dowry to be paid over a number of years, a method that appears often in Egyptian records of marriages among both rich and poor families:

> Sulaimān ibn ʿAmrān . . . married his betrothed the woman, daughter of Shihāta ibn ʿAbd Allāh . . . [for a dowry] valued at eight gold sulṭānī dinars . . . half the amount paid directly in gold and the rest to be paid by the husband to her over twenty years, guaranteed by two silver bracelets and a silver *hilāl bishūka* [crescent-shaped brooch] . . . as pawn under her hands.[17]

In a third case from the same *sijill*, the dowry reaches twelve gold sulṭānī dinars,[18] while in still another case, the dowry agreed upon was one goat at the time of contract followed by a payment of fifty *niṣf*s (a *niṣf fiḍa* was equivalent to a Turkish *para*, currency of the Ottoman empire) at the consummation of the marriage, which could be an indication of lesser affluence.[19]

Inheritance and other financial matters related to family relationships constituted an important source of income for Muslim women. Property left by women to heirs corroborates this and shows how women produced wealth even if they did not become involved in wage labor but rather gained money from investments. In her important research, *Women and Men in Late Eighteenth-Century Egypt*, Afaf Marsot gives details of property registered by women divided into class groups. Among "women of the artisanal class" she includes

> [the deceased] Sharīfa Zaynab Khātūn . . . [who] left an inheritance estimated at 24,249 *paras*, including 3,598 *paras* for a gold bracelet, 1101 *paras* for a silver anklet, 4330 *paras* in coin in her husband's keeping, 1210 paras in coin in her keeping, 1000 *paras* as the price of a *makān* (place/building), and 1100 *paras* as her back dowry.[20]

Here is also included Staita, the daughter of a "dealer in fodder" who married a cook. Together with her husband, Ḥāj Muḥammad, Staita "registered property jointly owned: two separate *makāns* [property] in different areas and half a *makān* next to one of the previous two *makāns*."[21]

Among "native elites," Marsot includes Badra, described as belonging to the merchant class, who set up a *waqf*

> comprising a property [*makān*] in Khatt al-Azbakiyya . . . described as a two-story building, each floor having a door and *hal* [hallway] and a *qaa* [workshop]. The property was surrounded on four sides by other properties which were described. The property belonged to Badra, who had bought it from Hanna. . . . Who had bought it from the woman Muna . . . according to a legal document.[22]

Badra also included in her registered *waqf* deed that she would act as *nāẓira* ("administrator") of the endowment to deal with all financial matters concerned with it. The case illustrates the keen knowledge and awareness that women had regarding personal and family finances and illustrates their role in investing and preserving family wealth. As for direct investments, Marsot includes the case of Fāṭima, who left

> 3 *qirats* and a fraction in two shops; 1 *qirat* and 4/9 *qirat* in a *maqaad* (part of a house); a little over 1 *qirat* in six businesses selling straw, over 1 *qirat* in a shop; weighing instruments deposited in one of the straw-selling establishments; over ½ *qirat* in two shops; less than 1 *qirat* in seven *hasils* [warehouse/place for storage], three floors of *wikalat al-sajai* [agency], and three shops; and over 1 *qirat* in a shop.[23]

Marsot notes that Fāṭima may have inherited some of this property, but another case she includes in this discussion, that of another Fāṭima, shows her registering a sale of half ownership of property storage facilities consisting of three floors that she had purchased from her brother's son for which "she paid the sum of 170 *riyal pataques* of 15,300 *paras*."[24]

The diversity of financial transactions that women were involved in, as registered in premodern courts, shows how integral women were to the economies of their communities and families. They inherited as well as left estates to their heirs after their death, some modest but others often quite substantial; they bought and registered property, invested the dowries they received and were keen on registering in court their shares and debts, even when it involved their husbands. They acted as guardians to their minor children as well as to other minor children within the family, watching out for their inheritance and investing it for them. Finally, they set up *waqfs* to preserve the fortunes or estates for future generations. In societies where both women and men had the right to own and hold property in their names, where women were given inheritance rights notwithstanding the unequal shares they received, and where the law did not forbid women from either working or from investing and holding wealth, one can only expect that they would be integral to the economy, doing well sometimes and getting hurt and robbed, as so many cases show, at other times.

Wage Labor or Women's Work

A father of a minor girl sued a woman by the name of Rakka in front of the court of Alexandria in 1865. The father alleged that Rakka, who identified herself as "the shaikha (female leader or chief) of a cotton *wābūr* (machine/factory)," enticed his daughter Fāṭima to come and work at the *wābūr*, where Fāṭima had an accident that cut off her fingers. He asked for financial compensation from Rakka. The court then listened to Rakka who explained:

> there is a *maḥḥal* (place/square) where women looking for work congregate, and any shaikha looking for workers goes to that *maḥḥal* and asks those who want to work; any who agree to work go with her. She went to that place and took back some women *shaghghālah* (workers) among whom was Fāṭima, daughter of the accuser, of their free will.[25]

Fāṭima worked for three days at the *wābūr* before the accident took place. This case informs us that there was already a local market for women's labor, a place where women and young girls like Fāṭima looking for work congregated. This was a time when manufacturing began in Egypt and deep structural changes included shifts in the economy and changing social patterns, but society was already quite familiar with the work of women and of women acting as *shaikhāt* (heads) of manufactories.

Teasing out information about women making a living shows that it seemed to be a natural part of women's lives throughout Islamic history and before that in ancient times. The Greek historian Herodotus (484–425 BCE), who visited Egypt in 445 BCE, had this to say about women: "The women attend the markets and trade, while the men sit at home at the loom . . . the women likewise carry burthens upon their shoulders, while the men carry them upon their heads."[26] The rich artistic heritage left by Ancient

Egyptians provides evidence of women who worked as weavers of textiles, laborers in fields, as priestesses and midwives, and in a number of other occupations. Such images fill museums worldwide in the form of paintings, wall carvings, and even actual statues, some of which are small and very detailed. Hatoon al-Fassi illustrated the economic power of women in her study of the tombs of Madā'in Ṣāliḥ in the Arabian Peninsula; she says, "two-thirds of the inscribed tombs mention women [which] suggests that they were wealthy and active in local affairs."[27] These inscriptions (dating from the first century BCE) showed women to be dedicators of the tomb, financing them to be the last resting place of members of their families.[28] It was not only the heavy financing of erecting and dedicating the tomb that illustrated the power of Nabataean women, but also the fact that "communal acceptance" was needed for this dedication. The story of Ḥalīma al-Sa'diyya, the Prophet Muḥammad's wet-nurse and foster mother,[29] tells us of the dependence of tribal women on both the earnings and patronage of chief tribes in Arabia by acting as wet-nurses and fostering their children. The poetess al-Khansā' (d. 24/645) famed for her eulogy of her two martyred brothers was also renowned for her veterinary abilities and was admired in lines penned by a suitor who witnessed her skill in healing dermatitis in camels.[30] Hind, wife of al- Ḥajjāj bin Yūsuf (d. 95/714), the Umayyad governor of Iraq, for example, was known to spin and weave even though she was married to the governor of Iraq.[31]

Like their pre-Islamic sisters, women in the Islamic period continued to be central to the economic life of their communities: They worked for a living, financed projects, bought and sold in the marketplace, and were active in setting up *waqf* endowments to preserve their families' wealth and/or establish endowments to serve the social needs of their communities. Women's investments in *waqf*s date to the early period of Islam, beginning with women closely associated with the Prophet Muḥammad, like his wife 'Ā'isha bint Abī Bakr (d. 58/678), who is said to have purchased a home to house a poor family with the condition that it be returned to her descendants after that. Her sister, Asmā' (d. 72/692), did the same with her home donated to charity, not to be sold or dispensed with.[32] While early information about *waqf*s consist mostly of short references primarily associated with females related to the Prophet's families, there are significant records of *waqf*s set up by women throughout Islamic history. Perhaps the most famous of the early medieval *waqf*s is that set up by Zubaida (d. 215/831), wife of the Abbasid caliph Harūn al-Rashīd, which extended water facilities from Baghdad to Mecca to make water available to pilgrims undergoing the long journey for *ḥājj*.[33]

Another charity meant to serve the larger public was established by Roxelana (d. 965/1558), the wife of the Ottoman sultan Sulaiman in Jerusalem. The *tikiyya* (Sufi hospice) of "Khasiki Sultan" (title used for Roxelana) served free meals to the poor and continues to do so until the present time.[34] Perhaps the most distinctive *waqf* established by important women is that of the Qarawiyyin mosque in the town of Fez in Morocco by Fāṭima al-Fihrī (d. 266/880) which became the University of al-Qarawiyyin, the oldest still-in-service university in the world. These activities continued into more recent years and among various levels of society. At the higher end can be found *waqf*s like the one set up in Cairo by another Zainab Khātūn (not to be confused with the previously mentioned Zainab, who died in 1836). This latter Zainab died in 1736, leaving behind her an "inheritance estimated at 24,249 *paras*, including 3,598 paras for a gold bracelet, 1,101 paras for a silver anklet, 4,330 paras in coin in her husband's keeping, 1,210 paras in coin in her keeping, 1,000 paras as the price of a *makān*, and 1,100 *paras* as her back dowry."[35]

The sources also provide information about women's involvement in trade both in the pre-Islamic and Islamic periods. Khadīja bint Khuwailid, first wife of the Prophet Muḥammad and the first to believe in him as God's Messenger, was a wealthy merchant in Mecca who hired Muḥammad to carry out trading expeditions to Syria and subsequently married him. Other women mentioned in the Prophet's *sīra* (biography) were merchants and possessed significant wealth. Perhaps Salma bint al-Najjār, the Prophet Muhammad's great-grandmother, mother of his grandfather Abū Ṭālib who raised him after his father's death, best exemplifies this. We know little about her, and the extant narratives concerning her can be extracted from the Prophet's sīra that give details of the origins of his family. Hāshim ibn ʿAbd Manāf, after whom the Hashemite branch of Quraish is named, led a caravan up north to trade in Gaza. On the way they stopped in Sūq al-Nabāṭ outside of Medina where merchants met to buy, sell, and exchange goods. There he saw a woman "standing in a prominent spot in the market issuing orders, purchasing and selling goods." Hāshim asked her to marry him even after learning that she kept *amraha biyadiha* (the right to marry and divorce herself); ʿAbd al-Muṯṭalib was the result of this marriage.[36] The Prophet's father is also said to have met with a woman, described by the sources as the woman who "accosted him" when he was on his way to offer marriage to the Prophet's mother, Āmina. The woman, identified as a "reader"(*qāriʾa*), meaning either a *kāhina* (priestess/soothsayer) or a literate person, asked him to marry her and offered a substantial dowry calculated at about 100 camels.[37] In other words, women traded, could command their own lives, and paid dowries similar to men. In fact, some narratives tell us that Khadīja actually gave Muḥammad the money to pay for her dowry.[38]

In later centuries, women guild heads are mentioned in the legal records of courts where they had to be certified, while women often appear as overseers of *waqf*.[39] Citations regarding women working as heads in guilds dominated by women appear often for guilds of physicians, weavers, beauticians, and entertainers.[40] Fariba Zarinebaf-Shahr records the case in 1778 of a flower-seller guild in Istanbul, where "women as well as elderly and handicapped men belonged to a branch of the gardeners' guild that planted flowers in Uskudar, a neighborhood of Istanbul on the Asiatic shore, and around the Bosphorus, and delivered them to boatmen and peddlers who sold them in baskets in the streets of Istanbul."[41]

The records of Islamic legal courts of the premodern period are filled with cases involving women who came to court to document legal and financial transactions, to sue for money lent or borrowed from others or dispute business partnerships, sell goods or property, pawn property, and various other matters. The archives from Jerusalem show women quite active in borrowing and extending credit, making money through pawning goods or loans at an interest. An example of this is a loan of

500 *qirsh*s (piasters) from Sarah to Yūsuf Zayn,[42] and a loan of 2,152 to Ibrāhim Rizq from Ammūna.[43] As evidence of interest being paid is a case in which a loan of 800 *qurūsh* was loaned with the stipulation, "I have given her for one year as security a room in a house I own against the loan . . . she may live in it or rent it out for the interest (*fā'iḍ*)."[44]

Fariba Zarinebaf-Shahr writes further about women who maintained "business relations as owners of urban property and workshops, and served as tax farmers. . . . They engaged in the rural economy as landowners, co-owners of private farms, and tax farmers . . . as managers of public endowments, owners and co-owners of public baths, and as moneylenders."[45] One such woman from Jerusalem was Badrī bint Ṭāhā, whose name first appears in connection with a pawn case in which she is said to have settled a pawn debt of four piasters to Esther Ibrāhīm who then turns over the pawned items, namely, "silver scissors, seven silver bracelets, two gold earrings."[46] But there is more to this case: the narrative continues by stating that Badrī also "sold the shares for two piasters and ten Egyptian pieces,"[47] receiving an amount that she then divides among her partners. We are not clear who the partners are or the nature of the shares or relationship with those who received shares.

Another case involving Badrī throws some light on her activities; she appears again in court a few weeks later. This time she was paying what she owed another lender in return for "attire (*atlas dhamm*), a bundle of embroidered clothes (*buqja*) and a right-hand (*yamin*) bundle (*buqja*) . . . a lot (*qism*) of silk."[48] From the items and quantity we are led to the conclusion that she was most probably in trade as a *dalāla* (seller/broker), a line of work quite frequently pursued by women in Jerusalem, sometimes working alone and more often forming groups supporting each other in buying and selling. When such groups were formed, they were expected to formally register their association in court where they received permission to work together as a group with joint liability.[49] A *kafīl* (sponsor) could also act as guarantor of repayment of losses incurred by such joint groups, a system that applied to male and female alike.[50] When *dalāla*s did not deliver goods they had been paid for or were found to cheat customers, the *qāḍī* (judge) forbade them from dealing; this was also the treatment received by male *dalāls*.[51]

In short, *shari'a* court records illustrate that women participated widely in their community's economy and that the *qāḍī*s (jurists/judges) did not question their right to work in particular jobs. This fits well with other *shari'a* sources, like the Qur'ān and *ḥadīth*, where there is no indication that women were forbidden from working. Women owned property and acted as landlords, coming often to court to demand late rent.[52] James Reilly had this to say about women and property, both residential and commercial property in nineteenth-century Damascus: "Women commonly acquired commercial properties, whether by consolidating family properties broken up by inheritance or by purchasing from strangers. . . . Women acquired a considerable variety of properties in this way, including coffee houses, greengrocer shops, herb and perfume shops, butcher shops, lumber warehouses, weaving shops, and others."[53]

Conclusion

To conclude, in this short survey about women as economic actors, I have tried to show that women's participation in the economic life of their communities was normative and that their contributions to their homes as wives and mothers were essential to the continuity and vitality of their communities and families. These contributions were recognized in financial terms through dowries and divorce settlements that amounted sometimes to substantial amounts often used by women to invest and produce an income. Their contributions also extended to multiple activities across the economic spectrum depending on class, place, and milieu. Some invested in agricultural land, others in housing and other urban instiutions, such as shops or coffee-houses, and many were involved in retail as *dalālas* or shop owners. Hard labor was also an area in which women participated, even though *fiqh* frowns on this activity and modern states have implemented laws limiting women's access to work labor, laws that have actually only impacted wages rather than stopped women from going into that market.

The chapter has also tried to show that when studying the life of women and their economic contributions, one needs to look at *fiqh* as the opinion of particular "*ulamā*" rather than as representing the lived realities of women or how the law dealt with women and the economic activities in which they were involved. In an earlier publication,[54] I pointed out how most jurists (*fuqahā'*) defined their outlook regarding women's lives based on considerations of class. Being largely middle-class themselves with upwardly mobile ambitions, they were in fact considering the situation of their own family members and those of the upper classes while their attitudes toward lower classes were quite different.

Looking at the sources—both archival and nonarchival—that deal with the actual lives of women also tells us that only taking cash-paid labor as a basis for economic agency is a mistake and highly misleading. Such a premise reflects modern conceptions propelled by ideas about economic development rather than the reality regarding how communities actually lived throughout history and in which women's work and productivity were a central part of the continuity and vitality of these societies, perhaps against all odds.

Notes

1. Sign was placed there by the Supreme Council of Antiquities of the government of Egypt, https://www.facebook.com/525699834244055/photos/a.1307719759375388/1307720549375309/?type=1&theater.
2. André Raymond, *Cairo* (Cambridge, MA: Harvard University Press, 2002), 283, 211.
3. Jerusalem court *sijill* no. 127, dating from 1670–1672 (1082–1083 AH) published in Zakariya 'Alawna, *Sijillāt maḥkamat al-Quds al-Shar'iyya al-'Uthmāniyya* (Ramallah, Palestine: Open University of Jerusalem, 2014). Of particular use are the tables published by

the authors itemizing cases being litigated before the Jerusalem court by page and case number, subject, date, and summary of proceedings that give an excellent overview of typical activities in these courts.

4. Ibid., 1081/1670, 9, case no. 10.
5. Ibid., 3, case no. 7.
6. Ibid., case no. 5.
7. Nablus Sharia Court, 1282–1284 [1864–1866], 2–14:157.
8. James Reilly, "Women in the Economic Life of Late-Ottoman Damascus," *Arabica* 42, no. 1 (1995): 86.
9. Ibid., 81–82.
10. University of Jordan Library, archival records, Sharīʿa court records, Nablus, Jerusalem, al-Salt, 1276–1277 [1860–1861] (Amman, Jordan), 2–13:27.
11. *Waṣī* is the guardian of a minor; as for *walī*, this is a person assigned the authority to oversee legal matters in particular situations. Generally speaking, a *walī* also supervises the *waṣī*, although the courts often reversed these responsibilities in specific case.
12. Egypt, Bāb al- ` Āli Court, Qiṣma ʿArabiyya, 1013–1604 [403–1012], 16:119–214.
13. Jerusalem, 1058 [1648], 28–140:317–2.
14. Beshara B. Doumani, *Family Life in the Ottoman Mediterranean* (Cambridge: Cambridge University Press, 2017).
15. Ibid., 91, case no. 5.
16. Egypt, Alexandria Sharīʿa Court, 957 [1550], 1:17–80.
17. Ibid., 1:15–74.
18. Ibid., 1:11–50.
19. Ibid., 1:408–1713.
20. Afaf Lutfi al-Sayyid Marsot, *Women and Men in Late Eighteenth-Century Egypt* (Austin: University of Texas Press, 2008), 186, discussing a court case from Egypt, Qisma ʿAskariyya (Q.A.), 1152 [1739], box 148, folder 128, 92–93.
21. Ibid., discussing court case: Q.A. 110, folder 795, 342.
22. Ibid., quoting court case: Egypt, Bab Al-ʿĀji, Shahr ʿAqāri, no. 232, item 144, pl. 110, 28 Rajab 1159.
23. Ibid., Q. A. 125, folder 63, p. 41.
24. Ibid., Egypt, Maḥfaẓa 7, no. 30/31, 1189 [1775].
25. Maḥkamat al-Askandariyya, no. 3, Daʿāwī, 1285–1293, 1. 143–144, case 167.
26. Herodotus, *The Histories*, trans. George Rawlinson (Digireads.com Publishing, 2010), 155.
27. Hatoon al-Fassi, "Women and Family in Nabataea," in *Women in Pre-Islamic Arabia: Nabataea*, BAR International Series, British Archaeological Reports, July 15, 2007, 94.
28. Ibid., 93.
29. Ibn Hishām, *al-Sīra al-Nabawiyya* (Beirut: Dār al-Kitāb al-ʿArabī, 1990), 1:178.
30. Zafar al-Qasimi, *al-ḥayāt al-Ijtimāʿiya ʿind al-ʿArab* (Beirut: Dār al-Nafāʾis, 1981), 12.
31. Ibn Hishām, *al-Sīra al-Nabawiyya*, 1:178; al-Tabarī, *Tārikh al-rusul wa-l-mulūk* (Cairo: Dār al-Maʿārif bi-Misr, 1990), 6:448.
32. Hussain Elasrag, "Toward a New Role for the Institution of Waqf," in MPRA, Munich Personal RePEc Archive, July 30, 2017, 13 (available online at https://mpra.ub.uni-muenchen.de/80513/ MPRA Paper no. 80513, 27 pages).

33. Darb Zubaida/Zubaida trail is a historical trail leading from Baghdad to Mecca that facilitated travel for pilgrimage, providing water through an accompanying canal; see "Zubaida Trail, a Historical Landmark and Ancient International Road to Makkah," *Arab News*, August 8, 2018, https://www.arabnews.com/node/1352141/saudi-arabia.
34. Amy Singer, "Serving up Charity: The Ottoman Public Kitchen," *Journal of Interdisciplinary History* 35, no. 3 (Winter 2005): 481–500.
35. Marsot, *Women and Men*, appendix C, no. 1.
36. Muḥammad ibn Sa'd al-Zuhrī, *Kitāb al-ṭabaqāt al-kābir* (Cairo: al-Khanjī Bookstore, 2001), 1: 60–61.
37. Ibn Hishām, *Al-Sīra al-Nabawiyya*, 1:178.
38. 'Alī ibn Burhān al-Dīn al-ḥalabī, *al-Sīra al-ḥalabiyya* (Cairo: al-Maṭba'a al-Azhariyya, 1932), 163–164; Qadriyya ḥusayn, *Shahīrat al-nisā' fī al-'alam al-islamī*, 2nd ed. (Cairo: Mu'assasat al-Mar'a wa al-Dhakīra, 2004), 35–36.
39. For example, Amna bint Muḥammad Kāmil who was the *nāzira* over her maternal grandfather's *waqf* in Jerusalem (15, case 4) published in 'Alawna, *Sijillāt mahkamat al-Quds, sijill* no. 127, 45.
40. Al-Quds Sharī'a Court, 972 [1564], 46:12–2; 939 [1532], 3:95–3; 1010 [1601], 83:156–6, 235–5; 937 [1530], 1:267–2; 939 [1532], 3:12–1; 957 [1550], 23:585–12 in al-Ya'qūbi, *Nāḥiyat al-Quds*, 1:127.
41. Fariba Zarinebaf-Shahr, "The Role of Women in the Urban Economy of Istanbul, 1700–1850," *International Labor and Working-Class History* 60 (Fall, 2001): 151.
42. Al-Quds Sharī'a Court, 1229 [1814], 297:94, in Ziyād 'Abd al-'Azīz al-Madanī, *Madīnat al-Quds wa-jiwāruhā khilal al-fatra 1215–1245H./1800–1830* (Amman, 1996), 112.
43. Al-Quds Sharī'a Court, 1228 [1812], 296:26, in al-Madanī, *Madīnat al-Quds*, 115.
44. Haifa Sharī'a Court, [1903/4], 1321: 274–42, quoted in Mahmoud Yazbak, *Haifa in the Late Ottoman Period. 1864–1914: A Muslim Town in Transition* (Leiden: E. J. Brill, 1998), 185.
45. Zarinebaf-Shahr, "Role of Women," 152.
46. 'Alawna, *Sijillāt maḥkamat al-Quds, sijill* no. 127 dating from 1670–1672 (1082–1083 AH), 4, case 2.
47. Ibid., 4, case 2.
48. Ibid., 5, case 5.
49. Al-Quds Sharī'a Court, 1041 [1632], 119:121–122, in Ibid., 175.
50. Al-Quds, 1040 [1631], 117:282–284 and 117:282–287, published in Maḥmūd 'Alī 'Aṭā' Allāh, *Wathā'iq al-ṭawā'if al-ḥirafiyya fi al-Quds fi al-qarn al-sābi' 'ashar al-milādī* (Nablus, al-Nagah University, 1991), 1:172.
51. Al-Quds Sharī'a Court, 1071 [1661], 151:603–1.
52. This was the case with Bint Ṣāliḥ, who sued Muḥammad ibn 'Umar for the rent of three *qirāṭ* of land that he rented from her; Ibid, p. 5, case 8.
53. Reilly, "Women in the Economic Life," 84–85.
54. Amira Sonbol, "Shari'a Court Records and Fiqh as Sources of Women's History," *Religion and Literature* 42 no.1–2 (Spring–Summer 2010): 229–246.

Bibliography

'Alawna, Zakariyya. *Sijillāt Maḥkamat al-Quds al-Shar'iyya al-'Uthmāniyya*. Ramallah, Palestine: Open University of Jerusalem, 2014.

ʻAtāʼ Allāh, Maḥmūd ʻ Ali. *Wathāʼiq al-ṭawāʼif al-ḥirafiyya fī al-Quds fī al-qarn al-sābiʻ ʻashar al-milādī*. Jordan: Nablus, al-Nagah University, 1991.
Beshara B. Doumani. *Family Life in the Ottoman Mediterranean*. Cambridge: Cambridge University Press, 2017.
Fassi, Hatoon al-. *Women in Pre-Islamic Arabia: Nabataea*. BAR International Series. British Archaeological Reports, July 15, 2007.
Herodotus. *The Histories*. Translated by George Rawlinson. Overland Park, KS: Digireads.com Publishing, 2010.
Ibn Hisham. *Al-sira al-nabawīyya*. Beirut: Dār al-Kitāb al-ʻArabī, 1990.
Madanī, Ziyād ʻAbd al-ʻAzīz al-. *Madīnat al-Quds wa-jiwāruhā khilal al-fatra 121–1245H./1800–1830*. Amman: n. pub., 1996.
Marsot, Afaf Lutfi al-Sayyid. *Women and Men in Late Eighteenth-Century Egypt*. Austin: University of Texas Press, 2008.
Qāsimi, Zafar al-. *Al-ḥayāt al-ijtimāʿiyya ʿind al-ʿarab*. Beirut: Dār al-Nafāʼis, 1981.
Raymond, André. *Cairo*. Cambridge, MA: Harvard University Press, 2002.
Reilly, James A. "Women in the Economic Life of Late-Ottoman Damascus." *Arabica* 42, no. 1 (1995): 79–106.
Singer, Amy. "Serving up Charity: The Ottoman Public Kitchen." *Journal of Interdisciplinary History* 35 (Winter, 2005):481–500.
Sonbol, Amira. "Shariʻa Court Records and Fiqh as Sources of Women's History." *Religion and Literature* 42 no.1–2 (Spring–Summer 2010): 229–246.
Supreme Council of Antiquities of the Government of Egypt. Al-Idārat al-markaziyya li-l-tasjīl wa al-tawthīq, Feb, 22, 2019 https://www.facebook.com/525699834244055/photos/a.1307719759375388/1307720549375309/?type=1&theater
Ṭabarī, Abū Jaʻfar ibn Jarīr al-. *Tārikh al-rusul wal-muluk*. Cairo: Dār al-Maʻārif bi-Miṣr, 1990.
Yazbak, Mahmoud. *Haifa in the Late Ottoman Period. 1864–1914: A Muslim Town in Transition*. Leiden: E. J. Brill, 1998.
Zarinebaf-Shahr, Fariba. "The Role of Women in the Urban Economy of Istanbul, 1700–1850." *International Labor and Working-Class History* 60 (Fall 2001).
Zuhrī, Muḥammad ibn Saʻd al-. *Kitāb al-ṭabaqāt al-kābir*. Cairo: al-Khanjī Bookstore, 2001.

Archival Sources

Amman, Jordan. University of Jordan Library. Archival records. Sharīʻa court records. Al-Salt, Nablus, Jerusalem, al-Quds.
Egypt, Alexandria Sharīʻa Court; Daʻāwī.
Egypt, Cairo. Bāb al- ʻĀli Court; Qiṣma ʻArabiyya; Shahr ʻAqāri; Mahfaẓa; Qisma ʻAskariyya.

E

WOMEN'S LIVED REALITIES AND THEIR RELIGIOUS AND SOCIAL ACTIVISM IN THE MODERN PERIOD

THROUGH the centuries, a significant part of women's lived realities has been shaped by their roles and status as mothers; "mothering" and "motherwork" often consume women's lives. Although everyone concedes their importance, at least rhetorically, cultural attitudes often do not match the appreciation that everyone claims to have for mothers and for the difficulties inherent in motherwork. One chapter traces the trajectory of cultural and social attitudes toward mothers and mothering and makes apparent the progressive transformations in the constructions of "womanhood" and conceptualizations of gendered identities, particularly of motherhood, in a number of Muslim-majority settings. More recently, Muslim mothers are having to endure sharp scrutiny by governmental and intelligence agencies in the wake of Islamist militancy in certain Muslim-majority societies, further enhancing their vulnerability to changing social and political attitudes about motherhood and its responsibilities.

In addition to their traditional roles as mothers, teachers, and benefactors of scholarship, elite and educated women in the modern period have also assumed positions of political authority, sometimes acceding to the position of president or prime minister in the modern nation-state. Several such female political personalities are studied in one chapter and bring to light the various historical and sociopolitical factors that have paved the way to their ascension to the highest echelons of political power in their respective societies and the lasting effects of their unique legacies.

A heightened "woman-centered" or "feminist" consciousness starts to become evident in the writings of women authors by the late nineteenth century and gains momentum through the twentieth century into our own time. A distinctive phenomenon that we may term "Islamic feminism" is discernible in the twentieth century that focuses particularly on scriptural hermeneutics in order to establish egalitarian, woman-friendly readings of the Qurʾān. This feminist/womanist consciousness helped spur women's activism in the political and national spheres in the Arab world starting in the nineteenth century, when the struggle against Western colonial occupation was underway. The Egyptian Women's Union led by Huda Shaarawi gained much prominence during the Egyptian independence struggle against British colonizers and gave legitimacy to women's public activism in the service of a noble cause. But the Egyptian Women's Union became much more under Shaarawi's leadership—it transformed itself into a women's rights organization that began to demand equal political and social rights for Egyptian women. Their influence would soon spread to other Arab countries.

This momentum continued through the twentieth century, galvanizing women activists from different backgrounds in many parts of the Muslim-majority world who began to demand enhanced civil and political rights, frequently in the name of Islam. In addition to focusing specifically on the activism of modern Muslim women in Egypt, this section goes on to describe the activities of feminist modernist reformers in Malaysia and the United States and those of sociopolitical activists in politically volatile areas, such as Palestine, Syria, and Iran, as well as the activism of social organizers and human rights activists in highly Islamophobic societies, such as in France and other parts of western Europe. Other chapters highlight the exercise of religious leadership by Muslim women in China, South Asia, and South Africa; by women exegetes of the Qurʾān and juridical reformers in Southeast Asia; by women social reformers in Saudi Arabia and the Gulf region and by female government officials in Turkey, among others. These countries and regions were chosen to be in the spotlight because of the visibility and robustness of Muslim women's activism there and the availability of scholars who study these areas and can write authoritatively about them. Other countries and regions were inevitably left out due to length constraints and also due to the paucity of studies conducted in these areas. Many of the reformers and activists of different stripes covered in these chapters are shown to invoke Islamic texts and history to empower themselves, whether explicitly or tacitly, creating for themselves a compelling mandate to (re)claim the larger social "public" sphere as the legitimate arena for their activities.

CHAPTER 15

WOMEN IN THE MOSQUE

Contesting Public Space and Religious Authority

MARION KATZ

THE "WOMEN'S MOSQUE MOVEMENT" AND ITS INTERPRETATION IN WESTERN SCHOLARSHIP

A group of women sitting in a circle recite the Qur'an in unison after a teacher sitting at the front of a mosque. A narrator intones,

> Women in the mosque—a revolution in Egypt, where the mosque has long been a bastion of men's power. Although Muslim women have the same religious duties as men, in the past women were expected to worship and pray at home. But these women represent a movement that is changing not only the face of the mosque, but the streets of Cairo itself.[1]

Thus begins Marilyn Gaunt and Elizabeth Fernea's influential 1982 documentary *A Veiled Revolution*. The remainder of the film, like much of the Western scholarship on Muslim women in that era, focuses on the emergence of new forms of modest Islamic dress among middle-class women in Egypt. Despite its brevity, however, the film's opening vignette prefigured (and perhaps contributed to) some of the themes that would predominate as scholars in Western academia gradually turned their attention to women's increasing presence in mosques in many parts of the Islamic world. Although the women represented are not engaged in overtly subversive activity, their presence in the mosque is construed as a "revolution" that challenges "men's power." While scholarly attention at that time was largely focused on the resurgence of veiling, the increased visibility of women in mosques raised the same underlying issue among Western academic observers as the spread of new forms of modest dress: the perceived contrast between the assertion of women's piety in the public sphere (which feminist scholars could hail as an expression of female agency) and the conservative gender ideology that frequently accompanied it.

In her groundbreaking 1992 survey *Women and Gender in Islam*, the Egyptian-American scholar Leila Ahmed represented the progressive exclusion of women from the mosque in the early Islamic period as a central element of the erosion of their rights in the post-Prophetic period (although veiling still receives more sustained attention).[2] Nevertheless, she was guarded about the feminist potential of women's reappearance in the mosque, cautiously observing,

> Some activities being pursued by some veiled women, such as reclaiming of the right to attend prayer in mosques, appear to support the view that some veiled women are to some extent challenging the practices of establishment Islam with respect to women. But little research is available on some Muslim women's return to the mosques and its significance.[3]

A decade later, Saba Mahmood's *Politics of Piety* placed the "women's mosque movement" and the challenge it posed to feminist scholarship's received conceptions of agency at the center of the conversation about women and contemporary Islam in the English-speaking academy. Mahmood's fundamental argument was that conservative women's project of cultivating a pious self should be understood as a form of agency even in the absence of any overt counterhegemonic content. This intervention makes sense of Gaunt and Fernea's intuition that women docilely perfecting their Qur'anic recitation were engaged in a form of self-actualization with deep political implications. Mahmood opens the book with the conundrum that

> [t]he burgeoning of this movement marks the first time in Egyptian history that such a large number of women have held public meetings in mosques to teach one another Islamic doctrine, thereby altering the historically male-centered character of mosques as well as Islamic pedagogy. At the same time, women's religious participation within such public arenas of Islamic pedagogy is critically structured by, and serves to uphold, a discursive tradition that regards subordination to a transcendent will (and thus, in many instances, to male authority) as its coveted goal.[4]

In this model, the perceived tension between the location and the overt content of women's mosque-based teaching lies in the mosque's character as a "public" and "male-centered" space; it is also a space that confers authority, such that women's presence there "alters the historically male-centered character of . . . Islamic pedagogy." Understood in this way, religious women's presence in mosques is inherently counterhegemonic, and thus contrasts with the overt content of their gender ideology.

Mahmood's study helped to inspire a vast body of research focusing on women and mosques. Much of this work has followed the lines of inquiry initiated by Mahmood, focusing on the ways in which the religiously conservative women who often operate within the context of mosques and madrasas nevertheless "show remarkable agency in trying to expand their sphere of authority."[5] This wealth of new research has also, however, both enriched and complicated the framework in which mosques are posited to be "public" venues distinctively associated with religious authority.

The Mosque as "Public" Space

As Jeff Weintraub has analyzed in a classic article, the public/private dichotomy is used in scholarly literature in multiple and sometimes contradictory ways. On a very basic level, it can reflect either of two intersecting but analytically distinct contrasts: that between the hidden and the revealed, and that between the individual and the collective.[6] At a higher level of theoretical elaboration, Weintraub identifies four distinct meanings that have emerged from different traditions of social and political analysis within the Western academy: one "which sees the public/private distinction primarily in terms of the distinction between state administration and the market economy"; a second "which sees the 'public' realm in terms of political community and citizenship, analytically distinct from both the market and the administrative state"; a third "which sees the 'public' realm as a sphere of fluid and polymorphous sociability"; and a fourth (associated with feminist analysis) that "conceive[s] of the distinction between 'private' and 'public' in terms of the distinction between the family and the larger economic and political order."[7]

Although the concept of the "public" is rarely theoretically elaborated in studies of women's presence in mosques, the routine description of mosques as "public" space suggests that women's presence in mosques both makes them and their religious activities visible and enables them to act collectively. The implicit contrast may be imagined as a woman praying alone in her home, her piety visible to none but God. Individual studies of women's activities inside and outside of mosques have offered greater insight into the "public" nature of mosques (and the ways in which they contrast with other religious venues) in several of the distinct senses identified by Weintraub. While the first approach (identifying the public in contrast with the market economy) has been marginal to this literature, there has been significant attention to the other three themes of "political community and citizenship," of sociability, and of the family.

The framing of the mosque as "public" space corresponds to some elements of the normative model historically developed by Muslim legal scholars. *Fiqh* (legal) texts conventionally articulated the issue of women's mosque attendance in terms of the legitimacy of women's "going out" (*khurūj*) to the mosque, creating a parallel with other activities (from grave visitation to grocery shopping) that could take a woman out of the house. In contrast with most modern discussions of women's mosque access, this suggests that classical Muslim jurists' attention was primarily directed not to the special qualities of mosque space, but to the legal status of (and justifications for) a woman's departure from her home. This ideal model is one of (elite) female seclusion, rather than of gender segregation involving both male and female "publics." Premodern legal scholars were concerned to mitigate a woman's isolation by affirming her right to some degree of female companionship and visiting with core kin, but were generally uninterested in the religious and social functions of pious activities that women pursued in their homes.

However, evidence from other kinds of sources suggests that this framing does not unproblematically reflect the historical reality of Muslim societies. In many places women were involved in grave-visitation practices that took them far from the home and involved pious sociability and the cultivation of kinship networks, defying any simple distinction between public and private. Religious scholars often deplored women's grave visitation more vigorously than they objected to their mosque attendance, suggesting that women's ritual preferences did not directly conform to legal norms. Although women's historical access to mosques appears to have been uneven, there is extensive evidence for their presence in many mosques over the centuries; however, the temporal rhythms and religious objectives of women's usage of mosque space diverged from those of men. Rather than being concentrated primarily in Friday congregational prayers, women's distinctive patterns of mosque usage could include discrete individual prayer between the times of congregational worship as well as distinctive forms of women's piety or single-sex sociability.[8] Thus, women's use of mosque space has not historically conformed to the model of "public" religious activity. Similarly, in a paper examining women's mosque groups in Sudan at the turn of the twenty-first century, Salma Nageeb describes how the women "domesticate" the mosque by using it as a venue for activities such as childcare and social gatherings.[9]

If women's activities in mosques have not been monolithically "public," neither were home-based activities necessarily "private." Domestic rituals such as commemorations of the birth of the Prophet Muḥammad (*mawlids*) have historically been particularly popular among women. In the Middle East beginning in the late medieval period, domestic *mawlids* involved hospitality and gift-giving; they activated social networks and contributed to the reputational profile of the household. Such rituals, which were often held in honor of lifecycle events, may have appealed to women because they responded to issues of familial well-being for which women were made particularly responsible, but they did not reflect women's isolation from the world outside of the family and the home.[10]

In the modern context as well, scholars have found that women's religious activities inside and outside of the mosque do not fit a simple public/private dichotomy. In her study of women in the Yemeni city of Zabid in the 1980s and 1890s, Anne Meneley focuses on the round of visiting that consumes much of their time and attention. (Significantly, the central social and ethical value of women's visiting is encapsulated in the concept of *khurūj*, "going out"[11]—precisely the word used by classical jurists to problematize women's excursions from the home.) Meneley emphasizes that "the sphere in which women socialize is not 'private,' although the venue is people's homes."[12] In this context, women generate honor and prestige not merely through their sociability and generosity but also through their piety. Although they do not attend mosques, they publicly display their religious devotion in each other's homes, whether by praying during visits or by leaving in order to pray.[13] *Mawlid*s and other domestic rituals similarly play a role in the public and political production of family honor.[14]

Rather than simply discarding the public/private dichotomy, Jaqueline Fewkes observes that it "is indeed a central spatial practice in a number of ethnographic cases"; it is thus necessary to "examine culturally specific assemblages of this 'public/private' divide, as the actual spatial practices and accompanying systems of social meaning that are mapped onto local geographies can vary significantly."[15] The anthropologist Niloofar Haeri points to the existence of "*degrees* of publicness and privateness in the performance of the *salat* [prayer]," observing of twenty-first century Iran:

> At one end of the scale, there is the mass Friday prayer on the grounds of Tehran University that is led by a senior cleric and . . . broadcast on television inside and outside of Iran. . . . Then there are group prayers in smaller mosques that are not televised. . . . There are individuals who pray at their local mosque by themselves. . . . are also group prayers at home on special occasions. . . . Finally, there is the most private prayer performed in one's room with no one else present except oneself and God.[16]

If we do not assume that religious activity outside of mosques is inherently "private" in the sense of being purely individual or socially invisible, then we must refine our sense of the factors that make mosque-based activities distinctive in any specific context. Both Haeri and Azam Torab offer insights into the criteria by which some women in postrevolutionary Iran evaluate prayer inside and outside of the mosque. Both find that some informants regard the mosque as a less desirable venue, in part because it is seen as less conducive to pious concentration. This perception is in part related to inadequate accommodations for women, but congregational prayers are also seen as a context where men's minds are likely to wander.[17] Conversely, in other contexts, the mosque may offer an atmosphere of quiet, sanctity, and separation from distractions of home and family. Fewkes notes that "[a]lthough women in the Maldives could pray at home, many *mudahim* [female mosque functionaries] noted in their interviews that women chose to come to the mosque as they find communal worship more personally satisfying and spiritually beneficial."[18]

In addition to complicating our understanding of the ways in which women's prayer may be socially visible, recent literature on women's mosque usage directs attention to two of the other iterations of the "public" enumerated by Weintraub: the mosque as a venue for active citizenship and debate and the mosque as an arm of the administrative state. The relationship between the mosque, politics, and the state has varied widely both in terms of historical experience and in terms of the ideals envisioned by Muslims. In the contemporary period, thinkers such as the Muslim Brotherhood–affiliated Egyptian scholar-activist Hiba Rāʾūf have argued that mosques should be multipurpose sites of social and political activity (as the Prophet's mosque was in his lifetime), and posited that this role is particularly important for the civic integration of Muslim women.[19] In contrast, the American Muslim leader Zaid Shakir asserts that "[o]ur homes, schools, campuses, offices, institutes, and meeting halls provide ample platforms for us to present our particular views concerning politics and society. The political neutrality of the mosque must be maintained."[20]

The varying relationship between mosques and the state can have a significant impact on women's use of mosque space. Haeri notes that the political valence of much contemporary mosque ritual in postrevolutionary Iran may deter some people (perhaps particularly women, for whom attendance is not traditionally obligatory) from attending.[21] On the other hand, the mosque is a site of political expression; Torab observes that "the political significance of sermons in the Islamic Republic is well-known so that barring women from the pulpit in effect denies them an influential political platform."[22] While the Islamic Republic of Iran may be a particularly striking case, parallel phenomena have been noted elsewhere. Noting the trend toward state funding and administration of mosques in Egypt since the 1970s, Mona Atia observes that increasing government control and surveillance have produced "a culture of fear and self-regulation inside mosques."[23] Atia also notes that in recent years "[m]osques and their associations [have] constituted a crucial space for the poor and the lower middle class to receive social services that formerly were provided by *awqaf* [charitable foundations] and the state," a situation that compels some poor women to attend mosque activities in order to receive needed aid.[24]

States may also directly encourage women's presence in mosques. The inclusion of architecturally distinct women's space in official state mosques has been a widespread, and symbolically resonant, practice since the 1950s.[25] As Kishwar Rizvi notes of the Ayatollah Khomeini Grand Muṣallā at Tehran University, "the visibility of women worshippers has an important ideological function."[26] State intervention may extend to much broader programs of education or indoctrination, such as the mosque-based literacy programs sponsored by the Moroccan government since 2001.[27] Women's access to and role within mosques may be conditioned by state projects in Western minority-Muslim contexts as well. In Sweden, mosques must adhere to "fundamental values" including gender equality in order to qualify for government grants; as a consequence, the main mosque of Stockholm faced a gender discrimination suit, raising issues such as the square footage of space available in the women's balcony.[28] In the United States in the post–September 11 period, mosques have become a major target of both government surveillance and social scrutiny; Leila Ahmed places the Women-Friendly Mosque Initiative sponsored by the Islamic Society of North America within this overall context (although it also clearly responds to widespread demands from American Muslim women).[29]

Some states have taken steps to promote women's religious leadership in mosques. The Moroccan government has instituted a program training and deploying female as well as male religious guides (*murshid/murshida*), with the objective in part of "promot[ing] the state's Islamic perspective."[30] In Turkey, where the official ideology of secularism (*laïklik*) has been accompanied by comprehensive state supervision of religious institutions, the Directorate of Religious Affairs has employed increasing numbers of officially appointed female preachers (*vaizeler*) over the last several decades.[31]

Fatma Tütüncü shows that the activities of these female preachers serve the interests of the Turkish state not only by asserting a "correct" rather than "superstitious" form of Islam, but (for instance) by "replicat[ing] the state discourse on the Kurdish question."[32] Nevertheless, these officially sanctioned female preachers have helped to increase Turkish women's access to mosques in many localities, sometimes in the face of resistance from imams and others who believe that women should pray at home.[33] As several studies note, the rising presence of state-sponsored female religious professionals does not simply reflect the introduction of female religious leaders where none existed before; rather, they may supplement or displace other forms of women's religious leadership.[34]

Diversity among Women: Age and Social Class

If recent studies have identified various factors conditioning the accessibility and appeal of mosques, they have also differentiated among different constituencies of women. Rather than positing that "women" as a homogeneous class have achieved greater visibility in mosques, scholars have increasingly pointed to the differential ways in which various groups of women have used (or avoided) mosque space. In historical and normative terms, the most obvious distinction has been among women of different age cohorts, with many classical Muslim legal authorities advocating that younger women avoid mosque attendance altogether. While some schools of law (particularly the Ḥanafīs) gradually extended this disapproval to all but the oldest women, the Mālikīs in particular have tended to maintain a normative distinction between young women (who are in principle discouraged from attending the mosque) and postmenopausal women whose presence is tolerated if not encouraged. Ethnographic evidence from historically Mālikī regions of North and West Africa suggests that this age distinction has persisted into the contemporary period in some areas, although the lack of uniformity across regions suggests that this pattern is not a direct or inevitable result of Mālikī legal teachings.[35] As Cleo Cantone has described for Senegal, in many places this pattern has been challenged since the 1980s or 1990s by a trend toward mosque attendance by young women members of Islamic reformist movements.[36]

In many places women's mosque usage is also deeply modulated by social class. Haeri notes not only that her female Iranian informants (all of whom are upper middle class) rarely pray in the mosque, but that "[e]ven their male relatives pray at home most of the time."[37] Without denying the increased magnitude of women's presence in Egyptian mosques in the 1970s and 1980s, it is worth asking whether the attention it attracted also had something to do with a shift in the social class of the women involved. The informal presence of lower-class women in mosques, which scattered evidence suggests had always been part of the mosque scene in Cairo, attracted less attention. Of course, class associations may also be specific to individual mosques; the mosque contexts studied by Mahmood varied widely in this regard.[38] The persisting classed valence of mosque space may also have played a role in the rise of the semiprivate religious salons that became popular in some circles of elite Egyptian women in the late twentieth century. Hiroko

Minesaki observes that since the late 1990s "salons and other nonmosque spaces . . . have been increasingly used by upper and upper-middle-class Egyptian women" who "felt lectures at the mosque were too crowded and included uneducated and unsophisticated participants."[39] Sofia Nehaoua notes that it is the socioeconomic homogeneity of these gatherings rather than their religious or ideological content that makes them distinctively appealing to the upper classes.[40] Conversely, however, the more open nature of mosques does not inevitably erase differences of access or opportunity; Salma Naguib's Sudanese informants describe how social class (and the resulting prevalence of formal education and domestic help) conditions the ability of members of women's mosque groups to pursue religious study and, ultimately, roles of pious authority.[41]

Mosque Space and Women's Religious Authority

The other central question that emerges from the scholarship on women in mosques produced in recent decades is the relationship between mosques and Muslim women's religious authority. In the Preface to their volume *Women, Leadership, and Mosques* (the single most substantive publication on the subject to date), Masooda Bano and Hilary Kalmbach describe "the mosque and the *madrasah*" as "the formal sphere of religious authority."[42] The scholarship they gather in this volume, as well as other work on the topic, both elaborates on and nuances the special role of mosques in this regard. From a broad historical point of view, it is not obvious that mosques per se play a central role in the generation of scholarly authority. Much Islamic teaching has occurred (and continues to occur) in mosques, but knowledge acquired in other venues, such as a teacher's home, is equally authoritative. The scholarly status of an imam or even of a *khaṭīb* has historically been modest in comparison with that of a mufti (jurisconsult).[43] Nevertheless, mosque teachers and preachers have traditionally enjoyed an unusual ability to disseminate their messages to a broader religious public. The degree to which this remains true in comparison with other venues and media for the dissemination of religious messages in the contemporary world can be determined only through focused studies of individual contexts.[44] More broadly, eligibility for the role of imam or *khaṭīb* can carry significant symbolic weight. As Uta Lehmann observes, "Ritual leadership is still regarded as the final expression of male 'ownership' of mosque space."[45]

Jacqueline Fewkes notes that the empirical diversity of titles and roles for Muslim women religious leaders across different cultural contexts defies any simple mapping onto the category of "imam." She also cautions, however, that a focus on the specificity of these local roles may obscure the fact that the term "imam" subsumes a wide variety of specific functions on the ground even when applied to men; there is thus no dichotomy between universal and normative male ritual roles and local and customary female ones.[46] Women's ritual leadership in mosques takes many different forms, which may or may not incorporate functions such as leadership of congregational prayer or the delivery of Friday sermons.

Margaret Rausch notes that, unlike their male counterparts, the Moroccan *murshidāt* do not lead prayers or deliver Friday sermons even as temporary replacements for imams.[47] Even in the celebrated women's mosques of western China, which have autonomous female religious personnel, leadership of congregational prayer is not a traditional core function of female mosque functionaries and the space does not traditionally include the *minbar* (pulpit) associated with the official delivery of the Friday sermon (although women sometimes do give a sermon).[48] In some cases, Muslim leaders creatively circumvent technical limitations on women's ritual roles; for instance, Halima Krausen (a German woman who has led Hamburg's Islamic Center since 1996) writes Friday sermons and disseminates them electronically, but has declined to deliver the *khuṭba* personally in the context of Friday prayers unless and until this move is unanimously supported by her congregation.[49] Similarly, the leadership of the Claremont Main Road Mosque in Cape Town redefined the address delivered there by amina wadud in August 1994 as a "pre-*khuṭba*" in order to defuse protests against women functioning as *khaṭībs*.[50]

In contrast, for other Muslim gender activists it is deeply important for women to inhabit the full range of ritual leadership roles defined by the Sharīʿa. Unlike her "pre-*khuṭba*" in 1994, wadud's leadership of a gender-mixed Friday prayer in New York City in 2005 fully affirmed her role as an imam. Juliane Hammer describes this event as representing "an embodied performance of gender justice in the eyes of organizers and participants."[51]

In addition, contemporary mosques may offer women a variety of new leadership roles. Women serve to various degrees on mosque boards and on mosque-based Sharīʿa councils.[52] Jamilla Karim observes of North America, that "[b]ecause mosques . . . follow the pattern of churches and synagogues and function as community organizations (not simply prayer spaces), there are multiple leadership opportunities for women in the areas of youth education, fundraising, public relations, and other activities."[53]

Directions for Further Inquiry

Much work remains to be done on the ways in which mosques in different places function as sacred spaces, and how this dimension affects gendered usage of that space. Notably, very little attention has yet been directed to such issues as *baraka* and merit in modern mosque contexts. It is unclear whether this lacuna results from a lack of focus on such issues among users of modern mosques, or whether these topics have simply been marginalized in the academic conversation. Similarly, much remains to be said about the way that the mosque is defined and elaborated as a local category in any given context, particularly in contrast with related categories such as tombs and shrines. The generic category of "mosque" may also elide the specificities of non-Sunni contexts; for instance, Maimuna Huq notes that although in rural regions of South Asia mosques usually lack accommodations for women, this is less true "in Shīʿī communities, where community centers called imambaras often serve as shrine/mosque/meeting-place complexes."[54]

To the extent that analysis of women's presence in mosques has revolved around the public/private distinction, it would be useful to see more analysis of the insider categories that may correspond to (or complicate) this distinction.[55] In the context of American history, Catherine Brekus has described how changing configurations of public and private conditioned attitudes toward women's roles within the Christian church, with women gaining greater latitude after the disestablishment of the churches following the American Revolution made them appear as "simply one more kind of voluntary association" rather than as the public arms of the state.[56] The existing literature on modern mosques suggests that in many contexts, changing political conditions have similarly shifted the location of the mosque within wider configurations of state and society. Scholars have only begun to explore the implications of these shifts on configurations of gender and ritual practice.

Finally, it is to be expected that as the study of Islamic masculinities continues to develop, studies on "women in the mosque" will be supplemented by a broader focus on gender. Work such as David Thurfjell's *Living Shi'ism: Instances of Ritualisation among Islamist Men in Contemporary Iran* (2005) already moves in this direction. Rather than regarding the mosque as a "bastion of men's power," as scholars did in the early days of Western academic inquiry into the women's mosque movement, there is increasing attention to the widely varying ways in which men as well as women may access the space of the mosque and the various kinds of authority it may confer.

Notes

1. "A Veiled Revolution," directed by Marilyn Gaunt (Brooklyn: Icarus Films, 1982), 00:00–00:55.
2. Leila Ahmed, *Women and Gender in Islam* (New Haven, CT: Yale University Press, 1992), 54–55, 60.
3. Ahmed, *Women and Gender*, 228.
4. Saba Mahmood, *Politics of Piety: The Islamic Revival and the Feminist Subject* (Princeton, NJ: Princeton University Press, 2005), 2–3.
5. See Masooda Bano and Hilary Kalmbach, eds., *Women, Leadership, and Mosques: Changes in Contemporary Islamic Authority* (Leiden: Brill, 2012), 365 (see also 509).
6. Jeff Weintraub, "The Theory and Politics of the Public/Private Distinction," in *Public and Private in Thought and Practice: Perspectives on a Grand Dichotomy*, ed. Jeff Weintraub and Krishan Kumar (Chicago: University of Chicago Press, 1997), 4–5. For critiques of the public/private dichotomy specifically in Middle Eastern and Islamic studies see, among many others, Abraham Marcus, "Privacy in Eighteenth-Century Aleppo: The Limits of Cultural Ideals," *International Journal of Middle Eastern Studies* 18 (1986): 165–183; Shampa Mazumdar and Sanjoy Mazumdar, "Rethinking Public and Private Space: Religion and Women in Islamic Society," *Journal of Architectural and Planning Research* 18, no. 4 (2001): 302–324.
7. Weintraub, "Theory and Politics," 7.

8. For a historical survey of legal doctrine and historical evidence on women's mosque attendance in the Middle East and North African, see Marion Katz, *Women in the Mosque: A History of Legal Thought and Social Practice* (New York: Columbia University Press, 2014). On the idea of acting "discretely," see Weintraub, "Theory and Politics," 6, n. 8.
9. Salma A. Nageeb, "Appropriating the Mosque: Women's Religious Groups in Khartoum," *Afrika Spectrum* 42 (2007): 17–21.
10. See Marion Katz, "Commemoration of the Prophet's Birthday as a Domestic Ritual in Fifteenth- and Sixteenth-Century Damascus," in *Domestic Devotions in the Early Modern World*, ed. Marco Faini and Alessia Meneghin (Leiden: Brill, 2018), 167–181.
11. See Anne Menely, *Tournaments of Value: Sociability and Hierarchy in a Yemani Town* (Toronto: University of Toronto Press, 2016), 22, 35.
12. Ibid., 4.
13. Ibid., 89, 162.
14. Ibid., 168–178.
15. Jacqueline H. Fewkes, *Locating Maldivian Women's Mosques in Global Discourses* (Cham, Switzerland: Palgrave Macmillan, 2019), 44–45.
16. Niloofar Haeri, "The Private Performance of Salat Prayers: Repetition, Time, and Meaning," *Anthropological Quarterly* 86, no. 1 (2013): 17–18.
17. See Haeri, "Private Performance," 16; Azam Torab, *Performing Islam: Gender and Ritual in Iran* (Leiden: Brill, 2007), 57.
18. Fewkes, *Locating Maldivian Women's Mosques*, 110–111.
19. See Katz, *Women in the Mosque*, 274–275.
20. Imam Zaid Shakir, *Scattered Pictures: Reflections of an American Muslim* (Hayward: Zaytuna Institute, 2005), 109.
21. Haeri, "Private Performance," 16.
22. Torab, *Performing Islam*, 96.
23. Mona Atia, *Building a House in Heaven: Pious Neoliberalism and Islamic Charity in Egypt* (Minneapolis: University of Minnesota Press, 2013), 80.
24. Atia, *Building a House in Heaven*, 59 (for recipient women's coerced participation in mosque activities, see 56).
25. See Renata Holod and Hasan-Uddin Khan, *The Contemporary Mosque: Achitects, Clients and Designs since the 1950s* (New York: Rizzoli, 1997), 19–20.
26. Kishwar Rizvi, *The Transnational Mosque: Architecture and Historical Memory in the Contemporary Middle East* (Chapel Hill: University of North Carolina Press, 2015), 126.
27. Michelle Rein, "Space: Mosques: North Africa," in *Encyclopedia of Women and Islamic Cultures*, vol. 4: *Economics, Education, Mobility, and Space*, ed. Suad Joseph (Leiden: Brill, 2007), 552.
28. Pia Karlsson Minganti, "Challenging from Within: Youth Associations and Female Leadership in Swedish Mosques," in *Women, Leadership and Mosques*, 375, 388.
29. Leila Ahmed, *A Quiet Revolution: The Veil's Resurgence, from the Middle East to America* (New Haven, CT: Yale University Press, 2011), 250. An example of the grassroots appeal of this issue among English-speaking Muslim women is Hind Makki's project "Side Entrance" (see Hind Makki, "Side Entrance," accessed August 24, 2018, http://sideentrance.tumblr.com/).
30. Margaret J. Rausch, "Women Preachers and Spiritual Guides in Morocco," in *Women, Leadership and Mosques*, 66.

31. See Mona Hassan, "Reshaping Religious Authority in Contemporary Turkey: State-Sponsored Female Preachers," in *Women, Leadership and Mosques*, 86.
32. Fatma Tütüncü, "The Women Preachers of the Secular State: The Politics of Preaching at the Intersection of Gender, Ethnicity and Sovereignty in Turkey," *Middle Eastern Studies* 46, no. 4 (2010): 607.
33. Tütüncü, "Women Preachers," 603; Hassan, "Reshaping Religious Authority," 89–90.
34. See, for instance, Hassan, "Reshaping Religious Authority," 91–92; Tütüncü, "Women Preachers," 598–600.
35. See Cleo Cantone, *Making and Remaking Mosques in Senegal* (Leiden: Brill, 2012), 327, 331–333, 336.
36. See Cleo Cantone, "Women Claiming Space in Mosques," *ISIM Newsletter* 11 (2002): 29.
37. Haeri, "Private Performance," 6.
38. See Mahmood, *Politics of Piety*, 40–43.
39. Hiroko Minesaki, "Gender Strategy and Authority in Islamic Discourses: Female Preachers in Contemporary Egypt," in *Women, Leadership and Mosques*, 397–398. On this theme, see also Samia Serageldin, "The Islamic Salon: Elite Women's Religious Networks in Egypt," in *Muslim Networks from Hajj to Hip Hop*, ed. miriam cooke and Bruce B. Lawrence (Chapel Hill: University of North Carolina Press, 2005), 155–168.
40. Sofia Nehaoua, "Prédicatrices de salon à Héliopolis: Vers la Salafisation de la bourgeoisie de Caire?" *Le Mouvement Social* 231 (2010), 63, n. 3.
41. Nageeb, "Appropriating the Mosque," 16–17.
42. "Preface," in Bano and Kalmbach, *Women, Leadership, and Mosques*, ix; see also Kalmbach's statement in the Introduction:"We focus particularly on women active in mosques and *madrasahs* because these spaces have long been central to the establishment and exercise of religious authority" (2–3).
43. Haeri notes that in a Twelver Shīʿī context, "Praying behind a prayer leader implies a hierarchy of knowledge and spiritual achievement" such that "one must consider [the prayer leader] as at least an equal"; See Haeri, "Private Performance," 17.
44. See Catharina Raudvere, "Textual and Ritual Command: Muslim Women as Keepers and Transmitters of Interpretive Domains in Contemporary Bosnia and Herzegovina," in *Women, Leadership, and Mosques*, 275.
45. Uta Christina Lehmann, "Women's Rights to Mosque Space: Access and Participation in Cape Town Mosques," in *Women, Leadership, and Mosques*, 504.
46. Fewkes, *Locating Maldivian Women's Mosques*, 164.
47. Rausch, "Women Mosque Preachers," 68–69.
48. Maria Jaschok, "Sources of Authority: Female *Ahong* and *Qingzhen Nüsi* (Women's Mosques) in China," in *Women, Leadership, and Mosques*, 45.
49. Riem Spielhaus, "Making Islam Relevant: Female Authority and Representation of Islam in Germany," in *Women, Leadership, and Mosques*, 442–443.
50. Lehmann, "Women's Rights to Mosque Space," 487–489, 497.
51. Juliane Hammer, "Activism as Embodied Tafsīr: Negotiating Women's Authority, Leadership, and Space in North America," in *Women, Leadership, and Mosques*, 476.
52. See Maimuna Huq, "Space: Mosques: South Asia," in *Encyclopedia of Women and Islamic Cultures*, 4:553; John R. Bowen, *On British Islam: Religion, Law, and Everyday Practice in Shari'a Councils* (Princeton, NJ: Princeton University Press, 2016).
53. Jamillah Karim, "Space: Mosques: North America," in *Encyclopedia of Women and Islamic Cultures*.

54. Huq, "South Asia," 553–554.
55. A promising effort in this direction for the early period is Yaseen Noorani, "Normative Notions of Public and Private in Early Islamic Culture," in *Harem Histories: Envisioning Places and Living Spaces*, ed. Marilyn Booth (Durham, NC: Duke University Press, 2010), 49–68.
56. Catherine Brekus, *Strangers and Pilgrims: Female Preaching in America, 1740–1845* (Chapel Hill: University of North Carolina Press, 1998), 14.

Bibliography

Ahmed, Leila. *A Quiet Revolution: The Veil's Resurgence, from the Middle East to America*. New Haven, CT: Yale University Press, 2011.

Ahmed, Leila. *Women and Gender in Islam*. New Haven, CT: Yale University Press, 1992.

Atia, Mona. *Building a House in Heaven: Pious Neoliberalism and Islamic Charity in Egypt*. Minneapolis: University of Minnesota Press, 2013.

Bano, Masooda, and Kalmbach, Hilary, eds. *Women, Leadership, and Mosques: Changes in Contemporary Islamic Authority*. Leiden: Brill, 2012.

Bowen, John R. *On British Islam: Religion, Law, and Everyday Practice in Shari'a Councils*. Princeton, NJ: Princeton University Press, 2016.

Brekus, Catherine. *Strangers and Pilgrims: Female Preaching in America, 1740–1845*. Chapel Hill: University of North Carolina Press, 1998.

Cantone, Cleo. *Making and Remaking Mosques in Senegal*. Leiden: Brill, 2012.

Fewkes, Jacqueline H. *Locating Maldivian Women's Mosques in Global Discourses*. Cham, Switzerland: Palgrave Macmillan, 2019.

Gaunt, Marilyn, dir. *A Veiled Revolution*. Brooklyn, NY: Icarus Films, 1982.

Haeri, Niloofar. "The Private Performance of Salat Prayers: Repetition, Time, and Meaning." *Anthropological Quarterly* 86, no. 1 (2013): 5–34.

Hassan, Mona. "Reshaping Religious Authority in Contemporary Turkey: State-Sponsored Female Preachers." In *Women, Leadership and Mosques: Changes in Contemporary Islamic Authority*, edited by Masooda Bano and Hilary Kalmbach, 85–104. Leiden: Brill, 2012.

Hammer, Juliane. "Activism as Embodied Tafsīr: Negotiating Women's Authority, Leadership, and Space in North America." In *Women, Leadership and Mosques: Changes in Contemporary Islamic Authority*, edited by Masooda Bano and Hilary Kalmbach, 457–480. Leiden: Brill, 2012.

Holod, Renata, and Hasan-Uddin Khan. *The Contemporary Mosque: Architects, Clients and Designs since the 1950s*. New York: Rizzoli, 1997.

Huq, Maimuna. "Space: Mosques: South Asia." In *Encyclopedia of Women and Islamic Cultures*, edited by Suad Joseph, 552–555. Leiden: Brill, 2007.

Jaschok, Maria. "Sources of Authority: Female *Ahong* and *Qingzhen Nüsi* (Women's Mosques) in China." In *Women, Leadership and Mosques: Changes in Contemporary Islamic Authority*, edited by Masooda Bano and Hilary Kalmbach, 37–58. Leiden: Brill, 2012.

Karim, Jamillah. "Space: Mosques: North America." In *Encyclopedia of Women and Islamic Cultures*, edited by Suad Joseph. Leiden: Brill, 2009.

Katz, Marion. "Commemoration of the Prophet's Birthday as a Domestic Ritual in Fifteenth- and Sixteenth-Century Damascus." In *Domestic Devotions in the Early Modern World*, edited by Marco Faini and Alessia Meneghin. Leiden: Brill, 2018, 167–181.

Katz, Marion. *Women in the Mosque: A History of Legal Thought and Social Practice.* New York: Columbia University Press, 2014.

Lehmann, Uta Christina. "Women's Rights to Mosque Space: Access and Participation in Cape Town Mosques." In *Women, Leadership and Mosques: Changes in Contemporary Islamic Authority*, edited by Masooda Bano and Hilary Kalmbach, 481–506. Leiden: Brill, 2012.

Mahmood, Saba. *Politics of Piety: The Islamic Revival and the Feminist Subject.* Princeton, NJ: Princeton University Press, 2005.

Makki, Hind. "Side Entrance." Accessed August 24, 2018. https://sideentrance.tumblr.com/

Marcus, Abraham. "Privacy in Eighteenth-Century Aleppo: The Limits of Cultural Ideals." *International Journal of Middle Eastern Studies* 18 (1986): 165–183.

Mazumdar, Shampa, and Mazumdar, Sanjoy. "Rethinking Public and Private Space: Religion and Women in Islamic Society." *Journal of Architectural and Planning Research* 18, no. 4 (2001), 302–324.

Menely, Anne. *Tournaments of Value: Sociability and Hierarchy in a Yemani Town.* Toronto: University of Toronto Press, 2016.

Minesaki, Hiroko. "Gender Strategy and Authority in Islamic Discourses: Female Preachers in Contemporary Egypt." In *Women, Leadership and Mosques: Changes in Contemporary Islamic Authority*, edited by Masooda Bano and Hilary Kalmbach, 393–412. Leiden: Brill, 2012.

Minganti, Pia Karlsson. "Challenging from Within: Youth Associations and Female Leadership in Swedish Mosques." In *Women, Leadership and Mosques: Changes in Contemporary Islamic Authority*, edited by Masooda Bano and Hilary Kalmbach, 371–392. Leiden: Brill, 2012.

Nageeb, Salma A. "Appropriating the Mosque: Women's Religious Groups in Khartoum." *Afrika Spectrum* 42 (2007): 5–27.

Nehaoua, Sofia. "Prédicatrices de Salon à Héliopolis: Vers la Salafisation de la Bourgeoisie de Caire?" *Le Mouvement Social* 231 (2010): 63–76.

Noorani, Yaseen. "Normative Notions of Public and Private in Early Islamic Culture." In *Harem Histories: Envisioning Places and Living Spaces*, edited by Marilyn Booth, 49–68. Durham, NC: Duke University Press, 2010.

Raudvere, Catharina. "Textual and Ritual Command: Muslim Women as Keepers and Transmitters of Interpretive Domains in Contemporary Bosnia and Herzegovina." In *Women, Leadership and Mosques: Changes in Contemporary Islamic Authority*, edited by Masooda Bano and Hilary Kalmbach, 259–278. Leiden: Brill, 2012.

Rausch, Margaret J. "Women Preachers and Spiritual Guides in Morocco." In *Women, Leadership and Mosques: Changes in Contemporary Islamic Authority*, edited by Masooda Bano and Hilary Kalmbach, 59–84. Leiden: Brill, 2012.

Rein, Michelle. "Space: Mosques: North Africa." In *Encyclopedia of Women and Islamic Cultures*. Vol. 4, *Economics, Education, Mobility, and Space*, edited by Suad Joseph, 550–552. Leiden: Brill, 2007.

Rizvi, Kishwar. *The Transnational Mosque: Architecture and Historical Memory in the Contemporary Middle East.* Chapel Hill: University of North Carolina Press, 2015.

Serageldin, Samia. "The Islamic Salon: Elite Women's Religious Networks in Egypt." In *Muslim Networks from Hajj to Hip Hop*, edited by miriam cooke and Bruce B. Lawrence. Chapel Hill: University of North Carolina Press, 2005.

Shakir, Imam Zaid. *Scattered Pictures: Reflections of an American Muslim.* Hayward, CA: Zaytuna Institute, 2005.

Spielhaus, Riem. "Making Islam Relevant: Female Authority and Representation of Islam in Germany." In *Women, Leadership and Mosques: Changes in Contemporary Islamic Authority*. Edited by Masooda Bano and Hilary Kalmbach, 437–456. Leiden: Brill, 2012.

Torab, Azam. *Performing Islam: Gender and Ritual in Iran*. Leiden: Brill, 2007.

Tütüncü, Fatma. "The Women Preachers of the Secular State: The Politics of Preaching at the Intersection of Gender, Ethnicity and Sovereignty in Turkey." *Middle Eastern Studies* 46, no. 4 (2010): 595–614.

Weintraub, Jeff. "The Theory and Politics of the Public/Private Distinction." In *Public and Private in Thought and Practice: Perspectives on a Grand Dichotomy*, edited by Jeff Weintraub and Krishan Kumar, 1–42. Chicago: University of Chicago Press, 1997.

CHAPTER 16

NEGOTIATING MOTHERHOOD, RELIGION, AND MODERN LIVED REALITIES

MARGARET AZIZA PAPPANO

Motherhood can be a challenging, creative, and fulfilling experience, a channel to social status and acceptance, and it can also be a position of isolation and marginalization, constricting women's identities and capacities. The recognition that motherhood is a massive and highly complex global and transhistorical social institution, important to every culture and society even when that importance is systematically obscured, has spawned extensive scholarship examining the multiple meanings, social formations, and diversity of practices associated with motherhood and mothering. Recent scholarship has reclaimed the position of motherhood from one of a biologically determined social role to the conception of an active mother-centered engagement with the critically important work of reproduction and childrearing. Andrea O'Reilly explains the terminology used to mark the distinction: "The term motherhood refers to the patriarchal institution of motherhood which is male-defined and controlled and is deeply oppressive to women, while the word mothering refers to women's experiences of mothering which are female-defined and potentially empowering to women."[1]

To some extent, Muslim scholars have participated in these scholarly endeavors, reconsidering the role of mothering from new, critical perspectives. Some would argue, however, that the Qur'ān and Islamic sources have always privileged mothering, according it a special role that distinguished and recognized the contributions of mothers to society.[2] "The Qur'ān does not merely hold up maternal specific exemplars but radiates a variety of maternal images that emphasize a woman's unique procreative power," Kathryn Kueny argues.[3]

Even if the Qur'ān may be read from a positive maternalist perspective, there is no doubt that many Muslim-majority communities have not conferred on mothers the kind of respect and status that the Qur'ān adumbrates. Moreover, while the Qur'ān may exhort followers to recognize mothers' unique qualities, interpreters may construe such statements in ways that reduce women to those very maternal or even reproductive identities. As amina wadud explains,

> Because woman's primary distinction [in the Qur'ān] is on the basis of her childbearing ability, it is seen as her primary function. . . . There is no term in the Qur'an that indicates that childbearing is "primary" to a woman. No indication is given that mothering is her exclusive role. It demonstrates the fact that a woman (though certainly not all women) is the exclusive human capable of bearing children.[4]

In other words, although only women can bear children, interpretive practices have construed sacred texts in such a way to suggest that women can only bear children. While the Qur'ān may be said to grant special recognition to mothers, the issue is how this recognition becomes a delimiting factor for women in defining social roles. For wadud, the Qur'ān is simply declaring that of the two biological sexes, only women are capable of reproduction, an essential mechanism for the future of humanity, and, therefore, women who do reproduce must be supported in this role—but nothing mandates that they *must* reproduce.

There is certainly substantial emphasis on childbearing in many Muslim communities, with women who fail to reproduce socially isolated and stigmatized, even subject to violence, while women who do give birth can be fused with their maternal roles, associated with self-sacrifice and self-abnegation. Jacqueline Rose speaks of the "impossible injunction" associated with motherhood—"be everything and be nothing, be life and death for your child"—an idea inflected in Aliah's Schleifer's conviction that "Islam views successful motherhood as the perfection of the Muslimah's religion."[5] While such emphases on restrictive reproductive identities for Muslim women might be traced to specific (mis)readings of the Qur'ān, they also must be seen within their socioeconomic locus. Indeed, most cultures associated with precarious economic situations are pronatalist, valuing children as a socioeconomic safety net and often circumscribing women's identity within their mothering role. "There is not a 'typical' pattern of reproductive behavior which would be considered 'Islamic' when considering global trends," Aisha J. Hutchinson and Patrick J. O'Leary write.[6] For instance, "[e]arly marriage, which is highly associated with Islamic communities is also considered an economic strategy often used by the poor whatever their religious affiliation."[7]

This chapter will examine the way that religion plays a role in forging maternal identities and practices, attempting to isolate ways that Islamic interpretive paradigms have been mobilized to negotiate mothering in both Muslim-majority and Muslim-minority contexts. While it is useful to be aware of Qur'ānic verses that bear on motherhood and women's roles, it is the ways in which these verses are commonly interpreted and deployed that structure the quotidian experiences of Muslims, many of whom may not have access to their own sources of religious authority. This chapter will focus on maternal identities, including issues of infertility; the structure of

Muslim households; the way that mothering practices may differ in Muslim contexts; and ways that Muslim motherhood have been mobilized in decolonization and nationalist projects. Finally, this chapter will discuss the current global climate in which fear of radicalization of children structures the lives of many Muslims, particularly mothers, who have been both implicated in and identified as critical to the struggle against extremism.

Maternal Identities and Muslim Household Dynamics

It is something of a truism that Islam is a sex-positive religion that acknowledges and addresses the role that sexuality plays in human relations. Marriage and procreation are frequently seen as religious duties by Muslims, based on readings of the Qur'ān and hadith,[8] among which Sūrat-al-Nahl is frequently cited: "And God has ordained mates for you among yourselves, and from your mates He has ordained for you children and grandchildren (72:16)."[9] In this way, Islam is consistent with the other Abrahamic faiths, which also emphasize the religious merits of childbearing. While medieval Catholicism advocated asceticism and associated spiritual virtue with celibacy, the Protestant reforms of Christianity in the early modern period promoted a married ministry and the patriarchal family unit as the cornerstone of a godly society.[10] Michael S. Berger writes of "the critical role the traditional family played in ensuring Jewish life in diaspora," given the long history of persecution and dispersal of Jewish communities.[11] In Islam, the centrality of marriage and family has been located within social formations that are concerned with kinship arrangements and protecting the paternal bloodline. Procreation within marriage is praised—as indeed is sex within marriage without procreation. However, any sexual activity outside of marriage is prohibited and associated with *fitna* (social disorder). By seeking to locate all sexual activity and reproduction within the framework of legal marriage, Muslim traditions organize social relations such that the status of women and children are circumscribed by a paternally controlled kinship structure, despite the positive role accorded to maternity in the Qur'ān. For instance, the Qur'ān provides the example of Maryam (Mary), whom God rewards for her faith with a miraculous pregnancy without a husband (19:19–21). Hence, in the Qur'ān, mothering a child need not involve a patriarchal family unit. Unlike in the Christian tradition, Maryam and the Prophet `Īsā are not placed within a "holy family," with Joseph the Carpenter as husband and head of household.

Feminist scholars and leaders of women's movements in Muslim societies have typically asked whether the family unit need be a patriarchal one; in other words, must male governance of familial structures be presumed? While the Qur'ān and hadith make clear that sexual activity is licit only within the frame of marital relations, could marriage be egalitarian? Or could a family have a female head? Must the location of sexual relations within marriage lead inexorably to the patriarchal organization of family life and a gender hierarchy?

The vision of family cited frequently by Muslims ascribes to a gendered division of labor and distinctive roles for fathers and mothers, often understood to be derived from Qur'ān 4:34. With translations varying widely, the verse is highly contested in contemporary scholarship. *The Study Quran* translates the first part of it as follows: "Men are the upholders and maintainers [*qawwāmūn*] of women by virtue of that in which God has favored some of them above others and by virtue of their spending from their wealth."[12] The interpretation of this verse that suggests male fiscal responsibility as family head underwrites the widespread conception among Muslims that the Qur'ān explicitly prescribes distinct gender roles for men and women: men as breadwinners and women as caretakers, homemakers, and mothers. However, while gender roles may be distinct in this conception, many consider them "complementary" and equal in importance.[13]

Family codes in many Muslim majority countries today reflect a belief in different spheres, deeming the man the legal head of the household. In the Middle East and North Africa "the mother is regarded as the child-minder and never as the legal guardian of her children, except where the father has died or in other very restricted cases."[14] In addition, mothers may have limited rights over the family home and cannot pass on citizenship to children. Women's movements in Muslim-majority countries have challenged the default status of fathers as legal head of family and feminist scholars contend that Islam provides the resources to imagine an egalitarian family framework with men and women sharing domestic duties, including childcare. In some cases, these movements have made gains. In Morocco, for instance, courts no longer automatically award custody to a father for a child past infancy, but are guided by "their perception of a child's 'best interests.'" Thus if a woman had a better employment situation than the man, judges would often award the former custody.[15]

Nonetheless, the widespread conception of the Muslim household in terms of a male-headed, multigenerational unit has spawned numerous theories of Muslim gender roles and family dynamics. Within the patriarchal orientation of this structure, women may have little power and what power they have is based on their reproductive identity: traditionally, their birthing and care of children, particularly sons, establishes their status in the household. According to this model of the patriarchal extended family, the most senior woman, the wife of the senior man and mother of grown sons, holds a position of power over the junior women, her sons' wives, and other women who live in the same dwelling place. In theory, she had herself once been in a powerless position as a daughter-in-law. Now, as a mother-in-law, she attains the most preeminent position available to a woman.

In such a familial organization, maternal identities are key to a woman's place in the power structure. Widowed, divorced, and "troubled women" (such as those seeking refuge from a disagreeable husband or familial arrangement involving a second wife) who live in the family home play roles in socializing children but are relatively powerless to fulfill any independent desires, according to Fatima Mernissi's well-known fictionalized memoir of her Moroccan childhood. In her depiction of her multigenerational family home in which spatial arrangements represent structures of power, Mernissi describes how these women "occupied a maze of small rooms" on the upper floors.[16]

The centrality of maternal identity to a woman's authority and status in the extended family structure is well represented in fiction, film, and scholarship; however, there are multiple adaptations of the extended family unit and the prevalence of such familial structures varies from region to region. In their recent article, Martin Latreille and Michel Verdon claim that while the patriarchal extended household may "represent a cultural ideal, the data shows that this type of living arrangement has never been statistically predominant in the recent past, neither in Tunisia nor elsewhere in the [Middle East and North Africa]."[17] They describe how younger women were the "main secessionist agents" in setting up their own household to create independent familial identities.[18]

Joint family systems continue to be prevalent in South and Southeast Asian Muslim communities, even enduring in various forms when migration occurs to Europe or North America. These familial structures tend to be patrilocal, in which women leave natal homes upon marriage to take up residence in their spouse's family home.[19] Hence, the presence of in-laws plays a large role in a woman's life in South and Southeast Asian communities and affects mothering identities and practices. Recent research has suggested that the phenomenon of patrilocal extended family arrangements are linked to numerous positive and negative social formations, such as shared domestic responsibilities, including childcare, but also a tendency to undervalue and undereducate girls because they are seen as temporary family members.[20]

Even outside of a joint household structure, maternal identities play a large role in how Muslim women negotiate their place in their communities. Marcia Inhorn's research on issues of fertility in contemporary Egypt demonstrates that women from urban, lower-class families experience their position as vulnerable if they are unable to bear children. Indeed, the identity of an unfertile woman is an anathema, according to her research. Inhorn's analysis of a specific population of women filters pronatalist views through class structure:

> Although Egyptian women of all classes are expected to become mothers, often abandoning their jobs permanently following the birth of their first child, motherhood expectations are exaggerated among the urban poor, who view motherhood as less a role than as a woman's primary identity. Because poor urban women have been stripped of the productive roles still held by women in the rural economy, they have been forced, in a sense, to focus exclusively on their reproductive roles.[21]

Although Inhorn identifies a convergence of geographic, economic, and religious factors in her study of the alienation of women experiencing infertility in urban Egypt, studies from other geographical regions find that women unable to have children experience similar issues. Zubia Mumtaz's study of infertile couples in rural Pakistan documents that women were blamed, even when medical evidence signified otherwise.

As such, these women were excluded from social rituals since they were considered to be bearers of bad luck; childless men, however, were not excluded. "Men in childless marriages view themselves and are seen by society as inert, usually innocent, partners. Pregnancy and childbirth are considered women's domain only."[22] Papreen Nahar's study of rural Bangladesh reveals that, as in urban Egypt, women without children tend not to work outside the home. Such women were considered untrustworthy, and, therefore, more available for extramarital relationships. A childless woman working also drew attention to the failure of the husband to uphold his role as a provider. Hence, a childless woman is considered to threaten a man from fulfilling his religiously ordained role as well as her own.[23]

Muslim Motherwork

Patricia Hill Collins has challenged the tendency in recent scholarship to draw from and reify the experiences of white middle-class women in Western societies as the norm in constructing theoretical models of mothering. Her multiple critiques of maternal theories have foregrounded the specific practices associated with Black and racialized motherhood in the US context, considering histories of slavery, racism, segregation, imprisonment, sterilization, impoverishment, unequal access to education, housing, healthcare, and work opportunities as well as the prevalence of female-headed households and nonnuclear family arrangements in the lives of racialized peoples.[24] Since about 20 percent of the total US Muslim population is composed of African Americans, her analysis is vital for considering how Black American Muslims negotiate motherhood. Wadud has examined how traditional Islamic paradigms of the family fail to account for the experience of African Americans. Since Islamic law is based on the principle that men will provide for women and children, either through the husband or extended family network, it ignores all of the other family arrangements that are increasingly prominent in today's world, including the presence of single mother households. "If an African-American articulation of Islamic identity is to be formed in a meaningful way, then our whole history shows the virtue of women surviving and helping children to survive," she argues,[25] calling on Muslims to reform family law and activate community services to extend systemic support to single mothers. A theory of Muslim motherwork must take into consideration the many single, divorced, and widowed mothers who encounter obstacles navigating Muslim communities that are organized around patriarchal family units but who seek to rear children in the faith, just like other Muslim mothers.

In addition, Collins's critiques are relevant for examining how other ethnic groups with Muslim identities in the United States negotiate the demands of mothering differently than those with a white middle-class experience. Sara Ruddick's landmark study of "maternal thinking" located three main categories through which mothers respond to and frame their practices of mothering: preservative love, nurturance of a child's development, and socialization.[26] Considering different emphases within these categories as well as the specific political and social contexts of Muslim lives suggests that one may be able to identify distinctive aspects associated with Muslim motherwork. However, given the expanse of and diversity within the Muslim population, such formulations are necessarily provisional and partial. For example, as discussed above, many, though not all, Muslims reside in joint family households; therefore, a large part of motherwork involves negotiating with and incorporating the values, beliefs, and practices of other family members in rearing children. Indeed, traditional Muslim mothering practices may differ from those prevalent in Western cultures that promote forms of child-centered and intensive mothering, like attachment mothering. When the child is conceptualized as belonging within larger kin and religious-cultural networks, the mother may focus less on fostering a child's expression of his/her individuality than on consciously and unconsciously transmitting the values of her social group. "Motherhood within the Arab-Islamic ethos is often interpreted through a framework of communitarianism, where family and community are overarching structures that often supersede individualism and individual rights," a study of mothers in Qatar explains.[27]

A concept of Muslim motherwork must also take into account the current global climate in which many millions of Muslims live in precarious situations: when mothers' lives are threatened daily by the realities of war, military occupation, natural disaster, extreme poverty, or famine, preserving their child's life is not something that she can expect to do, despite her best efforts. The dangers of mothering in these situations are evident: lack of access to basic necessities such as medical care, food, water, and secure shelter, plus the ever-present threat of physical violence. In addition, these dangerous conditions tend to reconfigure gender relations, with fathers and mothers forced to play unfamiliar roles, thus altering traditional modes of socialization. Fadwa al-Labadi describes how parental roles have changed in the context of the Israeli military occupation of Palestine: "During a time of conflict where men are deprived of access to mobility, forced to stay at home and not able any more to meet their traditionally ascribed roles as breadwinners and protectors of the family, women make a clear contribution as front liners: mothers, political prisoners, breadwinners."[28] For these mothers, there is no separation of the political from the familial and no such thing as a private home space in which mothering takes place.

For women living in many Muslim-majority states, motherwork must be understood within the context of histories of European colonization. In her memoir of growing up in Egypt "in the last days of the British Empire," Leila Ahmed captures something of the distinctive aura around motherhood in upper class Muslim society:

> Motherhood was mysterious. It was sacred, but it had little to do, apparently, with actually looking after or tending to one's children. It was, I supposed, about having one's children around one, under one's broad physical and moral guardianship and protection—even if, in the routines and practicalities of daily life, it was someone else who actually looked after them. And it connoted also some powerful, unseverable

> connection of the heart. Everything my mother did seemed to be an expression of this notion of motherhood from her apparent lack of interest in the dailiness of our lives to the scenes she made at the quayside in Alexandria, waving her large white handkerchief in a tear-drenched goodbye as one or another of us and sometimes several of us left for England.[29]

Ahmed here adumbrates the position of the mother—its revered place in the family undergirded by mystified and largely unacknowledged emotional commitments. While as a member of the elite, Ahmed's mother may not have been involved in daily childcare duties, she had an important social role in the traditional Muslim conception of the family. However, Ahmed also documents the way that colonialism infiltrates their family life, with her mother an Arabic speaker and connected to Arab culture while the children grew up speaking English, becoming educated in, and eventually settling in the West. The mother is thus aligned with native identity and traditional values that are displaced in the context of English colonization. "Among other things," Ahmed writes, "there were hard, practical consequences. The children would not be there in the way that children traditionally (and according to both the Bible and Quran) were supposed to be there when parents grew old and frail."[30] Traditional family life is fractured and reshaped by colonialism as the "modern" ideas associated with the West socialize children in new ways, leaving the mother isolated and deprived of the structures that support her maternal status and authority.

Hence in the context of Muslim-majority states struggling against colonial occupation, motherhood takes on iconic value. Woman is often represented as the repository of the national ideal, and the home exalted as a microcosm of the nation, a site of traditional cultural values that must be cleansed of colonial presence and protected. Thus, mothers frequently have been manipulated as symbols in claims for national belonging. Yet, in addition to symbolizing nation, women's reproductive capacity and maternal labor are also reified as central to nation-building and national stability. In Iran, for instance, women were called on to produce sons to contribute to the war effort in the context of the Iran–Iraq war. In Palestine, in the context of ongoing occupation, women's contribution to the resistance effort in the form of sons was exalted in official discourse. The cultivation of the mother as a symbol of national identity can even extend to the working mother. In Indonesia, the state encouraged mothers to leave their natal families to seek work as domestics in foreign countries in order to bolster the national economy through migrant remittances. Although, in this case, women were clearly functioning outside of their "traditional Islamic role" as caregivers to serve as breadwinners, the state "relied upon and reproduced an Islamic discourse of women's self-sacrifice to family and nation, in which the migratory income-earning woman becomes a provider of economic development for the 'national family.'"[31]

Although these formulations are widespread and fix women within the role of the sacrificing mother, mothers have not passively accepted these roles. Julie Peteet has documented how Palestinian mothers use their maternal martyr image to make political claims for themselves, provide critique, and otherwise participate in the political process.[32] In Iran, the mothers of martyrs are visible organizers, marking with their physical presence the personal nature of their sacrifice to demand recognition of their loss and concessions from the government.[33] These forms of motherwork demonstrate how mothering is intimately bound up with political processes for many Muslim mothers: the ability to mother is hardly ever assumed as natural and normative but is inseparable from the larger political and economic struggles in which women are engaged.

For Muslim women in Muslim-minority contexts, motherwork involves critical thinking skills that address the child's need for belonging, alongside the imperative to promote a positive Muslim identity and maintain Muslim practices as minorities who are systematically maligned in the media and culture at large. In her discussion of Black motherwork that seeks to equip Black children to contest the systems of racial oppression they encounter, Collins comments that the "push to assimilation is part of a larger effort to socialize racial ethnic children into their proper, subordinate systems of racial and class oppression."[34] Muslim motherwork involves teaching children similar strategies of resistance that instill pride in their Muslim identity when the dominant culture constructs them as terrorists, alien, oppressed, backward, etc. The socialization process is necessarily different for Muslim children than for those who are not religious and ethnic minorities: for Muslim children, the desire for social acceptability must be complicated by seeing themselves as unacceptable to some, while understanding how such politics of social acceptability operate. In addition, for Muslim communities in the West, exemplifying the values of the group can be more demanding given the challenges of maintaining a minority identity within a dominant culture. Children can be under pressure to "perform" as well as inhabit their religious identity.[35]

Mothers and the Politics of Extremism

Muslim mothers are targeted in the current climate of intensified fear over suspected and sometimes real radicalization of teenaged children. News specials produced by mainstream media outlets in Europe and North America focus on the dilemma of mothers of children who have left their family home to join ISIS forces in Syria. Such news stories are often marketed with and sometimes based on a prurient interest in uncovering what sort of mother could create a child capable of joining a heinous terrorist organization. What kind of woman mothers a terrorist? How is a terrorist created? As one mother explains, "people judge you. You're the mother. You must have done something wrong."[36] The focus on the mother more than the father speaks to the belief that a terrorist is someone so different from other people that there must be something fundamentally aberrant, inscribed at birth or in early childhood socialization that shapes his/her development. John G. Horgan references the erroneous but widespread belief that "terrorists (and in some cases, even the supporters of terrorists) are . . . psychologically 'different' or special," leading to a plethora of studies of the terrorist as "antisocial, narcissistic and paranoid personality types."[37]

The focus on the mother behind the radicalized child speaks also to the current emphasis on intensive mothering practices in Western cultures. As Lynda Rachelle Ross explains, "mothers are no longer just responsible for raising happy, healthy children but are accountable for more aspects of a child's intellectual, behavioral and emotional outcomes than has ever been the case before."[38] The news stories repeatedly ask the mothers to identify "what went wrong" and account for their child's actions. As one explains, "I looked at every moment what I have done wrong."[39] Yet the mothers interviewed also emphasize that the process of radicalization is both mysterious and quick. Mothers and other experts speak of months or even weeks in which such changes occur. Hence the mothers who gave their children "space" may be accused of improper mothering but in fact they responded to the phenomenon of unusual teenage behavior similarly to other parents, thinking that it was a phase and that it would pass like other phases. Although some of these mothers have organized to give support to other mothers who have lost children to ISIS and also to help families identify signs of radicalization, they emphasize that such signs are subtle, difficult to recognize, and can appear similar to the symptoms of depression and teenage moodiness. There is a common sense of bewilderment among the mothers: rejecting the role of omniscient mother implicated in contemporary notions of intensive mothering, they suggest that any mother could experience the loss of a child through radicalization. No one is immune.[40] The attempt to delink the actions of mothering from their children's participation in extremist movements shows them actively contesting dominant narratives of maternal blame, insisting that the mother is not the sole responsible agent in a child's development.

Indeed, what interviews with the mothers tend to expose is that the teens and young adults who have left home to join ISIS are as confused, emotionally opaque, and subject to aberrant behavior as teens anywhere. Omar Haque maintains, "for lonely young people in transition, ISIS provides a quick fix to the perennial problems of human life. . . . Specifically, the relief in question concerns the human desire for identity, certainty, social connection, meaning, the optimal amount of freedom and glory."[41] Particularly for socially marginal teens struggling to navigate those uncertain years between childhood and adulthood, sometimes in hostile, Islamophobic cultures, ISIS is attractive precisely because of its strict ideology and rules. A Belgian teenager who joined ISIS tried to enlist but was rejected for medical reasons by his nation's military a year previous to his departure,[42] challenging mainstream narratives that foreground the radical political and religious ideologies of such youth, and by extension, their familial environment that is believed to have fostered or supported such ideologies. Haque proposes that one motivation for joining ISIS may be a search for belonging and structure rather than any entrenched religious ideology. Indeed, many reports have documented the lack of religious knowledge among ISIS recruits, noting "how little your average Islamist knows about Islam."[43]

While these news stories purport to explore the origins of Islamic extremism, they tend to reify ossified, romanticized, and ultimately dangerous assumptions about mothering, as do initiatives like the "MotherSchools," a project of the European NGO

"Women without Borders," which seeks to train African and Asian mothers to detect and diffuse signs of radicalization in their children. Their website confidently declares that "mothers present a missing link in preventing the spread of violent extremism. Their unparalleled physical and emotional proximity make them witnesses of every stage in their child's development."[44] What are Muslim mothers imagined to be when they are positioned as the "missing link" in the deradicalization process, a process that has confounded experts across the globe?[45] As Rose observes, "because mothers are seen as our point of entry into the world, there is nothing easier than to make social deterioration look like something that it is the sacred duty of mothers to prevent—a type of socially upgraded version of the tendency in modern families to blame mothers for everything."[46] As Muslims face unprecedented oppression and violence around the world—from concentration camp–like conditions in China, India, and Palestine, to humanitarian crises in Myanmar, Syria, and Yemen, it should be clear that creating societies in which mothers thrive and have resources to support their children is the essential building block of peace, rather than imagining, to use Rose's words once more, that "the solution to the ills . . . could ever arise solely out of motherhood itself."[47]

Conclusion

This chapter has suggested that Muslim mothering practices should be considered within historically and geographically specific contexts. Despite traditions derived from religious texts that establish legal frameworks and influence beliefs concerning motherhood, mothering is dependent on familial structures and political systems, among other social institutions. Mothering cannot be abstracted from and examined outside of the societies in which mothers live. Investigating mothering practices is critical to the work of gender equity because, in both Muslim-majority and -minority contexts, ideals and realities of motherhood are closely linked to gender oppression. Despite some changes in modern parenting, in practice, most childcare continues to fall to mothers. Hence, motherhood can affect a women's ability to work outside the home (although, as argued above, infertility also can affect a women's ability to work). Motherhood also affects a woman's status within the family and society; while motherhood is often praised and exalted, expectations of maternal sacrifice continue to be normalized or promoted as religiously mandated in many Muslim contexts, a narrative reinforced by neocolonialist Western projects like the MotherSchools. In addition, a recent study by the World Health Organization found that "maternal mortality rates and infant and under five year mortality rates were almost twice as high in MMC [Muslim majority countries] as in non-MMC,"[48] suggesting that while motherhood continues to be valued by Muslims, infrastructure to support maternal health has not been prioritized. Scholars of mothering urge analysts and activists to consider mothers as a specific social category to draw attention to the inequities uniquely tied to motherhood. As Natalie Jolly writes, "Visualizing motherhood as a category of social oppression has the potential to sensitize us to not only the inequality that mothers face but also the intersectional nature of motherhood."[49] It is hence important to consider maternal identity alongside gender, religion, race, migrancy, poverty, etc., as a critical category of analysis for Muslim women.

Notes

1. Andrea O'Reilly, *Rocking the Cradle: Thoughts on Motherhood, Feminism, and the Possibility of Empowered Mothering* (Toronto: Demeter Press, 2006), 35.
2. See in particular Aliah Schleifer, *Motherhood in Islam* (Cambridge: Islamic Academy, 1986).
3. Kathryn M. Kueny, *Conceiving Identities: Maternity in Medieval Muslim Discourse and Practice* (Albany: State University of New York Press, 2013), 40.
4. Amina wadud, *Qur'an and Woman: Rereading the Sacred Text from a Woman's Perspective* (New York: Oxford University Press, 1999), 64.
5. Jacqueline Rose, *Mothers: An Essay on Love and Cruelty* (New York: Farrar, Straus and Giroux, 2018), 137; Schleifer, *Motherhood*, 88.
6. Aisha J. Hutchinson and Patrick J. O'Leary, "Young Mothers in Islamic Contexts: Implications for Social Work and Social Development," *International Journal of Social Work* 59, no. 3 (2016): 348.
7. Ibid., 352.
8. Abdel Rahim Omran, *Family Planning in the Legacy of Islam* (New York: Routledge, 1992), 13–15.
9. Seyyed Hossein Nasr, ed., *The Study Quran: A New Translation and Commentary* (New York: Harper Collins, 2015), 677.
10. Merry Weisner-Hanks, *Christianity and Sexuality in the Early Modern World: Regulating Desire, Reforming Practice*, 2nd ed. (New York: Routledge 2010), 73–97.
11. Michael S. Berger, "Marriage, Sex, and Family in the Jewish Tradition: A Historical Overview," in *Marriage, Sex, and Family in Judaism*, ed. Michael J. Broyde and Michael Ausubel (Toronto: Rowman and Littlefield, 2005), 8.
12. Nasr, *The Study Quran*, 206.
13. For a recent comprehensive discussion of this verse, see Ayesha Chaudhry, *Domestic Violence and the Islamic Tradition* (Oxford: Oxford University Press, 2014).
14. Rabéa Naciri and Isis Nusair, *The Integration of Women's Rights into the Euro-Mediterranean Partnership: Women's Rights in Algeria, Egypt, Israel, Jordan, Lebanon, Morocco, Palestine, Syria and Tunisia* (Copenhagen: Euro-Mediterranean Human Rights Network, 2003), 18.
15. Lawrence Rosen, "Revision and Reality in the Family Law of Morocco," in *Law and Religion in Multicultural Societies*, ed. Rubya Mehdi, Hanne Petersen, Erik Reenberg Sand, and Gordan R. Woodman (Copenhagen: DJØF, 2008), 135.
16. Fatima Mernissi, *Dreams of Trespass: Tales of a Harem Girlhood* (Don Mills, ON: Addison-Wesley, 1994), 16.
17. Martin Latreille and Michel Verdon, "Wives against Mothers: Women's Power and Household Dynamics in Rural Tunisia," *Journal of Family History* 32, no. 1 (2007), 69.
18. Ibid., 77.
19. Robina Mohammad discusses how new marriage practices in the diaspora reconfigure this tradition of the patrilocal home when British Muslim women marry men from Pakistan, who then take up residence in their natal home. "Transnational Shift: Marriage, Home,

and Belonging for British Pakistani Muslim Women," *Social and Cultural Geography* 16, no. 6 (2015): 593–614.

20. Riffat Moazam Zaman, "Parenting in Pakistan: An Overview," in *Parenting across Cultures: Childrearing, Motherhood and Fatherhood in Non-Western Cultures* (New York: Springer, 2014), 97.
21. Marcia C. Inhorn, *Infertility and Patriarchy: The Cultural Politics of Gender and Family Life in Egypt* (Philadelphia: University of Pennsylvania Press, 1996), 39.
22. Zubia Mumtaz et al., "Understanding the Impact of Gendered Roles on the Experiences of Infertility amongst Men and Women in Punjab," *Reproductive Health* 10, no. 3 (2013), 8.
23. Papreen Nahar and Annemiek Richters, "Suffering of Childless Women in Bangladesh: The Intersection of Social Identities of Gender and Class," *Anthropology and Medicine* 18, no. 3 (2011): 332.
24. Patricia Hill Collins, "Black Women and Motherhood," in *Black Feminist Thought: Knowledge, Consciousness, and the Politics of Empowerment*, 2nd ed. (New York: Routledge, 2000), 173–200; Collins, "Shifting the Center: Race, Class, and Feminist Theorizing about Motherhood," in *Mothering: Ideology, Experience, and Agency*, ed. Evelyn Nakono Glenn, Grace Chang, and Linda Rennie Forcey (New York: Routledge, 1994), 45–65.
25. Amina wadud, "A New Hajar Paradigm: Motherhood and Family," in *Inside the Gender Jihad: Women's Reform in Islam* (Oxford: Oneworld, 2006), 153.
26. Sara Ruddick, *Maternal Thinking: Toward a Politics of Peace* (Boston: Beacon, 1989).
27. Radhika Viruru and Ramzi Nasser, "'Wa'allah, the Woman She Should Go Direct to Paradise': Perceptions of Motherhood in Qatar." *Global Studies of Childhood* 7, no. 2 (2014): 151.
28. Fadwa al-Labadi, "Introduction from Abu Dis: Women Under Occupation," in *Stories from Our Mothers*, ed. Nandita Dowson and Abdul Wahab Sabbah (London: Camden Abu Dis Friendship Association, 2010), 5.
29. Leila Ahmed, *A Border Passage: From Cairo to America—A Woman's Journey* (New York: Penguin, 1992), 111.
30. Ibid., 111–112.
31. Rachel Silvey, "Transnational Islam: Indonesian Migrant Domestic Workers in Saudi Arabia," in *Geographies of Muslim Women: Gender, Religion, and Space*, ed. Ghazi-Walid Falah and Caroline Nagel (New York: Guildford, 2005), 140.
32. Julie Peteet, "Icons and Militants: Mothering in the Danger Zone," *Signs* 23, no. 1 (1997): 103–129.
33. Rachel Fox, "Mourning Mothers in Iran: Narratives and Counter-Narratives of Grievability and Martyrdom," in *Muslim Mothering: Global Histories, Theories, and Practices*, ed. Margaret Aziza Pappano and Dana M. Olwan (Bradford, ON: Demeter, 2016), 69–90.
34. Collins, "Shifting the Center," 57.
35. Yussef El Guindi's play, *Ten Acrobats in an Amazing Leap of Faith*, chronicling the struggles of an Egyptian-American family living in Los Angeles, offers a perceptive exploration of the performance of Muslim identities in a Muslim minority context. Holly Hill and Dina Amin, eds., *Salaam. Peace: An Anthology of Middle-Eastern American Drama* (New York: Theatre Communications Group, 2010), 3–91.
36. BBC Newsnight, "Mothers of ISIS Jihadis," YouTube video, 6:34, December 19, 2014, https://www.youtube.com/watch?v=yQwHDRnoDho.
37. John G. Horgan, *The Psychology of Terrorism* (New York: Routledge, 2005), 95.

38. Lynda Rachelle Ross, *Interrogating Motherhood* (Edmonton: Athabasca University Press, 2016), 128.
39. BBC Newsnight, "Mothers of ISIS Jihadis."
40. *The Atlantic*, "ISIS Radicalized My Son. It Can Happen to Anyone." Youtube video, 8:16, November 5, 2019.
41. Omar Sultan Haque, et al. "Why Are Young Westerners Drawn to Terrorist Organizations Like ISIS?" *Psychiatric Times* 32, no. 9 (2015).
42. Hind Elhinnawy, "Mothers of Intervention: Political Motherhood in the Battle against ISIS," YouTube video, 19:01, June 16, 2018, https://www.youtube.com/watch?v=oGTlzcV1lbg. (Paper presented at the "Emotional Politics" conference, University of Kent, May 31, 2018.)
43. Helen Lewis, "Why Extremists Need Therapy" *The Atlantic*, February 11, 2020.
44. Women Without Borders, "Activities," https://wwb.org/activities/
45. See studies such as John G. Horgan and Mary Beth Altier, "The Future of Terrorist De-Radicalization Programs," *Georgetown Journal of International Affairs* 13, no. 2 (Summer/Fall 2012): 83–90.; Elisabeth Zerofsky, "How to Stop a Martyr," *Foreign Policy* (September 1, 2016); Helen Lewis, "Why Extremists."
46. Rose, *Mothers*, 27.
47. Ibid., 97.
48. Razzak, J.A., et al. "Health Disparities between Muslim and Non-Muslim Countries," *Eastern Mediterranean Health Journal* 17, no. 9 (2011): 659.
49. Natalie Jolly, "Envisioning Mothers: Visualization and the Invisibility of Motherhood," *Journal of the Motherhood Initiative* 8, nos. 1–2 (2017): 86.

Bibliography

Ahmed, Leila. *A Border Passage: From Cairo to America—A Woman's Journey*. New York: Penguin, 1992.

Chaudhry, Ayesha. *Domestic Violence and the Islamic Tradition*. Oxford: Oxford University Press, 2014.

Collins, Patricia Hill. *Black Feminist Thought: Knowledge, Consciousness, and the Politics of Empowerment*. 2nd ed. New York: Routledge, 2000.

Collins, Patricia Hill. "Shifting the Center: Race, Class, and Feminist Theorizing about Motherhood." In *Mothering: Ideology, Experience, and Agency*, edited by Evelyn Nakono Glenn, Grace Chang, and Linda Rennie Forcey, 45–65. New York: Routledge, 1994.

Fox, Rachel. "Mourning Mothers in Iran: Narratives and Counter-Narratives of Grievability and Martyrdom." In *Muslim Mothering: Global Histories, Theories, and Practices*, edited by Margaret Aziza Pappano and Dana M. Olwan, 69–90. Bradford, ON: Demeter Press, 2016.

Haque, Omar Sultan, et al. "Why are Young Westerners Drawn to Terrorist Organizations Like ISIS?" *Psychiatric Times* 32, no. 9 (2015). Why Are Young Westerners Drawn to Terrorist Organizations Like ISIS? (psychiatrictimes.com); accessed May 28, 2023.

Hill, Holly and Dina Amin, eds. *Salaam. Peace: An Anthology of Middle-Eastern American Drama*. New York: Theatre Communications Group, 2010.

Horgan, John G. *The Psychology of Terrorism*. New York: Routledge, 2005.

Horgan, John G., and Mary Beth Altier. "The Future of Terrorist De-Radicalization Programs." *Georgetown Journal of International Affairs* 13, no. 2 (Summer/Fall 2012): 83–90.

Hutchinson, Aisha J., and Patrick J. O'Leary. "Young Mothers in Islamic Contexts: Implications for Social Work and Social Development." *International Social Work* 59, no. 3 (2016): 343–358.
Inhorn, Marcia C. *Infertility and Patriarchy: The Cultural Politics of Gender and Family Life in Egypt*. Philadelphia: University of Pennsylvania Press, 1996.
Jolly, Natalie. "Envisioning Mothers: Visualization and the Invisibility of Motherhood." *Journal of the Motherhood Initiative* 8, nos. 1–2 (2017): 74–88.
Kashani-Sabet, Firoozeh. *Conceiving Citizens: Women and the Politics of Motherhood in Iran*. Oxford: Oxford University Press, 2011.
Kueny, Kathryn M. *Conceiving Identities: Maternity in Medieval Muslim Discourse and Practice*. Albany: State University of New York Press, 2013.
Labadi, Fadwa al-. "Introduction from Abu Dis: Women Under Occupation." In *Stories from Our Mothers*, edited by Nandita Dowson and Abdul Wahab Sabbah, 4–5. London: Camden Abu Dis Friendship Association, 2010.
Latreille, Martin, and Michel Verdon. "Wives against Mothers: Women's Power and Household Dynamics in Rural Tunisia." *Journal of Family History* 32, no. 1 (2007): 66–89.
Mernissi, Fatima. *Dreams of Trespass: Tales of a Harem Girlhood*. Don Mills, ON: Addison-Wesley, 1994.
Mumtaz, Zubia, Umber Shahid, and Adrienne Levay. "Understanding the Impact of Gendered Roles on the Experiences of Infertility amongst Men and Women in Punjab." *Reproductive Health* 10, no. 3 (2013): 1–10.
Naciri, Rabéa, and Isis Nusair. *The Integration of Women's Rights into the Euro-Mediterranean Partnership: Women's Rights in Algeria, Egypt, Israel, Jordan, Lebanon, Morocco, Palestine, Syria and Tunisia*. Copenhagen: Euro-Mediterranean Human Rights Network, 2003.
Nahar, Papreen, and Annemiek Richters. "Suffering of Childless Women in Bangladesh: The Intersection of Social Identities of Gender and Class." *Anthropology and Medicine* 18, no. 3 (2011): 327–338.
Oh, Irene. "Motherhood in Christianity and Islam: Critiques, Realities, and Possibilities." *Journal of Religious Ethics* 38, no. 4 (2010): 638–653.
Omran, Abdel Rahim. *Family Planning in the Legacy of Islam*. New York: Routledge, 1992.
O'Reilly, Andrea. *Rocking the Cradle: Thoughts on Motherhood, Feminism, and the Possibility of Empowered Mothering*. Toronto: Demeter Press, 2006.
Peteet, Julie. "Icons and Militants: Mothering in the Danger Zone." *Signs* 23, no. 1 (1997): 103–129.
Razzak, J. A., U. R. Khan, I. Azam, M. Nasrullah, O. Pasha, et al. "Health Disparities between Muslim and Non-Muslim Countries." *Eastern Mediterranean Health Journal* 17, no. 9 (2011): 654–664.
Rose, Jacqueline. *Mothers: An Essay on Love and Cruelty*. New York: Farrar, Straus and Giroux, 2018.
Rosen, Lawrence. "Revision and Reality in the Family Law of Morocco." In *Law and Religion in Multicultural Societies*, edited by Rubya Mehdi, Hanne Petersen, Erik Reenberg Sand, and Gordan R. Woodman, 131–144. Copenhagen: DJØF, 2008.
Ross, Lynda Rachelle. *Interrogating Motherhood*. Edmonton: Athabasca University Press, 2016.
Ruddick, Sara. *Maternal Thinking: Toward a Politics of Peace*. Boston: Beacon Press, 1989.
Schleifer, Aliah. *Motherhood in Islam*. Cambridge: Islamic Academy, 1986.
Silvey, Rachel. "Transnational Islam: Indonesian Migrant Domestic Workers in Saudi Arabia." In *Geographies of Muslim Women: Gender, Religion, and Space*, edited by Ghazi-Walid Falah and Caroline Nagel, 127–146. New York: Guildford, 2005.

Viruru, Radhika, and Ramzi Nasser. "'Wa'allah, the Woman She Should Go Direct to Paradise': Perceptions of Motherhood in Qatar." *Global Studies of Childhood* 7, no. 2 (2014): 148–158.
Wadud, amina. *Inside the Gender Jihad: Women's Reform in Islam*. Oxford: Oneworld, 2006.
Wadud, amina. *Qur'an and Woman: Rereading the Sacred Text from a Woman's Perspective*. New York: Oxford University Press, 1999.
Zaman, Riffat Moazam. "Parenting in Pakistan: An Overview." In *Parenting across Cultures: Childrearing, Motherhood and Fatherhood in Non-Western Cultures*, edited by Helaine Selin, 91–104. Dordrecht: Springer Netherlands, 2014.

CHAPTER 17

WOMEN AS MODERN HEADS OF STATE

TAMARA SONN

Early Modern Women Heads of Government: The Begums of Bhopal

Among the early modern women leaders who felt their religion empowered them were some of the rulers of Bhopal.[1] Throughout the nineteenth century, central India's Bhopal, one of the "princely states" (principalities granted relative autonomy in return for political loyalty and various forms of tribute to Britain's colonial government at the time), was ruled by women. They were part of a dynasty of Afghans (Pashtuns, Pathans), who founded the state in 1707 following the death of Mughal Emperor Aurangzeb, in whose military the state's founder had served.

In earlier centuries, as in many royal courts, a number of Bhopali *begums* (*begum* is a title, borrowed from Turkic languages, indicating an elite woman) had wielded significant authority, but the first to actually reign was Qudsia (or Gohar) Begum (r. 1819–1837). Qudsia became regent upon the death of her husband, Nazar Mohammad Khan. The designated successor of Nazar was their daughter Sikander, but Sikander was still an infant when her father died. Qudsia was herself just nineteen, but she was preferable in the view of the majority of stakeholders to the older, male competitors for the throne.

Qudsia assumed her position, addressing a gathering of Bhopal's elites, without her veil, and promising that Sikander would eventually marry a designated fiancé who would then become the *nawab* (ruler). Until then, she—Qudsia—would govern. She had local religious authorities publicly confirm that there was nothing in Islam to bar women from political leadership, citing the example of the Prophet's widow ʿĀ'isha. Qudsia participated in military training, led the troops when necessary, and devoted significant energy to developing Bhopal, determining its needs by personally touring the countryside.

When Qudsia's daughter Sikander (r. 1847/1860–1868) married, Qudsia reluctantly ceded control to the husband, Jahangir Muhammad Khan. Sikander and he had one child, a daughter, Shah Jahan (b. 1838). When Jahangir died seven years into his tenure (1844), Sikander followed her mother's example, naming her young daughter ruler of Bhopal but promising that upon her marriage, the daughter's designated fiancé would assume the title. Until then she—Sikander—would govern as regent.

Like her mother, Sikander was also a skilled administrator. Besides modernizing Bhopal's bureaucracy, she established schools for both girls and boys. Sikander also maintained the alliance with India's British rulers, forged under previous *nawabs* as they struggled to defend Bhopal from regional Hindu powers. This entailed supporting the British in the 1857 Indian rebellion against the Raj. Sikander was rewarded by Britain with a knighthood, and was officially recognized as Nawab of Bhopal in 1860.

When both Shah Jahan's husband and her mother, Sikander, died, Shah Jahan, at age thirty, became the next Nawab of Bhopal. Shah Jahan emulated her mother's able administration. She continued her reforms as well as infrastructure and social services development projects. Her court patronized scholars and artists, male and female. Adept at diplomacy, she is perhaps best known outside of South Asia for establishing England's first mosque, the storied and still functioning Shah Jahan Mosque in Woking (1889).

Shah Jahan's skills and loyalty to the British Raj were also recognized with a knighthood (1872). But in a fascinating reflection of then-emerging anticolonial movements that stressed assertion of communal and national identities, Shah Jahan decided to publicly assert Muslim identity, retaking the veil. Given the dominant British perception of the veil as a symbol of the backwardness of Muslim society, Shah Jahan's donning the veil as the ruler of a princely state was indeed a bold assertion. But for her it was an assertion of identity, not submission or acceptance of segregation—as was her choice to remarry (against South Asian cultural taboos about widow remarriage), and to choose as her husband someone from outside Bhopal's leading families, Sayyid Siddiq Hasan.

Siddiq Hasan was deeply involved in one of the subcontinent's many developing reform movements, the Ahl-i Hadith. The Ahl-i Hadith movement advocated rejecting inherited customs, returning to Islam's foundational sources, and avoiding what it considered foreign influences. In view of anticolonial agitation throughout the British Empire, India's British rulers considered reformers potentially subversive. Siddiq Hasan's publications seemed particularly threatening to their control over India; as a result, they barred him from serving in government.[2] The British also reduced Shah Jahan's authority, relegating her to the position of a British agent in 1885.

But Shah Jahan continued to struggle to assert Bhopal's autonomy until her death in 1901. Then her daughter Sultan Jahan Begum (r. 1901–1926) duly ascended the throne and was recognized as Nawab by the British, provided she designate her eldest son as heir apparent. Sultan Jahan carried on her mother's and grandmother's work, promoting education in both Urdu and English, for rich and poor, female and male, Hindu and Muslim, in Bhopal and beyond. She established Aligarh Zenana Madrasa, the Muslims Girls' School in Lucknow, and patronized many others. She also patronized

Urdu-language women's journals and published works on women's rights and responsibilities, education, moral guidance for children, and women's health.

Sultan Jahan was also active at the national level. Agitation for independence had been developing in northern India, with the establishment of the Indian National Congress in Bombay in 1885, and the All-India Muslim League in Dhaka, Bengal in 1906. Sultan Jahan became president of the All-India Ladies Conference (Anjuman-i-Khawatin-i-Islam) in 1914, and supported the National Council of Women in India, established in 1925. Like her mother, Sultan Jahan joined the debate over women's rights. On the question of veiling, she came down strongly on the side of tradition but, again, calling for traditional Islamic dress codes did not mean accepting women's segregation. Like most reformers, Sultan Jahan insisted on women's rights to higher education, health, work, and travel. To wit: in 1924 her two elder sons died. She traveled to London and personally petitioned King George V to have her youngest son Hamidullah recognized as heir apparent. In 1926, at age sixty-eight, she stepped down, ending the run of women rulers of Bhopal. But she continued her engagement in public affairs until her death in 1930. To this day, the Begums of Bhopal remain powerful examples of Muslim women's leadership in the nineteenth and early twentieth centuries.[3]

Postcolonial Women Heads of Government

Pakistan

While the Begums of Bhopal may have been somewhat anomalous for their time, in the postcolonial era Muslim women are indeed well represented as political leaders. Major examples are the leaders of the countries that emerged from the 1947 partition of the Indian subcontinent by the departing British rulers: Pakistan and Bangladesh. Pakistan was created specifically for Muslims, leaving a clear majority of Hindus in India. Both countries struggled with postcolonial developmental challenges and various ethnic and communal tensions. Pakistan's ethnic tensions were so severe that they erupted into civil war in 1971. What had been West Pakistan became Pakistan and East Pakistan became Bangladesh at the end of the civil war on December 16, 1971.

Benazir Bhutto (1953–2007) was the first Muslim woman to become prime minister of a country. She was the daughter of Prime Minister Zulfikar Ali Bhutto, who was overthrown in a military coup in 1977 and subsequently hanged on questionable murder charges. With degrees from Harvard and Oxford universities, Benazir had returned to Pakistan just before the coup, and begun working for the restoration of democracy. She endured periods of detention, house arrest, and imprisonment before being released and going into exile in London in 1984, the same year she assumed leadership of the party founded by her father, the Pakistan People's Party (PPP). She returned to Pakistan in 1986, continuing to work for democracy and enduring further arrests and detention.

When democracy was reinstated following the death of military dictator Zia ul-Haq (1988), the PPP secured a slim majority in parliament and Benazir was invited to form a government. Zia had sought support for his military regime by allowing religious conservatives to roll back legal reforms that had been made in the 1960s, including those equalizing women's and men's legal status. Under his regime, not only were women's legal rights reduced but also gender segregation was enforced. Benazir's new government immediately sought and received a *fatwa* (authoritative but nonbinding religious legal opinion) affirming that while the head of state must be male, Islamic law does not preclude women serving as head of government (prime minister).

Benazir had campaigned on a platform of democracy and social justice, which, she argued in her posthumously published second autobiography, are Islamic values.[4] Once in power, echoing the 1979 United Nations Convention on the Elimination of All Forms of Discrimination Against Women (CEDAW), her government pledged to do just that. In addition to allowing trade unions to operate again and lifting press restrictions, it elevated Zia's Women's Department to ministerial level and appointed a woman to lead it, and also appointed women as heads of four other ministries dealing with social issues. Her government further established women's studies programs at four universities and a women's bank. But overall there was little progress on the intertwined economic and social fronts. Benazir's government was unable to deliver on its promises of economic and infrastructure development. Clashing with Pakistan's powerful military and intelligence establishment, in August 1990 her government was dismissed, and Benazir and her husband, Asif Ali Zardari, were charged with corruption.

New elections returned a majority for the Pakistan Muslim League (PML); its leader, Nawaz Sharif, became prime minister for the first of his three terms. But his government faced the same economic pressures, social strife, and uneasy relations with the military. Under allegations of corruption and mismanagement, Sharif resigned in 1993.

Another round of elections once again brought Benazir to the premiership. By her own account, she returned to her progressive agenda, dedicating foreign aid to energy development, health and family planning, and education especially for women. But with Pakistan's continued pursuit of its nuclear program and the resulting US sanctions, Benazir's economic policies again failed, giving rise to labor and ethnic tensions. Benazir and her husband became targets of more corruption charges, and her government was once again dismissed. New elections brought a second term for Nawaz Sharif, and Benazir again went into exile.

Nawaz's second term ended abruptly with a military coup in 1999 led by General Pervez Musharraf. Two years later, the 9/11 terrorist attacks in the United States resulted in another military dictatorship in Pakistan benefiting from US aid as Musharraf's government pledged support for the US-led invasion of Afghanistan.

But after several years, opposition to Musharraf mounted and Pakistanis agitated for a return to democracy. Elections were scheduled for early 2008. The government granted amnesty to all politicians charged with misconduct between 1986 and 1999, and Benazir Bhutto returned to Pakistan to campaign for the upcoming elections. Among her campaign themes was opposition to religious extremism, which she claimed was not only a perversion of Islam but also a result of the lack of democracy. But Pakistan's support for the US-led war in Afghanistan remained intensely unpopular. The violence in Afghanistan spread into Pakistan. The Government of Pakistan responded with military attacks, while Benazir spoke out against extremism. In December 2007, she was assassinated at a political rally in Rawalpindi. To date no one has been charged in the killing, although the government at the time blamed it on the leader of Pakistan's Taliban, Baitullah Mehsud, who was killed in a US drone strike in 2009.[5]

Bangladesh

Bangladesh has had two female prime ministers, one of whom is currently serving (at the writing of this chapter). Their political careers, like that of Benazir, have been characterized by enormous economic and social challenges, and marred by numerous charges of corruption. Like Pakistan, Bangladesh has struggled to maintain a functioning democracy. But unlike Pakistan, it adopted a constitution establishing a parliamentary government based on socialist and secular principles. The Awami League dominated the country's first general elections in 1973, confirming the premiership of Sheikh Mujibur Rahman, leader of the independence movement against Pakistan. But the country's already weak postcolonial economy and infrastructure had been devastated by the war for independence and further decimated by floods and widespread famine. Efforts by Mujib's government to curb mounting unrest included unpopular measures such as curtailing press freedom. Opposition to the government increased. A 1975 constitutional amendment calling for one-party rule led to Mujib's assassination and the young country's first period of martial law. In 1977, Army Chief of Staff Ziaur Rahman was installed as president. The constitution was changed, and Islam was made the state religion. Elections confirmed Ziaur Rahman as president in 1978, the same year he established the Bangladesh Nationalist Party (BNP). General elections were then held, and were dominated by the new party, but opposition escalated, culminating in Ziaur Rahman's assassination in 1981. The following year his successor, Abdus Sattar, was overthrown in another military coup, led by Army Chief of Staff Hussain Muhammad Ershad. Ershad, who was named president in 1983, allowed elections in 1986 and 1988. Those elections were widely boycotted, and in 1990 a popular uprising forced Ershad to resign.

Bangladesh's democracy was finally restored. Ziaur Rahman's BNP dominated the elections, resulting in the first of three terms as prime minister for his widow, Khaleda Zia (b. 1945). Her five-year term was marred by allegations of vote-rigging and demands for oversight of new elections by a caretaker government. The opposition then boycotted the February 1996 general elections, allowing Khaleda Zia a second term. But it was brief. Widespread protests led to passage of a constitutional amendment calling for parliament to cede power to a nonpartisan caretaker government until new general elections could be conducted. New elections were held in June, resulting in an Awami

League victory and the first of two terms for Bangladesh's second female prime minister, Sheikh Hasina Wazed (b. 1947).

Sheikh Hasina is the daughter of slain independence leader and former president Sheikh Mujibur Rahman (d. 1975). Like Benazir, Sheikh Hasina had lived several years in exile. Upon her return to her country in 1981, she became head of her father's party, the Awami League. Like Benazir Bhutto, Sheikh Hasina was subjected to numerous arrests and periods of detention. As prime minister she worked to resolve internal ethnic disputes and cooperate with neighboring countries on environmental measures and economic development. Her government signed a treaty with India to develop water-sharing in the Ganges basin, for example, and joined the Bay of Bengal Initiative for Multi-Sectoral Technical and Economic Cooperation.[6]

The results of general elections in 2001, though disputed by the Awami League, returned the BNP to a position of dominance, and Khaleda Zia's third term as prime minister. It was a period of escalating unrest in the country. Two Awami League ministers of parliament were assassinated in 2004; the same year Awami League members meeting in Dhaka were attacked, resulting in twenty-one deaths. The Jamaat-ul-Mujahideen (JMB) and Harakat-ul-Jihad al-Islami, both allegedly associated with al-Qaeda, launched a series of attacks in 2005, detonating bombs at government and other facilities across the country. Further unrest erupted in the runup to elections scheduled for January 2007. Following the end of parliament's term in October 2006, a state of emergency was declared.

During 2007 and 2008, charges of extortion, corruption, and murder were brought against Sheikh Hasina and some of her relatives. The High Court ultimately ruled that the emergency laws could not be used for most of these allegations; other charges were suspended or dropped. Sheikh Hasina was released from jail in mid-2008 for medical treatment. During the same period, corruption charges were also brought against Khaleda Zia and her sons. She was detained and briefly jailed.

The state of emergency was lifted in 2008. General elections again resulted in Awami League dominance and Sheikh Hasina's second term as prime minister, though the election results were again disputed. Her administration continued its efforts to develop and stabilize the country. In 2010 Bangladesh's Supreme Court outlawed martial law. But Sheikh Hasina was criticized in the aftermath of the 2012 Rakhine State anti-Muslim riots in Myanmar, when she prohibited tens of thousands of displaced Rohingya refugees from entering Bangladesh. She was also targeted in 2012 with more charges of corruption, this time brought by the World Bank.

An army coup against Sheikh Hasina was discovered and foiled. In 2013 she and members of her staff faced charges from the International Criminal Court. Nevertheless, the 2014 general election, boycotted by the opposition, confirmed Awami League's dominance and Sheikh Hasina began her third and current term as prime minister. She has continued to work with regional powers for cooperation on shared economic and environmental challenges. In 2017, as anti-Muslim campaigns erupted again in neighboring Myanmar, Sheikh Hasina reversed her position and granted the refugees temporary shelter. Like Benazir, she has also spoken out forcefully against religious extremism, stressing that it is antithetical to Islamic values. In early 2018 she inaugurated a project to build 560 mosques and cultural centers across Bangladesh with the goal of countering extremist influence and teaching what she considers authentic Islamic values of peace and religious pluralism.[7]

Like Pakistan, then, after a very difficult birth, the young country of Bangladesh continues its monumental struggle to establish a stable social, economic, and political culture. Like the men who have led those countries' governments, the women heads of state have failed to make marked progress in any of these areas. What they have done, however, is establish a firm precedent for Muslim women's places in the ranks of political leaders in the contemporary world.

Indonesia

Megawati Sukarnoputri is another woman who became head of a postcolonial government by way of her relationship to a man, but her career has been far less dramatic than those of Benazir Bhutto, Khaleda Zia, and Sheikh Hasina. Indonesia—the world's largest Muslim-majority country—has had a history of gradual democratization. Like Pakistan and Bangladesh, Indonesia was created after World War II within boundaries established by departing colonial powers. Its government has been "guided" toward democracy, as the country's first president put it, by the military, based on Pancasila (the "five principles"): Indonesian nationalism, international standards of justice, consultative/democratic governance, social welfare, and monotheism.[8]

That first president was the country's nationalist leader General Sukarno. Indonesia's first elections for a national representative legislature were held in 1955. In the face of struggles with opposition groups, particularly Communists, Sukarno's government quickly replaced the elected legislature with one comprising political appointees in equal number to elected members, and curtailed civil liberties. After attempting to negotiate with the Communist opposition, Sukarno was ousted by a military coup in 1967. The coup brought to power Major General Suharto.

Suharto initiated a massive and brutal backlash against Communists and alleged sympathizers, resulting in the deaths of hundreds of thousands. His government then established a "New Order" in 1971, attempting to continue the gradual development of democracy. Political parties and elections for the legislative assembly were organized by the government. The new system, and close alliance with the United States, led to significant economic development over the next quarter-century, but the 1997 Asian financial crisis devastated Indonesia's economy. That, in turn, exacerbated both ethnic tensions and opposition to Suharto's government. Suharto's reelection in March 1998 resulted in even greater social unrest, with ethnic rioting erupting in many areas. In May, student-led demonstrations, supported by the military, forced Suharto to resign. He appointed as successor his vice president, B. J. Habibie.

Habibie's government enacted some liberalization measures and ended the horrific war in East Timor, in which the Indonesian military had killed an estimated

100,000–300,000. But opposition remained strong. As in neighboring Malaysia around this time, a reform movement had developed, calling for greater political liberalization. Sukarno's daughter, Megawati Sukarnoputri, was a leading figure in the movement. She had taken over leadership of the Partai Demokrasi Indonesia (Indonesian Democratic Party-Struggle, or PDI-P). When Habibie announced elections in 1998, the opposition coalesced against him. Abdurrahman Wahid (d. 2009), leader of the prodemocracy organization of Muslim leaders Nahdatul Ulama (NU), was elected to the presidency in 1999—the first democratically elected president of the country. Megawati was his vice president. His government passed measures that limited the military's ability to interfere in politics and established a human rights tribunal to examine military abuses in East Timor, but charges of corruption undermined his popularity. In 2001 the national assembly removed him from office. His vice president, Megawati Sukarnoputri, became Indonesia's first woman president.

Megawati's presidency was opposed by some conservative Muslims on the basis of her gender, but the majority expressed strong support, especially given her alliance with Wahid's NU, an organization of traditional religious scholars. Her decisive actions against al-Qaeda-linked terrorists after the bombing of a nightclub in Bali that killed more than 200 people in 2002 were also extremely popular. But she was outcampaigned in the presidential elections held in 2004 and defeated by the popular Susilo Bambang Yudhoyono, a skilled administrator who focused on economic recovery, free trade, improvement of social services, and regional cooperation on environmental issues. He was reelected in 2009, again defeating Megawati. Her party backed Joko Widodo ("Jokowi"), the winning candidate in the 2014 elections. Megawati remains chairman of PDI-P.[9]

Turkey

Unlike Pakistan's, Bangladesh's, and Indonesia's Muslim women leaders, Turkey's Tansu Çiller (b. 1946) was avowedly secularist. Indeed, Turkey, born after World War I and the end of the religiously legitimated Ottoman Empire, was established as a secular state. Fears of the expansion of the neighboring USSR combined with domestic ethnic tensions created instability and resulted in military coups in 1960, 1972, and 1980. Democracy was restored in 1983, even as the country experienced continued ethnic strife centering on the rights of Turkey's large Kurdish minority.

By that time, popular discontent with authoritarianism was rising. The Democratic Party had been founded in 1946 to challenge Turkey's one-party rule by the Republican People's Party. Following the 1960 coup, the Democratic Party's legacy was picked up by the Justice Party (AP), founded by Süleyman Demirel. That party was dissolved with the 1981 coup and reemerged as the True Path Party (Doğru Yol Partisi, DYP) to lead the opposition, again with Demirel as leader, in 1983.

At the same time, popular opposition was also being expressed in terms of religious values, leading to another kind of polarization, the Turkish Constitution's official secularism versus political Islam. The National Order Party (Millî Nizam Partisi; MNP) was founded in 1970 by opposition leader Necmettin Erbakan but quickly banned for violating the constitutionally mandated prohibition of religious involvement in politics. It was succeeded by the National Salvation Party (Millî Selâmet Partisi, MSP), which was also banned, in 1981. In 1983 Erbakan established yet another iteration, the Refah Partisi (Welfare Party; RP). The same year, the Motherland Party (Anavatan Partisi, ANAP) was formed, echoing many of the themes of Islamist parties but maintaining a secular stance.

This is the context in which Tansu Çiller's political career developed in Turkey during the 1990s. Unlike the women leaders of Pakistan, Bangladesh, and Indonesia, Çiller did not come from a political family. An economics professor at Bogaziçi University in Istanbul, she became economic advisor to former True Path leader Demirel in 1990. She then ran for parliament and won a seat in 1991. Demirel, leading a coalition, was named prime minister, and gave her a ministerial position. The president, Turgut Özal, died suddenly in 1993, and the National Assembly elected Demirel president. Çiller then became leader of the True Path Party and prime minister.

Çiller's tenure as prime minister was marked by rising conflict with Kurdish separatists, leading to increased military spending and the establishment of controversial assassination squads. Her government was also implicated in a foiled coup attempt in neighboring Azerbaijan in 1995. Çiller did lead the country into a popular customs agreement with the European Union (the 1995 Ankara Agreement), but Turkey's economy struggled, further weakening confidence in her government. In 1996 her party formed a new coalition, with the former president's popular Motherland Party. Çiller was removed from the premiership, replaced by Motherland leader Ahmet Mesut Yilmaz, and became deputy prime minister. But the coalition soon collapsed. A new coalition was formed—this time with the Islamist Welfare Party. Welfare Party leader Erbakan was named prime minister; Çiller remained deputy prime minister and was also named minister of foreign affairs. But Çiller's reputation continued to decline, and the military's suspicion of Islamist activities continued to rise. In early 1997 the military intervened, pressuring President Erbakan to take measures against newly opened religious schools and Sufi orders. Erbakan resigned and was banned from politics. Çiller's party's efforts to form a new government failed. She retired from politics in 2002.[10]

Muslim Women Heads of State in Other Countries

One other woman, Sibel Siber (b. 1960), a physician and a public healthcare advocate, served a brief interim term as head of the government of the partially recognized Republic of Northern Cyprus (June 2013–September 2013) after a no-confidence vote brought down the previous government. Several other Muslim women have served as heads of state, if not heads of government. They achieved their positions primarily through careers in government and NGO service, rather than through family connections. Mame Madior Boye (b. 1940), for example, a leading international lawyer, served as prime minister (March 2001–November 2002) of Senegal. She was dismissed, along with several other appointed officials, over government mishandling of a maritime disaster. Aminata Toure (b. 1962) also briefly served as Senegal's prime minister (September 2013–July 2014). Cissé Mariam Kaidama Sidibé (b. 1948) served a brief term (April 2011–March 2012) as prime minister of the troubled former French colony of Mali. She was removed from office when President Touré's government was overthrown in a military coup. Ameenah Firdaus Gurib-Fakim served as president of the tiny island nation of Mauritius beginning in June 2015. She resigned in 2018 under allegations of financial impropriety. Roza Otunbayeva (b. 1950) briefly served as president of Kyrgyzstan (April 2010–December 2011). Following the 2010 uprising that ended the presidency of Kurmanbek Bakiyev, Otunbayeva was chosen to lead an interim government. The interim government oversaw the drafting of a new constitution, which limited presidents to a single term, preventing her from running in new elections. Atifete Jahjaga (b. 1975) served a term as president of the newly (2008) independent state of Kosovo. A professional in police management and law enforcement, Jahjaga was particularly active in dealing with militant religious extremism. And finally, Halimah Yacob (b. 1954) has served in the ceremonial role of president of Singapore since 2017. Her 2017 election resulted from a constitutional amendment that reserved the office for candidates from the Malay minority. Halimah ran unopposed and was therefore declared president.

Conclusion

The biographies of Muslim women political leaders reveal significant engagement with their religious identities. In the case of the nineteenth century Begums of Bhopal, religious authorities affirmed the legitimacy of their leadership, regardless of gender. Sikander Begum became the first Indian ruler to undertake pilgrimage to Mecca. She wrote an account of it that was later translated from the original Urdu into English and published by her daughter, Shah Jahan Begum. Shah Jahan in particular made a point of asserting her empowerment through Islam. In addition to works of poetry and a history of Bhopal, she published a manual for women, *Tahdhîb un-niswân wa tarbîyat ul-insân* (*The Reform of Women and the Cultivation of Humanity*, 1889). Dealing with women's work and legal rights in Islam, it presented empowering information on pregnancy, hygiene, and health, as well as practical advice regarding homemaking. The work is distinctive in its presentation of women as fully responsible participants in society. Shah Jahan also may be seen as an early representative of political Islam as she insisted on veiling publicly, shifting the symbolism of the veil from subservience to empowerment. Her daughter Sultan Jahan likewise stressed women's empowerment. She herself became a prolific author. Many of her speeches were compiled and published, including several on women's rights according to Islam.[11] Indeed, her erudition earned her the position of founding chancellor of Aligarh Muslim University (1920).[12]

Except for Turkey's Tansu Çiller, Muslim women political leaders in the postcolonial period engaged with Islam in more complex ways. While expressing belief that their religion both empowered them and encouraged them to work for democracy and social justice, they also felt compelled to condemn the religious extremism that emerged as a further challenge to postcolonial struggles for good governance. Only Benazir Bhutto has left behind an autobiographical work, but her positions well reflect those of the women rulers of Bangladesh and Indonesia, as indicated in their public remarks referenced above. Bhutto's first autobiography, *Daughter of Destiny: An Autobiography* (1989), mentions her religion several times, stressing that Islam teaches human equality, including between females and males, and upholds freedom and democracy. As noted above, her second autobiography, published twenty years later, focuses more intensely on opposition to religious extremism.

Overall, Muslim women's leadership reflects a strong tradition in classical Islamic history. Islam's foundational text, the Qur'an, expressly establishes equal female and male moral competence (33:35), insists that both women and men are entitled to earn wages (4:32), and that women may own and manage property. The Prophet Muḥammad first wife, Khadīja, for example, was a powerful businesswoman. She had been his employer, and it was she who proposed marriage to him. She is revered for supporting his prophetic calling and as the first person to embrace Islam. His last wife, ʿĀ'isha, is respected among Sunnī Muslims as a reliable source for oral traditions about Muḥammad (individually and collectively known as hadith; committed to written form by the ninth century), the most important religious literature in Islam after the Qur'an. She was also a warrior, leading supporters in a civil war against Muḥammad's cousin and son-in-law, Ali, who had been chosen to lead the community after the death of Muhammad's third successor. Khadīja and ʿĀ'isha are considered among the most important figures in Sunnī Islamic history. Despite these models, after the death of Muḥammad, Islam was institutionalized and politicized in a deeply patriarchal social context. As a result, legal opinion generally agreed that among the qualifications for political leadership was being male, a position that has prevailed throughout much of Islamic history. The modern political leaders described above may, therefore, be seen not as an innovation in Islamic history but as a reflection of some of its classical themes.

Notes

1. For a full bibliography on women in Islam, see Marcia Hermansen and Barbara von Schlegell, "Women in Islam," *Oxford Bibliographies Online*, www.oxfordbibliographies.com. For a study of premodern Muslim rulers, see Fatima Mernissi, *The Forgotten Queens of Islam* (Minneapolis: University of Minnesota Press, 1997); and Sher Banu A. L. Khan, *Sovereign Women in a Muslim Kingdom: The Sultanahs of Aceh, 1641–1699* (Singapore: NUS Press, 2017). Shahla Haeri covers some of the same material in *The Unforgettable Queens of Islam* (Cambridge: Cambridge University Press, 2020).

2. Metcalf, Barbara D. "Islam and Power in Colonial India: The Making and Unmaking of a Muslim Princess," American Historical Association Presidential Address, 2011, https://www.historians.org/about-aha-and-membership/aha-history-and-archives/presidential-addresses/barbara-d-metcalf.
3. For more information on the Begums of Bhopal, see Syed Ashfaq Ali, *Bhopal: Past and Present* (Bhopal: Jai Bharat Publishing House, 1970); Siobhan Lambert-Hurley, "Nawab Begums of Bhopal," *Oxford Dictionary of National Biography*, available at https://www.oxforddnb.com); Metcalf, "Islam and Power in Colonial India."
4. Benazir Bhutto, *Reconciliation: Islam, Democracy, and the West* (New York: Harper, 2008).
5. For an analysis of the UN investigation into Bhutto's assassination by its leader, see the publication by former Chilean ambassador to the UN Heraldo Muñoz, *Getting Away with Murder: Benazir Bhutto's Assassination and the Politics of Pakistan* (New York: W. W. Norton, 2013). Haeri, *Unforgettable Queens*, 141–182, provides further details on Benazir Bhutto's career.
6. See Home-The Bay of Bengal Initiative for Multi-Sectoral Technical and Economic Cooperation (BIMSTEC).
7. For a brief biography and further reading on Shaikh Hasina, see Maryam Khalid, "Wazed, Sheikh Hasina," in *The Oxford Encyclopedia of Islam and Women*, ed. Natana J. DeLong-Bas, available in John L. Esposito, ed., *Oxford Islamic Studies Online*, oxfordislamicstudies.com.
8. The Pancasila represented a compromise reached among various secularist and Islamist nationalists that allowed the country to be guided by Islamic principles but not bound by traditional interpretations of Islamic law; see Fred R. von der Mehden, "Indonesia," in *The Oxford Encyclopedia of the Modern Islamic World*, available in John L. Esposito, ed., *Oxford Islamic Studies Online*, oxfordislamicstudies.com.
9. For more information on Megawati Sukarnoputri, see Clinton Bennett, *Muslim Women of Power: Gender, Politics and Culture in Islam* (London: Bloomsbury, 2010), 164–194; and Haeri, *Unforgettable Queens of Islam*, 183–218.
10. For further information on Tansu Çiller, see Bennett, *Muslim Women of Power*, 10–136.
11. *Islam main 'Aurat ka Martaba'* [The Position of Women in Islam] (Bhopal: Hamidia Art, 1922); mentioned by Siobhan Lambert-Hurley, *Muslim Women, Reform and Princely Patronage, Nawab Sultan Jahan Begam of Bhopal* (Abingdon: Routledge, 2007), 144.
12. Aligarh Muslim University is the second iteration of the Muhammadan Anglo-Oriental College established in 1875 by reformer Sir Sayyid Ahmad Khan. For other works by Sultan Jahan, see: Her Highness Jahan, *Taj ul-Ikbal Tarikh Bhopal*, trans. H. C. Barstow (Kolkata: Thacker, Spink and Co., 1976); Jahan, *An Account of My Life (Gohur-i-Ikbal)*, trans. C. H. Payne (London: John Murray, 1912); Jahan, *Al-Hijab, or Why Purdah Is Necessary* (Calcutta: Thacker, Spink and Co. 1922); Jahan, *Hayat-i-Qudsi: Life of the Nawab Gauhar Begum, Alias the Nawab Begum Qudsia of Bhopal* (London: Paul, Trench, Trubner; New York: Dutton, 1918); Jahan, *Muslim Home* (Calcutta: Thacker, Spink and Co., 1916); and Jahan, *The Story of a Pilgrimage of Hijaz* (Calcutta: Thacker, Spink and Co., 1909, 1913).

BIBLIOGRAPHY

Ali, Syed Ashfaq. *Bhopal: Past and Present*. Bhopal: Jai Bharat, 1970.

Bennett, Clinton. *Muslim Women of Power: Gender, Politics and Culture in Islam*. London: Bloomsbury, 2010.

Bhutto, Benazir. *Daughter of Destiny: An Autobiography*. New York: Simon and Schuster, 1989.
Bhutto, Benazir. *Reconciliation: Islam, Democracy, and the West*. New York: Harper Perennial, 2008.
Haeri, Shahla. *The Unforgettable Queens of Islam*. Cambridge: Cambridge University Press, 2020.
Jahan. *An Account of My Life (Gohur-i-Ikbal)*. Translated by C. H. Payne. London: John Murray, 1912.
Jahan. *Hayat-i-Qudsi: Life of the Nawab Gauhar Begum, alias the Nawab Begum Qudsia of Bhopal*. London: Paul, Trench, Trubner; New York: Dutton, 1918.
Jahan. *Al-Hijab, or Why Purdah Is Necessary*. Calcutta: Thacker, Spink and Co. 1922.
Jahan. *Muslim Home*. Calcutta: Thacker, Spink and Co., 1916.
Jahan. *A Pilgrimage to Mecca*. Translated by Emma Laura Willoughby Osborne. 1870.
Jahan. *The Story of a Pilgrimage of Hijaz*. Calcutta: Thacker, Spink and Co., 1909, 1913.
Jahan. *Taj ul-Ikbal Tarikh Bhopal*. Translated by H. C. Barstow. Kolkata: Thacker, Spink and Co., 1976.
Khan, Shaharyar Muhammed. *The Begums of Bhopal: A History of the Princely State of Bhopal*. New York: I. B. Tauris, 2000, excerpted in https://scroll.in/article/875997/how-an-accidental-gunshot-at-a-family-picnic-led-to-the-107-year-long-rule-of-the-begums-of-bhopal.
Lambert-Hurley, Siobhan. *Muslim Women, Reform and Princely Patronage: Nawab Sultan Jahan Begam of Bhopal*. Abingdon: Routledge, 2007.
Lambert-Hurley, Siobhan. "Nawab Begums of Bhopal." In *Oxford Dictionary of National Biography*, https://doi-org.proxy.library.georgetown.edu/10.1093/ref:odnb/99719
Metcalf, Barbara D. "Islam and Power in Colonial India: The Making and Unmaking of a Muslim Princess." American Historical Association Presidential Address, 2011, https://www.historians.org/about-aha-and-membership/aha-history-and-archives/presidential-addresses/barbara-d-metcalf.
Muñoz, Heraldo. *Getting Away with Murder: Benazir Bhutto's Assassination and the Politics of Pakistan*. New York: W. W. Norton, 2013.
"PM Hasina for Real Teaching of Islam in Bangladesh." *Dhaka Tribune*, April 5, 2018, https://www.dhakatribune.com/bangladesh/nation/2018/04/05/pm-hasina-real-teaching-islam-bangladesh/.
von der Mehden, Fred R. "Indonesia." In *The Oxford Encyclopedia of the Modern Islamic World*, available at John L. Esposito, ed., *Oxford Islamic Studies Online*, oxfordislamicstudies.com.

CHAPTER 18

WOMEN'S RELIGIOUS AND SOCIAL ACTIVISM IN PALESTINE, LEBANON, AND SYRIA

ELIZABETH BROWNSON

SEVERAL intersecting debates have emerged in scholarship on Muslim women's activism in Palestine, Lebanon, and Syria in recent decades, with contested conceptions of empowerment and agency at the crux of the discourse. The emerging body of research in this field presents varied perspectives and evidence on these central questions: Has Islamic activism empowered women? To what extent? Can it potentially empower them? Most studies fall within the empowerment and agency camp at least in part, ranging from tentatively acknowledging that Islamist and Islamic activism has the potential to empower women to demonstrating that their activism is in fact empowering. A few outliers characterize this activism as inherently disempowering, offering tenuous or biased evidence for these claims while adhering to ideological misconceptions about Islamists and women.

The other major debate concerns the nature of the relationship between Islamist women activists and secular feminists and whether Islamists' versions of Islam are compatible with women's rights. Some scholars describe Islamist and secular feminists' convictions as posing an unbridgeable gap, while others show there has been dialogue in the past and suggest further common ground is possible. This chapter first examines studies on Islamist women's activism in Palestine and Lebanon that find varying extents of women's empowerment, then it turns to the debate on the Islamist-secular feminist divide among Palestinian activists. Finally, it analyzes scholarship on female religious teachers and their students in Syria, as well as a study conducted in Palestine, through the lens of women's empowerment.

Islamic Activism as Empowerment

Islah Jad's pioneering book *Palestinian Women's Activism: Nationalism, Secularism, Islamism* (2018) is the most comprehensive study of women in Hamas to date and shows multiple ways in which activism has empowered them. Based on interviews and observations of conferences from the late 1990s through 2004, Jad reveals Islamist women's tenacity in pushing Hamas leaders to expand their roles and reform the organization's initially restrictive gender ideology. She explains that Hamas needed women's support to transform into a political party in the mid-1990s; consequently, it recruited and incorporated them into all ranks of the organization, particularly college-educated women.[1]

Jad's research substantially widens analysis of women in Hamas by examining multiple factors affecting their empowerment and status. In doing so, she refutes studies that fixate on the ideal gender roles in Hamas's 1988 charter, assume Islamist women adhere to them, and depict Hamas's gender ideology as inflexible.[2] Jad argues that the traditional roles ascribed to women in the charter did not reflect reality because women were active in Hamas student blocs and other Islamist organizations.[3] She also emphasizes that the gender roles and ideals upheld in the charter are far from fixed; rather, they are constantly evolving. Jad's analysis of conferences organized by Hamas's women's department demonstrates a critical transformation in Hamas's gender ideology, from "the utter rejection of feminism" in 1997 to "selectively incorporating positions advocated by feminists" by 2000.[4] Finally, Hamas women made important gains by calling for "equal job opportunities and equal pay" for men and women performing the same jobs in the organization, progressive interpretations of Islamic texts, and a women's brigade in Hamas's military wing.[5]

The definitive study on women's religious and social activism in Lebanon is Lara Deeb's 2006 book *An Enchanted Modern: Gender and Public Piety in Shi'i Lebanon*, which likewise demonstrates empowering aspects of activism. Deeb's ethnography on pious Shīʿī women in south Beirut examines religious women's intertwined understandings of modernity and piety, as well as their centrality to the "normativization" of new forms of public religiosity that have emerged since the 1970s.[6] Most relevant for this chapter, Deeb's 2009 article shows how women's charitable volunteerism has become a central component of not only a woman's piety but also her identity: "Today, being a 'modern' woman (which is a highly desirable status) involves a combination of education, employment or volunteering, social-welfare work, and visibly expressed piety."[7] Deeb also illustrates various ways in which women volunteers are empowered by their work, such as being seen as role models for the people they serve, gaining increased self-confidence, and learning public speaking skills.[8] Perhaps most important for them is how their humanitarianism is "inextricably linked to piety" because helping one's community is considered a critical aspect of being pious; some women also express that the work makes them feel significantly closer to God.[9] Their work gives them pleasure from the "love of giving," as one woman puts it.[10]

Sara Ababneh's 2014 article on Palestinian Islamist women similarly but explicitly challenges feminist and Western assumptions about women's empowerment, showing how Islamist practices and "women's only spaces" can be empowering for women.[11] She argues that women's spaces are inherently more inclusive than mixed, in that they "enable women from all backgrounds to participate," particularly those from "more conservative and less privileged" families; in contrast, mixed spaces often effectively exclude women from these backgrounds.[12] To illustrate this, Ababneh first discusses the brief terms of Mariam Saleh and Amal Siyam, Hamas's ministers for women affairs, and how they shifted the ministry's raison d'être of espousing gender equality in the law to helping Palestinian women in need, such as those in refugee camps or prisoners' wives.[13] While they appear to have accomplished little beyond talking to women and organizing festivals for the families of imprisoned women, Saleh and Siyah had only fifteen months between them to realize their vision.[14] Ababneh is most convincing when she explains how the Islamic Bloc's women's section at Birzeit University has empowered women in a segregated context. The women members, for example, initiated and ran a female dormitory that enabled many young women to attend university because the "women's only space" reassured parents; furthermore, controlling an autonomous, gender-separated section enabled the female students "to focus on exclusively women's issues."[15] Ababneh also notes that the Islamic Bloc's women's structure is both equal and identical to the men's and it does not report to the men's section.[16]

As in Jad's work on Hamas women, Anne Baylouny's 2013 study attributes Hizbullah's progressive change on a range of issues to women's important position within the organization and provides convincing evidence indicating their empowerment through Islamic activism. Examining gender programming on Al-Manar, Hizbullah's television station, she argues that women's robust media presence instigated a "transformed vision" of women's roles in the organization and society.[17] Baylouny stresses that women's programs, which not only have been ignored in research but also air more frequently than other shows, are gender equal on many issues. For example, hosts encourage men to share more equally in household tasks and childcare and depict women's careers as important for self-fulfillment, not merely as a financial necessity.[18] These views indicate a considerable shift from the emphasis on complementary gender roles described by Victoria Firmo-Fontan (2004)[19] and by Deeb (2006), whose women volunteers "prioritized household responsibilities,"[20] perhaps because of the respective nine- and seven-year intervals between their studies and Baylouny's. Another reason for the different findings could be Baylouny's focus on professional women versus Deeb's more traditional demographic.

Firmo-Fontan's 2004 case study argues that aspects of Hizbullah women's activism are empowering but also underscores the patriarchal framework in which the Hizbullah Women's Association (HWA) functions. She maintains that while Al-Manar TV employs women and men equally in positions from correspondents to editors, its depiction of women "strictly adheres" to religious views regarding women's complementary roles with men.[21] This also reflects the founding ideology of the HWA, which she suggests has shaped Al-Manar's representations of women. Firmo-Fontan does not, however, support this argument beyond mentioning women's equal representation in "decision-making positions" within the television station.[22] An explanation of the links and power dynamics between the HWA and Al-Manar is needed as well. Finally, it would be instructive to discuss representations of women beyond their conservative dress and on Al-Manar's various programming.

In a similar way, Zeina Zaatari (2006) demonstrates empowering facets of Islamist women's activism as well as how they "are complicit" in the perpetuation of male-dominated systems.[23] Like Firmo-Fontan, she observes the HWA's stress on complementary gender roles but focuses on how it, along with secular women's organizations in South Lebanon, consistently associates women with motherhood. Zaatari argues that their emphasis of women's roles as mothers, "the culture of motherhood," is the prevailing discourse employed by Islamist and secular women alike, which enables them to participate politically and engage in civil society.[24] She observes that while her interviewees constantly exercise agency, from making their own decisions to resisting suppression and exploitation, they have also "contributed to the reproduction of oppressive patterns, including patriarchal structures," in stressing their roles as mothers.[25] It certainly seems worth the tradeoff for these activists because it increases their mobility and flexibility, allowing them to push for social change. Particularly for the Islamists, it would likely be more challenging to gain autonomy and approval from their male colleagues without emphasizing women's roles sanctioned by religious texts.

Aitemad Muhanna's 2015 case study of the head of the Women's Police Unit in Gaza likewise demonstrates that women can be empowered within an Islamist organization individually while supporting patriarchal systems and laws. Nariman, Muhanna's subject, disregards gendered restrictions for herself, however. In this respect she evokes a resemblance to the Egyptian activist Zaynab al-Ghazali (deceased in 2005), who founded the Muslim Ladies' Association in the 1930s as an independent counterpart to the Muslim Brotherhood.[26] Muhanna's microstudy supports Jad's findings, such as how "many educated and professional Hamas women have succeeded in gaining powerful autonomous positions within Hamas institutions" and have transformed some gender standards within the organization.[27] In this case, Hamas women galvanized the creation of an independent women's police unit, headed by a woman.[28]

Several scholars in related fields, whose work addresses Islamist women only tangentially, offer evidence of women's empowerment through Islamist groups and activism as well. In his 2009 book on Hamas's political success, Jeroen Gunning mentions that many women he met who supported Hamas commended the organization for "having given them the courage, opportunity and sometimes the financial aid to break with tradition and persuade their families to allow them to attend university."[29] Sara Roy's 2011 book on charitable organizations in Gaza speaks to the impact of activism on women, arguing that "the capacity to choose and participate was part of an ongoing effort among [Islamist Social Institutions] to empower individuals pragmatically, notably women."[30] Regarding activists, Cheryl Rubenburg's 2001 book on Palestinian women's status includes interviews with several Muslim Sisters that indicate they benefit from their religious and social activism, finding empowerment and meaning in their work.[31]

Islamist versus Secular Activists?

Another major debate in the scholarship on Islamist women's activism in Palestine concerns the relationship between Islamist activists and secular feminists. Scholars of Palestinian women's movements are divided regarding whether there has been room for dialogue and common ground in the past, as well as the potential for compromise between Islamist and secular views and convictions in the future. The compatibility of women's rights with Islamism is another aspect of this debate, with some secular feminists insisting that they are inherently incompatible and proponents of Islamic feminism arguing that religious texts can be interpreted in gender-equal ways.

Ababneh (2014), in addition to her arguments discussed above, describes the chasm that she observed in Palestine between secular feminists and Islamists in the wake of Hamas's electoral victory. While attending conferences in 2007, she was shocked to hear academics' "vilification of Islamists," characterizing Islamist women as "tools" of Hamas leaders and complicit in perpetuating "their own subordination."[32] Women's organizations boycotted Hamas's minister of women's affairs as well, refusing to meet, and even staff refused to cooperate with their new Islamist minister. Ababneh also addresses the rift in approaches to legal reform, with the Islamist ministers arguing that Islam should "provide the basic guiding principles" as opposed to the Universal Declaration of Human Rights.[33]

Fadwa al-Labadi (2008) well illustrates Ababneh's accounts of secular feminists' misgivings about and stereotyping of Islamist women. Al-Labadi claims that both Islamist women's activism and Islamic feminism "legitimize" Hamas's "gender policy," which "restricts personal freedom" and "ignores the repressive contexts of the social and political climate in Palestine."[34] She supports the latter assertion by repeating a few statements made by Hamas politicians that their own leaders have rejected, such as calling for mandatory headscarves. While al-Labadi acknowledges that Hamas gives affiliated women organizations "control over [its] educational and job training programs" and advocates higher education for women, she is skeptical that Islamic feminism, which aims to reinterpret the Qur'an and other Islamic texts to reflect gender equality in the law and society, "will resolve all women's issues" and lead to equal rights.[35]

Indeed, al-Labadi is most concerned about women's legal position and using sharīʿa as a source of law. She clearly believes that only a secular civil code will give Palestinian women full equality. Al-Labadi characterizes both Hamas and "the Islamist women's movement" as having "insisted on women's subordinate legal status."[36] Several points are important to note here. First, Hamas members are not homogeneous in their positions on family law reform. Al-Labadi's claim, for example, that Hamas "restricts" women's rights "to those laid out in the Qur'an" is not consistent with Jad's 2018 work outlined above.[37]

Jad's survey of conferences held by Hamas's women's department in the late 1990s shows a diversity of views among female and male participants, which included banning polygamy and upholding women's right to divorce. Second, as Jad observes in a 2018 edited book chapter, the law is but one of the "many power structures that affect women's political empowerment," and it is important to also consider "social, economic, and political factors," that influence women's status in a specific context.[38] Historical factors are imperative to examine as well.

Finally, there has not only been cooperation among Islamists and secular activists, but secular feminists have also influenced Hamas's gender ideology. Gunning (2009) shows how secular feminists and Islamist women were able to find common ground on specific human rights issues in the late 1990s. He describes the joint efforts of Hamas and secular women activists in organizing campaigns to increase awareness about and to denounce the practices of so-called honor killings and early marriage.[39] In the conferences organized by Hamas's women's department, Jad (2018) reveals that "meticulous attention was given to the concerns of Palestinian feminists related to legislation, work, education, political participation, communication, and women in the media."[40] Despite these collaborations and influences, women's status in Muslim family law, and particularly the acceptable methods for and extent of reform, remain a great impasse between many Islamist and secular activists. As al-Labadi stresses, most secular feminists prefer a universalist approach based on human rights, which is difficult to reconcile with many provisions of *fiqh*-based family laws.

Beverley Milton-Edwards and Stephen Farrell's 2010 book, which includes a chapter on women in Hamas, likewise depicts significant divisions between secular and Islamist women. They characterize the handful of Islamist women they interview as possessing little agency and emphasize aspects of Hamas that they assume are disempowering, such as gender segregation. Indeed, the authors dismiss their Islamist interviewees, describing PM Jamila al-Shanti as "less than convincingly" explaining the benefits of having male and female sectors of the organization, while acclaiming the nationalist activities of secular women whom they discuss extensively and neglect to fact-check.[41] Hanan Ashrawi, for example, states that Hamas's provision of social services comes with political pressure.[42] Roy's 2011 research on Islamic social institutions in Gaza, however, shows that they provide services regardless of political or religious affiliation and are in fact "highly decentralized."[43] The authors also fail to mention that few women actually became PLO guerrillas in the 1970s and that the Palestinian Authority has had an appalling record on women in political leadership. Jad points out that Hamas had twice the percentage of women's representation in its political organizations in 2003 at 15.3 percent compared to the secular Palestinian National Council in 2000, which was 7.5 percent.[44]

Milton-Edwards and Farrell argue that Hamas marginalizes its female associates, portraying them as powerless in the organization. They quote and discuss Hamas's 1988 charter at length and claim it "depicts women as passive bearers of future generations of jihadists."[45] Most significantly, they present these views as being observed by women and unchanged since 1988, rather than examining women's actual behavior and contributions. As discussed, Jad (2018) reveals that women were active participants in Hamas student blocs in the 1980s and that women have induced the organization to evolve its gender ideology considerably. Milton-Edwards and Farrell are also fixated on gender segregation and headscarves, mentioning them frequently and presuming them to be synonymous with women's oppression, whether describing election campaigns or the Islamic University. In essence, the authors discuss Hamas women in the manner of an ethnocentric Western journalist. Indeed, they discuss rare but fetishized incidents of female suicide bombers during the second intifada at great length, without offering a hint of possibility that Islamist women's activism could be empowering or offer contributions to society. These depictions contrast dramatically with Jad's description of Hamas's women's department welcoming "the 'new Islamic woman,' who is well educated, professional, politically active, and outspoken—in sum, modern—while also a good, committed Muslim."[46]

Female Mosque Teachers

Scholarship on women's religious and social activism in Syria has focused on female teachers who guide students in pursuit of Islamic knowledge, spirituality, and pious lives. Since the early 1980s, the state has suppressed Islamist activity, thus surviving movements have been careful to avoid politics or to espouse activism. In this context, religious movements with women leaders have been able to flourish, being subject to far less government scrutiny compared to their male counterparts. Regarding women's empowerment via Islamic activism, two of the three scholars below address the issue in various ways; only the first study, on Palestine, uses empowerment as the central lens of analysis, however.

Anne Sophie Roald's 2016 study of female Palestinian preachers and their students argues that Islamist and non-political Muslim women's religious activism in Palestine is "both disempowering and empowering."[47] She shows several respects in which preaching and attending Islamic lectures empowers women, particularly because of attendees' increased mobility, gaining "personal satisfaction" from charitable work, and improving one's economic situation through participation in groups that emphasize financial security through savings programs.[48] Roald also argues, however, that aspects of these activities are disempowering because female preachers' advice tends to reinforce patriarchal norms, such as instructing women to have patience with their husbands' bad behavior. She also references men's legal advantages in family issues as an example of "Islam" being "disempowering" and makes blanket statements such as "Islam creates oppressive situations for women . . . while offering the same women tools to endure these situations."[49] Conflating Islam with cultural constructs and practices oversimplifies and distorts the religion, but the ways in which male-privileged interpretations of Islam can restrict women's lives is a valid point.

Roald seems to minimize the empowerment that many women gain by participating in Islamic activities. How is it not a substantial improvement for a woman to go from "rarely" able to leave the house, to significantly increased mobility that includes networking with women, forming economic saving groups, and attending lectures?[50] Roald does note, however, that there is considerable potential for empowerment if female preachers were to use progressive teachings and interpretations. Another strength is that Roald contextualizes her study, discussing how "the socioeconomic situation limits women's independence from male domination," such as laws privileging men in child custody and women's economic dependence on husbands.[51]

In contrast, Hilary Kalmach (2008, 2012) shows how female mosque teachers can subtly push for more women-friendly interpretations of Islamic texts, which "has the *potential*" (her emphasis) to improve women's status, but they also need to carefully uphold the conservative social order.[52] She examines new types of women's religious authority in Syria since the late 1980s, illustrating this trend through a study of Huda al-Habash, a prominent mosque instructor in Damascus. Kalmbach explains how modern Islamist movements and women's increased access to education in the twentieth century has enabled female religious leaders to gain distinction in recent decades. Of particular importance has been Islamists' focus on personal piety and Muslims' authority to interpret religious texts themselves, which led to the "removal of many barriers to becoming religious instructors."[53] Al-Habash did not receive years of formal religious education; rather, her career as a religious instructor began at seventeen years of age when she began teaching Qur'an studies to girls. Kalmbach explains that al-Habash's religious authority is based on her family of preachers, her "quiet charisma," and her experience.[54]

Kalmbach characterizes al-Habash as a "staunch advocate" of complementary gender roles and men's predominant religious authority, as well as "a critic of feminism," but also explains that al-Habash's religious authority is contingent on these views.[55] Instead of claiming that complementary gender roles are distinct but equal, as is often argued,[56] al-Habash accepts inequalities as natural, citing the trope of women being more emotional and delicate than men.[57] Indeed, al-Habash legitimizes the need for women Islamic teachers by appealing to conservative arguments, such as female instructors being better suited to cultivate mothers and wives.[58] Al-Habash also points out that women were historically Sunna and Hadith preservers as well as instructors in mosques, "wistfully not[ing] that women were given even more religious authority in the past [because] they could teach both sexes."[59] Kalmbach confirms this, citing a new study that provides "biographical information for thousands of female instructors and Hadith transmitters from the early and medieval period."[60]

Al-Habash does, however, depart from conservative teachings in important ways. For example, a wife is required to ask her husband before leaving the house, but al-Habash "insists" that he must allow it, "especially if she is visiting her family or pursuing education."[61] She should request his permission only "in case he would prefer her to postpone her trip."[62] Al-Habash also strongly supports both secular and religious education for women, as well as women's public presence, arguing that women "should strive to be teachers, leaders, [and] even president of the country," although she accepts the status quo of the highest levels of Islamic leadership being closed to women.[63] Kalmbach argues that despite al-Habash and other mosque teachers' adherence to conservative mores, "their presence and activity are radically changing the streets and mosques."[64] They are also increasing women's knowledge of Islamic texts, which equips them to potentially demand their rights and increase their opportunities.[65] Indeed, Al-Habash's prominent presence and teachings that subtly challenge patriarchal guidelines may well have benefited thousands of women and girls.

Annabelle Bottcher (2002) similarly shows the important roles that Syrian women have played as Sufi and Sunni teachers and leaders of *dhikrs* (Sufi ceremonies) since the 1980s, but she does not address the content of their lessons. She also describes women's enthusiastic embrace of increased opportunities for Islamic learning and practice, suggesting that women's eager reception is partly because of women's limited options for leaving the home unaccompanied. Given that shopping and visiting family are considered "legitimate reason[s]," however, it seems they would have plenty of excuses to do so.[66]

Although Bottcher does not discuss empowerment explicitly, her descriptions of female teachers indicate that they exert agency. In fact, some are highly respected *shaykhas* with thousands of followers. It is worth noting that, as of 2002, women taught about half the religious classes among Sunnis in Syria.[67] The extent to which students are empowered from their lessons, however, is unclear. Like Roald, Bottcher describes a wide range of activities that take place along with women's religious lessons and rituals. A great deal involves social networking, such as discussing family issues, offering support to one another, sharing news of job opportunities, and even arranging marriages. They also trade all sorts of items, from clothing to apartments.[68] While these descriptions indicate that women benefit from the increased socializing that comes with attending lessons, it would have been instructive to discuss interpretations of Islamic texts taught in the lessons, as in Kalmbach's and Roald's studies. Bottcher also briefly describes women's charitable work, such as funding girls' education, in terms that suggest empowerment, but it appears to be a select group, "a tightly knit network," that provides these services.[69]

Conclusion

Even though women's empowerment and agency are analytical lenses employed frequently in Middle East women's studies, this chapter shows how academics can have different conceptions of the terms. Most of the scholarship analyzed demonstrates some extent of Muslim women's empowerment through religious and social activism. These studies range, however, from presenting compelling evidence of women's agency and empowerment, as we saw in Jad, Deeb, Ababneh, and Baylouny, to describing certain aspects of women's activism as empowering and others as adhering to patriarchal norms, as in Zaatari, Firmo-Fontan, Muhanna, Bottcher, Roald, and Kalmbach. Also, the latter two studies of female mosque teachers focus more on the potential for women's empowerment as opposed to empowerment already taking place.

Whether further dialogue and common ground is possible between Islamist activists and secular feminists in Palestine remains to be seen. While Jad and Gunning offer examples of discussion and collaborations among them in the past, Ababney and al-Labadi show there was also considerable acrimony and tension immediately after Hamas's landslide parliamentary victory in 2006. Divisions between the groups are certainly evident in terms of Muslim family law reform, given the discrepancies between universalist-human rights and traditional *fiqh*-based approaches on the issue. As my 2019 book on Palestinian women and Muslim family law discusses, however, the PA's Ministry of Women's Affairs, human rights groups, and particular *sharī'a* court judges began work on a new draft of family law in 2013.[70] Hopefully these efforts will eventually lead to a successful integration of the universalist and *fiqh*-based approaches in a unified Palestinian family law. More research is greatly needed on the extent of Islamists' participation on this and other issues.

Another critical avenue for further research concerns the extent to which Muslim women's activism influences nonactivist women. How do activists affect other women's views and behavior regarding piety, gender-equal interpretations of Islamic texts, family law reform, gender roles, and women's employment in traditionally male occupations, among other issues? Jad, for example, shows that Hamas women target both highly educated professional women with cultural programs, as well as women in need by providing vocational education and charitable aid.[71] How has their activism influenced both groups? Has it led to changes in their lives or opinions? More research on female preachers, and particularly their students, is also needed. To what extent do students benefit from their religious lessons and experience empowerment in their daily lives? The important studies discussed in this chapter can provide the foundation on which further scholarship can build.

Notes

1. Islah Jad, *Palestinian Women's Activism: Nationalism, Secularism, Islamism* (Syracuse, NY: Syracuse University Press, 2018), 73.
2. See Beverley Milton-Edwards and Stephen Farrell, *Hamas: The Islamic Resistance Movement* (Cambridge: Polity, 2010), chap. 10.
3. Jad, *Palestinian Women's Activism*, 134.
4. Ibid., 140.
5. Ibid., 151, 139, 142–143; Islah Jad, "Between Religion and Secularism: Islamist Women of Hamas," in *On Shifting Ground: Muslim Women in the Global Era*, ed. Fereshteh Nouraie-Simone (New York: Feminist Press, 2014), 276.
6. Lara Deeb, *An Enchanted Modern: Gender and Public Piety in Shi'i Lebanon* (Princeton, NJ: Princeton University Press, 2006), 5.
7. Deeb, "Emulating and/or Embodying the Ideal: The Gendering of Temporal Frameworks and Islamic Role Models in Shi'i Lebanon," *American Ethnologist* 36, no. 2 (2009): 253.

8. Deeb, *An Enchanted Modern*, 185–186.
9. Ibid., 193.
10. Ibid., 191.
11. Sara Ababneh, "The Palestinian Women's Movement versus Hamas: Attempting to Understand Women's Empowerment outside a Feminist Framework," *Journal of International Women's Studies* 15, no. 1 (2014): 39.
12. Ibid., 39.
13. Ibid., 49.
14. Ibid., 45.
15. Ibid., 48.
16. Ibid., 47.
17. Anne Marie Baylouny, "Hizbullah's Women: Internal Transformation in a Social Movement and Militia," in *Social Movements, Mobilization, and Contestation in the Middle East and North Africa*, 2nd ed., ed. Joel Beinin and Frederic Vairel (Stanford: Stanford University Press, 2013), 87.
18. Ibid., 97.
19. Victoria Firmo-Fontan, "Power, NGOs and Lebanese Television: a Case Study of Al-Manar TV and the Hezbollah Women's Association," in *Women and Media in the Middle East: Power through Self-Expression*, ed. Naomi Sakr (London: I. B. Tauris, 2004), 178–179.
20. Deeb, *An Enchanted Modern*, 210.
21. Firmo-Fontan, "Power, NGOs and Lebanese Television."
22. Ibid.
23. Zeina Zaatari, "The Culture of Motherhood: An Avenue for Women's Civil Participation in South Lebanon," *Journal of Middle East Women's Studies* 2, no. 1 (Winter 2006): 36.
24. Ibid., 34.
25. Ibid., 35.
26. Valerie Hoffman, "An Islamic Activist: Zaynab al-Ghazali," in *Women and the Family in the Middle East*, ed. Elizabeth Fernea (Austin: University of Texas Press, 1985), 236–237.
27. Aitemad Muhanna, "Women's Moral Agency and the Politics of Religions in the Gaza Strip," *Journal of Feminist Studies in Religion* 31, no 1 (2015): 6.
28. Ibid., 12.
29. Jeroen Gunning, *Hamas in Politics: Democracy, Religion, Violence* (New York: Columbia University Press, 2009), 149.
30. Sara Roy, *Hamas and Civil Society in Gaza: Engaging the Islamist Social Sector* (Princeton, NJ: Princeton University Press, 2011), 184.
31. Cheryl Rubenberg, *Palestinian Women: Patriarchy and Resistance in the West Bank* (Boulder: Lynn Rienner, 2001), 232–238.
32. Ababneh, "The Palestinian Women's Movement," 36.
33. Ibid., 44.
34. Fadwa al-Labadi, "Controversy: Secular and Islamist Women in Palestinian Society," *European Journal of Women's Studies* 15, no. 3 (2008): 193.
35. Ibid., 183, 198.
36. Ibid., 181.
37. Ibid., 183.
38. Islah Jad, "Palestine," in *Arab Family Studies: Critical Reviews*, ed. Suad Joseph (Syracuse, NY: Syracuse University Press, 2018), 225.
39. Gunning, *Hamas in Politics*, 169–170.

40. Jad, *Palestinian Women's Activism*, 145.
41. Milton-Edwards and Farrell, *Hamas*, 182.
42. Ibid., 194–195.
43. Roy, *Hamas and Civil Society*, 181.
44. Jad, *Palestinian Women's Activism*, 113.
45. Milton-Edwards and Farrell, *Hamas*, 183.
46. Jad, *Palestinian Women's Activism*, 110–111.
47. Anne Sofie Roald, "The Nuances of Islam: Empowerment and Agency for Palestinian Women in the West Bank," *Frontiers* 37, no. 3 (2016): 10.
48. Ibid., 7–8.
49. Ibid., 14.
50. Ibid., 7–8.
51. Ibid., 15.
52. Hilary Kalmbach, "Female Mosque Leadership and Islamic Authority in Syria and Further Afield," *Travail, genre et sociétés* 1, no. 27 (2012): XIV.
53. Hilary Kalmbach, "Social and Religious Change in Damascus: One Case of a Female Islamic Religious Authority," *British Journal of Middle Eastern Studies* 35, no. 1 (April 2008): 44.
54. Ibid., 48.
55. Ibid., 49.
56. For example, see Firmo-Fontan, "Power, NGOs, and Lebanese Television," 178–179.
57. Kalmbach, "Social and Religious Change," 50.
58. Ibid., 45.
59. Ibid., 46.
60. Ibid., 47.
61. Ibid., 52.
62. Kalmbach, "Female Mosque Leadership," XIII.
63. Ibid.
64. Kalmbach, "Social and Religious Change," 57.
65. Kalmbach, "Female Mosque Leadership," xiv.
66. Annabelle Bottcher, "Islamic Teaching among Sunni Women in Syria," in *Everyday Life in the Muslim Middle East*, ed. Donna Lee Bowen and Evelyn A. Early, 2nd ed. (Bloomington: Indiana University Press, 2002), 291. (Incidentally, I saw plenty of unaccompanied women on the streets of Damascus in 2001).
67. Ibid., 298.
68. Ibid., 291.
69. Ibid., 297.
70. Elizabeth Brownson, *Palestinian Women and Muslim Family Law in the Mandate Period* (Syracuse, NY: Syracuse University Press, 2019), 54, 61–62.
71. Jad, *Palestinian Women's Activism*, 115–116.

Bibliography

Ababneh, Sara. "The Palestinian Women's Movement versus Hamas: Attempting to Understand Women's Empowerment outside a Feminist Framework." *Journal of International Women's Studies* 15, no. 1 (2014): 35–53.

Baylouny, Anne Marie. "Hizbullah's Women: Internal Transformation in a Social Movement and Militia." In *Social Movements, Mobilization, and Contestation in the Middle East and North Africa*. 2nd ed. Edited by Joel Beinin and Frederic Vairel, 86–101. Stanford, CA: Stanford University Press, 2013.

Bottcher, Annabelle. "Islamic Teaching among Sunni Women in Syria." In *Everyday Life in the Muslim Middle East*. 2nd ed. Edited by Donna Lee Bowen and Evelyn A. Early, 290–299. Bloomington: Indiana University Press, 2002.

Deeb, Lara. "Emulating and/or Embodying the Ideal: The Gendering of Temporal Frameworks and Islamic Role Models in Shi'i Lebanon." *American Ethnologist* 36, no. 2 (2009): 242–257.

Deeb, Lara. *An Enchanted Modern: Gender and Public Piety in Shi'i Lebanon*. Princeton, NJ: Princeton University Press, 2006.

Firmo-Fontan, Victoria. "Power, NGOs and Lebanese Television: A Case Study of Al-Manar TV and the Hezbollah Women's Association." In *Women and Media in the Middle East: Power through Self-Expression*. Edited by Naomi Sakr, 162–179. London: I. B. Tauris, 2004.

Jad, Islah. "Between Religion and Secularism: Islamist Women of Hamas." In *On Shifting Ground: Muslim Women in the Global Era*. Edited by Fereshteh Nouraie-Simone, 256–293. New York: Feminist Press, 2014.

Jad, Islah. *Palestinian Women's Activism: Nationalism, Secularism, Islamism*. Syracuse, NY: Syracuse University Press, 2018.

Kalmbach, Hilary. "Female Mosque Leadership and Islamic Authority in Syria and Further Afield." *Travail, genre et sociétés* 1, no. 27 (2012): 1–17I.

Kalmbach, Hilary. "Social and Religious Change in Damascus: One Case of a Female Islamic Religious Authority." *British Journal of Middle Eastern Studies* 35, no. 1 (April 2008): 37–57.

Labadi, Fadwa, al-. "Controversy: Secular and Islamist Women in Palestinian Society." *European Journal of Women's Studies* 15, no. 3 (2008): 181–201.

Milton-Edwards, Beverley, and Farrell, Stephen. *Hamas: The Islamic Resistance Movement*. Cambridge: Polity, 2010.

Muhanna, Aitemad. "Women's Moral Agency and the Politics of Religion in the Gaza Strip." *Journal of Feminist Studies in Religion* 31, no. 1 (2015): 3–21.

Roald, Anne Sofie. "The Nuances of Islam: Empowerment and Agency for Palestinian Women in the West Bank." *Frontiers* 37, no. 3 (2016): 1–20.

Zaatari, Zeina. "The Culture of Motherhood: An Avenue for Women's Civil Participation in South Lebanon." *Journal of Middle East Women's Studies* 2, no. 1 (Winter 2006): 33–64.

CHAPTER 19

WOMEN'S RELIGIOUS AND SOCIAL ACTIVISM IN EGYPT AND NORTH AFRICA

NERMIN ALLAM

INTRODUCTION

WOMEN in the Middle East and North Africa have been actively engaged in multiple and diverse efforts toward change and reform. In Egypt, women's early activism was rooted in the social milieu and soon extended to the religious, national, and political spheres.[1] Their engagement in social welfare activities and/or Islamic inspired volunteerism often blurred the dichotomy between the social, the political, and the religious, since it took place against complex backgrounds and grounded itself in overlapping discourses. The influence of their activism further extended beyond Egypt, inspiring parallel efforts in the Middle East and North Africa. Notwithstanding the variations within and across groups in the region, in this chapter I survey some of the common themes that marked women's social and religious activism and shaped its trajectory. While the focus is primarily on Egypt, the analysis will occasionally include examples from North Africa and highlight the ways in which the priorities and foundations of different groups converge and diverge across the region.

The chapter specifically surveys the nature of early women's social and religious activities, the framing of their activism, the overlap between secular and Islamic discourses in their intellectual grounding, and tendencies to form nongovernmental organizations that has been called "NGO-ization." These themes are commonly identified in the literature and continue to figure squarely in discussions and debates on women's social and religious activism. The analysis presented does not intend to generalize the experiences of women, for, as Judith Tucker rightly notes, "women's lives—their access to power and economic resources as well as their social and legal standing—surely vary from one community or class to another."[2] I am rather interested in analyzing how the literature approached and theorized women's social and religious forms of participation and how they refashioned our thinking of activism. The analysis presented also focuses on how women's activities in these spheres figured in debates surrounding the authenticity, the ideological foundation, and the credibility of women's activism.

Charitable Agenda and Maternal Framework

Women's social activism in Egypt dates back to the late nineteenth and early twentieth centuries. Women from the upper and middle classes were highly engaged in philanthropic activities—they founded charitable organizations, such as hospitals, schools, and training centers for women and children.[3] The entrance of women into the public sphere and the expansion of their role in philanthropic and charitable organizations were byproducts of a global move toward industrialization and social reform. As Mohamed Ali Pasha (1805–1848)—often referred to as the founder of modern Egypt—attempted to introduce a systematic plan for industrialization and social restructuring, the topic of women's status and particularly their education gained prominence and became the subject of intense debates.[4] Religious leaders from al-Azhar University as well as some secular nationalists educated in the West opposed the education of women and grounded their position in religion and tradition.[5] They viewed the call for reform as a threat to the social fabric of the society and Islamic traditions. While some of the voices advocating for reform called for emulating the West, reformists, like their opponents, largely grounded their views in religion.

The literature often attributes the ideological foundation of women's early activism to Qāsm Amīn (1865–1908) and the influence of Muḥammad ʿAbduh (1849–1905) and Jamāl al-Dīn al-Afghānī (1838/1839–1897) on Amīn's intellectual formations.[6] In his controversial books *The Liberation of Women* (*Taḥrir al-Marʾa*, 1899) and *The New Woman* (*al-Marʾa al-Jadīda*, 1900), Amīn put forward a liberal view of Islam that does not clash with calls for reform; he used religion and the Qur'ān to refute traditions of female seclusion and veiling. A number of postcolonial feminists, however, challenge the overstated claim that male reformers—and predominantly Qāsim Amīn—inspired women's activism, they rather emphasize the influence of early writings by female intellectuals.[78] This is because, the omission of women's writings and the emphasis on male reformists in early analysis of women's activism not only create an "aporia in knowledge"—to borrow Gayatri Spivak's vocabulary—but also reproduce an essentialist view of women. According to postcolonial feminists Leila Ahmed and Beth Baron, the ideas put forward in Amīn's book *The Liberation of Women* reproduce colonial representations' of women and their status in Islamic societies.[9] The debate over the ideological foundation of women's early activism in Egypt thus opens up further discussions on the intellectual effect of colonialism and colonial encounters on women's studies and historical analyses.[10]

The framing of women's early activism gave rise to another enduring debate in the literature. Scholars note how members in the newly established philanthropic groups often framed and justified their demands and participation using maternal frames. This maternal framing had two aspects: First, it framed women's demand as a necessity for molding proper wives and mothers. For example, Nabawiya Mūsa (1890–1951), an Egyptian writer and pioneer of girls' education, believed that the education of women was a nationalist duty with great potential. In the same vein, the Egyptian feminist and Islamic modernist, Malak Ḥifnī Nāṣif (1886–1918) emphasized the significance of women's education and training for the welfare of the *umma* (the global Muslim community). Activists to date continue to tap into this discourse as it resonates with conservative segments in the society. Second, the maternal framing justified and encouraged women's participation in public volunteer work, as it was viewed as an extension of her caregiver role in the domestic sphere. This framing, notwithstanding its limitations in challenging gender stereotypes, often contributed to negotiating limitations that surrounded their activism in Egypt's early and modern history. The debate over the limits and opportunities that the maternal framing affords to women continues to figure in recent analysis of their participation in social welfare activities.[11] In my own research on women's engagement in welfare groups prior to the 2011 uprising in Egypt, women describe how their family often highly regarded the role of women as caregivers in social welfare and philanthropic organizations but not the role of women in labor unions or political organizations. This, undoubtedly, play on gender stereotypes and the essentialist representation of women as caregivers. However as Sunny Daly highlights in earlier studies, through women's participation in social welfare activities, women negotiate and mitigate social limits surrounding their public activism. Scholars as such view these spaces as important sites for the cultivation of agency and activism.[12]

Indeed, notwithstanding the seemingly apolitical nature of women's social and welfare activities, scholars trace their significant implications on the agenda of women's rights. Women's social activism primarily influenced the agenda of women's rights, I argue, in two broad ways. First, women's social activism in the area of women's health and education had important consequences on laws, legislations, and traditions.[13] Consider how recent efforts in the area of women's health resulted in the criminalization of female genital mutilation in Egypt in 2008. Second, though early and also more recent philanthropic organizations with secular or religious orientation did not always espouse an explicit gender or political agenda, they often functioned as dormant political organizations. Members in these organizations went on to form political movements and participate in political struggles during episodes of contentions.

The experiences of women's groups in Egypt, however, is not an exception. In Morocco, Mounira Charrad and Rita Stephan highlight, professional women leaders deployed the "power of presence"[14] to assert their voice and push for the 2004 reforms in the personal status code, the *Mudawwana*. By professional women leaders, the reference is to a social category of women who have entered the public sphere through their "college-education-based profession" and "by occupying positions in mainstream organizations that were not necessarily focused on women's issues."[15] These professional middle-class women were neither part of the women's rights grassroot organizations, nor the monarchy's entourage, they rather used their position in the society and their creditability in the eyes of the monarchy as reputable public figures and professionals to advocate for family law reforms for several years before the proclamation of the 2004 reforms.

Scholars also observed the political implications of women's seemingly apolitical organizations, theorizing it as "movement by implications,"[16] as Vania Carvalho Pinto remarked in the context of the Persian Gulf countries, or as "movements by consequence,"[17] according to Asef Bayat's theorization about women's groups in Iran.

Philanthropic Turn, Nationalist Turn, Feminist Turn

During periods of nationalist struggles, women's social and philanthropic organizations played an important role in mobilizing women to join liberation and independence movements. The literature on women's engagement in nationalist struggles in the region exposes the ways in which women's participation in these movements was instrumental in shifting the nature of women's activism from social and philanthropic to nationalist and political.[18] In Egypt's liberation struggle, women led protests and rallied for the release of male nationalist leaders and for Egypt's independence from British colonialism in 1919. Female leaders Ṣafiya Zaghloul (1876–1946) and Hudā Shaʿrāwī (1879–1947), among others, mobilized the masses; lower-class women participated in street protests with men; and rural women from the countryside provided food and assistance to male activists.

However, following the independence movement, demands raised by female nationalists were completely ignored. Instead their male nationalist colleagues called for their return to the domestic sphere and excluded them from the political landscape. Many scholars view this development as a turning point for female nationalists.[19] In the aftermath of their failed expectations, female leaders refashioned their vocabulary, activism, and work. This experience politicized women and led to the emergence of a well-articulated feminist agenda. Hudā Shaʿrāwī, then president of the Wafdist Women's Central Committee (WWCC), resigned, and with a number of other feminist nationalists established the Egyptian Feminist Union (EFU), on the fourth anniversary of the first women's public demonstration, in March 16, 1923.[20] Members in the EFU advocated for women's education, employment, and reforms in the Personal Status Law.

The failure of new nationalist regimes in the region to improve gender equality after independence is a defining character of women's experiences in liberation struggles in the Middle East and North Africa. For example, notwithstanding women's active participation in Algeria's liberation struggle against French colonizers (1954–1962), they were excluded from politics following liberation and their contributions often overlooked by historians as well as by the public.[21] Several feminist and nationalist studies draw attention to the ways in which the process of nation-building after the revolutions is premissed on particular gender identities and meanings.[22] Broadly speaking, this body of work acts as a *caveat emptor* for women who wish to participate in revolutions. Examining the process of nation-building and the construction of citizenship following major revolutions, scholars conclude by criticizing how women participated in national struggles only to be relegated to home and hearth after.[23]

The postindependence states, scholars note, brought further limitations to women's activism in both the social and political domain. In Egypt, women's activism came to a full halt following the Free Officers Revolution in 1952. Under the new nationalist regime of Gamal Abdel Nasser (1956–1970), the regime moved to adopting policies of state feminism. The policies extended limited gains for women; however, it completely crushed any independent social or political organizations and curtailed their role—even in social welfare initiatives. The status of women under the Nasserist model of state feminism is extensively debated in the literature, yielding various evaluations.[24] While most scholars claim that the 1952 revolution marked the end of independent feminism and women's activism in Egypt, others like Mervat Hatem, Nadje Al-Ali, and Laura Bier offer a qualified critique of Nasser's period by detailing the advancements in the agenda of women's rights.[25] They note the emergence of a younger generation of professionals and intellectuals who gained access to the newly established institutions.

The model of state-sponsored feminism carried out by Tunisian former president Ḥabīb Būrgība (1956 to 1987)—around the same time of Nasser—is extensively debated in the literature as well. While the literature identifies its limitations—specifically its failure to integrate religious women, the model is largely celebrated and credited for advancing women's status.[26] The experiences of women in liberation struggles and under the new nationalist regimes thus afforded women significant opportunities as well as limitations. The literature on the topic provides important insight for understanding how women's social activism gave rise to a feminist agenda. It further exposes the ways in which the new nationalist regime halted women's social activism and offers different assessments of the policies of state-sponsored feminism.

The Limits and Possibilities of the NGO-ization of Women's Groups

The internationalization of women's movements especially during the United Nations' Decade for Women (1976–1985), in addition to the dominance of state-sponsored feminism in recent years, has had important implications for the nature and structure of women's social activism in the Middle East. Together, these developments resulted in the NGO-ization of women's groups.[27] In her seminal work on women's movements, Islah Jad coined the term "NGO-ization" to refer to the increase in the number of NGOs that carry out research and advocacy work in the area of women's health, education, legal literacy, and economic participation.[28] Her work is instrumental in exposing the different ways in which the expansion in women's organizations created challenges and opportunities and shifted the character of social activism among women.

While the NGO-ization of women's groups can be noted across the Middle East and North African societies, scholars observe that, it was more pronounced in Yemen, Jordan, Palestine, and Lebanon, in addition to Egypt.[29] The variation is a function of the different regulations governing civil society, and is also intimately tied to the economic situation in different countries. As the government of Anwar Sadāt and that of his successor, Ḥusnī Mubārak, adopted policies of market liberalization, they had to renegotiate the role of NGOs in Egypt's public sphere. The social welfare activities carried out by women's groups were welcomed to ease the economic burden created by these neoliberal economic policies. The groups, some scholars hold, functioned as tools to maintain the status quo and dampen opposition by stepping in and carrying out what would otherwise be responsibilities of the state.[30] Islamic-oriented groups and their women-led organizations dedicated to piety, social services, and philanthropy benefited as well from this opening under Sadāt's regime. Their activities, however, came to a halt following the assassination of Sadāt by members of the militant group Egyptian Islamic Jihad.

Scholars further argue that the expansion in the number of NGOs is not necessarily a sign of democracy or decentralized power.[31] The number of civil society organizations, including women's organizations, increased under the former regime of Mubārak from around 10,000 in 1998 to almost 30,000 by 2008.[32] Civil society organizations, however, were closely monitored and controlled by the government through Law 32 of 1964 and its successor Law 84 of 2002 that placed them under the tight control of the Ministry of Social Solidarity.[33] A related limitation identified by scholars is the way in which the function and the funding of the social groups is often tied to international funding agencies and reflect the donors' agenda.[34] Given these limitations, the expansion in NGOs does extend narrow advancement for women. However, at the same time, they can perpetuate economic inequalities that are frequently associated with the neoliberal policies espoused by these organizations. The association between some of the independent women's groups and foreign funding agencies is also often used to discredit women's organizations and portray their members as agents of the West. This is particularly the case in dynamic authoritarian regimes: consider, for example, the recent crackdown on women's groups in Egypt under the regime of Abdel Fattāḥ al-Sisi. Scholars note how different regimes often use the issue of foreign funding to punish and tarnish the reputation of some independent women's groups.[35] The discussion over the NGO-ization of women's groups is thus, not surprisingly, a complicated one that is shot through with a number of conundrums and unresolved questions.

Religious Discourses and Women's Activism

The growing literature on women, Islam, and activism emphasizes how multiple religious discourses emerged and evolved in Egypt and in the region more broadly. It highlights the different ways in which these discourses aimed to ground women's rights in Islam and positioned the social activism of women against an explicit religious backdrop.[36] In Egypt, this faith-based movement developed and took shape in the early twentieth century with the rise and expansion of women's philanthropic activities. A prominent religious activist was Zaynab al-Ghazālī (1917–2005), whose early start was at the Egyptian Feminist Union established by Hudā Shaʿrāwī. Al-Ghazālī, however, soon became critical of what she perceived as attempts by feminists to "establish the civilization of the Western woman in Egypt, the Arab world and the Islamic world."[37] Al-Ghazālī created her own organization, The Muslim Women's Association (Jamaʿāt al-Sayyidāt al-Muslimāt) and focused her attention on the role of women in raising the future generation and their duty to the *daʿwa* (prosyletization).

The *daʿwa* movement by women gained wide acceptance and prominence since its inception and intensified during the last several decades—in late 1990s and early 2000s. The prominence of the movement can be traced to two main reasons. First, scholars argue that the *daʿwa* movement's view of society appealed to the marginalized strata who felt excluded from the social and economic transformations within Egyptian society.[38] The group's vision sought to ground Islamic principles in the practice of everyday life by disseminating religious knowledge and instruction and providing medical and welfare services to poor Egyptians.[39] Second, as the state retreated, the network of Islamic groups—including women's support groups—expanded and provided support and welfare for a broad swath of the population. This, Leslie Lewis, argues in her analysis of the mosque movement, created a shift in identity and allegiances.[40] Islam, thus, became not only one of the proposed answers to address societal ills and economic hardships, it, in fact, became the answer.

The influential work of the late Saba Mahmood on the piety movement in Egypt documented the growing influence of Islam in society and among women's groups.[41] Her analysis of the mosque movement and the role of *daʿiyat* (female missionaries) defied the long tradition of Western conception of agency and activism that have dominated the field of women's studies. According to Mahmood, the participation of women in these religious sites—often viewed in the literature as gendered and patriarchal—challenged simple categorization. Their participation, she holds, was grounded in a vocabulary of choice and agency.

Similarly in Morocco, the institutionalized role of woman preacher (*murshida*) further underscored how women in religious sites carve out a space for reform, activism, and authority.[42] While these forms of activism did not necessarily aim at challenging gender inequalities, they provided important venues for women to assert their agency and play important roles in the public and professional spheres.[43]

Parallel to the growth in women-centered Islamic spaces is the expansion in the number of female scholars who engage extensively with Islamic jurisprudence and hermeneutics. Female religious scholars, such as amina wadud, Asma Barlas, Fatima Mernissi, and Rifat Hassan, to name a few, articulate a "Muslima" theology. Their work focuses on grounding women's rights and gender equality within an Islamic framework. This movement developed and intensified throughout the latter part of the twentieth century and gave rise to what is called "Islamic feminism." Islamic feminism is a religiously-grounded discourse; it takes the Qur'ān as its central text and affirms that Islam has elevated the status of women. Examples of such scholars in Egypt are Heba Raouf Azzat and Omaima Abu Bakar. Raouf Azzat in particular has emphasized through her public life and prolific writing the role of women as the "soft force" (*quwāhā al-nāʿima*) in the awakening of Islamic sentiments, sensibilities, and senses in Egypt.[44]

Notwithstanding the ideological differences between secular and Islamic feminism, secular feminism, scholars observe, also anchors its approach within the discourse of religion and emphasizes its rootedness in Islamic teaching.[45] Margot Badran argues that the gap between secular and Islamic feminism is at best overstated, the two camps, she stresses, do not constitute and should not be viewed as oppositional forces.[46] Feminists and women's rights advocates often anchor their claims in Islamic teachings to ascribe indigeneity to their discourse and to avoid being labeled as Western agents of colonialism or imperialism. Lila Abu-Lughod thus rejects the Western versus Eastern opposition and rather argues for a "process of entanglement" to understand women's experiences and groundings.[47] These dynamics influence women's activism, refashion different forms of organization, and frame popular debates.

Even within societies like Tunisia, where the distinction between secular and religious is more profound, different regimes often sought to ground its progressive reforms within religion and Islamic teachings. The most salient example is the debate that surrounded the *Code du Statute Personnel* (Tunisian Code of Personal Status, or CPS). Tunisian former president Ḥabīb Būrgība introduced the CPS in the mid-1950s; it represented a major step toward reinterpreting classical Islamic law.[48] This reinterpretation of Islamic law and the sacred text, Būrgība often stressed, did not break away from religion. It was rather based on liberal *ijtihād* (independent legal reasoning) and imbued with the contributions of Taher Ḥaddad,[49] the reformist Tunisian scholar of Islam. Attempts to untangle the religious and the secular in women's activism in different spheres is thus complex and can be superficial. The historical and current analysis of women, Islamic practices, and social activism underscores how these discourses overlap and challenge our understanding of agency and activism in creative and productive ways.

Concluding Comments and Future Discussions

This chapter offered a brief survey of some of the major themes that marked women's religious and social activism specifically in Egypt, and, more broadly, in North Africa. It engaged with a wide range of literature and women's writings in diverse fields to trace the different debates surrounding women's religious and social welfare activities. The analysis presented underscored the ways in which political trajectories, historical contours, as well as social and religious dynamics influenced and shaped women's activism in social and religious spheres. Recent developments in the region following the 2010–2011 uprisings (Arab Spring) emphasized the need to attend to these dynamics and opened up new research venues and analytical ventures that are worthy of a close and detailed investigation.

Specifically, the experience of women's groups following the Arab Spring uprisings and the crackdown on their activities by the various governments in the region raises two overarching questions for our research agenda. First, how can women's groups sustain activism notwithstanding their disappointment in the political process and despite the constricted landscape? Second, how can the seemingly apolitical forms of activities carried out by women in the social milieu sustain the memory of resistance and remain a critical option for reform? The proposed questions are not intended to provide a complete or comprehensive picture of the field; rather my aim is to highlight some areas that are worth investigating while inviting the reader to expand on the list. The questions overlap, encouraging us to pursue a hopeful research agenda, that is to say, one that locates hope amid all the odds. This survey is significant, as the failure to consider and analyze the changing spaces for mobilization and activism in the Middle East and North Africa leads to stereotyping the region as stagnant[50] and women as passive. A focus on these subtle changes promises to enhance our understanding of the unfolding of events after the Arab Spring and opens up new ways of understanding women's activism in authoritarian contexts.

Notes

1. Leila Ahmed, *Women and Gender in Islam: Historical Roots of a Modern Debate* (New Haven, CT: Yale University Press, 1992); Amal Al-Sabaki and Kamel Bayoumi, *al- Ḥaraka al-Nisāʾiyya fi Maṣr bayn al-Thawratyn 1919–1953 (The Women's Movement in Egypt between the Two Revolutions 1919–1953)* (Cairo: Hay'at al-Kitāb al-'Āmma, 1987); Margot Badran, "Dual Liberation: Feminism and Nationalism in Egypt, 1870s–1925," *Feminist Issues* 8, no. 1 (1988): 15–34; Mervat F. Hatem, "Economic and Political Liberation in Egypt and the Demise of State Feminism," *International Journal of Middle East Studies* 24, no. 2 (1992): 231–251; Ijlal Khalifa, *al- Ḥaraka al-Nisaʾiyya al- ḥadītha (The Modern Women's Movement)* (Cairo: Dar al-Kutub, 1973); Cynthia Nelson, *Doria Shafik, Egyptian Feminist:*

A Woman Apart (Cairo: American University in Cairo Press, 1996); Thomas Philipp, "Feminism and Nationalist Politics in Egypt," in *Women in The Muslim World*, ed. Louis Beck and Nikki Keddie (Cambridge, MA: Harvard University Press, 1978), 277–294.

2. Judith E. Tucker, ed., *Arab Women: Old Boundaries, New Frontiers* (Bloomington: Indiana University Press, 1993).
3. Homa Hoodfar, "A Background to the Feminist Movement in Egypt," *Al-Raida* 10, no. 57 (1992): 11–13.
4. Ibid.; Nabila Ramdani, "Women in the 1919 Egyptian Revolution: From Feminist Awakening to Nationalist Political Activism," *Journal of International Women's Studies* 14, no. 2 (March 2013): 39–52.
5. Hoodfar, "A Background to the Feminist Movement."
6. Juan Ricardo Cole, "Feminism, Class and Islam in Turn-of-the-Century Egypt," *International Journal of Middle East Studies* 13 (1981): 387–407; Yvonne Y. Haddad, "Islam, Women and Revolution in Twentieth-Century Arab Thought," *Muslim World* 74, nos. 3–4 (October 1984): 137–160; Afaf Lutfi al-Sayyid Marsot Lotfi, "The Revolutionary Gentlewomen in Egypt," in *Women in the Muslim World*, ed. Lois Beck and Nikki Keddie (Cambridge, MA: Harvard University Press, 1978), 261–276; Robert L. Tignor, *Modernization and British Colonial Rule in Egypt, 1882–1914* (Princeton, NJ: Princeton University Press, 1966).
7. At the turn of the twentieth century, women established literary salons, magazines, and journals. By 1914, there were fourteen specialized magazines on women's issues, founded and edited by women.
8. Ahmed, *Women and Gender in Islam*; Beth Baron, *The Women's Awakening in Egypt: Culture, Society, and the Press* (New Haven, CT: Yale University Press, 1994); Margot Badran, *Feminists, Islam, and Nation: Gender and the Making of Modern Egypt* (Princeton, NJ: Princeton University Press, 1995).
9. Ahmed, *Women and Gender*.
10. Nadje Al-Ali, *Secularism, Gender and the State in the Middle East: The Egyptian Women's Movement* (Cambridge: Cambridge University Press, 2000); Frantz Fanon, *The Wretched of the Earth*, trans. Constance Farrington (New York: Grove Press, 1963).
11. Nermin Allam, *Women and the Egyptian Revolution: Engagement and Activism during the 2011 Arab Uprisings* (Cambridge: Cambridge University Press, 2017); Sunny Daly, "Young Women as Activists in Contemporary Egypt: Anxiety, Leadership, and the Next Generation," *Journal of Middle East Women's Studies* 6, no. 2 (2010): 59–85; Diane Singerman, *Avenues of Participation: Family, Politics, and Networks in Urban Quarters of Cairo* (Princeton, NJ: Princeton University Press, 1995).
12. Singerman, *Avenues of Participation*; Asef Bayat, *Life as Politics: How Ordinary People Change the Middle East* (Stanford, CA: Stanford University Press, 2010); Saba Mahmood, *Politics of Piety: The Islamic Revival and the Feminist Subject* (Princeton, NJ: Princeton University Press, 2005); Ellen Anne McLarney, *Soft Force: Women in Egypt's Islamic Awakening: Women in Egypt's Islamic Awakening* (Princeton, NJ: Princeton University Press, 2015); Jessica Winegar, "The Privilege of Revolution: Gender, Class, Space, and Affect in Egypt," *American Ethnologist* 39, no. 1 (2012): 67–70.
13. Leslie Lewis, "Convergences and Divergences: Egyptian Women's Activisms over the Last Century," in *Mapping Arab Women's Movements: A Century of Transformations from Within*, ed. Pernille Arenfeldt and Nawar Al-Hassan Golley (Cairo: American University in Cairo Press, 2012), 43–92.

14. Bayat, *Life as Politics*, 161.
15. Mounira M. Charrad and Rita Stephan, "The 'Power of Presence': Professional Women Leaders and Family Law Reform in Morocco," *Social Politics: International Studies in Gender, State and Society* 27, no. 2 (June 1, 2020): 337–360.
16. Vania Carvalho Pinto, "The 'Makings' of a Movement 'by Implication': Assessing the Expansion of Women's Rights in the United Arab Emirates from 1971 until Today," in *Mapping Arab Women's Movements: A Century of Transformations from within*, ed. Pernille Arenfeldt and Nawar Al-Hassan Golley (Cairo: American University in Cairo Press, 2012), 281–302.
17. Bayat, *Life as Politics*.
18. Baron, *Women's Awakening*; Baron, *Egypt as a Woman: Nationalism, Gender, and Politics* (Berkeley: University of California Press, 2005); Badran, *Feminists, Islam, and Nation*; Badran, "Dual Liberation."
19. Ahmed, *Women and* Gender; Badran, "Dual Liberation"; Baron, *Egypt as a Woman*; Nawal El Saadawi, *Woman at Point Zero* (London: Zed Books, 1997); Hudā Shaʿrāwī, *Harem Years: The Memoirs of an Egyptian Feminist (1879–1924)* (New York: Feminist Press, 1986).
20. Badran, "Dual Liberation," 28–29.
21. Djamila Amrane, *Des femmes dans la guerre d'Algérie: Entretiens* (Paris: Éditions Karthala, 1994); Assia Djebar, *Children of the New World: A Novel of the Algerian War* (New York: Feminist Press, 2005); Mildred Mortimer, "Tortured Bodies, Resilient Souls: Algeria's Women Combatants Depicted by Danièle Djamila Amrane-Minne, Louisette Ighilahriz, and Assia Djebar," *Research in African Literatures* 43, no. 1 (February 8, 2012): 101–117.
22. Jill Vickers, "Gendering the Hyphen: Gender Dimensions of Modern Nation-State Formation in Euro-American and Anti- and Post-Colonial Contexts," in Gendering the Nation-State: Canadian and Comparative Perspectives, ed. Yasmeen Abu-Laban (Vancouver: UBC Press, 2008), 21–45; Elleke Boehmer, *Stories of Women: Gender and Narrative in the Postcolonial Nation* (Manchester: Manchester University Press, 2005); Vanaja Dhruvarajan and Jill Vickers, *Gender, Race, and Nation: A Global Perspective* (Toronto: University of Toronto Press, 2002); Suad Joseph, *Gender and Citizenship in the Middle East* (Syracuse, NY: Syracuse University Press, 2000); Nira Yuval-Davis, *Gender and Nation*, 1st ed. (London: Sage, 1997).
23. Mervat F. Hatem, "The Pitfalls of the Nationalist Discourses on Citizenship in Egypt," in *Gender and Citizenship in the Middle East*, ed. Suad Joseph (Syracuse, NY: Syracuse University Press, 2000), 33–58; Joseph, *Gender and Citizenship*; Mary Ann Tétreault, *Women and Revolution in Africa, Asia, and the New World* (Columbia: University of South Carolina Press, 1994); Vickers, "Gendering the Hyphen"; Yuval-Davis, *Gender and Nation*.
24. Laura Bier, *Revolutionary Womanhood: Feminisms, Modernity, and the State in Nasser's Egypt* (Stanford, CA: Stanford University Press, 2011); Mervat F. Hatem, "Egyptian Discourses on Gender and Political Liberalization: Do Secularist and Islamist Views Really Differ?" *Middle East Journal* 48, no. 4 (1994): 661–676; Nadia Hijab, *Womanpower: The Arab Debate on Women at Work*, Cambridge Middle East Library (Cambridge, MA: Cambridge University Press, 1988); Nikki R. Keddie and Beth Baron, eds., *Women in Middle Eastern History: Shifting Boundaries in Sex and Gender* (New Haven, CT: Yale University Press, 1991); Nelson, *Doria Shafik*; Elie Podeh and Onn Winckler, eds., *Rethinking Nasserism: Revolution and Historical Memory in Modern Egypt* (Gainesville: University Press of Florida, 2004).

25. Ahmed, *Women and Gender*; Al-Ali, *Secularism, Gender and the State*; Bier, *Revolutionary Womanhood*; Hatem, "Pitfalls of the Nationalist Discourses."
26. Mounira Charrad, *States and Women's Rights: The Making of Postcolonial Tunisia, Algeria, and Morocco* (Berkeley: University of California Press, 2001); Elisabeth Johansson-Nogués, "Gendering the Arab Spring? Rights and (In)security of Tunisian, Egyptian and Libyan Women," *Security Dialogue* 44, nos. 5–6 (October 2013): 393–409.
27. Islah Jad, "The NGO-isation of Arab Women's Movements," in *Feminisms in Development: Contradictions, Contestations and Challenges*, ed. Andrea Cornwall, Elizabeth Harrison, and Anne Whitehead (London: Zed Books, 2007), 177–190; Hania Sholkamy, "Women Are Also Part of This Revolution," in *Arab Spring in Egypt: Revolution and Beyond*, ed. Bahgat Korany and Rabab El-Mahdi (Cairo: American University in Cairo Press, 2012), 153–174.
28. Jad, "The NGO-isation of Arab Women's Movements."
29. Arenfeldt and Golley, *Mapping Arab Women's Movements*.
30. Shahida El-Baz, "Globalisation and the Challenge of Democracy in Arab North Africa," *Africa Development*, no. 4 (2005): 1–33; Shahida El-Baz, "The Impact of Social and Economic Factors on Women's Group Formation in Egypt," in *Organizing Women: Formal and Informal Women's in the Middle East*, ed. Dawn Chatty and Annika Rabo (New York: Berg, 1997).
31. Jad, "The NGO-isation of Arab Women's Movements"; Lewis, "Convergences"; Sholkamy, "Women Are Also Part."
32. Nadine Sika and Yasmin Khodary, "One Step Forward, Two Steps Back? Egyptian Women within the Confines of Authoritarianism," *Journal of International Women's Studies* 13, no. 5 (December 20, 2012): 94.
33. The different activities of civil society organizations required the approval of the ministry, the ministry had the right to intervene in the internal affairs, and dissolve organizations receiving foreign funding or involved with international groups without prior official permission.
34. Al-Ali, *Secularism, Gender*; Lewis, "Convergences"; Sholkamy, "Women Are Also Part."
35. Nermin Allam, "Activism amid Disappointment: Women's Groups and the Politics of Hope in Egypt," *Middle East Law and Governance* 10, no. 3 (October 23, 2018): 291–316.
36. Ahmed, *Women and Gender*; Lila Abu-Lughod, "On- and Off-Camera in Egyptian Soap Operas: Women, Television, and the Public Sphere," in *On Shifting Ground: Muslim Women in the Global Era*, 2nd ed., ed. Fereshteh Nouraie-Simone (New York: Feminist Press, 2014), 67–87; Badran, *Feminists, Islam, and Nation*; Sherine Hafez, *An Islam of Her Own: Reconsidering Religion and Secularism in Women's Islamic Movements* (New York: New York University Press, 2011); Mahmood, *Politics of Piety*; Saba Mahmood, "Feminist Theory, Embodiment, and the Docile Agent: Some Reflections on the Egyptian Islamic Revival," *Cultural Anthropology* 16, no. 2 (November 11, 2012): 202–236; Moha Ennaji, Karen Vintges, and Fatima Sadiqi, *Moroccan Feminisms: New Perspectives*, 1st ed. (Trenton: Africa World Press, 2016).
37. Badran, *Feminists, Islam, and Nation*, 209.
38. Hafez, *An Islam of Her Own*.
39. Mahmood, *Politics of Piety*, 3.
40. Lewis, "Convergences."
41. Mahmood, *Politics of Piety*; Mahmood, "Feminist Theory, Embodiment, and the Docile Agent."

42. Fatima Sadiqi, *Women, Gender, and Language in Morocco* (Leiden: Brill, 2003); Sumayya Ahmed, "Learned Women: Three Generations of Female Islamic Scholarship in Morocco," *Journal of North African Studies* 21, no. 3 (May 26, 2016): 470–484.
43. Lewis, "Convergences," 29.
44. Heba Rauf Ezzat, *al-Mar'a wal'amal alsiyāsī: ru'ya islamiyya* (Herndon: Institute of Islamic Thought, 1995).
45. Nadje Al-Ali, *Secularism, Gender*; Lila Abu-Lughod, *Do Muslim Women Need Saving?* (Cambridge, MA: Harvard University Press, 2013), 199. Margot Badran, *Feminism in Islam: Secular and Religious Convergences*, (Oxford: Oneworld, 2009).
46. Badran, *Feminism in Islam*, 6.
47. Lila Abu-Lughod, ed., *Remaking Women: Feminism and Modernity in the Middle East*, Princeton Studies in Culture/Power/History (Princeton, NJ: Princeton University Press, 1998).
48. Alcinda Honwana, *Youth and Revolution in Tunisia* (London: Zed Books, 2013).
49. In 1929, Taher Ḥaddad published his infamous book *Our Women in the Sharia'a and Society*. In it, Ḥaddad criticized the lack of education for girls, and the veil. Ḥaddad condemned polygamy and repudiation; he also demanded special law courts for divorces. Even though he underlined that his work was based on a reinterpretation of the Qur'ān and the founding texts, Ḥaddad's book was highly condemned at the time of its publication.
50. Lina Khatib and Ellen Lust, *Taking to the Streets: The Transformation of Arab Activism* (Baltimore, MD: Johns Hopkins University Press, 2014).

Bibliography

Abu-Laban, Yasmeen. "Gendering the Hyphen: Gender Dimensions of Modern Nation-State Formation in Euro-American and Anti- and Post-Colonial Contexts." In *Gendering the Nation-State: Canadian and Comparative Perspectives*, edited by Yasmeen Abu-Laban, 1–20. Vancouver: UBC Press, 2008.

Abu-Lughod, Lila. *Do Muslim Women Need Saving?* Cambridge, MA: Harvard University Press, 2013.

Abu-Lughod, Lila. "On- and Off-Camera in Egyptian Soap Operas: Women, Television, and the Public Sphere." In *On Shifting Ground: Muslim Women in the Global Era*, 2nd ed., edited by Fereshteh Nouraie-Simone, 67–87. New York: Feminist Press, 2014.

Abu-Lughod, Lila, ed. *Remaking Women: Feminism and Modernity in the Middle East*. Princeton Studies in Culture/Power/History. Princeton, NJ: Princeton University Press, 1998.

Ahmed, Leila. *Women and Gender in Islam: Historical Roots of a Modern Debate*. New Haven, CT: Yale University Press, 1992.

Ahmed, Sumayya. "Learned Women: Three Generations of Female Islamic Scholarship in Morocco." *Journal of North African Studies* 21, no. 3 (May 26, 2016): 470–484.

Ali, Nadje al-. *Secularism, Gender and the State in the Middle East: The Egyptian Women's Movement*. Cambridge: Cambridge University Press, 2000.

Allam, Nermin. "Activism amid Disappointment: Women's Groups and the Politics of Hope in Egypt." *Middle East Law and Governance* 10, no. 3 (October 23, 2018): 291–316.

Allam, Nermin. *Women and the Egyptian Revolution: Engagement and Activism during the 2011 Arab Uprisings*. Cambridge: Cambridge University Press, 2017.

Al-Sabaki, Amal, and Bayoumi Kamel. *Al-Haraka al-Nissaiiyah Fi Misr Bayn al-Thawratayn 1919–1953 (The Women's Movement in Egypt between the Two Revolutions 1919–1953*. Cairo: Hay'at al-Kitāb al-'Āmma, 1987.

Amrane, Djamila. *Des femmes dans la guerre d'Algérie: Entretiens*. Paris: Éditions Karthala,1994.

Arenfeldt, Pernille, and Nawar Al-Hassan Golley. *Mapping Arab Women's Movements: A Century of Transformations from Within*. 2012. http://public.eblib.com/choice/publicfullrecord.aspx?p=1793187.

Badran, Margot. "Dual Liberation: Feminism and Nationalism in Egypt, 1870s–1925." *Feminist Issues* 8, no. 1 (1988): 15–34.

Badran, Margot. *Feminism in Islam: Secular and Religious Convergences*. Oxford: Oneworld, 2009.

Badran, Margot. *Feminists, Islam, and Nation: Gender and the Making of Modern Egypt*. Princeton, NJ: Princeton University Press, 1995.

Baron, Beth. *Egypt as a Woman: Nationalism, Gender, and Politics*. Berkeley and Los Angeles: University of California Press, 2005.

Baron, Beth. *The Women's Awakening in Egypt: Culture, Society, and the Press*. New Haven, CT: Yale University Press, 1994.

Bayat, Asef. *Life as Politics: How Ordinary People Change the Middle East*. Stanford: Stanford University Press, 2010.

Marsot, Afaf Lutfi al-Sayyid. "The Revolutionary Gentlewomen in Egypt." In *Women in the Muslim World*, edited by Lois Beck and Nikki Keddie, 261–276. Cambridge, MA: Harvard University Press, 1978.

Bier, Laura. *Revolutionary Womanhood: Feminisms, Modernity, and the State in Nasser's Egypt*. Stanford University Press, 2011.

Boehmer, Elleke. *Stories of Women: Gender and Narrative in the Postcolonial Nation*. Manchester University Press, 2005.

Botman, Salma. "Women's Participation in Radical Egyptian Politics 1939–1952." In *Women in the Middle East*, edited by the Khamsin Collective, 12–25. London: Zed Books, 1987.

Charrad, Mounira M., and Rita Stephan. "The 'Power of Presence': Professional Women Leaders and Family Law Reform in Morocco." *Social Politics: International Studies in Gender, State and Society* 27, no. 2 (June 1, 2020): 337–360. https://doi.org/10.1093/sp/jxz013.

Charrad, Mounira. *States and Women's Rights: The Making of Postcolonial Tunisia, Algeria, and Morocco*. Berkeley and Los Angeles: University of California Press, 2001.

Cole, Juan Ricardo. "Feminism, Class and Islam in Turn-of-the-Century Egypt." *International Journal of Middle East Studies* 13 (1981): 387–407.

Daly, Sunny. "Young Women as Activists in Contemporary Egypt: Anxiety, Leadership, and the Next Generation." *Journal of Middle East Women's Studies* 6, no. 2 (2010): 59–85.

Dhruvarajan, Vanaja, and Jill Vickers. *Gender, Race, and Nation: A Global Perspective*. Toronto: University of Toronto Press, 2002.

Djebar, Assia. *Children of the New World: A Novel of the Algerian War*. New York: Feminist Press, 2005.

Elbaz, Shahida. "Globalisation and the Challenge of Democracy in Arab North Africa." *Africa Development*, no. 4 (2005): 1–33.

Elbaz, Shahida. "The Impact of Social and Economic Factors on Women's Group Formation in Egypt." In *Organizing Women: Formal and Informal Women's Groups in the Middle East*, edited by Dawn Chatty and Annika Rabo. New York: Berg, 1997.

Elsadda, Hoda. "Women's Rights Activism in Post-Jan 25 Egypt: Combating the Shadow of the First Lady Syndrome in the Arab World." *Middle East Law and Governance* 3, nos. 1–2 (March 25, 2011): 84–93.

Ennaji, Moha, Karen Vintges, and Fatima Sadiqi. *Moroccan Feminisms: New Perspectives*. 1st ed. Trenton: Africa World Press, 2016.

Ezzat, Heba Rouf. *At, alMar'a Wa-l'Amal alSiyasi: Ru'ya Islamiyya*. Herndon, VA: Institute of Islamic Thought, 1995.

Fanon, Frantz. *The Wretched of the Earth. Trans. from the French by Constance Farrington*. New York: Grove Press, 1963.

Gallagher, Nancy, and Sondra Hale. "Editors' Introduction." *Journal of Middle East Women's Studies* 3, no. 1 (2007): 1–3..

Ghazali, Zainab al-, and Amr Farouk. *Days from My Life [Ayam Men Hayaty]*. Cairo: Kenouz, 2012.

Haddad, Yvonne Y. "Islam, Women and Revolution in Twentieth-Century Arab Thought." *Muslim World* 74, nos. 3–4 (October 1984): 137–160

Hafez, Sherine. *An Islam of Her Own: Reconsidering Religion and Secularism in Women's Islamic Movements*. New York: New York University Press, 2011.

Hatem, Mervat F. "Economic and Political Liberation in Egypt and the Demise of State Feminism." *International Journal of Middle East Studies* 24, no. 2 (1992): 231–251.

Hatem, Mervat F. "Egyptian Discourses on Gender and Political Liberalization: Do Secularist and Islamist Views Really Differ?" *Middle East Journal* 48, no. 4 (1994): 661–676.

Hatem, Mervat F. "The Pitfalls of the Nationalist Discources on Citizenship in Egypt." In *Gender and Citizenship in the Middle East*, edited by Suad Joseph, 33–58. Syracuse, NY: Syracuse University Press, 2000.

Hijab, Nadia. *Womanpower: The Arab Debate on Women at Work*. Cambridge Middle East Library. Cambridge: Cambridge University Press, 1988.

Honwana, Alcinda. *Youth and Revolution in Tunisia*. London: Zed Books, 2013. http://login.ezproxy.library.ualberta.ca/login?url=http://search.ebscohost.com/login.aspx?direct=true&db=cat03710a&AN=alb.6216085&site=eds-live&scope=site.

Hoodfar, Homa. "A Background to the Feminist Movement in Egypt." *Al-Raida* 10, no. 57 (1992): 11–13.

Ikhwanweb. "Muslim Brotherhood Statement Denouncing UN Women Declaration for Violating Sharia Principles—Ikhwanweb." Muslim Brotherhood's Official English website, March 14, 2013. http://www.ikhwanweb.com/article.php?id=30731.

Jad, Islah. "The NGO-isation of Arab Women's Movements." In *Feminisms in Development: Contradictions, Contestations and Challenges*, edited by Andrea Cornwall, Elizabeth Harrison, and Anne Whitehead, 177–190. London: Zed Books, 2007.

Jayawardena, Kumari. *Feminism and Nationalism in the Third World*. London: Zed Books, 1986.s

Johansson-Nogués, Elisabeth. "Gendering the Arab Spring? Rights and (In)security of Tunisian, Egyptian and Libyan Women." *Security Dialogue* 44, nos. 5–6 (October 2013): 393–409.

Joseph, Suad. *Gender and Citizenship in the Middle East*. Syracuse, NY: Syracuse University Press, 2000.

Keddie, Nikki R., and Beth Baron, eds. *Women in Middle Eastern History: Shifting Boundaries in Sex and Gender*. New Haven, CT: Yale University Press, 1991.

Khalifa, Ijlal. *Al-Haraka Al-Nissaíiyah Al-Haditha (The Modern Women's Movement)*. Cairo: Dar il-Kuttub, 1973.

Khater, Akram. "Egypt's Feminism." *Middle East Magazine* 148 (February 1987): 17–18.

Khater, Akram, and Cynthia Nelson. "Al-Harakah Al-Nissa'Iyah: The Women's Movement and Political Participation in Modern Egypt." *Women's Studies International Forum* 11, no. 5 (January 1, 1988): 465–483.

Khatib, Lina, and Ellen Lust. *Taking to the Streets: The Transformation of Arab Activism.* Baltimore, MD: Johns Hopkins University Press, 2014.

Lewis, Leslie. "Convergences and Divergences: Egyptian Women's Activisms over the Last Century." In *Mapping Arab Women's Movements: A Century of Transformations from Within*, edited by Pernille Arenfeldt and Nawar Al-Hassan Golley, 43–92. Cairo: American University in Cairo Press, 2012. http://public.eblib.com/choice/publicfullrecord.aspx?p=1793187.

Mahmood, Saba. "Feminist Theory, Embodiment, and the Docile Agent: Some Reflections on the Egyptian Islamic Revival." *Cultural Anthropology* 16, no. 2 (November 11, 2012): 202–236.

Mahmood, Saba. *Politics of Piety: The Islamic Revival and the Feminist Subject.* Princeton, NJ: Princeton University Press, 2005.

McLarney, Ellen Anne. *Soft Force: Women in Egypt's Islamic Awakening: Women in Egypt's Islamic Awakening.* Princeton, NJ: Princeton University Press, 2015.

Moghadam, Valentine, and Manilee Bagheritari. "Cultures, Conventions, and the Human Rights of Women: Examining the Convention for Safeguarding Intangible Cultural Heritage, and the Declaration on Cultural Diversity." *Museum International* 59, no. 4 (2007): 9–18.

Mortimer, Mildred. "Tortured Bodies, Resilient Souls: Algeria's Women Combatants Depicted by Danièle Djamila Amrane-Minne, Louisette Ighilahriz, and Assia Djebar." *Research in African Literatures* 43, no. 1 (February 8, 2012): 101–117.

Nelson, Cynthia. *Doria Shafik, Egyptian Feminist: A Woman Apart.* Cairo: American University in Cairo Press, 1996.

Philipp, Thomas. "Feminism and Nationalist Politics in Egypt." In *Women in The Muslim World*, edited by Louis Beck and Nikki Keddie, 277–294. Cambridge, MA: Harvard University Press, 1978.

Pinto, Vania Carvalho. "The 'Makings' of a Movement 'by Implication': Assessing the Expansion of Women's Rights in the United Arab Emirates from 1971 until Today." In *Mapping Arab Women's Movements: A Century of Transformations from within*, edited by Pernille Arenfeldt and Nawar Al-Hassan Golley, 281–302. Cairo: American University in Cairo Press, 2012. http://public.eblib.com/choice/publicfullrecord.aspx?p=1793187.

Podeh, Elie, and Onn Winckler, eds. *Rethinking Nasserism: Revolution and Historical Memory in Modern Egypt.* Gainesville: University Press of Florida, 2004.

Ramdani, Nabila. "Women in the 1919 Egyptian Revolution: From Feminist Awakening to Nationalist Political Activism." *Journal of International Women's Studies* 14, no. 2 (March 2013): 39–52.

Rauf Ezzat, Heba, *al-Mar'a wal'amal alsiyāsī: ru'ya islamiyya.* Herndon: Institute of Islamic Thought, 1995.

Rieker, Martina. "Introduction: Transnational Theory, National Politics, and Gender in the Contemporary Middle East/North Africa." *Journal of Middle East Women's Studies* 3, no. 1 (2007): 4–5.

Saadawi, Nawal El. *Woman at Point Zero.* London: Zed Books, 1997.

Sadiqi, Fatima. *Women, Gender, and Language in Morocco.* Leiden: Brill, 2003.

Shafik, Doria. "Egyptian Women." Speical issue of *Bint Al-Nil Journal* 132 (October 1956). http://dar.aucegypt.edu/bitstream/handle/10526/2235/oct%2056.pdf?sequence=1.

Sha'rāwī, Hudá. *Harem Years: The Memoirs of an Egyptian Feminist (1879–1924)*. Feminist Press, 1986.

Sholkamy, Hania. "Women Are Also Part of This Revolution." In *Arab Spring in Egypt: Revolution and Beyond*, edited by Bahgat Korany and Rabab El-Mahdi, 153–174. Cairo: American University in Cairo Press, 2012.

Sika, Nadine, and Yasmin Khodary. "One Step Forward, Two Steps Back? Egyptian Women within the Confines of Authoritarianism." *Journal of International Women's Studies* 13, no. 5 (December 20, 2012): 91–100.

Singerman, Diane. *Avenues of Participation: Family, Politics, and Networks in Urban Quarters of Cairo*. Princeton, NJ: Princeton University Press, 1995.

Tétreault, Mary Ann. *Women and Revolution in Africa, Asia, and the New World*. Columbia: University of South Carolina Press, 1994.

Tignor, Robert L. *Modernization and British Colonial Rule in Egypt, 1882–1914*. Princeton, NJ: Princeton University Press, 1966.

Tucker, Judith E., ed. *Arab Women: Old Boundaries, New Frontiers*. Bloomington: Indiana University Press, 1993.

Vickers, Jill. "Gendering the Hyphen: Gender Dimensions of Modern Nation-State Formation in Euro-American and Anti- and Post-Colonial Contexts." In *Gendering the Nation-State: Canadian and Comparative Perspectives*, edited by Yasmeen Abu-Laban, 21–45. Vancouver: UBC Press, 2008.

Weber, Charlotte. "Between Nationalism and Feminism: The Eastern Women's Congresses of 1930 and 1932." *Journal of Middle East Women's Studies* 4, no. 1 (2008): 83–106.

Winegar, Jessica. "The Privilege of Revolution: Gender, Class, Space, and Affect in Egypt." *American Ethnologist* 39, no. 1 (2012): 67–70.

Yuval-Davis, Nira. *Gender and Nation*. 1st ed. Sage Publications, 1997.

Zuhur, Sherifa. *Revealing Reveiling: Islamist Gender Ideology in Contemporary Egypt*. Albany: State University of New York Press, 1992.

CHAPTER 20

WOMEN'S RELIGIOUS AND SOCIAL ACTIVISM IN IRAN

SEEMA GOLESTANEH

WOMEN in Iran have been organizing, writing, reading, meeting, marching, and speaking out for change through disparate avenues, and in ways not always immediately legible as "activism," since the nineteenth century. They have championed gender rights explicitly or called for advancements in social justice or welfare issues more broadly, have worked alongside political groups such as the Communist Tudeh Party or guerrilla Marxist Fedayeen, and fought against both enforced unveiling and veiling.

Happily, there is a large corpus of literature on women's activism in Iran, although like all studies of non-Western women, the dangers of falling into tired binaries (Islamist vs. secular, modern vs. tradition, East vs. West, etc.) are ever present. There is also the more serious concern of using the observations surrounding the status of women in the Islamic world as a justification for intervention by foreign powers, military and otherwise. As Arzoo Osanloo has noted, Iranian women's activism has always been impacted by geopolitics.[1] Iranian women must attempt to navigate the opinions of those on the domestic front who deem feminism as an invention of the imperial powers, a foreign import meant to undermine the stability of the nation, and those outside Iran who argue that liberation through war or increased institutionalized secularization are the only viable alternative to "alleviate" women's suffering.

Before delving into the contemporary era, this chapter will first briefly examine histories of women's activism within Iran. These are typically organized vis-à-vis the associated ruling administration, namely the late Qajar and Constitutional Revolutionary Era, the Pahlavi Era, and the Islamic Republic; this overview will adhere to a similar layout. Following this, the rest of the chapter will analyze studies of women's activism during the Islamic Republic, covering such topics as legal battles, women's media, and religious activists in the seminaries.

Histories of Women's Activism

General Histories

Within the genre of histories of Iranian women's activism, there exist a few seminal monographs. The first is Parvin Paidar's thorough and exacting *Women and the Political Process in Twentieth Century Iran.*[2] Its interventions are twofold: (1) it provides information about key female political activists, including but not limited to those exclusively interested in women's issues, and (2) it is able to highlight the ways the question of gender influenced Iran's tumultuous twentieth-century political history, which is contrary to many earlier studies of the Islamic Revolution where the question of gender was presented as an afterthought.

Since Paidar's landmark study, histories of women's activism in Iran have often focused on a key question: why and how did the Iranian left fail to address questions of gender equity before and after the revolution? This question has been taken up by Paidar, but also by Eliz Sanasarian, Hammed Shahidian, Nikki Keddie, and Nozar Alaolmolki.[3] The most substantial study and only book-length work addressing this question is Haideh Moghissi's *Populism and Feminism in Iran*,[4] which sets itself apart with a large number of interviews with male and female leftists and revolutionaries. A former activist herself, Moghissi's most significant contribution is her close examination of the sexism within the Fedayeen Guerrilla Movement and their manipulation of the National Union of Women in the late 1960s and 1970s, as well as the perceived abandonment of women's issues during the postrevolutionary years of 1979–1981.[5] Although not intended to be a comprehensive history, Afasaneh Najmabadi's comparison of the "women question" (*masaliyi zan*) of two different time periods—the turn of the twentieth century and from the mid-1960s to the present—is an excellent introduction to key debates within studies of the role of women and women's activism in Iran.[6]

The Late Qajar Era (1851–1921)

A period of great political upheaval, this era is often described as the "birth" or "origins" of women's activism in Iran,[7] as it is during this time we see the emergence of the idea of women's rights (*hagh-e zanan*), as well as the first women-led publications and organizations. The fact that these developments occurred simultaneously with the Constitutional Revolution of 1905–1911[8] is not seen as inauspicious. In fact, one of the key questions within scholarship of this time period is the extent to which the general rise in political consciousness during the Constitutional Revolution era influenced women's activism. There are those who believe the initiatives of women at this time was a direct result of the exposure to such previously unheard of public dialogues, when growing political unrest against the Qajar dynasty and foreign influence directly influenced women to examine their own situation for the first time, a common narrative espoused by works such as Mangol Bayat-Phillip[9] and Bamadad.[10] Janet Afary,[11] who has written on women's councils and organizations of the era, also considers this period to be the "origin" of Iranian women's political consciousness and, in her words, "feminism." As her use of "feminism" goes undefined, however, the reader is left to unpack this anachronism for themselves. Moreover, the argument that the Tobacco Revolt and the Constitutional Revolution were the "origins" of the women's movements in Iran is problematic due to (1) the fact that it runs the risk of positioning the women's movements as simply derivative of the male-led social movements, and (2) the idea that a proliferation of female-led organizations, periodicals, and education suddenly emerge out of nowhere ignores the conversations and actions of nineteenth-century women. Certainly, these effective and very public political organizations influenced many women at the time and played a part in their considerations about their own role in the public sphere, but to ignore earlier conversations and actions is a disservice to the complexity of the situation.

One important exception to this narrative within the scholarship is the work of Susynne McElrone's.[12] McElrone provides original research on the propagation of women's educational opportunities in the nineteenth century, including both missionary and Muslim led schools, and emphasizes middle- and working-class women's presence in public places and employment in places like the bazaar. In doing so, she argues against the notion of a sui generis women's movement, connecting the proliferation of women-led organizations of the Constitutional Era to the gains and efforts of educations in the nineteenth century. Supporting this claim is the work of Jasmin Rostam-Koyali, who argues against the idea that women's education started in the 1920s and 1930s but rather took shape in the late nineteenth and early twentieth century with religious and ethnic minorities working outside of the Ministry of Education.[13]

In addition to general histories, there exists some scholarship devoted to the first women-run periodicals in Iran: namely *Dānish* (est. 1910), *Shukūfih* (est. 1913), and *Zabān-e Zanān* (est. 1919). Afsaneh Najmabadi provides an insightful close reading of poems and letters submitted to the periodicals by women, delineating the ways that women articulated citizenship rights for themselves, as well as analyzing parliamentary speeches from the era that wrestled with the ambiguities of the word *zan*, (meaning both "woman" and "wife"), and *millat* (meaning both "nation" and "household").[14]

Other investigations into the periodicals of this era are typically couched in broader discussions related to some aspect of the Constitutional Revolution or broader histories of women's rights activism in Iran. Roja Fazaeli's analyses are helpful in differentiating early periodicals that were "apolitical" but still advocated for women's literacy and respect in domestic situations.[15] There still does not exist a single monograph focused exclusively on these first publications by Iranian women activists, eight titles between 1910–1925 to be specific, despite the fact that many of the editions of these journals have been transferred to microfiche and now DVD. Articles by Ellen Fleischman, Ziba Mir-Hosseini, Eliz Sanasarian, and others provide helpful overviews, noting how these newspapers were related to women's organizations like the Women's Freedom Society

(*Anjuman-i Āzādiye Zanān*) and the Society of Women in Face Veils (*Anjuman-i Zanāni Niqābpūsh*), the proliferation of women's schools and education in the late nineteenth and twentieth centuries, and the broader nationalist movements occurring at the time.[16]

The Era of Reza Shah Pahlavi (1925–1941)

Scholarship that analyzes women's activism in the Reza Shah period typically focuses on his "Women's Awakening" (*Bidar-i Zanaan*) initiatives (1936–1941), a series of gender-focused laws, decrees, and programs designed to formulate and promote the state's ideal Iranian woman. This meant a woman who would be unveiled (but not too unveiled) in public, educated (but not too educated), and married (but not at too young or too old an age). Earlier research on the "Women's Awakening" initiatives tend to be highly critical of the movement. As the "Women's Awakening" project was a state-sponsored one, scholars like Paidar and Shahidian highlight the fact that, in the Reza Shah era, the project of women's advancement was taken away from the hands of women themselves and co-opted by the nation-state, ultimately transforming the entire endeavor into a patriarchal project.

While important to highlight the Reza Shah administration's interest and incorporation (and co-optation) of the "women question" into their aspirations for the ideal Iranian state, others counter that to understand these reform measures in such a way is a bit of a zero-sum game. At the forefront of this group is Camron Amin, whose close readings of Iranian press materials from the era re-evaluates earlier assessments of the Women's Awakening movement as being a wholly patriarchal project.[17] He argues instead that it was something more paradoxical: a project steeped in national patriarchy advocating a nationalist and standardized form of womanhood that still produced opportunities for women of various backgrounds, however limited they may have been. Moreover, through close examinations of the development of women's higher education and press materials, he demonstrates how Reza Shah's reforms were built on discourses already circulating in certain circles and periodicals prior to 1936, especially the state assuming the role of "the male guardian."[18] Jasmin Rostam-Koyali offers a similar analysis in her close reading of the influential newspaper *Women's World* (*Alam-i Nesvān*), whose subscribers included the female members of Reza Shah's immediate family. Ultimately, she demonstrates that some of the ideas and policies advocated by the state (education, love marriage) were first espoused by editorials in *Women's World*,[19] providing evidence that the state was not the only voice involved in formulating what was to become the "Women's Awakening" movement.

Another major concern within Iranian women's studies of the 1930s is Reza Shah's notorious unveiling decree of 1936. Given the decree's extreme and highly interventionist nature, it tends to lend itself to simplistic analyses; namely, that the order[20] was the result of a highly authoritarian, Western-obsessed despot. Without downplaying the oppressive elements of mandated unveiling, Rostam-Koyali and Afshin Matin-Asgar explain that a push for such a directive had been circulating in newspapers for some time. They flesh out the discourses surrounding the unveiling debates by discussing what was meant by "veiling" specifically, describing the difference between chadors, face veils/ *pīchih*, and *hijāb*, and whether veiling was meant as either head covering or mandated "revealing" of "hands, face, and feet."[21] Houchang Chehabi's analysis similarly looks not only at the immediate discussion surrounding the decree itself but also engages with debates of the era, noting that Reza Shah himself was more ambivalent and even uncomfortable about the matter, but felt it necessary after his visit to Turkey.[22] Chehabi documents remarkable instances of resistance of women to bypass the unveiling mandate, whether by traveling by rooftop to avoid police, going to *hamām* (bathhouse) at night, and in some instances even picking up and moving to Iraq.

The Era of Mohammad Reza Pahlavi (1941–1979)

Let us move now from the era of the father to that of the son, with women's activism in the Mohammad Reza Pahlavi era (1941–1979). Given how diverse the political landscape was in the 1940s and the comparative lack of press censorship,[23] it is surprising that there is not more research done on this time period in terms of gender studies focused especially on periodicals like *Bīdārī Mā* (Our Awakening) and *Jahān-I Zanān* (The World of Women), which were affiliated with the Communist Tudeh Party or more proestablishment publications such as *Zabān Zanān* (The Voices of Women).[24]

One exception to this is the work of the previously mentioned Camron Amin who, through an analysis of the political cartoons of two major newspapers, unpacks the phenomenon of "Mother Iran," portrayed in cartoon form as a glamourous damsel in distress that needs to be saved by the Iranian man.[25] More important to the topic of women's activism is Amin's "Globalizing Iranian Feminism, 1910–1950," which traces the first women's suffrage movements of Iran through an analysis of the Women's Party, the first independent organization whose primary focus was the advocacy of women's rights.

The Women's Party is also discussed in Hamideh Sedghi's comprehensive *Women and Politics in Iran: Veiling, Unveiling, and Reveiling*. In it, Sedghi traces the ideologies of grassroots organizations such as the Democratic Union of Women, who combined women's issues with discussion of class oppression, women's groups' ties to political organizations such as the Tudeh, and profiles of politically active women of the era such Fakhr Ozmā Arqun. Sedghi also traces the effects of urbanization, economic booms and busts, and other structural factors on women's activism through midcentury Iran.[26] Finally, she also analyzes the "state feminism" of the Pahlavi Regime, tracing the influence of the Women's Organization of Iran (WOI)[27] under Princess Ashraf with a focus on their construction of welfare centers, domestically and internationally.[28]

Women's Activism during the Islamic Republic

The most substantial subset of literature surrounding Iranian women's activism is, by a significant measure, research focused on the postrevolutionary era. The first works were written in the immediate aftermath of the revolution, focused primarily on the mandatory *hijāb* as well as the repeal of the Family Protection Law. These are works of a worried and contemplative nature, an understandable tone, given the momentousness of the event that had just transpired, as well as the swift and decisive actions and decrees of the Islamic Republic Party (IRP) during the Bazargan Era and Iran-Iraq war.[29] The concern over "women's issues" is often presented as part of a larger series of concerns over the increasingly authoritarian nature of the government during the Iran-Iraq War.[30] Essential reading on the revolutionary era also includes the thoughtful, powerful, and often devastating memoirs of political activists, including but not limited to Shahla Talebi's beautifully rendered *Ghosts of Revolution*.[31] Following the war, and as the status and policies of the Islamic Republic solidified, however, the scholarship began to become diversified.

Islamic Feminism in Iran

The field of Iranian Islamic feminism studies has produced sophisticated work from a variety of disciplines. While articles from the 1990s tended to work in unfortunate binaries, pitting "feminist" against "Islamic fundamentalism" or "Islamists" against "Secularists," the trend since has been to document the ways in which women, of varying personal pieties, have used religious discourses in order to influence legislation and issues they view as favorable to women.[32] As scholars like Najmabadi and Miriam Künkler demonstrate, these efforts often involve secular and religious feminists coming together to join forces on shared issues, and at times with Western feminists as well.[33] This tactic of theologically based argumentation, even for lawyers without any prior religious training or personal predilection, is perhaps unsurprising given the Islamic Republic's hybrid legal systems and structure. In a way, this insertion of Islam into the realm of civil law has led not only to the Islamicization of the legal system but also to the inverse, or, what Behrooz Ghamari-Tabrizi has described as the "secularization of Islam."[34] In other words, for activists looking to implement changes in legislation regarding women's issues, Islam is transformed from a form of faith into a practical means to an end.

This is seen perhaps nowhere more prominently than in one of the most preeminent arenas where the fight for women's rights takes place in postrevolutionary Iran: the courtroom. Indeed, perhaps the most popular avenue for advocating for women in contemporary Iran is through the legal system, where specific laws, ordinances, and grievances can be addressed head-on.

Scholarship surrounding the intersections of law and gender in Iran tends to focus on the issues of divorce, inheritance, child custody, and, to a lesser extent, abortion. With the exception of work focused on the 1963 Family Law, much of the research on legal challenges to laws perceived as restrictive to women is focused on postrevolutionary Iran. As such, it would be beneficial if there were more studies done on women's courtroom activism in the earlier part of the twentieth century,[35] especially if there could be some analyses of specific court cases, biographies of prominent female lawyers such as Mihrangīz Manūchihrīan and Shams al-Mūlūk Musāhib, or the process of allowing women to enter the legal professions.[36]

At the same time, much of the strengths of contemporary scholarship lies in the fact that researchers are able to combine historical evidence with ethnographic work, such as participant observation and interviews. One scholar who takes such an interdisciplinary approach is Arzoo Osanloo, whose masterful *The Politics of Women's Rights in Iran* combines extensive fieldwork in family court, legal offices, the Islamic Human Rights Commission, pro bono legal advisors, and women's Qur'anic readings groups to understand the ways that Iranian women understand and articulate their rights.[37] Ultimately, she traces how women must operate as both liberal subjects as citizens and also Muslim subjects who can perform the necessary legal reasoning (*ijtihād*) to approach the Islamic foundations of Iranian law.

Divorce has also emerged as a topic of contention among personal status laws due to the stipulation women must make a case for a divorce based on specific grounds, unless they have the "right to divorce" stipulation written into their marriage contracts.[38] The foremost expert on divorce in Iran is Ziba Mir-Hosseini, who carried out extensive fieldwork in family courts in Tehran in the 1980s and 1990s,[39] and traced the debates surrounding divorce laws in Iran from the era of Reza Shah through the post-2009 era. Ultimately, Mir-Hosseini posits that the Islamic Republic is trying to adhere to an "Islamic ideal" while still trying to attend to the social realities that characterize Iran, a stance that is achieved by carrying out Islamic legal scholarship that tailors interpretation of classical concepts to fit more easily into the contemporary era.

The Green Movement

The Green Movement—the protests that erupted in the wake of the 2009 presidential elections—was the largest demonstration in the Islamic Republic since 1979. Women participated in huge numbers, making their presence felt both within and in the extensive media coverage surrounding the protests. It is perhaps noteworthy how *unremarkable* it was that there were large numbers of women involved in the demonstrations, a fact that speaks to both to the extent of women in the workforce and the public sphere as well as their positions within activist movements during the era of the Islamic Republic.

In fact, the most ubiquitous symbol of the revolution was a woman, Nedā Aghā-Sultān, a twenty-six-year-old philosophy student who previously had not been particularly politically active. The heavily circulated video of Aghā-Sultān's tragic death is analyzed by Sasha Scott, who provides a formalist interpretation of the film clip, dissecting the affective and semantic dimensions of the video and highlighting the appeal of the woman victim, and the ways that Aghā-Sultān became a discursive marker for the Green Wave and its media narratives.[40]

Victoria Tahmasebi-Birgani's article on the Green Movement explores the ways that it was directly influenced by contemporary women's rights activists.[41] These similarities include the Green Movement's grassroots nature, use of rights talks, and, perhaps most compellingly, its borrowing from both religious and nationalist discourses, just as women activists do to further their cause in the legal system and beyond. On this point, Tahmasebi-Birgani highlights the protestors' criticisms of electoral politics and lack of transparency in Iran alongside the proclamations of "*Allah-u Akbar*" from people on their rooftops as a rallying cry for the reformers. Her comparison between the positionality of campaigns for gender equality in relation to broader reform movements prior to 1979 as opposed to today is also apt. In the 1970s, issues concerning women's rights were subsumed by the huge groundswell of efforts to end monarchical rule, whereas today women's rights campaigns and issues are not only recognized but also are at the forefront of any broader political and legal form.

Women's Media in the Islamic Republic

There is a substantial amount of writing devoted to the intersection of women's rights and the press in the post-1979 era, whether the scholarship is analyzing journalistic publications and practices directly or journalism's role within larger debates surrounding feminism in Iran. A helpful introductory overview of post-1979 women's activism within journalism can be found in Srebery and Khiabany,[42] which breaks down the shifting relationship between women and the media into four phases: (1) the revolutionary period 1979–1981; (2) the Gulf war and Islamization of the country 1980–1988; (3) the immediate post-Khomeini era of the late 1980s and early 1990s; and (4) the reform-minded Khatami era starting around 1997. While it unfortunately leans toward broad generalizations, the book thoroughly establishes ties between editors and electoral politics, a not insignificant trend as a number of editors later assumed government positions during the Khatami era.

Although there exists a diversity of publications directed toward a female readership in Iran,[43] most of the research on women and journalism in Iran has been focused on the bold and hard-hitting *Zanān* magazine. *Zanān* (Women) is a magazine that covers the ways that hard politics, theological debates, Qur'ānic exegesis, social issues, and more all affect women. Most notably they have also tried to reclaim the project of women's advancement/feminism as not inherently Western, tracing the history and nuances that exist within that which is called "Islamic feminism." Helpful introductions to *Zanān* include works by Shahidian and Fazeli[44] as well as Roza Eftekhari's essay "*Zanan*: Trials and Successes of a Feminist Magazine in Iran."[45] All three pieces describe the origins of the magazine out of the ashes of the government sponsored *Zanān -i Rūz* (Today's Woman) and give a basic description of their content and circulation. Eftekhari, an editor at *Zanān* since the third issue, offers a powerful insider view and thoughtful commentary. Essential reading is also a short article by Shahla Sherkat, the formidable founder of *Zanān*, who ran the magazine for sixteen years, on her new venture *Zanān-i Imrūz* (The Women of Today), a newsmagazine and site that picks up where *Zanān* left off.[46]

Zanān is mentioned within a broad array of scholarship concerning contemporary Iran: those interested in women's activism,[47] Islamic feminism[48] more broadly, the media, and Western works.

Islamist Women's Activism

The category of "Islamist" women in the context of Iran typically means women who consider themselves staunch supporters of the status quo within the Islamic Republic and the values and politics for which it stands. This is not to say they completely agree with all the policies of the state, especially regarding gender and women's rights, but unlike the Islamic feminists, they often view feminism as a foreign and/or harmful discourse, are sharply critical of the "West," and advocate for maintaining or increasing the role of religion in the public sphere. This is a demographic that has been studied significantly less than their more "liberal" counterparts.[49] While access to these groups plays a factor, there do exist conservative women's organizations, magazines, and publications that could be analyzed much more closely.

The limited, if rich, scholarship surrounding Islamist women largely involves female seminarians. Keiko Sakurai's "Shi'ite Women's Seminaries in Iran: Possibilities and Limitations"[50] provides an excellent overview of the growing popularity of the women's seminaries (*hauzih-ha*) through an analysis of the history, structure, and curriculum of women's seminaries since 1979. She also interviews female seminary students and clerics about their efforts to increase the number of women *mujtahids*, therein demonstrating these women's desires and actions to increase the number of female religious authority figures and hence the role of women in the public sphere. The most substantial study of Iranian women's seminaries is Amina Tawasil's dissertation,[51] based on fifteen months of research in Qom and with subjects including members of the *basīj* as well as students of the Supreme Leader and Chief Justice, Tawasil traces the way that the project of female-centered education and jurisprudence was seen by the women as a way to strengthen the Islamic Republic.

Outside of research on women's seminaries, Azadeh Kian[52] offers a comprehensive overview of the relationship between the state and Islamist women in Iran during the

1980s and 1990s. The article includes a portrait of the personal histories and politics of the first female parliamentarians, and the growth of Islamist women's organizations and magazines, and is generally a helpful source for identifying many of the key figures and political groups at the time. Discussions of the politicization of women's Qur'anic *jalasihs* (sessions) have also been discussed by Azam Torab,[53] although Niloofar Haeri has demonstrated that this is very frequently *not* the case.[54]

Regarding works centered around more specific subject matter, Künkler and Fazaeli have written short biographies of two prominent female *mujtahids* of the twentieth century: Nusrat Amin (1886–1983) and Zohreh Sefati (b. 1948), which is the only substantial material on these important clerics available in English.[55] Amin founded a women's *maktab* (school) during a time when secular education was growing, and even published religious opinions, often under the opaque nom de plume *yik banū-i irani* (an Iranian Gentlewoman). Sefati studied at Qom along with a handful of other young women who eventually began their own *maktab* after struggling to find teachers who would work with women. In the end, she educated hundreds of women, including Khomeini's daughter, and has been consulted by the Expediency Council.[56] Serati has been on record that she believes in "gender justice not gender equality" and is sometimes critical of women in the public sphere, although she supports the idea of a female president as well as female *marjā*.

Conclusion

From their earliest efforts to fight for a more representative form of government at the turn of the twentieth century to navigating the complex geopolitics ever present within domestic legal activism in the contemporary era, Iranian women have long taken charge of their own fate and that of their communities. In tracing these endeavors, this chapter has sought to envision "activism" as including those undertakings both traditionally understood to belong to activism—the formation of and participation in political groups like The Tudeh, the writing and distributing of manifestos and periodicals like *Zanān*, legal challenges to discriminatory government practices, etc.—as well as those endeavors not immediately legible as activism such as those early education advocates of the nineteenth century.

The latter must also include the actions of women whose dreams and aspirations do not so neatly fit into the model of Western-style feminism—including the seminary (*hawze*) students with whom Amina Tawwasil worked or conservative politicians like Marzieh Dastjerdi, both of whom work toward visions of womanhood focused more on family than the self. In embracing a broader view of women's religious and political activism, we might work toward a more inclusive, less teleological, and less Western-centric understanding of what it means to recognize the efforts of women. Within Iranian studies, there are still too many woman who have gone unnamed for their sacrifices, these women who have been participants in an incredibly tumultuous century and must currently endure pressures to be "saved" alongside pressures to "not be influenced" by foreign powers. Perhaps with a more inclusive understanding of activism we may begin to correct these shortcomings within the field.

Notes

1. Arzoo Osanloo, "Islamico-Civil "Rights Talk": Women, Subjectivity, and Law in Iranian Family Court," *American Ethnologist* 33, no. 2 (2006): 191–209.
2. Parvin Paidar, *Women and the Political Process in Twentieth-Century Iran* (Cambridge: Cambridge University Press, 1997).
3. Eliz Sanasarian, *The Women's Rights Movement in Iran: Mutiny, Appeasement, and Repression from 1900 to Khomeini* (New York: Praeger, 1982); Hammed Shahidian, *Women in Iran: Gender Politics in the Islamic Republic* (Westport, CT: Greenwood, 2000); Nikki R. Keddie, "Women in Iran since 1979," *Social Research* (2000): 405–438; Nikki R. Keddie, *Women in the Middle East: Past and Present* (Princeton, NJ: Princeton University Press, 2012).
4. Haideh Moghissi, *Populism and Feminism in Iran: Women's Struggle in a Male-Defined Revolutionary Movement* (New York: Springer, 2016).
5. The Fedayeen, or the Organization of Iranian People's Fedayeen, was an influential underground leftist organization with Marxist-Leninist leanings formed in 1971. The National Union of Women was an affiliate organization of the Fedayeen formed in March 1979 after, according to Haideh Moghissi, the group faced pressure from members to become more active in women's concerns.
6. Afsaneh Najmabadi, "Hazards of Modernity and Morality: Women, State and Ideology in Contemporary Iran," in *Women, Islam, and the State* (Philadelphia, PA: Temple University Press, 1991), 48–75.
7. Janet Afary. *The Iranian Constitutional Revolution, 1906–1911: Grassroots Democracy, Social Democracy, and the Origins of Feminism* (New York: Columbia University Press, 1996); "On the Origins of Feminism in Early 20th-Century Iran," *Journal of Women's History* 1, no. 2 (1989): 65–87; Mangol Bayat-Philipp, "Women and Revolution in Iran, 1905–1911," in *Women in the Muslim World* (1978): 295–308.
8. The Constitutional Revolution (*Enghelab-i Mashruteh*) of 1905–1911 was the culmination of years of struggle by disparate members of Iranian society—including merchants, clergy, and political activists—to implement a written constitution and parliament into the Iranian government. Taking place during the twilight years of the much-weakened Qajar dynasty, it was inspired not only by the need for a more representative form of government but also by the frustration toward the Qajar monarchies financial missteps, overall corruption, and acquiescence to the British and the Russians.
9. Bayat-Philip, "Women and Revolution in Iran," 295–308.
10. Badr al-Muluk Bamdad and Frank Ronald Charles Bagley, *From Darkness into Light: Women's Emancipation in Iran* (Hicksville, NY: Exposition, 1977).
11. Afary, *The Iranian Constitutional Revolution*.
12. Susynne M. McElrone, "Nineteenth-Century Qajar Women in the Public Sphere: An Alternative Historical and Historiographical Reading of the Roots of Iranian Women's Activism," *Comparative Studies of South Asia, Africa and the Middle East* 25, no. 2 (2005): 297–317.

13. Jasamin Rostam-Kolayi. "Origins of Iran's Modern Girls' Schools: From Private/National to Public/State," *Journal of Middle East Women's Studies* 4, no. 3 (2008): 58–88.
14. Afsaneh Najmabadi, "Zanhā -yi Millat: Women or Wives of the Nation?" *Iranian Studies* 26, nos. 1–2 (1993): 51–71.
15. Roja Fazaeli, *Islamic Feminisms: Rights and Interpretations across Generations in Iran* (New York: Taylor & Francis, 2016).
16. Ellen L. Fleischmann, "The Other "Awakening": The Emergence of Women's Movements in the Modern Middle East, 1900–1940," in *A Social History of Women and Gender in the Modern Middle East*, ed. Margaret Lee Meriwether (London: Routledge, 2018), 89–139; Ziba Mir-Hosseini, "Emerging Feminist Voices" in *Women's Rights: A Global View*, ed. Lynn Walter (Westport, CT: Greenwood, 2001), 113–126; Eliz Sanasarian, "Characteristics of Women's Movement in Iran," in *Women and the Family in Iran* (Boston: Brill, 1985), 38–86; and others.
17. Camron Michael Amin, "Propaganda and Remembrance: Gender, Education, and "The Women's Awakening" of 1936," *Iranian Studies* 32, no. 3 (1999): 351–386.
18. Camron Michael Amin, *The Making of the Modern Iranian Woman: Gender, State Policy, and Popular Culture, 1865–1946* (Gainesville: University Press of Florida, 2002).
19. See, for example, Jasamin Rostam-Kolayi, "Expanding Agendas for the 'New' Iranian Woman: Family Law, Work, and Unveiling," in *The Making of Modern Iran: State and Society under Riza Shah, 1921–1941*, ed. Stephanie Cronin (London: Routledge, 2003), 193–210.
20. The unveiling mandate was in fact an order or mandate, and never was enshrined into law. See Houchang Chehabi, "The Banning of the Veil and Its Consequences" for more.
21. Jasamin Rostam-Kolayi and Afshin Matin-Asgari, "Unveiling Ambiguities: Revisiting 1930s Iran's Kashf-i Hijab Campaign," in *Anti-Veiling Campaigns in the Muslim World*, ed. Stephanie Cronin (London: Routledge, 2014), 137–164.
22. Houchang Chehabi, "The Banning of the Veil and Its Consequences," in *The Making of Modern Iran: State and Society under Riza Shah, 1921–1941*, ed. Stephanie Cronin (London: Routledge, 2003), 203–221.
23. Gholam Khiabany, *Iranian Media: The Paradox of Modernity* (London: Routledge, 2009).
24. Parvin Paidar, *Women and the Political Process in Twentieth-Century Iran* (Cambridge: Cambridge University Press, 1997), 1:125.
25. Camron Michael Amin, "Selling and Saving "Mother Iran": Gender and the Iranian Press in the 1940s," *International Journal of Middle East Studies* 33, no. 3 (2001): 335–361.
26. Hamideh Sedghi, *Women and Politics in Iran: Veiling, Unveiling, and Reveiling* (Cambridge: Cambridge University Press, 2007), 61–193.
27. "High Council of Iranian Women's Organizations," later known as the Women's Organization of Iran (WOI), the umbrella group initiated by the Shah's twin sister Princess Ashraf and the Family Protection Law of 1967.
28. Ibid, 172.
29. Sanasarian, *The Women's Rights Movement in Iran*; Azar Tabari, "The Women's Movement in Iran: A Hopeful Prognosis," *Feminist Studies* 12, no. 2 (1986): 343; Farah Azari, *Women of Iran: The Conflict with Fundamentalist Islam* (Buford, GA: Evergreen, 1983); Jaqueline Rudolph Touba, "Effects of the Islamic Revolution on Women and the Family in Iran: Some Preliminary Observations," in *Women and the Family in Iran*, ed. Asghar Fathi (Leiden: Brill, 1985), 131–149.

30. Homa Hoodfar and Fatemeh Sadeghi, "Against All Odds: The Women's Movement in the Islamic Republic of Iran," *Development* 52, no. 2 (2009): 215–223; Guity Nashat, "Women in the Islamic Republic of Iran," *Iranian Studies* 13, nos. 1–4 (1980): 165–194.
31. Shahla Talebi, *Ghosts of Revolution: Rekindled Memories of Imprisonment in Iran* (Stanford, CA: Stanford University Press, 2011).
32. For those interested in an overview of the history of "Islamic Feminism" versus "Secular Feminism," see Valentine M. Moghadam, *Modernizing Women: Gender and Social Change in the Middle East* (Boulder, CA: Lynne Rienner, 2003).
33. Fereshteh Ahmadi, "Islamic Feminism in Iran: Feminism in a New Islamic Context," *Journal of Religion, Feminist Studies* 22, no. 2 (Fall 2006): 33–53.
34. Behrooz Ghamari-Tabrizi, "Women's Rights, Shari 'a Law, and the Secularization of Islam in Iran," *International Journal of Politics, Culture, and Society* 26, no. 3 (2013): 238.
35. Doreen Hinchcliffe, "The Iranian Family Protection Act," *International and Comparative Law Quarterly* 17, no. 2 (1968): 516–521; F. R. Bagley, "The Iranian Family Protection Law of 1967: A Milestone in the Advance of Women's Rights," in *Iran and Islam*, ed. C. E. Bosworth (Edinburgh: University of Edinburgh Press, 1971), 47–64.
36. Firoozeh Kashani-Sabet, *Conceiving Citizens: Women and the Politics of Motherhood in Iran* (Oxford: Oxford University Press, 2011), 180.
37. Arzoo Osanloo, *The Politics of Women's Rights in Iran* (Princeton, NJ: Princeton University Press, 2009).
38. Accessed January 2020, http://www.international-divorce.com/Iran-Family-Law.htm.
39. Mir Hosseini's other works on the topic include: "Divorce and Women's Options: Law and Practice in Iran," *Farzaneh: Journal of Women's Studies and Research* 2, no. 7 (1995/96): 65–82; "When a Woman's Hurt Becomes an Injury: 'Hardship' as Grounds for Divorce in Iran," *Hawwa: Journal of Women in the Middle East and the Islamic World* 5, no. 1 (2007): 111–126.
40. Sasha A. Q. Scott, *Social Media Memorialising and the Public Death Event* (PhD diss., Queen Mary University of London, 2017).
41. Victoria Tahmasebi-Birgani. "Green Women of Iran: The Role of the Women's Movement during and after Iran's Presidential Election of 2009," *Constellations* 17, no. 1 (2010): 78–86.
42. Annabelle Sreberny and G. Khiabany, *The Women's Press in Contemporary Iran: Engendering the Public Sphere* (London: I. B. Tauris, 2004).
43. See, for example, Niki Akhavan's, *Iran: The Cultural Politics of an Online Evolution* (New Brunswick, NJ: Rutgers University Press, 2014); which provides a close reading of blogs by Iranian women, highlighting their range of interests.
44. Roja Fazaeli, "Contemporary Iranian Feminism: Identity, Rights and Interpretations," *Muslim World Journal of Human Rights* 4, no. 1 (2007): 1–27.
45. Roza Eftekhari, "*Zanan*: Trials and Successes of a Feminist Magazine in Iran," in *Middle Eastern Women on the Move* (Washington, DC: Woodrow Wilson International Center for Scholars, 2003): 15–22.
46. Shahla Sherkat, Nazanin Shahrokni, and Frances Hasso, "Zanan-e Emrooz," *Journal of Middle East Women's Studies* 11, no. 3 (2015): 376–379.
47. Asef Bayat, "A Women's Non-Movement: What It Means to Be a Woman Activist in an Islamic State," *Comparative Studies of South Asia, Africa, and the Middle East* 27, no. 1 (2007): 160–172.
48. Fereshteh Ahmadi, "Islamic Feminism in Iran: Feminism in a New Islamic Context," *Journal of in Religion, Feminist Studies* 22, no. 2 (Fall 2006): 33–53.

49. Roksana Bahramitash, Atena Sadegh, and Negin Sattari, *Low-Income Islamist Women and Social Economy in Iran* (New York: Springer Publishing, 2018).
50. Keiko Sakurai, "Shi'ite Women's Seminaries (*howzeh-ye 'elmiyyeh-ye khahran*) in Iran: Possibilities and Limitations," *Iranian Studies* 45, no. 6 (2012): 727–744.
51. Tawasil, Amina, "The Howzevi (Seminarian) Women in Iran: Constituting and Reconstituting Paths" (PhD diss., Columbia University, 2013).
52. Azadeh Kian, "Women and Politics in Post-Islamist Iran: The Gender Conscious Drive to Change," *British Journal of Middle Eastern Studies* 24, no. 1 (1997): 75–96.
53. Azam Torab, "Piety as Gendered Agency: A Study of *Jalaseh* Ritual Discourse in an Urban Neighbourhood in Iran," *Journal of the Royal Anthropological Institute* (1996): 235–252.
54. Niloofar Haeri, "The Sincere Subject: Mediation and Interiority among a Group of Muslim Women in Iran," *HAU: Journal of Ethnographic Theory* 7, no. 1 (2017): 139–161; Haeri, *Say What Your Longing Heart Desires: Women, Prayer, and Poetry in Iran* (Stanford, CA: Stanford University Press, 2020).
55. Mirjam Künkler and Roja Fazaeli, "The Life of Two *Mujtahidahs*: Female Religious Authority in Twentieth-Century Iran," in *Women, Leadership, and Mosques: Changes in Contemporary Islamic Authority*, ed. Masooda Bano and Hilary Kalmbach (Boston: Brill, 2011): 127–160.
56. The Expediency Council is an assembly that is designated to act as mediator between various branches of government, particularly between the Parliament and the Guardian Council, and acts as an advisor to the Supreme Leader, who may also delegate certain responsibilities to them from time to time. Members of the council are appointed by the Supreme Leader for five-year terms.

Bibliography

Abbasgholizadeh, Mahboubeh. "'To Do Something We Are Unable to Do in Iran': Cyberspace, the Public Sphere, and the Iranian Women's Movement." *Signs: Journal of Women in Culture and Society* 39, no. 4 (2014): 831–840.

Abou Zahab, Mariam. "Between Pakistan and Qom: Shi'i Women's Madrasas and New Transnational Networks." In *The Madrasa in Asia*, edited by Farish Noor, Martin van Bruinessen, and Yoginder Sikand, 123–140. Amsterdam: Amsterdam University Press, 2008.

Afary, Janet. *The Iranian Constitutional Revolution, 1906–1911: Grassroots Democracy, Social Democracy, and the Origins of Feminism*. New York: Columbia University Press, 1996.

Afary, Janet. "On the Origins of Feminism in Early 20th-Century Iran." *Journal of Women's History* 1, no. 2 (1989): 65–87.

Afkhani, Mahnaz. "The Women's Organization of Iran: Evolutionary Politics and Revolutionary Change." In *Women in Iran from 1800 to the Islamic Republic*, edited by Lois Beck and Guity Nashat, 107–132. Chicago: University of Illinois Press, 2004.

Afshar, Haleh. "Women and Work in Iran." *Political Studies* 45, no. 4 (February 2002): 755–767.

Ahmadi, Fereshteh. "Islamic Feminism in Iran: Feminism in a New Islamic Context." *Journal of Feminist Studies in Religion* 22, no. 2 (Fall 2006): 33–53.

Agah, Azadeh, Sousan Mehr, and Shadi Parsi. *We Lived to Tell: Political Prison Memoirs of Iranian Women*. New York: McGilligan, 2007.

Aghajanian, Akbar, and Vaida Thompson. "Recent Divorce Trend in Iran." *Journal of Divorce and Remarriage* 54, no. 2 (February 2013): 112–125.

Akhavan, Niki. *Electronic Iran: The Cultural Politics of an Online Evolution*. New Brunswick: Rutgers University Press, 2013.
Akhavan, Niki. "Family Feuds: Digital Battles over the Place of Women in Contemporary Iran." *Middle East Critique* 23, no. 3 (August 2014): 349–362.
Amin, Camron Michael. "Propaganda and Remembrance: Gender, Education, and 'The Women's Awakening' of 1936." *Iranian Studies* 32, no. 3 (Summer 1999): 351–386.
Amin, Camron Michael. "Selling and Saving 'Mother Iran': Gender and the Iranian Press in the 1940s." *International Journal of Middle East Studies* 33, no. 3 (August 2001): 335–361.
Amin, Camron Michael. *The Making of the Modern Iranian Woman: Gender, State Policy, and Popular Culture, 1865–1946*. Gainesville: University Press of Florida, 2002.
Azari, Farah. *Women of Iran: The Conflict with Fundamentalist Islam*. Jaipur: Evergreen, 1983.
Bahramitash, Roksana, Atena Sadegh, and Negin Sattari. *Low-Income Islamist Women and Social Economy in Iran*. New York: Springer, 2018.
Bayat, Asef. "A Women's Non-Movement: What It Means to Be a Woman Activist in an Islamic State." *Comparative Studies of South Asia, Africa, and the Middle East* 27, no. 1 (2007): 160–172.
Bagley, F. R. C. "The Iranian Family Protection Law of 1967: A Milestone in the Advance of Women's Rights." In *Iran and Islam*, edited by C. E. Bosworth, 140–155. Edinburgh: Edinburgh University Press, 1971.
Bamdad, Badr al-Muluk, and Frank Ronald Charles Bagley. *From Darkness into Light: Women's Emancipation in Iran*. Hicksville, NY: Exposition, 1977.
Bayat-Philipp, Mangol. "Women and Revolution in Iran, 1905–1911." In *Women in the Muslim World*, edited by Lois Beck and Nikki Keddie, 295–308. Cambridge, MA: Harvard University Press, 1978.
Chehabi, Houchang E. "The Banning of the Veil and Its Consequences." In *The Making of Modern Iran: State and Society under Riza Shah, 1921–1941*, edited by Stephanie Cronin, 203–221. London: Routledge, 2003.
Doostdar, Alireza. "'The Vulgar Spirit of Blogging': On Language, Culture, and Power in Persian Weblogestan." *American Anthropologist* 106, no. 4 (2004): 651–662.
Esfandiari, Haleh. "The Role of Women Members of Parliament, 1963–88." In *Women in Iran from 1800 to the Islamic Republic*, edited by Lois Beck and Guity Nashat, 136–162. Chicago: University of Illinois Press, 2004.
Eftekhari, Roza. "Zanan: Trials and Successes of a Feminist Magazine in Iran." In *Middle Eastern Women on the Move*, 15–22. Washington, DC: Woodrow Wilson International Center for Scholars: 2003.
Fazaeli, Roja. "Contemporary Iranian Feminism: Identity, Rights and Interpretations." *Muslim World Journal of Human Rights* 4, no. 1 (2007): 297–321.
Fazaeli, Roja. *Islamic Feminisms: Rights and Interpretations across Generations in Iran*. New York: Taylor & Francis, 2016.
Farzanegan, Mohammad Reza, and Hassan Fereidouni Gholipour. "Divorce and the Cost of Housing: Evidence from Iran." *Review of Economics of the Household* 14, no. 4 (2016): 1029–1054.
Fleischmann, Ellen L. "The Other 'Awakening': The Emergence of Women's Movements in the Modern Middle East, 1900–1940." In *A Social History of Women and Gender in the Modern Middle East*, edited by Margaret Lee Merriweather, 89–139. London: Routledge, 2018.
Ghamari-Tabrizi, Behrooz. "Women's Rights, Shari 'a Law, and the Secularization of Islam in Iran." *International Journal of Politics, Culture, and Society* 26, no. 3 (2013): 237–253.

Haeri, Niloofar. *Say What Your Longing Heart Desires: Women, Prayer, and Poetry in Iran*. Stanford, CA: Stanford University Press, 2020.
Haeri, Niloofar. "The Sincere Subject: Mediation and Interiority among a Group of Muslim Women in Iran." *HAU: Journal of Ethnographic Theory* 7, no. 1 (2017): 139–161.
Hashemi, Nader. "If a Nation Want to Change Its Destiny: Zahra Rahnevard on Women's Rights and the Green Movement." In *The People Reloaded: The Green Movement and the Struggle for Iran's Future*, edited by Nader Hashemi and Danny Postel, 263–270. Brooklyn, NY: Melville House, 2010.
Hinchcliffe, Doreen. "The Iranian Family Protection Act." *International and Comparative Law Quarterly* 17, no. 2 (1968): 516–521.
Hoodfar, Homa. "Volunteer Health Workers in Iran: Social Activists?" Montpelier, France: WLUML Occasional Paper 10 (December 1998): 1–16.
Hoodfar, Homa. *The Women's Movement in Iran: Women at the Crossroads of Secularization and Islamization*. Waterloo: Grebels, 1999.
Hoodfar, Homa, and Fatemeh Sadeghi. "Against All Odds: The Women's Movement in the Islamic Republic of Iran." *Development* 52, no. 2 (2009): 215–223.
Hosseini, Mahrokhsadat. "Iranian Women's Poetry from the Constitutional Revolution to the Post-Revolution." PhD diss., University of Sussex, 2017.
Kamalkhani, Zahra. *Women's Islam: Religious Practice among Women in Today's Iran*. London: Routledge, 1998.
Kar, Mehranguiz. "Women's Strategies in Iran from the 1979 Revolution to 1999." In *Globalization, Gender, and Religion*, edited by Jane Bayes and Nayereh Tohidi, 177–201. New York: Palgrave Macmillan, 2001.
Kashani-Sabet, Firoozeh. *Conceiving Citizens: Women and the Politics of Motherhood in Iran*. Oxford: Oxford University Press, 2011.
Keddie, Nikki R. "Women in Iran since 1979." *Social Research* 67, no. 2 (2000): 405–438.
Keddie, Nikki R. *Women in the Middle East: Past and Present*. Princeton, NJ: Princeton University Press, 2012.
Kian, Azadeh. "Women and Politics in Post-Islamist Iran: The Gender Conscious Drive to Change." *British Journal of Middle Eastern Studies* 24, no. 1 (1997): 75–96.
Khiabany, Gholam. *Iranian Media: The Paradox of Modernity*. London: Routledge, 2009.
Künkler, Mirjam. "In the Language of the Islamic Sacred Texts: The Tripartite Struggle for Advocating Women's Rights in the Iran of the 1990s." *Journal of Muslim Minority Affairs* 24, no. 2 (2004): 375–392.
Künkler, Mirjam, and Roja Fazaeli. "The Life of Two *Mujtahidahs*: Female Religious Authority in Twentieth-Century Iran" in *Women, Leadership, and Mosques: Changes in Contemporary Islamic Authority*, edited by Masooda Bano and Hilary Kalmbach, 127–160. Boston: Brill, 2011.
Kurzman, Charles. "A Feminist Generation in Iran?" *Iranian Studies* 41, no. 3 (2008): 297–321.
Masserat, Amir-Ebrahimi. "Blogging from Qom, behind Walls and Veils." *Comparative Studies of South Asia, Africa and the Middle East* 28, no. 2 (2008): 235–249.
McElrone, Susynne M. "Nineteenth-Century Qajar Women in the Public Sphere: An Alternative Historical and Historiographical Reading of the Roots of Iranian Women's Activism." *Comparative Studies of South Asia, Africa and the Middle East* 25, no. 2 (2005): 297–317.
Mehryar, Amir, Farjadi, Gholamali, and Tabibian, Mohammad. "Labor-Force Participation of Women in Contemporary Iran." In *Women in Iran from 1800 to the Islamic Republic*, edited by Lois Beck and Guity Nashat, 182–203. Chicago: University of Illinois Press, 2004.

Mir-Hosseini, Ziba. "Divorce and Women's Options: Law and Practice in Iran." *Farzaneh: Journal of Women's Studies and Research* 2, no. 7 (1995/96): 65–82.
Mir-Hosseini, Ziba. "Iran: Emerging Feminist 'Voices'." In *Women's Rights: A Global View*, edited by Lynn Walters, 113–126. London: Greenwood, 2001.
Mir-Hosseini, Ziba. "Rethinking Gender: Discussions with Ulama in Iran." *Critique: Journal for Critical Studies of the Middle East* 7, no. 13 (1998): 45–59.
Mir-Hosseini, Ziba. "When a Woman's Hurt Becomes an Injury: 'Hardship' as Grounds for Divorce in Iran." *Hawwa: Journal of Women in the Middle East and the Islamic World* 5, no. 1 (2007): 111–126.
Mir-Hosseini, Ziba, and Kim Longinotto. "Divorce Iranian Style." Film. Directed by Ziba Mir-Hosseini and Kim Longinotto (1998).
Moghadam, Fatemeh "Women and Labor in the Islamic Republic of Iran." In *Women in Iran from 1800 to the Islamic Republic*, edited by Lois Beck and Guity Nashat, 163–181. Chicago: University of Illinois Press, 2004.
Moghadam, Valentine M. "Islamic Feminism and Its Discontents: Toward a Resolution of the Debate." *Signs: Journal of Women in Culture and Society* 27, no. 4 (2002): 1135–1171.
Moghadam, Valentine M. *Modernizing Women: Gender and Social Change in the Middle East.* Boulder, CO: Lynne Rienner, 2003.
Moghissi, Haideh. *Populism and Feminism in Iran: Women's Struggle in a Male-Defined Revolutionary Movement.* New York: Springer, 2016.
Najmabadi, Afsaneh. "Feminism in an Islamic Republic - Years of Hardship, Years of Growth." In *Islam, Gender, and Social Change*, edited by Yvonne Haddad and John Esposito, 59–84. Oxford: Oxford University Press, 1998.
Najmabadi, Afsaneh. "Hazards of Modernity and Morality: Women, State and Ideology in Contemporary Iran." In *Women, Islam, and the State*, edited by Deniz Kandiyoti, 48–75. Philadelphia, PA: Temple University Press, 1991.
Najmabadi, Afsaneh. "Power, Morality, and the New Muslim Womanhood." In *The Politics of Social Transformation in Afghanistan, Iran and Pakistan*, edited by Myron Weiner and Ali Banuazizi, 366–381. Syracuse, NY: Syracuse University Press, 1994.
Najmabadi, Afsaneh [Azar Tabari, pseud.]. "The Women's Movement in Iran: A Hopeful Prognosis." *Feminist Studies* 12, no. 2 (1986): 343–356.
Najmabadi, Afsaneh. "Zanha-yi Millat: Women or Wives of the Nation?" *Iranian Studies* 26, nos. 1–2 (1993): 51–71.
Nashat, Guity. "Women in the Islamic Republic of Iran." *Iranian Studies* 13, nos. 1–4 (1980): 165–194.
Natalie Nesvaderani. "Visualizing Vulnerability: Social Justice Filmmaking in Contemporary Iran." PhD diss., Cornell University, 2021.
Osanloo, Arzoo. "Islamico-Civil "Rights Talk": Women, Subjectivity, and Law in Iranian Family Court." *American Ethnologist* 33, no. 2 (2006): 191–209.
Osanloo, Arzoo. *The Politics of Women's Rights in Iran.* Princeton, NJ: Princeton University Press, 2009.
Paidar, Parvin. *Women and the Political Process in Twentieth-Century Iran.* Cambridge: Cambridge University Press, 1997.
Ringer, Monica M. "Rethinking Religion: Progress and Morality in the Early Twentieth-Century Iranian Women's Press." *Comparative Studies of South Asia, Africa and the Middle East* 24, no. 1 (2004): 47–54.
Rostam-Kolayi, Jasamin. "Expanding Agendas for the 'New' Iranian Woman: Family Law, Work, and Unveiling." In *The Making of Modern Iran: State and Society under Riza Shah, 1921–1941*, edited by Stephanie Cronin, 164–189. London: Routledge, 2003.

Rostam-Kolayi, Jasamin. "Origins of Iran's Modern Girls' Schools: From Private/National to Public/State." *Journal of Middle East Women's Studies* 4, no. 3 (2008): 58–88.
Rostam-Kolayi, Jasamin, and Afshin Matin-Asgari. "Unveiling Ambiguities: Revisiting 1930s Iran's Kashf-I Hijab Campaign." In *Anti-Veiling Campaigns in the Muslim World*, edited by Stephanie Cronin, 137–164. London: Routledge, 2014.
Sakurai, Keiko. "Shi 'ite Women's Seminaries (*howzeh-ye 'elmiyyeh-ye khahran*) in Iran: Possibilities and Limitations." *Iranian Studies* 45, no. 6 (2012): 727–744.
Sakurai, Keiko. "Women's Empowerment and Iranian-Style Seminaries in Iran and Pakistan." In *The Moral Economy of the Madrasa: Islam and Education Today*, edited by Keiko Sakurai and Fariba Adelkhah, 44–70. London: Routledge, 2011.
Sameh, Catherine. "Discourse of Equality, Rights, and Islam in the One Million Signatures Campaign in Iran." *International Feminist Journal of Politics* 12, nos. 3–4 (2010): 444–463.
Sanasarian, Eliz. *The Women's Rights Movement in Iran: Mutiny, Appeasement, and Repression from 1900 to Khomeini*. New York: Praeger, 1982.
Sedghi, Hamideh. *Women and Politics in Iran: Veiling, Unveiling, and Reveiling*. Cambridge: Cambridge University Press, 2007.
Shahidi, Hossein. "Women and Journalism in Iran." In *Women, Religion and Culture in Iran*, edited by Vanessa Martin and Sarah Ansari, 70–87. London: Routledge, 2014.
Shahidian, Hammed. *Women in Iran: Gender Politics in the Islamic Republic*. Westport, CT: Greenwood, 2002.
Sherkat, Shahla, Nazanin Shahrokni, and Frances Hasso. "Zanan-e Emrooz." *Journal of Middle East Women's Studies* 11, no. 3 (2015): 376–379.
Sreberny, Annabelle, and G. Khiabany. *Blogistan: The Internet and Politics in Iran*. London: I. B. Tauris, 2010.
Sreberny, Annabelle, and G. Khiabany. *The Women's Press in Contemporary Iran: Engendering the Public Sphere*. London: I. B. Tauris, 2004.
Tahmasebi-Birgani, Victoria. "Green Women of Iran: The Role of the Women's Movement during and after Iran's Presidential Election of 2009." *Constellations* 17, no. 1 (2010): 78–86.
Tajali, Mona. "Islamic Women's Groups and the Quest for Political Representation in Turkey and Iran." *Middle East Journal* 69, no. 4 (2015): 563–581.
Talebi, Shahla. *Ghosts of Revolution: Rekindled Memories of Imprisonment in Iran*. Stanford, CA: Stanford University Press, 2011.
Torab, Azam. "Piety as Gendered Agency: A Study of Jalaseh Ritual Discourse in an Urban Neighbourhood in Iran." *Journal of the Royal Anthropological Institute* (1996): 235–252.
Touba, Jaqueline, "Effects of the Islamic Revolution on Women and the Family in Iran: Some Preliminary Observations." In *Women and the Family in Iran*, edited by Asghar Fathi, 131–149. Leiden: Brill, 1985.
Vatandoust, Gholam-Reza. "The Status of Iranian Women during the Pahlavi Regime." In *Women and the Family in Iran*, edited by Asghar Fathi, 107–130. Leiden: Brill, 1985.
Zahedi, Ashraf. "Contested Meaning of the Veil and Political Ideologies of Iranian Regimes." *Journal of Middle East Women's Studies* 3, no. 3 (2007): 75–98.
Zakia, Salime. *Between Feminism and Islam: Human Rights and Sharia Law in Morocco*. Minneapolis: University of Minnesota Press, 2011.

CHAPTER 21

WOMEN'S RELIGIOUS AND SOCIAL ACTIVISM IN TURKEY

CHIARA MARITATO

INTRODUCTION

SINCE the 1990s, women's religious and social activism in Turkey has been at the core of a composite and fascinating literature. What has been labeled and examined as the 1980s' "second wave of feminism" was a watershed moment for the secular women's movement. It called into question Kemalist (state) feminism, its modernizing project, and its ability to liberate women from their subaltern condition within the family.[1] This critical approach promoted women's consciousness and made room for broadening the range of issues and including different demands. Muslim and Kurdish women claimed spaces and visibility against a homogenized and uniformized model of womanhood and found niches of cooperation with secular feminists. These transformations within the Turkish women's movement occurred at a time when Muslim women were actively protesting against the headscarf ban and asserting that the right to wear a headscarf was a human right and a religious freedom. Small groups of secular feminists and leftist activists also supported Muslim women's demand for the right to wear the headscarf, which contributed to shaping "militant"[2] Muslim women for whom protesting was becoming a "mode of survival and empowerment."[3] Scholars have focused particularly on the motivations that convinced young and educated women, often in opposition to the traditional and "reflexive" religiosity of their mothers, to actively engage in Islamist movements and their activism in support of the Islamist Welfare Party (*Refah Partisi*). This party had promised to remove the headscarf ban if it came to power. The women's struggle for the right to wear headscarves at public institutions increased democratic participation and required negotiations with the party's male hierarchies. It was through the female sections' (*kadin kolları*) activities that women helped spread the image of an urbanized and educated woman following Islamic principles in both the private and the public sphere.

Recent studies have examined the influences that strengthened this cooperation and the cross-fertilization between feminist values and Islamist discourse that characterized this period of contention and conflict with the Turkish state. Given that experience of coalition building, Yeşim Arat examines how feminist concerns have been appropriated by Islamist women and re-elaborated by Islamist columnists. According to the author, "feminist values and the secular women's movement in Turkey shaped the concerns of Islamist women despite differences in approach and priorities."[4] This cooperation has been institutionalized and was at its peak during the first two terms of the Justice and Development Party (AKP) in 2002–2007 and 2007–2011, when the party also co-opted feminist associations in the drafting of legal reforms and public policies. In 2004, the Penal Code was amended to increase the punishment for violence committed against women. In 2011, Turkey actively contributed to the drafting of the Council of Europe Convention on Preventing and Combating Violence Against Women and Domestic Violence (known as the Istanbul Convention), and a new law aimed at preventing violence against women was adopted in 2012. This was the occasion for both secular and Islamist women's associations and platforms to unite and engage in projects that would promote women's rights and gender equality. The dialogue with civil society organizations was the result of not only the European Union's conditions for membership but also the long-lasting synergy between Islamist women and feminist discourse. Another related aspect that has been investigated deals with the outcomes of women's activism in terms of positions granted to women in the AKP.[5] Ayşe Guneş Ayata and Fatma Tütüncü emphasize that even though women have become more visible in AKP politics, this visibility has not led to an increase in female representation, nor any other kind of structural change.[6] Moreover, scholars who have analyzed the incorporation of Islamist women into the state bureaucracy underline how this has deeply affected Islamist women's activism.[7] According to Berna Turam, the incorporation was selective: women who were "highly educated yet neither feminist nor active in women's groups" were incorporated into the bureaucracy.[8] Arat argues that interconnections between Muslim women's organizations and the secular women's movement shaped the concerns of Islamist women despite differences in approach and priorities[9]. The transition from pious women's activism to their bureaucratic role was shaped through cooperation between state institutions and civil society organizations, which included Muslim feminists (though only for a limited time).

Hence, it is worth investigating how these changes in circumstances have affected women's religious and social activism and their relations with the feminist movement. A perspective that considers women's religious activism beyond the feminism–antifeminism dichotomy makes it possible to illuminate the various forms of women's agency. I argue that in the past twenty years the Islamist women's *militant* position that characterized their engagement in political parties and contentious politics has evolved into a bureaucratic role promoting a passive defensive behavior that either complies with the government's gender regime or is unable to directly oppose it. The work stems from ethnographic research conducted between 2013 and 2019 into the forms and meanings of the increasing number of women employed as religious officers by the Presidency of Religious Affairs (Diyanet). The Diyanet women preachers were interviewed as part of that project. The interview with Hidayet Tuksal, who is a Muslim feminist theologian, activist, and well-known columnist, was conducted online in May 2021. In 2003 and the following years, the Diyanet was one of the first state agencies to employ women with headscarves. Women preachers, Qur'ān teachers, and vice-muftis[10] have contributed to redefining and expanding the notion of religious services to reach women and families. This process needs to be carefully assessed as it ostensibly speaks to the changes in the AKP's gender regime. Since 2010, the "silencing" of more innovative voices has accompanied the AKP's narrative aimed at restoring a religious-conservative gender climate[11] and hindering the legacies of cooperation with feminist and secular women.

The Bureaucratization of Muslim Women's Activism

Starting in 2003, under the presidency of Ali Bardakoğlu, the Diyanet increased the number of women employed as preachers, vice-muftis, and Qur'ān teachers in Turkish mosques. The number of women in its ranks totaled 2,696 in 2004 and had risen to 11,041 by 2010.[12] The feminization of an institution that had historically been dominated by men should be considered within the context of a broader redefinition of religious services as moral support and religious guidance provided by religious officers on various aspects of life. Women working as preachers were actively engaged in spreading Islamic morality, inviting women to mosques, and expanding religious services for women, children, and families.[13] This incorporation of Islamist women into the state bureaucracy has affected women's religious and social mobilization. In many conversations between 2013 and 2019 at Istanbul's Diyanet mosques, preachers and Qu'ran teachers described their current position as a "state invitation" resulting from decades of marginalization and oppression due to the headscarf ban in the education and public sector. In light of their experiences around the 1997 coup, they describe themselves as victims of a system that had prevented them from studying and working, unlike during the AKP era, which is defined as a "liberated" present full of opportunities to both work and serve the community.

The National Security Council met on February 28, 1997, to overthrow the government of Necmettin Erbakan, leader of the Welfare Party, reinstate laicism (*laiklik*), and reinforce the headscarf ban[14] at universities. This ban subsequently produced widespread unemployment among religiously educated women.[15] Although the data is not easy to verify, around 5,000 women were suspended, and 10,000 were fired from work for wearing a headscarf between 1998 and 2002.[16] On the one hand, the shared past is remembered with a sense of oppression and victimization by the women who are now civil servants or have served as state employees. On the other hand, that experience, which is often defined as "February 28" (*28 Şubat*), is an identity marker that defines a collective "we" and helps decipher the present. At the time, women who were still university students were not allowed to pursue their studies. Their self-realization is defined as completely linked to the rise to power of the AKP and what Sezen Yaraş defines as the "politics of service" to stress how the radical shift in the culture of politics in Turkey affected their professional lives. In this respect, the AKP played a historic role: "cleaning, morally purifying and changing the culture of politics."[17] Being the servants of society and serving our fellow citizens are some of the terms used to emphasize a mode of doing politics based on mutual care, proximity to society, and in opposition to the purportedly immoral politics of a past that should be cleansed. The notion of "service" and, in particular, the reference to the religious services (*din hizmetleri*) that they provide to their fellow citizens recur in women preachers' conversations to corroborate their decision to work outside the home after many years of study. On many occasions, the term *vatandaşlar* (compatriots, citizens) is replaced by *müminler* (believers). Zeynep, one of the preachers working in Istanbul's Beşiktaş district, describes her job as a service (*hizmet*) that she provides to the Muslim community:

> Working for the Diyanet, the most important thing is to illuminate *(anlatmak)* people (*halk*) and, in particular, women about our religion. [. . .] I work for the Diyanet, but I actually work for my Muslim brothers and sisters. There's a rule in our religion: Those who know should enlighten those who don't. I was educated in religious studies, so I report my knowledge to my Muslim brothers, and I try to meet their needs.
>
> This devotion to serving the community is also expressed when defining their jobs as religious officers and state employees. Similarly, Fatma, a preacher employed at the Ankara Diyanet Head Office, states the following about her employment within the Diyanet: I don't consider what I do a job for the Diyanet. I see it as work for my religion. I feel happy to enlighten people about true religious knowledge, to make them free by teaching them religion, to see them having more self-confidence.

In these conversations, the notion of service is also employed to qualify women's work outside the home. Emine, working as a Diyanet preacher in Istanbul's Üsküdar municipality, clearly expresses the link between women's education and work as a service to the community:

> I won't say that women must work (*çalismalılar*) outside the home. I would say, "If they want, they can work." These two expressions have different meanings. I have two grown-up daughters. Both are well educated. Because of their education, they're obliged (*borçlu olmak*) to society; to repay this, I think they should do something that could be helpful (*yararlı*) to other people.

Islamist women working at state institutions obtained a recognized status that, by protecting their right to participate in the public realm while wearing the headscarf, also means they no longer have to be on the defensive. Moreover, as state employees, they engaged in work activities outside the home by promoting a new form of female religious engagement: from pious militants to "pious bureaucrats." As Yaraş affirms:

> Women representatives desire to be active agents in this process to conduct the "cleaning" or purification of politics from the remnants of such practice of politics. Their exclusion from institutions of political representation in the past is attributed to a "moral" value in the sense that the more distant they were from the positions of power in the past, the more they are depicted as suitable actors for the purification of politics in the present. Being the "servants" of the people is the main rhetoric that is used to legitimize and naturalize their presence in various spheres of the constituency's social life.[18]

Although women included in state agencies seem to reproduce the role of compliant civil servants committed to executing the AKP's moralizing project, their agency should be carefully assessed to grasp how they react to the structure of dominations and patriarchal relationships. The incorporation of Islamist women into the state bureaucracy reached its peak after the repeal of the headscarf ban in 2013. This process has been analyzed to better understand women's participation in political institutions[19] and assess how the silencing of Muslim feminists and those critical voices outside the mainstream affected religious women's agency.[20] In both cases, women's religious and social activism has been examined by stressing points of convergence or distance between secular feminists and Islamist women. When the literature addresses Islamist women and their activism, their role is often framed as antifeminist and in opposition to women's liberation struggle in the region.[21] Women's intimate, personal, and emotional experience in prompting diverse forms of feminist resistance occurred because of their political experience and despite the overarching success or failure of the conflict. According to Kelsy Burke, religious women's agency can be described in four ways: "resistance agency," which is the agency of women attempting to challenge or change some aspects of religion; "empowerment agency," which defines how women reinterpret religious doctrine in ways that make them feel empowered in their everyday life; "instrumental agency," which focuses on nonreligious outcomes derived from religious practice; and, finally, "compliant agency," which focuses on the multiple and diverse ways in which women conform to the rules of gender-traditional religions.[22] This definition complexifies a notion of agency as necessarily manifested in resistance to include the possibility of agents to either reproduce forms of domination or partially challenge them. These typologies may be interrelated and shift according to the political context.

Since the 2010s, the focus on women's rights and gender equality has shifted to how men and women complement each other and how their bodies are considered different "by nature" because they were created that way. This perspective has been accompanied by what Simten Coşar and Metin Yeğenoğlu call a new mode of patriarchal configuration that is built on the sanctity of tradition, faith, and family values. According to the authors, the AKP's neoliberal-conservative version of patriarchy is familiar, for it defines "the familial sphere as the natural locus of women."[23] The content of this new gender regime has been presented through a widespread narrative about the traditional Turkish family, which has reinforced the implementation of policies and projects.[24] Betül Yarar analyzes this change in institutional and discursive strategies surrounding gender in relation to the global crisis of "neoliberalism with a human face" at the end of the 2000s, which in Turkey resulted in the rise to prominence of radical conservative and nationalist authoritarian forces. According to the author, during the first period of the AKP's rule, a "neoliberal feminism" made room for itself and brought together a coalition of actors in the common epistemic field of criticizing the Kemalist modernization project. The interaction among women's movements, neoliberals, and neoconservatives, as well as progressive-libertarian social movements, Islamic movements, and Kurdish movements, reinvigorated an Islamic feminism that is sensitive to women's rights. At that time, this was the "complex patchwork" that characterized the AKP's productive and constructive gender politics.[25] As we will show in the next section, it is precisely during that time that some of these feminists were included in the AKP's cadres and attempted to introduce feminist political arguments into the party's politics and state agencies. However, as Tuksal affirms:

> Between 2002 and 2013, women wearing headscarves were still fighting the bans. During this struggle, they received little support from women's rights organizations and feminists. They often had to wage their struggles alone or even against defenders of women's rights. For this reason, women wearing headscarves did not owe a debt of gratitude to other women's organizations, and there was no reason for them to fight together. Only a very small group of secular feminists (such as the *Amargi* and the *KAMER* Foundation[26]) actively engaged, while the mainstream feminists did nothing about it. Therefore, cooperation between the secular feminists and the religious feminists was not as strong or resilient as one might think.

The cooperation mostly occurred on specific issues such as improving gender equality and preventing violence against women, but it was largely affected by the AKP's increasingly polarizing language and policies in opposition to the women's rights movement and especially feminists.[27]

Women's Religious and Social Activism under the AKP's Gender Regime

Between 2003 and 2011, a group of Muslim feminists collaborated with the Diyanet's officials to design and coordinate projects targeting women. In 2006, one activity involved formulating a Friday prayer sermon (*Hutbe*) on the role of the woman as "daughter, spouse, and mother." The text sparked debate as it reaffirmed the equality of men and women before God and condemned how, in many circumstances, women are associated with dishonor and remain in the background.[28] In 2008, these feminists embarked on a project[29] to train women preachers and Qur'ān teachers about violence against women, and in 2010, in line with this project, the Diyanet promoted a campaign to condemn violence against women, distribute brochures, and organize seminars for both male and female personnel.[30] Moreover, in line with the approach taken by Islamic feminists, this group of women took part in propagating women's reading and interpretation of religious texts and adding women's rights and gender equality to the Diyanet's agenda. While feminist approaches have been more and more marginalized and ostracized by the Diyanet, those conservative positions have also collided with a reality in which women's right to study and work resonates with the personal experiences of the women officers. According to a Diyanet employee who in 2013 oversaw the activities directed toward women, children, and families, no one from the Diyanet's personnel would say "I am a Muslim feminist." In their daily activities, however, they share feminism's objectives, though not its philosophy.

In the aftermath of the 2011 elections, a new regime emerged in opposition to the previous attempt to present a conservative democracy that would meet the EU's expectations. The new state project delineated by the AKP's authoritarian turn was very gendered and resulted in the emergence of a progovernment civil society in parallel with its secular counterpart. The flourishing of government-organized nongovernmental organizations (GONGOs) and Islamic civic society associations is at the core of this transformation aimed at promoting a discourse of familialism.[31] In an attempt to read the AKP's new gender regime, Yarar analyzes how a "neoconservative feminism emerged in a very destructive and oppositional manner against secular queer and feminist politics in Turkey."[32] The latter resulted in a radical polarization that panders to radical right-wing groups' discourse on a patriarchal order threatened by "feminists." According to Yarar, "AKP politicians began to emphasize the conservative definition of femininity and feminine sexuality as a new affirmative strategy in attacking secular feminisms and replacing them with its highly illiberalized neoconservative feminist approach."[33]

The AKP's negative attitude toward women's rights affected the dialogue between secular and religious activists: Only Muslim feminists engaged to overtly oppose the government. Other women who also did not participate in the AKP's gender regime preferred to voice their opposition individually and behind closed doors. Tuksal further develops this point by affirming that:

> After the headscarf ban was lifted in 2013, women began to take part in the public sector. However, these women did not openly oppose the AKP in the practices that emerged later, which included threats to women's rights. Although some religious women were opposed, there was no loud opposition on an institutional basis.

It was during this process that organizations like "Women and Democracy" (*Kadın ve Demokrası Vakfı*, KADEM) were established. In 2011, women from KADEM and the AKP were also influential in the drafting of the Istanbul Convention. The convention marked significant cooperation between the Turkish women's movement and Muslim feminists. Turkey's withdrawal from the Istanbul Convention by presidential decree in March 2021 deeply divided the AKP's religious-conservative constituency. The party's women-centered branches intervened in support of the convention, as did some progovernment civil society organizations, such as KADEM. Women of the AKP also reacted, and many religious women columnists opposed the withdrawal. Such opposition coming from women within the party who are engaged in progovernment civil society activism can inform further theorization over what has been defined as "nonresistance" or a more quietist position of pious women living under the AKP.[34] Muslim feminist blogs like *Reçel* (meaning "marmalade" or "jam") and *Havle Kadın* (named in memory of Havle Bint-ii Salabe, a woman who lived at the time of the prophet Mohammed and opposed the injustice she was subjected to by her husband)[35] also expressed solidarity and engaged in cooperation with secular feminists.

Examining how Islamist women columnists disseminated feminist messages to a religious-conservative community, Arat affirms that, "Even though they were reluctant to criticize the AKP government, they did not restrain themselves from criticizing the conservative Muslim community with respect to women's rights."[36]

In deciphering the current situation, particularly in the aftermath of Turkey's withdrawal from the Istanbul Convention, Tuksal underlines some dissonance in this regard:

> Unfortunately, the freedom of women wearing headscarves to enter schools and workplaces did not result in women being sensitive toward or supportive of other women's demands for freedom. Only religious feminists have advocated the freedom they demand for everyone. However, women from other backgrounds, who were affiliated with religious communities or sects, continued to defend the narrow views of their communities disregarding the rights and freedoms of others.

The decades of societal polarization aimed at strengthening support for the AKP as a form of obedience to the head of state have greatly affected democratic opposition regarding both grassroots mobilization and coalition building. This concerned political opposition, as well as the mobilization of civic and social movements. The gradual democratic backsliding in Turkey under the rule of the AKP has led to heightened levels of political violence targeting dissent, especially after the 2016 coup attempt and, subsequently, the regime change with the 2017 constitutional referendum. These developments have fundamentally transformed the opposition in Turkey and, consequently, also the women's movement. The civic space has become densely populated by local and regional social movements organized to contest autocratic policymaking, particularly in opposition to social-conservative policies, the neoliberal exploitation of natural resources, and familial approaches designed to oppose women's rights.

Concluding Remarks

This chapter sheds light on how women's religious and social activism has been affected by two important changes: the lifting of the headscarf ban in 2013 and the opening of positions for women wearing headscarves in the public sector. The incorporation of women active in the Islamist movement into the Turkish state bureaucracy marked a shift from their status of activists to one of bureaucrats. This resulted in a redefinition of women's demands for rights and gender equality by pandering to a more compliant position vis-à-vis the AKP government. Therefore, while only a few groups of Muslim feminists have experienced multiple forms of cooperation with certain sections of the secular women's movement on specific issues, most women who wear the headscarf grasped the most from the opportunities deriving from the AKP's repeal of the ban but failed to mobilize for women's rights. Pious women bureaucrats have subscribed to what Deniz Kandiyoti describes as the same gender ideology of the AKP and accepted the oldest deal with patriarchal power; according to her, these women "opted for the comforts of what they see as protection and security traded against acquiescence and loyalty."[37] Further research should look into the experience of the feminist theologians and activists who have attempted to bring about change both inside religious institutions, such as the Diyanet, and enlarge the base of support for the women's movement.

Notes

1. Deniz A. Kandiyoti and Deniz Kandiyoti, "Emancipated but Unliberated? Reflections on the Turkish Case," *Feminist Studies* 13, no. 2 (July 1, 1987): 317–338; Nilüfer Göle, *The Forbidden Modern: Civilization and Veiling* (Ann Arbor: University of Michigan Press, 1996); Sibel Bozdoğan and Reşat Kasaba, *Rethinking Modernity and National Identity in Turkey* (Seattle: University of Washington Press, 1997).
2. I employ the term "militant" with a neutral connotation to indicate the brand of female activism within Islamic movements and parties during the 1980s and 1990s; the reinforcement of the headscarf ban sparked demonstrations and protests led by politically engaged religious women. These women were activists and militants in the sense that they were involved in political parties and took part in sit-ins and demonstrations for the right to access universities. Although it is commonplace to refer to militancy as leading to acts involving violence, the term is used here to designate a person actively supporting the group they belong to and are affiliated with.
3. Yeşim Arat, "Islamist Women and Feminist Concerns in Contemporary Turkey: Prospects for Women's Rights and Solidarity," *Frontiers: A Journal of Women Studies* 37, no. 3 (2016): 130.
4. Ibid., 127.
5. Ayşe Guneş Ayata and Fatma Tütüncü, "Party Politics of the AKP (2002–2007) and the Predicaments of Women at the Intersection of the Westernist, Islamist and Feminist Discourses in Turkey," *British Journal of Middle Eastern Studies* 35, no. 3 (2008): 363–384; Sezen Yaraş, "The Making of the 'New' Patriarch in Women's Self-Narrations of Political

Empowerment: The Case of Local Female AKP Politicians in the Aftermath of 2009 Elections," *Turkish Studies* 20, no. 2 (March 15, 2019): 273–296.

6. Ayata and Tütüncü, "Party Politics of the AKP," 366.
7. Berna Turam, "Turkish Women Divided by Politics," *International Feminist Journal of Politics* 10, no. 4 (December 1, 2008): 475–494; Selin Çağatay, "Women's Coalitions beyond the Laicism–Islamism Divide in Turkey: Towards an Inclusive Struggle for Gender Equality?" *Social Inclusion* 6, no. 4 (November 22, 2018): 48–58.
8. Turam, "Turkish Women Divided by Politics," 480.
9. Arat, "Islamist Women and Feminist Concerns," 127.
10. Women are employed as vice-muftis in Turkey's biggest cities. As deputy mufti, they support the activities of the muftis' offices issuing opinions in the form of *fatwas*, which in Turkey are not legally binding and defined as religious questions.
11. Ayşe Güneş-Ayata and Gökten Doğangün, "Gender Politics of the AKP: Restoration of a Religio-Conservative Gender Climate," *Journal of Balkan and Near Eastern Studies* 19, no. 6 (November 2, 2017): 610–627.
12. Chiara Maritato, "Expanding Religion and Islamic Morality in Turkey: The Role of the Diyanet's Women Preachers," *Anthropology of the Middle East* 13, no. 2 (2018): 43–60.
13. Chiara Maritato, "Performing *Irşad*: Female Preachers' (*Vaizeler*'s) Religious Assistance within the Framework of the Turkish State," *Turkish Studies* 16, no. 3 (July 3, 2015): 433–447.
14. Access to education for students wearing headscarves was restricted de jure by the "Dress and Appearance Regulation" passed by the Turkish Council of Higher Education in 1982 (*Yükseköğretim Kurulu*, YÖK).
15. Sultan Tepe, "Contesting Political Theologies of Islam and Democracy in Turkey," *Journal of Religious and Political Practice* 2, no. 2 (May 3, 2016): 175–192.
16. Richard Peres, "A History of the Headscarf Ban in Turkey," *Turkish Review* 2, no. 5 (2012): 44.
17. Yaraş, "The Making of the 'New' Patriarch," 280.
18. Ibid., 281.
19. Ayata and Tütüncü, "Party Politics of the AKP"; Yaraş, " Making of the 'New' Patriarch."
20. Turam, "Turkish Women Divided by Politics"; Arat, "Islamist Women and Feminist Concerns."
21. Valentine M. Moghadam, *Modernizing Women: Gender and Social Change in the Middle East* (Boulder, CO: Lynne Rienner, 2003); Haideh Moghissi, *Feminism and Radical Islamic Fundamentalism: The Limits of Postmodern Analysis* (London: Zed, 1999).
22. Kelsy C. Burke, "Women's Agency in Gender-Traditional Religions: A Review of Four Approaches," *Sociology Compass* 6, no. 2 (February 2012): 123–124.
23. Simten Coşar and Metin Yeğenoğlu, "New Grounds for Patriarchy in Turkey? Gender Policy in the Age of AKP," *South European Society and Politics* 16, no. 4 (December 1, 2011): 567.
24. Hikmet Kocamaner, "The Politics of the Family: Religious Affairs, Civil Society, and Islamic Media in Turkey," (PhD diss. University of Arizona, 2014) January 1, 2014, http://arizona.openrepository.com/arizona/handle/10150/333348; Hikmet Kocamaner, "Strengthening the Family through Television: Islamic Broadcasting, Secularism, and the Politics of Responsibility in Turkey," *Anthropological Quarterly* 90, no. 3 (September 26, 2017): 675–714; Hikmet Kocamaner, "Regulating the Family through Religion," *American Ethnologist* 46, no. 4 (2019): 495–508; Ayhan Kaya, "Islamisation of Turkey under the AKP Rule: Empowering Family, Faith and Charity," *South European Society and Politics* 20, no. 1 (January 2,

2015): 47–69; Güneş-Ayata and Doğangün, "Gender Politics of the AKP"; Zafer Yilmaz, "'Strengthening the Family' Policies in Turkey: Managing the Social Question and Armoring Conservative–Neoliberal Populism," *Turkish Studies* 16, no. 3 (July 3, 2015): 371–390.

25. Betül Yarar, "Neoliberal-Neoconservative Feminism(s) in Turkey: Politics of Female Bodies/Subjectivities and the Justice and Development Party's Turn to Authoritarianism," *New Perspectives on Turkey* 63 (November 2020): 123. See also Hürcan Aslı Aksoy, "Invigorating Democracy in Turkey: The Agency of Organized Islamist Women," *Politics and Gender* 11, no. 1 (2015): 146–170.
26. For more information, go to http://www.amargidergi.com/yeni/ and https://www.kamer.org.tr/eng/.
27. Çağatay, "Women's Coalitions."
28. For more on the *hutbe*, see: https://www.birgun.net/haber/diyanetten-8-mart-hutbesi-26328, accessed January 10, 2021.
29. In 2008, the "The Role of Religious Officers in the Fight against Violence against Women" (*Kadına Yönelik Şiddetle Mucadelede Din Görevlilerinin Katkısının Sağlanması*) project was carried out in cooperation with the United Nation Population Fund (UNFPA). The project's aim was twofold: to provide female preachers with training on what Islamic sources say about the issue and what kind of guidance preachers may give, and to provide female preachers with the information and contacts necessary to assist victims of violence, for example to direct them to police, psychologists, doctors, or shelters.
30. The name of the project, *Kadına şiddete son* ("Stop Violence against Women"), was changed to *Aile içi şiddete son* ("Stop Violence in the Family") in 2012.
31. Bilge Yabanci, "Work for the Nation, Obey the State, Praise the Ummah: Turkey's Government-Oriented Youth Organizations in Cultivating a New Nation," *Ethnopolitics* 20, no. 4 (2021): 467–499.
32. Yarar, "Neoliberal-Neoconservative Feminism(s)," 116.
33. Ibid., 131.
34. See "How Female Politicians in Turkey's Ruling Party Help Strengthen Patriarchy," accessed January 11, 2021, https://www.al-monitor.com/pulse/originals/2021/01/turkey-why-female-akp-lawmakers-strengthen-patriarchy.html.
35. More info about the two Muslim feminist blogs can be obtained here: for Reçel: http://recel-blog.com/ and for *Havle Kadın Derneği*: https://havlekadin.wordpress.com/hakkinda/. The life of Havle Bint-ii Salabe is also illustrated in the Diyanet's *Encyclopedia of Islam*, accessed June 23, 2021, https://islamansiklopedisi.org.tr/havle-bint-salebe.
36. Arat, "Islamist Women and Feminist Concerns," 144.
37. Deniz Kandiyoti, "No Laughing Matter: Women and the New Populism in Turkey," https://www.opendemocracy.net/en/5050/no-laughing-matter-women-and-new-populism-in-turkey/.

Bibliography

Aksoy, Hürcan Aslı. "Invigorating Democracy in Turkey: The Agency of Organized Islamist Women." *Politics and Gender* 11, no. 1 (2015): 146–170.

Arat, Yeşim. "Islamist Women and Feminist Concerns in Contemporary Turkey: Prospects for Women's Rights and Solidarity." *Frontiers: A Journal of Women Studies* 37, no. 3 (2016): 125–150.

Ayata, Ayşe Guneş, and Fatma Tütüncü. "Party Politics of the AKP (2002–2007) and the Predicaments of Women at the Intersection of the Westernist, Islamist and Feminist Discourses in Turkey." *British Journal of Middle Eastern Studies* 35, no. 3 (2008): 363–384.
Bozdoğan, Sibel, and Reşat Kasaba. *Rethinking Modernity and National Identity in Turkey*. Seattle: University of Washington Press, 1997.
Burke, Kelsy C. "Women's Agency in Gender-Traditional Religions: A Review of Four Approaches." *Sociology Compass* 6, no. 2 (February 2012): 122–133.
Çağatay, Selin. "Women's Coalitions beyond the Laicism–Islamism Divide in Turkey: Towards an Inclusive Struggle for Gender Equality?" *Social Inclusion* 6, no. 4 (November 22, 2018): 48–58.
Coşar, Simten, and Metin Yeğenoğlu. "New Grounds for Patriarchy in Turkey? Gender Policy in the Age of AKP." *South European Society and Politics* 16, no. 4 (December 1, 2011): 555–573.
Göle, Nilüfer. *The Forbidden Modern: Civilization and Veiling*. Ann Arbor: University of Michigan Press, 1996.
Güneş-Ayata, Ayşe, and Gökten Doğangün. "Gender Politics of the AKP: Restoration of a Religio-Conservative Gender Climate." *Journal of Balkan and Near Eastern Studies* 19, no. 6 (November 2, 2017): 610–627.
Kandiyoti, Deniz A., and Deniz Kandiyoti. "Emancipated but Unliberated? Reflections on the Turkish Case." *Feminist Studies* 13, no. 2 (July 1, 1987): 317–338.
Kaya, Ayhan. "Islamisation of Turkey under the AKP Rule: Empowering Family, Faith and Charity." *South European Society and Politics* 20, no. 1 (January 2, 2015): 47–69.
Kocamaner, Hikmet. "The Politics of the Family: Religious Affairs, Civil Society, and Islamic Media in Turkey." PhD diss., University of Arizona, 2014. http://arizona.openrepository.com/arizona/handle/10150/333348.
Kocamaner, Hikmet. "Regulating the Family through Religion." *American Ethnologist* 46, no. 4 (2019): 495–508.
Kocamaner, Hikmet. "Strengthening the Family through Television: Islamic Broadcasting, Secularism, and the Politics of Responsibility in Turkey." *Anthropological Quarterly* 90, no. 3 (September 26, 2017): 675–714.
Maritato, Chiara. "Expanding Religion and Islamic Morality in Turkey: The Role of the Diyanet's Women Preachers." *Anthropology of the Middle East* 13, no. 2 (2018): 43–60.
Maritato, Chiara. "Performing Irşad: Female Preachers' (Vaizeler's) Religious Assistance within the Framework of the Turkish State." *Turkish Studies* 16, no. 3 (July 3, 2015): 433–447.
Moghadam, Valentine M. *Modernizing Women: Gender and Social Change in the Middle East*. Boulder, CO: Lynne Rienner, 2003.
Moghissi, Haideh. *Feminism and Radical Islamic Fundamentalism: The Limits of Postmodern Analysis*. London: Zed, 1999.
OpenDemocracy. "No Laughing Matter: Women and the New Populism in Turkey." Accessed January 14, 2021. https://www.opendemocracy.net/en/5050/no-laughing-matter-women-and-new-populism-in-turkey/.
Peres, Richard. "A History of the Headscarf Ban in Turkey." *Turkish Review* 2, no. 5 (2012): 34–46.
Tepe, Sultan. "Contesting Political Theologies of Islam and Democracy in Turkey." *Journal of Religious and Political Practice* 2, no. 2 (May 3, 2016): 175–192.
Turam, Berna. "Turkish Women Divided by Politics." *International Feminist Journal of Politics* 10, no. 4 (December 1, 2008): 475–494.

Yabanci, Bilge. "Work for the Nation, Obey the State, Praise the Ummah: Turkey's Government-Oriented Youth Organizations in Cultivating a New Nation." *Ethnopolitics* 0, no. 0 (October 17, 2019): 1–33.

Yarar, Betül. "Neoliberal-Neoconservative Feminism(s) in Turkey: Politics of Female Bodies/Subjectivities and the Justice and Development Party's Turn to Authoritarianism." *New Perspectives on Turkey* 63 (November 2020): 113–137.

Yaraş, Sezen. "The Making of the "New" Patriarch in Women's Self-Narrations of Political Empowerment: The Case of Local Female AKP Politicians in the Aftermath of 2009 Elections." *Turkish Studies* 20, no. 2 (March 15, 2019): 273–296.

Yilmaz, Zafer. "'Strengthening the Family' Policies in Turkey: Managing the Social Question and Armoring Conservative–Neoliberal Populism." *Turkish Studies* 16, no. 3 (July 3, 2015): 371–390.

CHAPTER 22

WOMEN'S RELIGIOUS AND SOCIAL ACTIVISM IN SOUTH ASIA

ELORA SHEHABUDDIN

THIS chapter examines South Asian Muslim women's participation in different faith-based movements. While Muslim women across South Asia have mobilized on a wide range of issues since the late nineteenth century, such as women's education, suffrage, national liberation, legal reform, workers' rights, sexual rights and bodily autonomy, the environment, and in opposition to corruption and authoritarianism, I focus here on instances of activism in Pakistan and Bangladesh in which Muslim women's identity as Muslim women, their personal piety, or their reliance on an Islamic framework to resolve a problem have been paramount. These particular opportunities for activism have proven personally empowering to individual women or even small groups of women, for example, by enhancing their social networks and engagement, improving their access to religious texts, or allowing them to engage more deeply with their faith through adherence to strict dress codes and engagement in charitable deeds. I argue here, however, that such instances of empowerment notwithstanding, these movements have ultimately supported policies and laws that discriminate against women, especially Muslim women who do not dress or pray in ways the ideologues of the movements have prescribed.

THE WOMEN'S WINGS OF OLDER MOVEMENTS

The Tablighi Jamaat

Founded in Delhi in 1926 by Muhammad Ilyas, today the Tablighi Jamaat (TJ) has some 15 million followers in over 150 countries and its annual *bishwa ijtema* (world congregation) in Tongi, Bangladesh, is believed to be second only to the hajj in the number of participants it attracts. Although a minuscule portion of these visible participants are women, several recent studies clearly demonstrate that large numbers of women are actively involved in TJ around the world and work quietly to spread the movement's message. This movement is premised not on membership or political engagement, but rather a commitment to following the *sunna* or traditions and practices of the Prophet.[1]

Given his concern with inculcating Muslims with true knowledge of Islam, Ilyas was interested from the very beginning in bringing women into the fold. He wanted to send women out with the men to engage in *da'wa* (to call or invite people to embrace true Islam). His family had long been associated with both the Deoband and Aligarh Islamic reform movements, and he had grown up surrounded by pious and learned women.[2] He saw these female relatives as role-models for other women participants: they spoke to the children only about the Qur'ān and the great figures of early Islam and spent their spare time in prayer.[3] The Deobandi ulama of his time, however, vehemently opposed his plan to include women, arguing that *tabligh* work would give women a cover for leaving their homes, and that they would use *tabligh* tours as an "excuse" for "turning toward freedom." Ilyas persisted until a follower, Maulana Abdus Sobhan, agreed to let his wife take a small group of women—alongside their husbands—to engage in missionary work among Muslim women in Mewat, just outside Delhi, where the TJ had commenced work.[4] The term *masturat jamaat* (literally, unrevealed or hidden group or party) is used for female *jamaat* or tour groups, which work behind closed doors and are thus invisible.[5]

Women's responsibilities within the TJ are similar to those of men, and they are assessed on the basis of the same traits—humility, generosity, and piety. Like the men, women are encouraged to engage in self-improvement through education (specifically of Islamic topics) and enjoined to work in the *tariqa-i-tabligh* (the *tabligh* method), which requires leaving home for *tablighi* tours that last from three to forty days. Unlike the men, however, women who go on *tabligh* tours must be married. Also, they must be accompanied by their husband or other male *mahram* relative. Moreover, it is men who have the final say in any decision-making on these tours, including organizing the women's daily schedule of study and mission work.[6]

By the end of the twentieth century, TJ leaders had begun to articulate an expanded role for women in the movement. Women, they argued, were best suited to curb the dangers of emerging lifestyles as seen in new modes of dress, interaction, and leisure. TJ ideologues worried that women were both most vulnerable to new trends but also, as the mothers and thus the "first *madrasa* of their children," best positioned to direct their families away from un-Islamic activities.[7]

Unintentionally it would seem, what has somewhat disrupted traditional gender roles is the TJ's emphasis on humility, simplicity, and frugality, on spreading the message of Islam rather than the pursuit of material wealth, and its rejection of social indicators of status and hierarchy. These have helped to diminish differences not only between rich and poor but also, to a certain extent, between men and women. In the male tablighis' commitment to *khidmat* (service) by taking on a variety of roles from preaching to cooking and cleaning for the group when on tour—"actions associated with the lower-born and with women"—Barbara Metcalf discerned a suspension of traditional ideas about the division of labor by class and gender. Shaken by this erasure of boundaries, a critic of the Tabligh described a friend's son in the movement as behaving "abnormally," a statement he then clarified with, "He acts like a Pakistani girl!" The men's responsibilities when on tour has consequences often for the very nature of family dynamics when the couple is together at home. One young man reported to Metcalf that life at home was now "more cooperative and harmonious." Another explained that he now was more understanding at home and less likely to criticize his wife over her cooking "since he now knew how easy it was to do things like adding too much salt."[8]

Women, for their part, are also encouraged to take on new roles and responsibilities in the home during the men's extended periods of absence.[9] Tabligh Amir[10] Enamul Hassan, for instance, urged women to emulate the wives of the Prophet by spending their days in the service of Islam, not in the kitchen. As in the time of the Prophet, he declared, daily meals as well as marriage ceremonies should be much simpler, requiring far less sacrifice of time, money, and effort.[11]

Although encouraged to undertake *jamaats* alongside their male relatives, most TJ women have stayed closer to home and worked primarily with women in their neighborhoods. Some of these meetings occur fairly frequently, even daily, but because they are held in homes, women's contribution is typically not visible to outsiders, though there are occasional public appearances, such as that witnessed by Metcalf at Makki Masjid in Karachi, Pakistan, in July 1991 where around a thousand TJ women spoke.[12] Despite the strict rules about dress and conduct, TJ women appreciate the regular gatherings as a valuable opportunity to interact with women they might not otherwise meet in their fairly circumscribed daily lives. In one of the earliest studies on Tabligh women, in 1996 Yoginder Sikand interviewed a woman in Dhaka, Bangladesh, who recalled how much she had enjoyed going on her first tour or *jamaat* with her husband, both for the opportunity to travel to new places and for the "respite from the monotony of housework." While the women, like the men, are expected to devote their time to study, prayer, meditation, and discussion of Islamic topics while on tour, they have taken advantage of these gatherings to exchange ideas and offer advice to one another on such topics as children and family dynamics.[13] They also take pride in stories of TJ women who have brought their male relatives into the Tabligh rather than the other way around.[14]

Sarah White discusses the experience of Amma Huzur (which means revered teacher-mother and is used as a term of respect for female Tabligh leaders), a middle-aged, lower-middle-class *talim* (religious instruction) leader in rural Bangladesh. Amma Huzur's desire to read the meaning of the Qur'ān properly motivated her to learn Bengali, which further enhanced her standing in society and inspired others around her who now take pride in the leadership of, as they put it, "an illiterate woman like ourselves." In the end, however, what White refers to as Amma Huzur's "script" was a conservative, patriarchal one. Amma Huzur firmly believed that women's place was in the home, not in paid employment outside the home or in the voting booth, and she regarded the *sari*, the traditional female attire of the region, as insufficiently modest for good Muslim women.[15]

Bulbul Siddiqi reports that while TJ leaders in Bangladesh generally value women's contributions to the movement, they insist on traditional gender roles and a strict gender hierarchy. The main reason they encourage their wives' greater involvement is so that they might become more supportive of their own work.[16] While many women undoubtedly gain from the knowledge imparted at the TJ *talim* sessions and the networking and travel opportunities presented by the *masturat jamaat*, especially in the form of greater status within their families and communities, other women have felt restrained and sought to carve out new spaces for themselves within the Tabligh Jamaat.

The *Char Sathir Dal* (Group of Four Companions, or GFC) in Bangladesh studied by Momotaj Begum is one such alternative Tablighi women's group. Established in Dhaka in the 1980s and with branches throughout the country today, the group takes its name from the four close companions of the Prophet who became the first four Sunni caliphs. It emerged out of the frustration felt by women by the general dependence on and subordination to male tablighis that was expected of them. The GFC women consider themselves part of the TJ and, like traditional TJ women, observe strict *purdah* (literally, curtain, and refers to range of practices ranging from modest dress to seclusion). They insist, however, that they should be able to participate in tabligh activities even in the absence of appropriate male relatives and to organize their own events.[17]

Begum connects the emergence of the GFC to the dramatic political, social, and economic changes in Bangladesh in recent decades that have led to the greater visibility of women—in the prime minister's office, professional workplaces, educational institutions, and export-oriented factories.[18] While men make all important decisions in the TJ, the all-female GFC sought to establish a space of autonomy for themselves by constructing a *talim ghar*, a distinct physical space for education. It was "not just a place for preaching Tablighi lesson, but also . . . a mosque-like institution and community space for women and by women." They hold their own weekly meeting in the *talim ghar* with a ten-person *shura* (governing council) and any additional members present. According to Begum, it is this *ghar*—its very existence as well as the manner in which it is used—that distinguishes the GFC from not only mainstream TJ in South Asia, but also other female mosque movements, such as those studied by Saba Mahmood in Egypt and Sylva Frisk in Malaysia.[19] In a region where women have not historically prayed in mosques, GFC women appreciated being able to gather in their own *ghar* for communal prayers—on Fridays, for *tarawih* prayers during Ramadan,[20] and for the two major Eids. Built on donated land with contributions from the GFC women themselves, the *ghar* belongs to them all and they are all invested in maintaining and improving the structure. In this dedicated, sanctified place (women perform *wudu* or ablutions before entering even when meeting for a reading circle, discussion, or children's lessons), no single member has to take on the responsibility for hosting. This further helps GFC women separate their religious work from their domestic responsibilities.[21]

The Jamaat-I Islami

When Abul Ala Maududi (d. 1979) founded the Jamaat-i Islami in 1941 in India, his primary concern was to create a community of devout educated men to lead his movement for societal reform. He had already started writing about his concerns over changes in gender roles in the West and, to a certain extent, even in Muslim societies. He regarded women's place to be in the home, with responsibility for molding good Muslim children.[22] Nonetheless, in February 1947, just months before Partition, Hameeda Begum, who had been the first woman to join the Jamaat, helped to found the Halq-e-Khawateen, the Jamaat's women's wing. She was elected leader of the women's section in newly independent Pakistan the following year and went on to play a crucial role in shaping the nature of Jamaat women's interaction with the larger population for decades to come, in Bangladesh as in Pakistan. Given her own background as a school principal and the general restrictions of that era on middle-class women's mobility and visibility, Hameeda Begum identified "literary activism"—through writing and the distribution of inexpensive pamphlets and monthly magazines such as *Iffat*—as the primary mode of *dawa* and activism for Jamaat women.[23]

Worried that the new Pakistani state, "an irreligious state, with westernized people at its helm," would follow Kemalist Turkey in diminishing the public role of Islam, Maududi decided that the Jamaat would join formal politics and contest elections. For two more decades, however, the party continued to focus on educated men; there were, in any case, few democratic elections in Pakistan in that period. The party's poor results in the 1970 all-Pakistan elections led to another shift in policy, with Maududi exhorting party workers to expand beyond the educated minority to court the votes of women and rural and urban workers.[24]

Following the 1971 breakup of Pakistan, the Jamaat sought to take advantage of the reserved seats for women in the national parliament and provisional assemblies by fielding women candidates for election. In 1983, the Jamaat supported the establishment of a new organization of Islamist women, the Majlis-e-Khawateen. The following year, Pakistan's military ruler General Zia ul-Huq appointed the organization's president Nisar Fatima to the Commission on the Status of Women as well as the Council of Islamic Theology, and, in 1985, she took up one of the National Assembly seats reserved for women as a Jamaat representative. In each of these capacities, she cast herself in stark opposition to women's rights activists, especially those who were members of Khawateen Mahaz-e-Amal or Women's Action Forum (WAF), and, at the time, engaged in a battle against the Zia regime's Islamization of state, society, and the penal code. Since 1981, WAF activists, such as lawyer and human rights activist Asma Jehangir, had led the protests, in the words of two WAF founders, against "the growing trend to segregate women, which they saw as part of a larger move to push women out of public arenas and back in their homes" as well as new legal provisions such as the Hudood Ordinance (1979) and the Law of Evidence (1984), which blatantly discriminated against women and religious minorities. WAF cofounder Khawar Mumtaz later recalled that, throughout the Zia era, the women religious activists were most visible in their "immediate and vitriolic" reactions and responses to the statements and activities of "non-'fundamentalist'" women's organizations such as WAF, whom they repeatedly characterized as "westernized, alienated, and non-religious." When the Commission produced a report that the recent laws had been a "setback to women," Fatima wrote the sole dissenting report, arguing that only scholars of Islam were qualified to evaluate legal matters and that the Commission should have given priority to the central role of the family with a male breadwinner and female homemaker. The Commission's report was quickly shelved although Fatima's dissent received much publicity.[25] Although Zia would be killed in a suspicious plane crash in 1988, the laws he put in place remained on the books through succeeding governments, including those of Benazir Bhutto (1988–1990 and 1993–1996), the first female Muslim head of government in the world. They were finally amended in 2006.

An important development in the work of Jamaat women in Pakistan since the 1980s has been their forays beyond the urban elites to take their message to the urban and rural poor. In gatherings in shantytowns and rural communities, educated urban women impart lessons about religion as well as "health, hygiene, personal cleanliness, and other matters." The Jamaat women that sociologist Amina Jamal spoke with did not see these efforts as transgressions beyond Maududi's dictates regarding women's roles, but simply their contributions to help "establish the religion (*dīn*) of Allah on His land." Jamal notes that, unlike earlier generations of Jamaat women, today's Jamaat women activists recognize that they are competing against nonreligious Pakistani feminist activists in their efforts to bring about change in women's lives. As a result, they now expend more energy in publicizing their activities and their interest in women's issues.[26]

Given its own deeper engagement with the electoral process, the Jamaat's greater interest in women—as voters—was inevitable. General Pervez Musharraf, who came to power following a 1999 military coup, faced pressure from the UNDP to improve women's political participation, particularly through quotas for elected bodies at the local, provincial, and national levels. Following initial opposition to this dramatic expansion in women's visibility—on the grounds that it would violate gender roles and the family—as well as to Musharraf's plans for an approach to Islam that he characterized as "Enlightened Moderation," the Jamaat and its allies went on to nominate women candidates for those seats. Jamaat women pointed to the example of the Prophet himself to justify combining religion and politics in their activism. For the Jamaat women whom Jamal interviewed, politics was not an "avenue for a woman's self-empowerment or the exercise of the entitlements of citizenship," but rather, a "religious duty imposed on them by the party, necessitated by local and global political conditions." While all political parties took advantage of the new "women's seats," a 2005 UNDP report indicates the greater independence and internal democracy of the Women's Wing of the Jamaat compared to those of other parties.[27]

The same December 1970 general elections that persuaded the JI of the need to expand its voter base also galvanized the nationalist movement in East Pakistan when the central government refused to recognize the election results. The East Pakistan-based Awami League, led by Sheikh Mujibur Rahman, swept the polls in East Pakistan, giving the party a clear majority in the National Assembly. President Yahya Khan, Pakistan's military ruler, and Zulfiqar Ali Bhutto, head of the Pakistan People's Party, which had won 81 out of 138 seats in West Pakistan, deployed various tactics to prevent the new assembly from meeting, exacerbating civil unrest in the eastern wing. Bangladesh's declaration of independence three months later, in March 1971, was opposed by the East Pakistani wing of the JI, whose followers sided with West Pakistani forces in the ensuing nine-month war of independence and engaged in a range of atrocities against the local population. The Constitution of independent Bangladesh declared the new nation a secular democratic republic and the new government led by Sheikh Mujibur Rahman banned all religion-based political parties, including the JI. The ban was lifted following Sheikh Mujib's assassination in 1975 and, when formal democracy was restored in 1991 after fifteen years of military rule, the Jamaat contested the national elections. Understandably concerned with numbers, it nominated women for the reserved seats and courted women voters of all classes.[28]

Women's improved access to higher education in both Pakistan and Bangladesh, while small relative to the size of the population, created the larger readership on which Hameeda Begum's strategy of literary activism depended. The Jamaat encouraged the mobilization of young women on college and university campuses, with the Islami Jamiat-i-Talibat established in Pakistan in 1969 and the Bangladesh Islami Chatri Sangstha (BICSa) in 1978.[29] In her detailed study of BICSa, anthropologist Maimuna Huq notes the generation gap in the concerns of Islamist women that prompted the need for a distinct organization for students. Amina, as Huq calls the founder of BICSa, had become interested in Islamist activism in the early 1970s, but when she started recruiting, "she realized that the older women had an older style of talking, acting, and thinking that would not appeal to the younger women attending modern high schools and colleges in growing numbers." Given their different educational experiences, the older Jamaat women were "unable to advise Amina on strategies for offering effective Islamic competition with the attractions of secular entertainment increasingly available to college students. . . . There was clearly an emergent space for an organization run by and for young Muslim women students."[30]

The vast majority of the population of South Asia of course remains poor and uneducated, and as had happened in Pakistan, the women's wing of the Jamaat in Bangladesh took on the responsibility of taking the Jamaat's message beyond the party's educated core and to women in poor neighborhoods. Since literary activism would be of little use among women who could not read at all, educated Jamaat women developed new strategies: "We target women who read a little, tell them about the Qur'ān and *ḥadīth* and ask them to take the message to others, to explain to them our goals . . . orally, just as Islam was first preached orally."[31]

Unlike its counterparts in Bangladesh and Pakistan, the Jamaat-i Islami of India or Jamaat-e-Islami Hind (JIH) is not a political party. Its women's wings in different states have been visible at large public meetings at which they have discussed such issues as girls' education and women's legal rights. As senior JIH women's wing leader Nasira Khanum declared at a Hyderabad meeting in 2006 attended by some 30,000 people, "Islam advocates protection of women rights [*sic*] but men-dominated society hides the facts. Women themselves should know about their rights and learn to snatch them if denied!"[32]

Women-Only Groups

Militant Activism

Important examples of South Asian Muslim women's participation in what Swati Parashar labels "religio-political militant" Islamist movements are to be found in Kashmir, where some women are drawing on a specific interpretation of Islam to fight for their national Kashmiri identity. The founder of the all-women Dukhtaran-e-Millat (Daughters of Faith), Asiya Andrabi, has publicly declared that the group's primary objective is to help "Kashmiri women fight for their rights conferred on them by Islam." To that end, they have provided logistical support to male-dominated militant groups and occasionally engaged in acts of violence themselves—they have attacked cinema halls, beauty parlors, and unveiled women. Similarly, members of the women-only Muslim Khawateen Markaz have provided crucial financial support to male fighters, carried guns and messages, and provided medical assistance. These two organizations are widely believed to be the women's wings of the militant male dominated Hizbul Mujahideen and Jammu Kashmir Liberation Front, respectively, though the women in them insist they are independent. In Islamabad, a "burqa brigade" from the Jamia Hafsa seminary kidnapped three women and a baby and held them hostage, demanding in exchange that certain mosques be rebuilt and sharia law be enforced.[33]

Al-Huda in Pakistan

Very much in contrast to the women's sections of larger male-dominated organizations are the women-led and women-only movements that have emerged in recent decades. Perhaps the most visible female-run of these in the Pakistani context is the al-Huda (Guidance) Welfare Trust, with its founder Dr. Farhat Hashmi the most prominent Muslim woman leader and scholar of Islam in the country today. Armed with a doctorate in *Hadīth* Sciences from the University of Glasgow, Hashmi started to offer informal classes in Islamabad to teach women to read and understand Arabic and thereby gain "unmediated access" to the Qur'ān and *ḥadīth*. Since its start in the early 1990s as an affiliate of the International Islamic University, where Hashmi once taught, the movement has grown dramatically among educated women in Pakistan as well as in Pakistani diaspora communities around the world. The organization offers a formal curriculum with exams and diplomas, as well as multiday and even month-long seminars. Anita

Weiss describes the interpretation of women's rights espoused by al-Huda as drawing more from "globalized visions of Islamist thought" than what is "traditional in Pakistan." While Hashmi's Qur'ānic exegesis draws heavily on that of JI founder Maududi, she conveyed in an early interview with Weiss some openness to the minor blurring of traditional gender roles: "If they fulfill their responsibilities fully, they can do the others' tasks as well."[34] Upon receiving a diploma from al-Huda, a woman can begin offering classes herself. Hashmi's lectures are widely available on CDs and in books and pamphlets and she herself frequently appears on radio and TV. Although men cannot attend her lectures in person, many men regularly listen to her recordings and media appearances and are enrolled in al-Huda's distance-learning courses.[35]

The educated, urban women who are drawn to al-Huda see themselves as an educated vanguard in the movement to reclaim "true Islam" from those who have misinterpreted it over the centuries. They take pride in al-Huda's well-equipped schools and classrooms and their formal course of study, but most of all in Hashmi's own training in "modern" or secular, including Western, institutions, her doctoral degree, and facility in Arabic, Urdu, and English.[36] Hashmi, for her part, has been able to capitalize on the greater presence of women in higher education and the easier access to new forms of technology in order to grow her support base. Today the movement is truly transnational, offering online classes from its headquarters in Toronto, Canada, and with over 200 branches around the world.[37]

Shiʿi Women's Madrasas in Pakistan

The Shiʿi population of Pakistan, believed to be around a fifth of the country's population, has invested heavily in several women's madrasas in recent decades. These madrasas attract rural and urban women of different class backgrounds and, significantly, have helped produce female scholars of Islam, many of whom receive further training in seminaries in important Shiʿi religious centers such as Qom. According to Mariam Abou-Zahab, these Pakistani graduates from the Qom seminary constitute members of a new transnational elite, "a self-consciously new type of Shiʿi women," who enjoy "a considerable amount of prestige and a level of religious authority." They also "represent a form of Islamic feminism," given their commitment to using religious texts to improve "women's rights."[38]

Study Circles in Bangladesh

The Muslim wife of a foreign diplomat stationed in Dhaka initially mobilized the urban elite women's study circles in Bangladesh that anthropologist Samia Huq studied in the early years of the new century. At their peak, the weekly Qur'ānic reading classes in Urdu and, later, English, accommodated over forty women. The participants offered a variety of reasons for having joined the classes, including a degree of frustration at not understanding the Qur'ānic Arabic they had learned to recite and a desire for community. Energized by the changes they themselves experienced as members of the learning circle, they felt motivated to spread the message further in society and to "call for change," for a "return to the Islamic values that shape the Bengali Muslims." To achieve this goal, the women critiqued and rejected what they perceived to be un-Islamic elements in their personal lives and in the society around them and actively engaged in *dawa* to other women.[39]

Undoubtedly the most dramatic of the changes the women enacted in their personal lives was adopting the hijab. This, in turn, prompted changes in their conduct, including avoiding mixed company, removing from their homes any artwork depicting living beings, displaying a greater awareness around issues of wealth and consumption, and giving up singing and music. Many women also turned against the traditional religion-infused rituals common among Bengali Muslim women—and long dominated by women—such as visiting *pirs* (Sufi saints or spiritual guides) and shrines and organizing prayer gatherings to mark various occasions.[40]

It was, however, in their move beyond refashioning their personal lives and homes that the women of the discussion circles saw themselves as engaged in what can be described as activism, "a new kind of activism that renders them more vibrantly contributing members of society." The confidence, respectability, and "certainty" about religion, about themselves, that many women gained from their participation in the learning circle inspired them to "infect" others. These women thus "use *da'wa* as a medium of change that gives Islam a new public presence." Their understanding of dawa, accordingly, was an expansive one, ranging from "verbal calling to charity to community service."[41]

Agency, Piety, and Feminism

Recent scholarship on women engaged in religious activism has revolved around questions of agency, empowerment, and feminism. This brief survey of religious activism by Muslim women in South Asia highlights a variety of forms of engagement, from women's participation in the women's wings of longstanding movements to women's establishment of informal women-only organizations. In all instances, women have appreciated being part of a community, of the opportunities to interact with women beyond their families and travel outside their own neighborhoods. They have taken pride in working with others to deepen their own piety and submit to God and Islam through the way they dress, the practices they adopt, and the community service they perform, exercising what Saba Mahmood described as nonliberal agency.[42] Afiya Zia, however, provides an important reminder against overreading the agentive potential of such forms of activism, of portraying them as simply yet another form of feminism if we understand feminism as a movement with progressive means and goals.[43]

In the larger formal organizations, Jamaat-i Islami and Tablighi Jamaat, women members' pursuits are strictly circumscribed by the male leadership and dissent is infrequent and muted. Groups such as GFC, the TJ-affiliated women's organization, offers an example of the greater possibilities that emerge when women decide to take some control over their activities. The women-only, education-focused communities of al-Huda, BICSa, and the Study Circles that have received scholarly attention, for their part, have had greater leeway in choosing the topics of study and discussion for themselves, even though they rely largely on the same books—by Maududi—that have long been assigned to JI women. It is when such discussions have provided opportunities for questioning traditional interpretations or to broach topics that their male comrades might have deemed uninteresting or irrelevant that there has emerged the potential for changes in the larger community beyond individually empowering experiences. For now, women-centered interpretations of or critical engagements with religious texts that may be emerging from these discussion groups—the "pious critical agency" observed by Rachel Rinaldo in the Indonesian context—remain marginal.[44] Instead, the most visible effects have ranged from a greater visibility of Islamic practices, such as modest attire, prayer, and fasting, to the religious activists' organized defense of Pakistan's quarter-century-old, blatantly antiwomen Zina Ordinance—on the grounds that such a move would transform Pakistan into "a free sex zone"—and of other intolerant, exclusivist laws and measures in both Pakistan and Bangladesh. In the end, the nature of Muslim women's religious movements in South Asia, their relationship with the state as well as with secular feminist activists, and their ability and desire to transform their larger societies have been shaped not only by individual ideologues but also by the distinct histories and diverging political trajectories as well as their different locations in the larger transnational and geopolitical contexts.

Notes

1. Muhammad Khalid Masud, "The Growth and Development of the Tablighi Jamaat in India," in *Travellers in Faith: Studies of the Tablīghī Jamāʿat as a Transnational Islamic Movement for Faith Renewal*, edited by Muhammad Khalid Masud (Leiden: Brill, 2000), 4; Barbara D. Metcalf, "Living Hadith in the Tablighi Jama`at," *Journal of Asian Studies* 52, no. 3 (1993): 584–608; Barbara D. Metcalf, "Tablighi Jamaat and Women," in Masud, *Travellers in Faith*, 44–58.
2. Masud, "Growth and Development of the Tablighi Jamaat in India," 5.
3. Matthew J. Kuiper, *Da'wa and Other Religions: Indian Muslims and the Modern Resurgence of Global Islamic Activism* (London: Routledge, 2017), 142.
4. Yoginder S. Sikand, "Women and the Tablighi Jamaat," *Islam and Christian-Muslim Relations* 10, no. 1 (March 1999): 43.
5. Momotaj Begum, "Negotiation for Extended Gender Roles in Islam: Women in Tablighi Jamaat in Bangladesh" (PhD diss., Hiroshima University, 2015), 2; Meryem Fatima Zaman, "The Semiotics of Revivalist Islam: Women, Space, and Stories in Pakistan's Islamic Movements" (PhD diss., Michigan State University, 2014), 16.

6. Sikand, "Women and the Tablighi Jamaat," 43–44; Metcalf, "Tablighi Jamaat and Women," 50.
7. Sikand, "Women and the Tablighi Jamaat," 48–49.
8. Metcalf, "Tablighi Jamaat and Women," 45, 49, 53.
9. Metcalf, "Tablighi Jamaat and Women," 50.
10. Amir is the title given to the male leader of the TJ.
11. Sikand, "Women and the Tablighi Jamaat," 50.
12. Metcalf, "Tablighi Jamaat and Women," 50–51.
13. Sikand, "Women and the Tablighi Jamaat," 45–46.
14. Metcalf, "Tablighi Jamaat and Women," 52–53.
15. White, "Domains of Contestation," 341.
16. Bulbul Siddiqi, "Reconfiguring the Gender Relation: The Case of the Tablighi Jamaat in Bangladesh," *Culture and Religion* 13, no. 2 (June 2012), 183–184.
17. Begum, "Negotiation for Extended Gender Roles," chap. 6.
18. Begum, "Negotiation for Extended Gender Roles," 260–261.
19. Saba Mahmood, *Politics of Piety: The Islamic Revival and the Feminist Subject* (Princeton, NJ: Princeton University Press, 2005); Sylva Frisk, *Submitting to God: Women and Islam in Urban Malaysia* (Seattle: University of Washington Press, 2009).
20. The *tarawih* prayers refer to additional prayers offered during the fasting month of Ramadan after the Maghrib or sunset prayer.
21. Begum, "Negotiation for Extended Gender Roles," chap. 6.
22. Elora Shehabuddin, "Jamaat-i-Islami in Bangladesh: Women, Democracy and the Transformation of Islamist Politics," *Modern Asian Studies* 42, nos. 2–3 (2008): 577–603.
23. Seyyed Vali Reza Nasr, *The Vanguard of the Islamic Revolution: The Jamaat-i Islami of Pakistan* (Berkeley: University of California Press, 1994); Elora Shehabuddin, "Beware the Bed of Fire: Gender, Democracy, and the Jama'at-i Islami in Bangladesh," *Journal of Women's History* 10, no. 4 (1999): 148–171; Niloufer Siddiqui, "Gender Ideology and the Jamaat-e-Islami," *Current Trends in Islamist Ideology* 10 (July–September 2010), https://www.hudson.org/research/9797-gender-ideology-and-the-jamaat-e-islami (accessed October 10, 2018); Amina Jamal, *Jamaat-e-Islami Women in Pakistan: Vanguard of a New Modernity?* (Syracuse, NY: Syracuse University Press, 2013), 116–121; Meryem Zaman, "Religious Practices: Preaching and Women Preachers: Pakistan," in *Encyclopedia of Women and Islamic Cultures*, ed. Suad Joseph (2016), accessed October 10, 2018, http://www.brillonline.nl/browse/encyclopedia-of-women-and-islamic-cultures.
24. Nasr, *Vanguard of the Islamic Revolution*, 39, 90; Shehabuddin, "Beware the Bed of Fire," 150.
25. Khawar Mumtaz and Farida Shaheed, *Women of Pakistan: Two Steps Forward, One Step Back* (London: Zed Books, 1987), 74, 120; Khawar Mumtaz, "Identity Politics and Women: 'Fundamentalism' and Women in Pakistan," in *Identity Politics and Women: Cultural Reassertions and Feminisms in International Perspective*, edited by Valentine M. Moghadam (Boulder, CO: Westview, 1994), 238.
26. Amina Jamal, *Jamaat-e-Islami Women in Pakistan: Vanguard of a New Modernity?* (Syracuse, NY: Syracuse University Press, 2013), 132–134.
27. Jamal, *Jamaat-e-Islami Women in Pakistan*, 16–22, 87–94, 110–111.
28. Sarah Tasnim Shehabuddin, "Bangladeshi Politics since Independence," in *Routledge Handbook of Contemporary Bangladesh*, ed. Ali Riaz and Mohammad Sajjadur Rahman

(New York: Routledge, 2016); Navine Murshid, "The Genocide of 1971 and the Politics of Justice," in Riaz and Rahman, *Routledge Handbook of Contemporary Bangladesh*, 52–62.

29. Kathleen Fenner Laird, "Whose Islam? Pakistani Women's Political Action Groups Speak Out" (PhD diss., Washington University, St. Louis, 2007).
30. Maimuna Huq, "The Politics of Belief: Women's Islamic Activism in Bangladesh" (PhD diss., Columbia University, 2006), 84–86.
31. Elora Shehabuddin, *Reshaping the Holy: Democracy, Development, and Muslim Women in Bangladesh* (New York: Columbia University Press, 2008), 200–206.
32. Sylvia Vatuk, "Islamic Feminism in India: Indian Muslim Women Activists and the Reform of Muslim Personal Law," *Modern Asian Studies* 42, nos. 2–3 (March 2008): 518.
33. Swati Parashar, "The Sacred and the Sacrilegious: Exploring Women's 'Politics' and 'Agency' in Radical Religious Movements in South Asia," *Totalitarian Movements and Political Religions* 11, nos. 3–4 (2010): 435–455; Swati Parashar, "Gender, Jihad, and Jingoism: Women as Perpetrators, Planners, and Patrons of Militancy in Kashmir," *Studies in Conflict and Terrorism* 34, no. 4 (2011): 299.
34. Anita M. Weiss, *Interpreting Islam, Modernity, and Women's Rights in Pakistan* (New York: Palgrave Macmillan, 2014), 121–130.
35. Faiza Mushtaq, "A Controversial Role Model for Pakistani Women," *South Asia Multidisciplinary Academic Journal* 4 (December 2010), accessed October 11, 2018, available at *journals.openedition.org*; Sadaf Ahmad, "Al-Huda and Women's Religious Authority in Urban Pakistan," *Muslim World* 103, no. 3 (July 2013): 363–374; Zaman, "The Semiotics of Revivalist Islam," 16.
36. Sadaf Ahmad, *Transforming Faith: The Story of Al-Huda and Islamic Revivalism among Urban Pakistani Women* (Syracuse, NY: Syracuse University Press, 2009), 71.
37. Zaman, "Religious Practices," 16; Usha Sanyal, "Al-Huda International: How Muslim Women Empower Themselves through Online Study of the Qur'an," *Hawwa* 13, no. 3 (October 2015): 440–460.
38. Mariam Abou Zahab, "Shi'i Women's Madrasas and New Transnational Networks," in *The Madrasa in Asia: Political Activism and Transnational Linkages*, ed. Farish A. Noor, Yoginder Sikand, and Martin van Bruinessen (Amsterdam: Amsterdam University Press, 2008), 136–137.
39. Samia Huq and Sabina Faiz Rashid, "Refashioning Islam: Elite Women and Piety in Bangladesh," *Contemporary Islam* 2, no. 1 (March 2008): 7–22; Samia Huq, "Women's Religious Discussion Circles in Urban Bangladesh:Enacting, Negotiating and Contesting Piety" (PhD diss., Brandeis University, 2011), 7–12.
40. Huq and Rashid, "Refashioning Islam."
41. Samia Huq, "Religious Learning Circles and Da`wa: The Modalities of Educated Bangladeshi Women Preaching Islam," in *Proselytizing and the Limits of Religious Pluralism in Contemporary Asia*, ed. Juliana Finucane and R. Michael Feener (Singapore: Springer, 2014), 83–84.
42. Mahmood, *Politics of Piety*, 38.
43. Afiya Shehrbano Zia, "A State of Suspended Disbelief," *Economic and Political Weekly* 43, no. 23 (2008): 69–71; Afiya Shehrbano Zia, "Faith-Based Politics, Enlightened Moderation and the Pakistani Women's Movement," *Journal of International Women's Studies* 11, no. 1 (2009): 225–245.
44. Rachel Rinaldo, "Pious and Critical: Muslim Women Activists and the Question of Agency," *Gender and Society* 28, no. 6 (2014): 824–846.

Bibliography

Abou Zahab, Mariam. "Shi'i Women's Madrasas and New Transnational Networks." In *The Madrasa in Asia: Political Activism and Transnational Linkages*, edited by Farish A. Noor, Yoginder Sikand, and Martin van Bruinessen, 123–140. Amsterdam: Amsterdam University Press, 2008.

Ahmad, Irfan. "Cracks in the 'Mightiest Fortress': Jamaat-e-Islami's Changing Discourse on Women." *Modern Asian Studies* 42, nos. 2–3 (March 2008): 549–575.

Ahmad, Irfan. "Islam and Politics in South Asia." In *The Oxford Handbook of Islam and Politics*, edited by John L. Esposito and Emad El-Din Shahin, 324–339. Oxford: Oxford University Press, 2013

Ahmad, Sadaf. "Al-Huda and Women's Religious Authority in Urban Pakistan." *Muslim World* 103, no. 3 (July 2013): 363–374.

Ahmad, Sadaf. *Transforming Faith: The Story of Al-Huda and Islamic Revivalism among Urban Pakistani Women*. Syracuse, NY: Syracuse University Press, 2009.

Begum, Momotaj. "Negotiation for Extended Gender Roles in Islam: Women in Tablighi Jamaat in Bangladesh." PhD diss., Hiroshima University, 2015.

Frisk, Sylva. *Submitting to God: Women and Islam in Urban Malaysia*. Seattle: University of Washington Press, 2009.

Haniffa, Farzana. "Piety as Politics amongst Muslim Women in Contemporary Sri Lanka." *Modern Asian Studies* 42, nos. 2–3 (March 2008): 347–375.

Huq, Maimuna. "The Politics of Belief: Women's Islamic Activism in Bangladesh." PhD diss., Columbia University, 2006.

Huq, Maimuna. "Reading the Qur'an in Bangladesh: The Politics of 'Belief' among Islamist Women." *Modern Asian Studies* 42, nos. 2–3 (March 2008): 457–488.

Huq, Samia. "Religious Learning Circles and Da`wa: The Modalities of Educated Bangladeshi Women Preaching Islam." In *Proselytizing and the Limits of Religious Pluralism in Contemporary Asia*, edited by Juliana Finucane and R. Michael Feener, 81–102. Singapore: Springer, 2014.

Huq, Samia. "Women's Religious Discussion Circles in Urban Bangladesh: Enacting, Negotiating and Contesting Piety." PhD diss., Brandeis University, 2011.

Huq, Samia, and Sabina Faiz Rashid. "Refashioning Islam: Elite Women and Piety in Bangladesh." *Contemporary Islam* 2, no. 1 (March 2008): 7–22.

Jamal, Amina. *Jamaat-e-Islami Women in Pakistan: Vanguard of a New Modernity?* Syracuse, NY: Syracuse University Press, 2013.

Kuiper, Matthew J. *Da'wa and Other Religions: Indian Muslims and the Modern Resurgence of Global Islamic Activism*. London: Routledge, 2017.

Laird, Kathleen Fenner. "Whose Islam? Pakistani Women's Political Action Groups Speak Out." PhD diss., Washington University, 2007.

Manchanda, Rita. "Guns and Burqa: Women in the Kashmiri Conflict." In *Women, War and Peace in South Asia: Beyond Victimhood to Agency*, edited by Rita Manchanda, 42–101. New Delhi: Sage, 2001.

Mahmood, Saba. *Politics of Piety: The Islamic Revival and the Feminist Subject*. Princeton, NJ: Princeton University Press, 2005.

Masud, Muhammad Khalid. "The Growth and Development of the Tablighi Jamaat in India." In *Travellers in Faith: Studies of the Tablīghī Jamā'at as a Transnational Islamic Movement for Faith Renewal*, edited by Muhammad Khalid Masud, 3–43. Leiden: Brill, 2000.

Metcalf, Barbara D. "Living Hadith in the Tablighi Jama`at." *Journal of Asian Studies* 52, no. 3 (1993): 584–608.
Metcalf, Barbara D. "Tablighi Jamaat and Women." In *Travellers in Faith: Studies of the Tablīghī Jamā'at as a Transnational Islamic Movement for Faith Renewal*, edited by Muhammad Khalid Masud, 44–58. Leiden: Brill, 2000.
Mumtaz, Khawar. "Identity Politics and Women: 'Fundamentalism' and Women in Pakistan." In *Identity Politics and Women: Cultural Reassertions and Feminisms in International Perspective*, edited by Valentine M. Moghadam, 228–242. Boulder, CO: Westview, 1994.
Mumtaz, Khawar, and Farida Shaheed. *Women of Pakistan: Two Steps Forward, One Step Back*. London: Zed Books, 1987.
Murshid, Navine. "The Genocide of 1971 and the Politics of Justice." In *Routledge Handbook of Contemporary Bangladesh*, edited by Ali Riaz and Mohammad Sajjadur Rahman, 52–62. New York: Routledge, 2016.
Mushtaq, Faiza. "A Controversial Role Model for Pakistani Women." *South Asia Multidisciplinary Academic Journal* 4 (December 2010). https://journals.openedition.org/samaj/3030.
Nasr, Seyyed Vali Reza. *The Vanguard of the Islamic Revolution: The Jamaat-i Islami of Pakistan*. Berkeley: University of California Press, 1994.
Parashar, Swati. "Gender, Jihad, and Jingoism: Women as Perpetrators, Planners, and Patrons of Militancy in Kashmir." *Studies in Conflict and Terrorism* 34, no. 4 (2011): 295–317.
Parashar, Swati. "The Sacred and the Sacrilegious: Exploring Women's 'Politics' and 'Agency' in Radical Religious Movements in South Asia." *Totalitarian Movements and Political Religions* 11, nos. 3–4 (2010): 435–455.
Rinaldo, Rachel. "Pious and Critical: Muslim Women Activists and the Question of Agency." *Gender and Society* 28, no. 6 (2014): 824–846.
Sanyal, Usha. "Al-Huda International: How Muslim Women Empower Themselves through Online Study of the Qur'an." *Hawwa* 13, no. 3 (October 2015): 440–460.
Schneider, Nadja-Christina. "Islamic Feminism and Muslim Women's Rights Activism in India: From Transnational Discourse to Local Movement—or Vice Versa?" *Journal of International Women's Studies* 11, no. 1 (2009): 56–71.
Shehabuddin, Elora. "Beware the Bed of Fire: Gender, Democracy, and the Jama'at-i Islami in Bangladesh." *Journal of Women's History* 10, no. 4 (1999): 148–171.
Shehabuddin, Elora. "Jamaat-i-Islami in Bangladesh: Women, Democracy and the Transformation of Islamist Politics." *Modern Asian Studies* 42, no. 2/3 (2008): 577–603.
Shehabuddin, Elora. *Reshaping the Holy: Democracy, Development, and Muslim Women in Bangladesh*. New York: Columbia University Press, 2008.
Shehabuddin, Sarah Tasnim. "Bangladeshi Politics Since Independence." In *Routledge Handbook of Contemporary Bangladesh*, edited by Ali Riaz and Mohammad Sajjadur Rahman, 17–27. New York: Routledge, 2016.
Siddiqi, Bulbul. "Reconfiguring the Gender Relation: The Case of the Tablighi Jamaat in Bangladesh." *Culture and Religion* 13, no. 2 (June 2012): 177–192.
Siddiqui, Niloufer. "Gender Ideology and the Jamaat-e-Islami." *Current Trends in Islamist Ideology* 10 (July–September 2010). https://www.hudson.org/research/9797-gender-ideology-and-the-jamaat-e-islami.
Sikand, Yoginder S. "Women and the Tablighi Jamaat." *Islam and Christian-Muslim Relations* 10, no. 1 (March 1999): 41–52.

Vatuk, Sylvia. "Islamic Feminism in India: Indian Muslim Women Activists and the Reform of Muslim Personal Law." *Modern Asian Studies* 42, nos. 2–3 (March 2008): 489–518.
Weiss, Anita M. *Interpreting Islam, Modernity, and Women's Rights in Pakistan*. New York: Palgrave Macmillan, 2014.
White, Sarah C. "Domains of Contestation: Women's Empowerment and Islam in Bangladesh." *Women's Studies International Forum* 33, no. 4 (July 2010): 334–344.
Zaman, Meryem Fatima. "Religious Practices: Preaching and Women Preachers: Pakistan." In *Encyclopedia of Women and Islamic Cultures*, edited by Suad Joseph. Leiden: Brill, 2016. http://www.brillonline.nl/browse/encyclopedia-of-women-and-islamic-cultures.
Zaman, Meryem Fatima. "The Semiotics of Revivalist Islam: Women, Space, and Stories in Pakistan's Islamic Movements." PhD diss., Michigan State University, 2014.
Zia, Afiya Shehrbano. "Faith-Based Politics, Enlightened Moderation and the Pakistani Women's Movement." *Journal of International Women's Studies* 11, no. 1 (November 2009): 225–245.
Zia, Afiya Shehrbano. "A State of Suspended Disbelief." *Economic and Political Weekly* 43, no. 23 (2008): 69–71.

CHAPTER 23

WOMEN'S RELIGIOUS AND SOCIAL ACTIVISM IN SOUTHEAST ASIA

NELLY VAN DOORN-HARDER

Introduction

The largest Muslim community in the world lives in Southeast Asia. With around 240 million, Muslims make up about 42 percent of the total population of Southeast Asia. Indonesia, Malaysia, and Brunei are Muslim-majority countries, while there are Muslim minorities in Thailand, the Philippines, Singapore, Myanmar, Laos, Cambodia, and Vietnam.[1] Since the 1980s, many of these countries have witnessed a strengthening of Islamic influences and the rise of so-called *dakwah* or missionary movements that brought increased funding for religious schools and other Islamic institutions with money from oil-rich countries, such as Kuwait and Saudi Arabia.[2] Muslim guestworkers from the Philippines and Indonesia who work in the Gulf countries, have also contributed to increased visibility of Middle Eastern influences, among others, in the material culture.[3]

Certain historical moments generated new forms of feminist activism. In Indonesia, the fall of Present Suharto (1967–1998) generated the so-called era of *Reformasi*. In the same year, the firing of Anwar Ibrahim, the deputy prime minister of Malaysia, created the post-*Reformasi* state. The ensuing political ruptures allowed for radical-minded Muslim groups to add their voices to the debates about the place of Islam in society and resulted in increased demands for nationwide application of *Sharīʿa* laws. As these laws affected women's role and status, Muslim activists for women's rights had to adapt their agendas and strategies. As for the Philippines, activism was influenced by women's engagement in the aftermath of the recurring war between the State and the Moro National Liberation Front that strives for an independent Muslim region in the south.[4]

Across the region, women are active and present in the workplace, as well as in public life in general. Especially in Indonesia, and to a certain extent in Malaysia, women have gained access to religious education and now serve as religious scholars and leaders. Although the issues that are at stake differ depending on the local situations, Muslims advocating for gender and women's rights from Indonesia and Malaysia lead the debates and activities concerning the inequality of women based on interpretations of religious precepts. The rise of radical Muslim movements, especially in Malaysia and Indonesia, has created new challenges to their agendas with a renewed focus on issues related to violence against women, polygyny, child marriage, and, especially in Malaysia, Hudud laws, among others. Other areas of concern these advocates deal with include human trafficking, the rights of women guestworkers, political violence, and economic and environmental challenges.

Muslim Women's Text-Based Activism and Universal Human Rights

Muslim women's activism in Indonesia and Malaysia emerged in specific social, political, and economic contexts. These women activists belong to groups that represent a wide spectrum of Islamic interpretations with varying ideas about hotly debated issues, such as marital rape, polygyny, and child marriage. Some advocate for the application of *Sharīʿa* law, while others fight against it. Many Muslim women organizations do not strive for a level of gender equity but prefer forms of complementarity. This chapter discusses activism that looks at the rights of Muslim women through the lens of universal human rights. What connects these groups is that they propose "critical re-examination and reinterpretation of Islamic texts so that an Islamic tradition advocating women's rights, human rights, democracy, and modernity can be invoked."[5] In their view, the interpretation of religious texts and the process of codification of laws have been dominated by male jurists and scholars.[6] Central to the methodologies of Islamic feminists is the exercise of *ijtihād* (independent reasoning) when reading and interpreting religious texts.[7] This method offers Muslim women in Indonesia and Malaysia "strategic access to participate in religious discourse."[8] Participation is not just academic, however; in many cases activists seek to change national laws, mostly where it concerns personal status laws, in order to strengthen the rights of women and children. Furthermore, women-centered interpretations of religious texts aim to participate in the construction of Islamic jurisprudence (*fiqh*), the body of legal literature that is based on certain readings of the Qur'ān and the *ḥadīth* and transmits specific rules concerning women's rights and duties.

The Role of Nongovernmental and Islamic Organizations

Many Islamic activists work in religious nongovernmental organizations (NGOs). Aihwa Ong considers these NGOs as

> key agents that translate human rights principles into ethical gender regimes that are acceptable in local contexts, the activities of NGOs—religious, feminist, political, humanitarian, and economic—expand civil society in Southeast Asia, bringing about new values of human justice and good in society around which gender issues crystallize.[9]

In this context, activists stress that, in order to advocate reforms and change of laws, it is vital to foster mutual cooperation not just between groups but also between NGOs and Muslim intellectuals and scholars. Furthermore, women need to be "actively engaged with the project of interpretation of texts and laws."[10]

Large religious or political movements often have branches for women that can take on the character of an NGO. For example, the Indonesian organizations of Muhammadiyah and Nahdlatul Ulama operate as *organisasi masa* or Ormas, referring to organizations that work at the grassroots levels. To focus on certain issues or problems, these organizations have also set up their own NGOs. This synergy between Ormas and NGOs produces different forms of national and international cooperation.

Seeing the need to articulate women's agency and feminist solidarity as interconnected across national borders and cultures,[11] international cooperation between activist groups increased around the end of the twentieth century when NGOs, such as the Malaysian Sisters in Islam (SIS)[12] joined meetings organized by Indonesian activists. These forms of collaboration laid the foundation for international platforms, such as the online platform of Musawah[13] that was launched in Malaysia in 2009, and the first international congress of women Muslim scholars or ulama, called KUPI (Kongres Ulama Perempuan Indonesia) held in May 2017 in an Indonesian pesantren or Islamic boarding school.

Indonesia

In Indonesia, activism for Muslim women's rights, strictly speaking, started to develop during the first decades of the twentieth century, when it acquired several unique traits that continue to influence these movements today. During the late nineteenth and early twentieth centuries, pioneering women, such as the famous Raden Adjeng Kartini (1879–1905) and Rahmah El-Joenesijjah (1900–1969), promoted education for girls to advance their social and economic position. Women affiliated with the Muhammadiyah (founded in 1912) and Nahdlatul Ulama (NU, founded in 1926), organized their own groupings. The first was Muhammadiyah-related 'Aisyiyah (founded in 1917), followed by the Muslimat NU (founded in 1946). While initially promoting arguments that sought to increase respect for women based on biological differences, activists mostly lobbied for access to education (religious and nonreligious), worship spaces for women, and the protection of women's rights within the family as wives, mothers, and daughters. As these organizations were founded when Indonesia was still under Dutch colonial influence, promoting the education of women also took on a nationalist character in service of building a strong and independent Indonesian nation.

'Aisyiyah focused on creating a network of educational institutions for girls. While offering mixed curricula of religious and nonreligious subjects, these schools became part of the foundations for the current cohorts of female specialists of Islam. By the 1980s, increasing numbers of women started to study at the network of NU pesantren, where they engaged in deep studies of the Qur'ān, *ḥadīth*, *fiqh*, and their interpretations. Upon graduating, many continued to obtain a degree in Islamic Studies at one of the many Islamic universities.

Concerning the contemporary expressions of Islamic activism and feminism, the 1995 Beijing Fourth World Conference on Women inspired a new generation of activists to translate the conference's recommendations into Islamic-based projects that strengthened women's basic rights, for example, where it concerned reproductive rights. As women pursued higher degrees in Islamic studies, especially in Indonesia, large Islamic universities launched Women's Studies Centers, where scholars studied the writings of Islamic feminist and human rights activists, such as amina wadud, Riffat Hassan, Ali Asghar Engineer, and Abdullahi Ahmed An-Na'im. By the early 1990s, these initiatives generated new forms of Islamic feminist activism both in Indonesia and Malaysia, which promoted gender equality not just based on their readings of the Qur'ān but also through referencing human rights discourses.[14] Indonesian Muslim feminists firmly believe that this type of feminism is compatible with Islam and must be reflected in everyday life.[15] The term Islamic feminism in this context covers a range of frames of reference and methodologies. However, those identifying with this movement are united in their support of reinterpreting the Qur'ān and deploying "the tenets of Islam as a discursive reference for promoting gender equality and for eliminating oppression."[16] While this movement includes women as well as men, some propose that the term "Islamic feminist" should not be used to refer to male proponents of gender justice; "Muslim feminists" should be used instead, due to the reality that men do not experience what women do.[17]

Advocacy for the rights of women started during the 1980s, when NU activists (in cooperation with intellectuals from other Islamic organizations) launched NGOs, such as LP3ES (Institute for Economic and Social Research, Education, and Information), led by M. Dawam Rahardjo, and LSP (Institute for Development Studies). NU or Ormas's involvement within the NGO world took off toward the middle of the decade, when National NU Chair Abdurrahman Wahid (1984–1999), who later briefly served as Indonesia's president (1999–2001), spearheaded several community development projects that focused on educating pesantren leaders and students in order to transform the traditional educational models and train leaders who could be instrumental in social change.[18] One such project was Lakpesdam (Institute for Research and Development of Human Resources), which was tasked with creating developmental and educational activities tailored to parts of society where NU was strongly represented.[19]

In this context, a special NU initiative called P3M, Association for the Development of Pesantren and Society (Perhimpunan Pengembangan Pesantren dan Masyarakat, 1983), worked on creating awareness about issues such as Islam and democracy, women's reproductive rights, and gender awareness among teachers and students in the pesantren. For the NU, these schools provide a rigorous spiritual, religious, and secular formation that traditionally has been the backbone of strong NU leadership.[20] One of P3M's leading representatives, Muslim feminist Lies Marcoes-Natsir, led P3M's program on women's reproductive rights. In 2005, she went on to create the influential NU-related NGO called Rumah Kitab (Rumah Kita Bersama, meaning "our common home")[21] that has as its goal the transformation of Indonesia's Muslim society by addressing paradigms, moral and ethical norms, values, and teachings that have shaped current ways of thinking.[22]

During the 1990s, alumni from earlier projects launched several agencies focusing solely on women's issues. For example, Rifka Annisa (1993) was set up to assist victims of domestic violence.[23] Over the years, this NGO expanded its services to include the male perpetrators.[24] To cooperate closely with religious leaders, teachers, and government officials, former P3M activists established Rahima, the Center for Education and Information on Islam and Women's Rights Issues (2000). Rahima also became one of the international partners of the Sisters in Islam (SIS).[25] Around the same time (2000), two NGOs were launched that focused solely on the pesantren world. Puan Amal Hayati (established under the patronage of Abdurrahman Wahid's wife Sinta Nuriyah), sought to empower women students and teachers at the pesantren. In 2001, prominent religious leader and feminist, Kiai Husein Muhammad, set up the Fahmina project at his pesantren in Cirebon to empower women in the pesantren environment.[26]

Different religious leaders support these programs that each have their own priorities, structure, and constituencies. Many of them emerged from the NU educational networks; a fewer number are associated with organizations such as the Muhammadiyah, although individual Muhammadiyah members are active in several NGOs. If we look at the names of board and founding members of the different initiatives, we see several recurring, for example, those of Dawam Rahardjo, Kiai Husein Muhammad, and Sinta Nuriyah. They connect the large and complex organizations with their sprawling, nationwide programs to the NGOs. Sometimes the two types overlap. For example, the Fatayat NU, the NU branch for younger women, became a type of NGO by focusing on issues of women's rights and health.[27] They also started to teach about issues of gender and feminism as conceptual tools for women to understand their circumstances.[28] Quite a few active Fatayat members were previously or concurrently involved in Rahima, Lakpesdam, or other NGOs; Fatayat provided one of the main platforms through which Muslim feminist ideas could percolate down to the grassroots level.

Reinterpretation of the Qur'ān and *ḥadīth*, paired with analysis of the commentary literature and jurisprudence derived from these texts that affect women's lives resulted in numerous publications, most of them in Indonesian. Among others, the Fatayat have dealt with issues related to *fiqh* and abortion,[29] Fahmina has developed juridical interpretations to stop human trafficking,[30] and Rumah Kitab has published several books about child marriage.[31] These works are widely disseminated via discussions with advanced students at the pesantren, workshops for religious leaders, and teachers, and groups of women who lead Qur'an study circles for women (*pengajian*).

Several feminist activists went on to earn PhD degrees at Indonesian and international universities. Siti Musdah Mulia was the first Islamic feminist to earn a PhD at an Indonesian Islamic State University (1997). In 2001, the Indonesian government launched the National Action Plan to combat violence against women, and created a committee to review the marriage section of the Islamic legal Code (1974) with Siti Musdah Mulia as Chair. The current Legal Code is highly gender-biased, defining the role of the husband as "the head of the family' and that of the wife as "homemaker."[32] Under Mulia's guidance, the committee designed a Counter Legal Draft (2004), based on the principle that women are full equals within marriage, and prohibiting child marriage and polygyny.[33] According to committee member Husein Muhammad, a prominent Muslim leader and feminist, the Counter Legal Draft was one of the greatest contributions to the development of the feminist movement in Indonesia.[34] One of Siti Musdah Mulia's latest works, called *Ensiklopedia Muslimah Reformis: Pokok-pokok Pemikiran Untuk Reinterpretasi dan Aksi* (The Reformist Muslim Woman's Encyclopedia: Essential Ideas for Reinterpretation and Action), provides legal, theoretical, and religious foundations for Islamic feminism. In seventeen entries, totaling 865 pages, Mulia covers topics such as gender equality, education, justice, and religious pluralism, explaining how a Muslim feminist activist can combine faith and spirituality with activism.[35]

Other feminist scholars include Nina Nurmila, who published an in-depth study about Qur'ānic hermeneutics and the practice of polygyny,[36] and Eva Nisa, who has published widely on a range of topics concerning the status of women in Islam.[37] In fact, the movement of Islamic feminism is so well established in Indonesia that Indonesian feminist scholar Etin Anwar could frame and analyze it in her groundbreaking 2018 study *A Genealogy of Islamic Feminism: Pattern and Change in Indonesia*.[38]

A unique aspect of activism for women's rights is that it intersects with national governmental goals on crucial topics. KOMNAS Perempuan, referring to the Komisi Nasional Anti Kekerasan terhadap Perempuan (The National Commission against Violence against Women) is an example of such cooperation.[39] It is government-sponsored and was launched in 1998 after the collapse of the oppressive Suharto regime (1966–1998). Its mandate is to report gender-based human rights abuses and create awareness among the Indonesian public. Komnas Perempuan is a multilevel organization; its partners (called *mitra*) operate on the national, provincial, county, and local levels that represent a large spectrum of organizations advocating and protecting women's rights. Several of its commissioners have been and still are active in, for example, the Fatayat NU, 'Aisyiyah, and Fahmina. Its agenda emerges from the activities of the Ormas and NGOs and it supports, for example, antipolygyny and anti-child-marriage initiatives. In 2019, Komnas Perempuan's activities resulted in changing the minimum marriage age in the Marriage Law to nineteen years for women and men.[40]

Malaysia

Muslims make up 60 percent of the Malaysian population; since gaining independence from British colonial rule in 1957, Malay ethnicity is conflated with being Muslim and Islam is the official religion. The activities of Muslim feminists often focus on the judiciary that, based on the colonial system, is divided into secular courts that address civil and criminal law, and Islamic *Sharīʿa* courts, which deal with family matters. Secular laws and religious laws often intersect, and divisions between the two are unclear, particularly in cases involving gender and non-Muslims.[41] Through the Department of the Advancement of Islam (JAKIM), the State drafts legislation pertaining to Islam. However, each state has discretionary power to apply Islamic family law according to its own *Sharīʿa*-based personal status codes that cover matters of marriage, divorce, and inheritance.[42]

Women's activism started with initiatives to combat illiteracy among women. One of the first organizations was the Malay Women Teachers' Union (Johor, 1929), followed by a similar union founded in Malacca in 1938. Like developments in Indonesia, organizations, such as the United Malays National Organization (UMNO, 1949), created branches for women that focused on resisting the colonial powers and advancing women's literacy.[43]

While we find numerous NGOs and Islamic activist groups in Indonesia, the most prominent one in Malaysia is Sisters in Islam (SIS). This organization emerged from the local movements resisting global trends of revivalist Islam that gained strength during the 1970s and used women's agency as the benchmark for a strong Malay-Muslim identity.[44] By the late 1980s, these groups realized the importance of engaging with Islam. International networks, such as Women Living under Muslim Laws (WLUML), inspired Malaysian feminists to engage more deeply with Islamic law.[45] When the Islamic Family Law was introduced in 1984, the Joint Action Group against Violence against Women (JAG) was formed to make domestic violence a crime.[46] With each amendment of this law, which had started out as "one of the most enlightened personal status laws in the Muslim world," their efforts intensified.[47] Changes in the law during the 1990s made it easier for men to divorce and marry more than one wife and reduced their financial responsibilities toward women.

Another impulse to create SIS in the late 1980s came when professional women (lawyers, journalists, scholars) working in the *Sharīʿa* subcommittee of the Association of Women Lawyers (AWL), started to investigate cases of discrimination and injustice women experienced under the Islamic family law. When addressing court cases about custody, polygyny, and domestic violence, they faced a legal system based on the premise that men were superior to women.[48] Eight activists consisting of five Malays, an American, an Australian, and a Singaporean launched SIS, and the organization was officially registered in 1993. One of their main concerns was and remains discrimination against women under the application of *Sharīʿa* laws, with a focus on cases regulated by the Islamic Family law. Their founding principle was based on the notion of *muhibah* ("goodwill"); they pledged to work toward a Malay society that respects social and religious differences and in which the entire country benefits from gender justice.[49] One of the founding members was amina wadud, who taught Qur'ānic Studies at the Islamic University in Kuala Lumpur (1989–1992). Under her guidance, the early SIS members studied the Qur'ān, with a curriculum based on wadud's doctoral dissertation on reading the Qur'ān from a woman's perspective.[50]

SIS's main mission is to promote the principles of gender equality, justice, freedom, and dignity in Islam and empower women to be advocates for change. Its goal is to educate the public and create networks of likeminded groups and individuals. Its strategy is based on "faith-centered intellectual activism" that engages sources of the Islamic tradition.[51] Starting as a research and advocacy group, it focused on legal and policy matters concerning the rights of Muslim women via reinterpretations of the Qur'an, scrutiny of national law and policies, and support for international human rights principles. SIS advocacy has consisted of presenting letters and legal policy briefs to the government and submitting letters to the editors of journals and newspapers.[52] In 1990, this strategy brought them into the national discussion on the contentious topic of polygyny with a letter to the press, titled "Polygamy Is Not a Right in Islam."[53] In 2003, SIS became the secretariat for the Coalition for Women's Rights in Islam," an entity representing eleven women's rights groups.[54]

The networks SIS works with have initiated several media campaigns against polygamy with names such as: "Monogami, Pilihanku" (Monogamy, My Choice) aimed at educating women about their marital rights. Other campaigns that elicited much criticism from traditional Muslim leaders concerned domestic violence and the issue of marital rape. One of the concerns found in Malaysia that does not play a significant role in Indonesia, is the application of the so-called hudud laws in some states, such as Kelantan, where in 1990, the Islamist Pan-Malaysian Islamic Party (PAS) gained the majority vote. For example, the Kelantan Shari'ah Code (II, 1993), prescribes harsh punishments for six types of *hudud* offenses: *sariqah* (theft), *hirabah* (highway robbery), *zina* (adultery or sexual intercourse between a man and a woman who are not married), *qazaf* (improper accusation of *zina*), *syurb* (alcohol consumption), and *riddah* (apostasy). SIS was especially concerned with the *zina* matters, since the laws do not differentiate between adultery and rape. In case of pregnancy out of wedlock, a woman will be accused of committing *zina*, unless she can prove that she was raped.[55]

In order to build its cases, SIS cooperates closely with scholars specializing in matters of the *Sharīʿa*, such as Muhammad Khalid Masud and Mohammad Hashim Kamali.[56]

Apart from op-eds and letters to the press, SIS focuses on educating the public by publishing pamphlets, booklets, and books on topics such as domestic violence, wife beating, and gender equality.[57] Based on their readings of the Qur'ān, the women present their arguments, such as "The Qur'ān stresses love, kindness and justice in family relationships and prohibits cruelty of all kinds."[58] The organization furthermore initiates research projects that provide close studies of issues, such as religious fundamentalism and polygamy.[59]

Philippines

Around 5 percent of the Philippine population (around 107 million) is Muslim. The rest of the country is predominantly Christian. Filipino Muslim women's engagement was deeply influenced by a decades-long war between the military and the Moro National Liberation Front (MNLF) that aimed at establishing an Islamic state in the southern Philippines.[60] After several peace agreements (1996, 2006), Muslims live in a situation called "no war, no peace." At the same time, women's access to education and technology increased and NGOs designed to help women and children overcome the effects of the war started to appear. Among others, they focused on issues such as illiteracy and income-generation projects. At that time, campaigns for women's rights also started to increase.[61] One of the characteristics of Muslim women's activism is that it is connected to the traditional elites of the sultanate system that prioritizes male decision-making and forces women to operate within unofficial spaces and negotiate a "culture of patronage and the clan system that reinforce Islam and partisan politics."[62]

By the 2000s, NGOs dedicated to the study of Islam emerged. For example, the Philippine Center for Islam and Democracy (PCID) organized seminars and workshops promoting peace, democracy, and Islamic development, with Amina Rasul Bernardo becoming a prominent activist for women's rights.[63] The Philippines was among the first ASEAN countries to adopt CEDAW (1981) and participate in the Beijing Women's conference in 1995. The adoption of CEDAW led to the establishment of programs on gender equity and justice; one of the main legal instruments that emerged from this was the Philippine Plan for Gender-Responsive Development (1995–2025) that led to the creation of several initiatives.[64] Among others, in 1997, Yasmin Busran-Lao cofounded the Al-Mujadilah Development Foundation (AMDF) that aims at empowering women. Their vision is to create an Islamized society, based on the concept of *tawhid* (oneness of God), in which men and women serve as moral agents working toward enduring peace (*sakina*) and human development. This concept aligns with Muslim feminists worldwide who consider the responsibility of *khilafah*, or human vicegerency, to rest on men and women alike.[65] In order to educate Muslim Filipinos about the rights and duties of Muslim women, in 2005 they initiated a project to translate abstracts from the Code of Muslim Personal Laws (CMPL) that is enforced by Sharī'a courts. One of the problems with this law was that it included regulations that weakened women's position when compared to traditional (*adat*) rules.[66]

To address matters arising from the CMPL and to be connected with similar initiatives, the organization joined a confederation called *Nisa ul Haqq fi Bangsamoro* (Women for Truth and Justice in Bangsamoro), which is part of the Musawah network. Seeking to discourage, if possible forbid, the practice of polygamy, this association drafted amendments to the CMPL, organized workshops promoting CEDAW and the understanding of the CMPL.[67] Furthermore, they advocated against early and forced marriage.[68] Activist Busran-Lao supported the passage of the reproductive health bill as a measure to educate women on their reproductive rights.

The number of women who master Islamic sources is increasing. Some even studied at the famed al-Azhar university in Cairo. Women scholars of Islam are engaged in dakwah activities, especially aimed at creating awareness about Islamic teachings among Muslims. To host Muslim women scholars of Islam, Amina Rasul Bernardo's PCID created the Nur al Salam organization that advocates for issues on peace, health, and interreligious engagement.[69]

International Cooperation: Musawah and KUPI

Musawah (meaning "equality") is a transnational initiative launched and coordinated by SIS with the goal of realizing equality between women and men by reforming the Muslim family laws. It was founded during a 2009 international meeting in Kuala Lumpur. Its network consists of scholars, activists, lawyers and policymakers in forty-seven countries who cooperate to realize the Musawah framework of action, which holds "the principles of Islam to be a source of justice, equality, fairness and dignity for all human beings."[70] And that equality and justice within the family and family laws and practices are necessary and possible in Muslim countries and communities. While its agenda is large and ambitious, the organization's focus on issues related to child marriage, polygyny, and male guardianship (*qiwāma* and *wilāya*) intersects with Malaysian and Indonesian feminist priorities.[71]

To counter the practice of child marriage, Komnas Perempuan and Rumah Kitab decided to highlight the role of the girl's *wali* or guardian. Basically, marriage is a contract where the woman's *wali* transfers her to the protection of the husband. Rumah Kitab addressed this reality of inequality by studying the various parts of the Islamic family law, looking at issues such as lineage, sustenance, dowry, the head of the family, polygyny, the *mahram* (a woman's male companion when she has to leave the house), and the unequal valuation of male and female lives. While rereading religious texts and pairing them with international human rights values, Rumah Kitab also appealed to the Indonesian legal establishment. One of the main arguments advanced was that women and men are equal at the spiritual level and have similar rights and obligations.[72]

Research done by organizations such as Musawah, Rumah Kitab, Komnas Perempuan, and Fahmina, provided the foundational arguments against the practice of child marriage brought forward during the 2017 KUPI congress.[73] This congress, held at the campus of Kiai Hussein Mohammed's pesantren in Cirebon, was historic and groundbreaking: the majority of over five hundred feminists, male and female, were women authorities of Islam or ulama. According to one of the main organizers, Dr. Nur Rofiah, it was "a universal declaration of equality, a manifesto that women have the same spiritual and mental potentials as men."[74] Over the course of three days, the participants discussed the Islamic teachings influencing Islamic extremism, violence against women, and environmental problems. The main goal was to "build long-term perspectives on women's rights that are currently being ignored.[75] To conclude the Congress, the women jointly issued several statements, or recommendations, that equaled the religiolegal status of a fatwa. One of them was a decision to work toward total banning of child marriage.

Conclusion

In Indonesia, Malaysia, and the Philippines in particular, vibrant groups advocating for the rights of Muslim women are creating new models and repertoires of Muslim feminism. While facing different agendas in their respective countries, they not only propose new interpretations of the holy texts governing the rights and duties of women but also translate their new findings into social, cultural, legal, and political agendas. While focusing on the plight of women, in fact, they contribute to changing the face of Islam itself.

One of the more recent developments is that while addressing wide ranging agendas at home, they seek to connect globally with like-minded groups advocating overlapping issues. While legal systems differ, they are increasingly connected in their efforts to address abuses arising from applications of the Islamic family law they consider to be restrictive or harmful to women. Especially with increased opportunities to connect virtually, interconnectivity is growing and is bound to lead to unexpected changes that can affect Muslim-majority countries across the globe. While facing strong forces of resistance, locally and globally, emboldened by a register of activist and interpretive agendas, their religious advice no longer remains confined to informal platforms, such as women's Qur'an study groups and other gatherings. It is now reaching wider audiences. As a result, their activist interventions in traditional religious practices and interpretations can no longer be ignored, as slowly but steadily, they are making inroads into public conversations within their respective countries.

Notes

1. Imtiyaz Yusuf, "The Middle East and Muslim Southeast Asia: Implications of the Arab Spring," Oxford Islamic Studies Online, accessed July 20, 2020, http://www.oxfordislamicstudies.com/Public/focus/essay1009_southeast_asia.html. For information about the individual countries, also see: Greg Fealy and Virginia Hooker, *Voices of Islam in Southeast Asia: A Contemporary Sourcebook* (Singapore: Institute of Southeast Asian Studies, 2006), 19–90.
2. "Dakwah" is a term used in Malaysia and Indonesia. It refers to missionary work, and proselytization activities aimed at Islamizing society through the national application of Islamic laws and values. The term also is related to the political Islamist movement that emerged in the 1970s and seeks to strengthen Islamic influence in social, economic, and spiritual life. For further information, see: "Dakwah (Malaysia)," Oxford Islamic Studies Online, accessed January 27, 2021, http://www.oxfordislamicstudies.com/article/opr/t125/e480.
3. Vivienne S. M. Angeles, "Constructing Identity: Visual Expressions of Islam in the Predominantly Catholic Philippines," in *Identity in Crossroad Civilizations: Ethnicity, Nationalism, and Globalism in Asia*, ed. E. Kolig, V. S. Angeles, and S. Wong (Amsterdam: Amsterdam University Press, 2009), 159–177.
4. For the role of women in the conflict between the State and the MNLF, see: Vivienne S. M. Angeles, "Women and Revolution: Philippine Muslim Women's Participation in the Moro National Liberation Front," *Muslim World* 86, no. 2 (1996): 130–147.
5. Zainah Anwar, "What Islam? Whose Islam? Sisters in Islam and the Struggle for Women's Rights," in *The Politics of Multiculturalism: Pluralism and Citizenship in Malaysia, Singapore, and Indonesia*, ed. Robert W. Hefner (Honolulu: University of Hawaii Press, 2001), 228.
6. Cecilia Ng, Maznah Mohamad, Tan Beng Hui, *Feminism and the Women's Movement in Malaysia* (London: Routledge, 2006), 98.
7. Yasmin Moll, "Islamic Feminism between Interpretive Freedom and Legal Codification: The Case of Sisters in Islam in Malaysia," in *Contesting Feminisms: Gender and Islam in Asia*, ed. Huma Ahmed-Ghosh (New York: SUNY Press, 2015), 163.
8. Azza Basarudin, "In Search of Faithful Citizens in Postcolonial Malaysia: Islamic Ethics, Muslim Activism, and Feminist Politics," in *Women and Islam*, ed. Zayn R. Kassam (Oxford: Praeger, 2010), 117.
9. Aihwa Ong, "Translating Gender Justice in Southeast Asia: Situated Ethics, NGOs, and Bio-Welfare," *Journal of Women of the Middle East and the Islamic World* 9 (2011): 45.
10. Norani Othman, "Muslim Women and the Challenge of Islamic Fundamentalism/Extremism: An Overview of Southeast Asian Muslim Women's Struggle for Human Rights and Gender Equality," *Women's Studies International Forum* 29 (2006): 339.
11. See Chandra Mohanty, *Feminism without Borders: Decolonizing Theory, Practising Solidarity* (Durham, NC: Duke University Press, 2003).
12. "Homepage," Sisters in Islam, accessed May 2, 2021, https://sistersinislam.org/.
13. "Home," Musawah, accessed May 2, 2021, https://www.musawah.org/.
14. For a detailed study of the various movements in Indonesia, see Etin Anwar, *A Genealogy of Islamic Feminism: Pattern and Change in Indonesia* (Abingdon: Routledge, 2018).
15. Ibid., 188.
16. Ibid., 14.
17. Ibid., 15.

18. Pieternella van Doorn-Harder, *Women Shaping Islam: Reading the Qur'an in Indonesia* (Urbana: University of Illinois Press, 2006), 34, 189. Also see Martin van Bruinessen, "Overview of Muslim Organizations, Associations and Movements in Indonesia," in *Contemporary Developments in Indonesian Islam: Explaining the Conservative Turn*, ed. Martin van Bruinessen (Singapore: ISEAS, 2013), 45–49.
19. van Bruinessen, "Overview," 47; also see the Lakpesdam website: accessed May 24, 2021, http://www.lakpesdam.or.id/.
20. van Doorn-Harder, *Women Shaping Islam*, 189–202.
21. See the website "Rumah Kitab," accessed May 2, 2021, https://rumahkitab.com/en/.
22. For more details about the Rumah Kitab vision and goals, see the website of "Rumah Kitab."
23. "Rifka Annisa," accessed May 2, 2021, https://rifka-annisa.org/en/.
24. "Counseling for Men," Rifka Annisa, accessed May 2, 2021, https://rifka-annisa.org/en/services/counseling-for-men.
25. "About," Rahima, accessed May 2, 2021, https://swararahima.com/en/about-rahima/. As stakeholders the website mentions: *pesantren*, faith-based organizations, different levels of Islamic school, ranging from middle school to university, research centers, media outlets, governmental agencies, domestic and international donors, embassies, and the corporate world.
26. See website "Fahmina," accessed May 24, 2021, https://fahmina.or.id/.
27. For an analysis of the activism of the Fatayat NU, see chapters 1 and 3 in Rachel Rinaldo, *Mobilizing Piety. Islam and Feminism in Indonesia* (Oxford: Oxford University Press, 2013).
28. Anwar, *Genealogy*, 189.
29. Maria Ulfah Anshor, *Fikih Aborsi. Wacana Pengauatan Hak Reproduksi Perempuan* (Jakarta: Kompas, 2006).
30. Faqihuddin Abdul Kodir, Abd Moqsith Ghazali, Imam Nakha'I, K. H. Hussein Muhammad, and Marzuki Wahid, *Fiqh Anti-Trafficking. Jawaban atas Berbagai Kasus Kejahatan Perdagangan Manusia dalam Perspektif Hukum Islam* (Cirebon: Fahmina Institute, 2006).
31. Mukti Ali, Roland Gunawan, Jamaluddin Mohammad, and Ahmad Hilmi, *Aku, Kamu, End: Membaca ulang teks keagamaan kawin anak* (I, You, End: Rereading Religious Texts about Child Marriage) (Jakarta: Rumah Kitab, 2015); Mukti Ali, Roland Gunawan, Ahmad Hilmi, and Jamaluddin Mohammad, eds. *Fikh Kawin Anak: Mebaca Ulang Teks Keagamaan Perkawinan Usia Anak-Anak* (Jakarta: Rumah Kitab, 2015); and Roland Gunawan and Nur Hayati Aida, eds., *Fikih Perwalian, Membaca Ulang Hak Perwalian untuk Perlindungan Perempuan dari Kawin Paksa dan Kawin Anak* (Jakarta: Rumah Kitab, 2019).
32. Siti Musdah Mulia, "Toward a Just Marriage Law: Empowering Indonesian Women through a Counter Legal Draft to the Indonesian Compilation of Islamic Law," with Mark E. Cammack, in *Islamic Law in Contemporary Indonesia. Ideas and Institutions*, ed. R. Michael Feener and Mark E. Cammack (Cambridge, MA: Harvard University Press), 139.
33. Mulia, "Toward a Just Marriage Law," 140; Also see Musdah Mulia's Indonesian book about the Counter Legal Draft: *Posisi Perempuan Dalam Undang-Undang Perkawinan: Indonesia dan Kompilasi Hukum Islam* (The Position of Women in the Marriage Laws: Indonesia and the Compilation of Islamic Law) (Jakarta: LKAJ, Ministry for Religious Affairs, 2001).
34. Partogi, Sebastian, "Musdah Mulia: Injecting Spirituality into Human Rights Activism," *Jakarta Post*, February 18, 2021, accessed July 10, 2021, https://muslimahreformis.org/

beranda/post_profil_musdah/musdah-mulia-injecting-spirituality-into-human-rights-activism/.

35. Siti Musdah Mulia, *Ensiklopedia Muslimah Reformis: Pokok-pokok Pemikiran Untuk Reinterpretasi dan Aksi* (Jakarta: Mizan, 2020). In the following Youtube presentations, she explains the book's main tenets: "Review Buku Ensiklopedia Muslimah Reformis" https://www.youtube.com/watch?v=Z17RUPyzkck and Shahnaz Haque dkk dalam Bedah Buku Muslimah Reformis https://www.youtube.com/watch?v=WFb8W4cfj70 (accessed July 10, 2021).
36. Nina Nurmila, *Women, Islam and Everyday Life* (New York: Routledge, 2009).
37. For a list of publications, see "Dr. Eva Nisa," Australian National University, accessed May 2, 2021, https://researchers.anu.edu.au/researchers/nisa-e#related_websites.
38. Abingdon: Routledge, 2018.
39. See website of "Komnas Perempuan," accessed May 2, 2021, http://www.komnasperempuan.or.id/.
40. Adelia Putri, "Indonesian Court Says No to Raising Minimum Marrying Age for Girls," *Asia Pacific*, June 19, 2015, http://www.rappler.com/world/regions/asia-pacific/indonesia/96905-indonesian-court-rejects-judicial-review-marrying-age.
41. Azza Basarudin, *Humanizing the Sacred: Sisters in Islam and the Struggle for Gender Justice in Malaysia* (Seattle: University of Washington Press, 2016), 43–47, 50.
42. Judith Nagata, "Ethnonationalism vs. Religious Transnationalism: Nation-Building and Islam in Malaysia," *Muslim World* 17, no. 2 (2016): 129–150.
43. Meredith Weiss, "Malaysian NGOs. History, Legal Frameworks, and Characteristics," in *Social Movements in Malaysia: From Moral Communities to NGOs*, ed. Saliha Hassan and Meredith L. Weiss (London: Routledge, 2002), 28–29.
44. Ng, Mohamad, and Hui, *Feminism and the Women's Movement*, 23.
45. Ibid., 28.
46. Zainah Anwar, "Sisters in Islam and the Making of Musawah," in *Gender and Equality in Muslim Family Law*, ed. Ziba Mir-Hosseini, Kari Vogt, Lena Larsen, and Christian Moe (London: I. B. Tauris, 2013), 109.
47. Zainah Anwar, "Negotiating Gender Rights under Religious Law in Malaysia," in *New Directions in Islamic Thought: Exploring Reform and Muslim Tradition*, ed. Kari Vogt, Lena Larsen, and Christian Moe (New York: I. B. Tauris, 2009), 178.
48. Basarudin, "In Search of," 101.
49. Basarudin, *Humanizing the Sacred*, 99, 105.
50. Amina wadud, *Qur'an and Woman: Reading the Sacred Text from a Woman's Perspective* (Oxford: Oxford University Press, 1999).
51. Basarudin, "In Search of," 95.
52. See: Othman, "Muslim Women"; Basarudin, *Humanizing the Sacred*.
53. Basarudin, "In Search of," 107.
54. Basarudin, *Humanizing the Sacred*, 113.
55. Ibid., 123–124. The Arabic technical terms used here are rendered as they appear in the original Malay sources.
56. For example, see the position paper Mohammad Hashim Kamali, "Law, Morality and Religion: A Critique of the Syariah Criminal Offences (Federal Territories) Act 1997," Sisters in Islam, 2019, https://sistersinislam.org/position-papers/.
57. Basarudin, *Humanizing the Sacred*, 118–122. For all the available publications, see "Research Publications," Sisters in Islam, accessed May 24, 2021, https://sistersinislam.org/research-publications/.

58. Sisters in Islam, *Are Muslim Men Allowed to Beat Their Wives?* (Kuala Lumpur: SIS, 1991): 3–4.
59. Basarudin, *Humanizing the Sacred*, 115–116; and see "Our Work," Sisters in Islam, accessed May 24, 2021, https://sistersinislam.org/our-work/.
60. Angeles, "Women and Revolution," 130–147.
61. Vivienne S. M. Angeles, "From Secession to Social Activism: Muslim Women's Movements in the Philippines," in *Women and Asian Religions*, ed. Zayn R. Kassam (Santa Barbara, CA: Praeger, 2017), 72–73.
62. Francisco L. Gonzales, "Sultans in a Violent Land," in *Rebels, Warlords and Ulama: A Reader on Muslim Separatism and the War in the Southern Philippines*, ed. Eric Gutierrez (Quezon City: Institute for Popular Democracy, 2017), 132.
63. Angeles, "From Secession," 78.
64. For more detailed information, see the UN website: https://asiapacific.unwomen.org/en/countries/philippines/cedaw (accessed July 9, 2021).
65. Birte Brecht-Drouart, "The Influence of the National Question on Gender Issues in the Muslim Areas of the Southern Philippines: Maranao Muslim Women between Retraditionalization and Islamic Resurgence," in *Contesting Feminisms*, ed. Huma Ahmed-Ghosh (Albany: SUNY Press, 2015), 89–112.
66. Brecht-Douart, "The Influence," 97–98.
67. Angeles, "From Secession," 79.
68. Brecht-Douart, "The Influence," 99.
69. Angeles, "From Secession," 81.
70. "Musawah Framework for Action, English version," musawah.org, accessed May 24, 2021, https://www.musawah.org/wp-content/uploads/2018/11/MusawahFrameworkforAction_En.pdf.
71. Anwar, "Sisters in Islam," 121.
72. "Discussion: Wilayah (Guardianship) and Qiwamah (Protection) of Females," Rumah Kitab, Unpublished Activity Report, 2018.
73. Eva F. Nisa, "Muslim Women in Contemporary Indonesia: Online Conflicting Narratives behind the Women Ulama Congress," *Asian Studies Review* 43, no. 3 (2019): 434–454.
74. Dr. Nur Rofiah, Jakarta, interview with author, July 6, 2018.
75. Ibid.

Bibliography

Abdul Kodir, Faqihuddin, Abd Moqsith Ghazali, Imam Nakha'I, K. H. Hussein Muhammad, and Marzuki Wahid. *Fiqh Anti-Trafficking: Jawaban atas Berbagai Kasus Kejahatan Perdagangan Manusia dalam Perspektif Hukum Islam* (Anti-Trafficking Fiqh: An Answer to Several Cases of Evil; Human Trafficking from the Perspective of Islamic Law). Cirebon: Fahmina Institute, 2006.

Ali, Mukti, Roland Gunawan, Ahmad Hilmi, and Jamaluddin Mohammad, eds. *Fikh Kawin Anak: Mebaca Ulang Teks Keagamaan Perkawinan Usia Anak-Ana.* (The Fiqh concerning Child Marriage: Rereading Religious Texts about Child Marriage). Jakarta: Rumah Kitab, 2015.

Ali, Mukti, Roland Gunawan, Jamaluddin Mohammad, and Ahmad Hilmi. *Aku, Kamu, End: Membaca ulang teks keagamaan kawin anak* (I, You, End: Rereading Religious Texts about Child Marriage). Jakarta: Rumah Kitab, 2015.

Angeles, Vivienne S. M. "Constructing Identity: Visual Expressions of Islam in the Predominantly Catholic Philippines." In *Identity in Crossroad Civilizations: Ethnicity, Nationalism, and Globalism in Asia*, edited by E. Kolig, V. S. Angeles, and S. Wong, 159–177. Amsterdam: Amsterdam University Press, 2009.

Angeles, Vivienne S. M. "From Secession to Social Activism: Muslim Women's Movements in the Philippines." In *Women and Asian Religions*, edited by Zayn R. Kassam, 71–86. Santa Barbara: Praeger, 2017.

Angeles, Vivienne S. M. "Women and Revolution: Philippine Muslim Women's Participation in the Moro National Liberation Front." *Muslim World* 86, no. 2 (1996): 130–147.

Anwar, Etin. *A Genealogy of Islamic Feminism. Pattern and Change in Indonesia*. Abingdon: Routledge, 2018.

Anwar, Zainah. "Negotiating Gender Rights under Religious Law in Malaysia." In *New Directions in Islamic Thought: Exploring Reform and Muslim Tradition*, edited by Kari Vogt, Lena Larsen, and Christian Moe, 175–186. New York: I. B. Tauris, 2009.

Anwar, Zainah. "Sisters in Islam and the Making of Musawah." In *Gender and Equality in Muslim Family Law*, edited by Ziba Mir-Hosseini, Kari Vogt, Lena Larsen, and Christian Moe, 107–126. London: I. B. Tauris, 2013.

Anwar, Zainah. "What Islam? Whose Islam? Sisters in Islam and the Struggle for Women's Rights." In *The Politics of Multiculturalism: Pluralism and Citizenship in Malaysia, Singapore, and Indonesia*, edited by Robert W. Hefner, 227–252. Honolulu: University of Hawaii Press, 2001.

Basarudin, Azza. *Humanizing the Sacred. Sisters in Islam and the Struggle for Gender Justice in Malaysia*. Seattle: University of Washington Press, 2016.

Basarudin, Azza. "In Search of Faithful Citizens in Postcolonial Malaysia: Islamic Ethics, Muslim Activism, and Feminist Politics." In *Women and Islam*, edited by Zayn R. Kassam, 93–128. Oxford: Praeger, 2010.

Brecht-Drouart, Birte. "The Influence of the National Question on Gender Issues in the Muslim Areas of the Southern Philippines: Maranao Muslim Women between Retraditionalization and Islamic Resurgence." In *Contesting Feminisms*, edited by Huma Ahmed-Ghosh, 89–112. Albany: State University of New York Press, 2015.

Fealy, Greg, and Virginia Hooker. *Voices of Islam in Southeast Asia, A Contemporary Sourcebook*. Singapore: Institute of Southeast Asian Studies, 2006.

Gonzales, Francisco L. "Sultans in a Violent Land." In *Rebels, Warlords and Ulama: A Reader on Muslim Separatism and the War in the Southern Philippines*, edited by Eric Gutierrez, 87–143. Quezon City: Institute for Popular Democracy, 2017.

Gunawan, Roland, and Nur Hayati Aida, eds. *Fikih Perwalian, Membaca Ulang Hak Perwalian untuk Perlindungan Perempuan dari Kawin Paksa dan Kawin Anak* (The Jurisprudence Concerning Guardianship: Rereading Guardianship Rights to Protect Women from Forced and Child Marriage). Jakarta: Rumah Kitab, 2019.

Kamali, Mohammad Hashim. "Law, Morality and Religion: A Critique of the Syariah Criminal Offences (Federal Territories) Act 1997." Sisters in Islam, 2019, https://sistersinislam.org/position-papers/.

Maznah, Cecilia Ng, and Tan Beng Hui Mohamad. *Feminism and the Women's Movement in Malaysia*. London: Routledge, 2006.

Mohanty, Chandra. *Feminism without Borders: Decolonizing Theory, Practising Solidarity*. Durham, NC: Duke University Press, 2003.

Moll, Yasmin. "Islamic Feminism between Interpretive Freedom and Legal Codification: The Case of Sisters in Islam in Malaysia." In *Contesting Feminisms: Gender and Islam in Asia*, edited by Huma Ahmed-Ghosh, 159–180. New York: SUNY Press, 2015.

Mulia, Siti Musdah. "Review Buku Ensiklopedia Muslimah Reformis" https://www.youtube.com/watch?v=Z17RUPyzkck and Shahnaz Haque dkk dalam Bedah Buku Muslimah Reformis, https://www.youtube.com/watch?v=WFb8W4cfj70. Accessed July 10, 2021.

Mulia, Siti Musdah. *Ensiklopedia Muslimah Reformis: Pokok-pokok Pemikiran Untuk Reinterpretasi dan Aksi* (The Reformist Muslim Woman's Encyclopedia: Essential Ideas for Reinterpretation and Action). Jakarta: Mizan Publishers, 2019.

Mulia, Siti Musdah. *Muslimah Reformis: Perempuan Baru Keagamaan* (The Reformist Muslim Woman: The New Religious Woman). Jakarta: Mizan, 2005.

Mulia, Siti Musdah. *Posisi Perempuan Dalam Undang-Undang Perkawinan; Indonesia dan Kompilasi Hukum Islam* (The Position of Women in the Marriage Laws: Indonesia and the Compilation of Islamic Law). Jakarta: LKAJ, Ministry for Religious Affairs, 2001.

Mulia, Siti Musdah. "Toward a Just Marriage Law: Empowering Indonesian Women through a Counter Legal Draft to the Indonesian Compilation of Islamic Law." In *Islamic Law in Contemporary Indonesia. Ideas and Institutions*, edited by R. Michael Feener and Mark E. Cammack, 128–145. Cambridge, MA: Harvard University Press, 2007.

Nagata, Judith. "Ethnonationalism vs. Religious Transnationalism: Nation-Building and Islam in Malaysia." *Muslim World* 17, no. 2 (2016): 129–150.

Nisa, Eva F. "Muslim Women in Contemporary Indonesia: Online Conflicting Narratives behind the Women Ulama Congress." *Asian Studies Review* 43, no. 3 (2019): 434–454.

Nurmila, Nina. *Women, Islam and Everyday Life*. New York: Routledge, 2009.

Ong, Aihwa. "Translating Gender Justice in Southeast Asia: Situated Ethics, NGOs, and Bio-Welfare." *Hawwa* 9, nos. 1–2 (2011): 26–48.

Othman, Norani. "Muslim Women and the Challenge of Islamic Fundamentalism/Extremism: An Overview of Southeast Asian Muslim Women's Struggle for Human Rights and Gender Equality." *Women's Studies International Forum* 29, no. 4 (2006): 339–353.

Partogi, Sebastian. "Musdah Mulia: Injecting Spirituality into Human Rights Activism." *Jakarta Post*, February 18, 2021, https://muslimahreformis.org/beranda/post_profil_musdah/musdah-mulia-injecting-spirituality-into-human-rights-activism/.

Putri, Adelia Putri. "Indonesian Court Says No to Raising Minimum Marrying Age for Girls." *Asia Pacific*, June 19, 2015, accessed July 10, 2021, http://www.rappler.com/world/regions/asia-pacific/indonesia/96905-indonesian-court-rejects-judicial-review-marrying-age.

Rinaldo, Rachel. *Mobilizing Piety. Islam and Feminism in Indonesia*. Oxford: Oxford University Press, 2013.

Rofiah, Nur. Interview with author. Jakarta, July 6, 2018.

Kitab, Rumah. "Wilayah (Guardianship) and Qiwamah (Protection) of Females." Jakarta: Unpublished Activity Report, 2018.

Ulfah Anshor, Maria. *Fikih Aborsi: Wacana Pengauatan Hak Reproduksi Perempuan*. Jakarta: Kompas, 2006.

van Bruinessen, Martin, ed. *Contemporary Developments in Indonesian Islam: Explaining the Conservative Turn*. Singapore: ISEAS, 2013.

van Doorn-Harder, Pieternella. *Women Shaping Islam: Reading the Qur'an in Indonesia*. Urbana: University of Illinois Press, 2006.

Wadud, amina. *Qur'an and Woman: Reading the Sacred Text from a Woman's Perspective*. Oxford: Oxford University Press, 1999.

Weiss, Meredith. "Malaysian NGOs: History, Legal Frameworks, and Characteristics." In *Social Movements in Malaysia: From Moral Communities to NGOs*, edited by Saliha Hassan and Meredith L. Weiss, 17–44. London: Routledge, 2002.

Yusuf, Imtiyaz. "The Middle East and Muslim Southeast Asia: Implications of the Arab Spring." Oxford Islamic Studies Online, accessed July 20, 2020, http://www.oxfordislamicstudies.com/Public/focus/essay1009_southeast_asia.html.

Websites

Fahmina, accessed May 24, 2021, https://fahmina.or.id/.

Komnas Perempuan, accessed May 2, 2021, http://www.komnasperempuan.or.id/.

Lakpesdam, accessed May 24, 2021, http://www.lakpesdam.or.id/.

Musawah, accessed May 2, 2021, https://www.musawah.org/.

Oxford Islamic Studies Online, accessed January 27, 2021, http://www.oxfordislamicstudies.com/article/opr/t125/e480

Musawah, accessed May 2, 2021, https://www.musawah.org/.

Rahima, accessed May 2, 2021, https://swararahima.com/en/.

Rifka Annisa, accessed May 2, 2021, https://rifka-annisa.org/en/.

Rumah Kitab," accessed May 2, 2021, https://rumahkitab.com/en/.

Sisters in Islam, accessed May 2, 2021, https://sistersinislam.org/.

CHAPTER 24

MUSLIM WOMEN'S RELIGIOUS AND SOCIAL ACTIVISM IN CHINA

MARIA JASCHOK AND MAN KE

PREFACE

THIS short chapter is as much a contribution to the situation of China's Muslim women and their "activism" as it is about the very problematic of framing this contribution as "activism." That is, our presentation, based on the current state of relevant scholarship, with particular attention given to Chinese-language scholarship, seeks to clarify why discussion of "activities" is more pertinent than discussion of "activism" defined as "the policy or action of using vigorous campaigning to bring about political or social change" (*Oxford Dictionary*). At the same time, scholars and scholarship are reviewed through the critical prism of the researcher's positionality and its shaping of conceptualization and methodology.

DIVERSITY OF MUSLIM POPULATION IN CHINA

China's Muslim population is ethnically, culturally, and linguistically diverse, identifying with different Islamic traditions, organizations, and outward markers of Islamic piety. While Muslim settlements can be found scattered across the nation, they are most significantly concentrated in the borderlands of China, relating to the central state in historically and geopolitically contingent relationships. Gender regimes are thus both culturally specific as well as theologically inscribed. Informed by overarching global

Islamic precepts and injunctions, gender relations are ever translated at local level, in an interplay of continuity and change, into a familiar idiom. Thus any description of women's religious and social "activism"—and of the linkage between the religious and the social—must ask questions that acknowledge intersecting forces and influences that frame, facilitate, constrain, or obstruct religious and social engagement with the world in which they live.

Statistical Facts

China's Muslim population is made up of ten nationalities (out of fifty-five officially designated nationalities, also referred to as ethnic minorities) amounting in 2010 to a population of about 23,308,000 (or 1.8% of the total population of China).[1] Hui Muslims are the most numerous group, dispersed widely across China, living in majority-Muslim communities, especially in borderland areas or in close neighborhood with Han Chinese. The greatest concentration of Muslims, in the majority Uyghur, are to be found in Xinjiang Uyghur Autonomous Region in northwestern China, with other significant Muslim populations settled in the northwest regions and provinces of Ningxia, Gansu, and Qinghai. While the majority of Muslims belong to the Hanafi school of the Sunni tradition, with fewer identifying with Sufi, Salafi, and Shi'i traditions, all are marked by historical legacies of divisive internal schisms and intersectarian tensions.[2] Hui Muslims are considered among the most assimilated nationalities, leading to the reference of Hui Muslims as the Chinese state's "preferred Muslims." This is in stark contrast to the Uyghur ethnic group in Xinjiang, over which Xi Jinping's government has for many years exercised tight surveillance. However, the Chinese state has become wary of outside influences over all forms of Islam, making it increasingly difficult for Hui religious leaders to maintain a mutually beneficial relationship with the central government when in the recent past, at a superficial level at least, little appeared to separate Hui from Han Chinese. Increasingly all religions are at the receiving end of the state's regimentation of all aspects of religious affairs.[3]

Chinese Muslim Women and Religious Activities

As early as the 1990s, the Hui Muslim sociologist Shui Jingjun published an article on the history and significance of women's schools (*qingzhen nüxue*) and women's mosques (*qingzhen nüsi*),[4] arguing that their beginnings in the course of the sixteenth and seventeenth centuries had resulted from the need to educate non-Muslim Han women, married into Muslim families, in sufficient rudimentary knowledge to oversee the religious education of small children and avoid violation, or indeed forgetfulness, of fundamental Muslim discipline and practices. Women were thus the first converts to Islam, helping to sustain Islamic life and Muslim communities in China. Jaschok and Shui, in a later publication, related the appearance of women's schools and mosques to the existential crisis Chinese Muslims faced in the outgoing years of the Ming Dynasty (1368–1644), when the survival in China of Islam itself hung in the balance. Arguably, women played a crucial part in saving Islam from extinction, with incipient educational projects, ad hoc and temporary, leading in time to major and unique Islamic innovations, the establishment in central China's Hui communities of mosques for women, presided over and led by women, *nü ahong* (female imams). In some instances, these mosques developed near autonomy, coming under religious and administrative management of women.[5] These particular developments, internal to Islam, reflected the educational and cultural reforms that took place in the course of the twentieth century in the wider Chinese society, and which accelerated with the founding of the People's Republic of China in 1949 when emancipation of women, social reforms, and the changes of women's social and family status came to be hailed as main pillars of the Maoist revolution.

Writing related to Chinese Muslim women's religious activities emerged mainly after 2000, and this writing was nearly without exception focused on women in the northwestern areas of China, such as Gansu and Qinghai Provinces, including women living in the provincial capital of Lanzhou, in Linxia, the "Little Mecca" in northern Gansu, in Zhangjiachuan as well as in Xi'ning, capital of Qinghai Province and in the Ningxia Hui Autonomous Region. Women as subjects of study were on the whole Hui Muslims, with only a number of research projects devoted to women from the numerically smaller Salar and Dongxiang Muslim nationalities. Relatively little scholarship has been added in more recent years to this early upsurge of research, which featured in a review of studies of Chinese Muslim women after 2000.[6] What scarce studies there are tend to focus their findings on what is seen as continued dominance of a paradigmatic, traditionalist Muslim femininity. Women's primary responsibilities relate to domestic sphere and familial obligations; outside the house, only limited participation in mosque-based Islamic education is condoned. Young girls and adult women may be taking religious instruction or indeed fulfill honorable, and legitimate, roles as teachers and administrators of their local women's schools. This situation contrasts with trends notable in central China's Hui Muslim communities. More thorough investigation of continuity and persistence of Islamic injunctions on the proper gender division of labor is clearly needed, with its attendant assumptions of an ordained gender regime which is inscribed by a complex array of local sectarian and ethnic contexts that mark China's northern border regions.[7]

Generally speaking, scholarship after 2000 investigated women's involvement in relation to girls' and women's schools and to women's mosques. This scholarly focus took note of the poignant symbolism of *nüxue* and *nüsi* (women's school and mosques) in the lives of China's Muslim women, all too conscious of their distance from the heartland of Islamic faith. It is a distance compounded by the expenses of a *hajj* (pilgrimage) few women can afford and by a scriptural language to which access is acquired with difficulty and under manifold limitations. Learning of Arabic—or historically Farsi, the language of learning, until recently, in women's mosques in central China's Muslim institutions—is predicated on the presence of schools and/or mosques offering female education, whether in the form of extracurricular activities for young girls or further education classes for mature women. Only the availability of such institutions, active familial support, a husband's permission and knowledgeable guidance, offer women the chance of rudimentary religious education and, from the perspective of believing women, the possibility for a pathway to paradise, otherwise shrouded in uncertainty and fears of the consequences of lack of religious learning for afterlife.[8] It is of interest to note that male scholars[9] are inclined to emphasize the important role that women's schools and mosques, where they form part of the Islamic landscape in China, have played in the development of Islamic culture.[10] A saying, often quoted, stresses the central role of women to continuity of faith: "to educate a man one will only educate an individual; educating a woman is to educate a family and an entire community." Yang Wenjiong,[11] for example, holds the view that in the process of rapid modernization, Chinese Muslims expanded their options for instruction in religious education and enduring legacy of Muslim cultural traditions by establishing *nüxue*. Given dispersal in many cities and townships in recent years of Muslim populations away from old settlements to satellite towns and distant suburbs, these institutions continue to offer themselves as sites of identity and remembering in the midst of increasingly scattered faith communities.

Women scholars tend to place women's religious education and educational institutions at the core of their research, giving nuanced and comparative accounts of the emergence of educational/religious sites for women in different regions of the country. Studies embrace the history, size, economic support, management system, curriculum, daily life of a given school, and influence of religious education in a given institution for girls and women in different stages of their lifecycles. What emerges is a complex picture that does not allow for generalization as to the impact at both personal and societal levels. The nature of an educational institution and curriculum, its closeness to the mosque and degree of leadership exercised over the curriculum by the local *ahong* (imam), family support or obstruction, but also geopolitical location, among other factors, all influence educational objective and outcome for the recipients of education.[12] In pointing out the differences between Islamic female education in the south and in the north of China,[13] the Japanese anthropologist Matsumoto Masumi provides a local lens for understanding how local conditions shape educational norms and objectives. While Muslim girls enrolled in girls' schools in the southern province of Yunnan prepare themselves to acquire knowledge and skills useful for future employment in non-Muslim society as well, in Muslim girls' schools in China's northern border regions, preparation for the roles of Muslim wife and mother are at the forefront of education. Indeed, instrumentalizing education for the benefit of the entire community and for sustaining the religiocultural way of life of local Muslims has ever been the preferred means to safeguard the faith-based identity of China's Muslim population and find a sustainable collective response to crisis of identity.[14] It is a matter of historical record that during these moments of crisis, women have been provided with the chance of crossing gender lines, given roles of responsibility and societal value that were also openings to social and gender change. Matsumoto thus relates the impact on girls and women—what she calls an awakening of self-consciousness—as they answer the call of duty to proper education in the faith. Furthermore, in the course of this journeying beyond the family compound, they undergo a most subjective journey, an awareness of what education—whether in public or private schools—can bring about, and the beginning of independence that enrichment of knowledge promises. Rightly, critical voices are emphatic that such are incipient changes which may not ultimately shift the hard borders of gender marginalization in domestic and religious spheres of activities; that these changes are furthermore tentative and precarious because they are not the main driver of expansion of female (religious) education.[15]

Indeed, findings from a number of investigations conducted on female education have indicated how attendance of classes organized by women's schools and mosques strengthen the patriarchal grip on gender relations, resulting in pupils dropping out of schools to get married. Early termination of schooling is thus considered by their religious educators as successful accomplishment of the ultimate goal of female education, as preparation for the next stage in women's lifecycles.[16] Only a number of studies have paid closer attention to the complex relationship between traditional Islamic education as taught at Qur'anic women's schools and mosques and the formation of female subjectivity and agency.[17] For instance, Shui Jingjun and Maria Jaschok maintain in their history of Chinese women's mosques that women have been decisive agents and initiators of what became female-only spaces of Islamic education, worship and social congregation, in the course of the nineteenth century leading to women-only institutions as part of China's Islamic landscape, institutions moreover often built and maintained out of legacies bequeathed by pious women believers. Availability of women's own spaces, they argue, provided opportunities for women to transform an assigned space, assigned to women because of Confucian and Islamic injunctions on the imperative of gender segregation, into a space of transformation and intensification of religious piety. Moreover, female spiritual leadership which made possible religious and ritual guidance of largely illiterate women congregations helped to reframe a more positive women's self-image. Hope for afterlife could replace fear expressed by women of the consequences for their souls of ignorance and violation of basic Islamic precepts.

Collective worship, guided by their own *ahong*, enabled direct communication with God and reinforced their identities as practicing Muslim believers, creating meaning of life and identity as part of a global ummah from their busy domestic lives. In addition, the authors suggest, more comprehensively educated female *ahong* are starting to challenge the previously unquestioned authority of their male counterparts to interpret Qur'anic passages for influential interpretations on gender roles, conduct and aspirations, drawing attention to mainstream (non-Muslim) societal discourse on gender equality in secular life.

Ma Guifen and Hu Liping similarly hold the view that spatial gender segregation enabled the creation of women's schools as an exclusive and legitimate female space, making possible participation in Islamic learning and instruction in pious Muslim conduct, something which must be seen as of positive significance for the transmission of Muslim cultural traditions. Moreover, such developments, the authors say, facilitated the accumulation of women's personal capital and nurtured social communication and networking.[18]

Hu Meijuan likewise argues that the independent space created by women's schools for the exclusive benefit of women creates possibilities for affirmation of women's self-belief, gained through a direct pathway of faith to God, unmediated by expressions of patriarchy.[19] Occupying a space for women to make their voices heard, a space that endorses the right to speech, has undoubtedly facilitated and strengthened the capacities of religious women leaders to enter into critical conversations with male counterparts over limitations of women's religious education under the influence of patriarchal injunctions. But taboos remain, prohibiting women from touching the Qur'an directly and from reciting the scriptures during menstruation. Notions of impurity and unchallenged fears of contamination continue to justify a highly gendered reading of the hierarchical nature of spirituality and power.

All in all, researchers concerned with Chinese Muslim women's religious activities generally focus on aspects of female education offered by private or government schools and by mosques. Insight is provided into the impact of different types of education on girls and women and thus what might be the decisive factor leading families to support education for a daughter or indeed for an adult female member of the family. Moreover, students of Islamic female education agree that while women have played, and are playing, important roles in the development, teaching, and management of education for adults and children alike, Islamic female education in its organized form came out of a wider cultural and political crisis that threatened the very integrity of the faith of Islam and the survival of Muslim populations in China (see above). Male scholars and religious practitioners chose to confront these crises by co-opting wives and daughters into community-wide educational projects as primary educators and maternal authority figures. Without their participation, so Hui reformers argue, families would quickly lose touch with Islamic beliefs and Muslim ways of life and conduct. Families without religious education, on the other hand, would lead to a fatal amnesia and spell the end of Muslim life.

Men framed their incorporation of women into the educational project as necessitated by an existential crisis and unprecedented threat to collective survival of China's Muslim culture. As far as Muslim women of piety are concerned, historically or in contemporary society, the pursuit of religious knowledge and Muslim ritual life strengthens self-worth. At the same time, it contributes to the wider Muslim community the promise of a better future, the prospect of young Muslims being educated in their faith and a strong sense of belonging. It might furthermore be argued that availability of religious education, taught away from home, necessitate physical mobility, and enable women's legitimate appearance in public spaces hitherto the exclusive reserve of men. Entrenched gender relations and norms do not shift easily. Nevertheless, the greater fluidity of gender segregation through women's legitimate crossing of domestic thresholds out into public domains troubles received conventions. Historically, that these shifts came from within, indeed from requests by male Islamic scholars and practitioners for women to attend religious instruction, join study groups initially in private homes, later on in spaces especially set aside for female education (what became in the course of time *nüxue* and then *nüsi*), was of enduring impact because these developments were born of legitimate needs and had the approval of religious authorities.

Closer to home, the first steps taken by Muslim girls and women into "unguarded" space could only conceivably have taken place with the support of husbands and fathers. Their approval is needed to this day, in the more closed Muslim communities in China's borderlands, to make it possible for girls and women to leave their homes in order to acquire religious knowledge and familiarity with the language of the Qur'an, Arabic (*jingzi*). What motivates in particular older women to participate in education is interpreted differently by scholars. While some scholars argue that education turns the lives of Muslim girls and women around, raising their authority at home and reinforcing their standing in the wider community of Muslims, ultimately, so other scholars maintain, the ultimate driver of gaining religious knowledge remains a religiously informed agency, the goal of taking care of spiritual as well as material well-being of their family as respected members of their ethnoreligious communities. Extending thus what are traditional female roles as wives and mothers, the increasing numbers of female students and female teachers of Islamic knowledge consider this involvement in education as closely aligned to the paradigmatic educational functions of motherhood. There is thus no departure from traditional conceptions of femininity but a careful negotiation in case of any conflict with primary duties to family. Indeed, in certain more closed Muslim communities, the limited range of options open to women might enforce abandonment of a role outside the home, even if legitimate. The issue raised here, to be addressed briefly in the final section, is that of positionality of the researcher. These are questions that need to be asked, since in a number of studies on *nüxue* and *nüsi*, women's capacity to make choices in relation to roles outside the domestic sphere is seen by these scholars as heavily circumscribed, and female nature as essentially, and enduringly, passive and compliant.

Future scholarship needs to move away from widely held assumptions about the subjugation of Muslim women as a nonqueried fact. The growing feminization of Islamic education could serve research that would view women's choices and life-trajectories through their own lens. Rather than judging educational occupations where many women are found to work as mere replication of traditional care roles, reinforcing thus rather than querying stereotypes, other perspectives could highlight the initiatives and creativity of women in religious education and practice, whether breaking through restrictive injunctions in cultural interpretations of gender norms or through conventions in the way that women negotiate choices in their daily lives. Where closer observations and conversations are had by local researchers, engagement with Islamic feminist literature outside of China could bring into local discourses the radical questioning of western feminist epistemologies on agency and emancipatory processes that is taking place elsewhere, as for example represented by the scholarship of Saba Mahmood and Masooda Bano.[20]

Considering the intersectionality of gender identity and the multifaceted nature of Muslim women's participation in religious and social life, additional research must address relational and political nexus in which religious piety and activities are embedded. Indeed, as pointed out above, the use of "activism," rather than religious activities, must be a matter for problematization and discussion. "Activism" as widely understood refers to policy or action designed to achieve political or social change through robust campaigning. This is not currently the case. Instead, women's agency pertains to daily creative interaction and productive negotiations for collectively desirable outcomes rather than in radical mobilization for structural change.

To now proceed to a final example, the study of Chinese women *hajj*[21] has revealed that as a result of a growing and increasingly acknowledged religious piety and improved material resources, more and more women are making the pilgrimage to Mecca. On their return, these women pilgrims enjoy an enhanced social status on account of having completed an essential religious duty. It might however be argued that women's enhanced social status is not so much the consequence of pilgrimage but that the increase in the number of women undertaking the arduous and expensive journey to Mecca is itself the outcome of women's assertive agency and capacity—itself an indication of enhanced social status—so as to be able to marshal familial support and material resources needed. Religious activities and individual capacity, underlined by collective solidarity (as offered in the sociality of schools and mosques), are closely linked, enabling women's purposeful facilitation of existing spheres of religious activities as more heterogeneous and more gender-equal. This heterogeneity requires still more nuanced understanding of the diversity of women's activities that reflect their membership of a complex landscape of Islamic sects embedded in ethnic, regional, and political discourses. These both shape the faith of women and facilitate as well as circumscribe women's capacities to negotiate choices that are meaningful to them and their families.

Muslim Women's Social Activities in China to the Present

As in the foregoing discussion, the context of the Chinese state's tight control of all religion shapes the nature of religious practice, making studies of Chinese Muslim women's social "activism" (for social change) a rarity.

Among topics that have been identified as significant by Chinese researchers are possible explanations for enduring "low" level of political consciousness and lack of political participation on the part of Salar Muslim women in the northwestern province of Qinghai. Findings point to factors such as the strength of traditional customs and habits, to limited income and rudimentary education, but also to insufficient legal protection for women.[22] Other studies have provided different perspectives, allowing for alternative views of women's capacity for agency. As many men are obliged to leave their villages in search of work, becoming migrant workers in urban areas or in cities in southern China, women undoubtedly experience increased burden of work. But, so these researchers maintain, the absence of men also provides women with opportunities, born out of sheer necessity, for participation in village governance.[23] Other scholars have sought evidence for official claims that there has been much improvement in Muslim women's social participation due to the Chinese state's gender-equality legislation and the rapid development of the national economy during recent years.[24]

In this connection, a study was undertaken of strategies adopted by Hui Muslim women in the Ningxia Hui Autonomous Region to increase family income and involve members of their families to gain employment opportunities in the local tourist industry. Helped by relevant government policies, the women interviewed not only claimed to have gained economic benefits but also indicated that they increasingly asserted themselves within the household, taking part in important family decisions and generally receiving more attention and respect from male members of their families.[25] However, these developments are seen by researchers as indicative of very modest gains for women, with injunctions on adherence to traditional gender roles continuing too deeply entrenched in the minds of women to allow for structural change.[26] In the political area, women have so far only managed to act as deputy leaders, not breaking into top decision-making roles, the researcher Ma Guifen points out. In general, the overall level of political participation is persistently low, leading to recommendations by Ma to adopt robust countermeasures in order to change the situation. Public opinion itself must come out in support for Muslim women to play significant roles in the wider society. Another recommendation concerns education. Thus Ma argues for implementation of a gender-equality-sensitive education to enhance the wider societal support Muslim women require to make progress. In addition to such very basic demands for generally supportive means of giving women a public voice, emphasis is on the importance of granting additional legislative measures, providing specific tools for gender equality implementation and its protection.[27]

Other studies deal with the impact of change in macrosocial cultural circumstances on women's capacity to engage in societal activities. For example, Jia Yufei's study of Muslim women in Yiwu[28] reveals that women's motivation for settlement in Yiwu related to dissatisfaction with material conditions and restrictive norms back in their hometown. Early marriage and a lifecycle centered on domesticity defined their fate in the patriarchal milieu that characterizes much of Muslim culture in northwest China. In Yiwu, these women were able to take advantage of knowing some Arabic language to become independent entrepreneurs. Sharing the faith of Islam, they quickly accommodated themselves to life in Yiwu, building up translation services as a first step toward running their own companies; they also actively participate in social life. The move to another, more amenable, location but also individual effort and aspiration together produced this result, showing the influence of availability of social and cultural infrastructure, opportunities of a market economy and presence of more lenient gender norms on women's social participation. Su Muyu's study of immigrant Muslim women in Lanzhou[29] has found that in the national large-scale economic transformation and urbanization process, driven by constructive and relevant national policies, many Muslim women have chosen to migrate with their family to Lanzhou (provincial capital of Gansu Province) for the purpose of either work or study.

While many women are continuing traditional domestic roles, seen by researchers as a sign of passivity, on the other hand, it needs noting that because of the increase of economic (e.g., small business activities) and educational (cultural) capital, women are becoming visible in different spheres of society. The reason given for a noted broadening of women's vision of themselves as active in the world beyond the courtyard at home is the nature of urban culture, its more relaxed gender regime seen as more supportive of the country's policy of gender equality at all levels of society. Opportunities for escape from rural gender conservatism and patriarchal Islamic norms to the greater fluidity of urban surroundings are noted to heighten gender awareness and make for stronger incentives for social participation, for assertive voices in family decision-making and generally, for a more independent spirit. These findings are seen as indicative of the difference made by place of residence in the light of distinct urban/rural divides. The most effective way for Muslim women to escape from traditional lives and roles, such researchers maintain, is to leave behind the constraints of closed rural communities.

Finally, a very few studies take as their focus women's subjective states of mind. Questions are asked of the advantages of retaining cultural traditions in order to gain entry into a heavily male-dominated public space. For example, Ma Cijun found that in Yunnan Province the tradition of *bande*, which means taking responsibility for socializing, constructing, and maintaining interpersonal relationships, creates equal access to the public sphere and thus expands the space of legitimate public activity for local Hui Muslim women. Interestingly, a very similar activity may be observed among central China's women's mosque congregations, known as *zoufang* (paying strategic courtesy calls where it matters),[30] and it shares many of its salient features. In her paper, Ma Cijun argues that compared with the local Han community, there is an obvious gender division in the Hui community. Males take charge of public affairs in the village while females are completely invisible to outsiders or are placed in a subordinate position.

But is this indeed how women think, strategize, and make decisions? Might it be argued that evidence available to us also points to a number of creative ways in which local Hui women build and maintain social relations, expand their presence in the public space, even taking the initiative to develop new forms of social interaction? Women pay social visits, create opportunities for gift-giving, and explore the potential of new social relationships. Many occasions offer themselves when women are entertaining guests or accept invitations, when they are playing hosts or become part of an animated sociality during religious festivals, family anniversaries, family rituals, and numerous social gatherings associated with religious and secular calendars. Events are organized to pray for peace, to pray for the family in times of happiness or misfortune, and they offer opportunities to develop, and express, multiple identities among which religious membership is one—if for many women, the most important identity marker.[31] Through these numerous occasions, sociality consolidates, strengthening solidarity of faith and ethnicity. Women are at the heart of these activities. This is the significance of *bande*, enabling Hui women to bind together individuals, families, and indeed the whole Hui community. The private sphere of women, cemented by traditional gender norms, is here expanding outward, with the process of expansion certainly retaining Islamic and Confucian injunctions and gender norms but also adjusting these to make them fit for effective participation in public institutions and for societal (and their own) purposes. Interestingly, relatively little scholarship has been devoted to the ways that Muslim women change the nature of public society, introducing, however tentatively, the first building-blocks of civil society into their world as they create new relationships and foster local and translocal social/religious networks and in the process adjust public perceptions.[32]

The evidence presented has relied on scholarship in a sensitive field of investigation. A dominant scholarly trend is constituted by research into Chinese Muslim women's social activities in the northwest region. This is the case despite the nationwide distribution of Muslim settlements and the great diversity of Islamic schools and Muslim practices in China. The current situation thus points to problematic gaps in our knowledge of women, gender and Islam in Chinese society and the imperative for more research. Insufficient attention is paid by researchers to intersectional and multifaceted contexts in which women negotiate social mobility through family status, education, class, wealth, and membership of a given Islamic organization, making our appraisal of progress or obstruction when it comes to female participation in the political and social economies of their immediate and wider environments a difficult undertaking. Therefore, in the light of this discussion, the applicability to China of the concept of social "activism" which would allow us to interrogate the agency and action of Muslim women as responding to, as well as shaping, personal and collective fates, must be predicated on fuller and nuanced contextualization beyond the more commonly presented framework of Islamic gender norms and injunctions.

The researcher Su Muyu[33] discusses the implications of such conventional framing of China's Muslim women as leading to dominant, and widely accepted, tropes of passive and disenfranchised women. Within this framework, Muslim women may make small steps to improve their situation but will always be seen as falling short of attaining the feminist gold standard of empowerment, always staying within a mindset inscribed by Islamic religion, which by definition is held antithetical to expression of free agency and its pathway, activism. With religious agency and "activism" perceived by the researchers we referenced here, as largely oxymoronic, scholarship thus works under the sway of assumptions of Islam as uniformly engendering subjugated subjectivity and stifled capacities, negating individual effort as purposeful choice.

A discussion of Chinese Muslim women's "activism," given that the most comprehensive literature comes out of Chinese scholarship, must thus also reference the positionality of researchers and their standpoints in the production of new knowledge. When there is too little emphasis on probing fundamental issues of selfhood, the interplay of self and social norms and contingent nature of agency and its manifold social manifestations, it is not surprising that there are scarcely any studies treating fundamental questions of embedded epistemologies of women's subjectivities, aspirations and choices.[34] But this is needed, and only thus can we gain greater insights into issues surrounding the problematic of "activism" and its conceptual relevance to the nature of Chinese Muslim women's engagement in environments inscribed by gender, culture, time and place.

Notes

1. Pew Research Center, "The Future of the Global Muslim Population," accessed June 20, 2019, https://www.pewforum.org/2011/01/27/the-future-of-the-global-muslim-population/.
2. Dru C. Gladney, *Muslim Chinese: Ethnic Nationalism in the People's Republic* (Cambridge, MA: Harvard University Press,1996); Matthew S. Erie, *China and Islam: The Prophet, the Party, and Law* (Cambridge: Cambridge University Press, 2016); Kristian Petersen, *Interpreting Islam in China: Pilgrimage, Scripture, and Language in the Han Kitab* (Oxford: Oxford University Press, 2017).
3. Erik Durneika, "China's Favored Muslims? The Complex Relationship between the Chinese Communist Party and the Hui Ethnic Group," *Sociology of Islam* 6 (2018): 429–448.
4. Shui Jingjun, "A Brief Exposition of the Origin and Development of Women's Schools and Women's Mosques," *Huizu Yanjiu* 1 (1996): 51–59.
5. Maria Jaschok and Shui Jingjun, *The History of Women's Mosques in Chinese Islam* (Richmond: Curzon/Routledge, 2000). This study accounts for a complex history and a complex spectrum of female-only Islamic institutions between near-autonomy and close dependency on male religious and administrative leadership.
6. Maria Jaschok and Shui Jingjun, "The Study of Islam, Women, and Gender in China—Taking a Gender-Critical Turn," *Asian Culture* 37 (2013): 1–14.
7. For a recent general work on China's borderlands, see K. Mukherjee, *Conflict in India and China's Contested Borderlands: A Comparative Study*, Routledge Contemporary Asia Series (London: Routledge, 2019).
8. Jaschok and Shui, *History of Women's Mosques*.
9. See Jiang Bo and Fei Xiang, "Study of the Muslim Women's School in Linxia," *Xibei Shidi* 3 (1995): 75–84; Ma Qiang, "Women's Education and Cultural Self-Awareness: A Case Study of the Linxia Chinese-Arabic Women's School," *Zhongguo Musilin* 1 (2003): 15–17; Ma Qiang, "Fieldwork and Thinking on Hui Islamic Cultural Education," *Huizu Yanjiu* 4 (2003): 104–110.
10. Historically, the roots of organized female Islamic education go back to initiatives by scholars and religious practitioners engaged most closely in educational reforms in central China's Hui communities. Although, in the course of time, *nüxue* and *nüsi* were established in other parts of Muslim China, this has not been the case everywhere; nor were all *nüsi* restored in the years following radical uprooting of all religious life during the Cultural Revolution, 1966–1976; see Jaschok and Shui, *History of Women's Mosques*.
11. Yang Wenjiong, "*Nüxue*: the Extension of Mosque Education and Changes in the Important Role of Cultural Inheritance: Taking Lanzhou, Xi'an and Linxia as Examples," *Huizu Yanjiu* 1 (2002): 25–31; Yang Wenjiong, "Hui Traditional Culture and Modernization in Urban Society," *Huizu Yanjiu* 1 (2004): 58–64.
12. For example, Ma Wenmei, "A Case Study of Contemporary Muslim N*üxue:* Taking Sino-Arabic Women's school in Linxia as an Example" (MPhil thesis, Northwest Minzu University, 2008); Yang Mei, "Case Study of the Emergence of Women's Education in

Traditional Mosque Education—The Case of the Sino-Arabic Women's School in Xiguan, Lanzhou" (MPhil thesis, Northwest Minzu University, 2007); Ma Shuqin, "Case Study of a Muslim Women's School: Taking Zhangjiachuan Muslim School (Girls' Division) as an Example" (MPhil thesis, Northwest Minzu University, 2013).

13. Matsumoto Masumi, "Muslim Women Crossing Regions and States: Religious Education and Discussion of Women's Development in Yunnan Girls' Schools," in *Migration and Cultural Dynamics of Chinese Border Ethnic Groups* (Kunming: Yunnan People's Publishing House 2009), 89–112; Hu Liping, "Contemporary Muslim *Nüxue* from the Perspective of Gender—Taking a Female Hui School in Zhaotong, Yunnan Province as an Example," *Huizu Yanjiu* 2 (2013):109–114.
14. Matsumoto Masumi, "Islamic Women's Education in Northwest China—Taking the Sino-Arabic Women's School in Linxia and the Sino-Arabic Women's School in Weizhou as Examples," trans. Lu Zhonghui, *Huizu Yanjiu* 4 (2003): 111–115.
15. Ma Yan, "On the Cultural Self-Awareness of Hui Women Due to the Rise of Muslim Women's Schools—A Case Study of Urban Women's Schools in Tongxin County, Ningxia," *Ningxia Shehui Kexue* 2 (2007): 86–89; Yang Mei, "Case Study of the Emergence of Women's Education in Traditional Mosque Education—the Case of the Sino-Arabic Women's School in Xiguan, Lanzhou" (MPhil thesis, Northwest Minzu University, 2007); Ma Shuqin, "Case Study of a Muslim Women's School: Taking Zhangjiachuan Muslim School (Girls' Division) as an Example" (MPhil thesis, Northwest Minzu University), 2013; Hu Liping, "Contemporary Muslim *Nüxue* from the Perspective of Gender—Taking a Female Hui School in Zhaotong, Yunnan Province as an Example," *Huizu Yanjiu* 2 (2013): 109–114.
16. Han Shuzhen, "Study of Salar Women's Schools in Xunhua County, Qinghai Province—Taking Caotanba Village as an Example" (MPhil thesis, Shaanxi Normal University, 2018).
17. Jaschok and Shui, *History of Women's Mosques*; Shui Jingjun and Maria Jaschok, *The History of Women's Mosques in China*, Chinese-language edition (Beijing: SDX, 2002).
18. Ma Huifen and Hu Liping, "The Socio-Spatial Significance of Contemporary Muslim Female Education in Northwest China—Based on the Case Studies of Lanzhou and Linxia," *Huizu Yanjiu* 3 (2016): 13–19.
19. Hu Meijuan, "Body, Space and Gender: A Study of Muslim Women's Schools in Northwest China" (PhD diss., Lanzhou University, 2014).
20. Masooda Bano, *Female Islamic Education Movements: The Re-Democratisation of Islamic Knowledge* (Cambridge: Cambridge University Press, 2017); Saba Mahmood, "Feminist Theory, Embodiment, and the Docile Agent: Some Reflections on the Egyptian Islamic Revival," *Cultural Anthropology* 2 (2001): 202–236; Maria Jaschok, "Sources of Authority, Female *Ahong* and *Qingzhen Nüsi* (Women's Mosques) in China," in *Women, Leadership and Mosques: Changes in Contemporary Islamic Authority*, ed. Masooda Bano and Hilary Kalmbach (Leiden: Brill, 2012).
21. Han Xuyun, "Female Hajj and Rite of Passage—Based on the Investigation and Research of Xunhua Muslim Female Pilgrims in Qinghai Province," *Beifang Minzu Daxue Xuebao* 2 (2010): 70–74; Ma Xiaolin, "Anthropological Research on Hui Women's Pilgrimage: A Case Study of a Female Hajj Group" (MPhil thesis, Xinjiang Normal University, 2011).
22. Wang Lanxia, "An Investigative Report on Minority Women's Political Participation: Taking Salar in Xunhua County as an Example," *Zu Guo* 14 (2016): 132–133.
23. Gao Maosen and Zhang Xingnian, "Dilemmas and Suggestions for Female Salar Villagers' Political Participation," *Qinghai Minzu Daxue Xuebao* 2 (2014): 86–91.

24. Yan Guofang, "The Influence of Hui Women's Social Participation in Folklore in Transition," *Xibei Minzu Yanjiu* 2 (2003): 173–189.
25. Sha Aixia, "Study of Female Role Transformation in Rural Tourism Development in Hui Residential Areas—Taking Jingyuan County, Ningxia, as an Example," *Beifang Minzu Daxue Xuebao* 5 (2012): 107–110.
26. Ma Guifen, *Research on Muslim Women's Social Participation in Northwest China: Case Studies of Hui and Dongxiang Women in Gansu Province* (Beijing: Renmin, 2017).
27. Ibid.
28. Jia Yufei, "Study of Muslim Women in Yiwu" (MPhil thesis, Ningxia University, 2017).
29. Su Muyu, "Adjustments and Belonging: A Study of Social Adaptation of Migrant Muslim Women in Lanzhou" (PhD diss., Lanzhou University, 2018).
30. See Jaschok and Shui, "The Study of Islam, Women, and Gender."
31. Stephan Feuchtwang, *Popular Religion in China: The Imperial Metaphor* (Richmond, Surrey: Curzon, 2001). Feuchtwang argues that the Islamic revival ritualizes a diversity of relationships and loyalties that fashion and reconcile political, patriotic and dissenting, religious subjectivities.
32. Ma Cijun, "'Doing It'—The Construction of Public Space by Yongjian Hui Women in Lushan," in *Xinanbian Jiang Minzu Yanjiu* (Kunming: Yunnan University Press, 2018), 23:183–190.
33. Su Muyu, "Adjustments and Belonging: A Study of Social Adaptation of Migrant Muslim Women in Lanzhou" (PhD diss., Lanzhou University, 2018).
34. Saba Mahmood, *Politics of Piety: The Islamic Revival and the Feminist Subject* (Princeton, NJ: Princeton University Press, 2005). Most Chinese researchers are female and Muslims, according to Man Ke. Moreover, most come from conservative Muslim communities in northwest China. Empathy with the women they study, sharing origins and upbringing, makes it difficult at present to entirely "escape" from the "traditional" patriarchal religious structures, making "independent" viewpoints nearly impossible. Hence, we can see, like Man Ke, why the "subjectivity" of Muslim women in deeply religious communities is less a matter for study than of shared background.

Bibliography

Bano, Masooda, and Hilary Kalmbach, eds. *Women, Leadership and Mosques: Changes in Contemporary Islamic Authority*. Leiden: Brill, 2012.

Cone, Tiffany. *Cultivating Charismatic Power: Islamic Leadership Practice in China*. London: Palgrave Macmillan, 2018.

Durneika, Erik. "China's Favored Muslims? The Complex Relationship between the Chinese Communist Party and the Hui Ethnic Group." *Sociology of Islam* 6, no. 4 (2018): 429–448.

Edwards, Louise. "Women in the People's Republic of China: New Challenges to the Grand Gender Narrative." In *Women in Asia: Tradition, Modernity and Globalisation*, edited by Louise Edwards and Mina Roces, 59–84. Ann Arbor: University of Michigan Press, 2000.

Erie, Matthew S. *China and Islam: The Prophet, the Party, and Law*. Cambridge: Cambridge University Press, 2016.

Feuchtwang, Stephan. *Popular Religion in China: The Imperial Metaphor*. Richmond, Surrey: Curzon, 2001.

Gao, Maosen, , and Zhang Xingnian. "Dilemmas and Suggestions for Female Salar Villagers' Political Participation." *Qinghai Minzu Daxue Xuebao* 2 (2014): 86–91.

Gillette, Maris Boyd. *Between Mecca and Beijing: Modernization and Consumption among Urban Chinese Muslims*. Stanford, CA: Stanford University Press, 2000.

Gladney, Dru C. *Dislocating China: Muslims, Minorities, and Other Subaltern Subjects*. Chicago: University of Chicago, 2004.

Ha, Guangtian. "The Silent Hat: Islam, Female Labor, and the Political Economy of the Headscarf Debate." *Signs: Journal of Women in Culture and Society* 42, no. 3 (2017): 743–769.

Han, Shuzhen. "Study of Salar women's Schools in Xunhua County, Qinghai Province—Taking Caotanba Village as an Example." MPhil thesis, Shaanxi Normal University, 2018.

Han, Xuyun. "Female Hajj and Rite of Passage—Based on the Investigation and Research of Xunhua Muslim Female Pilgrims in Qinghai Province." *Beifang Minzu Daxue Xuebao* 2 (2010): 70–74.

Hu, Liping "Contemporary Muslim *Nüxue* from the Perspective of Gender—Taking a Female Hui School in Zhaotong, Yunnan Province as an Example." *Huizu Yanjiu* 2 (2013): 109–114.

Hu, Meijuan. "Body, Space and Gender: A Study of Muslim Women's Schools in Northwest China." PhD diss., Lanzhou University, 2014.

Jaschok, Maria, and Man Ke. "Covering Body, Uncovering Identity: Chinese Muslim Women's Vocabularies of Dress, Based on Fieldwork in Northwest and Central China." *Comparative Islamic Studies* 9, no. 2 (2016): 141–163. https://doi.org/10.1558/cis.28236.

Jaschok, Maria, and Shui Jingjun. "The Study of Islam, Women, and Gender in China—Taking a Gender-Critical Turn." *Asian Culture* 37 (2013): 1–14.

Jaschok, Maria, and Shui Jingjun. *The History of Women's Mosques in Chinese Islam*. Richmond: Curzon/Routledge, 2000.

Jaschok, Maria. "Religious Agency and Gender Complementarity: Women's Mosques and Women's Voices in Hui Muslim Communities in Central China." *Review of Religion and Chinese Society* 5 (2018): 83–207.

Jaschok, Maria. "Sound and Silence in Chinese Women's Mosques—Identity, Faith and Equality." *Performing Islam* 3, nos. 1–2 (2014): 59–82. https://doi.org/10.1386/pi.31-2.11_2.

Jia, Yufei. "Study of Muslim Women in Yiwu." MPhil thesis, Ningxia University, 2017.

Jiang Bo and Fei Xiang. "Study of the Muslim Women's School in Linxia." *Xibei Shidi* 3 (1995): 75–84.

Jin, Yijiu. *Localization and Nationalization of Islam in China*. Leiden: Brill, 2017.

Ma, Cijun " 'Doing It'—The Construction of Public Space by Yongjian Hui Women in Lushan." *Xinanbian Jiang Minzu Yanjiu*, 23 (2018):183–190.

Ma, Guifen. *Research on Muslim Women's Social Participation in Northwest China: Case Studies of Hui and Dongxiang Women in Gansu Province*. Beijing: Renmin Publishing House, 2017.

Ma, Huifen and Hu Liping. "The Socio-Spatial Significance of Contemporary Muslim Female Education in Northwest China—Based on the Case Studies of Lanzhou and Linxia," *Huizu Yanjiu* 3 (2016): 13–19.

Ma, Qiang "Fieldwork and Thinking on Hui Islamic Cultural Education." *Huizu Yanjiu* 4 (2003): 104–110.

Ma, Qiang. "Women's Education and Cultural Self-Awareness: A Case Study of the Linxia Chinese-Arabic Women's School." *Zhongguo Musilin* 1 (2003): 15–17.

Ma, Shuqin ."Case Study of a Muslim Women's School: Taking Zhangjiachuan Muslim School (Girls' Division) as an Example." MPhil thesis, Northwest Minzu University, 2013.

Ma, Wenmei. "A Case Study of Contemporary Muslim *Nüxue*: Taking Sino-Arabic Women's school in Linxia as an Example." MPhil thesis, Northwest Minzu University, 2008.

Ma, Xiaolin. "Anthropological Research on Hui Women's Pilgrimage: A Case Study of a Female Hajj Group." MPhil thesis, Xinjiang Normal University, 2011.
Ma, Yan. "On the Cultural Self-awareness of Hui Women Due to the Rise of Muslim Women's Schools—A Case Study of Urban Women's Schools in Tongxin County, Ningxia." *Ningxia Shehui Kexue* 2 (2007): 86–89.
Mahmood, Saba. *Politics of Piety: The Islamic Revival and the Feminist Subject.* Princeton, NJ: Princeton University Press, 2005.
Masumi, Matsumoto. "Islamic Women's Education in Northwest China—Taking the Sino-Arabic Women's School in Linxia and the Sino-Arabic Women's School in Weizhou as Examples." Translated by Lu Zhonghui. *Huizu Yanjiu* 4 (2003): 111–115.
Masumi, Matsumoto. "Muslim Women Crossing Regions and States: Religious Education and Discussion of Women's Development in Yunnan Girls' Schools." In *Migration and Cultural Dynamics of Chinese Border Ethnic Groups*, 89–112. Kunming: Yunnan People's Publishing House, 2009.
Mukherjee, Kunal. *Conflict in India and China's Contested Borderlands: A Comparative Study.* Routledge Contemporary Asia Series. London: Routledge, 2019.
Petersen, Kristian. *Interpreting Islam in China: Pilgrimage, Scripture, and Language in the Han Kitab.* Oxford: Oxford University Press, 2017.
Sha, Aixia. "Study of Female Role Transformation in Rural Tourism Development in Hui Residential Areas—Taking Jingyuan County, Ningxia, as an Example." *Beifang Minzu Daxue Xuebao* 5 (2012): 107–110.
Shui, Jingjun "A Brief Exposition of the Origin and Development of Women's Schools and Women's Mosques." *Huizu Yanjiu* 1 (1996): 51–59.
Shui, Jingjun. "In Search of Sacred Women's Organizations." In *Chinese Women Organizing*, edited by Ping-Chun Hsiung, Maria Jaschok, and Cecilia Milwertz, with Red Chan, 101–118. Oxford: Berg, 2001.
Stewart, Alexander. *Chinese Muslims and the Global Ummah: Islamic Revival and Ethnic Identity among the Hui of Qinghai Province.* London: Routledge, 2016.
Su, Muyu. "Adjustments and Belonging: A Study of Social Adaptation of Migrant Muslim Women in Lanzhou." PhD diss., Lanzhou University, 2018.
Wang, Lanxia "An Investigative Report on Minority Women's Political Participation: Taking Salar in Xunhua County as an Example." *Zu Guo* 14 (2016): 132–133.
Yan, Guofang. "The Influence of Hui Women's Social Participation in Folklore in Transition." *Xibei Minzu Yanjiu* 2 (2003): 173–189.
Yang, Mei. "Case Study of the Emergence of Women's Education in Traditional Mosque Education—the Case of the Sino-Arabic Women's School in Xiguan, Lanzhou." MPhil thesis, Northwest Minzu University, 2007.
Yang, Wenjiong. "Hui Traditional Culture and Modernization in Urban Society." *Huizu Yanjiu* 1 (2004): 58–64.
Yang, Wenjiong. "*Nüxue*: The Extension of Mosque Education and Changes in the Important Role of Cultural Inheritance: Taking Lanzhou, Xi'an and Linxia as Examples." *Huizu Yanjiu* 1 (2002): 25–31.

CHAPTER 25

MUSLIM WOMEN'S RELIGIOUS AND SOCIAL ACTIVISM IN SOUTH AFRICA

NINA HOEL

SHAMIMA Shaikh, one of the most notable and courageous gender-equality activists in South Africa, once remarked, "The fundamental principle of Islam is Tauhid—the unity of the human race under the sovereignty of the One and Only, Universal Divine Allah. Islam's message of peace affirms the equality of all human beings, and rejects all discrimination on the basis of race, class and gender."[1] Considered by many as a South African Joan of Arc,[2] Shaikh, who died in January 1998 when she was only thirty-seven years old, is remembered fondly by many for initiating a women's "rebellion" in 1993 so as to claim access for women to a mosque in Johannesburg during the month of Ramadan. Being a pioneer and a vigorous advocate for Muslim women's rights in South Africa, Shamima Shaikh's legacy is commemorated and carried forward through the work of the many women and men who share in her vision of social justice. The quotation above, taken from a talk she prepared seventeen days before she died, captures some of the central concerns of Muslim women's activism in South Africa that this chapter elaborates. Primarily, the quotation underlines the need to illuminate and respond to the overarching theological principle of *tawḥīd* (God's oneness or unicity)—a principle that subsumes all socially constructed and imaginary binaries. Moreover, the focus on broader Qur'anic ethical principles, such as social justice, resonates with much scholarly and activist work involving Muslim communities in South Africa. The quotation also calls attention to the need for intersectional lenses in the struggle for equality and social justice. In the context of South Africa, as in many other places, gender does not form the only basis of oppression. Race, together with class, sexuality, and religion, constitute central matrices of oppression and influence how people conceive of, embody, and experience their lived reality. The chapter argues that Muslim women's activism in

South Africa is informed by intersecting structures of oppression and that these, in turn, shape and configure the discourses wherein Muslim women live, imagine, and create possibilities for human flourishing. In this chapter, religion, race, gender, and sexuality are particularly emphasized as embodied categories that in different and imbricated ways give rise to activist initiatives that take seriously Muslim women's embodiment and diverse experiences.

The chapter presents three cases that all start from the epistemological priority of experience, and, furthermore, draw attention to the various ways in which Muslim women "*experientially* grapple with Islamic teachings," that is, engaging in a "*tafsīr* of praxis."[3] The first case engages the critical theme of women's access to mosques in South Africa and illustrates important academic debates that go beyond national borders. The second case considers the development of Muslim personal law, a legal framework that primarily involves family law. The case illustrates the importance of research that inextricably links academic scholarship with activism. Finally, the third case engages the topic of queer Muslim lives in South Africa. The case presents examples from the work of the organization The Inner Circle and highlights the many ways in which the organization's activist and knowledge-producing efforts inform the configuration of a discourse that holds a critically expansive understanding of human nature.

The next sections of the chapter explicate the three cases introduced. While describing particular historical moments and trajectories, the cases also illustrate the confluence of scholarship and activism at these critical junctures as well as some of the theoretical issues and strategies employed in research concerning the nexus of Islamic theology and lived experiences.[4]

Women in the Mosque

The "women in mosques" campaign was initiated by the Muslim Youth Movement (MYM) in the early 1990s. Stressing the priority of gender equality, the MYM bravely embarked on a campaign that was to make South African mosques more gender-inclusive. Noting that women's access to mosques was quite restrictive, particularly in the northern provinces, Na'eem Jeenah argues that the campaign generated much contestation within the South African ulama.[5] One of the most renowned activist initiatives took place in 1993, when a group of female MYM members, led by feminist-activist Shamima Shaikh, entered the 23rd Street mosque in Johannesburg, wishing to take part in the Tarāwīḥ (special evening prayers during Ramadan). Their disruption was met with disapproval and resulted in expulsion. The roughly 200 women who had wished to perform the Tarāwīḥ in the mosque, the space where the prayer traditionally is performed, were accommodated under a marquee *behind* the mosque.[6]

The following day, a pamphlet was produced and disseminated. Reflecting the experiences of the women who were denied access to the mosque space, the pamphlet also addressed the imbued androcentrism rendered visible by the event:

> It is about time that our community, especially the men, begins educating itself about issues that are crucial to our lives and survival as a community. Women and children are not second-class citizens to be denied access to mosques, to be hushed up whenever we begin talking, and to be shunted around at the whims of men.[7]

The statement highlights the need to address deeply rooted gendered beliefs. Given the normalization of racialized second-class citizenry under apartheid, the continuing existence of such systemic power dynamics was highly vexing. The MYM took action and established a Gender Desk later that year. The claim for women's "space in mosques" became replaced by the slogan "equal access to mosques."[8] The Gender Desk emphasized the importance of an equally shared space *in* the mosque, as opposed to the more typical practice of displacing women to basements, mezzanines, and backyards.

The achievement of women's equal access to mosques is a continuing struggle and, today, women's access and participation in mosques still remains a controversial issue.

With the notable exception of Claremont Main Road Mosque in Cape Town, most mosques throughout South Africa relegate women either to marginal spaces in the mosque (such as balconies, basements, and mezzanines) or to a space outside the mosque (such as backyards). Hence, there is still a long way to go before women's equal access to mosques becomes the normative standard. So what happened in the Claremont Main Road Mosque? It was 1994, the year of South Africa's first democratic election. The Claremont Main Road Mosque was, and still is, known for its progressive and inclusive approach to Islam under its imam-in-residence: Rashied Omar (who served as the president of the MYM from 1987 to 1990). Engaging sociopolitical issues through sermons, political activism, and community outreach programs, the Claremont Main Road Mosque urged the participation of women and were responsive to peoples' lived realities by including talks about HIV/AIDS, drugs, and gender violence.[9] It was August 12, 1994, and amina wadud delivered the Friday *khuṭbah* (sermon) in front of a mixed-gender congregation.

Prior to amina wadud's khuṭbah, it was decided that women should have equal access to the main prayer area.[10] Women, who normally accessed the upper mezzanine floor, were invited to occupy the one side of the main prayer area. The main prayer area was divided into two parallel sections by a rope, rendering the space shared and gender-inclusive. This is the way it has remained ever since.

Much has been written about this event as it received national and international media attention. Public debates tended to focus on two issues. First, the khuṭbah was given by a Muslim woman. And second, the space was gender-inclusive. As noted by amina wadud, in her own narration of "the Claremont Main Road Mosque Event," the *content* of her khuṭbah received scant attention in the media.[11] Academic debates ensuing from the event focused on critiquing the dualistic religious discourses that instill male normativity. Starting from patriarchal religious anthropology to assumptions concerning women's "nature" or "God-given" gender roles, theoretical discussions highlighted the sexual politics of the mosque space. Aptly titled "Sexual Men and Spiritual Women," Sa'diyya Shaikh's opinion piece published in *al-Qalam* (South African national Muslim newspaper) shortly after the event, problematizes the existing tensions between sexuality and spirituality. Arguing that the emphasis on sexuality in debates on women's religious leadership presents men as incapable of moral responsibility and spiritual dedication, she intelligibly deconstructs the dualism of spiritual men and sexual women.[12] In probing the question of what it means to be human in light of this event, *tawḥīd* emerges as a powerful concept bringing together females and males as equal subjects. Women's equal opportunity to occupy the mosque space or being purveyors of religious knowledge are indeed expressions of women's equal humanness. Shaikh movingly states, "it is only by breaking down oppressive categories and accepting responsibility for our own behavior that we—believing men and believing women, God-conscious men and women—can reclaim our full humanity, our Islam."[13] Calling attention to egalitarian constructs of religious anthropology, scholarly engagement is not about whether women can/should occupy the mosque space (as participants and as religious leaders) but that doing so is a truthful response to being fully Muslim, fully human. Indeed, both the statement issued in the pamphlet (quoted above) as well as scholarly engagement pertaining to the issue of women's full participation in the mosque is reflective of Shaikh's notion of a "*tafsīr* of praxis." Engaging in subversive acts and interpretations that is attentive to women's experiences and grappling with male-dominated Islamic norms, South African Muslim women create powerful ethical responses that are reflective of a profound commitment to egalitarianism, relationality, and *tawḥīd*.

The Struggle for Muslim Personal Law

Post-1994, it became a priority to both develop and integrate Muslim personal law (MPL) under the South African Constitution of 1996.[14] The debates that ensued in Muslim communities rendered visible diverse understandings of Islam along the progressive–conservative continuum. In particular, issues relating to Muslim women's rights and its relationship to the provision on gender equality set out in the Bill of Rights became vital points of contestation. Through mediums like *Al-Qalam* and *The Voice* (Muslim radio station), Muslim women became involved in the discussion and demanded that MPL needed to incorporate gender equality as a guiding principle. The radio programs "Saut al-Nisā'" (Women's Voice), "Lifting the Veil" (rereadings of foundational scriptures from a feminist perspective), and "Breaking the Silence" (a program focusing particularly on spousal abuse), did much to contribute to increased visibility of gender-related issues in Muslim communities, and, in effect, reinforced the need for women's protection under the law.[15]

Despite a host of activist initiatives, MPL is not yet implemented.[16] Customarily, various ulama bodies, situated in major cities in the country, tend to the needs of Muslim communities with issues pertaining to the contracting of marriages (including polygynous unions) and matters of divorce, custody, and inheritance. The non-recognition of Muslim marriages under South African Law constitutes an untenable situation for many Muslim women who are married according to Islamic rites *only* or who are in polygynous unions. Furthermore, the process of initiating and procuring divorce through Muslim ulama bodies, by women, has proven particularly difficult.[17]

In 2010, after many years of intense lobbying, the Department of Justice and Constitutional Development released the Muslim Marriages Bill (MMB)—a bill that seeks full legal recognition of Muslim marriages and includes provisions for regulation (e.g., pertaining to polygynous unions, matters of divorce, and maintenance). Although the release of the Bill revived some of the earlier contestations pertaining to women's rights, it also inspired the establishment of the Recognition of Muslim Marriages Forum. The Forum, consisting of a network of activists, legal scholars, and religious studies academics, shared a commitment to take seriously the experiences of South African Muslim women. The Forum's concerns, particularly related to the priority of gender equality in matters of Islamic law, were reflected in the Bill.

The release of the Bill also coincided with the finalization of a research project that aimed to provide information on and document the nature of South African Muslim women's experiences in relation to marriage, sexuality, and reproductive health, led by Sa'diyya Shaikh. The study—a first of its kind in the context of South Africa—employed both quantitative and qualitative approaches. The data, particularly from the qualitative research, indicates that Muslim women who had experiences with polygyny and/or divorce suffered severe marginalization when seeking recourse through religious authorities and were often subject to quite arbitrary, androcentric understandings of Islam. On the basis of these research results, the research team drew up a research report submitted to the minister of justice and constitutional development, in support of the Muslim Marriages Bill.[18] The submission outlined central research findings and consequently stressed the need for "relief and protection to Muslim women" and the need to "enable a practical implementation of the ethics of justice promised by the Shariah."[19] The research studies were extensively referred to in Court, which prompted an application made by the Women's Legal Centre Trust to the High Court of South Africa in 2017, to admit the research studies (qualitative and quantitative) not only as *submissions* (as previously done) but also as *evidence*.

Although the matter of implementing the Muslim Marriages Bill is currently unresolved,[20] the chapter finds it worth emphasizing the important intersections that can emerge between grassroots, research, and lawmaking—indeed, the importance of research that links academic scholarship with activism. Prioritizing women's experiences, as a research strategy and as a mode of activism undoubtedly produce knowledge that is socially relevant and meaningful. The case, the struggle for Muslim Personal Law, is an example of an ongoing endeavor that brings together the highest aspirations of the South African Constitution, gender-inclusive and egalitarian understandings of Islamic law, and the real life experiences of South African Muslim women.

Queer Muslim Lives in South Africa

Islam and queerness or being queer and Muslim, have received increased academic attention, nationally in South Africa and internationally—particularly since the publication of Scott Kugle's seminal book *Homosexuality in Islam: Critical Reflection on Gay, Lesbian and Transgender Muslims* in 2010.[21] Research and activism that focus on queer Muslims destabilize existing assumptions concerning the mutual exclusivity of being queer *and* Muslim. In South Africa, much work has been done pertaining to community awareness-raising and knowledge production. In particular, the organization, the Inner Circle, established as early as 1996, has done much to debunk heteronormativity in Islam. Being an organization dedicated to lending support to queer Muslims, the Inner Circle hosts workshops related to personal empowerment as well as to educate the wider community about sexual diversity. The organization also offers an Imamat training program and is authorized to conduct civil rights union marriages (same-sex unions) as well as interfaith marriages.[22]

It is not coincidental that the Inner Circle was founded in the wake of the new South African Constitution of 1996, which included a provision prohibiting discrimination based on sexual orientation.[23] Imam Muhsin Hendricks, the founder of the organization, who perhaps became best known internationally for his central role in Parvez Sharma's documentary *A Jihad for Love* (2007), has dedicated the greater part of his life to bringing about social justice for queer Muslims. Prioritizing *ijtihād* (independent reasoning), as a central interpretive strategy, while also foregrounding the experiences of queer Muslims in South Africa, the Inner Circle can safely be characterized as a pioneering activist organization. Among their many knowledge-producing achievements is the anthology of autobiographical writings by gay, lesbian, and trans Muslims, compiled in *Hijab: Unveiling Queer Muslim Lives* (2009).[24] The narratives in the book profoundly reflect deeply personal and embodied experiences that illuminate the wrestling for human wholeness. *Hijab* engages a multitude of themes related to the inextricable imbrication of religion and sexuality. One of the most significant themes relates to the organic rendering of sexual orientation as part of Divine Creation—a view that troubles traditional gender and sex binaries.[25] In many ways the autobiographical narratives resonate with Sa'diyya Shaikh's notion of a "*tafsīr* of praxis" in that narrators' experiences poignantly inform their engagement with the Islamic tradition. It is clear in many of the narratives that religiosity constitutes an important aspect of personhood. At the same time, traditional understandings of Islam prompt particular ethical quandaries relating to embodied sexualities that are commonly excluded from the fold of Islam.

Moreover, in addition to the intersections of religion and sexuality, *Hijab* also speaks to notions of race and national belonging.[26] As such, it complicates the embodiment of queer Muslim lives, marked by the heteropatriarchal legacies of apartheid. In the postapartheid era, *Hijab* renders visible the right to freedom from discrimination due to race, gender, religion, and sexual orientation. It disrupts contemporary masculinist discourses by rendering the life-stories of queerly situated subjects as part of an expansive national public.

The activist and knowledge-producing work of the Inner Circle reminds us that Muslim women's activism not only engages and subverts patriarchal norms and practices, but also the heterosexism that informs it and underlines it. Noting the prioritization of experience that seemingly informs activist discourses in South Africa, the diversity of experience and attention to intersectionality emerges as salient tropes.

Muslim Women's Activism in South Africa: Looking Back, Looking Forward

The three cases highlighted in this chapter cannot be said to be exhaustive when it comes to Muslim women's engagements in South Africa. They are, however, illustrative of some of the most noteworthy local activist initiatives. Relatedly, a variety of issues pertaining to Muslim women's equal access to mosques and religious leadership, the development of, and, impending implementation of an egalitarian Muslim Personal Law, and the dynamics of queer Muslim lives, have been fervently debated among activists and scholars of Islam in South Africa. Moreover, the cases in this chapter exemplify the coimbrication of activism and scholarship. Many scholars are activists, and many activists are scholars who through their work with grassroots produce invaluable knowledge that is taken up in scholarly discussions, informing the development of research projects and publications.

At the level of epistemology, the category of experience emerges both as a mode of activism and as a concept for theoretical analysis. Experience, it seems, importantly informs activist initiatives—experiences of being Muslim, experiences of being gendered, experiences of being queer, experiences of being racialized: that is to say, the experiences of embodiment. Experience also informs critical engagements, contemplation, and wrestling with Islam that leads to a realization of a *tafsīr* of praxis and recourse to *ijtihād*. Experience informs research strategies: ideologically, methodologically, conceptually, and theoretically. Experience acts as a useful heuristic device that destabilizes dominant patriarchal norms. Addressing experiences of marginalization, experiences of exclusion, experiences of injustice; and crafting discourses wherein inclusivity, reciprocity, and justice constitute central pinnacles. Experience informs an overall commitment to pursue research projects that are responsive to local dynamics and, as such, socially relevant.

Prioritizing experience also illuminates the diversity of experience in significant ways. Paying careful attention to intersectionality, which in this chapter is particularly foregrounded through the nexus of religion, gender, race, and sexuality, opens a portal to rich and complex notions of self, being, and embodiment. Arguably, the cases reflect experiences of marginalization that are complicated by the histories of colonialism and apartheid. Applying intersectional lenses to the case concerning equal access to mosques, it is possible to trace not only Muslim gendered regimes, but also connections to a racialized history wherein Muslims were displaced and denied access to previously embodied locations. The struggle for Muslim personal law can likewise be conceived not only as a struggle to regulate Muslim marital regimes so as to protect the rights of Muslim women, but also as a struggle for religious recognition. The vital work being done to craft spaces of inclusivity and belonging for queer Muslims navigates the dominant discourses of heteropatriarchy—not only within the Islamic tradition, but also within South Africa. In all of the three cases, embodiment is always multilayered, experienced, and imagined in ways that are relational and situated.

Importantly, Sa'diyya Shaikh's useful concept of a "*tafsīr* of praxis" emerges as a powerful trope in the cases presented, as they all, in slightly different ways, address the social worlds of religious texts. In other words, the cases exemplify the various ways in which religious texts—and particularly heteropatriarchal interpretations of religious texts—have rendered particularly situated subjects marginal, defined by lack, not fully human, sexualized, and disruptive. The cases gesture toward the various ways that a "*tafsīr* of praxis" is performed so as to negotiate, contest, and reconfigure societal, political, and interpersonal dynamics. Starting from the position of experience, a "*tafsīr* of praxis" is cognizant of both theoretical and embodied realities, and, as such, productive for the ways in which scholarship and activism are developed, envisioned, and embodied.

Highlighting experience, intersectionality, and "*tafsīr* of praxis" as three distinct, yet relational theoretical nodes, the chapter argues that complex embodied ways of knowing and experiencing religious discourses is a compelling and nascent avenue for further research and meaning-making. Recalling the "women's rebellion" in 1993, it would be worthwhile to examine the current situation of women's (and queer folks) perception of, access to, and use of mosques in South Africa. Or, researching the possible conceptualization of women's mosques—a phenomenon well-known in China. In light of broader conversations about gendered space, or, the contestation of space, what would a woman's mosque mean—ideologically, theoretically, experientially? Likewise, could Muslim personal law incorporate queer marital regimes? How can this be imagined—made real? Would it be responsive to the needs of Muslim communities? Also, as much research already have noted, there is a paucity of research pertaining to queer Muslim women. It would be valuable to investigate the experiences of queer Muslim women in South Africa, with a particular attention to embodiment and personhood. Finally, there exist a number of published novels, short stories, poetry, as well as a vibrant visual culture that importantly and critically engage the themes addressed in this chapter. A thorough study of the ways in which these mediums contribute to deeper understandings of Muslim selves would embellish the complexity and richness of the South African landscape.

Notes

1. Shamima Shaikh, "Women and Islam—The Gender Struggle in South Africa: The Ideological Struggle," https://shams.za.org/index.php/by-shamima/women-and-islam-the-gender-struggle-in-south-africa; (website dedicated to the memory of Shamima Shaikh).
2. Farid Esack, "Death of a Muslim Joan of Arc," *Mail and Guardian* (January 20, 1998), https://shams.za.org/index.php/about-shamima/death-of-a-muslim-joan-of-arc.

3. Nina Hoel and Sa'diyya Shaikh, "Sex as *Ibadah*: Religion, Gender and Subjectivity among South African Muslim Women," *Journal of Feminist Studies in Religion* 29, no. 1 (2013): 69–91; quotation at 70, my emphasis. The notion of a "*tafsīr* of praxis" was coined by Sa'diyya Shaikh in her invaluable chapter "A *Tafsir* of Praxis: Gender, Marital Violence, and Resistance in a South African Muslim Community," in *Violence against Women: Roots and Cures in World Religions*, ed. Dan Maguire and Sa'diyya Shaikh (Ohio: Pilgrim, 2007), 66–89. In the chapter, Shaikh elaborates that a "*tafsīr* of praxis" illustrates "how ordinary women engage, interpret, contest, and redefine the dominant understandings of Islam and how their engagement can inform some of the ethical quandaries that might emerge from ahistorical interpretations of the Qur'anic text," 70.
4. It is worth mentioning here that the critical themes explored by South African scholarship-activists have greatly inspired contemporaries as well as new generations of students to engage the intersecting nexus of Islamic theology and lived experiences. See for example, Fatima Noordien, "A Legacy of Struggle: Noorinhaar Mintin and the Empowerment of Women in Marriage and Divorce" (MA diss., University of KwaZulu-Natal, 2017); Farhana Ismail, "An Analysis of the Discursive Representations of Women's Sexual Agency in Online Fatwas: A Case Study of Askimam.org" (MA diss., University of KwaZulu-Natal, 2016); and, Zarina Hassem, "An Exploration of Women's Groups as a Tool of Empowerment for Muslim Women in South Africa" (MA diss., University of the Witwatersrand, 2008).
5. Na'eem Jeenah, "'A Degree Above . . .' The Emergence of Islamic Feminism in South Africa in the 1990s" (MA diss., University of the Witwatersrand, 2001, 13–14.
6. Jeenah, "A Degree Above," 30–32.
7. Ibid., 32.
8. Ibid., 30–32.
9. Fahmi Gamieldien, *The History of the Claremont Main Road Mosque, Its People and Their Contribution to Islam in South Africa* (Cape Town: Claremont Main Road Mosque, 2004), 53–68, 80–88.
10. Gamieldien, *The History of the Claremont Main Road Mosque.*
11. Which is also why a transcription of her *khuṭba* can be found in her book, *Inside the Gender Jihad* (2006).
12. Sa'diyya Shaikh, "Sexual Men and Spiritual Women," *Al-Qalam* 20, no. 9 (1994): 7.
13. Ibid.
14. This is not to say that conversations about the development of MPL were nonexistent prior to South Africa's first democratic election. Many efforts were made, particularly related to getting Islamic marriages recognized. However, due to the systemic discrimination against non-Christian beliefs and practices under apartheid, the process of developing MPL was constrained. For work dealing with the protracted process of developing MPL in South Africa, see Ebrahim Moosa, "Application of Muslim Personal and Family Law in South Africa: Law, Ideology and Socio-Political Implications" (MA diss., University of Cape Town, 1988); and Annie Leatt, "The State of Secularism: Constituting Religion and Tradition towards a Post-Apartheid South Africa" (PhD diss., University of the Witwatersrand, 2011).
15. Jeenah, "A Degree Above," 45–46.
16. However, it is important to point out here that aspects of Muslim marriages have been recognized by South African Law, as seen in the case of *Ryland v. Edros* in 1997. In this case, the court recognized "the contractual consequences" of a Muslim marital contract. In effect, the decision gestured toward the protection of Muslim wives (more specifically in

terms of maintenance) in the case of marital dissolution. For a more detailed engagement with the case, see Christa Rautenbach, "Some Comments on the Current (and Future) Status of Muslim Personal Law in South Africa," *PER* 2 (2004): 1–34.

17. See, Nina Hoel, "Engaging Religious Leaders: South African Muslim Women's Experiences in Matters Pertaining to Divorce Initiatives," *Social Dynamics* 38, no. 3 (2012): 184–200.
18. Sa'diyya Shaikh, Nina Hoel, and Ashraf Kagee, "The Minister of Justice and Constitutional Development, Submission on the Muslim Marriage Bill," Research report submitted to the Minister of Justice, South Africa, 2011.
19. Ibid., 24.
20. As of July 2023 the Divorce Amendment Bill has been tabled in Parliament. The draft bill seeks to amend the Divorce Act of 1979 so as to "insert a definition for a Muslim marriage; to provide for the protection and to safeguard the interests of dependent and minor children of a Muslim marriage; to provide for the redistribution of assets on the dissolution of a Muslim marriage; to provide for the forfeiture of patrimonial benefits of a Muslim marriage; and to provide for matters connected therewith" (Divorce Amendment Bill (B22-2023), https://www.parliament.gov.za/bill/2311444). The draft bill results from the Court judgment in Women's Legal Centre Trust v President of the Republic of South Africa and Others (2022) ZACC 23, which recognized the need for protecting Muslim women and children of Muslim marriages (Constitutional Court of South Africa, https://www.concourt.org.za/index.php/judgement/475-women-s-legal-centre-trust-v-president-of-the-republic-of-south-africa-and-others-cct24-21).
21. Scott Siraj al-Haqq Kugle, *Homosexuality in Islam: Critical Reflection on Gay, Lesbian and Transgender Muslims* (Oxford: Oneworld, 2010).
22. The Inner Circle website, available at http://www.theinnercircle.org.za/index.html.
23. This, of course, does not mean that discrimination based on sexual orientation does not occur. Regrettably, in South Africa, incidents of corrective rape—a hate crime that primarily targets queer women—is reflective of the disproportionate relationship between rights and the everyday experiences of queer folks. For more on corrective rape in South Africa, see the work of Zethu Matebeni, for example, "Exploring Black Lesbian Sexualities and Identities in Johannesburg" (PhD diss., University of the Witwatersrand, 2011).
24. Pepe Hendricks, ed., *Hijab: Unveiling Queer Muslim Lives* (Wynberg: Inner Circle, 2009).
25. Gabeba Baderoon, "States of Being: Public Selves and National Privacies," in "Theorising Experience, Subjectivity and Narrative in Studies of Gender and Islam," special thematic issue, ed. Sa'diyya Shaikh, Nina Hoel and Gabeba Baderoon, *Journal for Islamic Studies* 33 (2013): 77–100.
26. Baderoon, "States of Being," 83–84.

Bibliography

Baderoon, Gabeba. "States of Being: Public Selves and National Privacies." In "Theorising Experience, Subjectivity and Narrative in Studies of Gender and Islam," special thematic issue, guest edited by Sa'diyya Shaikh, Nina Hoel and Gabeba Baderoon, *Journal for Islamic Studies* 33 (2013): 77–100.

Constitutional Court of South Africa, https://www.concourt.org.za/index.php/judgement/475-women-s-legal-centre-trust-v-president-of-the-republic-of-south-africa-and-others-cct24-21.

Divorce Amendment Bill (B22-2023), https://www.parliament.gov.za/bill/2311444.

Esack, Farid. "Death of a Muslim Joan of Arc." *Mail and Guardian* (January 20, 1998). https://shams.za.org/index.php/about-shamima/death-of-a-muslim-joan-of-arc.

Gamieldien, Fahmi. *The History of the Claremont Main Road Mosque, Its People, and Their Contribution to Islam in South Africa*. Cape Town: Claremont Main Road Mosque, 2004.

Hassem, Zarina. "An Exploration of Women's Groups as a Tool of Empowerment for Muslim Women in South Africa." MA thesis, University of the Witwatersrand, 2008.

Hendricks, Pepe, ed. *Hijab: Unveiling Queer Muslim Lives*. Wynberg: Inner Circle, 2009.

Hoel, Nina. "Engaging Religious Leaders: South African Muslim Women's Experiences in Matters Pertaining to Divorce Initiatives." *Social Dynamics* 38, no. 3 (2012): 184–200.

Hoel, Nina, and Sa'diyya Shaikh. "Sex as *Ibadah*: Religion, Gender and Subjectivity among South African Muslim Women." *Journal of Feminist Studies in Religion* 29, no. 1 (2013): 69–91.

Ismail, Farhana. "An Analysis of the Discursive Representations of Women's Sexual Agency in Online Fatwas: A Case Study of Askimam.org." MA thesis., University of KwaZulu-Natal, 2016.

Jeenah, Na'eem. "'A Degree Above . . .' The Emergence of Islamic Feminism in South Africa in the 1990s." MA diss., University of the Witwatersrand, 2001.

Kugle, Scott Siraj al-Haqq. *Homosexuality in Islam: Critical Reflection on Gay, Lesbian and Transgender Muslims*. Oxford: Oneworld, 2010.

Leatt, Annie. "The State of Secularism: Constituting Religion and Tradition towards a Post-Apartheid South Africa." PhD diss., University of the Witwatersrand, 2011.

Matebeni, Zethu. "Exploring Black Lesbian Sexualities and Identities in Johannesburg." PhD diss., University of the Witwatersrand, 2011.

Moosa, Ebrahim. "Application of Muslim Personal and Family Law in South Africa: Law, Ideology and Socio-Political Implications." MA diss., University of Cape Town, 1988.

Noordien Fatima. "A Legacy of Struggle: Nourininhaar Mintin and the Empowerment of Women in Marriage and Divorce." MA diss., University of KwaZulu-Natal, 2017.

Rautenbach, Christa. "Some Comments on the Current (and Future) Status of Muslim Personal Law in South Africa." *PER* 2 (2004): 1–34.

Shaikh, Sa'diyya. "Sexual Men and Spiritual Women." *Al-Qalam* 20, no. 9 (1994): 7.

Shaikh, Sa'diyya. "A *Tafsir* of Praxis: Gender, Marital Violence, and Resistance in a South African Muslim Community." In *Violence against Women: Roots and Cures in World Religions*, edited by Dan Maguire and Sa'diyya Shaikh, 66–89. Cleveland, Ohio: Pilgrim, 2007.

Sa'diyya Shaikh, Nina Hoel, and Ashraf Kagee. "The Minister of Justice and Constitutional Development, Submission on the Muslim Marriage Bill." Research Report submitted to the Minister of Justice, South Africa, 2011.

Shaikh, Sa'diyya, Nina Hoel, and Ashraf Kagee. "South African Muslim Women: Sexuality, Marriage and Reproductive Choices, Research Report." *Journal for Islamic Studies* 31 (2011): 96–121.

Shaikh, Shamima. "Women and Islam—The Gender Struggle in South Africa: The Ideological Struggle." https://shams.za.org/index.php/by-shamima/women-and-islam-the-gender-struggle-in-south-africa.

Wadud, amina. *Inside the Gender Jihad: Women's Reform in Islam*. Oxford: Oneworld, 2006.

CHAPTER 26

MUSLIM WOMEN'S RELIGIOUS AND SOCIAL ACTIVISM IN THE UNITED STATES

JULIANE HAMMER

MUSLIM women, and more broadly, "gender issues in Islam" have been at the center of both scholarly and public attention since the dawn of European colonialism. They are still more often than not written about rather than spoken to or asked for their perspectives; and, they are perceived as being "over there" rather than present in societies across the globe, including the United States. Discussing Muslim women in the United States as participants and leaders in religious, social, and political activism then requires critical frames of inquiry as well as a sense of history. In my endeavor of writing about Muslim women's activism in the United States, I take inspiration from these words of Muslim feminist scholar Kecia Ali: "Not only is it easier to critique than to build, more importantly, Muslim women, Muslim families, Muslim communities are not identical. What works for some will not work for others."[1]

In this chapter, I present such a critical frame by offering four considerations that are necessary to recognize the historical process, diversity, and politics of Muslim women's activism as well as of any analysis of such activism. Those four theoretical considerations are the relationship of Islam and feminism; the role of anti-Muslim hostility in shaping activism and scholarship about it; the relationship between scholarship and activism (or from a slightly different angle, between practice and discourse); and the necessary consideration of women's activism as not limited to "women's issues." Taken together, they allow for a more grounded and complex picture of the history of American Muslim women's activism.

In the second part of the chapter, and following the development of this framework, I offer a number of examples of organizations, movements, and individuals, in order to illustrate the continuous negotiation of all three questions and the debates around them. This history-through-specific-examples approach has the advantage of allowing me to analyze in some depth the particularity of each example's historical context and specificity, while still arguing for broader patterns and a sense of cohesion among them. Much more work needs to be done to comprehensively document and thus preserve the histories of Muslim American communities, institutions, and individuals; and histories that do so with a focus on women are especially sparse. Telling the stories of people and the communities they helped build, as well as reflecting on the roles that individuals with agency play in a story that often focuses on how their contexts shaped them, is a monumental undertaking. I see histories, in the plural, emerging from precisely the interplay between agency and environment, with a focus on both intent and impact in activism. I draw on more than a decade of research on Muslim women's activism, in the United States and beyond, to offer the sketch that follows. My protagonists, Muslim women activists, are as diverse as American Muslim communities and they are both thoroughly American, despite claims to the contrary, and deeply transnational. National boundaries do not stop the travel and migration of ideas, movements, or people, and the religious, social, and political activism of American Muslim women is no exception. They are part of transnational Muslim women's movements for justice and equality; their ideas and actions are discussed and adopted in other contexts while they are inspired by women's activism elsewhere in the world, Muslim or otherwise. And their activism in the United States (and beyond) impacts perceptions of Islam and Muslims globally as well as in their local contexts.

Islam and Feminism

Can Muslims be feminist? Can feminists be Muslims? These are questions that I am asked frequently in presenting my research as well as in my teaching. The questioners perhaps have a point in that the mainstream feminist movement has tended to look at religion and religious people with suspicion because of the ways in which religious doctrines and institutions have, for the most part, supported patriarchal societal structures with reference to divine intent.[2] Feminism has inspired the work of some women activists because of its embrace of gender justice as a goal, as well as in its self-understanding of both a critique of patriarchy in theoretical form and an activist movement to transform society toward that goal. For Muslim women, feminism has also been, both in the past and in the present, a colonial and neocolonial tool for the advancement of an ideology that casts Islam and Muslim societies as uniquely patriarchal and unable to be modern because of gender inequality and the oppression of women. It is no wonder then that Muslim (women) activists have struggled with the adoption of feminist labels for themselves, both because they were accused of supporting an imperialist ideology through such adoption, and because they themselves rejected the feminist complicity in imperialist domination and discrimination.

As a result of the robust and thoughtful debate about the relationship between feminism and Islam, Muslim women have situated themselves on a spectrum from embracing the label to rejecting feminism as an idea and a practice and everything in between.[3] We will see in the examples below how one's placement on this spectrum can change over time and that it moves with and in response to broader debates about feminism in American society and the world at large. Some women activists are motivated by notions of change that deny any link to feminist ideas or even gender justice. Instead they embrace notions of benign patriarchy as well as certainty and preservation of historical societal norms and structures. One central question that is raised by this debate is how critique of Muslim communities, doctrines, and practices on the one hand, and neoimperialist power structures and practices on the other, can be possible without having to choose one over the other. Rochelle Terman's notion of "double critique" as well as Miriam Cooke's notion of "multiple critique" have become potent tools for negotiating this tension.[4] It is precisely the denial of this possibility that has become the hallmark of Islamophobic rhetoric and ideology with regard to "women in Islam."

Anti-Muslim Hostility and Gender in Islam

Anti-Muslim hostility (or Islamophobia[5]), like other phenomena, is gendered and takes on particular forms in its focus on Muslim women and in the particular context of the United States. There is a robust literature on Islamophobia in America that is both a testament to the enduring presence of a complex set of phenomena, actors, effects, and histories, and to the variety of approaches to analyzing and combatting this particular type of hostility and prejudice. Anti-Muslim hostility is now regularly identified as a specific form of racism that assumes the homogeneity of a diverse set of communities and individuals in the United States; describes Islam and Muslims as essentially foreign to the US and thus as not belonging; identifies Muslims, especially Muslim men, as uniquely prone to violence, radicalism, and terrorism; and assumes such propensity to be pseudo-genetic, thus racializing Muslims and placing them in an inferior position in the racist hierarchies of US society.[6] These negative and racist representations of Islam and Muslims are not limited to or produced only by different forms of media, but are rather the outcome of deliberate production in the triangle between state, media, and other political actors. While they may confirm existing biases in media consumers and citizens, the state as well as political pundits have a vested interest in deploying anti-Muslim hostility as a tool for political distraction, scapegoating, and the preservation of white and Christian supremacy in American society.[7]

Muslim women have been given center stage in these discourses and practices as oppressed and silent victims in need of saving and liberation from both Islam and Muslim men. They have also been represented as the reproducers of Muslim communities as a fifth column in the US civic body by birthing more Muslim children and thus growing the demographic threat of Muslims from within. More recently, new and different representations of Muslim women have emerged that have surpassed but not replaced the earlier "saving Muslim women victims" discourse: Muslim women as potential terrorists or supporters of terrorism, making them as prone as men to the assumed violence inherent in Islam; and Muslim women activists who advocate for progressive causes.[8] The latter points to a broader issue of what could be described as liberal Islamophobia, namely a set of discourses that do not exhibit open hostility or hate toward Muslims but rather set the limits of acceptable speech and action for Muslims and only accepts them when they stay within those parameters. Muslim women activists fighting against so-called honor killings, for equal leadership representation, and for gender equality more broadly are hailed as heroines who take great risks in the fight for gender equality, but their struggles in their communities and sometimes their rejection also confirm the oppressive and uniquely patriarchal nature of Muslim communities.

The strong and growing presence of Islamophobic sentiments, media representations, and government policies has had an ever-increasing impact on both the work and perception of Muslim women activists. When Muslim women advocate and work for change in their communities they first have to indicate issues in need of change, especially related to gender norms, thereby inadvertently confirming Islamophobic representations of Islam and Muslim men. This conundrum is in part manufactured by mainstream secular feminists, some of whom have been among the strongest supporters of anti-Muslim hostility.[9] American Muslim debates and conversations take place inside the American public square—thus making every internal critique automatically public. When Muslim women activists work for social justice in the broader American society, including issues such as poverty, racism, and women's rights, they are either accused of not being sufficiently American (or loyal to America) to criticize American society, or of treasonous intentions toward the US government. Multiple critique as introduced above is made difficult in such a political climate, which forms the backdrop for Muslim women's activism on a host of issues, including some that are not directly "gender issues."

Scholarship and Activism; Discourse and Practice

In a chapter on women's religious, social, and political activism it is important to define what I mean by "activism." To me, activism is that set of actions which aims to change any aspect of society through engagement in the social and political processes that form that society. This definition allows for the inclusion of activities such as production and distribution of knowledge, critiques of existing discourses and practices, and practices that transform society directly, such as legal advocacy and social services.

In much of the scholarship on women's activism there seems to be an underlying assumption that the relationship between discourse and practice is one of first and second. As a discourse is created, usually a critique of the existing condition or a description of a norm or vision, practice means applying that discourse to social and political circumstances or situations in an attempt to change them away from what has been critiqued and toward the described norm or vision. Based on my research on Muslim women and prayer leadership as well as American Muslim efforts against domestic violence, I have come to describe the relationship between discourse and practice as interdependent and at the very least in a continuous cycle.[10] In other words, experiences of injustice or discord inspire and compel activists to work for change, who then search for discursive frameworks that can put into words their critique or commitment. At times, scholars, intellectuals, and religious leaders are invited to help supply or produce the religious knowledge necessary to undergird social and political activism; at other times, the activists themselves are the producers of such discourse and thus knowledge.

In a slightly different approach, knowledge production and dissemination can be described as activism, in and beyond the academy. If the academic writings, books, and articles as well as conference presentations and public lectures are aimed at change in Muslim communities and the broader society, then writing, publishing, and disseminating knowledge are forms of activism themselves and scholars and intellectuals are simultaneously activists and producers of knowledge. At the same time, the knowledge produced by grassroots activists is in no way inferior to that of academics or traditional scholars, but is rather as situational and contextual as that of academics, a fact that needs to be acknowledged. This approach to knowledge production rejects the (patriarchal) notion that knowledge is superior to action, or that the mind is more important than the body. It helps address the existing tension between self-identified academics and grassroots activists, in which the latter feel compelled to defend themselves against charges that they lack broader understanding or intellectual sophistication. Rather, situational knowledge and focus on particular issues to be addressed through activism is a deliberate choice on the part of activists that needs to be taken seriously and that allows them to act efficiently in achieving change.

The abstract notion of knowledge should be made particular here by focusing on the ways in which scholars, activists and scholar-activists have focused on particular types of religious knowledge, namely reading and interpreting the Qur'ān (differently); engaging the *Sunna* of the Prophet Muhammad, including *Hadīth*; and debating the significance and application of Islamic Law in the secular context of the United States, both as self-imposed community law, and as a more general understanding of Muslim ethics.

Several women scholar-activists are noteworthy as pioneers, including Riffat Hassan, amina wadud, Asma Barlas, and Azizah al-Hibri as well as members of the next generation, such as Kecia Ali, Aysha Hidayatullah, and Ayesha Chaudhry. Their work revolves around gender-just interpretations of the Qur'ān in relation to critically rethinking readings of the *Sunna* as prophetic guidance, as well as the possibility of reframing and applying Islamic legal methodologies and rulings. Each of them, in addition to many others who could be added to this list, has negotiated in complex ways their relationship to the label "feminist" while being deeply and proudly identifying as scholar-activists.[11]

Women's Activism and Women's Issues

The last piece of the framework necessary for understanding the dynamics of American Muslim women's activism is related to the question of who is included in the notion of "Muslim women" on the one hand, and the scope of issues addressed by Muslim women activists on the other. On the former, I have included in my consideration anyone who identifies as a woman, regardless of sex assigned at birth, thereby recognizing the constructed nature of both sex and gender and the ongoing debate in the US context about the meaning of gender categories. Muslim women participate(d) in many different forms of activism, and regarding many different societal issues they want(ed) to change. Muslim women appear in the history of activism as individuals, in explicitly Muslim organizations and movements, and in other social and political movements, sometimes foregrounding their Muslimness as an important identity marker and at other times choosing not to identify directly as Muslim.

There is an interesting question here about the motivation for engaging in activism and whether someone's Muslimness or Islam is identified as an important or even primary driver for their activism. In other words, is Muslim women's activism necessarily "Muslim" because the women engaging in it share their Muslimness as part of their identity? Does someone's relationship with their faith provide the motivational basis for their activism and is such activism then automatically embedded in an "Islamic framework"? Part of the diversity in Muslim women's social, religious, and political activism in the United States lies precisely in the wide spectrum of possible answers to this question. Some women activists have identified Islamic ethics explicitly as lying at the core of their commitment to changing society and/or addressing injustice, while others have framed their activism less directly in those terms. And yet others see their engagement as a direct intervention in the deep and lasting conversation among Muslims about the Islamic tradition in relation to notions of stability and change, past and future, authority, and leadership.

This then provides the link to the second configuration of a spectrum, namely one of issues that can be identified as priorities in the work of women activists. At first, it may seem tempting to assume that women's activism should be geared toward "women's issues" such as women's leadership, women's rights in societies and communities, women's space, and perhaps also questions such as gender roles in marriage and women's sexuality. Indeed, a good number of projects and organizations have framed their efforts in these or similar terms. However, Saba Mahmoud has warned that feminist scholars will only recognize as activism what also reads as resistance to patriarchy, thereby obscuring those activist efforts by women that may not point in the direction of progressive feminist change.[12] This makes it difficult to recognize, for example, the work of organizations that support Muslim families; distribute charity for the poor, Muslim and non-Muslim alike; or offer gender-separated Islamic education to women and girls, as forms of activism because they do not conform to a progressive change paradigm. I argue that these are indeed also forms of women's activism and that it is important to think further and more critically about our own political commitments in evaluating Muslim women's work for change.

Similarly, women's activities related to environmental issues, against racism, on prison reform, for electoral and broader political participation (not only of women), for worker's rights, and even for conservative causes such as limits on abortion rights, need to be acknowledged as forms of activism. In a sense though, the participation of women activists in such activities, regardless of where they fall on the political spectrum, supports the claim of women to their full humanity, and illustrates the complicated nature of political, religious, and social commitments, as well as the fact that being women is only one facet of their identities.

All four of the theoretical considerations I have shared so far, are actualized and illustrated in the examples that follow. To my knowledge, no complete list of Muslim women's organizations in the United States has ever been created, with the above considerations providing some explanation as to why that might be the case. I have selected examples of formal and Muslim organizations and institutions but want to acknowledge the complexity of Muslim institution-building in the United States as well as the historical and continued presence of less formalized networks, communities of activism, and not least individuals. A difference perhaps also needs to be acknowledged between nationally recognized and operating organizations and many more that engage in various forms of activist work in local contexts and communities. And then there is the waxing and waning of organizations, activists involved in them, resulting in a rapidly changing landscape of women's activism that can only partially be tracked and documented through online archives and activities. This chapter can provide only a glimpse of the diversity, complexity, and relative prominence of organizations, movements, networks, and in all of these and beyond, the roles of individual activists as leaders.

Muslim Girls Training and General Civilization Class (MGT-GCC)

Created by the founder of the Nation of Islam (NOI), Fard Muhammad, and supported by the long-term leader Elijah Muhammad, MGT-GCC was a part of the NOI since the 1930s. Organized and run by the women of the NOI, MGT-GCC provided a broad range of classes, organized by age groups, to instruct NOI women of all ages in domestic tasks such as cooking, nutrition, sewing, house cleaning, child-rearing, personal hygiene, religious instruction, and self-defense. NOI sisters worked as instructors and inspectors in a hierarchical structure that allowed individual women to rise through the ranks based on their accomplishments. MGT-GCC also included career training at certain times and negotiated patriarchal gender norms with the changing conditions of American society from the 1930s to the 1970s. Ula Taylor has described the activism of women in the NOI as negotiating the "promise of patriarchy," thereby providing a framework for analyzing NOI women activists as more complex than women swayed by patriarchal certainty or actively working against it.[13] Instead, the NOI offered women the authenticity of a religious organization while also actively working for the empowerment of Black communities in a racist American society.

Muslim Women's League (MWL)

The Muslim Women's League was founded in 1992 in California, and has counted Muslim women's rights activist and medical doctor Laila al-Marayati among its most active spokespeople. Born of the commitment to provide support to women in Bosnia during the war, MWL has based its activist projects, both locally in California and across the United States, as well as internationally, on the need to reclaim "the status of women as free, equal and vital contributors to society" as one of the values of Islam.[14] Such projects included study circles for Muslim women, educating non-Muslims about women's rights in Islam, supporting grassroots efforts in Muslim communities and societies, and highlighting through research and publishing, alternative and gender-just interpretations of Islam. MWL has organized girls' sports summer camps and clinics to support women's reproductive health needs. The organization has also taken strong public stances in support of women's rights in marriage and against female genital cutting as well as recognizing the continuous need to combat negative stereotypes of Islam and Muslims.

Women in Islam (WI)

Women in Islam was also founded in 1992, in New York City, and also in response to the atrocities inflicted on Muslims in Bosnia. WI's founder, Aisha al-Adawiya, has been a prominent leader in Muslim communities in the United States, and has represented the organization at international events, such as the UN World Conference on Women in Beijing in 1995, and in domestic and international grassroots efforts. WI spearheaded campaigns in US Muslim communities in 2005 and 2015 to include women in communal leadership and provide better spaces for them in mosques and community centers. It supports Muslim women's training and participation in Islamic scholarship, advocates for "re-engagement" of Muslims, especially Muslim women, in mosque communities, and honors and supports Muslim women leaders and activists from other organizations.[15]

Karamah—Muslim Women Lawyers for Human Rights

Founded in 1993 by Muslim feminist legal scholar, Azizah al-Hibri, Karamah has engaged in knowledge-building and leadership training for Muslim women through various programs, both nationally and internationally, that are based on the argument that Islam and especially Islamic law is gender-just in principle and needs to be applied in order to improve Muslim societies and communities. Karamah has worked with international organizations, such as the UN, as well as human rights organizations, and in the United States with the State Department, the Department of Justice, and many Muslim and non-Muslim organizations. The organization, based in Washington, DC, provides educational events, community outreach, networking opportunities for activists and communities with shared goals, and training materials and Islamic legal resources on topics from domestic violence to participatory democracy.[16]

Peaceful Families Project (PFP)

The Peaceful Families Project was founded in 2000 by Sharifa Alkhateeb, a community activist in the Northern Virginia area to address domestic violence in Muslim communities. PFP emerged with support from the Department of Justice's Violence against Women (VAWA) program and was established as the Muslim program of the FaithTrust Institute, itself an interreligious organization dedicated to ending domestic and sexual violence in faith communities and the broader society. PFP and the FaithTrust Institute have developed programs that engage religious communities in developing and implementing religious resources against domestic violence (DV) while acknowledging that religious traditions can both be resources against DV and roadblocks to ending it. PFP has provided DV awareness trainings to Muslim communities, mainstream service providers, and law enforcement as well as to Muslim community leaders and scholars. After becoming independent in 2008, PFP joined the umbrella of United Muslim Relief, but by 2018 had yet again reestablished itself as an independent organization. It is noteworthy that PFP has thus engaged in its history both with an interreligious women's organization (FaithTrust) and a mainstream Muslim relief organization while maintaining its status as the leading Muslim anti-DV organization in the country. It has also functioned as an important node in a network of Muslim anti-DV organizations that has actively facilitated cooperation, resource sharing, and joint representation of Muslim efforts against DV.[17]

Women's Islamic Initiative in Spirituality and Equality (WISE)

WISE was founded in 2006 at a meeting of 200 Muslim women leaders, scholars, activists, and artists from 25 countries in New York. It was sponsored by the American Society for Muslim Advancement (ASMA), and came about through the initiative of Daisy Khan, a Muslim woman activist who is also WISE's executive director.[18] The organization embraces human and gender equality as Islamic principles and advocates for the full equality of men and women. WISE, too, emphasizes the production and dissemination of Islamic knowledge in support of gender equality, peace-building, and social justice. Its projects include leadership training programs and summits, the creation of a committee of women legal scholars known as the Shura Council, imam trainings in Muslim majority societies, awareness campaigns against female genital cutting, and work against domestic violence.[19] WISE has also engaged public education campaigns about Islam and Muslims in order to counter anti-Muslim hostility and prejudice in the United States.

HEART Women and Girls

HEART is a Muslim community organization, founded in 2009 in Chicago, by a local activist, Nadiah Mohajir. The organization focuses its efforts on countering sexual violence and offering faith-based sexual health literacy. To that end, a team of women activists, including trained counselors and social workers as well as Muslim women scholars, have developed educational resources, training programs, and media programming on sex education, sexual agency, and the need for Muslims to be educated on these issues and exercise agency in their own lives and the education of their children. HEART also provides support and resources for survivors of sexual assault, especially in Muslim communities. The organization emphasizes gender equity and the importance of educating especially Muslim women about their bodies, their sexuality, and their religion in relation to each other. The organization has been vocal on social media about the #MeToo movement and its connection to Muslim communities.[20]

Sapelo Square

Sapelo Square is a dynamic online resource and website focusing on the lives of Black Muslims in the United States. It was created by a group of Black Muslim women scholars and activists, including Su'ad Abdul Khabeer, the founding director senior editor and a leading scholar of Black Muslim culture, and, Nsenga Knight, Malikah A. Shabazz, and Rashida James-Saadiya, who are community activists, artists, and media professionals. Sapelo Square was created in early 2015 and has been curating content on topics from Ramadan reflections, to Black Muslim arts and culture, the deep and vast histories of Black Muslims in the United States, and racism, past and present, in American society. The project is an example of an organization that does not foreground women's issues or women's rights, but rather organically embraces the intersection between gender and race as a site for the preservation and appreciation of Black Muslim communities, including women's contributions to them, as well as women as contributors to the site, writers, activists, and storytellers.[21]

Muslim Anti-Racism Collaborative (MuslimARC)

The MuslimARC was launched in 2014 during Black History Month in order to address the intersection of anti-Muslim hostility and anti-Black racism. The cofounders, Namira Islam and Margari Aziza Hill, were joined by an initial steering committee that counted many prominent women community activists among its ranks. MuslimARC worked as a volunteer organization until 2017, when it hired its first full-time staff members and acquired a physical space to coordinate its activities. The organization has been active in cooperation with and support of the Black Lives Matter movement, and has focused many of its educational efforts, both resource building and outreach, on addressing anti-Black racism in Muslim communities.[22] MuslimARC draws on principles of human rights and social justice, as well as notions of equality and justice drawn from the Qur'ān, *Sunna*, and Black Muslim history, especially the legacy of Malcolm X.[23]

Conclusion

The nine organizations described in some detail in this chapter, framed by theoretical considerations of what constitutes activism, what makes it Muslim women's activism, and how the historical, political, and social context of the United States in the twentieth and twenty-first centuries has impacted such activism, have provided the beginning of a sketch. This sketch is a picture waiting to be filled in with more detail, but already in its current form pointing to the significance of context for activism and the ways in which Muslim women's efforts for change in their communities and the broader society rely on individual agency and effort on the one hand, and the dynamics of movement and organization building as a collective enterprise on the other. Women have and continue to play important roles in wider communal organizing, for a host of political goals that cannot be subsumed under the agenda of social justice, however tempting it may be to represent American Muslims, especially American Muslim women, as vanguards of a progressive political and social agenda.

One thing that has become clear to me in a decade of research on Muslim women's activism is that organizations, networks, and individuals are too deeply invested in their goal of transforming society and community, in literally changing lives and communities, to be able to pay attention to and reflect on their own histories. It is imperative for scholars as well as communities to create and maintain archives of activism, in order to reflect and learn from the past and develop strategies in a world that is constantly changing.

In this chapter I have argued that Muslim women's activism in the United States has to be considered, in no particular order, in light of the relationship of Islam and feminism; the role of anti-Muslim hostility in shaping activism and scholarship about it;

the relationship between scholarship and activism; and the analytical parameters we as scholars draw around the category of Muslim women's activism. The work of Muslim women activists is at once focused on local and national contexts and an integral part of broader transnational and international networks of Muslim women activists and scholars. Together, they not only change the world, they also actively participate in the discursive production of Islam as a living religious tradition.

Notes

1. Kecia Ali, *Sexual Ethics and Islam* (Oxford: Oneworld, 2016), 206.
2. See Sheila Briggs, "What Is Feminist Theology?" in *Oxford Handbook of Feminist Theology*, ed. Mary Fulkerson and Sheila Briggs (Oxford: Oxford University Press, 2012), 73–108; Lisbeth Mikaelsson, "Religion," in *Oxford Handbook of Feminist Theory*, ed. Lisa Disch and Mary Hawkesworth (Oxford: Oxford University Press, 2016), 761–780.
3. See Fatima Seedat, "When Islam and Feminism Converge," *Muslim World* 103, no. 3 (2013): 404–420; Fatima Seedat, "Islam, Feminism, and Islamic Feminism: Between Inadequacy and Inevitability," *Journal of Feminist Studies in Religion* 29, no. 2 (Fall 2013) 25–45; Ziba Mir Hosseini, "Beyond 'Islam' versus 'Feminism,'" *Institute for Development Studies Bulletin* 42, no. 1 (January 2011): 67–77; Margot Badran, *Feminism in Islam: Secular and Religious Convergences* (Oxford: Oneworld, 2009).
4. Rochelle Terman, "Islamophobia, Feminism, and the Politics of Critique," *Theory, Culture and Society* (2015): 1–26; Miriam Cooke, "Multiple Critique: Islamic Feminist Rhetorical Strategies," in *Postcolonialism, Feminism, and Religious Discourse*, ed. Laura E. Donaldson and Kwok Pui-Lan (New York: Routledge, 2002), 142–160.
5. The term "Islamophobia," while widely used, is problematic for several reasons, most important of which is that a phobia implies an individualized as well as a medical condition rather than capturing the systemic and constructed nature of a set of phenomena typically associated with Islamophobia. This reduction to a personal dislike or fear in place of acknowledgment of the deliberate production of Islamophobic discourse releases the producers of such discourses from responsibility, and severely limits the possibility of fighting it (rather than treating it in pseudo-medical terms). It is now also so widely applied as to risk losing meaning altogether: hate crimes against Muslims, pronouncements by media and politicians about Islam, racist discrimination and attacks, hate speech, and myriad forms of rhetorical and practical othering are all captured within it. While there is of course discursive power in a single term and the potential for unified political activism, this lumping together risks misreading the causes for these various phenomena and with it the assignation of political agency and responsibility.
6. See Carl Ernst, ed., *Islamophobia in America: The Anatomy of Intolerance* (New York: Palgrave, 2013); Todd Green, *The Fear of Islam* (Minneapolis: Fortress, 2015); and the #IslamophobiaIsRacism Syllabus (2017), https://islamophobiaisracism.wordpress.com/.
7. See for example, Juliane Hammer, "Muslim Women, Anti-Muslim Hostility, and the State in the Age of Terror," in *Muslims and Contemporary US Politics*, ed. Mohammad Khalil (Cambridge, MA: Harvard University Press and ILEX, 2019), 104–126; Khaled Beydoun, "'Muslim Bans' and the (Re)Making of Political Islamophobia," *University of Illinois Law Review* 5 (2017): 1733–1774.

8. See Juliane Hammer, "Gendering Islamophobia: (Muslim) Women's Bodies and American Politics, *Bulletin for the Study of Religion* 42, no. 1 (February 2013): 29–36; Hammer, "Muslim Women, Anti-Muslim Hostility"; Lila Abu-Lughod, "Do Muslim Women Really Need Saving?" *American Anthropologist* 104 (2002): 783–790; Lila Abu-Lughod, *Do Muslim Women Need Saving?* (Cambridge, MA: Harvard University Press, 2013).
9. For a good discussion, see Megan Goodwin, "'They Do That to Foreign Women': Domestic Terrorism and Contraceptive Nationalism in *Not without My Daughter*," *Muslim World* 106 (2018): 759–780.
10. Juliane Hammer, *American Muslim Women, Religious Authority, and Activism: More Than a Prayer* (Austin: University of Texas Press, 2012); Hammer, *Peaceful Families: American Muslim Efforts against Domestic Violence* (Princeton, NJ: Princeton University Press, 2019.
11. For further reading about these and other Muslim women scholar-activists, see Gisela Webb, ed. *Windows of Faith: Muslim Women Scholar-Activists in North America* (Syracuse, NY: Syracuse University Press, 2000); Juliane Hammer, "Gender, Feminism, and Critique in American Muslim Thought," in *Routledge Handbook of Islam in the West*, ed. Roberto Tottoli (London: Routledge, 2014), 395–410; Hammer, "Identity, Authority and Activism: American Muslim Women's Approaches to the Qur'an," in *Muslim World* 98, no. 4 (October 2008): 442–463. See also the many writings of these scholars themselves.
12. Saba Mahmoud, *Politics of Piety: The Islamic Revival and the Feminist Subject* (Princeton, NJ: Princeton University Press, 2006), 5–10.
13. Ula Taylor, *The Promise of Patriarchy: Women and the Nation of Islam* (Chapel Hill: University of North Carolina Press, 2017).
14. The MWL website was last updated in 2013, which I take as one sign that the organization may not be active any longer. https://www.mwlusa.org/about/about.html.
15. Information taken from WI's website, http://womeninislam.org/ (accessed September 2018).
16. Information taken from Karamah's constantly evolving website, http://karamah.org/ (accessed September 2018).
17. PFP is one of the organizations profiled in my book *Peaceful Families: American Muslim Efforts against Domestic Violence* (p. 58–60). See also https://www.peacefulfamilies.org/.
18. The ASMA Society was reorganized into Cordoba House, known from the 2010 and beyond Park51 controversy. See Rosemary Corbett, *Making Moderate Islam: Sufism, Service, and the "Ground Zero Mosque" Controversy* (Stanford, CA: Stanford University Press, 2017). See also http://www.asmasociety.org/.
19. https://www.wisemuslimwomen.org/.
20. http://heartwomenandgirls.org.
21. https://sapelosquare.com/.
22. http://www.muslimarc.org/.
23. See also Juliane Hammer, "Islam and Race in American History," in *Oxford Handbook of Religion and Race in American History*, ed. Kathryn Gin Lum and Paul Harvey (Oxford: Oxford University Press, 2018), 205–222.

Bibliography

Abu-Lughod, Lila. "Do Muslim Women Really Need Saving?" *American Anthropologist* 104 (2002): 783–790.

Abu-Lughod, Lila. *Do Muslim Women Need Saving?* Cambridge, MA: Harvard University Press, 2013.

Ali, Kecia. *Sexual Ethics and Islam*. Oxford: Oneworld, 2016.

Badran, Margot. *Feminism in Islam: Secular and Religious Convergences*. Oxford: Oneworld, 2009.

Cooke, Miriam. "Multiple Critique: Islamic Feminist Rhetorical Strategies." In *Postcolonialism, Feminism, and Religious Discourse*, edited by Laura E. Donaldson and Kwok Pui-Lan, 142–160. New York: Routledge, 2002.

Corbett, Rosemary. *Making Moderate Islam: Sufism, Service, and the "Ground Zero Mosque" Controversy*. Stanford, CA: Stanford University Press, 2017.

Ernst, Carl, ed. *Islamophobia in America: The Anatomy of Intolerance*. New York: Palgrave, 2013.

Goodwin, Megan. "'They Do That to Foreign Women": Domestic Terrorism and Contraceptive Nationalism in *Not without My Daughter*." *Muslim World* 106 (2018): 759–780.

Green, Todd. *The Fear of Islam*. Minneapolis, MN: Fortress, 2015.

Hammer, Juliane. *American Muslim Women, Religious Authority, and Activism: More Than a Prayer*. Austin: University of Texas Press, 2012.

Hammer, Juliane. "Gender, Feminism, and Critique in American Muslim Thought." In *Routledge Handbook of Islam in the West*, edited by Roberto Tottoli, 395–410. London: Routledge, 2014.

Hammer, Juliane. "Gendering Islamophobia: (Muslim) Women's Bodies and American Politics." *Bulletin for the Study of Religion* 42, no. 1 (February 2013): 29–36.

Hammer, Juliane. "Identity, Authority and Activism: American Muslim Women's Approaches to the Qur'an." *Muslim World* 98, no. 4 (October 2008): 442–463.

Hammer, Juliane. "Islam and Race in American History." In *Oxford Handbook of Religion and Race in American History*, edited by Kathryn Gin Lum and Paul Harvey, 205–222. Oxford: Oxford University Press, 2018.

Hammer, Juliane. "Muslim Women, Anti-Muslim Hostility, and the State in the Age of Terror." In *Muslims and Contemporary US Politics*, edited by Mohammad Khalil, 104–126. Cambridge, MA: Harvard University Press and ILEX, 2019.

Hammer, Juliane. *Peaceful Families: American Muslim Efforts against Domestic Violence*. Princeton, NJ: Princeton University Press, 2019.

Mahmoud, Saba. *Politics of Piety: The Islamic Revival and the Feminist Subject*. Princeton, NJ: Princeton University Press, 2006.

Mir-Hosseini, Ziba. "Beyond 'Islam' versus 'Feminism.'" *Institute for Development Studies Bulletin* 42, no. 1 (January 2011): 67–77.

Seedat, Fatima. "Islam, Feminism, and Islamic Feminism: Between Inadequacy and Inevitability." *Journal of Feminist Studies in Religion* 29, no. 2 (Fall 2013) 25–45.

Seedat, Fatima. "When Islam and Feminism Converge." *Muslim World* 103, no. 3 (2013): 404–420.

Taylor, Ula. *The Promise of Patriarchy: Women and the Nation of Islam*. Chapel Hill: University of North Carolina Press, 2017.

Terman, Rochelle. "Islamophobia, Feminism, and the Politics of Critique." *Theory, Culture and Society* 33, no. 2 (2015): 626.

Webb, Gisela, ed. *Windows of Faith: Muslim Women Scholar-Activists in North America*. Syracuse, NY: Syracuse University Press, 2000.

CHAPTER 27

MUSLIM WOMEN'S RELIGIOUS AND SOCIAL ACTIVISM IN WESTERN EUROPE

JEANETTE S. JOUILI

Introduction

A plethora of studies has emerged over the past thirty years on Muslim women's activism in Europe. Even if for a long time ignored, Muslim women have since their arrival in western Europe been involved in a range of organizations to better the lot of their families, communities, and society at large. This body of research has highlighted the multifaceted life-worlds of Muslim women activists, who, whether more, less, or nonreligious, are active beyond their professional and/or family life, in religious centers, in social, cultural, and political groups and movements.

This chapter charts the evolving academic research on Muslim women's activism in Europe. After a brief outline of the historical development of Muslim women's activism in the second half of the twentieth century, it will look at four fields of activism in particular and the specific challenges they pose: (1) activism concerned particularly with empowering women within Muslim communities and within the broader societies, and more recently, (2) women's religious activism within Islamic communities and institutions, (3) struggles around recognition and religious minority rights, and (4) activism on broader social and political issues.

What emerges from this overview is that Muslim women's activism in Europe (as elsewhere) circumscribes an extremely diverse field, with a number of different, even incommensurable concerns and agendas. These concerns and agendas are shaped in various ways by the particular socioeconomic conditions in which these women live and are often a response to the political discourses constructed about them in their respective societies. In all these struggles, Muslim women encounter particular difficulties in navigating a field that is saturated with fixed images of them, where only certain aspects of their subjectivities are allowed to enter the public domain, while others are consistently ignored and excluded.

Historical Overview of Muslim Women's Activism

Little research has been conducted on activism by women of Muslim background who migrated to Europe in the context of the post–World War II labor migration during the 1960s and 1970s. This is partially due to the fact that women did not constitute a large number in a migration dominated by single males. Only after the mid-1970s, when labor migration schemes came to an end and family reunification programs and paved the way for spouses and children to join male migrants, did women begin to constitute a significant population in countries like France, Great Britain, Netherlands, Belgium, or Germany. In spite of the small numbers of women who migrated in these earliest years, many of them took active part in community life and organizations, having often drawn "political inspiration, know-how and resources from national independence struggles in which their families were involved"[1] and also from family histories of workers, struggles.[2] They belonged, alongside men, to political movements in their home countries or organizations that were defined around their national or ethnic belongings.[3] In the latter case, they tackled especially problems related to their conditions as migrants, such as right of entry, family reunification, and employment discrimination.[4] There are almost no in-depth studies investigating women's activism during this earliest period. A noteworthy exception is Marc André, who has done archival work to document the activism of Algerian women in France in Algerian independence movements in the 1960s.[5]

Furthermore, because of the relatively small number of women among these early migrations, only a few organizations specifically set up for Muslim women existed, which only emerged from the 1970s onward. Women mainly organized around national affiliations, but also began, from the 1980s on, to establish migrant women's organizations that brought together women of different backgrounds. Most often, they did not emphasize religious identities then and subscribed to some form of feminist agenda.[6]

An important trend in the evolution of activism among women from Muslim communities is the coming of age of a generation born or raised in Europe. In countries like the United Kingdom or France, from the 1980s on, in other countries a decade later, these "second generation" women became actively involved in ethnic minority organizations.[7] In all these activisms Muslim women not only had to engage and responded to the different integration policies, which the countries they lived in employed, but they were also always at least partially shaped by those underlying political discourses and ideologies. Organization-mode and the language employed reflected whether so called multicultural models prevailed, such as in the United Kingdom, with some emphasis on antidiscrimination or strongly assimilationist models, such as in France or Germany. In France, for instance, the mobilization of French-Maghrebi youth in antiracist movements, also called the "Movement beur"[8] became very prolific, and not only were women prominently represented in these movements but they also formed many women's organizations.[9] Their languages mirrored in many ways republican egalitarian ideals even while critically engaging them. Young UK-raised South Asian Muslim women often became active in the 1980s with Black and other ethnic minority women. They organized under the umbrella term "black women," a term inspired partially by the US Black Power movement, but also framed by British race relations policies, even if the term was never endorsed unanimously within Muslim communities.[10]

Another context for Muslim women's activism in Europe were the new types of migrations from Muslim-majority countries since the 1980s. Women of Muslim background came as refugees and asylum-seekers from countries such as Iran, Somalia, Lebanon, Kurdistan, Sudan, or Algeria, as dependents of family members already residing in Europe, and as migrants in their own right. They also settled in countries in southern Europe or Scandinavia, which have not had a comparable history of post–World War II labor migration. In spite of their often very unstable status, these newly arrived women organized around politics relating to their country of origins or around migrants' and refugees' specific issues.[11]

Studies investigating these various women's activisms prior to the late 1990s have been mainly conducted from a (post)migration studies perspective, rarely employing religion as an analytical lens. Hence, these studies generally did not foreground these activist women as Muslim but rather as Moroccan, Somali, or Pakistani. This certainly corresponded often to the way the women had defined themselves and their activism. However, from the 1990s on, Islam as a mode of self-identification not only became increasingly discernible among European Muslims[12] but also transformed the institutional landscape of European Muslims, including women's organizations.[13] More and more women's groups emerged that underscored their Muslim identity. While religious instruction became an important aspect of their work, many of these associations continued their commitment to struggle against discrimination of Muslim women in the domain of education and economy as well as tackling issues such as domestic violence.[14]

Without a doubt, September 11 was a watershed moment in the history of Muslim women's activism. Now much more under the public gaze than ever before, Muslim women's organizations across Europe tackled the increasingly culturalist and aggressively assimilationist, even Islamophobic, discourses across Europe, especially in their gendered forms. At the same time, they had to cope with neoliberal reforms, which meant decreasing welfare measures and public funding for women's organizations.[15] It is also since this moment that literature focusing on the women's *Muslim* identity began to burgeon.

Struggling for Women's Rights

As already addressed briefly in the historical overview, women of Muslim background engage in a range of struggles—whether identified as part of a broader "religious" ethics or in terms of a more "secular" agenda—to increase women's rights within their own communities and also to respond to the social and economic marginalization Muslim women and their families face within the broader society. This can be part of a politically leftist or humanist agenda or stem from a religious conviction according to which service for social justice is an important part of Islamic ethics.

One aspect that the literature highlights recurrently is the common and enduring concern of many Muslim women's activists who pursue women's rights within their communities about how their own activism potentially reinforces reductive and essentializing public discourses about Muslim women. Women's organizations commonly experience that their work is sensationalized if they tackle certain issues such as, for instance, violence against women, which is, within mainstream society, culturalized as a specifically Muslim issue. At the same time, these women find that other forms of suffering such as those linked to socioeconomic marginalization are much harder to address and that interlocutors among the authorities on whom they might depend for funding are difficult to find for these matters.[16] Women at times try to make use of the public interest to advance their claims in the public sphere, simultaneously straining to "re-negotiate the terms of the conversation."[17] That this is not an easy task becomes especially visible in activism against highly contentious and publicized practices that are often considered to be rooted within Islam, such as female genital mutilation (FGM) or so-called honor killings. While women try to distance the Islamic religion from these practices, they often employ language that reifies religion and culture, with the result that the ethnic and regional cultures of the home countries become essentialized as backward, static, and incompatible with European values.[18]

This is even more prevalent in the way liberal or more outspokenly secular Muslim women's groups are frequently instrumentalized by the state. Those who employ simplistic culturalist discourses gain not only much more publicity than those who do not, but are also disproportionally better funded than any other organization even while they do less work on the ground. A particularly prolific example here is the French women's group *Ni Putes ni Soumises* (Neither Whores nor Submissives). While not an all-Muslim group, women of Muslim background were and are vocal speakers for the group and the issues they aspire to tackle are presented as concerning specifically women in Muslim communities. A rich body of literature critically documents not only the highly essentializing discourse the organization employs, reproducing common perceptions about the backwardness and misogyny of Muslim communities, but also the exceptional success this organization had in garnering public funding and media attention, leaving little place for women's groups that have more grounding in the community.[19] Similar exposure and success have been granted to other individual women speaking this type of language within European media landscapes, celebrated as Muslim women's spokespersons.[20] Other secular feminist groups, however, feel in this context trapped between "essentialist notions of Islam" and perceive little space in which to pursue a secular feminist agenda.[21]

Another related concern for many women activists in this field to which the literature regularly points is how to engage with the state and its resources while keeping an independent agenda. On the one hand, women's organizations consistently struggle with lack of funding, which limits their work. Especially in the wake of neoliberal reforms and further cuts to social programs, these organizations face even more structurally disadvantaged populations while also often having their own public funding reduced. On the other hand, accepting funding from the government, for which these associations are important sites for their integration policies, also means to develop initiatives and programs that respond to policy goals.[22] This is especially problematic because policy frameworks tend to employ assumptions that are stigmatizing for Muslim women, often reproducing the "Muslim women need saving" narrative.[23] Some studies show how often policies conceived around "emancipating" and "liberating" the "vulnerable"' Muslim woman are actually confined within conventional ideas of women's role as mothers and educators.[24] In these policies Muslim women are inevitably addressed in their roles as mothers and educators, with the underlying assumption that women are the vectors for change by educating "the household toward (cultural) change," thereby placing the burden of integration on women.[25] Thus, women's groups regularly have to decide between greater autonomy but less financial means or dependency on government agendas with more financial means for projects not defined by themselves.[26] In the United Kingdom, where government funding for Muslim women's organizations has been connected in recent years to security and counterterrorism programs, this poses serious questions.[27] Such a direct connection carries further risks, as for instance, the linking of FGM with counterextremism agendas, a connection that has made several activists concerned that the visibility of an issue to which they have contributed has also facilitated ever more intrusive surveillance of, and interventions into, Somali families through health, education, and security professionals.[28]

Women's Religious Activism

Resulting from the increased visibility of Islamic practices among European Muslims from the late 1990s on, a substantial number of more recent studies have investigated the apparently novel female piety, especially among European-raised women. This body of research documents how Muslim women, whether "first-generation" migrants or children of migrants but also women converts organize and participate in formal classes or informal study circles in Muslim institutions of learning, Muslim student organizations, mosque organizations, or in the private home.[29] The new emphasis on religion, along with participation in the institutional spaces of the Islamic revival has not necessarily meant a turn away from concerns with women's rights and welfare, as public discourses and commentators at times argued. Rather, this literature stresses that over the past two decades, this religious activism has often fostered empowering tendencies among these women, challenging certain practices and customs in their home environment but also among Muslim communities worldwide with recourse to the idea of an "authentic Islam," constructed especially around the Qur'ān, reliable *ḥadīth*, and a deeper knowledge of the extensive *fiqh* literature.[30]

At the same time, many authors show that this activism should not exclusively be looked at through the lens of an empowerment/oppression binary as often imposed by media and political discourses. Not only do women in their religious activism relate in very different degrees to patriarchal readings of the scriptures but also they vary in their challenges to male religious authority. The activism of Islamic feminists,[31] for instance, centered on laying claim to women's interpretive authority, including the right to exercise *ijtihād*, differs in this regard drastically from that of more mainstream Muslim women's circles,[32] let alone Salafi groups.[33] Other, more mainstream-aligned women claim positions to authority without however challenging head-on established gendered roles, seeking to "lead through consensus rather than assertion."[34] Often, while accepting limited roles, they might become prominent as speakers, addressing first and foremost a "female clientele."[35]

Furthermore, a range of scholars have pointed to the importance of posing a whole different set of questions beyond questions of empowerment: while crucially preoccupied with women's dignity, emancipation, and women's rights, their activism should not be captured exclusively through such a lens. Women's concerns in these groups often transcend these frameworks, focusing on realizing Muslim piety and spirituality and thus leading a life pleasing to God. In addition, their struggles seek to actualize a flourishing Muslim life compatible with their European identity. These aspirations are not the product of autonomous selves but have been shaped through complex operations of power as well as through mainstream discourses, governmental policies, and family and community norms.[36]

Nonetheless, for many religious Muslim women, the question of women's rights is intrinsically part of their religious activism, which is closely connected to the self-understanding that these women develop through their involvement in religious learning, which fashions their particular ideals of female Muslim piety. These ideals also intersect in complicated ways with demands and discourses of the mainstream society.

Within Islamic institutions, Muslim women have especially begun to challenge the conventional organization of these spaces, which have been historically dominated by men. In the beginnings, this could be rationalized with the history of male labor migration where the early prayer halls had been set up for the male workers.[37] Later, this became justified with patriarchal norms where mosques and other religious spaces were considered as primarily male spaces.[38]

One very basic struggle in which Muslim women have been and are involved, as documented in the literature in various European countries, relates to the lack of proper worship spaces for women in mosques. Not many statistics exist for this issue, but according to Katherine Brown, in 2008, for instance, only 40 percent of UK mosques had provisions for female worshippers.[39] Complaints about lack of access to mosques by women in France were registered as well.[40] Yet, significant variances exist among different European countries and cities. In some places, women's sections have become almost the rule, as Minganti discusses for the case of Sweden, or Spielhaus for Berlin/Germany.[41] Other studies discuss how women mobilize for better equipped and integrated women sections, while a few Muslim women activists contest the separation of women's prayer spaces all together, claiming for more radical changes in term of building mixed gender congregations.[42] Among these more radical challengers of traditional mosque organizations are also women who get involved in setting up mixed-gender nontraditional spaces that cater to women and to LGBTQ Muslims.[43] There, it becomes possible for women to lead mixed-gender prayers. Observing these manifold struggles, Katherine Brown argues that mosques, for women, often turn into "sites of political negotiation and representation beyond their devotional function."[44]

Another issue mentioned in the literature against which women increasingly rally is the exclusion of women from decision-making processes within Islamic institutions. Brown again documents for the United Kingdom, that in 2008, only 2 percent of trustees on mosque boards were women.[45] Theological and juridical arguments that prevent women from assuming leadership roles often serve the established male leadership to defend the status quo in mosques across Europe.[46] In these institutional settings, women are often in charge of female sections, with limited responsibilities reflective of a "naturalized notion of women's issues," usually related to childrearing and education.[47] Even so, the autonomy gained there from men might also become the starting point for women's further activism.[48] In the British case, Khadijah Elshayyal shows how women have succeeded in recent years in gaining increasing representation on mosque boards and in assuming leadership positions within some organizations that have begun to make the demanded changes.[49] Nonetheless, many women complain about men's unwillingness to consider them as equal partners within Islamic organizations, which causes many women to set up their own autonomous spaces.[50] Across Europe, the literature has documented a rising number of these types of initiatives. Female-led Islamic institutions target a range of activities, from women's religious education to social services, and, at times even the development of female-centric religious interpretations.[51]

The literature in the field has also discussed how the broader political context of Europe impacts religious Muslim women's activism. In a discursive climate where Islam is seen as the sexist religion per se, religious Muslim women are often isolated in their struggles, lacking support from the broader society. They are perceived as denigrators of their own community and regarded with mistrust not only by the male establishment within Muslim institutions but also by mainstream society which views them as "Islamists."[52] There seems to be a general lack of receptivity in European societies to the idea of a feminism that employs an Islamic language. Consequently, their efforts often remain invisible to mainstream society, ignored by media and the state.[53]

A quite distinct trend has been observed in Great Britain since the late 2000s, where religious Muslim women's activism has become coopted within a counterterrorism agenda that links cultural "integration" to security concerns. In this context, women's activism in Muslim spaces was actively promoted through government campaigns that pursued the increase of women's participation and inclusion in mosques.[54] Here, Muslim women did not suffer from a lack of visibility or absence of state support but were faced instead with the question of how to balance the need for support in challenging male-dominated Islamic institutions with their aversion to being instrumentalized by the state in the service of a highly stigmatizing security agenda.

Representation and Recognition Struggles

Two other aspects have become important fields of engagement for Muslim women in a post–September 11 environment in which Muslims are consistently negatively portrayed in political and media debates, something that coincides, furthermore, with a growing unwillingness by European states to accommodate Muslim religious practices. In this context, struggles around representation and for the recognition of minority religious rights have become central concerns for many women.

Even though Muslim women have grappled persistently with orientalist perceptions within European societies, after September 11, their scrutinization through a prejudiced public gaze has dramatically intensified. Muslim women, especially those made visible through head coverings, often feel strongly "interpellated" by public debates around women, Islam, and emancipation.[55] In this context, the question of representation of "the Muslim woman" became equally more urgent.[56] Many studies acknowledge the extent to which the aftermath of September 11 has worked as a trigger for motivating Muslim women, who were not previously engaged in activism, to struggle against these stereotypes.

One key obstacle to Muslim women's capacity to challenge these dominant accounts on Islam and Muslim women is, as the literature often notes, their limited access to the broader mainstream audiences. Activists especially are extremely aware of the importance of mainstream media to do this deconstructive work. Van Es documents, for instance, how religious Muslim women in the Netherlands and in Sweden find it difficult to convey nuanced stories in the media, finding themselves used to reconfirm preconceived stories.[57] One of the consequences of this difficulty is that Muslim women have become very active within alternative media[58] but have also searched for new forms of representation, through popular culture, music, comedy, fashion, or sports where they hope to be able to articulate their agenda on their own terms.[59] The difficulties addressed here, however, also point to a larger epistemological question, namely what languages can actually be employed to represent oneself differently. As Nadia Fadil and Sarah Bracke show for the headscarf debates, the hegemonic structure of the "liberal grammar" within debates on European Islam, multiculturalism, and integration makes it extremely difficult for many religious Muslim women to render themselves intelligible within this power structure.[60]

Other Social and Political Activisms

In spite of the significant number of Muslim women being preoccupied with recognition and representation struggles, many do engage in activism that tackles broader social and political issues—which is, as mentioned above, not always disconnected from representation issues, given that this type of activism is also viewed by Muslim women as an opportunity to represent, against common stereotypes, the socially and politically aware Muslim woman.[61] Connected to this is also sometimes the conscious expression of a refusal to be limited to the topics prescribed to them by the larger society.[62]

One field in which especially young Muslim women have become active and successful participants is the flourishing Muslim charity sector across Europe.[63] Here, women, alongside their male peers, are part of a global trend where young people, disenchanted with the reclining welfare state and growing inequality, search to act "concretely and immediately."[64] In that position, they have often become interlocutors to municipalities, public authorities, and state institutions. As citizens they deal with broader social justice issues that are not limited to Muslim issues, such as environment, poverty, education and so on, striving to be active participants in the society and pursuing the "common good."[65] While the charity sector might at times become a venue for an apolitical activism, William Barylo argues that the insights into structural inequalities and injustices gathered, is for many young Muslims—men and women—a trigger to get involved in other types of civic and political actions.[66]

Additionally, Muslim women mobilize in different mainstream political parties or independent political movements. While they often tend to be active within leftist-inclined political parties, they are also present across the political spectrum.[67] Within various organizations, Muslim women are engaged in a range of political struggles, but most of the literature points to activism around progressive issues, one of them being connected to the fragile status of many Muslim residents in various European countries. They mobilize for citizenship and proimmigration reforms, and, in regard to women, especially for independent residency for migrant women that should not be linked to the marriage that brought them to the country in the first place.[68] They are active in antiwar, pro-Palestine, and antiracist coalitions as well as in student politics,[69] but also defend environmental issues.[70]

In their activism on a broader social and political stage Muslim women face various challenges. At times, they feel that they are being used as the "token" Muslim figure, expected to perform the model Muslim woman, modern and integrated.[71] Visibly religious women have to cope with the stigma of being "Islamists" and of not having their political democratic stances being taken for sincere. In leftist movements particularly, they find that their allies often pose questions about the compatibility of leftist, progressive values and Islam.[72]

Conclusion

Muslim women have been involved in activism ever since their arrival in Western Europe, whether around social, political, or religious issues. Their activism evolved with the changing European political landscapes, political discourses on migrants and Muslims and especially recent policies around the so-called global War on Terror. Within their activism, Muslim women have to constantly negotiate the political agendas defined by the different European states they call their home as well as the negative perceptions of them within European mainstream societies. Furthermore, they have to resist their marginalization within male-dominated community spaces where they strive to articulate their own priorities, ambitions and concerns. In spite of the complicated terrain in which they function, these activist women continue to work for the positive transformation of the societies they live in, where Muslims, and more particularly Muslim women, can be accepted as full members.

Notes

1. Khursheed Wadia, "Women from Muslim Communities in Britain: Political and Civic Activism in the 9/11 Era," in *Muslims and Political Participation*, ed. Timothy Peace (London: Routledge, 2015), 91.
2. Danièle Joly and Wadia Khursheed, *Muslim Women and Power: Civic and Political Engagement in West European Societies* (London: Palgrave Macmillan, 2017), 147.
3. Ibid.
4. Joly and Wadia, *Muslim Women and Power*; Margaretha Van Es, *Stereotypes and Self-Representations of Women with a Muslim Background: The Stigma of Being Oppressed* (London: Palgrave Macmillan, 2016).
5. André Marc, *Femmes dévoilées: Des algériennes en France à l'heure de la décolonisation* (Lyon: ENS Editions, 2016).
6. See, for instance: Nadia Châabane, "Diversité des mouvements de 'femmes dans l'immigration,'" *Les Cahiers du CEDREF* 16 (2008): 231–250; Catherine Quiminal, "Un réseau d'associations de femmes africaines," *Hommes et Migrations* 1208 (1997): 24–29.
7. For example, Joly and Wadia, *Muslim Women and Power*.
8. "Beur" is a colloquial term that designates the French descendants of North African immigrants.
9. See, for instance, Cathie Lloyd, "Women Migrants and Political Activism in France," in *Gender and Ethnicity in Contemporary Europe* (Oxford: Berg, 2003), 97–116.
10. See, for instance: Sudbury, *Other Kinds of Dreams*.

11. Gill Allwood and Khursheed Wadia, *Refugee Women in Britain and France* (Manchester: Manchester University Press, 2013).
12. Tariq Modood, *Multicultural Politics: Racism, Ethnicity, and Muslims in Britain* (Minneapolis: University of Minnesota Press, 2005).
13. For example: Joly and Wadia, *Muslim Women and Power.*
14. Sudbury, *Other Kinds of Dreams.*
15. Conny Roggeband, "The Victim-Agent Dilemma: How Migrant Women's Organizations in the Netherlands Deal with a Contradictory Policy Frame," *Signs: Journal of Women in Culture and Society* 35, no. 4 (2010): 943–967.
16. Ibid.
17. Aleksandra Lewicki and Therese O'Toole, "Acts and Practices of Citizenship: Muslim Women's Activism in the UK," *Ethnic and Racial Studies* 40, no. 1 (2017), 60.
18. Katherine Pratt Ewing, *Stolen Honor: Stigmatizing Muslim Men in Berlin* (Stanford CA: Stanford University Press, 2008); Jeanette S. Jouili, *Pious Practice and Secular Constraints: Women in the Islamic Revival in Europe* (Stanford, CA: Stanford University Press, 2015).
19. See, for example, Mayanthi L Fernando, "Save the Muslim Woman, Save the Republic: Ni Putes Ni Soumises and the Ruse of Neoliberal Sovereignty," *Modern and Contemporary France* 21, no. 2 (2013): 147–165; Mayanthi L. Fernando, *The Republic Unsettled: Muslim French and the Contradictions of Secularism* (Durham, NC: Duke University Press, 2014).
20. Schirin Amir-Moazami, "Dialogue as a Governmental Technique: Managing Gendered Islam in Germany," *Feminist Review* 98, no. 1 (2011): 9–27; Rita Chin, "Turkish Women, West German Feminists, and the Gendered Discourse on Muslim Cultural Difference," *Public Culture* 22, no. 3 (2010): 557–581.
21. Van Es, *Stereotypes and Self-Representations*, 189.
22. Roggeband, "The Victim-Agent Dilemma."
23. Pojmann, "Muslim Women's Organizing."
24. Roggeband, "The Victim-Agent Dilemma," 943.
25. Ibid.
26. Ibid.
27. Katherine Brown, "The Promise and Perils of Women's Participation in UK Mosques: The Impact of Securitisation Agendas on Identity, Gender and Community," *British Journal of Politics and International Relations* 10, no. 3 (2008): 472–491.
28. Lewicki and O'Toole, "Acts and Practices of Citizenship," 162.
29. Schirin Amir-Moazami, *Politisierte Religion: Der Kopftuchstreit in Deutschland und Frankreich* (Bielefeld: Transcript, 2007); Jouili, *Pious Practice*; Nadine Weibel, *Par-delà le voile: Femmes d'Islam en Europe* (Paris: Complexe, 2000).
30. See, for instance, Zahra Ali, "Des musulmanes en France: féminisme islamique et nouvelles formes de l'engagement pieux," *Religioscope* 27 (2012): 1-15.; Jouili, *Pious Practice.*
31. Jeanette S. Jouili, and Melanie Kamp, "Islamic Education in Germany: The 'Institut für Internationale Pädagogik und Didaktik' and the 'Zentrum für Islamische Frauenförderung und Forschung,' " in *Islamic Movements of Europe* (London: I. B.Tauris, 2014), 287–291.
32. Jouili, *Pious Practice*; Nathal M. Dessing, "Thinking for Oneself? Forms and Elements of Religious Authority in Dutch Muslim Women's Groups," *Women, Leadership, and Mosques. Changes in Contemporary Islamic Authority* (Leiden: Brill, 2011), 217–234; Jouili and Kamp, "Islamic Education in Germany"; Els Vanderwaeren, "Muslimahs' Impact

on and Acquisition of Islamic Religious Authority in Flanders," *Women, Leadership, and Mosques: Changes in Contemporary Islamic Authority* (Leiden: Brill, 2011), 301–322.

33. Anabel Inge, *The Making of a Salafi Muslim Woman: Paths to Conversion* (Oxford: Oxford University Press, 2016); Fareen Z. Parvez, *Politicizing Islam: The Islamic Revival in France and India* (Oxford: Oxford University Press, 2017).
34. Riem Spielhaus, "Making Islam Relevant: Female Authority and Representation of Islam in German," in *Women, Leadership, and Mosques: Changes in Contemporary Islamic Authority* (Leiden: Brill, 2011), 438.
35. Amel Boubekeur, "Female Religious Professionals in France," *ISIM Newsletter* 14 (2004): 2.
36. Schirin Amir-Moazami and Jeanette S. Jouili, "Knowledge, Empowerment and Religious Authority among Pious Muslim Women in France and Germany," *Muslim World* 96, no. 4 (2006): 617–642; Sarah Bracke, "Subjects of Debate: Secular and Sexual Exceptionalism, and Muslim Women in the Netherlands," *Feminist Review* 98, no. 1 (2011): 28–46.
37. Khadijah Elshayyal, "The Gender Imbalance in British Muslim Organisations," 2014; http://www.publicspirit.org.uk/the-gender-imbalance-in-british-muslim-organisations/..
38. Ibid.
39. Brown, "The Promise and Perils of Women's Participation."
40. Ali, "Des Musulmanes en France," 8, fn. 9; Jouili, *Pious Practice*, 94.
41. Pia Karlsson Minganti, "Challenging from Within: Youth Associations and Female Leadership in Swedish Mosques," in *Women, Leadership, and Mosques: Changes in Contemporary Islamic Authority* (Leiden: Brill, 2011), 371–392; Spielhaus, "Making Islam Relevant."
42. Lewicki and O'Toole, "Acts and Practices of Citizenship," 165.
43. Ibid.
44. Brown, "The Promise and Perils of Women's Participation," 474.
45. Ibid.
46. Elshayyal, "The Gender Imbalance"; Joly and Wadia, *Muslim Women and Power*, 153ff.
47. Elshayyal, "The Gender Imbalance."
48. Spielhaus, "Making Islam Relevant."
49. Elshayyal, "The Gender Imbalance."
50. Joly and Wadia, *Muslim Women and Power*, 154.
51. Masooda Bano and Hilary E. Kalmbach, eds. *Women, Leadership, and Mosques: Changes in Contemporary Islamic Authority* (Leiden: Brill, 2011); Jouili and Kamp, "Islamic Education in Germany."
52. Spielhaus, "Making Islam Relevant."
53. Minganti, "Challenging from Within"; Kuppinger, "Women, Leadership, and Participation"; Spielhaus, "Interessen vertreten mit vereinter Stimme"; Van Es, *Stereotypes and Self-Representations.*
54. Rashid Naaz, "Giving the Silent Majority a Stronger Voice? Initiatives to Empower Muslim Women as Part of the UK's 'War on Terror,'" *Ethnic and Racial Studies* 37, no. 4 (2014): 589–604.
55. Bracke, "Subjects of Debate."
56. Sariya Contractor, *Muslim Women in Britain: De-Mystifying the Muslimah* (London: Routledge, 2012); Jouili, *Pious Practice.*
57. Van Es, *Stereotypes and Self-Representations.*
58. Claire Donnet, "Hijab and the city et la construction d'une feminité pieuse: Frontières identitaires et représentations de l'altérité," *Collection FIRA-HAL-SHS*, January 12, 2012, 1–9.

59. Asmaa Soliman, "European Muslims' Engagement in the Public Sphere Soft Counterpublics," *International Review of Sociology* 26, no. 1 (2016): 174–200; Asmaa Soliman, *European Muslims Transforming the Public Sphere: Religious Participation in the Arts, Media and Civil Society* (London: Routledge, 2017).
60. Sarah Bracke and Nadia Fadil, "Is the Headscarf Oppressive or Emancipatory?" *Religion and Gender* 2, no. 1 (2012): 52.
61. William Barylo, *Young Muslim Change-Makers: Grassroots Charities Rethinking Modern Societies*. London: Routledge, 2017; Narzanin Massoumi, *Muslim Women, Social Movements and the "War on Terror"* (New York: Palgrave Macmillan, 2015).
62. Van Es, *Stereotypes and Self-Representations*, 282.
63. Barylo, *Young Muslim Change-Makers*; Joly and Wadia, *Muslim Women and Power*, 130.
64. Barylo, *Young Muslim Change-Makers*, 138.
65. Ibid., 138.
66. Ibid., 159.
67. Alessia Belli, "Limits and Potentialities of the Italian and British Political Systems through the Lens of Muslim Women in Politics," in *Muslim Political Participation in Europe* (Edinburgh: Edinburgh University Press, 2013), 163–189.
68. Joly and Wadia, *Muslim Women and Power*; Roggeband, "The Victim-Agent Dilemma."
69. Fernando, *The Republic Unsettled*; Massoumi, *Muslim Women, Social Movements*.
70. Van Es, *Stereotypes and Self-Representations*.
71. Salima Bouyarden, "Political Participation of European Muslims in France and the United Kingdom," in *Muslim Political Participation in Europe* (Edinburgh: Edinburgh University Press, 2013), 102–125.
72. Fernando, *The Republic Unsettled*; Massoumi, "The Muslim Woman Activist"; Parvez, *Politicizing Islam*.

Bibliography

Afshar Haleh. "Muslim Women in West Yorkshire: Growing up with Real and Imaginary Values amidst Conflicting Views or Self and Society." In *The Dynamics of "Race" and Gender: Some Feminist Interventions*, edited by Haleh Afshar and Mary Maynard, 127–150. London: Taylor & Francis, 1994.

Ali, Zahra. "Des musulmanes en France: Féminisme islamique et nouvelles formes de l'engagement pieux." *Religioscope* 27 (2012): 1–15. https://www.religion.info/pdf/2012_09_Ali.pdf.

Amiraux, Valérie. "Jeunes musulmanes turques d'Allemagne: Voix et voies de l'individuation." In *Paroles d'Islam: Individus, sociétés et discours dans l'Islam contemporain*, edited by Felice Dassetto, 101–123. Paris: Maisonneuve & Larose, 2002.

Amir-Moazami, Schirin. "Dialogue as a Governmental Technique: Managing Gendered Islam in Germany." *Feminist Review* 98, no. 1 (2011): 9–27.

Amir-Moazami, Schirin. *Politisierte Religion: Der Kopftuchstreit in Deutschland und Frankreich*. Bielefeld: Transcript, 2007.

Amir-Moazami, Schirin, and Jouili, Jeanette S. "Knowledge, Empowerment and Religious Authority among Pious Muslim Women in France and Germany." *Muslim World* 96, no. 4 (2006): 617–642.

Allwood, Gill, and Khursheed Wadia. *Refugee Women in Britain and France*. Manchester: Manchester University Press, 2013.

André, Marc. *Femmes dévoilées: Des algériennes en France à l'heure de la decolonization. Lyon: ENS Editions, 2016.*
Bano, Masooda, and Hilary E. Kalmbach, eds. *Women, Leadership, and Mosques: Changes in Contemporary Islamic Authority*. Leiden: Brill, 2011.
Barylo, William. *Young Muslim Change-Makers: Grassroots Charities Rethinking Modern Societies*. London: Routledge, 2017.
Belli, Alessia. "Limits and Potentialities of the Italian and British Political Systems through the Lens of Muslim Women in Politics." In *Muslim Political Participation in Europe*, edited by Jorgen S. Nielsen, 163–189. Edinburgh: Edinburgh University Press, 2013.
Boubekeur, Amel. "Female Religious Professionals in France." *ISIM Newsletter* 14 (2004): 2.
Bouryarden, S. "Political Participation of European Muslims in France and the United Kingdom." In *Muslim Political Participation in Europe*, edited by Jorgen S. Nielsen, 102–127. Edinburgh: Edinburgh University Press, 2013.
Bracke, Sarah. "Subjects of Debate: Secular and Sexual Exceptionalism, and Muslim Women in the Netherlands." *Feminist Review* 98, no. 1 (2011): 28–46.
Bracke, Sarah, and Nadia Fadil. "Is the Headscarf Oppressive or Emancipatory?" *Religion and Gender* 2, no. 1 (2012): 36–56.
Brown, Katherine. "The Promise and Perils of Women's Participation in UK Mosques: The Impact of Securitisation Agendas on Identity, Gender and Community." *British Journal of Politics and International Relations* 10, no. 3 (2008): 472–491.
Châabane, Nadia. "Diversité des mouvements de femmes dans l'immigration." *Les Cahiers du CEDREF* 16 (2008): 231–250.
Chin, Rita. "Turkish Women, West German Feminists, and the Gendered Discourse on Muslim Cultural Difference." *Public Culture* 22, no. 3 (2010): 557–581.
Contractor, Sariya. *Muslim Women in Britain: De-Mystifying the Muslimah*. London: Routledge, 2012.
Danièle, Joly, and Wadia Khursheed. *Muslim Women and Power: Civic and Political Engagement in West European Societies*. London: Palgrave Macmillan, 2017.
Dessing, Nathal M. "Thinking for Oneself? Forms and Elements of Religious Authority in Dutch Muslim Women's Groups." In *Women, Leadership, and Mosques. Changes in Contemporary Islamic Authority*, edited by Masooda Bano and Hilary Kalmbach, 217–234. Leiden: Brill, 2011.
Donnet, Claire. "Hijab and the city et la construction d'une feminité pieuse: Frontières identitaires et représentations de l'altérité." *Collection FIRA-HAL-SHS*, January 2012, 1–9. https://halshs.archives-ouvertes.fr/halshs-00747420/document.
Elshayyal, Khadijah. "The Gender Imbalance in British Muslim Organisations," 2014. http://www.publicspirit.org.uk/the-gender-imbalance-in-british-muslim-organisations/.
Evolvi, Giulia. "Hybrid Muslim Identities in Digital Space: The Italian Blog Yalla." *Social Compass* 64, no. 2 (2017): 220–232.
Ewing, Katherine Pratt. *Stolen Honor: Stigmatizing Muslim Men in Berlin*. Stanford, CA: Stanford University Press, 2008.
Faure, Sylvia, and Daniel Thin. "Femmes des quartiers populaires, associations et politiques publiques." *Politix* 2 (2007): 87–106.
Fernando, Mayanthi L. *The Republic Unsettled: Muslim French and the Contradictions of Secularism*. Durham, NC: Duke University Press, 2014.

Fernando, Mayanthi L. "Save the Muslim Woman, Save the Republic: Ni Putes Ni Soumises and the Ruse of Neoliberal Sovereignty." *Modern and Contemporary France* 21, no. 2 (2013): 147–165.

Herding, Maruta. *Inventing the Muslim Cool: Islamic Youth Culture in Western Europe*. Bielefeld: Transcript, 2014.

Inge, Anabel. *The Making of a Salafi Muslim Woman: Paths to Conversion*. Oxford: Oxford University Press, 2016.

Jacobsen, Christine M. "Troublesome Threesome: Feminism, Anthropology and Muslim Women's Piety." *Feminist Review* 98, no. 1 (2011): 65–82.

Jouili, Jeanette S. "Islam and Culture: Dis/junctures in a Modern Conceptual Terrain." *Comparative Studies in Society and History* 60, no. 1 (2019: 207–237).

Jouili, Jeanette S. *Pious Practice and Secular Constraints: Women in the Islamic Revival in Europe*. Stanford, CA: Stanford University Press.

Jouili, Jeanette S., and Melanie Kamp. "Islamic Education in Germany: The 'Institut für Internationale Pädagogik und Didaktik' and the 'Zentrum für Islamische Frauenförderung und Forschung.'" In *Islamic Movements of Europe*, edited by Frank Peter and Rafael Ortega, 287–291. London: I. B.Tauris, 2014.

Kuppinger, Petra. "Pools, Piety, and Participation: A Muslim Women's Sports Club and Urban Citizenship in Germany." *Journal of Muslim Minority Affairs* 35, no. 2 (2015): 264–279.

Kuppinger, Petra. "Women, Leadership, and Participation in Mosques and Beyond: Notes from Stuttgart, Germany." In *Women, Leadership, and Mosques: Changes in Contemporary Islamic Authority*, edited by Masooda Bano and Hilary Kalmbach, 323–344. Leiden: Brill, 2011.

Lewicki, Aleksandra, and Therese O'Toole. "Acts and Practices of Citizenship: Muslim Women's Activism in the UK." *Ethnic and Racial Studies* 40, no. 1 (2017): 152–171.

Liberatore, Giulia. *Somali, Muslim, British: Striving in Securitized Britain*. London: Bloomsbury, 2017.

Lloyd, Cathie. "Women Migrants and Political Activism in France." In *Gender and Ethnicity in Contemporary Europe*, edited by Jacqueline Andall, 97–116. Oxford: Berg, 2003.

Massoumi, Narzanin. "'The Muslim Woman Activist': Solidarity across Difference in the Movement against the 'War on Terror.'" *Ethnicities* 15, no. 5 (2015): 715–741.

Massoumi, Narzanin. *Muslim Women, Social Movements and the 'War on Terror.'* London: Palgrave Macmillan, 2015

Mélis, Corinne. "Nanas-beurs, voix d'elles-rebelles et voix de femmes: Des associations au carrefour des droits des femmes et d'une redéfinition de la citoyenneté." *Revue Européenne des Migrations Internationales* 19, no. 1 (2003): 81–100.

Minganti, Pia Karlsson. "Challenging from Within: Youth Associations and Female Leadership in Swedish Mosques." In *Women, Leadership, and Mosques: Changes in Contemporary Islamic Authority*, edited by Masooda Bano and Hilary Kalmbach, 371–392. Leiden: Brill, 2011.

Modood, Tariq. *Multicultural Politics: Racism, Ethnicity, and Muslims in Britain*. Minneapolis: University of Minnesota Press, 2005.

Nökel, Sigrid. *Die Töchter der Gastarbeiter und der Islam. Zur Soziologie alltagsweltlicher Annerkennungspolitiken. Eine Fallstudie*. Bielefeld: Transcript, 2002.

Parvez, Z. Fareen. *Politicizing Islam: The Islamic Revival in France and India*. Oxford: Oxford University Press, 2017.

Pojmann, Wendy. "Muslim Women's Organizing in France and Italy: Political Culture, Activism, and Performativity in the Public Sphere." *Feminist Formations* 22, no. 3 (2010): 229–251.

Quiminal, Catherine. "Un réseau d'associations de femmes africaines." *Hommes et Migrations* 1208 (1997): 24–29.

Rashid, Naaz. "Giving the Silent Majority a Stronger Voice? Initiatives to Empower Muslim Women as Part of the UK's 'War on Terror.'" *Ethnic and Racial Studies* 37, no. 4 (2014): 589–604.

Roggeband, Conny. "The Victim-Agent Dilemma: How Migrant Women's Organizations in the Netherlands Deal with a Contradictory Policy Frame." *Signs: Journal of Women in Culture and Society* 35, no. 4 (2010): 943–967.

Rogozen-Soltar, Mikaela H. *Spain Unmoored: Migration, Conversion, and the Politics of Islam*. Bloomington: Indiana University Press, 2017.

Salih, Ruba. "Muslim Women, Fragmented Secularism and the Construction of Interconnected 'Publics' in Italy." *Social Anthropology* 17, no. 4 (2009): 409–423.

Shanneik, Yafa. "Gendering Religious Authority in the Diaspora: Shii Women in Ireland." In *Religion, Gender, and the Public* Sphere, 70–80. London: Routledge, 2014.

Soliman, Asmaa. "European Muslims' Engagement in the Public Sphere Soft Counterpublics." *International Review of Sociology* 26, no. 1 (2016): 174–200.

Soliman, Asmaa. *European Muslims Transforming the Public Sphere: Religious Participation in the Arts, Media and Civil Society*. London: Routledge, 2017.

Souilamas, Nacira Guénif, and Éric Macé. *Les féministes et le garçon arabe*. La Tour-d'Aigues: Editions de l'Aube, 2004.

Spielhaus, Riem. "Interessen vertreten mit vereinter Stimme: Der Kopftuchstreit als Impuls für die Institutionalisierung des Islams in Deutschland". In *Der Stoff, aus dem Konflikte sind. Debatten um das Kopftuch in Deutschland, Österreich und der Schweiz*, edited by Sabine Berghahn and Petra Rostock, 413–436. Bielefeld: Transcript, 2009.

Spielhaus, Riem. "Making Islam Relevant: Female Authority and Representation of Islam in Germany." In *Women, Leadership, and Mosques: Changes in Contemporary Islamic Authority*, edited by Masooda Bano and Hilary Kalmbach, 437–456. Leiden: Brill, 2011.

Sudbury, Julia. *"Other Kinds of Dreams": Black Women's Organisations and the Politics of Transformation*. London: Routledge, 1998.

Thiara, Ravi K. "South Asian Women and Collective Action in Britain." In *Gender and Ethnicity in Contemporary Europe*, edited by Jacqueline Andall, 79–96. Oxford: Berg, 2003.

Ticktin, Miriam. "Sexual Violence as the Language of Border Control: Where French Feminist and Anti-immigrant Rhetoric Meet." *Signs: Journal of Women in Culture and Society* 33, no. 4 (2008): 863–889.

Tissot, Sylvie. "Bilan d'un féminisme d'état." *Plein Droit* 4 (2007): 15–18.

Vanderwaeren, Els. "'Muslimahs' Impact on and Acquisition of Islamic Religious Authority in Flanders." In *Women, Leadership, and Mosques. Changes in Contemporary Islamic Authority*, edited by Masooda Bano and Hilary Kalmbach, 301–322. Leiden: Brill, 2011.

Van Es, Margaretha. *Stereotypes and Self-Representations of Women with a Muslim Background: The Stigma of Being Oppressed*. London: Palgrave Macmillan, 2016.

Wadia, Khursheed. "Women from Muslim Communities in Britain. Political and Civic Activism in the 9/11 Era." In *Muslims and Political Participation*, edited by Timothy Peace, 85–102. London: Routledge, 2015.

Weibel, Nadine. *Par-delà le voile: Femmes d'Islam en Europe*. Paris: Complexe, 2000.

Werbner, Pnina. "Political Motherhood and the Feminisation of Citizenship: Women's Activisms and the Transformation of the Public Sphere." In *Women, Citizenship and Difference*, edited by Nira Yuval-Davis and Pnina Werbner, 221–245. London: Zed Books, 1999.

CHAPTER 28

WOMEN'S RELIGIOUS AND SOCIAL ACTIVISM IN SAUDI ARABIA AND THE GULF COUNTRIES

ALAINNA LILOIA

Introduction

Women in the Arab Gulf states are outnumbering men in higher education enrollment rates, increasing their engagement and visibility in the public sphere, and skillfully renegotiating and redefining their societal roles. Some women are pursuing careers. Others are maintaining traditional domestic roles. Many are doing both. In Saudi Arabia, women activists are defying legal and social boundaries to fight for increased social and political rights. In Kuwait and Bahrain, women's political and social organizations are working closely with the state to affect gradual social change. In Qatar, women's professional organizations are pushing for women's increased involvement in the nation's economic development in line with the state's national agendas. As Gulf women shape the future trajectories of their nations through their personal and professional choices, they are also contending with the often contradictory and seemingly dualistic expectations promoted by state rulers and religious leaders and the pressures stemming from members of their own families and social communities.

This chapter analyzes women's religious and social activism in the Arab Gulf states, with attention to the varied ways Gulf women are negotiating religious, social and political norms and expectations and redefining their societal roles. Specifically, I examine the myriad strategies deployed by women in the Gulf to renegotiate and resist gender norms, focusing on women's religious and social activism in Saudi Arabia, Kuwait, and Bahrain. Before delving into how Gulf women are impacting their nation's social and political norms, I provide a brief historical overview of women's engagement with social, political, and religious gender norms in the Middle East since the late nineteenth century and important related scholarly debates. I also discuss the specificities of the Gulf's sociopolitical context and broad trends in the Gulf region related to gender roles, particularly the regulation of women's behavior in the public sphere and the implementation of gendered political initiatives requiring women's increased participation in higher education and the workforce.

Scholarship on Muslim Women's Religious and Social Engagement and Resistance

Throughout the history of the Gulf region and broader Middle East, states, religious institutions, and nationalist movements have commonly used representations of women as symbols of cultural and religious authenticity, or conversely, as markers of modernity and progress in pursuit of their political and social agendas.[1] As scholars have pointed out, particularly since the rise of nationalist movements in the region in the late nineteenth and early twentieth centuries, women have found themselves seemingly caught between competing agendas, as their roles in society and in the domestic sphere have become a site of negotiation for religious, nationalist, and political leaders vying for political and social power.[2]

In many Arab nations, competing anticolonial movements used representations of women to propagate their respective agendas, with secular nationalists on the one hand often representing women and their perceived advancement in society as proof of the "modern" values they promised to promote. On the other, conservative religious reformers represent women and their traditional roles in the domestic sphere as proof of the moral and religious values they promised to preserve.[3] While secular nationalists were accused by religious conservatives of caving to Westernization, religious conservatives were accused by secular nationalists of obstructing modern progress. Of course, women have not acted as passive recipients of the expectations imposed on them, but have actively contributed to the negotiation of their societal roles through a variety of strategies and choices, including participation in secular nationalist movements or religious reform movements and engagement in organized resistance against social and political inequalities.

Important scholarship has critiqued orientalist portrayals of Muslim women that fail to acknowledge their agency, highlighting the ways they have actively contributed to the formulation of their roles in nationalist and religious movements and in society at large.[4] However, while the participation of Muslim women in what are considered "secular" feminist or nationalist movements is often willingly acknowledged by scholars as a form of agency, women's participation in religious movements, particularly those characterized by conservative ideologies, has often been dismissed as a form of "false-consciousness."[5] The work of Lila Abu-Lughod and Sherine Hafez draws attention to the fact that the religious/secular binary does not adequately account for the crossover between secular and religious ideologies or the multiplicity of factors that impact Muslims women's subjectivities and experiences.[6] Hafez also emphasizes the heterogeneity of Muslim women's choices and subjectivities, challenging monolithic portrayals of Muslim women in various Islamic contexts.[7]

In addition, a number of scholars have analyzed Muslim women's participation in Islamic (and Islamist) movements in the Middle East, arguing that Muslim women seek to empower themselves and to advance their status in society through their strategic engagement with Islamic political and social movements.[8] Saba Mahmood questions the tendency in Western scholarship to represent women as exercising agency within Islamic movements only when their engagement in these movements involves resistance of social and political norms from a "progressivist point of view," reframing and broadening the concept of women's agency to include the choices of Muslim women that do not reflect liberal or progressive values or outright political or social resistance to patriarchal norms.[9]

Scholarship on women in the Arab Gulf is a growing area of study that highlights the variety of personal and professional choices Gulf women are making and the diversity of their responses to social, religious, and political expectations in their respective sociopolitical contexts.[10] The body of existing research acknowledges significant trends in the views of women in each of the Gulf states as well as certain regional trends, while also drawing attention to the fact that their views and actions are not monolithic. The intersection of political agendas, religious expectations, and social pressures have impacted women in the Gulf and shaped their subjectivities and identities in different ways, and their responses have included working within traditional structures to advance their status in society and/or shape gender norms, complying with traditional gender paradigms, exercising agency through religious engagement, and resisting norms through political activism. Much of the existing research on gender in the Gulf is ethnographic or sociological in nature and provides insight into women's expression of agency through their engagement in society, including their educational, religious, social, and political engagement. It has also analyzed the impact of state initiatives and agendas on women's engagement in the public sphere.[11]

It is worth nothing that scholars do not commonly associate women's "activism" with the Gulf states, with the exception of Saudi Arabia. There are not easily identifiable women's activist movements in many of the Gulf states, and in cases where there are, they do not necessarily look like what is commonly referred to as social or religious "activism." The women activists of Saudi Arabia have boldly defied legal boundaries in an effort to attain social and political equality, and scholars have rightly acknowledged how these women are exercising agency to advance their status in society. However, in Saudi Arabia and the other Gulf states, there are many women who have chosen to work within traditional structures of power to shape their roles in society and who have aligned their activities closely with the agendas of the state. There are women's organizations in all of the Gulf states, but these often function under the umbrella of the state or as branches of political parties. Yet, this does not diminish the significant ways that women are contributing to the formulation of gender roles, social and religious values, and political norms in their states. It is not only when women engage in political or social campaigns, such as Saudi women's campaign for the right to drive or Kuwaiti women's campaign for the right to vote, but when they are living their daily lives and engaging in their societies, that they are impacting the future trajectories of their nations and their roles within them.

The Arab Gulf Context

The historical context of the Gulf states differs from that of other Arab nations due to the fact that the nations transitioned peacefully from British protectorates into independent states and because their histories were not characterized by anticolonial nationalist struggles. However, scholars have demonstrated that nation-building and national identity are nonetheless useful categories of analysis for scholarship on women in the Gulf.[12] The construction of national identities is vital to the political and social agendas of state rulers and religious scholars, who commonly represent women as symbols of national and cultural identity, and the nation-building initiatives and rhetoric of the state significantly impact the context in which women make their personal and professional choices.

Particularly since the discovery of oil in the region in the 1930s, the Gulf states have experienced a rise in Western cultural and economic imperialism, including influxes of Western businesses and professionals looking to profit from the nations' newfound oil wealth, the establishment of Western oil companies, and the implementation of numerous capitalist infrastructures and projects. Since the Gulf states first acquired independence, Gulf rulers have prioritized nation-building agendas and the construction of national identities in an attempt to unify their populations and foster social stability. Increases in Western expatriate populations and Western influences have only increased the importance of these agendas. On the other hand, the economic and social pressures stemming from globalization and a desire to increase international political standing have also led Gulf nations to adopt certain Western paradigms related to modernization, social progress and economic development.

A conflict has arisen between religious conservatives seeking to preserve cultural and religious authenticity and political rulers seeking to implement social reforms and modernization projects. Unsurprisingly, women's roles have been central to the negotiations that take place between state rulers, religious leaders, and also citizens, with state rulers representing gender reform as proof of modern progress to domestic and international audiences and religious conservatives advocating for the preservation of women's traditional roles as a symbol of religious and cultural authenticity. State rulers have struggled to maintain a sense of national identity and alleviate concerns of religious leaders and citizens about Westernization while also fulfilling developmental agendas. In an attempt to simultaneously construct a national identity and facilitate economic and social development, Gulf rulers have implemented gendered political projects that promote women's increased participation in higher education and the workforce while simultaneously promoting social and cultural norms that restrict women's roles in society. In other words, the Gulf states have engaged in the regulation of women's behavior in the public sphere and the limitation of their political and social rights while also promoting women's increased public visibility and offering women increased opportunities to pursue higher education and careers. Workforce nationalization policies, which aim to increase the national workforce and provide more career opportunities for citizens, have targeted women in order to meet stated outcomes. New training programs, scholarship programs, and educational initiatives have been established to encourage women to pursue higher education and careers.

While the Gulf states differ in their legal codes, it is helpful to identify the commonalities that exist in their legal regulation of women's behavior, namely through personal status laws. Personal status laws are based on interpretations of Islamic law, and their codification in most of the Gulf states has served to standardize specific interpretations so that legal norms can be more uniformly followed and enforced. These laws impact women's rights in many areas, including areas of marriage, divorce, and child custody. With the exception of Saudi Arabia, all of the states of the Gulf Cooperation Council (GCC) have codified personal status laws. Qatar, Oman, the United Arab Emirates (UAE) and Bahrain codified their personal status laws on the basis of the same legal document, the "Muscat Document of the Uniform Code (the Law) of Personal Status for GCC Countries" that was issued in 1996 by the GCC, and Saudi jurists commonly use the document as a reference.[13] Despite the absence of a codified personal status law, similar legal norms are applied in Saudi as in the other states of the GCC. Patriarchal norms enforced through laws and even social codes serve to restrict women's roles in society and reinforce women's roles as symbols of the nations' religious and cultural values. Such norms elevate the role of the family, in which men are considered to have authority over the family and women are to act as caregivers, as the foundation of a moral society.[14] Personal status laws even consider women the caregivers and custodians of their children, though ultimate legal authority lies with the children's male guardians.[15]

Legal norms in the Gulf states restrict women in a number of areas. In order to marry, women in the Gulf states must receive the approval of a male guardian, who is a male relative granted authority in certain aspects of a woman's life. Once married, a woman's husband becomes her guardian. In marriage, women continue to be subject to male authority in a number of ways. For example, laws in Qatar, Kuwait, and Bahrain include provisions that allow women's husbands to stop them from working if they deem it is interfering with aspects of their domestic responsibilities or religious conduct.[16] In addition, women face inequalities in the area of divorce. In all of the Gulf states, men are generally granted a unilateral right to divorce, whereas women must either pursue a judicial divorce on the basis of specific marriage violations or *khul'*, a form of divorce allowed for personal reasons that requires a woman to pay a financial compensation.[17]

Women are also restricted in the areas of passing on citizenship to their children, inheritance, and freedom of movement. For example, in Saudi Arabia and Qatar, male guardians can prevent female relatives from traveling by filing a "disobedience" complaint or appearing before a court, respectively.[18] Some personal status laws also limit women's freedom to leave their homes.[19]

Norms prioritizing women's roles in the domestic sphere are not only promoted by the laws of the state. Religious institutions and women's own families and social communities often pressure women to fulfill traditional domestic responsibilities, and many women themselves are satisfied with maintaining traditional gender paradigms. Choosing to work outside the home is often viewed unfavorably, as women are expected to prioritize marriage and family responsibilities. At the same time, women in the Gulf states face increased pressure from the state to pursue educational opportunities and careers. New training programs, scholarship programs, and educational initiatives have been established to encourage women to pursue higher education and careers, and state documents and rhetoric highlight women's roles in modern development and national agendas.[20]

For example, in Saudi Arabia, the world's largest women-only university, Princess Nora bint Abdul Rahman University, was established in the capital city of Riyadh in 2010 to give women better opportunities to pursue male-dominated disciplines. The Gulf states have also established women's organizations that serve to encourage women's participation in the states' national agendas and their contribution to the states' economic development processes. In Qatar, the state's Chamber of Commerce and Industry established the Qatar Businesswomen Forum in 2001 to "assist Qatari businesswomen to practise their role in the economic development process."[21] Other examples include the Kuwaiti Union for Women Associations and the Bahrain Women Association for Human Development. However, these state-sanctioned organizations are often dominated by middle- and upper-class women and are not necessarily representative of the interests of women belonging to other social and economic classes.[22] In addition, all of the states have workforce nationalization policies, which aim to increase the national workforce and provide more career opportunities for citizens, and these have often targeted women in order to meet stated outcomes. Purported to curb the influence of expatriate populations, these policies are intentionally exclusionist and racialized. Migrant workers, many of whom originate from South Asian countries, are excluded from the economic and social benefits of citizenship through a discriminatory legal system. Moreover, Gulf women's identities are constructed by the state in opposition to those of female domestic workers, with their increased engagement in society symbolizing progress and modernity.

Women in the Gulf have responded to the opportunities available to them in a variety of ways, with some prioritizing domestic responsibilities, others prioritizing careers, and many balancing both. They have shaped their societies in a variety of ways, whether through participation in political structures and movements, their activities in state-sanctioned women's organizations, or their resistance to social and political norms through organized activism. The next sections will provide an overview of women's religious and social activism and engagement in a few of the Gulf states to highlight how Gulf women are shaping the future trajectories of their nations and renegotiating their roles in society.

The Saudi Women's Activist Movement

In Saudi Arabia, women activists have engaged in bold resistance to legal gender norms and developed an extensive women's movement to advance their status in society and fight gender inequalities. Their activism in the twenty-first century has involved direct defiance of state laws, social media campaigns, online petitions, and educational studies and workshops. Saudi women activists have garnered international media attention and skillfully utilized social media as a tool to raise international awareness, articulating their demands in global human rights language in an effort to gain the support of the international community. The movement has received the support of the global feminist movement and human rights organizations, and several women activists have written opinion pieces or appeared in television interviews for Western global media outlets. In 2016, through collaboration with Saudi women activists, Human Rights Watch (HRW) issued a report called "Boxed In" that described the inequalities Saudi women face under the guardianship system.[23]

Saudi women activists' most notable campaigns have included the Women-to-Drive Movement and anti-male-guardianship campaigns. The Women-to-Drive Movement was created to protest the state's ban on women drivers, which was in effect from the 1950s until 2018. The movement began in the 1990s when forty-seven Saudi women got behind the wheel and drove through the streets of Riyadh in protest of the ban. From the 1990s until the lifting of the ban in 2018, leaders of the movement, such as Manāl āl -Sharīf and Wajīha āl-Ḥūwaidar, continued to organize driving protests and activists began uploading videos of themselves driving to YouTube to raise public awareness. Leaders of the movement also sent a signed petition to King Abdullah in 2007 asking for women to be granted the right to drive. In 2011 they created a Facebook page called "Women2Drive" that was inspired by the Arab Spring protests.

Social media activism has been a particularly powerful tool to protest the guardianship system, a set of laws and social codes granting authority over women to their male relatives. In 2019, the state amended the guardianship system so that women no longer required guardian permission to travel or apply for a passport. However, women still require a guardian's permission to leave prison or domestic abuse shelters, and men can still report their female relatives missing for leaving their homes. The 2016 Twitter campaign with the hashtag "I Am My Own Guardian," which was coordinated to begin at the same time the HRW's "Boxed In" report was released, went viral on social media. Other campaigns to abolish the guardianship system included a petition to the Ministry of Labor in 2011 requesting that Saudi women be able to acquire employment without a guardian's permission, a letter-writing campaign in 2016 that involved over 2,000 women sending telegrams to King Salmān, and an online petition following the letter-writing campaign that was signed by almost 15,000 and delivered to the Royal Court directly by ʿAzīza āl-Yūsif, the activist who organized the petition. Activists have also conducted studies on the guardianship system related to its religious validity and held workshops to educate women on guardianship laws.

The Saudi state's response to women's activism has been characterized by repression, with the state initiating crackdowns to arrest and detain women activists. A particularly striking example of the state's repression of women activists occurred in the weeks leading up to the lifting of the driving ban in June of 2018, when the Saudi state arrested a number of Saudi women's rights activists, who had fought for the right to drive, in a crackdown supposedly initiated to enforce the state's security. The Saudi state's relationship to its female citizenry in the twenty-first century has been characterized by paradox in more ways than one. Particularly since September 11, the state has engaged in focused rebranding efforts to counter views of the nation as a hotbed for religious fundamentalism and terrorism and to alleviate international human rights concerns.[24] Gender reform has been central to these rebranding efforts, with the state implementing social reforms that ease restrictions on women, establishing initiatives to increase women's educational opportunities and participation in the workforce, and appointing women to highly visible public and political positions. Yet, the reform has been coupled with intense repression and continued regulation of women's behavior in the public sphere.

Particularly in the post–September 11 context, the state has presented women's increased engagement in the public sphere as a symbol of modernity and progress to the international community and represented itself as a patron of women's education and societal advancement. At the same time, state rulers have continued to elevate women's traditional roles as a symbol of the state's Islamic national identity and regulate women's behavior in the public sphere as proof of its preservation of religious morality.[25] Madawi Al-Rasheed argues that the Saudi state's close relationship to the Wahhabi religious tradition and the social and legal power granted to religious scholars have resulted in the emergence of a form of religious nationalism reliant on representations of women as symbols of religious piety and the regulation of women's behavior in the public sphere.[26]

However, political and social pressures faced by the Saudi state in the context of modern development and globalization have also led the state to implement gender reforms and encourage women's increased engagement in the public sphere, as well as promote more moderate religious interpretations and increase the state's regulation of religious scholars and their application of Islamic law.[27] Social reforms implemented under the Crown Prince Muḥammad bin Salmān have included lifting the driving ban on women, allowing women to attend public sporting events and join the military, and no longer requiring women to obtain a guardian's consent to open a business, apply for a passport, or travel abroad. Yet, while the state claims to advance women's status in society, state rulers continue to suppress the voices of women who criticize the state, seem only to appoint women to public positions if they are willing to echo the state's rhetoric and promote its agendas, and ignore many of women activists' concerns, such as those related to inequalities in inheritance practices, divorce, nationality rights, and access to governmental and social services, as well as continued concerns about the authority of male guardians. Thus, while state rulers may represent women as markers of modernity to international and domestic audiences, they do so while maintaining their control over women's roles in society and silencing and even jailing the women activists who fought for the very reforms they provide as proof of the nation's progress.

While Saudi women activists have received a great deal of attention in global media and gained the support of feminist and human rights organizations, there are many Saudi women who have chosen not to engage in direct resistance of state policies and gender norms. These women have chosen to navigate their existing social and political context rather than resist or attempt to dismantle it. As Amélie Le Renard has argued, many Saudi women have resisted social gender norms in more subtle ways, with urban Saudi women renegotiating gender norms by transgressing certain social expectations (such as forms of dress) in women-only, public spaces and by negotiating the forms of behavior permitted within their own families.[28] As the state represents itself as a patron of women's advancement while simultaneously repressing women's dissenting voices, women are shaping gender norms through their activism, their engagement in higher education and the workforce, and their subtle resistance of social norms in the public sphere.

Women's Activism in Kuwait and Bahrain

Gulf women are shaping the formulation of gender norms and cultural identities in their nations through their social, political and religious engagement and their increased involvement in the public sphere. It is impossible to cover fully the wide range of ways women are impacting the social and cultural fabric of their nations. However, I will provide a few examples through a discussion of women's activism in Kuwait and Shīʿī Bahraini women's political and religious engagement and activism.

In Kuwait, women's activism has included participation in Islamist movements as well as the development of secular feminist campaigns that opt for a more "liberal" approach to women's rights. Kuwaiti women's views on feminism and women's rights cannot be reduced to a dichotomy of religious versus secular. Kuwaiti women all across the political and religious spectrum have engaged with multiple feminist paradigms and utilized a variety of approaches to advancing their rights—including participation in women's organizations, political participation, and political and social media activism. Prominent activist campaigns in Kuwait today include Abolish 153, which aims to abolish the law that legally allows honor killings, as well as a campaign for women married to non-Kuwaitis to be allowed to pass on citizenship to their children.

State-funded women's organizations were first developed in Kuwait in the 1960s and were dominated largely by middle and upper-class women.[29] As second-wave feminism became a global phenomenon in the 1960s and 1970s, many upper-class Kuwaiti women adopted secular feminist views and approaches to women's rights. In the

1980s, the formation of Islamist women's organizations in Kuwait provided an alternative particularly for lower and middle-class women, whose ideologies and political leanings differed from those promoted by secular or nationalist women's movements popular among upper-middle and upper-class women.[30] Islamist propagation of religious values and opposition to Westernization resonated with many Kuwaiti women with strong religious and cultural identities. Many women in Kuwait and other Gulf states hold traditional views of gender equality, adopting a complementarian paradigm in which men and women naturally fulfill different roles. Many also use religious interpretations as justification of their views on gender equality, which range from traditional to liberal. Thus, it is often the case that Western feminist paradigms for gender equality and women's advancement do not align with their own views of gender equality.

After Kuwaiti women's enfranchisement in 2005, liberal and Islamist political parties found themselves competing to gain the women's vote in the 2006 election. The political need for women's votes led Islamist parties to strategically include women in their campaign efforts, and the success of Islamist candidates in the 2006, 2008, 2012, and 2016 parliamentary elections is partially a result of their successful incorporation of women into their political and social activities and the formation of women's groups under the umbrellas of their parties. Women's support for Islamist parties have often been viewed by Western and other secular feminists (including those in Kuwait) as opposed to women's rights, particularly because many Islamist candidates are not fully supportive of or were opposed entirely to women being granted political rights. However, Alessandra L. González argues that Islamist women in Kuwait have strategically yielded their political rights to advance their social rights and used political participation as a tool to reach greater goals of reform.[31] In her sociological research, González discovered that Kuwaiti women have voted for Islamist candidates because they believed these candidates would advance the causes most important to them.[32] Issues important to many Kuwaiti women, both Islamist and liberal, include gender inequalities in personal status laws, naturalization laws, divorce laws, guardianship laws, and inheritance laws, as well as issues related to women's property rights and maternity leave policies. Kuwaiti women across the religious and political spectrum have taken a variety of approaches to these issues, demonstrating that different women conceptualize and work to advance their own "interests" in different ways.

In Bahrain, women commonly articulate their understandings of women's rights in religious terms, upholding women-friendly interpretations of the Qur'an as a source of empowerment and gender equality. Women belonging to the nation's majority Shīʿī population have found religious engagement to be a source of empowerment and identity formation, and they have contributed to the formulation of their community's collective identities through their religious engagement in both mixed and women-only spaces.[33] They have also participated in the political activism of their communities, particularly in the wake of the Arab Spring protests of 2011. While Shīʿī women have often participated in male-led political activism by taking on traditional and supportive roles, they engaged in political activism in less traditional ways in the wake of increased political unrest in the 1990s.[34] As many male political activists were arrested by the government, women increased their public engagement in political activism, circulating petitions and organizing public demonstrations to demand the release of the men in their community and protest the undemocratic practices of the nation's rulers.

Since the 1990s, women-only *ma'tams* (Shīʿī religious centers) have sometimes functioned as spaces for political resistance and organizing. Shīʿī women also participated in the 2002 election boycott led by the Islamist party Āl Wufāq to protest the disproportionate power given to unelected officials, and they organized their own demonstration in Manama to protest the 2011 parliamentary elections which the Shīʿī opposition argued would result in the continued marginalization of the Shīʿī population. In addition, Sunnī and Shīʿī Bahraini women played an important role in the Arab Spring protests of 2011, joining the protestors storming Pearl Roundabout in the city of Manama and providing food and medical care to protestors. Bahraini women teachers also organized a strike. The government's repression of protests involved the arrest of men and women, including medics, doctors, nurses, and teachers believed to have been involved. Particularly since the Arab Spring, Shīʿī religious identity has become increasingly politicized, and in times of political organizing and unrest, Shīʿī women have supported male-led political activism in protest of the Shīʿī population's marginalization by the Sunni monarchy. Bahraini Shīʿī women have participated directly and played supportive roles in their community's fight for political and social equality, and their religious and political engagement has contributed to their community's formulation of collective identities and political and social aims.

Conclusion

Gulf women's navigation of their sociopolitical and religious contexts has been characterized by the skillful negotiation of political, religious and social norms as well and a variety of choices and strategies. As they face new pressures associated with modern development and social change alongside the expectations of their social and religious communities, their choices are impacting gender norms in both subtle and direct ways. Muslim women have never been a monolith, and the varied choices of women in the Gulf described in this chapter clearly exemplify the diversity of their views and actions. This chapter has analyzed a few of the many ways women in the Gulf states are redefining and renegotiating their societal roles, contributing to the formulation of gender norms, and shaping the future political and social trajectories. From the bold political activism of Saudi women to the strategic political participation of Kuwaiti Islamist women or the political and religious engagement of Bahraini Shīʿī women, women in the Gulf are impacting the social, cultural, and religious fabric of their nations in significant ways.

Notes

1. Lila Abu-Lughod, "Introduction: Feminist Longings and Postcolonial Conditions," in *Remaking Women: Feminism and Modernity in the Middle East*, ed. Lila Abu-Lughod, Princeton Studies in Culture/Power/History (Princeton, NJ: Princeton University Press, 1998), 3–32; P. Chatterjee, "Colonialism, Nationalism and Colonized Women: The Contest in India," *American Ethnologist* 16 (November 1989): 622–633; Suad Joseph, *Gender and Citizenship in the Middle East*, 1st ed., Contemporary Issues in the Middle East (Syracuse, NY: Syracuse University Press, 2000); Deniz Kandiyoti, "Identity and Its Discontents: Women and the Nation," *Millennium—Journal of International Studies* 20, no. 3 (1991): 429–443.
2. Abu-Lughod, "Introduction: Feminist Longings"; Joseph, *Gender and Citizenship*; Kandiyoti, "Identity and Its Discontents"; Deniz Kandiyoti, "The Politics of Gender and the Conundrums of Citizenship," in *Women and Power in the Middle East*, ed. Suad Joseph and Susan Slyomovics (Philadelphia: University of Pennsylvania Press, 2001), 52–60; Valentine M. Moghadam, "Gender, National Identity and Citizenship: Reflections on the Middle East and North Africa," *Comparative Studies of South Asia, Africa and the Middle East* 19, no. 1 (1999): 137–157.
3. Kandiyoti, "Identity and Its Discontents," 431–435.
4. Abu-Lughod, "Introduction: Feminist Longings and Postcolonial Conditions"; Lila Abu-Lughod, *Do Muslim Women Need Saving?* (Cambridge, MA: Harvard University Press, 2013); Joseph, *Gender and Citizenship in the Middle East*; Kandiyoti, "The Politics of Gender and the Conundrums of Citizenship"; Moghadam, "Gender, National Identity and Citizenship"; Saba Mahmood, *Politics of Piety: The Islamic Revival and the Feminist Subject* (Princeton, NJ: Princeton University Press, 2005).
5. Mahmood, *Politics of Piety*, 1–5.
6. Lila Abu-Lughod, "The Marriage of Feminism and Islamism in Egypt: Selective Repudiation as a Dynamic of Postcolonial Cultural Politics," in *Remaking Women: Feminism and Modernity in the Middle East* (Princeton, NJ: Princeton University Press, 1998), 243–269; Sherine Hafez, *An Islam of Her Own: Reconsidering Religion and Secularism in Women's Islamic Movements* (New York: New York University Press, 2011).
7. Hafez, *An Islam of Her Own*, 30–39.
8. Margot Badran, *Feminism in Islam: Secular and Religious Convergences*, Twentieth Century Religious Thought, Volume II: Islam (Oxford: Oneworld, 2011); Miriam Cooke, *Women Claim Islam: Creating Islamic Feminism through Literature* (New York: Routledge, 2001); Alessandra L. González, *Islamic Feminism in Kuwait the Politics and Paradoxes*, 1st ed. (New York: Palgrave Macmillan, 2013); Mahmood, *Politics of Piety*.
9. Mahmood, *Politics of Piety*, 15.
10. Madawi Al-Rasheed, *A Most Masculine State: Gender, Politics, and Religion in Saudi Arabia*, Cambridge Middle East Studies (New York: Cambridge University Press, 2013); Jane Bristol-Rhys, *Emirati Women: Generations of Change*, 2nd ed. (London: C. Hurst, 2016); Krystyna Golkowska, "Qatari Women Navigating Gendered Space," *Social Sciences* 6, no. 4 (October 16, 2017): 1–10; Laurie James-Hawkins, Yara Qutteina, and Kathryn M. Yount, "The Patriarchal Bargain in a Context of Rapid Changes to Normative Gender Roles: Young Arab Women's Role Conflict in Qatar," *Sex Roles* 77, nos. 3–4 (August 1, 2017): 155–168; Alainna Liloia, "Gender and Nation Building in Qatar: Qatari Women Negotiate Modernity," *Journal of Middle East Women's Studies* 15, no. 3 (November 1, 2019): 344–366; Mandana E. Limbert, *In the Time of Oil: Piety, Memory, and Social Life in an Omani*

Town (Stanford, CA: Stanford University Press, 2010); J. S. Mitchell et al., "In Majaalis Al-Hareem: The Complex Professional and Personal Choices of Qatari Women," *DIFI Family Research and Proceedings*, no. 4 (August 5, 2014): 1–12.

11. Al-Rasheed, *A Most Masculine State*; Golkowska, "Qatari Women"; James-Hawkins, Qutteina, and Yount, "The Patriarchal Bargain"; Liloia, "Gender and Nation Building in Qatar"; Mitchell et al., "In Majaalis Al-Hareem."
12. Al-Rasheed, *A Most Masculine State*, 8–22; Amélie Le Renard, *A Society of Young Women: Opportunities of Place, Power, and Reform in Saudi Arabia* (Stanford, CA: Stanford University Press, 2014), 29–33.
13. Hala Aldosari, "The Personal Is Political: Gender Identity in the Personal Status Laws of the Gulf Arab States," (The Arab Gulf States Institute Washington, August 29, 2016), 4, available at http://www.agsiw.org/wp-content/uploads/2016/08/Aldosari_ONLINE_updated.pdf.
14. Ibid., 6
15. Ibid., 13.
16. Ibid., 9.
17. Ibid., 1–2.
18. Al-Jazeera, "Loopholes Riddle Saudi Reforms on 'Guardianship' of Women: Report," October 23, 2019, https://www.aljazeera.com/news/2019/10/loopholes-riddle-saudi-reforms-guardianship-women-report-191023062306285.html; Ismaeel Naar, "Qatar Only Remaining GCC Country Restricting Travel for Women," August 4, 2019, https://english.alarabiya.net/en/features/2019/08/04/Qatar-remains-only-GCC-country-restricting-travel-for-women.
19. Aldosari, "The Personal Is Political," 9.
20. Qatar General Secretariat for Development Planning, "Qatar National Vision 2030," July 2008; Qatar General Secretariat for Development Planning, "National Development Strategy," March 2011, https://www.mdps.gov.qa/en/knowledge/HomePagePublications/Qatar_NDS_reprint_complete_lowres_16May.pdf; Kingdom of Saudi Arabia, "Saudi Vision 2030," accessed March 24, 2020, https://vision2030.gov.sa/en.
21. Qatar Businesswomen Forum, "Establishment—Page 554—Qatar Businesswomen Forum," accessed March 24, 2020, https://qbwf.org.qa/establishment/554/.
22. Haya Al-Mughni, "Women's Organizations in Kuwait," *Middle East Report* 26 (1996): 32; Haya Al Mughni, *Women in Kuwait: The Politics of Gender* (London: Saqi Books, 1993), 111.
23. Human Rights Watch, "Boxed In: Women and Saudi Arabia's Male Guardianship System," Human Rights Watch, July 16, 2016, https://www.hrw.org/report/2016/07/16/boxed/women-and-saudi-arabias-male-guardianship-system.
24. Al-Rasheed, *A Most Masculine State*, 134–174.
25. Al-Rasheed, 108–133; Le Renard, *A Society of Young Women*, 30–33; Eleanor A. Doumato, "Gender, Monarchy, and National Identity in Saudi Arabia," *British Journal of Middle Eastern Studies* 19, no. 1 (1992): 33–36, 41–44.
26. Al-Rasheed, *A Most Masculine State*, 43–51.
27. Ibid., 136–147.
28. Le Renard, *A Society of Young Women*, 107–129.
29. Al-Mughni, "Women's Organizations in Kuwait," 32–33.
30. Margot Badran, "Gender, Islam and the State: Kuwaiti Women in Struggle, Pre-Invasion to Postliberation," in *Islam, Gender, and Social Change*, ed. Yvonne Yazbeck Haddad and John L. Esposito (New York: Oxford University Press, 1998), 192.
31. González, *Islamic Feminism in Kuwait the Politics and Paradoxes*, 26.

32. Ibid., 27–28.
33. May Seikaly, "Women and Religion in Bahrain: An Emerging Identity," in *Islam, Gender, and Social Change*, ed. Yvonne Yazbeck Haddad and John L. Esposito (Oxford University Press, 1998), 169–189; Sophia Pandya, *Muslim Women and Islamic Resurgence: Religion, Education and Identity Politics in Bahrain* (Boca Raton: I. B.Tauris, 2013).
34. Pandya, *Muslim Women and Islamic Resurgence*, 65–99.

Bibliography

Abu-Lughod, Lila. *Do Muslim Women Need Saving?* Cambridge, MA: Harvard University Press, 2013.

Abu-Lughod, Lila. "Introduction: Feminist Longings and Postcolonial Conditions." In *Remaking Women: Feminism and Modernity in the Middle East*, edited by Lila Abu-Lughod, 3–32. Princeton Studies in Culture/Power/History. Princeton, NJ: Princeton University Press, 1998.

Abu-Lughod, Lila. "The Marriage of Feminism and Islamism in Egypt: Selective Repudiation as a Dynamic of Postcolonial Cultural Politics." In *Remaking Women: Feminism and Modernity in the Middle East*, edited by Lila Abu-Lughod, 243–269. Princeton Studies in Culture/Power/History. Princeton, NJ: Princeton University Press, 1998.

Aldosari, Hala. "The Personal Is Political: Gender Identity in the Personal Status Laws of the Gulf Arab States." The Arab Gulf States Institute Washington, August 29, 2016. http://www.agsiw.org/wp-content/uploads/2016/08/Aldosari_ONLINE_updated.pdf.

Al-Jazeera. "Loopholes Riddle Saudi Reforms on 'Guardianship' of Women: Report," October 23, 2019. https://www.aljazeera.com/news/2019/10/loopholes-riddle-saudi-reforms-guardianship-women-report-191023062306285.html.

Badran, Margot. *Feminism in Islam: Secular and Religious Convergences*. Twentieth Century Religious Thought, Volume II: Islam. Oxford: Oneworld, 2011.

Badran, Margot. "Gender, Islam and the State: Kuwaiti Women in Struggle, Pre-Invasion to Postliberation." In *Islam, Gender, and Social Change*, edited by Yvonne Yazbeck Haddad and John L. Esposito, 219–237. New York: Oxford University Press, 1998.

Bristol-Rhys, Jane. *Emirati Women: Generations of Change*. 2nd ed. London: C. Hurst, 2016.

Chatterjee, P. "Colonialism, Nationalism and Colonized Women: The Contest in India." *American Ethnologist* 16 (November 1989): 622–633.

Cooke, Miriam. *Women Claim Islam: Creating Islamic Feminism through Literature*. New York: Routledge, 2001.

Doumato, Eleanor A. "Gender, Monarchy, and National Identity in Saudi Arabia." *British Journal of Middle Eastern Studies* 19, no. 1 (1992): 31–47.

Golkowska, Krystyna. "Qatari Women Navigating Gendered Space." *Social Sciences* 6, no. 4 (October 16, 2017): 1–10.

González, Alessandra L. *Islamic Feminism in Kuwait the Politics and Paradoxes*. 1st ed. New York: Palgrave Macmillan, 2013.

Hafez, Sherine. *An Islam of Her Own: Reconsidering Religion and Secularism in Women's Islamic Movements*. New York: New York University Press, 2011.

Human Rights Watch. "Boxed In: Women and Saudi Arabia's Male Guardianship System." July 16, 2016. https://www.hrw.org/report/2016/07/16/boxed/women-and-saudi-arabias-male-guardianship-system.

James-Hawkins, Laurie, Yara Qutteina, and Kathryn M. Yount. "The Patriarchal Bargain in a Context of Rapid Changes to Normative Gender Roles: Young Arab Women's Role Conflict in Qatar." *Sex Roles* 77, nos. 3–4 (August 1, 2017): 155–168.

Joseph, Suad. *Gender and Citizenship in the Middle East*. 1st ed. Contemporary Issues in the Middle East. Syracuse, NY: Syracuse University Press, 2000.

Kandiyoti, Deniz. "Identity and Its Discontents: Women and the Nation." *Millennium—Journal of International Studies* 20, no. 3 (1991): 429–443.

Kandiyoti, Deniz. "The Politics of Gender and the Conundrums of Citizenship." In *Women and Power in the Middle East*, edited by Suad Joseph and Susan Slyomovics, 52–60. Philadelphia: University of Pennsylvania Press, 2001.

Kingdom of Saudi Arabia. "Saudi Vision 2030." Accessed March 24, 2020. https://vision2030.gov.sa/en.

Le Renard, Amélie. *A Society of Young Women: Opportunities of Place, Power, and Reform in Saudi Arabia*. Stanford, CA: Stanford University Press, 2014.

Liloia, Alainna. "Gender and Nation Building in Qatar: Qatari Women Negotiate Modernity." *Journal of Middle East Women's Studies* 15, no. 3 (November 1, 2019): 344–366.

Limbert, Mandana E. *In the Time of Oil: Piety, Memory, and Social Life in an Omani Town*. Stanford, CA: Stanford University Press, 2010.

Mahmood, Saba. *Politics of Piety: The Islamic Revival and the Feminist Subject*. Princeton, NJ: Princeton University Press, 2005.

Mitchell, J. S., C. Paschyn, S. Mir, K. Pike, and T. Kane. "In Majaalis Al-Hareem: The Complex Professional and Personal Choices of Qatari Women." *DIFI Family Research and Proceedings*, no. 4 (August 5, 2014): 1–12.

Moghadam, Valentine M. "Gender, National Identity and Citizenship: Reflections on the Middle East and North Africa." *Comparative Studies of South Asia, Africa and the Middle East* 19, no. 1 (1999): 137–157.

Mughni, Haya al-. *Women in Kuwait: The Politics of Gender*. London: Saqi Books, 1993.

Mughni, Haya al-. "Women's Organizations in Kuwait." *Middle East Report* 26 (1996): 32–35.

Naar, Ismaeel. "Qatar Only Remaining GCC Country Restricting Travel for Women," August 4, 2019. https://english.alarabiya.net/en/features/2019/08/04/Qatar-remains-only-GCC-country-restricting-travel-for-women.

Pandya, Sophia. *Muslim Women and Islamic Resurgence: Religion, Education and Identity Politics in Bahrain*. Boca Raton: I. B. Tauris, 2013.

Qatar Businesswomen Forum. "Establishment—Page 554—Qatar Businesswomen Forum." Accessed March 24, 2020. https://qbwf.org.qa/establishment/554/.

Qatar General Secretariat for Development Planning. "National Development Strategy," March 2011. https://www.mdps.gov.qa/en/knowledge/HomePagePublications/Qatar_NDS_reprint_complete_lowres_16May.pdf.

Qatar General Secretariat for Development Planning. "Qatar National Vision 2030," July 2008. Qatar National Vision 2030 - Government Communications Office (gco.gov.qa). Accessed May 25, 2023.

Rasheed, Madawi al-. *A Most Masculine State: Gender, Politics, and Religion in Saudi Arabia*. Cambridge Middle East Studies. New York: Cambridge University Press, 2013.

Seikaly, May. "Women and Religion in Bahrain: An Emerging Identity." In *Islam, Gender, and Social Change*, edited by Yvonne Yazbeck Haddad and John L. Esposito, 169–189. Oxford: Oxford University Press, 1998.

F

MODERN NARRATIVES OF THE GENDERED SELF

Women Writing about Women

WHEREAS women's lives and accomplishments during the premodern period can be retrieved from biographical and prosopographical works, devotional and literary texts to a certain degree, and less frequently from official chronicles, all composed by male scholars, women in the modern period write about their own lives or about the lives of other women and thereby offer us representations of feminine selves and identities generated by women authors themselves. These various literary works include biographies, fiction, novels, and memoirs that allow us to directly enter women's lives and thoughts without the mediation of the male recorder and redactor.

Some of these women authors focus on early generations of Muslim women, including the female Companions who figure in these writings as exemplary role models for feminine liberation and activism. Among the female Companions, the wives of Muḥammad occupy a special stature, and the details of their lives are carefully probed by modern women writers in their quest to justify their own quest for moral and social empowerment. The lives of these early women serve as a touchstone for highlighting contemporary treatments of women in Muslim-majority countries. By drawing an unfavorable contrast between current restrictions on women's behavior and the rights enjoyed by the early generations of Muslim women, these authors underscore the morally untenable nature of these restrictions and the "un-Islamic" nature of such gendered discrimination. Such “subversive” writings in which women express their explicit criticism of gendered perspectives that are otherwise held to be normatively binding have become powerful outlets for making these voices for social reform known to a larger reading public.

CHAPTER 29

MODERN REPRESENTATIONS OF THE WIVES OF THE PROPHET MUḤAMMAD

RUQAYYA Y. KHAN

THE Wives of the Prophet Muḥammad (*azwāj al-nabī*, henceforth "Wives"), also known as the Mothers of the Believers (*ummahāt al-muʾminīn*), loom large in the traditional biography of Muḥammad ibn ʿAbd Allāh, and these female figures occupy an important role in the foundational phase of Islam. They also continued to hold importance for subsequent debates and polemics in early Islamic history, society, and politics—even if through contested, refracted, and fragmented lenses. This chapter focuses on the analysis of these women as Wives, and less as the Mothers of the Believers, since undoubtedly these two different sobriquets, though they refer to the same subset of women, entail different associations and modes of assessments. It must be pointed out that few Muslims (and certainly far fewer non-Muslims) would be able to name a wife of the Prophet Muḥammad ibn ʿAbd Allāh beyond those of Khadīja and ʿĀʾisha. In Western sources, much ink has been spilled on perceptions of Muḥammad's polygamous household; this approach, often prejudicial, has largely shaped the examination of these women.

BACKGROUND

Historical Context

Muḥammad ibn ʿAbd Allāh: The Man Who Launched Islam

Muḥammad ibn ʿAbd Allāh was born in 570 CE and grew up as an orphan in Mecca, a pagan city in classical Arabian Peninsula, where he received no formal education, as the traditional sources inform us. He lived with his uncle, Abū Ṭālib, until he was twenty-five years old and worked as a caravan trader. It was through that job that he met his first wife-to-be, Khadīja bint Khuwaylid, a well-known and wealthy businesswoman. After their marriage, Muḥammad often retreated to Mount Hirāʾ to meditate, and it was there, in 610 CE, that he made his first claim to prophecy. Historical records suggest he immigrated to Medina, a neighboring city with his fledgling community of believers in approximately 622 CE. There he founded what is known as the first Islamic community, but Muḥammad never forgot Mecca. Contemporary biographer Karen Armstrong notes, "Muhammad was very proud of his city."[1] This ingrained love for Mecca would play a crucial part of the Islamic tradition in years to come. However, while the birthplace of Muḥammad, Mecca, is foundational, it is in the city-state of Medina where Muḥammad spent the last ten years of life and died (622–632 CE). Many (but not all) of his marriages took place in Medina. Historical, textual sources attest that the number of Muḥammad's wives ranged from nine to thirteen women during his lifetime.[2]

Rationale

Why the Wives Are Important

There are sundry reasons that warrant a renewed interest and innovative focus on the spousal women in this founder figure's life—namely, his Wives. First, and most importantly, these women are central to the foundational phase of Islam, as a quick inventory of some historical factors will demonstrate. Structurally, the domestic dwelling quarters with the Wives were adjacent to where the early community of believers worshipped and prayed, and where its public activities took place in Medina. The Prophet had ample female company and much of his time—day and night—must have been spent and passed amid this female company. Moreover, given that this was an Arab, Bedouin culture in which the oral medium prevailed—that is to say, the written word was uncommon—what was customary was verbal conversations, discussions, debates, and arguments, as well as the prevalence of oral modes of teaching and preaching. Often overlooked in the scholarship is that these women, i.e., his Wives, were as much conversation partners of and interlocutors with Muḥammad as they were his companions and bedfellows. Of the twenty-two years during which he experienced, received, and transmitted the Revelation of the Qurʾān, about half the years (again, 622–632 CE) were in Medina—the context within which the majority of his marriages took place. The implications of these historical circumstances for how these women possibly shaped and molded the prophet's receipt and transmission of the Revelation are worthy of reflection.

Furthermore, Muḥammad undertook a good deal of traveling when he lived first in Mecca and then in Medina. Hence, it is not surprising that he was often accompanied by one and sometimes more of his Wives during these travel expeditions. In fact, the traditional sources indicate that when he would embark on one of his expeditions, the Wives would cast lots to decide who would travel with him. Lastly, in the earliest written sources, many of the contexts within which the voices of women, especially those of the Wives, are featured consist of contexts involving communal and/or religious rituals, such as those of the pilgrimage. For instance, as demonstrated in the entries of the famous biographer, Muḥammad Ibn Saʿd (d. 230/845), on the Wives, it is often with regard to matters concerning Islamic domestic and communal rituals that the Wives make pronouncements or shape perception and practice.

Second, the importance of these women (as spouses of the founder figure of Islam) cuts across sectarian divides. As Wives, they are important to both Sunnīs and Shīʿa, although with some variation as to which ones are highly venerated and to which degree. Third, the Wives have been and continue to be immensely important in terms of norms and values. In other words, their religious status as Wives of the Prophet (*azwāj al-nabī*) and as Mothers of the Believers (*ummahāt al-muʾminīn*) establishes them as models for femininity and women's roles among Muslims across time and space. Hence, as central and idealized figures in Islamic tradition, the lives of the Wives and their narratives deserve much more attention. It is striking that this view is embraced alike by both progressives and conservatives in Islam. Put differently, their normativity, while interpreted and configured differently, is not a source of conflict among contemporary contesting orientations within Islam, e.g., Ṣufī, secular, Wahhābī, Salafī, fundamentalist, Islamist, progressive, etc. Finally, an enduring stereotype associated with Islam is that the religion is antithetical to women's interests and rights. A reexamination of these foundational women, an adoption of a fresh set of approaches, would perhaps contribute toward countering this stereotype and supporting a theology of egalitarianism within the religion. A crucial insight by Leila Ahmed, the well-known historian of women in Islam, comes to mind here: that there is a stark contrast between what she terms a strain of egalitarianism present in Islam's sacred text, the Qurʾān, and the cruel nonegalitarianism of the actuality of women's lived experiences in Muslim societies historically.[3]

In addition, there are other valid reasons. There continues to be widespread interest, polemics, and controversy surrounding Muḥammad ibn ʿAbd Allāh as the central religious figure and historical founder of Islam. Again, an innovative focus on a woman or the women in Muḥammad's life permits for a more nuanced and effective stocktaking and critique of the complexities of his life. For instance, the rich treasure trove of information, insights, and questions yielded by such a focus allows for a persuasive humanizing of the Prophet Muḥammad and for an honestly critical appraisal of him and his legacy. In other words, when dealing with the lives of the Wives, one is jarred into recognizing that the personal and private life of Muḥammad is not off-limits for the researcher—as one discovers that he certainly was not off-limits for his wives, who enjoyed loving intimacy with him.

Some feminists and others will inevitably level the charged question: why just focus on the "Women Worthies" in the Prophet Muḥammad's life? Why place the focus on these elite women whose status was "special" and "exceptional" simply by virtue of them being Muḥammad's Wives? In this sense, it could be argued that there is a tiresome traditionalism and predictability in focusing on the Wives. While this is a valid charge, with regard to Islam, far more ground needs tilling concerning its "Women Worthies" before relegating them to the historical bin. So much still needs to be reconstructed, recaptured, resurrected, reimagined, reexamined, and rewritten as regards these women. The ubiquitous "un"—the unspoken, unframed, untold, unimagined, unremembered, unasked—has to be spoken, narrated, and remembered concerning these women, lest what the feminist poet Adrienne Rich has eloquently proclaimed—

> Whatever is unnamed, un-depicted in images, whatever is omitted from biography, censored in collections of letters, whatever is misnamed as something else, made difficult-to-come-by, whatever is buried in the memory by the collapse of meaning under an inadequate or lying language—this will become, not merely unspoken, but unspeakable.[4]

—becomes true.

Moreover, in both classical and modern Muslim literatures and hagiographical corpus on the Wives, the primacy of place is exclusively assigned to Khadīja and/or ʿĀʾisha, and scant attention is given to his other Wives, even when there was still a dozen more. After all, who mattered most to the Prophet is what mattered most to Muslims who wrote about the Wives. With the Prophet being such a central and exemplary figure for Muslims throughout times, they hung on every word he uttered, every decision he made, and every example he set. As such, his thoughts, deeds, emotions, his likes and dislikes, whom and what he loved most, whom and what he detested most—all of this and more has been and continues to be what his followers seek to understand and emulate. These two women—Khadīja and ʿĀʾisha—merit and deserve the lion's share of attention because there is ample textual evidence to suggest that they were the dearest to the Prophet himself of all the Wives. Muḥammad married the mature and financially independent Khadīja when he was in Mecca during a time when he was vulnerable, young, and had not yet embarked on his mission as a prophet. Many Islamic sources showcase the importance of the confident and noble Khadīja, not only for Muḥammad's young adult life in Mecca, but also for the launch of his ministry as a preacher and prophet. Besides, his was a monogamous marriage to her, and they had six children—all in Mecca before he was forced to depart from it for Medina.

As for the witty and playful teenager ʿĀʾisha, she represents more the Medinan phase of Muḥammad's life because he married her soon after emigrating from Mecca to Medina. Both early and modern sources are fond of describing the Prophet's great affection for and attachment to her. She vies with Khadīja not just in these writings by mainly Muslims about the Wives, but also as evidence consequentially suggests, in the actuality of the Prophet's emotional life and lived experience. ʿĀʾisha understood just how much the Prophet loved his first wife Khadīja (and she was at times shown to be jealous of this fact), and yet she also knew that from among all his other Wives, she reigned supreme in his adoration of her. In the classical sources (see further below), it is ʿĀʾisha who surpasses even Khadīja in terms of being at the pinnacle of the Prophet's affections, but in modern Muslim sources (as explained elsewhere in my publications), it is Khadīja who has retaken this primacy of place. In any case, there is no reason to detract from the richness and complexities of the relationships Muḥammad had with these two women, nor is there any inclination to detract from their significance, historically and otherwise.

Yet, again, there is the need for a freshness in approaches and methods in the study and examination of the lives of the Wives; that is to say, there is the need for dismantling the tried and typical approaches. Evidently, as pointed out earlier, Muslims who wrote about the Wives replicated the preference given to Khadīja and ʿĀʾisha in the early sources. Nonetheless, Western scholarship—and even contemporary Muslim sources—cannot be bound to seriously consider only these two historical personalities and not the other women in Muḥammad's life. Being bound thus deprives one from consulting additional sources for knowing and comprehending more about the origins of this world religion and its founder. Western scholarship on Islam can be held more accountable in its academic output on the Wives for simply mimicking the hierarchy of the Prophet's affections found in traditional Islamic sources. It is detrimental to the interests of objective research and scholarship that Western academic and scholarly approaches situated in both the social sciences and the humanities often have reproduced the priorities and hierarchies of affection that Muslim sources have established and failed, to a considerable degree, to go beyond them.

Sources

Two Key Classical Sources

As indicated earlier, it is held that Muḥammad ibn ʿAbd Allāh married anywhere from nine to thirteen women during his lifetime.[5] These women are upheld and eulogized in the Islamic tradition as normative, female characters of virtue. Depicted as exemplary role-models for Muslim women, they nonetheless remain relatively unrecognized, unexamined, and unmentioned in Islamic history. Such obscurities have deep roots in the religious tradition and its intellectual history. There are two significant classical Islamic Arabic-language works that are especially helpful in plumbing the breadth and depth of the representations of the Wives: one is a religious story of the life of the Prophet Muḥammad and the other is a compilation of biographical entries on the most important personages (a premodern *Who's Who*) from the first several centuries of Islam. The standard hagiography or biographical work is titled *Sīrat Rasūl Allāh* (*Life of the Messenger of God*) composed by the biographer Ibn Isḥāq (second/eighth century) and redacted and transmitted by his student Ibn Hishām (third/ninth century). Ibn Isḥāq (d. 150/767) was an Arab biographer and historian who lived and died in Baghdad less than a century-and-a-half after the death of Muḥammad, and hence, this book consists of a remarkably early picture of the life and world of Muḥammad. Because of its prominence, one has to comb through it for content on the Wives despite the fact that there are only a few chapters that provide abundant information about them. This work has been translated into French and then into English under the title *The Life of Muḥammad: A Translation of Ibn Isḥāq's Sīrat Rasūl Allāh*, by Alfred Guillaume.[6] Less than a century after the death of Ibn Isḥāq, another historian from Baghdad, the aforementioned third/ninth century Muḥammad Ibn Sa'd compiled a second work, a multivolume compendium entitled *Kitāb al-Ṭabaqāt al-Kubrā* or *The Book of the Major Classes* (or *Tiers*).[7] This famous eight-volume biographical collection consists of life-stories of mainly early male Muslim figures. Seven volumes are dedicated to various Muslim men while women are featured only in the last volume (*Women of Medina*) in an abbreviated section. Most importantly, Ibn Sa'd presents rather vivid, detailed, and conservative accounts of the Wives of the Prophet.[8]

In addition to these two specific works, copious information on the Wives may be found and/or gleaned from other classical, Islamic textual sources including, but not limited to the Dicta of the Prophet (*Ḥadīth*); Qur'ān commentaries (*Tafsīr*); the "Causes for Revelation" accounts (*asbāb al-nuzūl*); the Prophet's biographical (*Sīra*) literature, and to some extent, from Islamic legal, jurisprudential (*Fiqh*) works).

Modern Secondary Scholarship on the Wives

Modern scholarship produced by both Muslim and non-Muslim authors on the Wives is found in at least two types of publications: (1) scholarship that is singly focused on the Wives, either as a collectivity or on an individual wife, and (2) scholarship and publications focused on various topics and representing many genres (e.g., histories of Islam; modern biographies [especially biographies of Muḥammad]; gender-based studies) that deal with aspects of the Wives in passing. Foremost among this second category are modern biographies of the Prophet Muḥammad. Among the modern biographers included whose writings contain extensive references to the Prophet's wives are the Egyptian scholar Muḥammad Haykal (1306–1375/1889–1956) and his famous *The Life of Muḥammad*; Martin Lings (who converted to Islam with the name Abū Bakr Sirāj al-Dīn) and his *Muḥammad: His Life Based on the Earliest Sources*;[9] and Karen Armstrong who produced the more recent *Muḥammad: A Biography of the Prophet*.[10] Muḥammad Haykal's biography of over six hundred pages has been translated by Ismā'īl al-Fārūqī (1339–1406/1921–1986).[11] Mention should also be made of the numerous *Encyclopedia of Islam* (second and third editions) entries and articles on the various wives of the Prophet under their individual names. Those may provide more elaboration and explanation of the hagiographical information as well as additional bibliography. In addition, there are myriad modern histories of early Islam (e.g., Asma Afsaruddin's *The First Muslims*)[12] which offer content on the Wives (or a given wife) in passing. In the case of all these sources, including the biographies, one may consult and search their bibliographies and indices under the names of the Prophet's Wives, and this would no doubt yield more information.

Three Trajectories

In the single-focus category, there are three trajectories concerning modern academic and what may be termed pseudo-academic sources on the Wives. The first trajectory consists of modern Western US-based scholarship regarding the Wives and it features both Muslim and non-Muslim names. Situated within the decade of the 1990s, these names include (in no particular order): Barbara Stowasser, Denise Spellberg, and Leila Ahmed; the list also features more recent publications by Asma Barlas, Asma Sayeed, Kecia Ali, and Ruqayya Khan, among others.[13] The second trajectory situated within the modern Islamic world features a pivotal figure Bint al-Shāṭi᾿ (meaning "Daughter of the [River] Bank," a pen name for her actual name ʿĀ᾿isha ʿAbd al-Raḥmān) from Egypt.[14] It also prominently features two North African francophone feminists, Fatima Mernissi and Assia Djebar. As for the last or third trajectory, it is produced largely by Muslim men—mainly English-speaking South Asian Muslim men, who themselves were products of British Colonial India—and hence, this stream consists of apologetic, pseudo-academic books, and pamphlets concerning the Wives in response to colonial and postcolonial dynamics and pressures.

In the English-language scholarship within the United States, Stowasser and Spellberg occupy primacy of place: their 1990s books—irrespective of whether they are devoted to the Wives as a group or to a single wife—are well recognized and often used in scholarly circles. Stowasser's 1996 book *Women in the Quran, Traditions, and Interpretation* is especially rich in mining the traditional, early Islamic textual material (e.g., *Ḥadīth*, *Tafsīr*, and *Asbāb al-Nuzūl*, etc.) in researching and writing about the Wives. It is also noteworthy for having two sections comprised of spousal figures represented in both the Judeo-Christian and Islamic traditions. Useful too is her seminal entry "Wives of the Prophet" in the second edition of the *Encyclopaedia of the Qur᾿ān*.[15] Denise Spellberg's important 1994 book titled *Politics, Gender and the Islamic Past: The Legacy of ʿA'isha bint Abi Bakr*[16] deserves praise for the nuanced historical methodology employed in stocktaking of the importance of this favored wife within early Islamic representations, which complements and supersedes to a certain extent the earlier work by Nabia Abbott on ʿĀ'isha.[17] Leila Ahmed's iconic historical work *Women and Gender in Islam: Historical Roots of a Modern Debate*, published in 1992,[18] contains several chapters in the first half of the book that set the stage for a sociohistorical evaluation of these figures. Delving into this category's scholarship in the 2000s onward, publications more engaged with textual hermeneutics as it pertains to the Wives include *Believing Women in Islam: Unreading Patriarchal Interpretations of the Qur'an*, published in 2002 by Asma Barlas,[19] and *Sexual Ethics and Islam: Feminist Reflections on Qur'an, Hadith and Jurisprudence* by Kecia Ali published in 2016.[20] Kecia Ali also authored *Marriage and Slavery in Early Islam* (2010),[21] which contains significant content on the Wives situated more within historical frameworks. In 2013 and 2014 respectively, Asma Sayeed (*Women and the Transmission of Religious Knowledge in Islam*)[22] and Ruqayya Khan ("Did a Woman Edit the Qur'ān? Hafṣa and Her Famed Codex" published in the *Journal of the American Academy of Religion*)[23] further nudged the consideration of the Wives toward historical and historiographical frameworks, the latter situated more within a feminist perspective.

In the modern Islamic world, the Arabic-language book simply entitled *Nisāʾ al-Nabī* (*Wives of the Prophet*) by the aforementioned Egyptian author Bint al-Shāṭiʾ,[24] consists of somewhat folksy narrative accounts using titillating storytelling techniques to illustrate the lives of the Wives and their domestic situations; it has been translated into English. It anthologizes each of the Wives chapter-by-chapter, with each wife meriting a chapter, and with some chapters being longer than others (e.g., the chapter on ʿĀʾisha is far longer than those on some lesser-known Wives). Both our two francophone authors—Fatima Mernissi from Morocco and Assia Djebar from Algeria—have written innovative books, often of a critical, theoretical nature, that attempt to reframe the inquiries regarding the Wives. While both authors composed and published in French, nearly all their books have been translated. Taking up Mernissi first, her iconic book, *The Veil and the Male Elite: A Feminist Interpretation of Women's Rights*, was groundbreaking within the context of women and gender studies in Islam when it was published in 1991;[25] half the book analyzes both the representations of the Wives in male-dominated genres (such as *Ḥadīth*) and the historical dimensions of their lives, as associated with Medina, with an eye to critiquing the patriarchal dimensions apparent through a feminist lens. As for Assia Djebar, her *Far from Medina*, published in the 1990s,[26] is eye-opening in how it reconstructs within a literary-historical framework the lives of the Wives in the city of Medina.

The British colonial context and the state of the Islamic world at the turn of the eighteenth and nineteenth centuries significantly shape the tenor of the third trajectory. When it comes to modern English-language scholarship, a number of Indo-Pakistani Muslim polemicists and scholars focus on the Wives of the Prophet through apologetic, traditional narratives; that is, works that attempt to justify and legitimate Muḥammad's domestic life and actions to a Western, non-Muslim audience, especially his polygamous marriages. Thus, this third trajectory partakes in the scholarship debating Muḥammad's polygamy—historically, politically, and theologically. Indeed, it would not be wrong to characterize many of these works as hagiographical. On the other hand, these works do represent a considerable portion of Muslim discourses about the Prophet's Wives, and it is in this respect that these are worth considering. Authors include Fida Hussain Malik and his work *Wives of the Holy Prophet* first published around 1952 in Pakistan[27] and Muhammad Saeed Ṣiddiqi and his book *The Blessed Women of Islam*, also published in Pakistan in 1982.[28] Worthy of attention is, furthermore, the pamphlet (also available on the internet) by Shahid Zafar Qasmi entitled *Questions and Answers on the Mothers of Believers*, which appeared in 1997.[29]

Conclusion

As central figures in the formative period of Islam, the Wives of the Prophet Muhammad have been venerated by the collectivity of Muslims, past and present. Besides Khadīja and ʿĀʾisha, these Wives nonetheless received very little attention in Islamic classical sources as well as in Western scholarship where their socio-religious status as Mothers of the Believers often obscured their status as wives in their own right. A survey of the classical and modern Muslim-authored works and biographies of Muḥammad show that some of these works are scholarly while others are not. As works bearing a distinctly "Islamic" imprint and character, they nonetheless offer the traditional, dominant narratives concerning the Prophet's Wives. These dominant narratives are salient as the starting point for most studies of these figures—at least, as far as most Muslims are concerned. Some of the relevant content and/or references stand alone, while others are embedded within a larger narrative, as is the case in the Prophet's biography (*Sīra*) literature. The apologetic works specifically on the wives are generally modern ones, while those representing the Prophet's biography often contain content translated from original classical sources, including some of the earliest ones. Often, the classical sources translated may represent the original tradition better than much later modern works that drew on that tradition.

In recommending that any and all of these aforementioned diverse sources be considered, no endorsement is being made as to their content. It should also be noted that what is not found in these multifarious, diverse sources—especially as regards the apologetic monographs specifically devoted to the Prophet's Wives—is material concerning their "after-lives." That is to say, while there is a good deal of content regarding the dominant Islamic narratives (or storylines) embracing the broad contours of the lives of the Wives, there is one exception to this: that exception consists of the somewhat scanty material on their lives after the Prophet's death in 632 CE.

On another level, the existing scholarship also pinpoints the need for fresh approaches and methodologies that examine the status of these women more as Wives during and after the demise of Prophet Muḥammad and less as Mothers of the Believers. This new articulation of the status of these women should be read through an egalitarian lens that can highlight the egalitarian undertones in the history and the biographical corpus of these prominent Muslim female figures. Such a new approach can yield a more nuanced appreciation of the different roles played by these women and further inform and transform the understanding of the contributions of these women to Islam and its founding figure. Hence, to view Muḥammad's Wives solely through the polemics of a debate on polygamy substantially neglects their importance in Islamic history and tradition. In order to fully understand and value the roles these women played in Islam, scholars and biographers need to look beyond the preconceived notions of the position of women in early Islam, and to examine the very stories behind the names in light of the origins of the religion and based on these women's own merits.

Notes

1. Karen Armstrong, *Muhammad: A Biography of the Prophet* (San Francisco, CA: Harper, 1992), 45.

2. In chronological order of marriage: Khadīja bint Khuwaylid, Sawda bint Zamʿa, ʿĀʾisha bint Abī Bakr, Hafṣa bint ʿUmar, Umm Salama, Umm Ḥabība, Zaynab bint Jaḥsh al-Asadiyya, Zaynab bint Khuzayma, Juwayriyya bint al-Ḥārith, Ṣafiyya bint Ḥuyayy, Rayḥana bint Zayd, Maria al-Qibṭiyya, and Maymūna bint al-Hārith; see Barbara Freyer Stowasser, "Wives of the Prophet," in *Encyclopaedia of the Qurʾān*, ed. Jane Dammen McAuliffe (Leiden: Brill, 2006), 506–521.
3. Leila Ahmed, *Women and Gender in Islam: Historical Roots of a Modern Debate* (New Haven, CT: Yale University Press, 1992), 64–67.
4. Adrienne Rich, *On Lies, Secrets, and Silence: Selected Prose, 1966–1978* (New York: W. W. Norton, 1995), 182.
5. See note 2 above for a list of the Wives in order of marriage.
6. ʿAbdal-Malik Ibn Hishām and Muḥammad Ibn Isḥāq, *The Life of Muhammad: A Translation of Isḥāq's Sīrat Rasūl Allāh*, trans. Alfred Guillaume (Karachi, Pakistan: Oxford University Press, 1955).
7. See, for example, Muḥammad Ibn Saʿd, *Kitāb al-ṭabaqāt al-kabīr*, ed. ʿUmar ʿAlī Muḥammad (Cairo: Maktabat al-Khānjī, 2001).
8. See Amira Naim Abou-Taleb, *Gender Discourse in Kitab al-Tabaqat al-Kubra: Deconstructing Ibn Saʿd's Portrayal of the Model Muslim Woman* (master's thesis, American University of Cairo, 2012).
9. Martin Lings, *Muhammad: His Life Based on the Earliest Sources* (New York: Inner Traditions International, 1983).
10. Armstrong, *Muhammad.*
11. Muḥammad Ḥusayn Haykal, *The Life of Muhammad*, trans. Ismail Ragi Al-Faruqi (Indianapolis, IN: North American Trust Publications, 1976).
12. Asma Afsaruddin, *The First Muslims: History and Memory*. Oxford: Oneworld, 2008.
13. They also include Asma Afsaruddin, Aisha Geissinger, Aisha Hidayatullah, and Roxanne Marcotte. The relevant publications of all these authors with full details are given in the bibliography.
14. See Bint al-Shāṭiʾ, *Nisāʾ al-Nabī ʿalayhi al-ṣalāh wa al-salām* (Cairo: Dār al-Hilāl, 1961).
15. Stowasser, "Wives of the Prophet."
16. Denise Spellberg, *Politics, Gender, and the Islamic Past: The Legacy of ʿAʾisha Bint Abi Bakr* (New York: Columbia University Press, 1994).
17. Nabia Abbott, *Aishah, the Beloved of Mohammed*. New York: Arno Press, 1973.
18. Leila Ahmed, *Women and Gender in Islam: Historical Roots of a Modern Debate* (New Haven, CT: Yale University Press, 1992).
19. Asma Barlas, *Believing Women in Islam: Unreading Patriarchal Interpretations of the Qurʾān* (Austin: University of Texas Press, 2002).
20. Kecia Ali, *Sexual Ethics and Islam: Feminist Reflections on Qurʾan, Hadith, and Jurisprudence* (Oxford: Oneworld, 2006).
21. Kecia Ali, *Marriage and Slavery in Early Islam* (Cambridge, MA: Harvard University Press, 2010).
22. Asma Sayeed, *Women and the Transmission of Religious Knowledge in Islam* (New York: Cambridge University Press, 2013).
23. Ruqayya Y. Khan, "Did a Woman Edit the Qurʾān? Hafṣa and Her Famed 'Codex,'" *Journal of the American Academy of Religion* 82, no. 1 (March 2014): 174–216.
24. Ruth Roded, "Bint Al-Shati's Wives of the Prophet: Feminist or Feminine?" *British Journal of Middle Eastern Studies* 33, no. 1 (2006): 51–66.

25. Fatima Mernissi, *The Veil and the Male Elite: A Feminist Interpretation of Women's Rights in Islam* (Reading, MA: Addison-Wesley, 1991).
26. Assia Djebar, *Far from Medina* (London: Quartet Books, 1994).
27. Fida Hussain Malik, *Wives of the Holy Prophet*, 1st ed. (Lahore, Pakistan: Muhammad Ashraf Publishers, 1952).
28. Muḥammad Saeed Siddiqi, *The Blessed Women of Islam* (Lahore, Pakistan: Kazi Publications, 1982).
29. Shahid Zafar Qasmi, *Question and Answers on the Mothers of Believers (May Allah Be Pleased with Them)*, revised by Muhammad Tahir Salafi (Riyadh: Darussalam, 1997); available at: Questions and Answers about Mothers of the Believers—(wordpress.com).

Bibliography

Abbott, Nabia. *Aishah, the Beloved of Mohammed*. New York: Arno, 1973.

Abou-Taleb, Amira Naim. *Gender Discourse in Kitab al-Tabaqat al-Kubra: Deconstructing Ibn Sa'd's Portrayal of the Model Muslim Woman*. Master's thesis, American University in Cairo, 2012.

Afsaruddin, Asma. *Contemporary Issues in Islam*. Edinburgh: Edinburgh University Press, 2015.

Afsaruddin, Asma, *The First Muslims: History and Memory*. Oxford: Oneworld, 2008.

Ahmed, Leila. *Women and Gender in Islam: Historical Roots of a Modern Debate*. New Haven, CT: Yale University Press, 1992.

Ali, Kecia. "'A Beautiful Example': The Prophet Muhammad as a Model for Muslim Husbands." *Islamic Studies* 43, no. 2 (Summer 2004): 273–291.

Ali, Kecia. *Marriage and Slavery in Early Islam*. Cambridge, MA: Harvard University Press, 2010.

Ali, Kecia. *Sexual Ethics and Islam: Feminist Reflections on Qur'an, Hadith, and Jurisprudence*. Oxford: Oneworld, 2006.

Armstrong, Karen. *Muhammad: A Biography of the Prophet*. San Francisco, CA: Harper, 1992.

Ascha, Ghassan. "The 'Mothers of the Believers': Stereotypes of the Prophet Muhammad's Wives." In *Female Stereotypes in Religious Traditions*, edited by Ria Kloppenborg and Wouter J. Hanegraaff, 89–107. Leiden: Brill, 1995.

Awde, Nicholas. *Women in Islam: An Anthology from the Qurān and Ḥadīths*. Richmond, Surrey, England: Curzon, 2000.

Barlas, Asma. *Believing Women in Islam: Unreading Patriarchal Interpretations of the Qur'ān*. Austin: University of Texas Press, 2002.

Djebar, Assia. *Far from Medina*. London: Quartet Books, 1994.

Geissinger, Aisha. *Gender and Muslim Constructions of Exegetical Authority: A Rereading of the Classical Genre of Qur'ān Commentary*. Boston: Brill, 2015.

Geissinger, Aisha. "Gendering the Classical Tradition of Quran Exegesis: Literary Representations and Textual Authority in Medieval Islam." PhD diss., University of Toronto, 2008.

Haykal, Muḥammad Ḥusayn. *The Life of Muhammad*. Translated by Ismail Ragi Al-Faruqi. Indianapolis, IN: North American Trust Publications, 1976.

Hidayatullah, Aysha A. *Feminist Edges of the Qur'an*. New York: Oxford University Press, 2014.

Hidayatullah, Aysha A. "Māriyya the Copt: Gender, Sex and Heritage in the Legacy of Muhammad's Umm Walad." *Islam and Christian-Muslim Relations* 21, no. 3 (July 2010): 221–243.

Ibn Hishām, ʿAbdal-Malik, and Ibn Isḥāq, Muḥammad. *The Life of Muhammad: A Translation of Isḥāq's Sīrat Rasūl Allāh*. Translated by Alfred Guillaume. Karachi, Pakistan: Oxford University Press, 1955.

Ibn Kathīr, Ismāʿīl ibn ʿUmar. *Al-Sīrah al-Nabawīyah*. Cairo: ʿIsá al-Bābī al-Ḥalabī, 1964.

Ibn Saʿd, Muḥammad. *Kitab al-ṭabaqāt al-kabīr*. Edited by ʿUmar ʿAlī Muḥammad. Cairo: Maktabat al-Khānjī, 2001.

Khan, Ruqayya Y. "Did a Woman Edit the Qur'ān? Hafṣa and Her Famed 'Codex.'" *Journal of the American Academy of Religion* 82, no. 1 (March 2014): 174–216.

Kahn, Tamam. *Untold: A History of* the *Wives of Prophet Muhammad*. Rhinebeck, NY: Monkfish, 2010.

Lings, Martin. *Muhammad: His Life Based on* the *Earliest Sources*. New York: Inner Traditions International, 1983.

Malik, Fida Hussain. *Wives of the Holy Prophet*. 1st ed. Lahore, Pakistan: Muhammad Ashraf Publishers, 1952.

Marcotte, Roxanne. "Muslim Women's Scholarship and the New Gender Jihad." In *Women and Islam*, edited by Zayn Kassam, 131–162. Santa Barbara, CA: Praeger, 2010.

Marcotte, Roxanne. "The Qur'ān in Egypt: Bint Al-Shāti on Women's Emancipation." In *Coming to Terms with the Qur' an: A Volume in Honor of Professor Issa Boullata*, edited by Khaleel Mohammed and Andrew Rippin, 179–208. North Haledon, NJ: Islamic Publications International, 2007.

Mernissi, Fatima. *The Veil and the Male Elite: A Feminist Interpretation of Women's Rights in Islam*. Reading, MA: Addison-Wesley, 1991.

Qasmi, Shahid Zafar. *Question and Answers on the Mothers of Believers (May Allah Be Pleased with Them)*. Revised by Muhammad Tahir Salafi. Riyadh: Darussalam, 1997.

Quṭb, Sayyid, M. A. Salahi, and A. A. Shamis. *In the Shade of the Qur' ān: Fī ẓilāl Al-Qur' ān*. Leicester, UK: Islamic Foundation, 1999.

Rich, Adrienne. *On Lies, Secrets, and Silence: Selected Prose, 1966–1978*. New York: W. W. Norton, 1995.

Roded, Ruth. "Bint Al-Shati's Wives of the Prophet: Feminist or Feminine?" *British Journal of Middle Eastern Studies* 33, no. 1 (2006): 51–66.

Sayeed, Asma, *Women and the Transmission of Religious Knowledge in Islam*. New York: Cambridge University Press, 2013.

Shāṭi', Bint al-. *Nisā' al-Nabī* ʿalayhi *al-ṣalāh wa al-salām*. Cairo: Dār al-Hilāl, 1961.

Ṣiddiqi, Muḥammad Saeed. *The Blessed Women of Islam*. Lahore, Pakistan: Kazi Publications, 1982.

Spellberg, Denise A. *Politics, Gender, and the Islamic Past: The Legacy of 'A' isha Bint Abi Bakr*. New York: Columbia University Press, 1994.

Stowasser, Barbara Freyer. "Wives of the Prophet." In *Encyclopaedia of the Qur'ān*, edited by Jane Dammen McAuliffe, 506–521. Leiden: Brill, 2006.

Stowasser, Barbara Freyer. *Women in the Qur'an, Traditions, and Interpretation*. New York: Oxford University Press, 1994.

Wadud, amina. *Qur' an and Woman:* Rereading *the Sacred Text from a Woman's Perspective*. 2nd ed. New York: Oxford University Press, 1999.

CHAPTER 30

MODERN AND CONTEMPORARY MUSLIM FEMINIST LITERATURE

An Overview

MIRIAM COOKE

IN this chapter, I review Arab, Iranian, and American novels, short stories, memoirs, and poems that engage with modern Muslim women's concerns about the ways in which they have been held back from enjoying their rights as equal members of the Muslim communities in which they live.

Although not without precedent, Muslim feminist literature is a modern phenomenon that was promoted in early twentieth-century Muslim women's journals. The word "feminism" took time to be accepted, especially in European colonies in Asia and Africa, where fear of association with the British colonizers, who pushed a feminist policy in their colonies in order to turn women against their men, made writers cautious about advocating an openly prowomen agenda. Moreover, women protesting oppressive gender norms and values were thought to threaten the status quo, i.e., men presiding over women to ensure a stable family life. In *Opening the Gates*, our coedited anthology of Arab feminist writings, Margot Badran and I explained that "historically, a term connoting feminism first appeared in the Arab world in 1909 when Malak Nasif under the penname Bāḥithat al-Bādiya published a collection of articles and speeches in a book titled *Al-Nisā'iyāt*."[1]

The word *al-Nisā'iyāt*, meaning "women's pieces," is derived from the adjective *nisā'ī*, referring ambiguously to anything female or feminist. Even if an explicit word for feminism did not exist at the time, the meaning did exist, as it had in the Bronze Age, if not before. To notice, reject, and do something about injustice is human. The issue is how to recognize injustice. In patriarchal societies, the degradation of women is so normalized it may not be marked as unjust. It may even be considered appropriate conduct in a hierarchy where status determines behavior and treatment.

In the 1920s, male short story writers like the Egyptians Maḥmūd Ṭāhir Lāshīn and Maḥmūd Taimūr of the *Madrasa Ḥadītha* ("Modern School" of literature) wrote angrily about stigmatized women. Their tales formed part of a wider social reform platform to eliminate discrimination against women. Reformists denounced child marriages, the toleration of women selling their bodies to pay for basic necessities, and so-called Islamic institutions like the "house of obedience" that gave men sanctioned rights to imprison "recalcitrant" wives.[2] These stories expanded on nineteenth- and early twentieth-century Muslim male reformers' demands that women be accorded rights to education, some participation in the public life of their communities, and dignity. Egyptians Qāsim Amīn (1865–1908) and Muḥammad 'Abduh (1849–1905), Iranian Mirza Aqa Khan Kirman (1853/4–1896),[3] Tunisian Ṭahār Ḥaddād (1899–1935/1317–1354) and Indonesian Haji Abdul Malik bin Abdul Karim Amrullah (1908–1981/1326–1401), aka Hamka,[4] argued that far from destroying the family, according women these rights would strengthen the nation. In the twentieth century, Muslim women launched their own reform campaigns demanding gender justice.[5]

In what follows, I concentrate on four topics broached by Muslim feminist writers. First, they have challenged two *ḥadīth*s that denigrate women by stating that (1) women lack in reason and religion; and (2) that women should be silent since their voices are *'awra,* a word meaning shame and commonly associated with women's mouths and genitalia that, like their voices, should be covered. Second, they have argued against the imposition of the veil without necessarily condemning women who choose to cover. Third, some have penned memoirs that trace paths through patriarchal mazes. Fourth, a few authors have protested the exclusion of women from ritual spaces. In each case, I provide an overview and then close readings of one or two exemplary texts.

Challenging Misogynistic Ḥadīth

Muslim feminists generally engage with the two textual sources of faith that form the bedrock of Islamic faith: the Qur'ān and *ḥadīth*, which refer to the words and statements concerning the deeds of the Prophet Muḥammad that his Companions witnessed and transmitted in the first/seventh century. Within two centuries of the Prophet's death, the number of orally transmitted *ḥadīth*s had swelled to almost half a million. In the third/ninth century, two Central Asian scholars, Muḥammad ibn Ismā`īl al-Bukhārī (d. 256/870) and Muslim ibn al-Ḥajjāj al-Naysabūrī (d. 261/875), collected and recorded what they determined were sound *ḥadīth*. Soundness depended on a reliable *isnād*, or chain of authorities going back to one of the narrating companions. Each found fewer than 9,000 trustworthy *ḥadīth* that they published in the *Sahīhān* (The Two Sound Collections of *ḥadīth*). Four contemporary scholars—al-Tirmidhī (d. 892/279), al-Sijistānī (d. 888/275), al-Qazwīnī (d. 887/274), and al-Nasā'ī (d. 915/303)—published their own collections of *ḥadīth* which, although less authoritative than the *Saḥīḥān*, along with them are considered to be the Six Books of the *Sunna*: "These collections are seen today as primary sources of both juridical and moral precedent and are second only to the Qur'ān in their practical significance and authority."[6]

Several of these *ḥadīth* relate negative stories about women. In the twentieth century, Muslim feminists began to critique some of the most misogynistic *ḥadīth*.[7] How, some wondered, could the Prophet Muḥammad, whom some have called the feminist founder of Islam and who counted women among the three most precious elements in life along with prayer and perfume, have said, "women are lacking in religion and reason?" How could he, who once said that paradise was under the feet of mothers, have even only thought that "woman is an *'awra*?"[8] Many Muslim feminists do not believe in the soundness of such *ḥadīth*.

One of the first recorded skeptics was a medieval Ottoman woman poet who had this to say about the infamous *ḥadīth*:

> Since they say women lack reason
> All their words should be excused.
> But as for Mihri, her well-wisher's supposition
> As well as, what an intelligent person would say, is this:
> A capable woman is much better than
> A thousand incapable men
> A clear-headed woman is much better than
> A thousand muddle-headed men.[9]

Mihri Hātūn (864–921/1460–1515) challenged her male contemporaries to accept a woman into their exclusive elite intellectual circles. Her defiant words touting not only women's intellectual and spiritual equality but also sometimes their superiority to men echo the descriptions of Muslim foremothers like the second/eighth-century pious woman Rābi'a al-'Adawiyya. Did seventh/thirteenth-century Farīduddīn `Aṭṭār's assessment of Rāb'a's superiority to men—"No, she wasn't a single woman / But a hundred men over"[10]—inspire Mihri Hātūn? She is not the first feminist Muslim writer but she is a good, if arbitrary, start to this chapter. To celebrate her tenth/sixteenth-century contribution to Muslim feminist literature and thought signals not a beginning but rather antecedents that might otherwise disappear with the touting of a later first.

In 1928, Lebanese Naẓīra Zeineddine (1908–1976) published what I have called a pioneering Islamic feminist text.[11] The first woman to write an entire book on Muslim women's rights, Zeineddine decried misogynist interpretations of Qur'ānic verses and the acceptance of *ḥadīth* such as the one describing women as lacking in reason and religion: "Gentlemen, you accuse us of lack of religion and reason. Why? Because you have blocked the paths of intellect and you have cast us into an ocean of humiliation and ignorance . . . can there be religion where there is ignorance?"[12] She reiterated what Mihri Hātūn had written three hundred years earlier: men, and she named Shaykhs Muṣṭafā al-Ghalaynī and Sa'īd al-Jābi' among others, cited the infamous *ḥadīth* without checking whether it was consonant with the Qur'ān. God's unmediated revelation, she argued, should take precedence over the human word, even if the speaker was the Prophet Muḥammad.[13]

The "woman is an *'awra*," a *ḥadīth* included in al-Tirmidhi's collection, has attracted the ire of Muslim feminist authors. In Nawal El Saadawi's *Memoirs of a Female Physician* (1980), a nine-year-old girl realizes that she has been taught to believe that everything in her is *'awra*. Not only her genitals and her mouth, but also her entire body has been branded: "the initial *'awra* of the private parts is made to expand and apply to the heroine's body in its entirety."[14]

From the genitalia the word moved to encompass the mouth, then the body and even the voice both physical and literary. Many have contested this *ḥadīth*, none more vigorously than the Nigerian Islamic Education Trust. In 2008, a group of scholars mounted a robust argument against the "prohibition of Muslim women speaking in public." Women's voices, they insisted, were far from taboo during the lifetime of the Prophet. Muhammad had often heard women singing, reciting Qur'ānic verses, praying and even giving the *adhān* (call to prayer) and he had not disapproved. They cite a *ḥadīth* from 'Ā'isha in which she proudly claimed that "she called the *adhān*, recited *iqamah* before prayers and led the women in prayers while standing in the middle of the row as their imam."[15] If the Prophet's wife 'Ā'isha—source of the largest number of sound *ḥadīths*—had, without her husband chastising her, called the *adhān*, how could women's voices be *'awra*? This is a question that Lebanese Zeina Ghandour (b.1966) addresses in her lyrical novel *The Honey* (1999).

Ghandour evokes the beauty of a woman's voice that is not *'awra* but honey. It is the honey that connects her to the Qur'ānic "Bee Chapter" that the villagers cited to console her mother at the birth of a girl:[16] "And they assign daughters for Allah, Glory be to Him!" (Qur'ān 16:57) Who is this honey-voiced woman?

> They call her the desert mermaid, and she performs the call to the dawn prayer. Those who have heard her say that her voice is so luminous, it was as though the sun and moon both had been arrested in it.[17]

This extraordinary voice evokes both joy and fear "dark and rare like black coral, and deep and mysterious as the sea which contains it."[18] She is Ruhiya, daughter of a desert village *muezzin* and sister of Yehya, a Palestinian militant who has been given weightless explosives that fragment his walk past the languid Israeli border police guarding the Wailing Wall (34). His sister's *adhān* reclaims him but also "creates a disorder and agitation inside me and I wish I could fly with the same grace and not choke with this despair."[19] Here is the *fitna*, or social disorder, that women embody and men fear women's voices will induce.[20] From a woman's perspective, however, calling the faithful to prayer was a blessing and permissible. Ruhiya called the *adhān* every time she prayed because

> I read that this was permissible, as long as it was performed in private. I like the way my voice sounded and unconsciously began to raise it. I raised it and raised it, aiming

> for the sky. And like our prophet, who once prayed to Jerusalem, I turned west to al-Quds, instead of south, to Mecca.[21]

Her confidence in her honey voice grew and with it her defiance of other injunctions against women's freedom. One dawn, the day that her brother blew himself up, she climbed the stairway of the yellow mosque from which her father had always called the *adhān*. Reaching the top of the minaret and preparing for the outrage of a woman singing out the *adhān*, she wonders why the great Egyptian singer Umm Kulthum's voice had not been considered *ʿawra*, but rather a miracle.

> "Allahu Akbar!" Her body was stiff. The yell had escaped from her. She stood steadfast as a volcano disgorging boiling liquid, dispensing words like ashes. . . . Ruhiya opened her eyes and put her hand on her heart. . . . Her mouth bore no traces of shame, despite the slight tremor and the tingling beneath her skin. . . . The villagers were willing to overlook the fact that it was being sung by a woman. But when they were woken that morning by Ruhiya's song, they stumbled out of bed and ran out into their gardens with dread and disbelief. For the women immediately knew she would pay for this pleasure, even though it had been so gracefully displayed. And the men? The men felt her song pierce through their hearts like a burning spear . . . nothing could have prepared them for the gratification and delight they felt on hearing her, or for the sweetness that lingered on in the atmosphere of her song at mid-morning.[22]

When a foreign journalist interviews the village women, they call what Ruhiya did "unbearable. Like pure sugar."[23] And the men are torn between believing it was a miracle, because it lifted her father's fever, and reaffirming that "our community has been polluted and must be cleansed. . . . A woman immodest enough to display her ecstasy to the entire world! She is obviously the perfect accessory for the Zionists."[24] This linking of women's ritual dissidence with Zionism and international conspiracies appears in other Muslim feminist writings.[25]

Contesting the Veil

From the late nineteenth century, Muslim reformers, both men and women, have focused on the veil and its role in keeping women out of public space and crippling the nation. In Iran, writes critic Farzaneh Milani, "Dehkoda, Malcolm Khan, Mirza Aqa Khan Kermani, Akhundzadeh, Lahuti, 'Eshqi, and Iraj Mirza, among others . . . attributed Iran's 'backwardness,' to use the prevalent term of the day, to women's condition and especially to their 'imprisonment' in veils . . . they maintained that the veil had prevented women from developing to their fullest potential." Poet 'Eshqi (1894–1924) asks, "What are these unbecoming cloaks and veils? / They are shrouds for the dead, not for those alive."[26]

In 1887/8, 'Ā'isha al-Taimūriyya (1840–1902), matriarch of an aristocratic literary family in Cairo, published an allegorical tale entitled *The Results of Circumstances in Words and Deeds* that warned of the loss to the nation when women are veiled and debarred from participation in society. She portrays a girl escaping her mother's insistence that she perfect women's occupations to join the "assemblages of writers, with no sense of embarrassment. And I found the screech of pen on paper the most inviting of melodies."[27] Her father supports her intellectual ambitions even though, like Mihri Hātūn three centuries earlier, she was not welcomed into men's gatherings:

> I was deprived of harvesting the fruits of their beneficial learning! What hindered me from realizing this hope was the tent-like screen of an all-enveloping wrap. And the lock on the private quarters of femaleness hid and secluded me from the radiance of those celestial moons.[28]

Exaggerated? Perhaps. But in her frustration, al-Taimūriyya gives voice to contemporary Arab women who had become aware of feminist writings and activism elsewhere that were forbidden to them. The veil and women's segregation, they argued, prevent the most accomplished and educated of women from contributing to their society.

Then in 1923, unveiling spread across Muslim societies after Hudā Sha'rāwī, founder and president of the Egyptian Feminist Union, stepped off a train in Cairo station her face uncovered. She was not the first to unveil, Iranian writer Qurrat al-'Ayn had discarded her veil over fifty years earlier, but Sha'rāwī's timing was better. So many intellectuals had opposed veiling and gender segregation by the early 1920s that the mood was right for such a revolutionary act to succeed. There were, however, hurdles along the way.

In 1927, some Syrian shaykhs called for veiling newly unveiled women, and Naẓīra Zeineddine reacted immediately. Her 1928 *Al-sufūr wa al-ḥijāb* (Unveiling and Veiling)[29] articulated a scholarly objection to the veil. Although many religious authorities have claimed the veil to be an Islamic mandate, she anticipated other Muslim feminists when she insisted that the veil is nowhere to be found in the Qur'ān beyond a verse telling women to cover their bosoms and not flaunt their charms. The book caused outrage among male traditionalists and she disappeared into domestic obscurity.[30] It took almost a century for feminists to retrieve her.

In her 1992 *Veils and Words*, Farzaneh Milani surveys over a century of modern Iranian women's literature, focusing on "writers whose works I consider to have marked important new beginnings concerning notions of veiling/unveiling."[31] Poets Forugh Farrokhzad (1935–1967), Simin Behbahani (1927–2014), and Tahereh Saffarzadeh (1939–2008), and novelists Simin Daneshvar (1921–2012) and Shahrnush Parsipur (b. 1946) form the core of her analysis. It is crucial to note that Iranian women's experience of veiling differs from other Muslim women's experiences because of the role of the state. In 1936, the Shah's government outlawed the veil, and in 1983, Khomeini's regime reimposed it. Milani follows the trajectory of Iranian feminist writing to what she calls the "birth of neo-traditional feminism" both inside and outside Iran.[32] The veil, whether explicitly invoked or not, colors the production of Iranian women's words.

Arab feminist writers have not had to contend with the same kind of official interference in women's public appearance. They are objecting to the emergence of Islamic fundamentalism and the accompanying pressure on women to disappear. Two Egyptian women have denounced the veil in fiction. "Eyes" (1988) by Nawal El Saadawi (b. 1931) and *Blue Aubergine* (1998) by Mirāl al- Ṭahāwī (b. 1970) disclose the whirlwind of emotions that pass unnoticed behind the thick cover of the *niqab* or face veil.

The doyen of twentieth-century Arab feminist writers, Nawal El Saadawi has devoted her life to fighting the many injustices women suffer. In over thirty novels, short story collections, and volumes of essays that have been translated into many languages, she connects class, religious patriarchy, and imperialism to women's oppression. *Innocence of the Devil* (1993), a novel set in what was once a Pharaonic palace and is now a psychiatric hospital, stages a battle between the women patients, supported by Iblis, a young male patient whose name means Devil, and "God," another male patient with delusions of grandeur. After the women defeat "God," he proclaims Iblis innocent and in the process destroys the binary that created him. The God of organized monotheistic religions who is knowable only through his opposite is a tyrant who must be resisted from within.[33] But the emergence of Islamic extremism renders such resistance difficult especially by a woman swathed in a veil since childhood.

The veiled protagonist of the short story "Eyes" illustrates the author's concern about the veil that does not merely shroud the body—it also highlights what is shameful and debilitating about a woman's body in a man's world. The protagonist consults a psychiatrist about her nightmares of death and abandonment, fearing that she has unwittingly committed a great sin. Fearing the *ʿawra* of her voice, she speaks with no one either in the university or in the museum basement storeroom where she catalogs mummies and ancient Egyptian statues. She does not ride public transport lest contact with men defile her. Living alone with her penniless, pseudo-pious father, she does not want to marry lest she suffer her mother's fate at her father's hands. One day, she notices "through the two narrow holes of the black cloth"[34] a little statue that she had not registered. The eyes of the statue seem alive and they rivet her attention. Fearful of losing "him," she looks around her in the streets in the hope of finding "a face that resembles his."[35] Two days in a row she "sees" him on her way to work, and she approaches him only to be rebuffed and shamed. She falls into a fever that none can cure: "That's how she came to me."[36] This woman closeted in cloth and panic drowns in a sea of longing, fears, and fantasies.

Another story of anguish behind the veil comes from Mirāl al- Ṭahāwī (b. 1968), a Bedouin woman from Sharqiyya in the Eastern Delta of Egypt. She has written several novels about the challenges tribal women face in a conservative, patriarchal society. Her most outspoken Islamic feminist work, *Blue Aubergine* published in Arabic in 1998, emerges out of her experience as an observant veiled student who rebels against the strictures Islamic fundamentalists impose on women.[37]

The blue aubergine of the title is Nadā, a woman caught in a whirlwind of surreal impressions, each one linking her to some malevolent person. Like the protagonist of

"Eyes," she ceases to speak and hides behind her veil. By the time she has matriculated in college, she has accustomed

> her eyes to making those submissive bows and curtsies with which she lives her life, humbly, as they had always wished her to be. She talks to herself about her mistakes and she forgets how speech can sound, because she has been silent for so long. All she sees in the lecture hall is the arrow pointing to the mosque. She weeps and ties back her hair. She lengthens her head covering every day so that no details are revealed. . . . She lengthens her dress, and starts to wear gloves, and becomes too chaste to shake hands or even speak.[38]

Silent for so long, Nadā no longer knows the sound of her voice. At night, she dreams about men's desires intersecting with her own. Her brother meanwhile is "collecting donations for the Afghan mujahideen. . . . He wants to travel to Afghanistan. He's talking about *jahiliya* and the necessity for jihad."[39] When she realizes that this is not the jihad she wants, she unveils and in her "heart is laughter, but your hand still stifles it as it rushes spontaneously to your mouth."[40] Traces of past anxieties, especially concerning her voice, haunt her newly liberated sense of self.[41]

In the end, throwing off her timidity, Nadā attends graduate school to write a dissertation on gender oppression. She accuses Islamists of "calling for woman, despite all the gains she has reaped in her struggle, to return obediently and of her own free will to her old position through adhering to tradition . . . with the idea that as a body she is useful but as a mind she is deficient."[42] Here again is a reference to the woman-lacking-reason-and-religion *ḥadīth* that has plagued Muslim women for well over a millennium.

Feminist Memoirs

Memoirs and autobiographies are latecomers to Muslim feminist literature. Concerns about the physical voice redouble when the literary voice unveils women's private lives. Muslim women's life stories frame some of the most powerful experiments in balancing faith with freedom. In 1976, Egyptian Islamist leader Zaynab al-Ghazālī (1917–2005) published her prison memoir *Ayyām min ḥayātī* (Days from My Life), in which she models the behavior of a good Muslim woman without obeying every patriarchal rule of how devout women should behave. The text revolves around her life before and during five years in prison. An associate of the Muslim Brothers but not a member of the organization, al-Ghazālī had retained her independence by establishing the Muslim Ladies Association in the 1930s. The Association collaborated on occasion with the mainstream Islamist movement and in the mid-1960s she was arrested along with Muslim Brother leaders for alleged participation in an anti-Nasser conspiracy. The prison memoir vaunts her superiority to these leaders whom she claims she instructed in correct Islam. She writes with some disdain of these men who could not withstand the kind of torture that her body so easily repulsed. So saintly was this body that witnessing its power over the torturers converted one of the prison guards from worship of Nasser to worship of God. Zaynab's disobedience to mortal men exploits the loophole of submission to God.[43]

Covering a similar period,[44] Egyptian-American academic Leila Ahmed (b. 1940) wrote a very different memoir that links her birthplace, Egypt, the country of her education, England, and her chosen home, America. Narrating the coming of age of a Muslim woman, the first half of *A Border Passage* (1999)[45] intertwines her stories of childhood and study at the University of Cambridge with those of her nanny, mother, and father during Egypt's struggle for independence from colonial rule and culture.

Ahmed grew up in a women's world that she alternately idealized and criticized:

> Our lives . . . were lived in women's time, women's space. And in women's culture. And the women had, too, I now believe, their own understanding of Islam . . . religion was an essential part of how they made sense of and understood their own lives. It was through religion that one pondered the things that happened, why they had happened.[46]

Religion helped women ponder life's complexities in a way men could not. Without access to ritual spaces, women's Islam was not regimented. Gender segregation, ironically, gave women privileged access to the heart of their religion:

> Generations of astute, thoughtful women, listening to the Quran, understood perfectly well its essential themes and its faith . . . and they knew what a travesty men had made of it. [She adds that] an emphasis on an oral and aural Islam is intrinsic to Islam and the Quran itself, and intrinsic even to the Arabic language. [Oral cultures] are the creations of living communities . . . and represent the ongoing interactions of these communities with their heritage of beliefs, outlook, circumstances and so on.[47]

However, when things went wrong, as in cases of divorce where women had rights they did not know they had or did not dare practice, these "women were powerless and acquiescent in a silence that seemed to me when I was young awfully like a guilty averting of the eyes, awfully like a kind of connivance."[48] Later, she criticizes her juvenile judgments, but they did indicate a burgeoning feminist awareness that she only acknowledged in name when reading Virginia Woolf as a student at the women-only Girton College in Cambridge that "represented the harem perfected" but rife with racism.[49] The greatest shock came on entry into the US academy. There she found that her starry-eyed notion of white American feminism was nothing but rhetoric. Why, Christian and Jewish feminists demanded, did Muslim women investigate their heritage and traditions, when Islam was "intrinsically, essentially, and irredeemably misogynist and patriarchal in a way that theirs (apparently) were not."[50] Christianity and Judaism could survive inspection and gender critique; Islam could not.

Throughout a memoir that rejects a binary epistemology, Ahmed practices the multiple critique I have discussed elsewhere.[51] Accepting her own ambivalence about people she may love at one moment and deplore at another, she condemns the many forces in society that restrict Muslim women's freedom to be who they want to be and to say what they want to say. She can do so because she has embraced her position on the margins of all the societies she has inhabited.[52]

Turning from Sunnī Egypt to post-1979 Shīʿī Iran, we encounter women who wrote about their experiences during and after the early days of Ayatollah Khomeini's Islamist experiment in statecraft. Their writings give insight into the sub rosa feminism that flowered despite Khomeini's misogynist rule in fundamentalist Iran. Zohreh Sullivan traces the ways Iranian women manipulated "gendered constructions of Islamic political discourse [to configure] new readings of Islam and feminism."[53] In 1992, Shahla Sherkat (b. 1956) founded *Zanān*, the first independent journal after 1979 to focus on women's issues. It embraced feminism, even using the English term to emphasize their belief that its global history was too important not to use a term that had succeeded in promoting gender justice. In 2005, Sherkat was awarded the Courage in Journalism Award from the International Women's Media Foundation (IWMF) and the Louis Lyons Award from the Nieman Foundation for Journalism at Harvard University. A short two years later, the Press Supervisory Board closed *Zanan* for "presenting a pessimistic picture of the situation for Iranian women" and publishing "morally questionable information."[54]

In her memoir *Iran Awakening* (2006), Nobel Peace laureate Shirin Ebadi (b. 1947) gives insight into what it felt like to live through and beyond the tumultuous 1979 Islamic Revolution and the subsequent eight-year war with Iraq. She grew up during the Shah's secular modernization agenda that celebrated women in liberated, i.e., Western, guise.[55] Secular upbringing notwithstanding, the family remained committed to Islamic values. Faith, she writes, "occupied a central role in our middle-class lives though in a quiet, private way."[56] From the youngest age, Ebadi writes, she had felt a deep love for God, and when Ayatollah Khomeini returned from his sixteen years of exile in Paris, she joined demonstrators who were calling for the Islamization of the state. The longed-for revolution brought her hardships, among them incarceration. Prison, where she prayed five times a day, strengthened her faith in God.[57] When her daughter left to study abroad, she "pulled out the Koran and held it high in the door frame . . . a ritual of departure we have performed too many times for our loved ones since the revolution."[58] It matters that she be viewed as a practicing and observant Muslim.[59]

One of the first female judges in Iran, president of the city court of Tehran from 1975 to 1979 and professor at the University of Tehran, Ebadi was forced to resign after the 1979 revolution and discovering a death squad list stating, "The next person to be killed is Shirin Ebadi."[60] The revolution she had backed demanded her defeat. When the Islamic penal code was imposed without consultation, she launched her opposition to a misogynistic code that she argued was not grounded in Islamic values and scriptures. She retooled as a lawyer focused on women and children's rights to "showcase the injustice of the Islamic Republic's laws . . . to advocate for female equality in an Islamic framework."[61] The only way to contest the ayatollahs' twisting of law and scripture was to work within their focus on the Muslim family.

Ebadi was not alone in her resistance. A friend of hers, condemned for walking with unrelated men in public, accused her judge of knowing nothing of the Qur'ān beyond lashing and whipping: "Did you skip that whole part at the beginning, about the mercy and compassion?" She reminded him that "only a woman can inflict corporal punishment on another woman," and that the flogger should hold a Qur'ān "under his arm, to soften the blows . . . the deterrent quality of a lashing lies in humiliation, not in wounding the flesh."[62] Like Zeineddine seventy years earlier, she accused religious authorities of not knowing Islamic law.

When chador-wearing girls from traditional families filled university classrooms, Ebadi was elated to note that young women were acquiring "a visceral consciousness of their oppression."[63] After the Nobel Peace Prize brought her global attention for her work on behalf of Muslim women, she realized that she could try to "make the system pay an international price for its refusal to reform its laws at home."[64] In 2003, fourteen progressive female MPs entered the legislature, and one of them approached Ebadi to draft a resolution on family law, relying on her ability and right to conduct *ijtihād*,

> My draft law which relied . . . on the central texts taught in the holy city of Qom's seminaries, showed that a basic right for women could be guaranteed within an Islamic framework of governance. . . . It is not religion that binds women, but the selective dictates of those who wish them cloistered.[65]

Ebadi's memoir affirms the power of individual narratives to protect women "from the tyrants of the day and from our own traditions."[66]

The memoirs of Zaynab al-Ghazālī, Leila Ahmed, and Shirin Ebadi forge paths between faith commitments, the search for freedom and the struggle to overcome a patriarchal structure so tight it chokes.

Trespassing on Men's Space

Some Muslim feminists have contested Muslim clerics' banishment of women from Islamic ritual life by writing about women's public roles during the lifetime of the Prophet Muḥammad or by revealing the erasure of women leaders from Islamic history. This Islamic feminist literature responded to the 1980s spread of political Islam and the imposition of misogynistic norms and values. In 1991, Algerian Assia Djebar (1936–2015) published *Loin de Médine*, a novel about strong women living in Arabia during the earliest period of Islam. Sharing public space with the men, some supported the Prophet Muḥammad against his detractors even while others were visible in their opposition. The visibility of women in the time of the Prophet continued well after his death but historians generally omitted them from the record. In *Sultanes Oubliées* (1990),[67] Moroccan Fatima Mernissi (1940–2015) unearths traces of women who had wielded great power only to be forgotten. What interests me more than such historically minded texts are the stories Muslim feminists tell of how their religious marginalization has affected their identities, agency, and faith commitments.

Women have confronted many barriers to full participation in their Muslim communities, none more difficult to overcome than their bodies and the *ʿawra* of their voices. Women are said not to be able to lead communal prayer, in other words they cannot be imams or deliver the Friday *khuṭba* or call the *adhān*. Many are barred from mosque space.

Muslim activists have taken on these taboos and shown them to be man-made. In August 1994, American scholar and activist amina wadud (b. 1952) shocked Muslims the world over when she delivered the Friday pre-*khuṭba* at the Cape Town Claremont Road mosque with women and men praying side by side separated only by a partition. In March 2005, after Suhayla al-ʿAttar had called the *adhān*, wadud took the next step when she led a New York City congregation in the Friday prayer, this time without any gender separation. She was called a heretic and received death threats.[68] Her daring inspired others so that in January 2018, K. Jamida Teacher became the first woman in India to lead the Friday communal prayer and deliver the *khuṭba* in Malappuram. Despite threats on her life, Jamida said, "I want to do things differently in a way that benefits my community in the long run."[69]

Women writers have joined their activist sisters in denouncing discrimination in religious spaces and rituals. Women, they insist, can lead the faithful in prayer; they can call them to prayer from the top of a minaret, as noted above in the discussion of Ghandour's novel. Above all, they must be given space in the communal mosque to pray with the same freedom that men enjoy.

Mohja Kahf (b. 1967), a Syrian-American poet and academic who has satirized Americans' and Arabs' views of each other has decried women's exclusion from Islamic public space. Her 2006 novel *The Girl in the Tangerine Scarf* paints the canvas of Middle American Muslim life. Through the eyes of Syrian-American Khadra, the reader observes the dailiness of women's challenges to live fully Muslim lives against the background of international events like the 1979 Islamic Revolution in Iran, Ḥāfiẓ Asad's 1982 brutal crackdown on the Muslim Brothers in Hama, the Israeli invasion of Lebanon, the Gulf War, and the war in former Yugoslavia during the early 1990s. From menarche to donning the hijab to the burial rituals for a raped and murdered Muslim student leader to marriage to the grandson of a Kuwaiti pearl diver—a seemingly open-minded Kuwaiti turned-tyrant whom she divorced—to college, Khadra negotiates the incompatible values of the two cultures to which she does and yet does not belong. Growing up in Islamophobic Indiana, Khadra leaves as soon as she can to work in Philadelphia as a reporter for *Alternative Americas*. To her dismay, she is sent to her hometown to give an insider's perspective on Muslims living far from the cities where most reside. The assignment flings her reeling into the past, and her struggles to be a strong, independent, even if not always orthodox, woman committed to Islam.

Khadra's first experience of gender discrimination comes during the family's Hajj trip to Mecca. Enchanted by the dawn call to prayer, she walks toward the mosque. The morality police stop her and take her back to the house where she and her family are staying. Why are women not allowed to pray in Saudi mosques when "women have always gone to the mosque. It's part of Islam?"[70] The next shock comes when some Saudi men try to take advantage of an American even though she keeps repeating that she is Arab. Khadra agonizes over her worry that the holiest of Islamic rituals, the Hajj, has been defiled. But it is not only in Saudi Arabia and other Muslim-majority countries that women are prevented from participating in public Islam. During a period of enchantment with Qur'ānic studies, her recitation tutor tells her she cannot participate in a competition for which she thought he was training her.[71] Adding insult to injury, her exquisite recitation opening a session of the Muslim Students' Association raises alarms about her gorgeous voice seducing men. Rather than fight the age-old insult that women's voices are *'awra*, she gives up Muslim student activities.[72]

During the newspaper assignment, she hears that a concert she was about to attend has been canceled. Why? Hijab Hip Hop with Nia Girls had tested the limits of local Muslim authorities, who pompously pronounced that women "are not to dance and not to make their voice suggestive and seductive."[73] Despite these setbacks for Muslim women, Khadra still cherishes her *ḥijāb*, her tangerine scarf from Syria.[74]

Mohja Kahf's poems titled "Little Mosque Poems" lament the loss of the generosity and openness that should characterize all Muslim women and men. How is it possible that the men should want to exclude women from Islam's ritual spaces?

> In my little mosque
> there is no room for me
> to pray. I am
> turned away faithfully
> five
> times a day
> My little mosque:
> so meager
> in resources, yet
> so eager
> to turn away
> a woman
> or a stranger[75]

Short staccato lines explode like bullets she is shooting at the mosque guards who refuse entry to women and strangers. She knows because she has been told to go away from the place where she rightfully belongs. A woman in a short skirt once dared to cross the mosque threshold in her search for help in a time of pain and despair. The men did not care about her physical needs, only about improper dress,

> Everyone rushed over to her
> to make sure
> she was going to cover her legs[76]

The only women the little mosque loves are those who "live like seventh-century Arabian women / or at least dress / like pre-industrial pre-colonial women."[77] Even for such pious women there is at best only a cordoned-off place where they can pray. Moreover, the congregation is expected to support the gender division of space with regular contributions for "another curtain to partition off the women."[78]

These women-despising men are infatuated with Arab men "with pure accents and beards" who are the source of Real Islam.[79] And for these men no luxury is too much: "My little mosque has a Persian carpet / depicting trees of paradise / in the men's section, which you enter / through a lovely classical arch.[80] The opulence of the men's sanctuary with its entry arch, magnificent columns, and carpet promising the pleasures of paradise contrasts shamefully with the women's section that is entered "through the back alley / just past the crack junkie here / and over these fallen garbage cans."[81] The injunction to cleanliness so central to Islamic belief and practice is overlooked when it comes to women and their prayer space. So cruel had the men become that she had no choice but to carry a little mosque "in the chambers of my heart / but it is closed indefinitely pending / extensive structural repairs."[82] Funny, ironic and despairing, Kahf flails around for a mosque that will welcome her. Failing to find one, she tries to build a little mosque in her heart, but despite her learning in Islamic sciences, her study of *Saḥiḥ al-Bukhārī*, and her religious commitment, her own little mosque falls into disrepair. Nowhere can she find a sanctified space to pray, not even in her heart.

Kahf knows that her charge of misogyny and apparently un-Islamic behavior and attitudes will not be believed. Did the little mosque's men not reject God's application for the job of janitor because they did not consider him a Muslim? They will also reject her poem, deriding it as

> written by the Devil
> in cahoots with the Zionists,
> NATO, and the current U.S. administration,
> as part of the Worldwide Orientalist Plot
> to Discredit Islam.[83]

Echoes from Ghandour's *The Honey* ring loud. The male authorities will never accept responsibility for what they have done wrong but will always blame others, the usual others. How can she persuade them that her criticism is the fruit of her love for Islam? Can they be persuaded to open the mosque doors to prevent the very real "bricks of bigots" from breaking the windows? She concludes with a plea for inclusiveness, not only for women, but also for all people of all religions, Christians, Jews, Buddhists and Hindus. She is not demanding the impossible: "only a few square inches of ground / that will welcome my forehead, / no questions asked."[84] Since these precious inches of ground are not to be hers she needs to remember, "The Mosque is under your feet, wherever you walk each day."[85] Better not to rail at the ignorant, but rather, understand that the whole of God's earth is a mosque for Muslims.

Conclusion

How better to conclude this chapter than with the words of another feisty Syrian-American, the *ḥijābī* poet Mona Haydar? In no uncertain terms, Mona (b. 1990), who calls herself a "rapper, poet, activist, practitioner of Permaculture, devotee, mountain girl, solar power lover, and a tireless God-enthusiast,"[86] informs the world in a 2017 video that her hijab empowers her against negative stereotyping in America. Surrounded by her energetic multiethnic veiled chorus, she belts out: "So even if you hate it I still wrap my hijab." Proudly pregnant while she was producing the YouTube video, she was deep into her MA in Islamic theology.

A year later, Mona Haydar produced another YouTube video that she titled "Dog." It sharply rebukes faux religious men who prey on women. "Shaikhs on the DL. Shaikhs in my DM begging me to shake it on my cam in the PM" she lilts, but the meaning is far from lilting. These shaikhs in her DM, or direct message app, beg Muslim women to arouse them online: "When the sun sets trying to hunt me down." But no luck with these women, they know that these kinds of men "might need Qur'ān," and with that Zeineddine's and Ebadi's voices resound over the decades telling ignorant shaikhs to read the Qur'ān before they presume to criticize any woman for un-Islamic behavior. Not only does she call out violent pious Muslim men, but, like the writers discussed in this chapter, she also mocks the way men have been calling women's voices *'awra* or shame: "Say my voice is haram / Cuz you getting turned on." No, she writes in capital letters across the screen, far from forbidden or a shame, "A woman's voice is REVOLUTION." After insulting the hypocrites, "the seedy sidis in their sidi suits . . . emotional terrorist. . . . If you please lower your gaze . . . you need a therapist / Boy, you need an exorcist." In the closing forty seconds of the video, the following words in caps flash up on the screen: "In the time it took you to watch this 27 women in the US have been assaulted or abused. 1 in 3 women worldwide has experienced physical sexual violence in their lifetime." Mona Haydar ends with a piece of advice to those ignorant men who use Islamic authority to abuse women: "O my God you need God."[87]

In this chapter, I have analyzed the words of some powerful Muslim women from around the world and across time who believe that Islam as a religion and a culture should welcome and empower everyone. These writers' daring self-assurance is remarkable. Mona Haydar's urban slang is far from the high-culture tone of Mihri Hātūn, or the scriptural erudition of Naẓīra Zeineddine, or the tender prose of Zeina Ghandour, or the postmodern pen of Mirāl al-Tahāwī, or the narrative legalese of Shirin Ebadi, or the down-to-earthness of Mohja Kahf. But in just over four minutes each, Haydar's two millennial videos each hit on topics that have absorbed Muslim feminist writers for centuries: misogynistic *ḥadīth*, the veil, self-appointed authorities' exploitation of women and the banning of a woman's voice that each woman in this chapter declares is not *'awra* but honey. Revolution even.

Notes

1. Margot Badran and miriam cooke, *Opening the Gates: An Anthology of Arab Feminist Writing*, 2nd ed. (Bloomington: Indiana University Press, 2004), xxv.
2. miriam cooke, *Anatomy of an Egyptian Intellectual Yahya Haqqi* (Washington, DC: Three Continents, 1984), 68–69.
3. Dealing with 150 years of Iranian women's literature, Farzaneh Milani writes, "ideologues and writers of the constitutional revolutionary period (1905–1911) felt compelled to challenge inequalities on all levels, including the sexual"; see Farzaneh Milani, *Veils and Words: The Emerging Voices of Iranian Women Writers* (Syracuse, NY: Syracuse University Press, 1992), 29.
4. Khairudin Aljunied, "Recasting Gendered Paradigms: An Indonesian Cleric and Muslim Women in the Malay World," *Islam and Christian-Muslim Relations* 27, no. 2 (2016): 175–193.
5. See, Margot Badran, *Feminists, Islam, and Nation: Gender and the Making of Modern Egypt* (Princeton, NJ: Princeton University Press, 1995); Marilyn Booth, *May Her Likes Be Multiplied: Biography and Gender Politics in Egypt* (Berkeley: California University Press, 2001); Afsahneh Najmabadi, "Crafting an Educated Housewife in Iran," in *Remaking Women: Feminism and Modernity in the Middle East*, ed. Lila Abu-Lughod (Princeton, NJ: Princeton University Press, 1998), 91–125; Janet Afary, "On the Origins of Feminism in Early Twentieth-Century Iran," *Journal of Women's History* 1, no. 2 (Fall 1989):65–87.
6. Vincent J. Cornell, "Fruit of the Tree of Knowledge: The Relationship between Faith and Practice in Islam," in *The Oxford History of Islam*, ed. John L. Esposito (Oxford: Oxford University Press, 1999), 74–75.
7. Mernissi provides a model of how sound *hadith* can and should be deconstructed so that even if the saying from the Prophet has been passed down through a reliable *isnād* that returns to a Companion it is not above scrutiny, especially when the Companion's character was questionable; see Fatima Mernissi, *The Veil and the Male Elite: A Feminist Interpretation of Women's Rights in Islam*, trans. Mary Jo Lakeland (New York: Addison-Wesley, 1991).
8. In his *Aḥkām al-Nisā'*, Aḥmad ibn Ḥanbal (d. 241/855) states, "Everything in a woman is *'awra.*" Al-Tirmidhī, author of one of the Six Books of *ḥadīth*, cites a report which states, "The woman is *'awra.*" (https://sunnah.com/search/?q=awra). Centuries later, lexicographers Ibn Manẓūr (d. 712/1312) and al-Zabīdī (d. 1205/1791) cite the *ḥadīth*: "Woman is an *'awra*"; see Fedwa Malti-Douglas, *Woman's Body, Woman's Word: Gender and Discourse in Arabo-Islamic Writing* (Princeton, NJ: Princeton University Press, 1991), 126–127; Hanadi Samman, *Anxiety of Erasure: Trauma, Authorship, and the Diaspora in Arab Women's Writings* (Syracuse, NY: Syracuse University Press, 2015), 47.
9. Didem Havlioglu, *Mihri Hatun: Performance, Gender Bending, and Subversion in Ottoman Intellectual History* (Syracuse, NY: Syracuse University Press, 2017), 95.
10. Naila Amat-un-Nur, "Rabi'a al-Adawiya, the Woman Mystic-Saint of Islam," accessed March 18, 2018, http://www.nazr-e-kaaba.com/rabia_al_adawiya.html.
11. miriam cooke, *Nazira Zeineddine: A Pioneer of Islamic Feminism* (Oxford: Oneworld, 2010).
12. Ibid., 55; Naẓīra Zeineddine, *al-sufūr wa al-ḥijāb: Muḥāḍarāt wa naẓarāt marmāhā taḥrīr al-mar'a wa al-tajaddud al-ijtimā'ī fī'l-'ālam al-islāmī* (Damascus: Al Mada, 1998), 136.
13. Zeineddine, *al-sufūr wa al-ḥijāb*, 234–235; see also cooke, *Nazira Zeineddine*, 32–38.
14. Malti-Douglas, *Woman's Body*, 121.

15. *Should a Muslim Woman Speak? A Comprehensive Introduction to the Islamic Textual Evidence against the Prohibition of Muslim Women Speaking in Public*; available at https://thequranblog.files.wordpress.com/2010/04/voice-book.pdf. See also https://www.al-islam.org/shiite-encyclopedia-ahlul-bayt-dilp-team/rules-modesty-according-five-islamic-schools-law.
16. Zeina Ghandour, *The Honey* (London: Quartet Books, 1999), 19.
17. Ibid., 6.
18. Ibid., 7.
19. Ibid., 37, 41.
20. Referring to Fatima Mernissi, *Beyond the Veil: Male-Female Dynamic in Modern Muslim Society* (Cambridge, MA: Schenkmann, 1995, Badran writes that she rejected the equivalence of *fitna* with women, and recently an online Muslim feminist group has called itself *FITNA*, redefining the term to mean "constructive disruption around gender issues in the Muslim community"; see Margot Badran, ed., "Islamic Feminism," *Samyukta* 17, no. 1 (2017): 8. In connection with Nawal El Saadawi's prison memoir and Algerian women's writings, Brinda Mehta discusses *fitna* as the "act of creating chaos in text [which] is a public intervention that brings the private art of writing to the open forum of readership and analysis"; see Brinda J. Mehta, *Dissident Writings of Arab Women: Voices against Violence* (London: Routledge, 2014), 7, 9, 79.
21. Ghandour, *The Honey*, 22–23.
22. Ibid., 23–28
23. Ibid., 64.
24. Ibid., 81.
25. See "My Little Mosque" below.
26. Milani, *Veils and Words*, 29.
27. Badran and cooke, *Opening the Gates*, 126.
28. Ibid., 127.
29. Zeineddine, *Al-sufūr wa al-ḥijāb*.
30. See cooke, *Nazira Zeineddine*.
31. Milani, *Veils and Words*, 15.
32. Ibid., 231–234
33. Fedwa Malti-Douglas, *Men, Women and God(s); Nawal El Saadawi and Arab Feminist Poetics* (Berkeley: California University Press, 1995), 118–140.
34. Nawal El Saadawi, "Eyes," in Badran and cooke, *Opening the Gates*, 206.
35. Badran and cooke, *Opening the Gates*, 208.
36. Ibid., 212.
37. Miral al-Tahāwī, *Blue Aubergine*, trans. Anthony Calderbank (Cairo: AUC Press, 2002).
38. Ibid., 45–46.
39. Ibid., 62.
40. Ibid., 100.
41. Ibid., 104.
42. Ibid., 106–107.
43. miriam cooke, *Women Claim Islam: Creating Islamic Feminism through Literature* (New York: Routledge, 2001), chap. 4.
44. Ahmed writes of her encounter with al-Ghazālī's memoir and how struck she was at its violence—she is surprised that al-Ghazālī's heroines were the fighters in Muḥammad's army—they were too violent for her taste.

45. Leila Ahmed, *A Border Passage from Cairo to America—A Woman's Journey* (New York: Farrar, Straus & Giroux, 1999).
46. Ibid., 120–121.
47. Ibid., 127, 280.
48. Ibid., 131.
49. Ibid., 180, 183, 225.
50. Ibid., 292.
51. See cooke, *Women Claim Islam*.
52. Ahmed, *A Border Passage*, 288.
53. Zohreh T. Sullivan, "Eluding the Feminist, Overthrowing the Modern? Transformations in Twentieth-Century Iran," in Abu-Lughod, *Remaking Women*, 234.
54. https://www.illustratedwomeninhistory.com/post/142289794640/shahla-sherkat-is-a-journalist-prominent-persian. May 15, 2018.
55. Shirin Ebadi, *Iran Awakening: One Woman's Journey to Reclaim her Life and Country*, with Azadeh Moaveni (New York: Random House, 2006), 68.
56. Ibid., 33.
57. Ibid., 165, 171.
58. Ibid., 183.
59. Ibid., 107.
60. Ibid., xv, 140.
61. Ibid., 111.
62. Ibid., 98–99.
63. Ibid., 106, 108.
64. Ibid., 127.
65. Ibid., 185–187, 190–191, 204.
66. Ibid., 209.
67. Fatima Mernissi, *Sultanes oubliées: Femmes chefs d'état en Islam* (Paris: Albin Michel, 1990).
68. For an account of the controversies surrounding wadud's ritual performances, see Harvard University's Pluralism Project, http://pluralism.org/research-report/amina-wadud/.
69. Deepa Soman, *Kochi Times*, January 29, 2018.
70. Mohja Kahf, *The Girl in the Tangerine Scarf* (New York: Carroll & Graf, 2006), 167–168.
71. Ibid., 199.
72. Ibid., 204.
73. Ibid., 413.
74. Ibid., 425.
75. Mohja Kahf, "Little Mosque Poems," in *Shattering the Stereotypes: Muslim Women Speak Out*, ed. Fawzia Afzal-Khan (Northampton, MA: Olive Branch, 2005), 116.
76. Ibid., 120.
77. Ibid., 116.
78. Ibid., 116–117.
79. Ibid., 121.
80. Ibid., 118.
81. Ibid., 118.
82. Ibid., 119.
83. Ibid., 120–121.
84. Ibid., 122–123.
85. Ibid., 123.

86. http://www.monahaydar.com/; last accessed March 26, 2018.
87. In an interview with *The Tempest*, she said, "Violence against women is something important to me as a woman, and the statistics that I feature are staggering. I feel that, as an artist, if I'm not pushing myself to do things for the betterment of the world, then I shouldn't do anything. I'm interested in using my art to explore the intersections of art, activism, music, and identity. I think to myself, 'How can I use my voice for the greatest good?' That culture of silence is so damaging because it allows those cycles of abuse to continue and we have to break them. . . . Hip-hop can be used as a global tool for liberation and the refinement of our selves and egos." Accessed March 26, 2018, https://thetempest.co/2017/07/27/entertainment/mona-haydar-smashing-patriarchy-hip-hop/.

Bibliography

Afary, Janet. "On the Origins of Feminism in Early Twentieth-Century Iran." *Journal of Women's History* 1, no. 2 (Fall, 1989): 65–87.

Ahmed, Leila. *A Border Passage from Cairo to America—A Woman's Journey*. New York: Farrar, Straus & Giroux, 1999.

Badran, Margot. *Feminists, Islam, and Nation: Gender and the Making of Modern Egypt* Princeton, NJ: Princeton University Press, 1995.

Badran, Margot. "Islamic Feminism." *Samyukta: A Journal of Gender and Culture* 17, no. 1 (2017); Introduction - Samyukta: A Journal of Gender and Culture (samyuktajournal.in)

Badran, Margot, and miriam cooke. *Opening the Gates: An Anthology of Arab Feminist Writing*. 2nd ed. Bloomington: Indiana University Press, 2004.

Booth, Marilyn. *May Her Likes Be Multiplied: Biography and Gender Politics in Egypt* Berkeley: California University Press, 2001.

cooke, miriam. *Anatomy of an Egyptian Intellectual Yahya Haqqi*. Washington, DC: Three Continents, 1984.

cooke, miriam. *Nazira Zeineddine: A Pioneer of Islamic Feminism*. Oxford: OneWorld, 2010.

cooke, miriam. *Women Claim Islam: Creating Islamic Feminism through Literature*. New York: Routledge, 2001.

Cornell, Vincent J. "Fruit of the Tree of Knowledge: The Relationship between Faith and Practice in Islam." In *The Oxford History of Islam*, edited by John L. Esposito, 63–105. Oxford: Oxford University Press, 1999.

Djebar, Assia. *Loin de Médine: Filles d'Ismael*. Paris: Albin Michel, 1991.

Ebadi, Shirin. *Iran Awakening: One Woman's Journey to Reclaim Her Life and Country*. With Azadeh Moaveni. New York: Random House, 2006.

Ghandour, Zeina. *The Honey*. London: Quartet Books, 1999.

Ghazālī, Zaynab al-. *Ayyām min ḥayātī*. Cairo: Dar al-Shuruq, 1976.

Havlioglu, Didem. *Mihri Hatun: Performance, Gender Bending, and Subversion in Ottoman Intellectual History*. Syracuse, NY: Syracuse University Press, 2017.

Aljunied, Khairudin. "Recasting Gendered Paradigms: An Indonesian Cleric and Muslim Women in the Malay World." *Islam and Christian-Muslim Relations* 27, no. 2 (2016): 175–193.

Kahf, Mohja. *The Girl in the Tangerine Scarf*. New York: Carroll & Graf, 2006.

Kahf, Mohja. "Little Mosque Poems." In *Shattering the Stereotypes: Muslim Women Speak Out*, edited by Fawzia Afzal-Khan, 116–122. Northampton, MA: Olive Branch Press, 2005.

Malti-Douglas, Fedwa. *Men, Women and God(s); Nawal El Saadawi and Arab Feminist Poetics*. Berkeley: California University Press, 1995.

Malti-Douglas, Fedwa. *Woman's Body, Woman's Word: Gender and Discourse in Arabo-Islamic Writing*. Princeton, NJ: Princeton University Press, 1991.

Mehta, Brinda J. *Dissident Writings of Arab Women: Voices against Violence*. London: Routledge, 2014.

Mernissi, Fatima. *Beyond the Veil: Male–Female Dynamic in Modern Muslim Society* Cambridge, MA: Schenkmann, 1995.

Mernissi, Fatima. *Sultanes oubliées: Femmes chefs d'état en Islam*. Paris: Albin Michel 1990.

Mernissi, Fatima. *The Veil and the Male Elite: A Feminist Interpretation of Women's Rights in Islam*. Translated by Mary Jo Lakeland. New York: Addison-Wesley, 1991.

Milani, Farzaneh. *Veils and Words: The Emerging Voices of Iranian Women Writers*. Syracuse, NY: Syracuse University Press, 1992.

Najmabadi, Afsahneh. "Crafting an Educated Housewife in Iran." In *Remaking Women: Feminism and Modernity in the Middle East*, edited by Lila Abu-Lughod, 91–125. Princeton, NJ: Princeton University Press, 1998.

Samman, Hanadi. *Anxiety of Erasure: Trauma, Authorship, and the Diaspora in Arab Women's Writings*. Syracuse, NY: Syracuse University Press, 2015.

Sullivan, Zohreh T. "Eluding the Feminist, Overthrowing the Modern? Transformations in Twentieth-Century Iran." In *Remaking Women: Feminism and Modernity in the Middle East*, edited by Lila Abu-Lughod, 215–242. Princeton, NJ: Princeton University Press, 1998.

Tahāwī, Mirāl al-. *Blue Aubergine*. Translated by Anthony Calderbank. Cairo: AUC Press, 2002.

Zeineddine, Naẓīra. *Al-sufūr wa al-ḥijāb: Muḥāḍarāt wa naẓarāt marmāhā taḥrīr al-mar'a wa al-tajaddud al-ijtimā'ī fī al-'ālam al-islāmī*. Damascus: Al Mada, 1998.

G

ISLAM, WOMEN, AND THE GLOBAL PUBLIC ARENA

MENTION "Muslim women" in Muslim-minority contexts, especially in the West, and specific stock images are conjured up by media pundits, television talking heads, and ideologues, both on the right and the left. Above all, Muslim women are associated with the *ḥijāb* or headscarf, which, for these groups, has become a synecdoche for all that is assumed to be wrong with "Islam" and "Muslims." Regardless of what some Muslim women themselves say about choosing to wear the headscarf or how empowering of their personhood they consider it to be, others insist on speaking for them and representing them as disenfranchised and relentlessly oppressed, all on account of a piece of clothing on their hair. The two excellent chapters in this final section skillfully dissect the multiple discourses that have emerged in the West since the period of European colonial occupation of a large part of the Muslim-majority world that has made "saving" Muslim women the "moral" justification in many cases for European military invasions of Muslim realms. Inheriting the imperial mantle in the post–World War II period, the United States has also borrowed this kind of "culture talk" to a certain degree from the Europeans and launched its own version of "*la mission civilatrice*."

After September 11, we witnessed a rising tide of Islamophobia generally in the West, but more acutely felt in the United States, which had been directly attacked. This fear and hatred of Islam went into overdrive during the presidency of Donald Trump, with his racial and religious slurs directed at Muslims. Islamophobes frequently target Muslim women in *ḥijāb* and play up their assumed "victimhood" in order to set up a contrast to "liberated" non-Muslim Western women, creating a "clash of civilizations" discourse that pits a reified "Muslim world" against a reified "West." The genealogy of this narrative is insightfully explored in this section, revealing its deep historical roots within

Orientalism, a phenomenon that has caricatured and demonized the Muslim East, not least through its fetishization of Muslim women and their attire. In the more recent past and continuing into the contemporary period, the clash of civilizations discourse has been deployed to stage the "War on Terror," which, at least in part, is being waged on the bodies of Muslim women.

CHAPTER 31

WOMEN'S SARTORIAL AGENCY

The History and Politics of Veiling

ANNA PIELA

INTRODUCTION

THE intense focus on the veil as a signifier of Islam has obscured the fact that the practice of veiling is not exclusively Islamic, as it was common in Europe, the Middle East, and Asia also before the advent of Islam. Head covering, and sometimes even face covering, has been practiced in Judaism, Christianity (in particular in Catholicism and Orthodox Christianity), and Hinduism.[1] Islamic veiling, however, has captured popular imagination to such a degree that it has become the central framework through which the position of women in Islam has been considered from theological, cultural, and sociological perspectives. This occurs in spite of many Muslim women's criticisms that the unrelenting focus on veiling obscures more important issues affecting their lives, such as access to education, employment, and political participation.[2] However, veiling is undeniably enmeshed with these aspects of life; in some contexts, veiled women report discrimination against them in educational spaces, the workplace and hiring process, and a variety of policies. In others, appearing unveiled may cause women to be harassed and belittled. The stereotypes of veiled women rely on ahistoricity, atemporality, and acontextuality, when in fact the practice of the veil, as is observed today, is the product of a combination of religious, political, social, and cultural processes.

The Islamic veil, through the processes of its adoption, imposition, discarding, or prohibition, has often functioned as a signifier of modern nation-making.[3] It referenced state "modernization" when it was legally prohibited or discouraged, and a turn to religious fundamentalism when it was decreed by the state. It also became greatly enmeshed in the colonial politics of the Middle East, and symbolized class boundaries, as the colonial policies led to the emergence of more pronounced socioeconomic classes. This expansion of the signification of the veil beyond religious piety, marked the emergence of the "discourse of the veil,"[4] which has, from late nineteenth century onward, resurfaced at transformative political moments, becoming the lens through which developments in global politics could be interpreted and understood. Given the enormous scope of the topic, in this chapter I focus on four historical turns during which the battle over the meaning of the veil became particularly consequential for articulation of Muslim women's agency embedded in the interwoven economic, social, and cultural contexts. These include the early twentieth century, when the veil became implicated in the emergence of feminism in the middle East; the last two decades of the twentieth century, when the veil made a global comeback on the wave of Islamic revival; the volatile post-9/11 decade when the veil became a hotly contested symbol in the context of the War on Terror; and, finally, the decade that started with the 2010 Belgian "*burqa*ʿ ban."

1920s: The Uneasy Relationship Between Unveiling and Feminism In The Middle East

The Muslim veil was an object of fascination of audiences of painters, writers, and travelers who visited the Middle East well before Western powers consolidated their presence in that region through colonial politics. Mohja Kahf describes how Muslim dress, then represented as sexually titillating, was used as a counterpoint to the normative European (and later, specifically Victorian) femininity, constructed as sexually submissive and home-bound.[5] It is no surprise then, that the veil was targeted by the British colonial administration of Egypt. As Leila Ahmed notes, Lord Cromer, the British consul in Egypt in the second half of the nineteenth century, was a firm advocate of Muslim women's unveiling as the path to improvement of women's lives (while opposing women's suffrage in Britain). The negative views of the veil espoused by Lord Cromer were shared by male Egyptian writers of the time, one of whom, Qāsim Amīn, a prominent lawyer, penned a work titled *The Liberation of Women* (1899).[6] In his book, he advocated for not only the rejection of the veil but also the introduction of mandatory primary education for women, along with some limited reforms in the family law. This was, however, framed by his general disdain for Egyptian women, which makes the proclamation that Amin is the "Father of Arab Feminism" highly debatable.[7] The notion contrasting veiled women as uneducated and backward, and unveiled women as modern and progressive thus became fundamental in the debate on women's rights, despite it being described as a red herring in a context where women's health and education reforms were required.[8] This reconfiguration of Egyptian women's priorities was recognized by Malak Ḥifnī Nāṣīf, a contemporary of Hudā Shaʿrāwī and advocate for a more indigenous-style Arab feminism, who argued that "the question of the veil was only central in the debate about woman's place in society because the west (personified in Egypt then by Lord Cromer) had made it so."[9] Nāṣīf did not advocate a forced unveiling, as she recognized that women are the best judges on the issue given that they know how to best navigate their lives and the social demands placed on them.[10]

Shaʿrāwī, the founder of the Egyptian Feminist Union in 1923, is known for staging a public unveiling (together with her two peer activists, Saizā Nabarāwī and Nabawiyya Mūsā, she discarded her face veil) in 1925 following her attendance at a women's conference in Rome. Taking Amīn's demands much further, they demanded that women be allowed to study at university. Such initiatives affected, first and foremost, the lives of upper- and middle-class women. It is notable that working-class women were largely unaffected by the notions of modernization through unveiling; for practical reasons, their lives had always been less restricted than those of urban women's.[11] Notably, a commitment to the veil was an important part of the political program of Zainab al-Ghazālī, one of the leaders of the Islamist movement in Egypt in the twentieth century, and often lauded as the mother of Islamic feminism.[12] Al-Ghazālī saw the domestic role as primary for women, but reserved the right to political participation for those women who desired it, herself rising in the ranks of the male-dominated Muslim Brotherhood to the very top.[13] In the postcolonial era, as women gained access to education and employment, chiefly in state administration, the veil lost much of its popularity among Egyptian women.

The erasure of religious signs and practices from the public realm was a part of the secular modernization project in Turkey led by Mustafa Kemal Atatürk. It began by the removal of the reference to Islam as a national religion in a 1928 constitutional amendment, and quickly evolved as the Swiss legal code was implemented, sharia courts were closed, and the Latin script replaced the Arabic one. As Yeğenoğlu noted ironically, the secular character of the new Turkish republic was sacralized through eradication of religion from the public sphere.[14] Men's traditional headgear, the fez, was replaced with the European hat, and traditional veiling was strongly discouraged, although not legally banned as in neighboring Iran. As the Westernization of the former Ottoman empire became the new goal for the secular elite, the Islamic practices and signifiers were "mapped onto backwardness."[15]

In Iran, the veil was present before the advent of Islam, and the ebb and flow in its popularity continued until it was abolished in 1936 by Rezā Shāh, who also established the new Pahlavi dynasty.[16] The forced unveiling, meant as a modernization effort, deeply divided Iranian society. To women who preferred to veil, it constituted violence, sometimes in a literal sense, as soldiers often made them unveil in public. As a result, many women were forced to stay within their homes and abandon public life. Many were forced to leave their employment, and veiled girls were prevented from continuing their education. After the ban was withdrawn in 1941, both veiled and unveiled women were present in the Iranian public sphere, although the negative meanings attached to the veil in the earlier period remained strong.[17]

Iranian women's movements in the early twentieth century focused on agitating for women's right to vote and girls' education. Rather than focusing on the veil, women activists published numerous newspapers and magazines that advocated for these issues as well as national unity in foreign affairs, in particular with Russia and Britain.[18] Similarly, in Turkey, the main thrust of women's political activity was on securing the right to vote (which they achieved in 1934). The veil did not feature within the early feminist agenda there.[19]

1979–2000: The Global Rise of Islamic Veiling

In the late 1970s, many Iranian women adopted the veil as a criticism of the modernization reforms of Shah Reza Pahlavi.[20] This, argues Homa Hoodfar, constituted a vastly different message to the compulsory veiling introduced as a result of the Islamic Revolution (strongly opposed by many women at mass demonstrations and sit-ins).[21] In its aftermath, critiques of the veil as a tool of patriarchal politics became more pronounced.[22] Haideh Moghissi quotes a number of studies that document coercive legislation and practices across the Middle East and North Africa region (in addition to Iran, she mentioned Sudan, Palestine, Kurdish territories, and Egypt) that required women to veil.[23] Lama Abu Odeh described the veil as dress worn in Egypt by "the followers of the current fundamentalist movements," an explicit signifier of the "completion of the already ambivalent segregation of the sexes," which however protected women from male violence within the family (honor crimes) and sexual harassment in the street.[24]

Complementing these mostly ethnographic studies, Fatima Mernissi, in her now classic feminist book *The Veil and the Male Elite*, insists that the veil, or the *ḥijāb*, must be considered as a notion whose original meaning was to divide in the spatial sense, conceal something from view, or, from the Ṣūfī perspective, to block the knowledge of the Divine.[25] In this latter case, she argues, the meaning of the *ḥijāb* is decidedly negative. In the Qur'ān, the *ḥijāb* denotes a separation or a curtain, rather than the veil.[26] To illustrate the historical context in which the original "*ḥijāb* verse" was revealed, she discussed the difficulties experienced by the Prophet and the early Muslim community in Medīna. She asserts that a lack of military success and subsequent loss of Muḥammad's standing in Medīna led to the revelation that placed his wives behind a curtain and prevented them from remarrying after his death. Mernissi ascribed the renewed preoccupation with the *ḥijāb as a head covering* in the MENA region to a political campaign conducted through publication of easily available conservative treatises on the role of women in Islam.[27] She observes that "hiding the female body seems to be an obsession" in this type of literature.[28] "Protecting women and shutting them out of the world"[29] is a means of resisting Western cultural influences; the understanding of how women's bodies came to symbolize the community in the early Islamic period throws light on the resurgence of the veil in modern day.

However, this conviction does not explain the sharp rise in the popularity of the veil both in the West and globally, as research shows that by no means are all women who adopt the veil conservative. Rather, it suggests that many women are keen to reap spiritual and social benefits that the veil offers. As a religious practice, it appears to sidestep the issue of potential male coercion and often frames the experience of personal engagement with tenets of Islamic ethics.[30] In addition, as argued Fadwa El Guindi[31] and, independently, Hoodfar,[32] it helps women safeguard opportunities effected by modernization by countering stereotypes associated with "the modernized woman," while protecting their traditional rights. In the 1970s, Papanek analyzed the *burqaʿ* as one of the practices that make up the complex system of purdah, or segregation of the sexes, in South Asia. However, she noted that for many women who practiced the *burqaʿ*, wearing it was preferable to being secluded within their homes, as they were able to enter the public space if they were fully covered.[33] This argument echoes in the modern-day narratives of women who wear the *niqāb* or the *burqaʿ*; facial covering does not necessarily signify social seclusion, but may actually be a vehicle of social engagement, despite the prevailing perceptions of this practice.

Sylvia Chan-Malik's analysis of American media's coverage of the Iranian chador (a combination of the headscarf and a cloak) during the Islamic Revolution indicates that in 1979, it quickly became a "central image" that communicated women's implied inferiority in Islam.[34] It provided a simple logic that helped Western subjects decode the unfolding of events in Iran. Chan-Malik noted that "American discourse of the veil that occurred around the women's protests in Iran certainly mimicked many of the discursive legacies of British colonial feminism, and undoubtedly utilized much of the same orientalist lexicon of phrases, terms, and ideas employed by Lord Cromer and his associates." However, the key rhetorical move in this case was based on rehashing the "modernized" (i.e., uncovered) Iranian women protesting the forced veiling as a variation of the second-wave American feminist movement protesting patriarchy in the 1970s. Thus, the feminist movement was co-opted into American nationalist pride that would culminate in the events of the "War on Terror."[35]

In the modern West, the veil gradually and unsurprisingly became a signifier for contested cultural politics. Claire Dwyer demonstrated early on how by adopting the veil, young British Muslim women oriented themselves to religious, ethnic, and national identities, continuously negotiating the boundaries drawn around the concepts of home, family, school, peer groups, and the public sphere.[36] School in particular became the stage for conflict over religious expression in France, Canada, and the United Kingdom. In particular, students were excluded, suspended, and expelled from school as a result of institutional prohibitions of "religious symbolism," or interpretations of religious dress as a violation of the school dress code. In 1989, three French Muslim girls who insisted on wearing the *ḥijāb* were expelled from a public school.[37] In subsequent years, the wearing of the *ḥijāb* was prohibited, formally or implicitly, in state educational institutions in many countries across Europe and North America, with the most restrictive bans in France, Turkey, Germany, and the Canadian province of Quebec, with "softer regulations" in the United Kingdom, the United States, the rest of Canada, and the Netherlands.[38] This wave of regulation of Islamic dress culminated at first in 2004 when the *ḥijāb* was delegalized in France in certain public spaces, such as the state schools. This situated the *ḥijāb* in various analytic frameworks of secularism, multiculturalism, gender equality, and international law. With public reception of the Islamic dress influenced by alarmist headlines, anti-Muslim hostilities and intercommunity tensions continued to rise.

Simultaneously, the interest in subjective constructions of the veil by its wearers became palpable in the academia, notably in Canada[39] and the United States.[40] Many of these pre-2001 studies signaled the notion that Muslim women were taking up the veil free of coercion, and, indeed, for reasons not immediately intelligible to Western secular audiences, namely piety. Simultaneously, it became obvious that the veil was quickly becoming a stand-in construct that ran the risk of obscuring other challenges faced by Muslim women. For example, Dwyer, having interviewed young British Muslim women, concluded that dress was an overdetermined marker of their identity in the dichotomous conceptualizations of "Western" versus "traditional," as well as "ethnic" versus "religious."[41] Indeed, young women are able to mobilize Islam as a resource in their everyday lives to advance their own gendered interests within the community to gain access to the urban public realm and greater mobility within it. Yet for these generations Islam is more than just a resource: it is also an identity for which they demand public recognition and validation.[42] It forms part of a "rejection of . . . [the] racialized coding of British civic and public culture."[43]

2001–2009: A Period of Volatile Change: New Perspectives and Perceptions of the Veil

The question of women's agency enacted through veiling became ubiquitous after the events of 9/11 and the "War on Terror," which culturally reconfigured Islamic dress. In the politically volatile period after 9/11, Western governments turned their attention to the Islamic veil, which became prominent in justifications for the "War on Terror," and in particular the attack on Afghanistan. Although the Ṭālibān regime imposed the *burqa*ʿ and severely limited Afghani girls' and women's access to education and employment many years earlier, the Western desire to "liberate" them was only made possible by the prospect of a successful military invasion and subsequent plundering of Afghanistan's natural resources (mainly oil) and humanitarian aid.[44] The *burqa*ʿ became a "synecdoche for fundamentalism, anti-modernism, and suddenly a ruthless pursuit of the terror network behind the September 11 events was transformed into a war of liberation with women as the main victors."[45] This narrative of salvation, mobilized by Western governments, delivered by figures such as Laura Bush, and recycled by media commentators on the left and right alike effectively became a cynical excuse for neocolonialism in the Middle East and beyond. Simultaneously, the veil began to increasingly signify the threatening Other internally. The securitization discourse has put Western

Muslims, and veiled Muslim girls and women in particular, in the crosshairs of discriminatory policies. As mentioned in the previous section, in addition to the 2004 French ban on the *ḥijāb* in public schools, many schools and workplaces in Europe and North America prohibited the *ḥijāb* and other forms of Islamic dress as part of their uniform, security, and health and safety regulations. It is characteristic of the discourse of the veil that it attempts to delineate the public from the private sphere through the parameter of women's bodily (in)visibility.[46]

Meanwhile, the increased popularity of the veil and associated media attention, particularly post-9/11, was mirrored by scholarly interest in the topic. Authors began to discuss the discrepancies between the ubiquitous stereotyping representations of the veil in policy and media on the one hand, and women's perspectives on the veil on the other.[47] Studies conducted in various global contexts indicated that for many women, veiling and modest comportment at large are considered to be religious obligations.[48] For others, it is a political statement signifying belonging to the Islamic community or a "passport" that allows them to move unhindered between different public and private spaces.[49] Importantly, it was also recognized, although this scenario received much less scholarly interest, that not veiling is a viable choice for many Muslim women living in the West. They may prefer to remain modest in a more inconspicuous manner, thereby facing a different set of dilemmas: while avoiding stereotypes ascribed by mainstream society to veiled women, they often have to navigate expectations regarding their conduct within their communities.[50]

Although the ultimate question regarding the "meaning of the veil" had been dissected by many academic and confessional scholars of gender and Islam, Faegheh Shirazi demonstrated in her landmark book, *The Veil Unveiled: The Hijab in Modern Culture*, that the veil operates as a polyvalent signifier, and its meanings change according to the context in which it is situated.[51] By discussing the veil's varied interpretations within contexts such as advertising (demonstrating differences between the ways in which the veil was positioned in Western and Saudi advertisements), cinematography, politics, poetry, and the state apparatus (as the veil is part of the military and police uniform in Iran, Iraq, and the UAE), Shirazi successfully exposed the Western narratives of the veil as limited in scope and depth. Although Shirazi's book was been critiqued for not engaging veiled women themselves, and, consequently, failing to include their own perspective on the practice,[52] it laid a foundation for more in-depth analyses of the veil by demonstrating its semantic versatility.

Since the publication of *The Veil Unveiled* there has been, indeed, a marked increase in inclusion of veiled Muslim women in research across humanities and social science disciplines, with the majority of work relying on interviews with women who wear the headscarf, the more common attire, and a scattering of articles analyzing firsthand experiences of face-covering as well. This literature has branched out in various directions, incorporating a plethora of theoretical perspectives illuminating the experiences of veil-wearing. The overarching argument proposed in this scholarship is that in the West, the wearing of the veil is based on women's choice as the exercise of their agency. This stands in contrast with Lama Abu Odeh's earlier assertion that the feminist possibilities of the veil are closed down by the dominant, patriarchal "rhetoric of the veil."[53] In other words, the narrative of the veil has been, to a large extent, recaptured from those who would see it as a mark of feminine submission by women who wear it with the aim of enhancing and promoting their faith. At the same time, conscious of the reductionist stereotyping of Muslim women as able to only speak out on the issue of the veil, scholars of gender and Islam contextualized this topic by addressing a number of challenges affecting Muslim women's lives, such as experiences of discrimination of higher education and employment[54] as well as local applications of Islamic family law.[55] In the United States, issues that gradually came to light included racial and class discrimination against African American Muslim women, who grappled with intersectional inequalities,[56] as well as inferior provisions for women in mosques—in particular, the low quality of women's prayer spaces and the lack of women in mosque governance structures.[57]

2010–2019: "Burqaʿ Bans," Female Muslim Voices Online, and Modest Fashion

The wave of nationwide legal prohibitions on the wearing of the veil began with the widely critiqued 2004 French ban that affected Muslim students attending French public schools. It was followed by "*burqa*ʿ bans," initially in Belgium in 2010, France in 2011, and subsequently instituted in Austria, Denmark, Tajikistan, Latvia, Bulgaria, Cameroon, Chad, the Republic of the Congo, Gabon, the Netherlands, China, and Sri Lanka. While the number of women affected by such bans in Europe was comparatively small,[58] these legislative acts gave rise to heated media and policy discussions on the possibility of women's agency in electing to wear such garments. In the case of the earlier bans, such as the French one, those advocating argued that the face-covering (niqāb) and all-enveloping, full-body garments are bound to be forced on Muslim women by their patriarchal relatives, referencing the Ṭālibān regime that required women to adopt the *burqa*ʿ. The counterarguments presented by several French Muslims who insisted that it was their own choice to cover were largely ignored.[59]

In later cases, such as in the Danish ban in 2018, the Islamic dress was framed less in terms of women's submission versus liberation, and more so as a signifier of "Islamic fundamentalism" or "extremism." Again, women's counterarguments that, for them, covering the face is simply a religious practice, went unheard by the legislators. Several challenges to the European *burqa*ʿ bans in the European Court of Human Rights were unsuccessful, but the rulings were widely criticized by legal scholars who insist that the Court's interpretation of the notion of religious practice was heavily biased toward Christian theology and should instead engage with interpretations offered by the women who wear Islamic dress in adjudicating cases that involve them, as it is the criminalization of the veil, rather than its adoption, that results in the erasure of veiled women from the public space. The complainant in *SAS vs. France* stated that as a result of the French *burqa*ʿ ban, "she is denied the right to exist as [an] individual in public."[60]

Again, as in the case of the increased media and academic focus on the *ḥijāb* post 9/11, the European wave of "*burqa*ʿ bans" triggered scholarly discussions about their legality and viability. In particular, two edited volumes *The Burqa Affair across Europe: Between Public and Private Space*[61] and *The Experiences of Face Veil Wearers in Europe and the Law*[62] brought together multiple analyses of the face veil from different disciplinary perspectives. The latter title stands out in that it actually contains chapters based on interviews with face veil wearers who are able to present their points of view. However, the literature that considers insider perspectives on the niqāb in the West often situates the analysis in one of two ways: the legal and sociopolitical contexts of the bans, or experiences of Islamophobia.[63] In other words, the bans and victimization, two types of power dynamic that disadvantage niqāb wearers, have become the key conceptual framework for interrogating them about their experiences,[64] even in national contexts where, as of 2019, no such bans have been introduced, such as the United Kingdom.[65]

Stepping outside these frameworks, many veiled women have claimed the authority to speak out about their experiences of veiling using digital text, still images, and videos on social media platforms. Various discursive strategies can be identified in online spaces, for example such as those examined by Heather Akou, who mapped the use of *ijtihād* (Islamic scholarly reasoning) in debates on what constitutes proper Islamic dress.[66] This is significant especially in the case of practices that have been touched on in the Qur'ān, but not elaborated fully. The significance of these debates is located in the encounter of different Islamic perspectives, for example from across the Sunnī-Shīʿī divide, various cultural and geographical contexts, and followers of different scholars. Such spaces operate as helpful communities of practice for women who veil, intend to veil, or are interested in the practice.[67] Some of them have actively cast Islamic dress as a type of dress characterized as "modest fashion," a global movement spearheaded by religious women preferring stylish fashion choices that allow them to avoid the often sexualized designs that have come to define mainstream fashion.[68] While at first glance, modest fashion styled by hijabistas (a *portmanteau* of *ḥijāb* and "fashionista") appears to function as a challenge to the stereotype of religious women as dowdy or frumpy, it is also an area in which women negotiate tensions between their interpretations of the faith, presentations of their personal politics, and demands of capitalism that frame their online performances (in which they may recommend a particular brand or review a halal beauty product). In so doing, they may transgress boundaries set by religious orthodoxy, and carve out alternative religious identities. For example, according to some orthodox interpretations, devout Muslim women should not appear made up. The fact that some hijabistas, like Amenakin or Dina Tokio, actually provide advice on how to look more attractive while wearing the veil, is an excuse for hostile commentators to question these women's authority to speak out on religious matters.[69] What is striking is the global reach of the hijabista movement, with Iran, Indonesia, and Turkey being important centers of modest fashion styles.[70]

Female Muslim online spaces are an arena where another central matter—the racialization of Islam—plays out. The frequent collapse between Islam and race, and, consequently, Islamophobia and racism, is currently a topic under much academic scrutiny.[71] The veil, understood as either *ḥijāb* or niqāb, is a vector that enables women to traverse the complex matrix of inequality defined by racism, classism, Islamophobia, and sexism. Depending on the context, adopting different degrees of coverage afforded by the veil allows the performance of different aspects of identity.

Discussion

This brief overview demonstrates that the Islamic veil, ostensibly a piece of cloth that some Muslim women use to wrap around their heads, or both their heads and faces, has become controversial due not to its religious but to its political nature, regardless of the intentions of women who wear it. Political actors, such as governments, legislators, political parties, movements, and individuals may define themselves through their alignment to the veil, whether through denouncing, encouraging, ignoring, or enforcing it. Their need to define, or sometimes establish themselves, and the functioning of the discourse of the veil driven by this need, have largely overshadowed the insights that veiled women have contributed to the debate on the veil.

When veiled women are genuinely engaged, they mobilize both religious and secular discourses to explain why have adopted this practice. However, as Fernando observes,[72] the religious discourse they employ may often be unintelligible to secular, culturally Judeo-Christian subjects, because veiling and other pious practices do not fit in with the binary through which religion is regulated under secular law that differentiates between the right to conscience, and the right to expression or manifestation of conscience. The former is perceived as a private, individualistic, interior experience of faith, while the latter is interpreted as external signifiers of that experience. In contrast to this binary, practices such as veiling are understood as the faith itself; this perspective has been elaborated on by Mahmood in her now classic book *Politics of Piety*.[73] This narrative is complemented by the secular narrative of personal autonomy, which frames the position that the veil is a matter of their choice. However, Fernando argues that this position (which arguably enables them to orient themselves as "modern religious subjects") severely limits their ability to argue that veiling is a religious duty within the ethical Islamic framework that they submit to. As women who veil in the West are embedded in these dominant narrative frameworks, they become competent in mobilizing secular ontologies and epistemologies in their engagement with the Islamic tradition, but simultaneously they deploy ethical practices and epistemologies of self central in Islam to "speak back to, disrupt, challenge, and reconfigure dominant secular–republican assumptions."[74]

The agency enacted by veiled Muslim women, especially those living in the West, is rooted in the ability to switch between discourses based on the requirements of the context: space, time, and audience. This kind of agency is constituted, so to speak, by the condition of secular-liberal polity, where religious argumentation, in both legal and everyday contexts, may be simply unintelligible. By formulating individualistic justifications for the veil (i.e., "it is my choice"), women attempt to engage with their secular audiences in order to safeguard their rights, claim their stake in the public sphere, and construct their position as rational individuals. This discursive position the women sometimes take does not, of course, preclude the religious (and, as participants in most studies argued, the foundational) aspect of the practice of veiling. The women who veil simply recognize that in order to be heard and understood, they need to translate this practice from religious into secular discourse. However, as Jacobsen notes, the binary between the religious and the secular is by no means clear-cut: " 'piety' cannot easily serve as a counter model to a liberal ethics of autonomy and authenticity. Rather, subjectivities and modes of agency are shaped at the intersection of different conceptions and techniques of the self, creating both convergences and tensions as people's relationship to norms and ethical conduct unfold over time."[75]

Talal Asad reflected that one's existence in the West is inevitably shaped by state interference in the life of an individual.[76] Consequently, covering in the liberal democratic context becomes denaturalized and ultimately stigmatized and unnatural, because it removes Muslim women from constant scrutiny of others. Covering up is seen as problematic in Western societies increasingly dependent on constant observation of others as well as self-scrutiny.[77] This argument is poignant in the context of how Muslim women were perceived historically, in particular in Orientalist art and literature, where they were eroticized and gazed at.[78] Khiabany and Williamson assert that "it has become impossible to talk about Islam without reference to women, and impossible to talk of Muslim women without reference to the veil."[79] Paradoxically, it is this triad that discursively produces the elusive European and American public spheres. By providing a negative reference point, imaginaries framed by progress, equality, and freedom, symbolically established in opposition to Islam, are mobilized in construction of European, British, and American identities. The veil triggers secular liberal frustrations that manifest themselves in unsurprising ways: under the guise of equality, progress, and common sense, the desire to control Muslim femininities, femininities of color, and immigrant, Asian, and nonnormative femininities takes the form of narrow racialized and cultural prescriptions. The veil is often misrepresented as inherently foreign, nonwhite, other, strange, anti-West. This otherness is often constructed on the basis of the veil portrayed as a foreign import, with no connection whatsoever to any forms of Western cultural expression. This approach is based on the notion of culture as singular and fixed, and needing preservation in a form it was encountered, partly, in the past. In this sense, this looking to the past for a source of its identity is a characteristic that the West shares with no other than many fundamentalist regimes it often claims superiority over.

Notes

1. Valeria Seigelshifer and Tova Hartman, "From Tichels to Hair Bands: Modern Orthodox Women and the Practice of Head Covering," *Women's Studies International Forum* 34, no. 5 (2011): 349–359; Elizabeth Kuhns, *The Habit* (New York: Doubleday, 2005); Janaki Abraham, "Veiling and the Production of Gender and Space in a Town in North India: A Critique of the Public/Private Dichotomy," *Indian Journal of Gender Studies* 17, no. 2 (June 2010): 191–222.
2. Yildiz Atasoy, "Muslim Organizations in Canada: Gender Ideology and Women's Veiling," *Sociological Focus* 36, no. 2 (2003): 143–158.
3. Margot Badran, *Feminists, Islam, and Nation: Gender and the Making of Modern Egypt* (Princeton, NJ: Princeton University Press, 1996); Valentine Moghadam, *Gender and National Identity: Women and Politics in Muslim Societies* (Helsinki: United Nations University World Institute for Development Economics Research, 1994); Joan Wallach Scott, *The Politics of the Veil* (Princeton, NJ: Princeton University Press, 2010).
4. Leila Ahmed, *Women in Islam: Historical Roots of a Modern Debate* (New Haven, CT: Yale University Press, 1992), 145.
5. Mohja Kahf, *Western Representations of the Muslim Woman from Termagant to Odalisque* (Austin: University of Texas Press, 1999).
6. Ahmed, *Women in Islam*, 144.
7. Ibid., 162–163.
8. Valerie Behiery, "A Short History of the (Muslim) Veil," *Implicit Religion* 16, no. 4 (2013): 413–441.
9. Ahdaf Soueif, *Mezzaterra Fragments from the Common Ground* (London: Bloomsbury, 2004), 269.
10. Ahmed, *Women in Islam.*
11. Homa Hoodfar, "Return to the Veil: Personal Strategy and Public Participation in Egypt," in *Working Women: International Perspectives on Labour and Gender Ideology*, ed. Nanneke Redclift and M. Thea Sinclair (London: Routledge, 2005), 105–126.
12. Pauline Lewis, "Zainab al-Ghazali: Pioneer of Islamist Feminism," *Journal of History* 4, no. 2 (2007): 1–47, https://michiganjournalhistory.files.wordpress.com/2014/02/lewis_pauline.pdf.
13. Miriam cooke, "Zaynab al-Ghazālī: Saint or Subversive?" *Die Welt des Islams* 34, no. 1 (1994): 1–20.
14. Meyda Yeğenoğlu, "Clash of Secularity and Religiosity: The Staging of Secularism and Islam through the Icons of Atatürk and the Veil in Turkey," in *Religion and the State: A Comparative Sociology*, ed. Jack Barbalet, Adam Possamai, and Bryan S. Turner (London: Anthem, 2011): 225–244.
15. Yeğenoğlu, "Clash of Secularity," 228.
16. Ashraf Zahedi, "Contested Meaning of the Veil and Political Ideologies of Iranian Regimes," *Journal of Middle East Women's Studies* 3, no. 3 (2007): 75–98.
17. Zahedi, "Contested Meaning," 84.
18. Kumari Jayawardena, *Feminism and Nationalism in the Third World* (London: Zed Books, 1986): 64.
19. Çagla Diner and Şule Tokaş, "Waves of Feminism in Turkey: Kemalist, Islamist and Kurdish Women's Movements in an Era of Globalization," *Journal of Balkan and Near Eastern Studies* 12, no. 1 (2010): 41–57.

20. Karen Armstrong, "My Years in a Habit Taught Me the Paradox of Veiling," *Guardian*, October 26, 2006, https://www.theguardian.com/commentisfree/2006/oct/26/comment.politics1.
21. Hoodfar, *Return to the Veil*, 105.
22. Haleh Afshar, "Epilogue," in *Iran: A Revolution in Turmoil*, ed. Haleh Afshar (Basingstoke: Macmillan, 1985): 244–253; Haideh Moghissi, *Feminism and Islamic Fundamentalism: The Limits of Postmodern Analysis* (London: Zed Books, 1999).
23. Moghissi, *Feminism*, 43–44.
24. Lama Abu Odeh, "Post-Colonial Feminism and the Veil: Thinking the Difference," *Feminist Review* 43, no. 1 (1993): 26.
25. Fatima Mernissi, *The Veil and the Male Elite: A Feminist Interpretation of Women's Rights in Islam* (New York: Perseus, 1991).
26. The earliest occurrence of *ḥijāb* in the Qur'ān is in reference to Mary and means a "curtain" or a "barrier (Qur'ān 19:17). for a fuller discussion of the term *ḥijāb* in the Qur'ān and its evolution in later centuries as a reference to women's apparel, see Barbara Freyer Stowasser, "The *Ḥijāb*: How a Curtain Became an Institution and a Cultural Symbol," in *Humanism, Culture and Language in the Near East: Studies in Honor of Georg Krotkoff*, ed. Asma Afsaruddin and Matthias Zahniser (Winona Lake, IN: Eisenbrauns, 1997), 87–104.
27. Mernissi, *The Veil*, 98.
28. Ibid., 99.
29. Ibid., 99.
30. Saba Mahmood, *Politics of Piety: The Islamic Revivalism and the Feminist Subject* (Princeton, NJ: Princeton University Press, 2005).
31. Fadwa El Guindi, "Veiling Infitah with Muslim Ethic: Egypt's Contemporary Islamic Movement," *Social Problems* 28, no. 4 (1981): 465–485.
32. Hoodfar, *Return to the Veil*, 106.
33. Hanna Papanek, "Purdah: Separate Worlds and Symbolic Shelter," *Comparative Studies in Society and History* 15, no. 3 (1973): 289–325.
34. Sylvia Chan-Malik, "Chadors, Feminists, Terror," *Annals of the American Academy of Political and Social Science* 637, no. 1 (2011): 112–140.
35. Chan-Malik, "Chadors," 121.
36. Claire Dwyer, "Veiled Meanings: Young British Muslim Women and the Negotiation of Differences," *Gender, Place and Culture* 6, no. 1 (1999): 5–26.
37. Sarah V. Wayland, "Religious Expression in Public Schools: Kirpans in Canada, Hijab in France," *Ethnic and Racial Studies* 20, no. 3 (1997): 545–561.
38. Hege Skjeie, "Headscarves in Schools: European Comparisons," in *Religious Pluralism and Human Rights in Europe: Where to Draw the Line?*, ed. Titia Loenen and Jenny Goldschmidt (Cambridge: Intersentia, 2007): 129–145; Anna Piela, *Wearing the Niqab: Muslim Women in the UK and the US* (London: Bloomsbury Academic, 2021).
39. Carmen Cayer, "Hijab, Narrative, and the Production of Gender among Second Generation, Indo-Pakistani, Muslim Women in Greater Toronto" (Master's thesis, York University, 1996). Jasmin Zine, "Muslim Students in Public Schools: Education and the Politics of Religious Identity" (Master's thesis, University of Toronto, 2007), https://tspace.library.utoronto.ca/bitstream/1807/11769/1/MQ28728.pdf.
40. Debra Reece, "Covering and Communication: The Symbolism of Dress among Muslim Women," *Howard Journal of Communications* 7, no. 1 (1996): 35–52.
41. Dwyer, "Veiled Meanings," 11.

42. Munira Mirza, "Multiculturalism, Religion and Identity," in *Pakistani Diaspora Culture, Conflict, and Change*, ed. Virinder Kalra (Oxford: Oxford University Press, 2009): 273–284.
43. Ash Amin, "Unruly Strangers? The 2001 Urban Riots in Britain," *International Journal of Urban and Regional Research* 27, no. 2 (2003): 462.
44. Gholam Khiabany and Milly Williamson, "Muslim Women and Veiled Threats: From 'Civilising Mission' to 'Clash of Civilisations,'" in *Pointing the Finger: Islam and Muslims in the British Media*, ed. Julian Petley (London: Oneworld, 2011): 173–200.
45. Annabelle Sreberny, "Unsuitable Coverage: The Media, the Veil, and Regimes of Representation," in *Global Currents: Media and Technology Now*, ed. Tasha G. Oren and Patrice Petro (New Brunswick, NJ: Rutgers University Press, 2004): 176.
46. Nilüfer Göle, "Secularism and Islamism in Turkey: The Making of Elites and Counter-Elites," *Middle East Journal* 51, no. 1 (1997): 46–58.
47. Katherine Bullock and Gul Joya Jafri, "Media (Mis)Representations: Muslim Women in the Canadian Nation," *Canadian Women's Studies* 20, no. 2 (2000): 35–40; Rachel Anderson Droogsma, "Redefining Hijab: American Muslim Women's Standpoints on Veiling," *Journal of Applied Communication Research* 35, no. 3 (2007): 294–319; Emma Tarlo, "Hijab in London: Metamorphosis, Resonance and Effects," *Journal of Material Culture* 12, no. 2 (2007): 131–156; Smeeta Mishra and Faegheh Shirazi, "Hybrid Identities: American Muslim Women Speak," *Gender, Place and Culture* 17, no. 2 (2010): 191–209; Nahed Eltantawy, "Above the Fold and beyond the Veil," in *The Routledge Companion to Media and Gender*, ed. Cynthia Carter, Linda Steiner, and Lisa McLaughlin (New York: Routledge, 2013): 384–394.
48. See Mahmood, *Politics of Piety*, 51.
49. Tabassum F. Ruby, "Listening to the Voices of Hijab," *Women's Studies International Forum* 29, no. 1 (2006): 54–66; Anicée Van Engeland, "What If? An Experiment to Include a Religious Narrative in the Approach of the European Court of Human Rights," *Journal of Law, Religion and State* 7, no. 2 (2019): 213–241.
50. Ruby, "Listening," 62.
51. Faegheh Shirazi, *The Veil Unveiled: The Hijab in Modern Culture* (Gainesville: University Press of Florida, 2001).
52. Katherine Bullock, "The Veil Unveiled: The Hijab in Modern Culture," review of *The Veil Unveiled*, by Faegheh Shirazi, in the *American Journal of Islamic Social Sciences* 19, no. 4 (2002): 118–121.
53. Odeh, "Post-Colonial Feminism," 36.
54. David Tyrer and Fauzia Ahmad, "Muslim Women and Higher Education: Identities, Experiences, and Prospects," unpublished report, European Social Fund, Liverpool John Moores University.
55. Ziba Mir-Hosseini, *Islam and Gender: The Religious Debate in Contemporary Iran* (Princeton, NJ: Princeton University Press, 1999); Ziba Mir-Hosseini, "Muslim Women's Quest for Equality: Between Islamic Law and Feminism," *Critical Inquiry* 32, no. 4 (Summer 2006): 629–645.
56. Jamillah Karim, *American Muslim Women: Negotiating Race, Class, and Gender Within the Ummah* (New York: New York University Press, 2008); Carolyn Moxley Rouse, *Engaged Surrender: African American Women and Islam* (Berkeley: University of California Press, 2004).

57. Jamila Hussain, "Finding the Women's Space: Muslim Women and the Mosque," in *Beyond the Hijab Debates: New Conversations on Gender, Race and Religion*, ed. Tanja Dreher and Christina Ho (Cambridge: Cambridge Scholars Publishing, 2009): 52–66.
58. Nilufar Ahmed, "So Few Muslim Women Wear the Burqa in Europe That Banning It is a Waste of Time," *Conversation*, August 30, 2017, https://theconversation.com/so-few-muslim-women-wear-the-burqa-in-europe-that-banning-it-is-a-waste-of-time-82957.
59. Mayanthi L. Fernando, "Reconfiguring Freedom: Muslim Piety and the Limits of Secular Law and Public Discourse in France," *American Ethnologist* 37, no. 1 (2010): 19–35.
60. Van Engeland, "What If," 219.
61. Alessandro Ferrari and Sabrina Pastorelli, eds., *The Burqa Affair across Europe: Between Public and Private Space* (London: Routledge, 2013).
62. Eva Brems, ed., *The Experiences of Face Veil Wearers in Europe and the Law* (Cambridge: Cambridge University Press, 2014).
63. Neil Chakraborti and Irene Zempi, "The Veil under Attack: Gendered Dimensions of Islamophobic Victimization," *International Review of Victimology* 18, no. 3 (2012): 269–284; Irene Zempi, "Veiled Muslim Women's Views on Law Banning the Wearing of the Niqab (Face Veil) in Public," *Ethnic and Racial Studies* 42, no. 15 (2019): 2585–2602; Irene Zempi and Neil Chakraborti, *Islamophobia, Victimisation and the Veil* (Houndmills: Palgrave Macmillan, 2014).
64. Eva Brems, Yaiza Janssens, Kim Lecoyer, Saïla Ouald Chaib, and Victoria Vanderstaan "Wearing the Face Veil in Belgium," unpublished report, University of Ghent, 2012, https://biblio.ugent.be/publication/8635340; Annelies Moors, "Face Veiling in the Netherlands: Public Debates and Women's Narratives," in *The Experiences of Face Veil Wearers in Europe and the Law*, ed. Eva Brems (Cambridge: Cambridge University Press, 2014): 19–41; Kate Østergaard, Margit Warburg, and Birgitte Schepelern Johansen, "Niqabis in Denmark: When Politicians Ask for a Qualitative and Quantitative Profile of a Very Small and Elusive Subculture," in *The Experiences of Face Veil Wearers in Europe and the Law*, ed. Eva Brems (Cambridge: Cambridge University Press, 2014): 42–76.
65. See Zempi, "Veiled Muslim Women."
66. Heather Akou, "Interpreting Islam through the Internet: Making Sense of Hijab," *Contemporary Islam* 4, no. 3 (2010): 331–346.
67. Anna Piela, "Online Islamic Spaces as Communities of Practice for Female Muslim Converts Who Wear the Niqab," *Hawwa* 13, no. 3 (2015): 363–382.
68. Reina Lewis, ed., *Modest Fashion: Styling Bodies, Mediating Faith* (London: Bloomsbury Academic, 2013); Elizabeth Bucar, *Pious Fashion: How Muslim Women Dress* (Cambridge, MA: Harvard University Press, 2017).
69. Kristin M. Peterson, "Beyond Fashion Tips and Hijab Tutorials: The Aesthetic Style of Islamic Lifestyle Videos," *Film Criticism* 40, no. 2 (2016), https://quod.lib.umich.edu/f/fc/13761232.0040.203/--beyond-fashion-tips-and-hijab-tutorials-the-aesthetic-style?rgn=main;view=fulltext.
70. Bucar, *Pious Fashion*, 1.
71. Sylvia Chan-Malik, *Being Muslim: A Cultural History of Women of Color in American Islam* (New York: New York University Press, 2017); Piela, *Wearing the Niqab*.
72. Fernando, "Reconfiguring Freedom," 20.
73. Mahmood, *Politics of Piety*, 51.
74. Fernando, "Reconfiguring Freedom," 20.

75. Christine M. Jacobsen, "Troublesome Threesome: Feminism, Anthropology and Muslim Women's Piety," *Feminist Review* 98, no. 1 (2011): 79.
76. Talal Asad, "The Idea of Anthropology of Islam," *Qui Parle* 17, no. 2 (2009): 19.
77. Michel Foucault, "Technologies of the Self," in *Technologies of the Self* (Amherst: University of Massachusetts Press, 1988), 16–49.
78. Kahf, *Western Representations*, 144.
79. Khiabany and Williamson, "Muslim Women," 173.

Bibliography

Abu-Lughod, Lila. "Do Muslim Women Really Need Saving? Anthropological Reflections on Cultural Relativism and Its Others." *American Anthropologist* 104, no. 3 (2002): 783–790.

Afshar, Haleh. "Epilogue." In *Iran: A Revolution in Turmoil*, edited by Haleh Afshar, 244–253. Basingstoke: Macmillan, 1985.

Ahmed, Leila. *Women in Islam: Historical Roots of a Modern Debate*. New Haven, CT: Yale University Press, 1992.

Ahmed, Nilufar. "So Few Muslim Women Wear the Burqa in Europe That Banning It Is a Waste of Time." *Conversation*, August 30, 2017, https://theconversation.com/so-few-muslim-women-wear-the-burqa-in-europe-that-banning-it-is-a-waste-of-time-82957.

Akou, Heather. "Interpreting Islam through the Internet: Making Sense of Hijab." *Contemporary Islam* 4, no. 3 (2010): 331–346.

Amin, Ash. "Unruly Strangers? The 2001 Urban Riots in Britain." *International Journal of Urban and Regional Research* 27, no. 2 (2003): 460–463.

Anderson Droogsma, Rachel. "Redefining Hijab: American Muslim Women's Standpoints on Veiling." *Journal of Applied Communication Research* 35, no. 3 (2007): 294–319.

Armstrong, Karen. "My Years in a Habit Taught Me the Paradox of Veiling," *Guardian*, October 26, 2006, https://www.theguardian.com/commentisfree/2006/oct/26/comment.politics1

Asad, Talal. "The Idea of Anthropology of Islam." *Qui Parle* 17, no. 2 (2009): 1–30.

Atasoy, Yildiz. "Muslim Organizations in Canada: Gender Ideology and Women's Veiling." *Sociological Focus* 36, no. 2 (2003): 143–158.

Badran, Margot. *Feminists, Islam, and Nation: Gender and the Making of Modern Egypt*. Princeton, NJ: Princeton University Press, 1996.

Behiery, Valerie. "A Short History of the (Muslim) Veil." *Implicit Religion* 16, no. 4 (2013): 413–441.

Brems, Eva, Yaiza Janssens, Kim Lecoyer, Saïla Ouald Chaib, and Victoria Vanderstaan. "Wearing the Face Veil in Belgium." Unpublished report, University of Ghent, 2012, https://biblio.ugent.be/publication/8635340.

Bucar, Elizabeth. *Pious Fashion: How Muslim Women Dress*. Cambridge, MA: Harvard University Press, 2017.

Bullock, Katherine. "The Veil Unveiled: The Hijab in Modern Culture." Review of *The Veil Unveiled*, by Faegheh Shirazi. *American Journal of Islamic Social Sciences* 19, no. 4 (2002): 118–121.

Bullock, Katherine, and Gul Joya Jafri, "Media (Mis)Representations: Muslim Women in the Canadian Nation." *Canadian Women's Studies* 20, no. 2 (2000): 35–40.

Brems, Eva, ed. *The Experiences of Face Veil Wearers in Europe and the Law*. Cambridge: Cambridge University Press, 2014.

Bullock, Katherine. *Rethinking Muslim Women and the Veil.* Herndon, VA: IIIT, 2002.
Cayer, Carmen. "Hijab, Narrative, and the Production of Gender among Second Generation, Indo-Pakistani, Muslim Women in Greater Toronto." Master's thesis, York University, 1996.
Chakraborti, Neil, and Irene Zempi. "The Veil under Attack: Gendered Dimensions of Islamophobic Victimization." *International Review of Victimology* 18, no. 3 (2012): 269–284.
Chan-Malik, Sylvia. "Chadors, Feminists, Terror." *Annals of the American Academy of Political and Social Science* 637, no. 1 (2011): 112–140.
Chan-Malik, Sylvia. *Being Muslim: A Cultural History of Women of Color in American Islam.* New York: New York University Press, 2017.
Cooke, miriam. "Zaynab al-Ghazālī: Saint or Subversive?" *Die Welt des Islams* 34, no. 1 (1994): 1–20.
Diner, Çagla, and Şule Tokaş. "Waves of Feminism in Turkey: Kemalist, Islamist and Kurdish Women's Movements in an Era of Globalization." *Journal of Balkan and Near Eastern Studies* 12, no. 1 (2010): 41–57.
Dreher, Tanja, and Christina Ho, eds. *Beyond the Hijab Debates: New Conversations on Gender, Race and Religion.* Cambridge: Cambridge Scholars, 2009.
Dwyer, Claire. "Veiled Meanings: Young British Muslim Women and the Negotiation of Differences." *Gender, Place and Culture* 6, no. 1 (1999): 5–26.
El Guindi, Fadwa. "Veiling Infitah with Muslim Ethic: Egypt's Contemporary Islamic Movement." *Social Problems* 28, no. 4 (1981): 465–485.
Eltantawy, Nahed. "Above the Fold and beyond the Veil." In *The Routledge Companion to Media and Gender*, edited by Cynthia Carter, Linda Steiner, and Lisa McLaughlin, 384–394. New York: Routledge, 2013.
Fernando, Mayanthi L. "Reconfiguring Freedom: Muslim Piety and the Limits of Secular Law and Public Discourse in France." *American Ethnologist* 37, no. 1 (2010): 19–35.
Ferrari, Alessandro, and Sabrina Pastorelli. *The Burqa Affair across Europe.* London: Routledge, 2013.
Foucault, Michel. "Technologies of the Self." In *Technologies of the Self*, 16–49. Amherst: University of Massachusetts Press, 1988.
Franks, Myfanwy. *Women and Revivalism in the West.* New York: Palgrave, 2001.
Freyer Stowasser, Barbara. "The *Ḥijāb*: How a Curtain Became an Institution and a Cultural Symbol." In *Humanism, Culture and Language in the Near East: Studies in Honor of Georg Krotkoff*, edited by Asma Afsaruddin and Matthias Zahniser, 87–104. Winona Lake, IN: Eisenbrauns, 1997.
Göle, Nilüfer. "Secularism and Islamism in Turkey: The Making of Elites and Counter-Elites." *Middle East Journal* 51, no. 1 (1997): 46–58.
Hoodfar, Homa. "Return to the Veil: Personal Strategy and Public Participation in Egypt." In *Working Women: International Perspectives on Labour and Gender Ideology*, edited by Nanneke Redclift and M. Thea Sinclair, 105–126. London: Routledge, 2005.
Hussain, Jamila. "Finding the Women's Space: Muslim Women and the Mosque." In *Beyond the Hijab Debates: New Conversations on Gender, Race and Religion*, edited by Tanja Dreher and Christina Ho, 52–66. Cambridge: Cambridge Scholars, 2009.
Inge, Annabel. *The Making of a Salafi Muslim Woman: Paths to Conversion.* Oxford: Oxford University Press, 2017.
Jacobsen, Christine M. "Troublesome Threesome: Feminism, Anthropology and Muslim Women's Piety." *Feminist Review* 98, no. 1 (2011): 65–82.

Janaki, Abraham. "Veiling and the Production of Gender and Space in a Town in North India: A Critique of the Public/Private Dichotomy." *Indian Journal of Gender Studies* 17, no. 2 (2010): 191–222.

Jayawardena, Kumari. *Feminism and Nationalism in the Third World*. London: Zed Books, 1986.

Kahf, Mohja. *Western Representations of the Muslim Woman from Termagant to Odalisque*. Austin: University of Texas Press, 2002.

Karim, Jamillah. *American Muslim Women: Negotiating Race, Class, and Gender within the Ummah*. New York: New York University Press, 2008.

Khiabany, Gholam, and Milly Williamson. "Muslim Women and Veiled Threats: From 'Civilising Mission' to 'Clash of Civilisations.'" In *Pointing the Finger: Islam and Muslims in the British Media*, edited by Julian Petley, 173–200. London: Oneworld, 2011.

Kuhns, Elizabeth. *The Habit*. Reprint, New York: Doubleday, 2005.

Lewis, Pauline. "Zainab al-Ghazali: Pioneer of Islamist Feminism." *Journal of History* 4, no. 2 (2007): 1–47, https://michiganjournalhistory.files.wordpress.com/2014/02/lewis_pauline.pdf.

Lewis, Reina, ed. *Modest Fashion: Styling Bodies, Mediating Faith*. London: Bloomsbury, 2013.

Mahmood, Saba. *Politics of Piety: The Islamic Revivalism and the Feminist Subject*. Princeton, NJ: Princeton University Press, 2005.

Mernissi, Fatima. *The Veil and the Male Elite: A Feminist Interpretation of Women's Rights in Islam*. New York: Perseus, 1991.

Mir-Hosseini, Ziba. *Islam and Gender: The Religious Debate in Contemporary Iran*. Princeton, NJ: Princeton University Press,1999.

Mir-Hosseini, Ziba. "Muslim Women's Quest for Equality: Between Islamic Law and Feminism." *Critical Inquiry* 32, no. 4 (Summer 2006): 629–645.

Mishra, Smeeta, and Faegheh Shirazi. "Hybrid Identities: American Muslim Women Speak." *Gender, Place and Culture* 17, no. 2 (2010): 191–209.

Moghadam, Valentine. *Gender and National Identity: Women and Politics in Muslim Societies*. Helsinki: United Nations University World Institute for Development Economics Research, 1994.

Moghissi, Haideh. *Feminism and Islamic Fundamentalism: The Limits of Postmodern Analysis*. London: Zed Books, 1999.

Moors, Annelies. "Face Veiling in the Netherlands: Public Debates and Women's Narratives." In *The Experiences of Face Veil Wearers in Europe and the Law*, edited by Eva Brems, 19–41. Cambridge: Cambridge University Press, 2014.

Moxley Rouse, Carolyn. *Engaged Surrender: African American Women and Islam*. Berkeley: University of California Press, 2004.

Mirza, Munira. "Multiculturalism, Religion and Identity." In *Pakistani Diaspora Culture, Conflict, and Change*, edited by Virinder Kalra, 273–284. Oxford: Oxford University Press, 2009.

Østergaard, Kate, Margit Warburg, and Birgitte Schepelern Johansen. "Niqabis in Denmark: When Politicians Ask for a Qualitative and Quantitative Profile of a Very Small and Elusive Subculture." In *The Experiences of Face Veil Wearers in Europe and the Law*, edited by Eva Brems, 42–76. Cambridge: Cambridge University Press, 2014.

Peterson, Kristin M. "Beyond Fashion Tips and Hijab Tutorials: The Aesthetic Style of Islamic Lifestyle Videos." *Film Criticism* 40, no. 2 (2016), https://quod.lib.umich.edu/f/fc/13761232.0040.203/--beyond-fashion-tips-and-hijab-tutorials-the-aesthetic-style?rgn=main;view=fulltext.

Piela, Anna. "Online Islamic Spaces as Communities of Practice for Female Muslim Converts Who Wear the Niqab." *Hawwa* 13, no. 3 (2015): 363–382.

Piela, Anna. *Wearing the Niqab: Muslim Women in the UK and the US*. London: Bloomsbury, 2021.
Reece, Debra. "Covering and Communication: The Symbolism of Dress among Muslim Women." *Howard Journal of Communications* 7, no. 1 (1996): 35–52.
Ruby, Tabassum F. "Listening to the Voices of Hijab." *Women's Studies International Forum* 29, no. 1 (2006): 54–66.
Scott, Joan Wallach. *The Politics of the Veil*. Princeton, NJ: Princeton University Press, 2010.
Seigelshifer, Valeria, and Tova Hartman. "From Tichels to Hair Bands: Modern Orthodox Women and the Practice of Head Covering." *Women's Studies International Forum* 34, no. 5 (2011): 349–359.
Shirazi, Faegheh. *The Veil Unveiled: The Hijab in Modern Culture*. Gainesville: University of Florida Press, 2001.
Soueif, Ahdaf. *Mezzaterra Fragments from the Common Ground*. London: Bloomsbury, 2004.
Sreberny, Annabelle. "Unsuitable Coverage: The Media, the Veil, and Regimes of Representation." In *Global Currents: Media and Technology Now*, edited by Tasha G. Oren and Patrice Petro, 171–185. New Brunswick, NJ: Rutgers University Press, 2004.
Tarlo, Emma. "Hijab in London: Metamorphosis, Resonance and Effects." *Journal of Material Culture* 12, no. 2 (2007): 131–156.
Tarlo, Emma, and Annelies Moors, eds. *Islamic Fashion and Anti-Fashion: New Perspectives from Europe and North America*. London: Bloomsbury Academic, 2013.
Tyrer, David, and Fauzia Ahmad, "Muslim Women and Higher Education: Identities, Experiences, and Prospects." Unpublished report, European Social Fund, Liverpool John Moores University, 2007, http://www.mywf.org.uk/uploads/projects/borderlines/Archive/2007/muslimwomen.pdf.
Van Engeland, Anicée. "What If? An Experiment to Include a Religious Narrative in the Approach of the European Court of Human Rights." *Journal of Law, Religion and State* 7, no. 2 (2019): 213–241.
Wayland, Sarah V. "Religious Expression in Public Schools: Kirpans in Canada, Hijab in France." *Ethnic and Racial Studies* 20, no. 3 (1997): 545–561.
Yeğenoğlu, Meyda. "Clash of Secularity and Religiosity: The Staging of Secularism and Islam through the Icons of Atatürk and the Veil in Turkey." In *Religion and the State: A Comparative Sociology*, edited by Jack Barbalet, Adam Possamai, and Bryan S. Turner, 225–244. London: Anthem, 2011.
Zahedi, Ashraf. "Contested Meaning of the Veil and Political Ideologies of Iranian Regimes." *Journal of Middle East Women's Studies* 3, no. 3 (2007): 75–98.
Zempi, Irene. "Veiled Muslim Women's Views on Law Banning the Wearing of the Niqab (Face Veil) in Public." *Ethnic and Racial Studies* 42, no. 15 (2019): 2585–2602.
Zempi, Irene, and Neil Chakraborti. *Islamophobia, Victimisation and the Veil*. Houndmills: Palgrave Macmillan, 2014.
Zine, Jasmin. "Muslim Students in Public Schools: Education and the Politics of Religious Identity." Master's thesis, University of Toronto, 2007.

CHAPTER 32

MUSLIM WOMEN AS A CULTURAL TROPE

Global Discourses and the Politics of Victimhood

KATHERINE BULLOCK

As a Muslim woman in *ḥijāb* who had been spat on after September 11 while walking with her three-year-old son in Birmingham, UK, Salma Yacoob began to feel less vulnerable once she became involved in the antiwar movement.[1] Yacoob experienced exclusion, hate, and activist resistance to negative stereotyping while opposing the War on Terror (WoT), all of which illustrate the nexus of several key themes related to the problematic of "Muslim Women as a Cultural Trope: Global Discourses and the Politics of Victimhood."

The politics of victimhood is not about Muslim women claiming to be victims and developing a politics around it. Rather it is about a monolithic concept of Muslim women as victims who need to be saved by the knight in shining armor—the white Western male and his female accomplice.

When an idea or image is used frequently it is called a "trope." When a trope occurs often it becomes a cliché—an overused and unoriginal idea. The notion that Muslim women are victims who need saving is now a cliché, having been a predominant image of Muslim women in the Western imagination since the late-1800s.[2] Orientalism in painting and literature depicted Muslim women as enslaved or imprisoned in a "harem." The "harem" was simply the women's quarters of their house; it became a trope signifying a gaggle of women with nothing to do but provide sexual enjoyment for their master. The veil signified their imprisonment when outside. Unfortunately, the cliché of the Muslim-woman-as-victim-needing-saving has not been confined to art. European colonialism partly justified itself during the nineteenth century as necessary to save Muslim women. The war on Afghanistan after September 11 was also justified as necessary to save Muslim women. Wars of conquest need galvanizing images of "the enemy." Tropes such as the Muslim-woman-as-victim-needing-saving play complex roles in the stories of self-delusion that societies tell themselves about their motivations as well as masking material interests that are always present in human motivation.

This chapter reviews the scholarly literature examining the production and utility of the Muslim-woman-as-victim-needing-saving cliché since September 11.[3] This is a narrow topic that is related to a vast scholarship in multiple disciplines that study the situation of Muslim women and/in/of the West. This topic sits at the intersections of anthropology, area studies, cultural studies, gender studies, history, Islamic studies, media studies, political science, and sociology. Because the manufacturing of a cliché involves multiple aspects of the human condition, each discipline spotlights a slightly different facet of the topic. My focus here is on Western cultural discourse production, although a cognate study would be how other cultures take up these tropes for their own political ends—China, India, Israel, Myanmar, and Russia are obvious candidates.

Previous review essays of academic literature related to gender and the Middle East found an absence of debate over key themes, except for two questions related to the possibility of feminism within Islam and the oppressive nature or not of the headscarf.[4] Scholars spoke in a "voice of unison"[5] that their work aimed to challenge negative stereotypes of Muslim women as "silent, passive, subordinate, victimized, and powerless."[6] This was true in Lila Abu-Lughod's pre–September 11 survey,[7] and in Mounira Charrad's 2011 one, though neither focused on the War on Terror literature.

Similarly, this review found that the academics who analyze global Western discourses about Muslim women in relation to the politics of Muslim women's victimhood, speak principally as one voice: They call out the racism in representations; they expose hypocrisy in imperial wars that justify themselves in feminist terms; they challenge the myth of a monolithic oppressed Muslim woman needing saving; and they trace the connections between colonial and contemporary representations, and between colonial and contemporary imperial politics. The most important differences of opinion revolve around how to respond to the connections between tropes of Muslim women's victimhood and the War on Terror. Should Muslim women embrace secularism and liberalism? Should all Muslim women unveil? Should we embrace or contest the "good Muslim/bad Muslim" dichotomy? What is the role of class, race, ethnicity, or regionalism in responding to the monolithic trope of the oppressed Muslim woman who needs saving? What are you saving her to, asks Abu-Lughod?[8]

No matter their home discipline, in addition to disciplinarily relevant theories and methodologies, there is a common pool of core sources. The scholars' objects for analysis are those who use the trope uncritically; they are the textual examples used to make the case that there is a "politics of victimhood" around Muslim women that masks imperial projects overseas and anti-Muslim racism at home.

Three relevant areas of study predate September 11: media representation of Muslim women; hate crimes and anti-Muslim racism; and studies of Muslim women and the headscarf. September 11 exists now as a backdrop to every conversation about Muslims and the West. Many post–September 11 articles on these topics mention the WoT only briefly, or not at all. The literature on media representations, Islamophobia, and headscarves is vast. It is included here only when an author connects their study explicitly to September 11 and the WoT.

This chapter will explore three core themes[9] related to the topic of "Muslim Women as a Cultural Trope: Global Discourses and the Politics of Victimhood":

1. The WoT's Tropes as a Continuation of Colonial and Orientalist Themes
2. The Role of Imperial Feminism
3. Continuities and Discontinuities in Representations of Muslim Women and Men.

The War on Terror's Tropes as a Continuation of Colonial and Orientalist Themes

George W. Bush launched the WoT on September 16, 2001, as a response to the September 11 attacks on the World Trade Center and the Pentagon by Muslim terrorists.[10] Soon after, in November, his wife, Laura Bush, addressed the nation via radio, explaining how an essential part of this campaign was bombing Afghanistan. Invoking the suffering of Afghan women under the Taliban regime, Laura Bush argued for the importance of the war between " 'the civilized people throughout the world' whose hearts break for the women and children of Afghanistan and the Taliban-and-the terrorists, the cultural monsters who want to . . . 'impose their world on the rest of us.' "[11] Laura Bush went on to explain, "Because of our recent military gains in much of Afghanistan, women are no longer imprisoned in their homes. They can listen to music and teach their daughters without fear of punishment. . . . The fight against terrorism is also a fight for the rights and dignity of women."[12] The wife of British prime minister, Cherie Blair, followed Laura Bush's November address a few days later, saying, "We need to free that spirit and give them their voice back, so they can create the better Afghanistan we all want to see."[13]

As scholars were quick to recognize, this was déjà vu for Muslims, as "saving Muslim women" had been part of the ideology of colonialism. Lord Cromer, the British Consul General for Egypt from 1883–1907, once said:

> The European reformer may instruct, he may explain, he may argue, he may devise the most ingenious methods for the moral and material development of the people, he may use his best endeavours to "cut blocks with a razor" and to graft true civilisation on a society which is but just emerging from barbarism, but unless he proves himself able, not only to educate, but to elevate the woman, he will never succeed in affording to the man, in any thorough degree, the only education which is worthy of Europe.[14]

To understand this aspect of the WoT, scholars often cite Gayatri Spivak's famous phrase of "white men saving brown women from brown men."[15] Spivak wrote this in 1988 due to her analysis of British colonial attempts at abolishing the Hindu practice of *sati* (burning widows on the funeral pyres of their husbands). Spivak's pithy phrase sums up the WoT in eight simple words.

We can see other important parallels between the Bushes' justifications of the war and Cromer's: the binary posed between the "civilized" West and the "barbaric" Muslim; the "superior" Westerner and the "inferior" Muslim; the "elevated" Western woman and the "suppressed" Muslim woman. These rigid binaries are examples of something called "culture talk"—a perspective exemplified in Samuel Huntington's clash of civilizations thesis[16]—and theorized before September 11 by Edward Said[17] and after September 11 by Abu-Lughod and Mahmood Mamdani.[18] Culture talk locates the explanations for Muslims' social and political behavior in religion or culture, rather than in history, socioeconomic relations, and power politics.

Huntington's heavily criticized 1993 theory, which saw a new lease on life after September 11, had divided the world into seven or eight major civilizations. Civilizations were divided on "basic" grounds of "history, language, culture, tradition" but most importantly: religion. The West was distinguished from the rest as having superior values, such as democratic governance, that was only found in other civilizations due to "colonialism or imposition."[19] Rather than considering history, economics, and politics, he claimed that conflict in the coming decades would be based on these basic cultural differences and that "Islam had bloody borders."[20] He proposed in the context of the fall of Communism (1989) that the next world war would be a civilizational war, likely between the West and a Confucian-Islamic alliance, the two cultures most unable to adopt Western "universal" civilizational values.

Huntington's paradigm of Islam versus the West was a major concept shaping foreign and domestic policy in many Western countries after September 11.[21] Unfortunately initially linking the WoT to a "crusade," Bush's language evolved to speak not of a crusade against Islam, but a war on terrorists, who were represented as "evil" and "fundamentalists" who had "hijacked" Islam.[22] Jill Steans suggests that this distinction between "Islam" and the "extremists" was a necessary part of the "war story," since they needed to portray the war as something "ordinary" Afghans would support, and thus what was involved was not so much a "clash of civilisations" but "fundamentalism . . . the 'enemy' of 'civilisation and freedom.'"[23] Sunaina Maira draws our attention to this shift from "clash" to "reform" as part of the war effort that sought to create a body of "moderate" Muslims at home and abroad who would not be opposed to US hegemony.[24] Nevertheless, this emphasis on civilization versus barbarism was predicated on a culturalist assumption that all the world's countries should evolve to be replicas of Western civilization. Bush asked, "Why do they hate us?" and the answer was not "because of our support for dictators that suppress them," or "because of their lack of economic opportunities due to western global capitalism," but because they "hate our freedoms" as they come from an "archaic culture" that hates "modernism."[25]

Said's *Orientalism*, published in 1979, is one of the most referenced works accessed by scholars to understand the connection between tropes of Muslim women as victims needing saving and the WoT. Orientalist scholarship is an example of "culture talk." It is predicated on rigid, unchanging, and monolithic categories of the superior Westerner and inferior Oriental, who are, above all, *different* due to their religion (nineteenth century) and (now) culture. The difference was captured in enduring tropes of Muslim men symbolizing "terror, devastation, the demonic, hordes of hated barbarians" whom Europeans had feared for centuries,[26] and the exoticized Muslim woman behind the veil. Orientalist imagery of the exotic but oppressed-in-her-veil Muslim woman was a staple metaphor for the "degraded East" in need of Western civilization. Colonial politicians and missionaries seized on this notion to explain why they were in the Orient. This parallels the contemporary focus explaining why the US military is in Afghanistan and why Western women are called on to support the war.[27]

The corporate media, rather than interrogating the political and historical motivations behind the September 11 attacks, produced reports replicating the binaries mentioned above.[28] According to Steans this is because they were less able to maintain "professional distance" in their reporting.[29] The "women of cover," as Bush called them,[30] became a focal point of media conversations about Muslim women. The Afghan burqa—in English reportage, a "veil"—became the symbol of Taliban extremism. Rather than understanding the clothing in its social context (Afghan women wore the burqa before the Taliban came to power, and they wore it after the Taliban lost power too[31]), a monolithic concept of "the veil" that all Muslim women wore was deterritorialized, becoming a symbol of Muslim's women's oppression compared to the "freedoms Western women enjoy [unveiled]."[32] Media stories celebrating Muslim women did so as long as they conformed to this image of empowerment.[33] In the colonial era Christian supersessionism had provided a rationale for the *mission civilisatrice* of European colonialism.[34] Unveiling women was as important then as it was for Bush's WoT.

Hunt and Rygiel theorize this obfuscating use of the "imperilled Muslim woman" needing rescue (in Sherene Razack's striking phrase[35]) through the concept of "camouflage politics."[36] Camouflage politics is the "official" war story told to "*camouflage* the interests, agendas, policies, and politics that underpin the war in order to legitimize and gain consent for the war on terror."[37] Lord Cromer, while co-opting the language of women's rights in order to justify conquest of Egypt, at the same time was a founding member and a president of the Men's League for Opposing Women's Suffrage in England.[38] Eisenstein, Stean, and others point to similar hypocrisies with Bush's WoT: prior to 9/11, the Bush administration was negotiating with the Taliban over developing oil pipelines; in post-Taliban Afghanistan they supported warlords from the Northern Alliance known to perpetrate violence against women. Coalition soldiers assaulted Iraqi and Afghan women as well as female coalition soldiers; Bush closed the Women's Bureau in the Labor Department, as well as the White House Women's office; repealed regulations allowing family leave, cut childcare funding; defunded battered women's programs, and selected nominees for judicial appointments who oppose protection in sexual harassment; and appointed as head of the Federal Drug Association someone who did not believe in birth control.[39] It is quite a list. No wonder Hunt and Rygiel concluded: "Far from being a war for women's rights, we conclude that the war is, in fact, a war on women's rights."[40]

Like the European colonial rulers who sought to discipline and manage their colonized populations, the WoT has inflicted the same kind of discipline and control on Muslim minority populations in the home country. In the literature reviewed for this chapter, many scholars connect the colonial and orientalist tropes of the WoT to domestic policies around asylum, immigration controls, border/airport experiences, surveillance, policing, detention, security certificates, values tests for immigrants, and unveiling laws.[41] Naz Rashid documents how the British Prevent antiterrorism program used the clash thesis by locating "radicalization" in "problematic interpretations of Islam . . . [that was] [d]ominated by a rescue paradigm in relation to Muslim women."[42] Narzanin Massoumi argued that focusing on Muslim women was due to a "counterterrorism strategy [that] assumed Muslim women to be more liberal and beneficial to fostering a Muslim mainstream than Muslim men, presenting women as the key to countering the disenfranchisement of Muslim radicalization and extremism."[43]

Role of Imperial Feminism

How can we support Muslim women's rights, and be critical of the Taliban and of the WoT's cynical use of women's rights to justify war, wonder many feminist scholars? The answers to this question might be complex, but one thing is clear: feminists who support the WoT and its domestic policy spinoffs do not have the right answer. The WoT did not make life better for Afghan women, it was often worse.[44] The WoT unleashed awful violence, destruction, and suffering in the Muslim world, and racist policies against Muslims at home that continue to this day; even if the WoT is officially over, its imperial project is not.

Shakira Hussein suggests the use of women's rights to justify the WoT is a "synthesis of militarism and feminism [that] had been laid down by the Feminist Majority Foundation's (FMF) 'Stop Gender Apartheid in Afghanistan' campaign [1997]."[45] Their campaign had scuttled an oil pipeline deal between the Taliban and Unocal that had had the support of the Clinton administration.[46] Post–September 11 FMF President Eleanor Smeal took the opportunity to rally feminist support for the WoT's mission to "save" Afghan women. This synthesis has many names in the literature: colonial feminism, orientalist feminism, imperial feminism, embedded feminism, gendered orientalism, or feminist orientalism. "Colonial feminism"/"feminist orientalism" is the use of feminist narratives in the service of the colonial project. "Imperial"/"embedded feminism," "gendered orientalism," and "orientalist feminism" are terms meaning modern feminism's resort to orientalist/colonial concepts in their theorizing of the struggle for women's equality. Roksana Bahramitash argues that in the post–September 11 era, orientalist feminism and feminist orientalism have come together in support of the WoT.[47] No matter the name, "imperial feminism" (as I call it) supports Western imperial hegemonic projects in the name of women's rights. These are feminists who inhabit the left pair of the rigid orientalist binaries mentioned above: the West as civilized and superior, Western women as empowered.

To understand imperial feminism in the post–September 11 period, many scholars turned again to early feminist works such as Chandra Mohanty's "Under Western Eyes: Feminist Scholarship and Colonial Discourses" from 1986.[48] Mohanty had called out Western feminists for a colonial discourse that homogenized Third World women into a single category of women, ignoring their specificities. First World women think of themselves "as educated, as modern, as having control over their own bodies and sexualities, and the freedom to make their own decisions," compared to the "third world" woman who leads an "essentially truncated life based on her feminine gender (read: sexually constrained) and her being 'third world' (read: ignorant, poor, uneducated, tradition-bound, domestic, family-oriented, victimized, etc.)."[49] In these discourses, the veil was depicted as oppressive, proving that Afghan women lack the agency to free themselves.[50] A multitude of high-profile political women, entertainers, and journalists strongly proclaimed this message, which was in turn criticized by several authors. For example, Roksana Bahramitash critically examined Geraldine Brooks's *Nine Parts of Desire* and Azar Nafisi's *Reading Lolita in Tehran*, bestsellers that reinforced the notion of an essentialized "Islam as a religion, portraying Muslim women only as victims."[51] Maryam Khalid examined three prominent images from the WoT—portrayal of the veil, and the Jessica Lynch and Lynndie England stories[52]—to show how they constructed masculinities and femininities to justify military invasion in Iraq and Afghanistan.[53] Sherene Razack reviewed Orianna Fallaci's *The Rage and the Pride*; Phyllis Chesler's *The New Anti-Semitism*, and Irshad Manji's *The Trouble with Islam*, all of which conveyed derogatory stock portrayals of the "oppressed" Muslim woman.[54]

These post–September 11 calls to support the WoT echoed nineteenth-century colonial discourses about Muslim women. M. E. Hume-Griffith, a British woman, lived in Persia and Arabia for several years around 1900 while her husband was employed as a doctor for a Christian Medical Mission. Hume-Griffith, who had often told the Muslim women she socialized with "Alhamd'llillah (thank God), I am not a Moslem woman!" described the *niqāb* as "a living grave. . . . The longer I live amongst Moslem women the more my heart yearns with love and pity for them, and the more thankful I am that their lot is not mine."[55] She articulated the following impassioned plea to save Muslim women: "Ought not the cries of distress and agony from the poor women of Persia so to rouse us, their sisters in England, that we shall determine to do all that lies in our power to lighten their burdens and to bring some rays of light into the dark lives of our Eastern sisters?" She went on, "Poor, blind, misguided Moslem women of Mosul and other Mohammedan lands! How my heart aches for them! Will no one heed the cry of anguish and despair which goes up from their midst? As we think of their lives our cry can only be, "How long, O Lord, how long will these things be?" It does not take much to transpose Hume-Griffith's words into WoT feminist supporters' language.

Scholars draw our attention to two more important aspects of imperial feminism. The first is ignoring Muslim women's own voices. One example: to legitimize the WoT campaign, Bush had partnered with the Revolutionary Association of Women of Afghanistan (RAWA), a secular liberal organization that opposed the Taliban. Yet RAWA went off script by criticizing Bush's support for the Northern Alliance to take down the Taliban and was opposed to the US military intervention.[56] Instead, there was a fixation with unveiling Afghan women.[57] Hussein notes this obsession with the veil, mentioning a dreadful moment "during a special performance of Eve Ensler's *Vagina Monologues* when Oprah Winfrey drew back a burqa to reveal the face of 'Zoya,' a young member of the Revolutionary Association of the Women of Afghanistan."[58] How different is this from the staged unveiling that took place in Algeria on May 13, 1958, when the French army brought a hundred women into a public square and unveiled them to the cries of "*Vive L'Algérie française!*"?[59] That it was a notable black woman doing the unveiling highlights the complicated relationship of class and race to orientalist tropes of Muslim women. Hussein rightly points out that "Afghan women were treated as exhibits rather than participants in the campaign that had been mounted on their behalf."[60]

The second aspect of imperial feminism is amnesia about the struggle for women's rights at home.[61] White Western feminists create an identity for themselves which is self-congratulatory as well as patronizing: constructing the self versus Muslim women through the orientalist binaries of superior/inferior; liberated/oppressed; and civilized/barbaric. Hunt argues that the effect of Western feminism "redirected outward [and] focused on the abuses of Other women by Other men" is twofold—it reinforces Western patriarchy at home, as well as in non-Western societies, as feminist discourse is forever tainted with imperialism, both of which must then be resisted.[62] Joan Scott suggests this "redirected outward" feminism was due to " 'exhaustion' of the militant feminism of the 1970s and 80s."[63] But the effect of "feminists turn[ing] to the salvation of their less fortunate immigrant sisters"[64] is support for racist policies at home, such as forced unveiling in France and Quebec.

Muslim and non-Muslim women have resisted imperial feminism abroad and at home. Muslim women activists, like Salma Yacoob, took leadership roles in the antiwar movement.[65] In the academy there are calls for a "more egalitarian language of alliances, coalitions, and solidarity, instead of salvation";[66] for a self-reflective feminism that abandons embedded feminism and builds solidarity by asking hard questions about any project feminists are asked to support;[67] for a pedagogy that unlearns imperialist feminism;[68] and for a theory around how to negotiate the common ground of difference, which is our "being-in-common,"[69] rather than requiring assimilation as the "basis for democratic politics in the twenty-first century."[70]

Continuities and Discontinuities in Representations of Muslim Women and Men

That the WoT's representations of Muslim women needing saving is a continuation of colonial and orientalist themes of oppression and rescue is thus evident. But continuation does not imply identicality in all aspects. There are permutations and refinements that developed in the post–September 11 political milieu. First, and among the most important, was Bush's initial differentiation between "Islam" and the "fundamentalists" who hijacked their religion for the purposes of "evil."[71] This produced a refinement in the concept of the "Muslim" and led to the development of the tropes of the "good Muslim" and the "bad Muslim." As Mamdani and Maira outline, the good/bad Muslim distinction reads [ignores] Islamic politics through the lens of culture—a right kind of Islam and a wrong kind. The "good Muslim" supported the WoT, American democracy and hegemony, and the "bad Muslim" resisted it. There was no gray area and no way, in the name of Islam, to be both against the violence of Muslims and that of the United States.

Second, September 11 also solidified a trend away from considering Muslims in the West through their ethnicity (Arab, Turk, or Asian) to seeing them through their religious identity alone: Muslim. Rita Chin tracks how German discourse about Turkish immigrants moved from largely ignoring them as temporary guestworkers to becoming in the 1980s/1990s a focal point as inassimilable to German nationhood due to their "oppression" of women. Turks were thought of as undermining post-Reich German efforts to be a modern, liberal society. Post–September 11 discourses about European identity and Muslims "have operated in a civilizational register [rather than a nation-state level], pitting an enlightened West against an antimodern Islam."[72] This has led to the "racialization of Muslims."[73]

Some scholars consider these variations large enough to need new names. Ivan Kalmar argues that the classical oriental harem woman, the odalisque, who is connected to an Orientalized image of the Jewess, notably through orientalized representations of Esther and Salome, is gone. He suggests that the contemporary images of Muslim women covered in burqas are not "the same thing" as the "reclining oriental nudes of Ingres, Delacroix, Manet, or Matisse," making Islamophobia, while connected genealogically to orientalism, a "new species." Kalmar submits that contemporary Islamophobia is a hatred of the Other that does not contain the wider "pallet" and here of orientalism that included fascination as well as fear; romanticized exoticness is replaced by contempt of migration and fears of terrorism.[74]

Katherine Allison argues that Orientalist binaries ignore pluralism in the "Occident." The post–September 11 moment sought out and promoted an image of the "agentic" Muslim woman that included women in headscarves. US pluralism was expanded to include such Muslim women who showed they could be both Muslim and participate fully in the "American way of life."[75]

Hussein maintains that the discourse justifying the WoT as a rescue mission for Muslim women was replaced over the decade by a discourse of discipline. The Muslim woman in the (Western) home country, especially if she wore a veil, signaled a refusal to be rescued and was "considered to be an agent of Islamisation by default."[76] Jane Freedman and Joan Scott highlight this transition from "rescue to threat" with respect to the antiveil debates and laws in France. Scott quotes the French philosopher André Glucksmann, who stated, "The veil is a terrorist operation."[77] Freedman quotes French feminist philosopher Elisabeth Badinter, who made a link between the "liberation" of women in Afghanistan and in Europe: "Soon feminists in the rest of Europe will realise the headscarf is a terrible symbol of submission. You cannot denounce what has been going on in Afghanistan while tolerating the veil in Europe—even if women claim they are wearing it voluntarily."[78]

Is this anti-Muslim racism discourse something new? While there might be discontinuities between an image of a harem girl and a woman in a burqa, or needing rescue and being disciplined, other scholars consider these differences to be variations on a theme, rather than something new. The continuity of colonial and orientalist tropes is established in the previous section. After all, the moves against the headscarf began in the late 1980s. Hussein herself concludes rescue is a "form of discipline."[79] Even Kalmar connects the image of the harem and the burqa through the concept of a desiring male gaze: the odalisque is already undressed, the aim is to undress the veiled woman.[80] Allison's "agentic Muslim woman" is actually, as Maira and Stabile and Kumar convincingly demonstrate, the rescued/disciplined Muslim woman at home, showing the benefits of US-style democracy that it sought to export around the world, so as to make smooth US hegemony in political and economic arenas.[81] The US needed the "good" Muslim woman at home to reinforce its claim that fighting the Taliban was necessary, and that it was doing it in the name of women's rights.

The WoT also amplified the orientalist image of the "camel-riding, terroristic, hook-nosed, venal lecher" Muslim man.[82] The War story is above all a gendered story. While it would be a separate chapter, the trope of the threatening Muslim male is linked to this literature review about global discourses on Muslim women because of the connection between masculinity, honor, protection, and war. The WoT is portrayed, as already mentioned, by political elites as the need for "white men to save brown women from brown men." Two different kinds of masculinity are at stake—the white male hero and the brown male oppressor. Several studies focus on the masculinity of the US military hero and its complicated relationship to the enemy male it was targeting, the enemy female it was saving, and the female back home it was protecting.[83] These studies also highlight how female soldiers, firefighters, and feminists back home did not fit into these narratives, so were either left out of the story or targeted as unwelcome.

Kalmar appears to be right that compared to the vitriol of today's anti-Muslim racism, orientalism centered on the desire for/fascination with the "Oriental despot," supreme master in his house resplendent with treasure and concubines, seems more benign. This seems to be far from the face of "evil" terrorist whose instinct is only to kill. And yet as Said pointed out in the 1970s the Arab in film and television was routinely portrayed as "oversexed . . . sadistic, treacherous, low," and "lurking behind all of these images is the menace of *jihad* [that had come to the fore in the 1979 Iranian revolution]. Consequence: a fear that the Muslims (or Arabs) will take over the world."[84] The Oriental despot may be admired out of a jealousy for his riches and women, but the "despot" in despotism—underscoring the possession of supreme political power—still evoked fear. The signifier may change over the centuries, but the signification remains the same.

Conclusion

This chapter has documented the continuation of colonialist and imperialist tropes of the Muslim-woman-in-need-of-rescue and its connection to imperialist feminism at home and abroad, with a specific focus on the scholarship around the post–September 11 WoT. My review of the academic literature found that rather than debates over key terms, scholars are working on variations of a few core themes. I explored the theme that the WoT is a continuation of colonial and orientalist themes of Muslim woman as oppressed members of a "backward" and "barbaric" civilization for whom the West felt a responsibility to save through military invasion and occupation. I looked at the role of Western feminists in supporting this neocolonial discourse and the WoT. I concluded by investigating continuities and discontinuities in the representations of Muslim women and men since the rise of Orientalism during the period of European colonialism through the post–September 11 period.

The WoT is officially over and supposedly winding down, so we can ask: What has happened since then? Has scholarly research that spotlighted problematic representations and links to anti-Muslim policy been able to move the needle to a more positive, less hostile, direction? Unfortunately, the large number of contemporary research papers that mention these issues of representation, anti-Muslim racism at home, and imperial policy abroad without mentioning September 11, suggest otherwise.

The WoT is but a moment in a continuum of anti-Muslim racism made intelligible through orientalism, colonialism, and imperialist feminism. While the geopolitics of the WoT may be changing, the ideologies that supported them remain unchanged: culturalist distinctions between a "progressive" modern West and a "retrograde" Muslim Other continue to buttress foreign policies aimed at ensuring Western global hegemony and "Western" cultural values at home. The rise of white nationalist movements, policies banning niqab, and calls for reduction in immigration and citizenship tests all indicate a worsening trend since September 11 in large swathes of the Western world. In North America, these trends are discernible despite the rise in numbers of Muslims as elected officials; the growing number of "firsts"—the first major, city councilor, judge, NFL coach; a widening interfaith movement; school boards recognizing Eid as a holiday;

and growing numbers of mosques and cities defending their right to be built. Eventually all of this will lead to the normalization and acceptance of Muslims, at least in North America.

In the meantime, scholars can continue to focus on these themes to demonstrate that they are not only historical, but also contemporary. In addition, spotlighting other aspects of Muslim women that are underresearched would contribute to a better understanding of their place and role in Western society: life histories of early Muslims; their participation in volunteer civic organizations; mosque and NGO leadership; charitable activities; and their role in the workplace, as scientists and entrepreneurs, for example. Knowledge production of this sort may also help challenge the unfortunate alliance between feminism and imperialist projects of various kinds in the Global North, which has by no means abated in the twenty-first century.

Notes

1. Salma Yacoob, "Muslim Women and War on Terror," *Feminist Review* 88 (2008): 150–161.
2. Katherine Bullock, *Rethinking Muslim Women and the Veil: Challenging Historical and Modern Stereotypes*, (Herndon, VA: International Institute of Islamic Thought, 2002); Ivan Kalmar, "The Jew and the Odalisque: Two Tropes Lost on the Way from Classic Orientalism to Islamophobia," *ReOrient: The Journal of Critical Muslim Studies* 4, no. 2 (Spring 2019): 186.
3. I am grateful for the research assistance support from Sophie Baalbaki and Humairaa Karodia.
4. Mounira Charrad, "Gender in the Middle East: Islam, State, Agency," *Annual Review of Sociology* 37 (2011): 430.
5. Ibid., 418.
6. Ibid., 418.
7. Lila Abu-Lughod, "'Orientalism' and Middle East Feminist Studies," *Feminist Studies* 27, no. 1 (2001): 101–113.
8. Lila Abu-Lughod, "Do Muslim Women Really Need Saving? Anthropological Reflections on Cultural Relativism and Its Others," *American Anthropologist* 104, no. 3 (Sept 2002): 788.
9. An overlapping but side theme investigates the connection between the WoT and hate crimes. Regrettably, space does not permit including these articles here. See for examples: Neil Chakraborti and Irene Zempi, "The Veil Under Attack: Gendered Dimensions of Islamophobic Victimization," *International Review of Victimology* 18, no. 3 (2012): 269–284;and Scott Poynting and Barbara Perry, "Climates of Hate: Media and State Inspired Victimisation of Muslims in Canada and Australia since 9/11," *Current Issues in Criminal Justice* 19, no. 2 (2007): 151–171.
10. Kenneth R. Bazinet, "A Fight vs. Evil, Bush and Cabinet Tell U.S.," *Daily News Washington Bureau*, September 17, 2001, https://web.archive.org/web/20100505200651/http://www.nydailynews.com/archives/news/2001/09/17/2001-09-17_a_fight_vs__evil__bush_and_c.html.
11. Abu-Lughod, "Do Muslim Women Really Need Saving," 784
12. Ibid.
13. Shakira Hussein, "From Rescue Missions to Discipline: Post-9/11 Western Political Discourse on Muslim Women," *Australian Feminist Studies* 28, no. 76 (2013): 145.

14. Evelyn Baring Cromer, *Modern Egypt*, 2 vols. (London: Macmillan, 1908), 2:542.
15. G. C. Spivak, "Can the Subaltern Speak?" in *Marxism and the Interpretation of Culture*, ed. C. Nelson and L. Grossberg (Urbana: University of Illinois Press, 1988), 297.
16. Samuel P. Huntington, "The Clash of Civilizations?" *Foreign Affairs* 72, no. 3 (1993): 22–49.
17. Edward Said, *Orientalism* (New York: Vintage Books, 1979).
18. Mahmood Mamdani, "Good Muslim, Bad Muslim: A Political Perspective on Culture and Terrorism," *American Anthropologist* 104, no. 3 (2002): 766–775.
19. Huntington, "Clash of Civilizations," 35.
20. Ibid., 32.
21. Cloud argues that a concept of superior/inferior civilizations concept has a long history in US imperialism, dating back at least to the nineteenth century; see Dana L. Cloud, "To Veil the Threat of Terror": Afghan Women and the ⟨Clash of Civilizations⟩ in the Imagery of the U.S. War on Terrorism," *Quarterly Journal of Speech* 90, no. 3 (August 2004): 286.
22. Mamdani, "Good Muslim, Bad Muslim," 111.
23. Jill Steans, "Telling Stories about Women and Gender in the War on Terror," *Global Society: Journal of Interdisciplinary International Relations* 22, no. 1 (2008), 161–163.
24. Sunaina Maira, "'Good" and 'Bad' Muslim Citizens: Feminists, Terrorists, and U.S. Orientalisms," *Feminist Studies* 35, no. 2 (2009): 650.
25. Mamdani, "Good Muslim, Bad Muslim," 110.
26. Said, *Orientalism*, 59.
27. Abu-Lughod, "Do Muslim Women Really Need Saving," 784.
28. Yasmin Jiwani, "Gendering Terror: Representations of the Orientalized Body in Quebec's Post-September 11 English-Language Press," *Critique: Critical Middle Eastern Studies* 13, no. 3 (2004): 265–291; and Lisa K. Taylor and Jasmin Zine, eds., *Muslim Women, Transnational Feminism and the Ethics of Pedagogy: Contested Imaginaries in Post-9/11 Cultural Practice* (New York: Routledge, 2014).
29. Steans, "Telling Stories about Women and Gender," 161.
30. Abu-Lughod, "Do Muslim Women Really Need Saving," 783; Steans, "Telling Stories about Women and Gender," 163.
31. Abu-Lughod, "Do Muslim Women Really Need Saving"; Hussein, "From Rescue Missions to Discipline"; Carol A. Stabile and Deepa Kumar, "Unveiling Imperialism: Media, Gender, and the War on Afghanistan," *Media, Culture and Society* 27, no. 5 (2005): 765–82.
32. Ralph Peters, "Global War on Women," *USA Today*, September 26, 2005, cited in Steans, "Telling Stories about Women and Gender," 163.
33. Ahlam Muhtaseb, "US Media Darlings: Arab and Muslim Women Activists, Exceptionalism and the 'Rescue Narrative,'" special double issue, *Arab Studies Quarterly* 42, no. 1/2 (Winter/Spring 2020): 7–24.
34. Kalmar, "The Jew and the Odalisque," 186, 193. Kalmar argues that contemporary Islamophobia has replaced supersessionism with the notion of the clash of civilizations. The Jew used to be orientalized in the Christian supersessionist ideology, and is a figure absent from contemporary Islamophobia.
35. Sherene H. Razack, *Casting Out: The Eviction of Muslims from Western Law and Politics* (Toronto: University of Toronto Press, 2008), 81.
36. Krista Hunt and Kim Rygiel, "(En)Gendered War Stories and Camouflaged Politics," in *(En)Gendering the War on Terror: War Stories and Camouflaged Politics*, ed. Krista Hunt and Kim Rygiel (Abingdon, Oxon: Taylor & Francis Group, 2016), 4.
37. Ibid.

38. Leila Ahmed, *Women and Gender in Islam: Historical Roots of a Modern Debate* (New Haven, CT: Yale University Press, 1992), 153.
39. Zillah Eisenstein, "Is 'W' for women?" in Rygiel and Hunt, *(En)Gendering the War on Terror*, 195–196; Stabile and Kumar, "Unveiling Imperialism," 777; Steans, "Telling Stories about Women and Gender," 164.
40. Hunt and Rygiel, "(En)Gendered War Stories," 11.
41. For example: Lalaie Ameeriar, "The Gendered Suspect: Women at the Canada-U.S. Border after September 11," *Journal of Asian American Studies* 15, no. 2 (2012): 171–195; Aneira J. Edmunds, "Precarious Bodies: The Securitization of the 'Veiled' Woman in European Human Rights," *British Journal of Sociology* 72, no. 2 (2021): 315–327; Taylor Markey, "Westernized Women? The Construction of Muslim Women's Dissent in U.S. Asylum Law," *UCLA Law Review* 64, no. 5 (2017): 1302–1327; Nandita Sharma, "White Nationalism, Illegality and Imperialism: Border Controls as Ideology," in Rygiel and Hunt, *(En) Gendering the War on Terror*, 121–143.
42. Naaz Rashid, *Veiled Threats: Representing the Muslim Woman in Public Policy Discourses* (Bristol, England: Policy Press, 2016), 131–133.
43. Narzanin Massoumi, *Muslim Women, Social Movements and the "War on Terror,"* (New York: Palgrave Macmillan, 2015), 36–50.
44. Cloud, "To Veil the Threat of Terror," 297; Krista Hunt, "'Embedded Feminism' and the War on Terror," in Rygiel and Hunt, *(En)Gendering the War on Terror*, 62–63; Stabile and Kumar, "Unveiling Imperialism," 775.
45. Hussein, "From Rescue Missions to Discipline," 145.
46. Abu-Lughod, "Do Muslim Women Really Need Saving," 787; Hussein, "From Rescue Missions to Discipline," 146.
47. Roksana Bahramitash, "The War on Terror, Feminist Orientalism and Orientalist Feminism: Case Studies of Two North American Bestsellers," *Critique: Critical Middle Eastern Studies* 14, no. 2, (2005): 221–222.
48. Chandra Talpade Mohanty, "Under Western Eyes: Feminist Scholarship and Colonial Discourses," in *Third World Women and the Politics of Feminism*, ed. C. Mohanty, Ann Russo, and Lourdes Torres (Bloomington: Indiana University Press, 1991), 51–80.
49. Ibid., 56.
50. Maryam Khalid, "Gender, Orientalism and Representations of the 'Other' in the War on Terror," *Global Change, Peace and Security* 23, no. 1 (2011): 25.
51. Bahramitash, "The War on Terror."
52. Jessica Lynch was a US soldier captured in Iraq in 2003. Her rescue by US marines was filmed, making her a media sensation. Much of the rescue narrative turned out to have been fabricated by the Pentagon. Lynndie England was one of the US soldiers convicted for prisoner abuse at Abu Ghraib prison in Baghdad in 2003.
53. Khalid, "Gender, Orientalism and Representations of the 'Other.'" For other analysis of the Lynch and England representations, see Melissa Brittain, "Benevolent Invaders, Heroic Victims and Depraved Villains: White Femininity in Media Coverage of the Invasion of Iraq," in Rygiel and Hunt, *(En)Gendering the War on Terror*, 73–96; Eisenstein, "Is 'W' for Women?"; Stabile and Kumar, "Unveiling Imperialism," 778.
54. Razack, *Casting Out*, 83–106.
55. M. E. Hume-Griffith, *Behind the Veil in Persia and Turkish Arabia: An Account of an Englishwoman's Eight Years' Residence amongst the Women of the East* (London: Seeley, 1909), 222–223.

56. Cloud, "To Veil the Threat of Terror," 289; Stabile and Kumar, "Unveiling Imperialism," 772; Steans, "Telling Stories about Women and Gender," 170.
57. Khalid, "Gender, Orientalism and Representations of the 'Other,'" 25.
58. Hussein, "From Rescue Missions to Discipline," 146.
59. After this, about 1,000 Algerian men, who had been bussed in from nearby villages to watch, sang the *Marseillaise* and the military *Chant des Africans*; see Frantz Fanon, *A Dying Colonialism*, trans. Haakon Chevalier (New York: Grove Press, 1967), 62.
60. Hussein, "From Rescue Missions to Discipline," 146.
61. Cloud, "To Veil the Threat of Terror," 289; Stabile and Kumar, "Unveiling Imperialism," 775; Steans, "Telling Stories about Women and Gender," 163; Sahar Aziz, *The Muslim Veil Post 9/11: Rethinking Muslim Women's Rights and Leadership* (Washington, DC: Institute for Social Policy and Understanding and the British Council, 2012).
62. Hunt, "Embedded Feminism," 54; Ahmed, *Women and Gender in Islam*, 167.
63. Joan Wallach Scott, *The Politics of the Veil* (Princeton, NJ: Princeton University Press, 2007), 98.
64. Ibid.
65. Massoumi, *Muslim Women*; Yacoob, "Muslim Women and War on Terror."
66. Abu-Lughod, "Do Muslim Women Really Need Saving," 789.
67. Hunt, "'Embedded Feminism," 66–67; Eisenstein, "Is 'W' for women?"; Jasmin Zine, "Between Orientalism and Fundamentalism: Muslim Women and Feminist Engagement," in Rygiel and Hunt, *(En)Gendering the War on Terror*, 45–46.
68. Diane Patricia Watt, "The Urgency of Visual Media Literacy in Our Post-9/11 World: Reading Images of Muslim Women in the Print News Media," *Journal of Media Literacy Education* 4, no. 1 (2012): 32–43; Lisa K. Taylor and Jasmin Zine, eds., *Muslim Women, Transnational Feminism and the Ethics of Pedagogy: Contested Imaginaries in Post-9/11 Cultural Practice* (New York: Routledge, 2014).
69. Scott, *The Politics of the Veil*, 20.
70. Ibid., 104.
71. Hunt and Rygiel, "(En)Gendered War Stories," 13.
72. Rita Chin, "Turkish Women, West German Feminists, and the Gendered Discourse on Muslim Cultural Difference," *Public Culture* 22, no. 3 (2010): 581.
73. Cloud, "To Veil the Threat of Terror," 292.
74. Kalmar, "The Jew and the Odalisque," 182–191.
75. Katherine Allison, "American Occidentalism and the Agential Muslim Woman," *Review of International Studies* 39 (2013): 665–684.
76. Hussein, "From Rescue Missions to Discipline," 147.
77. *L'Express*, 1994, cited in Scott, *The Politics of the Veil*, 64.
78. *The Observer*, 2004, cited in Jane Freedman, "The Headscarf Debate: Muslim Women in Europe and the 'War on Terror,'" in Rygiel and Hunt, *(En)Gendering the War on Terror*, 181.
79. Hussein, "From Rescue Missions to Discipline," 152.
80. Kalmar, "The Jew and the Odalisque," 190.
81. Maira, "'Good" and 'Bad' Muslim Citizens"; Stabile and Kumar, "Unveiling Imperialism."
82. Said, *Orientalism*, 108.
83. Brittain, "Benevolent Invaders"; Judith Lorber, "Heroes, Warriors, and *Burqas*: A Feminist Sociologist's Reflections on September 11," *Sociological Forum* 17, no. 3 (September 2002): 377–396; Khalid, "Gender, Orientalism and Representations of the 'Other,'" 25; Catherine V. Scott, "Rescue in the Age of Empire: Children, Masculinity, and the War on Terror," in

Rygiel and Hunt, *(En)Gendering the War on Terror*, 97–117; Steans, "Telling Stories about Women and Gender," 160, 166.

84. Said, *Orientalism*, 287. See also Jack Shaheen's classic work *Reel Bad Arabs: How Hollywood Vilifies A People* (Northampton, MA: Olive Branch Press, 2014) for a meticulous study of the negative depictions of Arabs and Muslims in Hollywood movies and their effects on the larger American population.

Bibliography

Abu-Lughod, Lila. "Do Muslim Women Really Need Saving? Anthropological Reflections on Cultural Relativism and its Others." *American Anthropologist* 104, no. 3 (Sept 2002): 783–790.

Abu-Lughod, Lila. "'Orientalism' and Middle East Feminist Studies." *Feminist Studies* 27, no. 1 (2001): 101–113.

Ahmed, Leila. *Women and Gender in Islam: Historical Roots of a Modern Debate*. New Haven: Yale University Press, 1992.

Allison, Katherine. "American Occidentalism and the Agential Muslim Woman." *Review of International Studies* 39 (2013): 665–684.

Ameeriar, Lalaie. "The Gendered Suspect: Women at the Canada–U.S. Border after September 11." *Journal of Asian American Studies* 15, no. 2 (2012): 171–195.

Aziz, Sahar. *The Muslim Veil Post 9/11: Rethinking Muslim Women's Rights and Leadership*. Washington, DC: Institute for Social Policy and Understanding and the British Council, 2012.

Bahramitash, Roksana. "The War on Terror, Feminist Orientalism and Orientalist Feminism: Case Studies of Two North American Bestsellers." *Critique: Critical Middle Eastern Studies* 14, no. 2 (2005): 221–235.

Bazinet, Kenneth R. "A Fight vs. Evil, Bush and Cabinet Tell U.S." *Daily News Washington Bureau*, September 17, 2001, https://web.archive.org/web/20100505200651/http://www.nydailynews.com/archives/news/2001/09/17/2001-09-17_a_fight_vs__evil__bush_and_c.html

Brittain, Melissa. "Benevolent Invaders, Heroic Victims and Depraved Villains: White Femininity in Media Coverage of the Invasion of Iraq." In *(En)Gendering the War on Terror: War Stories and Camouflaged Politics*, edited by Kim Rygiel and Krista Hunt, 73–96. Abingdon, Oxon: Taylor & Francis Group, 2016.

Bullock, Katherine. *Rethinking Muslim Women and the Veil: Challenging Historical and Modern Stereotypes*. Herndon, VA: International Institute of Islamic Thought, 2002.

Chakraborti, Neil, and Irene Zempi. "The Veil under Attack: Gendered Dimensions of Islamophobic Victimization." *International Review of Victimology* 18, no. 3 (2012): 269–284.

Charrad, Mounira. "Gender in the Middle East: Islam, State, Agency." *Annual Review of Sociology* 37 (2011): 417–437.

Chin, Rita. "Turkish Women, West German Feminists, and the Gendered Discourse on Muslim Cultural Difference." *Public Culture* 22, no. 3 (2010): 557–581.

Cloud, Dana L. "To Veil the Threat of Terror": Afghan Women and the ⟨Clash of Civilizations⟩ in the Imagery of the U.S. War on Terrorism." *Quarterly Journal of Speech* 90, no. 3 (August 2004): 285–306.

Cromer, Evelyn Baring. *Modern Egypt*, 2 vols. London: Macmillan, 1908.

Edmunds, Aneira J. "Precarious Bodies: The Securitization of the 'Veiled' Woman in European Human Rights." *British Journal of Sociology* 72, no. 2 (2021): 315–327.

Eisenstein, Zillah. "Is 'W' for women?" In *(En)Gendering the War on Terror: War Stories and Camouflaged Politics*, edited by Kim Rygiel and Krista Hunt, 191–199. Abingdon, Oxon: Taylor & Francis Group, 2016.

Fanon, Frantz. *A Dying Colonialism*. Translated by Haakon Chevalier. New York: Grove Press, 1967. French edition, 1959.

Freedman, Jane. "The Headscarf Debate: Muslim Women in Europe and the 'War on Terror.'" In *(En)Gendering the War on Terror: War Stories and Camouflaged Politics*, edited by Kim Rygiel and Krista Hunt, 169–189. Abingdon, Oxon: Taylor & Francis Group, 2016.

Hunt, Krista. "'Embedded Feminism' and the War on Terror." In *(En)Gendering the War on Terror: War Stories and Camouflaged Politics*, edited by Kim Rygiel and Krista Hunt, 51–71. Abingdon, Oxon: Taylor & Francis Group, 2016.

Hunt, Krista, and Kim Rygiel. "(En)Gendered War Stories and Camouflaged Politics." In *(En) Gendering the War on Terror: War Stories and Camouflaged Politics*, edited by Kim Rygiel and Krista Hunt, 4–24. Abingdon, Oxon: Taylor & Francis Group, 2016.

Huntington, Samuel P. "The Clash of Civilizations?" *Foreign Affairs* 72, no. 3 (1993): 22–49.

Hussein, Shakira. "From Rescue Missions to Discipline: Post-9/11 Western Political Discourse on Muslim Women." *Australian Feminist Studies* 28, no. 76 (2013): 144–154.

Jiwani, Yasmin. "Gendering Terror: Representations of the Orientalized Body in Quebec's post-September 11 English-Language Press." *Critique: Critical Middle Eastern Studies* 13, no. 3 (2004): 265–291.

Hume-Griffith, M. E. *Behind the Veil in Persia and Turkish Arabia: An Account of an Englishwoman's Eight Years' Residence amongst the Women of the East*. London: Seeley, 1909.

Kalmar, Ivan. "The Jew and the Odalisque: Two Tropes Lost on the Way from Classic Orientalism to Islamophobia." *ReOrient: The Journal of Critical Muslim Studies* 4, no. 2 (Spring 2019): 181–196.

Khalid, Maryam. "Gender, Orientalism and Representations of the 'Other' in the War on Terror." *Global Change, Peace and Security* 23, no. 1 (2011): 15–29.

Lorber, Judith. "Heroes, Warriors, and *Burqas*: A Feminist Sociologist's Reflections on September 11." *Sociological Forum* 17, no. 3 (September 2002).

Mamdani, Mahmood. "Good Muslim, Bad Muslim: A Political Perspective on Culture and Terrorism." *American Anthropologist* 104, no. 3 (2002): 766–775.

Maira, Sunaina. "'Good' and 'Bad' Muslim Citizens: Feminists, Terrorists, and U.S. Orientalisms." *Feminist Studies* 35, no. 3 (2009): 631–656.

Markey, Taylor. "Westernized Women? The Construction of Muslim Women's Dissent in U.S. Asylum Law." *UCLA Law Review* 64, no. 5 (2017): 1302–1327.

Massoumi, Narzanin. *Muslim Women, Social Movements and the "War on Terror."* New York: Palgrave Macmillan, 2015.

Mohanty, Chandra Talpade. "Under Western Eyes: Feminist Scholarship and Colonial Discourses." In *Third World Women and the Politics of Feminism*, edited by C. Mohanty, Ann Russo, and Lourdes Torres, 51–80. Bloomington: Indiana University Press, 1991.

Muhtaseb, Ahlam. "US Media Darlings: Arab and Muslim Women Activists, Exceptionalism and the 'Rescue Narrative.'" Special double issue, *Arab Studies Quarterly* 42, nos. 1–2 (Winter/Spring 2020): 7–24.

Poynting, Scott, and Barbara Perry. "Climates of Hate: Media and State Inspired Victimisation of Muslims in Canada and Australia since 9/11." *Current Issues in Criminal Justice* 19, no. 2 (2007): 151–171.

Rashid, Naaz. *Veiled Threats: Representing the Muslim Woman in Public Policy Discourses.* Bristol, England: Policy Press, 2016.
Razack, Sherene H. *Casting Out: The Eviction of Muslims from Western Law and Politics.* Toronto: University of Toronto Press, 2008.
Said, Edward. *Orientalism.* New York: Vintage Books, 1979.
Scott, Catherine V. "Rescue in the Age of Empire: Children, Masculinity, and the War on Terror." In *(En)Gendering the War on Terror: War Stories and Camouflaged Politics*, edited by Kim Rygiel and Krista Hunt, 97–117. Abingdon, Oxon: Taylor & Francis Group, 2016.
Scott, Joan Wallach. *The Politics of the Veil.* Princeton, NJ: Princeton University Press, 2007.
Shaheen, Jack. *Reel Bad Arabs: How Hollywood Vilifies a People.* Northampton, MA: Olive Branch Press, 2014.
Sharma, Nandita. "White Nationalism, Illegality and Imperialism: Border Controls as Ideology." In *(En)Gendering the War on Terror: War Stories and Camouflaged Politics*, edited by Krista Hunt and Kim Rygiel, 121–143. Abingdon, Oxon: Taylor & Francis Group, 2016.
Spivak, G. C. "Can the Subaltern Speak?" In *Marxism and the Interpretation of Culture*, edited by C. Nelson and L. Grossberg, 271–315. Urbana: University of Illinois Press, 1988.
Stabile, Carol A., and Deepa Kumar. "Unveiling Imperialism: Media, Gender, and the War on Afghanistan." *Media, Culture and Society* 27, no. 5 (2005): 765–782.
Steans, Jill. "Telling Stories about Women and Gender in the War on Terror." *Global Society: Journal of Interdisciplinary International Relations* 22, no. 1 (2008): 159–176.
Taylor, Lisa K., and Jasmin Zine, eds. *Muslim Women, Transnational Feminism and the Ethics of Pedagogy: Contested Imaginaries in Post-9/11 Cultural Practice.* New York: Routledge, 2014.
Yacoob, Salma. "Muslim Women and War on Terror." *Feminist Review* 88 (2008): 150–161.
Watt, Diane Patricia. "The Urgency of Visual Media Literacy in Our Post-9/11 World: Reading Images of Muslim Women in the Print News Media." *Journal of Media Literacy Education* 4, no. 1 (2012): 32–43.
Zine, Jasmin. "Between Orientalism and Fundamentalism: Muslim Women and Feminist Engagement." In *(En)Gendering the War on Terror: War Stories and Camouflaged Politics*, edited by Krista Hunt and Kim Rygiel, 27–49. Abingdon, Oxon: Taylor & Francis Group, 2016.

Index

For the benefit of digital users, indexed terms that span two pages (e.g., 52–53) may, on occasion, appear on only one of those pages.

Ababneh, Sara, 369, 371, 375–76
Abdoulkarim, Iman, 7
'Abduh, Muḥammad, 381, 550
Abou El Fadl, Khaled, 4–5, 93–94
Abou-Zahab, Mariam, 436
Abraham (Ibrāhīm), 23–27
Abū Bakr, 121–22, 125, 223, 245, 249–50, 254
Abū Bakr ibn al-ʿArabī, 44, 51, 85
Abū Dāwūd, 232
Abugideiri, Hibba, 2–3
Abū Hurayra, 99–100
Abu-Lughod, Lila, 91, 387, 520–21, 591, 593
Abū Mūsa al-Ash'arī, 27
Abū Muslim al-Iṣfahānī, 42
Abū Ṭalḥa al-Anṣārī, 227
Abū Ṭālib, 314, 537–38
Abū Tammām, 292
Abū Zahra, 120–21
Abū Zarʿ, 64–66
Afary, Janet, 398–99
Afghānī, Jamāl al-Dīn al-, 381
Africa, South. *See* South Africa
Afsaruddin, Asma, 235–36, 278–79, 542
agency
  classical exegeses and, 45
  devotional life and, 276–77, 279, 280–82, 285
  economic actors and, 305–6, 311
  feminist literature and, 559–60
  ḥadīth literature and, 69–70
  IFL and, 190
  littérateurs and, 291
  modern rereadings of *ḥadīth* and, 121, 122, 123–24, 125, 129–30, 131–32, 135, 139–40, 142
  modern rereadings of Qur'ān and, 90–91, 94, 96–97, 102, 103–4, 106, 107–8
  moral exemplars in Twelver Shī'ism and, 250
  mosques and, 324–25
  al-Mubashsharāt bi-l-janna and, 229
  overview of, 2
  rights and duties and, 205–6
  transmitters of knowledge and, 259, 268
  veiling and, 572–73, 576–78, 581
Aghaie, Kamran Scott, 254, 278–79
Aghā-Sultān, Nedā, 404
Ahl-i Hadith movement, 355
Aḥmad ibn Ḥanbal, 140, 232
Ahmed, Leila, 131–33, 203, 205–6, 275, 278–79, 282–83, 344–45, 381, 557, 572–73
'Ā'isha bint Abī Bakr
  adhan called by, 552
  authority of, 278, 364
  devotional life and, 282–83
  economic actors and, 313
  feminist literature and, 552
  interpretive preference given to, 540
  leadership role of, 278, 354
  legacy of, 278, 364
  marriage to Muḥammad of, 540–41
  modern rereadings of *ḥadīth* and, 125, 129, 131–32, 133
  as Muḥammad's favorite wife, 278
  traditional focus on, 14–15
  transmitters of knowledge and, 260–61, 262–63, 265, 282–83
'Ā'isha bint Ṭalḥa, 121–22, 260–61, 262
'Aisyiyah (organization), 446–47
Akhbārī revival, 268–69
al-Adawiya, Aisha, 496
al-'Attar, Suhayla, 560

al-ʿAyn, Qurrat, 554
al-Fassi, Hatoon, 312–13
al-Habash, Huda, 208–9
al-Hibri, Azizah, 203, 205, 207, 496–97
Al-Huda (organization), 283–85, 435–36
āl-Ḥūwaidar, Wajīha, 525
Ali, Kecia, 89–91, 102, 133–34, 136–37, 205–6, 278
Ali, Nadje al-, 384
Ali, Samer, 8
ʿAlī ibn al-Ḥusayn Zayn al-ʿĀbidīn, 251
Ali Pasham, Mohamed, 381
Allam, Nermin, 10–11
Al-Manar (television channel), 369–70
al-Marayati, Laila, 496
Al-Mujadilah Development Foundation (AMDF), 452–53
al-Mūlūk Musāhib, Shams, 403
al-Shanti, Jamila, 372
āl-Sharīf, Manāl, 525
Al-sufūr wa al-ḥijāb (Zeineddine), 554
al-Taimūriyya, Ā'isha, 554
American Society for Muslim Advancement (ASMA), 497–98
Amin, Camron, 400, 401
Amin, Nusrat, 260, 406
Amīn, Qāsim, 381, 572–73
Amin, Yasmin, 6
ʿAmra bint ʿAbd al-Raḥmān, 262
Annisa, Rifka, 448
Anṣār of Medina, 71
anti-Islamic sentiment. *See* Islamophobia
Arab Family Law Project, 190
Ardabīlī, Muḥammad b. ʿAlī al-, 268–69
Armstrong, Karen, 537–38, 542
Arqun, Fakhr Ozmā, 401
Asad, Talal, 581
Asia, South. *See* South Asia; Southeast Asia
Āsiya bint Muzāḥim, 66, 225
Asma'u, Nana, 262–63
Asmāʾ bint Abī Bakr, 226–27
Asmāʾ bint Yazīd, 71, 73
Association of Women Lawyers (AWL), 450–51
Association of Women of Afghanistan (RAWA), 597
Aṭāʾ ibn Abī Rabāḥ, 50–51, 84, 85
Atia, Mona, 328
Awami League, 358–60
Ayata, Ayşe Guneş, 416
Ayman, Umm, 230
Ayubi, Zahra, 7
ʿAyyāshī, Abū al-Naṣr al-, 42
Azam, Hina, 235
Azīz, 31–32
Azzat, Heba Raouf, 387

Badinter, Elisabeth, 599
Badr, Battle of, 232–33. *See* also Battle of Badr
Badran, Margot, 387
Badrī bint Ṭāhā, 315
Bahrain, women and girls in, 527–29
Bahrain Women Association for Human Development, 524
Bahramitash, Roksana, 595–96
Bakar, Omaima Abu, 387
Bangladesh, women and girls in, 358–60, 433–38
Bangladesh Islami Chatri Sangstha (BICSa), 434
Bano, Masooda, 330
Bāqir, Muḥammad al- (Abū Jaʿfar), 42, 47
Barazangi, Nimat, 132
Bardakoğlu, Ali, 417
Barlas, Asma, 21–22, 81–82, 87–88, 89–91, 133–34, 135, 141–42, 207, 387, 493, 543
Baron, Beth, 381
Baṣrī, al-Ḥasan al-, 30
Battle of Badr, 31, 232–33
Battle of Dhū Qār, 293–94
Battle of Karbala, 246–47, 252–55, 278–79
Bayat, Asef, 383
Bayat-Phillip, Mangol, 398–99
Bayḍāwī, ʿAbdallāh ibn ʿUmar al-, 41, 45–46, 48, 52, 83
Bayhaqī, al-, 231
Baylouny, Anne, 369
Bedouins, 291–94, 538, 555
Begum, Hameeda, 434
Begum, Momotaj, 431–32
"Believing Women" in Islam (Barlas), 81–82
Berger, Michael S., 340
Bernardo, Amina Rasul, 452–53

Betteridge, Anne, 281
Betul Yarar, 419–20
Bhutto, Benazir, 197, 356–58, 359, 360, 432–33
Bhutto, Zulfiqar Ali, 433–34
Bier, Laura, 384
Bilqīs, 27–30
Bint al-Shāṭi, 544
Booth, Marilyn, 235–36, 262–63
Border Passage, A (Ahmed), 557
Bottcher, Annabelle, 375
Bracke, Sarah, 510–11
Brown, Jonathan, 85
Brown, Katherine, 508–9
Brownson, Elizabeth, 10
Buḥturī, al-, 299
Bukhārī, Muḥammad ibn Ismāʿīl al-, 65, 224, 228, 229, 267, 550–51
Bullock, Katherine, 16
Būrgība, Ḥabīb, 384, 387
burqa. See veiling
Bush, George W., 592, 593, 597
Bush, Laura, 592–93
business. *See* economic actors
Buskens, Leon, 187
Busran-Lao, Yasmin, 452–53
Butorovic, Amila, 280–81

Calderini, Simonetta, 235
Cantone, Cleo, 329
Casanova, Jose, 208
Cavatorta, Francesco, 191–92
CEDAW (Convention on the Elimination of All Forms of Discrimination Against Women), 357, 452–53
Cesari, Jocelyne, 208
Chan-Malik, Sylvia, 279–80, 575
Charrad, Mounira, 382–83
Char Sathir Dal (Group of Four Companions, GFC), 431, 438
Chaudhry, Ayesha, 84–85
child marriage, 445, 449, 453–54, 550
China
  agency in, 466, 468–70, 472–73
  collective worship in, 466
  diversity of Muslim population in, 462–63
  economic actors in, 471
  education in, 463–68, 469–71, 472
  future research on, 468–69
  guardianship in, 468
  ḥajj in, 469
  Hui Muslim communities in, 463–64, 470, 471–72
  Ming Dynasty in, 463–64
  oppression and violence against Muslims in, 347–48
  overview of, 462
  People's Republic of China in, 463–64
  regional variation in, 472
  religious activities in, 463–69
  social activities in, 469–73
  statistical facts on, 463
  Uyghur communities in, 463
  women's mosques in, 331, 464–65, 466, 471, 485
Çiller, Tansu, 361–62
Claremont Main Road Mosque, 331, 480–81
classical exegeses on key Qur'ānic verses. *See also* rights and duties in classical legal texts
  agency and, 45
  compromise in, 52–53
  "degree" of men in, 46–49
  diversity of, 39–40
  divorce and, 43–45
  Qur'ān 4:1, 40–43
  Qur'ān 4:128, 49–50, 51–53
  Qur'ān 4:34, 49–51
  function of, 39–40
  gendered definitions of *nushūz* and, 49–50
  hitting of wife and, 50–51
  human creation narrative and, 40–43
  men's *nushūz* in, consequences of, 51–53
  obedience and, 47, 49–50
  outlier interpretations in, 42
  overview of, 39–40, 53–54
  polyvalence of, 39, 41, 48
  reciprocal yet unequal rights in, 43–46
  sexual responsibilities in, 46, 48, 49–50, 52
  Qur'ān 2:227, 43–46
  Qur'ān 2:228, 46–49
  women's *nushūz* in, consequences of, 50–51
Code of Muslim Personal Laws (CMPL), 452–53
Collins, Patricia Hill, 343–44

colonialism, 344–45, 381, 383–84, 520, 522, 590–95
commerce. *See* economic actors
complementarity, 22, 83–84, 86, 105, 245–46, 276–77, 283, 341, 369–70, 374, 419–20, 445, 527–28
Convention on the Elimination of All Forms of Discrimination Against Women (CEDAW), 357, 452–53
cooke, miriam, 15
Cornell, Rkia, 262, 280–81
Coşar, Simten, 419–20
Counter Legal Draft, 449
cultural trope of Muslim Women
  colonialism continued through, 590–95
  continuities and discontinuities in, 598–600
  feminism and, role of imperial, 591, 595–97
  Orientalism and, 590–96, 598–99
  overview of, 590–92, 600–1
  race and, 591, 597, 599
  September 11 attacks and, 590–92, 594, 598
  war on terror and, 590–95

Dakake, Maria, 6–7
Daly, Sunny, 382
daraja (degree), 43, 48–49, 90, 98, 101–2, 108
Dāraquṭnī, ʿAlī Ibn ʿUmar al-, 232–33
Dārimī, ʿAbd Allāh al-, 85
Decade for Women, 384–85
Deeb, Lara, 368–69
Delong-Bas, Natana, 6
Demirel, Suleyman, 361
Democratic Union of Women, 401
Department of the Advancement of Islam (JAKIM), 450
devotional life
  academics and, 282–85
  agency and, 276–77, 279, 280–82, 285
  alternative religious practices paradigm and, 275, 279, 280–82
  better than formula and, 277
  cultural context for, 277–78
  feminism and, 282
  gender roles and, 276, 278
  ḥadīth literature and, 277, 282–83
  insurgent domesticity and, 279–80
  Muharram rituals and, 278–79
  mysticism and, 280–81
  NGOs and, 283–85
  normative practices and spaces of, 277–80
  overview of, 275–77, 285
  pilgrimages and, 281
  popular revivalist movements and, 283–85
  recovery of religious learning and authority and, 282–85
  reformists and, 282–85
  reimagining of, 277–78, 282–85
  relation of women to the Divine and, 276, 281–85
  revivalists and, 282–85
  Sufism and, 280–81
  tawhidic paradigm and, 281–82
  in their own right paradigm and, 275
  transmitters of knowledge and, 282–83
Dhul-Rumma, 294
Dhū Qār, Battle of, 293–94
divorce. *See also* inheritance; marriage
  classical exegeses and, 43–45
  consensual separation, 162, 166–67
  contract stipulations in, 164–66
  delegated conditional divorce, 162, 164–66
  ḥadīth literature and, 64–66, 71
  Ḥanafī school and, 165, 167–68
  Ḥanbalī school and, 164–65, 167–68
  judicial divorce, 162, 164, 165, 167–68
  Mālikī school and, 162, 165, 167–68
  Shīʿī school and, 162–63, 164–65, 166
  Sunnī school and, 162, 163, 164, 166
  ṭalāq-divorce (unilateral repudiation), 162–64, 165–66, 167
  types of, 162
Djebar, Assia, 260–61, 544, 559–60
Doorn-Harder, Nelly van, 12
Doumani, Beshara, 171, 211
Dwyer, Claire, 575–76

Ebadi, Shirin, 558–59
economic actors
  agency and, 305–6, 311
  class differences and, 308–9
  dowry and, 310
  guardianship and, 306–12
  guilds and, 314
  inheritance and, 306–12

interconnected network of, 307
limited sources on, 305–6
marriage contracts and, 310
native elites and, 311
overview of, 304–6, 316
wage labor or women's work and, 312–15
EFU (Egyptian Feminist Union), 383, 386, 554, 573
Egypt and North Africa
agency in, 382, 386–87
charitable agenda in, 381–83
colonialism and, 381, 383–84
da'wa movement in, 386
early activism in, 381–82
female genital mutilation in, 382
feminism in, 383–84
future discussions for, 388
health and education in, 382
maternal framework in, 381–83
Morocco, 382–83, 386–87
Muslima theology in, 387
nationalist turn in, 383–84
NGO-ization in, 380–81, 384–85
overview of, 380–81, 388
philanthropic turn in, 383–84
religious discourses in, 386–87
Tunisia, 384, 387
woman preachers and, 386–87
Egyptian Feminist Union (EFU), 383, 386, 554, 573
El Guindi, Fadwa, 574–75
El-Joenesijjah, Rahmah, 446–47
El Saadawi, Nawal, 555
el-Sayyid, Hanan, 260–61
Elshayyal, Khadijah, 509
Enchanted Modern, An (Deeb), 368–69
Encyclopaedia of Islam, 542
Erbakan, Necmettin, 361–62, 417–18
'Eshqi, 553
Europe, Western. *See* Western Europe

faḍḍala (to prefer), 98–100
Fadel, Mohammad, 107
Fadil, Nadia, 510–11
FaithTrust Institute, 497
Farrell, Stephen, 372–73
Fatima, Nisar, 432–33
Fāṭima al-Fihrī, 313–14
Fāṭima bint Muḥammad
characteristics of Imams shared by, 249
as economic actor and, 311–12, 313–14
as exceptional and exemplary, 248–50
as exemplar of filial piety and devotion, 246–48
as having a special place in Muḥammad's heart, 68
marriage of, 247–48
martyr-like death of, 249
model for women and, 246
as moral exemplar in Twelver Shīʿīsm, 246–50, 253–55
as mother of her father, 68, 253–54
response to persecution and injustice by, 249–50
as woman of paradise, 225–26, 236
Fedayeen Guerrilla Movement, 398
Fekry, Ahmed, 189–90
femininity, 421, 464, 468, 539, 572–73
feminism
Arab feminism, 572–73
colonial feminism, 80–81, 575, 595–96
cultural trope of Muslim Women and, 591, 595–97
devotional life and, 282
imperial feminism, 591, 595–97
Islamic feminism, 80–81, 371, 387, 402–3, 405, 436, 447, 449, 573
modern representations of wives of the Prophet and, 539–40, 543
modern rereadings of Qur'ān and, 82–85
mosques and, 324
al-Mubashsharāt bi-l-janna and, 234–36
negotiating motherhood and, 340–41
overview of, 4, 31
rights and duties and, 204, 207
transmitters of knowledge and, 265
veiling and, 572–74
western feminism 597
feminist literature
agency and, 559–60
'Ā'isha and, 552
'awra and, 76, 550–51, 552–53, 555, 560, 563
challenging misogyny through, 550–53
ḥadīth literature and, 550–53

feminist literature (*cont.*)
memoirs in, 556–59
overview of, 549–50, 563
trespassing on men's space in, 559–62
veiling contested in, 553–56
Feminist Majority Foundation (FMF), 595–96
Fernando, Mayanthi, 580
Fernea, Elizabeth, 323–24
Fewkes, Jaqueline, 327, 330
Firmo-Fontan, Victoria, 369–70
First Muslims, The (Afsaruddin), 542
Fodio, Uthman dan, 262–63
France, veiling ban in, 575–76, 578, 597
Free Officers Revolution, 384

Gaunt, Marilyn, 323–24
Geissinger, Aisha, 235, 262
gender roles. *See* negotiating motherhood; rights and duties in classical legal texts
Ghamari-Tabrizi, Behrooz, 402
Ghandour, Zeina, 552
Ghazālī, Abū Ḥāmid al-, 39
Ghazālī, Zainab al-, 370, 386, 556–57, 573
Girl in the Tangerine Scarf, The (Kahf), 560–61
Glucksmann, Andre, 599
Goldziher, Ignaz, 201–2, 261
Golestaneh, Seema, 11
Gonzalez, Alessandra L., 528
Gulf Cooperation Council (GCC), 523
Gulf states. *See* Saudi Arabia and the Gulf
Gunning, Jeroen, 370–71, 372, 376

Habibie, B. J., 360–61
ḥadīth literature. *See also* modern rereadings of *ḥadīth*
Abū Zarʿ in, 64–65, 67
agency and, 69–70
ʿĀʾisha in, 61–66, 73
Anṣār of Medina in, 71
Āsiya in, 68–69
Asmāʾ bint Yazīd in, 71–73
companionship models in, 61–66
devotional life and, 277, 282–83
divorce and, 64–66, 71
Fāṭima in, 68
feminist literature and, 550–53
four women of paradise and, 66–70
Khadīja bint Khuwaylid in, 66–67
Khawla bint Thaʿlaba in, 70–71
Maryam in, 68–69
masculinity in, 67–68
models of virtue in, 68–69
Nusayba bint Kaʿb in, 73–74
overview of, 61, 76–77
public rituals in, 72–73
queries not answered by Qurʾān and, 70–74
short statements and, 74–76
transmitters of knowledge and, 261–62, 263–69
Umm Salama and, 70
Umm Zarʿ and, 61–66, 73
Ḥaḍramī, al-, 226
Haeri, Niloofar, 327, 328, 329–30, 405–6
Hafez, Sherine, 520–21
Ḥafṣa bint ʿUmar, 262
ḥajj (pilgrimages), *See* pilgrimages
Ḥalīma al-Saʿdiyya, 312–13
Hallaq, Wael, 202
Hamas, 368–69, 370–73
Hammer, Juliane, 13
Ḥanafī school, 157–58, 160–61, 165, 167–68
Ḥanbalī school, 157, 161, 164–65, 167–68
Ḥanna, 24
Haque, Omar, 347
Harakat-ul-Jihad al-Islami (organization), 359
Harūn al-Rashīd, 295, 313
Ḥasan ibn Qalawūn, 305
Hāshim ibn ʿAbd Manāf, 314
Hashmi, Farhat, 283–84, 435–36
Hassan, Riffat, 203–4
Hassan, Tabligh Amir Enamul, 430
Hassan II, 187, 191
Hatem, Mervat, 186–87, 384
Hātūn, Mihri, 551–52, 554
Haydar, Mona, 563
Haykal, Muḥammad, 542
heads of state. *See* modern heads of state
headscarf, 11, 15–16, 415, 417–18, 419, 421, 510–11, 569, 575, 591–92, 599
HEART women and girls, 498
Hendricks, Muhsin, 483
Herodotus, 312–13
Hidayatullah, Aysha, 89–90, 91–92, 96, 101–2, 135

ḥijāb. See headscarf; veiling
Hill, Margari Aziza, 499
hitting of wife, 50–51, 84–85, 93–94
Hizbullah, 369–70
Hizbullah Women's Association (HWA), 369–70
Hizbul Mujahideen, 435
Hoel, Nina, 13
Homosexuality in Islam (Kugle), 483
Hoodfar, Homa, 574
Horgan, John G., 346
Htun, Mala, 187–88, 190–91
Hudood Ordinance, 432–33
Ḥujayja, 290, 293–94, 296
human creation narrative, 40–43, 88–89, 127–28
human rights, 190, 371, 372, 376, 445, 525–26
Human Rights Watch (HRW), 525–26
Ḥumayd, 48
Hume-Griffith, M. E., 596–97
Hu Meijuan, 467
Hunt, Krista, 594–95, 597
Huntington, Samuel, 593
Huq, Maimuna, 331–32, 434
Huq, Samia, 436–37
Ḥurqa, al-, 293–94
Ḥusayn, Sukayna bint al-, 120
Hussein, Shakira, 595–96, 599
Hutchinson, Aisha J., 339
Huzur, Amma, 430

Ibn ʿAbbās, 29–30, 86–87
Ibn Abī Ḥātim al-Rāzī, 42–43
Ibn Abī Khaythama, 230
Ibn al-Athīr, 228–29
Ibn al-Ḥajj al-ʿAbdarī, 97
Ibn al-Jawzī, 232–33
Ibn al-Qayyim, 159
Ibn al-ʿArabī, 45, 48, 51
Ibn Bashkawāl, 228–29
Ibn Buṭlān, 299
Ibn Ḥajar, 27, 229, 232–33
Ibn Ḥanbal, 169–70, 230
Ibn Ḥazm of Cordoba, 27
Ibn Hishām, 231
Ibn Isḥāq, 541–42
Ibn Kathīr, 29–30, 42–43, 48–49, 99–100, 105, 106–7
Ibn Khallikān, 294–95
Ibn Qayyim al-Jawziyya, 107
Ibn Sa'd, 278–79
Ibn Saʿd, Muḥammad, 538–39
Ibn Taymiyya, 107
Ibn Ziyād, 251–52
Ibn ʿAbbās, 46–47, 48
Ibrahim, Anwar, 444–45
IFL. *See* Islamic family law (IFL)
ijtihād 138, 387, 403, 445, 483, 508, 559
Ilyas, Muhammad, 428–29
Imāmī Twelver Shīʿī, 157–58
Indonesia, women and girls in, 364, 444–45, 446–50, 451, 454
inheritance. *See also* divorce; marriage
economic actors and, 306–12
fictious sale and, 172
gifting and, 171–72
practice of, 170–72
science of the shares and, 168–70
sidestepping of, 171–72
social uses of, 171
system of, 170–72
Inhorn, Marcia, 342–43
Inside the Gender Jihad (wadud), 93–94
Iran
Constitutional Revolution in, 398–99
feminism in, 398–99, 401, 402–3, 404–5, 554–55, 558
Green Movement in, 403–4
guardianship in, 400
histories of women's activism in, 398
Islamic Republic era in, 402
Islamist women's activism in, 405–6
late Qajar era in, 398–400
legal reforms in, 402–3
Mohammad Reza Pahlavi era in, 401
overview of, 397, 406–7
periodicals in, 399–400
Reza Shah Pahlavi era in, 400–1
veiling in, 400–1, 574–75
Women's Awakening initiatives in, 400
women's media in, 404–5
Iran Awakening (Ebadi), 558
ISIS, 346–47

Islam, Namira, 499
Islamic family law (IFL). *See also* divorce; inheritance; marriage
  agency and, 190
  anthropological approach to, 185–86
  approaches to study of, 184–88
  Arab Family Law Project and, 190
  comparative analysis of, 187–88
  comparative reform to, 190–93
  eclecticism in, 189–90
  elements of application of, 185–86
  equity and quality reforms in, 188–89
  historical-legal approach to, 185
  history of, 182–84
  human rights and, 190
  Islamization and, 181
  Malaysia, 192–93
  mechanisms and strategies for reforms to, 188–90
  models of, 183
  Morocco and, 190–93
  NGOs and, 186–87, 190, 192
  OLFR and, 182
  overview of, 181–82, 193
  political science approach of, 187–88
  sociological approach to, 186–87
  Turkey and, 182, 187–88
Islamophobia, 491–92, 579, 580, 591–92, 598
Istanbul Convention, 416, 421–22

Jad, Islah, 369, 371–73, 384–85
Jahan, Shah, 355–56, 363–64
Jahan Begum, 355–56
Jamaat- e-Islami Hind (JIH), 434–35
Jamaat-i Islami (JI) (organization), 432–36
Jamaat-ul-Mujahideen (JMB) (organization), 359
Jamal, Amina, 433
James-Saadiya, Rashida, 498
Jammu Kashmir Liberation Front, 435
Jaschok, Maria, 12–13, 466
Jeenah, Na'eem, 479
Jihad for Love, A (film), 483
Joint Action Group against Violence against Women (JAG), 450
Joseph (Yūsuf), 30–33
Jouili, Jeannette, 13–14
Justice and Development Party (AKP), 416–18, 419–20

Kahf, Mohja, 560, 561, 572–73
Kalmar, Ivan, 598, 599–600
Kalmbach, Hilary, 330
Kamali, Mohammad Hashim, 451–52
Karamah, 496–97
Karbala, Battle of, 246–47, 252–55, 278–79
Kartini, Raden Adjeng, 446–47
Katz, Marion, 9, 280
Kaʿba, 66, 228–29
Ke, Man, 12–13
Khabeer, Su'ad Abdul, 279–80, 498
Khadīja bint Khuwailid
  bedrock of support provided by, 66–67
  character of, 66–67, 278
  dowry of, 314
  as economic actor, 314, 364
  as first convert to Islam, 67
  ḥadīth literature and, 66–67
  illness and death of, 246–47
  marriage to Muḥammad of, 537–38, 540–41
  traditional focus on, 30–31, 540–41
  as woman of paradise, 224–25
Khalid, Maryam, 596
Khan, Jahangir Muhammad, 355
Khan, Nazar Mohammad, 354
Khan, Ruqayya Y., 14–15, 262
Khansā', al-, 300, 312–13
Khawla bint Tha'laba, 70, 124–25
Khiabany, Gholam, 404, 581
Khirniq bint Badr, al-, 292–93, 296–97
Khomeini, 328, 554–55, 558
Kian, Azadeh, 405–6
Kitab, Rumah, 448, 449, 453–54
Knight, Nsenga, 498
knowledge transmission. *See* transmitters of knowledge
Komnas Perempuan (organization), 449–50, 453–54
Krausen, Halima, 331
Kueny, Kathryn, 338
Kugle, Scott, 280–81
Künkler, Miriam, 402
Kuwait, women and girls in, 527–29
Kuwaiti Union for Women Associations, 524

Labadi, Fadwa al-, 344, 371–72, 376
Lamrabet, Asma, 106
Lāshīn, Maḥmūd Ṭāhir, 550
Latreille, Martin, 342
law. *See* Islamic family law (IFL); rights and duties in classical legal texts
Law of Evidence, 432–33
Laylā al-Akhyaliyya, 294
Lebanon, women and girls in, 367, 368–69, 370
Lehmann, Uta, 330
Lewis, Leslie, 386
Liberation of Women, The (Amīn), 572–73
Life of Muḥammad; The (Haykal), 542
Life of Muḥammad (Guillaume), 541–42
Liloia, Alainna, 14
Liping, Hu, 466–67
littérateurs
  adab and, 291–92
  agency and, 291
  challenges in writing about, 289
  existential issues and, 293–94, 299
  gender norms and rituals in poetry and, 293
  Orientalism and, 289, 300
  overview of, 289, 300
  poetic crossdressing and, 293–94
  praise poetry, 294
  Rābiʿa al-ʿAdawiyya, 294–95
  reasons for robust legacy of, 290–91
  reorientations and, 291–92
  salons and, 297–300
  sources for writing about, 290–91
  survey of the literature and, 292–300
  types of persona of poetesses and, 296–97
  Ulayya, 295–97
  Wallāda bint al-Mustakfī, 290, 296–97, 298
"Little Mosque Poems" (Kahf), 561–62
Loin de Médine (Djebar), 559–60
L'Union de l'Action Feminine (UAF), 191

Maaruf, Mohammad, 279
Ma Cijun, 471
Mack, Beverly, 262–63
Ma Guifen, 466–67, 470
Mahmood, Saba, 324–25, 386, 494–95, 521
Maira, Sunaina, 598
Majlis-e-Khawateen (organization), 432–33
Majlisī, Muḥammad Taqī al-, 268–69
Malaysia
  comparative reform in, 192–93
  IFL in, 192–93
  polygamy in, 451
  sharīʿa in, 450–52
  social and political activism in, 445, 450–52
Malaysian Sisters in Islam (SIS), 446, 450–51
Malay Women Teachers' Union, 450
Mālikī school, 45, 157, 162, 165, 167–68
Mallat, Chibli, 189–90
Mamdani, Mahmood, 593, 598
Mamluk period, 42–43, 158–59, 163–64, 166–67, 168, 229, 265, 305
Manūchihrīan, Mihrangīz, 403
Maritato, Chiara, 11
marriage. *See also* divorce; inheritance
  bride's guardian and her consent, 156–58
  child marriage, 445, 449, 453–54, 550
  contract stipulations and, 164–66
  economic actors and, 310
  Ḥanafī school and, 157–58, 160–61, 165, 167–68
  Ḥanbalī school and, 157, 161, 164–65, 167–68
  Mālikī school and, 161, 167–68
  Mamluk period and, 157, 158–59, 162, 165, 166–68
  marital contract, 156–58
  Muḥammad and, 157, 166, 169
  Ottoman period and, 157–58, 162, 166–67, 168, 171–72
  overview of, 155–56, 173
  rights and obligations and, 158–62
  sexual responsibilities and, 159–61
  Shāfiʿī school and, 157, 161, 162, 167–68
  Sunnī school and, 162, 163, 164, 166
  Twelver Shīʿī school and, 155, 157–58, 160, 162–63, 164–65, 166, 170, 173
Marsot, Afaf, 311
Mary (Maryam), 23–27
Maryam bint ʿImrān, 66, 68–69, 225, 226
masculinity, 63, 65, 66, 67–68, 279–80, 599
Massad, Joseph, 91
Masud, Muhammad Khalid, 451–52
Matin-Asgar, Afshin, 400–1
Maududi, Abul Ala, 432
Mazumdar, Sanjoy, 277, 278–79
Mazumdar, Shampa, 277, 278–79

McElrone, Surynne, 399
Memoirs of a Female Physician (Saadawi), 552
Meneley, Anne, 326–27
Mernissi, Fatima, 121, 122–23, 125–26, 133, 134, 204, 341–42, 544, 559–60, 574
Metcalf, Barbara, 429–30
Milani, Farzaneh, 553, 554–55
Milton-Edwards, Beverley, 372–73
Minesaki, Hiroko, 329–30
Ming Dynasty, 463–64
modern family and personal law. *See* Islamic family law (IFL)
modern heads of state
 Bangladesh, 358–60
 begums of Bhopal and, 354–56
 early examples of, 354–56
 Indonesia, 360–61
 other country examples of, 362–63
 overview of, 363–64
 Pakistan, 356–58
 postcolonial examples of, 356–62
 Turkey, 361–62
modern representations of wives of the Prophet. *See also* ʿĀʾisha bint Abī Bakr; Khadīja bint Khuwailid
 background for, 537–41
 feminism and, 539–40, 543
 historical context of, 537–38
 importance of, 538–41
 overview of, 537, 544–45
 rationale for focus on, 538–41
 secondary scholarship on, 542–44
 sources of, 541–44
 three trajectories and, 543–44
modern rereadings of *ḥadīth*
 agency and, 121, 122, 123–24, 125, 129–30, 131–32, 135, 139–40, 142
 ʿĀʾisha and, 125, 129, 131–32, 133
 arguments from historical contexts and, 133–35
 bad omens, donkeys, dogs, and women and, 129
 definition of misogynistic reports and, 126
 definition of tension reports and, 123
 human creation narrative and, 127–28
 liberating memories and, 121, 125–26
 main stratagems for, 130–37
 majority of hellfire inhabitants and, 128–29
 misogynistic *ḥadīth* reports and, 127–30
 moments of possible liberation and, 120–23
 obedience and subservience reports and, 129–31
 overview of, 119, 139–42
 Qurʾānic guidance arguments and, 136–37
 responsibility in approaching, 137–39
 tension reports and, 120–25
 traditions of misogyny and, 125–27
 transmitters of knowledge and, 131–33
 veiling and, 126–27, 134
modern rereadings of Qurʾān
 agency and, 90–91, 94, 96–97, 102, 103–4, 106, 107–8
 assessing antipatriarchal position and its critiques, 92–93
 classical androcentrism challenged by, 85–88
 complementarity and, 83–84
 daraja as divine preference for men and, 101–2
 development of, 81–82
 faḍḍala as divine preference for men and, 98–100
 fault lines between feminists and traditionalists and, 82–85
 feminism and, 82–85
 *ḥadīth*s as exegetical reports and, 88–108
 hermeneutics of *tawhid*, 81
 hitting of wife and, 84–85, 93–94
 human creation narrative and, 88–89
 Qurʾān 2:282, 106–8
 Qurʾān 4:34, 84–85, 90, 91–92, 93–100
 Qurʾān 4:128, 84, 90
 Qurʾān 9:71, 93, 102–6
 Qurʾān 33:35, 93, 102–4
 nushūz and, 83, 84–85, 90
 obedience and, 83–84, 90, 93, 94, 96–97, 100
 one last attempt to restrict women and, 106–8
 overview of, 80–81, 108–9
 pioneers of nonpatriarchal exegesis and, 81–82
 premodern exegeses of 9:71, 104–6
 recent critiques of antipatriarchal readings and, 89–92

sexual responsibilities and, 86–87
women outside domestic sphere and, 102–4
Moghissi, Haideh, 574
Mohajir, Nadiah, 498
Mohanty, Chandra, 596
Moors, Annelies, 183–84
moral exemplars in Twelver Shīʿism
agency and, 250
commemoration of, 253
devotion to the family and, 250–52
exceptional nature of, 248–50
exemplary nature of, 248–50
Fāṭima, 246–50, 253–55
filial piety and, 246–48
overview of, 245–46, 253–55
relative lack of female participation and, 245
Zaynab bint ʿAlī, 250–52
Morocco, women and girls in, 190–93, 382–83, 386–87
Moro National Liberation Front (MNLF), 452
Moses, 27, 30, 69, 99–100
mosques
agency and, 324–25
class dimensions of, 329–30
directions for further inquiry on, 331–32
diversity of age and social class in, 329–30
feminism and, 324
political dimensions of, 327–29
as "public" space, 325–29
religious authority and, 328–29, 330–31
veiling and, 323–24
Western scholarship and, 323–31
women's mosque movement and, 323–31
motherhood. *See* negotiating motherhood
MotherSchools, 347–48
Mubarak, Hadia, 3, 85
Mubashsharāt bi-l-janna, al-
agency and, 229
al-Rabīʿ bint Maʿūdh al-Anṣāriyya, 230–31
Asmāʾ bint Abī Bakr, 226–27
Fāṭima, 225–26, 236
feminism and, 234–36
Khadīja bint Khuwaylid, 224–25
martyrs and, 231–32
modern scholarship on, 234–36
overview of, 223–24
Sumayya bint Khayyāṭ, 231
summary of exemplary traits of, 234
Umm Ayman, 230
Umm Ḥarām, 228
Umm Kulthūm, 233–34
Umm Rumān, 226
Umm Saʿd, 233
Umm Sulaym, 227
Umm Waraqa, 231–33, 235
Umm Zafar or Umm Zakhar and, 228–29
Umm ʿUmāra, 229–30
Mudawwana, 187, 191–92
Muḥaddithāt (Nadwi), 261–62
Muhalhil ibn Abī Rabīʿa, 293
Muḥammad. See also *ḥadīth literature*; *modern rereadings of ḥadīth*
background of, 537–38
Bilqīs and, 28
feminist sensibilities attributed to, 293–94
marriage and, 157, 166, 169
masculinity and, 67–68
political rule of women and, 28
Muḥammad (Armstrong), 542
Muḥammad (Haykal), 542
Muhammad, Elijah, 495–96
Muhammad, Fard, 495–96
Muhammad, Husein, 449
Muhammadiyah (organization), 446–47, 448–49
Muhammad VI, 191–92
Muhanna, Aitemad, 370
Mujahid (ibn Jabr), 86, 96–97
Mulia, Siti Musdah, 449
Mumtaz, Khawar, 432–33
Mumtaz, Zubla, 342–43
Muqātil ibn Sulaymān, 29–30, 83, 104–5
Mūsa, Nabawiya, 382
Musallam, Basim, 205–6, 208
Musharraf, Pervez, 357–58, 433
Muslimat NU, 446–47
Muslim Girls Training and General Civilization Class (MGT-GCC), 495–96
Muslim ibn Ḥajjāj, 228–29
Muslim Marriages Bill (MMB), 482
Muslim personal law (MPL), 481–82
Muslims Anti-Racism Collaborative (MuslimARC), 499
Muslim Studies (Goldziher), 261

Muslim Women's Association, 386
Muslim Women's League (MWL), 496
Muslim Youth Movement (MYM), 479
Muṯṯalib, 'Abd al- (Shayba ibn Hāshim), 314

Nābigha al-Ja'dī, al-, 294
Nadwi, Mohammad, 131–32
nafs, 31, 32–34, 41
Nahdlatul Ulama (NU), 446–48
Najmabadi, Afsaneh 398, 402
Nāṣīf, Malak Ḥifnī, 382, 549, 572–73
Nasser, Gamal Abdel, 384
National Action Plan (Indonesia), 449
National Order Party (Turkey), 361–62
National Union of Women, 398
Nation of Islam (NOI), 279–80, 495–96
Naysabūrī, Muslim ibn al-Ḥajjāj, al-, 550–51
negotiating motherhood
  active participation and, 345–46
  colonialism and, 344–45
  feminism and, 340–41
  household dynamics and, 340–43
  infertility and, 342–43
  joint family systems and, 342, 343–44
  maternal identities and, 341–43
  motherwork and, 343–46
  NGOs and, 347–48
  overview of, 338–40, 348–49
  parenting styles and, 343–44
  politics of extremism and, 346–49
  race and, 343–44
  war and, 344
Nehaoua, Sofia, 329–30
NGOs (Non-Governmental Organizations)
  devotional life and, 283–85
  IFL and, 186–87, 190, 192
  negotiating motherhood and, 347–48
  NGO-ization and, 380–81, 384–85
Nigerian Islamic Education Trust, 552
9/11 attacks, 505, 510, 526, 590–92, 594, 598
Nisa, Eva, 449
Nisā' al-Nabī, 544
North Africa. *See* Egypt and North Africa
Nurmila, Nina, 449
Nusayba bint Ka'b, 73–74
nushūz, 49–53, 83, 84–85, 90

obedience
  classical exegeses and, 47, 49–50
  modern rereadings of *ḥadīth* and, 129–31
  modern rereadings of Qur'ān and, 83–84, 90, 93, 94, 96–97, 100
Odeh, Lama Abu, 577–78
O'Leary, Patrick, 339
Ong, Aihwa, 446
O'Reilly, Andrea, 338
Organization of Islamic Cooperation (OIC), 181–82, 205
Orientalism
  cultural trope of Muslim Women and, 590–96, 598–99
  legal rights and duties and, 201
  littérateurs and, 289, 300
  politics of victimhood, 590, 592
Orientalism (Said), 594
Osanloo, Arzoo, 403
Ottoman Law of Family Rights (OLFR), 182
Ottoman period, 157–58, 162, 166–67, 168, 171–72, 182, 185–86, 265, 282–83, 291–92, 308
overview. *See* women and Islam overview
Özal, Turgut, 362

Pahlavi, Mohammad Reza, 401, 574
Pahlavi, Reza Shah, 400–1
Paidar, Parvin, 398
Pakistan, modern heads of state in, 356–58
Pakistan Muslim League (PML), 357
Pakistan People's Party (PPP), 356–57
Palestine, Lebanon, and Syria
  activism as empowerment in, 368–71
  agency in, 367, 370, 372, 375–76
  female mosque teachers in, 373–76
  feminism in, 371–73
  gender roles in, 368, 369–70, 374–75
  Hamas in, 368–69, 370–73
  Hizbullah in, 369–70
  human rights and, 371, 372, 376
  Islamist vs secular activists in, 371–73
  Lebanon, 367, 368–69, 370
  media portrayal of, 369–70
  overview of, 367, 375–76
  sharī'a and, 371–72
  Sufism and, 375
  Syria, 367, 373, 374, 375

women police in, 370
women's only spaces in, 369
Palestinian Women's Activism (Jad), 368
Pan-Malaysian Islamic Party (PAS), 451
Pappano, Margaret, 9
Parashar, Swati, 435
Partai Demokrasi Indonesia, 360–61
Peaceful Families Project (PFP), 497
Perempuan, Komnas, 453–54
Peteet, Julie, 345–46
Philippine Center for Islam and Democracy (PCID), 452–53
Philippine Plan for Gender-Responsive Development, 452–53
Philippines, women and girls in, 452–53
Piela, Anna, 15–16, 445
Pierce, Matthew, 246
pilgrimages, 71–72, 134–35, 277, 281, 363–64, 464–66, 538–39
Pinto, Vania Carvalho, 383
Politics of Piety (Mahmood), 324
Politics of Women's Rights in Iran, The (Osanloo), 403
Populism and Feminism in Iran (Moghissi), 398
Powers, David, 172, 203

qānitāt, 82–84, 90, 91–92, 94, 96, 100
Qatar Businesswomen Forum, 524
Qubaysī movement, 283–84
Qudsia Begum, 354
Queen of Sheba, 27–28, 29
Qur'ān. *See also* classical exegeses on key Qur'ānic verses; modern rereadings of Qur'ān
Abraham (Ibrāhīm) and, 23–27
annunication and, 24
archetypes and, 21, 23
'Azīz and, 31–32
Bilqīs and, 27–30
cunning and seduction and, 30–33
divine provenance of, 21–23, 34
Joseph (Yūsuf) and, 30–33
Mary (Maryam) and, 23–27
miracles and, 25
Moses and, 27
obedience to God and, 23
overview of, 21–22, 33–35
paradigmatization and, 23, 27–28
political models and, 27–30
prophethood and, 23–27
purification and, 24–26
queen of Sheba and, 27–28, 29
sight and, 29
Soloman (Sulaymān) and, 28–30
spiritual models and, 23–27
tawḥīdic approach and, 21–22, 23, 33–34
undifferentiated spirituality and, 22–23
Zulaykha and, 30–33
Qur'ān and Woman (wadud), 81, 92
Qur'ānic references
2:187, 87–88, 90, 94
2:223, 87–88, 90
2:227, 43–46
2:228, 46–49, 101–2, 103
2:253, 99, 100–1
2:282, 99, 106–8
3:195, 103–4
4:1, 33–34, 40–43
4:3, 95–96
4:8, 168–69
4:11-12, 95–96, 168–69
4:32, 98–99
4:34, 49–51, 84–85, 90, 91–92, 93–98, 100, 103, 161–62, 341
4:35, 94–95
4:128, 46, 49–50, 51–53, 84, 95
4:176, 168–69
9:20, 101
9:71, 93, 96–97, 102–6, 107–8
16:106, 231
17:55, 99
24:4, 94–95
24:6-9, 107–8
24:23, 94–95
27:34, 29–30
30:21, 87–88
30:26, 96
33:31, 96
33:32, 234–35
33:35, 93, 102–4, 107–8, 123–24
46:19, 101
58:1-2, 124
66:12, 23
81:8, 94–95

Qur'an of the Oppressed (Rahemtulla), 135
Qurṭubī, Muḥammad b. Aḥmad al-, 27, 29–30, 45, 46, 48, 52, 105
Quṭb, Sayyid, 83–84

Rābiʿa al-ʿAdawiyya, 253, 294–95, 296–97, 551
Rabīʿ bint Maʿūdh al-Anṣāriyya al-, 230–31
race, 91, 92, 136, 279–80, 343–44, 483, 498, 504–5, 591, 597, 599
Rahardjo, M. Dawam, 447–48
Rahemtulla, Shadaab, 135
Rahima (center), 448
Rahman, Mujibur, 358, 359, 433–34
Rahman, Ziaur, 358–59
Raouf Azzat, Heba, 387. *See also* Rāʾūf, Hiba
Rapoport, Yossef, 159, 163–64, 168, 211
Rashīd Riḍā, 83, 105
Rausch, Margaret, 331
Razak, Sherene, 596
Rāzī, Fakhr al-Dīn, al-, 29–30, 42, 44–45, 46, 47, 50, 51, 52, 83, 89, 106–7
Rāʾūf, Hiba, 327–28
Reda, Nevin, 235, 277
Reilly, James, 308, 315
rereadings of texts. *See* modern rereadings of *ḥadīth*;modern rereadings of Qur'ān
Results of Circumstances in Words and Deeds (al-Taimūriyya), 554
Rich, Andrienne, 539–40
Riḍā, Rashīd, 83
rights and duties in classical legal texts
  agency and, 205–6
  autonomy and, 206, 208
  "classical legal literature" deconstructed, 209–11
  constructing the field of Islamic law and, 201–3
  cultural context and, 203
  feminism and, 204, 207
  future trajectories of research on, 211–12
  gender roles and, 205–6, 208–9, 210
  Ḥanbalī school and, 209
  hermaphrodites and, 210
  mechanics of Islamic law and, 201–2
  methodological issues and, 204–9, 210
  Orientalism and, 201
  overview of, 200
  rediscovering foundational texts and, 203–4
  "rights and duties" deconstructed and, 207–9
  sexual rights and duties, 208
  slavery and, 206
  values within Islam and, 202
  "women" deconstructed and, 205–6
Rinaldo, Rachel, 438
Rizvi, Kishwar, 328
Roald, Anne Sophie, 373–74
Roded, Ruth, 236, 262–63
Rose, Jacqueline, 339, 347–48
Rosen, Lawrence, 185–86
Ross, Lynda Rachelle, 347
Rostam-Koyali, Jasmin, 399, 400–1
Roxelana, 313–14
Roy, Sara, 370–71, 372
Rubenburg, Cheryl, 370–71
Ruddick, Sara, 343–44
Rumān, Umm, 226
Rygiel, Kim, 594–95

Ṣafadī, al-, 227
Sakhāwī, al-, 265
Sakurai, Keiko, 405
Salāma bint al-Ḥurr, 265
Saleh, Mariam, 369
Salem, Feryal, 3–4, 97
Salmān al-Fārisī, 249–50
Sapelo Square, 498
Saudi Arabia and the Gulf
  agency and, 520–22
  Bahrain, 527–29
  colonialism and, 520, 522
  context of, 522–25
  education in, 524
  engagement and resistance in, 520–22
  guardianship in, 525–26
  identity in, 522–23
  inheritance in, 523–24
  Islamism in, 521
  Kuwait, 527–29
  marriage in, 523–24
  oil boom in, 522
  Orientalism and, 520–21
  overview of, 519–20, 529
  personal status laws in, 523–24

Saudi women's activist movement in, 525–27
scholarship on, 520–22
September 11 attacks and, 526
Women-to-Drive Movement in, 525–26
"saving" Muslim women 91, 491–92, 507, 590–91, 592, 598
Sayeed, Asma, 7, 132, 282–83
Schacht, Joseph, 201–2
Schimmel, Annemarie, 280–81
Schleifer, Aliah, 339
Scott, Joan, 91
Scott, Sasha, 404
Sedghi, Hamideh, 401
Sefati, Zohreh, 406
Sells, Michael, 34–35
September 11 attacks, 505, 510, 526, 590–92, 594, 598, *See also* 9/11 attacks
Sex and Secularism (Scott), 91
sexual responsibilities, 46, 48, 49–50, 52, 86–87, 159–61, 208
Sezgin, Yuksel, 182–84
Shabazz, Malikah A., 498
Shāfiʿī school, 157, 161, 162, 167–68
Shaikh, Khanum, 284–85
Shaikh, Saʿdiyya, 208, 485
Shaikh, Shamima, 478–79
Shajar al-Durr, 305
Shakir, Zaid, 327–28
Shaʿrāwī, Hudā, 383, 554, 572–73
shariʿa law, 137–38, 141, 308, 315, 371–72, 376, 444–45, 450–53. *See also* Islamic family law (IFL); rights and duties in classical legal texts
Sharif, Nawaz, 357
Shehabuddin, Elora, 11–12
Shehada, Nahda, 185–86
Sheibani, Mariam, 5
Sherkat, Shahla, 404–5, 558
Shīʿīsm, 155, 157–58, 160, 162–63, 164–65, 166, 170, 173, 245
Shui, Jingjun, 463–64, 466
Siddiq Hasan, Sayyid, 355
Siddiqi, Bulbul, 431
Siddiqui, Sohaira, 5
Sikander Begum, 354–55, 363–64
Sīrat Rasūl Allāh (Ibn Isḥāq), 541–42
Sisters in Islam (SIS), 192
Siyam, Amal, 369
Smith, Dorothy E., 93
Smith, Margaret, 280–81
Sobhan, Maulana Abdus, 429
Soloman (Sulaymān), 28–30
Sonbol, Amira, 8–9, 185–86
Sonn, Tamara, 9–10
South Africa
exegesis in, 479, 480–81, 483, 484–85
experience prioritized in, 484–87
ijtihād in, 483, 484
intersectionality in, 484–85
looking back, looking forward in, 484–85
marriage in, 482
mosques in, 479–81
Muslim personal law in, 481–82
overview of, 478–79
queer Muslim lives in, 483–84
struggle for personal law in, 481–82
tawḥīd approach in, 478–79, 480–81
South Asia
agency in, 437–38
Al-Huda in, 435–36
Bangladesh, 434, 436–38
feminism in, 437–38
gender roles in, 431, 432
Jamaat-i Islami in, 432–36, 438
literary activism in, 434
militant activism in, 435
overview of, 428
piety in, 437–38
Shi'i women's madrasas in Pakistan in, 436
study circles in, 436–38
Tablighi Jamaat in, 428–31, 438
veiling in, 437
women-only groups in, 435–36
Southeast Asia
agency in, 446, 450
child marriage in, 453–54
feminism in, 447, 448–49, 450, 452–53
guardianship in, 453–54
human rights in, 445
Indonesia, 444–45, 446–50, 451, 454
international cooperation in, 453–54
Islamic organizations in, 446
Malaysia, 445, 450–52
Musawah in, 453–54

Southeast Asia (*cont.*)
NGOs in, 446–49, 450, 452–53
overview of, 444–45, 454
Philippines, 452–53
tawhid approach in, 452–53
text-based activism in, 445
Spectorsky, Susan, 209
Spellberg, Denise, 262–63, 278, 543
Spivak, Gayatri, 381, 593
Steans, Jill, 593
Stephan, Rita, 382–83
Stewart, Devin, 260
Stowasser, Barbara, 543
Suddī, al-, 86–87
Sufism, 29, 156, 262, 270, 280–81, 375
Suharto, 360, 444–45, 449–50
Sukarno, 360
Sukarnoputri, Megawati, 360–61
Sukayna bint al-Ḥusayn, 120–22, 262
Sulaym, Umm, 227
Sullivan, Zohreh, 558
Sultanes Oubliées (Mernissi), 559–60
Sumayya bint Khayyāṭ, 231
Su Muyu, 470–71, 472
Syria, women and girls in, 367, 373, 374, 375

Ṭabaqāt (Ibn Saʿd), 66–67
Ṭabarānī, al-, 225–26, 232–33
Ṭabarī, Muḥammad ibn Jarīr al-, 29–30, 41, 44–45, 46–47, 49–51, 52, 83, 86–87, 89, 104–5, 106–7, 232–33
Ṭabarsī, Faḍl ibn Ḥasan al-, 42, 47
Tablighi Jamaat (TJ), 428–31
tafsīr (exegesis). *See* classical exegeses on key Qur'ānic verses
Ṭahāwī, Mirāl al-, 555–56
Taimūr, Maḥmūd, 550
Ṭālibān, 259, 357–58, 576–77, 592, 594, 595–96, 597, 599
Tanūkhī, al-, 297
Tapper, Nancy, 281
Tawasil, Amina, 405
tawḥīdic (unicity) approach, 21–22, 23, 33–34, 81, 136–37, 281–82
Taylor, Ula, 495–96
Teacher, K. Jamida, 560
Thaʿālibī, al-, 292
Thurfjell, David, 332
Torab, Azam, 328, 405–6
transmitters of knowledge
agency and, 259, 268
definition of knowledge, 263–64
definition of transmission, 263–64
devotional life and, 282–83
directions for future research on, 269–70
feminism and, 265
ḥadīth literature and, 261–62, 263–69
history and historicity and, 261–62
literature review of, 259–61
memory and, 262–63
modern period of, 267
modern rereadings of *ḥadīth* and, 131–33
navigating state of field on, 259–61
reception history and, 262–63
regional variation in, 260
representation and, 262–63
Shīʿī transmission and, 267–68
Sufism and, 262
Sunnī transmission and, 264–68
traditionalism and rationalism in, 268
uneven chronological coverage of, 260
True Path Party (formerly Justice Party), 361
Tucker, Judith, 185–86
Tuksal, Hidayet, 127, 416–17, 419–20, 421
Turam, Berna, 416
Turkey
agency in, 416–17, 419
AKP's gender regime in, 420–22
bureaucratization of activism in, 417–20
complementarity and, 419–20
feminism in, 415–17, 419, 420–21
IFL in, 182, 187–88
modern heads of state in, 361–62
NGOs in, 421
overview of, 415–17, 423
polarization in, 421–22
veiling in, 417–19
women preachers in, 417–18
Ṭūsī, Shaykh al-Ṭā'ifa Muḥammad ibn al-Ḥasan al-, 47
Tutuncu, Fatma, 416
Twelver Shīʿīsm, 155, 157–58, 160, 162–63, 164–65, 166, 170, 173, 245. *See also* moral exemplars in Twelver Shīʿīsm

ʿUbayd Allāh, Ṭalḥa ibn, 121–22
Ulayya, 295–96
ul-Huq, Zia, 432–33
ʿUmar ibn al-Khaṭṭābʾ, 122–23, 124–25
Umayyad ʿAbd al-Malik, 294
Umm Ayman, 230
Umm Ḥarām, 228
Umm Kulthūm bint Abī Bakr, 121–22
Umm Kulthūm bint ʿUqba, 233–34
Umm Rumān, 226
Umm Salama, 70, 123–24, 260–61
Umm Saʿd, 233
Umm Sulaym, 227
Umm ʿUmāra, 103–4, 229–30
Umm Waraqa, 231–33, 235, 278–79
Umm Zafar or Umm Zakhar, 228–29
Umm Zarʿ, 61–66, 73
United Malays National Organization (UMNO), 450
United States
- agency in, 489–90, 498, 499
- anti-Muslim hostility and gender in, 491–92
- definition of activism in, 492–93
- discourse and practice in, 492–93
- feminism in, 490–91, 493
- HEART women and girls in, 498
- identity in, 494
- Karamah in, 496–97
- Muslim Girls Training and General Cilization Class in, 495–96
- Muslims Anti-Racism Collaborative in, 499
- Muslim Women's League in, 496
- overview of, 489–90, 499–500
- Peaceful Families Project in, 497
- Sapelo Square in, 498
- saving Muslim women discourse in, 491–92
- scholarship on, 492–93
- Women in Islam in, 496
- women's activism and issues in, 492–99
- Women's Islamic Initiative in Spirituality and Equality in, 497–98

Van Ess, Josef, 510–11
Veil and the Male Elite, The (Mernissi), 133, 574
Veiled Revolution (film), 323–24
veiling
- agency and, 572–73, 576–78, 581
- burqa bans and, 578–80
- cultural politics of, 575–76
- discussion on, 580–81
- feminism and, 572–74
- feminist literature and, 553–56
- global rise of, 574–76
- modern rereadings of *ḥadīth* and, 126–27, 134
- modest fashion and, 578–80
- mosques and, 323–24
- 1920s, 572–74
- 1979-2000, 574–76
- online voices on, 578–80
- overview of, 571–72
- September 11th attacks and, 576–77, 579
- social media and, 579
- state interference and, 581
- 2001-2009, 576–78
- 2010-2019, 578–80
- uneasy relationships and, 572–74
- volatile change in perspectives and perceptions of, 576–78

Veils and Words (Milani), 554–55
Veil Unveiled (Shirazi), 577
Verdon, Michel, 342
Violence against Women (VAWA) program, 497

wadud, amina, 21–22, 23, 81, 89–91, 133–34, 281–82, 331, 338–39, 480, 560
Wafdist Women's Central Committee (WWCC), 383
Wahid, Abdurrahman, 360–61, 447–48
Wāḥidī, al-, 83, 105
Wallāda bint al-Mustakfī, 298
War of Basūs, 293
War on Terror (WoT), 512, 590–95
Wazed, Hasina, 358–60
Weintraub, Jeff, 325, 327–28
Weiss, Anita, 435–36
Welchman, Lynn, 182, 185
Weldon, Lauren, 187–88, 190–91
Western Europe
- counterterrorism in, 509–10
- empowerment paradigm in, 508

Western Europe (*cont.*)
  feminism in, 508, 509
  FGM in, 507
  historical overview of activism in, 504–5
  leadership in, 509
  mosques in, 508–9
  other social and political activisms in, 511–12
  overview of, 503–4, 512
  recognition struggles in, 510–11
  refugees and asylum-seekers in, 505
  religious activism in, 507–10
  representation struggles in, 510–11
  second generation in, 504–5
  September 11 attacks in, 505, 510
  state engagement in, 507
  struggling for women's rights in, 506–7
Western feminists, 16, 596, 597
  connivance with "war on terror" policies, 16, 595–96, 597, 600
White, Sarah, 430
wives of the Prophet. *See* 'Ā'isha bint Abī Bakr; Khadīja bint Khuwailid; modern representations of wives of the Prophet
Women and Democracy (KADEM), 421–22
Women and Gender in Islam (Ahmed), 324
women and Islam overview
  aims of current volume, 1
  biography and prospographical literature, 6
  broadness and complexity of topic, 1, 16–17
  chapter overview of current volume, 2–16
  devotional lives, 7
  economics, 8–9
  feminist exegeses, 4
  feminist literature, 15
  ḥadīth, 3–5, 7
  heads of state, 9–10
  historical approach of current volume, 1
  ideologization, 1
  Islamic law, 5
  Islamization, 5
  littérateurs, 8
  misogyny, 4
  modernization, 5
  mosque participation, 9
  motherhood, 9
  multidisciplinary methodological approach of current volume, 2
  patriarchy, 4–5
  Qur'ān, 2–3
  rights and duties, 6
  social and religious activism, 10–14
  sunna, 4–5
  tawḥīd approach, 2–3
  tension reports, 4
  transmission of knowledge, 7
  wives of Muḥammad, 14–15
  women promised paradise, 6–7
Women and Men in Late Eighteenth-Century Egypt (Marsot), 311
Women and Politics in Iran (Sedghi), 401
Women and the Political Process in Twentieth Century Iran (Paidar), 398
Women and the Transmission of Religious Knowledge in Islam (Sayeed), 261–62
Women in Islam (WI), 496
Women in Muslim Family Law (Eposito), 185
Women Living under Muslim Laws (WLUML), 450
Women's Action Forum (WAF), 432–33
Women's Awakening initiatives, 400
Women's Islamic Initiative in Spirituality and Equality (WISE), 497–98
Women's Organization of Iran (WOI), 401
Women-to-Drive Movement, 525
World Conference on Women, 447
writing. *See* feminist literature; littérateurs

Yacoob, Salma, 590
Yang Wenjiong, 464–65
Yaraş, Sezen, 417–18, 419
Yasār, Sulaymān ibn, 45
Yeğenoğlu, Metin, 419–20

Zaatari, Zeina, 370
Zaghloul, Ṣafiya, 383
Ẓāhirī school, 27
Zamakhsharī, al-, 45–46, 50, 52
Zanān (magazine), 404–5
Zarinebaf-Shahr, Fariba, 314–15

Zaynab bint ʿAlī
Battle of Karbala actions of, 251
commemoration of, 253
courage of, 251–52
devotion to the family and, 250–52
leadership of, 251–52
as moral exemplar in Twelver Shīʿism, 250–52, 253–55
transmitters of knowledge and, 260–61, 262–63
Zaynab Khātūn, 305
Zeineddine, Naẓīra, 551–52, 554
Zia, Khaleda, 358–59
Zia ul-Haq, 356–57
Zubaida, 313
Zulaykha, 30–33